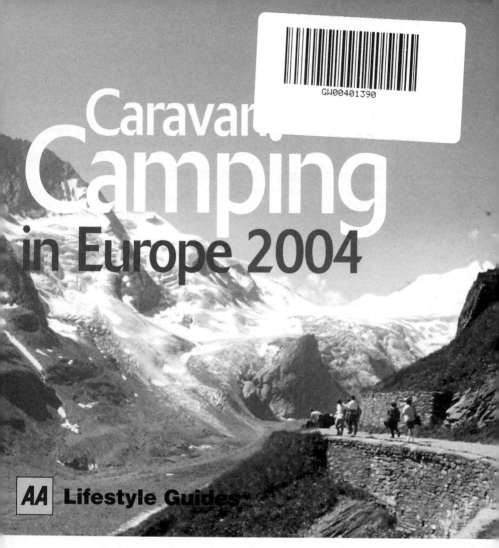

Caravan
Camping
in Europe 2004

AA Lifestyle Guides

GW00401390

This edition published 2004

© Automobile Association Developments Limited 2004

Automobile Association Developments Limited retains the copyright in the current edition © 2004 and in all subsequent editions, reprints and amendments to editions

Mapping produced by the Cartography Department of The Automobile Association from the Automaps database using electronic and computer technology

Maps © Automobile Association Developments Limited 2004

Typeset by: Keenes, Andover, Hampshire

Printed and bound by Printers Trento srl, Italy

Design by Kingswood Graphics, Reading, Berks

Advertisement Sales: advertisingsales@theAA.com

Editorial: lifestyleguides@theAA.com

A CIP catalogue record for this book is available from the British Library

ISBN 0749539291

Published by AA Publishing, a trading name of Automobile Association Developments Limited, whose registered office is Millstream, Maidenhead Road, Windsor, Berkshire, SL4 5GD.

Registered number 1878835

A02233

HanDPICKED

*Terms and Conditions

This offer is valid for new bookings taken between 1st October 2003 and 30th September 2004. Bookings are subject to availability and standard Classic Break terms and conditions apply (available in the Classic Breaks brochure). All bookings to be made via Central Reservations on 0845 458 0901 quoting AA-CV1. The number of rooms available at this special AA rate is limited and this offer cannot be used in conjunction with any promotion and excludes Christmas, New Year, Easter, Bank Holidays and major sporting events. This discount is only valid for a two night break booked on a dinner, bed and breakfast basis where two adults share a standard room.

Contents

How to Use This Guide

Each country in this guide is divided into regions, so that you can easily find all the sites in your chosen holiday area. Within the regions, place names are listed in alphabetical order, and details of site locations can be found on the country maps at the back of this book. If you need overnight stops on the way to your destination, the country maps should help you find something in the right place. Please remember that these maps are for town location purposes only and not for finding your way around. For route planning and use on the road, you should have a road atlas, such as the AA Big Road Atlas of Europe. Individual atlases of France, Germany and Italy are also available in the series.

ADVANCE BOOKING

Despite the carefree nature of a camping or caravanning holiday, it is best to book well in advance for peak holiday seasons, or for your first and last stop close to a ferry crossing point. However, we do find that some sites will not accept reservations. Although the AA cannot undertake to find sites or make reservations for you, we do include in this guide specimen booking letters in English, French, German, Italian and Spanish.

Please note that, although it is not common practice, some campsites may regard your deposit as a booking fee which is not deductible from the final account.

ON ARRIVAL

Look over the site if possible before you decide to stay. The information for any publication must be collected some time in advance, and ownership and standards may well have changed since our research was done. Even where standards are of the expected quality, the site may be very crowded and you may prefer to look elsewhere for more space and less noise. The descriptions in our guide are very brief, and are compiled from brochures provided by the sites. They are given only as a very loose guide.

The directions given to us by the campsites can also be very brief. If you have any difficulty locating a site, contact them directly for more comprehensive directions.

WHEN YOU LOOK OVER A SITE, CONSIDER THE FOLLOWING:

- Pleasant general situation, clean and tidy with plenty of refuse bins, site fenced and guarded.
- Sufficient and clean lavatories, washing facilities and showers with hot water.
- Well defined roads on site, preferably lit at night.
- Pitches should not be cramped.
- If you have a tent, make sure the surface is suitable for pegs; if you have a caravan, make sure the ground is firm enough.
- In hot weather there should be suitable shade, and if the weather is damp the ground should appear well drained.
- A good supply of safe drinking water.
- If you need the following facilities, confirm that they exist on the site: electric point for razors, Camping Gaz, a well stocked shop, laundry facilities, restaurant serving reasonably priced food, ice for sale.

Although most of the sites in this guide have been selected for the high standards they maintain, we have included, at the request of AA members, a number of sites along touring routes and others near the Channel ports which are suitable for overnight stops. These transit sites tend to become crowded at the height of the season, but provide the necessary amenities.

If you require information on additional sites, lists are free from most national tourist offices. In the introductions for each country we give details of local organisations which either publish a camping guide or provide more detailed information.

CAMPSITE ENTRIES

In order to update our information we send out questionnaires each year to every campsite. Inevitably a number of the questionnaires are not returned to us in time for publication, and where this is the case the campsite name is printed in italics. Most of the sites listed here take both tents and caravans unless otherwise stated.

PRICES

Prices are given in local currencies and are detailed per night, per adult, car, caravan and tent. Most prices will be in Euros, which will make things a lot simpler for those travelling to more than one country. We do not give charges relating to children, as these vary, but generally a 50 per cent reduction is made for children aged 3-14. To determine the cost of one night, simply add up the prices that apply to your party.

Some campsites do have different ways of structuring their prices. Whatever the variations may be, these should be reflected in the entry. Exceptions are:

pp Campsite charges per person. The charge for the vehicle and caravan/tent is included in the price for each person. For a party of four people, multiply the pp price by four for the total cost per night.

pitch This is the price per pitch, regardless of whether it is a caravan or a tent. Where the word pitch follows the ♠ for adult price, you should multiply the ♠ price by the number of adults in the party, then add the pitch price to that total to obtain the cost per night for your party.

OPENING TIMES

Dates shown are inclusive of opening dates. If the site is open all year, then 'All year' is written in the entry. All information was correct at the time of going to press, but we recommend you check with the site before arriving. Changes in opening times often occur because of demand and/or weather. Sometimes only restricted facilities are available between October and April.

COMPLAINTS

If you have any complaint about a site, do discuss the problem with the site proprietor immediately so that the matter can be dealt with promptly. If a personal approach fails, inform the AA when you return home. We regret, however, that the AA cannot act as intermediary in any dispute, or attempt to gain refunds or compensation. Your comments, however, help us to prepare new editions. Please use the Readers' Report form at the back of the guide.

WEBSITES

We including web addresses for the campsites where available. The AA cannot be held responsible for the content of any of these websites.

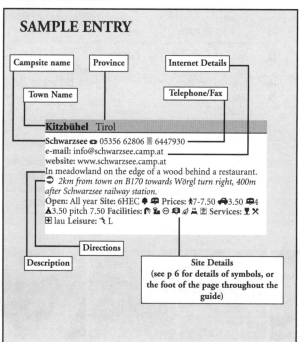

SAMPLE ENTRY

Campsite name · Province · Internet Details

Town Name · Telephone/Fax

Kitzbühel Tirol
Schwarzsee ☎ 05356 62806 📠 6447930
e-mail: info@schwarzsee.camp.at
website: www.schwarzsee.camp.at
In meadowland on the edge of a wood behind a restaurant.
➲ 2km from town on B170 towards Wörgl turn right, 400m
after Schwarzsee railway station.
Open: All year Site: 6HEC ♠ 🚐 Prices: ♠7-7.50 🚐3.50 🚐4
🏕3.50 pitch 7.50 Facilities: 🏠 🛁 ⊙ 🔄 ∅ 🚿 🅿 Services: ♀ ✕
⊞ lau Leisure: ⤵ L

Description · Directions

Site Details
(see p 6 for details of symbols, or
the foot of the page throughout the
guide)

5

Symbols and Abbreviations

For ease of use, the following symbols and abbreviations can also be found at the foot of each page throughout the campsite directory.

- 🧍 adult
- 🚗 car
- **pp** per person
- 🚐 caravan or motor caravan
- ⛺ tent
- ☎ telephone
- **HEC** 1 hectare (equals approx 2 acres)
- ▦ grass
- ∴ sand
- ⬧ stone
- 🌿 little shade
- 🌳 partly shaded
- ♣ mainly shaded
- ☂ shower
- 🛒 shop
- ✗ cafe/restaurant bar
- 🐕 no dogs
- ☉ electric points for razors
- 🔌 electric points for caravans
- ⌀ Camping Gaz International

- 🔥 gas other than Camping Gaz
- 🏠 bungalows for hire
- 🚐 caravans for hire
- ⛺ tents for hire
- 🏊 swimming:
  - L lake
  - P pool
  - R river
  - S sea
- 🅿 parking by tents permitted
- **P** compulsory separate car park
- ✚ first-aid facilities
- 🏰 site belongs to 'Castels & Camping Caravanning' chain (France only)
- **CM** camping municipal, parque municipal de campismo, or parque de la camara municipal (local authority site)

- **KC** Kommunens Campingplads (local authority site)
- **lau** laundry
- **pitch** pitch charge per night for car with tent or caravan (there is usually a charge per adult in addition to this)

Off-site: facilities not on site, but within 2km

contd Entry continued overleaf

Entries that have the campsite name in italics indicate that particulars have not been confirmed by management.

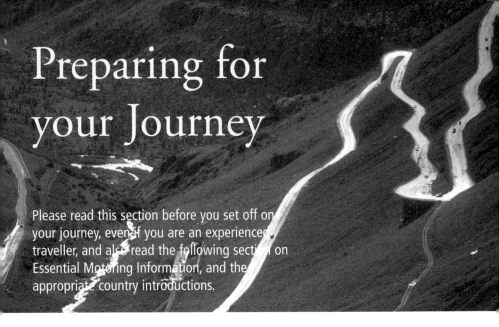

Preparing for your Journey

Please read this section before you set off on your journey, even if you are an experienced traveller, and also read the following section on Essential Motoring Information, and the appropriate country introductions.

Before setting off on your Continental holiday, there are certain preparations you should make and some regulations you should know about. Experienced campers and caravanners will, of course, be familiar with most of this, but we hope it will be a useful chapter for newcomers.

PREPARING YOUR CARAVAN

Your caravan should of course be regularly serviced, but the following tips could be useful, especially for the first trip after winter storage.

Just before your trip give the caravan a good airing. If you have a water pump fitted, check the flow and, after sterilising the system, flush with clean water to get rid of any staleness. Make sure that there are no leaks and replace any doubtful washers. Examine all potential leak spots, especially around window rubbers, rear light clusters and roof lights, applying sealing compound as necessary. Test all window, cupboard and locker catches to make sure that they shut firmly. Outside, clean rain gutters and make sure down-spouts and window channel drainpipes are clear.

BRAKES

Check that the caravan braking mechanism is correctly adjusted. If it has a breakaway safety mechanism, the cable between car and caravan must be firmly anchored so that the trailer brakes act immediately if the two part company.

LIGHTS

Make sure that all the lights are working - rear lights, stop lights, number-plate lights, rear fog guard lamps and flashers (check that the flasher rate is correct: 60-120 times a minute).

TYRES

Both tyres on the caravan should be of the same size and type. Make sure that the tread depth is well above the legal minimum (see Tyres p26) and that there is no uneven wear. Look also for cuts and for cracks that might have developed during the winter. Replace any suspect tyres and any tyres over five years old, irrespective of the amount of tread remaining. Remember, caravan tyres rarely wear out but do deteriorate with age.

PREPARING YOUR TENT

Some weeks before your holiday, choose a fine day, spread the tent on the lawn or some other space so that you can make a close inspection of all potential stress points: where guylines attach, where the ground sheet meets tent walls, and where the frame poles come into contact with fabric. The fabric of the tent can be damaged by branches or sharp objects and by mildew if it has not been stored correctly. Additionally, it can lose its proofing through long exposure to the weather, as a result of being splashed by cooking fat or by washing-up water containing detergent. If your tent is damaged in this way, consult a specialist camping supplier. Patch kits of different colours and materials are available, as are proofing preparations and sprays.

PREPARING YOUR CAMPING EQUIPMENT

Use this camping equipment check list when you are planning what to take:

- Air mattress and pump, or camp beds
- All-purpose knife
- Bucket
- Camp stove and fuel
- Clothes-line and pegs
- Cutlery, including cooking utensils
- Dishcloths, scouring pad, and tea towels
- First-aid kit
- Folding chairs or stools
- Folding table
- Food containers
- Ground sheet
- Icebox (portable)
- Kettle
- Mallet
- Matches
- Plastic bags or bags for litter
- Plates, cups and saucers, or mugs
- Rope
- Saucepans, frying pan
- Sleeping bags
- Small brush (useful when camping on sand)
- Teapot
- Tent, poles, tent pegs (spares), sand pegs and discs
- Tent-tidy (for scissors, string, needles, thread, etc.)
- Tin-opener, bottle-opener, and corkscrew
- Torch and batteries
- Washing powder
- Washing-up bowl and washing-up liquid
- Water and milk containers
- Water-purifying tablets
- Windshield

HOW TO ENSURE GOOD ROAD HANDLING

Before you load all your luggage and equipment into the caravan, check on the weight restrictions that apply to it and to the towing vehicle. The laden weight of the caravan should always be less than, and ideally no more than 85 per cent of the kerbside weight of the towing vehicle.

The kerbside weight is defined as: the weight of the vehicle plus fuel and other necessary liquids (e.g. water, oil, brake fluid, etc.) but with no passengers and no load other than normal tools and equipment.

The weight of the caravan is normally specified in the purchase literature, and usually refers to the weight 'ex works' or 'mass in running order (MIRO)'. This can be misleading because it is normally based on the standard model and may not take into account any fitted extras; one way to be certain is to take the caravan to your local public weighbridge. Once you have the accurate unladen weight, subtract that from the manufacturer's recommended gross weight, ('maximum technically permissible weight' - MTPW) and the figure you arrive at will be the amount of equipment you can safely load into the caravan. Remember that, ideally, the gross weight of

the caravan should not exceed 85 per cent of the kerbside weight of your car as given in the manufacturer's handbook. If in doubt, return the caravan to the weighbridge once fully loaded.

Loading can greatly affect the stability of the car-caravan combination on the road. Keep as much weight as possible near the trailer axle, and store heavy equipment on the caravan floor. Never store heavy items at the rear of the caravan in an attempt to counterbalance an excessive nose weight - this causes instability and can be very dangerous. Keep the roof lockers free of luggage if possible and ensure lockers, drawers and cupboards are securely closed so there are no loose items that could roll about.

After loading, check that the caravan, when coupled to the car, is level with the ground, or slightly nose down. If the nose is up, this can be corrected by a hitch height adjuster, available from caravan manufacturers or dealers. An adapter plate can be used to lower the tow-ball mounting, but it does put extra pressure on the bracket.

Check that the nose weight of the trailer complies with the car manufacturer's recommendations. As a guide, the nose weight should be heavier than the rear by about 40-50kg (90-119lbs). Check the nose weight of the laden caravan with bathroom scales and blocks of wood or a spring balance. A twin-axle trailer must be weighed when the coupling is at the exact towing height. Obtaining the ideal weight and weight distribution of the car-trailer combination helps prevent pitching and snaking. Pitching can also be prevented by stiffening the towing car's rear suspension - either fit a supplementary rubber or air spring unit to the rear spring, or use heavier duty shock absorbers, (more expensive) but always ensure first that the car's front and rear shock absorbers are in good condition.

Excessive pitching and/or bad weight distribution can lead to snaking as the vertical movement sways the caravan sideways. This can be particularly dangerous, since the first instinct is to steer against the movement, which only makes matters worse. The best course is to steer straight and gently decelerate. Stabilisers are available, but it is far better to cure the cause.

When choosing a car with which you intend to tow a caravan or trailer, remember that the amount of overhang - the distance between the car's rear axle and the towing ball - has an effect on the handling. The greater the overhang the more difficult handling will be.

A FEW FINAL CHECKS

- corner steadies are fully wound up and the brace is handy for when you arrive on site;
- windows, vents and doors are firmly shut;
- any fires or flames are extinguished and the tap on the gas cylinder is turned off;
- the coupling is firmly in position and the breakaway cable is attached;
- the over-run brake is working correctly;
- both car mirrors give good visibility;
- all the car and caravan lights are working;
- the safety catch on the hitch is on;
- the jockey wheel is raised and secured, the handbrake is released, and the fire extinguishers are operational and close at hand.

Much of the art of towing comes with experience, but many of the problems can be eliminated by being aware:

- Know your car well before attempting to tow.
- Stop before you get tired.
- Plan to use roads suitable for towing.
- Have the appropriate mirrors and use them.
- If traffic builds up behind you, pull up safely and let it pass.
- Keep a safe stopping distance between you and the vehicle in front.
- Switch on your headlights whenever visibility becomes poor.
- Make good use of the gears on hills.
- Allow plenty of time when overtaking or pulling across a main road.
- Never stop on narrow roads, bends, crests of hills, or anywhere that could be dangerous.
- In case of breakdown or accident, use hazard flashers and warning triangle(s).

OFF-ROAD HANDLING

On site you may encounter difficult ground. Try to avoid pitches liable to be waterlogged; sand that will not take the force of a driving wheel; and stone and shingle that provide no grip.

If you have to drive over difficult ground, keep moving slowly with a very light throttle. If you stop, do not accelerate hard or the wheels will spin and dig in. Move gently backwards and forwards to get out of a dip. If the driving wheels do dig in, put brushwood or sacks in front of and behind the wheels. To move the trailer manually, pull sideways on the drawbar and then work the trailer forwards by chocking alternate wheels.

CAMPING FUELS

(This information is intended as a guide only. Full safety regulations and legal information should be obtained from the suppliers or manufacturers of your equipment.)

Gas in cylinders or bottles, as used in caravans, is mainly of two types, butane and propane. Both are kept as liquid under pressure and become a combustible gas once the pressure is released. They are available on the Continent, but propane is more widely distributed in countries with low winter temperatures. Propane has a higher pressure than butane. See also the paragraph on Branded Gases, below.

CARRIAGE OF GAS BY CAR FERRIES

Vehicles carrying unsealed cylinders of liquefied petroleum gas (LPG) must report at both United Kingdom and European ports for a leakage test at least 30 minutes before the published reporting time. A maximum of three Home Office approved cylinders, not exceeding 35lb net weight each, or up to 12 small expendable cartridges, sealed and packed in an outer container, are allowed for each caravan. Cylinders should be securely fixed in or on the caravan as intended by the caravan manufacturer.

New users of LPG particularly should follow safety instructions and experienced people sometimes need reminding of the safety rules:

• change cylinders with care

• provide fresh air for safe combustion

• don't improvise or tamper with equipment

• have regular maintenance carried out by qualified engineers

GAS SAFETY RULES

1   Always use the right type and length of hose for connections If in doubt, ask the dealer's advice.

2   Replace worn hose. Never try repairs.

3   When fitting the hose, where applicable use worm-drive clips and ensure they are tight.

4   Always use a spanner when fitting connections - finger tightness is not enough. Before fitting a regulator or other screwed connection to a butane cylinder, always ensure that the sealing washer is there and in good condition. When fitting to switch-on or clip-on valves, refer to the manufacturer's or supplier's instructions.

5 Check for leaks by applying soapy water. Any leaks will be shown by bubbles.

6 Never check for leaks with a naked flame.

7 Always keep containers away from excessive heat or naked flames.

8 When starting, open container valve slowly.

9 If the container is not to be used for a while close the valve, remove the pressure regulator and replace the valve cover if fitted.

10 When changing a cartridge or container, keep away from any naked light, flame or source of ignition. Ensure good ventilation. With cartridge appliances, check that the sealing washer, usually housed in the appliance inlet connection, is in position and in good condition. Make sure that the valve on the container, where fitted, and the tap on the regulator are fully closed. Never try to change a pierceable cartridge (such as the Camping Gaz type) until you are sure all the gas has been expended. You can usually hear any gas remaining by gently shaking.

11 Once the pressure regulators are set they should not be tampered with. Adjustments or repairs should be left to a dealer.

12 Containers must always stand upright, valves uppermost, whether in use or not. Carry them upright, but not by the valve.

13 Whether full or empty, never store the containers below ground or near drains, as all these gases are heavier than air and will collect at the lowest point in the event of a leak.

14 Good ventilation is essential where gas burning appliances are used. Un-flued appliances must not be installed in sleeping areas. Only room-sealed appliances should be installed in bath or shower rooms.

15 When moving, turn off all appliances and cylinder valves.

16 Do not sleep in a room where gas cylinders are in use.

17 Permanent storage must always be outdoors.

18 When fitting cylinders, always check that the cylinder valve is fully closed in a clockwise direction before removing the valve-sealing cap or plug.

Camping: Single-burner picnic set or double-burner camp stove with 4.5kg butane cylinder

Motor Caravan: Two-burner hotplate or two-burner hotplate grill with 4.5kg butane cylinder

Caravan: Two-burner hotplate or small cooker, with 4.5kg butane cylinder with screw-on connections or 15kg butane cylinder or 7kg butane cylinder which will both accept the switch-on regulator. Take two 4.5kg or two 7kg.

If you follow the instructions a 4.5kg cylinder will last a month on either single or double-burner units.

If you cannot take enough Calor Gas cylinders in your outfit, you are advised to buy a Camping Gaz connecting tap before leaving this country.

PARAFFIN

Paraffin (petrole or kerosene) is not easily obtainable in country districts in Europe and you are advised to get supplies on arrival in large towns. Methylated spirit (alcoöl à brûler) is easier to get.

Safety

- Always make sure you have the right size and type of gas cartridge for the appliance.

- Never put a cartridge in a cartridge holder unless the upper part of the appliance has been unscrewed and completely removed.

- A cartridge with gas in it must never be removed from an appliance nor must the upper part of the appliance be unscrewed.

Online Resources

Here are a selection of useful websites that may offer relevant information to campers, caravanners and travellers generally. These addresses are provided for information only, and The AA cannot be held responsible for the content of these websites.

CAMPING:

www.calorgas.co.uk
Official site of Calor Gas

www.lpga.co.uk
Offical site of LP Gas, suppliers of Liquid Petroleum Gas

www.caravanclub.co.uk
Site of Britain's major caravan club.

www.gear-zone.co.uk
Major suppliers of camping gear

www.campingeurope.com
Homepage of the European Federation of Campingsite Organisations (EFCO)

OFFICIAL UK GOVERNMENT SITES:

www.fco.gov.uk/travel
Site of the Foreign and Commonwealth Office. Travellers' rights, & 'Know Before You Go' info.

www.hmce.gov.uk
Official HM Customs & Excise website

www.passport.gov.uk
Passport Agency Website

www.defra.gov.uk/animalh/quarantine/index.htm
Official Pet Travel Site of DEFRA and info on quarantine conditions

EUROPEAN UNION ISSUES / THE EURO ETC:

europa.eu.int
Official site of the European Union On-Line

TOURIST SITES:

Austria: www.austria-tourism.at
Official Site of the Austrian National Tourist Office

Belgium: www.belgium-tourism.net
Official Site of the OPT (Office for the Promotion of Tourism in Walloon + Brussels)

www.visitflanders.com
Official Site of Toerisme Vlaanderen (Tourism Flanders)

France: www.franceguide.com
Official Site of the French Government Tourist Board/Maison de la France

Germany: www.germany-tourism.de
Official Site of the German National Tourist Board

Italy: www.enit.it
Official Site of the Italian State Tourism Board

Luxembourg: www.ont.lu
Official Site of the Luxembourg Tourist Office

Netherlands: www.holland.com
Official Site of Netherlands Board of Tourism

Portugal: www.portugal.org
and **www.portugalinsite.pt**
Official tourist sites

Spain: www.okspain.org
Official Site of the Tourist Office of Spain

Andorra: www.turisme.ad
Official Site of the Ministry of Tourism and Culture

Switzerland: www.myswitzerland.com
Official Site of Switzerland Tourism

Essential Information for Motoring in Europe

This feature provides a general background of motoring regulations and useful information, and it designed to be read in combination with the relevant country introductions. The information is grouped under these headings: Your Car: (Technical Motoring Issues); Your Car and The Law (Legal Motoring Issues); Travel Information (Useful Things to Know While Travelling Abroad); and You and The Law (General Legal Info)

Motoring laws on the Continent should cause little difficulty to British motorists, but drivers should take more care and extend greater courtesy than they would normally do at home, and bear in mind the essentials of good motoring - avoiding any action likely to obstruct traffic, endanger persons or cause damage to property.

Road signs are mainly the familiar international ones, but in every country there are exceptions; watch especially for signs showing crossings and speed limits. Probably the most unfamiliar aspect of motoring abroad to British motorists is the rule giving priority to traffic coming from the right, and unless this priority is varied by signs, it must be strictly observed.

A tourist driving abroad should always carry a current passport, a full valid national driving licence (even when an International Driving Permit is held), the vehicle registration document and certificate of motor insurance. The proper international distinguishing sign should be displayed on the rear of the vehicle and any caravan or trailer. (See also 'International Distinguishing Sign' pg18) The appropriate papers must be carried at all times. The practice of spot checks on foreign cars is widespread; to avoid a police fine and/or confiscation of your vehicle, be sure that your papers are in order and readily available for inspection.

Make sure that you have clear all-round vision. See that your seat belts are securely mounted and undamaged, and remember that in most Continental countries their use is compulsory. If you carry skis remember that their tips should point to the rear. You must be sure that your vehicle complies with the regulations concerning dimensions for all the countries you intend to pass through (see below and relevant country introductions). This is particularly necessary if you are towing a trailer of any sort.

Mechanical repairs and replacement parts can be very expensive abroad and many breakdowns occur because the vehicle has not been properly prepared before the journey, which may involve many miles of hard driving over unfamiliar roads.

We recommend a major service for your vehicle before you go abroad - to find your local AA Service Centre call 0845 609 1641. You should also carry out your own general check for any audible or visible defects.

Also consult your manufacturer's handbook.

AA members can arrange a thorough check of their car by one of the AA's experienced engineers who will submit a written report, complete with a list of repairs required. There is a fee for this service. For more information or, if you wish to book an inspection, please telephone 0845 750 0610.

Your Car and the Law

ACCIDENTS

The country introductions give telephone numbers for the fire, police and ambulance services. International regulations are similar to those in the UK; the following action is usually required or advisable:

If you are involved in an accident you must stop. A warning triangle should be placed on the road at a suitable distance to warn following traffic of the obstruction. The use of hazard warning lights in no way affects the regulations governing the use of warning triangles. Get medical assistance for anyone injured in the accident. If the accident necessitates calling the police, leave the vehicle in the position in which it came to rest. If it seriously obstructs other traffic, mark the position of the vehicle on the road and get the details confirmed by independent witnesses before moving it.

The accident must be reported to the police in the following circumstances: if it is required by law, if the accident has caused death or bodily injury, or if an unoccupied vehicle or property has been damaged and there is no one present to represent the interests of the party suffering damage.

Be sure to notify your insurance company (by letter if possible), within 24 hours of the accident (see the conditions of your policy). If a third party is injured, contact your insurers for advice or, if you have a Green Card, notify the company or bureau given on the back of your Green Card; this company or bureau will deal with any compensation claim from the injured party. AA policy holders should refer to 'AA Policy Holders Driving Abroad' statement. Make sure that all essential particulars are noted, especially details concerning third parties, and co-operate with police or other officials taking on-the-spot notes by supplying your name, address or other personal details as required. It is also a good idea to take photographs of the scene. Try to get good shots of other vehicles involved, their registration plates and any background which might help later enquiries. This record may be useful when completing the insurance company's accident form.

BREAKDOWN

If your car breaks down, try to move it to the side of the road, or to a position where it will obstruct the traffic flow as little as possible. Place a warning triangle at the appropriate distance on the road behind the obstruction. Bear in mind road conditions and, if near or on a bend, the triangle should be placed where it is clearly visible to following traffic. If the car is fitted with hazard warning lights these may only be effective on straight roads, and will have no effect at bends or rises in the road. If the fault is electrical, the lights may not operate, which is why they cannot take the place of a triangle.

Motorists are advised to take out AA European Breakdown Cover, the overseas motoring emergency service. You can purchase breakdown assistance benefits, and personal travel insurance. It is available to all motorists, but AA members receive 10% off standard non-member prices for breakdown assistance.

For further information and/or brochures call: 0800 444500

(Republic of Ireland: 01 617 9988).

CLAIMS AGAINST THIRD PARTIES

The law and levels of damages in foreign countries are different to our own. Some types of claim present difficulties, the most common relating to recovery of car hire charges. Rarely are they fully recoverable, and in some countries they may be drastically reduced or not recoverable at all. General damages for pain and suffering will often be considerably less than awards made in the UK.

The negotiation of claims against foreign insurers is extremely protracted and translation of documents slows the process. A delay of three months between sending a letter and getting a reply is not uncommon.

Legal costs and expenses are not recoverable in many Continental countries. The AA's overseas motoring emergency packages, such as European Breakdown Cover, include a discretionary service in certain matters arising abroad requiring legal assistance. This includes the pursuit of uninsured loss claims against third parties arising from an accident involving the insured vehicle. Policy holders should seek assistance from the AA.

DRIVING LICENCE AND INTERNATIONAL DRIVING PERMIT

You should always carry your national driving licence with you even when you hold an International Driving Permit (IDP). A driving licence issued in the UK or Republic of Ireland is generally acceptable, subject to the minimum age requirements of the country concerned, but see also the individual country introductions for Italy and Spain, under 'Driving Licence', if you hold a UK licence.

If you wish to drive a hired or borrowed car in the country you are visiting, make local enquiries. If your licence is due to expire before your return, renew it in good time prior to your departure. The Driver and Vehicle Licensing Agency (DVLA) will accept an application two months before the expiry of your old licence; Driver and Vehicle Licensing Northern Ireland (DVLNI) will accept an application for renewal two months before expiry of your old licence, but also offer "Optional Renewal", unique to Northern Ireland. Under this option the holder of a valid licence may apply for renewal at any stage during its validity; in the Republic of Ireland, one month before expiry.

The IDP, for which a statutory charge is made, is issued by the AA to an applicant who holds a valid full British driving licence and who is over 18. Call the AA on 0870 5500 600 for advice or to get an application form.

VEHICLE LICENCE

When taking a vehicle out of the UK for a temporary visit remember that the vehicle licence (tax disc) needs to be valid on your return*. If it will expire while you are abroad, you can apply for a new one up to 42 days in advance of the expiry date on your present disc. Apply in writing to either a Post Office that deals with postal applications (if a vehicle registration document is enclosed) or to a DVLA Local Office. You should explain why you want it in advance, and ask for it to be posted to you before you leave, or to your address

abroad. However, your application form must always be completed with your UK address.

To find out which post office in your area offers this service, you should contact Post Office Customer Services Unit listed in your local telephone directory.

Residents of Northern Ireland must apply to Driver and Vehicle Licensing Northern Ireland, Vehicle Licensing Division, County Hall, Castlerock Road, Coleraine BT51 3TA. Residents of the Republic of Ireland should contact their Local Motor Tax Office.

*Agreement within the EU provides for the temporary use of foreign-registered vehicles within the member states. A vehicle which is properly registered and taxed in its home country should not be subject to the domestic taxation and registration laws of the host country during a temporary stay.

REGISTRATION DOCUMENT

You must take the registration document with you. The document should be in your name and kept with you. If you do not have a registration document, apply to a DVLA Local Office (in Republic of Ireland, Motor Tax) for a temporary certificate of registration (V379) to cover the period away. The address of your nearest DVLA Local Office is in the local telephone directory or in leaflet V100, available from post offices. You should apply well in advance of your journey, as it may take up to two weeks to issue the document if you are not already recorded as the vehicle keeper. Proof of identity (e.g. driving licence) and proof of ownership (e.g. bill of sale), should be produced for the DVLA Local Office.

In Northern Ireland contact Vehicle Licensing Division, County Hall, Castlerock Road, Colerain, BT51 3TA. Tel: 028 7034 1461 for further information.

If you plan to use a borrowed vehicle, the registration document must be accompanied by a letter of authority to use the vehicle from the registered keeper. If you plan to use a hired or leased vehicle, the registration document will not normally be available and you will need a Vehicle on Hire Certificate (VE103A). Generally the hiring/leasing operator or company transport manager will provide the certificate, but individual users may apply direct if necessary. For advice on the procedure to follow for personal or postal applications or for an application form, call the AA Information Centre on 0870 5500 600.

MOTOR INSURANCE

When driving abroad you must carry your certificate of motor insurance with you at all times. Third-party is the minimum legal requirement in most countries. Therefore, before taking a motor vehicle, caravan or trailer abroad, contact your motor insurer or broker to notify them of your intentions and ask their advice. Some insurers will extend your UK or Republic of Ireland motor policy to apply in the countries you plan to visit free of charge, others may charge an additional premium. It is most important to know the level of cover you will actually have and what documents you will need to prove it.

Of the countries covered by this guide, a Green Card is compulsory in Andorra. This document is issued by your motor insurer and provides instantly recognisable proof of insurance. The Green Card must be signed on receipt as it will not be accepted without the signature of the insured.

Motorists can obtain advice through AA Insurance Services for all types of insurance, including caravan. More information is available by contacting us on 0800 444 777 for a quotation; existing customers should contact 0870 533 6600, or alternatively visit our website at **www.theAA.com**.

Finally, do check to make sure that you are covered against damage in transit (e.g. on the ferry) when the vehicle is not being driven.

CARAVAN AND LUGGAGE TRAILERS

Take a list of contents, especially if any valuable or unusual equipment is being carried, as this may be required at a frontier. A towed vehicle should be readily identifiable by a plate in an accessible position showing the name of the maker of the vehicle and the production or serial number. See 'Identification Plate' (pg18) and also 'Principal Mountain Passes' (pg37).

CYCLE CARRIERS

If you intend taking your bicycles on a rear-mounted cycle rack, make sure that they do not obstruct rear lights and/or number plate, or you risk an on-the-spot fine. The AA recommends roof-mounted racks.

COMPULSORY EQUIPMENT

All countries have differing regulations as to how vehicles circulating on their roads should be equipped, but generally domestic laws are not enforced on visiting foreigners. However, where a country considers aspects of safety or other factors are involved, they will impose some regulations on visitors and these will be mentioned in the country introductions.

CRASH (SAFETY) HELMETS

All countries in this guide require visiting motorcyclists and their passengers to wear crash or safety helmets.

DIMENSIONS AND WEIGHT RESTRICTIONS

For an ordinary private car, a height limit of 4 metres and a width limit of 2.50 metres are generally imposed. However, see country introductions for full details. Apart from a laden-weight limit imposed on commercial vehicles, every vehicle has an individual weight limit. See 'Overloading' (pg19) and also 'Major Road and Rail Tunnels' (pg47) as some dimensions are restricted by the shape of the tunnels.

DRINKING AND DRIVING

There is only one safe rule – if you drink, don't drive. Laws are strict and the penalties severe.

HORN

In built-up areas, the general rule is that you should not use it unless safety demands it: in many large towns and resorts, and in areas indicated by the international sign (a horn inside a red circle, crossed through) use of the horn is totally banned.

IDENTIFICATION PLATE

If a boat trailer, caravan or trailer is taken abroad, it must have a unique chassis number for identification purposes. If yours does not have a number, you can buy an identification plate from the AA. Boats registered on the Small Ships Register (see 'Boats' (pg31)) have a unique number which must be permanently displayed on the boat.

INTERNATIONAL DISTINGUISHING SIGN

An international distinguishing sign of the approved pattern, and size (oval with black letters on a white background; GB at least 6.9in by 4.5in), must be displayed on a vertical surface at the rear of your vehicle (and caravan or trailer if you are towing one). These signs indicate the country of registration of the vehicle. On the Continent, fines are imposed for failing to display a distinguishing sign, or for not displaying the correct distinguishing sign. See also 'Police Fines' (pg21).

UK registration plates displaying the GB Euro-symbol (Euro-

Plates) became a legal option in March 2001, but must comply with the British standard (BS AU 145d). These plates make display of a conventional sticker unnecessary when circulating within the EU. The Euro-Plate is only legally recognised in the EU; it is still a requirement to display a GB sticker when travelling outside the EU.

A GB sign, or an AA Motoring Abroad Kit which includes one, may be purchased from the AA's Dover shop (Eastern Docks Terminal) or, if travelling via Eurotunnel, the AA's Folkestone shop (Eurotunnel Passenger Terminal).

MINIBUS

A minibus constructed and equipped to carry 10 or more persons (including the driver) and used outside the UK is subject to the regulations governing international bus and coach journeys, including controls on drivers' hours. Such vehicles must weigh no more than 3.5 tonnes (gross vehicle weight) or 4.25 tonnes including any specialist equipment for the carriage of disabled passengers. The vehicle must be fitted with a tachograph (except for journeys between UK and Republic of Ireland) and carry documentation to show the type of journey being made. The documentation requirements are determined by whether the vehicle is owned or hired and countries to be visited, as follows:

a) **Outside EU** (except Norway and Switzerland) - hired minibus taken outside EU into ASOR covered country requires model control document (set of translations) and ASOR waybills. For other kinds of tours or journeys to countries outside the EU, contact:

The Dept for Transport, Road Freight Operations Policy, Zone 2/23, Great Minster House, 76 Marsham Street, London SW1P 4DR, phone 020 7944 2774 for advice.

b) **Inside EU** - own account certificate (owned vehicle); (new type) EU passenger waybills (hired vehicle).

For vehicles registered and driven by holders of licences issued in UK (England, Scotland, Wales and Northern Ireland), contact:

a) Confederation of Passenger Transport

UK, Imperial House, 15-19 Kingsway, London WC2B 6UN phone 020 7240 3131 for model control document and waybills.

b) Department for Transport, International Road Freight Office, Eastgate House, Kings Manor, Newcastle-upon-Tyne, NE1 6PB phone 0191 201 4036 for own account certificate.

A person of 21 years or over and holding a car driving licence with D1 restricted entitlement (i.e. not for hire or reward) may drive a 17 seat (including the driver) minibus abroad, providing that it is not a hire or reward operation. See Section 1 (5) of the Public Passenger Vehicles Act 1981 for a definition of 'hire or reward'. As a result of subsequent court rulings, that definition has been further refined to encompass situations in which there is payment:

- of cash or kind

- whether paid directly or indirectly

- whether paid by the passenger or someone else on their behalf

- even when paid in the course of an arrangement which is a business activity or an activity which has a 'business-like' nature (i.e. is rather more than a 'one-off' social arrangement).

The effect of this is that most trips abroad by school or scout troops or similar organisations, running a minibus, could very likely be classed by the courts as 'hire or reward' operations for which full D1 driving licence entitlement is needed. In general, where an organisation is operating a minibus in the UK under a Section 19 'small bus' permit (as issued by the Traffic Area Offices) then this would almost certainly be regarded by the Courts as 'hire or reward'. Drivers involved in such operations are, therefore, advised to obtain a full D1 licence before taking the minibus abroad. To do this they will need to pass

separate driving and theory tests for minibus at their local driving tests centre. Drivers or organisers are also advised in any event to check the position with their insurance company.

For vehicles registered in the Republic of Ireland, contact the Department of Transport, Road Haulage Section, Setanta Centre, South Frederick Street, Dublin 2 for details about tachographs, and the Government Publications Sales Office, Molesworth Street, Dublin 2 for information on documentation.

BLUE (FORMERLY ORANGE) BADGE SCHEME FOR DRIVERS & PASSENGERS WITH DISABILITIES

A standard blue parking badge for disabled people has been introduced throughout the European Union. In the UK, the Blue Badge was introduced on 1 April 2000 and phased in over 3 years. This has now replaced the old style Orange Badge.

All EU Member States now operate the Blue Badge Scheme and there are reciprocal arrangements in place whereby badge holders across the EU can enjoy the parking concessions provided in the host country by displaying the badge issued under their own national scheme. To obtain a booklet outlining details of these reciprocal arrangements, call the AA on 0800 262050 or contact Department for Transport, Mobility and Inclusion Unit, 1/18 Great Minster House, 76 Marsham Street, London SW1P 4DR. The information is also available on the DFT website: http://www.mobility-unit.dft.gov.uk/bluebadge

However, the concessions do vary from country to country and you should always check local notices to ensure that you are parking within the law. As in the UK, these arrangements apply only to badge holders themselves and are not for the benefit of non-disabled companions. Wrongful display of the badge may incur whatever local penalties are imposed.

OVERLOADING

This can create risks, and in most countries the offence can involve on-the-spot fines (see Police fines pg21). You would also be made to reduce the load to an acceptable level before being allowed to continue your journey.

The maximum loaded weight, and its distribution between front and rear axles, is decided by the vehicle manufacturer, and if your owner's handbook does not give these facts, contact the manufacturer direct. There is a public weighbridge in all districts, and when the car is fully loaded (including driver and passengers) use this to check that the vehicle is within the limits.

Load your vehicle carefully so that no lights, reflectors, or number plates are masked, and the driver's view is not impaired. All luggage loaded on a roof-rack must be tightly secured, and should not exceed the manufacturer's recommended maximum limit. Any projections beyond the front, rear, or sides of a vehicle, that may not be noticed by other drivers, must be clearly marked. Limits apply to projections and may vary from country to country.

OVERTAKING

When overtaking on roads with two lanes or more in each direction, signal in good time, and also signal your return to the inside lane. Do not remain in any other lane. Failure to comply with this regulation, particularly in France, will incur an on-the-spot fine (immediate deposit in France) - see Police fines (pg21).

Always overtake on the left and use your horn to warn the driver (except where the use of a horn is banned). Do check the vehicles behind before overtaking. Do not overtake at level crossings, intersections, the crest of a hill or pedestrian crossings. When being overtaken, keep to the right and reduce speed if necessary.

PARKING

Parking is a problem everywhere in Europe, and the police are strict with offenders. Heavy fines are imposed and unaccompanied offending cars can be towed away. Heavy charges are imposed for the recovery of impounded vehicles. Find out about local parking regulations and make sure you understand all related signs. Always park on the right-hand side of the road or at an authorised place. If possible, park off the main carriageway, but not in cycle or bus lanes.

PASSENGERS

In many countries outside the UK, it is an offence to carry more passengers in a vehicle than the vehicle is constructed to seat, and some have regulations as to how the passengers should be seated. For information about regulations applied to visiting foreigners, see country introductions.

Special regulations (see Minibus pg18) apply to passenger-carrying vehicles constructed and equipped to carry more than 10 passengers, including the driver.

POLICE FINES

Some countries impose on-the-spot fines for minor traffic offences. Others (e.g. France) impose an immediate deposit, and subsequently levy a fine which may be the same as, or greater or lesser than, this sum. Fines are normally paid in cash in the local currency, either to the police or at a local post office against a ticket issued by the police. The amount can exceed the equivalent of £1000 for the most serious offences. The reason for the fines is to penalise, and to keep minor motoring offences out of the courts.

Disputing the fine usually leads to a court appearance, delays and expense. If the fine is not paid, legal proceedings will usually follow. Some countries immobilise vehicles until a fine is paid, and may sell it to pay the penalty.

Once paid, a fine cannot be recovered, but a receipt should always be obtained as proof of payment.

PRIORITY INCLUDING ROUNDABOUTS
(See also country introductions)

The general rule is to give way to traffic entering a junction from the right, but this is sometimes varied at roundabouts (see below). Road signs indicate priority or loss of priority, and tourists must be sure that they understand such signs.

Great care should be taken at intersections, and tourists should never rely on being ceded the right of way, particularly in small towns and villages where local, often slow moving, traffic - farm tractors etc., will assume right of way regardless of oncoming traffic. Always give way to public services and military vehicles, blind and disabled people, funerals and marching columns. Vehicles such as buses and coaches will expect, and should be allowed, priority.

Generally, priority at roundabouts is given to vehicles entering the roundabout unless signposted to the contrary (see France). This is a reversal of the UK and Republic of Ireland rule, and particular care should be exercised when circulating in an anti-clockwise direction on a roundabout. It is advisable to keep to the outside lane if possible, to make your exit easier.

RADIO TELEPHONE/CITIZENS' BAND RADIOS, TRANSMITTERS AND DETECTION DEVICES

Many countries control the temporary importation and use of radio telephones and radio transmitters. If your vehicle contains such equipment, whether fitted or portable, approach the AA for guidance before departure.

The use or even possession of devices, whether inside or outside vehicles, to detect police radar speed traps is illegal in most countries. Penalties are severe, including confiscation of the equipment, payment of an immediate deposit to serve as collateral against any fine subsequently levied, and/or a driving ban. Finally, if the case is viewed sufficiently seriously, confiscation of vehicle and even imprisonment may result.

ROAD SIGNS

Most road signs throughout Europe conform to international standards and most will be familiar. Watch for road markings - do not cross a solid white or yellow line marked on the road centre. In Belgium there are three official languages, and signs will be in Dutch, French or German, see Belgian country information under Roads for further information. In the Basque and Catalonian areas of Spain local and national place names appear on signposts, see the country introduction for Spain for further information.

RULE OF THE ROAD

In all countries in this guide, drive on the right and overtake on the left.

SEAT BELTS

All countries in this guide require wearing of seat belts.

SPEED LIMITS

It is important to observe speed limits at all times. Remember that it can be an offence to travel so slowly as to obstruct traffic flow without good reason. Offenders may be fined, and driving licences confiscated on the spot, causing great inconvenience and possible expense.

The standard legal limits are given in the appropriate country introductions for private cars, for motor cycles and for car-caravan-trailer combinations, but these may be varied by road signs, and where such signs are displayed the lower limit applies. At certain times, limits may also be temporarily varied, so watch out for the appropriate signs.

TRAFFIC LIGHTS

In principal cities and towns, traffic lights operate in a way similar to those in the United Kingdom, although they are sometimes suspended over the roadway. The density of the light may be so poor that lights could be missed - especially those overhead. There is usually only one set on the right-hand side of the road some distance before the road junction, and if you stop too close to the corner the lights will not be visible. Look out for 'filter' lights enabling you to turn right at a junction against the main lights. If you wish to go straight ahead, do not enter a lane leading to 'filter' lights or you may obstruct traffic trying to turn right.

TRAMS

Trams take priority over other vehicles. Always give way to passengers boarding and alighting. Never position a vehicle so that it impedes the free passage of a tram. Trams must be overtaken on the right, except in one-way streets.

You and Your Car

AUTOMATIC GEARBOXES

The fluid in an automatic gearbox does more work when it has to cope with the extra weight of a caravan. It becomes hotter and thinner, so there is more slip and more heat generated in the gearbox. Many manufacturers recommend the fitting of a gearbox oil cooler. Check with the manufacturer about what is suitable for your car.

AUTOMATIC TRANSMISSION FLUID

Automatic transmission fluid is not always readily available, especially in some of the more remote areas of Western Europe, so carry an emergency supply.

BRAKES

Car brakes must always be in peak condition. Check both the level in the brake fluid reservoir and the thickness of the brake lining/pad material. The brake fluid should be completely changed according to the manufacturer's instructions. It is always advisable to change the brake fluid before starting a Continental holiday, particularly if the journey includes travelling through a hilly or mountainous area.

COLD-WEATHER TOURING

If you are planning a winter tour, make sure that the strength of the antifreeze in your coolant is correct for low temperatures.

If travelling through snow-bound regions, it is important to remember that for many resorts and passes the authorities insist on wheel chains and/or winter tyres. However, chains should only be used when compulsory or necessary, prolonged use on hard surfaces may damage both the vehicle and the chains.

In fair weather, wheel chains are only necessary on the higher passes, but (as a rough guide) in severe weather you will probably need them at altitudes exceeding 610 metres (2000ft). Signposts usually indicate if wheelchains are compulsory.

Wheel or snow chains fit over the driving wheels to enable them to grip on snow or icy surfaces. Full-length chains which fit tightly round a tyre are the most satisfactory, but they must be fitted correctly. Check that they do not foul your vehicle bodywork; if your vehicle has front-wheel drive put the steering on full lock while checking. It is essential that you also check the vehicle's handbook

for the manufacturer's recommendations. On some vehicles there is insufficient clearance between the tyre and bodywork and wheel chains cannot be used. Wheel or snow chains may be purchased from the AA's Dover and Eurotunnel shops. To check that the required size of chain is in stock, telephone Dover on 01304 208122 or Eurotunnel on 01303 273576. Winter or snow tyres are tyres with rugged treads which provide extra grip on snow and ice. Some are designed to take spikes or studs which require specialist fitting and removal limiting their use. In practice, although regulations exist, spikes or studs are seldom used in countries such as Austria and Switzerland. A vehicle equipped with winter tyres without spikes or studs may be used in all conditions. However, the use of winter tyres does not remove the need to carry chains; such tyres are generally more effective, reducing the need to fit chains. If you travel regularly to Alpine regions it may be worth considering a set of winter tyres. Contact your local tyre dealer for more information.

NOTE: The above guidelines do not apply where extreme winter conditions prevail. For extreme conditions it is doubtful whether the cost of preparing a car normally used in the UK would be justified for a short period.

WARM-CLIMATE TOURING

In hot weather and at high altitude, excessive heat in the engine compartment can cause problems. If towing a caravan, consult the manufacturers of your vehicle about the limitations of the cooling system, and the operating temperature of the gearbox fluid for automatics (see Automatic Gearboxes pg23).

DIRECTION INDICATORS

All direction indicators should be working at between 60 and 120 flashes per minute. Most standard car-flasher units will be overloaded by the extra lamps of a caravan or trailer, and a special heavy duty unit or relay device should be fitted.

ENGINE AND MECHANICAL SERVICING

Consult your vehicle handbook for servicing intervals. Unless the engine oil has been changed recently, drain and refill it with fresh oil and fit a new filter. Deal with any leaks.

Brands and grades of engine oil familiar to the British motorist are usually available in Western Europe, but may be difficult to find in remote country areas. When available, they will be much more expensive than in the UK and are generally packed in 2-litre cans (3.5 pints). Motorists are strongly advised to carry a sufficient supply of oil, especially for modern makes of car that require special oils.

If you suspect that there is anything wrong with the engine - even if it seems insignificant - it should be dealt with immediately. And do not neglect such common-sense precautions as checking all drive belts and under bonnet levels.

Any obvious mechanical defects should be attended to at once. It is essential that all filters (fuel and air) should be cleaned or renewed.

The cooling system should be checked for leaks and the proportion of anti-freeze, and any perished hoses or suspect parts replaced.

Owners should seriously reconsider towing a caravan with a car that has already given appreciable service. Hard driving on motorways and in mountainous country puts an extra strain on ageing parts, and items such as a burnt-out clutch can be very expensive.

FIRE EXTINGUISHER

It is a wise precaution to take a fire extinguisher when motoring abroad. AA fire extinguishers may be purchased from the AA's Dover Shop (Eastern Docks Terminal) or, if travelling via Eurotunnel, the AA's Folkestone shop (Eurotunnel Passenger Terminal).

FIRST-AID KIT

It is a wise precaution (compulsory in Austria) to carry a first-aid kit when motoring abroad. An AA First-Aid Kit or an AA Motoring Abroad Kit, which includes a first-aid kit, can be purchased from the AA's Dover Shop (Eastern Docks Terminal) or, if travelling via Eurotunnel, the AA's Folkestone shop (Eurotunnel Passenger Terminal). See also 'Motoring Abroad Kit'. (pg25)

LIGHTS

(See also country introductions)

For driving abroad headlights should be adjusted so that the dipped beam does not dazzle oncoming drivers. For older vehicles this can be done using simple adhesive masks on the headlamp glass, but for newer vehicles with high intensity discharge (HID), xenon or many halogen headlamps things aren't so simple. Check out what you can do well before your intended departure by contacting your dealer.

Dipped headlights should also be used in fog, snowfall, heavy rain and in a tunnel, irrespective of its length and lighting. Police may wait at the end of a tunnel to check. Headlight flashing is used only to signal approach or as an overtaking signal at night. In other circumstances, it is taken as a sign of irritation, and may lead to misunderstandings.

Of the countries covered by the guide it is recommended (compulsory in Andorra and Spain) to carry a spare bulb kit. This will not avoid a fine if you are travelling with faulty lights, but being able to replace a bulb on the spot may avoid the cost and inconvenience of a garage call-out. On some cars it is inadvisable or indeed impossible for anyone other than a qualified technician to change a headlamp bulb or lamp unit (eg. High intensity discharge (HID) lamps), and carrying spare bulbs is not an option. However, it is recommended that spare bulbs are carried for any lights which may be easily and/or safely replaced.

AA Headlamp Beam Converters and/or AA Bulb Kits or an AA Motoring Abroad Kit, which includes converters and bulbs, may be purchased from the AA's Dover shop (Eastern Docks Terminal) or, if travelling via Eurotunnel, the AA's Folkestone shop (Eurotunnel Passenger Terminal). See also 'Motoring Abroad Kit'. (pg25)

LUGGAGE OR ROOF RACKS
Only use equipment suitable for your vehicle, i.e., approved by the vehicle manufacturer. Distribute the load evenly, taking care not to exceed the vehicle manufacturer's roof rack load limit. A roof rack laden with luggage increases fuel consumption, so remember this when calculating mileage per gallon, and it also reduces stability, especially when cornering.

MIRRORS
When driving or towing on the right, it is essential to have clear all-round vision. Ideally, external rear-view mirrors should be fitted to both sides of your vehicle, but certainly on the left, to allow for driving on the right.

When towing a caravan it is essential to fit mirror accessories for better rear vision. These include clip-on extensions, arms to extend wing mirrors, and long-arm wing or door mirrors. The longer the mirror arm, the

more rigid its mounting has to be. Some have supporting legs or extra brackets to minimise vibration. A mirror mounted on the door pillar gives a wide field of vision because it is close to the driver, but it is at a greater angle to the forward line of sight. Convex mirrors give an even wider field of vision, but practice is needed in judging distance due to the diminished image.

MOTORING ABROAD KIT
An AA Motoring Abroad Kit has all the essential motoring accessories you require for the countries covered by this guide. Available from the AA's Dover shop (Eastern Docks Terminal) or, if travelling via Eurotunnel, the AA's Folkestone shop (Eurotunnel Passenger Terminal); the kit comprises a nylon holdall with bulb kit, first-aid kit, GB sticker, headlamp beam converters and warning triangle.

PETROL/DIESEL
You will find familiar brands and comparable grades of petrol along the main routes in most countries. However, remember that leaded petrol is no longer generally available in northern European countries. If a lead-replacement petrol (LRP) is not on sale, an anti-wear additive may be bought from a filling station shop; this should be used in accordance with the instructions if your car requires this protection. The sale of leaded petrol continues in some southern European countries, but not in Italy, Portugal and Spain.

You will normally have to buy a minimum of 5 litres (just over a gallon) but it is wise to keep the tank topped up, particularly in more remote areas. When calculating mileage per gallon, don't forget that the extra weight of a caravan or roof rack increases petrol consumption. It is best to use a locking filler cap. Some garages may close between 12.00hrs and 15.00hrs, but petrol is generally available, with 24-hour service on motorways. Prices for petrol on motorways will normally be higher than elsewhere. Make sure you know the fuel requirement of the vehicle before you go (LRP, unleaded premium, unleaded super or diesel) and whether or not the car has an exhaust catalyst. Catalyst-equipped petrol cars will usually have a small fuel filler neck, to prevent the use of the larger sized nozzle dispensing LRP. If in doubt, check with a franchised dealer, or with the AA.

Some countries are supplying 97 octane unleaded petrol either in addition to, or instead of, 95 octane. The name may be 'super plus' or 'premium' but look for the octane rating 97. You should be careful to use the recommended type of fuel, particularly if your car has a catalytic converter, and the octane rating should be the same or higher. If you accidentally fill the tank of a catalyst-equipped car with LRP, it will do no harm; simply go back to normal petrol at the next fill. If your car requires LRP and you fill with unleaded, avoid hard use of the engine until about half the tank is used, then fill with an additised lead-substitute petrol or dose the fuel with an anti-wear additive.

Diesel fuel is generally known as 'diesel' or 'gas-oil'. Although readily available it is probably more inconvenient to run out of diesel, and it is wise to keep the tank topped up. If petrol is accidentally put into the tank of a diesel car (or vice versa), the action you need to take depends on the age and engine type of the vehicle. Some modern cars have no tolerance to such mis-fuelling and the tank must be drained and refilled with the correct fuel before the engine is started.

NOTE: Importing fuel.
While you may wish to carry a reserve supply of fuel in a can, remember that all operators (ferry, motorail etc.) will either forbid the carriage of fuel in spare cans or insist that spare cans must be empty. In Luxembourg motorists are forbidden to carry petrol in cans in the vehicle. If your vehicle has LPG or a dual fuel system - check. Eurotunnel and underground car parks in France don't allow LPG fuelled vehicles.

SPARES
The spares you should carry depend on the vehicle and how long you are likely to be away. Useful items include a pair of windscreen wiper blades, spare fuses, bulbs (see 'Lights' pg24) and a torch.

Remember that when ordering spare parts for dispatch abroad, you must be able to identify them clearly - by the manufacturer's part numbers if known. Always quote your engine and vehicle identification (VIN).

TYRES
Inspect your tyres carefully: if you notice uneven wear, scuffed treads, or damaged walls, get expert advice on whether the tyres are suitable for further use.

The regulations in the UK governing tyres requires a minimum tread depth of 1.6mm over the central three-quarters of the tyre around the whole circumference. Most western European countries have similar or stricter requirements. However, the AA strongly advises against using tyres with 2mm or less of tread, ideally changing any tyres worn down to 3mm before you go. Tyres wear out quickly when down to 3mm and wet grip is markedly reduced.

Check the car handbook for recommended tyre pressures. Different tyre pressures will be recommended for a fully loaded car travelling at motorway speeds. Remember pressures can only be checked accurately when the tyres are cold, and don't forget the spare wheel.

If towing a caravan find out the recommended tyre pressures from the caravan manufacturer. These will vary with the type and size of tyre. For winter or snow tyres see Cold-weather touring (pg23).

Tolls

Tolls are payable on most motorways in France, Italy, Portugal, Spain and on sections in Austria. Over long distances,

the toll charges can be quite considerable. Compare the cost against time and convenience (e.g., overnight stops), particularly as some of the all-purpose roads are often fast.

Always have some local currency ready to pay the tolls, as travellers cheques etc. are not acceptable at toll booths. Credit cards are accepted at toll booths in France and Spain.

In Austria and Switzerland authorities levy a tax for use of motorway netways in France, Italy, Portugal, Spain and on sections in Austria.

See under Motorway tax in the respective country introduction for further information.

Warning Triangles & Hazard Warning Lights

The use of a warning triangle is compulsory in most Continental countries. It should be placed on the road behind a stopped vehicle to warn traffic approaching from the rear. The triangle should be used when a vehicle has stopped for any reason - not just breakdowns. It should be clearly visible from up to 100m (109yds) by day and

night, about 60cm (2ft) from the edge of the road, but not in such a position as to be a danger to oncoming traffic. It should be set up about 30m (33yds) behind the obstruction, but this distance should be increased to 100m (109yds) on motorways.

A warning triangle is not required for two-wheeled vehicles.

An AA Warning Triangle, or an AA Motoring Abroad Kit, which includes a warning triangle, may be purchased from the AA's Dover shop (Eastern Docks Terminal) or, if travelling via Eurotunnel, the AA's Folkestone shop (Eurotunnel Passenger Terminal). See also 'Motoring Abroad Kit' (pg25).

Although four flashing indicators are allowed in the countries covered by this guide, they do not affect the regulations governing warning triangles. Generally, hazard warning lights should not be used in place of a triangle, although they may complement it. See the country introductions for France, Netherlands and Switzerland. See also Breakdown (pg15).

You and the Law

Travelling Within The EU

People travelling within the EU are free to take not only personal belongings but a motor vehicle, boat, caravan or trailer across the internal frontiers without being subject to Customs formalities. EU countries are: Austria, Belgium, Denmark, Finland, France, Germany, Greece, Republic of Ireland, Italy, Luxembourg, Netherlands, Portugal, Spain (but not the Canaries), Sweden, UK (but not the Channel Islands). Gibraltar is part of the EU, but Customs allowances for outside the EU apply.

When you return to the UK, use the blue exit reserved for EU travellers. You do not have to pay any tax or duty in the UK on goods you have bought in other EU countries for your own use, but you may be breaking the law if you sell alcohol or tobacco you have bought. If you are caught you face imprisonment, and/or confiscation of the goods and the vehicle in which they were transported. To help protect people in the UK, Customs carry out checks on some EU travellers to look for prohibited or restricted goods, including drugs, indecent or obscene material, firearms, ammunition, unlicensed animals and endangered species. This means they may ask you about your

baggage. The law sets out guidelines for the amount of alcohol and tobacco you can bring into the UK. If you bring in more, you must be able to satisfy the Customs Officer that the goods are for your own use. If you cannot, the goods may be taken from you, and your vehicle may also be seized. The guidelines are; 800 cigarettes, 400 cigarillos, 200 cigars, 1kg smoking tobacco, 10 litres spirits, 20 litres fortified wine, 90 litres wine, 110 litres beer. People under 17 are not allowed to bring in alcohol or tobacco.

Travelling to the UK from outside the EU

When you enter the UK from a non-EU country, or from an EU country having travelled through a non-EU country, you must pass through Customs. If you have any goods over the allowance, or if you are not sure what to declare you must use the Red Channel or the phone provided at the Red Point. If you do not declare items on which you should pay duty you are breaking the law and Customs may prosecute you. Customs allowances for travellers from outside the EU are:

Tobacco: 200 cigarettes or 100 cigarillos or 50 cigars or 250gms tobacco.

Wines & Spirits: 2 litres still table wine and 1 litre of spirits or strong liqueurs over 22% volume or 2 litres fortified wine, sparkling wine or other liqueurs.

Perfume: 60cc/ml of perfume and 250cc/ml of toilet water.

Other goods: £145 worth of all other goods including gifts and souvenirs.

All dutiable articles must be declared when you enter the UK from a non-EU country. Articles not properly declared may be forfeit, and if they are hidden in a vehicle that vehicle may also be forfeit. Customs Officers are legally entitled to examine your baggage and you are responsible for unpacking and repacking it. If you require further information, Customs Notice 1 "A Customs Guide for Travellers entering the UK" is available at UK points of entry and exit or by phoning 0845 010 9000. Additionally, information may be obtained from the HM Customs & Excise website at:

www.hmce.gov.uk

Travelling outside the EU

If, when leaving the UK, you take any items bought in the UK which are high value or look very new it is a good idea to carry the retailers' receipts with you as foreign Customs may wish to confirm where the goods were obtained.

Bona fide visitors to non-EU countries may generally assume

that they may temporarily import personal articles duty free, providing the following conditions are met:

- that the articles are for personal use, and are not to be sold or otherwise disposed of;

- that they may be considered as being in use, and in keeping with the personal status of the importer;

- that they are taken out when the importer leaves the country;

- that the goods stay for no more than 6 months in any 12 month period, whichever is the earlier.

All dutiable articles must be declared when you enter a country, or you will be liable to penalties. If you will be taking a large number of personal effects with you, it would be wise to prepare an inventory to present to the Customs authorities on entry. Customs officers may withhold concessions at any time and ask travellers to deposit enough money to cover possible duty, especially on portable items of apparent high value such as television sets, radios, cassette recorders, portable computers, musical instruments, etc., all of which must be declared. Any deposit paid (for which a receipt must be obtained) is likely to be high: it is recoverable on leaving the country and exporting the item but only at the entry point at which it was paid. Alternatively the Customs may enter the item in the traveller's passport; if this happens it is important to get the entry cancelled when the item is exported. Duty and tax-free

allowances may not apply if travellers enter the country more than once a month, or are under 17 years of age (other ages may apply in some countries). Residents of the Channel Islands and the Isle of Man do not benefit from EU allowances because of their fiscal policies.

A temporarily imported motor vehicle, boat, caravan, or any other type of trailer is subject to strict control on entering a country, attracting Customs duty and a variety of taxes: much depends upon the circumstances and the period of the import, and also upon the status of the importer. Non-residents entering a country with a private vehicle for holiday or recreational purposes who intend to export the vehicle within a short period enjoy special privileges, and minimal formalities in the interests of tourism.

A temporarily imported vehicle, etc., should not:

- be left in the country after the importer has left;

- be put at the disposal of a resident of the country;

- be retained in the country longer than the permitted period; or

- be lent, sold, hired, given away, exchanged or otherwise disposed of.

Generally, people entering a country with a motor vehicle to stay for a period of more than six months (see also Visa pg30), or who intend to take up residence, employment, any commercial activity or who intend to dispose of the vehicle should seek advice concerning their position well in advance of their departure. The AA Information Centre can give advice to members; for assistance, telephone 0870 5500 600.

Additionally the importation of certain goods into the UK is prohibited or restricted.

PASSPORTS

Each person must hold, or be named on, a valid passport. Always carry your passport and, as an extra precaution, a separate note of the number, date and place of issue. The only type of passport now is the standard UK passport.

Standard UK passports are issued to British Nationals, i.e. British Citizens, British Dependent Territories Citizens, British Overseas Citizens, British Nationals (Overseas), British Subjects, and British Protected Persons. A standard UK passport is valid for travel to all countries in the world - but you must check whether a visa is also required. From 5 October 1998 it has been necessary for all children to have their own passports; children entered on the existing passport of a parent before 5 October 1998 may remain until the passport expires or until they reach 16. All passports issued to children under the age of 16 years are for 5 years only. After 5 years a new application must be made.

Full information and application forms are available, on the UK mainland, from main Post Offices, Worldchoice Travel Agents, or from one of the Passport Offices in Belfast, Durham, Glasgow, Liverpool, London, Newport (Wales) and Peterborough. Alternatively, an application form pack may be obtained by calling the application form request hotline 0901 4700 110 or faxing 0901 4700 120. Application for a standard passport should be made to the appropriate area Passport Office. Allow 3 weeks for the processing of your application. NOTE: for personal callers who need their passports urgently (in less than 2 weeks) passport offices operate on an appointment only basis - call the UK's Adviceline below to make an appointment.

For any further information, visit the UK Passport Service website at: **www.passport.gov.uk**

or call the UKPS 24-hour helpline 0870 521 0410

Irish citizens who require an Irish Passport, and who are resident either in the Dublin metropolitan area or in Northern Ireland should apply to the Passport Office, Dublin; if, however, they are resident elsewhere in the Irish Republic, they should apply through the nearest Garda Station or Post Office. Irish citizens resident in Britain should apply to the Irish Embassy in London.

VISA

EU citizens travelling within the EU do not require visas. A visa is not normally required by United Kingdom and Republic of Ireland passport holders when visiting non-EU countries within Western Europe for periods of three months or less. However, if you hold a passport of any other nationality, a UK passport not issued in this country, or if you are in any doubt at all, check with the embassies or consulates of the countries you intend to visit.

VISITORS' REGISTRATION

In most countries registration formalities are to be undertaken by visitors spending up to three months. However, this formality is usually satisfied by completing a card or certificate when booking into a hotel, campsite or other accommodation. If you are staying with friends or relatives it is usually the responsibility of the host to seek advice from the police within 24 hours of the arrival of guests.

If you intend visiting a country for longer than three months and/or the circumstances are not as described above, then you should make the appropriate enquiries before your departure from the UK.

FOODSTUFFS

(See also country introductions)

Countries do have regulations governing the types and quantities of foodstuffs which may be imported. Although they are usually not strictly applied, visitors should know that they exist and only take reasonable quantities of food with them. See the country introductions for any specific regulations.

Tinned, frozen and dehydrated foods are useful for camping. It is best to take only as much as you need until you can shop locally. Good value for money will be found in supermarkets or in the open markets in towns.

NOTE: *The importation of food products of animal origin (meat, meat products not heat treated, milk and dairy products) into any country may be prohibited due to the risk of foot and mouth disease.*

BOATS

EU citizens may use their boats throughout the year in all EU countries provided VAT has been paid. However, the boats of non-EU citizens are still subject to temporary importation formalities.

All boats taken abroad by road should be registered in the UK, except for very small craft to be used close inshore in France. In France such craft are exempt from registration and the dividing line falls approximately between a Laser dinghy (which should be registered) and a Topper (which need not be); however, to avoid any confusion, registration is recommended. See also Identification Plate (pg18).

Registration is carried out by the Small Ships Register at the RSS. Currently the fee is £12 and provides registration for five years. The original Certificate of Registration is required - a photocopy is not acceptable. Application forms for Small Ships Registration, accompanied by notes on the purpose of the Register and eligibility for registration, are available from:

The Small Ships Register, Anchor Court, Keen Rd, Cardiff CF24 5JW. Tel: 02920 448800

Application forms are also available from some yacht/boat clubs, marinas and shipyards.

Of the countries in this guide, an International Certificate of Competence (ICC) is required or recommended for Belgium, France, Germany, Italy, the Netherlands, Portugal and Spain. For further information, contact the Royal Yachting Association, RYA House, Ensign Way, Hamble, Southampton, Hants, SO31 4YA.
telephone 0845 345 0370
www.rya.org.uk/faqs.asp

The UN agreement covering the ICC has been changed. Those renewing out-of-date certificates and wanting 'inland waters' endorsement must take a test on CEVNI rules. A rules booklet is obtainable from the RYA cost £5.99 plus postage.

On 16 June 1998 the Recreational Craft Directive came fully into force. This requires the CE mark on boats newly commissioned or imported into the EEA for the first time. Proof of use in EU waters before this date may become a useful document when visiting other EU countries.

The RYA recommends that all boats have marine insurance. Of the countries in this guide, third party insurance is compulsory for boats in Italy, Spain and Switzerland. A translation of the insurance certificate into the appropriate language is usually required. Check with your broker before you go.

OFF-SITE CAMPING

Off-site camping may contravene local regulations. You are strongly advised never to camp by the roadside and in isolated areas.

PET TRAVEL SCHEME

For information on how to bring pet cats and dogs back into the UK from certain countries without quarantine contact the Pets Helpline on 0870 2411710 or visit the Department for Environment, Food & Rural Affairs (DEFRA) website at:

**www.defra.gov.uk/
animalh/quarantine/index.htm**

Local DEFRA Animal Health Divisional Offices can also provide information on the requirements for taking pets from the UK to other countries.

Travel Information

BBC World Service

The international radio arm of the BBC broadcasts in 43 languages, including a 24-hour-a-day English Service. World news is on the hour every hour and there are regular bulletins of British news.

If you want to listen to World Service when you are abroad, write for information and a free programme guide to: BBC World Service, Audience Relations, Bush House, London WC2B 4PH. Remember to state the country or countries you are visiting.

A monthly magazine, BBC On Air, provides details of all World Service programmes and frequencies, with background information about features and personalities. It costs £20.00 for an annual subscription. If you would like to receive details, please write to 'On Air', at the above address or browse their website at **www.bbc.co.uk/worldservice/onair**

If you are buying a new radio to listen to the BBC abroad, the World Service recommends digitally tuned radios as they make finding frequencies easier.

Make sure your short-wave set can receive some of the key European frequencies such as 9410 and 12095 kHz.

World Service programmes can also be heard on the Internet at: **www.bbc.co.uk/worldservice**

British Embassies/Consulates

(See also country introductions)

Most Continental countries have more than one British consulate in addition to the British embassy. British consulates (and consular sections in embassies) aim to help British travellers in distress overseas but there are limitations to what they can do. For example, they cannot pay your hotel, medical or any other bills, nor will they do the work of a travel agent, information bureau or the police. Any loss or theft of property should, in the first instance be reported to the local police and not to consular offices as you will need to obtain a police report. If you still need help such as an emergency passport or guidance on how to transfer funds, contact the nearest British enbassy or consulate to you. See respective country introductions for British embassy and consulate details. Note that the hours and functions of Honorary Consuls are more restricted than full consular posts.

For hints on preparing for your travel abroad visit:
**www.fco.gov.uk/
knowbeforeyougo**

or telephone 0870 606 0290 for up-to-date travel advice.

Camping Card International

A Camping Card International (CCI) is recognised at most campsites in Europe; in some cases it is essential and you will not be allowed to camp without it. At certain campsites a reduction to the advertised charge may be allowed on presentation of the camping card. The camping card, which is valid for 12 months, provides third-party insurance cover for up to 11 people camping away from home or staying in rented accommodation or at a hotel.

On arrival at the campsite, report to the campsite manager who will tell you where you may pitch your tent or caravan. You may be asked to pay in advance, or alternatively, to give into charge the camping card for the length of your stay. Some campsite managers may also insist upon retention of all passports.

The AA no longer sells the CCI. However, personal AA members wishing to purchase a CCI may obtain one from the Caravan Club. AA members requiring further information should call the Caravan Club on 01342 327410 (09:15-17:15 Mon-Fri only), and be prepared to quote their AA membership number.

AA Ireland members who wish to obtain a CCI should call AA Dublin on 01 617 9988.

CURRENCY

(See also country sections)

There is no limit to the amount of sterling notes you may take abroad. However, it is recommended that you don't rely exclusively on any one payment method. A combination of a payment card, traveller's cheques and a small amount of local currency is suggested as the most practical arrangement.

Euro banknotes and coins were introduced on 1 January 2002 in the 12 countries of the Euro area* to replace national currencies. The banknotes have denominations of EUR 5, 10, 20, 50, 100, 200 and 500; the coins EUR 1 and 2 and cents 1, 2, 5, 10, 20 and 50. The old European currencies have now been withdrawn. Arrangements for exchanging old currencies differ between countries, with many restricting exchange to Central Bank offices. It is possible that banks in Europe will make a charge to non-customers making this exchange.

The 12 are Austria, Belgium, France, Germany, Italy, Luxembourg, Netherlands, Portugal, Spain (included in this guide) plus Finland, Greece and the Republic of Ireland.

ELECTRICAL

General: The electricity supply in Europe is usually 220 volts (50 cycles) AC (alternating current), but can be as low as 110 volts. In some isolated areas, low voltage DC (direct current) is provided. Continental circular two-pin plugs and screw-type bulbs are usually the rule. Check for correct polarity when using a mains hook-up on a touring caravan.

Electrical adapters (not voltage transformers) which can be used in Continental power sockets, shaver points and light bulb sockets are available in the UK from electrical retailers.

Vehicle: Check that all connections are sound, and wiring is in good condition. If problems arise with the charging system, you must consult a qualified auto-electrician.

EMERGENCY MESSAGES TO TOURISTS

In emergencies, the AA will assist in the passing on of messages to tourists when possible. Members wishing to use this service should telephone the AA Information Centre on 0870 5500 600.

The AA can arrange for messages to be published in overseas editions of the Daily Mail, and in an extreme emergency (death or serious illness of next-of-kin) pass on messages to the authorities so that they can be broadcast on overseas radio networks. Obviously the AA cannot guarantee that messages will be broadcast, nor can the AA or the Daily Mail accept responsibility for the authenticity of messages.

If you are expecting a message from home, it is best to contact the tourist office or motoring club of the country in which you're staying. They will advise you on radio frequencies, and at what time messages are normally broadcast. Before you leave home, make sure your relatives understand what to do if an emergency occurs.

Emergency 'SOS' messages about dangerous illness of a close relative may be broadcast on BBC Radio 4's long wave transmitters on 1515m/198Hz at the first opportunity before a news summary or bulletin. These should be arranged through the local police or hospital authorities.

EUROTUNNEL

Eurotunnel operates a fast frequent passenger service between Folkestone in Kent and Calais/Coquelles, for cars, motorcycles, camper vans, cars with caravans or trailers, cars with cycle racks, coaches and HGV trucks. A specific cycle service operates during the summer months. Vehicles powered by LPG or dual fuel cars are not permitted to travel at the moment.

The crossing takes 35 minutes from platform to platform and is just over one hour from the M20 in Kent to A16 in France. To get to the Eurotunnel Terminal in Kent take the M20 and leave at Jct11a, signed Channel Tunnel,

and arrive directly at Check-in. UK and French customs and immigration are cleared before travelling so there are no further checks on arrival in France.

Eurotunnel operates 24 hours a day 365 days a year, with up to four passenger shuttles an hour at peak times. Up-to-date travel information is available on the Eurotunnel website at www.eurotunnel.com or by calling the Eurotunnel call centre on 08705 35 35 35. Prices charged are per vehicale, all the passengers are included. It is possible to buy your ticket on arrival, however you might be subject to delay until there is space available.

Passengers stay with their vehicles for the crossing, although they can get out to stretch their legs or visit the cloakrooms on board. Visual display panels and onboard multilingual staff together with two in-car radio channels keep passengers up to date with information.

FERRY CROSSINGS

Before making ferry bookings, remember that the shortest sea crossing from a southern port to the Continent is not always the best choice; consider the roads and ease of travel from your home to a British port (an eastern British port might be easier if you are starting from the north of the country). Similarly consider the roads and travel from the Continental port to your final destination. Motorail services may be worth considering to save time.

LEVEL CROSSINGS

Almost all level crossings are indicated by international signs. Most guarded ones are the lifting barrier type, maybe with bells or flashing lights to warn of a train's approach.

MEDICAL TREATMENT

Travellers who normally take certain medicines should ensure they have a sufficient supply since they may be very difficult to get abroad.

Those with certain medical conditions (diabetes or coronary artery diseases, for example) should get a letter from their doctor giving treatment details. Some Continental doctors will understand a letter written in English, but it is better to have it translated into the language of the country you intend to visit. The AA cannot make translations.

Travellers who, for legitimate health reasons, carry drugs (see also Customs regulations for the United Kingdom) or appliances (e.g., a hypodermic syringe), may have difficulty with Customs or other authorities. They should carry translations which describe their special condition and appropriate treatment in the language of the country they intend to visit to present to Customs. Similarly, people with special dietary requirements may find translations helpful in hotels and restaurants.

The National Health Service is available in the UK only, and medical expenses incurred overseas cannot be reimbursed by the UK Government. There are bilateral health agreements with most of the countries in this guide, but you should not rely exclusively on these arrangements, as the cover provided under the respective national schemes is not always comprehensive. (For instance, the cost of bringing a person back to the UK in the event of illness or death is never covered). The full costs of medical care must be paid in Andorra. Therefore, you are strongly advised to take out adequate insurance cover before leaving the UK, such as the AA's Travel Insurance.

Urgent medical treatment in the event of an accident or unforeseen illness is available for most visitors at reduced costs, from the health care schemes of those countries with whom the UK has health-care arrangements. Details are in the Department of Health booklet "Health Advice for Travellers" which also gives advice about precautions and vaccinations. Free copies are available from main post offices or by ringing the Health Literature Line on 0800 555 777, free of charge. In some of these countries, visitors can obtain urgently needed treatment by showing their UK passport, but in some an NHS medical

card must be shown, and in most European Economic Area countries a certificate of entitlement (E111) is necessary. The E111 can be obtained at the post office on completion of the forms in booklet 'Health Advice for Travellers' (T6). The E111 must be stamped and signed by the post office clerk to be valid. Residents of the Republic of Ireland must apply to their Regional Health Board.

PAYMENT CARDS

Credit and debit cards are as easy and convenient to use abroad as they are at home. Their use is subject to the conditions set out by the issuing bank which, on request, will provide full information. Establishments display the symbols of cards that they accept. However, it is recommended that you don't rely exclusively on any one payment method. A combination of travellers cheques, a payment card and a small amount of local currency is suggested as the most practical arrangement.

TRAVELLERS CHEQUES

Local currency cheques can often be used like cash. Sterling cheques may be changed for local currency notes at banks, but charges can vary. Your bank will be able to recommend currency travellers cheques for the countries you are visiting. However, it is recommended that you don't rely exclusively on any one payment method. A combination of a payment card, travellers' cheques and a small amount of local currency is suggested as the most practical arrangement.

POLLUTION

Pollution of seawater at certain Continental coastal resorts,

including the Mediterranean, may still represent a health hazard, although the general situation is improving. Countries of the European Union publish detailed information on the quality of their bathing beaches, including maps, which are available from national authorities and the European Union. In most of the other Mediterranean countries, appropriate surveys regarding bathing water quality in populated beaches, are implemented every year. In many (though not all) popular resorts where the water quality may present risk, signs (generally small) are erected which forbid bathing:

FRENCH

No bathing
Défense de se baigner

Bathing prohibited
Il est défendu de se baigner

ITALIAN

No bathing
Vietato bagnarsi

Bathing prohibited
Evietato bagnarsi

SPANISH

No bathing
Prohibido bañarse

Bathing prohibited
Se prohibe bañarse

POSTE RESTANTE

If you are uncertain of having a precise address, you can be contacted through the local poste restante. Before leaving the UK notify family or friends of your approximate whereabouts abroad at given times. If you expect mail, call with your passport at the main post office of the town where you are staying. To ensure that the arrival of correspondence will coincide with your stay, your correspondent should check with the post office before posting, as delivery times differ throughout Europe. It is important that the recipient's name be written in full: Mr John Smith, Poste Restante, Sintra, Portugal. Do not use 'Esq'.

The Italian equivalent of 'Poste Restante' is 'Fermo in Posta' plus the name of the town or village and the province or region. The Spanish equivalent is 'Lista de Correos'.

Correspondence will be lodged at the main post office, and you will need proof of identity (e.g. a passport) to collect it.

TOURIST INFORMATION

National tourist offices are well equipped to deal with enquiries relating to their countries. They are particularly useful for information on current events, tourist attractions, car hire, equipment hire and specific activities such as skin-diving, gliding, horse-riding, etc. The offices in London (see country introductions for addresses) are helpful, but the local offices overseas merit a visit when you arrive at your destination for information not available elsewhere.

WEATHER AND TRAFFIC INFORMATION

The AA is one of Europe's largest traffic and travel information providers offering detailed and accurate reports for the whole of the UK.

Call 09003 401 100 (or '401 100'* from your mobile phone) for a range of valuable traffic and travel services which include

• The latest traffic information for your local area or any other region of the UK

• A traffic report on a specific UK motorway or 'A' road

• Local and national 5-day weather forecasts

For other weather information for the UK and the Continent (but not road conditions) please telephone the Met Office on 0845 300 0300, view their website at **www.metoffice.com** or contact:

> The Met. Office
> Customer Centre
> London Road
> Bracknell
> Berkshire RG12 2SZ

* Calls to 09003 numbers are charged at 60p per minute at all times. Availability and prices for mobile calls to 401 100 can vary - see your Service Provider for details.

Principal Mountain Passes

It is best not to attempt to cross mountain passes at night, and daily schedules should make allowances for the comparatively slow speeds inevitable in mountainous areas.

Gravel surfaces (such as dirt and stone chips) vary considerably; they are dusty when dry, slippery when wet. Where known to exist, this type of surface has been noted. Road repairs can be carried out only during the summer, and may interrupt traffic. Precipitous road sides are rarely, if ever, totally unguarded; on the older roads, stone pillars are placed at close intervals. Gradient figures take the mean figure on hairpin bends, and may be steeper on the inside of the curves, particularly on the older roads.

CONVERSION TABLE GRADIENTS

All steep hill signs show the grade in percentage terms. The following conversion table may be used as a guide:

30%=1 in 3	14%=1 in 7
25%=1 in 4	12%=1 in 8
20%=1 in 5	11%=1 in 9
16%=1 in 6	10%=1 in 10

Before attempting late evening or early morning journeys across frontier passes, check the times of opening of the frontier controls. A number close at night; for example the Timmelsjoch border is closed between 20.00 and 07.00hrs and throughout the winter.

Always engage a low gear before either ascending or descending steep gradients, and keep well to the right-hand side of the road and avoid cutting corners. Avoid excessive use of brakes. If the engine overheats, pull off the road, making sure that you do not cause an obstruction, leave the engine idling, and put the heater controls (including the fan) into the maximum heat position. Under no circumstances should you remove the radiator cap until the engine has cooled down. Do not fill the coolant system of a hot engine with cold water.

Always engage a lower gear before taking a hairpin bend, give priority to vehicles ascending and remember that as your altitude increases, so your engine power decreases. Always give priority to postal coaches travelling in either direction. Their route is usually signposted.

CARAVANS

Passes suitable for caravans are indicated in the table on the following pages. Those shown to be negotiable by caravans are best used only by experienced drivers in cars with ample power; the rest are probably best avoided. A correct power-to-load ratio is always essential.

CONDITIONS IN WINTER

Winter conditions are given in italics in the last column. UO means usually open, although a severe fall of snow may temporarily obstruct the road for 24 to 48 hours, and wheel chains are often necessary; OC means occasionally closed, UC, usually closed, between the dates stated. Dates for opening and closing the passes are approximate only. Warning notices are usually posted at the foot of a pass if it is closed, or if chains or snow tyres should or must be used.

Wheel chains may be needed early and late in the season, and between short spells (a few hours) of obstruction. At these times, conditions are usually more difficult for caravans.

In fair weather, wheel chains or snow tyres are only necessary on the higher passes, but in severe weather you will probably need to use them (as a rough guide) at altitudes exceeding 610 metres (2000ft).

Pass and height	From To	Distances from summit and max gradient	Min width of road	Conditions (see previous page for key to abbreviations)
*Albula 2312 metres (7585ft) Switzerland	Tiefencastel 851 metres (2792ft) La Punt 1687 metres (5535ft)	30km 1 in 10 18.6 miles 9km 1 in 10 5.6 miles	3.5 metres 11ft 6in	UC Nov - early Jun. An inferior alternative to the Julier; tar and gravel, fine scenery. Alternative rail tunnel.
Allos 2250 metres (7382ft) France	Barcelonnette 1132 metres (3714ft) Colmars 1235 metres (4052ft)	20km 1 in 10 12.4 miles 24km 1 in 12 14.9 miles	4.0 metres 13ft 1n	UC Early Nov - early Jun. Very winding, narrow mostly unguarded but not difficult otherwise; passing bays on southern slope, poor surface (maximum width vehicles 1.8 metres, 5ft 11in).
Aprica 1176 metres (3858ft) Italy	Tresenda 375 metres(1230ft) Edolo 699 metres (2293ft)	14km 1 in 11 8.7 miles 15km 1 in 16 9.3 miles	4.0 metres 13ft 1in	UO Fine scenery, good surface, well graded; suitable for caravans.
Aravis 1498 metres (4915ft) France	La Clusaz 1040 metres (3412ft) Flumet 917 metres (3009ft)	8km 1 in 11 5.0 miles 12km 1 in 11 7.4 miles	4.0 metres 13ft 1in	OC Dec - Mar. Outstanding scenery, and a fairly easy road.
Arlberg 1802 metres (5912ft) Austria	Bludenz 581 metres (1905ft) Landeck 816 metres (2677ft)	35km 1 in 8 21.7 miles 32km 1 in 7.5 20 miles	6 metres 19ft 8in	OC Dec - Apr. Modern road; short, steep stretch from west easing towards the summit; heavy traffic; parallel toll road tunnel. Suitable for caravans; using tunnel (see chapter on Major Road and Rail Tunnels). Pass road closed to vehicles towing trailers.
Aubisque 1710 metres (5610ft) France	Eaux Bonnes 750 metres (2461ft) Argelés-Gazost 463 metres (1519ft)	12km 1 in 10 7 miles 30km 1 in 10 19 miles	3.5 metres 11ft 6in	UC Mid Oct - Jun. A very winding road; continuous but easy ascent; the descent incorporates the Col de Soulor (1450 metres, 4757ft); 8km (5 miles) of very narrow, rough unguarded road, with a steep drop.
Ballon d'Alsace 1178 metres (3865ft) France	Giromagny 476metres (1562ft) St-Maurice-sur-Moselle 549 metres (1801ft)	17km 1 in 9 10.6 miles 9km 1 in 9 5.6 miles	4.0 metres 13ft 1in	OC Dec - Mar. A fairly straightforward ascent and descent, but numerous bends; negotiable by caravans.
Bayard 1248 metres (4094ft) France	Chauffayer 911 metres (2989ft) Gap 733 metres (2405ft)	18km 1 in 12 11.2 miles 8km 1 in 7 5.0 miles	6 metres 19ft 8in	UO Part of the Route Napoléon. Fairly easy, steepest on the southern side with several hairpin bends; negotiable by caravans from north to south.
*Bernina 2330 metres (7644ft) Switzerland	Pontresina 1805 metres (5922ft) Poschiavo 1019 metres (3343ft)	15.5km 1 in 10 10.5 miles 18.5km 1 in 8 11.5 miles	5 metres 16ft 5in	OC Dec - Mar. A good road on both sides; negotiable by caravans.
Bonaigua 2072 metres (6797ft) Spain	Viella 974 metres (3195ft) Esterri d'Aneu 957 metres (3140ft)	23km 1 in 12 14 miles 23km 1 in 12 14 miles	4.3 metres 14ft 1in	UC Nov - Apr. A sinuous and narrow road with many hairpin bends and some precipitous drops; the alternative route to Lleida (Lérida) through the Viella tunnel is open in winter.
Bracco 613 metres (2011ft) Italy	Riva Trigoso 43 metres (141ft) Borghetto di Vara 104metres (341ft)	15km 1 in 7 9.3 miles 18km 1 in 7 11.2 miles	5 metres 16ft 5in	UO A two-lane road with continuous bends; passing usually difficult; negotiable by caravans; alternative toll motorway available.
Brenner 1374 metres (4508ft) Austria - Italy	Innsbruck 574 metres (1883ft) Vipiteno 948 metres (3110ft)	36km 1 in 12 22miles 15km 1 in 7 9.3 miles	6 metres 19ft 8in	UO Parallel toll motorway open; heavy traffic; suitable for caravans using toll motorway. Pass road closed to vehicles towing trailers.
+Brünig 1007 metres (3304ft) Switzerland	Brienzwiler Station 575 metres (1886ft) Giswil 485 metres (1591ft)	6km 1 in 12 3.7 miles 13km 1 in 12 8.1 miles	6 metres 19ft 8in	UO An easy but winding road, heavy traffic at weekends; suitable for caravans.

* Permitted maximum width of vehicles 7ft 6in   + Permitted maximum width of vehicles 8ft 2.5in   ++ Maximum length of vehicle 30ft

Pass and height	From To	Distances from summit and max gradient	Min width of road	Conditions (see page 37 for key to abbreviations)
Bussang 721 metres (2365ft) France	Thann 340 metres (1115ft) St Maurice-sur-Moselle 549 metres (1801ft)	24km 1 in 14 15 miles 8km 1 in 14 5.0 miles	4 metres 13ft 1in	UO A very easy road over the Vosges; beautiful scenery; suitable for caravans.
Cabre 1180 metres (3871ft) France	Luc-en-Diois 580 metres (1903ft) Aspres sur Buëch 764 metres (2507ft)	24km 1 in 11 15 miles 17km 1 in 14 10.6 miles	5.5 metres 18ft	UO An easy pleasant road; suitable for caravans.
Campolongo 1875 metres (6152ft) Italy	Corvara in Badia 1568 metres (5144ft) Arabba 1602 metres (5256ft)	6km 1 in 8 3.7 miles 4km 1 in 8 2.5 miles	5 metres 16ft 5in	OC Dec - Mar. A winding but easy ascent; long level stretch on summit followed by easy descent; good surface; suitable for caravans.
Cayolle 2326 metres (7631ft) France	Barcelonnette 1132 metres (3714ft) Guillaumes 819 metres (2687ft)	30km 1 in 10 19 miles 33km 1 in 10 20.5 miles	4 metres 13ft 1in	UC early Nov - early Jun. Narrow and winding road with hairpin bends; poor surface and broken edges; steep drops. Long stretches of single-track road with passing places.
Costalunga (Karer) 1753 metres (5751ft) Italy	Cardano 282 metres (925ft) Pozza 1290 metres (4232ft)	24km 1 in 6 14.9 miles 11km 1 in 8 7 miles	5 metres 16ft 5in	OC Dec - Apr. A good well-engineered road but mostly winding; caravans prohibited.
Croix 1778 metres (5833ft) Switzerland	Villars-sur-Ollon 1253 metres (4111ft) Les Diablerets 1155 metres (3789ft)	8km 1 in 7.5 5.0 miles 9km 1 in 11 5.6 miles	3.5 metres 11ft 6in	UC Nov - May. A narrow and winding route but extremely picturesque.
Croix-Haute 1179 metres (3868ft) France	Monestier-de-Clermont 832 metres (2730ft) Aspres-sur-Buëch 764 metres (2507ft)	34km 1 in 14 21 miles 29km 1 in 14 18 miles	5.5 metres 18ft	UO Well engineered; several hairpin bends on the north side; suitable for caravans.
Envalira 2407 metres (7897ft) Andorra	Pas de la Casa 2091 metres (6860ft) Andorra 1029 metres (3376ft)	5km 1 in 10 3.1 miles 25km 1 in 8 16 miles	6 metres 19ft 8in	OC Nov - Apr. A good road with wide bends on ascent and descent; fine views; negotiable by caravans (maximum height vehicles 3.5 metres, 11ft 6in on northern approach near L'Hospitalet).
Falzárego 2117 metres (6945ft) Italy	Cortina d'Ampezzo 1224 metres (4016ft) Andraz 1428 metres (4685ft)	17km 1 in 12 10.6 miles 9km 1 in 12 5.6 miles	5 metres 16ft 5in	OC Dec - Apr. Well engineered bitumen surface; many hairpin bends on both sides; negotiable by caravans.
Faucille 1323 metres (4341ft) France	Gex 628 metres (2060ft) Morez 702 metres (2303ft)	11km 1 in 10 6.8 miles 27km 1 in 12 17miles	5 metres 16ft 5in	UO Fairly wide, winding road across the Jura mountains; negotiable by caravans, but it is probably better to follow La Cure-St-Cergue-Nyon.
Fern 1209 metres (3967ft) Austria	Nassereith 843 metres (2766ft) Lermoos 995 metres (3264ft)	10km 1 in 10 6 miles 10km 1 in 10 6 miles	6 metres 19ft 8in	UO An easy pass, but slippery when wet; heavy traffic at summer weekends; suitable for caravans.
Flexen 1784 metres (5853ft) Austria	Lech 1447 metres (4747ft) Rauzalpe (near Arlberg Pass) 1628 metres (5341ft)	6.5km 1 in 10 4 miles 3.5km 1 in 10 2.2 miles	5.5 metres 18ft	UO The magnificent 'Flexenstrasse', a well engineered mountain road with tunnels and galleries. The road from Lech to Warth, north of the pass, is usually closed between November and April due to danger of avalanches.

* Permitted maximum width of vehicles 7ft 6in   + Permitted maximum width of vehicles 8ft 2.5in   ++ Maximum length of vehicle 30ft

PRINCIPAL MOUNTAIN PASSES

Pass and height	From To	Distances from summit and max gradient	Min width of road	Conditions (see page 37 for key to abbreviations)
*Flüela 2383 metres (7818ft) Switzerland	Davos-Dorf 1563 metres (5128ft) Susch 1438 metres (4718ft)	14km 1 in 10 9 miles 14km 1 in 8 9 miles	5metres 16ft 5in	OC Nov - May. Easy ascent from Davos; some acute hairpin bends on the eastern side; bitumen surface; negotiable by caravans.
+Forclaz 1527 metres (5010ft) Switzerland France	Martigny 476 metres (1562ft) Argentière 1253 metres (4111ft)	13km 1 in 12 8.1 miles 19km 1 in 12 11.8 miles	5 metres 16ft 5in	UO Forclaz; OC Montets Dec - early Apr. A good road over the pass and to the frontier; in France, narrow and rough over Col des Montets (1461 metres, 4793ft); negotiable by caravans.
Foscagno 2291 metres (7516ft) Italy	Bormio 1225 metres (4019ft) Livigno 1816 metres (5958ft)	24km 1 in 8 14.9 miles 14km 1 in 8 8.7 miles	3.3 metres 10ft 10in	OC Nov - May. Narrow and winding through lonely mountains, generally poor surface. Long winding ascent with many blind bends; not always well guarded. The descent includes winding rise and fall over the Passo d'Eira (2200 metres, 7218ft).
Fugazze 1159 metres (3802ft) Italy	Rovereto 201 metres (660ft) Valli del Pasubio 350 metres (1148ft)	27km 1 in 7 16.4 miles 12km 1 in 7 7.4 miles	3.5 metres 11ft 6in	UO Very winding with some narrow sections, particularly on northern side. The many blind bends and several hairpin bends call for extra care.
*Furka 2431 metres (7976ft) Switzerland	Gletsch 1757 metres (5764ft) Realp 1538 metres (5046ft)	10km 1 in 9 6.2 miles 13km 1 in 10 8.1 miles	4 metres 13ft 1in	UC Oct - Jun. A well graded road, with narrow sections and several sharp hairpin bends on both ascent and descent. Fine views of the Rhône glacier. Alternative rail tunnel available.
Galibier 2645 metres (8678ft) France	Lautaret Pass 2058 metres (6752ft) St-Michel-de-Maurienne 712 metres (2336ft)	7km 1 in 9 4.4 miles 34km 1 in 8 21.1 miles	3 metres 9ft 10in	UC Oct - Jun. Mainly wide, well surfaced but unguarded. Ten hairpin bends on descent then 5km (3.1 miles) narrow and rough. Rise over the Col du Télégraphe (1600 metres, 5249ft), then 11 more hairpin bends. (The tunnel under the Galibier summit is closed.)
Gardena (Grödner-Joch) 2121 metres (6959ft) Italy	Val Gardena 1862 metres (6109ft) Corvara in Badia 1568 metres (5144ft)	6km 1 in 8 3.7 miles 10km 1 in 8 6.2 miles	5 metres 16ft 5in	OC Dec - Jun. A well engineered road, very winding on descent.
Gavia 2621 metres (8599ft) Italy	Bormio 1225 metres (4019ft) Ponte di Legno 1258 metres (4127ft)	25km 1 in 5.5 15.5 miles 18km 1 in 5.5 11 miles	3 metres 9ft 10in	UC Oct - Jul. Steep and narrow, but with frequent passing bays; many hairpin bends and a gravel surface; not for the faint-hearted; extra care necessary. (Maximum width for vehicles 1.8 metres, 5ft 11in.)
Gerlos 1628 metres (5341ft) Austria	Zell am Ziller 575 metres (1886ft) Wald 885 metres (2904ft)	29km 1 in 12 18 miles 15km 1 in 11 9.3 miles	4 metres 13ft 1in	UO Hairpin ascent out of Zell to modern toll road; the old, steep, narrow, and winding route with passing bays and 1-in-7 gradient is not recommended, but is negotiable with care; caravans prohibited.
+Grand St Bernard 2473 metres (8114ft) Switzerland - Italy	Martigny 476 metres (1562ft) Aosta 583 metres (1913ft)	46km 1 in 9 29 miles 34km 1 in 9 21 miles	4 metres 13ft 1in	UC Oct - Jun. Modern road to entrance of road tunnel (usually open; see chapter on Major Road and Rail Tunnels) then narrow over summit to frontier; also good surface in Italy; suitable for caravans using tunnel. Pass road closed to vehicles towing trailers.
*Grimsel 2164 metres (7100ft) Switzerland	Innerkirchen 630 metres (2067ft) Gletsch 1757 metres (5764ft)	26km 1 in 10 16.1 miles 6km 1 in 10 3.7 miles	5 metres 16ft 5in	UC mid Oct - late Jun. A fairly easy road, but heavy traffic weekends. A long winding ascent, finally hairpin bends; then a terraced descent (six hairpins) into the Rhône valley. Negotiable by caravans.
Grossglockner 2503 metres (8212ft) Austria	Bruck an der Glocknerstrasse 755 metres (2477ft) Heiligenblut 1301 metres (4268ft)	34km 1 in 8 21 miles 15m 1 in 8 9.3 miles	5.5 metres 18ft	UC late Oct - early May. Numerous well engineered hairpin bends; moderate but very long ascent, toll road; very fine scenery; heavy tourist traffic; negotiable preferably from south to north, by caravans. Road closed at night, 22.00 to 05.00 hrs.

* Permitted maximum width of vehicles 7ft 6in   + Permitted maximum width of vehicles 8ft 2.5in   ++ Maximum length of vehicle 30ft

PRINCIPAL MOUNTAIN PASSES

Pass and height	From To	Distances from summit and max gradient	Min width of road	Conditions (see page 37 for key to abbreviations)
Hochtannberg 1679 metres (5509ft) Austria	Schröcken 1269 metres(4163ft) Warth (near Lech) 1500 metres (4921ft)	5.5km 1 in 7 3.4 miles 4.5km 1 in 11 2.8 miles	4 metres 13ft 1in	OC Jan - Mar. A reconstructed modern road.
Ibañeta (Roncesvalles) 1057 metres (3468ft) France - Spain	St-Jean-Pied-de-Port 163 metres (535ft) Pamplona 415 metres (1362ft)	27km 1 in 10 17 miles 49km 1 in 10 30 miles	4 metres 13ft 1in	UO A slow and winding, scenic route; negotiable by caravans.
Iseran 2770 metres (9088ft) France	Bourg-St-Maurice 840 metres (2756ft) Lanslebourg 1399 metres (4590ft)	47km 1 in 12 29 miles 33km 1 in 9 20.5 miles	4 metres 13ft 1in	UC Mid Oct - late Jun. The second highest pass in the Alps. Well graded with reasonable bends, average surface; several unlit tunnels on northern approach.
Izoard 2360 metres (7743ft) France	Guillestre 1000 metres (3281ft) Briançon 1321 metres (4334ft)	32km 1 in 8 20 miles 22km 1 in 8 14 miles	5 metres 16ft 5in	UC Late Oct - mid Jun. A winding and sometimes narrow road with many hairpin bends. Care is required at several unlit tunnels near Guillestre.
*Jaun 1509 metres (4951ft) Switzerland	Broc 718 metres (2356ft) Reidenbach 845 metres (2772ft)	25km 1 in 10 15.5 miles 8km 1 in 10 5 miles	4 metres 13ft 1in	UO A modernised but generally narrow road; some poor sections on ascent, and several hairpin bends on descent; negotiable by caravans.
+Julier 2284 metres (7493ft) Switzerland	Tiefencastel 851 metres (2792ft) Silvaplana 1815 metres (5955ft)	35km 1 in 10 22miles 7km 1 in 7.5 4.4 miles	4 metres 13ft 1in	UO Well engineered road, approached from Chur by Lenzerheide Pass (1549 metres, 5082ft); negotiable by caravans, preferably from north to south.
Katschberg 1641 metres (5384ft) Austria	Spittal 554 metres (1818ft) St Michael 1068 metres (3504ft)	37km 1 in 5 23 miles 6km 1 in 6 3.7 miles	6 metres 19ft 8in	UO Steep though not particularly difficult, parallel toll motorway, including tunnel available; negotiable by light caravans, using tunnel (see chapter on Major Road and Rail Tunnels, Tauern Autobahn)
*Klausen 1948 metres (6391ft) Switzerland	Altdorf 458 metres (1503ft) Linthal 662 metres (2172ft)	25km 1 in 10 15.5 miles 23km 1 in 11 14.3 miles	5 metres 16ft 5in	UC Late Oct - early Jun. Narrow and winding in places, but generally easy, in spite of a number of sharp bends; no through route for caravans as they are prohibited from using the road between Unterschächen and Linthal.
Larche (della Maddalena) 1994 metres (6542ft) France - Italy	La Condamine-Châtelard 1308 metres (4291ft) Vinadio 910 metres (2986ft)	19km 1 in 12 11.8 miles 32km 1 in 12 19.8 miles	3.5 metres 11ft 6in	OC Dec - Mar. An easy, well graded road; narrow ascent, wider on descent; suitable for caravans.
Lautaret 2058 metres (6752ft) France	Le Bourg-d'Oisans 719 metres (2359ft) Briançon 1321 metres (4334ft)	38km 1 in 8 23.6 miles 28km 1 in 10 17.4 miles	4 metres 13ft 1in	OC Dec - Mar. Modern, evenly graded, but winding, and unguarded in places; very fine scenery; suitable for caravans.
Loibl (Ljubelj) 1067 metres (3500ft) Austria - Slovenia	Unterloibl 518 metres (1699ft) Kranj 385 metres (1263ft)	10km 1 in 5.5 6.2 miles 26km 1 in 8 16miles	6 metres 19ft 8in	UO Steep rise and fall over Little Loibl pass to tunnel (1.6km, 1 mile long) under summit. The old road over the summit is closed to through traffic.
*Lukmanier (Lucomagno) 1916 metres (6286ft) Switzerland	Olivone 893 metres (2930ft) Disentis 1133 metres (3717ft)	20km 1 in 11 12 miles 20km 1 in 11 12 miles	5 metres 16ft 5in	UC early Nov - late May. Rebuilt, modern road; suitable for caravans.

* Permitted maximum width of vehicles 7ft 6in   + Permitted maximum width of vehicles 8ft 2.5in   ++ Maximum length of vehicle 30f

41

PRINCIPAL MOUNTAIN PASSES

Pass and height	From To	Distances from summit and max gradient	Min width of road	Conditions (see page 37 for key to abbreviations)
+Maloja 1815 metres (5955ft) Switzerland	Silvaplana 1815 metres (5955ft) Chiavenna 333 metres (1093ft)	11km level 6.8 miles 32km 1 in 11 19.8 miles	4 metres 13ft 1in	UO Escarpment facing south; fairly easy, but many hairpin bends on descent; negotiable by caravans, possibly difficult on ascent.
Mauria 1298 metres (4258ft) Italy	Lozzo Cadore 753 metres (2470ft) Ampezzo 560 metres (1837ft)	13km 1 in 14 8 miles 31km 1 in 14 19.2 miles	5 metres 16ft 5in	UO A well designed road with easy, winding ascent and descent; suitable for caravans.
Mendola 1363 metres (4472ft) Italy	Appiano (Eppan) 411 metres (1348ft) Sarnonico 978 metres (3208ft)	15km 1 in 8 9.3 miles 9km 1 in 10 6 miles	5 metres 16ft 5in	UO A fairly straightforward but winding road, well guarded; suitable for caravans.
Mont Cenis 2083 metres (6834ft) France - Italy	Lanslebourg 1399 metres (4590ft) Susa 503 metres (1650ft)	11km 1 in 10 6.8 miles 28km 1 in 8 17.4 miles	5 metres 16ft 5in	UC Nov - May. Approach by industrial valley. An eas highway, with mostly very good surface; spectacular scenery; suitable for caravans. Alternative Fréjus road tunnel(see Major Road and Rail Tunnels).
Monte Croce di Comélico (Kreuzberg) 1636 metres (5368ft) Italy	San Candido 1174metres (3852ft) Santo Stefano di Cadore 908 metres (2979ft)	15km 1 in 12 9.3 miles 21km 1 in 12 13miles	5 metres 16ft 5in	UO A winding road with moderate gradients, beautiful scenery; suitable for caravans.
Montgenèvre 1850m (6070ft) France - Italy	Briançon 1321 metres (4334ft) Cesana Torinese 1344 metres (4409ft)	12km 1 in 14 7.4 miles 8km 1 in 11 5miles	5 metres 16ft 5in	UO An easy, modern road; suitable for caravans.
Monte Giovo (Jaufen) 2094 metres (6870ft) Italy	Merano 324 metres (1063ft) Vipiteno 948 metres (3110ft)	40km 1 in 8 24.8 miles 19km 1 in 11 11.8 miles	4 metres 13ft 1in	UC Nov - May. Many well engineered hairpin bends; caravans prohibited.
Montets (see Forclaz)				
Morgins 1369 metres (4491ft) France - Switzerland	Abondance 930 metres (3051ft) Monthey 424 metres (1391ft)	14km 1 in 11 8.7 miles 15km 1 in 7 9.3 miles	4 metres 13ft 1in	UO A lesser used route through pleasant, forested countryside crossing the French-Swiss border.
*Mosses 1445m (4740ft) Switzerland	Aigle 417 metres (1368ft) Château d'Oex 958 metres (3143ft)	16km 1 in 12 10 miles 15km 1 in 12 9.3 miles	4 metres 13ft 1in	UO A modern road; suitable for caravans.
Nassfeld (Pramollo) 1530m (5020ft) Austria - Italy	Tröpolach 601 metres (1972ft) Pontebba 568 metres (1864ft)	10km 1 in 5 6.2 miles 10km 1 in 10 6.2 miles	4 metres 13ft 1in	OC Late Nov - Mar. The winding descent in Italy has been improved.
*Nufenen (Novena) 2478 metres (8130ft) Switzerland	Ulrichen 1346 metres (4416ft) Airolo 1142 metres (3747ft)	13km 1 in 10 8.1 miles 24km 1 in 10 14.9 miles	4.0 metres 13ft 1in	UC Mid Oct - mid Jun. The approach roads are narrow, with tight bends, but the road over the pass i good; negotiable by caravans.
*Oberalp 2044 metres (6706ft) Switzerland	Andermatt 1447 metres (4747ft) Disentis 1133 metres (3717ft)	10km 1 in 10 6.2 miles 21km 1 in 10 13miles	5 metres 16ft 5in	UC Nov - late May. A widened road with a modern surface; many hairpin bends, but long level stretch or summit; negotiable by caravans. Alternative rail tunnel for winter (see chapter on Major Road and Rail Tunnels).

* Permitted maximum width of vehicles 7ft 6in   + Permitted maximum width of vehicles 8ft 2.5in   ++ Maximum length of vehicle 30ft

PRINCIPAL MOUNTAIN PASSES

Pass and height	From To	Distances from summit and max gradient	Min width of road	Conditions (see page 37 for key to abbreviations)
*Ofen (Fuorn) 2149 metres (7051ft) Switzerland	Zernez 1474 metres (4836ft) Santa Maria im Münstertal 1375 metres (4511ft)	22km 1 in 10 13.6 miles 14km 1 in 8 8.7 miles	4 metres 13ft 1in	UO Good, fairly easy road through the Swiss National Park; negotiable by caravans.
Petit St Bernard 2188 metres (7178ft) France - Italy	Bourg-St-Maurice 840 metres (2756ft) Pré St-Didier 1000 metres (3281ft)	30km 1 in 16 19 miles 23km 1 in 12 14.3 miles	5 metres 16ft 5in	UC Mid Oct - Jun. Outstanding scenery; a fairly easy approach, but poor surface and unguarded broken edges near the summit; good on the descent in Italy; negotiable by light caravans.
Peyresourde 1563 metres (5128ft) France	Arreau 704 metres (2310ft) Luchon 630 metres (2067ft)	18km 1 in 10 11.2 miles 14km 1 in 10 8.7 miles	4 metres 13ft 1in	UO Somewhat narrow with several hairpin bends, though not difficult.
*Pillon 1546 metres (5072ft) Switzerland	Le Sépey 974 metres (3196ft) Gsteig 1184 metres (3885ft)	15km 1 in 11 9 miles 7km 1 in 11 4.4 miles	4 metres 13ft 1in	OC Jan - Feb. A comparatively easy modern road; suitable for caravans.
Plöcken (Monte Croce-Carnico) 1362 metres (4468ft) Austria - Italy	Kötschach 706 metres (2316ft) Paluzza 600 metres (1968ft)	16km 1 in 7 10 miles 16km 1 in 14 10 miles	5 metres 16ft 5in	OC Dec - Apr. A modern road with long, reconstructed sections; heavy traffic at summer weekends; delay likely at the frontier; negotiable by caravans, best used only by experienced drivers in cars with ample power.
Pordoi 2239 metres (7346ft) Italy	Arabba 1602 metres (5256ft) Canazei 1465 metres (4806ft)	9km 1 in 10 5.6 miles 12km 1 in 10 7.4 miles	5 metres 16ft 5in	OC Dec - Apr. An excellent modern road with numerous hairpin bends; negotiable by caravans.
Port 1249 metres (4098ft) France	Tarascon 474 metres (1555ft) Massat 650 metres (2133ft)	18km 1 in 10 11.2 miles 12km 1 in 10 7.4 miles	4 metres 13ft 1in	OC Nov - Mar. A fairly easy road, but narrow on some bends; negotiable by caravans.
Portet-d'Aspet 1069 metres (3507ft) France	Audressein 508 metres (1667ft) Fronsac 472 metres (1548ft)	18km 1 in 7 11.2 miles 29km 1 in 7 18miles	3.5 metres 11ft 6in	UO Approached from the west by the easy Col des Ares (797 metres, 2615ft) and Col de Buret (599 metres, 1965ft); well engineered road, but calls for particular care on hairpin bends; rather narrow.
Pötschen 982 metres (3222ft) Austria	Bad Ischl 469 metres (1539ft) Bad Aussee 659 metres (2162ft)	19km 1 in 11 11.8 miles 9 km 1 in 11 5.6 miles	7 metres 23ft	UO A modern road; suitable for caravans.
Pourtalet 1792 metres (5879ft) France - Spain	Eaux-Chaudes 656 metres (2152ft) Biescas 860 metres (2822ft)	23km 1 in 10 14.3 miles 32km 1 in 10 20 miles	3.5 metres 11ft 6in	UC late Oct - early Jun. A fairly easy, unguarded road, but narrow in places.
Puymorens 1915 metres (6283ft) France	Ax-les-Thermes 720 metres (2362ft) Bourg-Madame 1130 metres (3707ft)	28km 1 in 10 17.4 miles 27km 1 in 10 16.8 miles	5.5 metres 18ft	OC Nov - Apr. A generally easy, modern tarmac road, but narrow, winding and with a poor surface in places; not suitable for night driving; suitable for caravans (max height vehicles 3.5 metres, 11ft 6in). Parallel toll road tunnel available.
Quillane 1714 metres (5623ft) France	Quillan 291 metres (955ft) Mont-Louis 1600 metres (5249ft)	63km 1 in 12 39.1 miles 6 km 1 in 12 3.5 miles	5 metres 16ft 5in	OC Nov - Mar. An easy, straightforward ascent and descent; suitable for caravans.

* Permitted maximum width of vehicles 7ft 6in   + Permitted maximum width of vehicles 8ft 2.5in   ++ Maximum length of vehicle 30ft

43

Pass and height	From To	Distances from summit and max gradient	Min width of road	Conditions (see page 37 for key to abbreviations)
Radstädter-Tauern 1738 metres (5702ft) Austria	Radstadt 862 metres (2828ft) Mauterndorf 1122 metres (3681ft)	21km 1 in 6 13.0 miles 17km 1 in 7 10.6 miles	5 metres 16ft 5in	OC Jan - Mar. Northern ascent steep, but not difficult otherwise; parallel toll motorway including tunnel; negotiable by light caravans, using tunnel (see chapter on Major Road and Rail Tunnels).
Résia (Reschen) 1504 metres (4934ft) Italy - Austria	Spondigna 885 metres (2903ft) Pfunds 970 metres (3182ft)	29km 1 in 10 18 miles 21km 1 in 10 13miles	6 metres 19ft 8in	UO A good, straightforward alternative to the Brenner Pass; suitable for caravans.
Restefond (La Bonette) 2802 metres (9193ft) France	Jausiers (near Barcelonnette) 1220 metres (4003ft) St-Etienne-de-Tinée 1144 metres (3753ft)	23km 1 in 8 14.3 miles 27km 1 in 6 16.8 miles	3 metres 9ft 10in	UC Oct - Jun. The highest pass in the Alps, completed in 1962. Narrow, rough, unguarded ascent with many blind bends, and nine hairpins. Descent easier, winding with 12 hairpin bends. Not for the faint-hearted; extra care required.
Rolle 1970 metres (6463ft) Italy	Predazzo 1018 metres (3340ft) Mezzano 637 metres (2090ft)	21km 1 in 11 13.0 miles 27km 1 in 14 17 miles	5 metres 16ft 5in	OC Dec - Mar. A well engineered road with many hairpin bends on both sides; very beautiful scenery; good surface; negotiable by caravans.
Rombo (see Timmelsjoch)				
Routes des Crêtes 1283 metres (4210ft) France	St-Dié 343 metres (1125ft) Cernay 296 metres (971ft)	- 1 in 8 - 1 in 8	4 metres 13ft 1in	UC Nov - Apr. A renowned scenic route crossing seven ridges, with the highest point at 'Hôtel du Grand Ballon'.
+St Gotthard (San Gottardo) 2108 metres (6916ft) Switzerland	Göschenen 1106 metres (3629ft) Airolo 1142 metres (3747ft)	18km 1 in 10 11miles 15km 1 in 10 9.3 miles	6 metres 19ft 8in	UC Mid Oct - early Jun. Modern, fairly easy two to three-lane road. Heavy traffic; negotiable by caravans. Alternative road tunnel (see chapter on Major Road and Rail Tunnels).
*San Bernardino 2066 metres (6778ft) Switzerland	Mesocco 790 metres (2592ft) Hinterrhein 1620 metres (5315ft)	21km 1 in 10 13miles 9.5km 1 in 10 5.9 miles	4 metres 13ft 1in	UC Oct - late Jun. Easy, modern roads on northern and southern approaches to tunnel(see chapter on Major Road and Rail Tunnels). Narrow and winding over summit, via tunnel suitable for caravans.
Schlucht 1139 metres (3737ft) France	Gérardmer 665 metres (2182ft) Munster 381 metres (1250ft)	15km 1 in 14 9.3 miles 18km 1 in 14 11miles	5 metres 16ft 5in	UO An extremely picturesque route crossing the Vosges mountains, with easy, wide bends on the descent; suitable for caravans.
Seeberg (Jezersko) 1218 metres (3996ft) Austria - Slovenia	Eisenkappel 555 metres (1821ft) Kranj 385 metres (1263ft)	14km 1 in 8 8.7 miles 33km 1 in 10 20.5 miles	5 metres 16ft 5in	UO An alternative to the steeper Loibl and Wurzen passes; moderate climb with winding, hairpin ascent and descent.
Sella 2240 metres (7349ft) Italy	Plan 1606 metres (5269ft) Canazei 1465 metres (4806ft)	9km 1 in 9 5.6 miles 12km 1 in 9 7 miles	5 metres 16ft 5in	OC Dec - Jun. A finely engineered, winding road; exceptional views of the Dolomites.
Semmering 985 metres (3232ft) Austria	Mürzzuschlag im Mürztal 672 metres (2205ft) Gloggnitz 457 metres (1499ft)	14km 1 in 16 8.7 miles 17km 1 in 16 10.6 miles	6 metres 19ft 8in	UO A fine, well engineered highway; suitable for caravans.
Sestriere 2033 metres (6670ft) Italy	Cesana Torinese 1344 metres (4409ft) Pinerolo 376 metres (1234ft)	12km 1 in 10 7.4 miles 55km 1 in 10 34.2 miles	6 metres 19ft 8in	UO Mostly bitumen surface; negotiable by caravan

* Permitted maximum width of vehicles 7ft 6in   + Permitted maximum width of vehicles 8ft 2.5in   ++ Maximum length of vehicle 30ft

Pass and height	From To	Distances from summit and max gradient	Min width of road	Conditions (see page 37 for key to abbreviations)
Silvretta (Bielerhöhe) 2032 metres (6666ft) Austria	Partenen 1051 metres (3448ft) Galtür 1584 metres (5197ft)	16km 1 in 9 9.9 miles 10km 1 in 9 6.2 miles	5 metres 16ft 5in	UC Late Oct - early Jun. For the most part reconstructed; 32 easy hairpin bends on western ascent; eastern side more straightforward. Toll road; caravans prohibited.
+Simplon 2005 metres (6578ft) Switzerland - Italy	Brig 681 metres (2234ft) Domodóssola 280 metres (919ft)	22km 1 in 9 13.6 miles 41km 1 in 11 25.5 miles	7 metres 23ft	OC Nov - Apr. An easy, reconstructed modern road, but 13 miles long, continuous ascent to summit; suitable for caravans.
Somport 1632 metres (5354ft) France - Spain	Bedous 416 metres (1365ft) Jaca 820 metres (2690ft)	31km 1 in 10 19.2 miles 32km 1 in 10 20miles	3.5 metres 11ft 6in	UO A favoured, old-established route; generally easy, but in parts narrow and unguarded; fairly well surfaced road; suitable for caravans.
*Splügen 2113 metres (6932ft) Switzerland - Italy	Splügen 1457 metres (4780ft) Chiavenna 330 metres (1083ft)	9km 1 in 9 5.6 miles 30km 1 in 7.5 18.6 miles	3.5 metres 11ft 6in	UC Nov - Jun. Mostly narrow and winding, with many hairpin bends, and not well guarded; care is also required at many tunnels and galleries (max height vehicles 9ft 2in).
++Stelvio 2757 metres (9045ft) Italy	Bormio 1225 metres (4019ft) Spondigna 885 metres (2903ft)	22km 1 in 8 13.6 miles 28km 1 in 8 12.9 miles	4 metres 13ft 1in	UC Oct - late Jun. the third highest pass in the Alps; the number of acute hairpin bends, all well engineered, is exceptional - from 40 to 50 on either side; the surface is good, the traffic heavy. Hairpin bends are too acute for long vehicles.
+Susten 2224 metres (7297ft) Switzerland	Innertkirchen 630 metres (2067ft) Wassen 916 metres (3005ft)	28km 1 in 11 12.9 miles 19km 1 in 11 11.8 miles	6 metres 19ft 8in	UC Nov - Jun. A very scenic and well guarded mountain road; easy gradients and turns; heavy traffic at weekends; negotiable by caravans - extra care required. Not for the faint-hearted.
Tenda (Tende) 1321 metres (4334ft) Italy - France	Borgo S Dalmazzo 641 metres (2103ft) La Giandola 308 metres (1010ft)	24km 1 in 11 14.9 miles 29km 1 in 11 18miles	6 metres 19ft 8in	UO Well guarded, modern road with several hairpin bends; road tunnel at summit; suitable for caravans; but prohibited during the winter.
+Thurn 1274 metres (4180ft) Austria	Kitzbühel 762 metres (2500ft) Mittersill 789 metres (2588ft)	19km 1 in 12 11.8 miles 10km 1 in 16 6.2 miles	5 metres 16ft 5in	UO A good road with narrow stretches; northern approach rebuilt; suitable for caravans.
Timmelsjoch (Rombo) 2509 metres (8232ft) Austria - Italy	Obergurgl 1910 metres (6266ft) Moso 1007 metres (3304ft)	14km 1 in 7 8.7 miles 23km 1 in 8 14miles	3.5 metres 11ft 6in	UC mid Oct - late Jun. Pass open to private cars (without trailers) only as some tunnels on the Italian side are too narrow for larger vehicles; toll road. Border closed at night 20.00 -07.00 hrs.
Tonale 1883 metres (6178ft) Italy	Edolo 699 metres (2293ft) Dimaro 766 metres (2513ft)	30km 1 in 12 18.6 miles 27km 1 in 10 16.7 miles	5 metres 16ft 5in	UO A relatively easy road; suitable for caravans.
Toses (Tosas) 1800 metres (5906ft) Spain	Puigcerdá 1152 metres (3780ft) Ribes de Freser 920 metres (3018ft)	26km 1 in 10 16miles 25km 1 in 10 15.5 miles	5 metres 16ft 5in	UO Now a fairly straightforward, but continuously winding, two-lane road with many sharp bends; negotiable by caravans.
Tourmalet 2114 metres (6936ft) France	Luz 711 metres (2333ft) Ste-Marie-de-Campan 857 metres (2812ft)	18km 1 in 8 11miles 17km 1 in 8 10.6 miles	4 metres 13ft 1in	UC Oct - mid Jun. The highest of the French Pyrenean routes; the approaches are good, though winding and exacting over summit; sufficiently guarded.
Tre Croci 1809 metres (5935ft) Italy	Cortina d'Ampezzo 1224 metres (4016ft) Auronzo di Cadore 864 metres (2835ft).	7km 1 in 9 4.4 miles 26 km 1 in 9 16 miles	6 metres 19ft 8in	OC Dec - Mar. An easy pass; very fine scenery; suitable for caravans.

* Permitted maximum width of vehicles 7ft 6in + Permitted maximum width of vehicles 8ft 2.5in ++ Maximum length of vehicle 30ft

PRINCIPAL MOUNTAIN PASSES

Pass and height	From To	Distances from summit and max gradient	Min width of road	Conditions (see page 37 for key to abbreviations)
Turracher Höhe 1763 metres (5784ft) Austria	Predlitz 922 metres (3024ft) Ebene-Reichenau 1062 metres (3484ft)	20km 1 in 5.5 12.4 miles 8km 1 in 4.5 5miles	4 metres 13ft 1in	UO Formerly one of the steepest mountain roads in Austria; now much improved. A steep, fairly straightforward ascent is followed by a very steep descent; good surface and mainly two-lane width; fine scenery.
*Umbrail 2501 metres (8205ft) Switzerland - Italy	Santa Maria im Münstertal 1375 metres (4511ft) Bormio 1225 metres (4019ft)	14km 1 in 11 9 miles 19km 1 in 11 11.8 miles	4.3 metres 14ft 1in	UC Early Nov - early Jun. Highest of the Swiss passes; narrow; mostly gravel surfaced with 34 hairpin bends, but not too difficult.
Vars 2109 metres (6919ft) France	St-Paul-sur-Ubaye 1470 metres (4823ft) Guillestre 1000 metres (3281ft)	8km 1 in 10 5miles 20km 1 in 10 12.4 miles	5 metres 16ft 5in	OC Dec - Mar. Easy winding ascent with seven hairpin bends; gradual winding descent with another seven hairpin bends; good surface; negotiable by caravans.
Wurzen (Koren) 1073 metres (3520ft) Austria - Slovenia	Riegersdorf 541 metres (1775ft) Kranjska Gora 810 metres (2657ft)	7km 1 in 5.5 4.5miles 6km 1 in 5.5 3.5 miles	4 metres 13ft 1in	UO A steep two-lane road, which otherwise is not particularly difficult; heavy traffic at summer weekends; delay likely at the frontier; caravans prohibited.
Zirler Berg 1009 metres (3310ft) Austria	Seefeld 1180 metres (3871ft) Zirl 622 metres (2041ft)	6km 1 in 7 3.5 miles 5km 1 in 6 3.1 miles	7 metres 23ft	UO An escarpment facing south, part of the route from Garmisch to Innsbruck; a good, modern road, but heavy tourist traffic and a long steep descent, with one hairpin bend, into the Inn Valley. Steepest section from the hairpin bend down to Zirl; caravans prohibited northbound.

* Permitted maximum width of vehicles 7ft 6in   + Permitted maximum width of vehicles 8ft 2.5in   ++ Maximum length of vehicle 30ft

Major Road and Rail Tunnels

ROAD TUNNELS

See Lights in the Essential Motoring Information. Minimum and maximum speed limits operate in the road tunnels.

During the winter wheel chains may occasionally be required on the approaches to some tunnels. However, you may not use them in tunnels. Use the laybys provided for removal and refitting. All charges listed are one-way and below should be used as a guide only.

BIELSA France-Spain

The trans-Pyrenean tunnel is 3km (2 miles) long, and runs nearly 1830 metres (6000ft) above sea level between Aragnouet and Bielsa.

SOMPORT France-Spain

The tunnel is over 1220 metres (4000ft) above sea level and runs between Les Forges d'Arbel and Canfranc. It is 4.5 metres (14ft 9in) high and the single carriageway is 10.15 metres (34ft 5in). There are no charges.

CADI Spain

The tunnel is 5km (3 miles) long and runs about 1220 metres (4000ft) above sea level under the Sierra del Cadi mountain range between the villages of Bellver de Cerdanya and Baga, and to the west of the Toses (Tosas) Pass.

Charges	(in Euros)
Motorcycles	8.55
Cars	8.55
Car/caravan	18.13

FREJUS France-Italy

This tunnel is over 1220 metres (4000ft) above sea level and runs between Modane and Bardonecchia. It is 12.8km (8 miles) long, 4.3 metres (14ft 2in) high, and the single carriageway is 9 metres (29ft 6in) wide. Minimum speed is 60km/h (37mph) and the maximum 70km/h (43mph).

Charges	(in Euros)
Motorcycles	18.60
Vehicle/vehicle combinations (front axle up to 1.30 metres and total height up to 2 metres)	28.10
Vehicle/vehicle combinations (front axle more than 1.30 metres and total height up to 3 metres)	37.20

MONT BLANC Chamonix (France) - Courmayeur (Italy)

The tunnel is over 1220 metres (4000ft) above sea level and is 11.6km (7 miles) long. The single carriageway is 7 metres (23ft) wide. Permitted dimensions of vehicles are: height 4.30 metres (14ft 1in); length 20 metres (65ft 7in); width 2.80 metres (9ft 2in). Larger vehicles, up to 4.70 metres (15ft 5in) high, by special arrangement. Minimum speed is 50km/h (31mph); maximum 70km/h (43mph). When exiting the tunnel the maximum speed is 50km/h (31mph) (exiting in France) or 40km/h (24mph) exiting in Italy. Do not stop, overtake, sound your horn or make U-turns. Use only side/rear lights not headlights and keep 150 metres (164yds) distance between vehicles.

Make sure you have sufficient fuel for the journey, 30km (19 miles). There are breakdown bays with telephones. From November to March, wheel chains may be required on the approaches.

Charges	(in Euros)
Motorcycle	18.60
Vehicle/vehicle combinations (front axle up to 1.30 metres and total height up to 2 metres)	28.10
Vehicle/vehicle combinations (front axle more than 1.30 metres and total height up to 3 metres)	37.20

GRAND ST BERNARD Switzerland - Italy

The tunnel is over 1925 metres (7570ft) above sea level and runs between Bourg-St-Pierre and St Rhémy. Although there are covered approaches, wheel chains may be needed in winter. Customs, passport control and toll offices are at the entrance. It is 5.9km (3.6 miles) long. Permitted maximum dimensions of vehicles are: height 4 metres (13ft 1in), width 2.5 metres (8ft 2.5in). Minimum speed is 40km/h (24mph); maximum 80km/h (49mph). Do not stop or overtake. Breakdown bays have telephones.

Charges*	(in Swiss francs)
Motorcycles	15
Cars	27
Car/caravan	40
Minibus, camper van (2 axles)	40
Vehicles with three axles	100
with four or more axles	150

*Motorway tax disc (see Switzerland Country Intro) must be displayed.

ST GOTTHARD Switzerland

This tunnel is 1154 metres (3786 ft) above sea level. It is 16.9km (10.5 miles) long and runs under the St Gotthard Pass from Göschenen, on the northern side in the Alps, to Airolo in the Ticino. The tunnel is 4.5 metres (14ft 9in) high, and the single carriageway is 7.5 metres (25ft) wide. Maximum speed is 80km/h (49mph). Forming part of the Swiss motorway network, the tunnel is subject to motorway tax, and the tax disc must be displayed (see Switzerland - Country Intro).

SAN BERNARDINO Switzerland

This tunnel is over 1644 metres (5396ft) above sea level. It is 6.6km (4 miles) long, 4.8 metres (15ft 9in) high; the carriageway is 7 metres (23ft) wide. Do not stop or overtake in the tunnel. Keep 100 metres (110yds) between vehicles. There are breakdown bays with telephones.

As part of the Swiss motorway network, the tunnel is subject to motorway tax (see Switzerland - Country Intro).

ARLBERG Austria

This tunnel is 14km (8.75 miles) long and runs at about 1220 metres (4000ft) above sea level, to the south of and parallel to the Arlberg Pass.

Charges*	(in Euros)
Motor vehicles up to 3.5 tonnes (motorcycle, car with or without caravan, minibus, van)	8.50

BOSRUCK Austria

This tunnel is 742 metres (2434ft) above sea level. It is 5.5km (3.4 miles) long and runs between Spital am Pyhrn and Selzthal, to the east of the Pyhrn Pass. Maximum speed is 80km/h (49mph). Do not overtake. Use of dipped headlights compulsory; occasional emergency laybys with telephones. With the Gleinalm Tunnel (see below) it forms part of the A9 Pyhrn Autobahn between Linz and Graz, being built in stages.

Charges*	(in Euros)
Motor vehicles up to 3.5 tonnes (motorcycle, car with or without caravan, minibus, van)	4.50

*Motorway tax disc (see Austria Country Intro) must be displayed.

FELBERTAUERN Austria

This tunnel, over 1650 metres (5415ft) above sea level, runs between Mittersill and Matrei, west of and parallel to the Grossglockner Pass. The tunnel is 5.2km (3.23 miles) long, 4.5 metres (14ft 9in) high, and the two-lane carriageway is 7 metres (23ft) wide. From November to April, wheel chains may be needed on the approach.

Charges	(in Euros)
Motorcycles	8.00
Car with or without caravan, camper van, minibus	10.00

GLEINALM Austria

This tunnel, part of the A9 Pyhrn Autobahn, is 817 metres (2680ft) above sea level, 8.3km (5 miles) long and runs between St Michael and Friesach, near Graz.

Charges*	(in Euros)
Motor vehicles up to 3.5 tonnes (motorcycle, car with or without caravan, minibus, van)	7.50

*Motorway tax disc (see Austria Country Intro) must be displayed.

KARAWANKEN Austria-Slovenia

This motorway tunnel under the Karawanken mountains between Rosenbach in Austria and Jesenice in Slovenia is about 610 metres (2000ft) above sea level and nearly 8km (5 miles) long.

Charges*	(in Euros)
Motor vehicles up to 3.5 tonnes (motorcycle, car with or without caravan, minibus, van)	6.50

*Motorway tax disc (see Austria Country Intro) must be displayed.

TAUERN AUTOBAHN (Katschberg and Radstädter) Austria

Two tunnels, the Katschberg and the Radstädter Tauern, form the key elements of this toll motorway between Salzburg and Carinthia.

The Katschberg tunnel is 1110 metres (3642ft) above sea level. It is 5.4km (3.5 miles) long, 4.5 metres (14ft 9in) high, and the single carriageway is 7.5 metres (25ft) wide.

The Radstädter Tauern tunnel is 1340 metres (4396ft) above sea level and runs east of the Tauern railway tunnel (see below). The tunnel is 6.4km (4 miles) long, 4.5 metres (14ft 9in) high; the single carriageway is 7.5m (25ft) wide.

Charges* (for the whole toll section between Flachau and Rennweg:)	(in Euros)
Motor vehicles up to 3.5 tonnes (motorcycle, car with or without caravan, minibus, van)	9.50

*Motorway tax disc (see Austria Intro) must be displayed.

MAJOR ROAD AND RAIL TUNNELS

LÖTSCHBERG Switzerland

This railway tunnel from Kandersteg to Goppenstein is 14km (8.7miles) in length. Duration of the actual journey is 15 minutes, but loading and unloading formalities can take some time.

Services

Frequent with no advance booking necessary

Charges	(in Swiss Francs)
Motorcycles	16
Cars (including driver)	25
Car/caravan	50

A full timetable and tariff is available from the Swiss National Tourist Office (see Switzerland - Tourist information for address) or at most Swiss frontier crossings.

ALBULA TUNNEL Switzerland

Thusis (723 metres, 2372ft) - Samedan (1722 metres, 5650ft). The railway tunnel is 5.9km (3.5 miles) long. It will accept vehicles, but you must give notice. Thusis telephone 081 6511113 and Samedan telephone 081 2886677. Journey time 90 minutes.

Services

9 trains daily southbound; 6 trains daily northbound.

Charges		(in Swiss franc)
Motorcycle/car (up to 5.40 metres) Mon-Thu		130
Fri-Sun		145
Car/caravan (up to 10 metres) Mon-Thu		260
Fri-Sun		290
Driver/passengers (per person) First class		38
Second class		23

FURKA TUNNEL Switzerland

Oberwald (1367 metres, 4482ft)-Realp (1539 metres, 5046ft). Railway tunnel is 15.4km (9.5 miles) long. Journey time 15 minutes.

Services

Hourly from 06.50-21.00

Charges	(in Swiss Francs)
Motorcycles	19
Cars (including driver) June-Sept	25
Oct-May	30
Car/caravan June-Sept	44
Oct-May	49

OBERALP RAILWAY Switzerland

Andermatt (1444 metres, 4737ft)-Sedrun (1441 metres, 4728ft). Journey duration 60 minutes.

Booking

Advance booking is necessary;

Andermatt telephone 041 8887511
Sedrun tel 041 819204711.

Services

2-4 trains daily, winter only (from October-April).

Charges	(in Swiss francs)
Cars	65
Minibus	99
Driver/passengers (per person)	10

TAUERN TUNNEL Austria

Bockstein (1131 metres, 3711ft)(near Badgastein)-Mallnitz, 8.5km (5.5 miles) long. Width 2 metres. Journey duration 13 minutes

Booking

Advance booking unnecessary (except for request trains), but motorists must report at least 20 minutes before departure. Drivers must drive their vehicles on and off the wagon.

Services

Regular services available.

Charges	(in Euros)
Motorcycles	8
Cars	15

Compulsory Equipment

Here are some items of equipment that are compulsory or recommended when travelling within areas of Europe. Alternatively, download our guide to compulsory equipment (www.theAA.com/allaboutcars/overseas/compulsory-equipment.html when driving in Europe for easy reference. In addition follow these tips for stress-free driving:

* ★ Display the appropriate identification letters.
* ★ In winter, remember that, authorities insist on wheel chains and/or winter tyres for many resorts and passes.
* ★ Ideally, fit external rear view mirrors to both sides of your vehicle.
* ★ Motorcyclists and passengers must wear crash helmets in all countries.

Country	First Aid Kit[1]	Fire Extinguisher[3]	Warning Triangle[3]	Spare Bulbs[1&2]	Headlamp Adjustment[4]
Andorra	Recommended	Recommended	Compulsory	Compulsory	Compulsory
Austria	Compulsory	Recommended	Compulsory	Recommended	Recommended
Belgium	Recommended	Recommended	Compulsory	Recommended	Compulsory
France	Recommended	Recommended	Compulsory[5/6]	Recommended	Compulsory
Germany	Recommended	Recommended	Compulsory[7]	Recommended	Compulsory
Italy	Recommended	Recommended	Compulsory	Recommended	Recommended
Luxembourg	Recommended	Recommended	Compulsory[7]	Recommended	Recommended
Netherlands	Recommended	Recommended	Compulsory[5]	Recommended	Compulsory
Portugal	Recommended	Recommended	Compulsory[5]	Recommended	Recommended
Spain	Recommended	Recommended	Compulsory[8]	Compulsory	Compulsory
Switzerland	Recommended	Recommended	Compulsory	Recommended	Recommended

NOTES

1. Applies to all vehicles including motorcycles unless stated otherwise.
2. A spare bulb kit will not avoid a fine if you are travelling with faulty lights, but replacing a bulb on the spot may avoid the cost and inconvenience of a garage call out. On some cars, only a qualified technician to change a headlamp bulb or lamp unit eg high-intensity discharge (HID) headlamps, so carrying spare bulbs is not an option. However, carry spare bulbs for any lights which can be easily and/or safely changed.
3. Excludes motorcycles.
4. Regardless of local requirements, it is wise to adjust headlamp beams for driving on the right. For older vehicles this can be done using simple adhesive masks on the headlamp glass, but for newer vehicles with high-density discharge (HID), xenon or many halogen headlamps it's not so easy. Check out what you need to do well before your intended departure by contacting a dealer for your make of vehicle. Without adjustment, dipped beams will dazzle oncoming drivers, and you could be fined. This adjustment is not required for two-wheeled vehicles as the beam pattern is more symmetrical, but check that any extra loading has not affected the beam height.
5. Hazard warning lights or a warning triangle are compulsory in an accident or breakdown situation. However, a warning triangle should always be carried as hazard warning lights have no effect at bends or rises in the road and may, of course, become damaged or inoperative.
6. Warning triangle compulsory for trailers with total authorised laden weight exceeding 500kg.
7. Although visitors don't have to carry warning triangles, it is compulsory to use them in an accident or breakdown situation.
8. One warning triangle compulsory for non-Spanish registered vehicles; two for Spanish registered vehicles. NOTE: Drivers of non-Spanish registered vehicles should consider carrying two triangles as regardless of the regulations, local officials may impose on the spot fine if only one is available.

SAMPLE BOOKING LETTERS FOR RESERVATIONS

Please use block capitals and enclose an International Reply Coupon, obtainable from post offices. Be sure to fill in your own name and address, including the post code and the country.

English

Dear Sir,

I intend to stay at your site for ....days, arriving on.............(date and month) and departing on...................(date and month).
We are a party of ....people, including....adults and ....children (aged...........) and would like a pitch for ....tent(s) and/or parking space for our car/caravan/caravan trailer.
We would like to hire a tent/caravan/bungalow.
Please quote full charges when replying and advise on the deposit required, which will beforwarded without delay.

French

Monsieur,
Je me propose de séjourner à votre terrain de camping pour ....jours, depuis le..... jusqu'au..........
Nous sommes........personnes en tout, y compris ....adultes et ....enfants (âgés de......) et nous aurons besoin d'un emplacement pour ....tente(s), et/ou un parking pour notre voiture/caravane/remorque.
Nous voudrions louer une tente/caravane/bungalow.
Veuillez me donner dans votre réponse une idée de vos prix, m'indiquant en même temps le montant qu'il faut payer en avance, ce qui vous sera envoyé sans délai.

German

Sehr geehrter Herr!
Ich beabsichtige, mich auf Ihrem Campingplatz ....Tage aufzuhalten, und zwar vom.....bis zum......
Wir sind im ganzen ....Personen, ...Erwachsene und ....Kinder (in Alter von......), und benötigen Platz für Zelt(e) und/oder unseren Wagen/Wohnwagen/Wohnwagenanhänger.
Wir möchten ein Zelt/Wohnwagen/Bungalow mieten.
Bitte, geben Sie mir in Ihrem Antwortschreiben die vollen Preise bekannt, und ebenso die Höhe der von mir zu leistenden Anzahlung, die Ihnen alsdann unverzüglich überwiesen wird.

Italian

Egregio Signore,
Ho intenzione di remanere presso di voi per .....giorni. Arriverò il.....e partirò il......
Siamo un gruppo di.......persone in totale, compreso ......adulti e ......bambini (de età.....) e vorrremo un posto per ......tenda(tende) e/o spazio per parcheggiare la nostra vetture/carovana/roulette.
Desideriamo affittare una tenda/carovana/bungalow.
Vi preghiamo di quotare i prezzi completi quando ci risponderete, e darci informazioni sul deposito richiesto, che vi sarà rimesso senza ritardo.

Spanish

Muy señor mio,
Desearia me reservara espacio por ......dias, a partir del.......hasta el......
Nuestro grupo comprende .....personas todo comprendido, ...adultos y ....niños (.......de años de edad). Necesitarimos un espacio por......tienda(s) y/o espacio para apacar nuestro choche/caravana/remolque.
Deseariamos alquilar una tienda de campana/caravan/bungalow.
Le ruego nos comunique los precios y nos informe sobre el depósito que debemos remitirle.

Key to Regions

The country directories, with the exception of Andorra and Luxembourg, are divided into regions, each introduced by a brief description, to help you to plan your touring holidays. Below is a list of the regional headings used in each country directory, followed by a list of the departments , districts or administrative areas that may be included within each region. See also the country maps at the end of the book.

AUSTRIA

TIROL
CARINTHIA = Kärnten
STYRIA = Steiermark
LOWER AUSTRIA - Niederösterreich,
Burgenland
UPPER AUSTRIA - Oberösterreich, Salzburg
VORARLBERG
VIENNA = Wien

BELGIUM

SOUTH WEST/COAST - Hainaut, West-
Vlaanderen
NORTH/CENTRAL - Brabant, Oost-Vlaanderen
NORTH EAST - Antwerpen, Limburg
SOUTH EAST - Liège, Luxembourg, Namur

FRANCE

ALPS/EAST - Ain, Doubs, Hautes-Alpes, Haute
Saône, Haute Savoie, Jura, Isère, Savoie, Territoire-
de-Belfort
ALSACE/LORRAINE - Bas-Rhin, Haut-Rhin,
Meurthe-et-Moselle, Meuse, Moselle, Vosges
BURGUNDY/CHAMPAGNE - Aube, Ardennes,
Côte-d'Or, Haute-Marne, Marne, Nièvre, Saône-
et-Loire, Yonne
SOUTH WEST/ PYRENEES - Ariège, Dordogne,
Gers, Gironde, Haute-Garonne, Hautes-Pyrénées,
Landes, Lot, Lot-et-Garonne, Pyrénées-Atlantiques,
Tarn, Tarn-et-Garonne
LOIRE/CENTRAL - Charente, Charente-
Maritime, Cher, Corrèze, Creuse, Deux-Sèvres,
Eure-et-Loir, Haute-Vienne, Indre, Indre-et-Loire,
Loire-Atlantique, Loiret, Loir-et-Cher, Maine-et-
Loire, Mayenne, Sarthe, Vendée, Vienne
BRITTANY/NORMANDY - Calvados, Côtes-
d'Armor, Eure, Finistère, Ille-et-Vilaine, Manche,
Morbihan, Orne, Seine-Maritime
PARIS/NORTH - Aisne, Essonne, Hauts-de-Seine,
Nord, Oise, Paris, Pas-de-Calais, Seine-et-Marne,
Seine-St-Denis, Somme, Val-de-Marne, Val d'Oise,
Yvelines
AUVERGNE - Allier, Aveyron, Cantal, Haute-
Loire, Loire, Lozère, Puy-de-Dôme, Rhône
SOUTH COAST/RIVIERA - Alpes-Maritimes,
Alpes-de-Haute-Provence, Ardèche, Aude,
Bouches-du-Rhône, Drôme, Gard, Hérault,
Monaco, Pyrénées-Orientales, Var, Vaucluse
CORSICA - Corse-du-Sud, Haute-Corse

GERMANY

SOUTH EAST - Bayern
SOUTH WEST - Baden-Württemberg
BERLIN AND EASTERN PROVINCES -
Brandenburg, Sachsen, Thüringen
CENTRAL - Hessen, Nordrhein-Westfalen,
Rheinland-Pfalz, Saarland
NORTH - Bremen, Hamburg, Niedersachsen,
Schleswig-Holstein

ITALY

NORTH WEST/ALPS/LAKES - Aosta,
Alessandria, Asti, Beramo, Bolzano, Brescia, Como,
Cremona, Cuneo, Mantova, Milano, Novara,
Pavia, Sondrio, Trento, Torino, Varese, Vercelli
VENICE/NORTH - Belluno, Gorizia, Padova,
Pordenone, Rovigo, Treviso, Trieste, Udine,
Venezia, Verona, Vicenza,
NORTH WEST/MED COAST - Arezzo, Firenze,
Genova, Grosseto, Imperia, Livorno, Lucca, Massa
Carrara, Pisa, Pistoia, Savona, Siena, La Spezia
NORTH EAST/ADRIATIC - Ancona, L'Aquila,
Ascoli Piceno, Bologna, Campobasso, Chieti,
Ferrara, Forli, Iserina, Macerata, Modena, Parma,
Perugia, Pescara, Pesaro & Urbino, Piacenza,
Ravenna, Reggio nell'Emilia, Teramo, Terni
ROME - Frosinone, Latina, Roma, Rieti, Viterbo
SOUTH - Avellino, Bari, Benevento, Brindisi,

Caserta, Catanzaro, Cosenza, Foggia, Lecce,
Matera, Napoli, Potenza, Reggio di Calabria,
Salerno, Taranto
SARDINIA - Cagliari, Nuoro, Oristano, Sassari
SICILY - Agrigento, Caltanissetta, Catania, Enna,
Messina, Palermo, Ragusa, Siracusa, Trapani

NETHERLANDS

NORTH - Ameland, Drenthe, Friesland,
Groningen
CENTRAL - Flevoland, Gelderland, Noord-
Holland, Overijssel, Utrecht
SOUTH - Limburg, Noord-Brabant, Zeeland,
Zuid-Holland

PORTUGAL

SOUTH - Algarve, Baixo-Alentejo
NORTH - Costa Verde, Douro Litoral, Minho,
Tras os Montes, Alto Douro
CENTRAL - Alto Alentejo, Beira Alta, Beira
Baixo, Beira Litoral, Costa de Prata, Estremadura,
Ribatejo

SPAIN

NORTH EAST COAST - Barcelona, Girona
CENTRAL - Albacete, Avila, Badajoz, Cáceres,
Ciudad Real, Cuenca, Guadalajara, Madrid,
Salamanca, Segovia, Soria, Teruel, Toledo
SOUTH EAST COAST - Alicante, Castellón,
Tarragona, Valencia
NORTH COAST - Asturias, Cantabria,
Guipúzcoa, La Coruña, Lugo, Vizcaya
NORTH EAST - Alava, Burgos, Huesca, Lleida,
La Rioja, Navarra, Zaragoza
NORTH WEST - Léon, Logrono Orense,
Palencia, Pontevedra, Valladolid, Zamora
SOUTH - Almeria, Cádiz, Cordoba, Granada,
Huelva, Jaén, Málaga, Murcia, Sevilla
ISLANDS - Ibiza, Mallorca Menorca

SWITZERLAND

NORTH - Aargau, Basel, Solothurn
NORTH EAST - Appenzell, Liechtenstein, St
Gallen, Schaffhausen, Thurgau, Zürich
NORTH WEST/CENTRAL - Bern, Jura, Luzern,
Neuchâtel, Nidwalden, Obwalden, Schwyz, Uri,
Zug
EAST - Glarus, Graubünden
SOUTH - Ticino
SOUTH WEST - Fribourg, Genève, Valais, Vaud

AUSTRIA

Austria is a land of chalet villages, beautiful cities and majestic mountains. It is bordered by eight countries: the Czech Republic, Germany, Hungary, Italy, Liechtenstein, Switzerland, Slovakia and Slovenia.

The scenery is predominantly Alpine, an inspiring mix of mountains, lakes and pine forests. The splendour of the mountains can be seen in the imposing Dachstein region of upper Austria and the massive Tyrolean peaks. The lakes of Burgenland and Salzkammergut, the River Danube, the forests and woods of Styria and the world-famous city of Wien (Vienna) are outstanding features of this majestic landscape.

Most of the country enjoys a moderate climate during the summer, although eastern areas are sometimes very hot. The heaviest rainfall occurs in midsummer. The language of Austria is German, and English is not widely spoken. The Austrians pride themselves on their informal and easy-going nature, a nature summed up by the word "gemütlich", one of those words that defies adequate translation.

Austria offers a variety of outdoor activities to suit everyone and there are numerous campsites throughout the country. Most are open from May to September, although a number remain open all year.

Off-site camping or caravanning is generally prohibited. In areas with no campsites contact local police to find out whether an overnight stay is possible. If permission is granted, no camping activity must be seen from outside, eg chairs, awnings etc. Open fires are generally prohibited in woodland areas. Campers not on an official site, eg private property, staying in Austria for more than three days should report to the police as soon as possible, and also inform them of subsequent changes of location. Within Wien (Vienna) and Tirol (Tyrol) any form of off-site camping or caravanning is prohibited.

HOW TO GET THERE

Apart from the crossing via the Channel Tunnel, the usual Continental Channel or this journey is Calais. From Calais drive through eastern France to Strasbourg, then via Karlsruhe and Stuttgart, crossing into Austria at Füssen for **Innsbruck and the Tirol**, and beyond München (Munich) for **Salzburg and central Austria**.

As an alternative, you could cross to Dieppe, Le Havre, Caen (Ouistreham) or Cherbourg and drive through northern France via **Strasbourg** and **Stuttgart**, or via **Basel** and northern Switzerland. But see 'Motorway tax' in this and the Swiss section.

DISTANCE

From the Continental Channel ports, Salzburg is about 1140km (708 miles) and Vienna is about 1310km (814 miles), and you will probably need one overnight stop on the way.

CAR SLEEPER TRAINS

Summer services are available from **Dortmund** and **Düsseldorf** (Germany) to Villach.

MOTORING AND GENERAL

The information given here is specific to Austria. It must be read in conjunction with the Essential Motoring Information at the front of the book, which covers those regulations which are common to many countries.

BRITISH EMBASSY/CONSULATES*

The British Embassy is located at 1030 Wien, Jaurèsgasse 12 ☎ (01) 716130; consular section, Jaurèsgasse 10 ☎(01) 71613 5151. There are British Consulates with Honorary Consuls, in Bregenz, Graz, Innsbruck and Salzburg.

CHILDREN IN CARS

Children under 12 and/or 1.5 metres in height are not permitted to travel as front or rear seat passengers unless using a suitable restraint system - see 'Passengers' and 'Seat Belts' in the Essential Motoring Information section.

CURRENCY

With the introduction of the Euro, the **Austrian Schilling (ATS)** ceased to be legal tender from 2002. However, ATS coins and notes may still be exchanged at the Austrian Central Bank (**Oesterreichische Nationalbank**) for an unlimited period.

DIMENSION AND WEIGHT RESTRICTION

Private **cars** and towed **trailers** or **caravans** are restricted to the following dimensions - height, 4 metres; width 2.55 metres; length, 12 metres. The maximum permitted overall length of vehicle/trailer or caravan combination is 18.75 metres.

DRIVING LICENCE*

A valid UK or Republic of Ireland licence is accepted in Austria. However, those licences which do not incorporate a photograph will not be recognised unless accompanied by photographic proof of identity, eg. a passport. The minimum age at which a visitor may use a temporarily imported motorcycle (exceeding 50cc) or car is 18 years.

FIRST-AID KIT*

In Austria all vehicles (including motorcycles) must be equipped with a first-aid kit by law and visitors are expected to comply. Spot checks are carried out by the police and, in addition, any motorist stopped at the scene of an accident must

be able to produce a first aid kit if this is requested by any competent authority; if this is not forthcoming the police may take action.

FOODSTUFFS*

If the imported foodstuffs are for personal use, there are no limits when travelling between EU countries. Visitors entering Austria from outside the EU may personally import 1kg of meat, all animal products (eg eggs, milk, honey) and all animal based products (eg milk products, sausages, fish and all sea animal products), 1kg of conserves made from meat or animal products as above, and 250g of caviar. Coffee (500g), coffee extract (200g), tea (100g), and tea extract (40g) are free of customs duties, but visitors under 15 cannot import coffee.

LIGHTS*

It is compulsory for motorcyclists to use dipped headlights during the day.

MOTORING CLUB

The **Österreichischer Automobil-, Motorrad- und Touring Club** (ÖAMTC) which has its headquarters at 1010 Wien, Schubertring 1-3 ☎ (01)71199-0, has offices at the major frontier crossings, and is represented in most towns either directly or through provincial motoring clubs.

The offices are usually open between 09.00 to 18.00hrs weekdays, 09.00 to 12.00hrs on Saturdays and are closed on Sundays and public holidays.

Website: **www.oamtc.at**

MOTORWAY TAX

All vehicles using Austrian motorways and expressways must display a tax sticker (Vignette). The stickers, valid for one year, two months or 10 days, may be purchased at many petrol stations located close to the border in neighbouring countries and in Austria, at the frontier or in ÖAMTC offices.

The cost of a 10-day sticker for vehicles up to 3.5 tonnes in weight, with or without a trailer is EUR 7.60.

ROADS

The motorist crossing into Austria from any frontier enters a network of well-engineered roads.

The main traffic artery runs from Bregenz in the west to Wien (Vienna) in the east, via the

Arlberg Tunnel (Toll: see *Major Road and Rail Tunnels p47*), Innsbruck, Salzburg, and Linz. Most of the major alpine roads are excellent, and a comprehensive tour can be made through the Tirol, Salzkammergut and Carinthia without difficulty. Service stations are fairly frequent, even on mountain roads.

In July and August, several roads across the frontier become congested. The main points are on the Lindau-Bregenz road; at the Brenner Pass (possible alternative - the Résia (Reschen) Pass); at Kufstein; on the München (Munich)-Salzburg *Autobahn* and on the Villach-Tarvisio road. Additionally, because of increasing traffic from Germany, Klingenbach and Nickelsdorf on the Austro/Hungarian border are very busy. For details of mountain passes consult page 37.

Austria has over 1000 miles of motorway *(autobahn)* with additional tolls payable on the Brenner, Karawanken Tunnel, Tauern, Pyhrn (Gleinalm and Bosruck Tunnels). Triangles marked on motorway posts indicate the nearest emergency telephone (every 2km). A flashing orange/yellow light at the top of telephone posts indicates danger ahead.

For details of mountain passes consult page 37.

SPEED LIMITS*

Car / Motorcycle
Built-up areas 50km/h (31mph)
Other roads 100km/h (62mph)
Motorways 130km/h (80mph)
Car towing caravan not exceeding 750kg (1,650lb)†
Built-up areas 50km/h (31mph)
Other roads 100km/h (62mph)
Motorways 100km/h (62mph)
Car towing caravan exceeding 750kg (1,650lb)†
Built-up areas 50km/h (31mph)
Other roads 80km/h (49mph)
Motorways 100km/h (62mph)

† If the total weight of the two vehicles exceeds 3,500kg the following speed limits apply:
Built-up areas 50km/h (31mph)
Other roads 60km/h (37mph)
Motorways 70km/h (43mph)

Notes
i. *To tow a caravan/trailer, the weight of any caravan/trailer equipped with over-run brakes must not exceed the maximum weight of towing vehicle.*
ii. *Driving licence must show entitlement to drive this kind of combination.*

WARNING TRIANGLE*

It is compulsory for a vehicle to be equipped with a warning triangle and to use it outside built-up areas in the event of an accident or breakdown. The triangle must be placed behind the vehicle at a distance that will allow the drivers of following vehicles sufficient time to react to the obstruction; it must be visible at a distance of 50 metres (55yds).

* Additional information will be found in the Essential Motoring Information at the front of the book.

St Gilgen's Town Hall

TIROL

ASCHAU TIROL

Aufenfeld Distelberg 1, 6274 ☎ 05282 2916 ▤ 05282 291611
e-mail: camping.fiegl@tirol.com
website: www.camping-zillertal.at
A well equipped family site on level meadowland backed by
thickly wooded slopes.
⮑ *Signposted from the Aschau road.*
Open: All year Site: 12HEC ⊞ Ϙ 🏠 Prices: ♦4.50-7 ▲6.60
pitch 6.60 Facilities: ⋔ 🏪 ⊙ 🗗 ⌀ 🛆 Services: 🍽 ✕ lau
Leisure: ⌇ LP Off-site: ⌇R ⊞

EHRWALD TIROL

International Dr-Ing E Lauth Zugspitzstr 34, 6632
☎ 05673 2666 ▤ 05673 26664
e-mail: camping-ehrwald@tirol.com
website: www.camping-ehrwald.at
On undulating grassland, surrounded by high conifers, below
the Wetterstein mountain range. Cars may park by tents in
winter.
⮑ *To the right of the access road to the Zugspitz funicular.*
Open: All year Site: 1HEC ⊞ ♦ Ϙ Facilities: ⋔ ⊙ 🗗 ⌀ 🛆
🛆 Services: 🍽 ✕ 🖫 lau Off-site: 🏪 ⌇P

Tiroler Zugspitzcamp Obermoos 1, 6632
☎ 05673 2309 ▤ 05673 230951
e-mail: ferienanlage@zugspitze.com
website: www.ferienanlage-zugspitze.at
A well equipped site on several grassy terraces surrounded by
woodland. Modern sanitary installations with bathrooms.
⮑ *Near the Zugspitz funicular station.*
Open: All year Site: 5HEC Ϙ Prices: ♦11.60-13.80 pitch 6-8
Facilities: ⋔ 🏪 ⊙ 🗗 ⌀ 🛆 🛆 Services: 🍽 ✕ Leisure: ⌇ P

FIEBERBRUNN TIROL

Tirol-Camp 6391 ☎ 05354 56666 ▤ 05354 52516
e-mail: office@tirol-camp.at
website: www.tirol-camp.at
A summer and winter site in pleasant Alpine surroundings.
Open: All year Site: 4.7HEC ⊞ Ϙ Prices: ♦7-10 pitch 10-
13 Facilities: ⋔ 🏪 ⊙ 🗗 ⌀ 🛆 🛆 Services: 🍽 ✕ 🖫 lau
Leisure: ⌇ LP Off-site: ⌇L

FÜGEN TIROL

Hell Gagering 212b, 6263 ☎ 05288 62203 ▤ 05288 64615
e-mail: camping.hell@tirol.com
website: www.tirol.com/camping-hell
In a meadow surrounding a farm with fine views of the
surrounding mountains.
⮑ *1km N of Fügen on the B169.*
Open: All year Site: 4HEC Ϙ 🚍 ⊘ Prices: ♦4.20-6.80
pitch 6-9 Facilities: ⋔ 🏪 ⊙ 🗗 ⌀ 🛆 🛆 Services: 🍽 ✕ lau
Leisure: ⌇ P Off-site: ⌇L

HAIMING TIROL

Center Oberland Bundestr 9, 6425
☎ 05266 88294 ▤ 05266 882949
e-mail: oberland@tirol.com
website: www.camping_oberland.at
On a sloping meadow in a picturesque mountain setting. A
wide variety of sporting facilities are available.
⮑ *Off B171 at Km485.*
Open: All year Site: 4HEC ⊞ Ϙ 🚍 Facilities: ⋔ 🏪 ⊙ 🗗 ⌀
🛆 🛆 Services: 🍽 ✕ 🖫 lau Leisure: ⌇ P Off-site: ⌇R

HEITERWANG TIROL

Heiterwangersee Hotel Fisher am See, 6611
☎ 05674 5116 ▤ 05674 5260
e-mail: fischer.am.see@tirol.com
In a quiet situation in a meadow beside lake behind the
hotel.
⮑ *By Hotel Fischer am See.*
Open: All year Site: 1HEC ⊞ ♦ ♠ Facilities: ⋔ ⊙ 🗗 ⌀ 🛆
🛆 Services: 🍽 ✕ 🖫 lau Leisure: ⌇ L

HOPFGARTEN TIROL

Schlossberg Itter 140, 6361 ☎ 05335 2181 ▤ 05335 2182
e-mail: info@camping-itter.at
website: www.camping-itter.at
A family site with good leisure facilities. In terraced
meadowland below Schloss Itter on the Brixental Ache.
⮑ *2km W on B170.*
Open: Dec-6 November Site: 4HEC ⊞ ∴∴ Ϙ
Prices: ♦4.72-5.50 🚍2.85-3.80 🚐2.85-3.80 ▲2.85-3.80
3.70-7.60 Facilities: ⋔ 🏪 ⊙ 🗗 ⌀ 🛆 🛆 Services: 🍽 ✕ lau
Leisure: ⌇ PR Off-site: ⌇L ⊞

HUBEN TIROL

Ötztaler Naturcamping 6444 ☎ 05253 5855 ▤ 05253 5538
e-mail: oetzt-naturcamp@utanet.at
website: www.oetztalernaturcamping.com
A well kept site in a beautiful wooded location beside a
mountain stream.
⮑ *S of the town. Signposted from Km27 on B186.*
Open: All year Site: 0.5HEC ⊞ Ϙ Prices: ♦4.70-4.90
🚍2.30-2.50 🚐4.20-5.90 ▲3.20-4.20 Facilities: ⋔ ⊙ 🗗 ⌀ 🛆
🛆 Services: ✕ 🖫 lau Off-site: 🏪 ✕ ⌀

IMST TIROL

Imst-West Langgasse 62, 6460
☎ 05412 66293 ▤ 05412 63364
e-mail: fink.franz@aon.at website: www.tiscover.at/ciw
On open meadowland in the Langgasse area.
⮑ *Off the bypass near the turn for the Pitztal.*
Open: All year Site: 1HEC ⊞ ♠ Prices: ♦4-5 pitch 5.50-
6.50 Facilities: ⋔ 🏪 ⊙ 🗗 ⌀ 🛆 🛆 Services: 🍽 lau Off-site: ✕
⌇LPR ⊞

INNSBRUCK TIROL

Innsbruck-Kranebitten Kranebitter Allee 214, 6020
☎ 0512 284180 ▤ 0512 284180
e-mail: campinnsbruck@hotmail.com
website: www.campinginnsbruck.at
In a pleasant location close to the city. An 'Innsbruck Card'
giving reductions to many places of interest and some forms
of public transport is available at the site.
⮑ *Signposted from A12/E60 (Innsbruck-Arlberg).*
Open: All year Site: 3HEC ⊞ Ϙ 🚐 ▲ Prices: ♦5.55-5.95
🚍3 🚐3 ▲3 Facilities: ⋔ 🏪 ⊙ 🗗 ⌀ 🛆 🛆 Services: 🍽 ✕ 🖫 lau
Leisure: ⌇ R Off-site: ⌇P

KITZBÜHEL TIROL

Schwarzsee 6370 ☎ 05356 62806 ▤ 6447930
e-mail: office@bruggerhof-camping.at
website: www.bruggerhof-camping.at
In meadowland on the edge of a wood behind a large
restaurant.
⮑ *2km from town on B170 towards Wörgl turn right, 400m
after Schwarzsee railway station.*
Open: All year Site: 6HEC ⊞ ♠ 🚐 Prices: ♦7.80-8.50 🚍4-
5 🚐3.70-3.70 pitch 7.70-7.70 Facilities: ⋔ 🏪 ⊙ 🗗 ⌀ 🛆 🛆
Services: 🍽 ✕ 🖫 lau Leisure: ⌇ L

Site: 6HEC-Site size ⊞-grass ∴∴-sand ♦-stone ᪷-little shade Ϙ-partly shaded ♠-mainly shaded
🏠-bungalows for hire 🚐-caravans for hire ▲-tents for hire ⊘-no dogs Prices: ♦-adult per night 🚍-car per night
pp-per person per night 🚐-caravan per night ▲-tent per night

KÖSSEN TIROL

Wilder Kaiser Kranebittau 18, 6345
☎ 05375 6444 ▤ 05375 2113
e-mail: info@eurocamp-koessen.com
website: www.eurocamp-koessen.com
Situated in a lovely position below Unterberg, this level site is adjoined on three sides by woodland.
⊃ *For access follow road to Unterberg Lift, then turn right and continue for 200m.*
Open: All year Site: 5HEC ⚏ ⛆ Prices: ⚐6-7 pitch 6-9 Facilities: ⚕ ⚑ ⊙ ⚐ ⚏ ⚐ Services: ⚐ ✗ ⊞ lau Leisure: ⚲ P

KRAMSACH TIROL

Stadlerhof 6233 ☎ 05337 63371 ▤ 05337 65311
e-mail: camping.stadlerhof@chello.at
website: www.camping-stadlerhof.at
A pleasant, year-round site on the Reintaler See with well defined pitches and good leisure facilities.
⊃ *Access via A12.*
Open: All year Site: 3HEC ⚏ ⚐ ⛆ Prices: ⚐4.60-5.80 pitch 14-24.50 (incl 2 persons) Facilities: ⚕ ⚑ ⊙ ⚐ ⚏ ⚐ Services: ⚐ ✗ ⊞ lau Leisure: ⚲ LP Off-site: ⚲R

KUFSTEIN TIROL

Kufstein Salurner Str 36, 6330
☎ 05372 62229 ▤ 05372 636894
e-mail: kufstein@hotelbaeren.at
website: www.hotelbaeren.at
In a pleasant location with a good variety of sporting facilities.
⊃ *1km W of Kufstein between River Inn and B171.*
Open: May-Oct Site: 1HEC ⚏ ⚐ Prices: ⚐4.95 ⛆4 ⛆4 ⚐3 pitch 5.50 Facilities: ⚕ ⚑ ⊙ ⚐ ⚏ ⚐ Services: ⚐ ✗ ⊞ lau Off-site: ⚲LPR

LANDECK TIROL

Riffler 6500 ☎ 05442 64898 ▤ 05442 648984
e-mail: riffler@aon.at website: www.camping-riffler.at
Site on meadowland between residential housing and the banks of the Sanna.
Site: 0.3HEC ⚏ ⚐ ⛆ Prices: ⚐4.40 ⛆2.30 ⚐7.10-8.30 ⚐4.50-7.10 Facilities: ⚕ ⊙ ⚐ ⚐ Services: ⊞ lau Leisure: ⚲ R Off-site: ⚐ ⚏ ⚲P

Sport Camp Tirol Mühlkanal 1, 6500
☎ 05442 64636 ▤ 05442 64037
e-mail: info@sportcamptirol.at
website: www.sportcamptirol.at
Meadowland site with many fruit trees.
⊃ *On B316.*
Open: All year Site: 1.5HEC ⚏ ⚐ Prices: ⚐5.20 ⛆3.40 ⚐7.80 ⚐3.30-7.80 Facilities: ⚕ ⊙ ⚐ ⚏ ⚐ Services: ⚐ ✗ ⊞ lau Leisure: ⚲ R Off-site: ⚲LP

LÄNGENFELD TIROL

Ötztal 6444 ☎ 05253 5348 ▤ 05253 5909
In meadowland with some tall trees on the edge of woodland.
⊃ *Turn right off E186 at fire station.*
Open: All year Site: 2.6HEC ⚏ ⚐ ⛆ Facilities: ⚕ ⊙ ⚐ ⚐ ⚏ ⚐ Services: ⚐ ✗ ⊞ lau Off-site: ✗ ⚲P

> **The AA cannot be held responsible for the content of third party websites**

LANGKAMPFEN TIROL

Hager Kufsteinerstrasse 38, 6336
☎ 05372 64170 ▤ 05332 7296635
Site situated on level meadowland.
Open: All year Site: 0.5HEC ⚏ ⚐ Prices: pitch 14 (incl 2 persons) Facilities: ⚕ ⚑ ⊙ ⚐ ⚐ ⚐ Services: ⚐ ✗ ⊞ lau Off-site: ⚲LR

LERMOOS TIROL

Happy Camp Hofherr Garmischer Str 21, 6631
☎ 05673 2980 ▤ 05673 29805
e-mail: info@camping-lermoos.com
website: www.camping-lermoos.com
Well equipped site in a wooded location with fine views of the surrounding mountains.
⊃ *500mtrs from the town, off B187 towards Ehrwald.*
Open: 15 Dec-Apr & Jun-Oct Site: 0.8HEC ⚏ ⚐ Facilities: ⚕ ⊙ ⚐ ⚏ ⚐ Services: ⚐ ✗ lau Off-site: ⚑ ⚐ ⚲PR ⊞

LEUTASCH TIROL

Holiday-Camping 6105 ☎ 05214 65700 ▤ 05214 657030
e-mail: info@holiday-camping.at
website: www.holiday-camping.at
A modern site on level grassland screened by trees on the Leutascher Ache.
⊃ *Turn off B313 (Mittenwald-Scharnitz) towards Leutasch.*
Open: 7 Dec-5 Nov Site: 2.6HEC ⚏ ⚐ ⛆ Prices: ⚐8.50 ⚐5 pitch 7-10.50 Facilities: ⚕ ⚑ ⊙ ⚐ ⚐ ⚏ ⚐ Services: ⚐ ✗ ⊞ lau Leisure: ⚲ PR

LIENZ TIROL

Falken Eichholz 7, 9900 ☎ 04852 64022 ▤ 04852 640226
e-mail: camping.falken@tirol.com
website: www.camping-falken.com
On open ground on the outskirts of the town with modern sanitary facilities.
⊃ *S of Lienz. Signposted from B100.*
Open: 21 Dec-19 Oct Site: 2.5HEC ⚏ ⚐ Prices: ⚐4.50-5.50 pitch 6-8 Facilities: ⚕ ⚑ ⊙ ⚐ ⚏ ⚐ Services: ⚐ ✗ lau Off-site: ⚲LPR ⊞

MAURACH TIROL

Karwendel 6212 ☎ 05243 6116 ▤ 05243 20036
e-mail: info@karwendel-camping.at
website: www.karwendel-camping.at
On a level meadow with fine views of the surrounding mountains.
⊃ *In town turn off the B181 and follow the Pertisau road.*
Open: All year Site: 1.8HEC ⚏ ⚐ ⛆ Prices: ⚐4.50 ⛆3 ⚐4.50 Facilities: ⚕ ⊙ ⚐ ⚐ ⚏ ⚐ Services: ⚐ ✗ lau Off-site: ⚑ ⚲LP ⊞

MAYRHOFEN TIROL

Mayrhofen Laubichl 125, 6290
☎ 05285 6258051 ▤ 05285 6258060
e-mail: camping@alpenparadies.com
website: www.alpenparadies.com
A modern site with good facilities, a few minutes walk from the centre of the village.
⊃ *Near a farm at N entrance to village.*
Site: 2HEC ⚏ ⚐ Facilities: ⚕ ⚑ ⊙ ⚐ ⚐ ⚏ ⚐ Services: ⚐ ✗ ⊞ Leisure: ⚲ P

Facilities: ⚑-shop ⚕-shower ⊙-electric points for razors ⚐-electric points for caravans ⚐-parking by tents permitted ⚐-compulsory separate car park **Services:** ✗-café/restaurant ⚐-bar ⚐-Camping Gaz International ⚏-gas other than Camping Gaz ⊞-first aid facilities lau-laundry **Leisure:** ⚲-swimming L-Lake P-Pool R-River S-Sea **Off-site:** All facilities within 2km

NATTERS TIROL

Natterer See Natterer See 1, 6161
☎ 0512 546732   ▤ 0512 54673216
e-mail: info@natterersee.com
website: www.natterersee.com
A terraced site beautifully situated amidst woodland and mountains on the shore of Natterersee. A wide variety of leisure facilities are available.
⤷ *Approach via Brenner Motorway, exit 'Innsbruck Süd', via Natters, onto B182 and follow signs.*
Open: 15 Dec-Oct Site: 7.5HEC ⸺ ⌇⌇ 🏠 🚐 🏕 Prices: ↑5.60-7.20 pitch 7.60-9.80 Facilities: ☂ ⅏ ⊙ 🚮 🏪 🍴 Services: 🍽 ✗ ⊞ lau Leisure: ⤳ L

NAUDERS TIROL

Alpencamping Nauders 6543
☎ 05473 87217   ▤ 05473 8721750
e-mail: alpencamping@tirol.com
website: www.camping-nauders.at
A year-round family site in a delightful Alpine location with good recreational facilities.
⤷ *Access via B315.*
Open: 17 Dec-Oct Site: 3HEC ⸺ ⅊ Prices: ↑5-6.90 ▲12.40-13.40 pitch 16-22.50 (incl 2 persons) Facilities: ☂ ⅏ ⊙ 🚮 🏪 Services: lau Off-site: 🍽 ✗ ⤳L

PILL TIROL

Plankenhof 6130 ☎ 05242 641950   ▤ 05242 72344
e-mail: m.khuen-belasi@tirol.com
Site in meadow.
⤷ *On B171 near Gasthof Plankenhof.*
Open: May-1 Oct Site: 0.6HEC ⸺ ⌇⌇ Prices: ↑3 ▲4.50 pitch 6.50 Facilities: ☂ ⊙ 🚮 🏪 Services: 🍽 ✗ ⊞ lau Leisure: ⤳ P Off-site: ⅏ ⤳LR

PRUTZ TIROL

Aktiv-Camping Prutz 6522 ☎ 05472 2648   ▤ 05472 2652
e-mail: info@aktiv-camping.at
website: www.aktiv-camping.at
A pleasant site in a beautiful mountain setting with good, modern facilities.
Site: 1.5HEC ⸺ ⅊ Prices: ↑5.50 🚐7-10 ▲4-9
Facilities: ☂ ⅏ ⊙ 🚮 🏪 🏕 Services: ✗ ⊞ lau Leisure: ⤳ R Off-site: ✗ ⤳LP

REUTTE TIROL

Seespitze A-6600 ☎ 05672 78121   ▤ 05672 63372
Open: May-15 Oct Site: 2HEC ⸺ ⅊ Facilities: ☂ ⅏ ⊙ 🚮 🏪 🏕 Services: ✗ ⊞ lau Leisure: ⤳ L Off-site: ✗

Sennalpe 6600 ☎ 05672 78115   ▤ 05672 63372
In a quiet situation next to the lake.
⤷ *On Reutte-Oberammergau road 200m from the Hotel Forelle.*
Open: 15 Dec-15 Oct Site: 4HEC ⸺ ⅊ Facilities: ☂ ⅏ ⊙ 🚮 🏪 🏕 Services: ✗ ⊞ lau Leisure: ⤳ L Off-site: 🍽

RIED BEI LANDECK TIROL

Dreiländereck 6531 ☎ 05472 6025   ▤ 05472 60254
e-mail: camping-drellandereck@tirol.com
website: www.tirolcamping.at
Level site in centre of village beside a lake with spectacular views.
Open: All year Site: 1HEC ⸺ ⅊ 🏠 Prices: ↑4.80-5.30 pitch 7.50-10 Facilities: ☂ ⅏ ⊙ 🚮 🏪 Services: 🍽 ✗ ⊞ lau Off-site: ✗ 🏕 ⤳LPR

RINN TIROL

Judenstein Judenstein 40, 6074 ☎ 05223 78620   ▤ 7887715
e-mail: kommunalgmbh@rinn.tirol.gv.at
website: www.tiscover.at/camping.judenstein
In a wooded location with fine views.
⤷ *Access via motorway exit Hall.*
Open: May-30 Oct Site: 0.6HEC ⸺ ⅊ Prices: ↑3 🚗2 🚐3 ▲3 Facilities: ☂ ⊙ 🚮 🏪 🏕 Services: ⊞ lau Off-site: ⅏ 🍽 ✗ ⤳LP

ST JOHANN TIROL

Michelnhof Weiberndorf 6, 6380
☎ 05352 62584   ▤ 05352 625844
e-mail: camping@michelnhof.at
website: www.camping-michelnhof.at
⤷ *1.5km S via B161 (St-Johann-Kitzbühel).*
Open: All year Site: 3HEC ⸺ ⅊ Prices: ↑4.20 🚗3.30 🚐3.60 ▲3-3.60 Facilities: ☂ ⅏ ⊙ 🚮 🏪 🏕 Services: ✗ ⊞ lau Off-site: ⅏ 🍽 ⤳PR

SCHWAZ TIROL
AT WEER (6KM W)

Alpencamping Mark Maholmhof, 6114
☎ 05224 68146   ▤ 05244 681466
e-mail: alpcamp.mark@aou.at
website: www.alpencampingmark.com
Situated on meadowland by a farm on the edge of a forest.
⤷ *Off B171.*
Open: Apr-Oct Site: 2HEC ⸺ 🍀 Prices: ↑5.50 🚐6 pitch 4.50-6 Facilities: ☂ ⅏ ⊙ 🚮 🏪 🏕 Services: 🍽 ✗ ⊞ lau Leisure: ⤳ P Off-site: ⤳L

SÖLDEN TIROL

Sölden 6450 ☎ 05254 26270   ▤ 05254 26275
e-mail: info@camping-soelden.com
website: www.camping-soelden.com
Situated on meadowland on left bank of Ötztaler tributary. Beautiful views of the surrounding mountains.
⤷ *By Grauer Bär Inn at Km36 on the B186.*
Open: 19 Jun-3 May Site: 1.3HEC ⸺ ⅊ Prices: ↑6-9 🚐6.70-11 pitch 6.70-11 Facilities: ☂ ⊙ 🚮 🏪 🏕 Services: ⊞ lau Off-site: ⅏ 🍽 ⤳P

STAMS TIROL

Eichenwald Schiessstand weg 10, 6422 ☎ 05263 6159
Well managed terraced site in oak wood.
⤷ *Turn off B171 at ESSO filling station in direction of abbey, onto a steep, narrow access road.*
Site: 2HEC ⸺ ⅊ 🏠 🚐 Facilities: ☂ ⅏ ⊙ 🚮 🏪 🏕 Services: 🍽 ✗ ⊞ lau Leisure: ⤳ P Off-site: ⤳R

THIERSEE TIROL

Rueppenhof Seebauern 8, 6335 ☎ 05376 5694
e-mail: atzl.barbara@tirol.com
Site made up of several meadows surrounding a farm that lies on the banks of the lake.
⤷ *Access via A12 exit Kufstein-Nord, then follow signs for Thiersee.*
Open: Apr-Oct Site: 1.5HEC ⸺ ⅊ Prices: ↑4 🚗2 🚐2.60 ▲1.60-2.20 Facilities: ☂ ⊙ 🚮 🏪 🏕 Services: ⊞ Leisure: ⤳ L Off-site: ⅏ 🍽 ✗

UMHAUSEN TIROL

Ötztal Arena Camp Krismer 6441
☎ 05255 5390   ▤ 05255 5390
e-mail: info@oetztal-camping.at
website: www.oetztal-camping.at

Site: 6HEC-Site size ⸺-grass ⌇⌇-sand ⅌-stone ⅊-little shade 🍀-partly shaded 🍂-mainly shaded
🏠-bungalows for hire 🚐-caravans for hire ▲-tents for hire 🐕-no dogs **Prices:** ↑-adult per night 🚗-car per night
pp-per person per night 🚐-caravan per night ▲-tent per night

➲ *Signposted from B186.*
Open: All year Site: 1HEC ⬛ 🔌 Prices: ♠5.60 pitch 3-8
Facilities: 🏪 🛒 ⊙ 🔋 🗑 🚿 🅿 Services: ⛾ ✕ ⊞ lau
Leisure: ⤜ LR

UNTERPERFUSS TIROL

Farm 6175 ☎ 05232 2209 ▮ 05232 22094
e-mail: brangeralm@aon.at
Modern site on gently sloping meadow in a beautiful
mountain setting.
➲ *W end of village near Amberg railway and main road.*
Open: All year Site: 1.5HEC ⬛ 🔌 Prices: ♠5 pitch 8.90
Facilities: 🏪 ⊙ 🔋 🚿 🅿 Services: ⛾ ✕ ⊞ Off-site: 🛒 ✕

VÖLS TIROL

Völs Bahnhofstr 10, 6176 ☎ 0512 303533
➲ *Access via motorway exit Innsbruck-Kranebitten.*
Open: Apr-Nov Site: 0.4HEC ⬛ 🔌 Facilities: 🏪 ⊙ 🔋 🅿
Services: ⛾ ✕ ⊞ lau Off-site: 🛒 🗑 ⤜LPR

WAIDRING TIROL

Steinplatte Unterwasser 43, 6384
☎ 05353 5345 ▮ 05353 5406
e-mail: camping-steinplatte@aon.at
website: www.camping-steinplatte.at
On a level meadow with fine panoramic views of the
surrounding mountains.
Open: All year Site: 4HEC ⬛ 🔌 🚐 Facilities: 🏪 🛒 ⊙ 🔋 🗑
🚿 🅿 Services: ⛾ ✕ ⊞ Leisure: ⤜ L Off-site: ⤜PR

WALCHSEE TIROL

Seespitz Wassersportzentrum, 6344
☎ 05374 5359 ▮ 05374 5845
e-mail: camping.seespitz@netway.at
website: www.watchsee.at
In pleasant surroundings beside the Walchsee with good
recreational facilities.
➲ *Between B172 and bank of lake.*
Open: All year Site: 3HEC ⬛ ⠿ 🔌 Facilities: 🏪 🛒 ⊙ 🔋
🗑 🅿 Services: ⛾ ✕ ⊞ lau Leisure: ⤜ L

Terrassencamping Süd-See Seestr 76, 6344
☎ 05374 5339 ▮ 05374 5529
e-mail: campingwalchsee@aon.at
website: www.camp-sud-see.com
A lakeside site in wooded surroundings with extensive
terracing and fine mountain views.
➲ *500m W on B172 turn into 'no through road' and continue
for 1500m.*
Open: All year Site: 11HEC ⬛ ⠿ 💧 🔌 Prices: ♠5-5.50
pitch 5.50-6.50 Facilities: 🏪 🛒 ⊙ 🔋 🗑 🚿 🅿 Services: ⛾ ✕ ⊞
lau Leisure: ⤜ L

WESTENDORF TIROL

Panorama Mühltal 70, A-6363 ☎ 05334 6166 ▮ 05334 6843
e-mail: info@panorama.camping.at
website: www.panorama.camping.at
In a beautiful Alpine setting with good modern facilities,
including well furnished studio apartments.
➲ *W towards Wörgl via B170.*
Open: All year Site: 2.2HEC ⬛ 🔌 Facilities: 🏪 🛒 ⊙ 🔋 🗑
🚿 🅿 Services: ⛾ ✕ ⊞ lau Leisure: ⤜P

ZELL AM ZILLER TIROL

Hofer Gerlossasstr 33, 6280 ☎ 05282 2248 ▮ 05282 2248
e-mail: office@campinghofer.at
website: www.campinghofer.at
On meadowland with some fruit trees.

➲ *Site lies to the end of Zillertal off the road leading to the
Gerlos Pass.*
Open: All year Site: 1.5HEC ⬛ 🔌 Prices: ♠4.50 pitch 5.50
Facilities: 🏪 🛒 ⊙ 🔋 🗑 🚿 🅿 Services: ⛾ ✕ ⊞ lau
Leisure: ⤜ P

ZIRL TIROL

Alpenfrieden Eigenhofen 11, 6170 ☎ 05238 53520
➲ *Terraced site with orchard surroundings.*
Near the B171.
Open: May-Sep Site: 1HEC ⬛ 🔌 🚐 Facilities: 🏪 ⊙ 🔋 🗑
🅿 Services: ⛾ ✕ ⊞ Leisure: ⤜ P Off-site: ⤜R

CARINTHIA

DELLACH KÄRNTEN

Neubauer 9872 ☎ 04766 2532 ▮ 04766 25324
website: www.tiscover.com/camping.neubauer
A terraced site with direct access to the Millstättersee.
➲ *Access from B100, Leinz-Spittal road. The turn-off is well
signposted in the village.*
Open: May-15 Oct Site: 1.5HEC ⬛ 🔌 Facilities: 🏪 ⊙ 🔋 🅿
Services: ⛾ ✕ lau Leisure: ⤜ L Off-site: 🛒 ✕ 🗑

DELLACH IM DRAUTAL KÄRNTEN

Waldbad 9772 ☎ 04714 288 & 234 ▮ 04714 2343
e-mail: dellach-drau@knt.gde.at
website: www.tiscover.com/dellach
A small site in a delightful wooded setting with two large
swimming pools.
➲ *Leave A10 at Spittal & turn onto B100.*
Open: May-Sep Site: 2HEC ⬛ 🔌 Prices: ♠4.50-7 pitch 11-
20 (incl 2 persons) Facilities: 🏪 🛒 ⊙ 🔋 🗑 🅿 Services: ✕ ⊞
lau Leisure: ⤜ P Off-site: ⛾ ⤜R

DÖBRIACH KÄRNTEN

Brunner am See Glanzerstr 108, 9873
☎ 04246 7189 ▮ 04246 7837
e-mail: camping.brunner@aon.at
website: www.camping-brunner.at
Tidily arranged with poplar trees. Private bathing area.
➲ *The access road is at the E end of Lake Millstatt.*
Open: All year Site: 3.5HEC ⬛ ⠿ 🔌 🚐 Prices: ♠5-7.50
pitch 6.60-10.90 Facilities: 🏪 🛒 ⊙ 🔋 🗑 🚿 🅿 Services: ⛾ ✕
⊞ lau Leisure: ⤜ L

Burgstaller Seefeldstr 16, 9873
☎ 04246 7774 ▮ 04246 77744
e-mail: deiter.burgstaller@campingpark.telecom.at
website: www.burgstaller.co.at/burgstaller
A quiet site situated 100m from the lake, with good modern
facilities.
➲ *At SE end of lake. From B98 continue towards Lake
Millstatt for 1km.*
Open: All year Site: 7.5HEC ⬛ 🔌 🚐 Facilities: 🏪 🛒 ⊙ 🔋
🗑 🚿 🅿 Services: ⛾ ✕ ⊞ lau Leisure: ⤜ LP

DÖLLACH KÄRNTEN

Zirknitzer 9843 ☎ 04825 451 ▮ 04825 45117
e-mail: camping.zirknitzer@utanet.at
Beside the River Möu.
➲ *Between Km8 and Km9 on the Glocknerstr (B107).*
Open: 21 Dec-4 Nov Site: 0.6HEC ⬛ 🔌 🚐 Prices: ♠3.20-4
🚗1.80-2 🚙1.80-2.50 ⛺1-2 Facilities: 🏪 🛒 ⊙ 🔋 🗑 🅿
Services: ⛾ ✕ ⊞ lau Leisure: ⤜ R Off-site: 🗑 ⤜P

Facilities: 🛒-shop 🏪-shower ⊙-electric points for razors 🔋-electric points for caravans 🅿-parking by tents permitted
🄿-compulsory separate car park **Services:** ✕-café/restaurant ⛾-bar 🗑-Camping Gaz International 🚿-gas other than Camping
Gaz ⊞-first aid facilities lau-laundry **Leisure:** ⤜-swimming L-Lake P-Pool R-River S-Sea **Off-site:** All facilities within 2km

FELDKIRCHEN KÄRNTEN

Seewirt-Spiess Maltschach am See 2, 9560
☎ 04277 2637   ▤ 04277 2637 - 4
e-mail: office@seewirl-spiess.com
website: www.seewirl-spiess.com
In a pleasant wooded location on the shore of the
Maltschacher See.
⊃ *Access via B95 towards Klagenfurt.*
Open: May-Sep Site: 1.2HEC ⬛⬛⬛ ⌁ ⊡ Facilities: ⬕ ⊙ ⬛ ⌀
⛺ Services: ⬗ ✗ lau Leisure: ⬚ L Off-site: ⬛ ⬚P ⊞

HEILIGENBLUT KÄRNTEN

Grossglockner 9844 ☎ 04824 2048   ▤ 04824 24622
e-mail: nationalpark-camping@heiligenblut.at
website: www.heiligenblut.at/nationalpark-camping
In a location on a meadow surrounded by woodland within
the National Park.
⊃ *Signposted.*
Open: 01 May-31Oct & 01 Dec-30 Apr Site: 2.5HEC ⬛⬛⬛ ⌁
Prices: ⚦5.90 ⚧2.20 ⚧2.20 Facilities: ⬕ ⬛ ⊙ ⬛ ⌀ ⛺ ⛺
Services: ⬗ ✗ ⊞ lau Leisure: ⬚ R Off-site: ⬚P

HERMAGOR KÄRNTEN

Schluga 9620 ☎ 04282 2051   ▤ 04282 288120
e-mail: camping@schluga.com
website: www.schluga.com
Well equipped family site in a rural setting 4km from
Presseger See.
Open: All year Site: 5.5HEC ⬛⬛⬛ ⌁ ⊡ ⛺ Prices: ⚦4.90-7.50
pitch 4-7.30 Facilities: ⬕ ⬛ ⊙ ⬛ ⌀ ⛺ ⛺ Services: ⬗ ✗ ⊞
Leisure: ⬚ LP

Schluga Seecamping 9620 ☎ 04282 2051   ▤ 04282 288120
e-mail: camping@schluga.com
website: www.schluga.com
A well equipped family site approx 300m N of lake in
meadowland with some terraces and fine views.
⊃ *6km E of Hermagor.*
Open: 20 May-20 Sep Site: 8.8HEC ⬛⬛⬛ ⌁ ⊡ ⛺
Prices: ⚦4.90-7.50 pitch 4-7.30 Facilities: ⬕ ⬛ ⊙ ⬛ ⌀ ⛺ ⛺
Services: ⬗ ✗ ⊞ lau Leisure: ⬚ L Off-site: ⬚R

KEUTSCHACH KÄRNTEN

Strandcamping Süd 9074 ☎ 04273 2773   ▤ 04273 27734
In a pleasant setting among shrubs and trees on south side of
the Keutschachersee.
⊃ *Access via motorway exit Valden towards Kreutschacher-
Seental.*
Open: 20 Apr-Sep Site: 2HEC ⬛⬛⬛ ⌁ Prices: ⚦5.50-6 pitch
7-8 Facilities: ⬕ ⬛ ⊙ ⬛ ⛺ Services: ✗ ⊞ lau Leisure: ⬚ L

KLAGENFURT KÄRNTEN

Strandbad 9020 ☎ 0463 21169   ▤ 0463 21193
e-mail: camping@stw.at
website: www.tiscover.at/camping-klagenfurt
Large site divided into sections by trees and bushes.
⊃ *From town centre take B83 towards Velden. Turn left just
outside town in direction of bathing area.*
Open: 15 Apr-5 Oct Site: 4HEC ⬛⬛⬛ ⌁ ⊡ Facilities: ⬕ ⬛ ⊙
⬛ ⛺ Services: ⬗ ✗ ⊞ lau Leisure: ⬚ L

KÖTSCHACH-MAUTHEN KÄRNTEN

Alpen 9640 ☎ 04715 429   ▤ 04715 429
e-mail: info@alpencamp.at website: www.alpencamp.at
On level meadowland beside River Gail with good facilities
for water sports.

⊃ *Turn off B110 in the S part of the village on the road to the
Plöcken Pass and drive 800m towards Lesachtal.*
Open: 15 Dec-Oct Site: 1.4HEC ⬛⬛⬛ ⌁ ⊡ Prices: ⚦3.40-5.30
pitch 4-6.30 Facilities: ⬕ ⬛ ⊙ ⬛ ⌀ ⛺ ⛺ Services: ⬗ ✗ ⊞ lau
Off-site: ✗ ⬚PR

MALTA KÄRNTEN

Maltatal 9854 ☎ 0043 4733 234   ▤ 4733 23416
e-mail: info@maltacamp.at website: www.maltacamp.at
On a gently rising alpine meadow with breathtaking views of
the surrounding mountains.
⊃ *In Gmünd turn off B99 and drive 5.5km through Malta
valley.*
Open: 12 Apr-Oct Site: 3.5HEC ⬛⬛⬛ ⌁ ⊡ Facilities: ⬕ ⬛ ⊙
⬛ ⌀ ⛺ Services: ⬗ ✗ ⊞ lau Leisure: ⬚ PR

MÖLLBRÜCKE KÄRNTEN

Rheingold Mölltalstr 65, 9813 ☎ 04769 2338
⊃ *Site on main road from Spittal to Mallnitz, next to
swimming pool.*
Open: All year Site: 2HEC ⬛⬛⬛ ⌁ Facilities: ⬕ ⊙ ⬛ ⛺
Services: ⬗ ✗ Leisure: ⬚ P Off-site: ⬛

OBERVELLACH KÄRNTEN

Sport Erlebnis 9821 ☎ 04782 2727   ▤ 04782 3183
e-mail: info@sporterlebnis.at
website: www.sporterlebnis.at
Open: May-Sep Site: 10HEC ⬛⬛⬛ ⌁ ⊡ Prices: ⚦5 ⚧1.50
⚧1.50 ⚠1.50 Facilities: ⬕ ⬛ ⛺ ⊞ Services: ⬗ ✗ ⊞ lau
Leisure: ⬚ R Off-site: ⬛ ⛺ ⬚P

OSSIACH KÄRNTEN

Ossiach 9570 ☎ 04243 436   ▤ 04243 8171
e-mail: martinz@camping.at
website: www.terrassen.camping.at
Divided into pitches with generally well-situated terraces.
⊃ *Off B94 on E bank of Kale Ossiacher.*
Open: May-Sep Site: 10HEC ⬛⬛⬛ ⌁ ⊡ ⛺ Prices: ⚦4.80-7.10
pitch 6.70-10.70 Facilities: ⬕ ⬛ ⊙ ⬛ ⌀ ⛺ ⛺ Services: ⬗ ✗
⊞ lau Leisure: ⬚ L

Parth 9570 ☎ 04243 2744
e-mail: camping@parth.at website: www.parth.at
On hilly ground on S shore of the lake. Steep, but there are
some terraces.
⊃ *Off B94 on S bank of Lake Ossiach.*
Open: Apr-Oct Site: 1.8HEC ⬛⬛⬛ ⬚⬚ ⊡ ⛺ Facilities: ⬕ ⬛
⊙ ⬛ ⌀ ⛺ ⛺ Services: ✗ ⊞ lau Leisure: ⬚ L

AT HEILIGEN GESTADE (5KM SW)

Seecamping Berghof Ossiachersee-Süduferstr 241, 9523
☎ 04242 41133   ▤ 04242 4113330
e-mail: ertl@camping.at
website: www.berghof.camping.at
Terraced meadowland in attractive setting. 800m long
promenade with bathing areas. Dogs not allowed Jul-Aug
⊃ *E shore of Lake Ossiacher.*
Open: Apr-Oct Site: 10HEC ⬛ ⬛ ⌁ ⛺ Prices: ⚦5.20-7.60
pitch 7.50-12.50 Facilities: ⬕ ⬛ ⊙ ⬛ ⌀ ⛺ ⛺ Services: ⬗ ✗
lau Leisure: ⬚ L

SACHSENBURG KÄRNTEN

Markt Sachsenburg Marktpl 12, 9751
☎ 04769 292522   ▤ 04769 292520
e-mail: gemeinde.sachsenburg@carinthia.com
website: www.discover.com/draucamping
A modern family site with good facilities in a delightful
mountain setting.

Site: 6HEC-Site size ⬛⬛⬛-grass ⬚⬚⬚-sand ⬥-stone ⬚⬚-little shade ⌁-partly shaded ⬥-mainly shaded
⊡-bungalows for hire ⛺-caravans for hire ⚠-tents for hire ⊘-no dogs Prices: ⚦-adult per night ⚧-car per night
pp-per person per night ⛺-caravan per night ⚠-tent per night

⮑ *Access via A10 between Spittal and Lienz.*
Open: 10 May-10 Oct Site: 1.3HEC ⬛ ⌂ Facilities: ↑ ⊙
⬛ ☎ Off-site: ⬛ ⬛ ✗ ⌀ ↻P ⊞

ST PRIMUS KÄRNTEN

Strandcamping Turnersee Breznik 9123
☎ 04239 2350 ▤ 04239 235032
e-mail: info@breznik.at website: www.breznik.at
A quiet site in a picturesque mountain setting with a good
variety of recreational facilities.
⮑ *Access via B70 Klagenfurt-Graz towards Kopenersee.*
Open: 30 Mar-Oct Site: 6HEC ⬛ ⬛ ⬛ ⬛ Facilities: ↑ ⬛
⊙ ⬛ ⌀ ⬛ ☎ Services: ⬛ ✗ Leisure: ↻ L Off-site: ⊞

SCHIEFLING KÄRNTEN

Weisses Rössl Auenstr 47, 9535
☎ 04274 2898 ▤ 04274 28984
e-mail: weisses.roessl@aon.at
website: members.aon.at/weisses.roessl
In a wooded setting with fine views of the surrounding
mountains on the shore of the Wörther See.
Open: May-Sep Site: 2.5HEC ⬛ ⬛ ⬛ ⬛ Prices: ⬛5.50-7
pitch 5-6 Facilities: ↑ ⬛ ⊙ ⬛ ⌀ ☎ Services: ✗ ⊞ lau
Leisure: ↻ L Off-site: ↻L

SEEBODEN KÄRNTEN

Ferienpark Lieseregg Kras 27, 9871
☎ 04762 2723 ▤ 04762 33857
e-mail: info@ferienpark-lieseregg.at
website: www.ferienpark-lieseregg.at
A family site on a large level meadow with terraces and
asphalt drives surrounded by woodland.
⮑ *B99 from Spittal north to B98, then left for 1.5km.*
Open: May-1 Oct Site: 3HEC ⬛ ⬛ ⬛ Prices: ⬛5.85-7.15
pitch 4-7.30 Facilities: ↑ ⬛ ⊙ ⬛ ⌀ ⬛ ☎ Services: ✗ ⊞ lau
Leisure: ↻ P

SPITTAL AN DER DRAU KÄRNTEN

Draufluss 9800 ☎ 04762 2466 ▤ 04762 2466
A long, narrow riverside site, partly surrounded by a hedge.
⮑ *From town centre follow road to river towards
Goldeckbahn.*
Open: Apr-Oct Site: 0.7HEC ⬛ ⌂ Facilities: ↑ ⊙ ⬛ ☎
Services: ⬛ ✗ ⊞ lau Leisure: ↻ PR Off-site: ⬛ ⌀ ⬛

STOCKENBOI KÄRNTEN

Ronacher Möse 6, 9714 ☎ 04761 256 ▤ 04761 2564
e-mail: terrassencamping.ronacher@net4you.at
website: www.campingronacher.at
Situated on meadow between forest slopes, gently sloping to
the shore of Lake Weissensee. Shop in high season only.
⮑ *Approach for caravans via Weissensee.*
Open: May-10 Oct Site: 1.7HEC ⬛ ⬛ Prices: ⬛7-8.50
pitch 5.60-8.20 Facilities: ↑ ⬛ ⊙ ⬛ ⌀ ⬛ ☎ Services: ⬛ ✗ ⊞
Leisure: ↻ L

VILLACH KÄRNTEN

Gerli St Georgenerstr 140, 9500
☎ 04242 57402 ▤ 04242 582909
e-mail: gerli.meidl@utanet.at
Level, quiet, isolated site, with heated swimming pool
annexed to it which is open to the public.
⮑ *From Spittal/Drau turn off B100, turn right just before
Villach and continue for 2km.*
Open: All year Site: 2.3HEC ⬛ ⬛ ⬛ ⬛ Prices: ⬛3.90-4.50
pitch 3.90-4.50 Facilities: ↑ ⬛ ⊙ ⬛ ⌀ ☎ Services: ✗ ⊞ lau
Off-site: ⬛ ↻P

AT FAAK AM SEE (10KM SE)

Strandcamping Arneitz A-9583
☎ 04254 2137 ▤ 04254 3044
On a wooded peninsula jutting into the Faakersee with good
sporting facilities.
Open: 28 Apr-Sep Site: 6HEC ⬛ ⬛⋮⋮ ⌂ ⬛ Facilities: ↑ ⬛
⊙ ⬛ ⌀ ⬛ ☎ Services: ⬛ ✗ ⊞ lau Leisure: ↻ L

Strandcamping Florian Badeweg 3, 9583
☎ 04254 2261 ▤ 04254 3943
e-mail: iris.effermann@eunet.at
website: www.camping-florian.at
A partially shaded site between the lakeside and the road.
⮑ *Access from road by Hotel Fürst.*
Open: May-25 Sep Site: 3.5HEC ⬛ ⌂ ⬛ ⬛ Facilities: ↑
⬛ ⊙ ⬛ ⌀ ☎ Services: ✗ ⊞ lau Leisure: ↻ L Off-site: ✗ ⬛

Strandcamping Gruber 9583 ☎ 04254 2298 ▤ 04254 2298-7
e-mail: info@strandcamping.at
website: www.strandcamping.at
On level ground beside the lake with fine views of the
surrounding mountains.
Open: May-Sep Site: 2.5HEC ⬛ ⬛⋮⋮ ⌂ Prices: ⬛6.30 ⬛12
⬛12-17.50 Facilities: ↑ ⬛ ⊙ ⬛ ☎ Services: ⬛ ✗ ⊞ lau
Leisure: ↻ L Off-site: ⌀ ⬛

WERTSCHACH KÄRNTEN

Alpenfreude 9612 ☎ 04256 2708 ▤ 04256 27084
e-mail: camping.alpenfreude@aon.at
website: www.alpenfreude.at
Open: May-Sep Site: 5HEC ⬛ ⌂ ⬛ ⬛ Prices: ⬛3.30-4.80
pitch 4.60-6.60 Facilities: ↑ ⬛ ⊙ ⬛ ⌀ ⬛ ☎ Services: ✗ ⊞
lau Leisure: ↻ P Off-site: ⬛

STYRIA

AUSSEE, BAD STEIERMARK

Traun Grundlseer Str 21, 8990
☎ 03622 54565 ▤ 03622 52427
e-mail: gh.staudnwirt@aussee.at
website: www.aussee.at/staudnwirt
In pleasant wooded surroundings.
⮑ *2.5km from Bad Aussee towards Grundlsee.*
Open: All year Site: 0.4HEC ⬛ ⌂ ⬛ Prices: ⬛6.20 pitch
2.90 Facilities: ↑ ⊙ ⬛ ☎ Services: ⬛ ✗ lau Leisure: ↻ R
Off-site: ⬛ ⌀ ⬛ ↻LP ⊞

GRAZ STEIERMARK

S C Central Martinhofstr 3, 8054
☎ 0316 281831 ▤ 0316 697824
e-mail: Freizeir@netway.at
website: tiscover.com/campingcentral
A site with many lawns separated by asphalt paths and partly
divided into pitches.
⮑ *Turn off the B70 in Strassgang S of Graz and continue for
300m.*
Open: Apr-Oct Site: 4HEC ⬛ ⬛ Prices: ⬛7.75 ⬛25.50
⬛13.75 Facilities: ↑ ⬛ ⊙ ⬛ ⬛ ☎ Services: ⬛ ✗ ⊞ lau
Leisure: ↻ P

HIRSCHEGG STEIERMARK

Hirschegg 8584 ☎ 03141 2201
e-mail: stoeklcamp@hotmail.com
website: www.camping-hirschegg.at
In a delightful Alpine setting.
⮑ *Access via A2 towards Klagenfurt, exit Modriach.*
Open: All year Site: 2HEC ⬛ ⌂ ⬛ Prices: ⬛3.20 ⬛2.20
⬛2.20 ⬛2.20 Facilities: ↑ ⊙ ⬛ ⌀ ☎ Services: lau
Off-site: ⬛ ⬛ ✗ ↻LPR ⊞

Facilities: ⬛-shop ↑-shower ⊙-electric points for razors ⬛-electric points for caravans ☎-parking by tents permitted
⬛-compulsory separate car park Services: ✗-café/restaurant ⬛-bar ⌀-Camping Gaz International ⬛-gas other than Camping
Gaz ⊞-first aid facilities lau-laundry Leisure: ↻-swimming L-Lake P-Pool R-River S-Sea Off-site: All facilities within 2km

LANGENWANG-MÜRTZAL STEIERMARK

Europa Siglstr 5, 8665 ☎ 03854 2950
e-mail: europa.camping.stmk@aon.at
On level meadow with some trees, surrounded by hedges.
The site occupies an attractive alpine setting.
➲ *The B306 (E7) by-passes the town, so be careful not to miss
the exit 6km S of Mürzzuschlag.*
Open: All year Site: 0.6HEC ⏛ 🈺 Prices: ♠4.15 🚗3 🚐3
🛆3 Facilities: 🏪 ⊙ 🚿 ♨ 🚽 Services: lau Off-site: 🛒 🍽 ✕ ⇘R
⊞

LEIBNITZ STEIERMARK

Leibnitz R-H-Bartsch-Gasse 33, 8430
☎ 03452 82463 🗏 03452 71491
e-mail: gde@leibnitz.steiermark.at
website: www.camping-steiermark.at
A well equipped site in pleasant wooded surroundings with
plenty of leisure facilities.
➲ *W of town. Signposted.*
Open: May-15 Sep Site: 0.7HEC ⏛ ♣ Prices: ♠4 🚗2.20
🚐3.60 🛆2.50 Facilities: 🏪 ⊙ 🚿 ♨ 🚽 Services: ✕ ⊞ lau
Leisure: ⇘ PR Off-site: 🛒 🍽 🌀 ♨ ⇘L

MARIA LANKOWITZ STEIERMARK

Piberstein Am See 1, 8591
☎ 03144 7095950 🗏 03144 7095974
e-mail: office@piberstein.at website: www.piberstein.at
Large well equipped site surrounding a series of lakes. Plenty
of sporting facilities.
➲ *S of Maria Lankowitz towards Pack.*
Open: May-15 Oct Site: 5.6HEC ⏛ 🈺 🚐 Prices: ♠6 pitch
7-9.50 Facilities: 🏪 🛒 ⊙ 🚿 🚽 Services: ✕ ⊞ lau Leisure: ⇘
L Off-site: 🍽 🌀 ♨

MITTERNDORF, BAD STEIERMARK

Grimmingsicht 8983 ☎ 03623 2985
e-mail: camping@grimmingsicht.at
website: www.grimmingsicht.at
A modern site in a picturesque mountain setting with a
variety of sporting facilities.
Open: All year Site: 0.6HEC ⏛ ♣ 🈺 🚐 Facilities: 🏪 ⊙ 🚿
🚽 Services: 🍽 ✕ ⊞ lau Leisure: ⇘ R Off-site: 🛒 ✕ ♨ ⇘P

MÜHLEN STEIERMARK

Badsee Hitzmannsdorf 2, 8822 ☎ 03586 2418
e-mail: office@camping-am-badesee.at
website: www.camping-am-badesee.at
Family site with direct access to the lake.
➲ *N via B92. Signposted.*
Open: May-Sep Site: 1.5HEC ⏛ 🈺 🈺 🚐 Facilities: 🏪 🛒 ⊙
🚿 🚽 Services: 🍽 ✕ ⊞ lau Leisure: ⇘ L Off-site: 🌀 ⇘P

OBERWÖLZ STEIERMARK

Burg Rothenfels 8832 ☎ 03581 8208 🗏 03581 82084
e-mail: rothenfels@aon.at
website: www.rothenfels.at
In picturesque Alpine surroundings in the grounds of a
castle, with good recreational facilities.
➲ *On SE outskirts.*
Open: Apr-Oct Site: 8HEC ⏛ ♣ 🈺 🚐 Facilities: 🏪 ⊙ 🚿
🚽 Services: lau Leisure: ⇘ L Off-site: 🛒 🍽 ✕ 🌀 ⇘PR ⊞

ST GEORGEN STEIERMARK

Olachgut 8861 ☎ 03532 2162 🗏 03532 2162
e-mail: olachgut@murau.at website: www.murau.at/olachgut
On a level meadow, surrounded by beautiful mountain
scenery.

➲ *Signposted.*
Open: All year Site: 10HEC ⏛ 🈺 🈺 🚐 🛆 Facilities: 🏪 🛒
⊙ 🚿 🌀 ♨ 🚽 Services: ✕ lau Leisure: ⇘ L Off-site: ⇘R

ST SEBASTIAN STEIERMARK

Erlaufsee Erlaufseestr 3, 8630
☎ 03882 4937 🗏 03882 214822
e-mail: gemeinde@st-sebastian.at
website: www.st-sebastian.at
In a picturesque Alpine setting in woodland, 100mtrs from
the lake.
➲ *Signposted.*
Open: May-15 Sep Site: 1HEC ⏛ ♣ Prices: ♠3.60 🚗2.50
🚐3 🛆3 Facilities: 🏪 ⊙ 🚿 🚽 Off-site: ✕ ⇘L ⊞

SCHLADMING STEIERMARK

Zirngast Linke Ennsau 633, 8970
☎ 03687 23195 🗏 03687 23495
e-mail: camping@zirngast.at website: www.zirngast.at
Site in meadow on left bank of River Enns next to railway.
➲ *Turn off B308 towards town as far as the petrol filling
station.*
Open: All year Site: 1.5HEC ⏛ 🈺 Prices: 🚐18.50 🛆17.50
Facilities: 🏪 🛒 ⊙ 🚿 🌀 ♨ 🚽 Services: 🍽 ✕ lau Leisure: ⇘
R Off-site: ⇘P ⊞

UNGERSDORF BEI FROHNLEITEN STEIERMARK

Lanzmaierhof Ungersdorf 16, 8130
☎ 03126 2360 🗏 03126 4174
e-mail: tourismus@frohnleiten.at
website: www.camping-steiermark.at
➲ *Signposted 2km S of Frohnleiten on the Graz road.*
Open: Apr-15 Oct Site: 0.5HEC ⏛ 🈺 🚐 Prices: ♠3.80
🚗2.40 🚐2.40 🛆1.20-2.40 Facilities: 🏪 ⊙ 🚿 🌀 ♨ 🚽
Services: 🍽 ✕ ⊞ lau Off-site: 🛒 ⇘P

WEISSKIRCHEN STEIERMARK

50Plus Campingpark Fisching Fisching 9, 8741
☎ 03577 82284 🗏 03577 8228440
e-mail: campingpark@fisching.at
website: www.camping50plus.at
A modern site with fine sanitary and sporting facilities, 6km
from the Formula 1 circuit (A1-Ring) in Zeltweg.
➲ *Leave S36 at Zeltweg-Ost exit, head towards Obdach and
follow signs for B78. Site well signposted in centre of Fisching.*
Open: Apr-15 Oct Site: 1.5HEC ⏛ 🈺 🈺 Prices: ♠3.60
pitch 5.80 Facilities: 🏪 ⊙ 🚿 🌀 ♨ 🚽 Services: 🍽 ✕ ⊞ lau
Leisure: ⇘ P Off-site: 🛒

WILDALPEN STEIERMARK

Wildalpen 8924 ☎ 03636 342 & 341 🗏 03636 313
e-mail: tourismus@wildalpen.at
website: www.wildalpen.at
Located in a nature reserve beside the River Salza with good
canoeing facilities.
Open: Apr-Oct Site: 0.8HEC ⏛ ⋰ 🈺 Facilities: 🏪 ⊙ 🚿
🌀 🚽 Services: lau Leisure: ⇘ R Off-site: 🛒 🍽 ✕ ⇘P ⊞

LOWER AUSTRIA
BREITENBRUNN BURGENLAND

Seebad 7091 ☎ 02683 5252 🗏 02683 5252
Open: May-Sep Site: 1HEC ⏛ 🈺 ⊘ Facilities: 🏪 ⊙ 🚿 🚽 🅿
Services: ⊞ lau Leisure: ⇘ L Off-site: 🛒 ✕ ⇘P

Site: 6HEC-Site size ⏛-grass ⋰-sand ♨-stone 🗻-little shade 🈺-partly shaded ♣-mainly shaded
🈺-bungalows for hire 🚐-caravans for hire 🛆-tents for hire ⊘-no dogs Prices: ♠-adult per night 🚗-car per night
pp-per person per night 🚐-caravan per night 🛆-tent per night

GMÜND NIEDERÖSTERREICH

Assangteich Albrechtser Str 10, 3950
☎ 02852 52506 📠 02852 52506500
e-mail: stadtgemeinde@gmuend.at
website: www.gmuend.at
In a pleasant location with a good variety of recreational facilities.
⮕ *Signposted from B41.*
Open: 5 Apr-6 Oct Site: 0.5HEC ⸺ ♣ Prices: ⋔4.06 pitch 6.20 Facilities: ⋔ ⅃ ⊙ ⬛ ☎ Services: ⬤ ✗ lau Off-site: ∅ ⚌ ⭲LP ⊞

HIRTENBERG NIEDERÖSTERREICH

Hirtenberg Leobersdorfefstr, 2552
☎ 02256 81111 📠 02256 8111117
⮕ *Take exit Leobersdorf on A2/E59 and continue W on B18 for approx. 0.8km.*
Open: 15 May-15 Sep Site: 1.5HEC ⸺ ♣ ⊘ Facilities: ⋔ ⊙ ⬛ ☎ Services: lau Off-site: ⅃ ✗ ∅ ⭲P ⊞

JENNERSDORF BURGENLAND

Jennersdorf Freizeitzentrum 3, 8380
☎ 03329 46133 📠 03329 4626121
e-mail: post@jennersdorf.bgld.gv.at
website: www.jennersdorf.net
A pleasant site in wooded surroundings.
⮕ *Access via A2 exit Fürstenfeld.*
Open: 16 Mar-Oct Site: 1HEC ⸺ ⅃ ⊙ ⬛ ☎ Services: ⊞ lau Leisure: ⭲ P Off-site: ⅃ ✗ ⬤ ∅ ⭲R

LAXENBURG NIEDERÖSTERREICH

Schlosspark Laxenburg Münchendorfer Str, 2361
☎ 02236 71333 📠 02236 73966
e-mail: camping.laxenburg@verkehrsbuero.at
website: www.wiencamping.at
On level meadowland with surfaced roads. The site lies in a recreation centre within the grounds of the historic Laxenburg Castle.
⮕ *Access 600m S on the road leading to the B16.*
Open: Apr-Oct Site: 2.4HEC ⸺ ⅃ Facilities: ⋔ ⅃ ⊙ ⬛ ∅ ☎ Services: ✗ ⊞ lau Leisure: ⭲ P Off-site: ✗

MARBACH NIEDERÖSTERREICH

Marbacher 3671 ☎ 0664 5581815 📠 07413 703533
e-mail: info@marbach-freizeit.at
website: www.marbach-freizeit.at
In a pleasant situation beside the River Danube.
⮕ *Access via A1 exit Ybbs.*
Open: Apr-Oct Site: 0.4HEC ⸺ ♣ Prices: ⋔5.30 ⬤3.50 ⬤4.50 ⋏4 Facilities: ⋔ ⊙ ⬛ ☎ Services: ✗ ⊞ lau Leisure: ⭲ R Off-site: ⭲P

MARKT ST MARTIN BURGENLAND

Markt St Martin Mühlweg 2, 7341
☎ 02618 2239 📠 02618 22394
e-mail: post@markt-st-martin.bgld.gv.at
On a level meadow with plenty of trees and bushes.
⮕ *Access via A2 exit Krumbach/Schäffern.*
Open: May-Sep Site: 0.5HEC ⸺ ♣ ⊘ Prices: ⋔4.70 ⬤4 ⋏1.50 Facilities: ⋔ ⊙ ⬛ ☎ Services: ⬤ ✗ ⊞ Leisure: ⭲ PR Off-site: ⅃ ✗

PODERSDORF BURGENLAND

Strandcamping Podersdorf am See Strandpl, 7141
☎ 02177 2279
Directly on the Neusiedler See next to the sportsground.
Open: Apr-Oct Site: 7HEC ⸺ ⸭ ⅃ ⬛ Facilities: ⋔ ⅃ ⊙ ⬛ ☎ Services: lau Leisure: ⭲ L Off-site: ⬤ ✗ ∅ ⊞

RAPPOLTENKIRCHEN NIEDERÖSTERREICH

Rappoltenkirchen Kreuthstr 5, 3443
☎ 02274 8425 📠 02274 8422
⮕ *Turn off B1 at Sieghartskirchen and continue S for 3km.*
Site: 2.2HEC ⸺ ⅃ Facilities: ⋔ ⊙ ⬛ ∅ ☎ Services: ⬤ ⊞ lau Off-site: ⅃ ✗

RECHNITZ BURGENLAND

GC Hauptpl 10, 7471 ☎ 03363 79202 📠 03363 7920222
e-mail: post@rechnitz.bgld.gr.at
On an artificial lake in the heart of the beautiful Faludi Valley.
Open: Jun-Aug Site: 1HEC ⸺ ⊁ Facilities: ⋔ ⊙ ⬛ ☎ Services: ✗ ⊞ Leisure: ⭲ L Off-site: ⅃ ⬤ ✗ ∅ ⚌

RUST BURGENLAND

Rust 7071 ☎ 02685 595 📠 02685 5952
e-mail: office@gmeiner.co.at
Situated on level meadowland with young trees.
⮕ *From Rust follow the lake road.*
Open: Apr-Oct Site: 56HEC ⸺ ⅃ Facilities: ⋔ ⅃ ⊙ ⬛ ∅ ☎ Services: ⬤ ✗ ⊞ lau Off-site: ⚌ ⭲LPR

SCHÖNBÜHEL NIEDERÖSTERREICH

Stumpfer 3392 ☎ 02752 8510 📠 02752 851017
e-mail: office@stumpfer.com website: www.stumpfer.com
A small site in a wooded location attached to a guesthouse close to the River Donau.
⮕ *SW of town.*
Open: Apr-Oct Site: 1.5HEC ⸺ ⅃ ⬛ Prices: ⋔4.40 ⬤5.50 ⋏2.50-5.50 Facilities: ⋔ ⅃ ⊙ ⬛ ∅ ☎ Services: ✗ ⊞ lau Leisure: ⭲ R

TRAISEN NIEDERÖSTERREICH

Terrassen-Camping Traisen Kulmhof 1, 3160
☎ 02762 62900 📠 02762 629004
e-mail: info@camping-traisen.at
website: www.camping-traisen.at
Set out in a circular formation around the main buildings with plenty of trees around the pitches.
⮕ *0.6km W via B20.*
Open: All year Site: 2.1HEC ⸺ ⅃ ⬛ Facilities: ⋔ ⅃ ⊙ ⬛ ∅ ⚌ ☎ Services: ⊞ lau Leisure: ⭲ P Off-site: ⬤ ✗

TULLN NIEDERÖSTERREICH

Donaupark-Camping Tulln Hafenstr, 3430
☎ 02272 65200 📠 02272 65201
e-mail: camptulln@oeamtc.at
website: www.campingtulln.at
A modern site in a peaceful location with good facilities close to the River Danube with a high season bus service to Vienna.
Open: 10 Apr-Oct Site: 10HEC ⸺ ⅃ ⬛ ⋏ Facilities: ⋔ ⅃ ⊙ ⬛ ∅ ⚌ ☎ Services: ⬤ ✗ ⊞ lau Leisure: ⭲ L Off-site: ⭲PR

WAIDHOFEN AN DER THAYA NIEDERÖSTERREICH

Thayapark Badgasse, 3830 ☎ 02842 50350 📠 02842 50399
e-mail: info@waidhofen-thaya-stadt.at
website: www.waidhofen-thaya.at
A family site in wooded surroundings close to the River Thaya.
⮕ *Signposted from village.*
Open: May-Sep Site: 10HEC ⸺ ⅃ ⊙ ⬛ ☎ Services: ⊞ lau Leisure: ⭲ R Off-site: ⅃ ⬤ ✗ ⭲P

Facilities: ⅃-shop ⋔-shower ⊙-electric points for razors ⬛-electric points for caravans ☎-parking by tents permitted ⬛-compulsory separate car park **Services:** ✗-café/restaurant ⬤-bar ∅-Camping Gaz International ⚌-gas other than Camping Gaz ⊞-first aid facilities lau-laundry **Leisure:** ⭲-swimming L-Lake P-Pool R-River S-Sea **Off-site:** All facilities within 2km

UPPER AUSTRIA/SALZBURG

ABERSEE SALZBURG

Wolfgangblick Seestr 24, A-5342
☎ 06227 3475 📠 06227 3218
e-mail: camping@wolfgangblick.at
website: www.wolfgangblick.at
In a pleasant position directly on the Wolfgangsee.
Camping Card Compulsory.
➲ *Access via B1598 6km from St Gilgen. Signposted from village.*
Open: May-1 Oct Site: 2HEC ⬛ ⊕ Facilities: ℝ ⌶ ⊙ ⊕ ⊘ ☎ Services: ⟐ ✕ ⊞ lau Leisure: ⟲ LR Off-site: ⊞

ABTENAU SALZBURG

Oberwötzhof Erlfeld 37, 5441
☎ 06243 2698 📠 06243 269855
e-mail: oberwoetzlhof@aon.at
website: www.go.to/oberwoetzlhof-camp
A summer and winter site on a level meadow with panoramic views of the surrounding mountains.
➲ *NW of Abtenau.*
Open: All year Site: 2HEC ⬛ ⊕ 🏠 Facilities: ℝ ⌶ ⊙ ⊕ ☎ Services: ✕ ⊞ Leisure: ⟲ P Off-site: ⟲R

ALTMÜNSTER OBERÖSTERREICH

Schweizerhof Hauptstr 17, 4813
☎ 07612 89313 📠 07612 872764
e-mail: office@schweizerhof.cc
website: www.schweizerhof.cc
A modern site on the shore of Lake Traunsee with plenty of sporting facilities.
➲ *Signposted from the motorway.*
Open: May-Sep Site: 0.6HEC ⬛ ⊕ Prices: ⚥4.60 🚗2.20 🚐5.90-8 ⛺3.50-5 Facilities: ℝ ⊙ ⊕ ☎ Services: ⟐ ✕ ⊞ lau Leisure: ⟲ L Off-site: ⌶ ⊘ ⟲P

BADGASTEIN SALZBURG

Kurcamping 'Erlengrund' Erlengrundstr 6, 5640
☎ 06434 2790
On meadowland below the road leading to the Tauern railway tunnel.
➲ *From Hofgastein turn left off B167 and descend for 100m.*
Open: All year Site: 4.5HEC ⬛ ⊕ Facilities: ℝ ⌶ ⊙ ⊕ ⊘ ☎ Services: ⊞ lau Leisure: ⟲ P Off-site: ⟐ ✕ ⟲LR

BRUCK AN DER GROSSGLOCKNERSTRASSE SALZBURG

Woferlgut Kroessenbach 40, 5671
☎ 06545 73030 📠 06545 73033
e-mail: info@sportcamp.at website: www.sportcamp.at
In a beautiful valley beside a lake with good recreational facilities. Some noise from the main road which bisects the site.
➲ *Access via Bruck-Süd or Grossglockner on B311.*
Open: All year Site: 17HEC ⬛ ⊕ 🏠 🚐 ⛺ Prices: ⚥4.60-5.90 🚗4.10-5.30 🚐4.80-6.20 ⛺4.80-6.20 Facilities: ℝ ⌶ ⊙ ⊕ ⊘ ☎ Services: ⟐ ✕ ⊞ Leisure: ⟲ LP Off-site: ⟲R ⊞

ESTERNBERG OBERÖSTERREICH

Pyrawang 4092 ☎ 07714 6504 📠 07714 6504
➲ *At Km45.5 on B130 (Passau-Linz).*
Open: Apr-Oct Site: 3HEC ⬛ ⊕ Prices: ⚥3 🚗3 🚐2.50 ⛺1.50 Facilities: ℝ ⊙ ⊕ ☎ Services: ⟐ ✕ ⊞ Off-site: ⟲R

GLEINKERAU OBERÖSTERREICH

Pyhrn Priel 4582 ☎ 07562 7066 📠 07562 7192
e-mail: pousek@aon.at website: www.pyhrn-priel.at
A year-round site with a wide variety of facilities.
➲ *Signposted from Windischgarsten towards Gleinkersee. 2.5km from town.*
Open: All year Site: 1HEC ⬛ ⊕ Prices: ⚥4.40-5.80 🚗2-2 🚐5.10-10.90 ⛺3.65 Facilities: ℝ ⊙ ⊕ ⌶ ☎ Services: ⟐ ✕ ⊞ lau Off-site: ⟲R

KAPRUN SALZBURG

Mühle N-Gassner Str 38, 5710
☎ 06547 8254 📠 06547 825489
e-mail: muehle@kaprun.at
website: www.kaprun.at/muehle
A pleasant family site on long stretch of meadow by the Kapruner Ache.
➲ *S end of village towards cable lift.*
Open: All year Site: 1.5HEC ⬛ ⊕ Facilities: ℝ ⌶ ⊙ ⊕ ⊘ ⌶ ☎ Services: ⟐ ✕ ⊞ lau Leisure: ⟲ P

MAISHOFEN SALZBURG

Kammerlander Oberreit 18, 5751 ☎ 06542 68755
➲ *On B168.*
Open: May-15 Sep Site: ⬛ ⊕ Prices: ⚥2.60 🚗1.50 🚐1.50 ⛺1.50 Facilities: ℝ ⊙ ⊕ ☎ Services: ⟐ ✕ Off-site: ⌶ ⟲L

MITTERSILL SALZBURG

Mittersill Klausgasse 49, 5730
☎ 06562 4811 📠 06562 4811-10
A modern, well-equipped site suitable for both summer and winter holidays.
➲ *0.5km from the centre of the town on the shores of the lake.*
Open: All year Site: 1.7HEC ⬛ ⊕ Facilities: ℝ ⌶ ⊙ ⊕ ⊘ ⌶ ☎ Services: ⟐ ✕ ⊞ lau

MONDSEE OBERÖSTERREICH

Mond-See-Land Punzau 21, 5310
☎ 06232 2600 📠 06232 27218
e-mail: austria@campmondsee.at
website: www.campmondsee.at
In a picturesque, peaceful location between Lake Mondsee and Lake Irrsee with good facilities.
➲ *From Mondsee exit on A1/E55/E60 take B154 towards Strasswalden for 1.5km, then take Haider-Mühle road for 2km.*
Open: Apr-Oct Site: 3HEC ⬛ ⊕ 🏠 Prices: ⚥4.80-5.30 ⛺3.15-3.30 pitch 6.30-6.70 Facilities: ℝ ⌶ ⊙ ⊕ ⊘ ⌶ ☎ Services: ⟐ ✕ ⊞ lau Leisure: ⟲ P

NUSSDORF OBERÖSTERREICH

Gruber Dortstr 63, 4865 ☎ 07666 80450 📠 07666 80456
On fairly long meadow parallel to the promenade.
➲ *S of village, access is at Km19.7. Turn off B151 towards lake (Attersee).*
Open: 15 Apr-15 Oct Site: 2.6HEC ⬛ ⊕ Facilities: ℝ ⌶ ⊙ ⊕ ☎ Services: ⟐ ✕ ⊞ lau Leisure: ⟲ LP Off-site: ⊘

PERWANG AM GRABENSEE OBERÖSTERREICH

Perwang 5163 ☎ 06217 8288 📠 06217 824715
e-mail: gemeinde@perwang.ooe.gv.at
website: www.tiscover.com/perwang
Site beside lake.
Open: May-Oct Site: 1.5HEC ⬛ ⊕ ⊗ Prices: ⚥3.80 ⛺4 Facilities: ℝ ⊙ ⊕ ☑ Services: ⟐ ✕ ⊞ lau Leisure: ⟲ L Off-site: ⌶

Site: 6HEC-Site size ⬛-grass ⸬-sand ⊘-stone ☀-little shade ⊕-partly shaded ♣-mainly shaded
🏠-bungalows for hire 🚐-caravans for hire ⛺-tents for hire ⊗-no dogs Prices: ⚥-adult per night 🚗-car per night
pp-per person per night 🚐-caravan per night ⛺-tent per night

PETTENBACH OBERÖSTERREICH

Almtal 4643 ☎ 07586 86270
On a level meadow in the grounds of a former castle,with good, modern facilities.
⊃ *Leave A1/E55/E60 at Sattledt exit and continue towards Graz.*
Open: All year Site: 12HEC ⬛ ⇔ 🏠 Facilities: 🅿 🚿 ⊙ 🖲
⌀ ♨ 🏢 Services: 🍽 ✖ 🖽 lau Leisure: ⇗ P

RADSTADT SALZBURG

Forellencamp Gaismairallee 51, 5550
☎ 06452 7861 🖹 06452 5092
e-mail: forellencamp@aon.at
website: www.forellencamp.com
Flat meadowland near town
⊃ *SW via B99.*
Open: All year Site: 1HEC ⬛ ⠿ ⇗ Prices: ♦4.50 ⇔2.40
🚐4.50 ▲2.20 Facilities: 🅿 🚿 ⊙ 🖲 ♨ 🏢 Services: 🍽 ✖ 🖽
Off-site: ⌀ ⇗PR

ST JOHANN IM PONGAU SALZBURG

Hirschenwirt Bundesstr 1, 5600
☎ 06412 6012 🖹 06412 60128
e-mail: hirschenwirt@aon.at
website: www.hirschenwirt.com
A small, pleasant site ideally placed for travelling on the Salzburg-Badgastein road or as a base for exploring this region of mountains and lakes. The flat open site has grass pitches on either side of gravel roads. There is a small pool for summer use. Being on a major road route there is traffic noise.
⊃ *Site is behind Gasthof Hirschenwirt at St Johann im Pongau on B311.*
Open: All year Site: 0.8HEC ⬛ ✂ Prices: ♦4-5 pitch 6-9 Facilities: 🅿 ⊙ 🖲 ⌀ ♨ 🏢 Services: 🍽 ✖ Leisure: ⇗ P

Wieshof Wieshofgasse 8, 5600
☎ 06412 8519 🖹 06412 82929
On gently sloping meadow behind pension and farmhouse. Modern facilities. Big spa house with sauna, massage facilities and health bars, adjacent to site.
⊃ *Off B311 towards Zell am Zee.*
Open: All year Site: 1.6HEC ⬛ ⇗ 🚐 Facilities: 🅿 🚿 ⊙ 🖲 ⌀
🏢 Services: lau Off-site: ✖ ⇗P 🖽

ST MARTIN BEI LOFER SALZBURG

Park Grubhof 5092 ☎ 06588 8237 🖹 06588 82377
e-mail: camping@lofer.net website: www.almdorf.com
Situated in meadowland on the banks of the River Saalach. Separate sections for dog owners, families, teenagers and groups.
⊃ *1.5km S of Lofer turn left off B311.*
Open: 25 Apr-5 Oct Site: 10HEC ⬛ ⇔ 🏠 🚐 Prices: ♦5
⇔2.20 🚐3.20-4 ▲2.20-3.20 Facilities: 🅿 🚿 ⊙ 🖲 ⌀ ♨ 🏢
Services: 🍽 ✖ 🖽 lau Leisure: ⇗ R Off-site: ⇗P

ST WOLFGANG OBERÖSTERREICH

Appesbach Au 99, 5360 ☎ 06138 2206 🖹 06138 220633
e-mail: camping@appesbach.at
website: www.appesbach.at
On sloping meadow facing lake with no shade at upper end.
⊃ *0.8km E of St Wolfgang between lake and Strobl road.*
Open: All year Site: 2HEC ⬛ ⇗ 🚐 Facilities: 🅿 🚿 ⊙ 🖲 ⌀
♨ 🏢 Services: 🍽 ✖ lau Leisure: ⇗ L Off-site: 🖽

Berau Schwarzenbach 16, 5360
☎ 06138 2543 🖹 06138 254355
e-mail: camping@berau.at website: www.berau.com
A family-run site in a picturesque setting on the edge of the Wolfgangsee. Spacious, level pitches and good, modern facilities.
⊃ *From A1 exit 'Talgau' follow signs for Hof and Bad Ischl on N158 through Strobl village towards St Wolfgang and follow signs.*
Open: All year Site: 2HEC ⬛ ⇗ Prices: ♦5.30-6.05 ⇔2-3.50 ▲4-5 pitch 7.50-10 Facilities: 🅿 🚿 ⊙ 🖲 ⌀ ♨ 🏢
Services: 🍽 ✖ 🖽 lau Leisure: ⇗ L

SALZBURG SALZBURG

Kasern C-Zuckmayerstr 26, 5101
☎ 0662 450576 🖹 0662 450576
e-mail: schwarzkopf@aon.at
website: www.camping-kasern-salzburg.com
⊃ *Access via exit 'Salzburg-Nord' on the A1.*
Open: Apr-Oct Site: 0.9HEC ⬛ ⇗ ▲ Facilities: 🅿 🚿 ⊙ 🖲
🏢 Services: ✖ lau Off-site: 🍽 ✖ ⌀

Nord Sam Samstr 22A, 5023 ☎ 0662 660494 🖹 0662 660494
e-mail: christinelex@camping-nord-sam.com
website: www.camping-nord-sam.com
Site divided into pitches.
⊃ *400m from Salzburg Nord Autobahn Exit.*
Open: May-Sep Site: 2HEC ⬛ ⠿ ⇗ Prices: ♦4.50-6 pitch 7-8.50 Facilities: 🅿 🚿 ⊙ 🖲 🏢 Services: ✖ 🖽 lau Leisure: ⇗ P Off-site: 🍽 ✖ ⌀ ♨

Schloss Aigen A5026 ☎ 0662 622079 🖹 0662 622079
e-mail: camping.aigen@elsnet.at
Site divided into pitches in partial clearing on mountain slope.
⊃ *From Salzburg-Süd motorway exit through Anif and Glasenbach.*
Open: May-Sep Site: 25HEC ⬛ ⇗ Prices: ♦4.60 pitch 5.50
Facilities: 🅿 🚿 ⊙ 🖲 🏢 Services: 🍽 ✖ 🖽 lau

Stadtblick Rauchenbichlerstr 21, 5020
☎ 0662 450652 🖹 0662 458018
e-mail: panorama.camping@utanet.at
website: www.panorama-camping.at
A terraced site affording spectacular views of the surrounding mountains.
⊃ *Leave motorway at exit Salzburg-Nord and follow signs.*
Open: 20 Mar-5 Nov Site: 0.8HEC ⬛ ⇗ 🚐 ▲
Facilities: 🅿 🚿 ⊙ 🖲 ⌀ ♨ 🏢 Services: 🍽 ✖ 🖽 lau

SCHLÖGEN OBERÖSTERREICH

Terrassencamping Pension Schlögen A-4083
☎ 07279 8241 🖹 07279 824122
e-mail: schloegen.freizeit@netway.at
website: www.schloegen.at
On level ground beside the River Donau, backed by woods and mountains.
Open: Apr-20 Oct Site: 2.8HEC ⬛ ⇔ Prices: ♦5 ▲3 pitch 6
Facilities: 🅿 🚿 ⊙ 🖲 🏢 Services: 🍽 ✖ 🖽 lau Leisure: ⇗ PR

SEEKIRCHEN SALZBURG

Strand Seestr 2, 5201 ☎ 06212 4088 🖹 06212 4088
Beside the Wallersee in beautiful meadow.
Open: 15 Apr-15 Oct Site: 2HEC ⬛ ⇗ Facilities: 🅿 🚿 ⊙
🖲 ⌀ 🏢 Services: 🍽 ✖ 🖽 lau Leisure: ⇗ LP Off-site: 🚿

Facilities: 🚿-shop 🅿-shower ⊙-electric points for razors 🖲-electric points for caravans 🏢-parking by tents permitted
🅿-compulsory separate car park **Services:** ✖-café/restaurant 🍽-bar ⌀-Camping Gaz International ♨-gas other than Camping
Gaz 🖽-first aid facilities lau-laundry **Leisure:** ⇗-swimming L-Lake P-Pool R-River S-Sea **Off-site:** All facilities within 2km

Zell am Wallersee 5201 ☎ 06212 4080 🗎 06212 4080
e-mail: franz.klampfer@aon.at
Level meadowland separated from the lake by the Lido.
➲ *Access from A1 exit Wallersee then via Seekirchen to Zell.*
Open: 11 May-19 Oct Site: 3HEC ⬛ 🔄 Facilities: ℝ ⊙ 🔾
🏠 Services: ✕ ⊞ lau Leisure: ᴿ LP

UNTERACH OBERÖSTERREICH

Insel 4866 ☎ 07665 8311 🗎 07665 7255
e-mail: camping@inselcamp.at
website: www.inselcamp.at
Quiet site on shore of Lake Attersee; divided into two
sections by River Seeache. Family site.
➲ *Entrance below B152 towards Steinbach at Km24.5; about
300m from fork with B151.*
Open: 15 May-15 Sep Site: 1.8HEC ⬛ 🔄 Facilities: ℝ 🔾 ⊙
🔾 🏠 Services: lau Leisure: ᴿ LR Off-site: 🍴 ✕ ∅ ⊞

WALD SALZBURG

S.N.P Lahn 65, 5742 ☎ 06565 84460 🗎 06565 84464
e-mail: snp.camping@utaney.at
website: www.snp-camping.at
A small family site in a beautiful Alpine setting.
➲ *W of town.*
Open: All year Site: 0.7HEC ⬛ 🔄 🔾 Facilities: ℝ 🔾 ⊙ 🔾
∅ 🏠 Services: 🍴 ✕ ⊞ lau Off-site: ✕ ᴿLP

WESENUFER OBERÖSTERREICH

Nibelungen 4085 ☎ 07718 7589 🗎 07718/7589
e-mail: nibelungen.camping@utanet.at
In a pleasant rural setting beside the River Donau.
➲ *500m from B130.*
Open: Apr-Sep Site: 1.2HEC ⬛ 🔄 Facilities: ℝ ⊙ 🔾 🏠
Services: ⊞ lau Leisure: ᴿ R Off-site: 🔾 ✕ ᴿP

ZELL AM SEE SALZBURG

Seecamp Zell am See Thumersbacherstr 34, 5700
☎ 06542 72115 🗎 06542 72115
e-mail: zell@seecamp.at website: www.seecamp.at
In a pleasant wooded location beside the lake with excellent
site and recreational facilities.
➲ *Access via B311, N of lake towards Thumersbach.
Signposted.*
Open: All year Site: 3HEC ⬛ ◕ 🔄 Prices: ⅄5.90-7.35 ⊘2-
2.50 🔺3.20-4 pitch 6.70-10.70 Facilities: ℝ 🔾 ⊙ 🔾 ∅ 🏠
Services: 🍴 ✕ ⊞ lau Leisure: ᴿ L Off-site: ᴿP

Südufer Thumersbach, Seeuferstr 196, 5700
☎ 06542 56228 🗎 06542 562284
e-mail: zell@camping-suedufer.at
website: www.camping-suedufer.at
A family site on level ground in a picturesque spot on the
southern bank of the Zeller See.
➲ *S via B311 towards Thumersbach.*
Open: All year Site: 0.6HEC ⬛ ◕ Prices: ⅄4.80-5.80
⊘2.10-2.50 ⊞4.60-5.40 🔺3.90-5.30 Facilities: ℝ 🔾 ⊙ 🔾 ∅
🔾 🏠 Services: ✕ lau Off-site: ✕ ᴿLPR

VORARLBERG

BEZAU VORARLBERG

Bezau Ach 206, 6870 ☎ 05514 2964
e-mail: camping.bezau@aon.at
website: www.campingfuehrer.at
Small family-owned site with modern sanitary facilities.

➲ *S via B200 (Dornbirn-Warth).*
Open: All year Site: 0.5HEC ⬛ 🔄 Prices: ⅄4 ⊞6.55-7.30
🔺5.80-7.30 pitch 5.80-7.30 Facilities: ℝ ⊙ 🔾 🔾 Off-site: 🔾
🍴 ✕ ᴿPR ⊞

BLUDENZ VORARLBERG

AT **BRAZ** (7KM SE)

Traube 6751 ☎ 05552 28103-0 🗎 05552 28103-40
e-mail: traube.braz@aon.at website: www.traubebraz.at
On sloping grassland in the picturesque Klostertal valley with
good, modern facilities.
➲ *7km SE of Bludenz via E17, S16 (Bludenz-Arlberg-
Innsbruck). Signposted. Near railway.*
Open: All year Site: 2HEC ⬛ ◕ ⊘ Prices: ⊞20.40-25.50
pitch 16-25.50 (incl 2 persons) Facilities: ℝ 🔾 ⊙ 🔾 ∅ 🛁 🏠
Services: ✕ ⊞ lau Leisure: ᴿ P Off-site: ᴿR

DALAAS VORARLBERG

Erne 6752 ☎ 05585 7223 🗎 05585 20049
e-mail: info@etpc.at website: www.etpc.at
In the town, attached to a guesthouse and next to the
swimming pool.
➲ *Access via S16, exit 'Dalass'.*
Open: All year Site: 0.6HEC ⬛ 🔄 Prices: pitch 17.50-19.50
(incl 2 persons) Facilities: ℝ ⊙ 🔾 ∅ 🛁 🏠 Leisure: ᴿ R
Off-site: 🔾 ✕ ᴿP ⊞

DORNBIRN VORARLBERG

In der Enz 6850 ☎ 05572 29119
e-mail: camping.spiegel@vol.at
A municipal site beside a public park, in a wooded area some
100m beyond the Karren cable lift.
➲ *Access via autobahn exit Dornbirn-Süd.*
Open: May-Sep Site: 10HEC ⬛ 🔄 Facilities: ℝ 🔾 ⊙ 🔾 ∅
🏠 Services: 🍴 ✕ ⊞ lau Off-site: ᴿPR ⊞

LINGENAU VORARLBERG

Feurstein Haidach 185, 6951 ☎ 05513 6114 🗎 05513 61144
A small site located in a meadow adjacent to some farm
buildings with sufficient facilities for a pleasant stay.
Open: All year Site: 1HEC ⬛ 🔄 Prices: ⅄6 ⊞7.70 ⊞3.50
🔺2-3.50 Facilities: ℝ ⊙ 🔾 ∅ 🛁 🏠 Services: ⊞ lau
Off-site: 🔾 🍴 ✕

NENZING VORARLBERG

Alpencamping Nenzing 6710 ☎ 05525 62491 🗎 635676
e-mail: josef.morik@vol.at
website: www.alpencamping.at
A well appointed site in magnificent Alpine scenery. There
are fine sporting facilities and modern sanitary blocks.
➲ *Signposted from B190 from Nenzing-2km towards Gurtis.*
Open: Jan-19 Apr & 8 May-Dec Site: 3HEC ⬛ 🔄 🏠 🔾
Prices: ⅄5.10-6.20 ⊞3.60 pitch 3.60-7 Facilities: ℝ 🔾 ⊙ 🔾
∅ 🏠 Services: 🍴 ✕ ⊞ lau Leisure: ᴿ P

AT **NÜZIDERS** (2.5KM NW)

Sonnenberg Hinteroferst 12, 6714
☎ 05552 64035 🗎 05552 33900
e-mail: camping.sonnenberg@eunet.at
website: www.camping-sonnenberg.com
Clean site with modern facilities in gently sloping
meadowland and splendid mountain scenery.
➲ *Access from Bludenz-Nüziders road, at first fork follow up
hill.*
Open: 24 May-2 Nov & 15 Dec-7 Apr Site: 1.9HEC ⬛ 🔄
Prices: ⅄5.20 ⊞7-10.70 🔺7-10.50 pitch 7-10.70 Facilities: ℝ
🔾 ⊙ 🔾 ∅ 🛁 🏠 Services: ⊞ lau Off-site: ✕ 🛁 ᴿR

Site: 6HEC-Site size ⬛-grass ⠿-sand ◕-stone ᴥ-little shade 🔄-partly shaded ◕-mainly shaded
🏠-bungalows for hire ⊞-caravans for hire 🔺-tents for hire ⊘-no dogs Prices: ⅄-adult per night ⊘-car per night
pp-per person per night ⊞-caravan per night 🔺-tent per night

RAGGAL-PLAZERA VORARLBERG

Grosswalsertal 6741 ☎ 05553 209
e-mail: contact@camping-grosswalsertal.at
website: www.camping-grosswalsertal.at
A family site in a quiet location on gently sloping terrain,
with pleasant views.
➲ *On NE outskirts.*
Open: 15 Apr-15 Nov Site: 0.8HEC ⬛⬛⬛⬛ ☀ Prices: ♠4.80
pitch 5-8 Facilities: ♗ ⚍ ⊙ 🖵 ∅ ☎ Services: lau Leisure: ⚓
P Off-site: ⚐ ✗ ⊞

TSCHAGGUNS VORARLBERG

Zelfen 6774 ☎ 0664 2002326 📠 05556 72326
e-mail: dsandrell@sandrell.vol.at
website: www.camping-zelfen.at
Partly uneven, grassy site in a wooded location beside River
Ill. Good recreational facilities.
➲ *Access via A14 to Bludenz, then B188 to Tschagguns.*
Open: All year Site: 2HEC ⬛⬛⬛⬛ ☀ Prices: ♠5.60-6.30 pitch
7.80-8.30 Facilities: ♗ ⚍ ⊙ 🖵 ∅ ⚌ ☎ Services: ⚐ ✗ ⊞ lau
Leisure: ⚓ R Off-site: ⚓P

VIENNA (WIEN)

WIEN (VIENNA) WIEN

Donaupark Klosterneuburg In der Au, 3400
☎ 02243 25877 📠 02243 25878
e-mail: campklosterneuburg@oeamtc.at
website: www.campingklosterneuburg.at
A modern site in delightful wooded surroundings with fine
recreational facilities and within easy reach of the city centre.

➲ *Signposted from A1.*
Open: 15 Mar-7 Nov Site: 2.2HEC ⬛⬛⬛⬛ ☀ 🚐 ⚐ Prices: ♠6
🚐4.50 🚐7.50-11 pitch 7.50-11 Facilities: ♗ ⚍ ⊙ 🖵 ∅ ⚌ ☎
Services: ✗ ⊞ lau Off-site: ⚓PR

Neue Donau Am Kaisermühlendamm 119, 1220
☎ 01 2024010 📠 01 2024010
e-mail: camping.neuedonau@verkehrsbuero.at
website: www.campingwien.at
Situated in a meadow surrounded by trees on the banks of
the Danube within a leisure park.
➲ *On E bank of the river with access to the A4 and A22.*
Open: Etr-Sep Site: 3.3HEC ⬛⬛⬛⬛ ☀ Prices: ♠5.50-6.50 🚐7-8
▲4-5 pitch 9-10 Facilities: ♗ ⚍ ⊙ 🖵 ∅ ☎ Services: ⚐ ✗ ⊞
lau Off-site: ⚓LPR

Wien-West Hüttelbergstr 80, 1140
☎ 01 9142314 📠 01 9113594
e-mail: camping.west@verkehrsbuero.at
website: www.campingwien.at
On slightly rising meadow with asphalt paths.
➲ *From end of A1/E5 (Linz-Wien) to Bräuhausbrücke, then
turn left and across road to Linz, continue for approx. 1.8km.*
Open: Jan & Mar-Dec Site: 2.4HEC ⬛⬛⬛⬛ ♠ 🚐 Prices: ♠5.50-
6.50 ▲4-5 pitch 9-10 Facilities: ♗ ⚍ ⊙ 🖵 ∅ ▣ Services: ⚐ ✗
⊞ lau

AT RODAUN (4KM SW)

Rodaun An der Au 2, 1230 ☎ 01 8884154 📠 01 8884154
➲ *Between An der Austr and Leising River dam. Access from
Breitenfürter Str N492.*
Open: 25 Mar-4 Nov Site: 0.8HEC ⬛⬛⬛⬛ ⚘ ♠ Prices: ♠5.45
🚐1.09 🚐4.36 ▲4.36 Facilities: ♗ ⊙ 🖵 ∅ ☎ Services: ⊞ lau
Off-site: ⚍ ⚐ ✗

*Looking across Vienna's Stephansplatz, past the ultra-modern Haas-Haus shopping centre
towards St Stephen's Cathedral*

Facilities: ⚍-shop ♗-shower ⊙-electric points for razors 🖵-electric points for caravans ☎-parking by tents permitted
▣-compulsory separate car park Services: ✗-café/restaurant ⚐-bar ∅-Camping Gaz International ⚌-gas other than Camping
Gaz ⊞-first aid facilities lau-laundry Leisure: ⚓-swimming L-Lake P-Pool R-River S-Sea Off-site: All facilities within 2km

BELGIUM

Belgium is a small, densely populated country bordered by France, Germany, Luxembourg and The Netherlands.

FACTS AND FIGURES
Area: 30,528 sq km (11,787 sq miles)
Population: 10,309,725 (2001)
Capital: Bruxelles (Brussel, Brussels)
Language: French, Dutch, German
IDD code: 32. To call the UK dial 00 44
Currency: Euro
Local time: GMT + 1 (summer GMT + 2)

Emergency Services:
Police 101; Fire 100; Ambulance 100. From a mobile phone dial 112 and ask for the service required.

Average daily temperatures: Bruxelles (Brussel, Brussels)
Jan 3°C   Jul 17°C
Mar 5°C   Sep14°C
May 13°C   Nov 5°C

Tourist Information:
UK Belgian National Tourist Office (Brussels-Ardennes) 225 Marsh Wall, London E14 9FW
Tel 0906 3020 245 (premium rate info line)
Belgian National Tourist Office (Flanders-Brussels) 31 Pepper Street, London E14 9RW.
Tel: 09001 887799 (premium rate info line)

USA
Belgian National Tourist Office, Suite 1501, 780 Third Ave, New York, NY10017
Tel (212) 758 8130

Tourist info website:
www.belgium-tourism.net
www.visitflanders.com
Business hours-
Banks: Mon-Fri 09.00-12.00, 14.00-16.00
Shops: Mon-Sat 09.00-18.00. (Supermarkets 20.00)

Despite the fact that it is heavily industrialised, Belgium possesses some beautiful scenery, notably the great forest of the Ardennes. The resorts in the Oostende (Ostend) area offer a selection of wide, safe, sandy beaches and cover about forty miles of coastline.

The climate is temperate and similar to that of Britain: the variation between summer and winter lessened by the effects of the Gulf Stream. Three main languages are spoken: French, Dutch and German. (See language opposite.)

Belgium is a varied, charming country in which to spend a camping holiday - the rivers and gorges of the Ardennes contrasting sharply with the rolling plains which make up the rest of the countryside. There are now over 800 campsites officially authorised by local authorities. They are normally open from April to October, but many are open throughout the year. Coastal sites tend to be very crowded at the height of the season.

Off-site camping (including sleeping) is prohibited beside public roads for more than 24 consecutive hours; on seashores; within a 100-metre radius of a main water point; or on a site classified for the conservation of monuments. Elsewhere, camping is permitted free of charge, as long as the stay does not exceed 24 hours and the camper has obtained authorisation from the landowner.

HOW TO GET THERE

The direct ferry service to Belgium operating to **Zeebrugge** from **Hull** takes 12 hrs 45 mins.

Alternatively, you could use Eurotunnel, or take a shorter crossing by ferry or catamaran to Calais, France, and drive along the coast road to Belgium.

MOTORING & GENERAL INFO

The information given here is specific to Belgium. It must be read in conjunction with the Essential Motoring Information at the front of the book, which covers those regulations which are common to many countries.

ACCIDENTS

The police must be called if an unoccupied, stationary vehicle is damaged, or if injuries are caused to persons; in the latter case, the car must not be moved. Please see the recommendations given under *Accidents* and also under *Warning triangle* in the Essential Motoring Information at the front of this guidebook.

BRITISH EMBASSY/CONSULATES*

The British Embassy is located at B-1040 Bruxelles, rue d'Aarlenstraat 85 ☎ (02) 2876211. There are British Consulates with Honorary Consuls in Antwerpen (Antwerp) and Liège.

CHILDREN IN CARS

Child under 3 must be in suitable restraint when travelling in the front and, if such a system is fitted, when travelling in the rear. Children over 3 and under 12 seated in front or rear must use seat-belt or child restraint appropriate to their size and weight. See Essential Motoring Information under 'Passengers' and 'Seat Belts'.

CURRENCY*

With the introduction of the Euro, the **Belgian Franc (BEF)** ceased to be legal tender from 2002. However, BEF coins and notes may still be exchanged at the Belgian Central Bank (**Nationale Bank van België/Banque National de Belgique**) and the Post Office for an unlimited period (banknotes) and until the end of December 2004 (coins).

DIMENSIONS AND WEIGHT RESTRICTIONS*

Private **cars** and towed **trailers** or **caravans** are restricted to the following dimensions: height, 4 metres; width, 2.55 metres; length, 12 metres.The maximum permitted overall length of vehicle/ trailer or caravan combination is 18 metres. Trailers without brakes may have a total maximum weight of 750kg.

DRIVING LICENCE*

A valid UK or Republic of Ireland licence is accepted in Belgium. The minimum age at which visitors from UK or Republic of Ireland may use a temporarily imported car or motorcycle is 18 years.

FOODSTUFFS*

If the imported foodstuffs are for personal use, there are no limits when travelling between EU countries. Visitors coming from other countries may import up to 1kg of meat for personal consumption. Coffee (500g), coffee extract (200g), tea (100g) and tea extract (40g) are free of customs duties, but visitors under 15 cannot import coffee.

LANGUAGE

There are *three* official languages in Belgium - *Dutch, French* and *German*. Dutch is spoken in the north, French in the south and, in the eastern provinces, German. Both Dutch and French are spoken in Brussels. These divisions are administrative but act as a rough guide to the areas in which the various languages are spoken.

Some of the town names in the directory are shown in both Dutch and French, and that shown first is the one used locally. However, Brussels (Bruxelles-Brussel) is officially bi-lingual.

The Dutch spoken in Belgium is different in many ways to the Dutch of the Netherlands, just as American English is different to the English spoken in the UK. It is regarded by some as a separate language (Flemish), but by most as a collection of Dutch dialects.

LIGHTS*

It is compulsory for motorcyclists to use dipped headlights during the day.

MOTORING CLUB

The **Touring Club Royal de Belgique** (TCB) has its office at 1040 Bruxelles, 44 rue de la Loi ☎(02) 2332211. The Bruxelles (Brussels) office is open 09.00-17.00hrs Mon-Fri.
Website: **www.touring.be**

PETROL

See Essential Motoring Information under 'Petrol/Diesel'.

ROADS

A good road system is available. However, one international route that has given more cause for complaints than any other is, without doubt, that from Calais (France) through Belgium to Köln/Cologne (Germany). The problem is aggravated by the fact that there are three official languages in Belgium (see language above).

In the Flemish part of Belgium the destination place names are in Dutch, in Wallonia they are in French and in the German part of Belgium they are in German and French or just in German. Brussels (Bruxelles-Brussel) seems to be the only neutral ground where the signs show the two alternative spellings of placenames (Antwerpen-Anvers; Gent-Gand; Liège-Luik; Mons-Bergen; Namur-Namen; Oostend-Ostende; Tournai-

Doornik.) From the Flemish part of the country, Dunkirk (Dunkerque) in France is signposted Duinkerke and Lille is referred to as Rijsel, and even Paris is shown as Parijs.

Belgium has a comprehensive system of toll-free motorways linking major towns and adjoining countries. Generally, signposts leading to and on motorways show foreign destination place-names in the language of the country concerned. The exceptions to this are on the E40 and E314 where cities such as Aachen and Köln may be given as Aken and Keulen (Dutch), and Aix-la-Chapelle and Cologne (French).

Car/motorcycle/car towing caravan/trailer
Built-up areas 50km/h (31mph)
Other roads 90km/h (56mph)
Motorways and 4-lane roads separated by central reservation 120km/h (74mph)†. Minimum speed on motorways on straight level stretches is 70km/h (43mph). Vehicles being towed due to accident or breakdown are limited to 25km/h (15mph) on all roads and, if on a motorway, must leave at the first exit.

†On dual carriageways separated only by road markings the limit is 90km/h (55mph).

WARNING TRIANGLE*

It is compulsory for a vehicle to be equipped with a warning triangle and to use it in the event of accident or breakdown. The triangle must be placed 30 metres (33yds) behind the vehicle on ordinary roads and 100 metres (109yds) on motorways to warn following traffic of any obstruction; it must be visible at a distance of 50 metres (55yds). In built-up areas the triangle may be placed close to or even on the vehicle if the 30 metre rule cannot be obeyed.

*Additional information on these topics will be found in the Essential Motoring Information at the front of the book.

The Arc de Triomphe in Brussels.

SOUTH WEST/COAST

BLANKENBERGE West-Vlaanderen

Bonanza I Zeebruggelaan 137, 8370
☎ 050 416658   ▤ 050 427349
e-mail: bonanza@kmonet.be
website: www.bonanza1.be
A family site in wooded surroundings 1km from both the village and the sea.
Open: 15Mar-15 Sep Site: 4.5HEC ⸺ ⸺ ꙮ Prices: ♦5 pitch 17-25 (incl 2 persons) Facilities: ⋔ ⚍ ⊙ ⊕ ⌀ ⚏ ⚊ Services: ☕ ✗ ⊞ lau Leisure: ⤳ P Off-site: ⤳LS

Dallas Ruzettelaan 191, 8370 ☎ 050 418157   ▤ 050 429479
Well equipped family site near a large department store 50mtrs from the beach.
Open: 15 Mar-1 Oct Site: 2.6HEC ⸺⸺ ꙮ Prices: ♦4.50 ⬟5 ▲3.27-4 Facilities: ⋔ ⚍ ⊙ ⊕ ⌀ ⚏ ⚊ Services: ⊞ lau Off-site: ☕ ✗ ⤳LPS

KNOKKE-HEIST West-Vlaanderen

De Vuurtoren Heistlaan 168, 8301 ☎ 050 511782
e-mail: kampvuurtoren@attglobal.net
website: www.knokke-heist.be
On level meadow with tarred roads.
➲ Turn S off Knokke-Oostende road 4km from Knokke and follow signposts.
Open: 15 Mar-15 Oct Site: 6.6HEC ⸺⸺ ꙮ Prices: ♦3.30 ⬟7.60-16.70 ▲6.25-14.20 Facilities: ⋔ ⚍ ⊙ ⊕ ⚏ Services: ☕ ✗ ⊞ lau Off-site: ⌀ ⚊ ⤳PS

Zilvermeeuw Heistlaan 166, 8301
☎ 050 512726   ▤ 050 512703
e-mail: info.campingzilvermeeuw@skynet.be
website: www.camping-zilvermeeuw.com
Level site in wooded surroundings.
➲ SW via N300.
Open: Mar-15 Nov Site: 7HEC ⸺⸺ ꙮ ⬟ Prices: ♦3-4 ⬟1 ⬟8-10 ▲6-8 Facilities: ⋔ ⚍ ⊙ ⊕ ⌀ ⚏ Services: ✗ ⊞ lau Off-site: ☕ ✗ ⤳LPS

At WESTKAPELLE (3km S)

Holiday Natienlaan 70-72, 8300
☎ 050 601203   ▤ 050 613280
A quiet family site with good modern facilities within easy reach of the sea.
➲ On S outskirts near the railway station.
Open: Apr-Sep Site: 1.5HEC ⸺⸺ ꙮ ⊛ Facilities: ⋔ ⊙ ⊕ ⌀ ⚏ Services: ⊞ lau Off-site: ⚍ ☕ ✗ ⤳PS

KOKSIJDE West-Vlaanderen

Blekker & Blekkerdal Jachtwakerstr 12, 8670
☎ 058 511633   ▤ 058 511307
e-mail: camping.deblekker@belgacom.net
website: blekker.hypermart.net
In a peaceful location, surrounded by trees, with good modern facilities.
➲ Situated between Dunkerque and Oostende, 5km from the Belgian frontier. Leave motorway and head towards Veurne.
Open: All year Site: 3HEC ⸺⸺ ꙮ ⊛ Prices: pitch 19-27 (incl 4 persons) Facilities: ⋔ ⊙ ⊕ ⚏ Services: ⊞ lau Off-site: ⚍ ☕ ✗ ⤳S

LOMBARDSIJDE West-Vlaanderen

Lombarde Elisabethlaan 4, 8434
☎ 058 236839   ▤ 058 239908
e-mail: info@delombarde.be website: www.delombarde.be
A well equipped family site 400mtrs from the sea and close to the centre of the village. Some facilities only available March to early November.

➲ From E40 exit Nieuwpoort and follow signs.
Open: All year Site: 8.5HEC ⸺⸺ ꙮ ⬟ Prices: ⬟13.50-27.90 Facilities: ⋔ ⚍ ⊙ ⊕ ⌀ ⚏ Services: ☕ ✗ ⊞ lau Leisure: ⤳ L Off-site: ⚊ ⤳PS

Zomerzon Elisabethlan 1, 8434 ☎ 058 237396   ▤ 232817
In a quiet location, 800mtrs from the sand dunes and beach with good facilities.
Open: 24 Mar-11 Nov Site: 10HEC ⸺⸺ ⊛ ⬟ ⊛ Facilities: ⋔ ⊙ ⊕ Services: ☕ ⊞ lau Off-site: ⚍ ✗ ⌀ ⤳PS

LOPPEM West-Vlaanderen

Lac Loppem 8210 ☎ 050 824262
Surrounded by fir trees on the edge of a lake.
➲ Leave A10/E40 at Torhout exit and turn right by the Esso service station.
Open: All year Site: 14HEC ⸺⸺ ⊛ Facilities: ⋔ ⚍ ⊙ ⊕ ⌀ ⚏ Services: ☕ ✗ ⊞ Leisure: ⤳ L

MIDDELKERKE West-Vlaanderen

Myn Plezier Duinenweg 489, 8430
☎ 059 300279   ▤ 059 314503
In wooded surroundings close to the castle. The camp shop only operates during high season.
Open: Apr-10 Sep Site: 3HEC ⸺⸺ ꙮ Facilities: ⋔ ⊙ ⊕ ⌀ ⚊ ⚏ Services: ☕ ✗ ⊞ lau Off-site: ⚍ ⤳S

MONS Hainaut

Waux-Hall av St-Pierre 17, 7000
☎ 065 337923   ▤ 065 363848
In a secluded position 1km from the town centre, with direct access to the Parc du Waux-Hall.
➲ From town ring road take exit for Beaumont/Binche, Charleroi. Turn right at lights, then take immediate right.
Open: All year Site: 1.4HEC ⸺⸺ ꙮ ⬟ Prices: ♦3.35 ⬟6.15 pitch 5.25-6.15 (incl 1 persons) Facilities: ⋔ ⊙ ⊕ ⚏ Services: ⊞ lau Off-site: ⚍ ☕ ✗ ⌀ ⚊ ⤳L

NIEUWPOORT West-Vlaanderen

Info Brugsesteenweg 49, 8620 ☎ 058 236037   ▤ 058 232682
e-mail: nieuwpoort@kompascamping.be
website: www.kompascamping.be
A family site in pleasant wooded surroundings. Plenty of recreational facilities including watersports.
➲ From E40 exit 4 head towards Diksmuide and Nieuwpoort. Signposted from St Joris.
Open: 26 Mar-8 Nov Site: 24HEC ⸺⸺ ꙮ ⬟ ⬟ Prices: pitch 18.50-28.75 (incl 4 persons) Facilities: ⋔ ⚍ ⊙ ⊕ ⌀ ⚏ Services: ☕ ✗ ⊞ lau Leisure: ⤳ P Off-site: ⚊ ⤳LRS

OOSTENDE (OSTENDE) West-Vlaanderen

Asterix Duinenstr 200, 8450 ☎ 059 331000   ▤ 324202
A family site in wooded surroundings, 500m from the sea.
Camping Card Compulsory.
➲ From Oostende follow N34 towards Knokke-Heist for 7km then right for Bredene-Dorp.
Open: All year Site: 3HEC ⸺⸺ ⬥ ⬟ ⬟ Prices: ♦9 Facilities: ⋔ ⚍ ⊙ ⊕ ⌀ ⚊ ⚏ Services: ☕ ✗ ⊞ lau Off-site: ⤳LPS

ST SAUVEUR Hainaut

Hauts r des Vertes Feuilles 13, 7912 ☎ 3269 768672
In a secluded, wooded situation within the Flemish Ardennes with fine facilities.
➲ Signposted from Renaix.
Open: All year Site: 1HEC ⸺⸺ ⬥ ⬟ ⬟ Facilities: ⋔ ⊙ ⊕ ⌀ ⚊ ⚏ Services: ⊞ lau Off-site: ⚍ ☕ ✗

Facilities: ⚍-shop ⋔-shower ⊙-electric points for razors ⊕-electric points for caravans ⚏-parking by tents permitted ⚏-compulsory separate car park **Services:** ✗-café/restaurant ☕-bar ⌀-Camping Gaz International ⚊-gas other than Camping Gaz ⊞-first aid facilities lau-laundry **Leisure:** ⤳-swimming L-Lake P-Pool R-River S-Sea **Off-site:** All facilities within 2km

TOURNAI HAINAUT

Orient Vieux Chemin de Mons 8, 7500
☎ 069 222635 ▤ 069 890229
e-mail: tourisme@tournai.be website: www.tournai.be
A pleasant site in an area of woodland with good recreational
facilities.
➲ From motorway exit 'Tournai Est' head towards the town
centre. Turn left at first crossroads and follow signs.
Open: All year Site: 20HEC ▦ ⬩ Prices: ♠2.50 ♣2.50 ♣3
▲2.50 Facilities: ⬩ ⊙ ⬩ ⬩ Services: ⬩ ✗ ⊞ lau Leisure: ⬩
LP Off-site: ⬩ ✗

WAREGEM WEST-VLAANDEREN

Gemeentelijk Sportstadion Zuiderlaan 13, 8790
☎ 056 609532 ▤ 056 621223
e-mail: toerisme@waregem.be website: www.waregem.be
In a sports and leisure centre SE of the town centre.
➲ Access via E17 (Kortrijk-Gent).
Open: Apr-Sep Site: 1HEC ▦ ⬩ Prices: pitch 15
Facilities: ⬩ ⊙ ⬩ ⬩ Services: ⊞ Off-site: ⬩ ⬩ ✗ ⬩ ⬩ ⬩P

WAUDREZ HAINAUT

Gloriettes r de la Résistance 98, 7131 ☎ 064 368269
Open: Apr-Oct Site: 3HEC ▦ ⬩ Prices: ♠2.25 ♣2.25
♣2.25 ▲2.25 Facilities: ⬩ ⊙ ⬩ ⬩ Services: ⊞ lau

WESTENDE WEST-VLAANDEREN

KACB Bassevillestr 81, 8434 ☎ 058 237343 ▤ 058 233505
e-mail: campingkacb\uesten@be. website: www.kacb.be
A well appointed site close to the beach.
Camping Card Compulsory.
➲ Situated between Westende and Lombardsijde towards the
sea.
Open: All year Site: 6.5HEC ▦ ⬩ ⬩ Facilities: ⬩ ⬩ ⊙ ⬩
⬩ ⬩ Services: ⬩ ✗ ⊞ lau Off-site: ⬩ ⬩LPS

NORTH/CENTRAL

BACHTE-MARIA-LEERNE OOST-VLAANDEREN

Groeneveld Groenevelddreef, 9800
☎ 09 3801014 ▤ 09 3801760
e-mail: info@campinggroeneveld.be
Well equipped site beside a lake.
➲ Approach via E17 or E40.
Open: 24 Mar-12 Nov Site: 1.7HEC ▦ ⬩ ⬩ Facilities: ⬩
⬩ ⊙ ⬩ ⬩ ⬩ Services: ⬩ ✗ ⊞ Leisure: ⬩ L Off-site: ⬩R

BEAUVECHAIN BRABANT

Arpents Verts r Longue 115, 1320
☎ 010 866993 ▤ 010 867457
e-mail: lesarpentsverts@msm.com
website: users.belgacombusiness.net/arpents.verts
➲ Access via E411 exit 8 towards Louvain or E40 exit 23
towards Bevekom.
Open: May-Aug Site: 1HEC ▦ ⬩ ⬩ Prices: ♠3.32 ♣3.32
▲3.35 pitch 11.16-37.19 Facilities: ⬩ ⬩ ⊙ ⬩ ⬩ ⬩
Services: ⬩ ⊞ lau

BEGYNENDYK BRABANT

Roygaerden Betekomsesteenweg 75, 3130
☎ 016 531087 ▤ 016 531087
e-mail: immo.vdb@pi.be
Pitches are in wooded surroundings beside a lake.
Open: All year Site: 5HEC ▦ ⬩ ⬩ Prices: ♠3.75 ♣2.50
♣8.70 ▲2.50 Facilities: ⬩ ⊙ ⬩ ⬩ ⬩ ⬩ ⬩ Services: ⬩ ✗ ⊞
lau Off-site: ⬩ ⬩L

BEVERE OOST-VLAANDEREN

Kompas Camping Oudenaarde Kortrijkstr 342, 9700
☎ 055 315473 ▤ 055 300865
e-mail: oudenaarde@kompascamping.be
website: www.kompascamping.be
A family site with good recreational facilities.
➲ Signposted from N453.
Open: Apr-mid Nov Site: 24HEC ▦ ⬩ ⬩ ⬩
Prices: ♣14.75-19.80 pitch 14.75-19.80 (incl 6 persons)
Facilities: ⬩ ⬩ ⊙ ⬩ ⬩ ⬩ ⬩ Services: ✗ ⊞ lau Leisure: ⬩ LP

GENT (GAND) OOST-VLAANDEREN

Blaarmeersen Zuiderlaan 12, 9000
☎ 92668160 ▤ 92668166
e-mail: camping.blaarmeersen@gent.be
website: www.gent.be/blaarmeersen
In pleasant wooded surroundings SW of Gent towards the
railway station.
Open: 01 Mar-15 Oct Site: 6HEC ▦ ⬩ ⬩ Prices: ♠3.25-4
♣1.75-2.25 ♣3.25-4 ▲3.25-4 Facilities: ⬩ ⬩ ⊙ ⬩ ⬩ ⬩
Services: ⬩ ✗ ⊞ lau Leisure: ⬩ L

GRIMBERGEN BRABANT

Grimbergen Veldkanstr 64, 1850
☎ 0473 760378 ▤ 02 2701215
➲ Access via exit 7 on Bruxelles ringroad.
Open: Apr-Oct Site: 1.5HEC ▦ ⬩ Prices: ♠3 ♣1.50 ♣3
▲3 Facilities: ⬩ ⊙ ⬩ ⬩ Services: ⊞ lau Off-site: ⬩ ⬩ ✗ ⬩P

HEVERLEE BRABANT

Ter Munck Sint Jansbergsesteenweg 152, 3001
☎ 016 228515
➲ Access via E40 or E413.
Open: 18 Jun-9 Sep Site: 1.5HEC ▦ ⬩ Facilities: ⬩ ⊙ ⬩
⬩ Services: ⬩ ✗ ⊞ lau Off-site: ⬩ ✗ ⬩ ⬩ ⬩P

JABBEKE OOST-VLAANDEREN

Klein Strand Varsenareweg 29, 8490 ☎ 050 811440
e-mail: kleinstrand@online.be website: www.kleinstrand.be
A lakeside site with good modern facilities and offering a
wide variety of leisure activities.
➲ Off the main Oostende-Brugge road.
Open: All year Site: 4HEC ▦ ⬩ ⬩ ⬩ Facilities: ⬩ ⬩ ⊙ ⬩
⬩ ⬩ ⬩ Services: ⬩ ✗ ⊞ lau Leisure: ⬩ L

See advertisement on page 75

ONKERZELE OOST-VLAANDEREN

Gavers Onkerzelestr 280, 9500 ☎ 054 416324 ▤ 054 410388
e-mail: gavers@oost-vlaanderen.be
website: www.althea.be/akdinnen/clients/noo21401.htm
A quiet, well equipped site beside a lake between the Dendre
Valley and the foothills of the Ardennes. There are good
sporting and sanitary facilities.
➲ NE of town towards the river.
Open: All year Site: 15HEC ▦ ⬩ ⬩ Facilities: ⬩ ⬩ ⊙ ⬩
⬩ ⬩ Services: ⬩ ✗ ⊞ lau Leisure: ⬩ LPR

STEKENE OOST-VLAANDEREN

Eurocamping Baudeloo Heirweg 183, 9190
☎ 03 7890663 ▤ 03 7890663
Open: All year Site: 4.5HEC ▦ ⬩ Facilities: ⬩ ⊙ ⬩ ⬩
Services: ⬩ ✗ ⊞ lau Leisure: ⬩ P Off-site: ⬩ ✗ ⬩

Reinaert Lunterbergstr 4, 9190
☎ 03 7798525 ▤ 03 7798525
Open: Apr-Oct Site: 2HEC ▦ ⬩ Facilities: ⬩ ⊙ ⬩ ⬩ ⬩
Services: ⬩ ✗ ⊞ lau Off-site: ⬩

Site: 6HEC-Site size ▦-grass ⫶⫶⫶-sand ⬩-stone ⬩-little shade ⬩-partly shaded ⬩-mainly shaded
⬩-bungalows for hire ⬩-caravans for hire ▲-tents for hire ✗-no dogs Prices: ♠-adult per night ♣-car per night
pp-per person per night ♣-caravan per night ▲-tent per night

WACHTEBEKE OOST-VLAANDEREN

Puyenbroeck Puyenbrug 1A, 9185
☎ 09 3424231 ▤ 09 3424258 website: www.puyenbroeck.be
Open: Apr-Sep Site: 500HEC ▦ ⁂ ⚘ Prices: pitch 500
Facilities: ⋒ ⊙ ⚑ 🏛 Services: ⊞ lau Off-site: 🏪 ⚑ ✕ ⤳LP

NORTH EAST

BRECHT ANTWERPEN

Floreal Het Veen Eekhoornlaan 1, St-Job In't Goor, 2960
☎ 03 6361327
A comfortable site in a pleasant wooded setting with
residential and touring pitches.
➲ *Leave Autoroute E19 at exit St Job In't Goor.*
Open: Mar-Oct Site: 7.5HEC ▦ ⚘ 🏠 Prices: ⬥3.10 ⚘8
⚘4.80 Facilities: ⋒ 🏪 ⊙ ⚑ 🏛 Services: ⚑ ✕ ⊞ lau
Leisure: ⤳ R Off-site: ⚘ 🏛

EKSEL LIMBURG

Lage Kempen Kiefhoek str 19, B-3941
☎ 011 402243 ▤ 011 348812
e-mail: info@lagekempen.be website: www.lagekempen.be
Situated in the middle of a forest with a variety of
recreational facilities.
➲ *From route 67 from Hasselt follow signs 'Lage Kampen' to
the left.*
Open: Etr-2 Nov Site: 3.8HEC ▦ ⁂ 🏠 Prices: ⬥3.75
⚘2.25 ⚘3.25 ⚘3.25 Facilities: ⋒ 🏪 ⊙ ⚑ ⚘ 🏛 🏛
Services: ⚑ ✕ lau Leisure: ⤳ P

GIERLE ANTWERPEN

Lilse Bergen Strandweg 6, 2275
☎ 014 557901 ▤ 014 554454
e-mail: info@lilsebergen.be website: www.lilsebergen.be
A very well equipped family site surrounding a private lake.
➲ *E39 exit 22.*
Open: All year Site: 60HEC ⁑ ⚘ 🏠 ⚘ Prices: pitch 16.50-
21 Facilities: ⋒ 🏪 ⊙ ⚑ ⚘ 🏛 🏛 🏛 Services: ⚑ ✕ ⊞ lau
Leisure: ⤳ L

HOUTHALEN LIMBURG

Hengelhoef Hengelhoefdreef 1, 3530
☎ 089 844583 ▤ 089 386940
e-mail: camp.hengelhoef@belgacom.net
A family site in pleasant wooded surroundings with good,
modern facilities.
➲ *Access via E314 exit 30.*
Open: All year Site: 15HEC ▦ ⚘ ⚘ Facilities: ⋒ ⊙ ⚑ 🏛
Services: ✕ ⊞ lau Off-site: 🏪 ✕

MOL ANTWERPEN

Zilvermeer Zilvermeerlaan 2, 2400
☎ 014 829500 ▤ 014 829501
e-mail: info@zilvermeer.provant.be
A pleasant lakeside site with good recreational facilities.
Site: 45HEC ▦ ⁘⁘⁘ ⚘ 🏠 Facilities: ⋒ 🏪 ⊙ ⚑ ⚘ 🏛 🏛 🏛
Services: ⚑ ✕ ⊞ lau Leisure: ⤳ L

OPGLABBEEK LIMBURG

Boseind Speeltuinstr 8, 3660 ☎ 089 854347 ▤ 089 854319
e-mail: info@hetlaer.be website: www.hetlaer.be
A family site adjoining a wood. A wide variety of recreational
facilities are available.
➲ *From town centre take N730 towards Bree and follow signs.*
Open: Apr-Sep Site: 8HEC ▦ ⚘ Facilities: ⋒ 🏪 ⊙ ⚑ 🏛
Services: ⚑ ✕ ⊞ Leisure: ⤳ P Off-site: ⚘

Wilhelm Tell Hoeverweg 87, 3660 ☎ 089 854444 ▤ 810010
e-mail: receptie@wilhelmtell.com
website: www.wilhelmtell.com
A family campsite situated in a vast nature reserve and
offering opportunities for walks in a varied area of
heathland, woodland and marshlands. A large variety of
water attractions on site including a water chute and a
swimming pool with a wave machine. Also an indoor family
pool and bubble bath.
➲ *E313 exit 32 in direction of Opglabbeek*
Open: All year Site: 4HEC ▦ ⚘ 🏠 ⚘ Prices: ⬥4.20-6
pitch 8.40-12 (incl 2 persons) Facilities: ⋒ ⊙ ⚑ ⚘ 🏛
Services: ⚑ ✕ ⊞ lau Leisure: ⤳ P

RETIE ANTWERPEN

Berkenstrand Brand 78, 2470 ☎ 014 377590 ▤ 014 375139
e-mail: info@berkenstrand.be
website: www.berkenstrand.be
In wooded surroundings beside a lake.
➲ *3km NE on road to Postel.*
Open: All year Site: 10HEC ▦ ⚘ 🏠 ⚘ Prices: ⬥3 ⚘2.50
⚘2.50 ⚘2.50 Facilities: ⋒ 🏪 ⊙ ⚑ ⚘ 🏛 🏛 Services: ⚑ ✕ ⊞
lau Leisure: ⤳ L

TURNHOUT ANTWERPEN

Baalse Hei Roodhuisstr 10, B-2300
☎ 014 421931 ▤ 014 420853
e-mail: info@baalsehei.be website: www.baalsehei.be
A family site in pleasant wooded surroundings with plenty of
recreational facilities.
Open: All year Site: 30HEC ▦ ⚘ ⚘ Prices: pitch 15-19
Facilities: ⋒ 🏪 ⊙ ⚑ 🏛 🏛 Services: ⚑ ✕ ⊞ lau Leisure: ⤳ L

Facilities: 🏪-shop **⋒**-shower **⊙**-electric points for razors **⚑**-electric points for caravans **🏛**-parking by tents permitted
🏛-compulsory separate car park **Services: ✕**-café/restaurant **⚑**-bar **⚘**-Camping Gaz International **🏛**-gas other than Camping
Gaz **⊞**-first aid facilities lau-laundry **Leisure: ⤳**-swimming L-Lake P-Pool R-River S-Sea **Off-site:** All facilities within 2km

VORST-LAAKDAL ANTWERPEN

Kasteel Meerlaer Verboekt 115, 2430
☎ 0475 808997 📠 013 667512
e-mail: camp.meerlaer@online.be website: www.camping.be
⮕ E313 exit 24 towards Hosselt or exit 24 towards Antwerp.
Open: All year Site: 6HEC 🛏 ♣ Prices: ♦2.50 ♠2.50
♠2.50 ▲2.50 Facilities: ⋔ ⊙ ♀ ∅ ♨ ☎ Services: ⬛ ✕ ⊞ lau
Off-site: ⬛ ✕

ZONHOVEN LIMBURG

Berkenhof Teutseweg 33, 3520 ☎ 011 814439 📠 011 812736
Open: Apr-Oct Site: 3.5HEC 🛏 ♣ � ♠ Facilities: ⋔ ⊙ ♀
∅ ♨ ☎ Services: ⬛ ✕ ⊞ Off-site: ⬛

Holsteenbron Hengelhoelseweg 9, 3520
☎ 011 817140 📠 011 817140
e-mail: camping.holsteenbron@skynet.be
website: www.holsteenbron.be
A rural family site in a wooded location.
⮕ Access via E314 exit 29 towards Zondhoven.
Open: Apr-11Nov Site: 4HEC 🛏 ♀ ♣ ♠ Prices: ♠14-17
pitch 14-17 Facilities: ⋔ ⊙ ♀ ☎ Services: ⬛ ✕ ⊞ lau

SOUTH EAST

AISCHE-EN-REFAIL NAMUR

Manoir de lá Bas rte de Gembloux 180, B-5310
☎ 081 655353
e-mail: europa-camping.sa@skynet.be
website: www.camping-manoirdelabas.be
In a beautiful situation within the wooded grounds of a
former manor house.
⮕ 5km W of Eghezée.
Open: Apr-Oct Site: 21HEC 🛏 ♀ Prices: ♦2.50 ♠3.75
▲3.75 pitch 3.75 Facilities: ⋔ ⊙ ♀ ∅ ♨ ☎ Services: ⬛ ✕ ⊞
lau Leisure: ⬥ P Off-site: ⬛

AMBERLOUP LUXEMBOURG

Tonny r Tonny 35-36, 6680 ☎ 061 688285 📠 061 688285
In a pleasant valley beside the River Ourthe with fine
sporting facilities.
⮕ Access via E25 or A4 to Bastogne, then N826.
Open: 15 Feb-15 Nov Site: 3HEC 🛏 ♀ 🚐 ♠ Facilities: ⋔
⬛ ⊙ ♀ ∅ ♨ 🅿 Services: ⬛ ✕ ⊞ lau Leisure: ⬥ R

AMONINES LUXEMBOURG

Val de l'Aisne Rue de TTA, 6997
☎ 086 470067 📠 086 470043
e-mail: info@levaldelaisne.be website: www.levaldelaisne.be
Open: All year Site: 25HEC 🛏 ♀ 🚐 ♠ ▲ Facilities: ⋔ ⬛
⊙ ♀ ∅ ♨ ☎ Services: ⬛ ✕ ⊞ lau Leisure: ⬥ LR

BARVAUX-SUR-OURTHE LUXEMBOURG

Hazalles Chainrue 77a, 6940 ☎ 086 211642 📠 086 211642
Situated in an orchard, this site is 600mtrs from the village
and sits beside a stream. Well maintained facilities.
Open: Apr-Sep Site: 0.4HEC 🛏 ♀ Facilities: ⋔ ⊙ ♀ ☎
Services: ⊞ lau Off-site: ⬛ ⬛ ✕ ∅ ♨ ⬥PR

Rives de l'Ourthe r Inzespres 70, 6940 ☎ 086 211730
A large site with plenty of touring pitches beside the River
Ourthe.
⮕ 200mtrs from the village towards the river.
Open: Apr-Sep Site: 2HEC 🛏 ♀ Facilities: ⋔ ⊙ ♀ ☎
Services: ⬛ ✕ ⊞ Leisure: ⬥ R Off-site: ⬛ ✕ ∅ ♨ ⬥LP

BERTRIX LUXEMBOURG

Kompas rte de Mortehan, 6880
☎ 061 412281 📠 061 412588
e-mail: bertrix@kompascamping.be
website: www.kompascamping.be
Well equipped family site in a pleasant wooded setting.
⮕ S of town beyond the church. Signposted from N884.
Open: 30 Mar-11 Nov Site: 14HEC 🛏 ♀ ♠ Prices: pitch
17.50-26.75 Facilities: ⋔ ⬛ ⊙ ♀ ♨ ☎ Services: ⬛ ✕ ⊞ lau
Leisure: ⬥ P

BÜLLINGEN (BULLANGE) LIÈGE

Hêtraie Rotheck 14, 4760 ☎ 080 642413 📠 080 642413
This site is situated on a sloping meadow near a fish pond
and is surrounded by groups of beautiful beech trees and
conifers.
⮕ Leave village in direction of Amel then left and continue for
2km. Signposted.
Open: Apr-15 Nov Site: 3HEC 🛏 ♀ 🚐 Facilities: ⋔ ⊙ ♀
☎ Services: ⊞ lau Leisure: ⬥ P Off-site: ⬥R

BURE LUXEMBOURG

Parc la Clusure 30 chemin de la Clusure, 6927
☎ 084 360050 📠 084 366777
e-mail: info@parclaclusure.be website: www.parclaclusure.be
Pleasant site with good facilities in the centre of the
Ardennes.
⮕ Access from E411 and N846 via Tellin.
Open: All year Site: 13HEC 🛏 ♀ 🚐 ♠ ▲ Prices: ♦3.15-
4.50 ▲3 pitch 15.40-22 (incl 2 persons) Facilities: ⋔ ⬛ ⊙ ♀
♨ ☎ Services: ⬛ ✕ ⊞ lau Leisure: ⬥ PR

BÜTGENBACH LIÈGE

Worriken Worriken Center 1, 4750
☎ 080 446358 📠 080 447089
e-mail: camping.worriken@swimp.be
website: www.tourist-info-butgenbach.be
Situated on the shores of a lake.
Site: 8HEC 🛏 ♀ Prices: ♠15.49 ▲9.30 pitch 15.49 (incl 4
persons) Facilities: ⋔ ⊙ ♀ ☎ Services: ⬛ ✕ ⊞ lau
Leisure: ⬥ L Off-site: ⬥ ∅ ♨ ⬥PR

CHEVETOGNE NAMUR

Domaine Provincial 5590 ☎ 083 687211
Located in the grounds of a castle and surrounded by fine
ornamental gardens. There is a wide variety of leisure
activities.
Open: All year Site: 0.5HEC 🛏 ♀ ♠ Facilities: ⋔ ⊙ ♀ ☎
🅿 Services: ⬛ ✕ ⊞ lau Leisure: ⬥ L Off-site: ⬥P

COO-STAVELOT LIÈGE

Cascade Chemin des Faravennes 5, 4970 ☎ 080 684312
A small touring and holiday site beside the River Amblève.
⮕ 3km from Trois-Ponts via motorway exit 10 or 11.
Open: Mar-Sep Site: 0.8HEC 🛏 ♀ Facilities: ⋔ ⊙ ♀ ☎
Services: ⬛ ✕ ⊞ lau Leisure: ⬥ R Off-site: ✕ ∅

EUPEN LIÈGE

`An der Hill' Hutte 46, 4700 ☎ 087 744617 📠 087 557232
In wooded surroundings with well defined pitches.
⮕ SW of town via N67 towards Monschau.
Open: All year Site: 0.6HEC 🛏 ♀ Facilities: ⋔ ⊙ ♀ ∅ ♨
☎ Services: ⬛ ✕ ⊞ lau Off-site: ⬛ ⬥P

Site: 6HEC-Site size 🛏-grass ⋮⋮⋮-sand ♦-stone ♨-little shade ♀-partly shaded ♣-mainly shaded
🚐-bungalows for hire ♠-caravans for hire ▲-tents for hire ✗-no dogs Prices: ♦-adult per night ♠-car per night
pp-per person per night ♠-caravan per night ▲-tent per night

FLORENVILLE LUXEMBOURG

Rosière Rive Gauche de la Semois, 6820
☎ 061 311937 ▤ 061 314873
e-mail: larosiere@pi.be website: www.larosiere.be
In wooded surroundings close to the town centre.
➲ *Access via E411 exit 26 for Verlaine/Nuefchâteau.*
Open: Apr-10 Nov Site: 10HEC ⊞ 🔾 Facilities: 🏠 🕿 ⊙ 🛱
🖉 �175 🕿 Services: 🍷 ✕ 🖪 lau Leisure: ⸄ PR

FORRIÈRES LUXEMBOURG

Pré du Blason r de la Ramée 30, 6953
☎ 084 212867 ▤ 084 223650
e-mail: predublason@freegates.be
website: www.camping-predublason.be
This well-kept site lies on a meadow surrounded by wooded
hills and is completely divided into pitches and crossed by
rough gravel drives.
➲ *Off N49 Masbourg road.*
Open: Apr-Oct Site: 3HEC ⊞ 🔾 🛱 Facilities: 🏠 🕿 ⊙ 🛱 🖉
🚍 🕿 Services: 🍷 ✕ 🖪 lau Leisure: ⸄ R

GEMMENICH LIÈGE

Kon Tiki Terstraeten 141, 4851 ☎ 087 785973
Open: All year Site: 12HEC ⊞ 🔾 Facilities: 🏠 🕿 ⊙ 🛱 🖉 🚍
🕿 Services: 🍷 ✕ 🖪 lau Leisure: ⸄ PR

GOUVY LUXEMBOURG

Lac de Cherapont Cherapont 2, 6670
☎ 080 517082 ▤ 080 517093
On an extensive lakeside tourist complex with a wide variety
of recreational facilities.
➲ *Access via E25 exit 51 or E42 exit 15.*
Open: Apr-Oct Site: 10HEC ⊞ 🔾 🛋 🛱 ⊙
🛱 🚍 🕿 Services: 🍷 ✕ 🖪 lau Leisure: ⸄ LR Off-site: 🖉

GRAND-HALLEUX LUXEMBOURG

Neuf Prés av de la Résistance, 6698 ☎ 080 216882
A family site in pleasant wooded surroundings beside a river.
➲ *Access via E42.*
Open: Apr-Sep Site: 4HEC ⊞ 🔾 Prices: 🅰2 🛱1.20 🛱3
🛖2.30 Facilities: 🏠 ⊙ 🛱 🕿 Services: 🍷 ✕ lau Leisure: ⸄ PR
Off-site: 🛒 ✕ 🖉 🚍 🖪

HABAY-LA-NEUVE LUXEMBOURG

Portail de la Forêt r du Bon-Bois 3, 6720
☎ 0497 907027 ▤ 063 423410
e-mail: athiry@belgacom.net
Parklike, terraced site on a hill surrounded by woodland.
➲ *Access via E25/E411 exit 29.*
Open: 15 Mar-15 Oct Site: 2.5HEC ⊞ 🔾 Prices: 🅰2.25
🛱2.25 🛖9 pitch 15 Facilities: 🏠 ⊙ 🛱 🕿 Off-site: 🛒 🍷 ✕ 🖉
🚍 ⸄PR 🖪

HAMOIR-SUR-OURTHE LIÈGE

CM Dessous Hamoir r du Moulin, 4180 ☎ 086 388925
A municipal site with well equipped pitches and good
facilities for children beside the River Ourthe.
➲ *From the Liège-Luxembourg motorway take exit
Werbomont and continue for 15km.*
Open: 15 Mar-15 Nov Site: 3.5HEC ⊞ 🔾 Facilities: 🏠 ⊙
🛱 🕿 Services: 🖪 lau Leisure: ⸄ R Off-site: 🛒 🍷 ✕ 🖉 🚍

HOGNE NAMUR

Relais 16 r de Serinchamps, 5377
☎ 084 311580 ▤ 084 312400
e-mail: bs825815@skynet.be
A pleasant site in a wooded park beside a lake.

➲ *Take N4 from Courrière to Hogne via Marche.*
Open: Mar-4 Jan Site: 12HEC ⊞ 🔾 🛱 🛱 Prices: 🅰3 🛖4
pitch 8 Facilities: 🏠 🕿 ⊙ 🛱 🖉 🚍 🕿 Services: 🍷 ✕ 🖪 lau
Leisure: ⸄ L

HOUFFALIZE LUXEMBOURG

Chasse et Pêche r de la Roche 63, 6660
☎ 061 288314 ▤ 061 289660
e-mail: info@cpbuitensport.com
website: www.cpbuitensport.com
A pleasant site attached to a café-restaurant with good
recreational facilities.
➲ *3km NW off E25.*
Open: All year Site: 2HEC ⊞ 🛋 🛱 Prices: 🅰4.50-4.50
🛱3.50-3.50 🛱4-40 🛖3.50-3.50 Facilities: 🏠 ⊙ 🛱 🖉 🕿 🖪
Services: 🍷 ✕ 🖪 lau Leisure: ⸄ R

Moulin de Rensiwez Moulin de Rensiwez 1, 6663
☎ 061 289027 ▤ 061 289027
A good transit site on a series of terraces beside the River
Ourthe close to an old water-mill.
Open: All year Site: 5HEC ⊞ 🔾 🛱 ⋫ Facilities: 🏠 🕿 ⊙
🛱 🖉 🕿 🖪 Services: 🍷 ✕ 🖪 lau Leisure: ⸄ R

LOUVEIGNÉ LIÈGE

Moulin du Rouge-Thier Rouge-Thier 8, 4141
☎ 04 3608341 ▤ 04 3608341
A well equipped site in a pleasant wooded location.
➲ *S of town towards Deigné.*
Open: Apr-30 Oct Site: 8HEC ⊞ 🔾 🛱 Prices: pitch 11.50
(incl 4 persons) Facilities: 🏠 ⊙ 🛱 🖉 🚍 🕿 Services: 🍷 ✕ 🖪
lau Leisure: ⸄ P

MALONNE NAMUR

Trieux r des Tris 99, 5020 ☎ 081 445583 ▤ 081 44 5583
e-mail: camping.les.trieux@skynet.be
website: www.campinglestrieux.be
Open: Apr-30 Oct Site: 2.2HEC ⊞ 🔾 🛱 Prices: 🅰2.50
🛱2.50 🛱8 🛖3.75-4.50 pitch 3.75 Facilities: 🏠 🕿 ⊙ 🛱 🚍
🕿 Services: 🖪 lau Off-site: 🍷 ✕ ⸄R

MARCHE-EN-FAMENNE LUXEMBOURG

Euro Camping Paola r du Panorama 10, 6900
☎ 084 311704 ▤ 084 314722
A long site on a hill with a beautiful view. The only noise
comes from a railway line, which passes right by the site.
➲ *Take road towards Hotton, turn right after cemetery and
continue 1km.*
Open: All year Site: 13HEC ⊞ 🖈 🛋 🛱 Prices: 🅰2.20
🛱2.50 🛱5 🛖3.70-5 Facilities: 🏠 ⊙ 🛱 🖉 🚍 🕿 Services: ✕ 🖪
Off-site: 🛒 🍷 ✕ ⸄P

NEUFCHÂTEAU LUXEMBOURG

International Spineuse r de Malome 7, rte de Florenville,
6840 ☎ 061 277320 ▤ 061 277104
e-mail: info@camping-spineuse.be
website: www.camping-spineuse.be
Camp shop operates July-Aug only.
➲ *Situated 2km from Florenville in the direction of
Neufchâteau.*
Open: All year Site: 2.5HEC ⊞ 🔾 🛱 Prices: 🅰3.75 pitch 9-
11.25 Facilities: 🏠 🕿 ⊙ 🛱 🖉 🚍 🕿 Services: 🍷 ✕ 🖪 lau
Leisure: ⸄ LPR

> A full guide to the Symbols &
> Abbreviations used in this book
> can be found on page 6

Facilities: 🛒-shop 🏠-shower ⊙-electric points for razors 🛱-electric points for caravans 🕿-parking by tents permitted
🖪-compulsory separate car park **Services:** ✕-café/restaurant 🍷-bar 🖉-Camping Gaz International 🚍-gas other than Camping
Gaz 🖪-first aid facilities lau-laundry **Leisure:** ⸄-swimming L-Lake P-Pool R-River S-Sea **Off-site:** All facilities within 2km

OLLOY-SUR-VIROIN NAMUR

Try des Baudets r de la Champagne, 5670
☎ 060 390108 ▤ 060 390108
e-mail: masson_p@yahoo.fr
website: http://home.freegates.be/campingtrydesbaudets
In a peaceful situation on the edge of a forest.
Open: All year Site: 11HEC ⟞⟞⟞⟞ ⌖ 🛏 Prices: ⋔0.50 ⛺12 ⛺7
Facilities: 🏠 ⊙ 🏪 🚿 🏧 Services: 🍴 ✕ ⊞ lau Off-site: 🏪 ✕

OTEPPE LIÈGE

Hirondelle r du Château 1, 4210
☎ 085 711131 ▤ 085 711021
e-mail: hirondelle@skynet.be
Ideal family site with modern facilities in the picturesque
Burdinale Valley.
➩ *N of town between E40 and E42. Signposted.*
Open: Etr-Sep Site: 65HEC ⟞⟞⟞⟞ ⌖ 🛏 Facilities: 🏠 🏪 ⊙ 🏪
🚿 🏧 Services: 🍴 ✕ ⊞ lau Leisure: ⭢ P

POLLEUR LIÈGE

Polleur r de Congrès 90, 4910 ☎ 087 541033 ▤ 087 542530
e-mail: info@campingpolleur.be
website: www.campingpolleur.be
A family site in a pleasant wooded location.
➩ *Signposted from A27/E42.*
Open: Apr-Oct Site: 3.7HEC ⟞⟞⟞⟞ 〰 🛏 Facilities: 🏠 🏪 ⊙
🏪 🚿 🏧 Services: 🍴 ✕ ⊞ lau Leisure: ⭢ PR

PURNODE NAMUR

Camping du Bocq av de la Vallée, 5530
☎ 082 612269 ▤ 082 646814
e-mail: campingdubocq@pi.be
website: www.camping-dubocq.be
In a beautiful wooded location beside the river.
➩ *Leave E411 at exit 19 (Spontin) towards Yvoir, exit
Purnode.*
Open: Apr-Oct Site: 3HEC ⟞⟞⟞⟞ ⌖ 🛏 Prices: ⋔3.25 ⛺2.50
⛺2.50 ⛺2.75 pitch 2.75 Facilities: 🏠 ⊙ 🏪 🚿 🏧 Services: 🍴
✕ ⊞ lau Leisure: ⭢ R Off-site: 🏪

REMOUCHAMPS LIÈGE

Eden r de Trois Ponts 92, 4920 ☎ 04 3844165 ▤ 3840055
e-mail: edencamping@swing.be
website: www.edencamping.be.tf
Open: Apr-Oct Site: 3.2HEC ⟞⟞⟞⟞ ⌖ ♣ 🛏 Facilities: 🏠 🏪 ⊙
🏪 🚿 🏧 Services: 🍴 ✕ ⊞ Leisure: ⭢ R Off-site: ✕

RENDEUX LUXEMBOURG

Festival rte de la Roche 89, 6987
☎ 084 477371 ▤ 084 477594
website: www.lefestival.be
In unspoiled surroundings beside the River Ourthe.
Open: Etr-Sep Site: 12HEC ⟞⟞⟞⟞ ⌖ 🛏 Prices: ⋔10-15 pitch
17-19 Facilities: 🏠 🏪 ⊙ 🏪 🚿 🏧 ⊞ Services: 🍴 ✕ ⊞ lau
Leisure: ⭢ R

ROBERTVILLE LIÈGE

Plage 33 rte des Bains, B-4950 ☎ 080 446658 ▤ 080 446178
Open: All year Site: 1.8HEC ⟞⟞⟞⟞ ⌖ 🛏 Facilities: 🏠 🏪 ⊙ 🏪
🚿 🏧 Services: 🍴 ✕ ⊞ lau Leisure: ⭢ LPR

ROCHE-EN-ARDENNE, LA LUXEMBOURG

Grillon r des Echarées, 6980 ☎ 084 412062 ▤ 084 412128
Well equipped family site in a pleasant wooded setting.
Open: Etr-Oct Site: 3.5HEC ⟞⟞⟞⟞ ⌖ Facilities: 🏠 🏪 ⊙ 🏪 🚿
🚿 🏧 Services: 🍴 ⊞ lau Leisure: ⭢ R Off-site: ✕ ⭢P

Lohan 20a rte de Houffalize, 6980 ☎ 084 411545
In a park surrounded by woodland, on N bank of the River
Ourthe.
➩ *3km E of La Roche towards Maboge and Houffalize.*
Open: Apr-1 Nov Site: 4HEC ⟞⟞⟞⟞ ⌖ 🛏 Facilities: 🏠 🏪 ⊙
🏪 🚿 🏧 Services: 🍴 ✕ ⊞ lau Leisure: ⭢ R

Ourthe 6980 ☎ 084 411459 ▤ 056 400050
e-mail: samatex@unicall.be
Well kept site, beside the River Ourthe.
➩ *On SW bank of the Ourthe below the N34.*
Open: 15 Mar-15 Oct Site: 2HEC ⟞⟞⟞⟞ ♣ 🛏 🛏 Facilities: 🏠
🏪 ⊙ 🏪 🚿 🏧 ⊞ Services: ⊞ lau Leisure: ⭢ R Off-site: 🍴 ✕ ⊞

SART-LEZ-SPA LIÈGE

Touring Club Stockay 17, 4845 ☎ 087 474400 ▤ 087 475277
e-mail: spador@pophost.elinet.be
website: www.campingspador.be
➩ *Signposted. The site lies to the E of Spa.*
Open: All year Site: 6HEC ⟞⟞⟞⟞ ⌖ 🛏 🛏 ⛺ Prices: pitch
17.50 (incl 2 persons) pp3.75 Facilities: 🏠 🏪 ⊙ 🏪 🚿 🏧 🏧
Services: 🍴 ✕ ⊞ lau Leisure: ⭢ R Off-site: ⭢L

SIPPENAEKEN LIÈGE

Vieux Moulin 114 Tebruggen, 4851 ☎ 087 784255
A family site with good recreational facilities, set in a pleasant
wooded location close to a nature reserve.
➩ *Access via E40 exit Battile towards Aubel-Hombourg-
Sippenaeken.*
Open: Apr-Sep Site: 6HEC ⟞⟞⟞⟞ ⌖ 🛏 Prices: ⋔3 pitch 3.50
Facilities: 🏠 🏪 ⊙ 🏪 🚿 Services: 🍴 ✕ ⊞ lau Leisure: ⭢ PR

Site: 6HEC-Site size ⟞⟞⟞⟞-grass ∵∴-sand ◔-stone 〰-little shade ⌖-partly shaded ♣-mainly shaded
🛏-bungalows for hire 🛏-caravans for hire ⛺-tents for hire ⊗-no dogs Prices: ⋔-adult per night ⛺-car per night
pp-per person per night ⛺-caravan per night ⛺-tent per night

SPA LIÈGE

Parc des Sources r de la Sauvenière 141, 4900
☎ 087 772311 📠 087 475965
e-mail: info@campingparc.be website: www.campingparc.be
On the outskirts of the town close to the forest.
⮕ *S of town centre on N32 towards Malmédy.*
Open: Apr-Nov Site: 2.5HEC 🎦 🔾 Prices: ⋔4.15 ⮔2
⮔4.40 ▲4.40 Facilities: 🅝 🝱 ⊙ 🝰 🝱 🏛 Services: ⬛ ✕ lau
Leisure: ⭐ P Off-site: ⬛ ✕ 🝱 ⊞

SPRIMONT LIÈGE

Tultay r de Tultay 22, 4140 ☎ 04 3821162 📠 04 3676397
e-mail: sprimont.r3cb@pi.be
website: www.ping.be/sprimont-r3cb
A pleasant site in wooded surroundings on the edge of a nature reserve.
⮕ *NE of Sprimont. Access via E9.*
Open: All year Site: 1.5HEC 🎦 🔾 Prices: ⋔3 pitch 5
Facilities: 🅝 ⊙ 🝰 🏛 Services: ⬛ ✕ ⊞ lau Off-site: 🝱 ✕ 🏛

STAVELOT LIÈGE

Domaine de l'Eau Rouge Cheneux 25, 4970
☎ 080 863075 📠 080 863075
website: www.campingleaurouge.be
A pleasant riverside site with good sporting facilities.
⮕ *Access via E42 to Francorchamps or Malmédy.*
Open: All year Site: 4HEC 🎦 🔾 🝰 Facilities: 🅝 ⊙ 🝰 🏛 🏛
🅟 Services: ⬛ ✕ ⊞ lau Leisure: ⭐ R Off-site: ⭐P

TENNEVILLE LUXEMBOURG

Pont de Berguème r Berguème 9, 6970
☎ 084 455443 📠 084 456231
e-mail: info@pontbergueme.be
website: www.pontbergueme.be
In a peaceful, wooded setting in the beautiful Ardennes area with good, modern facilities.

⮕ *Turn off E40/N4 towards Berguème then turn right.*
Open: All year Site: 3HEC 🎦 🔾 🝰 Prices: ⋔3 pitch 5
Facilities: 🅝 🝱 ⊙ 🝰 🝱 🏛 🅟 Services: ⬛ ✕ ⊞ lau
Leisure: ⭐ R

THOMMEN-REULAND LIÈGE

Hohenbusch Grüfflingen 44, 4791 ☎ 080 227523
website: users.swing.be/hohenbusch
A well appointed family site on a wooded meadow with plenty of recreational facilities.
⮕ *Off N26 SW of St-Vith.*
Open: Apr-Oct Site: 5HEC 🎦 🔾 🝰 Facilities: 🅝 🝱 ⊙ 🝰 🝰
🏛 Services: ✕ lau Leisure: ⭐ P

VIELSALM LUXEMBOURG

Salm chemin de la Vallée, B-6690 ☎ 080 216241
Open: All year Site: 2.5HEC 🎦 ♣ 🝰 Facilities: 🅝 ⊙ 🝰 🝰
🏛 Services: ⬛ ✕ ⊞ lau Leisure: ⭐ R Off-site: 🝱 ✕ 🝱 ⭐LP

VIRTON LUXEMBOURG

Vallée de Rabais r du Bonlieu, 6760
☎ 063 570144 📠 583342
e-mail: info@campingvalleederabais.be
website: www.campingvalleederabais.be
A secluded family site in the heart of the Gaume region close to a lake with good recreational facilities.
⮕ *NE of Virton between N87 and N82.*
Open: All year Site: 8HEC 🎦 🔾 🝰 🝰 ▲ Facilities: 🅝 🝱 ⊙
🝰 🝱 🏛 🅟 Services: ⬛ ✕ ⊞ lau Leisure: ⭐ P Off-site: ⭐L

WAIMES LIÈGE

Anderegg Bruyères 4, 4950
☎ 080 679393 📠 080 679396
e-mail: campinganderegg@skynet.be
website: www.campinganderegg.be
In a peaceful situation beside the Lac de Robertville.
Open: All year Site: 1.5HEC 🎦 🔾 Prices: ⋔3.50 ⮔5.50
▲5.50 Facilities: 🅝 🝱 ⊙ 🝰 🝱 🏛 Services: ⬛ ✕ ⊞ lau

The striking coastline of Flanders

Facilities: 🝱-shop 🅝-shower ⊙-electric points for razors 🝰-electric points for caravans 🏛-parking by tents permitted
🅟-compulsory separate car park **Services:** ✕-café/restaurant ⬛-bar 🝰-Camping Gaz International 🏛-gas other than Camping Gaz ⊞-first aid facilities lau-laundry **Leisure:** ⭐-swimming L-Lake P-Pool R-River S-Sea **Off-site:** All facilities within 2km

FRANCE

France, rich in history and natural beauty, is Europe's most popular camping destination. Its broad range of scenery offers something for everyone.

FACTS AND FIGURES
Area: 543,965 sq km (210,025 sq miles)
Population: 60,700,000 (1998)
Capital: Paris
Language: French
IDD code: 33.
To call the UK dial 00 44
Currency: Euro
Local time: GMT + 1 (summer GMT + 2)
Emergency Services:
Police 17; Fire 18;
Ambulance 15.
Alternatively, dial the

European emergency call number 112, and request the service you require.
Business hours-
Banks: 10.00-13.00 & 15.00-17.00 Mon-Fri (Paris area) and Tue-Sat elsewhere.
Shops: Mon-Sat 09.00-18.00 (times may vary for food shops)
Average daily temperature: Paris

Jan 3°C	Jul 18°C
Mar 6°C	Sep15°C
May 13°C	Nov 6°C

Tourist Information:
UK French Government Tourist Office
178 Piccadilly
London W1J 9AL
Tel 09068 244123 (Premium rate information line 0900-1700 Mon-Fri)
Monaco Government Tourist and Convention Office
The Chambers,
Chelsea Harbour
London SW10 0XF
Tel Freephone 0500 006 114 (Mon-Fri 9.30-17.30)

USA French Government Tourist Office
16th Floor,
444 Madison Ave
New York, NY 10022
Tel (212) 838 7800
Tourist info website:
www.franceguide.com

The country offers a great variety of scenery from the mountain ranges of the Alps and the Pyrénées to the attractive river valleys of the Loire, Rhône and Dordogne. And with some 1,800 miles of coastline, which includes the golden sands of the Côte-d'Azur, there is a landscape appealing to everyone's taste.

The climate of France is temperate but varies considerably. The Mediterranean coast enjoys a sub-tropical climate with hot summers, while along the coast of Brittany the climate is very similar to that of Devon and Cornwall. The language is, of course, French and this is spoken throughout the country, although there are many local dialects and variations, some of which may be impenetrable even to seasoned French speakers.

France has an enormous number of campsites, over 10,000 of them, under the auspices of the *French Federation of Camping and Caravanning*. During July and August, however, thery are heavily booked, especially on the Mediterranean coast and other popular holiday destinations.

There are *castels et camping* caravanning sites in the grounds of châteaux (castles) and many are included in this guide. On sites in state forests, *forêts domaniales,* it is necessary to apply to the *garde forestier* for permission to camp and evidence of insurance must be produced (such as the

camping card). Opening periods vary widely and some sites are open all year. Local information offices (see *Tourist information* above) can supply detailed information about sites in their locality.

All graded sites must display their official classification, site regulations, capacity and current charges at the site entrance. Some sites have inclusive charges per pitch, others show basic prices per person, vehicle and space, with extra facilities like showers, swimming pools and ironing incurring additional charges. In practice, most campsites charge from midday to midday, with each part day being counted as a full day. Reductions for children are usually allowed up to 7 years of age; there is generally no charge for children under 3.

Off-site camping in the South of France is restricted because of the danger of fire; in other parts, camping is possible, provided that permission has been obtained, although camping is seldom allowed near the water's edge, or at a large seaside resort. Casual camping is prohibited in state forests, national parks in the Landes and Gironde *départements* and in the Camargue. Camping in an unauthorised place renders offenders liable to prosecution or confiscation of equipment, or both, especially in the South. However, an overnight stop on parking areas of some motorways is tolerated, but make sure you do not contravene local regulations; overnight stops in a lay-by are not permitted. Camping is not permitted in *Monaco*. Caravans in transit are allowed but it is forbidden to park them.

HOW TO GET THERE

Apart from the direct crossing by Eurotunnel (Folkestone-Calais, 35 mins platform to platform), the following services are available:

Short ferry crossings

From **Dover** to **Calais** takes 60 mins (Seacat) or 75-90 mins (ferry).

From **Dover** to **Boulogne** takes 50 mins (Catamaran)

Longer ferry crossings

From **Dover** to **Dunkerque** takes 2hrs by ferry

From **Newhaven** to **Dieppe** takes 4hrs by ferry and 2hrs by Superseacat.

From **Portsmouth** to **Le Havre** takes 5hrs 30mins (day) - 7hrs 30mins (night): to **Caen** (**Ouistreham**) takes 6hrs; to **Cherbourg** takes 5hrs (day) – 7 hrs (night) or 2hrs 45mins (fast ferry); to **St Malo** takes 8hrs 45mins (day) – 10hrs 30 mins (night). From **Poole** to **Cherbourg** takes 4hrs 15mins (day) – 5hrs 45mins (night) or 2 hrs 15 mins (fast ferry - summer only). From **Plymouth** to **Roscoff** takes 6 hrs; to **St Malo** (winter only) takes 8hrs.

CAR SLEEPER TRAINS

Summer services are available from **Calais** to Avignon, Biarritz, Bordeaux, Brive, Narbonne, Nice and Toulouse.

MOTORING & GENERAL

The information given here is specific to France. It **must** be read in conjunction with the Essential Motoring Information at the front of the book, which covers those regulations which are common to many countries.

BRITISH EMBASSY/CONSULATES*

The British Embassy is located at 75383 Paris Cedex 08, 35 rue du Faubourg St-Honoré ☎ 0144513100; consular section 18 bis rue d'Anjou; phone as for Embassy. There are British Consulates in Bordeaux, Lille, Lyon and Marseille.

There are British Consulates with Honorary Consuls in Amiens, Biarritz, Boulogne-sur-Mer, Calais, Cherbourg, Clemont Ferrand, Dunkerque (Dunkirk), Le Havre, Lorient, Montpellier,

Nantes, Nice, St Malo-Dinard, Toulouse and Tours.

CHILDREN IN CARS

Child under 10 not permitted to travel as front seat passenger, with the exception of baby - up to 9 months and less than 9kg weight - in rear-facing seat. Children under 10 in rear must use restraint system appropriate to age and weight.
Note: Under no circumstances fit a rearward facing child restraint in a seat with a frontal airbag. See Essential Motoring Information under 'Passengers' and 'Seat Belts'.

CURRENCY*

With the introduction of the Euro, the French Franc (FRF) ceased to be legal tender from 2002. However, FRF coins and notes may still be exchanged at the French Central Bank (Banque de France) for 10 years (banknotes) and at least 3 years (coins).

DIMENSIONS AND WEIGHT RESTRICTIONS*

Private cars and towed trailers or caravans are restricted to the following dimensions - height, no restrictions, but 4 metres is a recommended maximum; width, 2.55 metres; length, 12 metres (excluding tow-bar). The maximum permitted overall length of vehicle/trailer or caravan combination is 18.75 metres.

Trailers without brakes have a maximum authorised weight of 750kg or 50% of unladen weight of the towing vehicle, whichever is lower. If the weight of the trailer exceeds that of the towing vehicle, see also Speed limits below.

DRIVING LICENCE*

(see also *Speed limits* below)
A valid UK or Republic of Ireland licence is accepted in France. The minimum age at which visitors from UK or Republic of Ireland may use a temporarily imported motorcycle (over 80cc) or car is 18. Visitors may use temporarily imported motorcycles of up to 80cc at 16.

FOODSTUFFS*

If the imported foodstuffs are for personal use, there are no limits when travelling between EU countries. Visitors entering France from Andorra should ensure that the following are not exceeded – 2.5kg milk powder, 3kg condensed milk, 6kg fresh milk, 1kg butter, 4kg cheese, 5kg

Café in Frejus.

sugar/sweets, 5kg meat. Coffee (1kg), coffee extract (400g), tea (200g) and tea extract (80g) are free of customs duties. Visitors coming from other countries may import up to 1kg of meat, but meat and meat products from Africa are prohibited. Coffee (500g), coffee extract (200g), tea (100g) and tea extract (40g) are free of customs duties, but visitors under 15 cannot import coffee.

LIGHTS*

Yellow tinted headlights are no longer necessary in France. It is compulsory for motorcyclists riding machines exceeding 125cc to use dipped headlights during the day.

MOTORING CLUB

The AA is affiliated to the **Fédération Française des Automobile-Clubs et des Usagers de la Route (FFAC)** whose office is at 76 avenue Marceau, 75008 Paris. ☎0156892070
Website: **www.automobileclub.org**

PARKING*

Parking restrictions are indicated by signs or yellow lines on the kerb. Stopping and parking is prohibited if the yellow line is continuous; parking if it is broken. In Paris parking is forbidden in many city centre streets, and wheelclamps are in use. It is absolutely forbidden to stop or park on a *red route.*

The east-west route includes the left bank of the Seine and the Quai de la Megisserie; the north-south route includes the Avenue du Général Leclerc, part of the Boulevard St Michel, the Rue de Rivoli, the Boulevards Sébastopol, Strasbourg, Barbès and Ornano, Rue Lafayette and Avenue Jean Jaurès.

PRIORITY INCLUDING ROUNDABOUTS*

In built-up areas, you must give way to traffic coming from the right - *priorité à droite.* However, at roundabouts with signs bearing the words *"Vous n'avez pas la priorité"* or *"Cédez le passage"* traffic on the roundabout has priority. Where no such sign exists, traffic **entering** the roundabout has priority.

Outside built-up areas, all main roads of any importance have right of way. This is indicated by a red-bordered triangle showing a black cross on a white background with the words "Passage Protégé" underneath; or a red-bordered triangle showing a pointed black upright with horizontal bar on a white background; or a yellow square within a white square with points vertical.

PETROL

See Essential Motoring Information under 'Petrol/Diesel'.

ROADS

France has more than 4000 miles of motorway (*autoroute*). With the exception of a few sections into or around large cities, tolls are payable. Emergency telephones which connect the caller to the police are located approximately every 2 kilometres. There is also a very comprehensive network of other roads, and surfaces are generally good; exceptions are usually signposted *Chauseé déformeé*. The camber is often severe and the edges rough.

During July and August, and especially at weekends, traffic on main roads is likely to be very heavy. Special signs are erected to indicate alternative routes with the least traffic congestion. Wherever they appear, it is usually advantageous to follow them, although you may not save time. The alternative routes are quiet, but they are not as wide as the main roads. They are not suitable for caravans.

A free road map showing the marked alternative routes, plus information centres and petrol stations open 24 hours, is available from service stations displaying the *Bison Futé* poster (a Red Indian chief in full war bonnet). These maps are also available from *Syndicats d'Initiative* and information offices.

SPEED LIMITS*

Built-up areas 50km/h (31mph)
Outside built-up areas on normal roads 90km/h (55mph); on dual-carriageways separated by a central reservation 110km/h (69mph).
On Motorways 130km/h (80mph). **Note** The minimum speed in the fast lane on a level stretch of motorway during good daytime visibility is 80km/h (49mph), and drivers travelling below this speed are liable to be fined. The maximum speed on the Paris ring road is 80km/h (49mph) and, on

other urban stretches of motorway, 110km/h (69mph).

In fog, when visibility is reduced to 50 metres (55yds), the speed limit on all roads is 50km/h (31mph). In wet weather speed limits outside built-up areas are reduced to 80km/h (49mph), 100km/h (62mph) and 110km/h (69mph) on motorways.

The above limits apply to private cars, motorcycles (exceeding 80cc) and private cars towing a trailer or caravan, if the latter's weight does not exceed that of the car and the total weight is less than 3.5 tonnes. However, if the weight of the trailer exceeds that of the car by less than 30%, the speed limit is 65km/h (40mph), if more than 30% the speed limit is 45km/h (28mph). Additionally these combinations must:

i Display a disc at the rear of the caravan/trailer showing the maximum speed.

ii Not be driven in the fast lane of a 3-lane motorway.

Those motorists who have held a full driving licence for less than two years, must not exceed 80km/h (49mph) outside built-up areas, 100km/h (62mph) on dual carriageways separated by a central reservation and 110km/h (69mph) on motorways.

WARNING TRIANGLE/HAZARD-WARNING*

The use of a warning triangle or hazard-warning lights† is compulsory in the event of accident or breakdown. As hazard-warning lights may be damaged or inoperative, it is recommended that a warning triangle be carried. The triangle must be placed on the road 30 metres (33yds) behind the vehicle and clearly visible from 100 metres (109yds). Note: A warning triangle is compulsory for trailers with a total authorised laden weight exceeding 500kg and for vehicles over 3500kg.

†If your vehicle is equipped with hazard warning lights, it is also compulsory to use them if you are forced to drive temporarily at a greatly reduced speed. However, when slow moving traffic is established in an uninterrupted lane or lanes, this only applies to the last vehicle in the lane(s).

*Additional information will be found in the Essential Motoring Information at the front of the book.

ALPS/EAST

ABRETS, LES ISÈRE

Coin Tranquille 38490 ☎ 476321348 ▤ 476374067
e-mail: contact@coin-tranquille.com
website: www.coin-tranquille.com
Completely divided into pitches with attractive flower beds
in rural surroundings.
➲ *2 km E of village, 500m off N6.*
Open: Apr-Oct Site: 7HEC ⸛⸛⸛ 🖙 🏠 Facilities: 🏕 🍴 ⊙ 🖾 🔌
🏛 Services: 🍴 ✕ 🖃 lau Leisure: 🏊 P

AILLON-LE-JEUNE SAVOIE

Jeanne et Georges Cher 73340 ☎ 479546032
On a level meadow with heated sanitary installations.
Situated close to the local ski station.
Open: All year Site: 2HEC ⸛⸛⸛ 🔆 Facilities: 🏕 ⊙ 🖾 🏛
Services: lau Off-site: 🍴 ✕

ALBENS SAVOIE

Beauséjour rte de la Rippe, 73410 ☎ 479541520
In a delightfully peaceful, wooded setting between Aix-les-
Bains and Annecy.
➲ *SW via rte de la Chambotte. Signposted*
Open: Jun-20 Sep Site: 2HEC ⸛⸛⸛ 🚐 Prices: ♦1.60 🚗3.50
🚐3.50 pitch 3.50 Facilities: 🏕 ⊙ 🖾 🔌 🏛 Services: lau
Off-site: 🔌 🍴 ✕ 🏊R 🖃

ALLEVARD ISÈRE

Clair Matin rte de Pommiers, 38580
☎ 476975519 ▤ 476458715
e-mail: jdavallet1@aol.com
website: www.ifrance.com/campingclairmatin
Gently sloping terraced area divided into pitches.
➲ *S of village, 300m off D525.*
Open: 10May-9 Oct Site: 5.5HEC ⸛⸛⸛ 🖙 🚐 Prices: ♦2.60
pitch 5-10 Facilities: 🏕 ⊙ 🖾 🔌 🏚 🏛 Services: 🍴 🖃 lau
Leisure: 🏊 P Off-site: 🔌 🍴 ✕ 🏊LR

ARBOIS JURA

CM Vignes av Gl-Leclerc, 39600 ☎ 384661412 ▤ 384661412
Terraced site. Shop open Jul-Aug only.
➲ *E on D107 Mesnay road at stadium.*
Open: Apr-Sep Site: 5HEC ⸛⸛⸛ ⁙⁙⁙ 🚐 Prices: pitch 9.90-
10.90 (incl 2 persons) Facilities: 🏕 🍴 ⊙ 🖾 🔌 🏛 Services: 🍴
🖃 lau Off-site: ✕ 🏚 🏊PR

ARGENTIÈRE HAUTE-SAVOIE

Glacier d'Argentière 161 chemin des Chosalets, 74400
☎ 450541736 ▤ 450540373
Set on sloping meadowland in a beautiful situation at the
foot of the Mont Blanc Massif.
➲ *Access is 1km S of Argentière, turn off N506 towards
Cableway Lognan et de Grandes Montets, then a further 200m
to site.*
Open: 15 May-Sep Site: 1.5HEC ⸛⸛⸛ 🖙 Prices: ♦4.20 🚗1.60
🚐3.10 ▲2.10 Facilities: 🏕 ⊙ 🖾 🔌 🏛 Services: 🖃 lau
Off-site: 🔌 🍴 ✕ 🏚

ARS-SUR-FORMANS AIN

Bois de la Dame Chemin du Bois de la Dame, 1480
☎ 474007723
Compulsory separate car park for arrivals after 22.00hrs.
➲ *Access from A6, exit Villefranche and continue towards
Jassans-Riottier.*
Open: Apr-Sep Site: 1.5HEC ⸛⸛⸛ 🚐 Prices: 🚐8 pitch 8 (incl
1 persons) Facilities: 🏕 ⊙ 🖾 🔌 🏛 🄿 Services: 🖃 lau
Off-site: 🔌 🍴 ✕ 🏊P

AUTRANS ISÈRE

Caravaneige du Vercors Les Gaillards, 38880
☎ 476953188 ▤ 476953682
e-mail: camping.le.vercors@wanadoo.fr
website: www.camping-du-vercors.fr
Ideal for summer or winter holidays, situated in the heart of
the Vercors with easy access to skiing.
➲ *0.6km S via D106 towards Méaudre.*
Open: 20 May-15 Sep, Nov-Apr Site: 1HEC ⸛⸛⸛ 🖙 🏠
Prices: ♦10.90 🚐3.50 🚐 pitch 10.67 (incl 2 persons)
Facilities: 🏕 ⊙ 🖾 🔌 🏛 Services: 🖃 lau Leisure: 🏊 P
Off-site: 🔌 🍴 ✕

Joyeux Réveil 38880 ☎ 476953344 ▤ 476957298
e-mail: camping-au-joyeux-reveil@wanadoo.fr
website: camping-au-joyeux-reveil.fr
In a beautiful location surrounded by woodland, with fine
mountain views.
➲ *NE of town via rte de Montaud.*
Open: Dec-Mar & 1May-Sep Site: 1.5HEC ⸛⸛⸛ 🖙 🏠
Prices: pitch 15-20 (incl 2 persons) Facilities: 🏕 ⊙ 🖾 🔌 🏚 🏛
Services: 🍴 ✕ 🖃 lau Leisure: 🏊 P Off-site: 🔌 🍴 ✕ 🔌

BARATIER HAUTES-ALPES

Verger 5200 ☎ 492431587 ▤ 4924981
e-mail: bresgilbert@minitel.net
website: www.campingleverger.fr
Terraced site in plantation of fruit trees with fine views of
Alps. Divided into pitches.
➲ *From N94 drive 2.5km S of Embrun, 1.5km E on D40.*
Open: All year Site: 4HEC ⸛⸛⸛ 🖙 🏠 🚐 Facilities: 🏕 ⊙ 🖾 🔌
🏚 🏛 Services: 🖃 lau Leisure: 🏊 P Off-site: 🔌 🍴 ✕ 🏊LR

BELFORT TERRITOIRE-DE-BELFORT

Étang des Forges r du Général Béthouart, 90000
☎ 384225492 ▤ 384227655
e-mail: contact@campings-belfort.com
website: www.campings-belfort.com
Situated by the side of the Malsaucy lake in the regional
nature reserve of "Ballons des Vosges". Ideal terrain for water
and hiking activities.
➲ *A36/E54 exit 2, situated off D13 Richtung-Offemont road*
Open: 10 Apr-Sep Site: 3.5HEC ⸛⸛⸛ 🖙 🚐 ▲ Prices: ♦3.10-
3.80 pitch 12.50-14 (incl 2 persons) Facilities: 🏕 🔌 ⊙ 🖾 🔌 🏚 🏛
Services: 🍴 ✕ 🖃 lau Leisure: 🏊 P Off-site: 🏚 🏊L

BELLEGARDE-SUR-VALSERINE AIN

Crêt d'Eau 2 av de Lattre-de-Tassigny, 01200
☎ 450566081 ▤ 450486209
In a pleasant mountain setting with good facilities.
➲ *3km N of town, 200m from N84.*
Open: All year Site: 5HEC ⸛⸛⸛ 🚐 🚐 Prices: ♦3.70 🚐4.50
pitch 4.50 Facilities: 🏕 ⊙ 🖾 🏛 🄿 Services: 🍴 ✕ 🖃 lau
Leisure: 🏊 P Off-site: 🔌 🔌 🏊R

BOURG-D'OISANS, LE ISÈRE

Caravaneige le Vernis 38520 ☎ 0476800268
e-mail: camping.vernis@online.fr
website: www.oisans.com/levernis
Well-kept site at foot of mountain in summer skiing area.
➲ *2.5km of N91, rte de BrianÅon.*
Open: Jun-10 Sept Site: 1.2HEC ⸛⸛⸛ 🚐 🚐 🚫 Prices: pitch
15 (incl 2 persons) Facilities: 🏕 ⊙ 🖾 🔌 🏛 Services: 🖃 lau
Leisure: 🏊 P Off-site: 🔌 🍴 ✕ 🔌 🏚

Site: 6HEC-Site size ⸛⸛⸛-grass ⁙⁙⁙-sand ◗-stone 🔆-little shade 🖙-partly shaded 🚐-mainly shaded
🏠-bungalows for hire 🚐-caravans for hire ▲-tents for hire 🚫-no dogs Prices: ♦-adult per night 🚗-car per night
pp-per person per night 🚐-caravan per night ▲-tent per night

Cascade rte de l'Alpe-d'Huez, 38520
☎ 476800242 🖷 476802263
e-mail: lacascade@wanadoo.fr
website: lacascade.cjb.net
Set at the foot of a mountain with a waterfall and modern,
very well-kept sanitary arrangements. Television lounge with
library, open fireplace. Booking essential.
➲ *From Grenoble follow signs 'Stations de l'Oisans' then from
Bourg-d'Oisans continue towards Alpe-d'Huez.*
Open: 15 Dec-Sep **Site:** 2.5HEC ⛭ ♙ 🏕 **Facilities:** ⋒ ⊙ 🖳
∅ 🚿 🛎 **Services:** 🍴 lau **Leisure:** ⚓ PR **Off-site:** 🛒 ✕ 🖽

Colporteur le Mas du Plan, 38520
☎ 476791144 🖷 476791149
e-mail: info@camping-colporteur.com
website: www.camping-colporteur.com
Situated 200mtrs from the centre of Bourg d'Oisans, a village
in the centre of a plain surrounded by mountains.
Open: 20 May-20 Sep **Site:** 4HEC ⛭ ♙ 🏕 **Prices:** pitch
11.25-15 (incl 1 persons) **Facilities:** ⋒ ⊙ 🖳 🛎 **Services:** 🍴 ✕
lau **Leisure:** ⚓ R **Off-site:** 🛒 ∅ ⚓P 🖽

Rencontre du Soleil rte de l'Alpe-d'Huez, 38520
☎ 476791222 🖷 476802637
e-mail: rencontre.soleil@wanadoo.fr
website: www.joliefrance.com/ais
Charming site in a lovely setting in the Dauphiny Alps at the
foot of a mountain. Fine rustic common room with open
fireplace. TV, playroom for children.
➲ *At the foot of the hairpin road to L'Alp-d'Huez, leave N91
(Grenoble-Briançon road) in Le Bourg d'Osians.*
Open: 11 May-15 Sep **Site:** 1.6HEC ⛭ ♙ 🏕 **Prices:** pitch
14.30-22.85 (incl 2 persons) **Facilities:** ⋒ ⊙ 🖳 🛎 **Services:** 🍴
✕ lau **Leisure:** ⚓ P **Off-site:** 🛒 ✕ ∅ 🚿 ⚓R

At Venosc (10km SE on N91 and D530)

Champ de Moulin 38520 ☎ 476800738 🖷 476802444
e-mail: christian.avallet@wanadoo.fr
website: www.champ-du-moulin.com
In a picturesque location with fine views of the surrounding
mountains and a direct cablecar connection to local ski
slopes. Separate car park for late arrivals.
Open: Jan-Sep & 15-31 Dec **Site:** 4HEC ⛭ ♙ 🔌 🏕 🖳
Prices: pitch 13-17.50 (incl 2 persons) **Facilities:** ⋒ 🛒 ⊙ 🖳
∅ 🛎 **Services:** 🍴 ✕ lau **Leisure:** ⚓ R **Off-site:** 🚿 ⚓P 🖽

Bourg-En-Bresse Ain

CM de Challes 5 allée du Centre Nautique, 01000
☎ 474455995 🖷 474224032
e-mail: camping_municipal_bourgenbresse@wanadoo.fr
In football ground near swimming pool.
➲ *Well signposted from outskirts of town.*
Open: Apr-14 Oct **Site:** 2.7HEC ⛭ ⠿ ♙ **Prices:** 🛉2.64
🛉4.82 pitch 5.75 **Facilities:** ⋒ 🛒 ⊙ 🖳 🛎 🄿 **Services:** 🍴 ✕ 🖽
lau **Leisure:** ⚓ P **Off-site:** ∅ 🚿

Bourget-du-Lac, le Savoie

CM Ile aux Cygnes 73370 ☎ 479250176 🖷 479253294
e-mail: camping@bourgetdulac.com
website: www.bourgetdulac.com
A family site on the shore of the Lac Bourdeau with plenty of
recreational facilities.
➲ *Access via N514.*
Open: 13 Apr-13 Oct, 1 May-30 Sept **Site:** 4.5HEC ⛭ ♙ 🏕
Prices: 🛉2.55-3.77 pitch 4.50-5.25 **Facilities:** ⋒ 🛒 ⊙ 🖳 ∅ 🛎
Services: 🖽 lau **Leisure:** ⚓ LR **Off-site:** 🍴 ✕

Bourg-St-Maurice Savoie

Versoyen rte des Arcs, 73700 ☎ 479070345 🖷 479072541
e-mail: leversoyen@wanadoo.fr
website: www.leversoyen.com
Two communal sanitary blocks - one heated. Skiing facilities.
Many secluded pitches in a wood.
➲ *On S outskirts of town. Access via N90.*
Site: 4HEC ⛭ ♙ 🏕 🖳 **Prices:** 🛉3.50-5.35 pitch 3.20-4.20
Facilities: ⋒ ⊙ 🖳 ∅ 🚿 🛎 **Services:** 🖽 lau **Off-site:** 🛒 🍴 ✕ ∅
🚿 ⚓PR

Bout-du-Lac Haute-Savoie

International du Lac Bleu rte d'Albertville, 74210
☎ 450443018 🖷 450448435
e-mail: lac-bleu@nwc.fr **website:** www.camping-lac-bleu.com
Modern, well-kept site. Overflow area with own sanitary
blocks.
➲ *On the southern shores of Lake Annecy via the N508,
opposite ANTAR Garage.*
Open: 15 Apr-25 Sep **Site:** 3.3HEC ⛭ ♙ 🏕 🖳 **Facilities:** ⋒
⊙ 🖳 🛎 **Services:** 🍴 ✕ 🖽 lau **Leisure:** ⚓ LP **Off-site:** 🛒 ∅ 🚿

Nublière 74210 ☎ 450443344 🖷 450443178
e-mail: nubliere@wanadoo.fr
Extensive site divided into pitches in attractive surroundings.
➲ *150m off N508 at S end of Lac d'Annecy.*
Open: May-Sep **Site:** 9HEC ⛭ ♙ 🏕 🅰 **Facilities:** ⋒ 🛒 ⊙
🖳 ∅ 🛎 **Services:** 🖽 lau **Leisure:** ⚓ L **Off-site:** 🍴 ✕ 🚿 ⚓R

Chalezeule Doubs

Plage 12 rte de Belfort, 25220 ☎ 381880426 🖷 381505462
e-mail: laplage.besancon@ffcc.asso.fr
website: www.ffcc.asso.fr
A modern site with good facilities near the main roads and
close to the River Doubs.
➲ *Access via N83 towards Belfort.*
Open: Apr-Sep **Site:** 1.8HEC ⛭ ♙ **Prices:** 🛉3.13-3.43
🏕1.60-2.30 pitch 4.28-4.78 **Facilities:** ⋒ ⊙ 🖳 ∅ 🛎
Services: 🍴 ✕ 🖽 lau **Leisure:** ⚓ PR **Off-site:** 🛒 ∅ 🚿

Chamonix-Mont-Blanc Haute-Savoie

Mer de Glace 200 Chemin de la Bagna, 74400
☎ 0450 450530863 🖷 450536083
e-mail: campingmdg@wanadoo.fr
website: www.chamonix_camping.com
In a forested setting with pitches divided by hedges. Enjoys
fine mountain views.
➲ *2km NE to Les Praz. On approach to village (from
Chamonix) turn right under railway bridge.*
Open: 19 May-Sept **Site:** 2.2HEC ⛭ ⠿ ♙ **Prices:** 🛉5.10-
5.90 pitch 4.80-6.70 **Facilities:** ⋒ ⊙ 🖳 🛎 **Services:** ✕ 🖽 lau
Off-site: 🛒 🍴 ✕ ∅ 🚿 ⚓P

Rosières 121 Clos des Rosières, 74400
☎ 450531042 🖷 450532955
e-mail: info@campinglesrosieres.com
website: www.campinglesrosieres.com
Picturesque site at the foot of the Mont Blanc range.
➲ *1.2km NE via N506.*
Open: 7 Feb-Oct **Site:** 1.6HEC ⛭ ⠿ ♙ 🏕 **Prices:** 🛉5-5.80
🅰2.50-3 pitch 4.30-5.70 **Facilities:** ⋒ ⊙ 🖳 ∅ 🛎
Services: 🍴 ✕ 🖽 lau **Off-site:** 🛒 🍴 ✕ ⚓P

At Bossons, Les (3km W)

Cimes 28 rte des Tissieres, 74400 ☎ 450535893
In a wooded meadow at the foot of Mont Blanc Massif. Ideal
for hiking and mountain tours.
Open: 15 Jun-20 Sep **Site:** 1HEC ⛭ ♙ 🖳 **Facilities:** ⋒ ⊙
🖳 ∅ 🛎 **Services:** lau **Leisure:** ⚓ R **Off-site:** 🛒 🍴 ✕ 🚿 ⚓L 🖽

Facilities: 🛒-shop ⋒-shower ⊙-electric points for razors 🖳-electric points for caravans 🛎-parking by tents permitted
🄿-compulsory separate car park **Services:** ✕-café/restaurant 🍴-bar ∅-Camping Gaz International 🚿-gas other than Camping
Gaz 🖽-first aid facilities lau-laundry **Leisure:** ⚓-swimming L-Lake P-Pool R-River S-Sea **Off-site:** All facilities within 2km

CAMPING JURA CLAIRVAUX-LES-LACS

Four Stars Campsite at the lake side / Heated swimmingpool / Kids'club, animation / Chalets, Mobil-homes, Fully equipped tent / Natur Campsite in the middle of the area of lake.

★ ★ ★ ★
FAYOLAN

yelloh! VILLAGE

Informations and reservations
Relaisoleil Jura BP 52 39130 Clairvaux-les-Lacs **FRANCE**
Tél.+33 (0) 3 84 25 26 19 Fax + 33 (0) 3 84 25 26 20
E.mail : relais.soleil.jura@wanadoo.fr **www.vacances-nature.com**

Deux Glaciers 80 rte des Tissières, 74400
☎ 450531584 🖷 450559081
e-mail: glaciers@clubinternet.fr
A glacial stream runs through the site. Pitches shaded by trees, very modern, well-kept sanitary installations. Rustic common room with open fires.
➾ *Leave N506 towards road underpass. 250m to site.*
Open: All year Site: 16HEC ⬛ 🔆 Facilities: 🖎 ⊙ 🖵 ⚍ 🖾 Services: 🍴 ✕ 🖃 lau Off-site: 🖾

CHAMPAGNOLE JURA

CM Boyse r G-Vallery, 39300 ☎ 384520032 🖷 384520116
e-mail: boyse@frce.fr
website: www.tourisme.champagnole.com
Clean and tidy site with asphalt drives and completely divided into pitches. In grounds of municipal swimming pool.
➾ *Turn onto D5 just before town and continue 1.3km to site.*
Open: 2 Jun-17 Sep Site: 7HEC ⬛ 🌳 🏠 Facilities: 🖎 🖳 ⊙ 🖵 ⚍ 🖾 Services: 🍴 ✕ 🖃 lau Leisure: 🏊 PR

CHÂTEAUROUX-LES-ALPES HAUTES-ALPES

Cariamas Fontmolines, 05380 ☎ 492432263
e-mail: p.tim@free.fr website: les.cariamas.free.fr
On a meadow in an attractive mountain setting beside the River Durance.
➾ *1.5km SE.*
Open: Apr-Oct Site: 6HEC ⬛ 🌳 🏠 🚐 🏕 Prices: ♠4.50 🚗5.25 🏕5.25 pitch 5.25 Facilities: 🖎 🖳 ⊙ 🖵 ⚍ 🖾 Services: lau Leisure: 🏊 P Off-site: 🍴 ✕

CHOISY HAUTE-SAVOIE

Chez Langin 74330 ☎ 450774165 🖷 450774101
In pleasant wooded surroundings.

➾ *1.3km NE via D3.*
Open: 14 Apr-Sep Site: 3HEC ⬛ 🔆 🏠 Prices: 🚐18 🏕1.60 pitch 18 (incl 2 persons) pp4.50 Facilities: 🖎 🖳 ⊙ 🖵 ⚍ 🖾 Services: 🍴 ✕ 🖃 lau Leisure: 🏊 P

CHORANCHE ISÈRE

Gouffre de la Croix 38680 ☎ 476360713 🖷 476360713
e-mail: camping.gouffre.croix@wanadoo.fr
In a quiet location beside the River Bourne with fine views of the surrounding mountains and good, modern facilities.
➾ *Access via A49 exit St-Marcellin or Hostun.*
Open: 15 Mar-15 Sep Site: 2.5HEC ⬛ 🌳 🏠 Prices: ♠3-4 🚗1.50-2 pitch 3-4 Facilities: 🖎 🖳 ⊙ 🖵 ⚍ 🖾 Services: 🍴 ✕ 🖃 lau Leisure: 🏊 R

CLAIRVAUX-LES-LACS JURA

Fayolan 39130 ☎ 384252619 🖷 384252620
e-mail: relais.soleil.jura@wanadoo.fr
website: www.vacances-nature.com
In a wooded location beside the lake.
➾ *1.2km SE via D118.*
Site: 17HEC ⬛ 🔆 🏠 🏕 Facilities: 🖎 🖳 ⊙ 🖵 ⚍ 🖾 Services: 🍴 ✕ lau Leisure: 🏊 LP Off-site: 🏊R 🖃

Grisière et Europe Vacances 39130
☎ 384258048 🖷 384252234
e-mail: la-grisiere.com website: www.la-grisiere.com
Fenced in meadowland with some trees, sloping down to the Grand Lac. The site is guarded during July and August.
➾ *From village centre turn off N78, follow D118 towards Châtel-de-Joux for 800m to the site.*
Open: May-Sep Site: 11HEC ⬛ 🔆 🏠 Prices: ♠3.20 pitch 6.80 Facilities: 🖎 🖳 ⊙ 🖵 ⚍ 🖾 Services: 🍴 ✕ lau Leisure: 🏊 L

CLUSAZ, LA HAUTE-SAVOIE

Plan du Fernuy route des Confins, 74220
☎ 450024475 🖷 450326702
e-mail: info@plendufernuy.com
website: www.plandufernuy.com
Airing rooms. 30 ski-lifts nearby. Several cable cars. Well-situated for skiing or walking.
➾ *At the road fork E of La Clusaz leave N50 the Col des Aravis road, and drive towards Les Confins from road fork 2km to site.*
Open: Jun-9 Sep & 20 Dec-Apr Site: 1.3HEC ⬛ 🔹 🔆 🏠 Prices: pitch 16-18 (incl 2 persons) Facilities: 🖎 🖳 ⊙ 🖵 ⚍ 🖾 Services: 🍴 ✕ lau Leisure: 🏊 P Off-site: ✕ 🖾 🖃

DIVONNE-LES-BAINS AIN

Fleutron Quartier Villard, 01220
☎ 450200195 🖷 450200035
e-mail: info@homair-vacances.fr
website: www.homair-vacances.fr
In wooded surroundings with large individual pitches.
➾ *3 km N.*
Open: Apr-28 Oct Site: 8HEC ⬛ 🔆 🏠 🚐 🏕 Facilities: 🖎 ⊙ 🖵 🖾 Services: 🍴 ✕ lau Leisure: 🏊 P Off-site: 🖾 ⚍ 🏊L 🖃

DOLE JURA

Pasquier 18 Chelin Theremot, 39100 ☎ 384720261
Meadow site near River Doubs.
➾ *900m SE of town centre.*
Open: 15 Mar-15 Oct Site: 2HEC ⬛ 🔹 🌳 🏠 🚐 Facilities: 🖎 🖳 ⊙ 🖵 ⚍ 🖾 Services: 🍴 ✕ 🖃 lau Off-site: ✕ ⚍ 🏊R

Site: 6HEC-Site size ⬛-grass ⋰⋰-sand ⬙-stone ✹-little shade 🔆-partly shaded ♣-mainly shaded
🏠-bungalows for hire 🚐-caravans for hire 🏕-tents for hire ✗-no dogs **Prices:** ♠-adult per night 🚗-car per night
pp-per person per night 🚐-caravan per night 🏕-tent per night

DOUCIER JURA

Domaine de Chalain 39130 ☎ 384257878 🖷 384249407
e-mail: chalain@chalain.com
website: www.chalain.com
A large site beside Lake Chalain with a wide variety of recreational facilities.
➲ *3km NE.*
Open: May-21 Sep Site: 20HEC ⚏ 🔌 � 🚐 Facilities: 🏪 🛁 ⊙ 🔌 ⌀ ♨ 🏚 Services: 🍴 ✕ 🏥 lau Leisure: ⚓ LP

DOUSSARD HAUTE-SAVOIE

Ravoire rte de la Ravoire, 74210 ☎ 450443780 🖷 45032960
e-mail: info@camping-la-ravoire.fr
website: www.camping-la-ravoire.fr
A well appointed, modern site on level ground 800mtrs from Lake Annecy. Spectacular mountain views.
➲ *Leave Autoroute at Annecy Sud exit towards Albertville and take N508 as far as Duingt to pick up signs.*
Open: 15 May-15 Sep Site: 2HEC ⚏ 🔌 🚐 Prices: pitch 25.92-28.97 (incl 2 persons) Facilities: 🏪 ⊙ 🔌 ⌀ ♨ 🏚 Services: 🍴 ✕ 🏥 lau Leisure: ⚓ P Off-site: ✕ ⚓L

Serraz r de la Poste, 74210 ☎ 450443068 🖷 450448107
e-mail: info@campinglaserraz.com
website: www.campinglaserraz.com
Modern site divided into pitches. Cosy bar in rustic style.
➲ *At E end of village 500m from N508 on D181.*
Open: 15 May-20 Sep Site: 4HEC ⚏ ♠ 🚐 Prices: ⚓3-5.50 pitch 8-4 Facilities: 🏪 ⊙ 🔌 🏚 Services: 🍴 ✕ 🏥 lau Leisure: ⚓ P Off-site: ⌀ ⚓L

EMBRUN HAUTES-ALPES

CM Clapière av du Lac, 05200 ☎ 492430183
Well-managed site with shaded pitches on stony ground, on N shore of lake. Site shop open during summer only.
➲ *2.5km SW on N94.*
Open: May-Sep Site: 5.3HEC ⚏ 🔌 Facilities: 🏪 ⊙ 🔌 🏚 Services: lau Off-site: 🛁 🍴 ✕ ⌀ ♨ ⚓LPR 🏥

ENTRE-DEUX-GUIERS ISÈRE

Arc en Ciel rue des berges, 38380
☎ 476660697 🖷 476668805
e-mail: info@camping-arc-en-ciel.com
website: www.camping-arc-en-ciel.com
In a wooded location on the river bank with well shaded pitches.
➲ *On D520 300m from N6.*
Open: Mar-Oct Site: 1.2HEC ⚏ ♠ 🚐 Facilities: 🏪 ⊙ 🔌 ⌀ ♨ 🏚 Services: 🏥 lau Leisure: ⚓ PR Off-site: 🛁 🍴 ✕

ÉVIAN-LES-BAINS HAUTE-SAVOIE

Clos Savoyard Maxilly sur Ciman, 74500
☎ 450752584 🖷 450753019
Attractive site with fine views of the lake and the mountains.
➲ *Turn onto D21 in town 1200m after Hôtel le Maximillien and continue uphill.*
Open: Jul-Aug Site: 2HEC ⚏ 🔌 🚐 Facilities: 🏪 ⊙ 🔌 🏚 Services: 🏥 lau Off-site: 🛁 🍴 ✕ ⌀ ⚓L

AT AMPHION-LES-BAINS (3.5KM W ON N5)

Plage 304 rue de la Garenne, Amphion les Bains, 74500
☎ 450700046 🖷 450700046
e-mail: info@camping-dela-plage.com
website: www.camping-dela-plage.com
A pleasant site with direct access to the lake. There are good recreational facilities and modern, well equipped bungalows and chalets are available for hire.

➲ *NW of town on N5, 150m from lake.*
Open: All year Site: 1HEC ⚏ 🔌 🚐 Prices: pitch 16-22 (incl 2 persons) Facilities: 🏪 ⊙ 🔌 🏚 Services: 🍴 ✕ 🏥 lau Leisure: ⚓ LP Off-site: 🛁 ✕ ⌀ ♨ ⚓R

FERRIÈRE-D'ALLEVARD ISÈRE

CM Neige et Nature chemin de Montarmand, 38580
☎ 476451984
e-mail: contact@neige-nature.fr
website: www.neige-nature.fr
In a beautiful situation with spectacular mountain views and good, modern facilities.
➲ *In Allevard take D525A towards Le Pleynet.*
Open: Jun-15 Sep Site: 1.2HEC ⚏ 🔌 🚐 Prices: ⚓4.30-4.50 pitch 4.30-4.50 Facilities: 🏪 ⊙ 🔌 🏚 Services: 🍴 ✕ 🏥 lau Leisure: ⚓ PR Off-site: 🛁 ♨

GRESSE-EN-VERCORS ISÈRE

4 Saisons 38650 ☎ 476343027 🖷 476343952
In a picturesque mountain setting with good facilities.
➲ *1.3km SW*
Open: May-Sept, 20 Dec- 15 Mar Site: 2.2HEC ⚏ ♨ ⛄ 🚐 Prices: ⚓4.75 pitch 13.40 (incl 2 persons) Facilities: 🏪 ⊙ ⌀ ♨ 🏚 Services: lau Leisure: ⚓ P Off-site: 🛁 🍴 ✕ ⚓R 🏥

GUILLESTRE HAUTES-ALPES

Villard Le Villard, 5600 ☎ 492450654 🖷 492450052
website: www.alpes_campings.com
In a magnificent location between the Ecrins national park and Queyras regional park. Good facilities, but bar and café operate July-Aug only.
➲ *2km W via D902A and N4, rte de Gap.*
Open: All year Site: 3HEC ⚏ 🔌 🚐 Prices: ⚓2.30-4.50 pitch 9.15-16.20 (incl 2 persons) Facilities: 🏪 🛁 ⊙ 🔌 ♨ 🏚 Services: 🍴 ✕ lau Leisure: ⚓ PR Off-site: ⌀ ⚓L 🏥

HAUTECOURT-ROMANÈCHE AIN

Ile Chambod 01250 ☎ 474372541 🖷 474372828
e-mail: camping.chambod@free.fr
website: www.campingilechambod.com
A well equipped site close to the River Ain where swimming is supervised by lifeguards. Good sanitary and recreational facilities.
➲ *From Bourg-en-Bresse take D979 towards Geneva.*
Open: May-Sep Site: 2.5HEC ⚏ 🔌 🚐 ⛺ Prices: ⚓4 🚐2.50 pitch 2.50 Facilities: 🏪 🛁 ⊙ 🔌 ⌀ ♨ 🏚 Services: 🍴 ✕ 🏥 lau Leisure: ⚓ P Off-site: ⚓LR

HUANNE-MONTMARTIN DOUBS

Bois de Reveuge 25680 ☎ 381843860 🖷 381844404
website: www.campingduboisdereveuge.com
A terraced site in a 20 hectare park surrounded by the Vosges and Jura mountains with good recreational facilities.
➲ *Access via A36 exit 'Baumes-les-Dames'.*
Open: 20 Apr-20 Sep Site: 20HEC ⚏ ⁘ ♨ 🔌 🚐 Facilities: 🏪 🛁 ⊙ 🔌 ⌀ ♨ 🏚 Services: 🍴 ✕ 🏥 lau Leisure: ⚓ LP

ISLE-SUR-LE-DOUBS, L' DOUBS

CM Lumes 10 r des Lumes, 25250
☎ 381927305 🖷 381927305
website: www.camping-des-lumes.com
The site lies close to the town. Common room with TV.
➲ *Off N83. Entrance near bridge over the Doubs.*
Open: May-Sep Site: 1.5HEC ⚏ 🔌 🚐 🚐 Prices: ⚓2.90 🚐4 ⛺3.80 Facilities: 🏪 🛁 ⊙ 🔌 🏚 Services: lau Leisure: ⚓ R Off-site: 🛁 🍴 ✕ ⌀ ♨

Facilities: 🛁-shop 🏪-shower ⊙-electric points for razors 🔌-electric points for caravans 🏚-parking by tents permitted
🅿-compulsory separate car park Services: ✕-café/restaurant 🍴-bar ⌀-Camping Gaz International ♨-gas other than Camping Gaz 🏥-first aid facilities lau-laundry Leisure: ⚓-swimming L-Lake P-Pool R-River S-Sea Off-site: All facilities within 2km

LANDRY SAVOIE

Eden 73210 ☎ 479076181 🗏 479076217
e-mail: info@camping-eden.net
website: www.camping-eden.net
A modern site with excellent sports and sanitary facilities, situated in the heart of the Savoie Olympic area.
Open: 18 Dec-26 Apr & 21 May-15 Sep **Site:** 2.7HEC � ♦
🚐 **Facilities:** 🏪 ⊙ 🚿 🛒 🏧 **Services:** ⛽ ✗ 🖃 lau **Leisure:** ⇗
PR **Off-site:** 🛒 ✗ ∅ 🛒

LONS-LE-SAUNIER JURA

Majorie 640 bd de l'Europe, 39000
☎ 384242694 🗏 384240840
e-mail: info@camping-marjorie.com
website: www.camping-marjorie.com
Clean, tidy site with tent and caravan sections separated by a stream. Caravan pitches (80 sq m) are gravelled and surrounded by hedges. Heated common room with TV, reading area, kitchen.
⮕ *Near swimming stadium on outskirts of town.*
Open: 1 Apr-15 Oct **Site:** 9HEC ⚑ ♦ 🕀 🏕 🚐
Prices: pitch 10-16 (incl 2 persons) **Facilities:** 🏪 🛒 ⊙ 🚿 ∅ 🛒
🏧 **Services:** ⛽ ✗ 🖃 lau **Off-site:** ✗ ⇗P

LUGRIN HAUTE-SAVOIE

Myosotis 28 chemin du Grand Tronc, 74500 ☎ 450760759
A terraced site with fine views over the lake and of the surrounding mountains.
⮕ *W of town. Signposted. 1km from Lac Leman*
Open: 4May-25 Sep **Site:** 0.9HEC ⚑ 🕀 🏕 🚐
Prices: ♠2.20-2.60 pitch 5.10-5.80 **Facilities:** 🏪 ⊙ 🚿 🏧
Services: 🖃 lau **Off-site:** 🛒 ⛽ ✗ ∅ ⇗L

Rys Route le Rys, 74500 ☎ 450760575 🗏 450760575
e-mail: jeanmichel.blanc@wanadoo.fr
Calm shady site with panoramic views of the lake and mountains. 10min walk from the beach
⮕ *W of town. Signposted.*
Open: 30 Apr-Oct **Site:** 1.5HEC ⚑ 🕀 🚐 **Prices:** ♠3 🚗1
pitch 4 **Facilities:** 🏪 🛒 ⊙ 🚿 ∅ 🛒 🏧 **Services:** 🖃 lau **Off-site:** 🛒
⛽ ✗ ⇗L

Vieille Église 74500 ☎ 450760195 🗏 450761312
e-mail: campingvieilleeglise@wanadoo.fr
On rising meadow between lake and mountains with good views. Close to lake Léman and its beaches.
⮕ *D24 to Neuvecelle, then take D21, 1km after Maxilly on right.*
Open: Apr-20 Oct **Site:** 1.5HEC ⚑ ♦ 🏕 🚐 **Prices:** pitch 12-15 (incl 2 persons) pp3.80-4.30 **Facilities:** 🏪 🛒 ⊙ 🚿 ∅
🏧 **Services:** ⛽ ✗ 🖃 lau **Leisure:** ⇗ P **Off-site:** 🛒 🛒 ⇗L

MALBUISSON DOUBS

Fuvettes 25160 ☎ 381693150 🗏 381697046
e-mail: les-fuvettes@wanadoo.fr
website: www.camping-fuvettes.com
Mainly level site with some terraces, gently sloping towards lake. At an altitude of 900mtrs in the Jura mountains.
⮕ *500m S on D437.*
Open: Apr-Sep **Site:** 6HEC ⚑ 🕀 🏕 **Prices:** pitch 13-17.80 (incl 2 persons) pp3-4.40 **Facilities:** 🏪 🛒 ⊙ 🚿 ∅ 🛒 🏧
Services: ⛽ ✗ 🖃 lau **Leisure:** ⇗ LP

MARIGNY JURA

Sunelia la Pergola 39130 ☎ 384257003 🗏 384257596
e-mail: contact@lapergola.fr
website: www.lapergola.com
A well equipped, terraced site with direct access to the lake.

⮕ *S of Marigny off D27.*
Open: 15 May- 19 Sep **Site:** 12HEC ⚑ ∴∴ 🕀 🏕
Prices: pitch 20-35 (incl 2 persons) **Facilities:** 🏪 🛒 ⊙ 🚿 ∅ 🛒
Services: ⛽ ✗ 🖃 lau **Leisure:** ⇗ LP **Off-site:** ⇗R

MATAFELON-GRANGES AIN

Gorges de l'Oignin r du Lac, 1580
☎ 474768097 🗏 474768097
e-mail: camping.lesgorgesdeloignin@wanadoo.fr
website: www.gorges-de-loignin.com
Campsite located in the heart of the countryside on the banks of a lake and surrounded by low mountains.
⮕ *A404 exit 11, site signed after 1m.*
Open: Apr-Sep **Site:** 2.6HEC ⚑ 🕀 🏕 **Prices:** pitch 10.60-13.20 (incl 2 persons) **Facilities:** 🏪 🛒 ⊙ 🚿 🏧 **Services:** ⛽ ✗
🖃 lau **Leisure:** ⇗ LP

MÉAUDRE ISÈRE

Buissonnets 38112 ☎ 476952104 🗏 476952614
e-mail: buissonnets@fr.st website: www.buissonnets.fr.st
A quiet, friendly site in the heart of the Vercors Regional Parc with modern sanitary blocks and a wide range of summer and winter recreational facilities.
⮕ *200m from village centre.*
Open: All year **Site:** 2.7HEC ⚑ 🕀 🏕 **Prices:** ♠8 pitch 12 (incl 2 persons) **Facilities:** 🏪 ⊙ 🚿 🛒 🏧 🅿 **Services:** lau
Off-site: 🛒 🛒 ✗ ∅ ⇗PR 🖃

MESSERY HAUTE-SAVOIE

Relais du Léman 74140 ☎ 450947111 🗏 450947766
e-mail: info@relaisduleman.com
website: www.relaisduleman.com
Well equipped site in a wooded location on the shore of Lac Léman.
⮕ *1.5km SW via D25.*
Open: Apr-Sep **Site:** 3.5HEC ⚑ ♦ 🏕 🚐 **Prices:** ♠5 🚗5
🚐5 **Facilities:** 🏪 ⊙ 🚿 ∅ 🏧 **Services:** ⛽ ✗ lau **Leisure:** ⇗ P
Off-site: 🛒 ⇗LP 🖃

MEYRIEU-LES-ÉTANGS ISÈRE

Moulin 38440 ☎ 474593034 🗏 474583612
e-mail: basedeloisirs.du.moulin@wanadoo.fr
In a quiet, rural setting with good recreational facilities.
⮕ *On D552 between Vienne and Bourgoin-Jallieu.*
Open: 15 Apr-Sep **Site:** 1.5HEC ⚑ ♦ 🏕 **Prices:** pitch 12-30 (incl 2 persons) **Facilities:** 🏪 🛒 ⊙ 🚿 🏧 **Services:** ⛽ ✗ 🖃
lau **Leisure:** ⇗ L **Off-site:** ✗

MIRIBEL-LES-ÉCHELLES ISÈRE

Bourdons 950 chemin de la foiet, 38380
☎ 476552853 🗏 476552582
e-mail: balcondechartreuse@wanadoo.fr
website: www.camping-balcondechartreuse.com
A peaceful site in the heart of the Parc Régional de Chartreuse, with fine views of the surrounding mountains.
⮕ *400m from village centre.*
Open: All year **Site:** 2.5HEC ⚑ 🕀 🏕 🚐 **Prices:** pitch 12.50 (incl 2 persons) **Facilities:** 🏪 ⊙ 🚿 🛒 🏧 **Services:** ⛽ ✗ lau
Leisure: ⇗ P **Off-site:** 🛒 🖃

MONTMAUR HAUTES-ALPES

Mon Repos 5400 ☎ 592580314
Generally well-kept site on wooded terrain with shaded pitches.
⮕ *1km E on D937 and D994.*
Open: May-Oct **Site:** 7HEC ⚑ ♦ 🏕 🚐 **Prices:** pitch 10 (incl 2 persons) pp3 **Facilities:** 🏪 🛒 ⊙ 🚿 ∅ 🏧 **Services:** ⛽ 🖃
lau **Leisure:** ⇗ LR **Off-site:** ✗

Site: 6HEC-Site size ⚑-grass ∴∴-sand ♦-stone 🌿-little shade 🕀-partly shaded ♠-mainly shaded
🏕-bungalows for hire 🚐-caravans for hire ⛺-tents for hire 🚫-no dogs **Prices:** ♠-adult per night 🚗-car per night
pp-per person per night 🚐-caravan per night ⛺-tent per night

MONTREVEL-EN-BRESSE AIN

Plaine Tonique Base de Plein Air, 01340
☎ 474308052 ▊ 474308077
e-mail: plaine.tonique@wanadoo.fr
website: www.laplainetonique.com
A well equipped site divided into a series of self contained
sections beside the lake. Entrance closed between 22.00 &
07.00 hrs. Booking advisable in July and August.
➲ *0.5km E on D28.*
Open: 19 Apr-26 Sep Site: 17HEC ▦ ♣ ⊞ Facilities: ♠ ⅏
⊙ 🖪 ∅ ⚱ 🏕 Services: ⵼ ✗ ⊞ lau Leisure: ⌇ LP Off-site: ⌇R

MOUCHARD JURA

Halte Jurassienne Bel Air, 39330 ☎ 384378392
Camping Card Compulsory.
➲ *NE, near the service station.*
Open: 25 Mar-Oct Site: 0.8HEC ▦ ⅑ ⊙ 🖪 ∅
⚱ 🏕 Services: ⊞ lau Off-site: ⅏ ⵼ ✗

MURS-ET-GELIGNIEUX AIN

Ile de la Comtesse rte des Abrets, 1300
☎ 479872333 ▊ 479872333
e-mail: camping.comtesse@wanadoo.fr
website: www.ile-de-la-comtesse.com
Situated right next to Lake Cuchet(part of the Rhone), with
direct access to the water. In a stunning natural setting
beneath the Alps.
➲ *From A43 Lyon to Chambery exit 10, take D592 to La
Bruyere and site is off route to Belley.*
Open: 26 Apr-5 Sep Site: 3HEC ▦ ⅑ ⊞ Prices: pitch 18-
22 (incl 2 persons) Facilities: ♠ ⅏ ⊙ 🖪 ∅ ⚱ 🏕 Services: ⵼
✗ lau Leisure: ⌇ PR Off-site: ⌇L

NEYDENS HAUTE-SAVOIE

Colombière 74160 ☎ 450351314 ▊ 450351340
e-mail: la.colombiere@wanadoo.fr
website: camping-la-colombiere.com
A pleasant, friendly site with good recreational facilities.
➲ *Access via A40.*
Open: Apr-Sep Site: 2.2HEC ▦ ⅑ ⊞ Facilities: ♠ ⅏ ⊙
🖪 ∅ ⚱ 🏕 Services: ⵼ ✗ lau Leisure: ⌇ P Off-site: ⅏ ⌇R

NOVALAISE SAVOIE

Charmilles Lac d'Aiguebelette, 73470
☎ 479360467 ▊ 479360467
e-mail: camping.les.charmilles@wanadoo.fr
website: www.marmotte.fr/charmilles
A terraced site in a beautiful mountain setting, 150m from
the lake.
➲ *On W shore of the lake on D941 towards St-Alban-de-
Montbel.*
Open: Jul-Aug Site: 2.3HEC ▦ ⋯ ⅑ Facilities: ♠ ⅏ ⊙ 🖪
∅ 🏕 Services: ⊞ lau Off-site: ⵼ ✗ ⌇L

ORNANS DOUBS

Chanet 9 chemin de Chanet, 25290
☎ 381622344 ▊ 381621397
e-mail: contact@lechanet.com
website: www.lechanet.com
Comfortable site with good facilities in the peaceful Loue
Valley.
➲ *1.5km SW on D241. Follow green signs.*
Open: Mar-Oct Site: 2.2HEC ▦ ⅑ ⊞ 🖾 A Facilities: ♠ ⅏
⊙ 🖪 ∅ 🏕 Services: ⵼ ✗ ⊞ lau Leisure: ⌇ P Off-site: ⚱ ⌇R

ORPIERRE HAUTES-ALPES

Princes d'Orange 05700 ☎ 492662253 ▊ 492663108
e-mail: campingorpierre@wanadoo.fr
website: www.campingorpierre.com
The site lies on a meadow with terraces.
➲ *Exit N75 at Eyguians and take D30.*
Open: Apr-28 Oct Site: 20HEC ▦ ⅑ ♣ ⊞ A Prices: pitch
19 (incl 3 persons) Facilities: ♠ ⊙ 🖪 ⚱ 🏕 Services: ⵼ ✗ ⊞
lau Leisure: ⌇ P Off-site: ⅏ ∅ ⌇R

OUNANS JURA

Plage Blanche 3 r de la Plage, 39380
☎ 384376963 ▊ 384376021
e-mail: reservation@la-plage-blanche.com
website: www.la-plage-blanche.com
In a pleasant location beside the River Loue with good
recreational facilities.
➲ *1.5km S via D71 (rte de Montbarcy).*
Open: Apr-Sep Site: 5HEC ▦ ⅑ ⊞ 🖾 A Prices: ⋔4.70
pitch 5.90 Facilities: ♠ ⊙ 🖪 🏕 Services: ⵼ ✗ lau Leisure: ⌇
PR Off-site: ⅏ ∅

PARCEY JURA

Bords de Loue Chemin du Val d'Amour, 39100
☎ 384710382 ▊ 384710342
e-mail: contact@jura-camping.com
website: www.jura-camping.com
A quiet site on the River Loue.
➲ *1.5km from the centre of the village via N5. Signposted.*
Open: 20 Apr-15 Sep Site: 18HEC ▦ ⅑ ⊞ 🖾 A
Facilities: ♠ ⊙ 🖪 ∅ 🏕 Services: ⵼ ✗ ⊞ lau Leisure: ⌇ PR
Off-site: ⅏ ✗

PATORNAY JURA

Moulin 39130 ☎ 384483121 ▊ 384447121
e-mail: feeries@club-internet.fr
website: www.camping-moulin.com
A modern site on a level meadow in a peaceful, wooded
location on the banks of the River Ain.
➲ *Access is NE via N78, rte de Clairvaux-les-Lacs.*
Open: 31May-14 Sep Site: 5HEC ▦ ♣ ⊞ A Prices: ⋔3
Facilities: ♠ ⅏ ⊙ 🖪 ∅ ⚱ 🏕 Services: ⵼ ✗ lau Leisure: ⌇ PR
Off-site: ✗ ⌇L ⊞

PLAGNE-MONTCHAVIN SAVOIE

Montchavin les Coches 73210 ☎ 479078323 ▊ 479078018
e-mail: montchavin@wanadoo.fr
website: www.montchavin-lescoches.com
A summer and winter site overlooking the Tarentaise Valley
with good, modern facilities.
Open: 19 Nov-Sep Site: 1.3HEC ▦ ♣ Prices: pitch 11.30
(incl 2 persons) Facilities: ♠ ⊙ 🖪 ⚱ 🏕 Services: ⊞ lau
Off-site: ⅏ ⵼ ✗ ∅ ⌇P

PONTARLIER DOUBS

Larmont r du Toulombief, 25300 ☎ 381462333
A mountain site with good facilities in an area associated
with winter sports.
Open: All year Site: ▦ ⅑ ⋇ ⊞ 🖾 Facilities: ♠ ⅏ ⊙ 🖪 ∅
⚱ 🏕 Services: ⵼ ✗ ⊞ lau Off-site: ✗ ⌇R

PONT-DE-VAUX AIN

Peupliers Port de Fleurville, 01190
☎ 385303365 ▊ 385303365
e-mail: camplier@worldonline.fr
website: www.perso.worldonline.fr
A family site beside the River Saône with good facilities.

contd.

Facilities: ⅏-shop ♠-shower ⊙-electric points for razors 🖪-electric points for caravans 🏕-parking by tents permitted
🖾-compulsory separate car park Services: ✗-café/restaurant ⵼-bar ∅-Camping Gaz International ⚱-gas other than Camping
Gaz ⊞-first aid facilities lau-laundry Leisure: ⌇-swimming L-Lake P-Pool R-River S-Sea Off-site: All facilities within 2km

⮩ *3km from Pont-de-Vaux via N6.*
Open: Apr-Sep Site: 7HEC ⬛ ⊕ ⬛ ⬛ ⬛ Prices: ⭡3.50-
4.50 ⬛2.50 ⬛25 ⬛3.50-4.50 Facilities: ⬛ ⊙ ⬛ ⬛ ⬛
Services: ⬛ ✗ ⊞ lau Leisure: ⬛ PR

PORT-SUR-SAÔNE HAUTE-SAÔNE

CM Maladière 70170 ⬛ 384915132 ⬛ 384781809
A quiet, comfortable site with modern facilities, close to the
River Saône.
⮩ *S on the D6, between the River Saône and the Canal*
Open: 15 May-15 Sep Site: 2HEC ⬛ ⬛ Facilities: ⬛ ⊙ ⬛
⬛ Services: ⊞ lau Off-site: ⬛ ⬛ ✗ ⬛ ⬛ ⬛PR

PRESLE SAVOIE

Combe Léat 73110 ⬛ 479255402
A quiet mountain site.
⮩ *Access via A43 and D207.*
Open: 15 Jun-5 Sep Site: 4HEC ⬛ ⬛ ⬛ Prices: ⭡2.50
⬛2.50 pitch 2.50 Facilities: ⬛ ⊙ ⬛ ⬛ Services: ⊞ lau

RENAGE ISÈRE

Verdon 185 av de la Piscine, 38140 ⬛ 476914802
⮩ *5km N of Tullins on D45.*
Open: Apr-15 Oct Site: 1.5HEC ⬛ ⬛ Facilities: ⬛ ⊙ ⬛ ⬛
⬛ Services: ⊞ lau Off-site: ⬛ ⬛ ✗ ⬛ ⬛PR

ROCHETTE, LA SAVOIE

Lac St-Clair 73110 ⬛ 479257355
At the foot of the Belledonne mountains, 1km from a lake
with good fishing.
⮩ *Access via D925B Grenoble-Albertville.*
Open: Jun-Aug Site: 3HEC ⬛ ⬛ ⬛ ⬛ Facilities: ⬛ ⊙ ⬛
⬛ Services: ⊞ lau Off-site: ⬛ ⬛ ✗ ⬛ ⬛ ⬛P

ROSIÈRE-DE-MONTVALEZAN, LA SAVOIE

Forêt 73700 ⬛ 79068621 ⬛ 79401625
e-mail: campinglaforet@free.fr
website: www.campinglaforet.free.fr
A peaceful site in pleasant wooded surroundings, with good,
modern facilities.
⮩ *2km S via N90 towards Bourg-St-Maurice.*
Open: 10 Jun-15 Sep & 15 Dec-1 May Site: 2.7HEC ⬛ ⬛
⬛ ⬛ ⬛ Facilities: ⬛ ⊙ ⬛ ⬛ Services: ⬛ ✗ ⊞ lau
Leisure: ⬛ P Off-site: ⬛ ✗ ⬛ ⬛R

ROUGEMONT DOUBS

⬛**Val de Bonnal** Bonnal, 25680 ⬛ 381869087 ⬛ 381860392
e-mail: val-de-bonnal@wanadoo.fr
Quiet woodland site beside the River Ognon. Supervised
swimming in lake with beach.
Open: 8 May-5 Sep Site: 15HEC ⬛ ⬛ ⬛ ⬛
Prices: ⬛3.50 pitch 8 Facilities: ⬛ ⬛ ⊙ ⬛ ⬛ ⬛ Services: ⬛
✗ ⊞ lau Leisure: ⬛ LPR

ST-AVRE SAVOIE

Bois Joli St Martin-sur-la-Chambre, 73130
⬛ 479562128 ⬛ 479562995
e-mail: camping-le-bois-joli@wanadoo.fr
Well kept site with pitches and individual washing cabins.
⮩ *1km N of St-Avre, off N6-E70 via La Chambre.*
Open: Apr-15 Sep Site: 4HEC ⬛ ⬛ ⬛ ⬛ Facilities: ⬛ ⊙
⬛ ⬛ Services: ⬛ ✗ ⊞ lau Leisure: ⬛ P Off-site: ⬛

ST-CLAIR-DU-RHÔNE ISÈRE

Daxia rte du Péage, 38370 ⬛ 474563920 ⬛ 474569346
A riverside site with good sanitary and recreational facilities.

⮩ *Access via N7/A7.*
Open: Apr-Sep Site: 7.5HEC ⬛ ⬛ ⬛ ⬛ Facilities: ⬛ ⊙ ⬛
⬛ Services: ✗ lau Leisure: ⬛ PR

ST-CLAUDE JURA

Martinet 39200 ⬛ 384450040
In a wooded location close to the Centre Nautique.
⮩ *2km SE, beside the river*
Open: May-Sep Site: 3HEC ⬛ ⬛ Facilities: ⬛ ⬛ ⊙ ⬛ ⬛
Services: ⬛ ✗ lau Leisure: ⬛ R Off-site: ⬛ ⬛P

ST-DISDILLE HAUTE-SAVOIE

St-Disdille av de St-Disdille, 74207
⬛ 450711411 ⬛ 450719367
e-mail: camping@disdille.com
website: www.disdille.com
In a peaceful, wooded location in the heart of the Chablais
region.
⮩ *N of N5. Signposted.*
Open: Apr-Sep Site: 12HEC ⬛ ⬛ ⬛ Prices: pitch 13 (incl
2 persons) Facilities: ⬛ ⬛ ⊙ ⬛ ⬛ ⬛ Services: ⬛ ✗ lau
Off-site: ⬛ ⬛LPR

ST-GERVAIS-LES-BAINS HAUTE-SAVOIE

Dômes de Miage 197 rte des Contamines, 74170
⬛ 450934596 ⬛ 450781075
e-mail: camping.st-gervais@wanadoo.fr
website: www.camping-mont-blanc.com
On a beautiful wooded plateau with fine views of the
surrounding mountains.
⮩ *2km S on D902.*
Open: Jun-15 Sep Site: 2.5HEC ⬛ ⬛ Prices: pitch 14-19
(incl 2 persons) Facilities: ⬛ ⬛ ⊙ ⬛ ⬛ ⬛ Services: ⬛ ✗ ⊞
lau Off-site: ⬛ ⬛P

ST-INNOCENT-BRISON SAVOIE

Rolande 24 chemin des Berthets, 73100 ⬛ 479543685
Situated on gently sloping terrain.
⮩ *Signposted from village centre.*
Open: May-Sep Site: 1.5HEC ⬛ ⬛ Facilities: ⬛ ⬛ ⊙ ⬛ ⬛
⬛ Services: ✗ ⊞ lau Off-site: ⬛L

ST-JEAN-DE-COUZ SAVOIE

International la Bruyère 73160 ⬛ 479657911 ⬛ 479657427
e-mail: bearob@libertysurf.fr
website: www.camping-labruyere.com
In wooded surroundings close to the Grande Chartreuse
range with a variety of sporting facilities.
⮩ *2km S via N6, towards Côte-Barrier*
Open: 15 Apr-15 Oct Site: 1HEC ⬛ ⬛ ⬛ Prices: ⭡2.80
pitch 2.70 Facilities: ⬛ ⬛ ⊙ ⬛ ⬛ ⬛ ⬛ Services: ⬛ ✗ ⊞ lau
Off-site: ⬛R

ST-JEAN-ST-NICOLAS HAUTES-ALPES

CM le Châtelard Pont-du-Fossé, 5260 ⬛ 492559431
Open: 15 Jun-15 Sep Site: 4HEC ⬛ ⬛ Prices: ⭡3.15 ⬛4.30
⬛3.50 Facilities: ⬛ ⊙ ⬛ ⬛ Services: ⊞ lau Leisure: ⬛ R
Off-site: ⬛ ⬛ ✗ ⬛ ⬛LP

ST-JORIOZ HAUTE-SAVOIE

Europa 1444 rte d'Albertville, 74410
⬛ 0033 450685101 ⬛ 450685520
e-mail: info@camping-europa.com
website: www.camping-europa.com
Well equipped site in picturesque surroundings close to Lake
Annecy.

Site: 6HEC-Site size ⬛-grass ⬛-sand ⬛-stone ⬛-little shade ⬛-partly shaded ⬛-mainly shaded
⬛-bungalows for hire ⬛-caravans for hire ⬛-tents for hire ⬛-no dogs **Prices:** ⭡-adult per night ⬛-car per night
pp-per person per night ⬛-caravan per night ⬛-tent per night

⊃ *1.4km SE*
Open: 7 May-15 Sep Site: 3.7HEC ⬛ 🐟 🏕 � Prices: pitch 14.20-22.80 (incl 2 persons) Facilities: 🆘 🛒 ⊙ 🔌 🅿 Services: 🍴 ✗ lau Leisure: ⭐ P Off-site: 🛁 ⌀ 🔥 ⭐L ⊞

International du Lac d'Annecy 74410
☎ 450686793 🗏 0450090122
website: www.campannecy.com
⊃ *N508 towards Albertville.*
Open: 20 May-20 Sep Site: 2.5HEC ⬛ 🌲 🏕 Prices: pitch 14.50-17.50 (incl 2 persons) pp3.40-3.60 Facilities: 🆘 ⊙ 🔌 🅿 Services: 🍴 ✗ ⊞ lau Leisure: ⭐ P Off-site: 🛒 ⌀ ⭐L

Belvédère de l'Obiou rte Napoléon, Lieu-dit les Egats, 38350
☎ 476304080 🗏 476304080
e-mail: info@camping-obiou.com
website: www.camping-obiou.com
Terraced meadow site at the foot of mountains with hedge surrounds.
⊃ *1m from Ortsteil Les Egats, on the N85, signed.*
Open: Apr-15 Oct Site: 1HEC ⬛ 🐟 🏕 � Prices: pitch 13.30-15.30 Facilities: 🆘 ⊙ 🔌 ⌀ 🔥 🅿 Services: ✗ ⊞ lau Leisure: ⭐ P Off-site: 🍴 ⊞

Martinière rte du Col de Porte, 38380
☎ 476886036 🗏 476886910
e-mail: brice.gaude@wanadoo.fr
website: www.campingdemartiniere.com
In pleasant position surrounded by the Chartreuse mountains and close to the famous monastery.
⊃ *2km SW off D512.*
Site: 2.5HEC ⬛ 🐟 🏕 Facilities: 🆘 🛒 ⊙ 🔌 ⌀ 🔥 🅿 Services: 🍴 ✗ ⊞ lau Leisure: ⭐ P Off-site: ✗

Champ-Long 38350 ☎ 476304181 🗏 476304721
e-mail: champ.long@tiscali.fr
In a beautiful Alpine setting at the entrance to the Ecrins Park at an altitude of 700mtrs.
⊃ *1.5km NW off N85.*
Open: Apr-Oct Site: 5HEC ⬛ 🐟 🏕 🧍 Prices: pitch 12.80-14.50 Facilities: 🆘 🛒 ⊙ 🔌 🅿 🏕 🅿 Services: 🍴 ✗ lau Leisure: ⭐ P Off-site: ⭐LR

Reclus rte de Tignes, 73700 ☎ 479410105 🗏 479410479
e-mail: campinglereclus@wanadoo.fr
website: www.campingsavoie.com
In a pleasant wooded location within easy reach of the ski slopes.
⊃ *NW on N90.*
Open: Dec-Oct Site: 1.8HEC ⬛ 🌲 � Facilities: 🆘 ⊙ 🔌 🅿 Services: ⊞ lau Leisure: ⭐ R Off-site: 🛒 🍴 ✗ ⌀ ⭐P

Barillons 05700 ☎ 492671735
Well-laid out with terraces.
⊃ *1km SE on N75.*
Open: End May- Mid Sep Site: 3HEC ⬛ 🌲 � Prices: pitch 12.50 (incl 2 persons) Facilities: 🆘 ⊙ 🔌 ⌀ 🅿 Services: 🍴 ✗ ⊞ lau Off-site: 🛒 ⭐LR

Domaine des 2 Soleils 05700 ☎ 492670133 🗏 492670802
e-mail: dom.2.soleils@wanadoo.fr
website: perso.wanadoo.fr/2soleils
Well-kept terraced site in Buéch Valley.

⊃ *S of town off N75. Signposted.*
Open: May-Sep Site: 12HEC ⬛ 🐟 🐟 🏕 � Prices: pitch 16.90-20.60 (incl 2 persons) Facilities: 🆘 🛒 ⊙ 🔌 ⌀ 🅿 Services: 🍴 ✗ ⊞ lau Leisure: ⭐ P Off-site: ⭐LR

International de Seyssel chemin de la Barotte, 01420
☎ 450592847 🗏 450592847
e-mail: camp.inter@wanadoo.fr
A quiet site on steep, terraced meadowland, with individual washbasins and clean sanitary installations.
⊃ *1km SW off Culoz road.*
Open: 15 Jun-15 Sep Site: 1.5HEC ⬛ 🌲 🏕 Facilities: 🆘 ⊙ 🔌 ⌀ 🔥 🅿 Services: 🍴 ✗ ⊞ lau Leisure: ⭐ P Off-site: 🛒 ⭐LR

Lanfonnet Angon, 74290
☎ 450607212 🗏 45060712/450233882
e-mail: camping.le.lanfonnet@wanadoo.fr
website: www.epernet-lanfonnet.com
A well equipped site 100mtrs from the lake.
⊃ *1.5km SE.*
Open: May-Sep Site: 2.5HEC ⬛ 🌲 � Prices: pitch 22.20 (incl 2 persons) Facilities: 🆘 🛒 ⊙ 🔌 ⌀ 🅿 Services: 🍴 ✗ ⊞ lau Leisure: ⭐ L

CM 01140 ☎ 474040425
e-mail: mairie.thoissey@wanadoo.fr
Situated between two rivers, the Saône and the Chalaronne.
⊃ *1km SW on D7.*
Open: 20 Apr-20 Sep Site: 15HEC ⬛ 🐟 � Facilities: 🆘 ⊙ 🔌 🅿 Services: 🍴 ✗ ⊞ lau Leisure: ⭐ PR Off-site: 🛒 ⌀ 🔥

Morcy 74200 ☎ 450704487 🗏 450704487
In a quiet location close to Lac Léman and the thermal spa.
⊃ *2.5km W of town.*
Open: 15 Apr-15 Sep Site: 1.2HEC ⬛ 🌲 🏕 �caravan Facilities: 🆘 🛒 ⊙ 🔌 ⌀ 🅿 Services: 🍴 ✗ ⊞ lau Off-site: ✗ 🔥 ⭐LR

Europeen dea Breviferes rte des Boisses, 73320
☎ 0479063032
e-mail: diane.taxi@wanadoo.fr
A well equipped site 1km from the centre of the village.
⊃ *Signposted from D902.*
Open: 15 Jun-29Sep Site: 4.5HEC ⬛ 🐟 Prices: 🧍3.20 �caravan1.60 �caravan2.20 🧍2.20 pitch 2.20 Facilities: 🆘 🛒 ⊙ 🔌 ⌀ 🅿 Services: ⊞ lau Off-site: 🍴 ✗ ⭐LPR

3 Lac La Plaine, 38460 ☎ 474929206 🗏 474929335
e-mail: leslacs@free.fr
website: www.camping-les-3-lacs.com
Situated at the gateway to the Alps, an undulating woody area with small lakes.
⊃ *On D517, 2.5km w.*
Open: May-10 Sep Site: 4HEC ⬛ 🐟 🏕 Facilities: 🆘 🛒 ⊙ 🔌 🅿 Services: 🍴 ✗ ⊞ lau Leisure: ⭐ LP

Bontemps 38150 ☎ 474578352 🗏 474578370
e-mail: info@campinglebontemps.com
website: www.campinglebontemps.com
A pleasantly landscaped site beside the River Varèze.
⊃ *Access via N7 and D131.*
Open: Apr-Sept Site: 8HEC ⬛ 🌲 🏕 Prices: pitch 6.50 Facilities: 🆘 🛒 ⊙ 🔌 ⌀ 🔥 🅿 Services: 🍴 ✗ ⊞ lau Leisure: ⭐ PR

Facilities: 🛒-shop 🆘-shower ⊙-electric points for razors 🔌-electric points for caravans 🅿-parking by tents permitted 🅿-compulsory separate car park Services: ✗-café/restaurant 🍴-bar ⌀-Camping Gaz International 🔥-gas other than Camping Gaz ⊞-first aid facilities lau-laundry Leisure: ⭐-swimming L-Lake P-Pool R-River S-Sea Off-site: All facilities within 2km

VILLARD-DE-LANS ISERE

L'Oursière 38250 ☎ 04 476951477 🖹 476955811
e-mail: info@camping-oursiere.fr
website: www.camping-oursiere.fr
Peaceful site in the natural park region of Vercors. Summer
and winter facilities.
➲ *N off D531 in direction of Grenoble.*
Open: Dec-Sep **Site:** 4.2HEC ⊞ ♠ ⊙ ⚑ 🚐 **Prices:** pitch
12.24-13.24 (incl 2 persons) **Facilities:** 🏠 🍴 ⊙ ⚑ ⊘ 🍴 🏕
Services: 🍴 ✗ 🗔 lau **Off-site:** ⚡PR

VILLARS-LES-DOMBES AIN

CM Autières 164 av des Nations, 01330 ☎ 474980021
e-mail: campingdesautieres@wanadoo.fr
Clean and tidy park-like site divided into plots and pitches.
Part reserved for overnight campers. Clean, modern sanitary
installations.
➲ *SW off N83.*
Open: 29 Mar-21 Sep **Site:** 4.5HEC ⊞ ♠ 🚐 **Facilities:** 🏠 ⊙
⚑ 🏕 **Services:** 🍴 ✗ lau **Leisure:** ⚡ PR **Off-site:** 🛒 ⊘ 🍴 🗔

VOIRON ISERE

Porte de la Chartreuse 33 ave du 8 Mai 45, 38500
☎ 476051420
On level terrain with some trees, divided into pitches. Much
traffic noise from nearby N75. Clean and modern sanitary
installations.
➲ *Access is NW of town next to the Esso garage.*
Open: All year **Site:** 1.5HEC ⊞ ♠ ⊙ ⚑ **Facilities:** 🏠 ⊙ ⚑
🏕 **Services:** 🍴 ✗ 🗔 **Off-site:** 🛒 ⊘ 🍴 ⚡P

ALSACE/LORRAINE

ANOULD VOSGES

Acacias 88650 ☎ 329571106 🖹 329571106
e-mail: contact@occaciascamp.com
website: www.occaciascamp.com
In pleasant surroundings with well defined pitches in the
heart of the Hautes-Vosges region.
➲ *NE of town centre towards the ski slopes.*
Open: Dec-10 Oct **Site:** 2.5HEC ♠ 🚐 **Prices:** ⚡3.50
🚗1.80 🚐1.80 🏕1.80 pitch 1.80 **Facilities:** 🏠 🍴 ⊙ ⚑ ⊘ 🍴 🏕
Services: 🍴 ✗ 🗔 lau **Leisure:** ⚡ P **Off-site:** 🛒 ⚡R

AUBURE HAUT-RHIN

CM La Ménère 68150 ☎ 389739299
e-mail: aubure@cc-ribeauville.fr
A peaceful site at an altitude of 800mtrs.
➲ *Access via N415 or D416, then D11.*
Open: 15 May-Sep **Site:** 1.8HEC ⊞ ∷ ⚑ 🚐 **Prices:** ⚡3.50
pitch 3 **Facilities:** 🏠 ⊙ ⚑ 🏕 **Services:** 🗔 lau **Off-site:** 🛒 ⚡ ✗

BAERENTHAL MOSELLE

Ramstein Plage Base de Baerenthal, Ramstein Plage, 57230
☎ 387065073 🖹 387066231
The River Zinsel runs through this rural wooded site close to
the border with Germany.
➲ *W via r du Ramstein.*
Open: Apr-Sep **Site:** 14HEC ⊞ ∷ ♠ 🚐 **Facilities:** 🏠 ⊙
⚑ 🏕 **Services:** 🍴 ✗ 🗔 lau **Leisure:** ⚡ LP **Off-site:** 🛒 ✗ ⊘ ⚡R

BIESHEIM HAUT-RHIN

Ile du Rhin Zone Touristique, 68600
☎ 389725795 🖹 389721421
e-mail: camping@shn.fr
On the Ile du Rhin, between the Canal d'Alsace and the River
Rhine in pleasant wooded surroundings.

➲ *From Colmar take N415 towards Germany as far as the
Rhine bridge.*
Site: 3HEC ⊞ ⚑ 🚐 **Prices:** pitch 12.51 (incl 2 persons)
pp3.83 **Facilities:** 🏠 🍴 ⊙ ⚑ 🏕 **Services:** ✗ 🗔 lau
Off-site: 🍴 ✗ ⚡PR

BRESSE, LA VOSGES

Belle Hutte Belle Hutte, 88250 ☎ 329254975 🖹 329255263
e-mail: camping-belle-hutte@wanadoo.fr
website: www.camping-belle-hutte.com
Terraced site beside the River Moselotte.
➲ *Access via D34 towards Col de la Schlucht.*
Open: All year **Site:** 3.2HEC ⊞ ⚑ 🚐 **Prices:** ⚡2.20-4.40
🚗1.30-1.70 🚐1.40-2.30 🏕1.30-2.10 **Facilities:** 🏠 🛒 ⊙ ⚑ ⊘
🍴 🏕 **Services:** lau **Leisure:** ⚡ PR **Off-site:** 🍴 ✗ ⚡L 🗔

BURNHAUPT-LE-HAUT HAUT-RHIN

Le Castor 4 rte de Guewenheim, 68520
☎ 389487858 🖹 389627466
e-mail: camping.les.castors@wanadoo.fr
A modern site in a rural setting close to a river and
surrounded by woodland.
➲ *E of Burnhaupt towards Guewenheim on D466.*
Open: 15 Feb-Dec **Site:** 2.5HEC ⊞ ♠ 🚐 **Prices:** ⚡3.40
🚐3.80 🚐3.80 pitch 3.80 **Facilities:** 🏠 ⊙ ⚑ 🏕 **Services:** 🍴 ✗
🗔 lau **Leisure:** ⚡ R **Off-site:** 🛒 ⊘ 🍴

BUSSANG VOSGES

Domaine de Champé 14 Les Champs Navés, 88540
☎ 329858645 🖹 329615690
e-mail: camping@bussang.com
website: www.bussang.com/camping
In pleasant surroundings beside the River Moselle.
➲ *On N57.*
Open: Apr-Oct **Site:** 1.5HEC ⊞ ✼ **Facilities:** 🏠 ⊙ ⚑ 🏕
Services: 🗔 lau **Off-site:** 🛒 🍴 ✗ ⊘ 🍴 ⚡L

CELLES-SUR-PLAINE VOSGES

Lac Base de Loisirs, Les Lacs de Pierre-Percée, 88110
☎ 329412800 🖹 329411869
e-mail: camping@sma-lacs-pierre-percee.fr
website: www.sma-lacs-pierre-percee.fr
Set among wooded hills in an extensive natural leisure area
around the Lakes of Pierre-Percée.
➲ *Access via D392A.*
Open: Apr-Sep **Site:** 3HEC ⊞ ✼ 🚐 **Facilities:** 🏠 🛒 ⊙ ⚑
⊘ 🏕 **Services:** 🍴 ✗ 🗔 lau **Leisure:** ⚡ PR
Off-site: ✗ 🍴 ⚡L

Site: 6HEC-Site size ⊞-grass ∷-sand ♠-stone ✼-little shade ⚑-partly shaded ♠-mainly shaded
🏠-bungalows for hire 🚐-caravans for hire 🏕-tents for hire ⊘-no dogs **Prices:** ⚡-adult per night 🚗-car per night
pp-per person per night 🚐-caravan per night 🏕-tent per night

CERNAY HAUT-RHIN

CM Acacias 16 rue Réne Guibert, 68700
☎ 389755697 ▤ 389397229
e-mail: lesacacias.cernay@ffcc.fr
Clean, quiet site on right bank of the River Thur.
➲ *Off N83 between Colmar and Belfort.*
Open: Apr-10 Oct Site: 4HEC ⬛⬛⬛ ♠ Prices: ⚑3.40 pitch
3.90 Facilities: ⚫ ⅒ ⊙ ⬛ ∅ 🅿 Services: lau Off-site: ⚡P ⊞

COLMAR HAUT-RHIN

Intercommunal de l'Ill 68180 ☎ 389411594 ▤ 389411594
website: www.camping.alseli.com
On a meadow beside the river with good, modern facilities.
Separate sections for campers in transit.
➲ *2km E on N415.*
Open: Mar-Dec Site: 2.2HEC ⬛⬛⬛ ⑭ Facilities: ⚫ ⅒ ⊙ ⬛ ∅
🅿 Services: ⚑ ✗ ⊞ lau Leisure: ⚡ R

CORCIEUX VOSGES

🏕*Domaine des Bains* r J-Wiese, 88430
☎ 329516467 ▤ 0329516465
e-mail: les-bans@domaine-des-bans.com
website: www.domaine-des-bans.com
On meadowland divided into pitches with a variety of
recreational facilities.
➲ *E of village off D8.*
Open: All year Site: 30HEC ⬛⬛⬛ ⑭ 🚐 🅿 Facilities: ⚫ ⅒ ⊙
⬛ ∅ ≞ 🅿 Services: ⚑ ✗ ⊞ lau Leisure: ⚡ LP Off-site: ✗

DABO MOSELLE

Rocher CD 45, 57850 ☎ 387074751 ▤ 387074773
e-mail: info@ot-dabo.fr
website: www.ot-dabo.fr
In a beautiful position close to the historic town of Dabo in
the Vosges mountains.
➲ *1.5km SW via D45.*
Open: 9 Apr-Oct Site: 0.5HEC ⬛⬛⬛ ⑭ 🚐 Prices: ⚑2.50 ⊞1
⊞2.30 ⚑1.50 Facilities: ⚫ ⊙ ⬛ 🅿 Off-site: ⅒ ⚑ ✗ ∅ ≞ ⊞

DAMBACH-LA-VILLE BAS-RHIN

CM rte d'Ebersheim, 67650 ☎ 388924860
e-mail: otdambach-la-ville@tourisme-alsace.info
website: www.pays-de-barr.com/dambach-la-ville
In a wooded location close to the town centre. Advance
booking recommended during July and August.
➲ *1km E via D120.*
Open: Jun-end Sep Site: 1.8HEC ⬛⬛⬛ ♠ Prices: ⚑2.50
⊞1.60 ⊞2 ⚑1.60 Facilities: ⚫ ⊙ ⬛ 🅿 Services: lau
Off-site: ⅒ ⚑ ✗ ∅ ≞ ⊞

EGUISHEIM HAUT-RHIN

CM Aux Trois Châteaux 10 r du Bassin, 68420
☎ 389231939 ▤ 389241019
In a peaceful location at an altitude of 210mtrs and
surrounded by vineyards.
➲ *6km S of Colmar on N83.*
Open: Apr-Sep Site: 1.8HEC ⬛⬛⬛ ⚭ ⑭ 🚐 Prices: ⚑3.30 pitch
3.50 Facilities: ⚫ ⊙ ⬛ ∅ 🅿 Services: lau Off-site: ⅒ ⚑ ✗ ⊞

FONTENOY-LE-CHÂTEAU VOSGES

Fontenoy rte de la Vierge, 88240
☎ 329363474 ▤ 329363474
e-mail: marliesfontenoy@hotmail.com
website: www.campingfontenoy.com
Set on a hill in peaceful, wooded surroundings.

➲ *2.2km S via D40.*
Open: 15 Apr-Sep Site: 1.2HEC ⬛⬛⬛ ♠ 🚐 Prices: ⚑2.60
⊞2.20 ⊞2.70 ⚑2.70 pitch 2.70 Facilities: ⚫ ⅒ ⊙ ⬛ ∅ 🅿
Services: ⚑ ✗ lau Leisure: ⚡ P Off-site: ≞ ⚡R ⊞

GEMAINGOUTTE VOSGES

CM 'Le Violu' 88520 ☎ 329577070 ▤ 329517260
e-mail: communedegemaingoutte@wanadoo.fr
➲ *W, beside the river, via N59.*
Open: May-Sep Site: 0.9HEC ⬛⬛⬛ ⑭ Facilities: ⚫ ⊙ ⬛ 🅿
Services: ⊞ lau Leisure: ⚡ R Off-site: ⅒ ⚑ ✗

GÉRARDMER VOSGES

Ramberchamp 21 chemin du Tour du Lac, 88400
☎ 329630382
website: www.camping-de-ramberchamp.com/fra.html
On a level meadow on S side of Lac de Gérardmer.
➲ *2km from the village centre via N417 or 486.*
Open: 20 Apr-20 Sep Site: 3.5HEC ⬛⬛⬛ ♠ Prices: pitch
15.25 (incl 2 persons) Facilities: ⚫ ⅒ ⊙ ⬛ ∅ 🅿 Services: ⚑
✗ lau Leisure: ⚡ L

GRANGES-SUR-VOLOGNE VOSGES

Château 2 Les Chappes, 88640 ☎ 329575083
e-mail: camping-du-chateau@wanadoo.fr
A terraced site with good sports facilities 1km from the
village,
Open: 15 Jun-15 Sep Site: 2HEC ⬛⬛⬛ ⑭ 🚐 Prices: ⚑2.90
pitch 3.20 Facilities: ⚫ ⅒ ⊙ ⬛ 🅿 Services: lau Leisure: ⚡ P
Off-site: ⚑ ✗ ⚡R

Gina-Park 88460 ☎ 0329514195 ▤ 0329575952
website: www.ginapark.com
In a pleasant park at the foot of a wooded mountain. Streams
cross the site and there is a lake and facilities for a variety of
sports.
➲ *1km SE of town centre.*
Open: All year Site: 4.5HEC ⬛⬛⬛ ♠ 🚐 🚐 Prices: ⚑2.90 pitch
3.05 Facilities: ⚫ ⅒ ⊙ ⬛ ∅ 🅿 Services: ⚑ ✗ lau
Leisure: ⚡ PR Off-site: ✗ ⚡L ⊞

HARSKIRCHEN BAS-RHIN

Étang Zone de Loisirs, r du Canal, 67260
☎ 388009365 ▤ 388009613
➲ *0.8km NW via D23 beside the lake.*
Open: All year Site: 12HEC ⬛⬛⬛ ⑭ Facilities: ⚫ ⊙ ⬛ 🅿
Services: ⚑ ✗ ⊞ lau Off-site: ⅒ ✗ ∅ ≞

HEIMSBRUNN HAUT-RHIN

Chaumière 62 r de la Galfingue, 68990
☎ 389819343 ▤ 389819343
e-mail: infos@camping-lachaumiere.com
website: www.camping-lachaumiere.com
In a pleasant wooded location with good, modern facilities.
➲ *Signposted from village centre.*
Open: All year Site: 1HEC ⬛⬛⬛ ∴ ♠ 🚐 Facilities: ⚫ ⅒ ⊙
⬛ ∅ 🅿 Services: ⊞ Leisure: ⚡ P Off-site: ⅒ ⚑ ✗ ⚡R

HOHWALD, LE BAS-RHIN

CM 67140 ☎ 388083090 ▤ 388083090
A well equipped terraced site in beautiful wooded
surroundings.
➲ *W via D425.*
Open: All year Site: 2HEC ⬛⬛⬛ ⑭ Facilities: ⚫ ⊙ ⬛ 🅿
Services: lau Off-site: ⅒ ⚑ ✗ ∅ ≞ ⊞

Facilities: ⅒-shop ⚫-shower ⊙-electric points for razors ⬛-electric points for caravans 🅿-parking by tents permitted
⬛-compulsory separate car park Services: ✗-café/restaurant ⚑-bar ∅-Camping Gaz International ≞-gas other than Camping
Gaz ⊞-first aid facilities lau-laundry Leisure: ⚡-swimming L-Lake P-Pool R-River S-Sea Off-site: All facilities within 2km

ISSENHEIM HAUT-RHIN

Florival rte de Soultz, 68500 ☎ 389742047 ▦ 389742047
e-mail: contact@camping-leflorival.com
website: www.camping-leflorival.com
Level meadowland site, situated in a Regional Park location
and surrounded by forest.
➲ *Off N83 (Colmar-Mulhouse), exit for Issenheim, site
signed.*
Open: Apr-Oct Site: 3.5HEC ⬛ ⚘ Prices: pitch 12 (incl 2
persons) Facilities: ⬧ ⊙ ⬛ 🏤 Services: lau Off-site: ⬧ ⬧ ✗
⬦ ⛄ ⬧P ⊞

KAYSERSBERG HAUT-RHIN

CM r des Acacias, 68240 ☎ 389471447
Between a sports ground and the River Weiss. Subdivided by
low hedges.
Camping Card Recommended.
➲ *200m from N415. Signposted.*
Open: Apr-Sep Site: 1.5HEC ⬛ ⚘ Facilities: ⬧ ⊙ ⬛ 🏤
Services: ⊞ lau Leisure: ⬧ R Off-site: ⬧ ⬧ ✗ ⬦ ⬧P

KRUTH HAUT-RHIN

Schlossberg r du Bourbach, 68820
☎ 389822676 ▦ 389822017
e-mail: contact@schlossberg.fr website: www.schlossberg.fr
In a quiet location in the heart of the Parc des Ballons with
good, modern facilities.
➲ *2.3km NW via D13b.*
Open: Etr-3 Oct Site: 5.2HEC ⬛ ⚘ ⬛ ⬛ Prices: ⬧3.60
⬧3.40 ⬧3.40 pitch 3.40 Facilities: ⬧ ⬧ ⊙ ⬛ ⬦ 🏤
Services: ⬧ ✗ ⊞ lau Leisure: ⬧ R Off-site: ✗ ⛄ ⬧L

LAUTERBOURG BAS-RHIN

CM des Mouettes chemin des Mouettes, 67630
☎ 388546860 ▦ 388546860
A level site on the shores of a lake.
➲ *Access via D63 from Haguenau.*
Open: 15 Mar-15 Dec Site: 3HEC ⬛ ⛙ ⬦ Facilities: ⬧
⊙ ⬛ 🏤 ⬧ Services: ⬧ ✗ ⊞ lau Leisure: ⬧ L Off-site: ⬧R

LUTTENBACH HAUT-RHIN

Amis de la Nature 4 r du Château, 68140
☎ 389773860 ▦ 389772572
e-mail: camping.an@wanadoo.fr
Situated on a long strip of land, in the heart of Luttenbach
countryside. Site is divided into pitches.
➲ *From Munster follow D10 for 1km.*
Open: All year Site: 7HEC ⬛ ⚘ Prices: ⬧2.45-3.15 ⬧1.30
pitch 1.70-1.70 Facilities: ⬧ ⬧ ⊙ ⬛ 🏤 Services: ⬧ ✗ ⊞ lau
Leisure: ⬧ R Off-site: ⬦ ⛄ ⬧P

MASEVAUX HAUT-RHIN

Camping Municipal de Masevaux 3 r du Stade, 68290
☎ 389824229 ▦ 389824229
In wooded surroundings beside the River Doller.
➲ *Off the main road to Ballon-d'Alsace.*
Open: Easter-Sep Site: 3.5HEC ⬛ ⚘ Prices: ⬧2.55 pitch
2.55 Facilities: ⬧ ⊙ ⬛ 🏤 Services: ⊞ lau Off-site: ⬧ ⬧ ✗ ⬦
⛄ ⬧PR

METZERAL HAUT-RHIN

AT **MITTLACH** (3KM SW)

CM 68380 ☎ 389776377 ▦ 389777436
e-mail: mairiemittlach@wanadoo.fr
website: http://commune-de-mittlach.ifrance.com
Situated in forested area in small village, very quiet.

➲ *From Munster follow signs for Metzeral then Mittlach D10.*
Open: May-Oct Site: 3HEC ⬛ ⚘ Prices: ⬧3.20 ⬧1.10
⬧2.30 ⬧1.40 Facilities: ⬧ ⬧ ⊙ ⬛ ⬦ 🏤 Services: lau
Leisure: ⬧ R

MOOSCH HAUT-RHIN

Mine d'Argent r de la Mine d'Argent, 68690 ☎ 389823066
e-mail: serge.sarribas@free.fr
A well established site in a peaceful wooded setting.
➲ *1.5km SW off N66.*
Open: May-Sep Site: 2.5HEC ⬛ ⚘ ⬛ ⬛ Prices: ⬧3.20
pitch 3.20 Facilities: ⬧ ⊙ ⬛ ⬦ ⛄ 🏤 Services: ⊞ lau
Leisure: ⬧ RS Off-site: ⬧ ⬧ ✗ ⬧R

MULHOUSE HAUT-RHIN

CM Ill av P-de-Coubertin, 68100
☎ 389062066 ▦ 389611834
e-mail: campingdelill@aol.com
website: www.camping-de-lill.com
In park between the canal and the River Ill, a few minutes
walk from the city centre.
➲ *From town centre follow Signs for 'Fribourg & Allemagne'.
At Ile Napoléon follow campsite signposts.*
Open: Apr-Oct Site: 6HEC ⬛ ⚘ ⬛ ⬛ ⬧ Prices: ⬧3.35
⬧3.35 pitch 3.35 Facilities: ⬧ ⬧ ⊙ ⬛ 🏤 Services: ⬧ ✗ ⊞ lau
Off-site: ⬧ ⬧ ✗ ⬧PR

MUNSTER HAUT-RHIN

CM Parc de la Fecht rte de Gunsbach, 68140
☎ 389773108 ▦ 389770455
e-mail: ville.munster@worldonline.fr
Well maintained site close to the town centre within a park-
like area surrounded by high walls and trees.
➲ *Access on D417, 200m after entering Munster town centre,
near the swimming pool.*
Open: Apr-Sep Site: 4HEC ⬛ ⚘ Facilities: ⬧ ⬧ ⊙ ⬛ ⬦ 🏤
Services: ⊞ lau Leisure: ⬧ R Off-site: ⬧ ✗ ⛄ ⬧P

OBERBRONN BAS-RHIN

CM Eichelgarten r de Zinswiller, 67110
☎ 388097196 ▦ 388096512
➲ *Follow signposts W from D28 (Oberbronn-Zinswiller).*
Open: 15 Mar-14 Nov Site: 4HEC ⬛ ⚘ ⬛ ⬛
Prices: ⬧3.13-3.30 ⬧1.50-1.60 ⬧1.99-2.10 pitch 2.09-2.20
Facilities: ⬧ ⬧ ⊙ ⬛ ⬦ 🏤 Services: ⬧ ✗ lau Leisure: ⬧ P
Off-site: ⬧ ✗ ⛄ ⊞

OBERNAI BAS-RHIN

CM rue de Berlin, 67210 ☎ 388953848 ▦ 388483147
e-mail: camping@obernai.fr
website: www.obernai.fr
Partly terraced site, situated in park.
➲ *W on D426 towards Ottrott.*
Open: All year Site: 3HEC ⬛ ⛙ Prices: ⬧3.30 ⬧4.40
pitch 4.40 Facilities: ⬧ ⬧ ⊙ ⬛ ⬦ 🏤 Services: ⊞ lau
Off-site: ⬧ ✗ ⬧P

RIBEAUVILLE HAUT-RHIN

Pierre de Coubertin 23 r de Landau, 68150
☎ 389736671 ▦ 389736671
e-mail: camping.ribeauville@wanadoo.fr
website: www.camping-alsace.com
In a peaceful location. Shop open in summer only.
➲ *Access via D106.*
Open: 15 Mar-14 Nov Site: 3.5HEC ⬛ ⚘ Prices: ⬧3.80
pitch 3.80 Facilities: ⬧ ⬧ ⊙ ⬛ ⬦ 🏤 Services: ⊞ lau
Off-site: ⬧ ✗ ⬧P

Site: 6HEC-Site size ⬛-grass ⁙-sand ⬧-stone ⛙-little shade ⚘-partly shaded ⬧-mainly shaded
⬛-bungalows for hire ⬛-caravans for hire ⬛-tents for hire ⬦-no dogs Prices: ⬧-adult per night ⬧-car per night
pp-per person per night ⬧-caravan per night ⬧-tent per night

RIQUEWIHR HAUT-RHIN

Inter Communal rte des Vins, 68340
☎ 389479008 ▤ 389490563
e-mail: camping.riquewihr@tiscali.fr
Extensive site overlooking vineyards.
⮑ *2km E on D16. Turn W off N83 (Colmar-Strasbourg) at Ostheim.*
Open: Apr-Dec **Site:** 4HEC ▦ ⊕ **Prices:** ⋔3.35-3.70 pitch 3.60-4 **Facilities:** ⋔ ⊾ ⊙ ⊕ ∅ ☎ **Services:** lau **Off-site:** ♀ ✕ ♨ ⊞

ST-MAURICE-SUR-MOSELLE VOSGES

Deux Ballons 17 r du Stade, 88560 ☎ 329251714
e-mail: vero@camping-deux-ballons.fr
website: www.camping-deux-ballons.fr
Well maintained site beside a stream and surrounded by woodland and mountains.
⮑ *1km W on N66.*
Open: 10 Apr-15 Sep **Site:** 4HEC ▦ ⊕ ⊞ **Prices:** pitch 19.80 (incl 2 persons) **Facilities:** ⋔ ⊙ ⊕ ♨ ☎ **Services:** ♀ ✕ ⊞ lau **Leisure:** ⭢ P **Off-site:** ⊾ ✕ ∅ ⭢R

ST-PIERRE BAS-RHIN

Beau Séjour r de l'Église, F.67140
☎ 388085224 ▤ 388085224
e-mail: commune.saintpierre@wanadoo.fr
website: www.pays-de-barr.com/beau-sejour/
Situated midway between Strasbourg and Colmar with good modern facilities.
Open: 15 May-1 Oct **Site:** 0.6HEC ▦ ⊕ **Prices:** pitch 13 (incl 2 persons) **Facilities:** ⋔ ⊙ ⊕ ☎ **Services:** ⊞ lau **Leisure:** ⭢ R **Off-site:** ⊾ ♀ ✕

STE-CROIX-EN-PLAINE HAUT-RHIN

Clair Vacances rte de Herrlisheim, 68127
☎ 389492728 ▤ 389493137
e-mail: clairvacances@wanadoo.fr
website: camping-alsace.com
In a pleasant woodland setting with good facilities for a family holiday.
⮑ *On D1 towards Herrlisheim.*
Open: Etr-17 Oct **Site:** 3.5HEC ▦ ⊕ ⊞ ⊗ **Prices:** ⊕12-16 **Facilities:** ⋔ ⊙ ⊕ ∅ ☎ **Services:** ⊞ lau **Leisure:** ⭢ P **Off-site:** ⊾ ♀ ✕

SAVERNE BAS-RHIN

CM 67700 ☎ 388913565 ▤ 388913565
A pleasant tourist site at the foot of the Rocher du Haut Barr.
⮑ *1.3km SW via D171*
Open: Apr-Sep **Site:** 2.5HEC ▦ ⊕ **Facilities:** ⋔ ⊙ ⊕ ☎ **Services:** ⊞ lau **Off-site:** ♀ ✕ ∅ ♨

SÉLESTAT BAS-RHIN

CM Cigognes r de la 1-er DFL, 67600 ☎ 388920398
In a rural setting at an altitude of 175mtrs.
⮑ *900mtrs from the town centre.*
Open: May-15 Oct **Site:** 0.7HEC ▦ ⊕ ▲ **Prices:** pitch 10-12.70 (incl 3 persons) **Facilities:** ⋔ ⊙ ⊕ ☎ **Services:** lau **Off-site:** ⊾ ⭢P ⊞

SEPPOIS-LE-BAS HAUT-RHIN

CM les Lupins r de l'Ancienne Gare, 68580
☎ 389256537 ▤ 389256537
e-mail: leslupins@wanadoo.fr
website: www.campingalsace.com
Picturesque site close to the German and Swiss borders.

⮑ *Access via A36, exit 'Burnhaupt' and continue towards Dannemarie.*
Open: Apr-Oct **Site:** 4HEC ▦ ⊕ **Prices:** ⋔3.40 ⊕3.40 pitch 3.40 **Facilities:** ⋔ ⊙ ⊕ ∅ ☎ ⊞ **Services:** ⊞ lau **Leisure:** ⭢ P **Off-site:** ⊾ ✕ ♨ ⭢R

SIVRY-SUR-MEUSE MEUSE

Brouzel 26 r du Moulin, 55110 ☎ 0329858645
Open: Apr-1 Oct **Site:** 1.5HEC ▦ ⊕ **Prices:** ⋔1.90 ⊕1.50 ⊕1.90 ▲1.90 pitch 1.90 **Facilities:** ⋔ ⊙ ⊕ ☎ **Services:** ⊞ lau **Off-site:** ⊾ ♀ ✕ ∅ ♨ ⭢R

THOLY, LE VOSGES

Noir Rupt chemin de l'Étang de Noirrupt, 88530
☎ 329618127 ▤ 329618305
e-mail: info@jpvacances.com
website: www.jpvacances.com
A peaceful site in a beautiful wooded location. Plenty of facilities.
⮑ *2km SE on D417.*
Open: 15 Apr-14 Oct **Site:** 3HEC ▦ ⊕ ⊞ **Prices:** pitch 5.81-8.30 **Facilities:** ⋔ ⊾ ⊙ ⊕ ∅ ☎ ☎ **Services:** ♀ ✕ lau **Leisure:** ⭢ P **Off-site:** ✕ ⭢R ⊞

TONNOY MEURTHE-ET-MOSELLE

Grande Vanné 54210 ☎ 383266236 ▤ 383266395
⮑ *W via D74, beside the River Moselle*
R **Open:** 15 Jun-15 Sep **Site:** 7HEC ▦ ⊕ **Prices:** pitch 8 **Facilities:** ⋔ ⊙ ⊕ ☎ **Services:** ♀ ✕ lau **Leisure:** ⭢ R **Off-site:** ⊾ ✕

TURCKHEIM HAUT-RHIN

Cigognes 7 quai de la Gare, 68230 ☎ 389270200
Camping Card Compulsory.
⮑ *From Colmar follow N417 to Wintzenheim, then to Turckheim. Before bridge turn left, continue past railway station and stadium.*
Open: 15 March -Oct **Site:** 2.5HEC ▦ ⊕ **Prices:** ⋔3.40 pitch 3.70 **Facilities:** ⋔ ⊾ ⊙ ⊕ ∅ ☎ ☎ **Services:** ♀ ⊞ lau **Leisure:** ⭢ R **Off-site:** ✕

URBÈS HAUT-RHIN

CM Benelux Bâle 68121 ☎ 389827876
A well maintained site with good facilities.
⮑ *W of rte de Bussang.*
Open: Apr-Oct **Site:** 2.4HEC ▦ ⊕ ⊕ ▲ **Prices:** ⋔2.70 ⊕1.40 ⊕1.40 pitch 1.40 **Facilities:** ⋔ ⊙ ⊕ ☎ **Services:** ⊞ lau **Off-site:** ⊾ ∅ ♨ ⭢R

VAGNEY VOSGES

CM du Mettey 88120 ☎ 329248135
⮑ *1.3km E on Gérardmer road.*
Open: 15 Jun-15 Sep **Site:** 2HEC ▦ ⊕ **Prices:** pitch 7.25 (incl 2 persons) pp2.65 **Facilities:** ⋔ ⊙ ⊕ ☎ **Services:** ⊞ lau **Off-site:** ∅ ♨

VERDUN MEUSE

Breuils allée des Breuils, 55100 ☎ 329861531 ▤ 329867576
e-mail: contact@camping-lesbreuils.com
website: www.camping-lesbreuils.com
A family site in peaceful surroundings. Pitches are divided by trees and bushes and the sanitary facilities are well maintained.
⮑ *SW via D34. Signposted.*
Open: Apr-Sep **Site:** 5.5HEC ▦ ⊕ **Prices:** ⋔4 pitch 4 **Facilities:** ⋔ ⊾ ⊙ ⊕ ♨ ☎ **Services:** ♀ ✕ ⊞ lau **Leisure:** ⭢ P **Off-site:** ⭢LR

Facilities: ⊾-shop ⋔-shower ⊙-electric points for razors ⊕-electric points for caravans ☎-parking by tents permitted ⊞-compulsory separate car park **Services:** ✕-café/restaurant ♀-bar ∅-Camping Gaz International ♨-gas other than Camping Gaz ⊞-first aid facilities lau-laundry **Leisure:** ⭢-swimming L-Lake P-Pool R-River S-Sea **Off-site:** All facilities within 2km

VILLERS-LÈS-NANCY MEURTHE-ET-MOSELLE

Touristique International de Nancy-Brabois av Paul Muller, 54600 ☎ 383271828 ▤ 383400643
e-mail: campeoles.brabois@wanadoo.fr
website: www.campeoles.fr
In beautiful wooded surroundings with well defined pitches and good recreational facilities.
➲ *SW in Brabois park.*
Open: Apr-15 Oct **Site:** 6HEC ▦ ⊕ 🏠 **Prices:** pitch 9.80-11.20 (incl 2 persons) **Facilities:** 🅟 🌡 ⊙ 🍴 ⊘ 🏧 **Services:** 🍴 ✗ 🔁 lau **Off-site:** 🌡 🍴 ✗ ⊘ 🔁

WASSELONNE BAS-RHIN

CM rte de Romanswiller, 67310 ☎ 388870008
On a level meadow adjoining the local sports complex.
➲ *1km W on D224.*
Open: Apr-15 Oct **Site:** 2.5HEC ▦ 🌡 ⊙ 🍴 ⊘ 🏧 **Services:** 🍴 ✗ 🔁 lau **Leisure:** ⤳ P **Off-site:** ✗ 🚿

WATTWILLER HAUT-RHIN

Sources rte des Crêtes, 68700 ☎ 389754494 ▤ 389757198
e-mail: camping.les.sources@wanadoo.fr
website: www.camping-les-sources.com
A family site on the edge of the Vosges forest close to the Route du Vin.
➲ *Approach via N83 exit Cernay Nord.*
Open: Apr-15 Oct **Site:** 14HEC ▦ ⋮⋮ ⊕ 🏠 🚐
Prices: pitch 17-19.70 (incl 2 persons) **Facilities:** 🅟 🌡 ⊙ 🍴
⊘ 🚿 🏧 **Services:** 🍴 ✗ 🔁 lau **Leisure:** ⤳ P

WIHR-AU-VAL HAUT-RHIN

Route Verte 13 r de la Gare, 68230 ☎ 389711010
e-mail: info@camping-routeverte.com
website: www.camping-routeverte.com
Near the centre of the village at an altitude of 320mtrs.
➲ *Approach via D10.*
Open: May-Sep **Site:** 1HEC ▦ 🌡 **Prices:** ⚲2.55 pitch 3.40
Facilities: 🅟 🌡 ⊙ 🍴 ⊘ 🏧 **Services:** 🍴 ✗ lau **Off-site:** 🌡 🍴 ✗
⤳PR 🔁

XONRUPT/LONGEMER VOSGES

L'Eau-Vive rte de Colmar, 88400
☎ 329630737 ▤ 329630737
On a meadow surrounded by trees, close to the ski slopes.
➲ *2km SE on D67A next to Lac de Longemer.*
Open: All year **Site:** 1HEC ▦ 🌡 ⊙ 🍴 ⊘
🚿 🏧 **Services:** 🍴 ✗ 🔁 lau **Leisure:** ⤳ R **Off-site:** 🌡 ⤳L

Jonquilles rte du Lac, 88400 ☎ 329633401 ▤ 329600928
In a delightful wooded lakeside setting. Advance booking necessary in July and August.
➲ *2km SE on D67A beside Lac de Longemer.*
Open: Apr-10 Oct **Site:** 4HEC ▦ 🌤 **Prices:** pitch 6.50-11 (incl 2 persons) **Facilities:** 🅟 🌡 ⊙ 🍴 ⊘ 🏧 **Services:** 🍴 ✗ 🔁
lau **Leisure:** ⤳ L **Off-site:** ✗ 🚿

BURGUNDY/CHAMPAGNE

ACCOLAY YONNE

Moulin Jacquot route de Bazarnes, 89460
☎ 386815687 ▤ 386815687
A well equipped site in a pleasant rural setting, close to the village.
➲ *W, beside the Canal du Nivernais.*
Open: Apr-Sep **Site:** 0.8HEC ▦ 🌡 **Facilities:** 🅟 ⊙ 🍴 🏧
Services: lau **Off-site:** 🌡 🍴 ✗ ⊘ 🚿 ⤳R 🔁

ANCY-LE-FRANC YONNE

CM rte de Cusy, 89160 ☎ 386751321
In a sheltered position just beyond the village.
➲ *Access via Montbard road.*
Open: Jun-15 Sep **Site:** 0.8HEC 🌡 **Facilities:** 🅟 ⊙ 🍴 🏧
Services: lau **Off-site:** 🌡 🍴 ✗ ⊘ 🚿 ⤳R 🔁

ANDRYES YONNE

Bois Joli 89480 ☎ 386817048 ▤ 386817048
A small site in pleasant Burgundian countryside.
➲ *0.6km SW via N151.*
Open: Apr-Sep **Site:** 5HEC ▦ 🌡 🏠 **Prices:** ⚲2.30-3.20
🚗2.10-4.50 🚐1.85-2.90 🔺1.25-1.85 pitch **Facilities:** 🅟 🌡 ⊙
🍴 🏧 **Services:** 🍴 ✗ 🔁 lau **Leisure:** ⤳ P **Off-site:** ⊘ 🚿 ⤳R

ARNAY-LE-DUC CÔTE-D'OR

CM de Fouché 21230 ☎ 380900223 ▤ 380901191
e-mail: camparnay@wanadoo.fr
website: www.arnay-le-duc.com
In a quiet location beside a lake with good recreational facilities close to the medieval town of Arnay-le-Duc.
➲ *0.7km E on CD17.*
Open: 15 Feb-15 Nov **Site:** 8HEC ▦ 🌡 🏠 **Prices:** pitch 8.50-11.70 (incl 2 persons) **Facilities:** 🅟 ⊙ 🍴 ⊘ 🏧 🔁
Services: 🍴 🔁 lau **Leisure:** ⤳ L **Off-site:** 🌡 🍴 ✗ 🚿

AUXERRE YONNE

CM 8 rte de Vaux, 89000 ☎ 386521115 ▤ 386511754
e-mail: sports@auxerre.com
➲ *SE towards Vaux*
Open: Apr-Sep **Site:** 3HEC ▦ 🌡 **Prices:** ⚲2.24-2.80 pitch 2.50 **Facilities:** 🅟 🌡 ⊙ 🍴 ⊘ 🏧 🔁 **Services:** 🔁 lau **Off-site:** 🍴 ✗ 🚿 ⤳PR

AUXONNE CÔTE-D'OR

Arquebuse rte d'Athée, 21130 ☎ 380310689
e-mail: camping.arquebuse@wanadoo.fr
Clean, well-equipped site on right bank of River Saône near bathing area.
➲ *From Auxonne travel W on N5 for 3km. Then turn northwards on D24 towards Athée and Pontailler-sur-Saône.*
Open: All year **Site:** 4HEC ▦ 🌡 🚐 🔺 **Prices:** ⚲3.20 🚗1
🚐3.10 🔺3.10 **Facilities:** 🅟 ⊙ 🍴 🏧 **Services:** 🍴 ✗ 🔁 lau
Off-site: 🌡 ✗ ⊘ 🚿 ⤳PR

AVALLON YONNE

CM Sous Roche 1 r Sous-Roche, 89200
☎ 386341039 ▤ 386341039
➲ *2km SE by D944 and D427.*
Open: 15 Mar-15 Oct **Site:** 2HEC ▦ 🌡 **Prices:** pitch 6.80-9.50 (incl 1 persons) **Facilities:** 🅟 🌡 ⊙ 🍴 🏧 **Services:** ✗ 🔁
lau **Leisure:** ⤳ R **Off-site:** ⤳P

BANNES HAUTE-MARNE

Hautoreille 52360 ☎ 325848340 ▤ 325848340
e-mail: campinghautoreille@free.fr
website: www.campinghautoreille.com
Small grassy site with modern facilities. Separate carpark for late arrivals.
➲ *Access via D74 towards Epinal.*
Open: All year **Site:** 3.5HEC ▦ 🌡 🚐 **Prices:** ⚲3.50-4 pitch 4 **Facilities:** 🅟 ⊙ 🍴 🏧 **Services:** 🍴 ✗ 🔁 lau **Off-site:** ⤳LR

Site: 6HEC-Site size ▦-grass ⋮⋮-sand 🌑-stone 🌤-little shade 🌡-partly shaded 🌳-mainly shaded
🏠-bungalows for hire 🚐-caravans for hire 🔺-tents for hire ⊘-no dogs Prices: ⚲-adult per night 🚗-car per night
pp-per person per night 🚐-caravan per night 🔺-tent per night

BAR-SUR-AUBE AUBE

Gravière av du Parc, 10200 ☎ 325271294
➲ *0.5km E of D13.*
Open: Apr-15 Oct Site: 2.8HEC ⊞⊞⊞ ♣ Facilities: ↑ ⊙ ➡ ☲
Services: lau Leisure: ↘ PR Off-site: ⊾ ♀ ✗ ∅ ⇌ ↘P

BAZOLLES NIÈVRE

Baye 58110 ☎ 386389033
Open: Apr-Oct Site: 1.5HEC ⊞⊞⊞ ♦ ⊖ ➡ Facilities: ↑ ⊙ ➡
☲ Services: ⊞ lau Leisure: ↘ L Off-site: ⊾ ♀ ✗ ∅ ⇌

BEAUNE CÔTE-D'OR

CM *Cent Vignes* 10 rue August Dubois, 21200 ☎ 380220391
On outskirts of town. Site divided into pitches, clean, well-looked after sanitary installations. From 20 Jun-Aug it is advisable to arrive before 1600 hrs.
➲ *On N74 on Savigny-les-Beaune road.*
Open: 15 Mar-Oct Site: 2HEC ⊞⊞⊞ ♦ ⊖ Prices: ↑3.05 pitch
4.20 Facilities: ↑ ⊾ ⊙ ➡ ∅ ☲ Services: ♀ ✗ ⊞ lau
Off-site: ⇌ ↘LP

BOURBON-LANCY SAÔNE-ET-LOIRE

St-Prix r du St-Prix, 71140 ☎ 385891485
e-mail: bourbon.loisirs@wanadoo.fr
A well equipped family site close to an extensive water sports centre.
➲ *By the swimming pool off the D979a.*
Open: Apr-Oct Site: 2.5HEC ⊞⊞⊞ ♦ ⊕ ➡ Facilities: ↑ ⊾ ⊙
➡ ☲ Services: ♀ ✗ lau Off-site: ✗ ∅ ⇌ ↘LP ⊞

BOURBONNE-LES-BAINS HAUTE-MARNE

Montmorency r du Stade, 52400 ☎ 325900864
A well equipped site in a pleasant natural setting.
Open: Apr-Oct Site: 2HEC ⊞⊞⊞ ⊖ ➡ Prices: ↑2.90 pitch
2.80 Facilities: ↑ ⊾ ⊙ ➡ ∅ ☲ Services: ♀ ⊞ lau Leisure: ↘
P Off-site: ↘P

BOURG HAUTE-MARNE

Croix d'Arles RN 74, 52200 ☎ 325882402 ▤ 325882402
e-mail: croix.arles@wanadoo.fr
website: perso.wanadoo.fr/escapecamping
A peaceful site in wooded surroundings close to Langres.
➲ *Access via N74 or A31.*
Open: 15 Mar-Nov Site: 7HEC ⊞⊞⊞ ⊖ ⊕ ➡ ▲
Prices: ↑2.50-4 pitch 5-6 Facilities: ↑ ⊾ ⊙ ⇌ ☲
Services: ♀ ✗ ⊞ lau Leisure: ↘ P

BOURG-FIDÈLE ARDENNES

Murée rte de Rocroi, 08230 ☎ 324542445
e-mail: barbara.maire@wanadoo.fr
website: www.campinglamuree.com
A lakeside site in wooded surroundings.
➲ *1km N via D22.*
Open: All year Site: 1.3HEC ⊞⊞⊞ ⊖ ⊕ ➡ Prices: ↑3 ➡1.60
pitch 4.60 Facilities: ↑ ⊙ ➡ ☲ Services: ♀ ✗ lau Off-site: ⊾
∅ ⇌ ↘P ⊞

BUZANCY ARDENNES

Samaritaine 8240 ☎ 33 324300888 ▤ 324302939
e-mail: info@campinglasamaritaine.com
website: www.campinglasamaritaine.com
Site set in a peaceful location in a small village in the heart of the Ardennes. The forests in the area are well suited for walking, horse-riding or cycling.

➲ *A203 from Charleville-Mezières, exit D977 at Sedan in direction of Vouziers. After 23km take D12 then D947 in direction of Buzancy for 17km*
Open: Apr-26 Sept Site: 2.5HEC ⊞⊞⊞ ⊖ ⊕ ➡ Prices: ↑3-4
➡2.50 pitch 7-9 Facilities: ↑ ⊾ ⊙ ➡ ☲ Services: ✗ ⊞ lau
Off-site: ♀ ✗ ∅ ⇌ ↘L

CHAGNY SAÔNE-ET-LOIRE

Pâquier Fané 20 Rue de Paquier, 71150 ☎ 385872142
A clean site 600m W of the church.
➲ *Follow the D974 from town centre.*
Open: 10 May-Oct Site: 1.8HEC ⊞⊞⊞ ♣ Prices: ↑3.35-3.35
➡4.70-4.70 pitch 4.70-4.70 Facilities: ↑ ⊾ ⊙ ➡ ∅ ⇌ ☲
Services: ♀ ✗ ⊞ lau Leisure: ↘ R Off-site: ↘P

CHÂLONS-EN-CHAMPAGNE MARNE

CM r de Plaisance, 51000 ☎ 326683800 ▤ 326683800
In a pleasant wooded location with good recreational facilities.
Open: Apr-Oct Site: 7.5HEC ⊞⊞⊞ ♦ ⊖ Prices: ↑4.40 ➡3
pitch 4.50 Facilities: ↑ ⊙ ➡ ∅ ☲ Services: ♀ ✗ ⊞ lau
Off-site: ⊾ ↘P

CHAROLLES SAÔNE-ET-LOIRE

CM rte de Viry, 71120 ☎ 385240490 ▤ 385240490
In pleasant wooded surroundings with good, modern sanitary facilities.
➲ *NE of town via D33 towards Viry. Follow signs.*
Open: Apr-05 Oct Site: 0.6HEC ⊞⊞⊞ ⠿ ⊖ Prices: ↑2
➡1.20 ➡2 ▲2 pitch 2 Facilities: ↑ ⊙ ➡ ☲ Services: ♀ ⊞
lau Leisure: ↘ PR Off-site: ⊾ ✗ ∅ ⇌

CHÂTILLON-SUR-SEINE CÔTE-D'OR

CM espl St-Vorles, 21400 ☎ 380910305 ▤ 380912146
e-mail: tourism-chatillon-sur-seine@wanadoo.fr
Hilly shaded site near the historic Renaissance church of St Vorles.
➲ *SE of town off rte de Langres (D928).*
Open: Apr-Sep Site: 0.8HEC ⊞⊞⊞ ♣ Prices: ↑2.80 ➡1
pitch 3 Facilities: ↑ ⊙ ➡ ∅ ☲ Services: ♀ ⊞ lau Off-site: ⊾
✗ ⇌ ↘P

CHATONRUPT HAUTE-MARNE

CM 52300 ☎ 325948007 ▤ 325948007
Open: May-Sep Site: 1.1HEC ⊞⊞⊞ ⊖ Prices: ↑1.10 ➡1 ➡1
▲1 pitch 1 Facilities: ↑ ⊙ ➡ ☲ Services: lau
Leisure: ↘ R Off-site: ⊾ ♀ ✗ ⇌

CHEVIGNY NIÈVRE

Hermitage de Chevigny 58230 ☎ 386845097
A pleasant site with good facilities in wooded surroundings within the Morvan Nature Reserve. There is direct access to the lake and most watersports are available.
Open: Apr-Sep Site: 2.5HEC ⊞⊞⊞ ♣ ⊕ ➡ Prices: ↑4 ➡2.50
pitch 2.50 Facilities: ↑ ⊾ ⊙ ➡ ∅ ⇌ ☲ Services: ♀ ✗ ⊞ lau
Leisure: ↘ LR

CLAMECY NIÈVRE

Pont Picot rte de Chenoches, 58500 ☎ 386270597
In a pleasant situation between the River Yonne and the Canal du Nivernais.
Open: May-Sep Site: 1.2HEC ⊞⊞⊞ ⠶ Facilities: ↑ ⊙ ➡ ☲
Services: lau Leisure: ↘ R Off-site: ⊾ ♀ ✗ ∅ ⇌ ↘P ⊞

COSNE-SUR-LOIRE NIÈVRE

Loire & Nohain Ile de Cosne, 18300
☎ 386282792 ▤ 386281810
e-mail: campingile18@aol.com
Site borders River Loire.

contd.

Facilities: ⊾-shop ↑-shower ⊙-electric points for razors ➡-electric points for caravans ☲-parking by tents permitted
⊟-compulsory separate car park **Services:** ✗-café/restaurant ♀-bar ∅-Camping Gaz International ⇌-gas other than Camping
Gaz ⊞-first aid facilities lau-laundry **Leisure:** ↘-swimming L-Lake P-Pool R-River S-Sea **Off-site:** All facilities within 2km

➲ *Follow D955 W towards Sancerre.*
Open: All year Site: 4HEC ⬛ ∴ ⬧ 🄰 🛖 🚐 Å
Prices: pitch 12 (incl 2 persons) Facilities: 🏕 🛏 ⊙ 🚽 🛒 🚿 🖂
Services: 🍴 ✕ 🔲 lau Leisure: 🗘 PR Off-site: 🚿 🗘P

CRÊCHES-SUR-SAÔNE SAÔNE-ET-LOIRE

CM Le Port d'Arciat 71680 ☎ 385371183 📠 385365157
e-mail: camping-creches.sur.saone@wanadoo.fr
In a wooded location beside the River Saône.
➲ *1.5km E via D31*
Open: 15 May-15 Sep Site: 6HEC ⬛ ♣ Prices: 🕴3.20
🚗3.10 pitch 6.50 Facilities: 🏕 🛏 ⊙ 🚽 🛒 🚿 🖂
lau Leisure: 🗘 LR Off-site: 🛏 🚿 🚿

DIGOIN SAÔNE-ET-LOIRE

CM Chevrette r de la Chevrette, 71160
☎ 385531149 📠 385885970
e-mail: lachevrette@wanadoo.fr
website: www.lachevrette.com
➲ *W of village on N79.*
Open: Mar-Oct Site: 1.5HEC ⬛ ⬧ ♣ 🛖 🚐 Å
Prices: 🕴2.80-3.15 pitch 5.40-6 Facilities: 🏕 🛏 ⊙ 🚽 🛒 🖂
Services: 🍴 ✕ 🔲 lau Leisure: 🗘 PR Off-site: 🚿 🚿

DIJON CÔTE-D'OR

Lac 3 bd Chanoine Kir, 21000 ☎ 0380435472 📠 0380435472
website: www.ville-dijon.fr
A well maintained site in natural surroundings, an ideal base
for exploring the historic town of Dijon.
➲ *1.5km W on N5.*
Open: Apr-15 Oct Site: 2.5HEC ⬛ ∴ 🄰 Prices: 🕴2.35
🚗1.45 pitch 2.05 Facilities: 🏕 ⊙ 🚽 🛒 🖂 Services: 🍴 ✕ 🔲 lau
Off-site: 🛏 🚿 🚿 🗘LP

DOMPIERRE-LES-ORMES SAÔNE-ET-LOIRE

Village des Meuniers 71520 ☎ 385503660 📠 385503661
e-mail: levillagedesmeuniers@wanadoo.fr
website: www.villagedesmeuniers.com
A well equipped site in the heart of the Southern Burgundy
countryside. Advance booking advisable in July and August.
➲ *Access via N79. Signposted.*
Open: 15 May-Sep Site: 4HEC 🄰 🛖 Prices: 🕴4.30-6
pitch 5-7 Facilities: 🏕 🛏 ⊙ 🚽 🛒 🚿 🖂 Services: 🍴 ✕ 🔲 lau
Leisure: 🗘 P

ÉCLARON-BRAUCOURT HAUTE-MARNE

Presqu'Île de Champaubert 52290
☎ 325041320 📠 325943351
e-mail: info@lacduder.com
Situated on lake peninsula.
Open: Etr-Sep Site: 3.5HEC ⬛ 🄰 Prices: 🕴4.50 🚗3.40
🚐4.40 Å4.40 pitch 4.40 Facilities: 🏕 🛏 ⊙ 🚽 🛒 🖂
Services: 🍴 ✕ 🔲 lau Off-site: 🗘L

EPINAC SAÔNE-ET-LOIRE

Pont Vert 71360 ☎ 385820026
In a wooded location on the banks of the river. Modern
facilities and motel within the site area.
➲ *S via D43 beside the River Drée.*
Open: Jun-Sep Site: 4HEC ⬛ ♣ 🛖 Facilities: 🏕 🛏 ⊙ 🚽 🛒
Services: 🍴 ✕ 🔲 lau Leisure: 🗘 R Off-site: ✕ 🚿 🚿

FRONCLES HAUTE-MARNE

Deux Ponts r des Ponts, 52320 ☎ 325023121 📠 325020980
In a peaceful location beside the River Marne.
Open: 15 Mar-15 Oct Site: 3HEC 🄰 Facilities: 🏕 🚽 🖂
Off-site: 🛏 🍴 ✕ 🗘R 🔲

GIBLES SAÔNE-ET-LOIRE

Château de Montrouant Montrouant, 71800
☎ 385845113 📠 385845430
A small site situated in the Charollais hill region with access
to extensive parkland.
➲ *1.6km NE beside the lake.*
Open: Jun-9 Sep Site: 1HEC ⬛ ∴ 🄰 🛖 Å Facilities: 🏕
🛏 ⊙ 🚽 🖂 Services: 🍴 ✕ 🔲 lau Leisure: 🗘 LPR Off-site: 🚿 🚿

GIFFAUMONT MARNE

Plage Chemin de la Cachotte, Station Nautique, 51290
☎ 326726184
A well maintained site situated at the Station Nautique.
➲ *2km from the village.*
Open: May-10 Sep Site: 1.5HEC ⬛ ♣ Prices: 🕴4 pitch 4
Facilities: 🏕 ⊙ 🚽 🛒 🖂 Services: 🍴 🔲 lau Off-site: 🛏 ✕ 🚿 🗘L

GIGNY-SUR-SAÔNE SAÔNE-ET-LOIRE

🛖Château de l'Epervière 71240 ☎ 385441690 📠 385941697
e-mail: domaine-de-leperviere@wanadoo.fr
website: www.domaine-eperviere.com
Quiet site in park surrounding 16th-century château. Close
to the River Saône for fishing and sailing.
➲ *N6 to Sennecey-le-Grand, then follow signs.*
Open: Apr-Sept Site: 10HEC ⬛ 🄰 Prices: 🕴5.40-6.40 pitch
6.90-9.60 Facilities: 🏕 🛏 ⊙ 🚽 🛒 🖂 Services: 🍴 ✕ 🔲 lau
Leisure: 🗘 LP Off-site: 🗘R

GRANDPRÉ ARDENNES

CM 8250 ☎ 324305071
A peaceful riverside site.
➲ *150m from village centre on D6.*
Open: Apr-Sep Site: 2HEC ⬛ ♣ 🚐 Prices: 🕴1.52 🚗0.75
🚐0.95 Å0.95 pitch 0.95 Facilities: 🏕 ⊙ 🚽 🛒 🖂 Services: 🖂 lau
Leisure: 🗘 R Off-site: 🛏 🍴 ✕ 🚿 🚿

ISSY-L'ÉVÊQUE SAÔNE-ET-LOIRE

CM de l'Étang Neuf 71760 ☎ 385249605 📠 385249605
e-mail: marc.pille@compaqnet.be
website: www.camping-etang-neuf.com
In a fine position beside the lake, overlooking the château.
Open: 15 May-Sep Site: 4HEC ⬛ 🄰 🛖 Å Prices: pitch 13.70-
16 (incl 2 persons) Facilities: 🏕 ⊙ 🚽 🛒 🚿 🖂 Services: 🍴 ✕ 🔲
lau Leisure: 🗘 LP Off-site: 🛏 🚿

LAIVES SAÔNE-ET-LOIRE

Lacs 'La Heronnière' Les Bois de Laives, 71240
☎ 385449885 📠 385449885
Compulsory separate car park for arrivals after 2200hrs.
➲ *Access via 'Châlon Sud' autoroute exit towards Mâcon.*
Open: 8 May-13 Sep Site: 1.5HEC ⬛ 🄰 🚐 Prices: 🕴4
🚗2.50 🚐8.20 pitch 4.50 Facilities: 🏕 🛏 ⊙ 🚽 🛒 🖂
Services: ✕ 🔲 lau Leisure: 🗘 P Off-site: 🍴 ✕ 🗘LR

MÂCON SAÔNE-ET-LOIRE

CM 71000 ☎ 385381622 📠 385381622
Divided into pitches. Water sports centre and pool nearby.
➲ *2km N on N6.*
Open: 15 Mar-Oct Site: 5HEC ⬛ ♣ Prices: pitch 9.50-
11.80 (incl 2 persons) Facilities: 🏕 🛏 ⊙ 🚽 🛒 🚿 🖂 Services: 🍴
✕ lau Leisure: 🗘 P Off-site: 🚿 🗘R

> A full guide to the Symbols &
> Abbreviations used in this book
> can be found on page 6

Site: 6HEC-Site size ⬛-grass ∴-sand ⬧-stone 🌿-little shade 🄰-partly shaded ♣-mainly shaded
🛖-bungalows for hire 🚐-caravans for hire Å-tents for hire 🐾-no dogs Prices: 🕴-adult per night 🚗-car per night
pp-per person per night 🚐-caravan per night Å-tent per night

MARCENAY CÔTE-D'OR

Grebes Laignes, 21330 ☎ 380816172 📠 380816199
e-mail: mairie.laignes@wanadoo.fr
A peaceful site in unspoiled contryside with separate hedged pitches. Direct access to lake.
Open: 30 Mar-15 Sep Site: 2.4HEC ⟿ ⊶ 🚐 Facilities: ⋔ ⚋ ⊙ 🚻 ⌀ 🏕 Services: ⊞ lau Leisure: ⚓ L Off-site: ⍮ ✕

MATOUR SAÔNE-ET-LOIRE

CM Le Paluet Le Paluet, 71520 ☎ 385597058 📠 385597454
e-mail: mairie.matour@.fr website: www.matour.com
In pleasant countryside beside the river.
Open: May-Sep Site: 2HEC ⟿ ⫶⫶⫶ ♠ 🏕 Facilities: ⋔ ⊙ 🚻 🏕 Services: ⍮ ✕ lau Leisure: ⚓ P Off-site: ⚋ ✕ ⌀ 🛒 ⊞

MESNIL-ST PÈRE AUBE

Voie Colette 10140 ☎ 325412715 📠 325412715
e-mail: voiecolette@yahoo.fr
Grassland, with trees, ornamental shrubs and flower beds. Slightly sloping, with a man-made lake nearby.
➭ About 2km from Mesnil-St-Père; signposted from centre.
Open: Apr-10 Oct Site: 4HEC ⟿ ⊶ 🚐 Prices: pitch 10.20-11.30 (incl 2 persons) Facilities: ⋔ ⊙ 🚻 ⌀ 🏕 Services: ⍮ ✕ ⊞ lau Off-site: ⚓ ⚓L

MEURSAULT CÔTE-D'OR

Grappe d'Or 2 rte de Volnay, 21190 ☎ 380212248 📠 380216574
Clean terraced site on an open meadow. Mountain bikes are available for hire.
➭ 700m NE on D11b.
Open: Apr-15 Oct Site: 5.5HEC ⟿ ♠ ♠ 🏕 Prices: pitch 11.50-15.50 (incl 2 persons) Facilities: ⋔ ⚋ ⊙ 🚻 ⌀ 🏕 Services: ✕ ⊞ lau Leisure: ⚓ P Off-site: ⍮

MONTAPAS NIÈVRE

CM La Chênaie La Chênaie, 58110 ☎ 386583432 📠 386582905
In a wooded location beside a lake with plenty of recreational facilities.
➭ 500m from town centre, beside the lake, via D259.
Open: Apr-Oct Site: 1HEC ⟿ ⊶ Prices: ⚶1.30 ♠1.30 ⛺1.30 pitch 1.30 Facilities: ⋔ ⊙ 🚻 🏕 Services: ⍮ ✕ lau Leisure: ⚓ L Off-site: ⚋ ⌀ 🛒 ⊞

MONTBARD CÔTE-D'OR

CM r M-Servet, 21500 ☎ 380922160 📠 380922160
website: www.montbard.com
➭ NW via rte de Laignes.
Open: Mar-Oct Site: 2.5HEC ⟿ ♠ 🏕 Prices: ⚶2.70 ♠4 pitch 5 Facilities: ⋔ ⊙ 🚻 🏕 Services: ⍮ ✕ lau Off-site: ⚋ ✕ ⌀ 🛒 ⚓R ⊞

MONTHERMÉ ARDENNES

Base de Loisirs Départementale 8800 ☎ 324328161 📠 0324323766
In a pleasant wooded situation.
➭ 0.8km NE beside the River Semoy.
Open: All year Site: 16HEC ⟿ ♠ 🏕 Prices: ⚶2.60 ♠1.40 ⛺1.40 ♠1.40 pitch 1.35 Facilities: ⋔ ⊙ 🚻 🏕 Services: lau Leisure: ⚓ R

MONTSAUCHE NIÈVRE

Mesanges Lac des Settons, Rive Gauche, 58230 ☎ 386845577
On the left bank of Lac des Settons.
Open: May-15 Sep Site: 5HEC ⟿ ⊶ Prices: ⚶3.70 ♠2.30 pitch 2.90 Facilities: ⋔ ⚋ ⊙ 🚻 🏕 Services: ⊞ lau Off-site: ⍮ ✕ ⌀ 🛒 ⚓LPR

Plage du Midi 58230 ☎ 386845197 📠 386845731
e-mail: plagedumidi@aol.com
website: www.settons-camping.com
In a wooded setting directly on the Lac des Settons with good facilities.
➭ From Salieu (on N6) follow D977. From town centre follow D193 to Les Sultons, then to site.
Open: Etr-15 Oct Site: 4HEC ⟿ ⊶ 🏕 Facilities: ⋔ ⚋ ⊙ 🚻 ⌀ 🏕 Services: ⍮ ✕ lau Leisure: ⚓ L Off-site: ✕ ⚋

PARAY-LE-MONIAL SAÔNE-ET-LOIRE

Mambré rte du Gué-Léger, 71600 ☎ 385888920 📠 385888781
On a level meadow with good, modern facilities.
➭ Well signposted from outskirts of town.
Open: Apr-Oct Site: 4HEC ⟿ ⊶ 🏕 Facilities: ⋔ ⚋ ⊙ 🚻 ⚋ 🏕 Services: ⍮ ✕ lau Leisure: ⚓ P Off-site: ⚋ ✕ ⌀ ⚓R ⊞

PONT-SAINTE-MARIE AUBE

CM de Troyes 7 r Roger Salengro, 10150 ☎ 325810264 📠 325810264
Wooded site a short walk from the town of Troyes.
Open: Apr-15 Oct Site: 3.8HEC ⟿ ⊶ Prices: ⚶4 pitch 5.50 Facilities: ⋔ ⚋ ⊙ 🚻 ⌀ 🏕 Services: ✕ ⊞ lau Off-site: ⍮ ✕

POUGUES-LES-EAUX NIÈVRE

CM Chanternes 58320 ☎ 386688618
➭ On N7 approx. 7km N of Nevers.
Open: Etr-Oct Site: 1.4HEC ⟿ ⊶ Facilities: ⋔ ⊙ 🚻 Services: ⊞ lau Off-site: ⚋ ⍮ ✕ ⚓P

PREMEAUX CÔTE-D'OR

Saule Guillaume 21700 ☎ 380612799 📠 380613519
Pleasant site beside a lake.
➭ 1.5km E via D109G.
Open: 15 Jun-5 Sep Site: 2.1HEC ⟿ ♠ 🏕 Prices: ⚶2.30 pitch 4.50 Facilities: ⋔ ⚋ ⊙ 🚻 🏕 Services: ⊞ lau Off-site: ⍮ ✕ ⌀ ⚓P

RADONVILLIERS AUBE

Garillon Rue des Anciens Combattants, 10500 ☎ 325922146 📠 325922134
Beside the river, 250m from the lake.
Open: May-15 Sep Site: 1HEC ⟿ ⊶ 🚐 Prices: ⚶2.20 pitch 2.80 Facilities: ⋔ ⊙ 🚻 🏕 Services: lau Off-site: ⍮ ✕ ⚓LR ⊞

RIEL-LES-EAUX CÔTE-D'OR

Riel-les-Eaux 21570 ☎ 380937276 📠 380937276
A lakeside site with fishing and boating facilities.
➭ 2.2km W via D13.
Open: Apr-Oct Site: 0.2HEC ⟿ ⊶ Facilities: ⋔ ⚋ ⊙ 🚻 ⌀ 🏕 Services: ⍮ ✕ lau Leisure: ⚓ L Off-site: ⚋

ST-HILAIRE-SOUS-ROMILLY AUBE

Domaine de La Noue des Rois chemin des Brayes, 10100 ☎ 325244160 📠 325243418
e-mail: michele.desmont@wanadoo.fr
website: www.lanouedesrois.com
A quiet site in a pine forest on the Basin d'Arcachon.
Booking recommended in July and August.
➭ 2km NE.
Open: All year Site: 30HEC ⟿ ⊶ 🏕 ⌁ Prices: ⚶5 ⛺18 Facilities: ⋔ ⚋ ⊙ 🚻 ⚋ 🏕 🄿 Services: ⍮ ✕ ⊞ lau Leisure: ⚓ LP

Facilities: ⚋-shop ⋔-shower ⊙-electric points for razors 🚻-electric points for caravans 🏕-parking by tents permitted 🄿-compulsory separate car park Services: ✕-café/restaurant ⍮-bar ⌀-Camping Gaz International ⚋-gas other than Camping Gaz ⊞-first aid facilities lau-laundry Leisure: ⚓-swimming L-Lake P-Pool R-River S-Sea Off-site: All facilities within 2km

ST-HONORÉ NIÈVRE

Bains 15 av J-Mermoz, 58360 ☎ 386307344 🗏 386306188
e-mail: camping-les-bains@wanadoo.fr
website: www.campinglesbains.com
A family site with good facilities close to the Morvan
National Park.
➲ *Access via A6 and D985.*
Open: 28 Apr-05 Oct **Site:** 4.5HEC ⊞ ♀ ♠ **Prices:** pitch
14.50 (incl 2 persons) **Facilities:** ⋔ ⅏ ⊙ �R ∅ ☎ **Services:** ⍾
✕ ⊞ lau **Leisure:** ⌇ P **Off-site:** ≞

ST-PÉREUSE NIÈVRE

Manoir de Bezolle 58110 ☎ 386844255 🗏 386844377
e-mail: info@bezolle.com website: www.bezolle.com
Situated in grounds of a manor house, at the edge of a
National Park. Well-kept site divided by hedges.
➲ *At 'X' roads of D11 and D978.*
Open: May-15 Sept **Site:** 8HEC ⊞ ♣ ♠ ⊞ ☬ **Prices:** pitch
15-25 (incl 2 persons) **Facilities:** ⋔ ⅏ ⊙ ⊠ ∅ ☎ **Services:** ⍾
✕ ⊞ lau **Leisure:** ⌇ P

STE-MENEHOULD MARNE

CM de la Grelette 51800 ☎ 326607389
A well equipped municipal site.
➲ *E of town towards Metz, beside the River Aisne*
Open: May-Sep **Site:** 1HEC ⊞ ♀ **Prices:** ⧍2 ⇔1 pitch 4.60
(incl 2 persons) **Facilities:** ⋔ ⊙ ⊠ ☎ **Services:** lau
Off-site: ⅏ ⍾ ✕ ∅ ≞ ⌇PR ⊞

SAULIEU CÔTE-D'OR

CM Perron 21210 ☎ 380641619 🗏 380641619
e-mail: saulieu.tourisme@wanadoo.fr
On level, open ground with good recreational facilities.
➲ *1 km NW on N6.*
Open: Apr-Sep **Site:** 4.5HEC ⊞ ♀ ♠ **Prices:** pitch 11.05-
12.05 **Facilities:** ⋔ ⅏ ⊙ ⊠ ☎ **Services:** ⍾ ⊞ lau **Leisure:** ⌇ P
Off-site: ⅏ ⍾ ✕ ∅ ≞ ⌇P

SEDAN ARDENNES

CM de la Prairie bd Fabert, 08200
☎ 324271305 🗏 324271305
A well equipped municipal site on the banks of the River
Meuse, close to the centre of the village.
Open: Apr-Sept **Site:** 1.5HEC ⊞ ♀ **Prices:** ⧍1.20-2.45
⊠2.05-2.75 pitch 2.05-2.75 **Facilities:** ⋔ ⊙ ⊠ ☎ **Services:** ⊞
lau **Off-site:** ⌇LP

SELONGEY CÔTE-D'OR

CM Les Courvelles r H-Jevain, 21260
☎ 380757074 🗏 380755665
e-mail: info@selongey.com website: www.selongey.com
In a rural location close to the river.
➲ *Access via A31 and N74.*
Open: May-Sep **Site:** 0.4HEC ⊞ ♀ **Prices:** ⧍2.10 ⇔1.35
⊠1.35 ⧍1.35 **Facilities:** ⋔ ⊙ ⊠ ☎ **Services:** lau **Off-site:** ⅏
⍾ ✕ ⌇LPR ⊞

SEURRE CÔTE-D'OR

Piscine 21250 ☎ 380204922 🗏 380203401
A well equipped municipal site with direct access to the river.
➲ *From town centre follow N73 W for 600m in the direction
of Beaune.*
Open: 15 May-15 Sep **Site:** ⊞ ♣ **Prices:** ⧍1.80 ⊠1.40
⧍1.40 pitch 2 **Facilities:** ⋔ ⊙ ⊠ ∅ ☎ **Services:** ⍾ ✕ ⊞ lau
Leisure: ⌇ PR **Off-site:** ⅏ ✕

SÉZANNE MARNE

CM rte de Launat, 51120 ☎ 326805700
e-mail: campingdesezanne@wanadoo.fr

➲ *1.5km W on D239, rte de Launat.*
Open: Apr-1 Oct **Site:** 1HEC ⊞ ☬ **Prices:** pitch 6.80-8.60
(incl 2 persons) pp1.94 **Facilities:** ⋔ ⊙ ⊠ ☎ **Services:** lau
Leisure: ⌇ P **Off-site:** ⅏ ⍾ ✕

SIGNY-LE-PETIT ARDENNES

Pré Hugon Base de Loisirs, 08380
☎ 324535473 🗏 324535132
e-mail: tourisme@signy-le-petit.fr
website: www.signy-le-petit.com
A pleasant site in wooded surroundings.
➲ *Access via N43.*
Open: 12 Apr-Sep **Site:** 0.8HEC ⊞ ♀ ♠ ⊞ **Prices:** ⧍2.50
⊕1.60 ⊠1.60 ⧍1.60 pitch 1.70 **Facilities:** ⋔ ⊙ ⊠ ☎
Services: lau **Leisure:** ⌇ P **Off-site:** ⅏ ⍾ ✕ ∅ ≞ ⌇LR ⊞

SOULAINES-DHUYS AUBE

CM La Croix Badeau 10200 ☎ 325927744
Open: May-Sep **Site:** 1.5HEC ⊞ ♠ ♀ **Prices:** ⧍1.52 pitch
4.57 **Facilities:** ⋔ ⊙ ⊠ ☎ **Services:** lau **Off-site:** ⅏ ⍾ ✕ ∅ ≞
⌇R ⊞

TAZILLY NIÈVRE

Château de Chigy 58170 ☎ 386301080 🗏 386309022
In a beautiful location within the extensive grounds of a
magnificent chateau. Good sporting facilities and
entertainment programme.
➲ *4km from Luzy on D973 Luzy-Moulins.*
Open: Apr-Sep **Site:** 7HEC ⊞ ♀ ♠ **Facilities:** ⋔ ⅏ ⊙ ⊠ ∅
☎ **Services:** ⍾ ✕ ⊞ lau **Leisure:** ⌇ LP

THONNANCE-LES-MOULINS HAUTE-MARNE

Forge de Ste-Marie 52230
☎ 0033 325944200 🗏 325944143
e-mail: la.forge.de.sainte.marie@wanadoo.fr
website: www.laforgedesaintemarie.com
Partially terraced, on the site of an 18th century forge
containing a lake.
➲ *Access via N67 and D427.*
Open: May-Sep **Site:** 11HEC ⊞ ♀ ♠ ⊞ **Prices:** ⧍3-6 pitch
15-25 (incl 2 persons) **Facilities:** ⋔ ⅏ ⊙ ⊠ ∅ ☎
Services: ⍾ ✕ lau **Leisure:** ⌇ PR

TOULON-SUR-ARROUX SAÔNE-ET-LOIRE

CM du Val d'Arroux rte d'Uxeau, 73120
☎ 0385795122 🗏 0385795276
On W outskirts beside the River Arroux.
➲ *Access via D985 then take Uxeau road.*
Open: 15 Apr-Oct **Site:** 0.6HEC ⊞ ♣ ⊞ **Facilities:** ⋔ ⊙ ⊠
☎ **Services:** ⊞ lau **Leisure:** ⌇ R **Off-site:** ⅏ ⍾ ✕ ∅ ≞

UCHIZY SAÔNE-ET-LOIRE

National 6 71700 ☎ 385405390 🗏 385405390
Site surrounded by poplar trees on banks of river.
➲ *Turn off N6 towards Saône 6km S of Tournus and continue
0.8km.*
Open: Apr-1 Oct **Site:** 6HEC ⊞ ♣ ♠ ⊞ **Facilities:** ⋔ ⅏ ⊙
⊠ ∅ ≞ ☎ **Services:** ⍾ ✕ ⊞ lau **Leisure:** ⌇ PR

VAL-DES-PRÉS MARNE

Gentianes La Vachette, 5100 ☎ 492212141 🗏 492212412
In a delightful wooded location backed by imposing
mountains and bordered by a river.
➲ *On the edge of the village, 3km SE of Briançon.*
Open: All year **Site:** 2HEC ⊞ ♠ ♀ ♠ ⊞ **Prices:** ⧍4.70
pitch 4.70 pp2.10 **Facilities:** ⋔ ⅏ ⊙ ⊠ ≞ ☎ **Services:** ⍾ ✕ ⊞
lau **Leisure:** ⌇ PR **Off-site:** ∅

Site: 6HEC-Site size ⊞-grass ∵-sand ⊕-stone ☬-little shade ♀-partly shaded ♣-mainly shaded
⊞-bungalows for hire ⊠-caravans for hire ⧍-tents for hire ⊗-no dogs **Prices:** ⧍-adult per night ⇔-car per night
pp-per person per night ⊠-caravan per night ⧍-tent per night

VANDENESSE-EN-AUXOIS CÔTE-D'OR

Lac de Panthier 21320 ☎ 380492194 ▤ 380492580
e-mail: info@lac-de-panthier.com
website: www.lac-de-panthier.com
In a wooded location beside Lake Panthier with a wide
variety of sporting facilities.
➲ 5km SE from Pouilly-en-Auxois on A6.
Open: 18 Apr-27 Sep Site: 6HEC ⬛⬛⬛ ♠ ⬛ Facilities: ⬛ ⬛
⊙ ⬛ ⬛ ⬛ Services: ⬛ ✕ ⬛ lau Leisure: ⬛ LP

Voiliers 21320 ☎ 380492194 ▤ 380492580
In a pleasant situation beside a lake with plenty of facilities
for families.
➲ 2.5km NE via D977.
Open: 18 Apr-27 Sep Site: 7HEC ⬛⬛⬛ ⬛ ♠ ⬛ A Prices: ⬛3.70-
6.20 pitch 4.10-7 Facilities: ⬛ ⬛ ⊙ ⬛ ⬛ ⬛ Services: ⬛ ✕ lau
Leisure: ⬛ LP

VENAREY-LES-LAUMES CÔTE-D'OR

Alésia r Dr-Roux, 21150 ☎ 380960776 ▤ 380960776
e-mail: mairie.vll@worldonline.fr
A peaceful site close to the lake and river.
Open: Apr-15 Oct Site: 2HEC ⬛⬛⬛ ⬛ Prices: ⬛2.50 pitch
1.60-4 Facilities: ⬛ ⊙ ⬛ ⬛ Services: ⬛ lau Off-site: ⬛ ⬛ ✕
⬛ ⬛LR ⬛

VERMENTON YONNE

Coulemières 89270 ☎ 386815302 ▤ 386815302
website: www.vermenton.fr
A peaceful site with good facilities set amongst the meadows
of Burgundy.
➲ On the N6 S of Auxerre.
Open: 10 Apr-10 Oct Site: 1.5HEC ⬛⬛⬛ ⬛ Prices: ⬛2.90
⬛1.50 pitch 1.90 Facilities: ⬛ ⬛ ⊙ ⬛ ⬛ ⬛ Services: ⬛ lau
Leisure: ⬛ R Off-site: ⬛

VILLENEUVE-LES-GENÊTS YONNE

Bois Guillaume 89350 ☎ 386454541 ▤ 386454920
e-mail: camping@bois-guillaume.com
website: www.bois-guillaume.com
In wooded surroundings with good, modern facilities.
➲ 2.7km NE.
Open: All year Site: 8HEC ⬛⬛⬛ ♠ ⬛ Prices: ⬛3.40-3.60
⬛2.35-2.35 ⬛2.35-2.35 pitch 2.35-2.35 Facilities: ⬛ ⊙ ⬛ ⬛
⬛ ⬛ Services: ⬛ ✕ ⬛ lau Leisure: ⬛ P Off-site: ⬛R

VINCELLES YONNE

Ceriselles rte de Vincelottes, 89290
☎ 386423939 ▤ 386423939
Rural situation beside the river Yonne, close to the village.
➲ Signed on exiting RN6 between Avallon and Auxerre.
Open: Apr-Sep Site: 21HEC ⬛⬛⬛ ⬛ ⬛ Prices: ⬛1.62-2.11
⬛1.62 ⬛5.04-5.86 ⬛3.10-3.74 Facilities: ⬛ ⊙ ⬛ ⬛
Services: ✕ lau Off-site: ⬛ ⬛ ⬛ ⬛ ⬛R ⬛

SOUTH WEST/PYRÉNÉES

ABZAC GIRONDE

Paradis rte de Périgueux, 33230 ☎ 557490510 ▤ 557491888
e-mail: campingleparadis@free.fr
website: www.campingleparadis.free.fr
In a centre of gastronomic importance, this site stands on
meadowland near an artificial lake. Pedal boats and fishing
nearby.

➲ Drive W on N89 from the direction of Périgueux. After St-
Médard-de-Guizières turn onto D17E and follow signposts.
Open: Feb-15 Nov Site: 5HEC ⬛⬛⬛ ⬛ ⬛ ⬛ Facilities: ⬛ ⬛
⊙ ⬛ ⬛ ⬛ Services: ⬛ ✕ ⬛ lau Leisure: ⬛ LR

AIGNAN GERS

Castex 32290 ☎ 562092513 ▤ 562092479
e-mail: gers.vacances@wanadoo.fr
Wooded site in peaceful surroundings. 800m from D48.
Open: 15 Mar-15 Oct Site: 3HEC ⬛⬛⬛ ♠ ⬛ ⬛ Prices: pitch
10-14 (incl 2 persons) Facilities: ⬛ ⬛ ⊙ ⬛ Services: ⬛ ✕ ⬛ lau
Leisure: ⬛ P Off-site: ⬛ ✕ ⬛ ⬛ ⬛R

AIRE-SUR-L'ADOUR LANDES

Ombrages de l'Adour r des Graviers, 40800
☎ 558717510 ▤ 0558713229
e-mail: hetaparsarl@yahoo.fr
A clean, tidy site next to a sports stadium beside the river.
Clean sanitary installations.
Open: Mar-Nov Site: 2HEC ⬛⬛⬛ ♠ ⬛ ⬛ A Prices: ⬛2.80-
3.80 ⬛1.80-2.30 ⬛3-3.80 ⬛3-3.80 pitch 3-3.80 Facilities: ⬛
⬛ ⊙ ⬛ ⬛ ⬛ Services: ⬛ ✕ ⬛ lau Leisure: ⬛ R Off-site: ⬛P

ALBI TARN

Languedoc allée du Camping Caussels, 81000
☎ 563603706 ▤ 563603706
The site is owned by the local automobile club. It lies on
terraced land in a forest next to municipal swimming pools.
Camping Card Compulsory.
➲ From village take N99 towards Millau, then turn left onto
D100 and left again into site.
Open: Apr-Oct Site: 1HEC ⬛⬛⬛ ⬛ Prices: pitch 66 (incl 2
persons) Facilities: ⬛ ⊙ ⬛ ⬛ Services: ⬛ lau Off-site: ⬛ ⬛
✕ ⬛P

ALLES-SUR-DORDOGNE DORDOGNE

Port de Limeuil 24480 ☎ 553632976 ▤ 553630419
e-mail: didierbonvallet@aol.com
website: www.leportdelimeuil.com
Situated in a conservation area at the confluence of the
Dordogne and Vézère rivers, with a 400 metre beach.
➲ Signed off D51
Open: May-Sept Site: 7HEC ⬛⬛⬛ ♠ Prices: pitch 13.51-19.30
(incl 2 persons) Facilities: ⬛ ⬛ ⊙ ⬛ ⬛ ⬛ ⬛ Services: ⬛ ✕ ⬛
lau Leisure: ⬛ PR

ANDERNOS-LES-BAINS GIRONDE

Fontaine-Vieille 4 bd du Colonel Wurtz, 33510
☎ 556820167 ▤ 556820981
e-mail: fontaine-vieille-sa@wanadoo.fr
website: www.fontaine-vieille.com
On level ground in sparse forest.
➲ S of village centre.
Open: Apr-Sep Site: 12.6HEC ⬛⬛⬛ ⬛ ♠ ⬛ Prices: pitch
16-24 (incl 2 persons) Facilities: ⬛ ⬛ ⊙ ⬛ ⬛ ⬛ ⬛
Services: ⬛ ✕ ⬛ lau Leisure: ⬛ PS

See advertisement on page 102

Pleine Forêt 33510 ☎ 556821718
Situated in a quiet location among pines.
➲ Off D106E or D106 Andernos-les-Bains-Bordeaux road.
Open: All year Site: 6HEC ⬛⬛⬛ ⬛ ♠ ⬛ ⬛ Facilities: ⬛ ⊙
⬛ ⬛ ⬛ Services: ⬛ ✕ ⬛ lau Leisure: ⬛ P Off-site: ⬛ ⬛ ⬛S

A Guide to Caravan & Camping
in Great Britain is also available
from **The AA**

Facilities: ⬛-shop ⬛-shower ⊙-electric points for razors ⬛-electric points for caravans ⬛-parking by tents permitted
⬛-compulsory separate car park Services: ✕-café/restaurant ⬛-bar ⬛-Camping Gaz International ⬛-gas other than Camping
Gaz ⬛-first aid facilities lau-laundry Leisure: ⬛-swimming L-Lake P-Pool R-River S-Sea Off-site: All facilities within 2km

ANGLARS-JUILLAC LOT

Floiras 46140 ☎ 565362739 ▤ 565214100
e-mail: campingfloiras@aol.com
A quiet, level site beside the River Lot surrounded by vineyards in a hilly landscape dotted with villages, castles and caves. Good facilities for boating etc.
➲ SW via D8.
Open: Apr-15 Oct Site: 1HEC ⸬⸬⸬ ⊙ ▲ Prices: ♠3.25-3.50 pitch 4.75-6 Facilities: ⋔ ⊙ ⊠ ⊘ ☎ Services: ☗ ✗ ⊞ lau Leisure: ⋟ R Off-site: ✗

ANGLES TARN

▦**Manoir de Boutaric** rte de Lacabarede, 81260
☎ 563709606 ▤ 563709605
e-mail: manoir@boutaric.com website: www.boutaric.com
Site lies in the grounds of an old Manor House in the heart of the Haute Languedoc region.
➲ S of village, on D52 towards Lacabarède.
Open: 30 Mar-10 Oct Site: 3.3HEC ⸬⸬⸬ ♣ ⊞ Prices: pitch 13-25 Facilities: ⋔ ⊙ ⊠ ⊘ ☎ Services: ☗ ✗ ⊞ lau Leisure: ⋟ P Off-site: ⋙ ⋟LR

ANGLET PYRÉNÉES-ATLANTIQUES

Parme Quartier Brindos, 64600
☎ 559230300 ▤ 559412955
e-mail: campingdeparme@wanadoo.fr
website: campingdeparme.com
In a wooded area with good facilities on the outskirts of Biarritz.
➲ 3km SW off N10
Open: 15 Mar- 15 Nov Site: 3.5HEC ⸬⸬⸬ ♣ ⊞ Prices: ♠4.20-6.50 pitch 6-7 Facilities: ⋔ ⊠ ⊙ ⊠ ⊘ ⛊ ☎ Services: ☗ ✗ ⊞ lau Leisure: ⋟ P Off-site: ⋟LRS

ARCACHON GIRONDE

Camping Club d'Arcachon av de la Galaxie, Les Abatilles, 33120 ☎ 556832415 📠 557522851
e-mail: camparcachon@hotmail.com
website: arcachon.cjb.net
In a delightful wooded position 800mtrs from the town and 1km from the beaches.
➲ *1.5 km S.*
Open: All year **Site:** 6HEC ∷∷ ♣ ⛺ ⌂ **Facilities:** ⋔ ⅙ ⊙ 🅰 🖉 🛒 🅿 🅿 **Services:** 🍸 ✕ 🕀 lau **Leisure:** ⌇ P **Off-site:** ⌇S

ARCIZANS-AVANT HAUTES-PYRÉNÉES

Lac 65400 ☎ 562970188 📠 562970188
e-mail: campinglac@campinglac65.fr
website: www.campinglac65.fr
Set in delightful Pyrenean surroundings on outskirts of village. Lakeside site close to a château.
➲ *S on N21 take D13 through St-Savin.*
Open: Jun-Sep **Site:** 3HEC ⚏ ♣ ⛺ **Prices:** ⋔5 pitch 5 **Facilities:** ⋔ ⅙ ⊙ 🅰 🖉 🛒 **Services:** 🕀 lau **Leisure:** ⌇ P **Off-site:** 🍸 ✕ 🔦 ⌇L

ARÈS GIRONDE

Canadienne rte de Lège, 82 r du Gl-de-Gaulle, 33740 ☎ 556602491 📠 557704085
e-mail: camping-la-canadienne@wanadoo.fr
website: www.lacanadienne.com
A family site surrounded by pine and oak trees with good facilities.
➲ *1 km N off D106.*
Open: Jan-Nov **Site:** 2HEC ⚏ ♣ ⛺ **Prices:** pitch 12-21 (incl 2 persons) **Facilities:** ⋔ ⊙ 🅰 🔦 🛒 **Services:** 🍸 ✕ 🕀 lau **Leisure:** ⌇ P **Off-site:** 🖉 ⌇L

Cigale rte de Lège, 33740 ☎ 556602259 📠 557704166
e-mail: campinglacigaleares@wanadoo.fr
Clean tidy site with good recreational facilities amongst pine trees. Grassy pitches.
➲ *0.5 km N on D106 between the sea and the Arcachon Basin.*
Open: 10 Apr-10 Oct **Site:** 2.8HEC ⚏ 🅰 ⛺ **Prices:** pitch 16.50-22.80 (incl 2 persons) **Facilities:** ⋔ ⅙ ⊙ 🅰 🛒 **Services:** 🍸 ✕ 🕀 lau **Leisure:** ⌇ P **Off-site:** 🖉 🔦

CM Goëlands av de la Libération, 33740 ☎ 556825564 📠 557760224
Situated among oak trees 200mtrs from the beach with good facilities.
➲ *1.7km SE*
Open: Apr-Sep **Site:** 10HEC ⚏ ∷∷ ♣ ⚲ **Facilities:** ⋔ ⅙ ⊙ 🅰 🖉 🔦 🛒 **Services:** 🍸 ✕ 🕀 lau **Off-site:** ⌇LP

Pasteur 1 r du Pilote, 33704 ☎ 556603333 📠 556600505
website: atlantic-vacances.com
➲ *S of D3, 300m from the sea.*
Open: Apr-Sep **Site:** 1HEC ⚏ 🅰 ⛺ ⚲ **Prices:** pitch 11.50-21 (incl 2 persons) **Facilities:** ⋔ ⊙ 🅰 🔦 🛒 **Services:** 🍸 ✕ 🕀 lau **Leisure:** ⌇ P **Off-site:** ⅙ ⌇S

ARGELÈS-GAZOST HAUTES-PYRÉNÉES
AT AGOS-VIDALOS (5KM NE)

Soleil du Pibeste 65400 ☎ 562975323
e-mail: info@campingpibeste.com
In a beautiful wooded setting in the heart of the Pyrénées.
➲ *S on N21.*
Open: All year **Site:** 1.5HEC ⚏ ♣ ⛺ **Facilities:** ⋔ ⅙ ⊙ 🅰 🖉 🔦 🛒 **Services:** 🍸 ✕ 🕀 lau **Leisure:** ⌇ P **Off-site:** ⌇R

ARREAU HAUTES-PYRÉNÉES

Refuge International route departemental 929, 65240 ☎ 562986334 📠 562986334
e-mail: camping.international.arreeau@wanadoo.fr
website: perso.wanadoo.fr/camping.international.arreau
Enclosed terrace site.
➲ *2km N on D929.*
Open: All year **Site:** 15HEC ⚏ 🅰 ⛺ ⚲ **Prices:** ⋔3.10 pitch 4.20 **Facilities:** ⋔ ⊙ 🅰 🖉 🔦 🛒 **Services:** 🍸 ✕ 🕀 lau **Leisure:** ⌇ PR **Off-site:** ⅙ ✕ 🖉 ⌇L

ASCAIN PYRÉNÉES-ATLANTIQUES

Nivelle 64310 ☎ 559540194 📠 559540195
e-mail: campiglanivelle@wanadoo.fr
In a picturesque location beside the River Nivelle.
➲ *2km N of town on D918 to St-Jean-de-Luz.*
Open: Apr-Oct **Site:** 2.8HEC ⚏ ♣ ⛺ ⚲ **Prices:** ⋔2.60-3.70 🚗1.45-1.70 ⚲4.20-6 pitch 4.20-6 **Facilities:** ⋔ ⅙ ⊙ 🅰 🖉 🛒 **Services:** ✕ 🕀 lau **Leisure:** ⌇ R **Off-site:** ⅙ 🍸 ✕ 🖉 🕀

ASCARAT PYRÉNÉES-ATLANTIQUES

Europ' Camping 64220 ☎ 559371278 📠 559372982
In rustic surroundings of mountains and vineyards, 300m from the River Nive.
➲ *1km W of St-Jean-Pied-de-Port on D918.*
Open: Etr-Sep **Site:** 1.7HEC ⚏ ♣ ⛺ **Prices:** ⋔5.40 🚗7.50 ⚲7.50 **Facilities:** ⋔ ⅙ ⊙ 🅰 🖉 🛒 **Services:** 🍸 ✕ 🕀 lau **Leisure:** ⌇ P **Off-site:** 🖉 🔦 ⌇R

ATUR DORDOGNE

Grand Dague 24750 ☎ 553042101 📠 553042201
e-mail: info@legranddague.fr website: www.legranddague.fr
Well equipped family site in the heart of the Dordogne region with pitches divided by bushes and hedges.
➲ *NE of Atur via D2.*
Open: Etr-Sep **Site:** 22HEC ⚏ 🅰 ⛺ ⚲ **Facilities:** ⋔ ⅙ ⊙ 🅰 🖉 🔦 🛒 **Services:** 🍸 ✕ 🕀 lau **Leisure:** ⌇ P

AUREILHAN LANDES

Aurilandes Camping 1001 promenade de l'Étang, 40200 ☎ 558091088 📠 558093823
e-mail: aurilandes@free.fr website: www.aurilandes.fr.fm
Quiet site separated by a small road on the banks of Lake Aureilhan.
➲ *D626, 2km before Mimizan, on the right.*
Open: Jun-20 Sep **Site:** 8HEC ⚏ ♣ ⛺ **Facilities:** ⋔ ⅙ ⊙ 🅰 🖉 🔦 🛒 **Services:** 🍸 ✕ 🕀 lau **Leisure:** ⌇ L **Off-site:** ⌇PS

Parc St-James Eurolac Promenade de l'Étang, 40200 ☎ 558090287 📠 558094189
e-mail: info@camping-parcstjames.com
website: www.camping-parcstjames.com
Well tended site under deciduous trees providing shade, partially on open meadow.
➲ *Turn right at Labouheyre off N10 on D626 to Aureilhan. Follow signs.*
Open: end Mar-end Sep **Site:** 13HEC ⚏ ♣ ⛺ ⚲ ⚑ **Facilities:** ⋔ ⅙ ⊙ 🅰 🖉 🛒 **Services:** 🍸 ✕ 🕀 lau **Leisure:** ⌇ LP

AZUR LANDES

Camping Azu' Rivage 720 Route des Campings, Au bord du lac, 40140 ☎ 558483072 📠 558483072
e-mail: azurivage@wanadoo.fr website: www.touradour.com
A family site in wooded surroundings close to the Lac de Soustons and 8km from the coast.
➲ *2 km S of Azur.*
Open: 15 June-15 Sep **Site:** 7HEC ⚏ ∷∷ 🅰 ⛺ **Prices:** pitch 10.10-16.70 (incl 2 persons) **Facilities:** ⋔ ⅙ ⊙ 🅰 🖉 🔦 🛒 **Services:** 🍸 ✕ 🕀 lau **Leisure:** ⌇ LPR

Facilities: ⅙-shop ⋔-shower ⊙-electric points for razors 🅰-electric points for caravans 🛒-parking by tents permitted 🅿-compulsory separate car park **Services:** ✕-café/restaurant 🍸-bar 🖉-Camping Gaz International 🔦-gas other than Camping Gaz 🕀-first aid facilities lau-laundry **Leisure:** ⌇-swimming L-Lake P-Pool R-River S-Sea **Off-site:** All facilities within 2km

BAGNÈRES-DE-BIGORRE HAUTES-PYRÉNÉES

Bigourdan rte de Tarbes, 65200 ☎ 0562951357
A level site recommended for caravans in a beautiful
Pyrenean setting.
➱ *2.5km NW at Pouzac.*
Open: 7 Apr-19 Oct **Site:** 1HEC ⭘⭘ ♣ 🚐 **Facilities:** ⬧ ⊙ 🖵
🏠 **Services:** lau **Leisure:** ⬧ P **Off-site:** 🛒 ⛾ ✗ ⊘ 🏊 ⬧R ⊞

Tilleuls 12 av Maréchal Alan Brooke, 65200 ☎ 562952604
A well equipped site at an altitude of 500mtrs. There are
good recreational facilities and a bakery operates during July
and August.
Open: May-Sep **Site:** 2.6HEC ⭘⭘ ♣ **Facilities:** ⬧ ⊙ 🖵 🏠
Services: lau **Off-site:** 🛒 ⛾ ✗ ⊘ ⬧P ⊞

AT TRÉBONS (4KM N ON D935)

Parc des Oiseaux RD26, 65200 ☎ 562953026
Clean, well-kept site with large pitches.
Open: All year **Site:** 2.8HEC ⭘⭘ ♣ 🚐 **Prices:** 🅰2.60-3 🚗1-1
🚐1-1 🅰1-1 pitch 3.50-3.50 **Facilities:** ⬧ ⊙ 🖵 ⊘ 🏊 🏠
Services: ⛾ 🖵 lau **Leisure:** ⬧ R **Off-site:** 🛒 ✗ ⬧P

BASTIDE-DE-SEROU, LA ARIÈGE

Arize rte de Nescus, 9240 ☎ 561658151 🖹 561658334
e-mail: camparize@aol.com
website: www.camping-arize.com
A well run site with a wide range of facilities in a peaceful,
wooded location at the foot of the Pyrénées.
Open: Apr-Oct **Site:** 1.8HEC ⭘⭘ 🔩 🚐 🅰 **Prices:** pitch
14.50-21.70 (incl 2 persons) **Facilities:** ⬧ 🛒 ⊙ 🖵 ⊘ 🏠
Services: ⛾ 🖵 lau **Leisure:** ⬧ PR **Off-site:** ✗ 🏊 ⬧R

BAYONNE PYRÉNÉES-ATLANTIQUES

Airotel la Chêneraie chemin de Cazenare, 64100
☎ 559550131 🖹 559551117
On gently sloping field divided by hedges.
➱ *4km NE off N117 (Pau) road.*
Open: Etr-1 Oct **Site:** 10HEC ⭘⭘ 🔩 🚐 🅰 **Facilities:** ⬧ 🛒 ⊙
🖵 ⊘ 🏠 **Services:** ⛾ ✗ lau **Leisure:** ⬧ LP **Off-site:** ⊞

BEAUCENS-LES-BAINS HAUTES-PYRÉNÉES

Viscos 65400 ☎ 562970545
In a secluded location at the foot of the Pyrénées.
➱ *1km N on D13, rte de Lourdes.*
Open: 15 May-Sep **Site:** 2HEC ⭘⭘ ♣ **Prices:** 🅰3 🚗3 🚐3
🅰3 pitch 3 **Facilities:** ⬧ 🛒 ⊙ 🖵 ⊘ 🏠 **Services:** ⊞ lau
Off-site: ⛾ ✗ ⬧R

BELVÈS DORDOGNE

Hauts de Ratebout 24170 ☎ 553290210 🖹 553290828
e-mail: camping@hauts-ratebout.fr
website: www.hauts-ratebout.fr
A well equipped site on an old Périgord farm, set in extensive
grounds on top of a hill.
➱ *D710 to Fumel. After Vaurez-de-Belvès, take D54 to Casals.*
Open: 27 Apr-6 Sep **Site:** 12HEC ⭘⭘ 🔩 🚐 🚐 ⊘
Prices: pitch 19-31 **Facilities:** ⬧ 🛒 ⊙ 🖵 ⊘ 🏠 **Services:** ⛾ ✗
⊞ lau **Leisure:** ⬧ P

Nauves Bos Rouge, 24170 ☎ 553291264 🖹 553291264
e-mail: campinglesnauves@hotmail.com
Located on a site of 40 hectares surrounded by forest
➱ *4.5km SW via D53.*
Open: 01 Apr- End of Sep **Site:** 7HEC ⭘⭘ 🔩 🚐 🚐
Prices: 🅰3.60-4.40 pitch 5-5.75 **Facilities:** ⬧ 🛒 ⊙ 🖵 ⊘ 🏊
🅿 **Services:** ⛾ ✗ ⊞ lau **Leisure:** ⬧ P

RCN Le Moulin de la Pique 24170
☎ 553290115 🖹 553282909
e-mail: info@rcn-lemoulindelapique.fr
website: www.rcn-campings.fr
A quiet well equipped site set out around an imposing villa
and a small lake. There are fine entertainment facilities and
modern sanitary installations.
➱ *500m S on D710.*
Open: 17 Apr-09 Oct **Site:** 12HEC ⭘⭘ 🔩 🚐 🚐 🅰
Prices: 🅰5.20-7.30 pitch 25-45 (incl 2 persons) **Facilities:** ⬧
🛒 ⊙ 🖵 ⊘ 🏊 🏠 **Services:** ⛾ ✗ ⊞ lau **Leisure:** ⬧ LPR

BEYNAC-ET-CAZENAC DORDOGNE

Capeyrou 24220 ☎ 553295495 🖹 553283627
e-mail: lecapeyrou@wanadoo.fr
Situated beside the River Dordogne close to the gates of the
picturesque medieval town of Beynac.
➱ *Access via D703.*
Open: 15 May-15 Sep **Site:** 5HEC ⭘⭘ 🔩 **Prices:** 🅰4.50 🅰6
pitch 6 **Facilities:** ⬧ ⊙ 🖵 🏠 **Services:** ⛾ ✗ lau
Leisure: ⬧ P **Off-site:** 🛒 ✗ ⊘ 🏊 ⬧R

BEZ, LE TARN

Plô 81260 ☎ 563740082
e-mail: info@leplo.com website: www.leplo.com
A pleasant site in wooded surroundings.
➱ *0.9km W via D30.*
Open: Jun-Aug **Site:** 3HEC ⭘⭘ 🔩 🚐 🅰 **Prices:** 🅰2.80 pitch
12.70 **Facilities:** ⬧ 🛒 ⊙ 🖵 🏠 **Services:** ⛾ ✗ ⊞ lau
Off-site: ✗ ⊘ ⬧LPR

BIARRITZ PYRÉNÉES-ATLANTIQUES

Biarritz 28 r d'Harcet, 64200 ☎ 559230012 🖹 559437467
e-mail: biarritz.camping@wanadoo.fr
website: www.biarritz-camping.fr
A pleasant site with spacious pitches 200m from beach.
➱ *2km from town centre on N10, follow signs 'Espagne'.*
Open: 10 May-21 Sep **Site:** 2.6HEC ⭘⭘ 🔩 🚐 🚐
Facilities: ⬧ 🛒 ⊙ 🖵 ⊘ 🏠 **Services:** ⛾ ✗ ⊞ lau **Leisure:** ⬧ P
Off-site: 🛒 ⛾ ✗ 🏊 ⬧S ⊞

AT BIDART (4KM SW)

Jean Paris Quartier M-Pierre, 64210
☎ 559265558 🖹 0559265558
600m from beaches.
➱ *S of town, cross railway line, site on S side of N10.*
Open: Jun-Sep **Site:** 1.1HEC ⭘⭘ ♣ **Facilities:** ⬧ 🛒 ⊙ 🖵 🏠
Services: ⛾ ✗ ⊞ lau **Off-site:** ✗ ⬧S

Oyam Ferme Oyamburua, 64210
☎ 559549161 🖹 559549161
e-mail: accueil@camping-oyam.com
website: www.camping-oyam.com/
Level meadow site near farm. Views of the Pyrénées. Simple
but pleasant site.
➱ *Turn off beyond the church in the direction of Arbonne, via
N10, for approx 1km.*
Open: Jun-Sep **Site:** 6HEC ⭘⭘ ♣ 🚐 🅰 **Prices:** pitch 10.30-
19 (incl 2 persons) **Facilities:** ⬧ ⊙ 🖵 🏠 **Services:** ⛾ ✗ lau
Leisure: ⬧ P **Off-site:** 🛒 ⊘ ⬧S ⊞

Pavillon Royal av Prince de Galles, 64210
☎ 559230054 🖹 559234447
e-mail: info@pavillon-royal.com
website: www.pavillon-royal.com
Beautiful, well-kept site, divided into pitches, most of which
have open view of sea. Beside rocky beach.

Site: 6HEC-Site size ⭘⭘-grass ⸪⸪-sand ◈-stone ❅-little shade 🔩-partly shaded ♣-mainly shaded
🏠-bungalows for hire 🚐-caravans for hire 🅰-tents for hire ⊘-no dogs **Prices:** 🅰-adult per night 🚗-car per night
pp-per person per night 🚐-caravan per night 🅰-tent per night

⊃ *2 km N.*
Open: 15 May-25 Sep Site: 5HEC ∷∷ ⊕ 🏠 ⊘ Prices: pitch 15-33 Facilities: ↑ ⅗ ⊙ 🖸 ⊘ ☎ Services: 🍷 ✕ 🖽 lau
Leisure: ⅋ P Off-site: ⅋S

Résidence des Pins rte de Biarritz, 64210
☎ 559230029 ▤ 559412459
e-mail: contact@campingdespins.com
website: www.campingdespins.com
Terraced site with numbered pitches, 800m from sea.
⊃ *2km N on N106 Biarritz road.*
Open: 15 May-30 Oct Site: 10HEC 🗔 🏠 Prices: pitch 14.10-22.90 Facilities: ↑ ⅗ ⊙ 🖸 ⊘ ☶ ☎ Services: 🍷 ✕ 🖽 lau
Leisure: ⅋ P Off-site: ⅋LS

Ruisseau rte d'Arbonne, 64210
☎ 559419450 ▤ 559419573
e-mail: francoise.dumont3@wanadoo.fr
website: www.camping-le-ruisseau.fr
A well equipped site in wooded surroundings set out around two lakes.
⊃ *2km E on D255.*
Open: 15 May-12 Sept Site: 15HEC 🗔 🏠 Prices: pitch 15-25 (incl 2 persons) Facilities: ↑ ⅗ ⊙ 🖸 ⊘ ☶ ☎
Services: 🍷 ✕ 🖽 lau Leisure: ⅋ LP

Sunelia Berrua rte Berrua, 64210
☎ 559549666 ▤ 559547830
e-mail: contact@berrua.com website: www.berrua.com
A well equipped family site 1km from the beach and 500mtrs from the village.
Open: 4 Apr-6 Oct Site: 5HEC 🗔 🏠 Prices: pitch 14.50-23.60 (incl 2 persons) Facilities: ↑ ⅗ ⊙ 🖸 ⊘ ☎ Services: 🍷 ✕ 🖽 lau Leisure: ⅋ P Off-site: ⅋RS

Ur-Onéa r de la Chapelle, 64210 ☎ 559265361 ▤ 559265394
e-mail: uronea@wanadoo.fr
website: www.uronea.com
A well equipped site lying at the foot of the Pyrénées with good recreational facilities.
⊃ *0.6km E.*
Open: 3 Apr-19 Sep Site: 5HEC 🗔 ⊕ 🏠 🖼 Prices: pitch 11.50-18.50 (incl 2 persons) Facilities: ↑ ⅗ ⊙ 🖸 ⊘ ☎ 🄿
Services: 🍷 ✕ 🖽 lau Leisure: ⅋ P Off-site: ✕ ☶ ⅋RS

BIAS LANDES

CM Le Tatiou 40710 ☎ 558090476 ▤ 558824430
e-mail: campingletatiou@wanadoo.fr
website: www.campingletatiou.com
Family site in a forested setting 4km from the sea.
⊃ *2km W towards Lespecier.*
Open: 4 Apr-14 Oct Site: 10HEC 🗔 ∷∷ 🏠 🏠 🖼
Prices: pitch 12 (incl 2 persons) Facilities: ↑ ⅗ ⊙ 🖸 ⊘ ☎
Services: 🍷 ✕ lau Leisure: ⅋ P Off-site: ☶ ⅋S

BIRON DORDOGNE

Sunêlia le Moulinal 24540 ☎ 553408460 ▤ 553408149
e-mail: lemoulinal@perigord.com
website: www.lemoulinal.com
In a pleasant situation beside a lake close to the former mill of Biron Castle. This is a modern holiday village with a wide variety of recreational facilities.
⊃ *2km S on the Lacapelle-Biron road.*
Open: 3 Apr-18 Sep Site: 18HEC 🗔 ⅍ ⊕ 🏠 🛆
Prices: pitch 12-35 (incl 2 persons) Facilities: ↑ ⅗ ⊙ 🖸 ⊘ ☶ ☎ Services: 🍷 ✕ 🖽 lau
Leisure: ⅋ LP

BISCARROSSE LANDES

Bimbo 176 chemin de Bimbo, 40600
☎ 558098233 ▤ 558098014
e-mail: camping.bimbo@free.fr
website: camping.bimbo.free.fr
In delightful wooded surroundings 500mtrs from the lake and 10 minutes from the sea. Reservations recommended.
⊃ *3.5km N towards Sanguinet.*
Open: All year Site: 6HEC 🗔 🏠 Facilities: ↑ ⅗ ⊙ 🖸 ⊘ ☶ ☎ Services: 🍷 ✕ 🖽 lau Leisure: ⅋ P Off-site: ⅋L

Ecureuils Port Navarrosse, 40600 ☎ 558098000
e-mail: camping.les.ecureuils@wanadoo.fr
In a pleasant wooded location 200mtrs from the lake shore. Plenty of recreational facilities.
⊃ *Access via D652.*
Open: Apr-Sep Site: 7HEC 🗔 🏠 Facilities: ↑ ⊙ 🖸 ⊘
Services: 🍷 ✕ lau Leisure: ⅋ P Off-site: ⅗ ⊘ ⅋L

Rive rte de Bordeaux, 40600 ☎ 558781233 ▤ 558781292
e-mail: larive@wanadoo.fr
website: www.camping-de-la-rive.fr
Level site in tall pine forest on E side of lake. Private port and beach.
⊃ *N of town off 652 Sanguinet road.*
Open: Apr-Sep Site: 15HEC 🗔 ∷∷ 🏠 🖼 Prices: pitch 20-35 (incl 2 persons) Facilities: ↑ ⅗ ⊙ 🖸 ⊘ ☶ ☎ Services: 🍷 ✕ 🖽 lau Leisure: ⅋ LP

BLAYE GIRONDE
AT MAZION (5.5KM NE ON N937)

Tilleuls 33390 ☎ 557421813 ▤ 557421301
⊃ *5.5km NE on N937.*
Open: May-Oct Site: 0.5HEC 🗔 ⊕ Prices: ↟3.50 pitch 2.50 Facilities: ↑ ⊙ 🖸 ☎ Services: 🖽 lau Off-site: ⅗ 🍷 ✕

BOURNEL LOT-ET-GARONNE

Ferme de Bourgade 47210 ☎ 553366715
e-mail: bourgade47@libertysurf.fr
website: www.bourgade-holidays.co.uk
A small, tranquil site with good, clean facilities.
⊃ *Signposted from N21 between Castillonnès and Villeréal.*
Open: June-Mid Oct Site: 1HEC 🗔 🏠 Prices: ↟1.50 ⚶1.50 pitch 3 Facilities: ↑ 🖸 ☎ Services: 🖽 lau
Leisure: ⅋ L Off-site: 🍷 ✕

BRETENOUX LOT

Bourgnatelle 46130 ☎ 565384407
e-mail: bourgnatel@aol.com
website: www.bourgnatelle.fr.fm
In a pleasant location beside the River Cére. Separate car park for arrivals after 22.30hrs.
⊃ *Access via D940 towards Rocamadour.*
Open: May-Sep Site: 2HEC 🗔 🏠 🖼 Facilities: ↑ ⊙ 🖸 ⊘ ☎ Services: lau Leisure: ⅋ R Off-site: ⅗ 🍷 ✕ ☶ ⅋P 🖽

BUGUE, LE DORDOGNE

Rocher de la Granelle rte du Buisson, 24260 ☎ 53072432
Surrounded by woodland with pitches set out among trees and bushes on the banks of the Vézère with a wide variety of leisure facilities.
⊃ *From Le Bugue centre cross the bridge and follow signs.*
Open: Apr-Sep Site: 8HEC 🗔 ⊕ 🏠 🖼 Facilities: ↑ ⅗ ⊙ 🖸 ⊘ ☶ ☎ Services: 🍷 ✕ 🖽 lau Leisure: ⅋ PR

Facilities: ⅗-shop ↑-shower ⊙-electric points for razors 🖸-electric points for caravans ☎-parking by tents permitted 🄿-compulsory separate car park Services: ✕-café/restaurant 🍷-bar ⊘-Camping Gaz International ☶-gas other than Camping Gaz 🖽-first aid facilities lau-laundry Leisure: ⅋-swimming L-Lake P-Pool R-River S-Sea Off-site: All facilities within 2km

St-Avit Loisirs St-Avit-de-Vialard, 24260
☎ 553026400   ▤ 553026439
e-mail: contact@saint-avit.loisirs.com
website: www.saint-avit-loisirs.com
A pleasant site in natural wooded surroundings.
➔ *W of town via C201.*
Open: Apr-Sep Site: 7HEC ⛺ ⊕ ⊞ Prices: pitch 11
Facilities: ⋔ ⅏ ⊙ ⊖ ∅ ≞ ☎ Services: ⏧ ✕ ⊞ lau Leisure: ⌇
P Off-site: ⌇R

CAHORS LOT

Rivière de Cabessut r de la Rivière, 46000
☎ 565300630   ▤ 565239946
e-mail: camping/riviere/cabessut@wanadoo.fr
website: www.cabessut.com
➔ *N of town via the Cabessut Bridge over the River Lot.*
Open: Apr-Sep Site: 3HEC ⛺ ⊕ ⊞ Facilities: ⋔ ⅏ ⊙ ⊖ ∅
☎ Services: ⏧ ✕ ⊞ lau Leisure: ⌇ PR Off-site: ✕ ≞

AT ESCLAUZELS (18KM SE)

Pompit 46090 ☎ 565315340   ▤ 565317800
Situated in the heart of a large forest close to the magnificent
Lot Valley.
➔ *5km NW of Esclauzels village.*
Open: All year Site: 3.5HEC ⛺ ⊕ ⊕ ⊞ ⊞ Prices: ⋔3.40
🚗3.60 ⊞3.60 pitch 3.60 Facilities: ⋔ ⅏ ⊙ ⊖ ∅ ☎
Services: ⏧ ✕ ⊞ lau Leisure: ⌇ P

CALVIAC LOT

Chênes Verts rte de Sarlat, Souillac, 24370 ☎ 553592107
In a beautiful wooded setting within the Périgord countryside.
A wide variety of recreational facilities are available.
➔ *On D704A between Sarlat and Calviac.*
Open: May-Sep Site: 6HEC ⛺ ⊕ ⊞ Facilities: ⋔ ⅏ ⊙ ⊖
∅ ☎ Services: ⏧ ✕ ⊞ lau Leisure: ⌇ P Off-site: ⌇LR

Trois Sources Le Peyratel, 46190 ☎ 565330301   ▤ 565330645
e-mail: l3s@wanadoo.fr website: www.les-trois-sources.com
Wooded location, family site with plenty of leisure facilities.
➔ *Access via D653, then D25 to Calviac.*
Open: May-Sep Site: 6.4HEC ⛺ ⊕ ⊞ ⊞ A
Facilities: ⋔ ⅏ ⊙ ⊖ ∅ ☎ Services: ⏧ ✕ ⊞ lau
Leisure: ⌇ LPR

CAMBO-LES-BAINS PYRÉNÉES-ATLANTIQUES

Bixta Eder rte de St-Jean-de-Luz, 64250
☎ 5559299423   ▤ 559292370
e-mail: camping.bixtaeden@wanadoo.fr
website: www.camping-bixtaeder.com
Modern site with good sports facilities.
➔ *Near the junction of D932 and D10.*
Open: 15 Apr Site: 1HEC ⛺ ⊕ ⊞ Prices: ⋔3.20 🚗1.52
Facilities: ⋔ ⊙ ⊖ ☎ Services: lau Off-site: ⌇LP ⊞

CAPBRETON LANDES

Pointe Quartier la Pointe, 40130
☎ 558721498   ▤ 558723197
Family site in a wooded location on the banks of a river,
800mtrs from the sea. Good recreational facilities.
➔ *2km S towards Labenne on N652.*
Open: Apr-Oct Site: 13HEC ⠿ ⊕ ⊞ Prices: pitch 18
Facilities: ⋔ ⊙ ⊖ ∅ ≞ ☎ ⊞ Services: ⏧ ✕ ⊞ lau
Leisure: ⌇ PRS

*The AA cannot be held
responsible for the content of
third party websites*

CAP FERRET GIRONDE

Truc Vert rte Forestière, 33970
☎ 556608955   ▤ 556609947
e-mail: camping.trvc-vert@worldonline.fr
website: www.trvcvert.com
In a very pleasant location on a slope in a pine wood close to
the beach.
➔ *On D106 in the direction of Cap Ferret to Petit Piquey.
Turn right and follow signs.*
Open: May-Sep Site: 11HEC ⠿ ⊕ Prices: pitch 12-17.90
(incl 2 persons) Facilities: ⋔ ⅏ ⊙ ⊖ ∅ ☎ Services: ⏧ ✕ ⊞
lau Off-site: ⌇S

CARLUCET LOT

Château de Lacomté 46500 ☎ 565387546   ▤ 565331768
e-mail: chateaulacomte@wanadoo.fr
website: www.camping-chateau-lacomte.com
In wooded surroundings with good sized pitches and a
variety of recreational facilities.
➔ *Follow signposts from D677/D32.*
Open: 15 May-Sep Site: 12HEC ⛺ ⊕ ⊕ ⊞ ⊞ A
Prices: ⋔3.77-5.80 A3.70 pitch 4.80-7.40 Facilities: ⋔ ⅏ ⊙ ⊖
☎ Services: ⏧ ✕ ⊞ lau Leisure: ⌇ P

CASTELJALOUX LOT-ET-GARONNE

Club de Clarens rte de Mont-de-Marsan, 47700
☎ 553930745   ▤ 553939309
A large site with direct access to a 17 hectare Lac de Clarens
and good recreational facilities.
Open: Jun-Sep Site: 2HEC ⠿ ⊕ ⊞ Facilities: ⋔ ⊙ ⊖ ☎
Services: ⏧ ✕ ⊞ lau Leisure: ⌇ LR Off-site: ⅏ ✕ ⌇P

CM de la Piscine rte de Marmande, 47700
☎ 553935468   ▤ 553891325
➔ *NW on D933 Marmande road.*
Open: Apr-3 Nov Site: 1HEC ⛺ ⊕ Prices: ⋔2 A2 pitch 2-
3.35 Facilities: ⋔ ⊙ ⊖ ☎ Services: lau Leisure: ⌇ P
Off-site: ⅏ ⏧ ✕ ∅ ≞ ⌇R ⊞

CASTELNAUD-LA-CHAPELLE DORDOGNE

Maisonneuve 24250 ☎ 553295129   ▤ 553302706
e-mail: campmaison@aol.com
website: www.campingmaisonneuve.com
In picturesque surroundings, 800mtrs from the village, close
to the River Céou in the heart of the Périgord Noir region.
➔ *10kms S of Sarlat on D57.*
Open: 29 Mar-Sep Site: 6HEC ⛺ ⊕ ⊞ Prices: ⋔3.40-4.80
pitch 4.40-6.30 Facilities: ⋔ ⅏ ⊙ ⊖ ☎ Services: ⏧ ✕ ⊞ lau
Leisure: ⌇ PR Off-site: ∅ ≞

CAUTERETS HAUTES-PYRÉNÉES

Mamelon-Vert 32 av du Mamelon-Vert, 65110
☎ 562925156   ▤ 562925156
e-mail: info@mamelon-vert.com
website: www.mamelon-vert.com
In a beautiful wooded mountain setting close to the local
winter sports facilities.
Open: Dec-Sep Site: 2HEC ⛺ ⊕ ⊞ ⊞ Prices: ⋔2.80-3.40
🚗1.25-1.50 A1-1.20 pitch 8.60-9.90 (incl 2 persons)
Facilities: ⋔ ⊙ ⊖ ≞ ☎ Services: ⊞ lau
Off-site: ⅏ ⏧ ✕ ∅ ≞ ⌇PR

CLAOUEY GIRONDE

Airotel les Viviers rte du Cap Ferret, 33950
☎ 556607004   ▤ 556607614
e-mail: lesviviers@wanadoo.fr
website: www.airotel.les.viviers.com
Beautiful, widespread site in a forest divided by seawater
channels.

Site: 6HEC-Site size ⛺-grass ⠿-sand ◈-stone ⋎-little shade ⊕-partly shaded ⊞-mainly shaded
⊞-bungalows for hire ⊞-caravans for hire A-tents for hire ⊘-no dogs Prices: ⋔-adult per night 🚗-car per night
pp-per person per night ⊞-caravan per night A-tent per night

➲ *On the D106, 1km S of the town.*
Open: Apr-Sep Site: 33HEC ⠿ ♦ ⛺ 🚐 Prices: ⚑2.75-7.05
⛟1.50-4.60 🚐21.10-35.10 ▲15.10-30.10 Facilities: ⋒ ⚄ ☉
🔌 ☎ Services: ⚧ ✗ ⊞ lau Leisure: ⇲ LPS

CONTIS-PLAGE LANDES

Lous Seurrots 40170 ☎ 558428582 ▤ 558424911
e-mail: info@lous-seurrots.com
website: www.lous-seurrots.com
Well equipped site in a pine forest on outskirts of village
between road and stream.
➲ *Access via D41.*
Open: Apr-Sep Site: 15HEC ⠿ ♦ ⛺ Prices: pitch 15-24
(incl 2 persons) Facilities: ⋒ ⚄ ☉ 🔌 ⚄ ㅗ ☎ Services: ⚧ ✗ ⊞
lau Leisure: ⇲ PRS

CORDES TARN

Moulin de Julien 81170 ☎ 563561110 ▤ 563561110
website: www.cordes-sur-ciel.org
In a beautiful valley with good pitches for caravans and tents
and plenty of modern facilities.
➲ *900m E on D600 and D922.*
Open: Apr-Sep Site: 6HEC ⠿ ⚄ ⛺ 🚐 Prices: pitch 13.50-
15 Facilities: ⋒ ☉ 🔌 ⚄ ☎ Services: ⚧ ⊞ lau Leisure: ⇲ LP

COUX-ET-BIGAROQUE DORDOGNE

Clou Meynard, 24220 ☎ 553316332 ▤ 553316933
e-mail: leclou@perigord.com
website: www.camping-le-clou.com
Separate section for dog owners.
➲ *Access via D703 (Le Bugue-Delve road).*
Open: Easter-29 Sep Site: 3.5HEC ⠿ ♦ ⛺ ▲
Prices: ⚑3.50-4.65 🚐4-7.25 ▲4-7.25 pitch 4-7.25 Facilities: ⋒
⚄ ☉ 🔌 ⚄ ㅗ ☎ Services: ⚧ ✗ ⊞ lau Leisure: ⇲ P

Faval 24220 ☎ 553316044 ▤ 553283971
e-mail: camping.la.faval@libertysurf.fr
website: www.lafaval.com
In a wooded location 200m from River Dordogne. A family
site with good recreational facilities.
➲ *1km E of village on D703, near junction with D710.*
Open: Apr-Sep Site: 3HEC ⠿ ♦ ⛺ Prices: ⚑3.50-4.70
🚐4.60-6.10 ▲3.45-4.60 Facilities: ⋒ ⚄ ☉ 🔌 ⚄ ☎ Services: ⚧
✗ ⊞ lau Leisure: ⇲ P Off-site: ✗ ㅗ ⇲R

Valades Les Valades, 24220 ☎ 553291427 ▤ 553281928
e-mail: camping.valades@wanadoo.fr
website: perso.wanadoo.fr/les-valades
In wooded surroundings within a pleasant valley. Well
equipped pitches available.
➲ *5km N of town off N703.*
Open: Apr-Sept Site: 11HEC ⠿ ⚄ ⛺ Prices: ⚑4.20-4.20
pitch 5.50-5.50 Facilities: ⋒ ⚄ ☉ 🔌 ⚄ ☎ Services: ⚧ ✗ ⊞ lau
Leisure: ⇲ LP

CRÉON GIRONDE

Bel Air 33670 ☎ 556230190 ▤ 556230838
e-mail: info@camping-bel-air.com
website: www.camping-bel-air.com
A well equipped, roomy site on a level meadow shaded by tall
trees.
➲ *1 mile W of Créon on D671.*
Open: Apr-Sep Site: 2HEC ⠿ ⚄ ⛺ Prices: ⚑2.60 ⛟1.55
pitch 4.60 Facilities: ⋒ ⚄ ☉ 🔌 ⚄ ㅗ ☎ Services: ⚧ ✗ ⊞
Leisure: ⇲ P

DAGLAN DORDOGNE

Moulin de Paulhiac 24250 ☎ 553282088 ▤ 553293345
e-mail: francis.armagnac@wanadoo.fr
website: www.moulin-de-paulhiac.com
In picturesque wooded surroundings with wide, well marked
pitches and good, modern facilities.
➲ *4km N via D57 beside the Céou*
Open: 15 May-15 Sep Site: 5HEC ⠿ ♦ 🚐 Facilities: ⋒ ⚄
☉ 🔌 ⚄ ㅗ ☎ Services: ⚧ ✗ ⊞ lau Leisure: ⇲ PR

DAX LANDES

Chênes Au Bois-de-Boulogne, 40100
☎ 558900553 ▤ 558904243
e-mail: camping-chenes@wanadoo.fr
website: www.camping-les-chenes.fr
In a wooded park on the edge of the Bois-de-Boulogne with
good facilities.
➲ *1.5km W of town beside River Adour.*
Open: 27 Mar-6 Nov Site: 5HEC ⠿ ♦ ⛺ Prices: pitch
10.50-18 (incl 2 persons) Facilities: ⋒ ⚄ ☉ 🔌 ⚄ ☎
Services: lau Leisure: ⇲ P Off-site: ⚧ ✗ ⇲R

DURAVEL LOT

Club de Vacances Port de Vire, 46700 ☎ 565246506
A pleasant site with good facilities beside the River Lot.
Camping Card Compulsory
➲ *2.3km S via D58.*
Open: 25 Apr-Sep Site: 7HEC ⠿ ⚄ ⛺ 🚐 ▲ Facilities: ⋒
⚄ ☉ 🔌 ⚄ ☎ Services: ⚧ ✗ ⊞ lau Leisure: ⇲ PR

DURFORT ARIÈGE

Bourdieu 09130 ☎ 561673017 ▤ 561672900
e-mail: lebourdieu@wanadoo.fr
website: www.lebourdieu.com
Well equipped site in a picturesque setting with fine views
over the Pyrénées.
➲ *Off D14 Le Fossat-Saverdun.*
Open: All year Site: 20HEC ⠿ ⚄ ⛺ 🚐 Prices: ⚑2.10-3
🚐6.30-9 ▲4.90-7 pitch 4.90-7 Facilities: ⋒ ⚄ ☉ 🔌 ⚄ ㅗ ☎
Services: ⚧ ✗ ⊞ lau Leisure: ⇲ PR

ESTAING HAUTES-PYRÉNÉES

🏔Pyrénées Natura rte du Lac, 65400
☎ 562974544 ▤ 562974581
e-mail: sarl.ruysschaert@wanadoo.fr
website: www.camping-pyrenees-natura.com
A well run site at an altitude of 1000mtrs, situated on the
edge of the National Park with fine views of the surrounding
mountains.
➲ *From Argelès-Gazost take road towards Arrens, then D13
for Lac d'Estaing.*
Open: May-Sep Site: 2.5HEC ⠿ ⚄ ⛺ Facilities: ⋒ ⚄ ☉ 🔌
⚄ ☎ Services: ⚧ ✗ ⊞ lau Leisure: ⇲ R Off-site: ✗

ÉYZIES-DE-TAYAC, LES DORDOGNE

Pech Charmant 24620 ☎ 553359708 ▤ 553359709
e-mail: info@lepech.com
website: www.lepech.com
Located on the side of a wooded hill and contains a small
farm with donkeys, goats, horses and chickens.
Open: Apr-Sep Site: 7HEC ⠿ ⚄ ♦ ⛺ ▲ Prices: ⚑3-4.50
pitch 5-8 Facilities: ⋒ ⚄ ☉ 🔌 ⚄ ☎ Services: ⚧ ✗ ⊞ lau
Leisure: ⇲ P Off-site: ㅗ ⇲R

Facilities: ㅗ-shop ⋒-shower ☉-electric points for razors 🔌-electric points for caravans ☎-parking by tents permitted
🅿-compulsory separate car park Services: ✗-café/restaurant ⚧-bar ⚄-Camping Gaz International ㅗ-gas other than Camping
Gaz ⊞-first aid facilities lau-laundry Leisure: ⇲-swimming L-Lake P-Pool R-River S-Sea Off-site: All facilities within 2km

La Réserve

A stunningly beautiful lakeside location, set among scented pines - perfect for lovers of nature, beautiful beaches and watersports.

- 100m² standard pitch size
- Superb spring & autumn prices
- Ferry inclusive package
- High standard facilities open all season
- Free use of superb indoor & outdoor pools
- Free use of 3 childrens clubs for all ages
- Bilingual friendly staff
- Site open from: 30 April - 19 September

La Réserve, Gastes, 40160, Parentis-en-Born, France
Tel: 00 33 558 09 74 79 Fax: 00 33 558 09 78 71
To book please call the number above, quoting code TOAA01
or request a brochure by calling 0870 242 6666
ABTA
V2819

FIGEAC LOT

Rives du Célé Domaine du Surgie, 46100 ☎ 565345900
In a pleasant wooded location on the banks of the River Célé with plenty of leisure facilities, the site lies within a large recreation area. Separate carpark for late arrivals.
Open: Apr-Sep Site: 2HEC ⛺ ♣ ⭑ Facilities: �📶 ⛽ ⊙ 🚰 🖿 🏪 Services: ▮ ✕ ⊞ lau Leisure: ⮑ LPR Off-site: ∅

FOIX ARIÈGE

Lac RN 20, 09000 ☎ 561651158 ▤ 561651998
e-mail: camping-du-lac@wanadoo.fr
website: www.campingdulac.com
On well-kept meadow beside the Lac de Labarre.
⤳ *3km N on N20.*
Open: All year Site: 5HEC ⛺ ♣ ⭑ Prices: pitch 10-15 (incl 2 persons) Facilities: 📶 ⊙ ⛽ ∅ 🏪 Services: ✕ lau Leisure: ⮑ LP Off-site: 🛒 ▮ ✕ ∅ ⊞

GASTES LANDES

Réserve 40160 ☎ 0870 242 7777 ▤ 0870 242 9999
website: www.haveneurope.com
A large, popular site situated in one of the largest forests in Europe. Plenty of sporting and entertainment facilities.
⤳ *3km SW via D652*
Open: 28 Apr-14 Sep Site: 32HEC ⛺ ♣ ⭑ ▲ ⊘
Prices: pitch 12-34 (incl 2 persons) Facilities: 📶 🛒 ∅ 🖿 🏪
Services: ▮ ✕ ⊞ lau Leisure: ⮑ LP

GAUGEAC DORDOGNE

Moulin de David 24540 ☎ 553226525 ▤ 553239976
e-mail: courrier@moulin-de-david.com
website: moulin-de-david.com
Situated in a wooded valley alongside a small stream with well defined pitches and good recreational facilities.

⤳ *3km from town towards Villeréal.*
Open: 15 May-11 Sep Site: 14HEC ⛺ ♣ ⭑ 🐾 ▲
Prices: ▲3.88-6.63 ♠5-9.30 ♠5-9.30 pitch 5-9.30
Facilities: 📶 🛒 ⊙ ⛽ ∅ 🖿 🏪 Services: ▮ ✕ ⊞ lau
Leisure: ⮑ LP

GOURDON LOT

Paradis La Peyrugue, 46300 ☎ 565416501 ▤ 565416501
e-mail: gilles@campingparadis.com
On a pleasant wooded meadow surrounded by hills.
⤳ *1.6km SW off N673.*
Open: 15 May-15 Sep Site: 2HEC ⛺ ♣ ⭑ 🐾 Prices: ▲4.75
pitch 2.50 Facilities: 📶 ⊙ ⛽ ∅ 🖿 🏪 Services: ⊞ lau
Leisure: ⮑ LP Off-site: 🛒 ▮ ✕ ⮑LR

AT GROLÉJAC (15KM N ON D704)

Granges 24250 ☎ 553281115 ▤ 553285713
e-mail: lesueur.francine@wanadoo.fr
Beautifully situated terraces on a hill with big pitches. The site has been constructed around a disused railway station, incorporating the old ticket office and the bridge into its modern design. Facilities for sports and entertainment.
⤳ *Turn off D704 in village towards Domme.*
Open: 2 May-14 Sep Site: 6.5HEC ⛺ ♣ 🐾 Prices: pitch
14.80-25.20 (incl 2 persons) pp6.20 Facilities: 📶 ⊙ ⛽ 🏪
Services: ▮ ✕ ⊞ lau Leisure: ⮑ PR Off-site: 🛒 ∅ ⮑L

AT ST-MARTIAL-DE-NABIRAT (6KM W)

Carbonnier 24250 ☎ 553284253 ▤ 553285131
Family site in a small, wooded valley with a variety of recreational facilities.
⤳ *Off the D46.*
Open: Etr-15 Sep Site: 8HEC ⛺ ♣ ⭑ Facilities: 📶 🛒 ⊙ ⛽
∅ 🖿 🏪 Services: ▮ ✕ ⊞ lau Leisure: ⮑ LP

GOURETTE PYRÉNÉES-ATLANTIQUES

Ley 64440 ☎ 559051147 ▤ 559051147
Terraced site with gravel and asphalt caravan pitches. TV, common room.
⤳ *From Laruns drive E to Eaux-Bonnes and drive uphill to Gourette.*
Open: Dec-Apr & Jul-Sep Site: 2HEC ⛺ ⭒ ⭑ 🐾
Prices: pitch 10.70 (incl 2 persons) pp3.85 Facilities: 📶 ⊙ ⛽
🖿 🏪 Services: ▮ ✕ ⊞ lau Leisure: ⮑ R Off-site: 🛒 ∅

GRAULGES, LES DORDOGNE

Crozes les Graulges 24340 ☎ 553607473
e-mail: info@lesgraulges.com
website: www.lesgraulges.com
In a picturesque setting in woodland beside a lake.
⤳ *Off D939 between Angoulême and Périgueux.*
Open: May-Oct Site: 8HEC ⛺ ♣ 🐾 Prices: ▲3.75-4.25
♠4.50-5.50 Facilities: 📶 🛒 ⊙ ⛽ 🏪 Services: ▮ ✕ ⊞
Leisure: ⮑ LPR

GRISOLLES TARN-ET-GARONNE

Aquitaine rte Nationale 20, 82170 ☎ 563673322
e-mail: campingaquitaine@aol.com
⤳ *1.5km N off 'X' roads N20/N113.*
Open: All year Site: 3HEC ⛺ ♣ ⭑ 🐾 Facilities: 📶 ⊙ ⛽ 🏪
Services: ⊞ lau Leisure: ⮑ P Off-site: 🛒 ▮ ✕ ∅ 🖿 ⮑R

> A full guide to the Symbols & Abbreviations used in this book can be found on page 6

Site: 6HEC-Site size ⛺-grass ∵-sand ♣-stone ⭒-little shade 🐾-partly shaded ♠-mainly shaded
⭑-bungalows for hire 🐾-caravans for hire ▲-tents for hire ⊘-no dogs Prices: ▲-adult per night ♠-car per night
pp-per person per night ♠-caravan per night ▲-tent per night

HASPARREN PYRÉNÉES-ATLANTIQUES

Chapital rte de Cambo, 64240 ☎ 559296294 ▤ 559296971
On level ground, surrounded by woodland. Good facilities
for families.
➲ *0.5km W via D22. Access via A64 towards Hasparren.*
Open: Etr-Oct Site: 2.6HEC ⚌ ⊙ ⊕ ⊕ Facilities: ⋔ ⊙ ⊕
⊘ ⊞ Services: ⊞ lau Off-site: ⋤ ⋏ ⋄P

HAUTEFORT DORDOGNE

Moulin des Loisirs L'etang du Coucou, 24390 ☎ 553504655
e-mail: moulin.des.loisirs@wanadoo.fr
website: www.moulin-des-loisirs.fr
➲ *2km SW via D72 & D71, 100m from Coucou lake.*
Open: Etr-Sep Site: 4HEC ⚌ ⊕ ⊕ Prices: pitch 9.20-11.80
(incl 2 persons) Facilities: ⋔ ⊙ ⊕ ⊘ ⋏ ⊞ Services: ⊤ ✗ lau
Leisure: ⋄ P Off-site: ⊘ ⋏ ⋄L ⊞

HENDAYE PYRÉNÉES-ATLANTIQUES

Acacias 64700 ☎ 559207876 ▤ 559207876
e-mail: camping.acacias@oreka.com
website: www.les-campings.com/acacias
A pleasant family site in parkland, 5 minutes from the beach.
➲ *1.8km E (rte de la Glacière).*
Open: Apr-Sep Site: 5HEC ⚌ ⊕ ⊕ Prices: pitch 13.20-16
(incl 2 persons) Facilities: ⋔ ⊙ ⊕ ⋏ ⊞ ⊞ ⊞ Services: ⊤ ✗ ⊞
lau Off-site: ⋄ L Off-site: ⊤ ✗ ⋄S

Airotel Eskualduna rte de la Corniche (D-912), 64700
☎ 559200464 ▤ 559200464
website: www.camping-eskualduna.fr
On gently sloping meadow.
➲ *2km from village on N10c.*
Open: 15 Jun-Sep Site: 10HEC ⚌ ⊕ ⊕ ⊕ Facilities: ⋔ ⋤
⊙ ⊕ ⊘ ⋏ ⊞ Services: ⊤ ✗ ⊞ lau Leisure: ⋄ PR Off-site: ⋄S

HOURTIN GIRONDE

Acacia Ste-Hélène, 33990 ☎ 556738080
website: www.acacia-lac.com
Pleasant, quiet site on the edge of a forest with good sanitary
facilities. Compulsory car park for arrivals after 2330hrs.
➲ *Off D3 towards the lake.*
Site: 5HEC ⚌ ⊕ ⊕ Prices: ⋄3.50 pitch 3.35 Facilities: ⋔ ⊙
⊕ ⊞ ⊞ Services: ⊤ ⊞ lau Off-site: ⋄L

Mariflaude 33990 ☎ 556091197 ▤ 556092401
Level meadowland, shaded by pines, in rural setting 2km
from one of the biggest lakes in the country.
➲ *Turn onto D4 at the chemist and continue E towards
Pauillac.*
Open: May-15 Sep Site: 7HEC ⚌ ⊕ ⊕ Facilities: ⋔ ⋤ ⊙
⊕ ⊘ ⋏ ⊞ Services: ⊤ ✗ ⊞ lau Leisure: ⋄ P Off-site: ⋄L

Ourmes av du Lac, 33990 ☎ 556091276 ▤ 556092390
e-mail: lesourmes@free.fr website: www.lesourmes.com
In wooded surroundings close to the beach and 500mtrs
from the largest freshwater lake in France.
➲ *Follow D4 towards lake.*
Open: Apr-Sep Site: 7HEC ⚌ ⊕ ⊕ Prices: pitch 14-20.90
(incl 2 persons) Facilities: ⋔ ⋤ ⊙ ⊕ ⊘ ⊞ Services: ⊤ ✗ lau
Leisure: ⋄ P Off-site: ⋏ ⋄LS ⊞

HOURTIN-PLAGE GIRONDE

Côte d'Argent 33990 ☎ 556091025 ▤ 556092496
e-mail: info@camping-cote-dargent.com
website: www.camping-cote-dargent.com
In a pine and oak forest 500m from beach with good facilities.
➲ *Access via D101 from Hourtin.*
Open: mid May-mid Sep Site: 20HEC ⋯ ⊕ ⊕ ⊕
Prices: pitch 15-25 (incl 2 persons) Facilities: ⋔ ⋤ ⊙ ⊕ ⊘ ⋏
⊞ Services: ⊤ ✗ ⊞ lau Leisure: ⋄ PS

LABENNE LANDES

Pins Bleus av de l'Océan, 40530
☎ 559454113 ▤ 559454470
e-mail: ville.labenne@wanadoo.fr website: www.labenne.fr
➲ *On RN10.*
Open: All year Site: 6HEC ⚌ ⋯ ⊕ ⊕ ⊼ Prices: pitch 7-
14 (incl 2 persons) Facilities: ⋔ ⊙ ⊕ ⊞ Services: ⊤ ✗ ⊞ lau
Off-site: ⋤ ⊘ ⋏ ⋄LRS ⊞

LABENNE-OCÉAN LANDES

Boudigau 40530 ☎ 559454207 ▤ 559457776
Situated in pine forest.
➲ *Turn right into site after bridge.*
Open: 15 May-15 Sep Site: 6HEC ⚌ ⋯ ⊕ ⊕ ⊕
Facilities: ⋔ ⊙ ⊕ ⊘ ⊞ Services: ⊤ ✗ ⊞ lau Leisure: ⋄ P
Off-site: ⋏ ⋄S

Côte d'Argent av de l'Océan, 40530
☎ 559454202 ▤ 559457331
e-mail: info@camping-cotedargent.com
website: www.camping-cotedargent.com
Very well-managed modern site attached to holiday village.
➲ *3km W on D126.*
Open: Apr-Oct Site: 4HEC ⚌ ⋯ ⊕ ⊕ Prices: pitch 9.10-
20.50 Facilities: ⋔ ⊙ ⊕ ⋏ ⊞ Services: ⊤ ✗ ⊞ lau Leisure: ⋄
P Off-site: ⋤ ⊘ ⋄RS

Mer rte de la Plage, 40530 ☎ 559454209 ▤ 559454307
e-mail: campinglamer@wanadoo.fr
website: www.campinglamer.com
In a pine forest 700mtrs from the beach.
➲ *On D126 (rte de la Plage).*
Open: Etr-Sep Site: 6.5HEC ⋯ ⊕ ⊕ ⊕ ⊼ Prices: pitch 9-
19.90 (incl 2 persons) Facilities: ⋔ ⊙ ⊕ ⊘ ⊞ Services: ⊤ ✗
⊞ lau Leisure: ⋄ PR Off-site: ⋤ ⋄S

Airotel Camping Caravaning
de la **Côte d'Argent** ★★★

Water complex of 3500 sq. m. with
water slides and Jacuzzi's

♥ ALL SHOPS
♥ SPORTS
♥ ACTIVITIES
♥ SAILING
♥ SURFING
♥ TENNIS
♥ HORSE RIDING
♥ ARCHERY
♥ MINI CLUB
♥ GAMES ROOM

Discounts
out of
season
20% to 50%
on week
rentals and
special
rates for
weekends

Caravans and
mobile homes
to let

Airotel Camping Caravaning de la Côte d'Argent
33990 Hourtin Plage • Tél : +33 5.56.09.10.25
Fax : +33 5.56.09.24.96 • www.camping-cote-dargent.com

Facilities: ⋤-shop ⋔-shower ⊙-electric points for razors ⊕-electric points for caravans ⊞-parking by tents permitted
⊞-compulsory separate car park Services: ✗-café/restaurant ⊤-bar ⊘-Camping Gaz International ⋏-gas other than Camping
Gaz ⊞-first aid facilities lau-laundry Leisure: ⋄-swimming L-Lake P-Pool R-River S-Sea Off-site: All facilities within 2km

Lacanau-Océan Gironde

Airotel de l'Océan 24 r du Répos, 33680
☎ 556032445 ▤ 557700187
website: www.airotel-ocean.com
On rising ground in pine forest. 800m from beach.
Open: May–Sep Site: 9.5HEC ∷∴ ♣ ♛ ♨ Facilities: ⋔ ≞ ☉ ♨ ⌀ ☷ ☷ ☎ Services: ⍩ ✗ ⊞ lau Leisure: ⏃ P Off-site: ⏃S

Grands Pins Plages Nord, 33680
☎ 556032077 ▤ 557700389
e-mail: lesgrandspins@yellohvillage.com
website: www.lesgrandspins.com
On very hilly terrain in woodland. 350m from the beach, access to which is through dunes.
➲ Approach via exit 7 on A10, then D6 to Lacanau.
Open: 24 Apr–25 Sep Site: 12HEC ∷∴ ♣ ♨ Prices: pitch 15–34 Facilities: ⋔ ≞ ☉ ♨ ⌀ ☷ ☎ Services: ⍩ ✗ ⊞ lau Leisure: ⏃ P Off-site: ⏃S

At Medoc (8km E)

Talaris rte de l'Océan, 33680 ☎ 556030415 ▤ 556262156
e-mail: talarisvacances@free.fr
website: www.talaris-vacances.fr
A family site in delightful wooded surroundings 1.2km from the lake. Separate car park for arrivals after 22.30hrs.
➲ 2km E on rte de Lacanau.
Open: May–12 Sep Site: 8.2HEC ⊞ ♣ ♛ Å Prices: pitch 15.60–23 (incl 2 persons) Facilities: ⋔ ≞ ☉ ♨ ⌀ ☷ ☷ Services: ⍩ ✗ lau Leisure: ⏃ P Off-site: ⏃L ⊞

At Moutchic (5km E)

Lac 33680 ☎ 556030026

➲ On D6 rte de Lacanau, 60m from lake.
Open: Apr–15 Oct Site: 1HEC ⊞ ♣ ♛ ♨ Prices: pitch 11.43–15.24 (incl 2 persons) Facilities: ⋔ ≞ ☉ ♨ ⌀ ☷ Services: ⍩ ✗ ⊞ lau Off-site: ⏃L

Tedey rte de Longarisse, 33680 ☎ 55603015 ▤ 556030190
e-mail: campingletedey@wanadoo.fr
Quiet site in pine forest, on edge of Lake Lacanau. Private bathing area.
➲ Turn off D6 and continue along narrow track through forest for 0.5km.
Open: 15 May–18 Sep Site: 14HEC ∷∴ ♣ ♨ ⊗ Prices: pitch 15.50–18.30 (incl 2 persons) Facilities: ⋔ ≞ ☉ ♨ ⌀ ☷ Services: ⍩ ✗ ⊞ lau Leisure: ⏃ L

Lacapelle-Marival Lot

CM Bois de Sophie Route d'Aymac, 46120
☎ 565408259 ▤ 565408259
In a pleasant wooded location with a variety of sporting facilities.
➲ 1km NW via D940
Open: 15 May–Sep Site: 1HEC ⊞ ♣ ♛ ♨ Prices: ⋏2–3 pitch 3–4 Facilities: ⋔ ☉ ♨ ☷ Services: lau Leisure: ⏃ P Off-site: ≞ ⍩ ✗ ⌀ ☷ ⏃LR ⊞

Lanton Gironde

Roumingue 33138 ☎ 556829748 ▤ 556829609
e-mail: info@roumingue.com website: www.roumingue.com
Level terrain under a few deciduous trees partially in open meadow on the Bassin d'Arcachon.
➲ 1km NW of village towards sea.
Open: All year Site: 10HEC ⊞ ∷∴ ♺ ♛ ♨ Facilities: ⋔ ≞ ☉ ♨ ⌀ ☷ Services: ⍩ ✗ ⊞ lau Leisure: ⏃ PS Off-site: ☷

Site: 6HEC-Site size ⊞-grass ∷∴-sand ♦-stone ᠅-little shade ♺-partly shaded ♣-mainly shaded ♛-bungalows for hire ♨-caravans for hire Å-tents for hire ⊗-no dogs Prices: ⋏-adult per night ♠-car per night pp-per person per night ♨-caravan per night Å-tent per night

LARNAGOL LOT

Ruisseau de Treil Le Ruisseau, 46160
☎ 565312339 🖩 565219970
e-mail: mkanter@emsgroup.com
website: www.lotcamping.com
A quiet site situated within a small valley with well defined pitches and good leisure facilities.
➲ *0.6km E via D662*
Open: May-Sep Site: 4.3HEC ⊞⊞⊞ ⊕ ♣ 🏠 🚐 Prices: ⋔3.90-5.25 pitch 5.10-6.80 Facilities: ⋔ ☎ ☉ ☒ 🖾 🏠 Services: ⋔ ✗ 🖶 lau Leisure: ⋔ P Off-site: ⋔R

LARUNS PYRÉNÉES-ATLANTIQUES

Gaves 64440 ☎ 559053237 🖩 559054714
e-mail: campingdesgaves@wanadoo.fr
website: www.camping-desgaves.com
On the bank of the Gave d'Ossan amid beautiful Pyreneean scenery. Some pitches reserved for caravans.
➲ *1km S.*
Open: All year Site: 2.5HEC ⊞⊞⊞ ⊕ 🏠 🚐 Prices: ⋔2.90-3.51 ▲5.64-8.38 pitch 7.32-9.15 Facilities: ⋔ ☉ 🖾 ⌀ 🖾 🏠
Services: ⋔ ✗ lau Leisure: ⋔ R Off-site: ☎ ✗ ⋔P 🖶

LARUSCADE GIRONDE

Relais du Chavan 33620 ☎ 557686305
On well-kept meadow edged by a strip of forest. Some traffic noise.
➲ *6.5km NW on N10 near Km20.3.*
Open: 15 May-15 Sep Site: 3.6HEC ⊞⊞⊞ ♣ 🏠 🚐 Prices: ⋔3 pitch 3.50 Facilities: ⋔ ☎ ☉ 🖾 ⌀ 🖾 🏠 Services: 🖶 lau Leisure: ⋔ P

LECTOURE GERS

⋔Lac des Trois Vallées 32700 ☎ 562688233 🖩 562688882
e-mail: lac.des.trois.vallees@wanadoo.fr
website: lac-des-3-vallees.com
This rural site is part of a large park and lies next to a lake. It has spacious marked pitches.
➲ *3km SE on N21.*
Open: 15 May-12 Sep Site: 40HEC ⊞⊞⊞ ♣ 🏠 ▲ Prices: pitch 15-40 (incl 2 persons) Facilities: ⋔ ☎ ☉ 🖾 ⌀ 🖾 🏠 Services: ⋔ ✗ 🖶 lau Leisure: ⋔ LP

LÉON LANDES

Lou Puntaou Av du Lau, 40550 ☎ 558487430
e-mail: reception@loupuntaou.com
website: www.loupuntaou.com
In oak wood with separate sections for caravans.
➲ *Turn off N652 in village and continue towards lake for 1.5km on D142.*
Open: Apr-Sep Site: 8HEC ⊞⊞⊞ ⠿⠿⠿ ♣ 🏠 Prices: pitch 11-33 (incl 2 persons) Facilities: ⋔ ☎ ☉ 🖾 ⌀ 🏠 Services: ⋔ ✗ 🖶 lau Leisure: ⋔ P Off-site: ⌸ ⋔LRS

St-Antoine St-Michel-Escalus, 40500
☎ 558487850 🖩 558487190
A pleasant, well equipped site beside a river in peaceful wooded surroundings.
Open: Mar-Sep Site: 6HEC ⊞⊞⊞ ♣ 🏠 🚐 Prices: ⋔3 pitch 5 Facilities: ⋔ ☎ ☉ 🖾 ⌀ 🏠 Services: ⋔ ✗ 🖶 lau Leisure: ⋔ R

LESCAR PYRÉNÉES-ATLANTIQUES

Terrier av du Vert Galant, 64230
☎ 559810182 🖩 559812683
e-mail: camping.terrier@wanadoo.fr
On meadowland split in two with pitches surrounded by hedges in foreground.

➲ *From Pau take N117 towards Bayonne for approx. 6.5km, then turn left onto D501 towards Monein to site towards bridge.*
Open: All year Site: 4HEC ⊞⊞⊞ ⊕ ♣ Prices: ⋔3.80-3.80 pitch 5-5 Facilities: ⋔ ☉ 🖾 ⌀ 🖾 🏠 Services: ⋔ ✗ 🖶 lau Leisure: ⋔ P Off-site: ☎ 🖶

LINXE LANDES

CM Le Grandjean rte de Mixe, 40260 ☎ 558429000
A modern site situated on the edge of a forest. Ideal for family holidays.
➲ *From the Castets road, take the D42 towards Linxe.*
Open: 29 Jun-Aug Site: 2.7HEC ⊞⊞⊞ ⠿⠿⠿ ♣ 🏠 Prices: ⋔2.70 16 pitch 3.16 Facilities: ⋔ ☉ 🖾 🏠 Services: lau Off-site: ☎ ✗

LIT-ET-MIXE LANDES

Vignes rte du Cap de l'Homy, 40170
☎ 558428560 🖩 558427436
e-mail: contact@les-vignes.com
website: www.les-vignes.com
In a pine forest with good sanitary and sports facilities.
➲ *3km S via D652 and D89.*
Open: Jun-15 Sep Site: 15HEC ⊞⊞⊞ ⠿⠿⠿ ⊕ 🏠 🚐 ▲ Prices: pitch 14.50-33 (incl 2 persons) Facilities: ⋔ ☎ ☉ 🖾 ⌀ 🖾 🏠 Services: ⋔ ✗ 🖶 lau Leisure: ⋔ P

LIVERS-CAZELLES TARN

Rédon 81170 ☎ 563561464 🖩 563561464
e-mail: campingcampredon@wanadoo.fr
A quiet site with fine views over the surrounding area and good modern facilities.
➲ *4km SE of Cordes on D600.*
Open: 28 Mar-30 Oct Site: 2HEC ⊞⊞⊞ ♣ 🚐 Facilities: ⋔ ☎ ☉ 🖾 ⌀ 🏠 Services: ⋔ ✗ 🖶 lau Leisure: ⋔ P

LOURDES HAUTES-PYRÉNÉES

Arrouach 9 r des Trois Archanges, Quartier Biscaye, 65100
☎ 562421143 🖩 562420527
e-mail: camping.arrouach@wanadoo.fr
In pleasant wooded surroundings on N outskirts.
➲ *Situated on D947 Soumoulou road.*
Open: All year Site: 13HEC ⊞⊞⊞ ♣ Prices: ⋔3.50 pitch 4.20 Facilities: ⋔ ☉ 🖾 ⌀ 🖾 🏠 Services: ⋔ 🖶 lau Off-site: ☎ ✗ ⌸ ⋔LPR

Domec rte de Julos, 65100 ☎ 562940879 🖩 562940879
➲ *Off N21 Tarbes road N of town centre.*
Open: Etr-Oct Site: 2.5HEC ⊞⊞⊞ ♣ 🚐 Facilities: ⋔ ☎ ☉ 🖾 ⌀ 🏠 Services: 🖶 lau Off-site: ⋔ ✗ ⌸ ⋔PR

LUZ-ST-SAUVEUR HAUTES-PYRÉNÉES

Bergons rte de Barèges, 65120 ☎ 562929077
e-mail: abordenave@club-internet.fr
In a beautiful setting on a level meadow surrounded by woodland close to the main Pyreneean ski resorts.
➲ *600m E on D618 Barèges road.*
Open: 1 Dec-20 Oct Site: 1HEC ⊞⊞⊞ ♣ 🏠 Prices: ⋔2.90 pitch 2.70 Facilities: ⋔ ☉ 🖾 ⌀ 🏠 Services: lau Off-site: ☎ ⋔ ✗ ⋔PR 🖶

Pyrénées International rte de Lourdes, 65120
☎ 562928202 🖩 562929687
e-mail: camping.international.luz@wanadoo.fr
In a wooded valley at an altitude of 700mtrs with panoramic views of the surrounding mountains.
➲ *1.3km NW on N21.*
Open: 15 Dec-20 Apr & Jun-Sep Site: 4HEC ⊞⊞⊞ ⊕ 🏠 Facilities: ⋔ ☎ ☉ 🖾 ⌀ 🏠 Services: ⋔ ✗ 🖶 lau Leisure: ⋔ P Off-site: ⋔R

Facilities: ☎-shop ⋔-shower ☉-electric points for razors 🖾-electric points for caravans 🏠-parking by tents permitted 🖿-compulsory separate car park **Services:** ✗-café/restaurant ⋔-bar ⌀-Camping Gaz International ⌸-gas other than Camping Gaz 🖶-first aid facilities lau-laundry **Leisure:** ⋔-swimming L-Lake P-Pool R-River S-Sea **Off-site:** All facilities within 2km

CAMPING
ALBRET PLAGE ★★★
40660 MESSANGES
STE DULER PIERRE
Tel: 00 33 (0)5 58 48 03 67
Fax: 00 33 (0)5 58 48 21 91
A 3-star family campsite, with direct access to the beach (300m), with lifeguard. 1km from the town centre of Vieux Boucau (all shops).

On site: bar, restaurant, foodstuffs, launderette, playground for children, French boules, table tennis, entertainment.

Mobile homes and cottages to let

Pyrénévasion rte de Luz-Ardiden, Sazos, 65120
☎ 562929154 🗐 562929834
e-mail: camping-pyrenevasion@wanadoo.fr
website: www.campingpyrenevasion.com
A quiet site in an idyllic mountain setting close to the ski-runs. The pitches are well defined and all facilities are clean and modern.
➲ *2km from town on Luz-Ardiden road.*
Open: All year Site: 2HEC ⊞ ⌵ �� Facilities: ℝ ⊙ 🖭 ⌀ ⌐ 🖭 Services: ⌐ ✕ 🖭 lau Leisure: ⌐ P Off-site: ✕ ⌐R 🖭

MARCILLAC-ST-QUENTIN DORDOGNE

Tailladis 24200 ☎ 553591095 🗐 553294756
e-mail: tailladis@aol.com website: www.tailladis.com
Well maintained family site with good recreational facilities.
➲ *2km N near D48.*
Open: All year Site: 4HEC ⊞ ⌵ 🚌 🛆 Prices: ⌂3.08 pitch 4.19-6.45 Facilities: ℝ 🖭 ⊙ 🖭 ⌀ ⌐ 🖭 Services: ⌐ ✕ 🖭 lau Leisure: ⌐ LP

MARTRES-TOLOSANE HAUTE-GARONNE

Moulin 31220 ☎ 561988640 🗐 561986690
e-mail: info@campinglemoulin.com
website: www.campinglemoulin.com
In a beautiful wooded location beside the River Garonne at the foot of the Pyrénées. Well maintained, with a wide variety of recreational facilities.
➲ *1.5km SE off N117.*
Open: Etr-Sep Site: 7HEC ⊞ ⌵ 🚌 🖭 Prices: ⌂3.60 pitch 4.80-6 Facilities: ℝ ⊙ 🖭 ⌀ ⌐ 🖭 🖭 Services: ⌐ lau Leisure: ⌐ PR Off-site: 🖢 ✕ ⌐ 🖭

MAULÉON-LICHARRE PYRÉNÉES-ATLANTIQUES

Saison rte de Libarrenx, 64130
☎ 559281879 🗐 559280623
e-mail: camping.uhaitza@wanadoo.fr
A peaceful site beside the river, near the town centre.
➲ *1.5km S on D918.*
Open: Apr-Oct Site: 1.1HEC ⊞ ⌵ 🚌 🖭 Prices: ⌂3.30 pitch 3.80 Facilities: ℝ 🖭 ⊙ 🖭 ⌀ ⌐ 🖭 Services: ⌐ ✕ 🖭 lau Leisure: ⌐ R Off-site: ✕ ⌐P

MESSANGES LANDES

Albret Plage 40660 ☎ 558480367 🗐 558482191
Site with direct access to beach (300m). 1km from town of Vieux Boucau.
Site: 🚌 🖭 Facilities: ℝ 🖭 ⊙ 🖭 Services: ⌐ ✕ lau Leisure: ⌐ S

Côte rte de Vieux Boucau, 40660
☎ 558489494 🗐 558489444
e-mail: lacote@wanadoo.fr
website: www.campinglacote.com
In a picturesque wooded area 1km from the beach.
➲ *2.3km S via D652.*
Open: Apr-Sep Site: 4HEC ⊞ ⌵ 🚌 Prices: ⌂2.30-3 pitch 8.50-11.90 Facilities: ℝ 🖭 ⊙ 🖭 ⌀ ⌐ 🖭 Services: 🖭 lau Off-site: ⌐ ✕ ⌀ ⌐LS

Moïsan rte de la Plage, 40660 ☎ 558489206 🗐 558489206
website: www.camping-moisan.com
In a pine forest, 800mtrs from the sea with good modern facilities.
Open: 15 May-Sep Site: 7HEC ⊞ ⌵ ⌂⌂ ⌵ ⌐ 🚌 🖭 Facilities: ℝ 🖭 ⊙ 🖭 ⌀ ⌐ 🖭 Services: ⌐ ✕ 🖭 lau Off-site: ⌐PS

Vieux Port Plage Sud, 40660 ☎ 558482200 🗐 558480169
e-mail: contact@levieuxport.com
website: www.levieuxport.com
A family site in the heart of the Landes forest with direct access to the beach. Good recreational facilities.
➲ *2.5 km SW via D652.*
Open: Apr-Sep Site: 30HEC ⌂⌂ ⌵ ⌐ 🚌 🖭 Prices: pitch 12-31 (incl 2 persons) Facilities: ℝ 🖭 ⊙ 🖭 ⌀ ⌐ 🖭 Services: ⌐ ✕ 🖭 lau Leisure: ⌐ PS Off-site: ⌐ ⌐LR 🖭

MÉZOS LANDES

Sen Yan 40170 ☎ 558426005 🗐 558426456
e-mail: reception@sen-yan.com
website: www.sen-yan.com
A pleasant site in exotic tropical gardens, surrounded by a pine wood.
➲ *1km E*
Open: Jun-15 Sep Site: 8HEC ⌂⌂ ⌵ 🚌 Prices: ⌂5 🖭16.50-31 ⌂3.15 Facilities: ℝ 🖭 ⊙ 🖭 ⌀ 🖭 🖭 Services: ⌐ ✕ 🖭 lau Leisure: ⌐ PS Off-site: ⌐ ⌐R

Site: 6HEC-Site size ⊞-grass ⌂⌂⌂-sand ⌵-stone ⌵-little shade ⌵-partly shaded ⌵-mainly shaded
🚌-bungalows for hire 🖭-caravans for hire 🛆-tents for hire ⌀-no dogs Prices: ⌂-adult per night ⌐-car per night
pp-per person per night 🖭-caravan per night 🛆-tent per night

MIERS LOT

Pigeonnier 46500 ☎ 565337195 ▯ 565337195
e-mail: veronique.bouny@wanadoo.fr
website: www.campingdupigeonnier.com
Peaceful, shady site close to the River Dordogne amid some
of France's most spectacular scenery.
➲ *400m E via D91.*
Open: Apr-15 Oct Site: 1HEC ⊞ ♣ ⌂ ⟷ Prices: pitch
3.51-3.90 Facilities: ⋔ ⊙ ⊕ ⚲ 🅿 Services: ⟶ ✕ ⊞ lau
Leisure: ⟋ P Off-site: ⛟ ✕

MIMIZAN LANDES

AT MIMIZAN-PLAGE (6KM E BY D626)

CM de la Plage bd de l'Atlantique, 40200
☎ 558090032 ▯ 558094494
e-mail: contact@mimizan-camping.com
Open: 16 Apr-02 Oct Site: 16HEC ⦂⦂⦂ ⊕ ♣ ⌂ Prices: pitch
12-16 (incl 2 persons) Facilities: ⋔ ⊙ ⊕ ⚲ 🅿 Services: ✕
lau Off-site: ⟶ ⟋LPS   *See advertisement on page 112*

Marina-Landes 40202 ☎ 558091266 ▯ 558091640
e-mail: contact@clubmarina.com
In a pinewood. 500m from beach.
➲ *Take D626 from Mimizan Plage.*
Open: 15 May-15 Sep Site: 9HEC ⦂⦂⦂ ⊕ ⌂ ⟷ ⛰
Prices: pitch 12.95-28.50 (incl 3 persons) Facilities: ⋔ ⛟ ⊙
⊕ ⚲ 🅿 Services: ⟶ ✕ ⊞ lau Leisure: ⟋ P Off-site: ⟋LRS

MIRANDOL-BOURGNOUNAC TARN

Clots Les Clots, 81190 ☎ 563769278 ▯ 563769278
e-mail: campclots@wanadoo.fr website: www.tron.be/clots
In a wooded area within the Viaur Valley with good facilities.
➲ *5.5km N via D905, rte de Rieupeyroux.*
Open: May-Sep Site: 7HEC ⊞ ♣ ⌂ ⟷ ⛰ Facilities: ⋔ ⛟
⊙ ⊕ ⚲ 🅿 Services: ⟶ lau Leisure: ⟋ PR

MOLIÈRES DORDOGNE

Grande Veyière 24480 ☎ 553632584 ▯ 553631825
e-mail: la_grande_veyiere@wanadoo.fr
Wooded site with good sporting facilities in the heart of
Périgord's Bastides country.
➲ *2.4km SE.*
Open: Apr-5 Nov Site: 4HEC ⊞ ⊕ ♣ ⌂ ⟷ Facilities: ⋔ ⛟
⊙ ⊕ ⚲ 🅿 Services: ⟶ ✕ lau Leisure: ⟋ P

MOLIÈRES TARN-ET-GARONNE

Lac du Malivert Centre de Loisirs du Malivert, 82220
☎ 0563677637 ▯ 0563676216
e-mail: molieres.82@wanadoo.fr
website: www.cdg82.fr/molieres
In a pleasant lakeside setting.
➲ *Approaching Molières from the south, head towards Centre
de Loisirs and Lac Malivert.*
Open: 15 Jul-15 Sep Site: 0.7HEC ⊞ ⊕ ⟷ Facilities: ⋔ ⛟
⊙ ⊕ ⚲ 🅿 Services: ⟶ lau Leisure: ⟋ L Off-site: ⛟ ⟶ ✕ ⊞

MOLIETS-PLAGE LANDES

Airotel St-Martin av de l'Océan, 40660
☎ 558485230 ▯ 558485073
e-mail: contact@camping-saint-martin.fr
website: www.camping-saint-martin.fr
Large site on the Atlantic coast with direct access to the
largest sandy beach in the region.
➲ *Between the village and the beach.*
Open: Etr-12 Oct Site: 18.5HEC ⊞ ⦂⦂⦂ ♣ ⌂
Prices: ⬆16.50-36 pitch 16.50-36 (incl 2 persons)
Facilities: ⋔ ⛟ ⊙ ⊕ ⚲ 🅿 Services: ⟶ ✕ lau Leisure: ⟋ P
Off-site: ⛰ ⟋S ⊞

Facilities: ⛟-shop ⋔-shower ⊙-electric points for razors ⊕-electric points for caravans 🅿-parking by tents permitted
⊡-compulsory separate car park Services: ✕-café/restaurant ⟶-bar ⚲-Camping Gaz International ⛰-gas other than Camping
Gaz ⊞-first aid facilities lau-laundry Leisure: ⟋-swimming L-Lake P-Pool R-River S-Sea Off-site: All facilities within 2km

Cigales av de l'Océan, 40660 ☎ 558485118 ▤ 558483527
e-mail: camping-les-cigales@wanadoo.fr
website: www.camping-les-cigales.fr
On undulating ground in pine trees.
➜ *300m from beach.*
Open: Apr-Sep Site: 23HEC ▦ ∴ ♣ ⛺ 🚐 Facilities: 🛈
🛱 ⊙ 🚻 ⌀ 🚿 🖾 Services: 🍴 ✕ 🖃 lau Off-site: ⚓LRS

MONCRABEAU LOT-ET-GARONNE

CM Mouliat 'Le Nouliat', 47600 ☎ 553654328 ▤ 553652178
website: www.nosnerabeau.fr.st
A small site in a wooded location on the banks of the River
La Baïse.
➜ *On D219, 200m from D930.*
Open: 15 Jun-15 Sep Site: 1.3HEC ▦ ♣ ⛺ Facilities: 🛈 ⊙
🚻 🖾 Services: 🖃 lau Off-site: 🛱 🍴 ✕ ⚓PR

MONTAUBAN-DE-LUCHON HAUTE-GARONNE

Lanette 31110 ☎ 561790038
On gently sloping ground surrounded by pastures.
➜ *1.5km E of Luchon. Off D27.*
Open: All year Site: 4.3HEC ▦ 🌤 ⛺ 🚐 Facilities: 🛈 🛱 ⊙
🚻 ⌀ 🖾 Services: 🍴 ✕ 🖃 lau Off-site: ⚓PR

MONTESQUIOU GERS

Château le Haget 32320 ☎ 562709580 ▤ 562709483
e-mail: info@lehaget.com
website: www.lehaget.com
In grounds of Château.
Open: Apr-Oct Site: 12HEC ▦ ♣ ⛺ 🚐 Facilities: 🛈 🛱 ⊙
🚻 ⌀ 🖾 🖾 Services: 🍴 ✕ 🖃 lau Leisure: ⚓ P Off-site: ⚓LR

MONTIGNAC DORDOGNE

Moulin du Bleufond av Aristide Briand, 24290
☎ 553518395 ▤ 553511992
e-mail: le.moulin.du.bleufond@wanadoo.fr
website: www.bleufond.com
Situated beside a river in the grounds of an ancient 17th
century mill.
➜ *0.5km off D65 Montignac to Sergeac road.*
Open: Apr-15 Oct Site: 1.3HEC ▦ 🌤 ⛺ 🚐 Prices: pitch
4.05-5.40 Facilities: 🛈 🛱 ⊙ 🚻 🖾 Services: 🍴 ✕ 🖃 lau
Leisure: ⚓ P Off-site: ⚓R

MUSSIDAN DORDOGNE

CM Le Port 24400 ☎ 553812009
Open: 15 Jun-15 Sep Site: 0.5HEC ▦ ♣ Prices: ⚥2.60 pitch
1 Facilities: 🛈 ⊙ 🚻 🖾 Services: 🖃 lau Off-site: 🛱 🍴 ✕ ⚓PR

NAGES TARN

Rieu Montagné Lac du Laouzas, 81320
☎ 563372671 ▤ 563371542
e-mail: rieumontagne@camping-indigo.com
website: www.camping-indigo.com
In a wooded location beside the Laouzas lake with good
recreational facilities.
➜ *4.5km S via D62*
Open: 12 Jun-12 Sep Site: 9HEC ▦ ♣ ⛺ ⛺ Prices: ⚥4.50
pitch 13-22 (incl 2 persons) Facilities: 🛈 🛱 ⊙ 🚻 ⌀ 🖾 🖾
Services: 🍴 ✕ 🖃 lau Leisure: ⚓ P Off-site: ⚓LR

OLORON-STE-MARIE PYRÉNÉES-ATLANTIQUES

Val du Gave-d'Aspe rte du Somport, Gurmençon, 64400
☎ 559360507 ▤ 559360052
e-mail: chalet.aspe@wanadoo.fr
website: www.chalet-aspe.com
A pleasant site situated in the Aspe Valley amid picturesque
Pyrenean scenery.
Open: All year Site: 0.5HEC ▦ ♣ ⛺ Prices: ⚥3 pitch 12-15
Facilities: 🛈 ⊙ 🚻 🖾 Services: 🍴 🖃 lau Leisure: ⚓ P
Off-site: ✕ 🖾 ⚓R

ONESSE-ET-LAHARIE LANDES

CM Bienvenu 259 route de Mimizan, 40110
☎ 558073049 ▤ 558073078
A family site situated within a forest.
➜ *500m from village centre on D38.*
Open: 15 Jun-15 Sep Site: 1.2HEC ▦ 🌤 Prices: ⚥2.60
♣1.40 🚐2.20 ⛺2.20 Facilities: 🛈 ⊙ 🚻 🖾 Services: 🍴 ✕ 🖃
lau Off-site: 🛱 ✕ ⚓R

OUSSE PYRÉNÉES-ATLANTIQUES

Sapins 64320 ☎ 559817421
➜ *Access via N117, exit 'Pau' or A64, exit Soumoulou.*
Open: All year Site: 1HEC ▦ 🌤 ⛺ 🚐 Prices: ⚥3 pitch 3.50
Facilities: 🛈 ⊙ 🚻 🖾 Services: 🍴 ✕ 🖃 lau Off-site: 🛱 ✕

PADIRAC LOT

Chênes rte du Gouffre, 46500
☎ 565336554 ▤ 565337155
e-mail: les_chenes@hotmail.com
website: www.campingleschenes.com
In a fine position in the centre of the Haute-Quercy with
good facilities.
➜ *1.5km NE via D90 towards Gouffre.*
Open: May-14 Sep Site: 5HEC ▦ ♣ ⛺ ⛺ Prices: ⚥3-6.50
pitch 4-8 Facilities: 🛈 🛱 ⊙ 🚻 ⌀ 🖾 🖾 Services: 🍴 ✕ 🖃 lau
Leisure: ⚓ P

PAMIERS ARIÈGE

Ombrages rte d'Escosse, 9100 ☎ 561671224 ▤ 561601823
A pleasant site in wooded surroundings beside the River
Ariège, 1.5km from the town centre.
➜ *NW on D119 beside river.*
Open: All year Site: 2.5HEC ▦ ♣ 🚐 Facilities: 🛈 🛱 ⊙ 🚻
⌀ 🖾 🖾 Services: 🍴 ✕ 🖃 lau Off-site: ⚓PR

PAUILLAC GIRONDE

CM Les Gabarreys rte de la Rivière, 33250
☎ 556591003 ▤ 556733068
e-mail: camping.les.gabarreys@wanadoo.fr
website: www.pauillac-medoc.com
A municipal site with good sports facilities.
➜ *S of town. Follow signposts.*
Open: 05 Apr-09 Oct Site: 2HEC ▦ 🌊 🌤 ⛺ Prices: pitch
11-12 (incl 2 persons) Facilities: 🛈 ⊙ 🚻 🖾 Services: lau
Off-site: 🛱 🍴 ✕ ⌀ 🖾 ⚓P 🖃

PAYRAC LOT

Panoramic rte de Loupiac, 46350
☎ 565379845 ▤ 565379165
e-mail: camping.panoramic@wanadoo.fr
A peaceful family site 5km from the River Dordogne with
good recreational facilities.
➜ *Off N20 N of Payrac.*
Open: All year Site: 1.5HEC ▦ ♣ ⛺ 🚐 ⛺ Prices: ⚥2.50
pitch 3-3 Facilities: 🛈 ⊙ 🚻 🖾 🖾 Services: 🍴 ✕ 🖃 lau
Off-site: 🛱 ⌀ ⚓P

Site: 6HEC-Site size ▦-grass ∴-sand ♣-stone 🌤-little shade 🌤-partly shaded ♣-mainly shaded
⛺-bungalows for hire 🚐-caravans for hire ⛺-tents for hire ⌀-no dogs **Prices:** ⚥-adult per night ♣-car per night
pp-per person per night 🚐-caravan per night ⛺-tent per night

Pins rte de Cahors, 46350 ☎ 565379632 ▤ 565379108
e-mail: info@les-pins-camping.com
website: www.les-pins-camping.com
A well-managed site, partly in forest, partly on meadowland.
Sheltered from traffic noise.
➲ *S of village off N20.*
Open: Apr-30 Oct Site: 3.5HEC ⸬⸬⸬ ⓐ ⊞ ⊞ Prices: ⚹2.75-
5.50 pitch 6.70-10.70 Facilities: ⓡ ⊙ ⓔ ⓩ Services: ⓨ ✕ lau
Leisure: ⸸ P Off-site: ⓛ ⓓ ⊞

PÉRIGUEUX DORDOGNE

Barnabé 80 r des Bains, Boulazac, 24750
☎ 553534145   ▤ 553541662
A well appointed site in a wooded park-like location beside
the river.
➲ *Signposted from N89, 2km E of town centre.*
Open: All year Site: 1.5HEC ⸬⸬⸬ ♣ Prices: ⚹3.30 ⇢1.95
🚐3.20 ▲2.90 Facilities: ⓡ ⊙ ⓔ ⓩ Services: ⓨ ✕ ⊞ lau
Off-site: ⓛ ✕ ⓓ ⸸P

PETIT-PALAIS GIRONDE

Pressoir Queyrai Petit-Palais, 33570
☎ 557697325   ▤ 557697736
e-mail: camping.le.pressoir@wanadoo.fr
website: www.campinglepressoir.com
An old farm in the rolling countryside around St-Emilion.
➲ *On N89 Bordeaux-Périgeux road, exit at St-Médard de
Guizières & follow signs.*
Open: Apr-Sep Site: 2HEC ⸬⸬⸬ ♣ ▲ Prices: pitch 6.90-9.90
Facilities: ⓡ ⊙ ⓔ ⓩ Services: ⓨ ✕ ⊞ lau Leisure: ⸸ P

PEZULS DORDOGNE

Forêt 24510 ☎ 553227169   ▤ 553237779
e-mail: camping.laforet@wanadoo.fr
website: www.camping-dordogne.com/la-foret
In extensive grounds on the edge of the forest with modern
facilities.
➲ *600m off D703. 3km from the village centre.*
Open: Apr-01 Oct Site: 9HEC ⸬⸬⸬ ⓐ ♣ ⊞ ⊞ Prices: ⚹3.80-
4.80 pitch 3.50-4.50 Facilities: ⓡ ⓛ ⊙ ⓔ ⓓ ⸿ ⓩ Services: ⓨ
⊞ lau Leisure: ⸸ P

PONT-ST-MAMET DORDOGNE

Lestaubière Pont-St-Mamet, 24140
☎ 553829815   ▤ 553829017
e-mail: lestaubiere@cs.com website: www.lestaubiere.com
Peaceful and secluded site in attractive part of the Dordogne,
occupying the former outbuildings and wooded grounds of
the adjacent château. Site commands fine views of the
surrounding countryside.
➲ *Between Perigueux and Bergerac on RN21, take exit Pont-
St-Mamet, 500m N of Pont-St-Mamet is the campsite*
Open: 26 Apr-1 Oct Site: 22HEC ⸬⸬⸬ ♣ 🚐 ▲ Prices: ⚹4.70-
5.40 pitch 6.90-8 Facilities: ⓡ ⓛ ⊙ ⓔ ⓓ ⓩ Services: ⓨ ✕ ⊞
lau Leisure: ⸸ LP

PUYBRUN LOT

Sole 46130 ☎ 565385237   ▤ 565109109
e-mail: la-sole@wanadoo.fr website: www.la-sole.com
A well run site in pleasant wooded surroundings with good
facilities.
➲ *On D703 leave village in the direction of Bretenoux and
take the first turning after the garage.*
Open: Apr-Sep Site: 3HEC ⸬⸬⸬ ♣ ⊞ 🚐 Facilities: ⓡ ⊙ ⓔ ⓓ
⸿ ⓩ Services: ⓨ ✕ ⊞ lau Leisure: ⸸ P Off-site: ⓛ ⸸LR

SEA, SUN, FOREST

325 shady and marked
pitches. Mobile homes and
chalets to let, 4-6 persons.
Swimming pool – tennis –
all shops – daycare center
– entertainment – service
point for motorhomes.

ROUTE DE BISCARROSSE – 33115 PYLA/MER
Tel: 05 56 22 72 17 – Fax: 05 56 22 72 17

Unique site at the foot of
the highest dune in Europe.

www.campingdeladune.fr · campingdeladune@wanadoo.fr

PUY-L'ÉVÊQUE LOT
AT MONTCABRIER (7 KM NW)

Moulin de Laborde 46700 ☎ 565246206   ▤ 565365133
e-mail: moulindelaborde@wanadoo.fr
website: www.moulindelaborde.com
Well equipped site surrounded by woods and hills, in a
picturesque valley on the River Thèze.
➲ *NW off D673.*
Open: May-14 Sep Site: 9HEC ⸬⸬⸬ ♣ ⊗ Prices: ⚹5.50 pitch
7 Facilities: ⓡ ⓛ ⊙ ⓔ ⓓ ⓩ Services: ⓨ ✕ ⊞ lau Leisure: ⸸
LPR Off-site: ⸿

PYLA-SUR-MER GIRONDE

Dune rte de Biscarrosse, 33260 ☎ 556227217   ▤ 556227217
e-mail: campingdeladune@wanadoo.fr
website: campingdeladune.fr
A beautifully situated and quiet site partly on terraced sandy
fields. Opposite a dune of over 100m in height, which
separates the site from the sea.
➲ *Follow the road between Pilat-Plage.*
Open: May-Sep Site: 6HEC ⸬⸬⸬ ♣ ⊞ Prices: pitch 10-23
(incl 2 persons) Facilities: ⓡ ⓛ ⊙ ⓔ ⓓ ⸿ ⓩ Services: ⓨ ✕ ⊞
lau Leisure: ⸸ P Off-site: ⸸S

Forêt rte de Biscarrosse, 33115 ☎ 556227328   ▤ 556227050
e-mail: camping.foret@wanadoo.fr
website: www.campinglaforet.fr
A well equipped site surrounded by pine trees and with
direct access to the fine sandy beaches at the mouth of the
Arcachon Basin. There are good sporting facilities and
evening entertainment is provided on a regular basis.

contd.

Facilities: ⓛ-shop ⓡ-shower ⊙-electric points for razors ⓔ-electric points for caravans ⓩ-parking by tents permitted
ⓟ-compulsory separate car park Services: ✕-café/restaurant ⓨ-bar ⓓ-Camping Gaz International ⸿-gas other than Camping
Gaz ⊞-first aid facilities lau-laundry Leisure: ⸸-swimming L-Lake P-Pool R-River S-Sea Off-site: All facilities within 2km

LA FORÊT
CAMPING CARAVANING
★ ★ ★ ★

**Open from Easter
to All Saints**
Bar
Restaurant
Snacks
**Cottages and mobile
homes to let.**
Route de Biscarrosse
- 33115 Pyla sur Mer
Tel 05 56 22 73 28
Fax 05 56 23 70 50
www.campinglaforet.fr
camping.foret@wanadoo.fr

⮑ *Access via N250 then D218.*
Open: Apr-Oct Site: 12HEC ⸛⸛⸛ ♣ 🏠 Facilities: ⬛ 🛏 ☉ 🔲 ∅ ♨ 🏠 Services: 🍴 ✗ 🔲 lau Leisure: ⮌ PS

Panorama rte de Biscarrosse, 33260
☎ 556221044 🗎 556221012
e-mail: mail@camping-panorama.com
website: www.camping-panorama.com
Partially terraced site amongst dunes, on the edge of the 100m high 'Dune de Pyla'. Views of the sea from some pitches.
⮑ *On the D218. Signposted.*
Open: 25 Apr-Sep Site: 15HEC ⠭⠭⠭ ♣ 🏠 🔲 🅰
Prices: ⭡3.50-8 pitch 8-17 Facilities: ⬛ 🛏 ☉ 🔲 ∅ ♨ 🏠 🅿 Services: 🍴 ✗ 🔲 lau Leisure: ⮌ PS

Pyla rte de Biscarrosse, 33115 ☎ 556227456
e-mail: pylacamping@free.fr
website: www.pyla-camping.com
A well equipped family site with good recreational facilities and direct access to the sea.
Open: May-Sep Site: 8HEC ⸛⸛⸛ ⠭⠭⠭ ⮲ 🏠 ☉ 🔲 ∅ ♨ 🏠 Services: 🍴 ✗ 🔲 lau Leisure: ⮌ PS

Sunêlia Petit Nice rte de Biscarrosse, 33115
☎ 556227403 🗎 556221431
e-mail: camping.petit.nice@wanadoo.fr
website: www.petitnice.com
Sandy terraced site, mainly suitable for tents; in parts sloping steeply in pine woodland. Paths and standings are strengthened with timber. 220 steps down to the beach.
⮑ *6 km S on D218.*
Open: Apr-Sep Site: 5.5HEC ⸛⸛⸛ ⠭⠭⠭ ⮲ 🏠 🅰 Prices: ⭡3.50-6 pitch 13-26 Facilities: ⬛ 🛏 ☉ 🔲 ∅ 🏠 Services: 🍴 ✗ 🔲 lau Leisure: ⮌ PS

RAUZAN GIRONDE

Vieux Château Route de par tementale 123, 33420
☎ 557841538 🗎 557841834
e-mail: hoekstra.camping@wanadoo.fr
website: www.vieux-chateau.com
A family site situated in a peaceful valley surrounded by vineyards and overlooked by the ruined 12th century Rauzan castle.
⮑ *200mtrs N, 1500mtrs from N670.*
Open: Apr-Oct Site: 2.5HEC ⸛⸛⸛ ♣ 🏠 🔲 Prices: ⭡2.95-3.95 pitch 3.95-5 Facilities: ⬛ 🛏 ☉ 🔲 ♨ 🏠 Services: ✗ lau Leisure: ⮌ P

REYREVIGNES LOT

Papillon 46320 ☎ 565401240 🗎 565401718
e-mail: info@domaine-papillon.com
website: www.domaine-papillon.com
In a wooded park in the heart of the Haut-Quercy region with good, modern facilities.
⮑ *Access via N653.*
Open: Apr-Oct Site: 3HEC ⸛⸛⸛ ◔ 🏠 🔲 Prices: ⭡2.80-4 pitch 3.50-5 Facilities: ⬛ ☉ 🔲 🏠 Services: 🍴 ✗ 🔲 lau Leisure: ⮌ P Off-site: ⮌LR

ROCAMADOUR LOT

Cigales 46500 ☎ 565336444 🗎 565336960
e-mail: camping.cigales@wanadoo.fr
website: www.camping-cigales.com
A peaceful, well equipped site with shaded pitches and good, modern facilities. Fine views of Rocamadour.
Open: 21 Jun-31 Aug Site: 3HEC ⸛⸛⸛ ◔ 🏠 🔲 Facilities: ⬛ 🛏 ☉ 🔲 🏠 🅿 Services: 🍴 ✗ 🔲 lau Leisure: ⮌ P

Relais du Campeur l'Hospitalet 46500 ☎ 565336328
Shady, level site with well marked pitches and good facilities. Fine views of Rocamadour.
⮑ *On D36.*
Open: Apr-Sep Site: 1.7HEC ⸛⸛⸛ ◔ Facilities: ⬛ 🛏 ☉ 🔲 ∅ 🏠 Services: 🍴 🔲 lau Leisure: ⮌ P Off-site: ✗ ♨

ROCHE-CHALAIS, LA DORDOGNE

Gerbes r de la Dronne, 24490 ☎ 553914065 🗎 553903201
e-mail: camping.la.roche.chalais@wanadoo.fr
Well appointed family site on banks of River Dronne.
⮑ *Off D674 in village centre. Signposted.*
Open: 15 Apr-30 Sep Site: 3.5HEC ⸛⸛⸛ ♣ 🔲 Prices: ⭡2.10 pitch 2.60 Facilities: ⬛ ☉ 🔲 🏠 Services: 🔲 lau Leisure: ⮌ R Off-site: 🛏 🍴 ✗ ∅ ♨ ⮌P

ROMIEU, LA GERS

Camp de Florence 32480 ☎ 562281558 🗎 562282004
e-mail: info@campdeflorence.com
website: www.campdeflorence.com
Well equipped site in rural surroundings.
⮑ *Take D931 in direction Agen-Condom. 3km before Condom turn left to La Romieu.*
Open: Apr-12 Oct Site: 15HEC ⸛⸛⸛ ♣ 🏠 🅰 Prices: pitch 15-27.50 (incl 2 persons) Facilities: ⬛ ☉ 🔲 🏠 Services: 🍴 ✗ 🔲 lau Leisure: ⮌ P Off-site: 🛏

ROQUEFORT LANDES

CM de Nauton Cité Nauton, 40120
☎ 558455046 🗎 558455363
A small municipal site with good facilities.
⮑ *1.6km N via D932 towards Bordeaux.*
Open: Jun-Sep Site: 1.4HEC ⸛⸛⸛ ⠭⠭⠭ ♣ Facilities: ⬛ ☉ 🔲 🏠 Services: 🔲 Off-site: 🛏 🍴 ✗ ⮌PR

Site: 6HEC-Site size ⸛⸛⸛-grass ⠭⠭⠭-sand ◍-stone ⭍-little shade ◔-partly shaded ♣-mainly shaded
🏠-bungalows for hire 🔲-caravans for hire 🅰-tents for hire ⊗-no dogs Prices: ⭡-adult per night ♠-car per night
pp-per person per night 🔲-caravan per night 🅰-tent per night

ROQUELAURE GERS

Talouch 32810 ☎ 562655243 ▤ 562655368
e-mail: info@camping-talouch.com
website: www.camping-talouch.com
A family site in picturesque wooded surroundings, situated
in the heart of Gascony. There are fine sports and
entertainment facilities.
➲ *Access via N21 and D148.*
Open: Apr-Sep Site: 9HEC ▦ ⌑ ⌂ ⚓ Prices: ♠5.35 pitch
17.15 (incl 2 persons) Facilities: ⚑ ⚏ ⊙ ⚇ ⌀ ⚞ ☷ Services: ☂
✗ ⊞ lau Leisure: ⸾ P

ROUFFIGNAC DORDOGNE

Cantegrel 24580 ☎ 553054830 ▤ 553052787
e-mail: info@camping-bleusoleil.com
website: www.camping-bleusoleil.com
In a peaceful location in the heart of the Périgord Noir, with
good recreational facilities.
➲ *1.5km N via D31, rte de Thenon.*
Open: Apr-20 Oct Site: 60HEC ▦ ⌑ ⌂ ⚓ Prices: ♠2.20
pitch 5.20-6.80 Facilities: ⚑ ⚏ ⊙ ⚇ ⌀ ☷ ⚞ Services: ☂ ✗ ⊞
lau Leisure: ⸾ P

ST-ANTOINE-DE-BREUILH DORDOGNE

CM St-Aulaye St Aulaye, 24230
☎ 553248280 ▤ 553248280
e-mail: info@la-riviere-fleurie.com
website: www.la-riviere-fleurie.com
➲ *Access via D936. Take a right turn before the village and
travel 3km in the direction of the Dordogne.*
Open: Apr-Sep Site: 2.4HEC ▦ ⌑ ⌂ ⚓ Prices: ♠3.80
pitch 13 Facilities: ⚑ ⚏ ⊙ ⚇ ⚞ Services: ☂ ✗ ⊞ lau
Leisure: ⸾ PR

ST-ANTONIN-NOBLE-VAL TARN-ET-GARONNE

Trois Cantons 82140 ☎ 563319857 ▤ 563312593
e-mail: info@3cantons.fr website: www.3cantons.fr
Divided into pitches, partly on sloping ground within an oak
forest. Separate section for teenagers.
➲ *8.5km NW near D926. Signposted.*
Open: 15 Apr-Sep Site: 15HEC ⚬ ⌑ ⌂ ⚓ Prices: ♠4.10-5.35
pitch 4.80-6.70 Facilities: ⚑ ⚏ ⊙ ⚇ ⌀ ⚞ Services: ☂ ✗ ⊞
lau Leisure: ⸾ P

ST-BERTRAND-DE-COMMINGES HAUTE-GARONNE

Es Pibous chemin de St-Just, 31510
☎ 561883142 ▤ 561956383
A quiet, shaded site in an elevated position with good
facilities.
Open: All year Site: 1.8HEC ▦ ⌑ ⌂ ⚓ Prices: ♠3.16 pitch
3.50 Facilities: ⚑ ⚏ ⊙ ⚇ ⌀ ⚞ Services: lau Leisure: ⸾ P
Off-site: ⚏ ☂ ✗ ☷ ⸾R

ST-CÉRÉ LOT

CM de Soulhol quai A-Salesse, 46400
☎ 565381237 ▤ 565106175
e-mail: info@campinglesoulhol.com
website: www.campingsoulhol.com
A family site bordered by two rivers with good recreational
facilities.
➲ *200m SE on D940.*
Open: May-20 Sep Site: 5HEC ▦ ⌑ ⌂ Prices: ♠3.80-4.20
pitch 4.10 Facilities: ⚑ ⊙ ⚇ ⌀ ⚞ Services: ☂ ⊞ lau
Leisure: ⸾ R Off-site: ⚏ ✗ ⌀ ⸾P

ST-CIRQ DORDOGNE

Brin d'Amour Saint Cirq, 24260
☎ 553072373 ▤ 553072373
In a fine location overlooking the Vézère Valley with good
facilities.
Open: Apr-Sept Site: 3.8HEC ▦ ⌑ ⌂ Prices: ♠3.10-3.95
pitch 4-4.50 Facilities: ⚑ ⚏ ⊙ ⚇ ⌀ ☷ ⚞ Services: ☂ ✗ ⊞ lau
Leisure: ⸾ P Off-site: ⸾LR

ST-CIRQ-LAPOPIE LOT

Plage 46330 ☎ 565302951 ▤ 565302333
e-mail: camping-laplage@wanadoo.fr
website: www.la-plage-camping.com
In an ideal location beside the River Lot with well defined
pitches and good, modern facilities. Boat and bicycle hire
available.
➲ *Access via D41 from N or D42 from S.*
Open: All year Site: 3HEC ▦ ⌑ ⌂ ⚓ Prices: ♠5 pitch 5
Facilities: ⚑ ⊙ ⚇ ⌀ ☷ ⚞ Services: ☂ ✗ ⊞ lau Leisure: ⸾ R
Off-site:

ST-CRICQ GERS

Lac de Thoux 32440 ☎ 562657129 ▤ 562657481
e-mail: lacdethoux@cacg.fr
A family site with good facilities situated on the edge of the
lake, 50mtrs from the beach.
➲ *On D654 between Cologne and L'Isle Jourdain.*
Open: Apr-15 Oct Site: 3HEC ▦ ⌑ ⌂ ⚓ ⚐ Facilities: ⚑
⚏ ⊙ ⚇ ⌀ ☷ ⚞ Services: ☂ ✗ ⊞ lau Leisure: ⸾ LP

ST-CYBRANET DORDOGNE

Bel Ombrage 24250 ☎ 553283414 ▤ 553596464
e-mail: belombrage@wanadoo.fr
website: www.belombrage.com
Quiet holiday site in wooded valley.
Open: Jun-5 Sep Site: 6HEC ▦ ⌑ Prices: ♠4.90 ⚓6.50
Facilities: ⚑ ⊙ ⚇ ⚞ Services: ⊞ lau Leisure: ⸾ PR
Off-site: ⚏ ☂ ✗ ⌀ ☷

ST-CYPRIEN DORDOGNE

Ferme de Campagnac Castels, 24220
☎ 553292603 ▤ 553292603
e-mail: maboureau@libertysurf.fr
A quiet site situated 200mtrs from the farm in a sheltered
position.
➲ *Access from town on D25. Signposted.*
Open: Apr-Oct Site: 0.8HEC ▦ ⌑ ⌂ ⚓ Prices: ♠2 pitch 5
Facilities: ⚑ ⊙ ⚇ ⚞ Services: lau Off-site: ⚏ ☂ ✗ ⌀ ☷ ⊞

CM Garrit 24220 ☎ 553292056 ▤ 553292056
e-mail: pbecheau@aol.com
website: www.campings-dordogne.com/du-garrit
In a peaceful location beside the River Dordogne with safe
bathing.
➲ *1.5km S on D48.*
Open: May-15 Sep Site: 2HEC ▦ ⌑ ⌂ ⚓ Facilities: ⚑ ⚏
⊙ ⚇ ⚞ Services: ☂ ⊞ lau Leisure: ⸾ PR Off-site: ⚏ ✗ ⌀ ☷
⸾R

Plage Vezac, 24220 ☎ 553295083
Modest but attractive site in a pleasant riverside setting.
➲ *Access via D703 beyond La Roque Gageac.*
Open: Apr-Sep Site: 3.5HEC ▦ ⁙ ⌑ Facilities: ⚑ ⚏ ⊙
⚇ ⌀ ⚞ Services: ☂ ⊞ lau Leisure: ⸾ R Off-site: ✗

Facilities: ⚏-shop ⚑-shower ⊙-electric points for razors ⚇-electric points for caravans ⚞-parking by tents permitted
⊟-compulsory separate car park **Services:** ✗-café/restaurant ☂-bar ⌀-Camping Gaz International ☷-gas other than Camping
Gaz ⊞-first aid facilities lau-laundry **Leisure:** ⸾-swimming L-Lake P-Pool R-River S-Sea **Off-site:** All facilities within 2km

St-Émilion Gironde

Barbanne route de Montagne, 33330
☎ 57247580 🖷 57246968
e-mail: barbanne@wanadoo.fr
website: www.camping-saint-emilion.com
In a peaceful country setting among vineyards, close to a 12 acre lake.
➲ *3km N via D122.*
Open: Apr-19 Sep Site: 10HEC ⸺ ⊕ 🏠 Prices: ♦4-6.50 pitch 14-21 (incl 2 persons) Facilities: 🌳 🕍 ⊙ 🖾 🖉 🖭 Services: ✗ 🖽 lau Leisure: ⋋ LPR

St-Genies Dordogne

Bouquerie 24590 ☎ 553289822 🖷 553291975
e-mail: labouquerie@wanadoo.fr
website: www.labouquerie.com
A family site in wooded surroundings with a good variety of facilities.
➲ *N of village on D704.*
Open: 10 Apr-25 Sep Site: 8HEC ⸺ ♠ 🏠 Prices: ♦4.60-6.50 pitch 9.30-12 Facilities: 🌳 🕍 ⊙ 🖾 🖉 🖳 🖭 Services: 🍸 ✗ 🖽 lau Leisure: ⋋ LP

St-Girons Ariège

Pont du Nert rte de Lacourt (D33), 09200 ☎ 561665848
e-mail: dmmadre@aol.com
Grassy site between road and woodland.
➲ *Approx 3km SE at the junction of the D33 and the D3.*
Open: 12 Jun-15 Sep Site: 1.5HEC ⸺ ♠ Prices: ♦3 pitch 2 Facilities: 🌳 ⊙ 🖾 🖭 Off-site: 🖉 ⋋R

St-Jean-de-Luz Pyrénées-Atlantiques

Atlantica Quartier Acotz, 64500 ☎ 559477244 🖷 559547227
e-mail: campinga@club-internet.fr
website: www.campingatlantica.com
A family site with good facilities close to the Spanish border at the foot of the Pyrénées and only 500mtrs from the beach.
➲ *Leave N10 at St-Jean-de-Luz Nord exit and continue towards Biarritz. Site 1km on left.*
Open: 15 Mar Site: 3.5HEC ⸺ ⊕ 🏠 🖳 Prices: pitch 13-22 (incl 2 persons) pp3-5 Facilities: 🌳 🕍 ⊙ 🖾 🖉 🖳 🖭 Services: 🍸 ✗ 🖽 lau Leisure: ⋋ P Off-site: ⋋S

International d'Erromardie 64500
☎ 559263426 🖷 559512602
Site is situated by the sea and consists of several sections divided by roads and low hedges. Take away food.
➲ *If approached from N to N10, cross railway bridge and turn immediately right and follow signs.*
Open: 15 Mar-15 Oct Site: 2HEC ⸺ ⊕ 🏠 Prices: pitch 11-18 (incl 2 persons) Facilities: 🌳 🕍 ⊙ 🖾 🖳 🖭 Services: 🍸 ✗ 🖽 lau Leisure: ⋋ RS Off-site: 🖉

Iratzia ☎ 559261489 🖷 559266969
➲ *1km NE off N10. Leave autoroute, signed St-Jean-de-Luz Nord and follow directions for Plage d'Erromardie.*
Open: May-Sep Site: 4HEC ⸺ ♠ 🏠 Facilities: 🌳 🕍 ⊙ 🖾 🖉 🖭 Services: 🍸 ✗ 🖽 lau Off-site: ⋋S

Tamaris Plage quartier d'Acotz, 64500
☎ 559265590 🖷 559477015
e-mail: tamaris1@wanadoo.fr
website: www.tamaris-plage.com
Level family site with good facilities divided into sections by drives and hedges.
➲ *Signposted from N10 towards the sea.*
Open: Apr-Sep Site: 1.3HEC ⸺ ⊕ 🏠 🖳 Prices: ♦3.70 pitch 22-29 (incl 2 persons) Facilities: 🌳 ⊙ 🖾 🖭 Services: lau Off-site: 🕍 ✗ 🖉 🖳 ⋋S 🖽

At Socoa (3km SW)

Juantcho rte de la Corniche, 64122
☎ 559471197 🖷 559471197
website: www.juantcho.com
➲ *2km W on D912.*
Open: 10 Apr-30 Sep Site: 6HEC ⸺ ⊕ 🏠 Facilities: 🌳 ⊙ 🖾 🖭 🖭 Services: lau Off-site: 🕍 🍸 ✗ 🖳 ⋋RS 🖽

St-Jean-Pied-de-Port Pyrénées-Atlantiques

Narbaïtz rte de Bayonne, Ascarat, 64220
☎ 559371013 🖷 559372142
e-mail: camping-narbaitz@wanadoo.fr
website: www.camping-narbaitz.com
A quiet, comfortable site beside the River Berroua.
➲ *2km NW towards Bayonne.*
Open: 15 Mar-Sep Site: 2.5HEC ⸺ ♠ 🏠 Prices: pitch 11-14.50 (incl 2 persons) Facilities: 🌳 🕍 ⊙ 🖾 🖉 🖭 Services: ✗ lau Leisure: ⋋ PR Off-site: 🕍 🍸 🖳

St-Julien-En-Born Landes

Lette Fleurie 40170 ☎ 558427409 🖷 558424151
e-mail: mairie40170@wanadoo.fr
On undulating ground in a pine wood with good facilities, 5 minutes from the beach.
Open: Apr-Sep Site: 18HEC ⸺ ⋰⋱ ♠ 🖳 Prices: ♦3.35 ♠1.25 🖳3.50 ▲3.40 Facilities: 🌳 🕍 ⊙ 🖾 🖉 🖳 🖭 Services: 🍸 ✗ 🖽 lau Leisure: ⋋ P Off-site: ⋋R

St-Justin Landes

Pin rte de Roquefort, 40240 ☎ 558448891 🖷 358448891
e-mail: camping.lepin@wanadoo.fr
website: www.campinglepin.com
A quiet family site beside the lake. Bar and café open May to 15 September only.
➲ *2.3km N on D626.*
Open: Apr-Sep Site: 3HEC ⸺ ⋰⋱ ♠ 🏠 🖳 Prices: ♦3-4.50 pitch 5-8 Facilities: 🌳 ⊙ 🖾 🖭 Services: 🍸 ✗ lau Leisure: ⋋ P Off-site: 🕍

St-Léon-sur-Vézère Dordogne

Paradis 24290 ☎ 553507264 🖷 553507590
e-mail: le-paradis@perigord.com
website: www.le-paradis.com
Situated on the river bank in the picturesque Vézère valley.
S of village off D706 Les Éyzies road.
Open: 01 Apr-25 Oct Site: 7HEC ⸺ ♠ 🖳 Prices: ♦4.76-6 pitch 7.49-10.70 Facilities: 🌳 🕍 ⊙ 🖾 🖉 🖳 🖭 Services: 🍸 ✗ 🖽 lau Leisure: ⋋ PR

At Tursac (7km SW)

Pigeonnier 24620 ☎ 553069690 🖷 553069690
e-mail: le-pigeonnier-tursac@wanadoo.fr
A small, peaceful site in the heart of the Dordogne countryside.
➲ *Acces via D706 between Le Moustier and Les Éyzies.*
Open: Jun-30 Sep Site: 1.1HEC ⸺ ♠ 🖳 Prices: ♦3.80 pitch 4.80 Facilities: 🌳 🕍 ⊙ 🖾 🖉 🖭 Services: 🍸 ✗ 🖽 lau Leisure: ⋋ P Off-site: ✗ ⋋R

Vézère Périgord route de Montignac, 24620
☎ 553069631 🖷 553067966
website: www.le-vezere-perigord.com
A well equipped site in wooded surroundings close to the river.
➲ *0.8km NE on D706.*
Open: Etr-Oct Site: 6HEC ⸺ ♠ 🏠 Prices: ♦3-6 pitch 5-7 Facilities: 🌳 🕍 ⊙ 🖾 🖭 Services: 🍸 ✗ 🖽 lau Leisure: ⋋ P Off-site: 🖉 ⋋R

Site: 6HEC-Site size ⸺-grass ⋰⋱-sand ⊕-stone ⋎-little shade ⊕-partly shaded ♠-mainly shaded
🏠-bungalows for hire 🖳-caravans for hire ▲-tents for hire ⊘-no dogs Prices: ♦-adult per night ♠-car per night
pp-per person per night 🖳-caravan per night ▲-tent per night

St-Martin-de-Seignanx LANDES

Lou P'tit Poun 40390 ☎ 559565579 ▤ 559565371
e-mail: ptitpoun@club-internet.fr
website: www.les-campings.com/lou-ptit-poun
A quiet site with well defined pitches on terraces.
➲ *Access via A63 exit Bayonne Nord towards Pau.*
Open: 15 Jun-15 Sep Site: 7HEC ▥▥ ⊶ ⚐ ⚘ ▲
Facilities: ⚑ ⊙ ⚐ ∅ ≟ 🛁 ▣ Services: ⚌ ✕ lau Leisure: ⟊ P

St-Martory HAUTE-GARONNE

CM rte de St-Girons, 31360 ☎ 561902224
Open: All year Site: ▥▥ ⊶ Prices: ⚑5 Facilities: ⚑ ⊙ ⚐ 🛁
Services: ⊞ lau Off-site: 🛒 ⚌ ✕ ∅ ≟ ⟊R

St-Nicolas-de-la-Grave TARN-ET-GARONNE

Plan d'Eau Base de Plein Air, et de Loisirs, 82210
☎ 563955002 ▤ 563955001
e-mail: basedeloisirs.stnicolas@cg82.fr
➲ *2.5km N via D15.*
Open: 15 Jun-15 Sep Site: 1.5HEC ▥▥ ⚘ Prices: pitch 9.10
(incl 2 persons) Facilities: ⚑ ⊙ ⚐ 🛁 Services: lau Off-site: ⚌
✕ ⟊LPR ⊞

St-Pardoux-la-Rivière DORDOGNE

⚑**Château le Verdoyer** 24470 ☎ 553569464 ▤ 553563870
e-mail: chateau@verdoyer.fr website: www.verdoyer.fr
A small, well equipped site in the grounds of a restored
castle.
➲ *3km N via D96.*
Open: 19 Apr-18 Oct Site: 17HEC ▥▥ ⊶ ⚐ ⚐ ▲
Facilities: ⚑ 🛒 ⊙ ⚐ ∅ 🛁 Services: ⚌ ✕ ⊞ lau Leisure: ⟊ LP

St-Paul-les-Dax LANDES

Pins du Soleil RD459, 40990 ☎ 558913791 ▤ 558910024
e-mail: pinsoleil@aol.com website: www.pinsoleil.com
On a hotel complex with good modern facilities.
➲ *SW via D954.*
Open: 03 Apr-30 Oct Site: 6HEC ▥▥ ⊶ ⚐ Prices: pitch 15-
23 (incl 2 persons) Facilities: ⚑ 🛒 ⊙ ⚐ ∅ 🛁 ▣ Services: ⚌
✕ lau Leisure: ⟊ P Off-site: ✕ ∅ ≟ ⟊LRS

St-Pée-sur-Nivelle PYRÉNÉES-ATLANTIQUES

Goyetchea 64310 ☎ 559541959
e-mail: c-goyetchea@wanadoo.fr
website: www.camping-goyetchea.com
Quiet, peaceful site in a wooded location at the foot of the
Pyrénées.
➲ *0.8km N on rte d'Ahetze.*
Open: Jun-20 Sep Site: 3HEC ▥▥ ⊶ ⚐ Prices: pitch 12.50-
17.50 (incl 2 persons) Facilities: ⚑ 🛒 ⊙ ⚐ ∅ 🛁 Services: ✕
⊞ lau Leisure: ⟊ P Off-site: ⚌ ✕ ⟊R

Ibarron 64310 ☎ 0559541043
e-mail: campingdibarron@wanadoo.fr
website: www.camping-ibarron.com
In a pleasant wooded location with level pitches and good,
modern facilities.
➲ *2km W on D918.*
Open: May-Sep Site: 2.8HEC ▥▥ ⚘ ⚐ ⚐ Prices: pitch
4.48-5.50 Facilities: ⚑ 🛒 ⊙ ⚐ ∅ 🛁 Services: ✕ ⊞ lau
Off-site: 🛒 ⚌ ✕ ∅ ≟ ⟊LPR

St-Pierre-Lafeuille LOT

Graves 46090 ☎ 565368312 ▤ 565368312
e-mail: lesgravescamping@ninitel.net
On a small hill on the northern outskirts of the village
providing fine views over the surrounding countryside.

➲ *10km N of Cahors.*
Open: Mar-15 Oct Site: 1HEC ▥▥ ⊶ ⚐ Facilities: ⚑ ⊙ ⚐
🛁 Services: ✕ lau Leisure: ⟊ P Off-site: 🛒 ⚌ ✕

Quercy-Vacances Le Mas de Lacombe, 46090
☎ 565368715 ▤ 565360239
e-mail: quercyvacances@wanadoo.fr
website: www.quercyvacances.com
A well equipped site in pleasant wooded surroundings.
➲ *On N20. 12km N of Cahors.*
Open: May-Sep Site: 3HEC ▥▥ ⊶ ⚘ ⚐ ⚐ Prices: ⚑3.94-
4.92 pitch 6.77-8.46 Facilities: ⚑ ⊙ ⚐ ∅ 🛁 Services: ⚌ ✕
⊞ lau Leisure: ⟊ P Off-site: ⟊LR

St-Rémy-sur-Lidoire DORDOGNE

Tuilière 24700 ☎ 553824729 ▤ 553824729
e-mail: la-tuiliere@wanadoo.fr
website: www.campinglatuiliere.com
In pleasant wooded surroundings beside a lake. Separate car
park for arrivals after 22.00hrs.
➲ *6km from Montpon on D708 towards Ste-Foy-la-Grande.*
Open: Jun-15 Sep Site: 8HEC ▥▥ ⚘ ⚘ ⚐ Prices: ⚑2.50-
3.10 pitch 3.60-4.50 Facilities: ⚑ 🛒 ⊙ ⚐ ∅ 🛁 ▣ Services: ⚌
✕ ⊞ lau Leisure: ⟊ LP

St-Sernin-de-Duras LOT-ET-GARONNE

Moulin de Borie Neuve 47120 ☎ 553207073
e-mail: info@borieneuve.com
website: www.borieneuve.com
A pleasant site in the Dourdèze valley close to an old mill.
➲ *Access via D244 towards St-Astier-de-Duras.*
Open: 15 May-15 Oct Site: 1HEC ▥▥ ⊶ ⚐ Prices: ⚑3.85
⚐5.30 pitch 5.30 Facilities: ⚑ ⊙ ⚐ ∅ 🛁 Services: ⚌ ⊞ lau
Leisure: ⟊ PR Off-site: 🛒 ✕ ∅ ≟ ⟊L

St-Seurin-de-Prats DORDOGNE

Plage 24230 ☎ 553586107 ▤ 553586267
e-mail: campdelaplage@aol.com
In a peaceful, wooded setting beside the Dordogne with a
variety of recreational facilities.
➲ *0.7kms on D11.*
Open: 26 May-20 Sep Site: 3.9HEC ▥▥ ⚘ ⚐ Facilities: ⚑
🛒 ⊙ ⚐ 🛁 Services: ⚌ ✕ lau Leisure: ⟊ PR Off-site: ∅ ≟ ⊞

Ste-Eulalie-En-Born LANDES

Bruyères chemin Laffont, 40200 ☎ 558097336 ▤ 558097558
e-mail: bonjour@camping-les-bruyeres.com
website: www.camping-les-bruyeres.com
In the middle of the Landes forest close to lakes and the sea.
➲ *2.5km N via D652*
Open: 14 May-29 Sep Site: 3HEC ▥▥ ⚘ ⚐ ⚐ Facilities: ⚑
🛒 ⊙ ⚐ ∅ ≟ 🛁 Services: ⚌ ✕ ⊞ lau Leisure: ⟊ P
Off-site: ⟊LR

Salignac DORDOGNE

'Les Peneyrals' Le Poujol, St-Crépin Carlucet, 24590
☎ 553288571 ▤ 553288099
e-mail: camping.peneyrals@wanadoo.fr
website: www.peneyrals.com
Quiet site among trees between the Vézère and Dordogne
rivers.
➲ *10 km N of Sarlat on D60.*
Open: 15 May-11 Sep Site: 12HEC ▥▥ ⊶ ⚐ ⚐
Prices: ⚑4.20-6.60 pitch 6-9.70 Facilities: ⚑ 🛒 ⊙ ⚐ ∅ 🛁 🛁
Services: ⚌ ✕ ⊞ lau Leisure: ⟊ P

Facilities: 🛒-shop **⚑**-shower **⊙**-electric points for razors **⚐**-electric points for caravans **🛁**-parking by tents permitted
▣-compulsory separate car park **Services: ✕**-café/restaurant **⚌**-bar **∅**-Camping Gaz International **≟**-gas other than Camping
Gaz **⊞**-first aid facilities **lau**-laundry **Leisure: ⟊**-swimming **L**-Lake **P**-Pool **R**-River **S**-Sea **Off-site:** All facilities within 2km

Mobile homes and chalets to let

Camping Park du Val de l'Eyre ★★★

Situated in a hilly, 213 ha. park with many trees and a pond, a swimming pool and bordering the tranquil river the Eyre, where you can make canoe trips with the whole family. Many activities, cozy and quiet ambience, relaxation and cleanliness guaranteed by our friendly staff.

www.valdeleyre.com

8, route du Minoy - 33770 SALLES
Tel : 33 5 56 88 47 03   Fax : 33 5 56 88 47 27

SALLES GIRONDE

Val de l'Eyre 8 rte de Minoy, 33770
☎ 556884703   ▤ 556884727
e-mail: levaldeleyre@free.fr
website: www.valdeleyre.com
A well equipped family site in a pleasant wooded location between the Landes forests and the Bordeaux vineyards.
➲ *SW on D108, rte de Lugos.*
Open: Mar-Oct Site: 13HEC ⠿ ∴ ⊕ ▲ Facilities: ⬧ ⊙ �R ⚑ ≞ ⌂ Services: ⬤ ✗ ⊞ lau Leisure: ⬩ LR Off-site: ⚑ ∅ ⬩P

SALLES LOT-ET-GARONNE

Bastides 47150 ☎ 553408309   ▤ 553408176
e-mail: info@campingdesbastides.com
website: www.campingdesbastides.com
In peaceful wooded surroundings overlooking the Lède Valley with good sporting and entertainment facilities.
➲ *1km N via D150.*
Open: Etr-Sep Site: 6HEC ⠿ ♣ ⊞ ▲ Prices: ⚑4-5.25 pitch 12-21 (incl 2 persons) pp4-5.25 Facilities: ⬧ ⚑ ⊙ ⊑ ∅ ≞ ⌂ Services: ⬤ ✗ ⊞ lau Leisure: ⬩ P

SARLAT-LA-CANÉDA DORDOGNE

Maillac Ste-Nathalène, 24200 ☎ 553592212   ▤ 553296017
e-mail: campingmaillac@wanadoo.fr
website: www.campingmaillac.fr
In wooded surroundings in the heart of the Périgord Noir region with good facilities for a family holiday. Separate car park for arrivals after 23.00hrs.
➲ *7km NE on D47.*
Open: 15 May-Oct Site: 6HEC ⠿ ♣ ⊞ Prices: ⚑4.50 pitch 5.50 Facilities: ⬧ ⚑ ⊙ ⊑ ∅ ≞ ⌂ Services: ⬤ ✗ ⊞ lau Leisure: ⬩ P Off-site: ⬩LR

☀Moulin du Roch rte des Éyzies, 24200
☎ 553592027   ▤ 553592095
e-mail: moulin.du.roch@wanadoo.fr
website: www.moulin-du-roch.com
In a picturesque location between the Dordogne and Vézère valleys.
➲ *10km NW via D704-D6-D47.*
Open: 01 May-19 Sep Site: 8HEC ⠿ ⚑ ⊞ ▲ ⚘ Prices: pitch 13-24 (incl 2 persons) Facilities: ⬧ ⚑ ⊙ ⊑ ∅ ⌂ Services: ⬤ ✗ ⊞ lau Leisure: ⬩ P

Périères 24203 ☎ 553590584   ▤ 553285751
e-mail: les-perieres@wanadoo.fr
website: www.lesperieres.com
Very well kept terraced site situated in 12 acres of parkland and woods in the heart of the Périgord Noir with fine views over the Sarlat valley. There are good recreational facilities and modern, well equipped bungalows are available for hire.
➲ *1km N of town on D47.*
Open: Etr-Sep Site: 11HEC ⠿ ⚑ ⊞ Prices: ⚑5.80 pitch 18-31 Facilities: ⬧ ⚑ ⊙ ⊑ ∅ ⌂ Services: ⬤ ✗ ⊞ lau Leisure: ⬩ P

Val d'Ussel La Fond d'Ussel, 24200
☎ 553592873   ▤ 553293825
e-mail: valdussel@online.fr website: www.valdussel.com
A well equipped site in woodland in the heart of the Périgord Noir region. Separate car park for late arrivals.
➲ *Off D704 or D56.*
Open: 15 Jun-Sep Site: 7.5HEC ⠿ ♣ ⊞ ⚑ ▲ Facilities: ⬧ ⚑ ⊙ ⊑ ∅ ⌂ Services: ⬤ ✗ lau Leisure: ⬩ P

AT CARSAC-AILLAC (7KM SE VIA D704A)

Aqua Viva 24200 ☎ 553314600   ▤ 553293637
e-mail: aqua-viva@perigord.com website: www.aquaviva.fr
Site with numerous terraces in beautiful wooded surroundings in the heart of the Dordogne.
➲ *Along the main road Sarlat/Souillac D704A*
Open: Etr-Sep Site: 11HEC ⠿ ∴ ⚑ ♣ ⊞ Prices: ⚑3.90-6.40 pitch 4.80-9.50 Facilities: ⬧ ⚑ ⊙ ⊑ ∅ ⌂ Services: ⬤ ✗ ⊞ lau Leisure: ⬩ LP Off-site: ⬩R

Rocher de la Cave 24200 ☎ 553281426   ▤ 553282710
e-mail: rocher.de.le-cave@wanadoo.fr
website: www.rocherdelecave.com
Pleasant family site on a level meadow beside the Dordogne, set in beautiful countryside.
➲ *Access via D703 & D704.*
Open: 15 May-15 Sep Site: 4HEC ⠿ ∴ ♣ ⊞ ⚑ ▲ Prices: ⚑3.48-4.35 pitch 4.56-5.70 Facilities: ⬧ ⚑ ⊙ ⊑ ∅ ⌂ Services: ⬤ ✗ ⊞ lau Leisure: ⬩ PR

SAUVETERRE-DE-BÉARN PYRÉNÉES-ATLANTIQUES

CM Gave av de la Gare, 64390 ☎ 559385330
➲ *Turn left before bridge on St-Palais road.*
Open: Jun-Sep Site: 1.5HEC ⠿ ⚑ Facilities: ⬧ ⊙ ⊑ ⌂ Services: ⊞ lau Leisure: ⬩ R Off-site: ⚑ ⬤ ✗ ∅ ≞

SAUVETERRE-LA-LÉMANCE LOT-ET-GARONNE

Moulin du Périé rte de Loubejac, 47500 ☎ 553406726
In a wooded valley close to an 18th century watermill with good, modern facilities.
➲ *3km E of town off D710. Follow signposts from the entrance to the village and keep to the valley road.*
Open: Apr-Sept Site: 5HEC ⠿ ♣ ⊞ ⚑ ▲ Facilities: ⬧ ⚑ ⊙ ⊑ ∅ ≞ ⌂ Services: ⬤ ✗ ⊞ lau Leisure: ⬩ PR Off-site: ⬩L

SEIGNOSSE LANDES

Chevreuils rte de Hossegor, 40510
☎ 558433280 📠 558433280
e-mail: chevreuils@wanadoo.fr website: www.chevreuils.com
In a pine forest close to the sea with good recreational
facilities.
➲ *On CD79 rte de Hossegor.*
Open: Jun-15 Sep Site: 8HEC ⬛ ::: ♦ 🏠 🚐
Prices: ♠3.30-4.71 pitch 11.90-17 Facilities: 🅡 🅛 ⊙ 🖳 ∅ 🚿
🅟 Services: 🍴 ✗ 🅗 lau Leisure: ↝ P Off-site: ↝S

CM Hourn Naou av des Tucs, 40510
☎ 558433030 📠 558416421
e-mail: camping.municipal@ville-seignosse.fr
Very clean and tidy site situated in a pine forest 600mtrs
from the sea.
➲ *200mtrs from Seignosse town centre.*
Open: 6 Apr-Sep Site: 16HEC ::: 🅠 🏠 Facilities: 🅡 🅛 ⊙
🖳 ∅ 🅟 Services: 🍴 ✗ 🅗 lau Off-site: 🚿 ↝LPS

Oyats rte de la Plage des Casennes, 40510
☎ 558433794 📠 0558432329
Level site, subdivided into fields and surrounded by woods.
Separate section for young people. Children's play area.
➲ *Turn off D79 in N outskirts towards Plage des Casernes.*
Open: 11 May-15 Sep Site: 17HEC ::: ♦ 🏠 ⚑ Prices: pitch
10-19.80 (incl 2 persons) Facilities: 🅡 🅛 ⊙ 🖳 ∅ 🚿 🅟
Services: 🍴 ✗ 🅗 lau Leisure: ↝ P Off-site: ↝S

AT SEIGNOSSE-LE-PENON (5KM W)

Forêt 40510 ☎ 558416850 📠 558432326
A pleasant, quiet site 300m from the sea.
Open: 29 Jun-2 Sep Site: 11HEC ::: ♦ 🏠 ⚘ Facilities: 🅡
⊙ 🖳 🅟 Services: 🍴 ✗ 🅗 lau Leisure: ↝ P Off-site: 🅛 🚿
↝LS

SEIX ARIÈGE

Haut Salat 09140 ☎ 561668178 📠 561669417
e-mail: camping.le-haut-salat@wanadoo.fr
website: www.ariege.com/campinglehautsalat
Very clean, well kept site beside stream. Big gravel pitches for
caravans. Common room with TV.
➲ *0.8km NE on D3.*
Open: All year Site: 2.5HEC ⬛ ♦ 🚐 Prices: ♠15.90
⚑13.90 Facilities: 🅡 🅛 ⊙ 🖳 ∅ 🚿 🅟 Services: 🍴 ✗ 🅗 lau
Leisure: ↝ PR Off-site: ✗

SÉRIGNAC-PÉBOUDOU LOT-ET-GARONNE

Vallée de Gardeleau 47410 ☎ 553369696 📠 553369696
e-mail: valleegardeleau@wanadoo.fr
In a shaded wooded position, offering peace and comfort in
relaxing surroundings. *Situated between Lauzun and
Castilonnès on RN21*
Open: 29 Apr-18 Sep Site: 2HEC ⬛ ♦ 🅐 ⚘
Prices: ♠2.40-3.70 pitch 3.65-5.65 Facilities: 🅡 ⊙ 🖳 🅟
Services: 🍴 ✗ 🅗 lau Leisure: ↝ P

SOUILLAC LOT

🏠**Domaine de la Paille Basse** 46200
☎ 565378548 📠 565370958
e-mail: paille.basse@wanadoo.fr
website: www.lapaillebasse.com
A family site in a picturesque wooded location in the
grounds of a former château.
➲ *6.5km NW off D15 Salignac-Eyvignes road.*
Open: 15 May-15 Sep Site: 12HEC ⬛ ♠ 🅠 Prices: ♠4.60-
5.80 pitch 8.70-10.90 Facilities: 🅡 🅛 ⊙ 🖳 ∅ 🅟 Services: 🍴 ✗
🅗 lau Leisure: ↝ P

SOULAC-SUR-MER GIRONDE

Océan L'Amélie, 33780 ☎ 556097610 📠 556097475
A level site in a pine forest, 300mtrs from the beach.
➲ *3.5km S.*
Open: Jun-15 Sep Site: 6HEC ⬛ ::: 🅠 🚐 Facilities: 🅡 🅛
⊙ 🖳 ∅ 🅟 Services: 🍴 ✗ 🅗 lau Off-site: ↝S

Sables d'Argent 33BD de l'Amélie, 33780
☎ 556098287 📠 556099482
e-mail: camping.sables.d.argent@wanadoo.fr
website: www.sables-d-argent.com
In a pine forest, bordered by sand dunes with direct access to
the beach.
➲ *1.5km SW of village.*
Open: Apr-Sep Site: 2.6HEC ⬛ ::: 🅠 🏠 Prices: pitch
13.95-18.20 Facilities: 🅡 🅛 ⊙ 🖳 ∅ 🚿 🅟 Services: 🍴 ✗ 🅗 lau
Leisure: ↝ S Off-site: ↝P

AT AMÉLIE-SUR-MER, L' (4.5KM S)

Amélie-Plage 33780 ☎ 556098727 📠 556736426
e-mail: camping.amelie.plage@wanadoo.fr
website: www.camping-amelie-plage.com
In hilly wooded terrain. Lovely sandy beach.
➲ *3km S on the Soulac road.*
Open: Mar-Dec Site: 8.5HEC ⬛ ::: ♦ Prices: pitch 15-18
(incl 2 persons) Facilities: 🅡 🅛 ⊙ 🖳 ∅ 🚿 🅟 Services: 🍴 ✗ 🅗
lau Leisure: ↝ S

At LILIAN (4.5KM S)

Pins 33780 ☎ 556098252 📠 5577365558
e-mail: contact@campingdispins.fr
website: www.campingdespins.fr
Situated in beautiful pine forest close to the beach with
plenty of sporting facilities.
➲ *S on D101.*
Open: May-Oct Site: 3.2HEC ⬛ ::: ♦ 🏠 🅐 ⚑
Facilities: 🅡 🅛 ⊙ 🖳 ∅ 🅟 Services: 🍴 ✗ 🅗 lau
Off-site: ↝RS

SOUSTONS LANDES

CM Airial 40140 ☎ 558411248 📠 558415383
e-mail: contact@camping-airial.com
website: www.camping-airial.com
Situated in a shady park with plenty of recreational facilities
and modern installations.
➲ *2km W on D652.*
Open: Apr-15 Oct Site: 17HEC ⬛ ::: 🅠 🏠 🚐
Prices: ♠3.35-4.65 pitch 4.10-5 Facilities: 🅡 🅛 ⊙ 🖳 ∅ 🅟
Services: 🍴 ✗ 🅗 lau Leisure: ↝ P

TARASCON-SUR-ARIÈGE ARIÈGE

Pré Lombard rte d'Ussat, 9400 ☎ 561056194 📠 561057893
e-mail: leprelombard@wanadoo.fr
website: www.prelombard.com
In beautiful wooded surroundings beside the River Ariège
with good, modern facilities.
➲ *1.5km SE on D23.*
Open: All year Site: 3.5HEC ⬛ ♦ 🏠 Prices: ♠4-9 pitch 15-
23 (incl 2 persons) Facilities: 🅡 ⊙ 🖳 ∅ 🚿 🅟 Services: 🍴 ✗
🅗 lau Leisure: ↝ PR Off-site: 🅛

TEILLET TARN

Relais de l'Entre Deux Lacs 81120
☎ 563557445 📠 563557565
e-mail: contact@camping-entredeuxlacs.com
website: www.camping-entredeuxlacs.com
Shady terraced site. Various activities arranged. Beautiful
views.

contd.

Facilities: 🅛-shop 🅡-shower ⊙-electric points for razors 🖳-electric points for caravans 🅟-parking by tents permitted
🅟-compulsory separate car park Services: ✗-café/restaurant 🍴-bar ∅-Camping Gaz International 🚿-gas other than Camping
Gaz 🅗-first aid facilities lau-laundry Leisure: ↝-swimming L-Lake P-Pool R-River S-Sea Off-site: All facilities within 2km

↪ *Off D81 towards Lacaune.*
Open: All year Site: 4HEC ⬛ ♣ 🏠 Prices: ⚑4 pitch 13
(incl 2 persons) Facilities: ʰ ☉ 🖭 🏠 Services: ⏸ ✕ ⊞ lau
Leisure: ⟍ P Off-site: ⚍ ⍥ ⚍ ⟍LR

TESTE-DE-BUCH, LA GIRONDE

Village de Loisirs Domaine de la Forge rte Sanguinet, 33260
☎ 556660772 ▤ 556667897
e-mail: domainedelaforge@bigfoot.com
website: www.domainedelaforge.com
Secluded site in very quiet woodland.
↪ *3km S on D652.*
Open: All year Site: 20HEC ⬛ ⠿ ♣ 🏠 Facilities: ʰ ⚍ ☉
⚍ 🏠 🅿 Services: ⏸ ✕ ⊞ lau Leisure: ⟍ P Off-site: ⟍R

THIVIERS DORDOGNE

CM Le Repaire 24800 ☎ 553526975 ▤ 553526975
In a wooded valley, this well appointed family site lies in the
'Périgord Vert' region of the Dordogne some ten minutes
walk from the ancient village of Thiviers.
↪ *1500mtrs along D707 towards Lanouaille.*
Open: May-Sep Site: 11HEC ⬛ ⋇ 🏠 Prices: ⚑3.20-4
pitch 4-6 Facilities: ʰ ⚍ ☉ 🖭 🏠 Services: ⏸ ✕ ⊞ lau
Leisure: ⟍ P Off-site: ✕ ⍥ ⚍ ⟍L

TONNEINS LOT-ET-GARONNE

CM Robinson 47400 ☎ 553790228
↪ *500m from town centre on N113 Agen road.*
Open: Jun-Sep Site: 0.7HEC ⬛ ⅄ 🖭 Facilities: ʰ ☉ 🖭 🏠
Services: lau Leisure: ⟍ R Off-site: ⟍P ⊞

TOUZAC LOT

Ch'Timi 46700 ☎ 565365236 ▤ 565365323
e-mail: info.lechtimi@wanadoo.fr
website: www.campinglechtimi.com
A well equipped site overlooking the River Lot.
Entertainment available in high season.
↪ *800m from Touzac on D8.*
Open: Apr-Sep Site: 3.5HEC ⬛ ⅄ 🏠 🖭 Prices: ⚑3.30-4.40
pitch 4.50-6 Facilities: ʰ ⚍ ☉ 🖭 🏠 Services: ⏸ ✕ ⊞ lau
Leisure: ⟍ PR

Clos Bouyssac 46700 ☎ 565365221 ▤ 565246851
e-mail: camping.leclosbouyssac@wanadoo.fr
website: monsite.wanadoo.fr/leclosbouyssac
On the fringe of a wooded hillside by the sandy shore of the
River Lot. Good for walking.
↪ *S of Touzac on D65.*
Open: Apr-Oct Site: 15HEC ⬛ ♣ 🏠 🖭 Prices: ⚑5 ⊕1.20
Facilities: ʰ ⚍ ☉ 🖭 ⍥ 🏠 Services: ⏸ ✕ ⊞ lau Leisure: ⟍ PR

URRUGNE PYRÉNÉES-ATLANTIQUES

Larrouleta 64122 ☎ 559473784 ▤ 559474254
e-mail: larrouleta@wanadoo.fr website: www.larrouleta.com
Hilly meadow with young trees.
↪ *1.5 km N of Urrugne on N1 to Spain.*
Open: All year Site: 10HEC ⬛ ♣ Prices: ⚑3.50-4.80 pitch
4-4.50 Facilities: ʰ ⚍ ☉ 🖭 🏠 Services: ⏸ ✕ ⊞ lau
Leisure: ⟍ L Off-site: ⍥ ⟍PS

URT PYRÉNÉES-ATLANTIQUES

Etche Zahar allée de Mesplès, 64240
☎ 559562736 ▤ 559562962
e-mail: camping.etche-zahar@wanadoo.fr
website: www.etche-zahar.fr
A small, privately owned site in a wooded location and
within easy reach of local tourist areas. Separate car parking
for arrivals between 22.00hrs and 7.00hrs.

↪ *Access via exit 8 on A63 or exit 4 on A64.*
Open: 15 Mar-15 Nov Site: 2.5HEC ⬛ ⋇ 🏠 ⚑
Prices: ⚑1.75-3.50 ⊕2 pitch 3.50-7 Facilities: ʰ ⚍ ☉ 🖭 ⍥ ⚍
🏠 Services: ✕ ⊞ lau Leisure: ⟍ P Off-site: ⏸ ✕ ⟍R

VALEUIL DORDOGNE

Bas Meygnaud D393 Brantome, 24310 ☎ 553055844
e-mail: camping-du-bas-meygnaud@wanadoo.fr
website: www.basmeygnaud.com
A quiet, shady site in the Dronne Valley.
↪ *Access via D939, turning off at Lasserre.*
Open: Apr-Sep Site: 1.7HEC ⬛ ♣ 🏠 ⚑ Prices: ⚑2.50 ⊕2
🖭4 ⚑4 Facilities: ʰ ⚍ ☉ 🖭 🏠 Services: ⏸ ✕ ⊞ lau
Leisure: ⟍ P Off-site: ⟍R

VARILHES ARIÈGE

CM Parc du Château av du 8 Mai 45, 9120
☎ 561674284 ▤ 561605554
On the banks of the river and close to the town.
↪ *N on N20.*
Open: All year Site: 1HEC ⬛ ♣ Facilities: ʰ ☉ 🖭 🏠
Services: ⊞ lau Off-site: ⚍ ⏸ ✕ ⍥ ⚍ ⟍P

VAYRAC LOT

Domaine de Bourzolles Condat, 46110 ☎ 565321632
↪ *Off D20 between Condat and Vayrac.*
Open: May-30 Oct Site: 4HEC ⬛ ♣ Facilities: ʰ ☉ 🖭 🏠
Services: ⊞ lau Leisure: ⟍ P Off-site: ⏸ ✕ ⍥ ⚍

VENDAYS-MONTALIVET GIRONDE

Mayan 3 route de Mayan, 33930 ☎ 556417651
A small site situated in a pine wood.
↪ *Access from Bordeaux direction via N215 and D102.*
Open: Jul-Aug Site: 1HEC ⬛ ⅄ 🏠 Prices: ⚑1.90 pitch 1.91
Facilities: ʰ ☉ 🖭 🏠 Services: ⊞ lau Off-site: ⚍

VERDON-SUR-MER, LE GIRONDE

Royannais 88 rte de Soulac, 33123
☎ 556096112 ▤ 556737067
e-mail: camping.le.royannais@wanadoo.fr
Level, sandy terrain under high pine and deciduous trees.
↪ *S of Le Verdon-sur-Mer in Le Royannais district on D1.*
Open: 15 Jun-15 Sep Site: 2HEC ⬛ ⠿ ♣ 🏠 🖭
Facilities: ʰ ⚍ ☉ 🖭 ⍥ ⚍ 🏠 Services: ⏸ ✕ ⊞ lau
Off-site: ⟍RS

VERGT-DE-BIRON DORDOGNE

Patrasses 24540 ☎ 553630587 ▤ 6553248895
Situated in the heart of the Périgord Noir region with good
facilities.
↪ *3.6km S via D2E.*
Open: Jun-Sep Site: 4.7HEC ⬛ ⅄ 🏠 🖭 ⚑ Facilities: ʰ ⚍
☉ 🖭 🏠 Services: ⏸ ✕ ⊞ lau Leisure: ⟍ P

VEYRINES-DE-DOMME DORDOGNE

Pastourels Le Brouillet, 24250 ☎ 553295249
A quiet site in a pleasant rural setting near the Château des
Milandes.
↪ *3.6km N off D53 towards Belvès.*
Open: Apr-Sep Site: 3.5HEC ⬛ ⠿ ♣ 🖭 ⚑ Facilities: ʰ
⚍ ☉ 🖭 ⍥ 🏠 Services: ⊞ lau Leisure: ⟍ P

VÉZAC DORDOGNE

Deux Vallées 24220 ☎ 553295355 ▤ 553310981
e-mail: les2v@perigord.com
website: www.les-2-vallees.com
A level site in a picturesque location in the Dordogne Valley.
Good facilities for families.

➲ *Access via D57 from Sarlat or D703 from Bergerac.*
Open: All year Site: 3.2HEC ⛺ ♠ Prices: ♦3.50 pitch 3
Facilities: ↟ ⚍ ⊙ ⊞ ∅ 囵 Services: ♈ ✗ lau Leisure: ⇝ P
Off-site: ⇝R

VIELLE-ST-GIRONS LANDES

Eurosol rte de la Plage, 40560
☎ 558479014 & ▤ 558477674
e-mail: contact@camping-eurosol.com
website: www.camping-eurosol.com
Well maintained family site in a pine forest, 700mtrs from
one of the finest beaches in the country.
➲ *Access via A63 exit Castets.*
Open: 08 May-18 Sep Site: 18HEC ⛺ ⠿ ♠ 🏠 Prices: ♦4
pitch 2-16 Facilities: ↟ ⚍ ⊙ ⊞ ∅ 囵 Services: ♈ ✗ ⊞ lau
Leisure: ⇝ P Off-site: ⇝S

Sunelia Col Vert Lac de Léon, 40560
☎ 558429406 ▤ 558429188
e-mail: contact@colvert.com
website: www.colvert.com
Quiet site on lakeside in sparse pine woodland. Small natural
harbour in the mouth of a stream.
➲ *Turn off D652 on N side of village and continue towards
lake.*
Open: Apr-Sep Site: 30HEC ⛺ ⚏ 🏠 ⊞ ⸜ Prices: ♦2-5.90
pitch 6.50-16.10 Facilities: ↟ ⚍ ⊙ ⊞ ∅ 峠 囵 Services: ♈ ✗
⊞ lau Leisure: ⇝ LP

VIEUX-BOUCAU-LES-BAINS LANDES

CM des Sablères bd du Marensin, 40480
☎ 558481229 ▤ 558482070
e-mail: camping-lessableres@wanadoo.fr
website: www.lessableres.com
A family site with modern facilities and direct access to
beach.
➲ *Access via N10 and D652.*
Open: Apr-15 Oct Site: 11HEC ⛺ ⚏ ♠ Prices: pitch
10.10-15.50 (incl 2 persons) Facilities: ↟ ⊙ ⊞ 囵 Services: ⊞
lau Off-site: ⚍ ♈ ✗ ∅ 峠 ⇝LS

VIGAN, LE LOT

Rêve Revers, 46300 ☎ 565412520 ▤ 565416852
e-mail: info@campinglereve.com
website: www.campinglereve.com
A modern family site in wooded surroundings.
➲ *From Payrac take D673 towards Le Vigan and follow signs.*
Open: 26 Apr-15 Sep Site: 8HEC ⛺ 🏠 Prices: ♦2.80-4
pitch 4.20-6 Facilities: ↟ ⚍ ⊙ ⊞ ∅ 囵 Services: ♈ ✗ ⊞ lau
Leisure: ⇝ P

VILLEFRANCHE-DU-QUEYRAN LOT-ET-GARONNE

Moulin de Campech 47160 ☎ 553887243 ▤ 553880652
e-mail: campech@wanadoo.fr
website: www.moulindecampech.co.uk
A beautiful site in a peaceful location beside a small lake
stocked with trout.
➲ *Access via D11 towards Casteljaloux.*
Open: Apr-10 Oct Site: 4HEC ⛺ ♠ ⸜ Prices: ♦3.45-4.85
pitch 6.80-8.50 Facilities: ↟ ⚍ ⊙ ⊞ 囵 Services: ♈ ✗ ⊞ lau
Leisure: ⇝ LPR

VILLENAVE-D'ORNON GIRONDE

Gravières 35 ave Mirieu de Labarre, 33140 ☎ 556870036
➲ *2km NE*
Open: All year Site: 3.5HEC ⛺ ⠿ ◊ ♠ 🏠 ⊞ ⸜
Facilities: ↟ ⚍ ⊙ ⊞ ∅ 峠 囵 Services: ♈ ✗ ⊞ lau Leisure: ⇝
L Off-site: ∅

VILLERÉAL LOT-ET-GARONNE

Château de Fonrives Rives, 47210
☎ 553366338 ▤ 553360998
e-mail: chateau.de.fontives@wanadoo.fr
website: www.campingchateaufonrives.com
In a beautiful natural park in the grounds of a château with
good facilities for all ages.
➲ *2.2km NW via D207*
Open: Apr-Sep Site: 20HEC ⛺ ♠ 🏠 ⊞ ⸜ Prices: pitch
16-23 (incl 2 persons) Facilities: ↟ ⚍ ⊙ ⊞ ∅ 峠 囵
Services: ♈ ✗ ⊞ lau Leisure: ⇝ LP

VITRAC DORDOGNE

Bouysse Caudon, 24200 ☎ 553283305 ▤ 553303852
e-mail: la-bouysse.24@wanadoo.fr
website: www.labouysse.com
Well appointed site in a wooded valley beside the Dordogne.
➲ *2km E, near the River Dordogne.*
Open: Apr-Sep Site: 3HEC ⛺ ♠ 🏠 Prices: ♦4.08-5.10
pitch 5.44-6.80 Facilities: ↟ ⚍ ⊙ ⊞ ∅ 囵 Services: ♈ ✗ lau
Leisure: ⇝ PR Off-site: ✗ 峠 ⊞

Soleil Plage 24200 ☎ 553283333 ▤ 553283024
e-mail: soleil.plage@wanadoo.fr
website: www.camping-soleilplage.fr
Set out around an old farmhouse bordering the Dordogne
with excellent facilities.
➲ *4km E on D703, turn by 'Camping Clos Bernard'.*
Open: 10 May-20 Sep Site: 8HEC ⛺ ♠ 🏠 Facilities: ↟ ⚍
⊙ ⊞ ∅ 囵 Services: ♈ ✗ ⊞ lau Leisure: ⇝ PR

LOIRE/CENTRAL

AIGUILLON-SUR-MER, L' VENDÉE

Bel Air 85460 ☎ 251564405 ▤ 251971558
e-mail: camping.belair@wanadoo.fr
website: www.camping-belair.com
A long, level stretch of meadowland in rural surroundings.
➲ *1.5 km NW on D44 then turn left.*
Open: Apr-Sep Site: 7HEC ⛺ ⚏ 🏠 ⊞ ⸜ Prices: ♦6.94
pitch 18 Facilities: ↟ ⚍ ⊙ ⊞ ∅ 峠 囵 Services: ♈ ✗ ⊞ lau
Leisure: ⇝ P Off-site: ⇝LRS

AIRVAULT DEUX-SÈVRES

Courte Vallée Courte Vallée, 79600
☎ 549647065 ▤ 549647065
e-mail: camping@caravanningfrance.com
website: www.caravanningfrance.com
A modern site, situated in a river valley, with large pitches
and good facilities.
➲ *On the outskirts of the town, 0.5km NW towards Availles.*
Open: May-Sep Site: 12HEC ⛺ ♠ Prices: ♦5-6 pitch
7.50-10.50 Facilities: ↟ ⚍ ⊙ ⊞ 囵 Services: ⊞ lau
Leisure: ⇝ P Off-site: ⚍ ♈ ✗ ∅ 峠 ⇝P

ALLONNES MAINE-ET-LOIRE

Pô Doré Le Pô Doré, 49650 ☎ 241387880 ▤ 241387881
e-mail: camping.le.po.dore@wanables.fr
website: campinglepodore.monsite.wanadoo.fr
A family site in a pleasant rural setting in the heart of the
Anjou region with good recreational facilities. Separate car
park for arrivals 22.00hrs.
➲ *Access via D35 from Tours or N147 from Angers.*
Open: Apr-Oct Site: 2HEC ⛺ ⚏ 🏠 ⊞ Prices: ⊞12-15
⸜12-15 Facilities: ↟ ⚍ ⊙ ⊞ 囵 Services: ♈ ✗ lau
Leisure: ⇝ P

Facilities: ⚍-shop ↟-shower ⊙-electric points for razors ⊞-electric points for caravans 囵-parking by tents permitted
⊞-compulsory separate car park Services: ✗-café/restaurant ♈-bar ∅-Camping Gaz International 峠-gas other than Camping
Gaz ⊞-first aid facilities lau-laundry Leisure: ⇝-swimming L-Lake P-Pool R-River S-Sea Off-site: All facilities within 2km

ANCENIS LOIRE-ATLANTIQUE

Ile Mouchet La Charbonnière, 44150
☎ 240830843 🗏 240831619
e-mail: efberthelot@wanadoo.fr
Peaceful, wooded site located on the banks of the Loire. *Off N23 from Nantes-Ancenis*
Open: Apr-13 Oct **Site:** 3HEC ⊞ 🔾 🛏 🚐 **Prices:** ♠1.90-2.20 pitch 5.40-6.10 **Facilities:** 🖍 🖭 ⊙ 🖾 🖺 **Services:** 🛒 ✗ lau **Leisure:** 🔾 P **Off-site:** ⊘ 🚿

ANDONVILLE LOIRET

Domaine de la Joullière rte de Richerelles, 45480
☎ 238395846 🗏 238396194
e-mail: domaine.joulliere@wanadoo.fr
website: www.domaine.joulliere.com
Spread over a series of small, wooded valleys with good sports and leisure facilities.
➲ *1km E on road to Richerelles.*
Open: 15 Feb-15 Dec **Site:** 10HEC ⊞ ♣ **Prices:** ♠5 pitch 5 **Facilities:** 🖍 🖭 ⊙ 🖾 🖺 **Services:** 🛒 ✗ 🖽 lau **Leisure:** 🔾 P

ANGERS MAINE-ET-LOIRE

Lac de Maine av du Lac de Maine, 49000
☎ 241730503 🗏 241730220
e-mail: camping@lacdemaine.fr
website: www.lacdemaine.fr
In pleasant rural surroundings on the shore of the 100 hectares Lac de Maine. There are fine sporting and entertainment facilities and the historic town of Angers is within easy reach.
➲ *Access via A11 (Angers/Nantes) at Lac de Maine exit.*
Open: 25 Mar-10 Oct **Site:** 4HEC ⊞ ⠿ 🔾 🛏
Prices: pitch 10-14 (incl 2 persons) **Facilities:** 🖍 ⊙ 🖾 ⊘ 🚿 🖺 **Services:** 🛒 ✗ lau **Leisure:** 🔾 P **Off-site:** 🖭 🔾LR 🖽

ANGLES VENDÉE

Moncalm-Atlantique 85750 ☎ 251975550 🗏 251289109
e-mail: camping-apv@wanadoo.fr
website: www.camping-apv.com
Two distinct sites, but sharing the same recreational facilities in a wooded setting close to the beach.
Open: Apr-Sep **Site:** 10HEC ⊞ ♣ 🛏 🚐 🅰 **Facilities:** 🖍 🖭 ⊙ 🖾 ⊘ 🚿 🖺 **Services:** 🛒 ✗ lau **Leisure:** 🔾 LP **Off-site:** 🔾R 🖽

ANGOULINS-SUR-MER CHARENTE-MARITIME

Chirats rte de la Platère, 17690 ☎ 546569416
Modern site with good facilities 100m from a small sandy beach and providing panoramic views over the Bay of Fouras. The more popular, larger beaches of the area are some 3km away. Reservations are strongly recommended.
➲ *7km S of La Rochelle.*
Open: Apr-Sep **Site:** 4.5HEC ⊞ 🔾 🛏 🚐 **Facilities:** 🖍 🖭 ⊙ 🖾 ⊘ 🚿 🖺 🅿 **Services:** 🛒 ✗ 🖽 lau **Leisure:** 🔾 S

APREMONT VENDÉE

Prairies du Lac rte de Maché RD40, 85220
☎ 251557058 🗏 251557604
e-mail: infos@les-prairies-du-lac.com
website: www.camping-les-prairies-du-lac.com
Site located in a country setting but near the Vendée beaches and the lake of Apremont with its water slide.
➲ *D58 from Challans*
Open: May-Sep **Site:** 6HEC ⊞ 🔾 **Prices:** pitch 17 (incl 2 persons) **Facilities:** 🖍 ⊙ 🖾 🖺 **Services:** 🛒 lau **Leisure:** 🔾 P **Off-site:** 🖭 🔾LR 🖽

ARCES CHARENTE-MARITIME

Chez Filleux 17120 ☎ 546908433 🗏 546908433
e-mail: laferme.chezfilleux@wanadoo.fr
website: www.camping-chezfilleux.com
On a level meadow partly shaded by trees and bushes with good, modern facilities. 10 minutes from the local beaches.
Open: Apr-Sep **Site:** 3HEC ⊞ 🔾 🛏 🚐 **Prices:** ♠12 pitch 12 (incl 3 persons) **Facilities:** 🖍 🖭 ⊙ 🖾 ⊘ 🖺 **Services:** 🛒 ✗ 🖽 lau **Leisure:** 🔾 P

ARGENTAT CORRÈZE

Gibanel Le Gibanel, 19400 ☎ 555281011 🗏 555288162
e-mail: contact@camping-gibanel.com
website: www.camping-gibanel.com
Pleasant site situated in grounds of a château next to a lake. Some facilities are only available in high season.
➲ *S from Tulle on N120.*
Open: Jun-14 Sep **Site:** 6.5HEC ⊞ 🔾 🚐 **Prices:** ♠3.60-4.50 **Facilities:** 🖍 🖭 ⊙ 🖾 ⊘ 🖺 **Services:** 🛒 ✗ 🖽 lau **Leisure:** 🔾 LP **Off-site:** 🚿

Saulou Vergnolles, 19400 ☎ 555281233 🗏 555288067
e-mail: le.saulou@wanadoo.fr website: www.saulou.com
A peaceful site in a wooded location beside the River Dordogne. Ideal for families.
➲ *6km S on D116.*
Open: Apr-Sep **Site:** 7.5HEC ⊞ ♣ 🛏 **Prices:** pitch 11.40-18 (incl 2 persons) **Facilities:** 🖍 🖭 ⊙ 🖾 ⊘ 🚿 🖺 **Services:** 🛒 ✗ 🖽 lau **Leisure:** 🔾 PR

AT MONCEAUX-SUR-DORDOGNE (3KM SW)

Vaurette 19400 ☎ 555280967 🗏 555288114
e-mail: camping.le.vaurette@wanadoo.fr
website: www.vaurette.com
On the banks of the River Dordogne with a beach, swimming pool & tennis court.
➲ *On D12 between Argentat and Beaulieu.*
Open: May-21 Sep **Site:** 4HEC ⊞ ♣ 🛏 **Prices:** pitch 13-19 (incl 2 persons) **Facilities:** 🖍 🖭 ⊙ 🖾 ⊘ 🚿 🖺 **Services:** 🛒 ✗ 🖽 lau **Leisure:** 🔾 PR

ARGENTON-CHÂTEAU DEUX-SÈVRES

CM du Lac d'Hautibus 79150
☎ 549659508 🗏 549657084
e-mail: marie-argenton-chateau@wanadoo.fr
➲ *0.4km S on D748.*
Open: Apr-Oct **Site:** 16.2HEC ⊞ 🔾 🛏 **Prices:** ♠1.80 pitch 1.65 **Facilities:** 🖍 ⊙ 🖾 🖺 **Services:** lau **Off-site:** 🖭 🛒 ✗ ⊘ 🚿 🔾LPR 🖽

AVRILLÉ VENDÉE

Forges Domaine Les Forges, 85440
☎ 251223885 🗏 251223885
e-mail: contact@domaine-des-forges.net
website: www.domaine-des-forges.net
In a pleasant position beside a lake, 300m from the town centre. Close to beach, the site has a variety of leisure facilities.
Open: Etr-end Sep **Site:** 8HEC ⊞ 🔾 🛏 🚐 **Prices:** ♠12-15.50 **Facilities:** 🖍 🖭 ⊙ 🖾 🚿 🖺 **Services:** 🛒 ✗ 🖽 lau **Leisure:** 🔾 LP **Off-site:** ⊘

Mancelières rte de Longeville-sur-Mer, 85440
☎ 251903597 🗏 251903931
e-mail: camping.mancellieres@tiscali.fr
website: www.lesmancellieres.com
A pleasant site in a wooded park approx. 5km from the fine beaches of South Vendée. Separate car park for arrivals after 23.00hrs.

➲ *1.7km S via D105 towards Longeville*
Open: Easter-15 Sep **Site:** 2.6HEC ⊞ ⊕ 🏠 🏠 Å
Prices: pitch 10.15-14.50 (incl 2 persons) **Facilities:** 🏕 🏪 ⊙
🔌 𝚍 🏠 **Services:** ✗ ⊞ lau **Leisure:** ⌇ P **Off-site:** ⚐ ✗

AZAY-LE-RIDEAU INDRE-ET-LOIRE

Parc du Sabot r du Stade, 37190
☎ 247454272   🗏 247454911
e-mail: marie.azayleideau@free.fr
Site lies in large meadow on bank of River Indre.
➲ *Near château in town centre.*
Open: 11 Apr-30 Nov **Site:** 9HEC ⊞ ♠ **Prices:** pitch 11.40-
12.40 (incl 2 persons) **Facilities:** 🏕 🏪 ⊙ 🔌 🏠 **Services:** ⊞ lau
Leisure: ⌇ R **Off-site:** 🏪 ⚐ ✗ 𝚍 🏔 ⌇P

BARRE-DE-MONTS, LA VENDÉE

Grande Côte 85550 ☎ 251685189   🗏 251492557
website: www.campeoles.fr
In pine forest behind dunes with direct access to the beach.
Plenty of recreational facilities.
➲ *3 km from village beside Noirmoutier toll bridge.*
Open: 7Apr-23Sep **Site:** 22HEC ⁙ ♠ 🏠 Å **Facilities:** 🏕 🏪
⊙ 🔌 🏠 **Services:** ⚐ lau **Leisure:** ⌇ P **Off-site:** ✗ 𝚍 🏔 ⌇S

BATZ-SUR-MER LOIRE-ATLANTIQUE

Govelle rte de la Côte Sauvage, 44740 ☎ 240239163
Direct access to the sea. Supervised beach and sea-fishing
nearby.
➲ *On D45 between Le Pouliguen and Batz.*
Open: 15 Jun-15 Sep **Site:** 6.8HEC ⊞ ☀ 🏠 **Facilities:** 🏕
⊙ 🔌 🏠 🅿 **Services:** ⚐ ✗ ⊞ lau **Leisure:** ⌇ S

BAULE, LA LOIRE-ATLANTIQUE

Ajoncs d'Or chemin du Rocher, 44500
☎ 240603329   🗏 240244437
e-mail: contact@ajoncs.com website: www.ajoncs.com
In a large wooded park, close to the beach with well defined
pitches.
➲ *Signposted from the entrance to the town.*
Open: Apr-Sep **Site:** 6HEC ⊞ ♠ 🏠 **Prices:** ⚑6 pitch 18-23
Facilities: 🏕 🏪 ⊙ 🔌 𝚍 🏔 🏠 **Services:** ⚐ ✗ ⊞ lau **Leisure:** ⌇
P **Off-site:** ⌇S

CM av de Diane, 44505 ☎ 240601740   🗏 240601148
e-mail: campi-boisamour@wanadoo.fr
website: www.campingdefrance.com/boisdamour/
Site consists of two sections, one for caravans, one for tents,
each with separate entrance.
➲ *On NE outskirts near the railway.*
Open: Feb-Oct **Site:** 5HEC ⊞ ⁙ ♠ 🏠 ⌇ **Prices:** pitch
10.30-14.10 (incl 2 persons) **Facilities:** 🏕 🏪 ⊙ 🔌 𝚍 🏔 🏠
Services: ⚐ ✗ ⊞ lau **Leisure:** ⌇PRS

Eden 1315 Route De Ker Rivaud, 44500
☎ 240119425   🗏 240600323
e-mail: eden-caravaning@wanadoo.fr
website: www.ledencaravaning.com
In pleasant rural surroundings with good sports and sanitary
facilities.
➲ *1km NW via N171 exit 'La Baule-Escoublac'.*
Open: 9 Apr-15 Oct **Site:** 4.7HEC ⊞ ⊕ 🏠 **Prices:** ⚑3.65-
5.35 pitch 5.50-7.80 **Facilities:** 🏕 🏪 ⊙ 🔌 🏠 **Services:** ⚐ ✗ ⊞
lau **Leisure:** ⌇ LP **Off-site:** 𝚍 🏔 ⌇S

Roseraie 20 av J-Sohier, 44500 ☎ 240604666   🗏 240601184
e-mail: camping@laroserie.com
website: www.laroseraie.com
A well planned site in wooded surroundings with good
recreational facilities.

➲ *E of N171 towards the bay.*
Open: Apr-Sep **Site:** 5HEC ⊞ ⊕ 🏠 **Prices:** ⚑4.50-6.50
pitch 8-12 **Facilities:** 🏕 🏪 ⊙ 🔌 𝚍 🏔 🏠 **Services:** ⚐ ✗ ⊞ lau
Leisure: ⌇ P **Off-site:** ⌇S

BAZOUGES-SUR-LE-LOIR SARTHE

CM rte de Cré-sur-Loir, 72200 ☎ 243459580   🗏 243453826
On the bank of the River Loir with well defined pitches.
➲ *Approach off A11 towards La Flèche.*
Open: 15 May-Oct **Site:** 0.8HEC ⊞ ⊕ 🏠 **Facilities:** 🏕 ⊙
🔌 🏠 **Services:** ⊞ lau **Off-site:** 🏪 ⚐ ✗ 𝚍 🏔 ⌇RS

BEAULIEU-SUR-DORDOGNE CORRÈZE

Îles 19120 ☎ 555910265   🗏 555910519
e-mail: jycastanet@aol.com
website: www.camping-des-iles.net
On an island in the River Dordogne, within easy reach of all
facilities.
Open: 15 Apr-15 Oct **Site:** 4.5HEC ⊞ ♠ 🏠 🏠 Å
Prices: ⚑3.90-4.30 pitch 4.70-5.70 **Facilities:** 🏕 ⊙ 🔌 🏔 🏠
Services: ⚐ ✗ ⊞ lau **Leisure:** ⌇ PR **Off-site:** 🏪 𝚍

BESSINES-SUR-GARTEMPE HAUTE-VIENNE

At **MORTEROLLES-SUR-SEMME** (4.5KM N ON N20)

CM 87250 ☎ 0555766018
➲ *100m from N20; in town centre.*
Open: All year **Site:** 8HEC ⊞ ⊕ **Prices:** pitch 6 (incl 2
persons) **Facilities:** 🏕 ⊙ 🔌 🏠 **Services:** lau **Off-site:** ⚐ ✗ 𝚍
⌇R ⊞

BEYNAT CORRÈZE

Étang de Miel 19190 ☎ 555855066   🗏 0555855796
e-mail: camping.lac.de.miel@wanadoo.fr
A family site in a picturesque wooded setting close to the lake
within the 'Green Valley'.
➲ *4km E on N121 Argentat road.*
Open: Apr-Oct **Site:** 9HEC ⊞ ⊕ 🏠 🏠 **Prices:** pitch 11-13
Facilities: 🏕 🏪 ⊙ 🔌 𝚍 🏠 **Services:** ⚐ ✗ ⊞ lau **Leisure:** ⌇ LR

BIGNAC CHARENTE

Marco de Bignac Lieudit "Les Sablons", 16170
☎ 0545217841   🗏 0545215237
website: www.camping-marco-bignac.com
In a beautiful wooded location set out around the shore of a
5 acre lake with fine entertainment and sporting facilities.
➲ *N of Angoulême off N10. Take D11 W at La Touche
through Vars to Basse then right onto D117 to Bignac. Site well
signposted close to the River Charente.*
Open: 15 May-15 Sep **Site:** 8HEC ⊞ ♠ **Prices:** pitch 12-
17 (incl 2 persons) **Facilities:** 🏕 🏪 ⊙ 🔌 🏠 **Services:** ⚐ ✗ ⊞
Leisure: ⌇ LP **Off-site:** ⌇R

BLÉRÉ INDRE-ET-LOIRE

CM r de la Gatine, 37150 ☎ 0247579260   🗏 0247579260
e-mail: marie@blere-touraine.com
website: www.blere-touraine.com
Well-kept site beside River Cher. Two entrances.
Open: 7 Apr-15 Oct **Site:** 4HEC ⊞ ⊕ **Prices:** pitch 8.40
(incl 2 persons) **Facilities:** 🏕 ⊙ 🔌 🏠 🅿 **Services:** lau
Off-site: 🏪 ⚐ ✗ ⌇P ⊞

BONNAC-LA-CÔTE HAUTE-VIENNE

🏠Château de Leychoisier 87270
☎ 555399343   🗏 555399343
e-mail: leychoisier@wanadoo.fr website: www.leychoisier.fr.st
Well-managed site on ground sloping gently towards the
woods. Divided into roomy pitches.

contd.

Facilities: 🏪-shop 🏕-shower ⊙-electric points for razors 🔌-electric points for caravans 🏠-parking by tents permitted
🅿-compulsory separate car park **Services:** ✗-café/restaurant ⚐-bar 𝚍-Camping Gaz International 🏔-gas other than Camping
Gaz ⊞-first aid facilities lau-laundry **Leisure:** ⌇-swimming L-Lake P-Pool R-River S-Sea **Off-site:** All facilities within 2km

⇨ *1km S off N20.*
Open: 15 Apr-20 Sep Site: 4HEC ⊞⊞ ⊕ ⬛ ⬛ Prices: ⭢5.50-7 pitch 8-9.50 Facilities: ⬛ ⬛ ⊙ ⬛ ⬛ Services: ⬛ ✕ ⊞ lau Leisure: ⬛ LP

BONNES VIENNE

CM r de la Varenne, 86300 ☎ 549564434 ▥ 549564851
e-mail: camping-bonnes@hotmail.com
website: www.camping.bonnes86.free.fr
A quiet site with plenty of recreational facilities.
⇨ *S beside the River Vienne.*
Open: May-15 Sep Site: 1HEC ⬛ ⬿ Facilities: ⬛ ⊙ ⬛ ⬛
Services: lau Leisure: ⬛ PR Off-site: ⬛ ⬛ ✕ ⬛ ⬛L ⊞

BONNY-SUR-LOIRE LOIRET

Val 45420 ☎ 238315771 ▥ 238315771
e-mail: maisonpays-bonny@wanadoo.fr
Woodland site situated by the side of the Loire, near the town centre
⇨ *At the junction of N7 and D965.*
Open: mid May-30 Oct Site: 0.8HEC ⊞⊞ ⊕ Prices: ⭢2 pitch 2 Facilities: ⬛ ⊙ ⬛ ⬛ Services: lau Leisure: ⬛ R Off-site: ⬛
⬛ ✕ ⬛ ⬛

BOURGES CHER

CM de Bourges 26 bd de l'Industrie, 18000
☎ 248201685 ▥ 248503239
e-mail: tourisme@wellbourges.fr
website: www.wellbourges.fr
In the town near Lake Auron.
⇨ *Access via A71, N144 or N76.*
Open: 15 Mar-15 Nov Site: 2.2HEC ⊞⊞ ⬿⬿ ⊕ Prices: ⭢3.20
⬛4.50 ⬛3.20 Facilities: ⬛ ⊙ ⬛ ⬛ Services: ⊞ lau
Off-site: ⬛ ⬛ ✕ ⬛ ⬛ ⬛LPR

BOUSSAC-BOURG CREUSE

⬛Château de Poinsouze rte de La Châtre - BI 12, 23600
☎ 555650221 ▥ 555658649
e-mail: info.camping-de.poinsouze@wanadoo.fr
website: www.camping-de-poinsouze.com
In a picturesque location in the grounds of a château with good, modern facilities.
⇨ *2km N via D917.*
Open: 15 May-12 Sep Site: 22HEC ⊞⊞ ⊕ ⬛ ⬛ Prices: pitch 19-25 (incl 2 persons) Facilities: ⬛ ⬛ ⊙ ⬛ ⬛ ⬛
Services: ⬛ ✕ ⊞ lau Leisure: ⬛ P

BRACIEUX LOIR-ET-CHER

CM des Châteaux 11 rue Roger Brun, 41250
☎ 254464184 ▥ 254464121
In a pleasant, shady park close to the town centre and conveniently situated for visiting the castles of Chambord, Cheverny and Villesavin.
Open: 1Apr- 3 Nov Site: 8HEC ⊞⊞ ⊕ ⬛ Facilities: ⬛ ⊙ ⬛
⬛ Services: ⊞ lau Leisure: ⬛ PR Off-site: ⬛ ⬛ ✕ ⬛ ⬛

BRAIN-SUR-L'AUTHION MAINE-ET-LOIRE

CM Caroline 49800 ☎ 241804218
A modern site in a pleasant wooded setting close to the river.
Open: 15 Mar-Oct Site: 3.5HEC ⊞⊞ ⬿ Facilities: ⬛ ⊙ ⬛ ⬛
Services: ⊞ lau Off-site: ⬛ ⬛ ✕ ⬛ ⬛

BRÉTIGNOLLES-SUR-MER VENDÉE

Dunes Plage des Dunes, 85470 ☎ 251905532 ▥ 251905485
e-mail: campinglesdunes@freesurf.fr
website: www.campinglesdunes.com
Direct access to the beach. All plots surrounded by hedges.

⇨ *2km S turn right off D38 and proceed for 1km across the dunes. 150m from beach.*
Open: 1 Apr-11 Nov Site: 12HEC ⬿⬿ ⬿ ⬛ Facilities: ⬛ ⬛
⊙ ⬛ ⬛ ⬛ Services: ⬛ ✕ ⊞ lau Leisure: ⬛ P Off-site: ⬛S

Motine 4 r des Morinières, 85470
☎ 251900442 ▥ 251338052
e-mail: campinglamotine@wanadoo.fr
Pleasant site situated 350m from the town centre and 400m from the beach with good facilities.
Open: Apr-Sep Site: 1.8HEC ⊞⊞ ⊕ ⬛ Prices: pitch 17-24.50 (incl 2 persons) Facilities: ⬛ ⊙ ⬛ ⬛ ⬛ Services: ⬛ ✕
⊞ lau Leisure: ⬛ P Off-site: ⬛ ⬛LRS

Trevilliere rte de Bellevue, 85470
☎ 251900965 ▥ 251900965
e-mail: camping-chadotel@wanadoo.fr
website: www.chadotel.com
⇨ *900mtrs from the town centre and 2km from the beach.*
Open: 15 Apr-30 Sep Site: 3.5HEC ⊞⊞ ⬿ ⬛ ⬛ ⬿ ⬿
Prices: pitch 12-22 (incl 2 persons) Facilities: ⬛ ⬛ ⊙ ⬛ ⬿ ⬿
⬛ Services: ⬛ ✕ ⊞ lau Leisure: ⬛ P Off-site: ✕ ⬛S

Vagues 20 bd du Centre, 85470
☎ 251901948 ▥ 240024988
e-mail: lesvagues@free.fr
website: www.campinglesvagues.fr
A family site situated on the Côte de Lumière in a delightful rural setting.
⇨ *N on D38 towards St-Gilles-Croix-de-Vie*
Open: Apr-Sep Site: 5HEC ⊞⊞ ⬿ ⬛ ⬛ Prices: ⭢3.29-4.70
pitch 12.95-18.50 Facilities: ⬛ ⊙ ⬛ ⬛ Services: ⬛ ✕ ⊞ lau
Leisure: ⬛ P Off-site: ⬛ ✕ ⬛ ⬛LRS

BRISSAC-QUINCÉ MAINE-ET-LOIRE

L'Étang rte de St Mathurin, 49320
☎ 241917061 ▥ 241917265
e-mail: info@campingetang.com
website: www.campingetang.com
A lakeside site in the heart of the Anjou countryside with good recreational facilities.
⇨ *Access via D748 towards Poitiers.*
Open: 19 May-04 Sept Site: 3.5HEC ⊞⊞ ⊕ ⬛ ⬛ ⬛
Prices: pitch 17-22 (incl 2 persons) Facilities: ⬛ ⬛ ⊙ ⬛ ⬛ ⬛
Services: ⬛ ✕ ⊞ lau Leisure: ⬛ P Off-site: ✕

BRÛLON SARTHE

Brûlon-le-Lac 72350 ☎ 243956896 ▥ 243926036
In attractive wooded surroundings beside a lake.
⇨ *Access via N157 towards Sable-sur-Sarthe.*
Open: 15 Apr-Sep Site: 3.5HEC ⊞⊞ ⬿ Facilities: ⬛ ⬛ ⊙ ⬛
⬛ ⬛ ⬛ Services: ⬛ ✕ ⊞ lau Leisure: ⬛ LPR

CANDÉ-SUR-BEUVRON LOIR-ET-CHER

Grande Tortue 3 rte de Pontlevoy, 41120
☎ 254441520 ▥ 254441945
e-mail: info@la-grande-tortue.com
website: www.la-grand-tortue.com
A family site in a peaceful wooded setting.
⇨ *D751, between Blois and Amboise, on the left bank of the river.*
Open: 15 Apr-25 Sep Site: 5.8HEC ⊞⊞ ⬿ ⬛ Prices: pitch 12.50-22.50 (incl 2 persons) Facilities: ⬛ ⬛ ⊙ ⬛ ⬛ ⬛ ⬛
Services: ⬛ ✕ ⊞ lau Leisure: ⬛ P

A full guide to the Symbols &
Abbreviations used in this book
can be found on page 6

Site: 6HEC-Site size ⊞⊞-grass ⬿⬿-sand ⬿-stone ⬿-little shade ⊕-partly shaded ⬿-mainly shaded
⬛-bungalows for hire ⬛-caravans for hire ⬛-tents for hire ⬿-no dogs Prices: ⭢-adult per night ⬿-car per night
pp-per person per night ⬛-caravan per night ⬛-tent per night

CHALARD, LE HAUTE-VIENNE

Vigères Les Vigères, 87500 ☎ 555093722 ▤ 555099339
e-mail: lesvigeres@aol.com
website: www.lesvigeres.com
Generally level site in peaceful surroundings in an elevated position with fine views. English management.
➲ *Between Châlus and Le Chalard on D901.*
Open: All year Site: 20HEC ⊞ ⊕ ☎ Prices: ♠2.50-3 pitch 2.50-3.50 Facilities: ⋒ ⊾ ⊙ ⊝ ⊞ ⚏ ☎ Services: ⊞ lau
Leisure: ⊰ LP Off-site: ⊻ ✕

CHALONNES-SUR-LOIRE MAINE-ET-LOIRE

CM Candais rte de Rochefort, 49290 ☎ 241780227
On the banks of the River Loire at its confluence with the River Louet.
➲ *NE off D751 towards Rochefort.*
Open: 15 May-Sep Site: 3HEC ⊕ ⊙ ⊝ ☎ Facilities: ⋒ ⊙ ⊝ ☎
Services: ⊞ lau Off-site: ⊾ ⊻ ✕ ⊘ ⚏ ⊰P

CHAPELLE HERMIER, LA VENDÉE

Pin Parasol Lac du Jaunay, Chateaulong, 85220
☎ 251346472 ▤ 251346462
e-mail: pinparasol@freesurf.fr
website: www.pinparasol.freesurf.fr
In the heart of the Vendée countryside on the shore of Lac du Jaunay with good, modern facilities.
➲ *Between D6 and D12.*
Open: 01 May-20 Sep Site: 7HEC ⊞ ⊕ ☎ Prices: pitch 13-22 (incl 2 persons) Facilities: ⋒ ⊾ ⊙ ⊝ ⊘ ⚏ ☎
Services: ⊻ ✕ ⊞ lau Leisure: ⊰ P

CHARTRES EURE-ET-LOIR

CM des Bords de l'Eure 9 r de Launay, 28000
☎ 237287943 ▤ 237282943
e-mail: camping-mousell-chartres@wanadoo.fr
In wooded surroundings beside the river.
➲ *Signposted towards Orléans.*
Open: 10 Apr-10 Nov Site: 3.9HEC ⊞ ⊁ Prices: pitch 8-11.50 (incl 2 persons) Facilities: ⋒ ⊾ ⊙ ⊝ ⊘ ⚏ ☎
Services: ⊻ ✕ ⊞ lau Off-site: ⊘ ⚏ ⊰PR

CHARTRE-SUR-LE-LOIR, LA SARTHE

Vieux Moulin av des Déportés, 72340 ☎ 243444118
e-mail: campingvieuxmoulin@worldonline.fr
Open: 15 Apr-Sep Site: 2.4HEC ⊞ ⊕ ⊙ ⊝ ☎ Facilities: ⋒ ⊙ ⊝ ☎
Services: ⊞ lau Leisure: ⊰ PR Off-site: ⊾ ⊻ ✕ ⊘ ⚏ ⊰LP

CHARTRIER-FERRIÈRE CORRÈZE

Magaudie La Magaudie Ouest, 19600
☎ 555852606 ▤ 555852606
e-mail: camping@lamagaudie.com
website: www.lamagaudie.com
A peaceful site covering 8 hectares with half consisting of forest, 3km from Lac du Causse which has beaches and facilities for water sports. The 18th century buildings on the site have been converted to give hygenic sanitary facilities.
➲ *A20 Limoges-Toulouse exit 53, take N20 in direction of Cahors. At roundabout take D19 in direction of Chasteaux and after railway viaduct 4th left for D154 in direction of Chartrier and remain on road towards Nadaillac. Third right for La Magaudie and then 1st right, site on left.*
Open: All year Site: 8HEC ⊞ ⊛ ⊕ ⚏ Prices: ♠3.25 pitch 3.80-4.25 Facilities: ⋒ ⊾ ⊙ ⊝ ☎ Services: ⊻ ✕ ⊞ lau
Leisure: ⊰ P Off-site: ⊘ ⚏

CHASSENEUIL-SUR-BONNIEURE CHARENTE

CM Les Charmilles r des Écoles, 16260
☎ 545395536 ▤ 545225245
e-mail: mairie.chasseneuil@wanadoo.fr
website: http://membres.lycos.fr/ville16260/
➲ *W of town via D27, beside the River Bonnieure.*
Open: All year Site: 1.5HEC ⊞ ⊛ ⚏ ⚠ Prices: ♠1.55 pitch 0.92 Facilities: ⋒ ⊙ ⊝ ☎ Services: lau Off-site: ⊾ ⊻ ✕ ⊘
⊰P ⊞

CHÂTEAU D'OLONNE, LE VENDÉE

Pirons r des Marchais, La Pironnière, 85180
☎ 251952675 ▤ 251239317
e-mail: contact@camping-les-pirons.com
website: www.camping-les-pirons.com
Site 300m from beach with three swimming pools and an aquatic chute.
➲ *off D949*
Open: Apr-Oct Site: 7HEC ⊕ ☎ ⚏ ⚠ ⊗ Facilities: ⋒ ⊾ ⊙
⚏ ⊘ ⚏ ☎ Services: ⊻ lau Leisure: ⊰ P Off-site: ⊰S

CHÂTEAU-DU-LOIR SARTHE

CM de Coemont 72500 ☎ 243794463
Shady site on the bank of the Loir.
Open: 01 Jun-30 Sep Site: 0.6HEC ⊞ ⊛ Prices: ♠1.39 pitch 4.02 Facilities: ⋒ ⊙ ⊝ ☎ Services: lau Leisure: ⊰ R
Off-site: ⊾ ⊻ ✕ ⊘ ⊰LP ⊞

CHÂTELAILLON-PLAGE CHARENTE-MARITIME

Clos des Rivages av des Boucholeurs, 17340 ☎ 546562609
Level, well-kept site with pitches divided by trees and bushes, 500mtrs from the sea.
➲ *500mtrs from the village. Signposted.*
Open: 15 Jun-5 Sep Site: 2.5HEC ⊞ ⊛ Prices: pitch 16.50-19 (incl 2 persons) Facilities: ⋒ ⊙ ⊝ ⊘ ⚏ ☎ Services: ⊻ ⊞
lau Leisure: ⊰ P Off-site: ✕ ⊰S

Deux Plages 17340 ☎ 546562753 ▤ 546435118
e-mail: reception@2plages.com
website: www.2plages.com
In pleasant wooded surroundings 200mtrs from the beach.
Open: May-Sep Site: 4.5HEC ⊞ ⸬ ⊛ ☎ Facilities: ⋒ ⊾
⊙ ⚏ ☎ Services: ⊻ ✕ ⊞ lau Leisure: ⊰ P Off-site: ⊘ ⚏ ⊰S

CHÂTELLERAULT VIENNE

Relais du Miel rte d'Antran, 86100
☎ 549020627 ▤ 549932576
e-mail: camping@lerelaisdumiel.com
website: www.lerelaisdumiel.com
In the grounds of the Château de Valette, beside the River Vienne.
➲ *Access via A10 exit 26 (Châtellerault Nord).*
Open: 15 May-31 Aug Site: 7HEC ⊞ ⊛ ☎ ⚏ Facilities: ⋒
⊙ ⚏ ☎ Services: ⊻ ✕ ⊞ lau Leisure: ⊰ PR Off-site: ⊾ ⊻ ✕
⊘ ⚏

CHÂTRES-SUR-CHER LOIR-ET-CHER

CM des Saules 41320 ☎ 254980455
➲ *On N76 near bridge.*
Open: 01 May-31 Aug Site: 2HEC ⊞ ⊛ Facilities: ⋒ ⊙ ⊝
☎ Services: lau Off-site: ⊾ ⊻ ✕ ⊘ ⚏ ⊰R ⊞

CHAUFFOUR-SUR-VELL CORRÈZE

Feneyrolles 19500 ☎ 555253143
e-mail: feneyrolles@aol.com
In a quiet, wooded location with good facilities. Ideal for exploring the Dordogne Valley and surrounding area.

contd.

Facilities: ⊾-shop ⋒-shower ⊙-electric points for razors ⚏-electric points for caravans ☎-parking by tents permitted
⊟-compulsory separate car park **Services:** ✕-café/restaurant ⊻-bar ⊘-Camping Gaz International ⚏-gas other than Camping
Gaz ⊞-first aid facilities lau-laundry **Leisure:** ⊰-swimming L-Lake P-Pool R-River S-Sea **Off-site:** All facilities within 2km

⊃ *2.2km E.*
Open: 15 Apr-15 Sep Site: 4HEC ⊞ ♠ ⛺ 🚐 Facilities: ⋔ 🍴 ⊙ 🚿 🛒 Services: ⱅ ✕ ⊞ lau Leisure: ⤳ P

CHEF-BOUTONNE DEUX-SÈVRES

Moulin Treneuillet, rte de Brioux, 79110
☎ 549297346   🖩 549297346
e-mail: campingchef@infonie.fr website: campingchef.com
Small, secluded family site in a rural setting.
⊃ *1km NE via D740.*
Open: All year Site: 2.5HEC ⊞ 🏕 ⛺ Prices: ⋔2-2.30 pitch 4.60-7 Facilities: ⋔ ⊙ 🚿 🛒 🛒 Services: ⱅ ✕ lau
Leisure: ⤳ PR Off-site: 🚿

CHENONCEAUX INDRE-ET-LOIRE

Moulin Fort 37150 ☎ 247238622   🖩 247238093
e-mail: lemoulinfort@wanadoo.fr
website: www.lemoulinfort.com
⊃ *2km SE*
Open: Etr-15 Oct Site: 3HEC ⊞ 🏕 🚐 Prices: pitch 12-18 (incl 2 persons) Facilities: ⋔ 🍴 ⊙ 🚿 🚿 🛒 Services: ⱅ ✕ ⊞ lau Leisure: ⤳ PR

CHÉVERNY LOIR-ET-CHER

Les Saules rte de Contres, 41700
☎ 254799001   🖩 254792834
In the heart of the Châteaux-du-Val-de-Loire, bordered by a golf course and the Cheverny forest.
⊃ *1.5km from town towards Contres on D102.*
Open: Apr-Oct Site: 10HEC ⊞ ♠ ⛺ Prices: pitch 18 (incl 2 persons) Facilities: ⋔ 🍴 ⊙ 🚿 🚿 🛒 🛒 Services: ⱅ ✕ ⊞ lau Leisure: ⤳ P

CHINON INDRE-ET-LOIRE

CM 37500 ☎ 247930835
On the banks of the river opposite the Château.
⊃ *Off D951.*
Open: Apr-Oct Site: 6HEC ⊞ ∷∷ 🏕 🚐 Facilities: ⋔ ⊙ 🚿 🛒 Services: ⊞ lau Leisure: ⤳ PR Off-site: 🚿 ⱅ ✕ ⤳S

CHOLET MAINE-ET-LOIRE

Lac de Ribou av L-Mandin, 49300
☎ 241497430   🖩 241582122
Well set-out site bordering a lake, with fishing, boating, tennis and volleyball.
⊃ *3km from town centre.*
Open: Apr-Oct Site: 5HEC ⊞ ♠ ⛺ 🚐 Facilities: ⋔ ⊙ 🚿 🛒 Services: ⱅ ✕ ⊞ lau Leisure: ⤳ P Off-site: 🚿 🛒 🚿 ⤳L

CLOYES-SUR-LE-LOIR EURE-ET-LOIR

Parc des Loisirs rte du Montigny, 28220
☎ 237985053   🖩 237983384
e-mail: info@parc-de-loisirs.com website: www.parc-de-loisirs.com
On the bank of the River Loir. Extensive leisure facilities. Separate section for teenagers. Shop only available in July and August, bar and restaurant only May-September.
⊃ *Access from Châteaudun S on N10 towards Cloyes, then right onto Montigny-le-Gamelon road.*
Open: 15 Mar-15 Nov Site: 5HEC ⊞ 🏕 ⛺ Prices: ⋔4-5 pitch 6.10-7.65 Facilities: ⋔ 🍴 ⊙ 🚿 🚿 🛒 Services: ⱅ ✕ ⊞ lau Leisure: ⤳ P Off-site: 🚿 ⱅ ✕

COGNAC CHARENTE

Cognac rte de Ste-Sévère, bd de Chatenay, 16100
☎ 545321332   🖩 545365529
e-mail: ccdc-camping@wanadoo.fr
website: www.campingdecognac.com
In wooded surroundings beside the River Charente with good, modern facilities.
⊃ *2km N on D24.*
Open: May-15 Oct Site: 1.6HEC ⊞ 🏕 ⛺ Prices: pitch 11-13 (incl 2 persons) Facilities: ⋔ 🍴 ⊙ 🚿 🛒 Services: ⱅ ✕ lau Leisure: ⤳ PR Off-site: ⱅ ✕ ⤳P ⊞

CONTRES LOIR-ET-CHER

Charmoise Sassay, 41700 ☎ 254795515   🖩 254795515
On a level meadow with good facilities.
⊃ *N956.*
Open: Apr-Oct Site: 1HEC ⊞ 🏕 Facilities: ⋔ ⊙ 🚿 🛒 Services: lau Off-site: 🚿 ⱅ ✕ 🚿 🚿

COUHÉ-VERAC VIENNE

Peupliers 86700 ☎ 549592116   🖩 549379209
e-mail: info@lespeupliers.fr
website: www.lespeupliers.fr
A family site in a forest beside the river.
⊃ *N of village on N10 Poitiers road.*
Open: 2 May-Sep Site: 16HEC ⊞ 🏕 ⛺ 🚐 Prices: ⋔4.20-6 pitch 5.25-7.50 Facilities: ⋔ 🍴 ⊙ 🚿 🚿 🛒 Services: ⱅ ✕ ⊞ lau Leisure: ⤳ PR Off-site: 🚿

COURÇON-D'AUNIS CHARENTE-MARITIME

Garenne 21 r du Stade, 17170 ☎ 546016050   🖩 46016359
Open: Jun-Sept Site: ⊞ ♠ Prices: ⋔1.80-10 pitch 1.65-9 Facilities: ⋔ ⊙ 🚿 🛒 Services: lau Off-site: 🚿 ⱅ ✕ 🚿 ⤳P ⊞

COUTURES MAINE-ET-LOIRE

Européen Montsabert, 49320 ☎ 241579163   🖩 241579002
e-mail: anjoucamp@wanadoo.fr
website: www.camping-european.com
In a picturesque wooded park with mature trees.
⊃ *Access via left bank of the River Loire (D751) between Angers and Saumur.*
Open: 24 Apr- 19 Sept Site: 10HEC ⊞ 🏕 ⛺ Prices: pitch 13.50-19.50 (incl 2 persons) Facilities: ⋔ 🍴 ⊙ 🚿 🛒 Services: ⱅ ✕ ⊞ lau Leisure: ⤳ P Off-site: 🚿 ✕ 🚿 🚿

CROISIC, LE LOIRE-ATLANTIQUE

Océan 44490 ☎ 240230769   🖩 240157063
e-mail: camping-ocean@wanadoo.fr
website: www.camping-ocean.fr
A quiet, well appointed site situated 150m from the sea.
⊃ *1.5km NW via D45*
Open: Apr-Sep Site: 7.5HEC ⊞ 🏕 ⛺ 🚐 Prices: pitch 16-32 (incl 3 persons) Facilities: ⋔ 🍴 ⊙ 🚿 🚿 🚿 🛒 Services: ⱅ ✕ ⊞ lau Leisure: ⤳ P Off-site: ⤳S

DISSAY VIENNE

Bois de Chaume Chemin des Meuniers, 86130 ☎ 549623630
Situated on N10 within easy reach of the Futuroscope.
Open: Mar-Oct **Site:** 1.7HEC ᛗᛗ ⌀ 🏠 🚐 **Facilities:** 🏕 ☉
🔌 🅿 **Services:** lau **Off-site:** ✕ ⚡R

CM du Parc 86130 ☎ 549628429 📠 549625872
Quiet, shady site at the foot of a 15th century castle, with
close proximity to Futuroscope, lake of St-Cyr and the Forest
of Mouliere.
Open: Jun-15 Sep **Site:** 1HEC ᛗᛗ **Facilities:** 🏕 ☉ 🔌
Services: lau

DURTAL MAINE-ET-LOIRE

International 9 r du Camping, 49430
☎ 0241763180 📠 0241763267
e-mail: mairie@ville-durtal.fr
website: www.ville-durtal.fr
A pleasant site beside the River Loire.
➲ *Near the centre of the town. Access via N23 or A11.*
Open: Apr-Sep **Site:** 3HEC ᛗᛗ ⌀ 🏠 🚐 ⚠ **Prices:** pitch 9.20
(incl 2 persons) **Facilities:** 🏕 ☉ 🔌 🅿 **Services:** 🍷 ✕ ⊞ lau
Leisure: ⚡ R **Off-site:** 🛒 ✕ ⚡P

EGLETONS CORRÈZE

Egletons-Lac 19300 ☎ 555931475
A lakeside site in wooded surroundings with a fine range of
recreational facilities.
➲ *2km from Egletons towards Ussel.*
Open: All year **Site:** 9HEC ᛗᛗ ⌀ 🚐 **Facilities:** 🏕 ☉ 🔌 🅿 ⚒
🅿 **Services:** 🍷 ✕ ⊞ lau **Off-site:** ⚡LP

EYMOUTHIERS CHARENTE

Gorges du Chambon 16220 ☎ 545707170 📠 545708002
e-mail: gorges.chambon@wanadoo.fr
website: www.gorgesduchambon.fr
In a beautiful location on a wooded hilltop.
➲ *3km N via D163.*
Open: 27 Apr-14 Sep **Site:** 7HEC ᛗᛗ ⌀ 🏠 🅰 ⚘
Prices: pitch 12-18.50 (incl 2 persons) **Facilities:** 🏕 🛒 ☉ 🔌
🅿 ⚒ 🅿 **Services:** 🍷 ✕ ⊞ lau **Leisure:** ⚡ PR

FAUTE-SUR-MER, LA VENDÉE

Fautais 18 rte de la Tranche, 85460 ☎ 251564196
Situated in centre of village. Numbered pitches.
➲ *On D46.*
Open: Apr-Sep **Site:** 1HEC ᛗᛗ ⌀ 🏠 **Prices:** ⚡6.50 pitch 20
Facilities: 🏕 ☉ 🔌 🅿 **Services:** lau **Off-site:** 🛒 🍷 ✕ ⚒ ⚒
⚡LPS ⊞

Flots Bleus av des Chardons, 85460
☎ 251271111 📠 251294076
Family site only 100m from the sea.
➲ *In La Faute, cross Pont de l'Aiguillons-sur-Mer and follow
Route de la Pointe d'Arçay to site.*
Open: 08 May-08 Sep **Site:** 1.5HEC ᛗᛗ ⁙ ⌀ 🏠 🚐
Facilities: 🏕 ☉ 🔌 🅿 ⚒ 🅿 **Services:** 🍷 ✕ ⊞ lau **Off-site:** 🛒 ✕
⚡LRS

FENOUILLER, LE VENDÉE

SAS SHH Le Pas Opton rte de Nantes, 85800
☎ 251551198 📠 251554494
website: www.springharvestholidays.com
Well equipped family site a few minutes from the beach and
close to the "Des Vallées" sailing centre.

➲ *2km N beside the River Vie on D754.*
Open: May-Nov **Site:** ᛗᛗ ⌀ 🏠 🅰 ⚘ **Facilities:** 🏕 🛒 ☉ 🅿
🔌 🅿 **Services:** 🍷 ✕ ⊞ lau **Leisure:** ⚡ PR

FOURAS CHARENTE-MARITIME

Charmilles St Laurent de la Pree, 17450
☎ 546840005 📠 546840284
e-mail: charmilles17@wanadoo.fr
website: www.domainedescharmilles.com
Open: Apr-Sep **Site:** 7HEC ᛗᛗ ⌀ 🏠 **Prices:** pitch 12-25
(incl 2 persons) **Facilities:** 🏕 🛒 ☉ 🔌 🅿 ⚒ 🅿 **Services:** 🍷 ✕
lau **Leisure:** ⚡ P **Off-site:** ✕ ⚡S

FRESNAY-SUR-SARTHE SARTHE

CM Sans Souci r de Haut Ary, 72100 ☎ 243973287
e-mail: camping-fresnay@wanadoo.fr
website: http://membres.tripod.fr/fresnay
A family site with good facilities and access to the river.
➲ *1km SE on D310.*
Open: Apr-Sep **Site:** 2HEC ᛗᛗ ⌀ 🏠 **Prices:** pitch 4.10
(incl 2 persons) **Facilities:** 🏕 🛒 ☉ 🔌 🅿 ⚒ 🅿 **Services:** lau
Leisure: ⚡ PR **Off-site:** 🍷 ✕ ⚒

FRIAUDOUR HAUTE-VIENNE

Freaudour 87250 ☎ 555765722 📠 555712393
website: www.lac-saint-pardoux.com
A well equipped site beside Lac de St-Pardoux.
➲ *Access via A20 exit 25.*
Open: 05 Jun-11 Sep **Site:** 3.5HEC ᛗᛗ ⌀ 🏠 🚐
Prices: 🅿11.20-17.30 **Facilities:** 🏕 🛒 ☉ 🔌 🅿 ⚒ 🅿 **Services:** 🍷
✕ ⊞ lau **Leisure:** ⚡ LP **Off-site:** ⚒

FROSSAY LOIRE-ATLANTIQUE

Migron Le Square de la Chaussée, 44320 ☎ 240397783
In a pleasant location beside the canal.
Open: Jun-Sep **Site:** 2.5HEC ᛗᛗ ⌀ 🏠 🚐 **Facilities:** 🏕 ☉ 🔌
⚒ 🅿 **Services:** ⊞ lau **Leisure:** ⚡ R **Off-site:** 🛒 🍷 ✕

GENNES MAINE-ET-LOIRE

Bord de l'Eau r des Cadets de Saumur, 49350 ☎ 241380467
In a peaceful location on the river bank.
➲ *N beside the River Loire*
Open: 01 May-15 Sep **Site:** 2.5HEC ᛗᛗ ⌀ 🅰
Facilities: 🏕 ☉ 🔌 🅿 **Services:** ✕ lau **Leisure:** ⚡ R **Off-site:** 🛒
🍷 ✕ ⚒ ⚡P ⊞

GIEN LOIRET

Bois du Bardelet rte de Bourges, Poilly, 45500
☎ 238674739 📠 238382716
e-mail: contact@bardelet.com
website: www.bardelet.com
A family site with a good variety of sporting facilities.
➲ *Access via D940 SW of Gien.*
Open: Apr-Sep **Site:** 12HEC ᛗᛗ ⌀ 🏠 **Prices:** pitch 23-28
(incl 2 persons) **Facilities:** 🏕 🛒 ☉ 🔌 🅿 ⚒ 🅿 **Services:** 🍷 ✕ ⊞
lau **Leisure:** ⚡ LP

GIVRAND VENDÉE

Europa Le Petit Bois, 85800 ☎ 251553268 📠 251558010
A pleasant family site with a wide variety of recreational
facilities and modern sanitary blocks.
➲ *W from St-Gilles-Croix-de-Vie via D6 for 2.5km, then S for
0.2km.*
Open: Apr-Sep **Site:** 4HEC ᛗᛗ ⌀ 🏠 **Facilities:** 🏕 🛒 ☉ 🔌 🅿
⚒ 🅿 **Services:** 🍷 ✕ ⊞ lau **Leisure:** ⚡ P **Off-site:** ⚡LRS

Facilities: 🛒-shop 🏕-shower ☉-electric points for razors 🔌-electric points for caravans 🅿-parking by tents permitted
🅿-compulsory separate car park **Services:** ✕-café/restaurant 🍷-bar ⌀-Camping Gaz International ⚒-gas other than Camping
Gaz ⊞-first aid facilities lau-laundry **Leisure:** ⚡-swimming L-Lake P-Pool R-River S-Sea **Off-site:** All facilities within 2km

Au Petit Port de l'Houmeau ★★★ **Camping-Caravaning**

200m away from the sea, at 3,5km from the bridge of Ile de Ré

Tél. 05 46 50 90 82 • Fax 05 46 50 01 33
www.aupetitport.com • E-mail : info@aupetitport.com
17137 L'Houmeau - La Rochelle

GUÉMENÉ-PENFAO LOIRE-ATLANTIQUE

Hermitage 36 av du Paradis, 44290
☎ 240792348 ▤ 240515 1187
e-mail: contact@campinglhermitage.com
website: www.campinglhermitage.com
In a beautiful setting overlooking the Don Valley with good,
modern facilities.
➲ 1.5km E on rte de Châteaubriant.
Open: All year Site: 2.5HEC ⟱ ⚲ ⊞ ⊞ ⚑ Prices: pitch
8.15-9.60 (incl 2 persons) Facilities: ⋔ ⚴ ⊙ ⚵ ⌀ ⚑
Services: ⚑ ✗ lau Leisure: ⚲ P Off-site: ⚑ ✗ ⚶ ⚶R ⊞

GUÉRANDE LOIRE-ATLANTIQUE

Bréhadour 44350 ☎ 240249312 ▤ 24024+277
e-mail: info@homair-vacances.fr
website: www.homair-vacances.fr
A well equipped family site with good facilities, a few
kilometres from the sea.
➲ 2km NE on D51, rte de St-Lyphard.
Open: 15 Apr-30 Sep Site: 7HEC ⟱ ⚲ ⊞ ⊞ ⚑
Facilities: ⋔ ⚴ ⊙ ⚵ ⚑ Services: ⚑ ✗ lau Leisure: ⚲ P
Off-site: ⌀ ⚶ ⊞

Parc de Lévéno rte de l'Étang de Sandun, 44350
☎ 240247930 ▤ 240620123
e-mail: domaine.leveno@wanadoo.fr
website: www.domaine-leveno.com
In a pleasant location with good facilities.
➲ 3km E via rte de Sandun.
Open: 27 Apr- 28 Sep Site: 12HEC ⟱ ⚲ ⊞ Facilities: ⋔ ⚴
⊙ ⚵ ⌀ ⚶ ⚑ Services: ⚑ ✗ ⊞ lau Leisure: ⚲ P

⚑**Pré du Château de Careil** Careil, 44350
☎ 240602299 ▤ 240602299
e-mail: chateau.careil@free.fr
website: www.pays-blanc.com/camping-careil
Divided into pitches. Caravans only. Booking recommended
for Jul & Aug.
➲ 2km N of La Baule on D92.
Open: 22 May-12 Sep Site: 2HEC ⟱ ⚲ Prices: pitch 18-22
(incl 2 persons) Facilities: ⋔ ⊙ ⚵ ⚑ Services: ⊞ lau
Leisure: ⚲ P Off-site: ⚴ ⚑ ✗ ⌀ ⚶

HÉRIC LOIRE-ATLANTIQUE

Pindière 44810 ☎ 240576541 ▤ 228022543
e-mail: patrick.ara@wanadoo.fr
website: www.camping-la-pindiere.com
A family site on a level meadow with good facilities.
➲ 1km from town on D16.
Open: All year Site: 3HEC ⟱ ⚲ ⊞ Prices: ⚑3.05 pitch 3.81
Facilities: ⋔ ⊙ ⚵ ⚶ ⚑ Services: ⚑ ✗ ⊞ lau Leisure: ⚲ P
Off-site: ⚴

HOUMEAU, L' CHARENTE-MARITIME

Trépied au Plomb 17137 ☎ 546509082 ▤ 546500133
e-mail: au.petit.port@wanadoo.fr
➲ NE via D106
Open: Apr-Sep Site: 2HEC ⟱ ⚲ ⊞ ⚑ Facilities: ⋔ ⊙ ⚵
⚑ Services: ⚑ ⊞ lau Off-site: ⚴ ✗ ⌀ ⚶S

INGRANDES VIENNE

AT ST-USTRE (2KM NE)

⚑**Petit Trianon de St-Ustre** 86200
☎ 549026147 ▤ 549026881
e-mail: chateau@petit-trianon.fr
website: www.petit-trianon.fr
In a beautiful park surrounding a small 18th-century castle,
the site has good entertainment and recreational facilities.
➲ Turn off N10 at signpost N of Ingrandes and continue for 1km.
Open: 20 May-20 Sep Site: 7HEC ⟱ ⚲ ⊞ ⚑
Prices: ⚑5.84-6.60 pitch 3.50-3.95 Facilities: ⋔ ⚴ ⊙ ⚵ ⌀ ⚑
Services: ⊞ lau Leisure: ⚲ P Off-site: ⚑ ✗ ⚶

JARD-SUR-MER VENDÉE

Écureuils rte des Goffineaux, 85520
☎ 251334274 ▤ 251339114
e-mail: camping-ecureuils@wanadoo.fr
website: www.camping-ecureuils.com
Quiet woodland terrain 500yds from the sea. Large pitches
surrounded by hedges.
➲ Signposted.
Open: 15 May-15 Sep Site: 4.3HEC ⟱ ⚬⚬ ⚲ ⚑ ⚒
Prices: ⚑6 pitch 11.50-15.50 Facilities: ⋔ ⚴ ⊙ ⚵ ⌀ ⚶ ⚑
Services: ⚑ ✗ ⊞ lau Leisure: ⚲ P Off-site: ✗ ⚶S

La Mouette Cendrée Les Malecots, St-Vincent-sur-Jard,
85520 ☎ 251335904
e-mail: camping.mc@free.fr
website: www.mouettecendree.com
Open: May-15 Sep Site: 1.2HEC ⟱ ⚶ ⊞ ⚑ Prices: pitch
10-16 (incl 2 persons) Facilities: ⋔ ⊙ ⚵ ⚶ ⚑ Services: ⊞ lau
Leisure: ⚲ P Off-site: ⚴ ⚑ ✗ ⌀ ⚶S

Océano d'Or r G-Clemenceau, 85520
☎ 251336508 ▤ 251339404
e-mail: chadotel@wanadoo.fr website: camping.chadotel.com
A well maintained site 1km from the beach and 500mtrs
from the town centre.
➲ Access via D19.
Open: Apr-Sep Site: 7.8HEC ⟱ ⚲⚢ ⊞ ⚑ Prices: pitch 12-
22.50 (incl 2 persons) Facilities: ⋔ ⚴ ⊙ ⚵ ⌀ ⚶ ⚑
Services: ⚑ ✗ ⊞ lau Leisure: ⚲ P Off-site: ✗ ⚶S

Pomme de Pin r Vincent Auriol, 85520
☎ 251334385 ▤ 251339404
e-mail: info@pommedepin.net website: www.pommedepin.net
Situated in a pine forest
➲ 300mtrs from the town centre and 150mtrs from the beach.
Open: 06 Apr-20 Sep Site: 3HEC ⟱ ⚲ ⊞ ⚑ Prices: pitch 14-
21.50 (incl 2 persons) Facilities: ⋔ ⚴ ⊙ ⚵ ⌀ ⚶ ⚑
Services: ⚑ ✗ ⊞ lau Leisure: ⚲ PS Off-site: ✗

JARGEAU LOIRET

Isle aux Moulins r du 44ème RI, 45150
☎ 238597004 ▤ 238591223
e-mail: kas@wanadoo.fr
In a wooded location on the bank of the Loire.
Open: Mar-15 Nov Site: 7HEC ⟱ ⚲ ⊞ ⊞ Facilities: ⋔ ⚴
⊙ ⚵ ⚶ ⚑ Services: ⊞ lau Leisure: ⚲ R Off-site: ⚑ ✗ ⌀

Site: 6HEC-Site size ⟱-grass ⚬⚬-sand ⚴-stone ⚢-little shade ⚲-partly shaded ⚑-mainly shaded
⊞-bungalows for hire ⚑-caravans for hire ⚑-tents for hire ⚒-no dogs **Prices:** ⚑-adult per night ⚑-car per night
pp-per person per night ⚑-caravan per night ⚑-tent per night

JAUNAY CLAN VIENNE

Croix du Sud rte de Neuville, 86130 ☎ 549625814
e-mail: camping@la-croix-du-sud.fr
website: www.la-croix-du-sud.fr
Within easy reach of 'Futuroscope', the European Park of the
Moving Image.
⊃ *Access via A10 and D62.*
Open: 29 Mar-13 Sep Site: 4HEC ▦ ↗ 🏠 Facilities: ⬤ ⬤
⊙ ⬤ ⚏ ☎ Services: ♀ ✕ lau Leisure: ⸕ P

LAGORD CHARENTE-MARITIME

CM Parc r du Parc, 17140 ☎ 546676154 ▤ 546006201
e-mail: mairie.lagord@wanadoo.fr
Pleasant municipal site within easy reach of the coast.
⊃ *Access via N137/D735.*
Open: Jun-Sep Site: ▦ ⬤ ⬤ Facilities: ⬤ ⊙ ⬤ ☎
Services: ☎ lau Off-site: ⬤ ♀ ✕ ⬤ ⚏ ⸕P

LANDEVIEILLE VENDÉE

Pong r du Stade, 85220 ☎ 251229263 ▤ 251229925
A family site with spacious pitches surrounded by trees and
bushes. Good recreational facilities.
Open: Etr-Sep Site: 3HEC ▦ ⬤ 🏠 ⬤ Facilities: ⬤ ⬤ ⊙ ⬤
⬤ ⚏ ☎ Services: ♀ ✕ ☎ lau Leisure: ⸕ P Off-site: ☎

LESSAC CHARENTE

Roufferies 16500 ☎ 545302126 ▤ 545302126
Extremely rural situation; 20 acres of grassland surrounded
by trees hidden from the road with a large lake for
swimming.
⊃ *From Potiers take road to Confolens, through Preesac and
take left turn for Leesac. Continue for approx 3m, signed on
right.*
Open: Apr-Sep Site: 20HEC ▦ ↗ ⬤ Facilities: ⬤ ☎
Leisure: ⸕ L Off-site: ⬤ ♀ ✕ ⚏

LINDOIS, LE CHARENTE

Étang 16130 ☎ 545650267 ▤ 545650896
website: www.campingdelatang.com
Well shaded site with a natural lake, ideal for swimming and
fishing with a small beach.
⊃ *From Rochefocauld take D13 towards Montemboeuf.*
Open: 01 Apr-01Nov Site: 10HEC ▦ ⬤ 🏠 Prices: ↟2.75-
3.65 pitch 5.50-6.90 Facilities: ⬤ ⊙ ⬤ ☎ Services: ♀ ✕ ☎
lau Leisure: ⸕ L Off-site: ⬤ ⬤ ⚏

LION D'ANGERS, LE MAINE-ET-LOIRE

CM Frénes 49220 ☎ 241953156
A municipal site on the banks of the River Oudon, 300mtrs
from the town centre.
⊃ *NE on N162.*
Open: May-Aug Site: 2HEC ▦ ⬤ Prices: ↟11 pitch 11
Facilities: ⬤ ⊙ ⬤ ☎ Services: lau Off-site: ⬤ ♀ ✕ ⬤ ⚏ ⸕P
☎

LONGEVILLE VENDÉE

Brunelles Le Bouil, 85560 ☎ 251335075 ▤ 251339821
e-mail: camping@les-brunelles.com
A well appointed site in a wooded location 700mtrs from the
beach.
⊃ *On the coast between Longeville and Jard-sur-Mer.*
Open: 03 Apr-18 Sep Site: 4.8HEC ▦ ⬤ 🏠 ⬤ A
Prices: pitch 14-20 (incl 2 persons)
Facilities: ⬤ ⬤ ⊙ ⬤ ⬤ ⚏ ☎ Services: ♀ ✕ ☎ lau
Leisure: ⸕ P Off-site: ⸕S

Clos des Pins Les Conches, 85560
☎ 251903169 ▤ 251903068
e-mail: philip.jones@freesbee.fr
website: campinginfrance.com
A family run site with good facilities, 250yds from a sandy
beach.
⊃ *Between Longeville and La Tranche.*
Open: 1 Apr-2 Oct Site: 1.6HEC ▦ ⸪⸪ ⬤ ⬤ 🏠 A
Prices: ↟4.40-5.50 pitch 16.80-24 Facilities: ⬤ ⬤ ⊙ ⬤ ⚏ ☎
Services: ♀ ✕ ☎ lau Leisure: ⸕ P Off-site: ⬤ ⸕S

Jarny Océan Le Bouil, 85560 ☎ 251334221 ▤ 251339537
e-mail: jarny-ocean@wanadoo.fr
Subdivided well tended meadow, with a holiday complex of
the same name where shopping facilities are provided. 800m
to sea via forest path.
⊃ *Turn off D105 about 3km S of Longeville.*
Open: May-Sep Site: 7.6HEC ▦ ⬤ 🏠 ⬤ Prices: pitch
8.95-19.45 (incl 2 persons) Facilities: ⬤ ⬤ ⊙ ⬤ ⚏ ☎
Services: ♀ ✕ ☎ lau Leisure: ⸕ P Off-site: ✕ ⬤ ⸕S

AT CONCHES, LES (4KM S)

Dunes av de la Plage, 85560 ☎ 251333293 ▤ 251903861
e-mail: contact@camping-lesdunes.com
website: www.camping-lesdunes.com
Well-kept site amongst sand dunes in pine forest.
⊃ *6km S of Longeville on D105.*
Open: May-Sep Site: 5HEC ⸪⸪ ⬤ 🏠 Facilities: ⬤ ⬤ ⊙ ⬤ ⬤
☎ Services: ♀ ✕ ☎ lau Leisure: ⸕ P Off-site: ✕ ⸕PRS

Camping Les Dunes - Les Conches
85560 Longeville sur Mer
Phone : 02 51 33 32 93
Fax : 02 51 90 38 61
E-mail:contact@campinglesdunes.com
Website: www.camping-lesdunes.com

CAMPING★★★
DE MAYENNE
53100 – ☎ (33) 243 04 57 14(33) 243 04 19 37
ON SITE

LUCHÉ-PRINGÉ SARTHE

CM de la Chabotière Place des Tilleuls, 72800
☎ 243451000 ▤ 243451000
e-mail: lachabotiere@ville-luche-pringe.fr
website: www.ville-luche-pringe.fr
Site by a river just 100 metres from the village and a short
drive from several Loire chateaux. Large marked sites are set
on terraces above the river and most cars are kept in a private
car park to ensure play areas are safe for children.
Open: Apr-15 Oct Site: 2HEC ⬛ ⌇ ⊞ ⚑ Facilities: ↑ ⊙
⛻ ₱ Services: ⊞ lau Leisure: ⭢ PR Off-site: ⚍ ⚐ ✕ ⌀ ⚏ ⚍

LUSIGNAN VIENNE

CM Vauchiron Vauchiron, 86600
☎ 549433008 ▤ 549436119
e-mail: lusignan@cg86.fr
In a quiet wooded location beside the River Vonne with good
facilities.
⮕ *500m NE on N11.*
Open: 15 Apr-14 Oct Site: 4HEC ⬛ ⌇ ⊞ Prices: ⭡1.70
pitch 1.20 Facilities: ↑ ⊙ ⛻ ₱ Services: lau Leisure: ⭢ R
Off-site: ⚍ ⚐ ✕ ⌀ ⚏ ⊞

LUYNES INDRE-ET-LOIRE

CM Granges Les Granges, 37230 ☎ 247556085
Quiet site close to the village. Ideal for visiting historical sites,
fishing, and wine tasting
⮕ *S via D49.*
Open: 8 May-15 Sep Site: 0.8HEC ⬛ ⌇ ⊞ Facilities: ↑ ⊙
⛻ ⌀ ⚏ Services: ⊞ lau Off-site: ⚍ ⚐ ✕ ⭢P

MACHÉ VENDÉE

Val de Vie r du Stade, 85190 ☎ 251602102 ▤ 251602102
e-mail: campingvaldevie@aol.com
Open: 01 May-30 Sep Site: 2.2HEC ⬛ ⌇ ⊞ Prices: pitch
13.60-17 (incl 2 persons) Facilities: ↑ ⊙ ⛻ ⚏ Services: ⊞
lau Leisure: ⭢ P Off-site: ⚍ ⚐ ✕ ⌀ ⚍ ⭢LR

MAGNAC-BOURG HAUTE-VIENNE

Écureuils rte de Limoges, 87380 ☎ 555008028 ▤ 555004909
e-mail: mairie.magnac-bourg@wanadoo.fr
A grassy site close to the historic village
⮕ *25 kms S on N20.*
Open: Apr-Sep Site: 1.3HEC ⬛ ⌇ Prices: ⭡2.50 pitch 2.50
Facilities: ↑ ⊙ ⛻ ⚏ Services: lau Off-site: ⚍ ⚐ ✕ ⌀ ⚍ ⊞

MANSIGNÉ SARTHE

CM de la Plage rte du Plessis, 72510
☎ 243461417 ▤ 243461665
e-mail: campingmansigne@wanadoo.fr
A holiday complex set in extensive parkland around a 60 acre
lake with good recreational facilities.
⮕ *On D13, 4km from D307 (Le Mans-Le Lude).*
Open: Etr-Oct Site: 3.4HEC ⬛ ⌇ ⚑ ⊞ Prices: ⭡3.50 ⚑2.70
Facilities: ↑ ⊙ ⛻ ⚏ Services: ⚐ ✕ ⊞ lau Leisure: ⭢ LP
Off-site: ⚍ ⌀ ⚍

MARANS CHARENTE-MARITIME

CM Le Bois Dinot rte de Nantes, 17230
☎ 546011051 ▤ 546011051
e-mail: campingboisdinot.marans@wanadoo.fr
website: www.ville-marans.fr
Separate car park for arrivals after 22.00hrs.
⮕ *Access via N137 (Nantes-Bordeaux).*
Open: May-Sep Site: 6HEC ⬛ ⌇ Prices: ⭡2.80 pitch 2
Facilities: ↑ ⊙ ⛻ ⚏ Services: ⊞ lau Off-site: ⚍ ⚐ ✕ ⌀ ⚍
⭢PR

MARÇON SARTHE

Lac des Varennes 72340 ☎ 243441372 ▤ 243445431
e-mail: camping.des.varennes.marcon@wanadoo.fr
An attractive site bordering the lake in the heart of the Loire
Valley, with spacious pitches and well maintained
installations.
Open: 25 Mar-19 Oct Site: 7HEC ⬛ ⌇ ⊞ ⚑ Prices: ⭡3-
4.10 pitch 2.40-3.80 Facilities: ↑ ⚍ ⊙ ⛻ ⚏ Services: ⚐ ✕ ⊞
lau Leisure: ⭢ LR Off-site: ⌀

MATHES, LES CHARENTE-MARITIME

Charmettes av de la Palmyre, 17570
☎ 546225096 ▤ 546236970
website: www.camping-lescharmettes.com
Large site with plenty of organised activities. 5km from
beach.
⮕ *1km SW via D141.*
Open: 15 Apr-Sep Site: 34HEC ⬛ ⁙ ⌇ ⊞ ⚑ ⊗
Facilities: ↑ ⚍ ⊙ ⛻ ⚍ ⚏ ₱ Services: ⚐ ✕ ⊞ lau
Leisure: ⭢ PS

Orée du Bois 225 rte de la Bouverie, La Fouasse, 17570
☎ 546224243 ▤ 546225476
e-mail: info@camping-oree-du-bois.fr
website: www.oree-du-bois.fr
A family site situated in a pine and oak forest, 5 minutes
from the beach.

Site: 6HEC-Site size ⬛-grass ⁙-sand ⚐-stone ⌇-little shade ⌇-partly shaded ⚑-mainly shaded
⊞-bungalows for hire ⚑-caravans for hire ⚑-tents for hire ⊗-no dogs **Prices:** ⭡-adult per night ⚑-car per night
pp-per person per night ⚑-caravan per night ⚑-tent per night

➲ *3.5km NW.*
Open: 27 Apr-27 Sep **Site:** 6HEC ∷∵ ♦ 🚐 🚑 **Prices:** pitch 15-28 (incl 2 persons) **Facilities:** 🏕 🏪 ⊙ 🔌 ⌀ 🚿 🏚 🅿 **Services:** 🍸 ✗ 🏥 lau **Leisure:** ⤳ P **Off-site:** ⤳S

Pinède rte de la Fouasse, 17570
☎ 546224513 📠 546225021
e-mail: campinglapinede@free.fr
website: www.campinglapinede.com
A modern family site in a wooded area around the large Aquatic Park. Excellent sporting facilities. Entertainment available in July and August.
➲ *3km NW.*
Open: Apr-Sep **Site:** 7HEC 🏚🏚 ∷∵∷ ♦ 🚐 🚑 **Prices:** pitch 18.50-35 (incl 2 persons) **Facilities:** 🏕 🏪 ⊙ 🔌 🏚 **Services:** 🍸 ✗ 🏥 lau **Leisure:** ⤳ P

MAYENNE MAYENNE

CM du Gue St Leonard r St-Léonard, 53100
☎ 243045714 📠 243302110
e-mail: webmestre@mairie-mayenne.fr
website: www.mairie-mayenne.fr
In a wooded location on the banks of the River Mayenne.
➲ *800m from town centre near N12.*
Open: 15 Mar-Sep **Site:** 1.8HEC 🏚🏚 ♦ 🚐 **Prices:** pitch 4.60-9.70 (incl 3 persons) **Facilities:** 🏕 🏪 ⊙ 🔌 🏚 **Services:** ✗ 🏥 lau **Leisure:** ⤳ P **Off-site:** 🏪 🍸 ✗ ⌀ 🚿 🏥

See advertisement on page 132

MEMBROLLE-SUR-CHOISILLE, LA INDRE-ET-LOIRE

CM rte de Foudettes, 37390 ☎ 247412040
On level meadow in sports ground beside River Choisille.
➲ *N on N138 Le Mans road.*
Open: 01 May-30 Sep **Site:** 1.5HEC 🏚🏚 🔩 **Prices:** pitch 8.80 (incl 2 persons) **Facilities:** 🏕 ⊙ 🔌 🏚 **Services:** 🏥 lau **Leisure:** ⤳ R **Off-site:** 🏪 🍸 ✗ ⤳L

MERVENT VENDÉE

Chêne Tord 34 chemin du Chêne Tord, 85200
☎ 251002063 📠 251002794
A well appointed site 200mtrs from a large artificial lake in the heart of the Mervent Forest.
➲ *Access via D99.*
Open: All year **Site:** 4HEC 🏚🏚 🔩 **Prices:** ⋔2.20-2.70 pitch 4.50-6 **Facilities:** 🏕 ⊙ 🔌 ⌀ 🏚 **Services:** lau **Off-site:** 🏪 🍸 ✗ 🚿 ⤳LPR 🏥

MESLAND LOIR-ET-CHER

Parc du Val de Loire rte de Fleuray, 41150
☎ 254702718 📠 254702171
In a sheltered position in the heart of the Touraine vineyards with good recreational facilities.
Camping Card Compulsory.
➲ *1.5km W between the A10 and the N152.*
Open: 28 Apr-15 Sep **Site:** 13.6HEC 🏚🏚 🔩 🚐 **Facilities:** 🏕 🏪 ⊙ 🔌 ⌀ 🚿 🏚 🅿 **Services:** 🍸 ✗ 🏥 lau **Leisure:** ⤳ P **Off-site:** ⤳L

MESQUER LOIRE-ATLANTIQUE

Au Soir d'Été 44420 ☎ 240425726 📠 251739776
e-mail: nadine-houssass@wanadoo.fr
website: www.camping-soirdete.com
Open: 3 Apr-31 Dec **Site:** 1.5HEC 🏚🏚 ♦ 🚐 **Prices:** pitch 11.50-17 (incl 2 persons) **Facilities:** 🏕 ⊙ 🔌 🚿 🏚 **Services:** 🍸 ✗ 🏥 lau **Leisure:** ⤳ P **Off-site:** 🏪 ⌀ ⤳S

Beaupré rte de Kervarin, Kercabellec, 44420
☎ 240426748 📠 2440426672
e-mail: camping.beaupre@wanadoo.fr
Well equipped site 500mtrs from the beach.
➲ *On road between Mesquer and Quimiac. Entrance signposted.*
Open: 15 Jun-15 Aug **Site:** 0.6HEC 🏚🏚 🔩 🚐 🚑 **Facilities:** 🏕 ⊙ 🔌 🏚 **Services:** 🏥 lau **Off-site:** 🏪 🍸 ✗ ⌀ 🚿 ⤳S

Château de Petit Bois 44420 ☎ 240426877 📠 240426558
e-mail: camping-du-petit-bois@wanadoo.fr
website: www.paysblanc.com/camping-du-petit-bois
In the extensive grounds of an 18th century castle with shaded, well defined pitches.
Open: Apr-Sep **Site:** 10HEC 🏚🏚 ♦ 🚐 **Prices:** pitch 14.25-17.80 (incl 2 persons) **Facilities:** 🏕 🏪 ⊙ 🔌 🚿 🏚 **Services:** 🍸 ✗ lau **Leisure:** ⤳ P **Off-site:** ⌀ ⤳S 🏥

Praderoi allée des Barges, Quimiac, 44420
☎ 240426672 📠 240426672
e-mail: camping.praderoi@wanadoo.fr
website: http://perso.wanadoo.fr/mtger.debonne
On level ground 70mtrs from Lanseria Beach.
➲ *300mtrs from Quimiac.*
Open: 15 Jun-15 Sep **Site:** 0.5HEC 🏚🏚 ♦ 🚑 **Prices:** pitch 9-14.20 (incl 2 persons) **Facilities:** 🏕 ⊙ 🔌 🏚 **Services:** 🏥 lau **Off-site:** 🏪 🍸 ✗ ⌀ 🚿 ⤳S

Welcome r de Bel-Air, 44420 ☎ 240425085 📠 251739984
e-mail: lewelcom@club-internet.fre
website: perso.club-internet.fr/lewelcom/
In pleasant wooded surroundings, 600mtrs from the coast. Separate car park for arrivals after 22.30 hrs.
➲ *1.8km NW via D352*
Open: Apr-Sep **Site:** 2HEC 🏚🏚 ♦ 🚐 🚑 **Facilities:** 🏕 🏪 ⊙ 🔌 🚿 🏚 **Services:** lau **Leisure:** ⤳ P **Off-site:** 🍸 ✗ ⌀ ⤳S 🏥

MESSE DEUX-SÈVRES

Grande Vigne 79120 ☎ 549059615
e-mail: admin@grande-vigne.com
website: www.grande-vigne.com
Flat orchard site bordered by fruit trees and set in rural countryside. No boundaries or marked pitches as only 5 pitches are let at any one time.
➲ *Off RN10 between Poitiers and Anguleme*
Open: All year **Site:** 0.5HEC 🏚🏚 🔩 🚐 ⌘ **Prices:** pitch 10-15.50 **Facilities:** 🏕 ⊙ 🔌 🏚 **Services:** lau **Leisure:** ⤳ P

MISSILLAC LOIRE-ATLANTIQUE

CM des Platanes 10 r du Château, 44780 ☎ 240883888
➲ *1km W via D2, 50m from the lake.*
Open: Jul-Aug **Site:** 2HEC 🏚🏚 🔩 **Facilities:** 🏕 ⊙ 🔌 🏚 **Services:** lau **Off-site:** 🏪 🍸 ✗ 🏥

MONTARGIS LOIRET

CM de la Forêt rte de Paucourt, 45200 ☎ 238980020
In the Forest of Montargis.
➲ *1.5km NE near the station and the stadium.*
Open: Feb-Nov **Site:** 5.5HEC 🏚🏚 ∷∵∷ ♦ **Facilities:** 🏕 ⊙ 🔌 🏚 **Services:** 🏥 lau **Off-site:** 🏪 🍸 ✗ ⌀ 🚿 ⤳LPR

MONTGIVRAY INDRE

CM Solange Sand 2 r du Pont, 36400
☎ 254061036 📠 254061039
e-mail: mairie.montgivray@wanadoo.fr
A pleasant, riverside site in the grounds of a château.
Open: 15 Mar-15 Oct **Site:** 1HEC 🏚🏚 🔩 **Prices:** ⋔1.80 pitch 2.55 **Facilities:** 🏕 ⊙ 🔌 ⌀ 🏚 **Services:** lau **Leisure:** ⤳ R **Off-site:** 🏪 🍸 ✗ 🚿

Facilities: 🏪-shop 🏕-shower ⊙-electric points for razors 🔌-electric points for caravans 🏚-parking by tents permitted 🅿-compulsory separate car park **Services:** ✗-café/restaurant 🍸-bar ⌀-Camping Gaz International 🚿-gas other than Camping Gaz 🏥-first aid facilities lau-laundry **Leisure:** ⤳-swimming L-Lake P-Pool R-River S-Sea **Off-site:** All facilities within 2km

MONTLOUIS-SUR-LOIRE INDRE-ET-LOIRE

CM Peupliers 37270 ☎ 247458585 ▤ 247451574
e-mail: mairie@ville-montlouis-loire.fr
website: www.ville-montlouis-loire.fr
On level meadow.
➔ *1.5km W on N751, next to swimming pool near railway bridge.*
Open: 15 Mar-15 Oct Site: 6HEC ⬛⬛⬛ ♣ Prices: pitch 7.39-7.80 (incl 2 persons) Facilities: ⋒ ⅃ ⊙ ⊟ ∅ ☎ Services: ⊞ lau Leisure: ⇃ P Off-site: ⅃ ✗ ⇃R

MONTMORILLON VIENNE

CM Allochon av F-Tribot, 86500
☎ 549910233 ▤ 549915826
e-mail: montmorillon@cg86.fr
A well equipped municipal site close to the river and 1.5km from the town centre.
➔ *SE via D54*
Open: Apr-Oct Site: 2HEC ⬛⬛⬛ ♣ Facilities: ⋒ ⊙ ⊟ ☎ Services: lau Off-site: ⅃ ⅃ ✗ ∅ ⅃ ⇃PR ⊞

MONTSOREAU MAINE-ET-LOIRE

Isle Verte av de la Loire, 49730 ☎ 241517660 ▤ 241510883
e-mail: isleverte@wanadoo.fr
website: www.cvtloisirs.com
In wooded surroundings beside the River Loire.
➔ *On D947 between road and river.*
Open: Apr-Sep Site: 2HEC ⬛⬛⬛ ♣ ⊞ ⊿ Prices: pitch 13.50-16 (incl 2 persons) Facilities: ⋒ ⊙ ⊟ ⅃ ☎ Services: ⅃ ✗ ⊞ lau Leisure: ⇃ P Off-site: ⅃ ∅ ⇃R

MOUTIERS-EN-RETZ, LES LOIRE-ATLANTIQUE

Domaine du Collet 44760 ☎ 240214092 ▤ 240214512
e-mail: info@domaine-du-collet.com
website: www.domaine-du-collet.com
Open: May-Sep Site: 12HEC ⬛⬛⬛ ♣ ⊞ ⊟ ⅃ Prices: pitch 13-20 (incl 2 persons) Facilities: ⋒ ⅃ ⊙ ⊟ ∅ ☎ Services: ⅃ ✗ lau Leisure: ⇃ LPS

Village de la Mer 18 r de Prigny, 44760
☎ 240646590 ▤ 251746317
e-mail: info@le-village-de-la-mer.com
website: www.village-mer.com
Quiet site close to a village and the beach
➔ *on D97, 9kms S of Pornic*
Open: 15 Jun-15 Sep Site: 7HEC ⬛⬛⬛ ⊿ ⊞ Prices: pitch 16-26 (incl 2 persons) Facilities: ⋒ ⊙ ⊟ ⅃ ☎ Services: ⅃ ✗ lau Leisure: ⇃ P Off-site: ⅃ ✗ ∅ ⇃S

NANTES LOIRE-ATLANTIQUE

Petit Port bd du Petit Port 21, 44300
☎ 240744794 ▤ 240742306
e-mail: camping-petit-port@nge-nantes.fr
On modern well kept park by a river.
➔ *In N part of town near Parc du Petit Port. From town centre follow Rennes road (N137) then signs to camp site.*
Open: All year Site: 6.5HEC ⬛⬛⬛ ⊿ Facilities: ⋒ ⅃ ⊙ ⊟ ☎ Services: ⊞ lau Off-site: ⅃ ✗ ⅃ ⇃PR

NEUVILLE-SUR-SARTHE SARTHE

Vieux Moulin 72190 ☎ 243253182 ▤ 243253811
e-mail: vieux.moulin@wanadoo.fr
website: perso.wanadoo.fr/camping
A pleasant site with good recreational facilities, close to the village.
➔ *Access via N138 and D197.*
Open: Jul-Aug Site: 4.8HEC ⬛⬛⬛ ♣ ⊞ Prices: pitch 11 (incl 2 persons) Facilities: ⋒ ⅃ ⊙ ⊟ ∅ ⅃ ☎ Services: ⊞ lau Leisure: ⇃ P Off-site: ⅃ ✗ ⇃R

NIBELLE LOIRET

Nibelle rte de Boiscommun, 45340
☎ 238322355 ▤ 238320387
Level site in the clearing of an oak woodland.
➔ *Access via D921 turning off to Nibelle in an easterly direction. Signposted.*
Open: Mar-Nov Site: 12HEC ⬛⬛⬛ ⊿ ⊞ ⅃ Prices: ⋔12 ⬥2-3 ⅃3.50-3 ⬥3 Facilities: ⋒ ⊙ ⊟ ⅃ ☎ Services: ⅃ ✗ lau Leisure: ⇃ P Off-site: ⅃ ✗ ∅

NIORT DEUX-SÈVRES

Niort-Noron 21 bd Salvador-Allendé, 79000
☎ 05 549790506 ▤ 549790506
Shady site by a river.
Open: Apr-Sep Site: 3HEC ⬛⬛⬛ ⊿ Prices: ⋔2.75 pitch 1.10 Facilities: ⋒ ⅃ ⊙ ⊟ ☎ Services: ⊞ lau Leisure: ⇃ R Off-site: ⅃ ✗ ∅ ⅃ ⇃P

NOIRMOUTIER, ÎLE DE VENDÉE

BARBÂTRE

Onchères 85630 ☎ 251398131 ▤ 251397365
In quiet setting on sand dunes. S of village on D95.
Open: Apr-Sep Site: 10HEC ⁞⁞⁞ ⊿ Facilities: ⋒ ⅃ ⊙ ⊟ ∅ ⅃ ☎ Services: ⅃ ✗ ⊞ lau Leisure: ⇃ PS

GUERINIERE, LA

Caravan'Ile BP N4, 85680 ☎ 251395029 ▤ 251358685
e-mail: camping.caravanile@wanadoo.fr
website: www.caravanile.com
Located near fine sand beaches. Swimming pool with aquatic toboggan.
Open: 01 Mar-15 Nov Site: 9HEC ⁙ ⁙ 🛲 🛏 🚐
Facilities: ⋔ 🖩 ⊙ 🖾 ☎ Services: ⛽ ✖ lau Leisure: ↘ PS

NOIRMOUTIER-EN-L'ILE

Vendette rte des Sableaux, 85330 ☎ 251390624
A well equipped site in a pine wood close to the beach.
➲ From town centre continue towards Plage des Sableaux.
Open: 1 Mar-Sep Site: 12HEC ⁙ 🛲 🔵 Facilities: ⋔ ⊙
🖾 ☎ Services: ⛽ ✖ 🖽 lau Leisure: ↘ S Off-site: 🖩 ⌀ ⛰ ↘P

NOTRE-DAME-DE-MONTS VENDÉE

Beauséjour 85690 ☎ 251588388
➲ 2km NW on D38.
Open: Etr-Sep Site: 1.3HEC ⁙ 🔵 🛲 Prices: pitch 9.80 (incl 2 persons) Facilities: ⋔ ⊙ 🖾 ⌀ ☎ Services: 🖽 lau Off-site: 🖩 ⛽ ↘S

Grand Jardin Le Grand Jardin, 50 r de la Barre, 85690
☎ 0228112175
website: www.legrandjardin.net
A family site in a picturesque location facing the Ile d'Yeu. Modern sanitary installations and plenty of sporting facilities. 1km from the beach.
➲ 0.6km N
Open: All year Site: 4HEC ⁙ ♣ 🛲 🛏 🚐 Prices: pitch 14.20-17.50 (incl 2 persons) Facilities: ⋔ ⊙ 🖾 ⛰ ☎ 🅿 Services: ⛽ ✖ 🖽 lau Leisure: ↘ PR Off-site: 🖩 ↘S

NOZAY LOIRE-ATLANTIQUE

CM 'Henri Dubourg' rte de Rennes, 44170
☎ 240879433 ▤ 240793564
e-mail: marie@nozay.fr
A small site in a quiet location.
➲ Access via N137 and N171.
Open: 15 May-15 Sep Site: 1HEC ⁙ 🔵 🛲 Prices: ♠2 pitch 2 Facilities: ⋔ ⊙ 🖾 ☎ Services: lau Off-site: 🖩 ⛽ ✖ ⌀ ⛰ ↘P 🖽

OLÉRON, ILE D' CHARENTE-MARITIME

BOYARDVILLE

Signol 17190 ☎ 546470122 ▤ 546472346
e-mail: contact@signol.com website: www.signol.com
In attractive surroundings within a pine forest, close to the village centre and 800mtrs from the beach.
➲ W of town, leave D126 by the AVIA service station and follow signs for 0.6km.
Open: Apr-Sep Site: 8HEC ⁙ ♣ 🛲 🚐 Facilities: ⋔ ⊙ 🖾 ☎
Services: ⛽ 🖽 lau Leisure: ↘ P Off-site: 🖩 ↘S

CHÂTEAU-D'OLÉRON, LE

Airotel d'Oléron Domaine de Montreavail, 17480
☎ 546476182 ▤ 546477967
e-mail: info@camping-airotel-deron.com
website: www.camping-airotel-deron.com
In a peaceful, parklike setting 1km from the beach and the town centre.
➲ Signposted from town centre.
Open: Mar-01 Nov Site: 4HEC ⁙ ♣ 🛏 Facilities: ⋔ 🖩 ⊙
🔵 ⌀ ⛰ ☎ Services: ⛽ ✖ 🖽 lau Leisure: ↘ LPS

Brande rte des Huîtres, 17480 ☎ 546476237 ▤ 546477170
e-mail: info@camping-labrande.com
website: www.camping-labrande.com
A family site with good facilities in beautiful surroundings.
➲ 2.5km NW, 250m from the sea.
Open: 15 Mar-15 Nov Site: 5.5HEC ⁙ ⁙ 🔵 🛏
Prices: pitch 17-32 (incl 2 persons) Facilities: ⋔ 🖩 ⊙ 🔵 ⌀ ⛰
☎ Services: ⛽ ✖ 🖽 lau Leisure: ↘ P Off-site: ↘S

COTINIÈRE, LA

Tamaris 72 av des Pins, 17310 ☎ 546471051 ▤ 546472796
About 150m from sea. Level site in pleasant olive grove.
➲ W side of island. N of town.
Open: 15 Mar-15 Nov Site: 5HEC ⁙ 🔵 🛏 🅰 Facilities: ⋔
⊙ 🔵 ⛰ ☎ Services: ⛽ ✖ 🖽 lau Leisure: ↘ P Off-site: 🖩 ⌀ ↘S

DOLUS-D'OLÉRON

Ostréa rte des Huîtres, 17550 ☎ 546476236 ▤ 546752001
A well equipped site in wooded surroundings close to the beach.
➲ 3.5km NE
Open: Apr-Sep Site: 2HEC ⁙ ⁙ 🔵 🛏 🚐 Prices: pitch 12.25-17.50 (incl 2 persons) Facilities: ⋔ 🖩 ⊙ 🔵 ⌀ ⛰ ☎
Services: ⛽ ✖ 🖽 lau Leisure: ↘ S

DOMINO

International Rex Domino, 17190
☎ 546765597 ▤ 546766788
Pleasant seaside site with good recreational facilities and access to the beach.
Open: May-14 Sep Site: 0.8HEC ⁙ ◑ 🔵 🛏 Facilities: ⋔ 🖩
⊙ 🔵 ⌀ ☎ Services: ⛽ ✖ 🖽 lau Leisure: ↘ PS Off-site: ✖

ST-DENIS-D'OLÉRON

Phare Ouest 7 Impasse des Beaupins, 17650
☎ 251975550 ▤ 0251289109
e-mail: camping-apv@wanadoo.fr
website: www.camping-apv.com
On level ground with direct access to the beach.
➲ 1km NW towards the lighthouse.
Open: Apr-Sep Site: 3.5HEC ⁙ 🔵 🛏 🚐 Facilities: ⋔ 🖩 ⊙
🔵 ⌀ ⛰ ☎ Services: ⛽ ✖ lau Leisure: ↘ S Off-site: 🖽

ST-GEORGES-D'OLÉRON

Gautrelle Plage des Saumonards, 17190 ☎ 546472157
In a pine wood close to the beach.
Open: 27 Mar-Sep Site: 6HEC ⁙ 🔵 Facilities: ⋔ ⊙ 🔵 ☎
Services: 🖽 lau Leisure: ↘ S

Gros Joncs 17190 ☎ 546765229 ▤ 546766774
e-mail: camping.gros.joncs@wanadoo.fr
website: www.les-gros-joncs.fr
Quiet location on undulating land in the midst of lovely pine woodland.
➲ On tourist route from La Cotinière about 5km NW in the direction of Domino, 1km SW of St-Georges-d'Oléron.
Open: end of Mar - Oct Site: 5.2HEC ⁙ ⁙ 🔵 🛏
Prices: pitch 12.50-32.50 (incl 2 persons) Facilities: ⋔ 🖩 ⊙
🔵 ☎ Services: ⛽ ✖ 🖽 lau Leisure: ↘ PS

Quatre Vents La Jousselinière, 17190
☎ 546756547 ▤ 546361566
e-mail: 4vents.oleron@wanado.fr
A peaceful site with good facilities.
➲ 3km E via N739.
Open: Mar-Nov Site: 7.2HEC ⁙ 🛲 🛏 Prices: 🚐15-21
🅰2.30-3 Facilities: ⋔ 🖩 ⊙ 🔵 ⛰ ☎ Services: ⛽ ✖ 🖽 lau
Leisure: ↘ P Off-site: ↘S

Facilities: 🖩-shop ⋔-shower ⊙-electric points for razors 🔵-electric points for caravans ☎-parking by tents permitted
🅿-compulsory separate car park Services: ✖-café/restaurant ⛽-bar ⌀-Camping Gaz International ⛰-gas other than Camping Gaz 🖽-first aid facilities lau-laundry Leisure: ↘-swimming L-Lake P-Pool R-River S-Sea Off-site: All facilities within 2km

Signol av de Albatros, Boyardville, 17190
☎ 546470122   ▤ 546472346
e-mail: contact@signol.com
website: www.signol.com
Situated among pine and oak trees, half a mile from a sandy beach.
Open: Apr-Sep Site: 8HEC ⠿ ♣ ⊡ ⊗ Facilities: ⋒ ⊡ ⊟
Services: ⦿ Leisure: ⦚ P

Suroit rte Touristique Côte Ouest, l'Ileau, 17190
☎ 546470725
e-mail: info@camping-lesuroit.com
website: www.camping-lesuroit.com
On level ground, sheltered by sand dunes with fine, modern facilities.
➲ *5km SW of town.*
Open: Apr-Sep Site: 5HEC ⠿ ⠿ ◔ ♣ ⊡ Prices: pitch 14-20 (incl 2 persons) Facilities: ⋒ ⊡ ⊙ ⊡ ⌀ ⊡
⊞ lau Leisure: ⦚ PS Off-site: ⊟

Verébleu La Jousselinière, 17190 ☎ 546765770   ▤ 546767056
e-mail: verebleu@wanadoo.fr
website: www.verebleu.tm.fr
➲ *1.7km SE via D273*
Open: 3 Apr-20 Sep Site: 7.5HEC ⠿ ◔ ⊡ Facilities: ⋒ ⊡
⊙ ⊡ ⌀ ⊡ ⊡ Services: ⦿ ✕ ⊞ lau Leisure: ⦚ P Off-site: ✕ ⊟

Pierrière 18 rte de St-Georges, 17310
☎ 546470829   ▤ 546751282
e-mail: camppier@club-internet.fr
website: www.camping-la-pierriere.com
A pleasant site in wooded surroundings with well defined pitches.
➲ *NW towards St-Georges-d'Oléron*
Open: 4 Apr-28 Sep Site: 4HEC ⠿ ♣ ⊡ Facilities: ⋒ ⊡ ⊙
⊡ ⊡ Services: ⦿ ✕ lau Leisure: ⦚ P Off-site: ✕ ⌀ ⊟ ⦚S ⊞

Trois Masses Le Marais Doux, 17310
☎ 546472396   ▤ 546751554
A well equipped site in a picturesque location 2.5 km from the beach.
Open: Etr-Sep Site: 3HEC ⠿ ◔ ⊡ ⊡ Facilities: ⋒ ⊡ ⊙ ⊡
⌀ ⊡ Services: ⦿ ✕ ⊞ lau Leisure: ⦚ P Off-site: ⦚S

OLIVET   LOIRET

CM Olivet r du Pont Bouchet, 45160
☎ 238635394   ▤ 238635896
Site lies partly on shaded peninsula, partly on open lawns beside river.
➲ *2km E. Signposted from village.*
Open: Apr-Oct Site: 1HEC ⠿ ♣ Prices: ⋔2.80 pitch 4
Facilities: ⋒ ⊡ ⊙ ⊡ ⌀ ⊡ Services: ⊞ lau

OLONNE-SUR-MER   VENDÉE

Loubine 1 rte de la Mer, 85340
☎ 251331292   ▤ 251331271
e-mail: camping.la.loubine@wanadoo.fr
website: la.loubine.fr
Situated on the edge of a forest bordering the beach.
➲ *N via D87/D80.*
Open: 03 Apr-26 Sep Site: 8HEC ⠿ ◔ ⊡ ⊗ Prices: pitch 16-25 (incl 2 persons) Facilities: ⋒ ⊡ ⊙ ⊡ ⌀ ⊟ ⊡
Services: ⦿ ✕ ⊞ lau Leisure: ⦚ P Off-site: ⦚S

Moulin de la Salle r.des Moulin de la salle, 85340
☎ 251959910   ▤ 251969613
In pleasant surroundings close to the beach with good facilities.

⊃ *2.7km W.*
Open: Apr-Oct Site: 3.1HEC ⊞ ♣ ⌂ Facilities: ⋔ ⊙ ⌷ ≞
⌺ Services: ⍢ ✗ ⊞ lau Leisure: ⌇ P Off-site: ≞

Oreé rte des Amis de la Nature, 85340
☎ 251331059 ▤ 251331516
e-mail: loree@free.fr website: www.l-oree.com
⊃ *3km N*
Open: Apr-29 Sep Site: 7HEC ⊞ ⌷ ⌂ ⌷ ⚑ Facilities: ⋔
≞ ⊙ ⌷ ⌀ ≞ ⌺ Services: ⍢ ✗ ⊞ lau Leisure: ⌇ P
Off-site: ⌇RS

See advertisement on page 136

ONZAIN LOIR-ET-CHER

Dugny rte de Chambon-sur-Cisse, 41150
☎ 254207066 ▤ 254337169
e-mail: info@camping-de-dugny.fr
website: www.camping-de-dugny.fr
On a small lake, surrounded by farmland with well marked
pitches shaded by poplars.
⊃ *From Onzain follow direction Chambon-sur-Cisse (CD45).*
Open: All year Site: 10HEC ⊞ ⌷ ⌂ ⌷ ⚑ Prices: ⚑5.80-
8.90 pitch 3.10-3.60 Facilities: ⋔ ≞ ⊙ ⌷ ⌀ ≞ ⌺ Services: ⍢
✗ ⊞ lau Leisure: ⌇ P

PALMYRE, LA CHARENTE-MARITIME

Beausoleil 20 av de la Coubre, 17570
☎ 546223003 ▤ 546223004
Situated in a pine forest, 400 metres from the beach.
Open: Apr-Sep Site: 4.4HEC ⊞ ∷∷ ⌷ ⚑ Prices: pitch 11-
21 (incl 3 persons) Facilities: ⋔ ≞ ⊙ ⌷ ⌀ ≞ ⌺ Services: ⍢
✗ ⊞ lau Leisure: ⌇ PS

Bonne Anse Plage 17570 ☎ 546224090 ▤ 546224230
e-mail: bonne.anse@wanadoo.fr
website: www.campingbonneanseplage.com
An extensive, gently undulating site in a pine wood, 400m
from the beach.
⊃ *1km from La Palmyre roundabout. Follow signs for Ronce-
les-Bains.*
Open: 19 May-5 Sep Site: 17HEC ⊞ ∷∷ ♣ ⌂ ⊘
Prices: ⚑28 pitch 30 (incl 3 persons) Facilities: ⋔ ≞ ⊙ ⌷ ⌀
⌺ Services: ⍢ ✗ ⊞ lau Leisure: ⌇ P Off-site: ⌀ ≞ ⌇S

Palmyre Loisirs 28 des Mathes, 17570
☎ 546236766 ▤ 546224881
Well equipped family site with plenty of recreational facilities
and well supervised activities for children.
⊃ *From Les Mathes take the La Palmyre road.*
Open: 16 May-12 Sep Site: 20HEC ⊞ ∷∷ ♣ ⌂ ⚑
Facilities: ⋔ ≞ ⊙ ⌷ ⌀ ≞ ⌺ Services: ⍢ ✗ ⊞ lau Leisure: ⌇ P

Palmyr Océana 26 av des Mathes, 17570
☎ 546224035 ▤ 546236476
e-mail: palmyr-oceana@wanadoo.fr
website: www.palmyr-oceana.fr
A well equipped family site in a delightful wooded setting
close to the beach. A wide variety of recreational facilities are
available.
Open: 15 Jun-15 Sep Site: 17HEC ⊞ ∷∷ ⌷ ⌂ ⚑
Prices: pitch 13-23 (incl 2 persons) Facilities: ⋔ ≞ ⊙ ⌷ ⌀ ≞
⌺ Services: ⍢ ✗ ⊞ lau Leisure: ⌇ P Off-site: ⌇RS

PERRIER, LE VENDÉE

CM de la Maison Blanche 85300
☎ 251493923 ▤ 251493923
A family site on level ground, with pitches divided by trees.
6km from the coast.
Open: 01May-15 Sep Site: 3.2HEC ⊞ ♣ ⌂ Prices: pitch
7.55-8.40 (incl 2 persons) Facilities: ⋔ ⊙ ⌷ ⌺ Services: lau
Leisure: ⌇ PR Off-site: ≞ ⍢ ✗ ⌀ ≞ ⊞

PEZOU LOIR-ET-CHER

CM "Les Ilots" rte de Renay, 41100
☎ 254234069 ▤ 254236240
e-mail: commune.pezou@wanadoo.fr
A well equipped site 400mtrs from the town centre.
⊃ *SE via D12, 50m from the River Loir*
Open: 02 May-8 Sept Site: 1HEC ⊞ ⌷ Prices: ⚑2.40 pitch
2.40 Facilities: ⋔ ⊙ ⌷ ⌺ Services: lau Off-site: ⊞

PIRIAC-SUR-MER LOIRE-ATLANTIQUE

Parc du Guibel 44420 ☎ 240235267 ▤ 240155024
e-mail: camping@parcduguibel.com
website: www.parcduguibel.com
On level ground in a delightful wooded setting with good
recreational facilities.
⊃ *3.5km E via D52*
Open: 05 Apr-27Sep Site: 14HEC ⊞ ♣ ⌂ ⚑ Facilities: ⋔
≞ ⊙ ⌷ ≞ ⌺ Services: ⍢ ✗ ⊞ lau Leisure: ⌇ P Off-site: ⌇PS

PLAINE-SUR-MER, LA LOIRE-ATLANTIQUE

Tabardière 44770 ☎ 603003417 ▤ 240210268
e-mail: info@camping-la-tabardiere.com
website: www.camping-la-tabardiere.com
A wooded, terraced site 3km from the sea.
⊃ *Situated between Pornic and La Plaine-sur-Mer off D13.*
Open: Apr-Sep Site: 6HEC ⊞ ⌷ ⌂ Prices: ⚑3.30-5.10
Facilities: ⋔ ≞ ⊙ ⌷ ⌀ ≞ ⌺ Services: ⍢ ✗ ⊞ lau Leisure: ⌇
P Off-site: ✗

PONS CHARENTE-MARITIME

Chardon Chardon, 17800 ☎ 546950125
e-mail: chardon2@wanadoo.fr
Quietly situated on the edge of a small village next to a farm.
⊃ *From Pons take D732 westwards towards Royan. The site is
2.5km on the left. Alternatively from exit 36 of the Autoroute
A10 and turn towards Pons. Site is 800m on right.*
Open: Apr-Oct Site: 1.6HEC ⊞ ⌷ ⌂ ⚑ Facilities: ⋔ ≞ ⊙
⌷ ⌺ Services: ⍢ ✗ lau Off-site: ⌇R ⊞

PONT-L'ABBÉ-D'ARNOULT CHARENTE-MARITIME

Parc de la Garenne 24 av Brenard Chambenoit, 17250
☎ 546970146 ▤ 546955278
e-mail: info@lagarenne.net
website: www.lagarenne.net
Peaceful site in a parkland setting. Shady individual pitches.
⊃ *Access via A10, N137 and D18.*
Open: 19 Apr-4 Oct 2003 Site: 2.8HEC ⊞ ⌷ ⌂
Prices: ⚑3.28-4.10 pitch 11.04-13.80 Facilities: ⋔ ⊙ ⌷ ⌺
Services: ⍢ ✗ lau Leisure: ⌇ P Off-site: ≞ ⍢ ✗ ⌀ ≞ ⌇R ⊞

Facilities: ≞-shop ⋔-shower ⊙-electric points for razors ⌷-electric points for caravans ⌺-parking by tents permitted
⌷-compulsory separate car park Services: ✗-café/restaurant ⍢-bar ⌀-Camping Gaz International ≞-gas other than Camping
Gaz ⊞-first aid facilities lau-laundry Leisure: ⌇-swimming L-Lake P-Pool R-River S-Sea Off-site: All facilities within 2km

PONTS-DE-CÉ, LES MAINE-ET-LOIRE

Ile du Château rte de Cholet, av de la Boire Salée, 49130
☎ 241446205 📠 241446205
e-mail: ile-du-chateau@wanadoo.fr
Situated on a small island in the River Loire close to the
Château des Ponts-de-Cé. Separate car park for arrivals after
9pm.
⊃ *SW of Angers towards Cholet.*
Open: Apr-Sep Site: 2.3HEC ⟱ ♣ ⊞ 🏕 ▲ Prices: pitch
9.90-11.60 (incl 2 persons) Facilities: 🏕 🖳 ⊙ 🖾 🗗 🚄 🖾
Services: 🍴 ✕ ⊞ lau Leisure: ⟱ PR

PORNIC LOIRE-ATLANTIQUE

Boutinardière 44210 ☎ 240820568 📠 240824901
e-mail: info@boutinardiere.com
website: www.camping-boutinardiere.com
The site has three outdoor pools with water slides. Also a
heated indoor pool.
Open: Apr-Sep Site: 7.5HEC ⟱ ⊙ ⊞ Prices: pitch 12-26
(incl 2 persons) Facilities: 🏕 🖳 ⊙ 🖾 🗗 🚄 🖾 Services: 🍴 ✕ ⊞
lau Leisure: ⟱ P Off-site: ⟱S

Patisseau 29 rue de Patisseau, 44210
☎ 240821039 📠 240822281
e-mail: contact@lepatisseau.com
website: www.lepatisseau.com
In wooded surroundings close to the beach with fine
recreational facilities.
⊃ *3km E via D751.*
Open: 03 Apr-12 Sep Site: 4.3HEC ⟱ ⊙ ⊞ ▲ Prices: pitch
19-33 (incl 2 persons) pp5-7 Facilities: 🏕 🖳 ⊙ 🖾 🗗 🚄 🖾
Services: 🍴 ✕ ⊞ lau Leisure: ⟱ P Off-site: ⟱S

PORNICHET LOIRE-ATLANTIQUE

Bel Air 150 av de Bonne Source, 44380
☎ 33240611078 📠 33240612618
website: www.belairpornichet.com
In a pleasant, wooded location 50 metres from the beach.
Open: 27 Mar-3 Oct Site: 6HEC ⠿ ⊙ ⊞ Prices: pitch
9.20-26.20 (incl 2 persons) Facilities: 🏕 🖳 ⊙ 🖾 🗗 🖾
Services: 🍴 ✕ lau Leisure: ⟱ P Off-site: 🚄 ⟱S ⊞

Forges 98 rte de Villes Blais, 44380
☎ 240611884 📠 240601184
In wooded surroundings with well defined pitches and good
recreational facilities.
⊃ *Access via N171.*
Open: All year Site: 2HEC ⟱ ♣ ⊞ Facilities: 🏕 🖳 ⊙ 🖾 🗗
🚄 🖾 Services: ⊞ lau Leisure: ⟱ P Off-site: ⟱L

PORT-DE-PILES VIENNE

Bec des Deux Eaux rte de Marigny, 86220 ☎ 247650271
Wooded family site located close to the confluence of the
Vienne and Creuse rivers with easy access to the Futuroscope.
⊃ *E off N10.*
Open: Apr-Sep Site: 3.5HEC ⟱ ♣ ⊞ Facilities: 🏕 ⊙ 🖾 🖾
Services: 🍴 ✕ lau Leisure: ⟱ PR

PRAILLES DEUX-SÈVRES

Lambon Plan d'eau du Lambon, 78370
☎ 549799041 📠 549797862
e-mail: comcanton.celles@wanadoo.fr
website: www.paysmellois.com/lambon
Peaceful rural site situated by a stretch of water with a beach
for bathing.
⊃ *Take D948 from Niort towards Limoges. Follow signs for
Celle-sur-Belle, site 6kms N*

Site: 6HEC-Site size ⟱-grass ⠿-sand ♦-stone ♣-little shade ⊙-partly shaded ♣-mainly shaded
⊞-bungalows for hire 🖾-caravans for hire ▲-tents for hire ✕-no dogs **Prices:** ♠-adult per night ♠-car per night
pp-per person per night 🖾-caravan per night ▲-tent per night

Open: Jun-Sep Site: 1HEC ⚏ 👥 🏠 Facilities: 🅟 ☺ 🚰 🚿 🏕
Services: 🍸 ✗ ⊞ lau Leisure: ⬎ L Off-site: ⬎R

RÉ, ILE DE CHARENTE-MARITIME

ARS-EN-RÉ

Cormoran rte de Radia, 17590 ☎ 546294604 📠 546292936
e-mail: info@cormoran.com
Situated on the edge of a forest, 500 metres from village of Ars.
Facilities: 🅟 ☺ 🚰 Services: 🍸 ✗ Leisure: ⬎ P

Soleil 57 r de la Plage, 17590 ☎ 546294062
On level, shaded meadow 150mtrs from the beach and
500mtrs from the village.
➲ *Signposted from the N735 shortly before reaching Ars.*
Open: Mar-16 Nov Site: 2HEC ⚏ ♣ Facilities: 🅟 🚰 ☺ 🚰
🚿 🏕 Services: 🍸 ✗ ⊞ lau Off-site: ⬎S

BOIS-PLAGE-EN-RÉ, LE

Antioche 17580 ☎ 546092386 📠 546094334
In quiet, wooded area among dunes with direct access to the beach.
➲ *3.5km SE of village towards the beach.*
Open: 27 Mar-Sep Site: 2.7HEC ⚏ 👥 🏠 🚐 Facilities: 🅟 🚰
☺ 🚿 🏕 Services: 🍸 ✗ ⊞ lau Leisure: ⬎ S Off-site: 🚿

Camping Interlude-Gros-Jonc rte de Gros Jonc, 17580
☎ 546091822 📠 546092338
e-mail: info@interlude.fr website: www.interlude.fr
In a pleasant, wooded location 50mtrs from the beach, this site has
a fitness centre and can arrange guided tours of the area.
Open: 3 Apr-19 Sep Site: 7.5HEC ⚏ 👥 🏠
Prices: pitch 17-38.50 (incl 1 persons) pp3.90-9.15
Facilities: 🅟 🚰 ☺ 🚿 🏕 Services: 🍸 ✗ lau Leisure: ⬎ P
Off-site: ⚒ ⬎S ⊞

Facilities: 🚰-shop 🅟-shower ☺-electric points for razors 🚰-electric points for caravans 🏕-parking by tents permitted
🅿-compulsory separate car park **Services:** ✗-café/restaurant 🍸-bar 🚿-Camping Gaz International ⚒-gas other than Camping
Gaz ⊞-first aid facilities lau-laundry **Leisure:** ⬎-swimming L-Lake P-Pool R-River S-Sea **Off-site:** All facilities within 2km

COUARDE-SUR-MER, LA

Océan 50 Route d'Ars, 17670 ☎ 546298770 ▤ 546299213
e-mail: campingdelocean@wanadoo.fr
website: www.campingocean.com
In a fine position facing the sea with good modern facilities.
➲ *3km NW on N735.*
Open: Apr-Sep Site: 7HEC ⬛ ⋮⋮ ♣ 🏠 Prices: pitch 23.50-34 Facilities: �📷 🛒 ⊙ 🍴 🗻 🏠 Services: ⛴ ✕ ⊞ lau
Leisure: ⚓ P Off-site: ⚓S

FLOTTE, LA

Blanche Deviation de la Flotte, 17630
☎ 546095243 ▤ 546093694
website: www.ileblanche.com
A popular family site in a wooded location.
➲ *N on D735 towards St-Martin.*
Open: Apr-Sept Site: 4HEC ⋮⋮ 🔆 🏠 Facilities: ⚓ ⊙ 🍴 🐾 🏠
Services: ⛴ ✕ ⊞ lau Leisure: ⚓ P Off-site: 🛒 ⚓S

Peupliers 17630 ☎ 546096235
e-mail: contact@les-peupliers.com
website: www.camp-atlantique.com
Situated in a large, wooded park 800mtrs from the sea with good sporting facilities.
➲ *1.3km SE*
Open: 3 Apr-18 Sept Site: 4.4HEC ⋮⋮ 🔆 🏠 Prices: pitch 15-28 (incl 2 persons) Facilities: ⚓ 🛒 ⊙ 🍴 🐾 🗻 🏠
Services: ⛴ ✕ ⊞ lau Leisure: ⚓ P Off-site: ⚓S

LOIX

Ilates Le Petit Boucheau, rte du Grouin, 17111
☎ 546290543 ▤ 546290679
e-mail: ilates@wanadoo.fr
➲ *Access E towards Pointe du Grouin, 500mtrs from the sea.*
Open: Apr- 12 Nov Site: 4.5HEC ⬛ 🔆 🏠 Prices: ♠3-5 pitch 5-23 (incl 1 persons) Facilities: ⚓ ⊙ 🍴 🏠 Services: ⛴ ✕ ⊞ lau Leisure: ⚓ P Off-site: 🛒 ⛴ ✕ 🐾 🗻 ⚓S

ST-MARTIN-DE-RÉ

CM r du Rempart, 17410 ☎ 546092196 ▤ 546099418
In pleasant wooded surroundings at the foot of the 17th century ramparts.
➲ *N, beyond La Flotte.*
Open: Mar-15 Oct Site: 4HEC ⬛ 🔆 ♣ 🏠 Prices: ♠3.90 pitch 14-17 (incl 3 persons) Facilities: ⚓ ⊙ 🍴 🏠 Services: ⛴ ✕ lau Off-site: 🛒 ⚓S ⊞

RONCE-LES-BAINS CHARENTE-MARITIME

Pignade av des Monards, 17390
☎ 0870 2427777 ▤ 0870 2429999
website: www.haveneurope.com
A family site with good recreational facilities.
➲ *1.5km S*
Open: 28 Apr-16 Sep Site: 16HEC ⬛ ⋮⋮ ♣ 🍴 ⛺ ⊘
Facilities: ⚓ 🛒 🍴 🗻 🏠 Services: ⛴ ✕ ⊞ lau Leisure: ⚓ P
Off-site: ⚓S

ROSIERS, LES MAINE-ET-LOIRE

Val de Loire 6 r Ste-Baudruche, 49350
☎ 241519433 ▤ 241518913
A comfortable site partly on the banks of the River Loire with good recreational facilities.
➲ *N via D59*
Open: Apr-15 Oct Site: 4HEC ⬛ 🔆 🏠 🍴 ⛺ Facilities: ⚓ 🛒 ⊙ 🍴 🏠 ⊞ Services: ✕ ⊞ lau Leisure: ⚓ P Off-site: ⛴ ✕ 🐾 🗻 ⚓R

ROYAN CHARENTE-MARITIME
AT MÉDIS (4KM NE)

Chênes La Verdonneric, 17600 ☎ 546067138
In a wooded location with good facilities. Separate late
arrivals car park after 22.00hrs.
⮕ *2km from Royan on the Saintes-Royan road.*
Open: All year Site: 6.5HEC ▦ ♠ ⊞ ⊕ Facilities: 🅝 🅛 ⊙
🅡 🅐 🅟 🖭 Services: 🍽 ✕ ⊞ lau Leisure: ⬎ P

AT PONTAILLAC (2KM NE ON D25)

Clairfontaine allée des Peupliers, 17200
☎ 546390811 ▤ 546381379
e-mail: camping.clairfontaine@wanadoo.fr
website: www.camping-clairfontaine.com
A well equipped site in wooded surroundings 300mtrs from
the beach with a variety of recreational facilities.
Open: 20 May-15 Sep Site: 5HEC ▦ ⊕ Facilities: 🅝 🅛 ⊙
🅡 🅐 🖭 🅟 Services: 🍽 ✕ ⊞ lau Leisure: ⬎ PS

SABLES-D'OLONNE, LES VENDÉE

Dune des Sables La Paracou, 85100
☎ 251323121 ▤ 251323121
e-mail: camping-chadotel@wanadoo.fr
website: www.chardotec.com
In a fine location facing the sea and close to the beach.
Open: Apr-Sep Site: 6HEC ▦ ⤬ ⊞ ⊕ Prices: ⬆5.50 pitch
14-22.50 (incl 2 persons) Facilities: 🅝 🅛 ⊙ 🅡 🅐 🚿 🖭
Services: 🍽 ✕ ⊞ lau Leisure: ⬎ PS Off-site: ⬎S

Roses 1 r des Roses, 85100 ☎ 251951042 ▤ 251339404
e-mail: camping@chadotel.fr
website: www.chadotel.com
A level site, shaded by trees and bushes, 500mtrs from the
Remblai beach.

⮕ *Close to the town centre off D949.*
Open: Apr-3 Nov Site: 3.5HEC ▦ ⊕ ⊞ ⊕ Prices: ⬆5.50
pitch 14-22.50 (incl 2 persons) Facilities: 🅝 🅛 ⊙ 🅡 🅐 🚿 🖭
Services: 🍽 ✕ ⊞ lau Leisure: ⬎ P Off-site: ✕ ⬎S

SABLÉ-SUR-SARTHE SARTHE

Hippodrome allée du Quebec, 77233
☎ 243954261 ▤ 243927473
e-mail: camping-sable@wanadoo.fr
website: www.sable-sur-sarthe.com
In a peaceful wooded setting with a great variety of
recreational facilities.
⮕ *Situated 450 yards from the town.*
Open: Apr-Oct Site: 3HEC ▦ ⊕ ⊞ ⊕ Prices: ⬆1.62-2.08
pitch 3.04-4.08 Facilities: 🅝 🅛 ⊙ 🅡 🅐 🖭 Services: 🍽 ✕ ⊞
lau Leisure: ⬎ P Off-site: 🍽 ✕ 🚿

ST-AIGNAN-SUR-CHER LOIR-ET-CHER

CM Cochards 41110 ☎ 254751559 ▤ 254754472
e-mail: camping@les_cochards.com
website: www.lescochards.com
On beautiful meadowland, completely surrounded by hedges.
⮕ *1km from bridge on D17 towards Selles.*
Open: Apr-15 Oct Site: 4HEC ▦ ⊕ ⊞ ⊕ 🅐 Prices: ⬆2.60-
3.20 pitch 11-13.70 (incl 3 persons) Facilities: 🅝 🅛 ⊙ 🅡 🚿
🖭 Services: 🍽 ✕ ⊞ lau Leisure: ⬎ P Off-site: ⬎R

ST-AMAND-MONTROND CHER

CM Roche chemin de la Roche, 18200
☎ 248960936 ▤ 248960591
e-mail: mairie-sam@wanadoo.fr
website: www.st-amand-tourisme.com
In a lovely wooded location between the River Cher and the
Berry Canal with good modern facilities.

contd.

**Facilities: 🅛-shop 🅝-shower ⊙-electric points for razors 🅡-electric points for caravans 🖭-parking by tents permitted
🅟-compulsory separate car park Services: ✕-café/restaurant 🍽-bar 🅐-Camping Gaz International 🚿-gas other than Camping
Gaz ⊞-first aid facilities lau-laundry Leisure: ⬎-swimming L-Lake P-Pool R-River S-Sea Off-site: All facilities within 2km**

⮩ *1.5km SW near river and canal.*
Open: Apr-Sep Site: 4HEC ⸬⸬⸬⸬ ♣ Prices: ⋔2.80 ⊕3.80
⊕3.80 ▲1.80 pitch 3.80 Facilities: ⋔ ⊙ ⊑ ⬚ Services: ⊞ lau
Leisure: ⬚ R Off-site: ⬚ ⚊ ✕ ⬚ ⬚P

ST-ANDRÉ-DES-EAUX LOIRE-ATLANTIQUE

CM Les Chalands Fleuris r du Stade, 44117
☎ 240012040 ▤ 240915424
e-mail: chalfleu@club-internet.fr
website: www.chalandsfleuris.com
A peaceful site with good facilities in the middle of a natural
park.
⮩ *1km NE.*
Open: Apr-15 Oct Site: 4HEC ⸬⸬⸬⸬ ⋰⬚ ⬚ ▲ Prices: ⋔18
Facilities: ⋔ ⬚ ⊙ ⊑ ⬚ ⬚ Services: ⚊ ✕ ⊞ lau Leisure: ⬚ P
Off-site: ⬚

ST-AVERTIN INDRE-ET-LOIRE

CM Rives du Cher 61 r de Rochepinard, 37550
☎ 247272760 ▤ 247258289
e-mail: contact@camping-lesrivesducher.com
website: www.camping-lesrivesducher.com
Municipal site on the banks of the River Cher. Only caravans
weighing less than 1000kg accepted.
⮩ *400mtrs N of the town centre and 4km from Tours.*
Open: Apr-15 Oct Site: 3HEC ⸬⸬⸬⸬ ⋰⬚ ⬚ ⬚ Prices: ⋔3 ⊕2
⊕5.50 Facilities: ⋔ ⬚ ⊙ ⊑ ⬚ ⬚ ⬚ Services: ⊞ lau
Off-site: ⚊ ✕ ⬚LPR

ST-BRÉVIN-LES-PINS LOIRE-ATLANTIQUE

CM Courance 100/110 av Ml-Foch, 44250
☎ 240272291 ▤ 240272459
e-mail: francecamping@wanadoo.fr
website: www.francecamping.fr
In a pine forest with direct access to the beach.

Camping & Renting ★★★★
Les Pierres Couchées
300 m from the sea!
Spoil Yourself!
l'Ermitage • 44250 Saint-Brévin-les-pins
Tél : 33 (0)2 40 27 85 64 - Fax : 33 (0)2 40 64 97 03
www.pierres-couchees.com
SOUTH BRITTANY

⮩ *S off D305.*
Open: All year Site: 4HEC ⸬⸬⸬⸬ ⸬⸬⸬ ♣ ⬚ ▲ Facilities: ⋔ ⬚
⊙ ⬚ ⬚ ⬚ Services: ⚊ ✕ ⊞ lau Leisure: ⬚ S Off-site: ⬚ ⬚P

Fief 57 chemin du Fief, 44250
☎ 240272386 ▤ 240644619
website: www.lefief.com
A family site adjacent to a long sandy beach. The pitches are
surrounded by trees and bushes and there are good modern
facilities.
⮩ *In town follow 'Route Bleue' to Centre Leclerc then take 2nd
on right to site.*
Open: 3 Apr-16 Oct Site: 7HEC ⸬⸬⸬⸬ ⋰⬚ ⬚ ▲ Prices: ⋔3.50-6
pitch 12-26 (incl 2 persons) Facilities: ⋔ ⬚ ⊙ ⊑ ⬚ ⬚
Services: ⚊ ✕ ⊞ lau Leisure: ⬚ S Off-site: ⬚ ⬚S
See advertisement on page 141

ST-BRÉVIN-L'OCÉAN LOIRE-ATLANTIQUE

Village Club des Pierres Couchées L'Ermitage, 44250
☎ 240278564 ▤ 240849703
e-mail: contact@pierres-couchees.com
website: www.pierres-couchees.com
Extensive, well screened terrain made up of 3 sites, 2 of
which are open all year.
⮩ *300mtrs from the sea, 2km on D213 toward Pornic.*
Open: Apr-15 Oct Site: 14HEC ⸬⸬⸬⸬ ⸬⸬⸬ ♣ ⬚ Prices: pitch
10-24 (incl 2 persons) pp3.50-5.50 Facilities: ⋔ ⬚ ⊙ ⊑ ⬚ ⬚
Services: ⚊ ✕ ⊞ lau Leisure: ⬚ P Off-site: ⬚S

ST-CYR VIENNE

Parc de Loisirs 86130 ☎ 549625722 ▤ 549522858
e-mail: contact@parcdesaintcyr.com
website: www.parcdesaintcyr.com
In a delightful setting in a spacious park beside a lake. The
Futuroscope is within easy reach via the A10.
⮩ *1.5km NE via D4/D82.*
Open: Apr-Sep Site: 5HEC ⸬⸬⸬⸬ ⋰⬚ ⬚ Prices: ⋔2.50-5 ⊕1.50
pitch 6-12 Facilities: ⋔ ⬚ ⊙ ⊑ ⬚ ⬚ ⬚ Services: ⚊ ✕ ⊞ lau
Leisure: ⬚ L

SAINTES CHARENTE-MARITIME

Au Fill de l'Eau 6 r de Courbiac, 17100
☎ 546930800 ▤ 546936188
On the banks of the River Charente, 900mtrs from the town
centre.
⮩ *1km on D128.*
Open: 15 May-15 Sep Site: 7HEC ⸬⸬⸬⸬ ♣ ⬚ ⬚
Prices: ⋔3.35-4.20 pitch 4.30-4.30 Facilities: ⋔ ⬚ ⊙ ⊑ ⬚ ⬚
Services: ⚊ ✕ ⊞ lau Leisure: ⬚ PR Off-site: ⬚

ST-FLORENT-LE-VIEIL MAINE-ET-LOIRE

Ile Batailleuse 44370 ☎ 240834501
e-mail: ilebatailleuse@wanadoo.fr
⮩ *6km SE. N of Lac du Boudon.*
Open: Apr-16 Nov Site: 2.5HEC ⸬⸬⸬⸬ ♣ ⬚ ▲ Prices: ⋔7.50-
8.50 ⊕5-5.50 pitch 5-7 Facilities: ⋔ ⬚ ⊙ ⊑ ⬚ Services: ⚊
✕ ⊞ lau Leisure: ⬚ R Off-site: ⬚ ⚊ ✕ ⬚P ⊞

ST-GAULTIER INDRE

Village Vacances 'La Matronnerie' r de la Pierre Plate, 36800
☎ 254471704
e-mail: campoasisduberry@aol.com
website: www.campoasisduberry.com
Open: All year Site: 2.5HEC ⸬⸬⸬⸬ ⋰⬚ ⬚ ⬚ ▲ Prices: ⋔3.50
⊕1.50 pitch 11.50 (incl 2 persons) Facilities: ⋔ ⊙ ⊑ ⬚
Services: ⚊ ✕ ⊞ lau Leisure: ⬚ P Off-site: ⬚ ⬚R

St-Georges-de-Didonne Charente-Maritime

Bois Soleil 2 av de Suzac, 17110
☎ 546050594 ▤ 546062743
e-mail: camping.bois.soleil@wanadoo.fr
website: www.bois-soleil.com
Pitches lie on different levels. Direct access to the beach.
➲ *2.5km S of town on Meschers road (D25).*
Open: 3 Apr-Nov Site: 8.5HEC ⁙ ⊕ ⚍ ✍ Prices: pitch
17-31 (incl 2 persons) pp3.50-6 Facilities: ⋔ ⚊ ⊙ ⚑ ⌀ ⚌ ⌕
⊡ Services: ⚓ ✕ ⊞ lau Leisure: ⤳ PS

Ideal Camping No 1 Av de Suzac, 17110
☎ 546052904 ▤ 546063236
e-mail: info@ideal-camping.com
website: www.ideal-camping.com
A well equipped, peaceful site in a pine forest 200mtrs from
Suzac beach.
➲ *W of St-Georges-de-Didonne via D25.*
Open: 30 Apr-12 Sep Site: 8HEC ⁙ ⊕ ⚍ ✍
Prices: ⋔3.10-3.85 pitch 13.85-17.30 (incl 3 persons)
Facilities: ⋔ ⚊ ⊙ ⚑ ⌀ ⚌ ⌕ Services: ⚓ ✕ ⊞ lau Off-site: ⤳S

St-Georges-lès-Baillargeaux Vienne

Futuriste 86130 ☎ 549524752 ▤ 549524752
e-mail: d.radet@libertysurf.fr
website: www.camping-le-futuriste.fr
In an elevated position offering fine views over the Parc du
Furturoscope and the Clain valley. Advance booking is
advisable from June to August.
Open: All year Site: 4HEC ⚌ ⊕ ⚍ Prices: ⋔1.60-2.28
pitch 12.35-17 (incl 3 persons) Facilities: ⋔ ⚊ ⊙ ⚑ ⌀ ⌕
Services: ⚓ ✕ lau Leisure: ⤳ LP Off-site: ⊞

St-Gilles-Croix-de-Vie Vendée

Bahamas Beach 168 rte des Sables, 85800
☎ 251546916 ▤ 251546916
e-mail: camping-chadotel@wanadoo.fr
website: www.chadotel.com
➲ *2km from centre of town and 600mtrs from the beach.*
Open: Apr-Sep Site: 5HEC ⚌ ⤲ ⚑ Prices: ⋔5.50 pitch
14-22.50 (incl 2 persons) Facilities: ⋔ ⚊ ⊙ ⚑ ⌀ ⌕
Services: ⚓ ⊞ lau Leisure: ⤳ PS Off-site: ⤳S

Domaine de Beaulieu Givrand, 85800 ☎ 251555946
e-mail: info@camping.chadotel.com
website: www.chadotel.com
➲ *4km from the town and 1km from the beach.*
Open: 5 Apr-28 Sep Site: 7HEC ⚌ ⬥ ⚍ ⚑ ⚐
Prices: pitch 12.50-17.50 (incl 2 persons) Facilities: ⋔ ⚊
⊙ ⚑ ⌀ ⚌ ⌕ Services: ⚓ ✕ ⊞ lau Leisure: ⤳ PS Off-site: ⤳R

Pas Opton rte de Nantes, Le Fenouiller, 85800 ☎ 251551198
Well tended garden-like site in rural surroundings.
➲ *On D754 Nantes Road.*
Open: 20 May-10 Sep Site: 6.5HEC ⚌ ⊕ ⚍ ✍
Facilities: ⋔ ⚊ ⊙ ⚑ ⌀ ⌕ Services: ⚓ ✕ ⊞ lau Leisure: ⤳ PR

St-Hilaire-de-Riez Vendée

Biches rte de Notre-Dame-de-Riez, 85270
☎ 251543882 ▤ 251543074
e-mail: campingdesbiches@wanadoo.fr
website: www.campingdesbiches.com
A well equipped site in a pine forest and close to the sea.
➲ *2km N*
Open: 15 May-15 Sep Site: 10HEC ⚌ ⊕ ⚍ Prices: ⋔10
⚐2 pitch 37 (incl 3 persons) Facilities: ⋔ ⚊ ⊙ ⚑ ⌀ ⚌ ⌕
Services: ⚓ ✕ ⊞ lau Leisure: ⤳ P

Bois-Soleil
★★★★
CHARENTE MARITIME
Open from 4/4 till 2/11
240 M2
AQUATIC PARK

Rental
2, Avenue de Suzac
17110 St-Georges de Didonne
Tél. : 05 46 05 05 94
Fax : 05 46 06 27 43

Cottages
"Les Pieds dans l'Eau"
Chalets, Studio apartments,
Mobil-homes.

email : camping.bois.soleil@wanadoo.fr
Site Web: www.camping.bois.soleil.com

Bois Tordu 84 av de la Pège, 85270
☎ 251543378 ▤ 2515400829
e-mail: leboistordu@wanadoo.fr website: www.leboistordu.fr
In a wooded location with good facilities.
➲ *5.3km NW.*
Open: 15 May-15 Sep Site: 2HEC ⚌ ⬥ ⚍ Prices: ⋔5.60
⚐2 pitch 29.50 (incl 3 persons) Facilities: ⋔ ⚊ ⊙ ⚑ ⌀ ⚌ ⌕
Services: ⚓ ✕ ⊞ lau Leisure: ⤳ P Off-site: ✕ ⤳S

Chouans 108 av de la Faye, 85270
☎ 251543490 ▤ 251540592
e-mail: info@sunmarina.com website: www.sunmarina.com
In a wooded location on the edge of the National Forest.
➲ *2.5 km NW.*
Open: 15 May-15 Sep Site: 5HEC ⚌ ⊕ ⚍ Prices: pitch
21.60-27 (incl 3 persons) Facilities: ⋔ ⚊ ⊙ ⚑ ⌀ ⌕
Services: ⚓ ✕ lau Leisure: ⤳ P Off-site: ⤳S

Ecureuils 100 av de la Pège, 85270
☎ 251543371 ▤ 251556908
e-mail: info@camping-aux-ecureuils.com
In pleasant surroundings, 250mtrs from a fine sandy beach,
with good recreational facilities.
➲ *From A11 to Nantes, then via D178 and D753 to St-
Hilaire-de-Riez.*
Open: 15 May-15 Sep Site: 3HEC ⚌ ⁙ ⊕ Prices: ⋔4.10-
4.70 pitch 22.80-30 (incl 3 persons) Facilities: ⋔ ⊙ ⚑ ⌕
Services: ⚓ ✕ ⊞ lau Leisure: ⤳ P Off-site: ⚊ ⤳S

Padrelle 1 r Prévot, La Corniche de Sion/l'Océan, 85270
☎ 251553203
In a rural setting 50mtrs from the beach and within 5
minutes of the town.
Open: May-Sep Site: 1.5HEC ⚌ ⤲ ⚑ Prices: ⋔2.80 ⚐2
pitch 9.70 (incl 2 persons) Facilities: ⋔ ⊙ ⚑ ⌕ Services: lau
Off-site: ⚊ ⚓ ✕ ⌀ ⚌ ⤳PS ⊞

Facilities: ⚊-shop ⋔-shower ⊙-electric points for razors ⚑-electric points for caravans ⌕-parking by tents permitted
⊡-compulsory separate car park **Services:** ✕-café/restaurant ⚓-bar ⌀-Camping Gaz International ⚌-gas other than Camping
Gaz ⊞-first aid facilities lau-laundry **Leisure:** ⤳-swimming L-Lake P-Pool R-River S-Sea **Off-site:** All facilities within 2km

Plage 106 av de la Pège, 85270 ☎ 251543393 📠 251559702
e-mail: campinglaplage@campingscollinet.com
website: www.campingscollinet.com
On a meadow with trees. Access to beach via dunes.
➲ *5.7km NW.*
Open: 15 Apr-10 Sep Site: 5.5HEC ⼐ ⌁ ⊕ ⚏ ▲
Prices: ♠4.23-4.70 pitch 18.09-20.10 (incl 2 persons)
Facilities: ↾ ⊙ ⚏ ⌀ ♨ 🏠 Services: ♀ ✗ ⊞ lau Leisure: ⅃ PS
Off-site: ⚏

Prairie chemin des Roselières, 85270
☎ 251540856 📠 251559702
e-mail: campinglaprairie@campingscollinet.com
website: www.campingscollinet.com
A family site with pitches shaded by trees. Advance booking
recommended in high season.
➲ *5.5km NW, 500m from the beach*
Open: 15 May-10 Sep Site: 4.7HEC ⼐ ⌁ ⊕ ⚏
Prices: ♠3.87-4.30 pitch 20.70-23 (incl 2 persons) pp4.30
Facilities: ↾ ⊙ ⚏ ⌀ ♨ 🏠 Services: ♀ ✗ lau Leisure: ⅃ P
Off-site: ⚏ ⅃S

Puerta del Sol Les Borderies - D59, 85270
☎ 251491010 📠 251498484
e-mail: puerta-del-sol@wanadoo.fr
website: campinglapuertadelsol.com
A peaceful site with well defined pitches in a wooded
location. Good facilities for family recreation.
➲ *4.5km N.*
Open: Apr- 29 Sep Site: 5HEC ⼐ ⌁⁚⁚ ♣ ⊕ ⚏
Facilities: ↾ ⚏ ⊙ ⚏ 🏠 Services: ♀ ✗ ⊞ lau Leisure: ⅃ P
Off-site: ⊞

Sol-à-Gogo 61 av de la Pège, 85270
☎ 251542900 📠 251548874
e-mail: solagogo@wanadoo.fr
website: www.solagogo.com
A family site with good recreational facilities, including an
aquaslide, with direct access to the beach.
➲ *4.8km NW of St-Hilaire, 6km S of St-Jean-de-Monts.*
Open: 15 May-15 Sep Site: 4HEC ⼐ ⌁⁚⁚ ⌁ ⚏
Prices: pitch 24.80-31 (incl 3 persons) Facilities: ↾ ⚏ ⊙ ⚏
🏠 Services: ♀ ✗ ⊞ lau Leisure: ⅃ PS Off-site: ⌀ ♨

ST-HILAIRE-LA-FORÊT VENDÉE

Batardières 85440 ☎ 251333385
In a pleasant location, surrounded by mature trees and
shrubs with large individual pitches, separated by hedges.
➲ *W on D70.*
Open: Jul-5 Sep Site: 1.6HEC ⼐ ♣ Facilities: ↾ ⊙ ⚏ 🏠
Services: lau Off-site: ⚏ ♀ ✗ ⌀ ♨

Grand' Métairie 8 r de la Vineuse en Plaine, 85440
☎ 251333238 📠 251332569
e-mail: grand-metairie@wanadoo.fr
website: www.la-grand-metairie.com
Site with flowers and trees with clearly marked sites.
Entertainment for children and teenagers. Free shuttle
available to nearby sandy beach.
Open: Apr-Sep Site: 3.8HEC ⼐ ♣ ⌁ ▲ Facilities: ↾ ⊙ ⚏
⌀ 🏠 ⊞ Services: ♀ ✗ ⊞ lau Leisure: ⅃ P Off-site: ⚏ ⅃LS

ST-HILAIRE-PEYROUX CORRÈZE

Le Chazal 19560 ☎ 555257296
e-mail: camping.lechazal@wanadoo.fr
website: perso.wanadoo.fr/camping.lechazal/
A peaceful site on the edge of the Massif Central with fine
views over the Couze valley.
➲ *N89 Brive to Tulle. At Malemort take D141 left off
roundabout to Venarsal and then proceed 1.5m for St-Hilaire-
Peyroux. Turn left onto C13 for campsite.*
Open: Apr-1 Nov Site: 1.5HEC ⼐ ⌁ ⚏ ▲ Facilities: ↾
⊙ ⚏ ⌀ 🏠 Services: ⊞ lau

ST-JEAN-DE-MONTS VENDÉE

Abri des Pins rte de Notre-Dame-de-Monts, 85160
☎ 251588386 📠 251593047
e-mail: abridespins@aol.com
website: www.abridespins.com
A family site on level grassland with pitches subdivided by
hedges, bushes and trees. 10 minutes walk from the beach.
➲ *4km N on D38 Notre-Dame-de-Monts road.*
Open: 3 May-12 Sep Site: 3HEC ⼐ ⌁⁚⁚ ⌁ Facilities: ↾ ⚏
⊙ ⚏ 🏠 Services: ♀ ✗ ⊞ lau Leisure: ⅃ P Off-site: ⌀ ♨ ⅃S

Amiaux 223 rte de Notre-Dame de Monts, 85160
☎ 251582222 📠 251582609
e-mail: accueil@amiaux.fr
website: www.amiaux.fr
A well equipped site on the edge of a forest, 700mtrs from
the beach.
➲ *3.5km NW of D38.*
Open: Etr-Sep Site: 16HEC ⼐ ⌁⁚⁚ ⌁ ⚏ Prices: ♠3.50 ♠♠2
pitch 11.20-21.40 Facilities: ↾ ⚏ ⊙ ⚏ ⌀ 🏠 ⊞ Services: ♀ ✗
⊞ lau Leisure: ⅃ P Off-site: ⅃S

Avenhiriers de la Calypso rte de Notre-Dame-de-Monts, Les
Tonnelles, 85160 ☎ 251975550
e-mail: camping_apv@wanadoo.fr
A holiday village with good, modern facilities, 700mtrs from
Tonnelles beach.
Open: Apr-Sep Site: 5HEC ⼐ ⌁ ⌁ ⚏ ▲ Facilities: ↾ ⚏
⊙ ⚏ ⌀ ♨ 🏠 Services: ♀ ✗ ⊞ lau Leisure: ⅃ P Off-site: ⅃S

Bois Dormant 168 r des Sables, 85160
☎ UK Central Res 0870 242 7777
▤ 0870 242 9999 (Central Res)
website: www.haveneurope.com
Open: Apr-14 Sep Site: 11.5HEC ▦ ∷ ♠ ⌂ ⌾ ▲ ⌁
Facilities: ⋔ ℤ ☉ ⊞ ∅ ⌘ ▦ Services: ☕ ✗ ⊞ lau

Bois Joly 46 r de Notre-Dame-de-Monts, BP 507, 85165
☎ 251591163 ▤ 251591106
e-mail: boisjoly@compuserve.com
website: www.camping-leboisjoly.com
A pleasantly landscaped, terraced site set among pine trees.
Good facilities. Close to the beach and the town centre.
Open: Apr-26 Sep 2004 Site: 7.5HEC ▦ ⌾ ⌂
Prices: ⋔2.20-4 pitch 15-24 (incl 2 persons) Facilities: ⋔ ℤ ☉
⊞ ∅ ▦ Services: ☕ ✗ ⊞ lau Leisure: ⌁ PR Off-site: ⌘ ⌁S

Bois Masson 149 r des Sables, 85160
☎ 251586262 ▤ 251582997
A family site with a wide variety of facilities. In a wooded
setting, just a few minutes from the beach. Aquatic complex
includes covered and outdoor pools, water chutes, jacuzzi
and sauna.
➲ 2km SE
Open: 3 Apr-2 Oct Site: 7.5HEC ∷ ⌾ ⌂ Prices: pitch 34
(incl 2 persons) Facilities: ⋔ ℤ ☉ ⊞ ∅ ▦ Services: ☕ ✗ lau
Leisure: ⌁ P Off-site: ⌁S

Clarys Plage av des Epines, 85160
☎ 251581024 ▤ 251595196
e-mail: leclarys@wanadoo.fr
website: www.leclarys.com
A family site with good facilities including an indoor
swimming pool and an outdoor pool with a water slide.
➲ S of town 300mtrs from the beach.
Open: 15 May-15 Sep Site: 8HEC ▦ ∷ ♠ ⌂
Prices: pitch 24-30 (incl 3 persons) Facilities: ⋔ ℤ ☉ ⊞ ▦
Services: ☕ ✗ ⊞ lau Leisure: ⌁ P Off-site: ⌘ ⌁S

Sirenes av des Demoiselles, 85160
☎ 251580131 ▤ 251590367
In a forested location 500mtrs from the beach with good
facilities.
➲ SE off D38.
Open: 27 Mar-Oct Site: 15HEC ▦ ∷ ♠ Facilities: ⋔ ☉
⊞ ▦ ⊡ Services: ⊞ lau Off-site: ℤ ☕ ✗ ∅ ⌘ ⌁PS

Forêt 190 chemin de la Rive, 85160
☎ 251588463 ▤ 251588463
e-mail: camping-la-foret@wanadoo.fr
website: www.chez.com/campinglaforet
A well equipped family site in a pleasant rural setting.
➲ 5.5km NW.
Open: 15 Apr-Sep Site: 1HEC ▦ ∷ ♠ ⌂ Prices: ⋔3-5
pitch 16-23.50 (incl 2 persons) Facilities: ⋔ ℤ ☉ ⊞ ▦
Services: ⊞ lau Leisure: ⌁ P Off-site: ☕ ✗ ⌘ ⌁S

Zagarella rte des Sables, 85160 ☎ 251581982 ▤ 251593528
Open: 15 May-15 Sep Site: 4.2HEC ∷ ⌾ Prices: pitch
27.50 Facilities: ⋔ ℤ ☉ ⊞ Services: ☕ ✗ lau Leisure: ⌁ P
Off-site: ⌁S

AT OROUET (6KM SE)

Yole chemin des Bosses, 85160
☎ 251586717 ▤ 251590535
e-mail: contact@la-yole.com
website: www.la-yole.com
In rural surroundings 1km from a fine sandy beach.
➲ Signposted from D38 in Orouet.
Open: 8 May-15 Sep Site: 6HEC ▦ ∷ ⌾ ⌾ ⌁
Prices: pitch 17-28.20 (incl 2 persons) Facilities: ⋔ ℤ ☉ ⌾
∅ ▦ Services: ☕ ✗ ⊞ lau Leisure: ⌁ P Off-site: ⌘ ⌁S

Le Bois Masson

One of two great parcs
with swimming pools,
sports & family activities.
Enjoy the lively life at
Le Bois Masson, or relax
at the more peaceful sister
- Le Bois Dormant.

■ 80m² standard pitch size
■ Superb spring & autumn prices
■ Ferry inclusive package
■ High standard facilities open all season
■ Free use of superb indoor & outdoor pools
■ Free use of 3 childrens clubs for all ages
■ Bilingual friendly staff
■ Site open from: 3 April - 2 October

Le Bois Masson, 168 Rue des Sables, 85167 St Jean de Monts, France
Tel: 00 33 251 58 62 62 Fax: 00 33 251 58 29 97
To book please call the number above, quoting code TOAA01
or request a brochure by calling 0870 242 6666
V2819

ST-JULIEN-DES-LANDES VENDÉE

Fôret 85150 ☎ 251466211 ▤ 251466087
e-mail: camping@domainelaforet.com
website: www.domainelaforet.com
In a picturesque setting in the grounds of a château with well
defined pitches and modern facilities.
➲ NE on D55, rte de Martinet.
Open: 15 May-15 Sep Site: 50HEC ▦ ⌾ ⌂ Facilities: ⋔ ℤ
☉ ⌾ ∅ ▦ Services: ☕ ✗ ⊞ lau Leisure: ⌁ P

Garangeoire 85150 ☎ 251466539 ▤ 251466985
e-mail: garangeoire@wanadoo.fr
website: www.camping-la-garangeoire.com
Family site set in 200 hectare estate. Pitches separated by
hedges. A good variety of recreational facilities.

contd.

Rental Chalets - Mobile homes
Heated and covered swimming pool, with Jacuzzi.
Outdoors swimming pool with water slide, bar, restaurant,
entertainment programme and children's club.
Route des Sables, 85160 Saint-Jean-de-Monts
Phone.: 02 51 58 19 82 • Fax: 02 51 59 35 28
zagarella@wanadoo.fr • http://www.zagarella.fr

Facilities: ℤ-shop **⋔**-shower **☉**-electric points for razors **⌾**-electric points for caravans **▦**-parking by tents permitted
⊡-compulsory separate car park **Services: ✗**-café/restaurant **☕**-bar **∅**-Camping Gaz International **⌘**-gas other than Camping
Gaz **⊞**-first aid facilities lau-laundry **Leisure: ⌁**-swimming L-Lake P-Pool R-River S-Sea **Off-site:** All facilities within 2km

⮱ *2km N of the village.*
Open: 3 Apr-25 Sep Site: 15HEC ⊞ ⊙ 🏠 Prices: ⚑4.50
🚐3 pitch 17-30 (incl 2 persons) Facilities: ⭐ ⅃ ⊙ 🗷 ⊘ 🛉
Services: ⚑ ✗ 🗷 lau Leisure: ⚓ LP

Guyonnière La Guyonnière, 85150
☎ 251466259 🗎 251466289
e-mail: info@laguyonniere.com
website: www.laguyonniere.com
A pleasant site with pitches divided by hedges with good
sanitary and recreational facilities.
⮱ *2km from the town centre towards St-Gilles-Croix-de-Vie.*
Open: May-Oct Site: 30HEC ⊞ ⊙ 🏠 ▲ Prices: pitch 21
(incl 2 persons) Facilities: ⭐ ⅃ ⊙ 🗷 ⊘ ≞ 🛉 Services: ⚑ ✗ 🗷
lau Leisure: ⚓ LP

Séquoia Parc La Josephtrie, 17320
☎ 546855555 🗎 546855556
e-mail: sequoia.parc@wanadoo.fr
website: www.sequoiaparc.com
Situated in a spacious park on the 'La Josephtrie' estate
containing an attractive château some 5km from the coast.
⮱ *Access via A10 exit 'Saintes' then D728 towards Ile
d'Oléron and follow signs from St-Just.*
Open: 15 May-11 Sep Site: 45HEC ⊞ ∿ 🏠 Prices: ⚑6-8
🚐4 ▲4 pitch 15-35 (incl 2 persons) Facilities: ⭐ ⅃ ⊙ 🗷 ⊘
🛉 Services: ⚑ ✗ lau Leisure: ⚓ P

Amitié r du Camping, 41220 ☎ 254870152 🗎 254870993
On the shore of the River Loire between Blois and Orléans.
⮱ *On D951.*
Open: All year Site: 2HEC ⊞ ∿ Facilities: ⭐ ⊙ 🗷 🛉
Services: lau Leisure: ⚓ R Off-site: ⅃ ⚑ ✗ ⊘ ≞

CM Beaufort 87400 ☎ 555560279
In pleasant wooded surroundings with good facilities.
⮱ *Access from the D39.*
Open: 15 Jun-15 Sep Site: 2HEC ⊞ ⊙ 🏠 Prices: ⚑2.04
pitch 7.15-8.15 (incl 2 persons) Facilities: ⭐ ⅃ ⊙ 🗷 ⊘ 🛉
Services: ⚑ ✗ 🗷 lau Off-site: ✗ ≞

La Vallee de Poupet 85590 ☎ 251923145 🗎 251923865
e-mail: camping@valleedepoupet.com
website: www.valleedepoupet.com
In a picturesque location beside the River Sèvre Nantaise,
surrounded by woodland.
⮱ *From village take D72 for 1km, then take left fork and
follow signs.*
Open: 15 May-15 Sep Site: 3HEC ⊞ ⊙ 🏠 ⊞ Prices: ⚑2.70-3
🚐1.80-2 pitch 11.25-12.50 (incl 2 persons) Facilities: ⭐ ⊙ 🗷 🛉
Services: 🗷 lau Leisure: ⚓ PR Off-site: ⅃ ⚑ ✗ ⊘

Ormeaux 44 av de Bernezac, 17420
☎ 546390207 🗎 546385666
Well equipped site in wooded surroundings, 500mtrs from
the beach.
⮱ *1km N.*
Open: Apr-Oct Site: 3.5HEC ⊞ ⚑ 🏠 ⊞ ▲ Facilities: ⭐ 🛉
⊙ 🗷 ⊘ ≞ 🛉 Services: ⚑ ✗ 🗷 lau Leisure: ⚓ P Off-site: ⚓LS

Puits de l'Auture La Grande Côte, 17420
☎ 546232031 🗎 546232638
e-mail: camping-lauture@wanadoo.fr
website: www.camping-puitsdelauture.com
A family site in a picturesque location at the edge of a forest
facing the sea.

⮱ *2km NW on D25 La Palmyre road.*
Open: May-Sep Site: 5HEC ⊞ ⚑ ⊘ Prices: pitch 15.50-31
(incl 2 persons) Facilities: ⭐ ⅃ ⊙ 🗷 ⊘ 🛉 Services: ⚑ ✗ 🗷
lau Leisure: ⚓ P Off-site: ⚓S

Pont Rouge av Georges Clémenceau, 85220
☎ 251546850 🗎 251546850
e-mail: camping.pontrouge@wanadoo.fr
Quiet site situated in the Vendee countryside within easy
reach of the sea.
⮱ *From La Roche sur Yon, take D948 Noirmoutier-St Hilaire.
Exit for Aizenay and take D6 towards Saint Gilles. Pass Coex
and turn off at Saint Reverend*
Open: Apr-Oct Site: 1.6HEC ⊞ ⚑ 🏠 ⊞ Prices: pitch
11.05-13 (incl 2 persons) Facilities: ⭐ ⅃ ⊙ 🗷 ≞ 🛉
Services: lau Leisure: ⚓ PR Off-site: ⊘

'Bolée d'Air' rte du Bouil, 85520
☎ 251903605 🗎 251339404
e-mail: chadotel@wanadoo.fr website: camping.chadotel.fr
A family site on level ground with pitches divided by hedges.
Good recreational facilities, including a water slide, and
900mtrs from Bouil beach.
⮱ *2km E via D21.*
Open: Apr-Sep Site: 6.5HEC ⊞ ⊙ 🏠 ⊞ ⊘ ≞ 🛉 ▲ Prices: ⚑5.50
pitch 15-22 (incl 2 persons) Facilities: ⭐ ⅃ ⊙ 🗷 ⊘ ≞ 🛉
Services: ⚑ ✗ 🗷 lau Leisure: ⚓ P Off-site: ✗ ⚓S

Parc de Fierbois 37800 ☎ 247654335 🗎 274655375
e-mail: parc.fierbois@wanadoo.fr website: www.fierbois.com
Beside artificial lake; good bathing area.
⮱ *Follow D101 off N10, 1.5km SE.*
Open: 15 May-14 Sep Site: 20HEC ⊞ ⚑ 🏠 Prices: pitch
15-30 (incl 2 persons) Facilities: ⭐ ⅃ ⊙ 🗷 ⊘ ≞ 🛉 Services: ⚑
✗ 🗷 lau Leisure: ⚓ LP

Jamica la Sablière Ferme de Magne, 17250 ☎ 546229099
In a pleasant situation beside a lake within a country park.
⮱ *Access via A10 exit 25 (Saintes) and D728 towards Ile
d'Oléron.*
Open: May-15 Oct Site: ⊞ ⚑ 🏠 ⊞ Facilities: ⭐ ⅃ ⊙ 🗷 ⊘
≞ 🛉 Services: ⚑ ✗ 🗷 lau Leisure: ⚓ L

Château du Deffay BP 18, 44160
☎ 240880057 🗎 240016655
e-mail: campingdudeffay@wanadoo.fr
website: camping-le-deffay.com
Situated in the beautiful Parc de Brière providing fishing,
walking and horse riding. Games and TV rooms.
⮱ *4.5km W on D33 rte de Pontchâteau.*
Open: 8 May-17 Sep Site: 8HEC ⊞ ⊙ 🏠 Prices: ⚑2.80-
4.55 pitch 10.40-13.90 Facilities: ⭐ ⅃ ⊙ 🗷 🛉 Services: ⚑ ✗
🗷 lau Leisure: ⚓ LP

Santrop 87640 ☎ 555710808 🗎 555712393
website: www.lac-saint-pardoux.com
A well equipped family site on the shore of Lac de St-
Pardoux with good facilities for water sports.
⮱ *Access via A20 exit 25.*
Open: 18 May-21 Sep Site: 4.5HEC ⊞ ⚑ 🏠 Prices: ⚑3.10-
4.10 pitch 9.70-15.80 (incl 2 persons) Facilities: ⭐ ⊙ 🗷 ⊘
≞ 🛉 Services: ⚑ ✗ 🗷 lau Leisure: ⚓ L

Site: 6HEC-Site size ⊞-grass ∷-sand ⊘-stone ∿-little shade ⊙-partly shaded ⚑-mainly shaded
🏠-bungalows for hire ⊞-caravans for hire ▲-tents for hire ⊘-no dogs Prices: ⚑-adult per night 🚐-car per night
pp-per person per night ⊞-caravan per night ▲-tent per night

SAUMUR MAINE-ET-LOIRE

Chantepie 49400 ☎ 241679534 📠 241679585
e-mail: info@campingchantepie.com
website: www.campingchantepie.com
A pleasant site with a fine view over the River Loire.
➲ Access via D751 towards Gennes.
Open: 27 Apr-14 Sep Site: 10HEC ⚏ ⚐ ▲ Facilities: ℝ ➋
⊙ ⚑ ⊘ ☎ Services: ⍾ ✕ ⊞ lau Leisure: ⚓ P

Ile d'Offard av de Verden, 49400
☎ 241403000 📠 241673781
e-mail: iledoffard@wanadoo.fr
website: www.cvtloisirs.com
On island in the middle of the Loire near municipal stadium.
Some facilities are only available during the high season.
Open: Mar-Oct Site: 4.5HEC ⚏ ♣ ⚐ ▲ Prices: pitch
14.50-14.50 (incl 2 persons) Facilities: ℝ ➋ ⊙ ⚑ ☕ ☎
Services: ⍾ ✕ ⊞ lau Leisure: ⚓ P Off-site: ⊘ ⚓R

SELLE CRAONNAISE, LA MAYENNE

Rincerie Base de Loisirs la Rincerie, 53800
☎ 243061752 📠 243075020
website: www.la-rincerie.com
A modern site offering a good selection of sporting facilities.
Separate carpark for arrivals after 22.00hrs.
➲ N of La Selle-Craonnaise towards Ballots.
Open: All year Site: 5HEC ⚏ ⚐ ⊙ Prices: pitch 9 (incl 2
persons) Facilities: ℝ ⊙ ⚑ ☎ Services: ⊞ lau

SILLÉ-LE-GUILLAUME SARTHE

Privé du Landereau 72140 ☎ 243201269
➲ 1.5km NW via D304
Open: Etr-15 Oct Site: 2.5HEC ⚏ ⚐ ☕ ⊙ Facilities: ℝ ⊙
⚑ ⊘ ☎ Services: ⍾ ✕ ⊞ lau Off-site: ✕ ☕ ⚓LR

SILLÉ-LE-PHILIPPE SARTHE

⌂Château de Chanteloup 72460
☎ 243275107 📠 243890505
e-mail: chanteloup.souffront@wanadoo.fr
website: www.chateau-de-chanteloup.com
Set partly in wooded clearings and open ground within the
park surrounding an old mansion. Good sanitary
installations.
➲ 17km NE of Le Mans on D301.
Open: 31 May-6 Sep Site: 20HEC ⚏ ⚐ Prices: ⌂5-6.50
pitch 7-10.50 Facilities: ℝ ➋ ⊙ ⚑ ☎ Services: ⍾ ✕ ⊞ lau
Leisure: ⚓ P

SOUTERRAINE, LA CREUSE

Suisse Océan Le Cheix, 23300 ☎ 555633332
➲ 1.8km E via D912 near the lake.
Open: All year Site: 2HEC ⚏ ⚐ ☕ ⊙ Facilities: ℝ ⊙ ⚑ ☎
Services: ⍾ ✕ ⊞ lau Off-site: ➋ ⚓L

SUÈVRES LOIR-ET-CHER

⌂Château de la Grenouillère 41500
☎ 254878037 📠 254878421
e-mail: la.grenouillere@wanadoo.fr
website: www.camping-loire.fr
Completely divided into pitches. Castle now hotel with
common room for campers. Each pitch 150sq mtr. Separate
area for overnight campers.
➲ 3km from village towards Orléans.
Open: May-05 Sep Site: 11HEC ⚏ ⚐ ☕ Prices: ⌂4.40-6.50
⚑18.40-28 Facilities: ℝ ➋ ⊙ ⚑ ⊘ ☎ Services: ⍾ ✕ ⊞ lau
Leisure: ⚓ P

SULLY-SUR-LOIRE LOIRET

CM chemin de la Salle Verte, 45600 ☎ 238362393
Near Château, adjacent to River Loire.
➲ 100mtrs from town.
Open: 26 Apr-29 Sep Site: 1.5HEC ⚏ ☷ ⊙ ⊘ ⚑
Facilities: ℝ ⊙ ⚑ ☎ Services: ⊞ lau Off-site: ➋ ⍾ ✕ ⚓P

AT ST-PÈRE-SUR-LOIRE

St-Père rte d'Orléans, 45600 ☎ 238363594
On a level meadow on the right bank of the River Loire.
➲ W on D60 towards St-Benoît-sur-Loire.
Open: 12 Apr-29 Sep Site: 2.7HEC ⚏ ⚐ ☕ ⚑
Facilities: ℝ ⊙ ⚑ Services: ⊞ lau Leisure: ⚓ P
Off-site: ➋ ⍾ ✕ ⚓P

TALMONT-ST-HILAIRE VENDÉE

Littoral Le Porteau, 85440 ☎ 251220464 📠 251220537
e-mail: info@campinglelittoral.fr
website: www.campinglelittoral.fr
Situated near Port Bourgenay, 80mtrs from the sea. Good
facilities and entertainment available during the season.
Open: Apr-Sep Site: 8.5HEC ⚏ ⚐ ☕ Prices: pitch 17-29
(incl 2 persons) pp4-5.60 Facilities: ℝ ➋ ⊙ ⚑ ⊘ ☷ ☎
Services: ⍾ ✕ ⊞ lau Leisure: ⚓ P Off-site: ⚓S

TOURS INDRE-ET-LOIRE

AT BALLAN-MIRÉ (8.5KM W D751)

Mignardière 22 av des Aubepines, 37510
☎ 247733100 📠 247733101
e-mail: info@mignardiere.com
website: www.mignardiere.com
A well maintained site with a variety of sporting facilities.
➲ 2.5km NE.
Open: 10 Apr-Sep Site: 3.5HEC ⚏ ⚐ ☕ ⚑ Prices: ⌂4-5
pitch 13.50-19 (incl 2 persons) Facilities: ℝ ➋ ⊙ ⚑ ⊘ ☷ ☎
Services: ⊞ lau Leisure: ⚓ P Off-site: ⍾ ✕

TRANCHE-SUR-MER, LA VENDÉE

Bale d'Aunis 10 r du Pertuis, 85360
☎ 251274736 📠 251274454
e-mail: info@camping-baiedaunis.com
website: www.camping-baiedaunis.com
On level land on sea-shore, 50mtrs from the beach and
400mtrs from the town centre with a variety of leisure
activities.
➲ 300mtrs E on D46.
Open: May-19 Sept Site: 2.4HEC ⚏ ☷ ⚐ ♣ ⚐ ⚶
Prices: pitch 22.20-25.80 (incl 2 persons) Facilities: ℝ ⊙ ⚑
⊘ ☎ Services: lau Leisure: ⚓ PS Off-site: ➋ ⍾ ✕ ☷ ⊞

Bel r du Bottereau, 85360 ☎ 251304739 📠 251277281
A quiet, family-run site 500mtrs from a magnificent beach
and a marine lake. Plenty of sports and entertainment
facilities.
➲ 400mtrs from town centre.
Open: 29 May-7 Sep Site: 3.5HEC ⚏ ☷ ♣ ⚶
Prices: pitch 24 (incl 2 persons) Facilities: ℝ ➋ ⊙ ⚑ ☎
Services: ⍾ ✕ ⊞ lau Leisure: ⚓ PS Off-site: ✕ ⊘ ☷ ⊞

Cottage Fleuri La Grière-Plage, 85360
☎ 251303457 📠 251277477
A level site with modern facilities.
➲ 2.5km E, 500mtrs from the beach
Open: Apr-15 Oct Site: 7.5HEC ⚏ ⚐ Facilities: ℝ ⊙ ⚑
☷ ☎ Services: ⍾ ✕ ⊞ lau Leisure: ⚓ P Off-site: ⚓S

**Facilities: ➋-shop ℝ-shower ⊙-electric points for razors ⚑-electric points for caravans ☎-parking by tents permitted
⚐-compulsory separate car park Services: ✕-café/restaurant ⍾-bar ⊘-Camping Gaz International ☷-gas other than Camping
Gaz ⊞-first aid facilities lau-laundry Leisure: ⚓-swimming L-Lake P-Pool R-River S-Sea Off-site: All facilities within 2km**

Escale du Perthuis 120 bd Tassigny
☎ 251303896 📠 251277148
In meadowland by the sea and a lovely sandy beach. Site only offers mobile homes to let.
➔ *On D46 about 4.5 km in the direction of L'Aiguillon.*
Open: 15 Apr-15 Sep **Site:** 6HEC ∴ ⚶ ♣ 🚐 **Facilities:** ↑ 🏖 🏕 🏫 **Services:** 🍽 ⊞ lau **Leisure:** ↖ PS

Jard 123 bd de Lattre-de-Tassigny, 85360
☎ 251274379 📠 251274292
e-mail: info@camping-du-jard.fr
A family site on level ground with clearly defined pitches, 700mtrs from the beach, with plenty of recreational facilities.
➔ *Access via D747.*
Open: 23 May-15 Sep **Site:** 6HEC ⚿ ⛄ 🚐 ⚘ **Prices:** pitch 21.50 **Facilities:** ↑ 🏖 ⊙ 🔌 🏕 **Services:** 🍽 ✕ ⊞ lau **Leisure:** ↖ P **Off-site:** ⚘ 🏫

Repos du Pêcheur rte de La Roche-sur-Yon, 85400
☎ 251303694 📠 251303704
Situated on the banks of a canal approx 3km from the sea.
Open: May-Sep **Site:** 6HEC ⚿ ⛺ 🚐 **Facilities:** ↑ 🏖 ⊙ 🔌 ⚘ 🏕 **Services:** 🍽 ✕ ⊞ lau **Leisure:** ↖ PR

Savinière 85360 ☎ 251274270 📠 251274048
Set in a beautiful natural park with good, modern facilities.
➔ *1.5km NW via D105.*
Open: Apr-Sep **Site:** 2.5HEC ∴ ♣ ⛺ **Facilities:** ↑ 🏖 ⊙ 🔌 🏕 **Services:** 🍽 ✕ ⊞ lau **Leisure:** ↖ P **Off-site:** ⚘ ↖S

TROGUES INDRE-ET-LOIRE
Château de la Rolandière 37220
☎ 247585371 📠 247585371
Situated in the parkland surrounding a fine chateau. Ideal for visiting the chateaux of the Loire valley.
➔ *A10 exit 25, follow road for Chinon for 6km*
Open: May-26 Sep **Site:** 4HEC ∷ ♣ 🚐 **Prices:** ⚹6 pitch 8.50 **Facilities:** ↑ 🏖 ⊙ 🔌 🏕 **Services:** 🍽 ⊞ lau **Leisure:** ↖ P **Off-site:** ↖R

TURBALLE, LA LOIRE-ATLANTIQUE
Parc Ste-Brigitte Domaine de Bréhet, 44420
☎ 240248891 📠 240156572
e-mail: saintebrigitte@wanadoo.fr
website: www.campingsaintebrigitte.com
Site in grounds of old Château. Parkland divided into pitches and surrounded by hedges.
➔ *E of village on D99 Guérande road.*
Open: Apr-Sep **Site:** 6HEC ∷ ⚿ ♣ **Prices:** ⚹5.25 🚐9.80 🚐5.50-11 **Facilities:** ↑ 🏖 ⊙ 🔌 ⚘ 🏕 **Services:** 🍽 ✕ ⊞ lau **Leisure:** ↖ P

VALENÇAY INDRE
CM Chènes rte de Loches, 36600
☎ 254000392 📠 254000392
A quiet site on level ground with well defined pitches.
➔ *1km W on D960*
Open: 27 Apr-29 Sep **Site:** 5HEC ∷ ⚿ **Facilities:** ↑ ⊙ 🔌 🏕 **Services:** ⊞ lau **Leisure:** ↖ LP **Off-site:** 🏖 🍽 ✕ ⚘ 🏫 ↖R

VARENNES-SUR-LOIRE MAINE-ET-LOIRE
Étang de la Brèche 5 Impasse de la Brèche, 49730
☎ 241512292 📠 241512724
e-mail: etang.breche@wanadoo.fr
website: www.etang-breche.com
Relaxing site in the heart of the Loire Valley, ideal base for visiting sites of historical interest.
➔ *4.5km NW via N152.*
Open: 15 May-15 Sep **Site:** 12HEC ∷ ♣ **Prices:** ⚹4-6 🚐4 pitch 16.50-27 (incl 2 persons) **Facilities:** ↑ 🏖 ⊙ 🔌 ⚘ 🏫 🏕 **Services:** 🍽 ✕ ⊞ lau **Leisure:** ↖ P

VEILLON, LE VENDÉE
St-Hubert av de la Plage, Bourgenay Le Veillon, 85440
☎ 251222230 📠 251222230
e-mail: campingsthubert@free.fr
website: www.campingsainthubert.com
In a wooded location with well defined pitches, 300mtrs from the sea.
➔ *From Talmont-St-Hilaire head towards Bourgenay and Veillon.*
Open: Apr-Sep **Site:** 1HEC ∷ ♣ ⛺ **Facilities:** ↑ ⊙ 🔌 ⚘ 🏫 🏕 **Services:** 🍽 ⊞ lau **Off-site:** 🏖 ✕ ↖LPS

VELLES INDRE
Grands Pins Les Maisons Neuves, 36330
☎ 254366193 📠 254361009
e-mail: contact@les-grands-pins.fr
website: www.les-grands-pins.fr
The site has individual pitches and has easy access to the countryside. Swimming pool available July-August only.
➔ *7km S of Châteauroux on N20.*
Open: All year **Site:** 5HEC ∷ ∴ ♣ **Prices:** ⚹4 pitch 4 **Facilities:** ↑ ⊙ 🔌 🏕 **Services:** 🍽 ✕ lau **Leisure:** ↖ P

VENDÔME LOIR-ET-CHER	**AUDIERNE** FINISTÈRE

Grand Prés r G-Martel, 41100 ☎ 254770027 ▤ 254834358
e-mail: camping.vendome@free.fr
Site lies on a meadow, next to a sports ground.
➲ *E of town on right bank of Loire.*
Open: 28 May-Aug Site: 2.5HEC ⛺ ⌗ ⊞ Prices: ⚑2.02
⚑1.25 pitch 7 (incl 2 persons) Facilities: ⓝ ⊙ ⬛ ⚐
Services: ⊞ lau Leisure: ⸙ PR Off-site: ⬛ ⾙ ✕ ⊘ ⽱

VINEUIL LOIR-ET-CHER

Châteaux-Lac de Loire 41350
☎ 254788205 ▤ 254786203
Level site on left bank of River Loire with modern buildings.
Boating. Bathing not recommended.
➲ *From Blois drive towards St-Dye. After modern bridge
continue towards 'Lac de Loire' for 1.5km.*
Open: June-15 Sept Site: 30HEC ⛺ ⌗ Prices: ⚑1.50 pitch
7-11 (incl 2 persons) Facilities: ⓝ ⊙ ⬛ ⚐ Services: ⊞ lau
Leisure: ⸙ P

BRITTANY/NORMANDY

ALENÇON ORNE

CM de Guéramé 65 r de Guéramé, 61000 ☎ 233263495
Situated in open country near a stream, 500mtrs from town
centre.
➲ *Access via the Boulevard Périphérique in the SW part of
town.*
Open: All year Site: 1.5HEC ⛺ ⚐ Facilities: ⓝ ⊙ ⬛ ⚐
Services: ⊞ lau Leisure: ⸙ R Off-site: ⬛ ⾙ ✕ ⊘ ⸙P

Jacques Fould av H-Chanteloup, 61000 ☎ 233292329
➲ *On N12.*
Open: All year Site: 1HEC ⛺ ⚐ Facilities: ⓝ ⊙ ⬛ ⚐
Services: ⊞ lau Off-site: ⬛ ⾙ ✕ ⊘ ⸙PR

ALLINEUC CÔTES-D'ARMOR

Lac de Bosméléac Bosméléac, 22460 ☎ 296288788
Wooded site situated by the sides of a lake with a beach.
➲ *Off RN 12 Brest-Paris road, exit for Loudéac.*
Open: 14 Jun-15 Sep Site: 1.2HEC ⛺ ⦂⦂⦂ ⌗ ⊞
Prices: ⚑2.30 ⚑2.80 ⚑2.80 pitch 2.80 Facilities: ⓝ ⊙ ⬛ ⚐
Services: ⾙ ✕ ⊞ lau Leisure: ⸙ L Off-site: ⸙R

ARRADON MORBIHAN

Penboch 9 chemin de Penboch, 56610
☎ 297447129 ▤ 297447910
e-mail: camping.penboch@wanadoo.fr
website: www.camping-penboch.fr
An exceptionally well appointed site in a pleasant wooded
location 200mtrs from the beaches of the Gulf of Morbihan.
➲ *Signposted from N165.*
Open: 3 Apr-25 Sep Site: 4HEC ⛺ ⌗ ⊞ ⚑ Prices: ⚑3-4.60
pitch 3.95-18.20 (incl 2 persons) Facilities: ⓝ ⬛ ⊙ ⬛ ⊘ ⚐
Services: ⾙ ✕ ⊞ lau Leisure: ⸙ PS Off-site: ⬛ ⸙S

ARZANO FINISTÈRE

⬛Ty Nadan rte d'Arzano, 29310
☎ 298717547 ▤ 298717731
e-mail: infos@camping-ty-nadan.fr
website: www.camping-ty-nadan.fr
A quiet riverside site in attractive parkland in the Ellé valley.
➲ *3km W. Leave N165 at Quimperlé exit and drive towards
Arzano.*
Open: 15 May-16 Sep Site: 12HEC ⛺ ⌗ ⊞ ⚑ ⚑
Prices: ⚑6.04-7.10 pitch 13 Facilities: ⓝ ⬛ ⊙ ⬛ ⊘ ⚐
Services: ⾙ ✕ ⊞ lau Leisure: ⸙ PR

Loquéran BP 55, 29770 ☎ 298749506 ▤ 298749114
e-mail: campgite.loqueran@free.fr
A terraced woodland site in calm and peaceful surroundings,
a short distance from the sea.
Open: May-Sep Site: 1HEC ⛺ ⌗ ⊞ ⚑ Prices: ⚑3 ⚑1.50
pitch 3 Facilities: ⓝ ⊙ ⬛ ⚐ Services: ⊞ lau Off-site: ⬛ ⾙
✕ ⸙S

AVRANCHES MANCHE

AT GENÊTS (10KM W ON D911)

Coques d'Or 14 rte du Bec d'Andaine, 50530
☎ 233708257 ▤ 233708683
A well equipped site 1km from the sea.
Open: Apr-Sep Site: 5HEC ⛺ ⌗ ⚑ Facilities: ⓝ ⊙ ⬛ ⚐ ⊞ ⚐
Services: ⾙ ⊞ lau Leisure: ⸙ P Off-site: ⬛ ✕ ⊘

BADEN MORBIHAN

Mané Guernehué 56870 ☎ 297570206 ▤ 297571543
e-mail: mane-guernehue@wanadoo.fr
website: mane-guernehue.com
In a pleasant situation at the head of the Gulf of Morbihan
with good recreational facilities.
➲ *1km SW via Mériadec road.*
Open: 3 Apr-Sep Site: 8HEC ⛺ ⌗ ⊞ ⚑ Prices: ⚑3.10-5.80
pitch 10.50-16 Facilities: ⓝ ⬛ ⊙ ⬛ ⊞ ⚐ Services: ⾙ ✕ ⊞ lau
Leisure: ⸙ P Off-site: ⊘ ⽱ ⸙S

BAYEUX CALVADOS

CM Calvados bd d'Eindhoven, 14400
☎ 231920843 ▤ 231920843
Very clean and tidy site with tarmac drive and hardstanding
for caravans. Adjoins football field.
➲ *N side of town on Boulevard Circulaire.*
Open: May-Sep Site: 2.9HEC ⛺ ⌗ Prices: ⚑2.97 ⚑3.67
⚑3.67 pitch 3.67 Facilities: ⓝ ⊙ ⬛ ⚐ Services: ⊞ lau
Off-site: ⬛ ⾙ ✕ ⊘ ⽱ ⸙P

BEG-MEIL FINISTÈRE

Kervastard chemin de Kervastard, 29170
☎ 298949152 ▤ 298949983
e-mail: camping.le.kervastard@wanadoo.fr
In a pleasant wooded area close to a fine sandy beach with
plenty of leisure facilities.
➲ *Within the village, 250mtrs from the beach.*
Open: May-Sep Site: 2HEC ⛺ ⌗ ⊞ ⚑ Facilities: ⓝ ⊙ ⬛
⽱ ⚐ Services: ⊞ lau Leisure: ⸙ P Off-site: ⬛ ⾙ ✕ ⊘ ⸙S

Roche Percée 29170 ☎ 298949415 ▤ 298944805
e-mail: info@campingbrittany.com
website: www.campingbrittany.com
Wooded family site with 400mtrs from the Roche Percée beach.
➲ *1km from Beg Meil towards Fouesnant.*
Open: 8 Apr-26 Sep Site: 2HEC ⛺ ⚐ ⊞ Prices: ⚑3-4.50
pitch 8.50-11.50 Facilities: ⓝ ⬛ ⊙ ⬛ ⊘ ⚐ Services: ⾙ ✕ ⊞
lau Leisure: ⸙ P Off-site: ✕ ⊘ ⸙S

BÉNODET FINISTÈRE

Letty 29950 ☎ 298570469 ▤ 298662256
e-mail: reception@campingduletty.com
website: www.campingduletty.com
Site bordering beach, divided into sectors. Good sanitary
installations, ironing rooms and games room. Good beach
for children. Use of car park compulsory after 11pm.
➲ *By the sea 1km SE.*
Open: 15 Jun-6 Sep Site: 10HEC ⛺ ⌗ ⚑ Prices: ⚑5
⚑1.70 pitch 7 Facilities: ⓝ ⬛ ⊙ ⬛ ⊘ ⊞ ⚐ ⚐ Services: ⾙ ✕ ⊞
lau Leisure: ⸙ S

Facilities: ⬛-shop ⓝ-shower ⊙-electric points for razors ⬛-electric points for caravans ⚐-parking by tents permitted
⚐-compulsory separate car park **Services:** ✕-café/restaurant ⾙-bar ⊘-Camping Gaz International ⽱-gas other than Camping
Gaz ⊞-first aid facilities lau-laundry **Leisure:** ⸙-swimming L-Lake P-Pool R-River S-Sea **Off-site:** All facilities within 2km

Pointe St-Gilles r du Poulmic, 29950
☎ 298570537 🖷 298572752
e-mail: information@camping-stgilles.fr
website: www.camping-stgilles.fr
Holiday site south of village, on fields by beach. Divided into several sectors; individual pitches. Well-equipped sanitary blocks.
Open: 19 Apr-20 Sep Site: 7HEC ⏍ ♃ ⊗ Facilities: ⋔ 🝙 ⊙ 🖳 ⌀ ♨ 🏛 Services: ⏍ 🖾 lau Leisure: ⚓ PS Off-site: ✗

Port de Plaisance 7 rte de Quimper, Prad Poullou, 29950
☎ 298570238 🖷 298572525
e-mail: info@camping-benodet.fr
website: www.camping-benodet.fr
A well equipped family site on the outskirts of the town, 500mtrs from the harbour.
➲ NE off D34 at the entrance to the town.
Open: 15 Apr-Sep Site: 10HEC ⏍ ♃ 🏕 ⚓ Prices: ⚹4.30-6 pitch 9.15-12.50 Facilities: ⋔🝙 ⊙ 🖳 ⌀ 🏛 Services: ⏍ ✗ 🖾 lau Leisure: ⚓ P Off-site: ⌀ ⚓RS

Hautes Coutures rte de Ouistréham, 14970
☎ 231447308 🖷 231953080
e-mail: camping-hautes-coutures@wavadoo.fr
Pleasant site with good facilities near the Canal Maritime and within easy reach of the Caen-Portsmouth ferry.
➲ From Caen, driving toward Ouistréham on the dual carriageway, Camping Les Hautes Coutures has its own exit shortly after the Pegasus Bridge exit. It can be clearly seen on the R of the dual carriageway.
Open: Apr-Sep Site: 8HEC ⏍ ♃ 🏕 Prices: ⚹6.50 pitch 7.20 Facilities: ⋔ 🝙 ⊙ 🖳 ⌀ ♨ 🏛 Services: ⏍ ✗ 🖾 lau Leisure: ⚓ PR Off-site: ⚓S

Palmiers Kerviarc'h, 22520 ☎ 296737259 🖷 296737259
website: www.campingpalmiers.com
A well equipped site within the Parc Tropical de Bretagne, just over one kilometre from the town centre.
➲ Access via N12/D786.
Open: 15 Jul-Sep Site: 2HEC ⏍ ♃ 🏕 Prices: pitch 14 (incl 2 persons) pp4 Facilities: ⋔ 🝙 ⊙ 🖳 🏛 Services: ⏍ ✗ 🖾 lau Leisure: ⚓ P Off-site: ✗ ⚓RS

Senéquet 50910 ☎ 233472311
A family site with plenty of recreational facilities.
➲ 2km NW on D651.
Open: Mar-early Dec Site: 13HEC ⏍ ⋯⋯ ☳ ⊗ Facilities: ⋔ 🝙 ⊙ 🖳 🏛 Services: ⏍ ✗ lau Leisure: ⚓ PS Off-site: 🖾

🏠**Brévedent** 14130 ☎ 231647288 🖷 231643341
e-mail: castelcamp.lebrevedent@mageos.com
Situated in the grounds of an 18th century manor house with good facilities.
➲ 3km SW on D51 beside lake.
Open: May-25 Sep Site: 5.5HEC ⏍ ♃ ⊗ Prices: ⚹4.10-5.50 pitch 6-8 Facilities: ⋔ 🝙 ⊙ 🖳 ⌀ 🏛 Services: ⏍ ✗ 🖾 lau Leisure: ⚓ P Off-site: ✗

Domaine du Lac 14130 ☎ 231646200 🖷 231641591
Open: Apr-Oct Site: 4HEC ⏍ ☳ Facilities: ⋔ 🝙 ⊙ 🖳 ⌀ ♨ 🏛 Services: ⏍ ✗ 🖾 lau Leisure: ⚓ LR

CM r des Étangs, 76340 ☎ 235945565 🖷 235940614
In the middle of the local Leisure Park comprising 80 hectares of woodland, lakes and streams.

➲ 300mtrs on N28.
Open: 15 Mar-15 Oct Site: 8HEC ⏍ ♃ Prices: ⚹2.20 🚐1.35 🖳1.80 ⚑1.80 Facilities: ⋔ ⊙ 🖳 🏛 🖭 Services: 🖾 lau Off-site: ⌀ ♨ ⚓R

Village Club le Lieu Bill Le Lieu Bill, 14910
☎ 231879727 🖷 231814715
e-mail: info@villageclub.fr website: www.villageclub.fr
A family site in a convenient location for Le Havre and other ferry ports.
➲ Off D118 Villers-sur-Mer-Pont-l'Évêque
Open: Apr-Sep Site: 7HEC ⏍ ♃ Prices: ⚹5.70-25 🚐1 Facilities: ⋔ ⊙ 🖳 🏛 Services: ⏍ ✗ 🖾 lau Leisure: ⚓ P Off-site: 🝙 ⚓S

Clos Normand 235 rte de Pont-Audemer, 27310
☎ 232563484
In a peaceful location within an apple orchard.
➲ 1km from A13 exit Bourg-Achard.
Open: Apr-Sep Site: 1.5HEC ⏍ ♣ 🖳 Prices: ⚹3.30-3.90 🚐1.50 pitch 2.70-3 Facilities: ⋔ ⊙ 🖳 🏛 Services: ⏍ ✗ 🖾 lau Leisure: ⚓ P Off-site: 🝙 ⌀ ♨

CM Verte Vallée 22160 ☎ 296455850
➲ W via D28 towards Morlaix
Open: 15 Jun-15 Sep Site: 1HEC ⏍ ♃ 🖳 Prices: ⚹2.20 🚐1.10 pitch 1.70 Facilities: ⋔ ⊙ 🖳 🏛 Services: lau Off-site: 🝙 ⏍ ✗ ⌀

Grand Large Lambezen, 29570 ☎ 298279141 🖷 298279372
Situated at the tip of the Armorique Natural Park, facing the sea.
➲ On entering Camaret, at roundabout take right turn (D355), then right again after 2km
Open: 29 Mar-Sep Site: 2.8HEC ⏍ ♃ 🏕 🖳 Prices: ⚹3.80-4.85 pitch 6-11.50 pp2.50-3.10 Facilities: ⋔ 🝙 ⊙ 🖳 ⌀ ♨ 🏛 Services: ⏍ ✗ 🖾 lau Leisure: ⚓ P Off-site: ⚓S

Lambézen 29570 ☎ 298277733 🖷 298273838
e-mail: contact@campingarmorique.com
website: www.campingarmorique.com
Situated beside the sea on the edge of the Armorican Natural Park with a wide variety of recreational facilities.
➲ 2km NE on rte de Roscanvel (D355).
Open: 29 Mar-Sep Site: 2.5HEC ⏍ ♃ 🏕 🖳 Prices: ⚹3.40-4.80 pitch 5.50-9 Facilities: ⋔ 🝙 ⊙ 🖳 ⌀ ♨ 🏛 Services: ⏍ ✗ 🖾 lau Leisure: ⚓ P Off-site: ⚓S

Plage de Trez Rouz 29570 ☎ 298279396 🖷 298278454
e-mail: camping-plage-de-trez-rouz@wanadoo.fr
On level ground 50mtrs from the beach.
➲ 3km from Camaret-sur-Mer via D355 towards Pointe-des-Espagnols.
Open: Etr-Sep Site: 3.1HEC ⏍ ♃ 🖳 Prices: ⚹3.70-4 🚐1.30-1.60 pitch 3-3.60 Facilities: ⋔ ⊙ 🖳 ⌀ 🏛 Services: ⏍ 🖾 lau Off-site: 🝙 ✗ ⚓S

Notre Dame du Verger 35260 ☎ 299897284 🖷 299896011
Terraced site overlooking the sea with direct access to the beach.
➲ 2km from Pointe-du-Grouin on D201.
Open: 29 Mar-28 Sep Site: 2.2HEC ⏍ ♃ Prices: ⚹3-3.50 pitch 12-18 (incl 2 persons) Facilities: ⋔ 🝙 ⊙ 🖳 ⌀ 🏛 Services: ⏍ ✗ 🖾 lau Off-site: ⚓S

Site: 6HEC-Site size ⏍-grass ⋯⋯-sand ◬-stone ☳-little shade ♃-partly shaded ⊗-mainly shaded
🏕-bungalows for hire 🖳-caravans for hire ⚑-tents for hire ⊗-no dogs Prices: ⚹-adult per night 🚐-car per night
pp-per person per night 🖳-caravan per night ⚑-tent per night

CARANTEC FINISTÈRE

Mouettes Grande Grève, 29660 ☎ 298670246 ▤ 298783146
e-mail: camping@lesmouettes.com
website: www.les-mouettes.com
Level site divided by low shrubs and trees.
➔ 1.5km SW on rte de St-Pol-de-Léon, towards the sea.
Open: May-13 Sep Site: 7HEC ⨅ ⌗ ⊞ Å Facilities: ⋔ ⅏
☉ ⬛ ⌀ ⌗ 🄿 Services: ⏻ ⊞ lau Leisure: ⤳ P Off-site: ⤳S

CARENTAN MANCHE

CM le Haut Dick 30 chemin du Grand-Bas Pays, 50500
☎ 233421689 ▤ 233421689
e-mail: lehautdick@aol.com
website: www.camping-municipal.com
A level site in wooded surroundings with well defined
pitches.
➔ Take village road off N13 towards Le Port.
Open: All year Site: 2.5HEC ⨅ ⌗ ⊞ 🄿 Prices: ⚬2.30
⚘1.10 🚐2.90 Å2.90 Facilities: ⋔ ☉ ⬛ 🄿 Services: ⊞ lau
Off-site: ⅏ ⏻ ✕ ⌀ ⛬ ⤳PR

CARNAC MORBIHAN

Bruyères Kerogile, 56340 ☎ 297523057 ▤ 297523057
e-mail: camping.les.bruyeres@wanadoo.fr
Partly wooded site with modern facilities close to the local
beaches.
➔ N of Carnac on C4, 2km from Plouharnel.
Open: Apr-15 Oct Site: 2HEC ⨅ ⌗ ⊞ Prices: ⚬2.75-3.45
pitch 5.35-6.70 Facilities: ⋔ ⅏ ☉ ⬛ ⌀ ⛬ Services: ⊞ lau
Off-site: ⏻ ✕

Étang 67 rte de Kerlann, 56340 ☎ 297521406 ▤ 297522319
In a rural setting with pitches divided by hedges, 2.5km from
the coast.
➔ 2km N at Kerlann on D119.
Open: Apr-15 Oct Site: 2.5HEC ⨅ ⚘ ⊞ 🄿 Prices: ⚬3.10-
4.50 pitch 4.80-6.50 Facilities: ⋔ ⅏ ☉ ⬛ ⌀ ⛬ Services: ⏻ ✕
⊞ lau Leisure: ⤳ P

Grande Métairie rte des Alignements, de Kermario, 56342
☎ 297522401 ▤ 297528358
e-mail: info@lagrandemetairie.com
website: www.lagrandemetairie.com
Holiday site with modern amenities, completely divided into
pitches.
➔ 2.5km NE on D196.
Open: 3 Apr-11 Sep Site: 15HEC ⨅ ⌗ ⊞ 🄿 Prices: ⚬6.50
pitch 14.10-23.50 Facilities: ⋔ ⅏ ☉ ⬛ ⌀ ⛬ Services: ⏻ ✕ ⊞
lau Leisure: ⤳ PS

Moulin de Kermaux 56340 ☎ 297521590 ▤ 297528385
e-mail: moulin-de-kermaux@wanadoo.fr
website: www.camping-moulinkermaux.com
In a quiet location, surrounded by trees and bushes, with
good facilities. Within easy reach of the coast and the local
megaliths.
➔ 2.5km NE.
Open: 3 Apr-15 Sep Site: 3HEC ⨅ ⌗ ⊞ Prices: ⚬4 pitch
13.50 Facilities: ⋔ ⅏ ☉ ⬛ ⌀ ⛬ Services: ⏻ ✕ ⊞ lau Leisure: ⤳
P Off-site: ✕ ⌀ ⤳RS

Moustoir rte du Moustoir, 56340
☎ 297521618 ▤ 297528837
e-mail: info@lemoustoir.com website: www.lemoustoir.com
Well equipped site in a rural setting close to the sea.
➔ 3 km NE of Carnac.
Open: May-10 Sept Site: 5HEC ⨅ ⚘ ⊞ Å Prices: ⚬2.50-4
pitch 7.20-12 Facilities: ⋔ ⅏ ☉ ⬛ ⌀ ⛬ Services: ⏻ ✕ ⊞ lau
Leisure: ⤳ P Off-site: ✕ ⤳R

CAMPING LE HAUT DICK
50500 CARENTAN Tel: 02.33.42.16.89
www.camping-municipal.com
OPEN ALL YEAR
In the heart of "Parc des Marais", near the
historic landing-zones in Normandy, quiet –
shady – marked pitches. Free Hot showers.
Games hall: table tennis, pinball, table tennis for
children, reading material. Curved slide –
French boules – Minigolf.
Nearby: Tennis – swimming pool – Harbour:
canoe – fishing. 500m. Away from centre of
town, with shopping available.

Ombrages 56430 ☎ 297521652
In a wooded location with shaded pitches divided by hedges.
➔ Take rte Carnac to Auray and turn left at SHELL filling
station.
Open: 15 Jun-15 Sep Site: 1HEC ⨅ ⌗ 🄿 Prices: ⚬3.80
pitch 5.20 Facilities: ⋔ ⅏ ☉ ⬛ ⌀ ⛬ Services: ⊞ lau
Off-site: ⤳LS

Rosnual rte d'Auray, 56340 ☎ 297521457
A pleasant site in a wooded rural setting with good
recreational facilities.
➔ 1.5km from village, 2.5km from the sea.
Open: Apr-Sep Site: 4HEC ⨅ ⌗ ⊞ 🄿 ⚙ Facilities: ⋔ ⅏
☉ ⬛ ⌀ ⛬ Services: ⏻ ✕ ⊞ lau Leisure: ⤳ P Off-site: ⌀

Saules rte de Rosnual, 56340 ☎ 297521498 ▤ 297526584
Grassland family site with good facilities site between road
and deciduous woodland, subdivided by hedges and shrubs.
➔ 2.5km N on D119.
Open: Apr-Sep Site: 2.5HEC ⨅ ⌗ ⊞ ⊞ Å Facilities: ⋔ ⅏
☉ ⬛ ⌀ ⛬ Services: ⊞ lau Leisure: ⤳ P Off-site: ⏻ ✕

AT **CARNAC-PLAGE** (1KM S)

Druides 55 chemin de Beaumer, 56340
☎ 297520818 ▤ 297529613
e-mail: camping-les-druides@wanadoo.fr
website: www.camping-le-druides.com
Family site with well defined pitches, 400mtrs from a fine
sandy beach.
➔ SE of town centre. Approach via D781 or D119.
Open: 19 May-10 Sep Site: 2.5HEC ⨅ ⚘ ⊞ Prices: pitch
16.50-27.30 (incl 2 persons) Facilities: ⋔ ☉ ⬛ ⛬ Services: ⊞
lau Leisure: ⤳ P Off-site: ⅏ ⏻ ✕ ⌀ ⛬ ⤳S

Men Dû r de Beaumer, 56340 ☎ 297520423
Peaceful site in a wooded setting close to the beach.
➔ 1km from Carnac Plage via D781 and D186.
Open: Apr-Sep Site: 1.5HEC ⨅ ⚘ ⊞ Facilities: ⋔ ☉ ⬛ ⛬
⛬ Services: ✕ lau Off-site: ⅏ ⏻ ⤳PRS ⊞

Menhirs allée St-Michel, 56340
☎ 297529467 ▤ 297522538
e-mail: campinglesmenhirs@free.fr
website: www.lesmenhirs.com
A family site near the beach and shops with good
recreational facilities and modern sanitary blocks, including
toilets suitable for the disabled.
Open: 30 Apr-12 Sep Site: 6HEC ⨅ ⚘ ⊞ Prices: ⚬3.60-
7.20 pitch 13.50-27 Facilities: ⋔ ⅏ ☉ ⬛ ⛬ Services: ⏻ ✕ ⊞
lau Leisure: ⤳ P Off-site: ✕ ⌀ ⛬ ⤳S

Facilities: ⅏-shop ⋔-shower ☉-electric points for razors ⬛-electric points for caravans 🄿-parking by tents permitted
⬛-compulsory separate car park Services: ✕-café/restaurant ⏻-bar ⌀-Camping Gaz International ⛬-gas other than Camping
Gaz ⊞-first aid facilities lau-laundry Leisure: ⤳-swimming L-Lake P-Pool R-River S-Sea Off-site: All facilities within 2km

CAUREL CÔTES-D'ARMOR

Nautic International rte de Beau Rivage, 22530
☎ 296285794 📠 296260200
e-mail: contact@campingnautic.fr.st
website: www.campingnautic.fr.st
A terraced site in woodland on the edge of Lake Guerlédan
with a variety of recreational facilities.
➲ *N164 in the direction of Beau Rivage.*
Open: 15 May-25 Sep **Site:** 3.6HEC ⸬⸬⸬ ↺ 🏠 **Prices:** ⚥3.30-
4.60 🚗1.60 pitch 5.40-6.90 **Facilities:** ℞ 🏪 ⊙ 🛈 🚰 **Services:** ⊞ lau **Leisure:** ⸮ LP **Off-site:** ⚑ ✗

CHAPELLE-AUX-FILZMÉENS, LA ILLE-ET-VILAINE

Camping du Logis 35190 ☎ 299452545 📠 299453040
e-mail: domainedeslogis@wanadoo.fr
A quiet, pleasant site in the wooded grounds of an 18th
century château.
➲ *NE of town towards Combourg.*
Open: All year **Site:** 20HEC ⸬⸬⸬ ♣ 🏠 **Prices:** ⚥3-4 pitch 10-
14 **Facilities:** ℞ 🏪 ⊙ 🛈 ⚑ 🚰 **Services:** ⚑ ✗ ⊞ lau
Leisure: ⸮ P **Off-site:** ⸮R

CHÂTEAULIN FINISTÈRE

La Pointe Superbe rte St-Coulitz, 29150
☎ 298865153 📠 298865153
In a wooded valley close to the town with good modern
facilities. Pitches divided by hedges. British owners.
➲ *From centre of Châteaulin take D770 S to Quimper for
1km, then left to St-Coulitz. Site 100mtrs on right.*
*SE of Chateaulin. From bridge in town centre follow signs for St
Coulitz/Quimper. After 700mtrs turn left at sign for St Coulitz.
Site signed and is a further 100mtrs on right.*
Open: 15 Mar-Oct **Site:** 2.5HEC ⸬⸬⸬ ↺ **Prices:** 🚐10-12
Facilities: ℞ ⊙ 🛈 🚰 **Off-site:** 🏪 ⚑ ✗ ⚑ 🚰 ⸮PRS ⊞

CLOÎTRE-ST-THEGONNEC, LE FINISTÈRE

Bruyères 29410 ☎ 298797176
A small, secluded site in a picturesque setting within the
Amorique Nature Park.
➲ *12km S of Morlaix via D769.*
Open: Jul-Aug **Site:** 2.5HEC ⸬⸬⸬ ↺ **Prices:** ⚥3 🚗2 pitch 3
pp3 **Facilities:** ℞ ⚑ 🚰 **Services:** ⊞ lau **Off-site:** 🏪 ⚑ ✗ 🚰

COMBOURG ILLE-ET-VILAINE

Bois Coudrais Cuguen, 35270 ☎ 299732745 📠 299731308
e-mail: info@vacancebretagne.com
website: www.vacancebretagne.com
A small, level site with fine views.
➲ *Access via D83 (Combourg-Mont-St-Michel).*
Open: Apr-30 Oct **Site:** 1HEC ⸬⸬⸬ 🌤 🏠 **Prices:** ⚥1.50
pitch 6.50 **Facilities:** ℞ ⊙ 🛈 🚰 **Services:** ⚑ ✗ ⊞ lau
Off-site: 🏪

CONCARNEAU FINISTÈRE

Prés Verts Kernous Plage, 29900 ☎ 298970974 📠 298973206
e-mail: pres-verts-camp@wanadoo.fr website: pres-verts.com
A landscaped site with good facilities overlooking
Concarneau Bay.
➲ *1.2km NW.*
Open: May-22 Sep **Site:** 2.5HEC ⸬⸬⸬ ↺ 🏠 **Prices:** ⚥4.76-
5.95 pitch 16.48-20.60 (incl 2 persons) **Facilities:** ℞ 🏪 ⊙ 🛈 🚰 🄿 **Services:** lau **Leisure:** ⸮ PS **Off-site:** 🏪 ⚑ ✗ ⚑ 🚰 ⸮S

COUTERNE ORNE

Clos Normand rte de Bagnoles, 61410 ☎ 233379243
A pleasant site in rural surroundings in a sheltered position
close to the thermal spa of Bagnoles-de-l'Orne.

➲ *Approach D916.*
Open: May-Sep **Site:** 1.3HEC ⸬⸬⸬ ♣ 🚐 **Prices:** ⚥2.65 pitch 7
(incl 2 persons) **Facilities:** ℞ ⊙ 🛈 🚰 **Services:** ⚑ ✗ lau
Off-site: ⚑ 🚰 ⸮LPR

CRACH MORBIHAN

Fort Espagnol rte de Fort Espagnol, 56950
☎ 297551488 📠 297300104
e-mail: fort-espagnol@wanadoo.fr
website: www.fort-espagnol.com
In a secluded, wooded location, this is a family site with a
wide variety of recreational facilities.
➲ *Due E of Crac'h towards the coast.*
Open: 19 Apr **Site:** 4.5HEC ⸬⸬⸬ ↺ 🏠 ▲ **Prices:** ⚥3.20-4.40
pitch 6-8.40 **Facilities:** ℞ 🏪 ⊙ 🛈 ⚑ 🚰 🚰 **Services:** ⚑ ✗ ⊞ lau
Leisure: ⸮ P **Off-site:** ⸮R

CRIEL-SUR-MER SEINE-MARITIME

Mouettes r de la Plage, 76910 ☎ 235867073 📠 235867073
website: camping-lesmouettes.com
Small grassy site overlooking the sea.
Open: Apr-2 Nov **Site:** 2HEC ⸬⸬⸬ 🌤 🏠 **Prices:** ⚥7.50-8.50
pitch 7.50-8.50 **Facilities:** ℞ 🏪 ⊙ 🛈 ⚑ 🚰 **Services:** ⚑ lau
Off-site: ✗ ⸮RS ⊞

CROZON FINISTÈRE

Pen ar Menez bd de Pralognan, 29160 ☎ 298271236
On fringe of a pinewood. Water sport facilities 5km away.
Cycles for hire.
Open: All year **Site:** 2.6HEC ⸬⸬⸬ ↺ 🏠 🚐 **Facilities:** ℞ ⊙ 🛈
🚰 **Services:** ⚑ ✗ lau **Off-site:** 🏪 ✗ ⚑ 🚰 ⸮S ⊞

Plage de Goulien Kernaveèno, 29160
☎ 298271710 📠 298272195
e-mail: camping.goulien@presquile-crozon.com
website: www.presquile-crozon.com
Grassy site in wooded surroundings 150mtrs from the sea.
➲ *5km W on D308.*
Open: 10 Jun-15 Sep **Site:** 2.5HEC ⸬⸬⸬ ↺ 🏠 🚐
Prices: ⚥3.80 🚗2.05 🚐3.95 ▲3.95 pitch 3.95 **Facilities:** ℞ 🏪
⊙ 🛈 🚰 🚰 **Services:** ⊞ lau **Off-site:** ⚑ ✗ ⸮S

DEAUVILLE CALVADOS

AT ST-ARNOULT (3KM S)

Vallée route de Beaumont, 14800
☎ 231885817 📠 231881157
e-mail: loreca@free.fr
In a pleasant wooded setting with plenty of recreational facilities.
➲ *1km S via D27 and D275*
Open: Apr-3 Nov **Site:** 19HEC ⸬⸬⸬ 🌤 🏠 **Facilities:** ℞ ⊙ 🛈
🚰 🚰 **Services:** ⚑ ✗ lau **Leisure:** ⸮ LPR **Off-site:** 🏪 ⸮S ⊞

AT TOUQUES (3KM SE)

Haras chemin du Calvaire, 14800
☎ 231884484 📠 231889708
e-mail: les.haras@wanadoo.fr
website: www.region-normandie.com/lesharas
A partially residential site in pleasant surroundings. Ideal for
overnight stops, but reservations recommended in July and
August.
➲ *N on D62, to Honfleur.*
Open: Feb-Nov **Site:** 4HEC ⸬⸬⸬ ↺ 🏠 🚐 **Facilities:** ℞ ⊙ 🛈
⚑ 🚰 🚰 **Services:** ⚑ ✗ ⊞ lau **Off-site:** 🏪 ⸮P

DÉVILLE-LÈS-ROUEN SEINE-MARITIME

CM r Jules-Ferry, 76250 ☎ 235740759 📠 235763521
Open: All year **Site:** 1.5HEC ⸬⸬⸬ 🌤 🏠 **Prices:** ⚥4 🚗1.45
🚐2.80 ▲1.55 **Facilities:** ℞ ⊙ 🛈 🚰 **Services:** ⊞ lau
Off-site: 🏪 ⚑ ✗ ⸮PR

Site: 6HEC-Site size ⸬⸬⸬-grass ⸬⸬⸬-sand ⚭-stone 🌤-little shade ↺-partly shaded ♣-mainly shaded
🏠-bungalows for hire 🚐-caravans for hire ▲-tents for hire 🚫-no dogs **Prices:** ⚥-adult per night 🚗-car per night
pp-per person per night 🚐-caravan per night ▲-tent per night

DIEPPE SEINE-MARITIME

AT HAUTOT-SUR-MER (6KM SW)

Source Petit Appeville, 76550 ☎ 235842704 ▤ 235842704
Open: 15 Mar-15 Oct Site: 2.5HEC ⊞ ⊞ ④ ⊞ Prices: ♠4.40
♠1 ⊞7 ▲5 Facilities: ℕ ⊙ ⊞ ⊞ Services: ⊉ ✕ ⊞ lau
Leisure: ⊰ PR Off-site: ⊾ ∅ ⊰S

DINAN CÔTES-D'ARMOR

AT TADEN (3.5KM NE)

CM Hallerais 22100 ☎ 296391593
Beautiful clean site with level pitches on gentle slope near a
country estate. Asphalt drives. Good sanitary installations.
Shop, bar and restaurant are only open in July and August.
➲ *SW of Taden off D12.*
Open: 15 Mar-Oct Site: 6HEC ⊞ ♣ ⊞ ⊞ Facilities: ℕ ⊾
⊙ ⊞ ∅ ⊞ Services: ⊉ ✕ lau Leisure: ⊰ PR Off-site: ⊞

DINARD ILLE-ET-VILAINE

See also St-Lunaire

Mauny 35800 ☎ 299469473
A family site in pleasant wooded surroundings with a variety
of recreational facilities.
➲ *Off St-Briac road (CD603).*
Open: 3 Mar-25 Sep Site: 5HEC ⊞ ♣ ⊞ Facilities: ℕ ⊾ ⊙
⊞ ∅ ⊞ Services: ⊉ ✕ ⊞ lau Leisure: ⊰ P Off-site: ⊰S

DOL-DE-BRETAGNE ILLE-ET-VILAINE

⊞Château des Ormes 35120 ☎ 299735300 ▤ 299735355
e-mail: info@lesormes.com website: www.lesormes.com
Site in grounds of château, within a large leisure complex
with excellent facilities.
➲ *7km S on N795 Rennes road.*
Open: 22 May-12 Sep Site: 160HEC ⊞ ♣ ⊞ Prices: ♠6.50-
7.20 ⊞9-21 ▲19-21 Facilities: ℕ ⊾ ⊙ ⊞ ∅ ⊞ Services: ⊉
✕ ⊞ lau Leisure: ⊰ LP

CM Les Tendieres r des Tendieres, 35120 ☎ 299481468
On level meadow.
➲ *SW on rte de Dinan 400mtrs from town centre.*
Open: 15 May-15 Sep Site: 1.7HEC ⊞ ④ Facilities: ℕ ⊙
⊞ ⊞ Services: lau Leisure: ⊰ R Off-site: ⊾ ⊉ ✕ ⊰P

AT BAGUER-PICAN (4KM E ON N176)

Camping du Vieux Chêne 35120
☎ 299480955 ▤ 299481337
e-mail: vieux.chene@wanadoo.fr
website: www.camping-vieuxchene.fr
Spacious site in pleasant lakeside situation. Farm produce
available.
➲ *5km E of Dol-de-Bretagne on D576.*
Open: 3 Apr-26 Sep Site: 12HEC ⊞ ④ ⊞ Prices: ♠5 pitch
5.50-14 Facilities: ℕ ⊾ ⊙ ⊞ ∅ ⊞ Services: ⊉ ✕ ⊞ lau
Leisure: ⊰ P

DOUARNENEZ FINISTÈRE

Kerleyou Tréboul, 29100 ☎ 298741303 ▤ 298740961
e-mail: camp-kerleyou@infonie.fr
website: www.camping-kerleyou.com
Family site in wooded surroundings near the beach. Separate
car park for arrivals after 23.00hrs.
➲ *1km W on r de Préfet-Collignon towards the sea.*
Open: 5 Apr-27 Sep Site: 3HEC ⊞ ④ ⊞ ⊞ Prices: ♠3.10-
3.70 ♠0.95-1.70 pitch 3.25-6.20 Facilities: ℕ ⊾ ⊙ ⊞ ⊞
Services: ⊉ ✕ ⊞ lau Leisure: ⊰ P Off-site: ✕ ∅ ⊰S

AT POULLAN-SUR-MER (5KM W ON D765)

Pil Koad 29100 ☎ 298742639 ▤ 298745597
e-mail: camping.pil.koad@wanadoo.fr
website: www.pil-koad.com
In a natural wooded setting with a variety of recreational
facilities.
➲ *E via D7 towards Douarnenez.*
Open: Apr-Sep Site: 5.5HEC ⊞ ④ ⊞ ▲ Prices: ♠3-4.50
♠6.20-13 pitch 6.20-13 Facilities: ℕ ⊾ ⊙ ⊞ ∅ ⊞ ⊞
Services: ⊉ ✕ ⊞ lau Leisure: ⊰ P Off-site: ✕ ⊰S

ERDEVEN MORBIHAN

Sept Saints 56410 ☎ 297555265 ▤ 297552267
e-mail: campingseptsaints@wanadoo.fr
website: www.sept-saints.com
In wooded surroundings with good recreational facilities.
➲ *2km NW via D781 rte de Plouhinec.*
Open: 15 May-15 Sep Site: 5HEC ⊞ ♣ ⊞ Prices: ♠4-6
pitch 10-17 Facilities: ℕ ⊾ ⊙ ⊞ ∅ ⊞ Services: ⊉ ⊞ lau
Leisure: ⊰ P Off-site: ✕ ⊰LRS

ERQUY CÔTES-D'ARMOR

Hautes Greés 123 r St-Michel, 22430
☎ 296723478 ▤ 296723015
e-mail: hautesgrees@wanadoo.fr
website: www.camping-hautes-grees.com
Good family site, 2km from the town centre and 400mtrs
from the sea.
➲ *500mtrs from the sea.*
Open: Apr-Sep Site: 3HEC ⊞ ④ ⊞ Facilities: ℕ ⊾ ⊙ ⊞ ∅
⊞ ⊞ Services: ⊞ lau Off-site: ⊉ ✕ ∅ ⊞ ⊰S

Roches Caroual Village, 22430 ☎ 296723290 ▤ 296635784
e-mail: camping.les.roches@wanadoo.fr
website: www.camping-les-roches.com
In a rural setting with well marked pitches, 800mtrs from the
beach.
➲ *3km SW.*
Open: Apr-15 Sep Site: 3.1HEC ⊞ ④ ⊞ Prices: ♠3.06-3.40
♠1.98-2.40 pitch 3.06-3.40 Facilities: ℕ ⊾ ⊙ ⊞ ⊞ ⊞
Services: ⊞ lau Off-site: ⊰S

St-Pabu 22430 ☎ 296722465 ▤ 296728717
On big open meadow with several terraces in beautiful,
isolated situation by sea. Divided into pitches.
➲ *W on D786 then follow signposts from La Coutre.*
Open: Apr-10 Oct Site: 5.5HEC ⊞ ④ ⊞ Prices: ♠4.20
pitch 8 Facilities: ℕ ⊾ ⊙ ⊞ ∅ ⊞ Services: ⊉ ✕ ⊞ lau
Leisure: ⊰ S

Vieux Moulin r des Moulins, 22430
☎ 296723423 ▤ 296723663
e-mail: camp.vieux.moulin@wanadoo.fr
website: www.campingvieuxmoulin.com
Clean tidy site divided into pitches and surrounded by a pine
forest. Suitable for children.
➲ *On D783.*
Open: May-11 Sep Site: 6.5HEC ⊞ ④ ⊞ ▲ Prices: ♠4.20-
5.30 ♠4-4.50 pitch 9-12 Facilities: ℕ ⊾ ⊙ ⊞ ∅ ⊞
Services: ⊉ ✕ ⊞ lau Leisure: ⊰ P Off-site: ⊞ ⊰S

ÉTABLES-SUR-MER CÔTES-D'ARMOR

Abri Côtier 22680 ☎ 296706157 ▤ 296706523
e-mail: camping.abricotier@wanadoo.fr
website: perso.wanadoo.fr/abricotier
A pleasant family site in a wooded location close to the sea.
➲ *1km N of town centre on D786.*
Open: 15 Apr-9 Sep Site: 2HEC ⊞ ④ ⊞ Prices: ♠4-4.50
pitch 6-7 Facilities: ℕ ⊾ ⊙ ⊞ ∅ ⊞ Services: ⊉ ✕ lau
Leisure: ⊰ P Off-site: ✕ ⊰S

Facilities: ⊾-shop ℕ-shower ⊙-electric points for razors ⊞-electric points for caravans ⊞-parking by tents permitted
⊞-compulsory separate car park Services: ✕-café/restaurant ⊉-bar ∅-Camping Gaz International ⊞-gas other than Camping
Gaz ⊞-first aid facilities lau-laundry Leisure: ⊰-swimming L-Lake P-Pool R-River S-Sea Off-site: All facilities within 2km

NORMANDY BETWEEN CABOURG AND DEAUVILLE, 900 M. FROM THE BEACH

CAMPING - CARAVANING

LA VALLÉE

Camping Qualité France

FRANCE

Grocery · Bar · Children's playground · Heated swimming pool · Paddling pool · Organized leisure · Bikes and cross bikes for hire · Ponies · Mobile homes to let · Golf course at 1 km. 10% discount.

88, rue de la Vallée – 14510 HOULGATE
Tel: 00 33 (0)2 31 24 40 69 Fax: 00 33 (0)2 31 24 42 42
www.campinglavallee.com · camping.vallee@wanadoo.fr

ETRÉHAM CALVADOS

Reine Mathilde 14400 ☎ 231217655 ▤ 231221833
e-mail: camping.riene_mathilde@wanadoo.fr
website: campingreinemathilde.com
In a quiet rural setting 4km from the sea.
⮑ 1km W via D123
Open: Apr-Sep Site: 6.5HEC ⬚⬚⬚ ⌖ ⊞ Prices: ⭡5.08-5.67
pitch 4.76-5.35 Facilities: ⬚ ⊙ ⬚ ∅ ⚊ ☎ Services: ⬚ ✗ ⊞
lau Leisure: ⭢ P

FAOUËT, LE MORBIHAN

Beg Er Roch rte de Lorient, 56320
☎ 297231511 ▤ 297231166
In pleasant surroundings on the banks of a river. A popular
site with modern sanitary facilities and a wealth of
opportunities for all kinds of sport.
Open: 10 Mar-Sep Site: 3.5HEC ⬚⬚⬚ ⌖ ⊞ Å Prices: ⭡2.55-
3.55 ⭠1-2.05 pitch 2.05-3.10 Facilities: ⬚ ⊙ ⬚ ☎
Services: lau Leisure: ⭢ R Off-site: ⬚ ⬚ ✗ ∅ ⚊ ⊞

FORËT-FOUESNANT, LA FINISTÈRE

Kérantérec 29940 ☎ 298569811 ▤ 298568173
e-mail: info@camping-keranterec.com
website: www.camping-keranterec.com
Well-kept terraced site, divided into sections by hedges and
extending to the sea.
⮑ 3km SE.
Open: 10 Apr-19 Sep Site: 6.5HEC ⬚⬚⬚ ⌖ ⊞ ⬚
Prices: ⭡5.25-7 pitch 6.75-9 Facilities: ⬚ ⊙ ⬚ ∅ ⚊ ☎ ▣
Services: ⬚ ✗ ⊞ lau Leisure: ⭢ PS Off-site: ⬚ ✗

Manoir de Pen Ar Steir 29940 ☎ 298569775 ▤ 298568049
e-mail: info@camping-penarsteir.com
website: www.camping-penarsteir.com
Well-tended site close to Port La Forêt, a major yachting arena.

⮑ *NE off D44.*
Open: Feb-15 Nov Site: 3HEC ⬚⬚⬚ ⌖ ⊞ Prices: ⭡3.76-4.70
pitch 6.08-7.60 Facilities: ⬚ ⊙ ⬚ ⚊ ☎ ▣ Services: ⊞ lau
Off-site: ⬚ ⬚ ✗ ∅ ⭢PS

Plage Plage de Kerleven, rte de Port la Forêt, 29940
☎ 298569625 ▤ 298369625
e-mail: laplage.camp@wanadoo.fr
website: www.camping-en-finistere.com
⮑ *2.5km SE on D783.*
Open: May-Dec Site: 1HEC ⬚⬚⬚ ⁚⁚⁚ ⬚ Facilities: ⬚ ⊙ ⬚
☎ Services: lau Off-site: ⬚ ✗ ∅ ⚊ ⭢S ⊞

Pontérec Pontérec, 29940 ☎ 298569833 ▤ 298569347
A modern site with well defined pitches separated by hedges,
2.5km from the beach.
⮑ *0.5km on D44 towards Bénodet.*
Open: Apr-Sep Site: 3HEC ⬚⬚⬚ ⌖ ⊞ ⬚ Prices: ⭡3.10
⭠1.55 pitch 3.70 Facilities: ⬚ ⊙ ⬚ ☎ Services: ⊞ lau
Off-site: ⬚ ⬚ ✗ ∅

St-Laurent Kerleven, 29940 ☎ 298569765 ▤ 298569251
e-mail: info@camping-du-saint-laurent.fr
website: www.camping-du-saint-laurent.fr
On rocky coast. Divided into pitches.
⮑ *3.5km SE of village.*
Open: 3 May-13 Sep Site: 5.2HEC ⬚⬚⬚ ⬘ ⊞ Facilities: ⬚ ⬚
⊙ ⬚ ☎ Services: ⬚ ✗ lau Leisure: ⭢ PS Off-site: ∅ ⚊ ⊞

FOUESNANT FINISTÈRE

Atlantique rte de Mousterlin, 29170
☎ 298561444 ▤ 298561867
e-mail: information@camping-atlantique.fr
website: www.camping-atlantique.fr
Modern site with plenty of amenities 400mtrs from the beach.
⮑ *4.5km S on the road to Mousterlin.*
Open: ⬚⬚⬚-15 Sep Site: 9HEC ⬚⬚⬚ ⌖ ⊞ ⬚ ⬚ Facilities: ⬚ ⬚
⊙ ⬚ ∅ ⚊ ☎ Services: ⬚ ✗ ⊞ lau Leisure: ⭢ P Off-site: ✗ ⭢S

Grand Large Pointe de Mousterlin, 29170
☎ 298560406 ▤ 298565826
e-mail: info@campingsbretagnesud.com
website: www.campingsbretagnesud.com
A family site in a wooded setting with direct access to the
beach. Plenty of modern facilities.
⮑ *S of Fouesnant via D145.*
Open: 15 May-8 Sep Site: 6HEC ⬚⬚⬚ ⌖ ⊞ Å Prices: ⭡4-6
⭠2 pitch 15-36 (incl 2 persons) Facilities: ⬚ ⬚ ⊙ ⬚ ∅ ☎
Services: ⬚ ✗ ⊞ lau Leisure: ⭢ PR Off-site: ⭢S

Piscine 51 Hent Kerleya, 29170 ☎ 298565606 ▤ 298565764
e-mail: contact@campingdelapiscine.com
website: www.campingdelapiscine.com
In a beautiful location 1.5km from the beach.
⮑ *4km NW towards Kerleya.*
Open: 15 May-15 Sep Site: 5HEC ⬚⬚⬚ ⌖ ⊞ Prices: ⭡3.50-5
pitch 7-10 Facilities: ⬚ ⬚ ⊙ ⬚ ∅ ☎ Services: ⊞ lau
Leisure: ⭢ PS

FOUGÈRES ILLE-ET-VILAINE

CM Paron rte de la Chapelle Janson, 35300 ☎ 299994081
A well managed site suitable for overnight stays.
⮑ *1.5km E via D17*
Open: Mar-Oct Site: 2.5HEC ⬚⬚⬚ ⬘ Facilities: ⬚ ⊙ ⬚ ☎
Services: lau Off-site: ⬚ ⬚ ✗ ∅ ⭢PR ⊞

GUILLIGOMARC'H FINISTÈRE

Bois des Ecureuils 29300 ☎ 298717098 ▤ 298717098
e-mail: price.reed@wanadoo.fr website: bois-des-ecureuils.fr
Tranquil four acre wooded site set among oak, chestnut and
beech trees. An ideal base for walking, cycling, horse-riding
and fishing.

Site: 6HEC-Site size ⬚⬚⬚-grass ⁚⁚⁚-sand ⬥-stone ⬚-little shade ⌖-partly shaded ⬘-mainly shaded
⊞-bungalows for hire ⬚-caravans for hire Å-tents for hire ⬚-no dogs **Prices:** ⭡-adult per night ⭠-car per night
pp-per person per night ⬚-caravan per night Å-tent per night

⮡ *2km W from D769 (Roscoff to Lorient). N of Plouay, turn W to Guilligomarc'h*
Open: 15 May-15 Sep Site: 2.5HEC ⬛ ♣ Prices: ⋔2.50 ⬛4.10 pitch 4.10 Facilities: ⋔ ⧉ ⊙ ⬛ ∅ ⧈ Services: ⊞ lau

GUILVINEC FINISTÈRE

Plage rte de Penmarc'h, 29730 ☎ 298586190 ▤ 298588906
e-mail: info@campingsbretagnesud.com
website: www.campingbretagnesud.com
On level meadow. Divided into pitches. Flat beach suitable for children.
⮡ *2km W of village on the Corniche towards Penmarc'h.*
Open: 15 May-8 Sept Site: 14HEC ⦂⦂⦂ ⊕ ⬛ ▲ Prices: ⋔4-6 ⬛2 pitch 15-36 Facilities: ⋔ ⧉ ⊙ ⬛ ∅ ⧈ ⧈ Services: ▾ ✗ ⊞ lau Leisure: ⭢ PS

HAYE-DU-PUITS, LA MANCHE

Étang des Haizes 50250 ☎ 233460116 ▤ 233472380
e-mail: etang.des.haizes@wanadoo.fr
website: www.etang-des-haizes.com
A well equipped family site bordering a lake, shaded by apple trees.
⮡ *Access via D903 from Carentan.*
Open: 10 Apr-15 Oct Site: 5HEC ⬛ ⊕ ⬛ ⬛ Prices: ⋔2-4 pitch 15-28 (incl 2 persons) Facilities: ⋔ ⊙ ⬛ ⧈ Services: ▾ ✗ ⊞ lau Leisure: ⭢ LP Off-site: ⧉ ✗

HOULGATE CALVADOS

Vallée 88 r de la Vallée, 14510 ☎ 231244069 ▤ 231244242
e-mail: camping.lavallee@wanadoo.fr
website: campinglavallee.com
Site with good recreational facilities, 900mtrs from the beach.
⮡ *1km S.*
Open: Apr-Sep Site: 11HEC ⬛ ⊕ ⬛ Facilities: ⋔ ⧉ ⊙ ∅ ⧈ ⧈ Services: ▾ ✗ ⊞ lau Leisure: ⭢ P Off-site: ⭢S

IFFENDIC ILLE-ET-VILAINE

Domaine de Trémelin 35750 ☎ 299097379 ▤ 299097069
A lakeside site in beautiful wooded surroundings with good sports and entertainment facilities.
⮡ *S of town towards Plélan-le-Grand.*
Open: Apr-Sep Site: 2HEC ⬛ ⊕ ⬛ Facilities: ⋔ ⊙ ⬛ ⧈ Services: ▾ ✗ ⊞ Leisure: ⭢ L

JULLOUVILLE MANCHE

Chaussée 1 av de la Libération, 50610 ☎ 233618018 ▤ 233614526
website: www.campinglachaussee
On large meadow, completely divided into pitches. Separated from beach and coast road by row of houses.
Open: 7 Apr-23 Sep Site: 6HEC ⬛ ⊕ ⬛ Facilities: ⋔ ⧉ ⊙ ⬛ ∅ ⧈ Services: ▾ ✗ ⊞ lau Off-site: ⧉ ✗ ⭢S ⊞

AT ST-MICHEL-DES-LOUPS (4KM SE)

Chaumière 50740 ☎ 233488293
⮡ *4km SE on D21 via Bouillon.*
Site: 2HEC ⬛ ⊕ ⬛ ⬛ ▲ Facilities: ⋔ ⊙ ⬛ ⧈ Services: ▾ ✗ lau Leisure: ⭢ LS

JUMIÈGES SEINE-MARITIME

Forêt rue Mainberthe, 76480 ☎ 235379343 ▤ 235377648
e-mail: ci.jumieges@free.fr
website: www.campinglaforet.com
Located in the heart of the Broetonne Regional Natural Park on the banks of the Seine.
⮡ *10km from A13 Caen-Paris road, exit Bourg-Achard*
Open: 3 Apr-Oct Site: 2.5HEC ⬛ ⊕ ⬛ ⬛ Prices: pitch 14.20-15 (incl 2 persons) Facilities: ⋔ ⧉ ⊙ ⬛ ∅ ⧈ Services: ⊞ lau Leisure: ⭢ P Off-site: ▾ ✗ ⭢R

KERLIN FINISTÈRE

Étangs de Trévignon Pointe de Trévignon, Kerlin, 29910
☎ 298500041 ▤ 298500409
e-mail: camp.etangsdetrevignon@wanadoo.fr
website: www.camping-etangs.com
A family site with good, modern facilities 800mtrs from the beach, reached by a short pathway.
Open: Jun-15 Sep Site: 3.5HEC ⬛ ⊕ ⬛ ▲ Prices: ⋔5.05 ⬛1.60 pitch 6.10 Facilities: ⋔ ⧉ ⊙ ⬛ ∅ ⧈ Services: ▾ ⊞ lau Leisure: ⭢ P Off-site: ✗ ⭢S

LANDAUL MORBIHAN

Le Pied-à-Terre Branzého, 56690
☎ 297245270 ▤ 297245271
e-mail: jimrolland@wanadoo.fr
website: www.lepiedaterre.net
In a pleasant, quiet location, 15 minutes from the sea.
⮡ *1km from N165. Signposted from Landaul.*
Open: Apr-Sep Site: 1.5HEC ⬛ ♣ Prices: ⋔4 ⬛2 ⬛3 ▲3 pitch 3 Facilities: ⋔ ⊙ ⬛ ⧈ Services: ▾ ⊞ lau Off-site: ⧉ ✗

LANDÉDA FINISTÈRE

Abers Dunes de Ste-Marguerite, 29870
☎ 298049335 ▤ 298048435
e-mail: camping-des-abers@wanadoo.fr
website: www.camping-des-abers.com
Very quiet beautiful site among dunes. Ideal for children.
⮡ *2.5km NW on a peninsula between bays of Aber-Wrac'h and Aber Benoît.*
Open: May-26 Sep Site: 4.5HEC ⬛ ⊕ ⬛ Prices: ⋔2.79-3.10 ⬛1.35-1.50 pitch 4.95-5.50 Facilities: ⋔ ⧉ ⊙ ⬛ ∅ ⧈ Services: ⊞ lau Leisure: ⭢ S Off-site: ▾ ✗ ⭢R

• NEW 2004: Covered Water Park •

Camping ★★★★
"Le Ty Nadan"

the only campsite where you can do this...

www.camping-ty-nadan.fr

LESCONIL FINISTÈRE

Dunes 7 r P-Langevin, 29740 ☎ 298878178 🗐 298822705
A family site on slightly sloping landscaped ground, 800mtrs
from the town centre and the harbour.
➲ *Access via D53, turning S in Plobannalac. Signposted.*
Open: end May-15 Sep **Site:** 2.8HEC ⚏ 🕀 **Prices:** ⭡4.25
pitch 9.90 **Facilities:** ⎰ ⊙ 🖴 🖻 **Services:** 🖽 lau **Off-site:** 🖦 🍽
✕ ⭠RS

Grande Plage 71 r P-Langevin, 29740
☎ 298878827 🗐 298878827
Well equipped site on level ground, surrounded by
woodland, 300mtrs from the sea.
Open: Etr-Sep **Site:** 2.5HEC ⚏ 🕀 🚐 🖭 **Facilities:** ⎰ ⊙ 🖴
🖻 🖻 **Services:** 🖽 lau **Off-site:** 🖦 🍽 ✕ ⭠S

LOCUNOLE FINISTÈRE

🏠**Ty Nadan** 29310 ☎ 298717547 🗐 298717731
e-mail: ty-nadan@wanadoo.fr
Located in 60 acres surrounding an old Breton village and
situated in a riverside position.
➲ *off D22(Quimperle to Plouay), take W exit at Arzano and
3 kms to site*
Open: 24 May-6 Sep **Site:** 20HEC ⚏ 🕀 🚐 🖭 **Facilities:** ⎰
🖦 ⊙ 🖴 🖻 **Services:** 🍽 ✕ 🖽 lau **Leisure:** ⭠ R **Off-site:** ⭠S
See advertisement on page 155

LOUVIERS EURE

Bel Air Hameau de St-Lubin, rte de la Haye Malherbe, 27400
☎ 232401077 🗐 232401077
e-mail: le.belain@wanadoo.fr **website:** www.lebelair.fr.st
Small site on the edge of a forest with landscaped pitches and
good facilities.
➲ *3km from the town centre via D81.*
Open: Mar-Oct **Site:** 2.5HEC ⚏ 🕀 🚐 **Prices:** ⭡3.15-3.80
pitch 3.90-4.70 **Facilities:** ⎰ 🖦 ⊙ 🖴 🖻 🖻 **Services:** 🖽 lau
Leisure: ⭠ P

LUC-SUR-MER CALVADOS

Capricieuse 2 r Brummel, 14530
☎ 231973443 🗐 231968278
e-mail: info@campinglacapricieuse.com
A large family site 100mtrs from the beach.
➲ *On W outskirts, access via A13 exit Douvres.*
Open: Apr-Sep **Site:** 4.5HEC ⚏ 🏝 🕀 🚐 **Facilities:** ⎰ ⊙ 🖴
🖻 **Services:** 🖽 lau **Off-site:** 🖦 🍽 ✕ 🖴 🖴 ⭠PS

MARTIGNY SEINE-MARITIME

2 Rivières 76880 ☎ 235856082 🗐 235859516
e-mail: martigny76@wanadoo.fr
website: www.camping-2-rivieres.com
On the shore of a lake in pleasant surroundings 8km from
Dieppe.
➲ *Access via D154.*
Open: 28 Mar-12 Oct **Site:** 6.8HEC ⚏ 🕀 🚐 **Prices:** pitch
13.45 (incl 3 persons) **Facilities:** ⎰ 🖦 ⊙ 🖴 🖻 **Services:** 🖽 lau
Off-site: ⭠P

MARTRAGNY CALVADOS

🏠**Château de Martragny** 14740 ☎ 231802140 🗐 231081491
e-mail: chateau.martragny@wanadoo.fr
website: www.chateau-martragny.com
Family site in grounds of a château which also offers
accommodation.
➲ *From N13 take exit for Martragny. Drive through St-Léger
and campsite is on the right as you leave the village.*
Open: May-15 Sep **Site:** 15HEC ⚏ 🕀 **Prices:** ⭡3.90-4.50
pitch 9-10.50 **Facilities:** ⎰ 🖦 ⊙ 🖴 🖴 🖻 **Services:** 🍽 🖽 lau
Leisure: ⭠ P **Off-site:** ⭠R

MAUPERTUS-SUR-MER MANCHE

Anse du Brick 50330 ☎ 233543357 🗐 233544966
e-mail: welcome@anse-du-brick.com
website: www.anse-du-brick.com
Terraced site in a landscaped park between the sea and the
forest.
➲ *200mtrs from beach.*
Open: Apr-Sep **Site:** 17HEC ⚏ 🕀 🚐 🖭 **Prices:** ⭡3-5.10
pitch 8.20-11.50 **Facilities:** ⎰ 🖦 ⊙ 🖴 🖴 🖴 🖻 🖻 **Services:** 🍽
✕ 🖽 lau **Leisure:** ⭠ P **Off-site:** ⭠S

MERVILLE-FRANCEVILLE CALVADOS

Peupliers Allée des Pins, 14810 ☎ 231240507 🗐 231240507
e-mail: asl_mondeville@wanadoo.fr
website: www.asl-mondeville.com
Situated in a rural setting, 300 metres from the beach. The
sanitary arrangements include a bathroom for babies. Shop,
bar and café available high season.
➲ *Approx 2km E from sign on D514*
Open: Apr-Oct **Site:** 2HEC ⚏ 🏝 🕀 🚐 🖭 🅰 **Prices:** ⭡5.05
pitch 5.65 **Facilities:** ⎰ ⊙ 🖴 🖴 🖻 **Services:** lau **Leisure:** ⭠ S
Off-site: 🖴 ⭠R

MONTERBLANC MORBIHAN

Haras Aérodrome Vannes-Meucon, Vannes-Meucon, 56250
☎ 297446606 🗐 297444941
e-mail: campingvannes@free.fr
website: www.campingvannes.free.fr
➲ *Situated 4kms from Vannes in the direction Aerodrome
Vannes-Meucon.*
Open: All year **Site:** 1HEC ⚏ 🕀 🚐 🖭 🅰 **Prices:** ⭡3 🚗1
🖭3 🅰3 pitch 1.50 **Facilities:** ⎰ 🖦 ⊙ 🖴 🖴 🖻 **Services:** 🍽 ✕ 🖽
lau **Leisure:** ⭠ P

MONT-ST-MICHEL, LE MANCHE

Gué de Beauvoir 5 rte du Mont-St-Michel, Beauvoir, 50170
☎ 233600923
A level site in an orchard close to the River Couesnon.
➲ *4km S of Abbey on D776 Pontorson road.*
Open: Etr-Sep **Site:** 0.6HEC ⚏ 🕀 **Prices:** ⭡2.50 🚗1.20
🖭2.50 🅰2 **Facilities:** ⎰ ⊙ 🖴 🖻 **Services:** 🍽 ✕ 🖽 lau
Off-site: 🖦 ✕

MORGAT FINISTÈRE

Bruyeres Le Bouis, 29160 ☎ 298261487
e-mail: camping.les.bruyeres@presquile-crozon.com
website: www.presquile-crozon.com
On a meadow surrounded by woodland with pitches divided
by hedges on the extremity of the Parc Naturel Régional
d'Armorique.
➲ *From Morgat follow D255 towards Cap de la Chèvre for
1.5km then right towards Bouis.*
Open: May-Sept **Site:** 3HEC ⚏ 🕀 **Prices:** ⭡3.35 🚗1.20
pitch 3.35 **Facilities:** ⎰ ⊙ 🖴 🖻 **Services:** 🖽 lau **Off-site:** 🍽 ✕
🖴 ⭠S

MOYAUX CALVADOS

🏠**Colombier** 14590 ☎ 231636308 🗐 231631597
e-mail: chateau@camping-lecolombier.com
website: www.camping-lecolombier.com
Well-kept site in grounds of manor house.
Camping Card Compulsory.
➲ *3km NE on D143.*
Open: May-15 Sep **Site:** 10HEC ⚏ 🕀 **Prices:** ⭡5-7 pitch 8-
13 **Facilities:** ⎰ 🖦 ⊙ 🖴 🖴 🖻 **Services:** 🍽 ✕ 🖽 lau
Leisure: ⭠ P

Site: 6HEC-Site size ⚏-grass ⫶⫶⫶-sand ◈-stone �293-little shade 🕀-partly shaded ♠-mainly shaded
🏠-bungalows for hire 🚐-caravans for hire 🅰-tents for hire ⽆-no dogs **Prices:** ⭡-adult per night 🚗-car per night
pp-per person per night 🖭-caravan per night 🅰-tent per night

NÉVEZ FINISTÈRE

Deux Fontaine Raguènes, 29920
☎ 298068191 ▤ 2980697180
e-mail: info@les2fontaines.fr
website: www.les2fontaines.fr
Mainly level site, subdivided into several fields surrounded by woodland with good recreational facilities including an aquaslide.
➲ 700mtrs from Ragunès Beach.
Open: 15 May-11 Sep **Site:** 7HEC ⊞ ⌯ ☎ **Prices:** ↟3.85-5.50 ♠2.17-3.10 pitch 7.35-10.50 **Facilities:** ⋔ ⌾ ⊙ ☢ ∅ ☎
Services: ⦿ ✗ ⊞ lau **Leisure:** ⭢ P **Off-site:** ⭢RS

NOYAL-MUZILLAC MORBIHAN

Moulin de Cadillac Moulin de Cadillac, 56190
☎ 297670347 ▤ 297670002
e-mail: infos@moulin-cadillac.com
website: www.camping-moulin-cadillac.com
A well equipped family site in a pleasant wooded location with good facilities.
➲ Access via N165, N through Muzillac.
Open: May-Sep **Site:** 3HEC ⊞ ♣ ☎ ☎ Å **Prices:** ↟2.74-3.65 pitch 3.75-5 pp1.43-1.90 **Facilities:** ⋔ ⌾ ⊙ ☢ ⩩ ☎
Services: ⦿ ⊞ lau **Leisure:** ⭢ P

OUISTREHAM CALVADOS

Prairies de la Mer rte de Lion, Riva-Bella, 14150
☎ 231976161
A camping area attached to a larger static caravan site with good recreational facilities, 400mtrs from the sea.
➲ Access via D514.
Open: 13 Mar-17 Oct **Site:** 80HEC ⊞ ⌯ ☎ ☎
Facilities: ⋔ ⌾ ⊙ ☢ ∅ ☎ **Services:** ⦿ ✗ ⊞ lau **Leisure:** ⭢ P
Off-site: ⌾ ✗ ⭢S

PÉNESTIN-SUR-MER MORBIHAN

Airotel-Inly 56760 ☎ 299903509 ▤ 299904093
e-mail: inly-info@wanadoo.fr
website: www.camping-inly.com
Situated in the centre of a nature reserve and close to the coast, with good recreational facilities.
➲ 2km SE via D201
Open: 29 Mar-26 Sep **Site:** 30HEC ⊞ ⌯ ☎ ☎ Å
Facilities: ⋔ ⌾ ⊙ ☢ ☎ **Services:** ⦿ ✗ lau **Leisure:** ⭢ LP
Off-site: ∅ ⩩ ⭢RS ⊞

Cénic 56760 ☎ 299904565 ▤ 299904505
e-mail: info@lecenic.com website: www.lecenic.com
In a forested area 2km from the sea. Spacious grassy pitches ideal for families.
➲ Access via D34 from La Roche-Bernard.
Open: Apr-Sep **Site:** 7HEC ⊞ ♣ ☎ ☎ Å **Prices:** ↟4-5.50
pitch 5-8.50 **Facilities:** ⋔ ⌾ ⊙ ☢ ∅ ⩩ ☎ **Services:** ⦿ ✗ ⊞ lau
Leisure: ⭢ P **Off-site:** ✗ ⭢S

Iles La Pointe du Bile, 56760 ☎ 299903024 ▤ 299904455
e-mail: contact@camping-des-iles.fr
website: www.camping-des-iles.fr
A family site with direct access to the beach and a separate residential section.
➲ 3km S on D201.
Open: Apr-3 Oct **Site:** 4HEC ⊞ ⌯ ☎ Å **Prices:** ↟3.20-5
pitch 19.50-31.50 (incl 2 persons) **Facilities:** ⋔ ⌾ ⊙ ☢ ∅ ☎
Services: ⦿ ✗ ⊞ lau **Leisure:** ⭢ PS

PENTREZ-PLAGE FINISTÈRE

Tamaris 29550 ☎ 298265395 ▤ 298265248
e-mail: camping-kerys@wanadoo.fr
website: www.ker-ys.com
Level site divided into pitches 20mtrs from the beach.

➲ Access via D887.
Open: May-14 Sep **Site:** 3HEC ⊞ ⌯ ☎ ☎ **Prices:** ↟3.70
♠1.60 **Facilities:** ⋔ ⌾ ⊙ ☢ ∅ ⩩ ☎ ⊡ **Services:** ⊞ lau
Off-site: ⦿ ✗ ⭢S

PERROS-GUIREC CÔTES-D'ARMOR

Claire Fontaine Toul ar Lann, 22700
☎ 296230355 ▤ 296490619
website: www.camping-claire-fontaine
Spacious, level site in a rural setting.
➲ 1.2km SW of town centre, 800mtrs from Trestraou beach.
Open: Etr-Sep **Site:** 3HEC ⊞ ⌯ ☎ ☎ **Prices:** pitch 12-15
(incl 2 persons) **Facilities:** ⋔ ⊙ ☢ ∅ ☎ **Services:** ⦿ ⊞ lau
Off-site: ⌾ ⭢S

AT LOUANNEC (3KM SE)

CM Ernest Renan rte de Perros-Guirec, 22700
☎ 296231178 ▤ 293490447
e-mail: mairie-lovannec@wannadoo.com
Well situated site next to the sea. Take away food, games room.
➲ 1km W.
Open: May-Sep **Site:** 4.5HEC ⊞ ⋇ ☎ ☎ **Facilities:** ⋔ ⌾
⊙ ☢ ∅ ☎ **Services:** ⦿ ✗ lau **Leisure:** ⭢ LRS **Off-site:** ✗

AT PLOUMANACH (2KM NW)

▥Ranolien 22700 ☎ 296916565 ▤ 296914190
e-mail: leranolien@wanadoo.fr
website: www.leranolien.com
The site is divided into pitches by hedges; separate sections for caravans.
➲ 500mtrs from the village.
Open: Apr-Sep **Site:** 16HEC ⊞ ⌯ ☎ **Facilities:** ⋔ ⌾ ⊙ ☢
∅ ⩩ ☎ **Services:** ⦿ ✗ ⊞ lau **Leisure:** ⭢ P **Off-site:** ⭢S

PIEUX, LES MANCHE

Grand Large 50340 ☎ 233524075 ▤ 233525820
e-mail: Le-grand-Large@wanadoo.fr
website: legrandlarge.com
In an unspoilt location with direct access to the beach.
➲ 3km from the town centre on D117.
Open: 3 Apr-19 Sep **Site:** 4HEC ⊞ ⋯ ⌯ ☎ ☎
Prices: pitch 17-23.50 (incl 2 persons) pp4-5.20 **Facilities:** ⋔
⌾ ⊙ ☢ ∅ ☎ **Services:** ⦿ ✗ ⊞ lau **Leisure:** ⭢ PS

PLÉRIN CÔTES-D'ARMOR

Mouettes Les Rosaires les Mouettes, 22190 ☎ 296745148
Open: Jul-Aug **Site:** 1HEC ⊞ ⌯ ☎ **Prices:** ↟3 ♠2 pitch 10
Facilities: ⋔ ⊙ ☢ ☎ **Services:** ⊞ lau **Off-site:** ⌾ ⦿ ✗ ∅
⭢PRS

PLEUBIAN CÔTES-D'ARMOR

Port la Chaîne 22610 ☎ 296229238 ▤ 296228792
e-mail: info@portlachaine.com
website: www.portlachaine.com
A peaceful, terraced site on the 'Wild Peninsula', with direct access to the sea, with good facilities.
➲ 2km N via D20.
Open: May-Sep **Site:** 5HEC ⊞ ♣ ☎ Å **Prices:** ↟4.20-5.20
pitch 7.20-9 **Facilities:** ⋔ ⌾ ⊙ ☢ ∅ ⩩ ☎ **Services:** ⦿ ✗ ⊞ lau
Leisure: ⭢ PS

PLOBANNALEC FINISTÈRE

Manoir de Kerlut 29740 ☎ 298822389 ▤ 298822649
e-mail: info@campingsbretagnesud.com
website: www.campingsbretagnesud.com
A peaceful site located in the grounds of a manor house some 2km from the beach.

contd.

Facilities: ⌾-shop **⋔**-shower **⊙**-electric points for razors **☢**-electric points for caravans **☎**-parking by tents permitted
⊡-compulsory separate car park **Services: ✗**-café/restaurant **⦿**-bar **∅**-Camping Gaz International **⩩**-gas other than Camping
Gaz **⊞**-first aid facilities lau-laundry **Leisure: ⭢**-swimming L-Lake P-Pool R-River S-Sea **Off-site:** All facilities within 2km

◐ *1.6km S via D102.*
Open: 15 May-8 Aug Site: 12HEC ⛺ ⚬ 🏠 ▲ Prices: ♠3-6
♠2 pitch 15-36 (incl 2 persons) Facilities: 🏪 🛁 ⊙ 🍴 ⊘ 🏛
Services: ♟ ✕ ⊞ lau Leisure: ⌇ PS Off-site: ✕

PLOÊMEL MORBIHAN

Kergo 56400 ☎ 297568066
e-mail: camping.kergo@wanadoo.fr
website: www.members.lycos.fr/campingkergo
In pleasant wooded surroundings, close to the neighbouring
beaches.
◐ *2km SE via D186*
Open: 15 Apr-Sep Site: 2.5HEC ⛺ ⚬ 🏠 Prices: ♠3.20
♠1.70 🏠3.20 ▲3.20 pitch 3.20 Facilities: 🏪 🛁 ⊙ 🍴 🏛
Services: ⊞ lau Off-site: ♟ ✕

PLOEMEUR MORBIHAN

Ajoncs Beg Minio, 56270 ☎ 297863011 ▤ 297863011
e-mail: secretariat@campingclub.200.fr
website: www.campingclub.2000.fr
A rural site situated in an orchard.
◐ *From town centre continue towards Fort-Bloqué.*
Open: 18 Mar-Sep Site: 2HEC ⛺ ⚬ Prices: pitch 12.16
Facilities: 🏪 ⊙ 🍴 🏛 Services: lau Off-site: ⌇LPS

PLOÊRMEL MORBIHAN

Lac Les Belles Rives, Taupont, 56800
☎ 297740122 ▤ 297740122
website: www.le-camping-du-lac.com
A lakeside family site with plenty of facilities for water sports.
◐ *2km from village centre, beside the lake.*
Open: Apr-Oct Site: 3HEC ⛺ ♠ 🏠 Prices: ♠2.90 🏠3 ▲3
pitch 3 Facilities: 🏪 🛁 ⊙ 🍴 ⊘ 🏛 Services: ♟ ✕ ⊞ lau
Leisure: ⌇ L Off-site: ⌇P

Vallée du Ninian Le Rocher, 56800
☎ 297935301 ▤ 297935727
e-mail: info@camping-ninian.com
website: www.camping-ninian.com
Peaceful family site at the heart of Brittany which specialises
in homemade cider beside the River Ninian.
◐ *W of Taupont towards the river.*
Open: May-Sep Site: 2.7HEC ⛺ ⚬ 🏠 🏠 Prices: ♠2.50-
3.10 🏠4-5 Facilities: 🏪 🛁 ⊙ 🍴 ⊘ 🏛 Services: ♟ ⊞ lau
Leisure: ⌇ PR Off-site: ✕

PLOMEUR FINISTÈRE

Torche Pointe de la Torche, Roz an Tremen, 29120
☎ 298586282 ▤ 298588969
e-mail: info@campingdelatorche.fr
website: www.campingdelatorche.fr
A family site with pitches surrounded by trees and bushes,
1.5km from the beach.
◐ *3.5km W*
Open: 3 Apr-25 Sep Site: 4HEC ⛺ ∴ ⚬ 🏠 Prices: ♠2.20-
4.30 ♠1-2 pitch 3.50-7 Facilities: 🏪 🛁 ⊙ 🍴 ⊘ 🏛
Services: ♟ ✕ ⊞ lau Leisure: ⌇ P Off-site: ✕ ⌇S

PLOMODIERN FINISTÈRE

Iroise Plage de Pors-ar-Vag, 29550
☎ 298815272 ▤ 298812610
e-mail: campingiroise@aol.com
website: www.camping-iriose.com
A family site with fine recreational facilities, providing
magnificent views over the Bay of Douarnenez.
◐ *5km SW, 150mtrs from the beach.*
Open: 10 Apr-20 Sep Site: 2.5HEC ⛺ ⚬ 🏠 Prices: ♠4.35-
5.80 pitch 8.25-11 Facilities: 🏪 🛁 ⊙ 🍴 ⊘ 🏛 Services: ♟ ✕
⊞ lau Leisure: ⌇ P Off-site: ✕ ⌇S

PLONÉVEZ-PORZAY FINISTÈRE

International de Kervel 29550 ☎ 298925154 ▤ 298925496
e-mail: camping.kervel@wanadoo.fr
website: www.kervel.com
One of the best sites in the region. Ideal for families. 800mtrs
from the sea.
◐ *SW of the village on the D107 Douarnenez road for 3km,
then towards coast at 'X' roads.*
Open: Apr-12 Sep Site: 7HEC ⛺ ⚬ 🏠 🏠 ▲ Prices: ♠4.30-
5.50 pitch 9.15-11.50 Facilities: 🏪 🛁 ⊙ 🍴 ⊘ 🏛
Services: ♟ ✕ ⊞ lau Leisure: ⌇ P Off-site: ⌇S

Tréguer-Plage Ste-Anne-la-Palud, 29550
☎ 298925352 ▤ 298925489
e-mail: camping-treguer-plage@wanadoo.fr
website: www.camping-treguer-plage.com
A level site with direct access to the beach.
◐ *1.3km N*
Open: 15 Jun-15 Sep Site: 6HEC ⛺ ∴ 🍂 🏠
Prices: ♠3.30 ♠2.60 pitch 3.30 Facilities: 🏪 🛁 ⊙ 🍴 ⊘ 🏛
🅿 Services: ♟ ✕ lau Leisure: ⌇ S Off-site: ⌇S ⊞

PLOUÉZEC CÔTES-D'ARMOR

Cap Horn Port Lazo, 22470 ☎ 296206428 ▤ 296206388
e-mail: lecaphorn@hotmail.com
website: lecaphorn.com
In an elevated position overlooking the Ile de Bréhat with
direct access to the beach.
◐ *2.3km NE via D77 at Port-Lazo.*
Open: Apr-10 Sep Site: 5HEC ⛺ 🍂 🏠 Prices: ♠4.50 pitch
7.50 Facilities: 🏪 🛁 ⊙ 🍴 ⊘ 🏛 Services: ♟ ✕ lau Leisure: ⌇
PS Off-site: 🍂

PLOUEZOCH FINISTÈRE

Baie de Térénez 29252 ☎ 298672680 🗏 298672680
e-mail: camping@libertysurf.fr website: www.aucamping.com
A well equipped site in a pleasant rural setting.
➲ 3.5km NW via D76.
Open: 5 Apr-Sep Site: 3HEC ⚏ 🔾 🛖 🖩 🍃 Prices: ♠4.20
♣5.80 pitch 5.80 Facilities: 🖍 ⊙ 🖳 🖉 🚈 🖭 Services: ♀ ✕ 🖽
lau Leisure: 🔾 P Off-site: 🔾RS

PLOUGASNOU FINISTÈRE

CM Mélin-ar-Mésqueau 29630 ☎ 298673745
Large municipal site with good recreational facilities.
➲ 3.5km S via D46
Open: 15 Jun-Aug Site: 15HEC ⚏ 🔾 Facilities: 🖍 ⊙ 🖳 🖭
🄿 Services: ♀ ✕ 🖽 lau Leisure: 🔾 LR

Trégor Kerjean, 29630 ☎ 298673764
e-mail: bookings@campingdutregor.com
website: www.campingdutregor.com
A sheltered site with numbered, grassy pitches. Surrounded
by hedges.
➲ Off D46 towards Morlaix.
Open: Etr-Oct Site: 1HEC ⚏ 🔾 🖩 Prices: ♠2.40-2.90
🚗1-1.20 🚐1.80-2.10 🏕1.80-2.10 Facilities: 🖍 ⊙ 🖳 🚈 🖭
Services: lau Off-site: 🛒 ♀ ✕ 🖽

PLOUHA CÔTES-D'ARMOR

AT TRINITÉ, LA (2KM NE)

Domaine de Keravel rte de Port Moguer, 22580
☎ 296224913 🗏 296224713
e-mail: keravel@wanadoo.fr website: www.keravel.com
Forested site built around an elegant country mansion, 1km
from the sea.
Open: 15 May-Sep Site: 5HEC ⚏ 🔾 🖩 Prices: ♠4.20-5.30
pitch 6.44-8.05 Facilities: 🖍 🛒 ⊙ 🖳 🖉 🖭 Services: 🖽 lau
Leisure: 🔾 P Off-site: 🔾S

PLOUHARNEL MORBIHAN

Étang de Loperhet 56340 ☎ 297523468 🗏 297523468
e-mail: info@camping-loperhet.com
website: www.camping-loperhet.com
➲ 1km NW via D781
Open: Apr-30 Oct Site: 6HEC ⚏ ⋮⋮⋮ 🔾 🖩 🖩
Prices: ♠3.96 pitch 7.32 Facilities: 🖍 🛒 ⊙ 🖳 🖉 🖭 Services: ♀
✕ lau Leisure: 🔾 P Off-site: ✕ 🚈 🔾S 🖽

Kersily Ste-Barbe, 56340 ☎ 297523965 🗏 297524476
Open: Apr-Oct Site: 3HEC ⚏ ♠ 🖩 🖩 Prices: ♠2.60-4
🚗1.30-1.60 pitch 3.50-5 Facilities: 🖍 🛒 ⊙ 🖳 🖭 Services: ♀
✕ 🖽 lau Leisure: 🔾 P Off-site: 🔾S

Lande Kerzivienne, 56340 ☎ 297523148 🗏 297523148
e-mail: campdelalande@aol.com
On partially shaded terrain, 600mtrs from the beach
Site: 1HEC ⚏ 🔾 🖩 🖩 Prices: ♠11 Facilities: 🖍 ⊙ 🖳 🖉 🚈
🖭 Services: 🖽 lau Off-site: 🛒 ♀ ✕ 🖉 🔾S

PLOUHINEC MORBIHAN

Moténo rte du Magouer, 56680 ☎ 297367663 🗏 297858184
e-mail: camping-moteno@wanadoo.fr
website: www.camping-le-moteno.com
On slightly sloping ground, subdivided into several fields in a
wooded area 600mtrs from the beach.
➲ S beside the Mer d'Etel.
Site: 4HEC ⚏ 🔾 🖩 🖩 Prices: ♠2.60-4.20 pitch 4.50-9.50
Facilities: 🖍 🛒 ⊙ 🖳 🖉 🚈 🖭 Services: ♀ ✕ 🖽 lau
Off-site: 🔾PS

Domaine de Kerlann

Enjoy the relaxed atmos-
phere at the beautiful
Domaine de Kerlann
- a lovely wooded parc in a
perfect location for making
the most of Southern
Brittany.

■ 80m² standard pitch size
■ Superb spring & autumn
prices
■ Ferry inclusive package
■ High standard facilities
open all season
■ Free use of superb indoor
& outdoor pools
■ Free use of 3 childrens
clubs for all ages
■ Bilingual friendly staff
■ Site open from:
2 April - 29 October

Domaine de Kerlann, Land Rosted, 29930 Pont Aven, France
Tel: 00 33 298 06 01 77 Fax: 00 33 298 06 18 50
To book please call the number above, quoting code TOAA01
or request a brochure by calling 0870 242 6666

ABTA
V2819

PLOZÉVET FINISTÈRE

Corniche rte de la Corniche, 29710
☎ 298913394 🗏 298914153
e-mail: info@campinglacorniche.com
website: www.campinglacorniche.com
Peaceful rural site 1.5km from the sea.
Open: Apr-Sep Site: 2HEC ⚏ 🔾 🖩 Facilities: 🖍 🛒 ⊙ 🖳 🖉
🖭 Services: ♀ ✕ 🖽 lau Leisure: 🔾 P Off-site: ♀ ✕ 🚈 🔾LRS

PONTAUBAULT MANCHE

Vallée de la Sélune 7 rue Mal Leclerc, 50220
☎ 233603900 🗏 233603900
e-mail: campselune@wanadoo.fr
This site is in a quiet village near the River Sélune. Ideal base
for exploring the Normandy/Brittany area.
➲ Access via N175 Portorson-Caen.
Open: Apr-20 Oct Site: 1.6HEC ⚏ 🔾 🖩 🖩 Prices: ♠2.50
🚗2.50 🚐2.50 🏕1.50-2.50 Facilities: 🖍 🛒 ⊙ 🖳 🖉 🖭
Services: ♀ ✕ Off-site: 🚈 🔾R

PONT-AVEN FINISTÈRE

Domaine de Kerlann 29930
☎ 298060177 🗏 0870 242 9999
e-mail: kerlann@haven.fr
website: www.haveneurope.com
A wooded park with shady pitches featuring an indoor pool
complex with waterslide and spa bath.
➲ Approx 3m E of Pont Aven.
Open: 2 Apr-22 Oct Site: 26HEC ⚏ ♠ 🖩 🏕 🍃
Prices: pitch 11-29 (incl 2 persons) Facilities: 🖍 🛒 ⊙ 🖳 🚈 🖭
Services: ♀ ✕ 🖽 lau Leisure: 🔾 P Off-site: 🛒 ♀

PONT-L'ABBÉ FINISTÈRE

Écureuil 29120 ☎ 298870339 📠 298870339
Shady site set in a wooded park with good recreational facilities.
➲ 3.5km NE onD44.
Open: May-Sep Site: 3HEC ⬛⬛⬛ ♣ 🏠 Prices: ⚹3.20-3.50 �car1.60-1.80 pitch 4-4.40 Facilities: ⬥ 🦁 ⊙ 🏪 🖉 🛒 🖀 Services: 🍷 ✗ 🎫 lau Leisure: ⚓ P

PORDIC CÔTES-D'ARMOR

Madières rte de Vau Madec, 22590
☎ 296790248 📠 296794667
e-mail: lesmadieres@wanadoo.fr
website: www.campinglesmadieres.com
A quiet coastal site in a well shaded position.
➲ 1500mtrs from village on St-Brieuc road (D786).
Open: 01 May-30 Sep Site: 2HEC ⬛⬛⬛ 🌿 🏠 🏪 Facilities: ⬥
🦁 ⊙ 🏪 🖉 🛒 🖀 Services: 🍷 ✗ 🎫 lau Leisure: ⚓ P
Off-site: ⚓S

PORT-EN-BESSIN CALVADOS

Port'land 14520 ☎ 231510706 📠 231517649
e-mail: campingportland@wanadoo.fr
website: www.camping-portland.com
Situated near Omaha beach in rural surroundings with an indoor heated swimming pool on site.
Open: Apr-3 Nov Site: ⬛⬛⬛ 🌿 🌿 🏠 Prices: ⚹4.80-7.30 🚗2
pitch 19.20-27.30 Facilities: ⬥ 🦁 ⊙ 🏪 🖀 Services: 🍷 ✗ 🎫
lau Leisure: ⚓ LP Off-site: 🦁 🍷 ✗ 🖉 🛒 ⚓S

PORT-MANECH FINISTÈRE

St-Nicolas 29920 ☎ 298068975 📠 298067461
e-mail: info@campinglesaintnicolas.com
website: www.campinglesaintnicolas.com
Divided into hedge-lined pitches in beautiful surroundings close to the beach.
Open: May-Sep Site: 3.5HEC ⬛⬛⬛ 🌿 🏠 Prices: ⚹4.25 pitch
7.60 Facilities: ⬥ ⊙ 🏪 🖀 Services: 🍷 ✗ 🎫 lau Leisure: ⚓ P
Off-site: 🦁 🍷 ✗ 🖉 🛒 ⚓S

POSES EURE

Ile Adeline 27740 ☎ 232593581 📠 232598895
A well equipped site situated close to the Lery-Poses leisure centre.
➲ Access via A13 exit 19 towards Val-de-Reuil.
Open: Apr-Sep Site: 2.5HEC ⬛⬛⬛ 🌿 🏪 Facilities: ⬥ 🦁 ⊙ 🏪
🖀 Services: 🍷 ✗ 🎫 lau Off-site: ⚓LR

POULDU, LE FINISTÈRE

Embruns r du Philosophe Alain, 29360
☎ 298399107 📠 298399787
e-mail: camping-les-embruns@wanadoo.fr
website: www.camping-les-embruns.com
A pleasant site with good facilities and easy access to the beach. Separate car park for arrivals after 22.00hrs.
Open: 3 Apr-15 Sep Site: 5HEC ⬛⬛⬛ 🌿 🏪 Prices: ⚹3.50-
4.60 pitch 9-20.50 Facilities: ⬥ 🦁 ⊙ 🏪 🖉 🛒 🖀 🖀 Services: 🍷
✗ 🎫 lau Leisure: ⚓ P Off-site: ✗ ⚓RS

QUETTEHOU MANCHE

Rivage rte de Morsalines, 50630 ☎ 233541376
e-mail: camping.lerivage@wanadoo.fr
website: www.camping-lerivage.com
Quiet, sheltered site, 400mtrs from the sea.
➲ Access via D14.
Open: Apr-Sept Site: 1.6HEC ⬛⬛⬛ 🌿 🏠 Prices: ⚹3.50-4.50
pitch 12.20-15.50 (incl 2 persons) Facilities: ⬥ ⊙ 🏪 🖉 🛒 🖀
Services: 🍷 ✗ 🎫 lau Leisure: ⚓ P Off-site: 🦁 🍷 ✗ ⚓S 🎫

QUIBERON MORBIHAN

Bois d'Amour rue St-Clement, 56170
☎ 297504267 📠 297501352
e-mail: info@homair-vacances.fr
website: www.homair-vacances.fr
A family site with plenty of recreational facilities close to the area's fine beaches.
➲ 1.5 km SE at La Pointe de la Presqu'île, close to beach.
Open: Apr-Oct Site: 4.5HEC ⬛⬛⬛ ∴ 🌿 🏠 🏪 Facilities: ⬥
🦁 ⊙ 🏪 🖀 Services: 🍷 ✗ lau Leisure: ⚓ P Off-site: 🦁 🍷 ✗ 🖉
🛒 ⚓S 🎫

Conguel bd Teignouse, 56170 ☎ 297501911
Directly on the beach, with fine recreational facilities.
➲ Near the aerodrome towards Pointe de Conguel.
Open: Apr-Oct Site: 5HEC ⬛⬛⬛ 🌿 🏪 Facilities: ⬥ 🦁 ⊙ 🏪
🖀 Services: 🍷 ✗ 🎫 lau Leisure: ⚓ P Off-site: ⚓S

QUIMPER FINISTÈRE

🏠Orangerie de Lanniron Chateau de Lanniron, 29336
☎ 298906202 📠 298521556
e-mail: camping@lanniron.com
website: www.lanniron.com
In the grounds of the former residence of the Bishops of Quimper, beside the River Odet and surrounded by tropical vegetation.
➲ 2.5km from town centre via D34.
Open: 15 May-15 Sep Site: 27HEC ⬛⬛⬛ 🌿 🏠 🏪
Prices: ⚹4.20-6 pitch 14.70-21 Facilities: ⬥ 🦁 ⊙ 🏪 🖉 🛒 🖀
Services: 🍷 ✗ 🎫 lau
Leisure: ⚓ PR

RAGUENÈS-PLAGE FINISTÈRE

Airotel International Raguenès-Plage 19 r des Iles,
Raguenez, 29920 ☎ 298068069 📠 298068905
e-mail: info@camping-le-raguenes-plage.com
website: www.camping-le-raguenes-plage.com
Asphalt drives; 400mtrs from beaches.
➲ Leave Pont-Aven and take the road to Nevez. At Nevez follow directions to Raguenès.
Open: 9 Apr-1 Oct Site: 7HEC ⬛⬛⬛ ♣ 🏠 🏪 Prices: ⚹3.80-
5.30 🚗2 pitch 6.80-13.40 Facilities: ⬥ 🦁 ⊙ 🏪 🖉 🛒 🖀 🖀
Services: 🍷 ✗ 🎫 lau Leisure: ⚓ PS

RAVENOVILLE-PLAGE MANCHE

Cormoran 50480 ☎ 233413394 📠 233951680
e-mail: lecormoran@wanadoo.fr
website: www.lecormoran.com
A pleasant family site with well defined pitches, 20mtrs from the sea.
➲ 300mtrs from the town towards Utah Beach.
Open: 2 Apr-26 Sept Site: 6.5HEC ⬛⬛⬛ 🌿 🏠 Prices: pitch
15.75-22 (incl 2 persons) Facilities: ⬥ 🦁 ⊙ 🏪 🖉 🛒 🖀
Services: 🍷 ✗ 🎫 lau Leisure: ⚓ PS Off-site: ✗

RIEC-SUR-BÉLON FINISTÈRE

Château de Bélon Port de Bélon, 29340 ☎ 298064143
Situated in wooded parkland by the sea with facilities for sailing and fishing.
➲ 3.5km S
Open: Apr-15 Nov Site: 8HEC ⬛⬛⬛ ♣ 🏠 Facilities: ⬥ 🦁 ⊙
🏪 🖉 🖀 Services: 🎫 lau Leisure: ⚓ S Off-site: 🍷 ✗

ROCHE-BERNARD, LA MORBIHAN

CM Patis 3 chemin du Patis, 56130
☎ 299906013 📠 299908828
On banks of River Vilaine.

Site: 6HEC-Site size ⬛⬛⬛-grass ∴∴∴-sand ⬗-stone 🌿-little shade 🌿-partly shaded ♣-mainly shaded
🏠-bungalows for hire 🏪-caravans for hire ⚠-tents for hire ⊘-no dogs Prices: ⚹-adult per night 🚗-car per night
pp-per person per night 🏪-caravan per night ⚠-tent per night

➾ *100mtrs from village centre.*
Open: Apr-Sep Site: 1HEC ⬜ ⊕ 🚐 Prices: ♦3 ➡1.50
🚐2.50 pitch 3.50 Facilities: ☂ ⊙ ⛽ 🎪 Services: ⊞ lau
Leisure: ⚓ R Off-site: 🛒 🍴 ✗ ⌀ ⚓P

ROCHEFORT-EN-TERRE MORBIHAN

Moulin Neuf 56220 ☎ 297433752 ▤ 297433545
A well equipped site in wooded surroundings. The shop
contains only basic items but there is a supermarket nearby.
Camping Card compulsory.
➾ *Signposted from D744 in village.*
Open: May-Sep Site: 2.5HEC ⬜ ⊕ Prices: ♦4.30-5 pitch 7-
8 Facilities: ☂ ⊙ ⛽ 🎪 🅿 Services: ⊞ lau Leisure: ⚓ P
Off-site: 🍴 ✗ ⌀ ⚓LR ⊞

ROSTRENEN CÔTES-D'ARMOR

Fleur de Bretagne Kerandouaron, 22110 ☎ 296291645
e-mail: aharrison@hotmail.com
A spacious site in a picturesque, sheltered valley with good,
modern facilities.
➾ *1.5km from Rostrenen on D764 towards Pontivy.*
Open: Apr-Sep Site: 6HEC ⬜ ⊕ Prices: ♦3.25 pitch 5
Facilities: ☂ ⊙ ⛽ 🎪 Services: 🍴 ✗ lau Leisure: ⚓ P
Off-site: 🛒 ⌀ 🔥 ⊞

ST-ALBAN CÔTES-D'ARMOR

St-Vrêguet St-Vréguet, 22400 ☎ 296329021
e-mail: vrguet@wanadoo.fr
A peaceful site in a pleasant park with good sanitary and
recreational facilities.
Open: Jun-Sep Site: 1HEC ⬜ ⊕ 🚐 Facilities: ☂ 🛒 ⊙ ⛽ ⌀
🎪 Services: 🍴 ⊞ lau Off-site: ⚓R

ST-AUBIN-SUR-MER CALVADOS

Côte de Nacre 17 r du Major Moulton, 14750
☎ 231971445 ▤ 231972211
A pleasant site with good recreational facilities. Reservations
recommended in high season. Separate car park for arrivals
after 22.00hrs.
Open: Apr-Oct Site: 6HEC ⬜ ☀ Facilities: ☂ 🛒 ⊙ ⛽ ⌀
🔥 🎪 Services: 🍴 ✗ ⊞ lau Leisure: ⚓ P Off-site: ⚓S

CM Mesnil 76740 ☎ 235830283
A family site attached to a typical Norman farm.
➾ *2 km W on D68.*
Open: Apr-Oct Site: 2.3HEC ⬜ ⊕ Prices: ♦4.93 ➡1.90
pitch 2.67 Facilities: ☂ ⊙ ⛽ 🎪 Services: ✗ ⊞ lau
Off-site: 🛒 ⚓S

ST-BRIAC ILLE-ET-VILAINE

Emeraude 7 chemin de la Souris, 35800 ☎ 299883455
e-mail: camping.emeraude@wanadoo.fr
website: www.camping-emeraude.com
Well-kept site in pleasant quiet situation and divided into
pitches.
➾ *Turn left off D786 and continue for 0.8 km.*
Open: Apr-Sep Site: 2HEC ⬜ ⊕ 🔥 🎪 Facilities: ☂ 🛒 ⊙
⛽ ⌀ 🔥 🎪 Services: 🍴 ⊞ lau Off-site: ✗ ⚓S

ST-BRIEUC CÔTES-D'ARMOR

Vallées Parc de Brézillet, 22000 ☎ 296940505
e-mail: campingdesvallees@wanadoo.fr
Situated on the edge of the town in a plateau criss-crossed by
wooded valleys. Restaurant open July and August only.
Open: Etr-15 Oct Site: 4.8HEC ⬜ ☀ 🔥 🎪 Prices: ♦4-3.20
➡2.20-2.60 pitch 8-10 (incl 1 persons) Facilities: ☂ 🛒 ⊙ ⛽
🎪 Services: 🍴 ✗ ⊞ lau Leisure: ⚓ R Off-site: ⌀ ⚓PS

Camping de la
Côte de Nacre

14750 ST-AUBIN-SUR-MER
Tél. : 33 (0) 231 971 445 Fax : 33 (0) 231 972 211
e mail : camping-cote-de-nacre wanadoo.fr
www.camping-cote-de-nacre.com

ST-CAST-LE-GUILDO CÔTES-D'ARMOR

Château de Galinée 22380 ☎ 296411056 ▤ 296410372
e-mail: chateaudegalinee@wanadoo.fr
website: www.chateaudegalinee.com
A family site in a 5 acre wood incorporating the buildings of
an old farm, 3km from the local beaches.
➾ *1km from CD786. Well signposted.*
Open: 7 May-5 Sep Site: 14HEC ⬜ ⊕ 🏕 ♠ Prices: ♦3.85-
5.45 pitch 8.40-13.80 Facilities: ☂ 🛒 ⊙ ⛽ 🎪 Services: 🍴 lau
Leisure: ⚓ P Off-site: ⌀ ⚓LS

Châtelet r des Nouettes, 22380 ☎ 296419633 ▤ 296419799
e-mail: chateletcp@aol.com website: www.lachatelet.com
In superb landscaped surroundings overlooking the sea with
good sporting facilities.
➾ *1km W, 250mtrs from the beach*
Open: 8 May-11 Sep Site: 8HEC ⬜ ⊕ 🚐 Prices: ♦4-5.80
pitch 11-16 Facilities: ☂ 🛒 ⊙ ⛽ ⌀ 🎪 Services: 🍴 ✗ ⊞ lau
Leisure: ⚓ LPS Off-site: 🔥

Crique r de la Mare, 22380 ☎ 296418919
A tiered camp site with exceptional views across Fort Lalette
and the sea. Direct access to the beach.
Open: 15 Mar-2 Jan Site: 2.8HEC ⬜ ⊕ 🏕 Prices: ♦2.40-
3.70 ➡1.10-1.70 pitch 3.20-5.60 Facilities: ☂ ⊙ ⛽ ⌀ 🎪
Services: 🍴 ✗ ⊞ lau Off-site: ⚓S

Mielles 22380 ☎ 296418760 ▤ 296810477
Ideally positioned at the heart of the resort and within
walking distance of the beach. Spacious defined pitches.
➾ *500 mtrs NE on coast.*
Open: 15 Mar-2 Jan Site: 3.5HEC ⬜ ⋯ ⊕ 🏕
Prices: ♦2.60-4.40 ➡1.50-2.30 pitch 4.40-8.20 Facilities: ☂
⊙ ⛽ ⌀ 🎪 Services: ✗ ⊞ lau Leisure: ⚓ P

Facilities: 🛒-shop ☂-shower ⊙-electric points for razors ⛽-electric points for caravans 🎪-parking by tents permitted
🅿-compulsory separate car park **Services:** ✗-café/restaurant 🍴-bar ⌀-Camping Gaz International 🔥-gas other than Camping
Gaz ⊞-first aid facilities lau-laundry **Leisure:** ⚓-swimming L-Lake P-Pool R-River S-Sea **Off-site:** All facilities within 2km

Camping-Caravaning
Le P'tit Bois ★★★★

St Malo
35430 St Jouan des Guérêts

Sunêlia
open style

|Le P'tit Bois

Saint Malo
City of the sea

Booking :
Tél. 33 (0)2 99 21 14 30
Fax 33 (0)2 99 81 74 14
E-mail: camping.ptitbois@wanadoo.fr

www.ptitbois.com

ST-EFFLAM CÔTES-D'ARMOR

CM r de Ian-Carré, 22310 ☎ 296356215 ▤ 296350975
e-mail: camping-municipal@plestinlesgreves.com
website: www.plestinlesgreves.com
On a level meadow with well defined pitches 100mtrs from a
magnificent beach.
Open: Apr-Sep Site: 4HEC ▦ ⋇ ⚑ Prices: ⋔2.21-2.60
🚗1.30-1.53 pitch 2.86-3.36 Facilities: ⓘ ⊙ ▨ ☎ Services: ⚑
✕ lau Off-site: ✕ ⌀ ⭣S

ST-GERMAIN-SUR-AY MANCHE

Aux Grands Espaces 50430 ☎ 233071014 ▤ 233072259
website: www.aux-grand-espaces.com
On slightly sloping ground among dunes. Children's play
area. Lunchtime siesta 12.30-14.30 hrs. 500mtrs from sea.
➲ Leave D650 W of town and follow signs 'Plage' on D306.
Open: May-15 Sep Site: 15HEC ▦ ⚓ ⚑ ⚑ Prices: ⋔4.50
pitch 5.30 Facilities: ⓘ ⚑ ⊙ ▨ ⌀ ⛺ ☎ Services: ⚑ ✕ lau
Leisure: ⭣P Off-site: ⭣S

ST-GILDAS-DE-RHUYS MORBIHAN

Menhir rte de Port Crouesty, 56730
☎ 297452288 ▤ 297453718
e-mail: campingmenhir@aol.com
website: www.campingdumenhir.com
A family site with good facilities situated 1km from the
beach.
➲ 3.5km N.
Open: 26 May-5 Sep Site: 3HEC ▦ ⚓ ⚑ Prices: ⋔5.50
pitch 14.50 Facilities: ⓘ ⚑ ⊙ ▨ ☎ Services: ⚑ ✕ ⊞ lau
Leisure: ⭣ PS Off-site: ⌀ ⭣S

ST-JOUAN-DES-GUÉRÊTS ILLE-ET-VILAINE

P'tit Bois 35430 ☎ 299211430 ▤ 299817414
e-mail: camping.ptitbois@wanadoo.fr
website: www.ptitbois.com
A pleasant family site in quiet wooded surroundings.
➲ Access via N137.
Open: 15 May-11 Sep Site: 6HEC ▦ ⚑ ⚑ Prices: ⋔7 pitch
10-18 Facilities: ⓘ ⚑ ⊙ ▨ ☎ Services: ⚑ ✕ ⊞ lau Leisure: ⭣
P Off-site: ⌀ ⛏ ⭣RS

ST-LÉGER-DU-BOURG-DENIS SEINE-MARITIME

Aubette 23 r Vert Buisson, 76160
☎ 235084769 ▤ 0235084769
In a wooded valley, 3km E of Rouen.
Open: All year Site: 0.8HEC ▦ ⚑ ⚑ Prices: ⋔15 pitch 16
Facilities: ⓘ ⊙ ▨ ⛏ ☎ Services: ⊞ lau
Off-site: ⚑ ✕ ⌀ ⭣R

ST-LUNAIRE ILLE-ET-VILAINE

Longchamp bd de St-Cast, 35800
☎ 299463398 ▤ 299460271
In a beautiful wooded setting in the heart of the Emerald
coast with a good range of facilities.
➲ Turn off D786 towards St-Briac at end of village, site is on
left. 100mtrs from the sea.
Open: 15 May-10 Sep Site: 5HEC ▦ ⚑ Facilities: ⓘ ⚑ ⊙
▨ ⌀ ☎ Services: ⚑ ✕ ⊞ lau Off-site: ⭣S

Touesse 35800 ☎ 299466113 ▤ 299160258
e-mail: camping.la.touesse@wanadoo.fr
website: www.campinglatouesse.com
A well equipped family site, 300mtrs from the beach.
➲ 2km E via D786.
Open: Apr-Sep Site: 2.8HEC ▦ ⚑ ⚑ ⚑ Prices: ⋔3.50-4.50
🚗2.50-3 pitch 4.60-5.90 Facilities: ⓘ ⚑ ⊙ ▨ ⌀ ⛏ ☎
Services: ⚑ ✕ ⊞ lau Off-site: ⭣PS

ST-MALO ILLE-ET-VILAINE

CM le Nicet av de la Varde Rotheneuf, 35400 ☎ 299402632
e-mail: camping@ville-saint-malo.fr
website: www.ville-saint-malo.fr/campings
100mtrs from the beach; direct access via staircase. Water
sports and other activities available.
Open: 15 Jun-1 Sept Site: 2.9HEC ▦ ⚑ Prices: ⋔5.10
🚗14.40 pitch 10.80 (incl 2 persons) pp5.10 Facilities: ⓘ ⊙
▨ ☎ Services: ⊞ lau Leisure: ⭣ S Off-site: ⚑ ✕ ⌀ ⛏ ⭣S

Ville Huchet rte de la Passagère, 35400
☎ 299811183 ▤ 299815189
e-mail: info@lavillehuchet.com website: www.lavillehuchet.com
➲ 5km S via N137.
Open: 30 Apr-15 Sep Site: 6HEC ▦ ⚓ ⚑ Prices: ⋔4.25-
4.80 🚗10.35-11.50 ⚑10.35-11.50 Facilities: ⓘ ⚑ ⊙ ▨ ⛏ ☎
Services: ⚑ ✕ ⊞ lau Leisure: ⭣ P Off-site: ⭣RS

ST-MARCAN ILLE-ET-VILAINE

Balcon de la Baie 35120 ☎ 299802295 ▤ 299802295
In a beautiful location overlooking the bay of Mont-St-
Michel.
➲ 10km NW of Pontorson on D797.
Open: Apr-Oct Site: 2.7HEC ▦ ⚑ ⚑ Prices: ⋔3.50 pitch
4.10 Facilities: ⓘ ⊙ ▨ ⌀ ☎ Services: ⚑ ✕ lau Leisure: ⭣ P
Off-site: ✕

A full guide to the Symbols &
Abbreviations used in this book
can be found on page 6

Site: 6HEC-Site size ▦-grass ⋯-sand ⚬-stone ⋇-little shade ⚑-partly shaded ⚓-mainly shaded
⚑-bungalows for hire ⚑-caravans for hire ⚑-tents for hire ⊗-no dogs Prices: ⋔-adult per night ⚑-car per night
pp-per person per night ⚑-caravan per night ⚑-tent per night

ST-MARTIN-DES-BESACES CALVADOS

Puits 14350 ☎ 231678002 🖳 231678002
e-mail: camping.le.puits@wanadoo.fr
website: www.lepuits.com
A small family run site surrounded by a pleasant garden and
lush fields.
�’ *Access via N175 Caen/Mont-St-Michel.*
Open: Feb-Oct Site: 3.6HEC 〰〰 ☼ 🚐 Prices: ⛺3 pitch 6
Facilities: 🚿 ⊙ 🗨 🏕 Services: ♣ ✗ 🖽 lau Off-site: ✗ ⌀ ⅏

ST-MARTIN-EN-CAMPAGNE SEINE-MARITIME

Goelands r des Grèbes, Saint Martin Plage, 76370
☎ 235838290 🖳 235861799
e-mail: info@camping-les-goelands.com
website: www.camping-les-goelands.com
Site with good recreational facilities in an area of woodland,
100mtrs from a small lake. Shop and bar open in high season
only.
�’ *NE of Dieppe, 2km from D925.*
Open: 30 Mar-30 Oct Site: 4HEC 〰〰 ☼ 🚐 Prices: ⛺11-15
pitch 20-21 (incl 4 persons) Facilities: 🚿 🅿 ⊙ 🗨 ⌀ 🏕
Services: ✗ 🖽 lau Leisure: ⚓ S Off-site: ⅏ ⚓P

ST-MICHEL-EN-GRÈVE CÔTES-D'ARMOR

Capucines Kervourdon, 22300
☎ 296357228 🖳 296357898
e-mail: les.capucines@wanadoo.fr
website: lescapucines.fr
In a peaceful setting near the beach with a large variety of
facilities.
�’ *On D786 Lannion-Morlaix road.*
Open: May-11 Sep Site: 4HEC 〰〰 🄰 🚐 🕸 Prices: ⛺3.60-5
13-24.50 (incl 2 persons) Facilities: 🚿 🅿 ⊙ 🗨 🏕
Services: ♣ ✗ 🖽 lau Leisure: ⚓ P Off-site: ✗ ⌀ ⚓S

ST-PAIR-SUR-MER MANCHE

Ecutot 50380 ☎ 233502629 🖳 233506494
e-mail: camping.ecutot@wanadoo.fr
website: www.ecutot.com
Situated in an orchard 1km from the sea.
�’ *On the main road between Granville and Avranches.*
Open: Jun-15 Sep Site: 5HEC 〰〰 🄰 🚐 Prices: ⛺9 ⛺3.60
pitch 5 Facilities: 🚿 ⊙ 🗨 🏕 Services: ♣ lau Leisure: ⚓ P
Off-site: 🛒 ✗ ⌀ ⅏ ⚓S 🖽

🏠Lez-Eaux St-Aubin-des-Preaux, 50380
☎ 233516609 🖳 233519202
e-mail: lez.eaux@wanadoo.fr website: www.lez-eaux.com
Situated in grounds of an old Château. Bank, TV and reading
room. Fishing available.
�’ *7km SE via D973 rte d'Avranches.*
Open: May-15 Sep Site: 12HEC 〰〰 🄰 🚐 Prices: ⛺7 pitch
15-26 (incl 2 persons) Facilities: 🚿 🛒 ⊙ 🗨 ⌀ ⅏ 🏕
Services: ♣ ✗ 🖽 lau Leisure: ⚓ P

Mariénée 50380 ☎ 233906005
2km from sea; situated in grounds of old farm.
�’ *2km S of town on D21.*
Open: Apr-Sep Site: 1.2HEC 〰〰 🄰 Facilities: 🚿 ⊙ 🗨 ⅏ 🏕
Services: 🖽 lau Off-site: 🛒 ♣ ✗ ⌀ ⚓PS

ST-PHILIBERT-SUR-MER MORBIHAN

Vieux Logis Kernivilit, 56470 ☎ 297550117 🖳 297300391
e-mail: campvieuxlogis@aol.com
website: www.camping-au-vieux-logis.com
Beautiful, well-kept site divided by hedges.

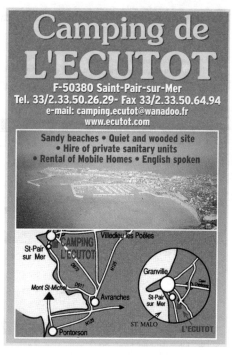
�’ *2km W via D781.*
Open: All year Site: 2.5HEC 〰〰 🄰 🚐 Prices: ⛺3.60-4.50
⛺2-2.60 pitch 6-7.90 Facilities: 🚿 ⊙ 🗨 ⌀ ⅏ 🏕 Services: ♣
✗ 🖽 lau Leisure: ⚓ P Off-site: ⚓RS

ST-PIERRE-DU-VAUVRAY EURE

St-Pierre 1 r du Château, 27430
☎ 232610155 🖳 232610155
In wooded surroundings with pitches divided by hedges,
50mtrs from the River Seine.
�’ *Access via A13/N15.*
Open: All year Site: 3HEC 〰〰 🄰 Prices: ⛺3.20 ⛺5 ⛺5
pitch 5 Facilities: 🚿 ⊙ 🗨 🏕 Services: lau Leisure: ⚓ P
Off-site: 🛒 ♣ ✗ ⅏ ⚓R 🖽

ST-PIERRE-QUIBERON MORBIHAN

Park-er-Lann 56170 ☎ 297502493 🖳 297502493
�’ *1.5km S on D768.*
Open: Etr-Sep Site: 2.5HEC 〰〰 🄰 🚐 Facilities: 🚿 ⊙ 🗨
⅏ 🏕 Services: ♣ ✗ 🖽 lau Off-site: ⌀ ⚓S

ST-QUAY-PORTRIEUX CÔTES-D'ARMOR

Bellevue 68 bd du Littoral, 22410
☎ 296704184 🖳 269705546
e-mail: campingbellevue@free.fr
website: www.campingbellevue.net
A terraced site adjacent to the sea with numbered pitches.
�’ *800mtrs from town centre off D786.*
Open: 01 May-15 Sep Site: 4HEC 〰〰 🄰 🚐 Prices: ⛺3.40-
4.35 pitch 5-6.40 Facilities: 🚿 🛒 ⊙ 🗨 ⌀ 🏕 Services: 🖽 lau
Leisure: ⚓ PS Off-site: 🛒 ♣ ✗ ⌀ ⅏

Facilities: 🛒-shop 🚿-shower ⊙-electric points for razors 🗨-electric points for caravans 🏕-parking by tents permitted
🅿-compulsory separate car park Services: ✗-café/restaurant ♣-bar ⌀-Camping Gaz International ⅏-gas other than Camping
Gaz 🖽-first aid facilities lau-laundry Leisure: ⚓-swimming L-Lake P-Pool R-River S-Sea Off-site: All facilities within 2km

ST-VAAST-LA-HOUGUE MANCHE

Gallouette r de la Gallouette, 50550
☎ 233542057   ▤ 233541671
e-mail: contact@camping-lagallouette.fr
website: www.camping-lagallouette.fr
A well equipped site, 300mtrs from the town centre and with
direct access to the beach.
Open: Apr-Sept Site: 2.3HEC ⊞ ♁ 🏠 🚐 Prices: ♦4-4.55
pitch 5-6 Facilities: 🏧 ⚡ ⊙ ⚑ ⊘ ♨ 🏫 Services: ♀ ✗ lau
Leisure: ⚓ S Off-site: ✗

STE-MARIE-DU-MONT MANCHE

Utah Beach La Madeleine, 50480
☎ 233715369   ▤ 233710711
e-mail: utah.beach@wanadoo.fr
website: www.campingutahbeach.com
On a level meadow 100mtrs from the beach.
➲ 6km NE via D913 and D421.
Open: Apr-Sep Site: 3HEC ⊞ ♁ ⦂⦂⦂ ㇇ 🏠 Prices: ♦3.80-
4.50 pitch 13.70-16.40 Facilities: 🏧 ⚡ ⊙ ⚑ 🏫 Services: ♀
✗ lau Leisure: ⚓ PS

STE-MARINE FINISTÈRE

Hellès 29120 ☎ 298563146   ▤ 298563683
e-mail: contact@le-helles.com
website: www.le-helles.com
➲ 400mtrs from the beach
Open: May-15 Sep Site: 3HEC ⊞ ♁ 🏠 🚐 Prices: 🚐11.50-
15.50 Facilities: 🏧 ⊙ ⚑ ⊘ 🏫 Services: ⊞ lau Leisure: ⚓ P
Off-site: ⚓S

STE-MÈRE-ÉGLISE MANCHE

Cormoran Ravenoville-Plage, 50480
☎ 233413394   ▤ 233951608
e-mail: lecormoran@wanadoo.fr website: www.lecormoran.com
A quiet site with well defined pitches, 20mtrs from the sea.
➲ Drive towards Ravenoville Plage, then take Utah Beach
road for 500mtrs.
Open: 30 Mar-22 Sep Site: 6.5HEC ⊞ ♁ 🏠 Prices: ▲4-5
pitch 14.50-19 (incl 2 persons) Facilities: 🏧 ⚡ ⊙ ⚑ ⊘ ♨ 🏫
Services: ♀ ✗ ⊞ lau Leisure: ⚓ P Off-site: ⚓S

SARZEAU MORBIHAN

Ferme de Lann Hoedic rte du Roaliguen, 56370
☎ 297480173   ▤ 297417287
e-mail: contact@camping-lannhoedic.fr
website: www.camping-lannhoedic.fr
Quiet site situated 800 metres from a sheltered beach,
accessible by foot or bike through a shady forest path. Pitches
in sunny or shady locations, some surrounded by landscaped
hedges.
➲ From Vannes, take the exit for Sarzeau, continue in the
direction for Arzon. Turn left at 1st roundabout, next to the
Super U, after 2kms take turning on left in direction for Lann
Hoedic.
Open: Apr-Oct Site: 3.6HEC ⊞ ♁ 🏠 🚐 ▲ Prices: ♦4-4
pitch 7-7 Facilities: 🏧 ⊙ ⚑ ♨ 🏫 Services: ⊞ lau Off-site: ⚡
♀ ✗ ⊘ ⚓S

Treste rte de la Plage du Roaliguen, 56370
☎ 297417960   ▤ 297413621
e-mail: letreste@campingletreste.com
website: www.campingletreste.com
A family site with good facilities 800mtrs from the Roaliguen
beach.
➲ 2.5km S
Open: 15 May-9 Sep Site: 5HEC ⊞ ♁ 🏠 ▲ Prices: ♦4.95
pitch 8.90 Facilities: 🏧 ⚡ ⊙ ♨ ⊘ 🏫 Services: ♀ lau
Leisure: ⚓ P Off-site: ✗ ♨ ⚓S

AT POINTE-ST-JACQUES (5.5KM S)

CM St-Jacques 56370 ☎ 297417929   ▤ 297480445
e-mail: camping-stjacques.com
website: www.camping-stjacques.com
On beach protected by dunes. Well kept site with asphalt
drives in a pleasant wooded location.
Open: Apr-Sep Site: 7.6HEC ⊞ ♁ 🏠 🚐 ▲ Prices: ♦2.88-
3.60 pitch 4.32-5.40 Facilities: 🏧 ⊙ ⚑ ⊘ ♨ 🏫 Services: ♀ ✗
⊞ lau Leisure: ⚓ S Off-site: ⚡ ✗

SASSETOT-LE-MAUCONDUIT SEINE-MARITIME

Trois Plages 76540 ☎ 235274011   ▤ 235282320
Well equipped site 3km from the coast.
➲ 1.3km S near D925.
Open: 25 Apr-15 Sep Site: 4HEC ⊞ ♁ Facilities: 🏧 ⚡ ⊙
⚑ ⊘ ♨ 🏫 Services: ⊞ lau Off-site: ✗

SUBLIGNY MANCHE

Grand Chemin 50870 ☎ 233513096
Small site in a rural setting with well defined pitches within
easy reach of the village.
➲ Access via N175 towards Avranches, then D39 and follow
signs.
Open: All year Site: ⊞ ♁ 🚐 Prices: ♦2.28 🚐3.75 ▲1.22
Facilities: 🏧 ⊙ ⚑ 🏫 Services: lau

TELGRUC-SUR-MER FINISTÈRE

Panoramic rte de la Plage, 29560
☎ 298277841   ▤ 298273610
e-mail: info@camping-panoramic.com
website: www.camping-panoramic.com
Quiet terraced site with views across a wide sandy beach.
Secluded pitches.
➲ W on D887 and then S on D208.
Open: Jun-15 Sept Site: 4HEC ⊞ ♣ 🏠 🚐 Prices: ♦5 🚗2
pitch 8 Facilities: 🏧 ⚡ ⊙ ⚑ ⊘ 🏫 Services: ♀ ✗ ⊞ lau
Leisure: ⚓ P Off-site: ⚓S

THEIX MORBIHAN

Rhuys Le Poteau Rouge, Atlantheix, 56450
☎ 297541477   ▤ 297759854
Directly on the sea, with good modern facilities.
➲ 3.5km NW via N165
Open: Apr-15 Oct Site: 2HEC ⊞ ⦂⦂⦂ ♁ 🏠 🚐 Facilities: 🏧
⊙ ⚑ ♨ ⊞ 🏫 Services: ⊞ lau Leisure: ⚓ P Off-site: ⚡ ♀ ✗

THURY-HARCOURT CALVADOS

Vallée du Traspy 14220 ☎ 231796180   ▤ 231525354
Level meadow site near a small reservoir, 250mtrs from
Centre Aquatique de la Suisse Normande.
Open: 15 Apr-15 Sep Site: 1.5HEC ⊞ ♁ Facilities: 🏧 ⊙ ⚑
🏫 Services: ⊞ lau Leisure: ⚓ LPR Off-site: ⚡ ♀ ✗ ⊘ ♨

TINTÉNIAC ILLE-ET-VILAINE

Peupliers La Besnelais, 35190 ☎ 299454975   ▤ 299455298
e-mail: camping.les.peupliers@wanadoo.fr
A peaceful site in a wooded location with good facilities.
➲ 2km SE via N137.
Open: Mar-Oct Site: 4.5HEC ⊞ ♁ 🏠 Prices: ♦4.30 pitch
5.95 Facilities: 🏧 ⚡ ⊙ ⚑ ♨ 🏫 Services: ♀ ✗ ⊞ lau
Leisure: ⚓ P Off-site: ✗ ⊘

TOLLEVAST MANCHE

Village Vert 50470 ☎ 233430078
A peaceful site situated in a pine grove within an extensive
park.

⮕ *From Cherbourg car ferry terminal follow N13 to the Auchan Hypermarket and then continue for 200mtrs for site on left-hand side of the road.*
Open: All year Site: 5.5HEC ⚏ ⊕ 🚐 Prices: ↟2.80-4 🚐3-4.50 pitch 3-4.50 Facilities: ⋔ 🚿 ⊙ 🚐 🏖 🖾 Services: 🖽 lau Off-site: 🍽 ✕ ∅ 🏖 ↴R

TOURLAVILLE MANCHE

Espace Loisirs de Collignon 50110 ☎ 233201688 🖷 233205303
e-mail: VPT50@wanadoo.fr
A pleasant site with good facilities, 1km from town centre.
Site: 2HEC ⚏ 🌿 🎪 Facilities: ⋔ 🚿 ⊙ 🚐 ∅ 🏖 🖾
Services: 🍽 ✕ lau Leisure: ↴ S Off-site: ✕ ↴PS 🖽

TOURNIÈRES CALVADOS

Picard Holidays 14330 ☎ 231228244 🖷 231517028
e-mail: paul.palmer@wanadoo.fr
website: www.camp-france.com
A quiet site with pleasant, sheltered pitches conveniently situated between Cherbourg and Caen.
⮕ *Access via N13 and D15/D5.*
Open: All year Site: 2HEC ⚏ 🌿 🚐 ⚒ Prices: ↟5.10 pitch 5.10 Facilities: ⋔ 🚿 ⊙ 🚐 🖾 🖾 Services: 🍽 ✕ 🖽 lau
Leisure: ↴ LP Off-site: ↴R

TRÉBEURDEN CÔTES-D'ARMOR

Armor-Loisirs rue de Kernevez-Lors-Mabo, 22560
☎ 296235231 🖷 296154036
e-mail: info@armorloisirs.com
website: www.armorloisirs.com
Modern site with individual pitches surrounded by hedges. Hardstandings for caravans.
⮕ *500mtrs S of the Kernévez road.*
Open: Apr-Sep Site: 2.2HEC ⚏ ⊕ 🚐 Prices: ↟3-5 🚐2-2.50 pitch 5-7.50 Facilities: ⋔ 🚿 ⊙ 🚐 🏖 🖾 Services: 🍽 ✕
🖽 lau Leisure: ↴ P Off-site: ↴RS

TRÉGUNC FINISTÈRE

Pommeraie St-Philibert, 29910 ☎ 298500273 🖷 298500791
e-mail: pommeraie@club-internet.fr
website: www.campingdelapommeraie.com
A well equipped site with good facilities for children, 1.2km from the beach.
⮕ *S via D1.*
Open: May-5 Sep Site: 7HEC ⚏ ⊕ 🎪 Prices: ↟3.50-5 🚐5-9 Facilities: ⋔ 🚿 ⊙ 🚐 🏖 🖾 Services: 🍽 ✕ 🖽 lau Leisure: ↴
P Off-site: ∅ ↴S

TRÉLÉVERN CÔTES-D'ARMOR

Port l'Epine Pors-Garo, 22660 ☎ 296237194 🖷 296237783
e-mail: camping-de-port-lepine@wanadoo.fr
website: www.camping-port-lepine.com
Well shaded site directly on the sea.
Open: Apr-Sep Site: 3HEC ⚏ ⊕ 🎪 ⛺ Facilities: ⋔ 🚿 ⊙ 🚐
∅ 🏖 🖾 Services: 🍽 ✕ 🖽 lau Leisure: ↴ PS

TRÉPORT, LE SEINE-MARITIME

CM les Boucaniers r Mendes-France, 76470 ☎ 235863547
Well-kept site on flat meadow on E edge of village. Sports and games nearby.
Open: Etr-Sep Site: 5.5HEC ⚏ 🌿 🎪 Facilities: ⋔ ⊙ 🚐 🖾
Services: 🖽 lau Off-site: 🏖 🍽 ✕ ↴PRS

Parc International du Golf rte de Dieppe, 76470
☎ 227280150 🖷 227280151
In a park on the cliffs.
⮕ *1km W on D940.*
Open: Apr-20 Sep Site: 5HEC ⚏ ⊕ Prices: ↟5-6
Facilities: ⋔ ⊙ 🚐 🖾 Services: 🖽 lau Off-site: 🏖 🍽 ✕ ∅ ↴PS

AT MESNIL-VAL

Parc Val d'Albion 1 r de la Mer, 76910
☎ 235862142 🖷 235867851
Terraced site in wooded parkland next to the sea.
⮕ *3km S from Le Tréport on D126.*
Open: Jun-15 Sep Site: 3HEC ⚏ ⊕ Prices: ↟7 Facilities: ⋔
⊙ 🚐 🖾 Services: 🖽 lau Off-site: 🏖 🍽 ✕ ∅ ↴S

TRÉVOU-TRÉGUIGNEC CÔTES-D'ARMOR

Mât 38 r de Trestel, 22660 ☎ 296237152
e-mail: camping-le-mat@wanadoo.fr
A family site on level ground, close to beach.
⮕ *Access via D38.*
Open: 15 Apr-15 Sep Site: 1.6HEC ⚏ ⊕ 🎪 🚐
Prices: ↟4.20 pitch 5.30 Facilities: ⋔ ⊙ 🚐 ∅ 🏖 🖾
Services: 🖽 lau Leisure: ↴ P Off-site: 🏖 🍽 ✕ ↴LS

TRINITÉ-SUR-MER, LA MORBIHAN

Baie Plage de Kervilen, 56470 ☎ 297557342 🖷 297558881
e-mail: camping@camping-la-baie-com
website: www.camping-la-baie.com
Several strips of land divided by tall trees on the edge of a fine sandy beach.
⮕ *Signposted in the direction of Kerbihan.*
Open: 15 May-15 Sep Site: 2.4HEC ⚏ ⊕ 🚐 Prices: ↟1.95-5.40 pitch 11.25-20 Facilities: ⋔ ⊙ 🚐 ∅ 🖾 Services: 🍽 ✕
🖽 lau Leisure: ↴ P Off-site: ↴S

Kervilor 56470 ☎ 297557675 🖷 297558726
e-mail: ebideau@camping-kervilor.com
website: www.camping-kervilor.com
In a pleasant wooded location 1.5km from the port. Plenty of recreational facilities.

contd.

Facilities: 🚿-shop ⋔-shower ⊙-electric points for razors 🚐-electric points for caravans 🖾-parking by tents permitted 🅿-compulsory separate car park **Services:** ✕-café/restaurant 🍽-bar ∅-Camping Gaz International 🏖-gas other than Camping Gaz 🖽-first aid facilities lau-laundry **Leisure:** ↴-swimming L-Lake P-Pool R-River S-Sea **Off-site:** All facilities within 2km

➲ *1.6km N*
Open: 9 May-15 Sep Site: 4.8HEC ⟰ ⌴ ⌂ Prices: ⋔3.53-
4.70 ⌘2.25-3 ⩘3 pitch 8.63-11.50 Facilities: ⋒ ⚍ ⊙ ⌑ ∅ ⌂
Services: ⵟ ✕ ⊞ lau Leisure: ⇝ P Off-site: ✕ ♨

Plage Plage de Kervilen, 56470 ☎ 297557328   ▤ 297558831
e-mail: laplage@club-internet.fr
website: www.camping-plage.com
A family site divided into pitches and lying behind sand
dunes which give direct access to the beach.
➲ *1km S towards Carnac-Plage.*
Open: 8 May-15 Sep Site: 3HEC ⟰ ⌴ ⌂ Prices: ⋔4 pitch
8.40-23.10 Facilities: ⋒ ⊙ ⌑ ⌂ Services: ⊞ lau Leisure: ⇝ P
Off-site: ⚍ ⵟ ✕ ∅ ⇝S

VEULES-LES-ROSES SEINE-MARITIME

Mouettes av J-Moulin, 76980 ☎ 235976198
Open: 15 Feb-Nov Site: 3.6HEC ⟰ ⌴ Facilities: ⋒ ⚍ ⊙ ⌑
∅ ⌂ Services: ⊞ lau Off-site: ⚍ ⵟ ✕ ∅ ⇝S

Paradis chemin de Manneville, 76980 ☎ 235976142
A municipal site on the southern outskirts of the town.
Open: mid May-mid Sep Site: 0.9HEC ⟰ ⌴ Facilities: ⋒
⊙ ⌑ ⌂ Services: ⊞ lau Off-site: ⚍ ⵟ ✕ ∅ ♨ ⇝PRS ⊞

VILLERS-SUR-MER CALVADOS

Ammonites rte de la Corniche, 14640
☎ 231870606   ▤ 231871800
e-mail: camping-lesammonites@wanadoo.fr
website: www.camping-les-ammonites.com
➲ *4km SW on rte de Cabourg and D163 towards Auberville.*
Open: Apr-Oct Site: 3HEC ⟰ ⌴ ⌂ Facilities: ⋒ ⚍ ⊙ ∅
∅ ♨ ⌂ Services: ⵟ ✕ ⊞ lau Leisure: ⇝ P

PARIS/NORTH

ACY-EN-MULTIEN OISE

Ancien Moulin 60620 ☎ 344872128   ▤ 344872128
e-mail: secretariat@campingclub.2000.fr
website: www.campingclub.2000.fr
Situated beside a river and a small lake with good sporting
facilities.
Open: All year Site: 5HEC ⟰ ⌴ Prices: ⌘18.76
Facilities: ⋒ ⊙ ⌑ ⌂ Services: lau Leisure: ⇝ LR Off-site: ⚍
ⵟ✕ ∅ ⌂

AMBLETEUSE PAS-DE-CALAIS

Beaucamp 10 r de Ferquent, 62164
☎ 321326210   ▤ 321306377
A useful overnight stop between Boulogne and Calais.
Open: All year Site: 9HEC ⟰ ⌴ ⌂ ⌘ Prices: ⋔4.80 ⌘3.40
⌘3.40 ⩘4.90-5.50 pitch 6.80 Facilities: ⋒ ⚍ ⊙ ⌑ ♨
Services: ⵟ ✕ lau Off-site: ⇝RS

AMPLIER PAS-DE-CALAIS

Val d'Authie 93 r du Marais, 62760
☎ 321485707   ▤ 321580860
e-mail: a.boulanger@free.fr
website: a.boulanger.free.fr/index/
In wooded surroundings beside a small lake.
➲ *Access via N25 and D24 or D938.*
Open: 16 Apr-14 Oct Site: 2HEC ⟰ ⌴ ♣ Facilities: ⋒ ⚍ ⊙
⌑ ⌂ Services: ⵟ ✕ lau Leisure: ⇝ R

ARDRES PAS-DE-CALAIS

AT AUTINGUES (2KM S)

St-Louis 223 r Leulène, 62610 ☎ 321354683   ▤ 321001978
website: www.campingstlouis.com
A well equipped site in pleasant wooded surroundings.

➲ *Turn off N43 approx 1km SE of Ardres onto D224 and
follow signs.*
Open: Apr-Oct Site: 1.7HEC ⟰ ⌴ ⌘ Prices: ⋔2.50 pitch
5.50-5 Facilities: ⋒ ⚍ ⊙ ⌑ ♨ ⌂ Services: ✕ ⊞ lau
Off-site: ⵟ ✕ ⇝L

AUDRUICQ PAS-DE-CALAIS

CM Les Pyramides 62370 ☎ 321355917
A site with good sanitary and sports facilities beside the
canal.
Open: Apr-Sep Site: ⟰ ⌴ Facilities: ⋒ ⊙ ⌑ ⌂ ⌂ ▣
Services: ⊞ lau Off-site: ⚍ ⵟ ✕ ∅ ⇝P

BEAUVAIS OISE

Clos Normand 1 r de l'Abbaye, St-Paul, 60650 ☎ 344822730
A small site on a lake with facilities for fishing.
➲ *6km W via N31 towards Rouen.*
Open: May-Sept Site: 1.3HEC ⟰ ⌴ ⌂ Prices: ⋔2.50
pitch 7 Facilities: ⋒ ⊙ ⌑ ♨ ⌂ Services: lau Leisure: ⇝ L
Off-site: ⵟ ✕

BERCK-SUR-MER PAS-DE-CALAIS

Orée du Bois chemin Blanc 251, Rang-du-Fliers, 62180
☎ 321842851   ▤ 321842856
e-mail: oree.du.bois@wanadoo.fr
website: www.loreedubois.com
A modern site in wooded surroundings with good sports
facilities.
➲ *2km NE.*
Open: 29 Mar-20 Oct Site: 18HEC ⟰ ⌴ ⌂ Facilities: ⋒ ⊙
⌑ ♨ ⌂ Services: ⵟ ✕ ⊞ lau Off-site: ⚍ ∅

BERNY-RIVIÈRE AISNE

Croix du Vieux Pont 2290 ☎ 323555002   ▤ 323550513
e-mail: lacroixdúvieuxpont@wanadoo.fr
website: www.la-croix-du-vieux-pont.com
In wooded surroundings beside the River Aisne with ample
facilities.
➲ *N of N31; cross River Aisne, site is 500mtrs E of Vic-sur-
Aisne on D91.*
Open: All year Site: 19HEC ⟰ ⌴ ⌂ Prices: ⋔9.50-11.50
Facilities: ⋒ ⚍ ⊙ ⌑ ∅ ⌂ Services: ⵟ ✕ ⊞ lau Leisure: ⇝ P
Off-site: ♨

BERTANGLES SOMME

Château r du Château, 80260 ☎ 322933773   ▤ 322936836
e-mail: camping.bertangles@wanadoo.fr
website: perso.wanadoo.fr/chateau.de.bertangles
Site in old orchard of Château.
➲ *Signed off Amiens-Doullens road.*
Open: 23 Apr-6 Sep Site: 0.8HEC ⟰ ⌴ ♣ Prices: ⋔3 ⌘2 ⌘3
⩘3 Facilities: ⋒ ⊙ ⌑ ∅ ⌂ Services: lau Off-site: ⵟ ✕

BEUVRY PAS-DE-CALAIS

CM r Victor-Dutériez, 62660 ☎ 321650800
Open: 15 May-15 Sep Site: 1HEC ⟰ ⌴ ♣ Prices: ⋔1.90
⌘2.55 ⩘2.55 pitch 2.55 Facilities: ⋒ ⊙ ⌑ ⌂ Services: lau
Off-site: ⚍ ⵟ ✕ ∅ ♨ ⇝P

BLANDY-LES-TOURS SEINE-ET-MARNE

Pre de L'Etang 34 r St Martin, 77115
☎ 160669634   ▤ 160669634
On the outskirts of the village, surrounded by fields in a calm
and peaceful location and containing a large pond.
➲ *Take autoroute A5 exit 16 for Chatillon La Borde and
follow directions for Blandy-Les-Tours. On reaching town, take
direction for St Martin*
Open: 15 Feb-15 Dec Site: 2HEC ⟰ ⌴ ⌂ ⌘ Prices: pitch
12.50 Facilities: ⋒ ⊙ ⌑ ∅ ⌂ Services: lau Off-site: ⚍ ⵟ ✕

Site: 6HEC-Site size ⟰-grass ⋮⋮⋮-sand ♦-stone ⵊⵊ-little shade ⌴-partly shaded ♣-mainly shaded
⌂-bungalows for hire ⌘-caravans for hire ⩘-tents for hire ⌀-no dogs Prices: ⋔-adult per night ⌘-car per night
pp-per person per night ⌘-caravan per night ⩘-tent per night

BOIRY-NOTRE-DAME PAS-DE-CALAIS

Flandres Artois 1 r Verte, 62156 ☎ 321481540 📠 321220724
On a level meadow with a good variety of recreational
facilities.
➲ *On D34. Access via A1 exit 15 towards Cambrai or A26 exit
8 towards Arras.*
Open: 26 Mar-Oct Site: 3.4HEC ⊞ ⊕ Facilities: ⋒ ⊙ 🖳 ⓩ
Services: ⬤ ✗ lau Off-site: ⅏ ∅ ♨

BOISSY-LE-CUTTE ESSONNE

Boulinière La Boulinière, 91590 ☎ 164576523 📠 145448516
e-mail: secretariat@campingclub.asso.fr
website: www.campingclub.asso.fr
Situated in a wood 800mtrs from the village.
➲ *Access via N20 and D148.*
Open: All year Site: 4HEC ⊞ ∵ ⊕ Facilities: ⋒ ⊙ 🖳 ⓩ
Services: lau Off-site: ⅏ ⬤ ✗ ∅ ♨ ⅊R ⊞

BOUBERS-SUR-CANCHE PAS-DE-CALAIS

Flore 27 rue de Frevent, 62270
☎ 321048520 📠 321048520
e-mail: arielle.triart@wanadoo.fr
website: perso.wanadoo.fr/camping.loisir/
In a peaceful, rural setting within easy reach of the village.
➲ *E via D340 towards Frévent.*
Open: Apr-15 Oct Site: 1HEC ⊞ ⊕ 🔄 Prices: ⋔3.50 🚐2
pitch 2.29 Facilities: ⋒ ⊙ 🖳 ♨ ⓩ Services: ⊞ lau
Off-site: ⅊PR

BOULANCOURT SEINE-ET-MARNE

Ile de Boulancourt 6 allée des Marronniers, 77760
☎ 164241338 📠 164241043
e-mail: camping-ile-de-boulancourt@wanadoo.fr
website: www.camping.paris.com
A peaceful site shaded by mature trees in a convenient
situation in the Essonne valley.
➲ *Access via D410.*
Open: All year Site: 5HEC ⊞ ⊕ 🏠 🔄 Prices: ⋔4 pitch 4
Facilities: ⋒ ⊙ 🖳 ⓩ Services: ⊞ lau Leisure: ⅊ R
Off-site: ⅏ ⬤ ✗ ∅ ♨

BRAY-DUNES NORD

Perroquet-Plage 59123 ☎ 328583737 📠 328583701
e-mail: camping-perroquet@wanadoo.fr
website: www.campingduperroquet.com
An above average site situated among sand dunes with direct
access to the beach.
➲ *3km NE towards La Panne*
Open: Apr-Sep Site: 28HEC ⊞ ∵ ⊕ 🏠 🔄 Prices: ⋔4.60
🚐1.90 🚐2.60 ⚑2 Facilities: ⋒ ⅏ ⊙ 🖳 ∅ ♨ ⓩ Services: ⬤ ✗
⊞ lau Leisure: ⅊ S

CAMIERS PAS-DE-CALAIS

Sables d'Or 62176 ☎ 321849515
In a wooded location with good recreational facilities.
Open: All year Site: 10HEC ⊞ ∵ ⬤ 🏠 Facilities: ⋒ ⊙ 🖳
ⓩ Services: ⬤ ⊞ lau Leisure: ⅊ P Off-site: ⅊S

CAYEUX-SUR-MER SOMME

Voyeul rte des Canadiens, 80410 ☎ 322266084 📠 322266084
In pleasant surroundings, 400mtrs from the sea, with pitches
enclosed by hedges and flowerbeds.
➲ *1.5km S on D140.*
Open: Apr-15 Oct Site: 1.7HEC ⊞ ⊕ Facilities: ⋒ ⅏ ⊙ 🖳
∅ ♨ ⓩ Services: ⬤ ✗ ⊞ lau Off-site: ⅊S

CHAMOUILLE AISNE

Parc de l'Ailette Parc Nautique de l'Ailette, 02860
☎ 323246686 📠 323246687
e-mail: ailette@wanadoo.fr
On the shore of a lake within an extensive leisure park and
nature reserve.
➲ *2km SE via D19.*
Open: Apr-Oct Site: 6HEC ⊞ ⊕ 🏠 🔄 ⚑ Prices: ⋔9-15
Facilities: ⋒ ⅏ ⊙ 🖳 ∅ ⓩ Services: ⬤ ✗ ⊞ lau Leisure: ⅊ L
Off-site: ✗

CONDETTE PAS-DE-CALAIS

Château 21 r Nouvelle, 62360 ☎ 321875959 📠 321875959
e-mail: campingduchateau@libertysurf.fr
website: camping-caravaning-du-chateau.com
On pleasant parkland, bordered by a forest, 500mtrs from the
town centre. Separate car park for arrivals after 23.00hrs.
➲ *Access via D940 towards Hardelot.*
Open: Apr-Oct Site: 1.2HEC ⊞ ⊕ 🏠 🔄 Prices: ⋔2.30
pitch 1 Facilities: ⋒ ⊙ 🖳 ⓩ Services: ⊞ lau Off-site: ⅏ ⬤ ✗
∅ ♨ ⅊L

COUDEKERQUE NORD

Bois des Forts 59280 ☎ 328610441
➲ *0.7km NW on D72.*
Open: All year Site: 4HEC ⊞ ∿ 🏠 🔄 Facilities: ⋒ ⊙ 🖳
♨ ⓩ Services: ⬤ ✗ lau Off-site: ⅏ ∅

CROTOY, LE SOMME

Aubépines r de la Maye, Saint Firmin, 80550
☎ 322270134 📠 322270134
e-mail: contact@camping-lesaubepines.com
website: www.camping-lesaubepines.com
Situated on the Picardy coast at the heart of the Somme
estuary in a peaceful verdant location surrounded by
hawthorn trees. The nearest beach, a kilometre away, is part
of a nature reserve.
➲ *D940 from Abbeville*
Open: Apr-Oct Site: 4HEC ⊞ ∿ 🏠 Prices: ⋔3.25-3.60
🚐2.25-2.50 ⚑1.35-1.50 pitch 12.60-15 Facilities: ⋒ ⅏ ⊙ 🖳
♨ ⓩ Services: ⊞ lau Off-site: ⬤ ✗ ∅ ⅊S

DUNKERQUE (DUNKIRK) NORD

CM bd de l'Europe, 59240 ☎ 328692668 📠 328695621
e-mail: campinglalicorne@wanadoo.fr
Open: Apr-Nov Site: 10HEC ⊞ ∿ Prices: ⋔4.50 🚐2.50
🚐5.10 ⚑2.60 Facilities: ⋒ ⊙ 🖳 ∅ ⓩ ⓟ Services: ⬤ ✗ ⊞ lau
Off-site: ⅏ ⬤ ✗ ∅ ♨ ⅊PS ⊞

ÉPERLECQUES PAS-DE-CALAIS

Château de Gandspette 62910 ☎ 321934393 📠 321957498
e-mail: contact@chateau_gandspette.com
website: www.chateau-gandspette.com
A peaceful site, surrounded by woodland.
➲ *11.5km NW on N43 and D207.*
Open: Apr-Sep Site: 11HEC ⊞ ⊕ Prices: ⋔4.30-5.30 pitch
7.40-10.40 Facilities: ⋒ ⊙ 🖳 ∅ ⓩ Services: ⬤ ✗ ⊞ lau
Leisure: ⅊ P Off-site: ⅏

EQUIHEN-PLAGE PAS-DE-CALAIS

CM la Falaise r C-Cazin, 62224 ☎ 321312261
e-mail: mairie.equinhen.plage@wanadoo.fr
website: www.ville-equinhen-plage.fr
150mtrs between Boulogne and Le Touquet.
Open: 28 Mar-4 Nov Site: 8HEC ⊞ ∿ 🏠 Facilities: ⋒ ⊙
🖳 ⓩ Services: ⊞ lau Off-site: ⅏ ⬤ ✗ ∅ ♨ ⅊S

Facilities: ⅏-shop ⋒-shower ⊙-electric points for razors 🖳-electric points for caravans ⓩ-parking by tents permitted
ⓟ-compulsory separate car park Services: ✗-café/restaurant ⬤-bar ∅-Camping Gaz International ♨-gas other than Camping
Gaz ⊞-first aid facilities lau-laundry Leisure: ⅊-swimming L-Lake P-Pool R-River S-Sea Off-site: All facilities within 2km

ÉTAMPES ESSONNE

Vauvert Ormoy La Rivière, 91150
☎ 164942139 🖳 169927259
In a pleasant woodland situation beside the river.
⮕ *2km S via D49.*
Site: 11HEC ⸽⸽⸽⸽ ◖ Prices: ⚲4 🚐5 ▲5 pitch 5 Facilities: ⋔ ⊙
🔲 ∅ ⚏ ☎ Services: ⚒ ✗ ⊞ Leisure: ⬝ R Off-site: ⬝LP

ÉTAPLES PAS-DE-CALAIS

Pinède 62630 ☎ 321943451
A well equipped site situated amongst sand dunes and
surrounded by pine trees close to the yacht basin and local
shopping facilities.
Open: 15Feb-15Dec Site: 3HEC ⸽⸽⸽⸽ ◖ 🏠 Facilities: ⋔ ⌿ ⊙
🔲 ☎ Services: ⚒ ✗ lau Off-site: ∅ ⌿ ⬝R ⊞

FELLERIES NORD

CM La Boissellerie r de la Place, 59740
☎ 327590650 🖳 327590288
Open: 15 Apr-Sep Site: 1HEC ⸽⸽⸽⸽ ◖ Prices: ⚲2 🚐1 🚐1 ▲1
pitch 1 Facilities: ⋔ ⊙ 🔲 ☎ 🄿 Off-site: ⌿ ⚒ ✗ ∅ ⬝ ⊞

FERTÉ-SOUS-JOUARRE, LA SEINE-ET-MARNE

Bondons 47/49 r des Bondons, 77260
☎ 160220098 🖳 160229701
e-mail: chateau-des-bondons@club-internet.fr
Set in a beautiful wooded park. Reserved for caravans.
⮕ *2km NE via D402 & D70.*
Open: All year Site: 28HEC ⸽⸽⸽⸽ ᶰᵉ Prices: ⚲7 pitch 10
Facilities: ⋔ ⊙ 🔲 ☎ Services: ⚒ ✗ ⊞ lau Off-site: ⌿ ⚒ ✗ ⌿
⬝PR

FORT-MAHON-PLAGE SOMME

Royon rte de Quend, 80790 ☎ 322234030 🖳 322236515
e-mail: barbara.dutot@wanadoo.fr
website: www.campingleroyon.com
A family site with good facilities and well marked pitches,
2.5km from the beach.
Open: 6 Mar-2 Nov Site: 5.5HEC ⸽⸽⸽⸽ ◖ 🏠 Prices: ⚲6.50
pitch 15-28 (incl 3 persons) Facilities: ⋔ ⌿ ⊙ 🔲 ∅ ⚏ ☎
Services: ⚒ ✗ ⊞ lau Leisure: ⬝ P Off-site: ⬝S

FRIAUCOURT SOMME

CM Au Chant des Oiseaux Ruelle du Grand Patis, 80460
☎ 322264954
In pleasant surroundings with good sanitary and sporting
facilities 2km from the sea. Separate carpark for arrivals after
22.00hrs.
⮕ *NE via D63.*
Open: Apr-15 Oct Site: 1.4HEC ⸽⸽⸽⸽ ◖ 🏠 Facilities: ⋔ ⊙ 🔲
☎ Services: lau

GOUVIEUX OISE

César rte de Toutevoie 10, 60270 ☎ 344571273
On a hill overlooking the River Oise.
⮕ *Access via A1 to Gouvieux town centre, then towards Creil.*
Open: All year Site: 6HEC ⸽⸽⸽⸽ ◖ Facilities: ⋔ ⊙ 🔲 ☎
Services: ⊞ lau Off-site: ⚏ ⚒ ✗ ∅ ⌿ ⬝P

GRAND-FORT-PHILIPPE NORD

CM de la Plage r Ml-Foch, 59153 ☎ 328653195
On a level meadow separated from the beach (500mtrs away)
by sand dunes.
⮕ *On the seaward extremity of Grand-Fort Philippe.*
Open: Apr-Oct Site: 1.5HEC ⸽⸽⸽⸽ ◖ Prices: ⚲3.70 🚐1.45
🚐2.90 ▲2.90 Facilities: ⋔ ⊙ 🔲 ☎ Services: lau Off-site: ⚏
⚒ ✗ ∅ ⌿ ⬝S ⊞

GREZ-SUR-LOING SEINE-ET-MARNE

CM Près chemin des Près, 77880 ☎ 164457275 🖳 16445727
website: camping-grez@wanadoo.fr
⮕ *NE towards Loing*
Open: end Mar-11 Nov Site: 6HEC ⸽⸽⸽⸽ ◖ 🚐 Prices: ⚲2.45
🚐1.70 🚐2.45 ▲2.45 Facilities: ⋔ ⚏ ⊙ 🔲 ☎ Services: lau
Off-site: ⚒ ✗ ∅ ⬝R ⊞

GUINES PAS-DE-CALAIS

▦Bien Assise 62340 ☎ 321352077 🖳 321367920
e-mail: castel@bien-assise.com website: www.bien-assise.com
A nice site in the country near to a large forest and a
charming little town.
⮕ *Access via D231 towards Marquise.*
Open: 19 Apr-21 Sep Site: 12HEC ⸽⸽⸽⸽ ◖ 🏠 🚐
Prices: ⚲4.50 pitch 11.30 Facilities: ⋔ ⚏ ⊙ 🔲 ∅ ☎
Services: ⚒ ✗ ⊞ lau Leisure: ⬝ P

HIRSON AISNE

Cascade Site de Blangy, 2500 ☎ 323581897 🖳 323587451
e-mail: tourisme.info.hirson@wanadoo.fr
In a picturesque woodland setting with good, modern facilities.
⮕ *1.8km N via N43 towards La Capelle.*
Open: 20 Apr-20 Sep Site: 1.6HEC ⸽⸽⸽⸽ ◖ Prices: ⚲3
🚐1.50 pitch Facilities: ⋔ ⚏ ⊙ 🔲 ∅ ☎ Services: ⚒ ⊞ lau
Leisure: ⬝ P Off-site: ⚏

HOUDAIN PAS-DE-CALAIS

Parc d'Olhain 62150 ☎ 321279179 🖳 321641795
website: www.parcdolhain.com
Situated in an extensive leisure park on the edge of a forest.
⮕ *1.5 km S.*
Open: Apr-Sep Site: 1HEC ⸽⸽⸽⸽ ⌿ ◖ Facilities: ⋔ ⚏ ⊙ 🔲 ☎
🄿 Services: ⊞ Leisure: ⬝ P Off-site: ⚒ ✗

ISQUES PAS-DE-CALAIS

Cytises r de l'Église, 62360 ☎ 321311110
In a pleasant rural setting beside the River Liane.
⮕ *4km S of Boulogne-sur-Mer towards Abbeville, 100mtrs
from N1.*
Open: Apr-15 Oct Site: 2.5HEC ⸽⸽⸽⸽ ◖ 🏠 🚐 Prices: ⚲2.85-
3.10 🚐2.85-3.10 pitch 2.45-2.90 Facilities: ⋔ ⊙ 🔲 ☎
Services: ⚒ ✗ ⊞ lau Off-site: ⚏ ∅ ⌿ ⬝R

JABLINES SEINE-ET-MARNE

International 77450 ☎ 160260937 🖳 160265333
e-mail: welcome@camping-jablines.com
website: www.camping-jablines.com
Only 9km from Disneyland Paris.
⮕ *Access via A1 or A3 towards Marne-la-Vallée, then N3.*
Open: 28 Mar-2 Nov Site: 3.5HEC ⸽⸽⸽⸽ ᶰᵉ 🏠 Prices: ⚲4.50-
5.50 🚐2.50 Facilities: ⋔ ⚏ ⊙ 🔲 ☎ Services: ⚒ ✗ lau
Leisure: ⬝ L

LAON AISNE

CM La Chênaie allée de la Chênâie, 02000
☎ 323202556 🖳 323202556
A peaceful family site with good facilities close to the city centre.
⮕ *W of the city centre towards N44.*
Open: May-Sep Site: 3.3HEC ⸽⸽⸽⸽ ◖ Prices: 🚐1.60 ▲1.42
Facilities: ⋔ ⊙ 🔲 ☎ Services: ⊞ lau Off-site: ⚏ ∅ ⌿ ⬝LPR

LICQUES PAS-DE-CALAIS

Canchy r de Canchy, 62850 ☎ 321826341 🖳 321826341
A quiet site on an open, level meadow well situated for access
to the ferries and the Channel Tunnel.
Open: 15 Mar-Oct Site: 1HEC ⸽⸽⸽⸽ ◖ Facilities: ⋔ ⚏ ⊙ 🔲
∅ ☎ Services: ⚒ ✗ ⊞ lau Leisure: ⬝ R

Site: 6HEC-Site size ⸽⸽⸽⸽-grass ⸰⸰⸰-sand ◈-stone ᶰᵉ-little shade ◖-partly shaded ◆-mainly shaded
🏠-bungalows for hire 🚐-caravans for hire ▲-tents for hire ⊗-no dogs Prices: ⚲-adult per night 🚗-car per night
pp-per person per night 🚐-caravan per night ▲-tent per night

LYNDE NORD

Becquerel 1396 r du Becquerelle, 59173 ☎ 328432037
In a rural setting surrounded by woodland and hedges.
Open: Mar-Nov Site: 1.5HEC ⚏ ⚘ Facilities: ⋔ ⊙ ⚑ ⚈
Services: ⚑ ⊞ Off-site: ⌀ ⛰

MAISONS-LAFFITTE YVELINES

International 1 r Johnson, 78600
☎ 139122191 ▥ 139127050
e-mail: ci.mlaffitte@wanadoo.fr website: www.campint.com
A well-kept site in a residential area on the banks of the
Seine. Modern installations, heated in cold weather.
➲ For access, 8 km N of St-Germain-en-Laye; alternatively
follow N308 from Porte Champerret or from Colombos-Ouest
exit of Autoroute A86.
Open: Apr-Oct Site: 7HEC ⚏ ⚘ ⚑ Prices: ⋔5-5.60 pitch
21-24 (incl 2 persons) Facilities: ⋔ ⚊ ⊙ ⚑ ⛰ ⚈ Services: ⚑
✕ ⊞ lau Off-site: ⋔P

MARNE-LA-VALLÉE SEINE-ET-MARNE

Davy Crockett Ranch Disneyland Paris, 77777
☎ 160456900 ▥ 160456933
A modern site in wooded surroundings on the Disneyland
Paris complex.
➲ Access via A4 Serris exit (no 13).
Open: Apr-Oct Site: 57HEC ⚏ ⦂⦂ ⚘ ⚑ ⚗ Facilities: ⋔
⚊ ⊙ ⚑ ⚈ Services: ⚑ ✕ ⊞ lau Leisure: ⋔ P Off-site: ✕

MAUBEUGE NORD

Camping Municipal de Clair de Lune rte de Mons, 59600
☎ 327622548 ▥ 327622548
➲ 1.5km N via N2 (Bruxelles road).
Open: All year Site: 2.1HEC ⚏ ⚘ ⚑ Facilities: ⋔ ⊙ ⚑ ⚈
Services: ⊞ lau Off-site: ⚊ ⚑ ✕ ⌀ ⛰

MELUN SEINE-ET-MARNE

Belle Étoile Quai Joffre, 77000 ☎ 164394812 ▥ 164372555
e-mail: info@camp-la-belle-etoile.com
website: www.camp-la-belle-etoile.com
Pleasant grassy site with two central blocks.
➲ At La Rochette, on left bank of River Seine 1km from the
town.
Open: Apr-Oct Site: 3.5HEC ⚏ ⚘ ⚘ ⚑ Prices: ⋔4.65-5
pitch 4.70-5 Facilities: ⋔ ⚊ ⊙ ⚑ ⌀ ⚈ Services: ⚑ ✕ ⊞ lau
Leisure: ⋔ P Off-site: ⌀ ⋔LPR

MERLIMONT PAS-DE-CALAIS

St-Hubert RD 940, 62155 ☎ 321891010 ▥ 321891012
e-mail: sthubert62@wanadoo.fr website: www.sthubert62.com
In pleasant wooded surroundings with good recreational
facilities.
➲ 3km S via D940, near Parc de Bagatelle.
Open: Apr-Oct Site: 16HEC ⚏ ⚘ Prices: pitch 14-26 (incl
2 persons) Facilities: ⋔ ⚊ ⊙ ⚑ ⌀ ⛰ ⚈ Services: ⚑ ✕ ⊞ lau
Leisure: ⋔ P

MILLY-LA-FORÊT ESSONNE

Musardière rte des Grandes Vallées, 91490
☎ 164989191 ▥ 164989191
e-mail: lamusardiere@infonie.fr
In pleasant wooded surroundings.
➲ 4km SE via D948.
Open: 16 Feb-Nov Site: 12HEC ⚏ ⦂⦂ ⚘ ⚘ ⚑ Prices: ⋔5
⚘3 ⚑5.50 ⚊3 pitch 3 Facilities: ⋔ ⊙ ⚑ ⚈ Services: ⊞
Leisure: ⋔ P

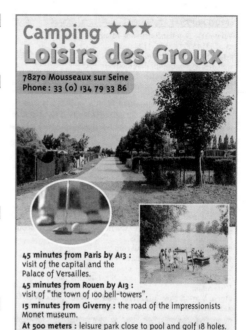

Camping ★★★
Loisirs des Groux

78270 Mousseaux sur Seine
Phone : 33 (0) 134 79 33 86

45 minutes from Paris by A13 :
visit of the capital and the
Palace of Versailles.
45 minutes from Rouen by A13 :
visit of "the town of 100 bell-towers".
15 minutes from Giverny : the road of the impressionists
Monet museum.
At 500 meters : leisure park close to pool and golf 18 holes.

infos@loisirsdesgroux.com • www.loisirsdesgroux.com

MONNERVILLE ESSONNE

Bois de la Justice 91930 ☎ 164950534 ▥ 164951731
Pitches separated by trees and hedges in beautiful natural
woodland with good facilities.
➲ N20 Orléans to Étampes.
Open: Mar-Nov Site: 5.5HEC ⚏ ⚘ Facilities: ⋔ ⊙ ⚑ ⛰ ⚈
Services: ⚑ ✕ ⊞ lau Leisure: ⋔ P

MONTIGNY-LE-BRETONNEUX YVELINES

Parc Étang Base de Loisirs-de-St Quentin, 78180
☎ 130585620 ▥ 134600714
In beautiful rural surroundings within a leisure centre with
easy access to Paris and Versailles.
➲ SE of town centre towards the Centre de Volle.
Open: Mar-Oct Site: 12HEC ⚏ ⚘ ⚘ Facilities: ⋔ ⚊ ⊙ ⚑
⌀ ⛰ ⚈ Services: ⚑ ✕ ⊞ lau Off-site: ✕ ⋔LP

MONTREUIL-SUR-MER PAS-DE-CALAIS

CM 1, Rue de L'eglise, 62170 ☎ 321060728
e-mail: freddy.monchaux@wanadoo.fr
➲ N of town on N1.
Open: All year Site: 2HEC ⚏ ⚘ ⚑ ⚊ Facilities: ⋔ ⊙ ⚑ ⚈
Services: ⊞ lau Leisure: ⋔ R Off-site: ⚊ ⚑ ✕ ⌀ ⛰ ⋔P

MOUSSEAUX SUR SEINE YVELINES

Loisirs des Groux chemin de Vetheuil, 78270 ☎ 134793382
e-mail: infos@loisirsdesgroux.com
website: www.loisirsdesgroux.com
Conveniently situated for visiting Paris, Giverny and
Versailles.
Open: Feb-Dec Site: 3.5HEC ⚘ ⚑ Prices: ⚑14.20
Facilities: ⋔ ⚑ ⚈ Services: lau Leisure: ⋔ LR Off-site: ⚊ ⚑
✕ ⋔L ⊞

Facilities: ⚊-shop ⋔-shower ⊙-electric points for razors ⚑-electric points for caravans ⚈-parking by tents permitted ⚑-compulsory separate car park **Services:** ✕-café/restaurant ⚑-bar ⌀-Camping Gaz International ⛰-gas other than Camping Gaz ⊞-first aid facilities lau-laundry **Leisure:** ⋔-swimming L-Lake P-Pool R-River S-Sea **Off-site:** All facilities within 2km

MOYENNEVILLE Somme

Val de Trie Bouillancourt-sous-Miannay, 80870
☎ 322314888 🗎 322313533
e-mail: raphael@camping-lavaldetrie.fr
website: www.camping-levaldetrie.fr
A small site in a picturesque wooded location with good facilities including a lake for fishing.
➲ 1km from the D925 (Abbeville-Le Tréport).
Open: 28 Mar-1 Nov Site: 3HEC ⏛ ♠ ⊞ Prices: ⚑2.90-3.90 ⚐2.90-3.90 pitch 1.30-2.60 Facilities: ⋔ ⅃ ⊙ ⬛ ∅ ⌗ ☎ Services: ⚑ ✕ ⊞ lau Leisure: ⚓ PR Off-site: ⌗

NEMOURS Seine-et-Marne

ACCCF 77140 ☎ 64281062 🗎 64281062
On well-kept meadow. Clean sanitary installations.
➲ 200mtrs from N7.
Open: 15 Mar-11 Nov Site: 4.8HEC ⏛ ♣ Facilities: ⋔ ⊙ ⬛ ☎ Services: lau Leisure: ⚓ R Off-site: ⅃ ⚑ ✕ ∅ ⌗ ⊞

NESLES-LA-VALLÉE Val-d'Oise

Parc de Séjour de l'Étang 10 Chemin des Belles Vues, 95690
☎ 134706289 🗎 134706289
e-mail: brehinier1@hotmail.com
website: www.campingparcset.com
Level site near a small lake.
➲ A15 exit 10, then D927 and D79. From N1 take exit for L'Isle Adam.
Open: Mar-15 Nov Site: 6HEC ⏛ ♣ ⚐ Facilities: ⋔ ⊙ ∅ ☎ Services: ⊞ lau Off-site: ⅃ ⅃ ✕ ∅ ⌗

NEUVILLE, LA Nord

Leu Pindu 2 r du Gl-de-Gaulle, 59239
☎ 320865087 🗎 320865177
➲ N on D8.
Open: All year Site: 1.2HEC ⏛ ♣ ⚐ Facilities: ⋔ ⊙ ⬛ ∅ ⌗ ☎ Services: ⅃ ✕ ⊞ lau Off-site: ⅃ ✕ ⚓L

ORVILLERS-SOREL Oise

Sorel 60490 ☎ 344850274 🗎 34485027
Divided into pitches. Local tradesmen supply provisions.
➲ Leave A1 at N17, turn right and continue 400mtrs.
Open: Feb-15 Dec Site: 3HEC ⏛ ♣ ⚐ Prices: ⚑5 pitch 12.20 (incl 2 persons) Facilities: ⋔ ⅃ ⊙ ⬛ ∅ ☎ Services: ✕ ⊞ lau

OYE-PLAGE Pas-de-Calais

Oyats 272 Digue Vert, 62215 ☎ 321851540 🗎 328603833
e-mail: bnilliet.nicolas@wanadoo.fr
4.5km NW directly on the beach.
Open: May-Sep Site: 5HEC ⏛ ♣ Facilities: ⋔ ⅃ ⊙ ⬛ ☎ Services: ✕ ⊞ lau Leisure: ⚓ PS

PARIS

Bois de Boulogne 2 allée du Bord de l'Eau, 75016
☎ 145243000 🗎 142244295
Much of this site's popularity stems from its location close to the city centre and it can become crowded during high season as it is the only site actually in Paris.
Open: All year Site: 7HEC ⏛ ♦ ♠ ⊞ Prices: ⚑5-8 ⚑2-3 pitch 18-24 (incl 2 persons) pp4.40-6.10 Facilities: ⋔ ⅃ ⊙ ⬛ ∅ ☎ Services: ⅃ ✕ ⊞ lau

PLESSIS-FEU-AUSSOUX Seine-et-Marne

Château-de-Chambonnières 77540
☎ 164041585 🗎 164041336
➲ On D231 towards Provins, 23km from Disneyland Paris.
Open: All year Site: 5HEC ⏛ ♣ ⊞ ⚐ Facilities: ⋔ ⅃ ⊙ ⬛ ∅ ☎ Services: ⊞ lau

POIX-DE-PICARDIE Somme

Bois des Pêcheurs rte de Forges-les-Eaux, 80290
☎ 322901171 🗎 322903291
e-mail: mairie.poix.de.picardie@wanadoo.fr
In a quiet riverside location with a high standard of sanitary facilities.
➲ W via D919 towards Forges-les-Eaux.
Open: Apr-Sep Site: 2.4HEC ⏛ ♣ Prices: pitch 10 (incl 2 persons) Facilities: ⋔ ⊙ ⬛ ∅ ☎ Services: lau Off-site: ⅃ ⅃ ✕ ∅ ⌗ ⚓PR ⊞

PROYART Somme

Loisir la Violette rte de Mericourt, 80340
☎ 322858136 🗎 322851737
Open: Mar-Oct Site: 1.8HEC ⏛ ♣ ⊞ Prices: ⚑2.10 ⚑1 pitch 1.30 Facilities: ⋔ ⊙ ⬛ ☎ Services: lau Off-site: ⅃ ⅃ ✕ ⌗ ⚓P ⊞

QUEND-PLAGE-LES-PINS Somme

At Monchaux-les-Quend (3.5km E via D102E)

Roses 80120 ☎ 322277617 🗎 322239306
e-mail: sandrine.bruyelle@wanadoo.fr
website: www.campingdesroses.com
Well-kept site with trees and hedges surrounding individual pitches. Only recommended site in area.
➲ Turn off D940 at Quend, site 500mtrs on left of D102.
Open: 15 Mar-27 Oct Site: 9HEC ⏛ ♣ ⊞ ⚐ Prices: pitch 21 (incl 2 persons) Facilities: ⋔ ⊙ ⬛ ⌗ ☎ Services: ⅃ ✕ ⊞ lau Leisure: ⚓ P Off-site: ⅃ ∅ ⚓S

RAMBOUILLET Yvelines

CM de l'Étang d'Or r du Château d'Eau, 78120
☎ 130410734 🗎 130410017
e-mail: ramboulillet.tourisme@wanadoo.fr
website: www.ot-rambouillet.fr
In a pleasant situation. Shop, bar etc only open Jun-Aug.
➲ From railway station follow road SE for 1.3km passing Camping Pont Hardy.
Open: Feb-19 Dec Site: 4.7HEC ⏛ ♣ Prices: ⚑3.90-4.30 pitch 4.30-4.90 Facilities: ⋔ ⅃ ⊙ ⬛ ☎ Services: ⅃ ✕ ⊞ lau Off-site: ⚓P

ST-AMAND-LES-EAUX Nord

Mont des Bruyères 806 r Basly, 59230
☎ 327485687 🗎 327485687
➲ 3.5km SE in the forest of St-Amand
Open: Mar-Nov Site: 3.5HEC ⏛ ♣ Prices: ⚑3.40 pitch 8.40 (incl 2 persons) Facilities: ⋔ ⅃ ⊙ ⬛ ⌗ ☎ Services: ⅃ ⊞ lau Off-site: ✕ ∅ ⚓LPR

Site: 6HEC-Site size ⏛-grass ∴-sand ❀-stone ❊-little shade ♣-partly shaded ♠-mainly shaded ⊞-bungalows for hire ⚐-caravans for hire ⚑-tents for hire ⊗-no dogs Prices: ⚑-adult per night ⚑-car per night pp-per person per night ⚐-caravan per night ⚑-tent per night

St-Chéron Essonne

Parc des Roches La Petite Beauce, 91530
☎ 164566550 ▥ 164565450
e-mail: parc.des.roches@free.fr
website: www.parc.des.roches.free.fr
In a wooded park.
Open: 15 Apr-15 Sep Site: 23HEC ⵘ ⌕ ⊞ Facilities: ⋔ ☉
⊞ ⌑ Services: ⵏ ✕ ⊞ lau Leisure: ⌇ P Off-site: ⌀

St-Cyr-sur-Morin Seine-et-Marne

Choisel rte de Rebais, 77750 ☎ 160238493
e-mail: campingduchoisel@wanadoo.fr
In a pleasant situation. Separate carpark for arrivals after
22.00hrs.
➲ *2km W via D31.*
Open: Mar-Nov Site: 3.5HEC ⵘ ♣ Facilities: ⋔ ☉ ⊞ ⌕ ⌑
Services: ⵏ ✕ ⊞ lau Off-site: ⌀ ⌇PR

St-Jans-Cappel Nord

Domaine de la Sablière Le Mont Noir, 59270
☎ 328494634 ▥ 328426290
A pleasant family site in a wooded location with large, well
defined pitches.
➲ *3.5km NE via D10 and D318.*
Open: 15 Apr-15 Oct Site: 3.6HEC ⵘ ⌕ Facilities: ⋔ ☉ ⊞
⌕ ⌑ Services: ⊞ lau Off-site: ⌕ ✕ ⌀ ⌇LP

St-Leu-d'Esserent Oise

Campix ☎ 44560848
In wooded surroundings, within easy reach of Chantilly.
➲ *3.5km NE via D12.*
Open: 7 Mar-1 Dec Site: 6HEC ⵘ ⦂ ♣ Facilities: ⋔ ☉
⊞ ⌀ ⌑ Services: ⊞ lau Off-site: ⌕ ⵏ ✕ ⌇L

St-Quentin Aisne

CM bd J-Bouin, 02100 ☎ 323626866
A good site in pleasant wooded surroundings near the canal.
Open: Mar-Nov Site: 1.9HEC ⵘ ⦂ ⌕ Facilities: ⋔ ⊞ ⌑
Off-site: ⌀ ⌕ ⌇PR ⊞

St-Valéry-sur-Somme Somme

⌕*Domaine du Château de Drancourt* 80230 ☎ 322269345
In open countryside, surrounded by woods, fields and lakes,
within the grounds of a former hunting lodge.
➲ *3.5km S via D48.*
Open: Apr-Sep Site: 15HEC ⵘ ⌕ ⊞ Facilities: ⋔ ⌕ ☉ ⊞
⌀ ⌕ ⌑ Services: ⵏ ✕ ⊞ lau Leisure: ⌇ P Off-site: ✕ ⌇L

Salency Oise

Étang du Moulin 54 r du Moulin, 60400 ☎ 344099981
A small site opposite a trout fishing lake and recreational
area under the ownership of the site proprietors.
➲ *3km from Noyon on the N32 towards Chauny.*
Open: All year Site: 0.4HEC ⵘ ⌕ Prices: ⋔1.90 ⌕2.30
⌕3.85 ▲3.85 Facilities: ⋔ ☉ ⊞ ⌕ ⌑ Services: ⵏ ✕
Off-site: ⌇PR

Seraucourt-le-Grand Aisne

Pêche du Vivier aux Carpes 10 r Ch-Voyeux, 02790
☎ 323605010 ▥ 323605169
e-mail: camping.du.vivier@wanadoo.fr
A peaceful site bordered by lakes. Separate car park for
arrivals after 22.00hrs.
➲ *A26 exit 11-left on D1 exit Essigny-D72.*
Site: 3HEC ⵘ ☉ ⌕ Prices: ⋔3.30 pitch 250 (incl 2 persons)
Facilities: ⋔ ☉ ⊞ ⌀ ⌕ ⌑ Services: ⊞ lau
Off-site: ⌕ ⵏ ✕ ⌇R

Soissons Aisne

CM av du Mail, 02200 ☎ 323745269 ▥ 323596772
e-mail: officedetourisme@ville-soissons.fr
website: www.ville-soissons.fr
In pleasant surroundings with good, modern facilities.
Open: All year Site: 1.8HEC ⵘ ⌕ Prices: ⋔2 ⌕2 ⌕2 pitch
2 Facilities: ⋔ ☉ ⊞ ⌕ ⌑ Services: ⊞ lau Off-site: ⌕ ⵏ ✕ ⌀
⌕ ⌇P ⊞

Thiembronne Pas-de-Calais

Pommiers rte de Desvres, 62560
☎ 321395019 ▥ 321957920
A family site in pleasant wooded surroundings
➲ *NW on D132.*
Open: 15 Mar-15 Oct Site: 1.8HEC ⵘ ⌕ Prices: ⋔3.30-
4 ⌕1.65-2.60 ⌕3.30-4 pitch 3.30-4 Facilities: ⋔ ☉ ⊞ ⌀ ⌑
Services: ⊞ lau Leisure: ⌇ P Off-site: ⌕ ⵏ ✕ ⌇R

Tollent Pas-de-Calais

Val d'Authie CD 119 Rt de Berck, 62390
☎ 321471427 ▥ 321471427
In a pleasant wooded location with wide, well marked
pitches.
➲ *SE via D119*
Open: Apr-Sep Site: 3.5HEC ⵘ ⌕ ⌑ Prices: pitch 12 (incl
3 persons) Facilities: ⋔ ☉ ⊞ ⌑ Services: ⵏ ✕ ⊞ lau
Leisure: ⌇ LP Off-site: ⌇R

Torcy Seine-et-Marne

Parc de la Colline rte de Lagny, 77200
☎ 160054232 ▥ 164800517
e-mail: camping.parc.de.la.colline@wanadoo.fr
website: camping-de-la-colline.com
An ideal base for visiting Paris (30 minutes from the centre
by Metro). Separate car park for arrivals after 22.00 hrs.
➲ *Access via exit 10 on the A104 and D10E.*
Open: All year Site: 10HEC ⵘ ♣ ⌑ ▲ Facilities: ⋔ ⌕ ☉
⌑ ⌀ ⌑ Services: ⵏ ✕ ⊞ lau Off-site: ⌇LP

Touquin Seine-et-Marne

Étangs Fleuris rte de la Couture, 77131
☎ 164041636 ▥ 164041228
website: www.etangs.fleuris@libertysurf.fr
In wooded surroundings with well defined pitches and
modern facilities.
➲ *E of town towards Provins.*
Open: Mar-Oct Site: 5.5HEC ⵘ ⌕ Prices: ⋔8 Facilities: ⋔
⌕ ☉ ⌑ Services: ⵏ ✕ lau Leisure: ⌇ P Off-site: ✕

Tournehem Pas-de-Calais

Bal Parc 500 r du Vieux Château, 62890
☎ 321356590 ▥ 321351857
e-mail: balparc@wanadoo.fr
A peaceful site in rural surroundings with good, modern
facilities.
➲ *Access via D218 from village centre.*
Open: All year Site: 1.6HEC ⵘ ⌕ ⌑ ▲ Facilities: ⋔ ⌕ ☉
⌑ ⌀ ⌑ Services: ⵏ ✕ ⊞ lau Off-site: ⌇R

Vailly-sur-Aisne Aisne

Domaine de la Nature chemin de Boufaud, Pont de Vailley,
02370 ☎ 323547455 ▥ 326883465
In a pleasant rural setting alongside the canal with well
defined pitches and modern sanitary facilities.
➲ *4km W via D144 near the canal and lake.*
Open: All year Site: 3HEC ⵘ ⌕ ⌑ ⌕ ▲ Prices: pitch
11.50 (incl 2 persons) Facilities: ⋔ ☉ ⊞ ⌀ ⌕ ⌑ Services: ⵏ
✕ ⊞ lau Off-site: ⌕ ✕ ⌇LPR

Facilities: ⌕-shop ⋔-shower ☉-electric points for razors ⊞-electric points for caravans ⌑-parking by tents permitted
⊞-compulsory separate car park Services: ✕-café/restaurant ⵏ-bar ⌀-Camping Gaz International ⌕-gas other than Camping
Gaz ⊞-first aid facilities lau-laundry Leisure: ⌇-swimming L-Lake P-Pool R-River S-Sea Off-site: All facilities within 2km

VERNEUIL-SUR-SEINE YVELINES

Val de Seine chemin du Rouillard, 78480
☎ 139281620 ▤ 139711860
Situated on the outskirts of Paris in a pine forest.
Open: Apr-Sept Site: 3.5HEC ⊞ ♣ Prices: ♠2.50 ♠2.50 ♣5 ▲4 Facilities: ♠ ⅃ ⊙ ⬛ ☎ Services: ✖ Leisure: ⇗ L

VILLENNES-SUR-SEINE YVELINES

Club des Renardières rte de Vernouillet, 78670 ☎ 139758897
Site for caravans only, in beautiful hilly park laid out with hedges, lawns and flower beds. Fully divided into completely separated pitches.
⮕ Follow D113 to Maison Blanche turn right and continue 3km.
Open: All year Site: 7HEC ⊞ ♣ Facilities: ♠ ⊙ ⬛
Services: lau Off-site: ⅃ ▾ ✖ ⇗LPR

VILLERS-HÉLON AISNE

Castel des Biches Chateau Alexandre Dumas, 2600
☎ 323729393 ▤ 323729333
e-mail: pacal.ginailhac@wanadoo.fr
website: castel-des-biches.com
Attractive site in grounds of an old castle.
⮕ Turn off N2 onto D2 between Soissons and Villers-Cotterêts and continue for 7km via Longport.
Open: All year Site: 10HEC ⊞ ♁ ♞ ♠ ▲ Prices: ♠2.90 pitch 11.10-13.10 Facilities: ♠ ⊙ ⬛ ☎ Services: ⬚ lau Off-site: ⅃ ⇗ ▴ ⇗LR

VILLERS-SUR-AUTHIE SOMME

Val d'Authie 20 rte de Vercourt, 80120
☎ 322299247 ▤ 3222299220
e-mail: camping@valdauthie.fr website: www.valdauthie.fr
A well designed site situated between the Forest of Crécy and the sea. Bar and café open in high season only.
⮕ Access via N1.
Open: Apr-Oct Site: 7HEC ⊞ ♁ ♞ Prices: ♠6-6 ♠4.50 ▲4.50 Facilities: ♠ ⅃ ⊙ ⬛ ☎ Services: ▾ ✖ lau Leisure: ⇗ P Off-site: ⇗R

VIRONCHAUX SOMME

Peupliers 221 r du Cornet, 80150
☎ 322235427 ▤ 322290519
e-mail: les-peupliers2@wanadoo.fr
A peaceful site 3km from the Forest of Crécy.
⮕ Approach via N1 and D938.
Open: Apr-Oct Site: 1.5HEC ⊞ ♞ Prices: ♠3 ♠2.50 pitch 3.50 Facilities: ♠ ⅃ ⊙ ⬛ ⬛ ☎ Services: ▾ ✖ ⬚ lau Off-site: ✖

WACQUINGHEN PAS-DE-CALAIS

Éscale 62250 ☎ 321320069 ▤ 321320069
In a pleasantly landscaped park with modern facilities 5 minutes from the coastal resorts.
⮕ Access via A16 and D231.
Open: 15 Mar-15 Oct Site: 11HEC ⊞ ♁ ♞ Prices: ♠3.65 ♠2 ♠4 ▲3 Facilities: ♠ ⅃ ⊙ ⬛ ⬛ ☎ Services: ▾ ✖ ⬚ lau Off-site: ⬛ ⬛

AUVERGNE

ALLANCHE CANTAL

CM Pont Valat 15160 ☎ 471204587
⮕ 1km S on D679 towards St-Flour.
Open: 15 Jun-15 Sep Site: 3HEC ⊞ ♁ Facilities: ♠ ⊙ ⬛ ☎ Services: lau Off-site: ⅃ ▾ ✖ ⇗ ▴ ⬚

ALLEYRAS HAUTE-LOIRE

CM 43580 ☎ 471575686
In pleasant surroundings on level ground beside the River Allier.
⮕ 2.5km NW.
Open: May-Sep Site: 1HEC ⊞ ♆ ♞ Prices: ♠7 pitch 7 (incl 2 persons) Facilities: ♠ ⊙ ⬛ ⬛ ☎ Services: ⬚ lau Off-site: ⅃ ▾ ✖ ▴ ⇗R

AMBERT PUY-DE-DÔME

Trois Chênes rte du Puy, 63600 ☎ 473823468 ▤ 473823468
e-mail: tourisme-ambert@wanadoo.fr
Open: May-Sep Site: ⊞ ♁ ♞ Prices: ♠2.90 ♠2 pitch 2.50 Facilities: ♠ ⊙ ⬛ ☎ Services: ⬚ lau Off-site: ⅃ ▾ ✖ ⇗ ⇗LP

ANSE RHÔNE

Porte du Beaujolais chemin des Grandes Levées, 69480
☎ 474671287 ▤ 474099097
e-mail: campingbeaujolais@wanadoo.fr
A pleasant, modern site in the heart of the Beaujolais country beside the River Saône.
⮕ Access via A6 or N6 then D39.
Open: 15 Mar-30 Oct Site: 7HEC ⊞ ♁ ♞ ⬛
Prices: ♠4.33-4.80 ♠16.90-18.67 pitch 1.92 (incl 2 persons) Facilities: ♠ ⅃ ⊙ ⬛ ⬛ ☎ Services: ▾ ✖ ⬚ lau Leisure: ⇗ PR Off-site: ✖ ⬚

ARNAC CANTAL

Gineste 15150 ☎ 471629190 📠 471629272
e-mail: lagineste@mairie-arnac.fr
website: www.mairie-arnac.fr
Situated on a peninsula in Lake Enchanet with good, modern facilities and access to local ski slopes.
➜ *NW of Arnac towards the lake.*
Open: All year Site: 3HEC ▦ ⊕ ♿ 🚐 Facilities: 🏪 🚿 ⊙ 🅿
Services: ▮ ✕ ⊞ lau Leisure: ⚓ LP

ARPAJON-SUR-CÈRE CANTAL

Cère r F-Ramond, 15130 ☎ 471645507
➜ *S towards Rodez via D920, beside the river.*
Open: Jun-Sep Site: 2HEC ▦ ⊕ Prices: 🚐11 ▲8.50
Facilities: 🏪 ⊙ 🚐 🅿 Services: lau Leisure: ⚓ R
Off-site: 🛒 ▮ ✕ ∅ ⊞

AUBIN AVEYRON

CM 12110 ☎ 565630386
➜ *100mtrs from the lake.*
Open: 15 Apr-Sep Site: 4HEC ▦ ⠿ ♣ Facilities: 🏪 ⊙ 🚐
🅿 Services: lau Off-site: 🛒 ▮ ✕ ∅ 🔥 ⚓PR

AT BELLERIVE-SUR-ALLIER (3KM W)

Acacias r Claude-Decloître, 03700
☎ 470323622 📠 470598852
e-mail: campingacacias@club-internet.fr
website: www.camping-acacias.com
Well-managed site, sub-divided into numbered pitches by hedges. Clean sanitary installations. Library, billiard room. Water sports are available nearby on lake.
➜ *From Vichy turn left after bridge beside ESSO garage and follow river for 500mtrs.*
Open: 5 Apr-15 Oct Site: 3HEC ▦ ♣ 🚐 Prices: 🚐2.60-4.60 pitch 2.60-4.60 Facilities: 🏪 🛒 ⊙ 🚐 ∅ 🔥 🅿 🅿 Services: ⊞
lau Leisure: ⚓ LPR Off-site: ▮ ✕

Beau Rivage r Claude Decloitre, 03700
☎ 470322685 📠 470320394
e-mail: camping-beaurivage@wanadoo.fr
website: www.camping-beaurivage.com
Neat meadowland with marked out pitches. Well kept sanitary installations. TV.
➜ *Watch for turning over bridge onto left bank of River Allier.*
Open: 15 May-15 Sep Site: 1.5HEC ▦ ♣ 🚐 🚐 Prices: 🚐3-4.20 🚐3-4.20 pitch 3-4.20 Facilities: 🏪 🛒 ⊙ 🚐 ∅ 🅿
Services: ▮ ✕ ⊞ lau Leisure: ⚓ PR

BELMONT-SUR-RANCE AVEYRON

Val Fleuri 12370 ☎ 565999513
A peaceful site beside the River Rance with good, modern facilities.
➜ *Access via N9 and D999.*
Open: Jun-Aug Site: 1HEC ▦ ⊕ 🚐 Facilities: 🏪 ⊙ 🚐 ∅ 🔥
🅿 Services: ▮ ✕ ⊞ lau Leisure: ⚓ R Off-site: 🛒 ⚓P

BOURBON-L'ARCHAMBAULT ALLIER

CM Parc Bignon Parc Jean Bignon, 03160
☎ 470670883 📠 470673535
➜ *1km SW on N153, rte de Montluçon, turn right.*
Open: Mar-Oct Site: 3HEC ▦ ♣ Prices: 🚐2 🚐0.75 🚐1.15
▲1.15 pitch 1.15 Facilities: 🏪 ⊙ 🚐 🅿 Services: lau
Off-site: 🛒 ▮ ✕ ∅ 🔥 ⚓LP

BOURG-ARGENTAL LOIRE

Astrée 'L'Allier', 42220 ☎ 477397297 📠 477397621
e-mail: prl@bourgargental.fr
In pleasant surroundings with good recreational facilities.

AVEYRON
To know everything about:
– camping & caravanning
– rental of chalets, mobile homes, tent bungalows
– service areas for motor caravans
and to organise your holiday
Visit our website:
www.camping-aveyron.com
the homepage for campsites in Aveyron

➜ *Access via N82.*
Open: All year Site: 2HEC ▦ ⊕ 🚐 Prices: 🏕2.50-3.50
🚐1.25-1.75 🚐5-7 ▲2.50-3.50 Facilities: 🏪 ⊙ 🚐 🅿
Services: ▮ lau Leisure: ⚓ R Off-site: 🛒 ▮ ✕ ∅ 🔥 ⚓P ⊞

BRAIZE ALLIER

Champ de la Chapelle 03360 ☎ 470061545 📠 470061545
e-mail: ccdlp@aol.com
A family site in the centre of the Tronçais Forest with good recreational facilities.
➜ *7km SE via D28 and D978.*
Open: 17 Apr-19 Sep Site: 5.6HEC ▦ ♣ 🚐 Prices: pitch 9.90-9.90 (incl 1 persons) Facilities: 🏪 ⊙ 🚐 🅿 Services: ✕ ⊞
lau Leisure: ⚓ P

BRUSQUE AVEYRON

VAL Camping Les Pibouls Domaine de Céras, 12360
☎ 565495066
Open: Jul-Aug Site: 1HEC ▦ ⊕ Facilities: 🏪 ⊙ 🚐 🅿
Services: ▮ ✕ lau Leisure: ⚓ L Off-site: 🛒 ⊞

CANET-DE-SALARS AVEYRON

Caussanel Lac de Pareloup, 12290
☎ 565468519 📠 565468985
e-mail: info@lecaussanel.com
website: www.lecaussanel.com
Well equipped site on the shore of Lake Pareloup.
➜ *Access via D911.*
Open: May-25 Sep Site: 10HEC ▦ ⊕ 🚐 Prices: 🏕4.40-5.40 pitch 13.20-19.20 (incl 2 persons) Facilities: 🏪 ⊙ 🚐 ∅ 🅿
Services: ▮ ✕ ⊞ lau Leisure: ⚓ LP Off-site: 🔥

Soleil Levant Lac de Pareloup, 12290
☎ 565460362
e-mail: contact@camping-le-soleil-levant.com
website: www.camping-le-soleil-levant.com
A family site set on terraces on the shores of Lac de Pareloup with good recreational facilities.
➜ *S of Canet-de-Salars via D933 towards Salles-Curan.*
Open: Apr-Oct Site: 11HEC ▦ ♣ 🚐 ▲ Prices: 🏕3.80 🚐16
Facilities: 🏪 ⊙ 🚐 ∅ 🔥 🅿 Services: ▮ ✕ ⊞ lau Leisure: ⚓ L

CAPDENAC-GARE AVEYRON

Diège Vallée de la Diège, Sonnac, 12700 ☎ 565646125
Level, sub-divided terrain located in a narrow valley of La Diège river.
➜ *From Figeac on N140 travel 7km, in the direction of Capdenac-Gare. Turn sharp right after the bridge and continue on D558 for about 7km in the direction of Naussac.*
Open: May-1 Nov Site: 7HEC ▦ ⊕ 🚐 ▲ Facilities: 🏪 🛒
⊙ 🚐 ∅ 🔥 🅿 Services: ▮ ✕ ⊞ lau Leisure: ⚓ R

Facilities: 🛒-shop 🏪-shower ⊙-electric points for razors 🚐-electric points for caravans 🅿-parking by tents permitted
🅿-compulsory separate car park **Services:** ✕-café/restaurant ▮-bar ∅-Camping Gaz International 🔥-gas other than Camping
Gaz ⊞-first aid facilities lau-laundry **Leisure:** ⚓-swimming L-Lake P-Pool R-River S-Sea **Off-site:** All facilities within 2km

CM Rives d'Olt bd Paul-Ramadier, 12700 ☎ 565808887
A quiet site on level ground with pitches divided by hedges on the bank of a river.
➲ *7km from Figeac via N140 towards Rodez, then D35 to Capendac.*
Open: Apr-Sep Site: 1.3HEC ⟿ ⌾ ⊞ Prices: ⚲2.50 ⏚1.60 ⏚2.60 ⚲1.80 Facilities: ⟨ ⊙ ⨀ ⊠ ⊞ Services: ⊞ lau Leisure: ⥿ R Off-site: ⟐ ⚲ ✗ ⦿ ⚲ ⥿P

CHAMPAGNAC-LE-VIEUX HAUTE-LOIRE

Chanterelle Le Plan d'Eau, 43440
☎ 471763400 ▦ 471763400
e-mail: camping@es-conseil.fr
website: www.champagnac.com
Situated in the heart of the Auvergne beside a wooded lake.
➲ *1km N via D5.*
Open: Apr-Oct Site: 4HEC ⟿ ♣ ⊞ ⨀ Ⓐ Facilities: ⟨ ⊙ ⨀ ⊠ Services: ⊞ lau Leisure: ⥿ L Off-site: ⟐ ⚲ ✗ ⦿ ⥿R ⊞

CHAMPS-SUR-TARENTAINE CANTAL

Tarentaine 15270 ☎ 471787125
In an attractive location surrounded by lakes and woodland.
➲ *1km SW via D679 and D22 beside the River Tarentaine.*
Open: 15 Jun-15 Sep Site: 4HEC ⟿ Ⓐ Facilities: ⟨ ⊙ ⨀ ⊠ Services: lau Off-site: ⟐ ⚲ ✗ ⥿P ⊞

CHÂTEL-DE-NEUVRE ALLIER

Deneuvre Les Graves, 03500
☎ 470420451 ▦ 470420451
e-mail: campingdeneuvre@wanadoo.fr
website: www.deneuvre.com
In pleasant surroundings within a nature reserve beside the River Allier.
➲ *0.5km N via D9.*
Open: Apr-Sep Site: 1HEC ⟿ ⌾ ⨀ Ⓐ Prices: ⚲3.10-3.85 pitch 3.10-3.85 Facilities: ⟨ ⊙ ⨀ ⦿ ⊠ Services: ⚲ ✗ ⊞ lau Leisure: ⥿ R Off-site: ⟐

CHÂTEL GUYON PUY-DE-DÔME

Clos de Balanède r de la Piscine, 63140
☎ 473860247 ▦ 473860564
e-mail: closde.pougheon@wauado.fr
website: www.balanede.com
A pleasant site, situated in an orchard.
➲ *Access via A71 and D685.*
Open: 14 Apr-Sep Site: 4HEC ⟿ ♣ ⊞ Prices: ⚲2.60-3.65 ⏚0.90-1.25 ⚲0.90-1.25 Ⓐ0.90-1.25 pitch 1.85-2.45 Facilities: ⟨ ⊙ ⨀ ⦿ ⚲ ⊠ Services: ⚲ ✗ ⊞ lau Leisure: ⥿ P Off-site: ⥿R

CHÂTEL-MONTAGNE ALLIER

Croix Cognat 03250 ☎ 470593138
e-mail: campinglacroixcognat@wanadoo.fr
website: perso.wanadoo.fr/mairie-chatel-montagne
Well equipped site at an altitude of 540mtrs.
➲ *0.5km NW via D25 towards Vichy.*
Open: May-1 Oct Site: 1HEC ⟿ ♣ ⊞ Prices: pitch 10 (incl 2 persons) Facilities: ⟨ ⊙ ⨀ ⦿ ⚲ ⊠ Services: ⚲ ✗ ⊞ lau Leisure: ⥿ P Off-site: ⚲ ⥿R

CHAUDES-AIGUES CANTAL

CM du Couffour 15110 ☎ 471235708 ▦ 471235708
website: www.chaudesaigues.com
Tastefully sited around the town football pitch in the local leisure area.
➲ *2km S via D921.*
Open: May-20 Oct Site: 2.5HEC ⟿ ⌾ ⨀ Prices: ⚲2 ⏚1 Ⓐ1 pitch 1 Facilities: ⟨ ⊙ ⨀ ⊠ Services: ⊞ lau Off-site: ⟐ ⚲ ✗ ⦿ ⥿PR

CONDRIEU RHÔNE

Belle Rive La Plaine, 69420 ☎ 474595108
In wooded surroundings bordering the Rhône.
➲ *11km S of Vienne on N86.*
Open: Apr-Sep Site: 5HEC ⟿ ⌾ ⊞ ⨀ Prices: ⚲3.30 ⚲1.60 pitch 3.80 Facilities: ⟨ ⟐ ⊙ ⨀ ⦿ ⊠ Services: ⚲ ✗ ⊞ lau Leisure: ⥿ PR

CONQUES AVEYRON

Beau Rivage 12320 ☎ 565698223 ▦ 565728929
Peaceful site beside the river with spacious, well marked pitches.
➲ *On D901.*
Open: Apr-Sep Site: 1HEC ⟿ ♣ ⊞ ⨀ Prices: ⚲3.50-4 ⚲2.50-3 pitch 3-4 Facilities: ⟨ ⟐ ⊙ ⨀ ⦿ ⊠ Services: ⚲ ✗ lau Leisure: ⥿ PR Off-site: ⟐ ⊞

COURNON-D'AUVERGNE PUY-DE-DÔME

CM Plage r de Laveuses, 63800 ☎ 473848130 ▦ 473846590
e-mail: camping@cournon-auvergne.fr
website: www.cournon-auvergne.fr/camping
In a rural setting on the shore of a 7 hectare lake, close to the River Allier.
➲ *1.5km E towards Billom.*
Open: All year Site: 5HEC ⟿ ⧫ ⌾ ⊞ Prices: ⚲2.90-3.20 pitch 4-4.35 Facilities: ⟨ ⟐ ⊙ ⨀ ⦿ ⊠ Services: ⚲ ✗ ⊞ lau Leisure: ⥿ LR Off-site: ⦿ ⟐ ⥿P

DALLET PUY-DE-DÔME

Ombrages rte de Pont-du-Château, 63111
☎ 473831097 ▦ 473831097
e-mail: lesombrages@hotmail.com
website: www.lesombrages.nl
In a wooded location beside the River Allier.
Open: Jun-15 Sep Site: 3.5HEC ⟿ ⌾ ⨀ Ⓐ ⧬ Prices: ⚲5 pitch 13 (incl 2 persons) Facilities: ⟨ ⊙ ⨀ ⊠ Services: ⚲ ✗ ⊞ lau Leisure: ⥿ PR Off-site: ⟐

DARDILLY RHÔNE

International de Lyon Porte de Lyon, 69570
☎ 478356455 ▦ 472170426
e-mail: camping.lyon@mairie-lyon.fr
website: www.camping-lyon.com
Generously arranged and equipped site divided into pitches. Ideal for overnight stays near motorway. Concrete platforms for caravans.
➲ *9km N of Lyon La Garde exit off A6.*
Open: All year Site: 6.5HEC ⟿ ♣ ⊞ Prices: ⚲3.10 ⚲7.60 Ⓐ6.10 Facilities: ⟨ ⊙ ⨀ ⦿ ⊠ Services: ⚲ ✗ ⊞ lau Leisure: ⥿ P Off-site: ⟐ ⦿ ⟐

EBREUIL ALLIER

Filature de la Sioule Ile de Nieres, 3450
☎ 470907201 ▦ 470907948
e-mail: camping.filature@libertysurf.fr
website: www.campingfilature.com
A peaceful, well equipped in an orchard beside the River Sioule.
➲ *Access signposted from exit 12 on A71.*
Open: 30 Mar-Sep Site: 3.6HEC ⟿ ♣ ⊞ Prices: pitch 14 (incl 2 persons) Facilities: ⟨ ⟐ ⊙ ⨀ ⦿ ⊠ Services: ⚲ ✗ ⊞ lau Leisure: ⥿ R Off-site: ✗ ⟐

FERRIÈRES-ST-MARY CANTAL

Vigeaires 15170 ☎ 471206188
A level site surrounded by woodland close to the River Allagnon with good, modern facilities.

Site: 6HEC-Site size ⟿-grass ⠿-sand ⦿-stone ⧬-little shade ⌾-partly shaded ♣-mainly shaded
⊞-bungalows for hire ⨀-caravans for hire Ⓐ-tents for hire ⧬-no dogs Prices: ⚲-adult per night ⏚-car per night
pp-per person per night ⨀-caravan per night Ⓐ-tent per night

➲ *Access via A75 exit Massiac towards Aurillac.*
Open: 15 Jun-Aug Site: 0.6HEC ⬛ ♣ ♠ Prices: ♠1.55
♠1.10 ♠1.20 ♠1.20 Facilities: ⬛ ⊙ ⬛ ⬛ Services: ⊞ lau
Leisure: ⬩ R Off-site: ⬛ ♥ ✗ ⬛ ⬛

FLAGNAC AVEYRON

Port de Lacombe 12300 ☎ 565601097 ▦ 565601688
e-mail: info@campingportdelacombe.com
website: www.campingportdelacombe.com
A shady site in the Lot valley. Water activities including
fishing and canoeing on the river and an aquatic area
incorporating a large water chute.
➲ *Follow A75 autoroute in the direction of Rodez, turn off for
Decazeville/Flagnac.*
Open: 15 May-15 Sep Site: 4HEC ⬛ ♣ ♠ Facilities: ⬛ ⬛
⊙ ⬛ ⬛ ⬛ ⬛ Services: ♥ ✗ ⊞ lau Leisure: ⬩ R

FLEURIE RHÔNE

CM la Grappe Fleurie 69820 ☎ 474698007 ▦ 474698571
e-mail: info@fleurie.org website: www.fleurie.org
A good quality municipal site in a picturesque setting in the
heart of the Beaujolais region.
➲ *0.6km SE on D119 E.*
Open: mid Mar-mid Oct Site: 2.5HEC ⬛ ♣ Prices: ♠3.50
pitch 10 (incl 2 persons) Facilities: ⬛ ⊙ ⬛ ⬛ ⬛ Services: lau
Off-site: ⬛ ♥ ✗ ⬛ ⊞

GOUDET HAUTE-LOIRE

Bord de l'Eau Plaine du Chambon, 43150
☎ 471571682 ▦ 471571288
Well equipped site in wooded surroundings below the ruins
of the castle.
➲ *W via D49, beside the River Loire.*
Open: 15 Jun-5 Sep Site: 4HEC ⬛ ♣ ♠ Prices: ♠4.27
♠4.27 ♠4.27 Facilities: ⬛ ⬛ ⊙ ⬛ ⬛ ⬛ Services: ♥ ✗ ⊞ lau
Leisure: ⬩ PR

ISLE-ET-BARDAIS ALLIER

Écossais 3360 ☎ 470666257 ▦ 470066399
In a peaceful location in the heart of the Forest of Tronçais,
beside the Pirot Lake.
➲ *Access via A71-E11.*
Open: Apr-Sep Site: 25HEC ⬛ ♣ ♠ Prices: ♠2-2.40 ♠1-
1.15 pitch 1-1.15 Facilities: ⬛ ⬛ ⊙ ⬛ ⬛ ⬛ Services: ♥ ⊞ lau
Leisure: ⬩ L Off-site: ✗

JASSAT PUY-DE-DÔME

Ribeyre 63790 ☎ 473886429 ▦ 473886841
e-mail: laribeyre@free.fr website: laribeyre.free.fr
Situated in the heart of the Auvergne amid lakes and
mountains, a flat grassy site with access to a private beach
with swimming.
➲ *Autoroute A71 exit 6, then take D978/D996 to Murol, then
D5 southwards*
Open: May-15 Sep Site: 10HEC ⬛ ♣ ♠ ♠ Prices: ♠3.60-
4.90 ♠5.10-7.10 pitch 12.30-16.90 (incl 2 persons)
Facilities: ⬛ ⬛ ⊙ ⬛ ⬛ ⬛ Services: ♥ ✗ lau Leisure: ⬩ LPR
Off-site: ✗ ⬛ ⊞

JENZAT ALLIER

Champ de Sioule rte de Chantelle, 03800
☎ 470568635 ▦ 470568538
e-mail: mairie-jenzat@pays-alliu.com
Open: 10 Apr-19 Sep Site: 1HEC ⬛ ♣ Prices: ♠2.30 ♠1
♠2.30 ♠1.30 pitch 4 Facilities: ⬛ ⊙ ⬛ ⬛ Services: ⊞ lau
Off-site: ⬛ ♥ ✗ ⬛ ⬛ ⬩R

LACAPELLE-VIESCAMP CANTAL

Puech des Ouilhes 15150 ☎ 471464238 ▦ 471464738
e-mail: campingpuech@infonie.fr
website: www.campingpuech.chez.tiscali.fr
On a wooded peninsula on Lake St-Étienne-Cantalès.
Open: 15 Jun-5 Sep Site: 2HEC ⬛ ♣ ♠ ♨ Prices: ♠3.40
♠1.50 pitch 12 (incl 2 persons) Facilities: ⬛ ⬛ ⊙ ⬛ ⬛ ⬛
Services: ⊞ lau Leisure: ⬩ LP Off-site: ♥ ✗

LANGEAC HAUTE-LOIRE

Gorges de l'Allier Domaine du Prad'Eau, 43300
☎ 471770501 ▦ 471772734
e-mail: langeac@wanadoo.fr
In wooded surroundings within a natural park, 800mtrs
from the river. Good recreational facilities.
➲ *Access via N102.*
Open: Apr-30 Oct Site: 14HEC ⬛ ♣ ♠ ♠ Å Facilities: ⬛
⊙ ⬛ ⬛ Services: ♥ lau Leisure: ⬩ PR Off-site: ⬛ ♥ ✗ ⬛ ⬛
⊞

LAPEYROUSE PUY-DE-DÔME

CM Les Marins La Loge, 63700 ☎ 473520273 ▦ 473520389
A modern, lakeside site with good facilities set among the
rolling hills of the Combtaille.
➲ *2km E via D998.*
Open: 15 Jun-1 Sep Site: 2HEC ⬛ ♣ ♠ Prices: pitch 13
Facilities: ⬛ ⊙ ⬛ ⬛ Services: ♥ ✗ ⊞ lau Leisure: ⬩ L
Off-site: ⬛ ✗ ⬛

LEMPDES HAUTE-LOIRE

Club A.Tou.Vert 43410 ☎ 471765369 ▦ 467363542
e-mail: a.tou.vert@net-up.com
Open: May-30 Oct Site: 2HEC ⬛ ♣ ♠ Prices: ♠6.50-7
pitch 9-11 (incl 2 persons) Facilities: ⬛ ⊙ ⬛ ⬛ ⬛
Services: ♥ ⊞ lau Leisure: ⬩ R Off-site: ⬛ ♥ ✗ ⬛ ⬩P

LOUBEYRAT PUY-DE-DÔME

Colombier 63410 ☎ 473866694
➲ *1.5km S via D16.*
Open: May -14 Oct Site: 1.3HEC ⬛ ♣ ♠ ♠ Prices: ♠1.50-
2.30 ♠0.75-1.15 ♠0.75-1.15 pitch 1.50-2.30 Facilities: ⬛ ⊙
⬛ ⬛ Services: ⊞ lau Leisure: ⬩ P Off-site: ♥ ✗ ⬛

MALZIEU-VILLE, LE LOZÈRE

Piscine 48140 ☎ 66314763
Peaceful shaded site on the banks of a river near to the
municipal sports complex.
➲ *A75 Clermont-Ferrand-Millau road, exit for St Chély
D'Apcher, at Malzieu turn right before the bridge over the
river.*
Open: May Sep Site: 1HEC ⬛ ♣ ♠ Prices: ♠9.10-12.50
pitch 9.10-12.50 Facilities: ⬛ ⬛ ⊙ ⬛ ⬛ Services: ♥ lau
Off-site: ✗ ⬩PR

MARTRES-DE-VEYRE, LES PUY-DE-DÔME

Camping la Font de Bleix r des Roches, 63730
☎ 473392649 ▦ 473392011
e-mail: ailes_liobres@infonie.fr
website: goeland03.chez.tiscali.fr/
A pleasant site beside the River Allier. A good centre for
touring the surrounding area.
➲ *SE via D225 beside the River Allier.*
Open: All year Site: 1.3HEC ⬛ ♣ ♠ ♠ Prices: ♠2.50-
2.80 ♠1.60 ♠1.60 pitch 1.60 Facilities: ⬛ ⬛ ⊙ ⬛ ⬛
Services: lau Leisure: ⬩ R Off-site: ♥ ✗ ⬛ ⊞

Facilities: ⬛-shop ⬛-shower ⊙-electric points for razors ⬛-electric points for caravans ⬛-parking by tents permitted
⬛-compulsory separate car park Services: ✗-café/restaurant ♥-bar ⬛-Camping Gaz International ⬛-gas other than Camping
Gaz ⊞-first aid facilities lau-laundry Leisure: ⬩-swimming L-Lake P-Pool R-River S-Sea Off-site: All facilities within 2km

HEATED AQUATIC PARK (28°)
Bar – Take-away meals - New mobile homes
8 to 12 entertainment activities daily
Hiking trips to the mountains with guide

CAMPING ★★★★
l'EUROPE
MUROL
de Paradis Aquatique

Disco evenings
Karaoke
Children's club

Canoe-kayak, Sailing,
Horse-riding, Parapente,
Archery, Water-polo, Aquagym,
Basketball ground, Quad
Big screen TV.

63790 MUROL
Tel.: 00 33 (0)4 73 39 76 66 - Fax: 00 33 (0)4 73 39 76 61
Website: www.camping-europ.com (on-line booking)

MASSIAC CANTAL

CM Allagnon av de Courcelles, 15500 ☎ 471230393
A riverside site with plenty of facilities.
➲ 0.8km W on N122.
Open: May-Sep Site: 2.5HEC ⊞ ♣ Facilities: ↑ ⊙ ▣ ⌀ ☎
Services: ⊞ lau Leisure: ↘ R Off-site: ▨ ♥ ✗ ♨ ↘P

MAURS CANTAL

AT ST-CONSTANT (4.5KM SE VIA N663)

Moulin de Chaules rte de Calvinet, 15600
☎ 471491102 ▤ 471491363
website: www.eurocampings.net
Terraced site in a valley by the stream of a former watermill
with good, modern facilities.
➲ 3km E via D28.
Open: 20 Apr-Oct Site: 3HEC ⊞ ⚙ ☎ Facilities: ↑ ▨ ⊙
▣ ▣ Services: ♥ ✗ ⊞ lau Leisure: ↘ PR

MENDE LOZÈRE

Tivoli av des Gorges-du-Tarn, 48000
☎ 466650038 ▤ 466650038
e-mail: tivoli.camping@libertysurf.fr
website: www.campingtivoli.com
A level site in wooded surroundings beside the river.
➲ 2km from the town via A75 or N88.
Open: All year Site: 1.8HEC ⊞ ♣ ☎ Prices: ♠4.20-4.20
♠2.70-2.70 ♣2.30-2.30 ▲2.30-2.30 pitch 2.30-2.30
Facilities: ↑ ⊙ ▣ ⌀ ▨ ☎ Services: ♥ ✗ ⊞ lau Leisure: ↘ PR

MEYRUEIS LOZÈRE

Ayres rte de la Brèze, 48150 ☎ 466456051 ▤ 466456051
e-mail: campinglechampdayres@wanadoo.fr
website: www.campinglechampdayres.com
On a wooded meadow with well defined pitches and modern
sanitary installations within easy reach of the picturesque
Gorges de la Jonte. Plenty of recreational facilities.
➲ 0.5km E via D57
Open: Apr-Sep Site: 1.5HEC ⊞ ⚙ ☎ Prices: ♠2.50-3.50
pitch 5-8 (incl 2 persons) Facilities: ↑ ▨ ⊙ ▣ ⌀ ☎
Services: ♥ ✗ ⊞ lau Leisure: ↘ P Off-site: ✗ ♨ ↘R

Capelan 48150 ☎ 466456050 ▤ 466456050
e-mail: camping.le.capelan@wanadoo.fr
website: www.campingcapelan.com
In picturesque surroundings alongside the Gorges de la Jonte
with good facilities.
➲ Access via D986 from Ste-Enimie.
Open: 30Apr-17Sep Site: 4HEC ⊞ ♣ ☎ Prices: ♠2.70-3.70
pitch 12-18 (incl 2 persons) Facilities: ↑ ▨ ⊙ ▣ ⌀ ☎
Services: ♥ ✗ ⊞ lau Leisure: ↘ PR Off-site: ✗ ♨

MILLAU AVEYRON

Millau Graufesenque av de L'Aigoual, 12100
☎ 565611883 ▤ 565611883
➲ 1 km E on D591 next to River Dourbe.
Open: 15 Apr-Sep Site: 3.5HEC ⊞ ♣ ☎ Facilities: ↑ ▨ ⊙
▣ ⌀ ☎ Services: ♥ ✗ Leisure: ↘ PR

CM Millau Plage rte de Millau Plage, 12100
☎ 565601097 ▤ 565601688
e-mail: info@campingmillauplage.com
website: www.campingmillauplage.com
Beside the River Tarn, flat shady parkland.
➲ Access via D187.
Open: 30 Mar-Sep Site: 5HEC ⊞ ♣ ☎ Facilities: ↑ ▨ ⊙
▣ ⌀ ♨ ☎ Services: ♥ ✗ ⊞ lau Leisure: ↘ PR

Rivages av de l'Aigoual, 12100 ☎ 565610107 ▤ 565590356
e-mail: campinglesriveages@wanadoo.fr
website: www.campinglesrivages.com
A family site with good facilities beside the River Dourbie.
➲ 1.7km E via D991.
Open: May-Sep Site: 7HEC ⊞ ⚙ ☎ ▲ Facilities: ↑ ▨ ⊙
▣ ⌀ ☎ Services: ♥ ✗ ⊞ lau Leisure: ↘ PR Off-site: ♨

MIREMONT PUY-DE-DÔME

Confolant 63380 ☎ 473799276
➲ 7km NE via D19 and D19E.
Open: Jun-10 Sep Site: 2.5HEC ⊞ ♣ ☎ ▣ Facilities: ↑ ▨
⊙ ▣ ⌀ ☎ Services: ♥ ✗ ⊞ lau Leisure: ↘ L

MONTAIGUT-LE-BLANC PUY-DE-DÔME

CM Le Bourg, 63320 ☎ 473967507
e-mail: montaigut-le-blanc@wanadoo.fz
website: www.ville-montaigut-le-blanc.fr
A quiet, level municipal site with good recreational facilities.
Open: May-Sep Site: 1.5HEC ⊞ ♣ ☎ Prices: ♠2.15-3.50
pitch 2.75 Facilities: ↑ ⊙ ▣ ☎ Services: ⊞ lau Leisure: ↘
PR Off-site: ▨ ♥ ✗

MONT-DORE, LE PUY-DE-DÔME

CM du L'Esquiladou rte des Cascades, 63240
☎ 473652374 ▤ 473652374
e-mail: camping.esquiladou@wanadoo.fr
Mountainous situation in the heart of a national park region
Open: May-20 Oct Site: 2HEC ⫶ ⚘ Prices: ♠2.80 pitch
2.50 Facilities: ↑ ⊙ ▣ ☎ Services: ⊞ lau Off-site: ▨ ♥ ✗ ⌀
♨ ↘R

MORNANT RHÔNE

CM de la Trillonière bd du Général-de-Gaulle, 69440
☎ 478441647 ▤ 478449170
e-mail: mairiemornant@wanadoo.fr
website: www.ville-mornant.fr
In a rural setting on the southern outskirts of the town at an altitude of 333mtrs.
⊃ *Off D30 towards La Condamine.*
Open: May-Sep Site: 1.6HEC ⏛ ⊶ ⊗ Prices: ⋔2.70-3.80 pitch 2.86 Facilities: ⋔ ⊙ ⊟ ⚑ 🛆 Services: ⊞ lau Leisure: ⋋ R Off-site: ⏛ ⊻ ✕ ⌀ ⚏ ⋋P

MUROL PUY-DE-DÔME

Plage Plage du Lac Chambon, 63790
☎ 473886027 ▤ 473888008
Busy site beside lake. Caravan section divided into pitches, terraced area for tents. Asphalt drive.
⊃ *1.2km from centre of village. Turn off into allée de Plage before entering village and follow signposts.*
Open: May-Sep Site: 7HEC ⏛ ⦂⦂⦂⦂ ⚑ 🏕 Facilities: ⋔ ⏛ ⊙ ⚑ ⌀ 🛆 Services: ⊻ ✕ ⊞ lau Leisure: ⋋ LR Off-site: ⚏

Pré-Bas Lac Chambon, 63790 ☎ 473886304 ▤ 473886593
e-mail: prebas@lac-chambon.com
website: www.campingauvergne.com
On the side of Lake Chambon with direct access to the beach and windsurf beach.
⊃ *SW off D996.*
Open: May-Sep Site: 3.5HEC ⏛ ⊶ 🏕 Prices: ⋔3.50-4.50 pitch 8.30-13 Facilities: ⋔ ⊙ ⚑ 🛆 Services: ⊻ ✕ lau Leisure: ⋋ LP Off-site: ⏛ ⊻ ⌀ ⋋LR

Ribeyre Jassat, 63790 ☎ 473886429 ▤ 473886841
e-mail: laribeyne@free.fr
website: www.laribeyne.free.fr
A modern site in a beautiful mountain location 1km from Lac Chambon.
⊃ *1.2km S on rte de Jassat.*
Open: May-15 Sep Site: 10HEC ⏛ ⚑ 🏕 🚐 Facilities: ⋔ ⏛ ⊙ ⚑ ⌀ 🛆 Services: ⊻ ✕ lau Leisure: ⋋ LPR Off-site: ⚏ ⊞

NANT AVEYRON

🏠Val de Cantobre 12230 ☎ 565584300 ▤ 565621036
e-mail: info@valdecantobre.com
website: www.valdecantobre.com
Beside the river in the picturesque Gorges de la Dourbie with fine views from the terraced pitches.
⊃ *4km N of Nant, towards Millau off D591.*
Open: 15 May-13 Sep Site: 6.5HEC ⏛ ⚬ 🏕 Prices: ⋔4-7 ⊶2 pitch 19-29 (incl 2 persons) Facilities: ⋔ ⏛ ⊙ ⚑ ⌀ 🛆 Services: ⊻ ✕ ⊞ lau Leisure: ⋋ PR

NAUCELLE AVEYRON

Lac de Bonnefon L'etang de Bonnefon, 12800
☎ 565593320 ▤ 56693209
e-mail: campingdulac@hotmail.com
A peaceful site in a wooded location beside a lake with good modern facilities and well marked pitches.
⊃ *NW of N88. Signposted.*
Open: Apr-Oct Site: 2.6HEC ⏛ ⊶ 🏕 ⊗ Facilities: ⋔ ⊙ ⚑ 🛆 Services: ⊻ ✕ ⊞ lau Leisure: ⋋ P Off-site: ⏛ ✕ ⌀ ⚏

A Guide to Caravan & Camping
in Great Britain is also available
from **The AA**

NAUSSAC LOZÈRE

Terrasses du Lac Lac de Naussac, 48300
☎ 466692962 ▤ 466692478
e-mail: naussac@club-internet.fr
website: www.naussac.com
Situated within a few metres of the lake at an altitude of 1000 metres with fine views.
⊃ *Take Autoroute 75, exit 88 for Langogne*
Open: Mar-Sep Site: 5.8HEC ⏛ ⊶ 🏕 Prices: pitch 12.50 (incl 2 persons) pp3.50 Facilities: ⋔ ⊙ ⚑ 🛆 Services: ⊻ ✕ ⊞ lau Leisure: ⋋ LP Off-site: ⏛ ⌀ ⚏

NÉBOUZAT PUY-DE-DÔME

Domes Les Quatre routes de Neébouzat, 63210
☎ 473871406 ▤ 473871881
e-mail: camping.les-domes@wanadoo.fr
website: www.les-domes.com
A comfortable site with hard-standing for caravans. Advance reservations recommended.
⊃ *On D216 towards Orcival.*
Open: 15 May-15 Sep Site: 1HEC ⏛ ⚑ 🏕 🚐 Prices: ⋔9 ⊶5.50 ⊟3 pitch 3.50 (incl 2 persons) pp5.50 Facilities: ⋔ ⏛ ⊙ ⚑ ⌀ ⚏ 🛆 Services: ⊞ lau Leisure: ⋋ P Off-site: ⊻ ✕ ⋋R

NÉRIS-LES-BAINS ALLIER

du Lac av Marx-Dormoy, 03310 ☎ 470032470 ▤ 470037999
website: www.ville-neris-les-bains.fr
Situated in a spa town, close to the town centre. Some of the pitches are close to a road with the remainder in the shaded hollow of a valley by the side of a stream.
Open: 4 Apr-24 Oct Site: 7HEC ⏛ ⊶ 🏕 Prices: ⋔3.32 🚐8.76 ▲7.05 Facilities: ⋔ ⊙ ⚑ 🛆 🅿 Services: ⊻ ✕ ⊞ lau Off-site: ⏛ ⊻ ✕ ⋋P

NEUVÉGLISE CANTAL

Belvédère du Pont de Lanau 15260
☎ 471235050 ▤ 471235893
e-mail: belvedere.cantal@wanadoo.fr
website: perso.wanadoo.fr/belvedere.cantal/
⊃ *5km S on D921.*
Open: Apr-Oct Site: 5HEC ⏛ ⚑ 🏕 🚐 ▲ Prices: pitch 10.90-17 (incl 2 persons) Facilities: ⋔ ⏛ ⊙ ⚑ ⌀ ⚏ 🛆 Services: ⊻ ✕ ⊞ lau Leisure: ⋋ P Off-site: ⋋LR

OLLIERGUES PUY-DE-DÔME

Chelles 63880 ☎ 473955434
e-mail: camping.les.chelles@wanadoo.fr
website: www.camping-les-chelles.com
A family site in wooded surroundings with good leisure facilities.
⊃ *5km from town centre.*
Open: May-Sep Site: 3.5HEC ⏛ ⚑ 🏕 Prices: ⋔2.80 pitch 9.30 (incl 2 persons) Facilities: ⋔ ⏛ ⊙ ⚑ 🛆 Services: ⊻ ✕ ⊞ lau Leisure: ⋋ P

ORCET PUY-DE-DÔME

Clos Auroy r de la Narse, 63670 ☎ 473842697 ▤ 473842697
e-mail: camping.le.clos.auroy@wanadoo.fr
website: www.camping-le-clos-auroy.com
Terraced site in a green valley next to a small river.
⊃ *From Clermont-Ferrand take A75 towards Montpellier, then exit 5 to Orcet (signposted)*
Open: All year Site: 2.5HEC ⏛ ⊶ 🏕 🚐 Prices: ⋔1.90-3.80 pitch 15 (incl 2 persons) Facilities: ⋔ ⏛ ⊙ ⚑ ⌀ 🛆 Services: ⊻ lau Leisure: ⋋ PR Off-site: ✕ ⚏ ⊞

Facilities: ⏛-shop ⋔-shower ⊙-electric points for razors ⚑-electric points for caravans 🛆-parking by tents permitted 🅿-compulsory separate car park Services: ✕-café/restaurant ⊻-bar ⌀-Camping Gaz International ⚏-gas other than Camping Gaz ⊞-first aid facilities lau-laundry Leisure: ⋋-swimming L-Lake P-Pool R-River S-Sea Off-site: All facilities within 2km

PARAY-SOUS-BRIAILLES ALLIER

CM *Le Moulin du Pré* 3500 ☎ 470450514   ▤ 470456514
A small municipal site beside the river.
➔ *N via D142.*
Open: Etr-Sep **Site:** 1.5HEC ▦ ♀ **Facilities:** ⋒ ⊙ ▣ ⚑
Services: lau **Leisure:** ⋋ R **Off-site:** ▮ ✕ ∅ ♨ ⊞

POLLIONNAY RHÔNE

Col de la Luère Col de la Luere, 69290
☎ 478458111   ▤ 478458947
e-mail: contact@camping-coldelaluere.com
website: camping-coldelaluere.com
Situated in the Monts du Lyonnais, 20 minutes from Lyon.
Open: All year **Site:** 5HEC ▦ ♣ ⚏ ▦ ⚑ **Prices:** ⋌3
⛺2.50 ⚏2.50 ▲2.50 pitch 2.50 **Facilities:** ⋒ ⚏ ⊙ ▣ ∅ ♨ ⚑
Services: ▮ ✕ ⊞ lau **Leisure:** ⋋ P

PONT-DE-SALARS AVEYRON

Lac 12290 ☎ 565468486   ▤ 565743310
e-mail: camping.du.lac@wanadoo.fr
website: camping-du-lac.fr.st
A terraced site on the shore of a 200hect lake with good
water sports facilities.
➔ *1.5km N via D523.*
Open: Jun-15 Sep **Site:** 4.8HEC ▦ ♣ ⚏ ▦ ▲ ⊗
Prices: pitch 11-18 **Facilities:** ⋒ ⚏ ⊙ ▣ ∅ ♨ ⚑ **Services:** ▮
✕ ⊞ lau **Leisure:** ⋋ LP

Terrasses du Lac rte du Vibal, 12290
☎ 565468818   ▤ 565468538
e-mail: terrasses12@aol.com website: www.terrasses.fr.st
Pleasant lake-side site with terraced pitches overlooking the
Pont-de-Salars lake.
➔ *4km N via D523.*
Open: Apr-Sep **Site:** 6HEC ▦ ♣ ⚏ ▦ ▲ **Prices:** pitch 11-
18.90 (incl 2 persons) pp3.50-4.20 **Facilities:** ⋒ ⚏ ⊙ ▣ ∅ ♨
⚑ **Services:** ▮ ✕ lau **Leisure:** ⋋ LP

PONTGIBAUD PUY-DE-DÔME

CM rte de la Miouze, 63230 ☎ 473889699   ▤ 473887777
In a wooded area beside the River Sioule.
➔ *0.5km SW via D986 towards Rochefort-Montagne.*
Open: 15 Apr-15 Oct **Site:** 4.5HEC ▦ ♀ ⚏ ▦
Prices: ⋌2.20-2.70 pitch 2.70-3.10 **Facilities:** ⋒ ⊙ ▣ ⚑
Services: ✕ ⊞ lau **Leisure:** ⋋ R **Off-site:** ⚏ ▮ ✕ ∅ ♨ ⋋L

PRADEAUX, LES PUY-DE-DÔME

Châteaux la Grange Fort 63500 ☎ 473710593   ▤ 473710769
e-mail: chateau@grangefort.com
website: www.grangefort.com
Parklike area surrounding an old château on the bank of the
River Allier.
➔ *From A75 take exit 13 for Parentignat, then take D999.
Signposted.*
Open: Mar-Oct **Site:** 22HEC ▦ ∷ ♀ ⚏ ▦ ▲
Prices: ⋌3.75-4.95 ⛺1.75 ⚏4.80-7.60 ▲4.80-7.60
Facilities: ⋒ ⊙ ▣ ∅ ⚑ **Services:** ▮ ✕ ⊞ lau **Leisure:** ⋋ PR
Off-site: ⚏ ♨

PUY, LE HAUTE-LOIRE

Camping du Puy-en-Velay 43000 ☎ 615082359
On a wooded meadow with a section reserved for motor
caravans.
➔ *From the town centre follow sign for Clermont-Ferrand; at
traffic lights by church of St-Laurent, turn right following
'camping' signpost, site is 500mtrs on left of road.*
Open: Etr-Sep **Site:** 1HEC ▦ ♀ **Facilities:** ⋒ ⊙ ▣ ⚑
Services: ⊞ lau **Off-site:** ⚏ ▮ ✕ ∅ ♨ ⋋P

AT BLAVOZY (9KM E)

Moulin de Barette 43700 ☎ 471030088   ▤ 471030051
website: www.lepuyenvelay.com/lemoulindebarette
A pleasant site situated in woodland beside a picturesque
stream.
➔ *Access via D156 off N88.*
Open: Apr-15 Oct **Site:** 2HEC ▦ ♀ ⚏ **Facilities:** ⋒ ⚏ ⊙
▣ ♨ ⚑ **Services:** ▮ ✕ lau **Leisure:** ⋋ PR

AT BRIVES-CHARENSAC (4.5KM E)

Audinet Av des Sports, 43700 ☎ 471091018   ▤ 471091018
website: www.brives-charensac.fr
A peaceful site in a wooded setting beside the River Loire
with good recreational facilities.
➔ *E on N88.*
Open: 14 Apr-15 Sep **Site:** 4.5HEC ▦ ♣ ⚏ ▦
Prices: ⋌2.50 ⛺1.20 ⚏5.40 ▲3.20 pitch 3.20 **Facilities:** ⋒ ⚏
⊙ ▣ ⚑ **Services:** ▮ ✕ ⊞ lau **Off-site:** ⋋R

RIOM-ÈS-MONTAGNES CANTAL

Sédour rte de Condat, 15400 ☎ 471780571
In a pleasant situation beside the River Véronne.
➔ *Access via D678.*
Open: May-Sep **Site:** 1.5HEC ▦ ♀ ⚏ **Facilities:** ⋒ ⊙ ▣ ⚑
Services: ⊞ lau **Leisure:** ⋋ R **Off-site:** ⚏ ▮ ✕ ∅ ♨ ⋋LP

RIVIÈRE-SUR-TARN AVEYRON

Peyrelade rte des Gorges-du-Tarn, 12640
☎ 565626254   ▤ 565626561
e-mail: campingpeyrelade@wanadoo.fr
website: www.campingpeyrelade.com
In wooded surroundings close to the Gorges du Tarn.
➔ *2km E via D907, beside the River Tarn.*
Open: 15 May-15 Sep **Site:** 4HEC ▦ ♣ ⚏ ▲ **Prices:** ⋌3.50-
5 pitch 14-20 (incl 2 persons) **Facilities:** ⋒ ⚏ ⊙ ▣ ∅ ⚑
Services: ▮ ✕ ⊞ lau **Leisure:** ⋋ PR

RODEZ AVEYRON

CM Layoule 12000 ☎ 565670952   ▤ 565671143
Clean, tidy site in valley below town, completely divided into
pitches.
➔ *NE of town centre. Well signposted.*
Open: Jun-Sep **Site:** 3HEC ▦ ∷ ♀ ⚏ **Prices:** ⋌2 pitch 12
(incl 3 persons) **Facilities:** ⋒ ⊙ ▣ ⚑ **Services:** ⊞ lau
Off-site: ⚏ ▮ ✕ ∅ ♨

ROYAT PUY-DE-DÔME

Indigo Royat rte de Gravenoire, 63130
☎ 330 473359705   ▤ 473356769
e-mail: royat@camping-indigo.com
website: www.camping-indigo.com/royat
In a unique natural setting, at the foot of the Puy de Dome,
and overlooking Clermont Ferrand, this site has high quality
sites, comfortably shaded and laid out in terraces.
➔ *Off D941 SW of Royat*
Open: Jun-Sep **Site:** 7HEC ▦ ∷ ♣ ⚏ **Prices:** pitch
12.50-19 (incl 2 persons) **Facilities:** ⋒ ⚏ ⊙ ▣ ∅ ⚑
Services: ▮ ✕ lau **Leisure:** ⋋ P **Off-site:** ✕ ⋋R

RUYNES-EN-MARGERIDE CANTAL

CM Petit Bois 15320 ☎ 471234226   ▤ 467363542
e-mail: a.tou.vert@net-up.com
A pleasant, well equipped, parklike site on the bank of the
River Charente.
➔ *0.5km SW on D13, rte de Garabit. Signposted.*
Open: Apr-15 Oct **Site:** 7HEC ▦ ♣ ⚏ **Prices:** pitch 9-11
Facilities: ⋒ ⊙ ▣ ⚑ **Services:** ⊞ lau
Off-site: ⚏ ▮ ✕ ∅ ♨ ⋋P

Site: 6HEC-Site size ▦-grass ∷-sand �‐stone ⊗-little shade ♀-partly shaded ♣-mainly shaded
⚏-bungalows for hire ▦-caravans for hire ▲-tents for hire ⊗-no dogs Prices: ⋌-adult per night ⛺-car per night
pp-per person per night ⚏-caravan per night ▲-tent per night

Saignes Cantal

Bellevue 15240 ☎ 471406840 📠 471406165
e-mail: saignes-mairie@wanadoo.fr
A pleasant rural site in the Sumène Valley.
Open: Jul-Aug Site: 0.9HEC ⚒ ♣ Facilities: ↑ ⊙ ⚑ 🏕
Services: ✗ lau Off-site: 🛒 🍽 ✗ ∅ 🚿 ⚑P ⊞

St-Alban-sur-Limagnole Lozère

Galier 48120 ☎ 466315880 📠 466314183
Well equipped site beside the river.
➣ Access via A75 exit 34.
Open: Mar-15 Nov Site: 4HEC ⚒ ⚑ 🏕 🚽 Prices: ↟7.40-
9.20 pitch 10-12.40 (incl 2 persons) Facilities: ↑ ⊙ ⚑ ∅ 🚿 🏕
Services: 🍽 ✗ ⊞ lau Leisure: ⚓ PR Off-site: 🛒 ✗

St-Amant-Roche-Savine Puy-de-Dôme

CM Saviloisirs 63890 ☎ 73957360 📠 73957360
Run by the local tourist authoriry with plenty of sporting
facilities within easy reach.
Open: May-Sep Site: 1.5HEC ⚒ ⚑ 🏕 Facilities: ↑ ⊙ ⚑ 🚿 🏕
Services: ⊞ lau Off-site: 🛒 🍽 ✗ ⚓R

St-Bonnet-Tronçais Allier

Champ-Fossé 3360 ☎ 470061130 📠 470061501
In the Forest of Tronçais beside a lake with plenty of
recreational facilities.
➣ Access via A71-E11.
Open: Apr-Sep Site: 35HEC ⚒ ⚑ 🏕 Prices: ↟2.10-2.70
♠1 pitch 0.80 Facilities: ↑ 🛒 ⊙ ⚑ ∅ 🏕 Services: 🍽 ✗ lau
Leisure: ⚓ L

St-Clément-de-Valorgue Puy-de-Dôme

Narcisses 63660 ☎ 473954576
e-mail: nobilet.catherine@wanadoo.fr
website: www.campinglenarcisses.com
In a beautiful natural setting within the Livradois Forez
national park area.
Open: Apr-Oct Site: 1.3HEC ⚒ ⚑ 🏕 Prices: ↟2.40-3
♠1.28-1.60 🚙2.32-2.90 ▲2.32-2.90 pitch 2.32-2.90
Facilities: ↑ 🛒 ⊙ ⚑ 🏕 Services: 🍽 ✗ ⊞ lau Leisure: ⚓ PR
Off-site: ∅ 🚿 ⚓L

St-Gal-sur-Sioule Puy-de-Dôme

Pont de St-Gal 63440 ☎ 473974471
A pleasant site with well defined, shaded pitches and access
to the river for boating, fishing etc.
➣ E via D16 towards Ebreuil, beside the River Sioule.
Open: May-Sep Site: 1HEC ⚒ ⚑ 🚙 ▲ Facilities: ↑ ⚑ ⊙
⚑ ∅ 🚿 🏕 Services: 🍽 ✗ ⊞ lau Leisure: ⚓ R

St-Geniez-D'Olt Aveyron

Campéole La Boissière rte de la Cascade, 12130
☎ 565704043 📠 565475639
website: www.campeoles.fr
A comfortable site in wooded surroundings with good
facilities. Entertainment provided in July and August.
➣ Access via A75 exit 41 towards St-Geniez-d'Olt.
Open: 20 Apr-Sep Site: 4.5HEC ⚒ ⚑ 🏕 Facilities: ↑ 🛒 ⊙
⚑ ∅ 🏕 Services: 🍽 ✗ ⊞ lau Leisure: ⚓ PR Off-site: ✗ 🚿

Marmotel 12130 ☎ 565704651 📠 565474138
website: www.marmotel.com
Grassy family site on River Lot with a wide variety of
recreational facilities.
➣ On D19 about 1km NW of St Geniez-d'Olt.
Open: May-19 Sep Site: 5HEC ⚒ ⚑ 🏕 Prices: pitch 23
(incl 2 persons) Facilities: ↑ ⊙ ⚑ 🚿 🏕 Services: 🍽 ✗ ⊞ lau
Leisure: ⚓ PR Off-site: 🛒 ∅

St-Germain-de-Calberte Lozère

Garde 48370 ☎ 466459482 📠 466459518
e-mail: camping-lagarde@wanadoo.fr
In a pleasant situation on the edge of the Cevennes National
Park.
➣ Access via A7 or A75.
Open: Jun-15 Sep Site: 2.4HEC ⚒ ⚖ ♣ Facilities: ↑ ⊙ ⚑
🏕 Services: ✗ lau Leisure: ⚓ P Off-site: 🛒 🍽 ∅ 🚿 ⚓R ⊞

St-Gérons Cantal

Presqu'île d'Espinet 15150 ☎ 471622890
e-mail: camping.despinet@wanadoo.fr
website: www.perso.wanadoo.fr/campingdespinet/camping
On a wooded peninsula jutting into the lake with fine views
of the Cantal mountains.
➣ 8.5km SE, 300m from Lake St-Étienne-Cantalès.
Open: 15 Jun-Aug Site: 3HEC ⚒ ⚑ 🏕 Prices: ↟3 ♠1.60
pitch 11 (incl 2 persons) Facilities: ↑ 🛒 ⊙ ⚑ 🏕 🏕
Services: 🍽 ✗ ⊞ lau Leisure: ⚓ LP Off-site: 🚿

St-Gervais-D'Auvergne Puy-de-Dôme

CM de l'Étang Philippe rte de St-Eloy-les-Mines, 63390
☎ 473857484
e-mail: camping.stgervais-auvergne@wanadoo.com
website: www.ville-stgervais-auvergne.fr
A small municipal site beside a small lake.
➣ Access via N987.
Open: Etr-Sep Site: 5HEC ⚒ ⚌⚌ ⚑ 🏕 Prices: pitch 8.80
Facilities: ↑ ⊙ ⚑ 🏕 Services: 🍽 ⊞ lau Leisure: ⚓ L
Off-site: 🛒 ✗ ∅

St-Hippolyte Aveyron

CM La Rivière 12140 ☎ 565661450
A small site in wooded surroundings with good sporting
facilities.
➣ Access via D904.
Open: 15 Jun-15 Sep Site: 0.7HEC ⚒ ♣ 🏕 Facilities: ↑ ⊙
⚑ 🏕 Services: ⊞ lau Leisure: ⚓ PR Off-site: 🛒 🍽 ✗ ∅ 🚿

St-Jacques-des-Blats Cantal

CM rte de la Gare, 15800 ☎ 471470590 📠 471470709
e-mail: i-tourisme-st-jacques@wanadoo.fr
A small site on the banks of the River Cère. A good centre for
exploring the surrounding Volcanic Park area.
Open: May-Sep Site: 1HEC ⚒ ⚑ Prices: ♠1.30 pp2.40
Facilities: ↑ ⊙ ⚑ 🏕 Services: ⊞ lau Leisure: ⚓ R
Off-site: 🛒 🍽 ✗

St-Jodard Loire

CM 42590 ☎ 477634242 📠 477634001
Open: May-Sep Site: 0.3HEC ⚒ ♣ 🚙 Prices: ↟1.24-1.70
♠0.62-0.85 🚙17 pitch 0.62-0.85 Facilities: ↑ ⊙ ⚑ 🏕
Services: lau Off-site: 🛒 🍽 ✗ ∅ 🚿 ⚓P

St-Just Cantal

CM Le Bourg, 15320 ☎ 471737257 📠 471737144
e-mail: commune.stjust@wanadoo.fr
website: www.saintjust.com
In the centre of the village beside the river.
Open: Etr-Sep Site: 2HEC ⚒ ♣ 🏕 🚙 Prices: 🚙8 pp1.60
Facilities: ↑ ⊙ ⚑ 🏕 Services: ⊞ lau Leisure: ⚓ P Off-site: 🛒
🍽 ✗ ∅ 🚿 ⚓R

St-Martin-Valmeroux Cantal

Moulin du Teinturier rte de Loupiac, 15140
☎ 471694312 📠 4719692452
Wooded valley site close to medieval market town.

contd.

Facilities: 🛒-shop ↑-shower ⊙-electric points for razors ⚑-electric points for caravans 🏕-parking by tents permitted ⚑-compulsory separate car park **Services:** ✗-café/restaurant 🍽-bar ∅-Camping Gaz International 🚿-gas other than Camping Gaz ⊞-first aid facilities lau-laundry **Leisure:** ⚓-swimming L-Lake P-Pool R-River S-Sea **Off-site:** All facilities within 2km

Off D922 Aurillac-Mauriac.
Open: May-Sep Site: 2.8HEC ⬛ ⬛ 🏕 Facilities: ⬛ ☺
⬛ ⬛ Services: lau Leisure: ⬛ R Off-site: ⬛ ⬛ ✕ ⬛ ⬛ ⬛P ⬛

ST-NECTAIRE PUY-DE-DÔME

Vallée Verte rte des Granges, 63710
⬛ 473885268 ⬛ 473885262
e-mail: lavalleeverte@libertysurf.fr
website: www.campinglavalleeverte.com
In wooded surroundings by a river within the Auvergne
Natural Volcanic Park.
➲ *On R146, 400 mtrs from R996.*
Open: 15 Apr-Sep Site: 2HEC ⬛ ⬛ ⬛ ⬛ Prices: ⬛3 pitch
8-10 (incl 2 persons) Facilities: ⬛ ☺ ⬛ ⬛ ⬛ ⬛ Services: ⬛ ✕
lau Leisure: ⬛ R Off-site: ⬛ ⬛PR ⬛

ST-OURS PUY-DE-DÔME

Bel-Air 63230 ⬛ 473887214 ⬛ 173722044
e-mail: camping.belair@free.fr
website: camping.belair.free.fr
➲ *1km SW on D941.*
Open: 15 May-15 Oct Site: 2HEC ⬛ ⬛ ⬛ ⬛ Prices: ⬛3.75
pitch 3.50 Facilities: ⬛ ☺ ⬛ ⬛ ⬛ ⬛ Services: ⬛ ⬛ lau
Off-site: ✕

ST-PIERRE-COLAMINE PUY-DE-DÔME

Ombrage 63610 ⬛ 473967787 ⬛ 473963040
e-mail: campombrage@infonie.fr
website: www.campombrage.com
A pleasant site in peaceful wooded surroundings at an
altitude of 800 metres on the edge of the Auvergne Volcano
Park. All the usual services are provided and there are good
recreational facilities.
➲ *300mtrs from D978.*
Open: All year Site: 2HEC ⬛ ⬛ ⬛ ⬛ Prices: ⬛3.60 ⬛1
pitch 3.30 Facilities: ⬛ ⬛ ☺ ⬛ ⬛ ⬛ ⬛ Services: ⬛ ⬛ lau
Leisure: ⬛ P Off-site: ✕ ⬛R

ST-RÉMY-SUR-DUROLLE PUY-DE-DÔME

CM Chanterelles 63550 ⬛ 473943171 ⬛ 473943171
website: www.saint-remy-sur-durolle.fr
In pleasant wooded surroundings close to the lake.
➲ *3km NE via D201*
Open: May-Sep Site: 6HEC ⬛ ⬛ Prices: ⬛2.55 ⬛1.35
⬛1.65 ⬛1.35 Facilities: ⬛ ☺ ⬛ ⬛ ⬛ Services: ⬛ lau
Off-site: ⬛ ⬛ ✕ ⬛ ⬛LP

ST-ROME-DE-TARN AVEYRON

Cascade 12490 ⬛ 565625659 ⬛ 565625862
e-mail: campingdelacascade@wanadoo.fr
Terraced site beside the River Tarn.
➲ *0.3km N via D993.*
Open: All year Site: 4HEC ⬛ ⬛ ⬛ ⬛ Prices: pitch 13-18
pp5 Facilities: ⬛ ⬛ ☺ ⬛ ⬛ ⬛ Services: ⬛ ✕ lau
Leisure: ⬛ LPR Off-site: ✕ ⬛

ST-SALVADOU AVEYRON

Muret 12200 ⬛ 565818069 ⬛ 565818066
e-mail: campinglemuret@hotmail.com
website: www.campinglemuret.com
A modern site in peaceful, rural surroundings beside the
lake.
➲ *3km SE.*
Open: 15 Jun-Aug Site: 3HEC ⬛ ⬛ ⬛ Facilities: ⬛ ⬛ ☺
⬛ ⬛ ⬛ Services: ⬛ ✕ ⬛ lau Leisure: ⬛ L Off-site: ⬛

STE-CATHERINE RHÔNE

CM du Châtelard 69440 ⬛ 478818060 ⬛ 478818773
e-mail: ste.catherine@coteaux-lyonnais.com
A quiet, well equipped site providing magnificent views over
the surrounding countryside.
➲ *2km S.*
Open: Mar-Nov Site: 4HEC ⬛ ⬛ Prices: ⬛1.90 ⬛2.20
⬛2.20 pitch 2.20 Facilities: ⬛ ☺ ⬛ ⬛ ⬛ Services: ⬛ lau
Off-site: ⬛ ⬛ ✕ ⬛ ⬛ ⬛R

STE-SIGOLÈNE HAUTE-LOIRE

Vaubarlet Vaubarlet, 43600 ⬛ 471666495 ⬛ 471661198
e-mail: vaubarlet@aol.com
website: www.vaubarlet.com
In a beautiful wooded valley beside the River Dunières with a
variety of supervised family activities.
➲ *Exit for Ste-Sigolène on D44, then towards Grazac on D43.*
Open: May-Sep Site: 3.5HEC ⬛ ⬛ ⬛ ⬛ Facilities: ⬛ ⬛ ☺
⬛ ⬛ ⬛ Services: ⬛ ✕ lau Leisure: ⬛ PR Off-site: ✕

SALLES-CURAN AVEYRON

Beau Rivage Route des Vernhes, Lac de Pareloup, 12410
⬛ 565463332 ⬛ 565463396
e-mail: camping-beau-rivage@wanadoo.fr
website: www.beau-rivage.fr
A terraced site located on the shore of Lac de Pareloup. There
are facilities for all kinds of water sports and the site's
popularity makes advance booking advisable.
➲ *3.5km N via D993n and D243.*
Open: Jun-15 Sep Site: 2HEC ⬛ ⬛ ⬛ ⬛ Prices: pitch 11-
20 (incl 2 persons) Facilities: ⬛ ⬛ ☺ ⬛ ⬛ ⬛ ⬛ Services: ⬛
✕ ⬛ lau Leisure: ⬛ LP

Genêts 12410 ⬛ 565463534 ⬛ 565780072
e-mail: contact@camping-les-genets.fr
website: www.camping-les-genets.fr
On the edge of the Papeloup lake.
➲ *7 km W via D577.*
Open: Jun-Sep Site: 3HEC ⬛ ⬛ ⬛ 🏕 Facilities: ⬛ ⬛ ☺ ⬛
⬛ ⬛ ⬛ Services: ⬛ ✕ ⬛ lau Leisure: ⬛ LP

SAZERET ALLIER

Petite Valette 03390 ⬛ 470076457 ⬛ 470072548
e-mail: la.petite.valette@wanadoo.fr website: www.valette.nl
A well equipped site attached to a farm with well defined
pitches and organised activities for children.
➲ *Access via A71 exit 11 and follow signs.*
Site: 4HEC ⬛ ⬛ ⬛ ⬛ 🏕 Facilities: ⬛ ☺ ⬛ ⬛
Services: ✕ ⬛ lau Leisure: ⬛ LP

SEMBADEL-GARE HAUTE-LOIRE

Casses 43160 ⬛ 471009472
A family site in a rural setting at an altitude of 1000mtrs,
2km from a lake.
➲ *1km W via D22.*
Open: Jul-20 Sep Site: 2.4HEC ⬛ ⬛ Facilities: ⬛ ☺ ⬛ ⬛
Services: lau Off-site: ⬛ ✕ ⬛ ⬛LR

SÉNERGUES AVEYRON

Étang du Camp 12320 ⬛ 565796225 ⬛ 565728158
e-mail: conques@conques.com
website: www.conques.com
Well equipped site in a wooded setting beside the lake.
➲ *6km SW via D242.*
Open: 15 Jun-15 Sep Site: 3HEC ⬛ ⬛ ⬛ Facilities: ⬛
☺ ⬛ ⬛ ⬛ Services: ⬛ lau

Site: 6HEC-Site size ⬛-grass ⬛-sand ⬛-stone ⬛-little shade ⬛-partly shaded ⬛-mainly shaded
⬛-bungalows for hire ⬛-caravans for hire ⬛-tents for hire ⬛-no dogs Prices: ⬛-adult per night ⬛-car per night
pp-per person per night ⬛-caravan per night ⬛-tent per night

SÉVÉRAC-LE-CHÂTEAU AVEYRON

CM av J-Moulin, 12150 ☎ 565476482
A quiet, well equipped municipal site close to the town centre. In a good location for visiting the Gorges du Tarn.
➲ *1.2km S via N9 towards Millau.*
Open: Jun-Sep Site: 1.3HEC ⊞ ♀ Facilities: ♠ ⊙ ☷ ⊞
Services: lau Off-site: ☲ ♥ ✕ ∅ ♨ ⦁PR ⊞

SÉVÉRAC-L'ÉGLISE AVEYRON

Grange de Monteillac Monteillac, 12310
☎ 565702100 ▦ 565702101
e-mail: info@la-grange-de-monteillac.com
website: www.la-grange-de-monteillac.com
A family site in a quiet wooded location with good recreational facilities.
➲ *Access via A75 and N88.*
Open: May-15 Sep Site: 4.5HEC ⊞ ♀ ⊞ ☷ ⅄
Prices: pitch 21.50 (incl 2 persons) Facilities: ♠ ☲ ⊙ ☷ ⊞
Services: ♥ ✕ lau Leisure: ⦁ P Off-site: ♨

SINGLES PUY-DE-DÔME

Moulin de Serre D 73 Vallee de la Burande, 63690
☎ 473211606 ▦ 473211256
e-mail: moulin-de-serre@wanadoo.fr
website: www.moulindeserre.com
A well equipped site beside the River Burande.
➲ *1.7km S of La Guinguette via D73.*
Open: 10 Apr-26 Sep Site: 6.5HEC ⊞ ♀ ⊞ ☷ ⅄
Prices: ⅄1.65-2.20 pitch 10.40-13.90 (incl 2 persons)
Facilities: ♠ ☲ ⊙ ☷ ∅ ♨ ⊞ Services: ♥ ✕ lau Leisure: ⦁ PR

THÉRONDELS AVEYRON

Source Presqu'ile de Laussac, 12600
☎ 565660562 ▦ 565662100
e-mail: campinglasource@:wanadoo.fr
website: camping-la-source.com
In a beautiful situation beside Lake Sarrans.
Open: 18 Jun- 03 Sep Site: 4.5HEC ⊞ ♀ ⊞ ⅄ Prices: ⅄3-4
pitch 11-18 (incl 2 persons) Facilities: ♠ ☲ ⊙ ☷ ∅ ⊞
Services: ♥ ✕ lau Leisure: ⦁ LP

TRIZAC CANTAL

Pioulat 15400 ☎ 471786420 ▦ 471786540
e-mail: mairie.trizac@wanadoo.fr
Open: 16 Jun-16 Sep Site: 4.7HEC ⊞ ⚹ ⊞ Prices: ⅄10
⦁8 ☷8 ⅄8 Facilities: ♠ ⊙ ☷ ⊞ Services: lau Leisure: ⦁ LR
Off-site: ☲ ♥ ✕ ∅ ♨ ⊞

URÇAY ALLIER

CM r de la Gare, 3360 ☎ 470069144 ▦ 470069330
Open: 15 May-Aug Site: 0.7HEC ⊞ ⠿ ♀ Facilities: ♠ ⊙
☷ ⊞ Services: lau Leisure: ⦁ R Off-site: ☲ ♥ ✕ ∅ ♨ ⊞

VARENNES-SUR-ALLIER ALLIER

⌂Château de Chazeuil 03150
☎ 470450010 ▦ 470450010
e-mail: camping-de-chazeuil@ifrance.com
website: www.camping-de-chazeuil.com
On well-kept meadow within the château park.
➲ *3km NW on N7.*
Open: 15 Apr-15 Oct Site: 1.5HEC ⊞ ♀ Prices: ⅄4.50
⦁2.75 pitch 4.50 Facilities: ♠ ⊙ ☷ ⊞ Services: ⊞ lau
Leisure: ⦁ P Off-site: ☲ ♥ ✕ ∅ ⦁R

VERRIÈRES-EN-FOREZ LOIRE

Ferme Le Soleillant Le Soleillant, 42600 ☎ 477762273
e-mail: camille.rival@wanadoo.fr
A small terraced site within the grounds of a farm.
➲ *Access via A47.*
Open: All year Site: 3.2HEC ⊞ ♣ ☷ Prices: ⅄2.90 ⦁0.80
pitch 2.20 Facilities: ♠ ⊙ ☷ ⊞ Services: ✕ ⊞ lau Off-site: ☲
♥ ✕ ♨ ⦁R

VIC-SUR-CÈRE CANTAL

Pommeraie 15800 ☎ 471475418 ▦ 471496330
e-mail: pommeraie@wanadoo.fr
website: camping-la-pommeraie.com
A well equipped family site in a peaceful situation with good recreational facilities.
➲ *2km SE.*
Open: Apr-15 Sep Site: 4HEC ⊞ ♣ ⊞ ☷ ⅄ Facilities: ♠
☲ ⊙ ☷ ♨ ⊞ Services: ♥ ✕ ⊞ lau Leisure: ⦁ P
Off-site: ∅ ⦁R

VIEILLE-BRIOUDE HAUTE-LOIRE

Dintillat Dintillat, 43100 ☎ 471509336 ▦ 471509336
e-mail: elie.sicard@wanadoo.fr
website: http://perso.wanadoo.fr/elie.sicard
A terraced site with good modern facilities at an altitude of 500mtrs.
➲ *Access via N102 and D16.*
Open: May-Sep Site: 1HEC ⊞ ♀ ⊞ ☷ ⅄ Facilities: ♠ ⊙
☷ ⊞ Services: lau Off-site: ⦁R

VILLEFORT LOZÈRE

Palhère rte du Mas de la Banque, 48800 ☎ 466468063
A well equipped, peaceful site on the edge of the Parc National des Cévennes.
➲ *4km SW via D66 beside the river.*
Open: May-Sep Site: 2HEC ⊞ ♣ ♣ Prices: ⅄3.20 ⦁1 ☷12
⅄1.55 pitch 9 (incl 2 persons) Facilities: ♠ ⊙ ☷ ⊞
Services: ♥ ✕ ⊞ lau Leisure: ⦁ PR Off-site: ☲ ∅ ♨ ⦁L

VILLEFRANCHE-DE-PANAT AVEYRON

Cantarelles Alrance, 12430 ☎ 565464035 ▦ 565464035
e-mail: cantarelles@wanadoo.fr
On level grassland by Lac de Villefranche-de-Panat.
➲ *On the D25 about 3km N.*
Open: 15 June-15 Sep Site: 3.5HEC ⊞ ♣ ⊞ ☷
Prices: pitch 15 (incl 2 persons) Facilities: ♠ ☲ ⊙ ☷ ∅ ♨ ⊞
Services: ♥ ✕ ⊞ lau Leisure: ⦁ L

VILLEFRANCHE-DE-ROUERGUE AVEYRON

Rouergue 12202 ☎ 565451624 ▦ 565455558
e-mail: infos@villefranche.com
website: villefranche.com
A comfortable site in a pleasant, shady situation beside the River Aveyron.
➲ *1.5km SW via D47 rte de Monteils.*
Open: 20 Apr-Sep Site: 1.8HEC ⊞ ♣ ⊞ ☷ ⅄ Prices: pitch
10.50-13.50 (incl 2 persons) Facilities: ♠ ☲ ⊙ ☷ ∅ ♨ ⊞
Services: lau Off-site: ♥ ✕ ♨ ⦁P ⊞

YSSINGEAUX HAUTE-LOIRE

CM Choumouroux 43200 ☎ 471655344
➲ *800m S of town off the rte de Puy.*
Open: May-Sep Site: 0.8HEC ⊞ ♀ ☷ Prices: ⅄1.90
⦁2.50 ☷2.50 pitch 2.50 Facilities: ♠ ⊙ ☷ ⊞ Services: ⊞
lau Off-site: ☲ ♥ ✕ ∅ ♨ ⦁P

Facilities: ☲-shop ♠-shower ⊙-electric points for razors ☷-electric points for caravans ⊞-parking by tents permitted ⊟-compulsory separate car park **Services:** ✕-café/restaurant ♥-bar ∅-Camping Gaz International ♨-gas other than Camping Gaz ⊞-first aid facilities lau-laundry **Leisure:** ⦁-swimming L-Lake P-Pool R-River S-Sea **Off-site:** All facilities within 2km

SOUTH COAST/RIVIERA

AGAY VAR

Agay Soleil 1152 bd de la Plage, rte de Cannes RN 98, 83530
☎ 494820079 ▦ 494828870
e-mail: camping-agay-soleil@wanadoo.fr
website: www.agaysoleil.com
A small site in a shady position directly on a sandy beach.
The facilities are good and all kinds of watersports are
available nearby.
➲ *Between N98 and the sea.*
Open: 15 Mar-3 Nov **Site:** 0.7HEC ▦ ⠿ ♠ ⬛
Prices: pitch 20.50-24.50 (incl 2 persons) **Facilities:** ⋒ ⊙ ⍾
⌀ ☎ **Services:** ⍾ ✗ ⊞ lau **Leisure:** ⥾ S **Off-site:** ⍾

⚫Estérel rte de Valescure, 83530 ☎ 494820328 ▦ 494828737
e-mail: contact@esterel_caravaning.fr
website: www.esterel_caravaning.fr
A pleasant family-site of provincial architecture. There is
plenty to entertain all age groups day and evening. Riding
and cycling can be enjoyed in the nearby in the surrounding
hills and woods.
➲ *3km from Agay-Plage towards Valescure. N of Agay near
the golf course.*
Open: Apr-Sep **Site:** 12.5HEC ▦ ♠ ⠿ ⬛ **Facilities:** ⋒ ⍾ ⊙
⍾ ⚱ ☎ **Services:** ⍾ ✗ ⊞ lau **Leisure:** ⥾ P **Off-site:** ⥾R

AGDE HÉRAULT

Escale Rte de la Tamarissière, 34300 ☎ 467212109 ▦ 467211024
e-mail: camping.escale@wanadoo.fr
A riverside site, 900mtrs from the sea, with good recreational
facilities.
Open: Apr-Sep **Site:** 3HEC ▦ ♠ ⬛ **Prices:** pitch 15-27.20
(incl 2 persons) **Facilities:** ⋒ ⍾ ⊙ ⍾ ⚱ ☎ **Services:** ⍾ ✗ ⊞
lau **Leisure:** ⥾ PRS **Off-site:** ⌀ ⥾S

Camping Airotel CHANTECLER
Exit Nr 31- Val St André
13100 AIX-EN-PROVENCE
Tel : 00 33 4 42 26 12 98
Fax : 00 33 4 42 27 33 53
E-mail : chanteclerc@wanadoo.fr
www.airotel-chanteclerc.com

8 ha surface park, only 2 km from the centre of Aix, the
city of Cézanne. Swimming pool, launderette, shop,
restaurant, children's club. Motor homes welcome.
Many organized activities. Discounts from November
to February. Ideally situated to relax and discover the
Provence. Mobile homes and bungalows to let.
OPEN ALL YEAR

International de l'Hérault rte de la Tamarissière, 34300
☎ 467941283
A grassy site on W bank of the River Hérault. There are fine
sporting and recreational facilities and free transport is
provided to the beach 3km away.
➲ *Take the exit for 'Agde' off autoroute A9, then continue via
D13 and D32E.*
Open: Etr-Sep **Site:** 11HEC ▦ ⠿ ⬛ ⍾ **Facilities:** ⋒ ⍾ ⊙
⍾ ⌀ **Services:** ⍾ ✗ lau **Leisure:** ⥾ P **Off-site:** ⚱ ⥾RS

Mer et Soliel rte de Rochelongue, 34300
☎ 467942114 ▦ 467948194
e-mail: contact@camping-mer-soleil.com
website: www.camping-mer-soleil.com
A modern, well equipped family site within easy reach of the
beach.
Open: Apr-15 Oct **Site:** 7.9HEC ▦ ⠿ ♠ ⬛ ⍾ ⯈
Prices: ⥼3-6 ⟲3 ⯌3 ⯈3 **Facilities:** ⋒ ⍾ ⊙ ⍾ ⌀ ⚱ ☎
Services: ⍾ ✗ ⊞ lau **Leisure:** ⥾ P **Off-site:** ⥾RS

AT ROCHELONGUE-PLAGE (4KM S)

Champs Blancs rte de Rochelongue, 34300
☎ 467942342 ▦ 467948781
e-mail: champs.blancs@wanadoo.fr
website: www.champs-blancs.fr
Quiet shady site with hedged pitches and surrounded by
exotic vegetation. Good sporting and entertainment facilities.
➲ *Situated between Agde and Cap d'Agde on route de
Rochelongue.*
Open: Apr-Sep **Site:** 4HEC ▦ ⠿ ♠ ⬛ **Prices:** ⥼8 pitch 30-
40 **Facilities:** ⋒ ⍾ ⊙ ⍾ ⚱ ☎ **Services:** ⍾ ✗ lau **Leisure:** ⥾
P **Off-site:** ✗ ⌀ ⥾RS

AIGUES MORTES GARD

Camping Village La Petite Camargue 30220
☎ 466539898 ▦ 466539880
e-mail: petite.camargue@yellohvillage.com
website: www.la-petite-camargue.fr
A grassy site lying amongst vineyards on the D62. 3.5 km
from the sea.
➲ *Access via autoroute exit Gallargues in direction of La
Grande Motte.*
Open: 24 Apr-19 Sep **Site:** 10HEC ⠿ ⍾ ⬛ **Prices:** pitch
15-38 (incl 2 persons) **Facilities:** ⋒ ⍾ ⊙ ⍾ ⌀ ⚱ ☎
Services: ⍾ ✗ ⊞ lau **Leisure:** ⥾ P **Off-site:** ⥾S

AIX-EN-PROVENCE BOUCHES-DU-RHÔNE

Arc en Ciel Pont de Trois Sautets, rte de Nice, 13100
☎ 442261428
A pleasant terraced site on both sides of a stream.
➲ *Near motorway exit 3 Sautets on N7 towards Toulon. 3km
SE near Pont des Trois Sautets.*
Open: Apr-Sep **Site:** 3HEC ▦ ⠿ ⠿ ♠ **Prices:** ⥼5.80 pitch
5.20 **Facilities:** ⋒ ⊙ ⍾ ⌀ ⚱ **Services:** ⊞ lau **Leisure:** ⥾ PR
Off-site: ⍾ ⍾ ✗ ⚱

Chantecler Val St Andre, 13100 ☎ 442261298 ▦ 442273353
Widespread, uneven site on hill. Terraced pitches.
➲ *Access off motorway exit Aix-Est on A8.2.5 km SE of town.*
Open: All year **Site:** 8HEC ▦ ♠ ⬛ ⍾ **Prices:** ⥼5.40 pitch
19.80 (incl 2 persons) **Facilities:** ⋒ ⍾ ⊙ ⍾ ⌀ ⚱ ⚱
Services: ⍾ ✗ ⊞ **Leisure:** ⥾ P **Off-site:** ⥾S

ALET-LES-BAINS AUDE

Val d'Aleth chemin de la Paoulette, 11580
☎ 468699040 ▦ 468699460
e-mail: camping@valdaleth.com website: www.valdaleth.com
In picturesque surroundings beneath the ancient ramparts,
on the banks of the River Aude. English owners.

Site: 6HEC-Site size ▦ -grass ⠿ -sand ⠿ -stone ⥾⥾-little shade ⠿-partly shaded ♠-mainly shaded
⬛-bungalows for hire ⬛-caravans for hire ⚠-tents for hire ⥾-no dogs **Prices:** ⥼-adult per night ⟲-car per night
pp-per person per night ⬛-caravan per night ⚠-tent per night

➲ *From Carcassonne take D118 towards Quillan. Site 8km beyond Limoux.*
A61 then D118 to Limoux **Open:** All year **Site:** 0.5HEC ⊞⊞⊞
⊕ ⊞ ⊞ **Prices:** ⋔2.60 ⊞9.50 Å1.30 pitch 9.50 (incl 2 persons) **Facilities:** ⋔ ⋢ ⊙ ⊞ ⊘ ⊞ ⊞ **Services:** ⊞ lau
Leisure: ⋡ R **Off-site:** ⋢ ⊞ ✕ ⋡P

ANDUZE GARD

Arche 30140 ☎ 466617408 ▦ 466618894
e-mail: resa@camping-arche.fr
website: www.camping-arche.fr
In a beautiful situation on the River Gard with fine views of the surrounding Cevennes scenery.
➲ *Access via A7 exit Bollène and D907.*
Open: Apr-Sep **Site:** 10HEC ⊞⊞⊞ ⁖⁖⁖ ♣ ⊞ Å **Prices:** ⋔2.60-4.20 pitch 10.90-17.50 (incl 2 persons) **Facilities:** ⋔ ⋢ ⊙ ⊞ ⊘ ⊞ ⊞ **Services:** ⊞ ✕ ⊞ lau **Leisure:** ⋡ R

Brise des Pins rte de St-Félix de Pallières, 30140
☎ 466616339
A terraced site offering fine panoramic views over the surrounding countryside.
➲ *3km from Anduze.*
Open: Jun-15 Sep **Site:** ⊞⊞⊞ ♣ **Prices:** ⋔8 pitch 11 (incl 2 persons) **Facilities:** ⋔ ⊙ ⊞ ⊞ **Services:** lau

Castel Rose 610 chemin de Recoulin, 30140 ☎ 466618015
e-mail: castelrose@wahadoo.fr website: www.castelrose.com
A well equipped site on the banks of the River Gardon.
➲ *1 km NW on D907.*
Open: 29 Mar-21 Sep **Site:** 7HEC ⁖⁖⁖ ♣ ⊞ ⊞ **Facilities:** ⋔
⊙ ⊞ ⊘ ⊞ **Services:** ⊞ ✕ lau **Leisure:** ⋡ R **Off-site:** ⋢ ⊞ ⊞

Cévennes Provence 30140 ☎ 466617310 ▦ 466616074
e-mail: marais@camping-cevennes-provence.com
website: www.camping-cevennes-provence.com
Situated in a valley bordered by two rivers and offering a choice of pitches in varying levels of shade and terrain.
➲ *Near railway station.*
Open: 20 Mar-2 Nov **Site:** 30HEC ⊞⊞⊞ ♣ ⊞ **Prices:** pitch 11.55-16.50 (incl 2 persons) **Facilities:** ⋔ ⋢ ⊙ ⊞ ⊘ ⊞ ⊞ **Services:** ⊞ ✕ ⊞ lau **Leisure:** ⋡ R

AT ATTUECH (5KM SE ON D907)

Fief 30140 ☎ 466618171 ▦ 466618171
On level meadow, divided by flowerbeds and shrubs.
➲ *Turn off D982 E of Attuech and continue for 400mtrs on partially rough track.*
Open: Apr-Sep **Site:** 4.5HEC ⊞⊞⊞ ♣ ⊞ **Facilities:** ⋔ ⋢ ⊙ ⊞
⊘ ⊞ **Services:** ⊞ ✕ ⊞ lau **Leisure:** ⋡ P **Off-site:** ⋡LR

ANTHÉOR-PLAGE VAR

Azur Rivage RN 98, 83530 ☎ 494448312 ▦ 494448439
Well-equipped site only a few metres from the sea and a sandy beach.
Open: Etr-Sep **Site:** 1HEC ⊞⊞⊞ ♣ ⊞ **Facilities:** ⋔ ⋢ ⊙ ⊞ ⊘
⊞ ⊞ **Services:** ⊞ ✕ ⊞ lau **Leisure:** ⋡ P **Off-site:** ⋡S

Viaduc bd des Lucioles, 83530 ☎ 494448231 ▦ 494448231
A quiet site 150mtrs from a sandy beach, with good facilities.
➲ *Access via N98.*
Open: 15 May-15 Sep **Site:** 1.1HEC ⊞⊞⊞ ♣ **Prices:** ⋔3.50 pitch 22-29 (incl 2 persons) **Facilities:** ⋔ ⊙ ⊞ ⊞ **Services:** ⊞ lau **Leisure:** ⋢ ⊞ ✕ ⊘ ⋢ ⋡S

ANTIBES ALPES-MARITIMES

Logis de la Brague 1221 rte de Nice, 06600 ☎ 493335472
website: www.camping-logis-brague.com
On a level meadow beside a small river.

➲ *On N7.*
Open: 2 May-Sep **Site:** 1.7HEC ⊞⊞⊞ ⊕ ⊞ **Prices:** ⊞15 pitch 12 (incl 2 persons) pp4.40 **Facilities:** ⋔ ⋢ ⊙ ⊞ ⊘ ⊞ **Services:** ⊞ ✕ ⊞ lau **Leisure:** ⋡ RS **Off-site:** ⋢

AT BIOT (7KM N ON N7 AND A8)

Eden chemin du Val-de-Pome, 06410
☎ 493656370 ▦ 493655422
Site on level meadowland, no tents allowed.
➲ *On D4.*
Open: Apr-30 Oct **Site:** 2.5HEC ⊞⊞⊞ ⁖⁖⁖ ♣ ⊞ ⊞ ⊗ **Prices:** ⋔3.80-5.40 ⊞3.10-3.90 pitch 15.50-18.30 (incl 2 persons) **Facilities:** ⋔ ⋢ ⊙ ⊞ ⊞ **Services:** ⊞ ✕ ⊞ lau **Leisure:** ⋡ P **Off-site:** ⋡S

AT BRAGUE, LA (4KM N ON N7)

Pylône av du Pylone, 06600 ☎ 493335286 ▦ 493333054
e-mail: contact@campingpylone.com
website: www.campingpylone.com
In an ideal location between Cannes and Nice, the Pylône is a family site with good facilities.
➲ *From N7 take D4 for Biot. First turning on left.*
Open: All year **Site:** 16HEC ⊞⊞⊞ ♣ ⊞ ⊞ ⊗ **Prices:** ⋔5 ⊞4 Å3 **Facilities:** ⋔ ⋢ ⊙ ⊞ ⊘ ⋢ ⊞ **Services:** ⊞ ✕ ⊞ lau **Leisure:** ⋡ PR **Off-site:** ⋡S

ARGELÈS-SUR-MER PYRÉNÉES-ORIENTALES

Criques de Porteils La Corniche de Collioure, 66700
☎ 468811273 ▦ 468958576
e-mail: criques.costa@wanadoo.fr website: lescriques.com
Terraced site with beautiful view of sea.
➲ *4km S on N114 turn left through railway underpass and continue for 0.3km.*
Open: Mar-Oct/Nov **Site:** 5HEC ◈ ⊘ ⊞ **Prices:** ⋔3.45-5.35
⊞3.35 ⊞3.05 Å3.05 pitch 18.35-26.45 (incl 2 persons) **Facilities:** ⋔ ⋢ ⊙ ⊞ ⊘ ⊞ **Services:** ⊞ ✕ ⊞ lau **Leisure:** ⋡ S

Dauphin rte de Taxo d'Avall, 66701
☎ 468811754 ▦ 468958260
e-mail: camping.ledauphin6t6@wanadoo.fr
On a long stretch of grassland shaded by poplars, 1500mtrs from sea.
➲ *3km N of town; at Taxo d'Avall turn right onto unclass road.*
Open: May-Sep **Site:** 5.5HEC ⊞⊞⊞ ♣ ⊞ **Prices:** pitch 20-28.50 (incl 2 persons) **Facilities:** ⋔ ⋢ ⊙ ⊞ ⊘ ⊞ **Services:** ⊞ ✕ ⊞ lau **Leisure:** ⋡ P **Off-site:** ⋡LRS

Galets rte de Taxo a la Mer, 66700
☎ 468810812 ▦ 468816876
e-mail: lesgalets@wanadoo.fr website: www.campmed.com
A well equipped family site with trees, bushes and exotic plants.
➲ *4km N*
Open: 3 Apr-2 Oct **Site:** 5HEC ⊞⊞⊞ ⊕ ⊞ **Prices:** ⋔4.10-6.70 pitch 21-29.50 (incl 2 persons) **Facilities:** ⋔ ⋢ ⊙ ⊞ ⋢ ⊞ **Services:** ⊞ ✕ ⊞ lau **Leisure:** ⋡ P **Off-site:** ⊘ ⋡S

Marsouins chemin de la retirada, 66702
☎ 468811481 ▦ 468959358
e-mail: marsouins@campmed.com
website: www.campmed.com
A large family site with good facilities.
➲ *2km NE towards Plage Nord.*
Open: Apr-Sep **Site:** 10HEC ⊞⊞⊞ ♣ ⊞ **Prices:** pitch 12-25 (incl 2 persons) **Facilities:** ⋔ ⋢ ⊙ ⊞ ⊘ ⋢ ⊞ **Services:** ⊞ ✕ ⊞ lau **Leisure:** ⋡ P **Off-site:** ⋡S

Massane 66702 ☎ 468810685 ▦ 468815918
e-mail: camping.massane@infonic.fr
website: camping-massane.com
Well laid-out site in shady garden 1km from sea.

contd.

Facilities: ⋢-shop ⋔-shower ⊙-electric points for razors ⊞-electric points for caravans ⊞-parking by tents permitted ⊞-compulsory separate car park **Services:** ✕-café/restaurant ⊞-bar ⊘-Camping Gaz International ⋢-gas other than Camping Gaz ⊞-first aid facilities lau-laundry **Leisure:** ⋡-swimming L-Lake P-Pool R-River S-Sea **Off-site:** All facilities within 2km

⤵ *Beside D618 near the municipal sports field.*
Open: 15 Mar-15 Oct **Site:** 3HEC ▦ ∴ ♨ � 🚐 🚐
Prices: pitch 11.50-23 (incl 2 persons) pp2.50-5 **Facilities:** 🏪
🛒 ⊙ 🅿 ∅ 🚿 🏪 **Services:** 🍴 ⊞ lau **Leisure:** ⚓ P
Off-site: 🛒 🍴 ✗ ⚓S

Neptune Plage Nord, 66702 ☎ 468810298 🖷 468810041
e-mail: neptune@parcpemin.com
Flat site with both sunny and shady pitches 350mtrs from the
northern beach. Modern sanitary facilities. Water-slide.
Separate car park for arrivals after 23.00 hrs.
Open: May- 15 Sep **Site:** 4.5HEC ▦ 💥 ♨ ♣ **Prices:** ⚲7.50
🚗2.50 pitch 30.50 **Facilities:** 🏪 🛒 ⊙ 🅿 ∅ 🚿 🏪 🅿
Services: 🍴 ✗ ⊞ lau **Leisure:** ⚓ P **Off-site:** ∅ ⚓LS

Ombrages av du Général-de-Gaulle, 66702
☎ 468812983 🖷 468812983
e-mail: les-ombrages@freesurf.fr
website: www.les-ombrages.com
In a picturesque wooded setting, 300mtrs from the beach. A
well equipped site with good recreational facilities and clearly
defined pitches.
Open: Jun-Sep **Site:** 4HEC ▦ ♣ 🚐 **Prices:** ⚲10-21.30
🚗12.90-17.50 **Facilities:** 🏪 ⊙ 🅿 ∅ 🏪 **Services:** lau
Off-site: 🛒 🍴 ✗ ⚓LPRS ⊞

Pujol rte du Tamariguer, 66700 ☎ 468810025 🖷 468812121
Set amid rich vegetation with a wide variety of recreational
facilities.
⤵ *1km from the beach and 500mtrs from the village.*
Open: Jun-Sep **Site:** 4.5HEC ▦ ♣ **Facilities:** 🏪 🛒 ⊙ 🅿 ∅
🚿 🏪 **Services:** 🍴 ✗ ⊞ lau **Leisure:** ⚓ P **Off-site:** ⚓S

CM Roussillonnais bd de la Mer
☎ 468811042 🖷 468959611
On a long stretch of sandy terrain adjoining a fine sandy
beach.
⤵ *In N part of town. Well signposted.*
Open: mid Apr-mid Oct **Site:** 10HEC ▦ ∴ ♨ 🚐 🚐
Facilities: 🏪 🛒 ⊙ 🅿 ∅ 🏪 **Services:** 🍴 ✗ ⊞ lau **Leisure:** ⚓ S

Sirène rte de Taxo d'Avall, 66702
☎ 468810461 🖷 468816974
e-mail: contact@camping.lasirene.fr
website: www.camping-lasirene.fr
A well appointed family site with good facilities in a
delightful wooded setting.
⤵ *4km NE.*
Open: 9 Apr-25 Sep **Site:** 17HEC ▦ ♨ 🚐 **Prices:** pitch 23-
40 (incl 3 persons) **Facilities:** 🏪 🛒 ⊙ 🅿 ∅ 🏪 **Services:** 🍴 ✗
⊞ lau **Leisure:** ⚓ P **Off-site:** 🚿 ⚓S

AT ARGELÈS-PLAGE (2.5KM E VIA D618)

Pins av du Tech, 66703 ☎ 468811046
A peaceful family site situated on a narrow stretch of
grassland with some poplar trees.
Open: 15 May-21 Sep **Site:** 4HEC ▦ ♣ 🚐 **Facilities:** 🏪 ⊙
🅿 🏪 **Services:** ✗ lau **Off-site:** 🛒 ∅ 🚿 ⚓PS

Soleil rte du Littoral, Plage Nord, 66702
☎ 468811448 🖷 468814434
e-mail: camping.soleil@wanadoo.fr
website: campmed.com
Peaceful site in wide meadow surrounded by tall trees.
Private beach, natural harbour. Best site in region, but
pitches must be booked in advance.
⤵ *Follow rte du Littoral N out of town then 1.5km towards
beach.*
Open: 15 May-Sep **Site:** 16HEC ▦ ♣ 🚐 🐾 **Prices:** ⚲7
pitch 11 **Facilities:** 🏪 🛒 ⊙ 🅿 ∅ 🏪 **Services:** 🍴 ✗ ⊞ lau
Leisure: ⚓ PRS

ARLES BOUCHES-DU-RHÔNE

Rosiers Pont de Crau, 13200 ☎ 490960212 🖷 490933672
e-mail: camping-rosiers@wanadoo.fr
website: www.arles-camping.com
On level ground, shaded by bushes.
⤵ *Access via autoroute exit `Arles Sud' or N443.*
Open: 15 Mar-15 Nov **Site:** 3.5HEC ▦ ♣ 🚐 🚐
Prices: ⚲3.45 🚗1.50 🚐3.45 ▲3.45 pitch 3.42 **Facilities:** 🏪 ⊙
🅿 ∅ 🏪 **Services:** 🍴 ✗ ⊞ lau **Leisure:** ⚓ P **Off-site:** 🛒 🚿 ⚓R

ARLES-SUR-TECH PYRÉNÉES-ORIENTALES

Riuferrer 66150 ☎ 468391106 🖷 468391209
e-mail: campingriuferrer@libertysurf.fr
website: www.campingriuferrer.fr.st
Quiet holiday site on gently sloping ground in pleasant area.
Clean sanitary installations. Separate area reserved for
overnight stops. Bar, ice for iceboxes and nearby municipal
swimming pool are available in summer only.
⤵ *Signposted from N115.*
Open: All year **Site:** 4.5HEC ∴ ♨ 🚐 **Prices:** ⚲2.80-3.80
pitch 3.10-3.60 **Facilities:** 🏪 ⊙ 🅿 ∅ 🚿 🏪 **Services:** 🍴 ⊞ lau
Leisure: ⚓ R **Off-site:** 🛒 ✗ ⚓P

ARPAILLARGUES GARD

Mas de Rey rte d'Anduze, 30700 ☎ 466221827 🖷 466221827
e-mail: masderey@hvtour.fr
In quiet wooded surroundings with pitches divided by trees
and bushes. There are good facilities for sports and modern
sanitary arrangements.
⤵ *3km from Uzès towards Anduze.*
Open: 10 Apr-10 Oct **Site:** 3HEC ▦ ♨ 🚐 🚐 **Prices:** pitch
16 (incl 2 persons) **Facilities:** 🏪 🛒 ⊙ 🅿 ∅ 🏪 **Services:** 🍴 ✗
⊞ lau **Leisure:** ⚓ P **Off-site:** 🚿

AUBIGNAN VAUCLUSE

Intercommunal du Brégoux chemin du Vas, 84810
☎ 490626250 🖷 490626521
e-mail: camping-lebregoux@wanadoo.fr
A level site with good views of Mt.Ventoux.
⤵ *On southern outskirts of town turn off D7 onto D55 and
continue towards Caromb for 0.5km.*
Open: Mar-Oct **Site:** 3.5HEC ▦ ♣ **Prices:** ⚲2.70 pitch 2.60
Facilities: 🏪 ⊙ 🅿 🏪 **Services:** ⊞ lau **Off-site:** 🛒 🍴 ✗ ∅ 🚿
⚓PR

AUPS VAR

International rte de Fox-Amphoux, 83630
☎ 494700680 🖷 494701051
e-mail: camping-aups@internationalcamping-aups.com
website: www.internationalcamping-aups.com
In wooded surroundings with well defined pitches and good
recreational facilities. An ideal centre for exploring the
magnificent Gorges du Verdon.

➲ *0.5km W via D60 towards Fox-Amphoux*
Open: Apr-Sep Site: 4HEC ⏚⏚⏚ ⌖ 🏠 Prices: ⚑5.30 ⚑4.50
⚑4.50 pitch 4.50 Facilities: ⟦ ⊙ 🖭 🖭 🅿 Services: 🍴 ✗ lau
Leisure: 🏊 P Off-site: 🛒 ✗ ∅ 🚰 ⊞

AURIBEAU ALPES-MARITIMES

Parc des Monges 635 Chemin du Gabre, 06810
☎ 493609171 📠 493609171
In a wooded setting on the banks of a 1st category fishing
river, surrounded by mimosa fields.
➲ *Leave A8 at Mandelieu exit and head towards Grasse.*
Open: 28 Mar-1 Oct Site: 1.3HEC ⏚⏚⏚ ⌖ 🏠 ⚑ Prices: pitch
14.50-19 (incl 2 persons) Facilities: ⟦ ⊙ 🖭 🅿 Services: 🍴 ✗
⊞ lau Leisure: 🏊 PR Off-site: 🛒 ∅ 🚰

AVIGNON VAUCLUSE

Bagatelle Ile de la Barthelasse, 84000
☎ 490863039 📠 490271623
e-mail: camping.bagatelle@wanadoo.fr
Pleasant site with tall trees on the Isle of Barthelasse. All
pitches are numbered; on hard standing and divided by
hedges. Separate section for young people.
➲ *Travel alongside the old town wall and the Rhône onto the
Rhône bridge (Nîmes road). About halfway along turn right
and follow signs.*
Open: All year Site: 4HEC ⏚⏚⏚ ⚑ 🏠 ⚑ Prices: ⚑11.30-15
⚑9.60-14 Facilities: ⟦ 🛒 ⊙ 🖭 ∅ 🚰 🅿 Services: 🍴 ✗ lau
Off-site: 🏊P

CM Pont St-Bénézet Ile de la Barthelasse, 84000
☎ 490806350 📠 490852212
e-mail: info@camping-avignon.com
website: www.camping-avignon.com
On island opposite bridge with fine views of town. Several
tiled sanitary blocks with individual wash cabins. Individual
pitches. Common room with TV, souvenir shop, car wash.
Several playing fields for volleyball and basketball. Definite
divisions for tents and caravans.
➲ *NW of the town on the right bank of the Rhône, 370mtrs
upstream from bridge on right. (N100 leading to Nîmes).*
Open: Mar-Oct Site: 7.5HEC ⏚⏚⏚ ⚑ ⚑ Prices: pitch 9.60-
20.50 (incl 2 persons) Facilities: ⟦ 🛒 ⊙ 🖭 ∅ 🅿 Services: 🍴
✗ ⊞ lau Leisure: 🏊 P

AXAT AUDE

Crémade 11140 ☎ 468205064
A shady, peaceful site, ideal for water sports.
Open: Etr-end Sep Site: 4HEC ⏚⏚⏚ ⚑ ⚑ Facilities: ⟦ 🛒 ⊙
🖭 ∅ 🅿 Services: ✗ ⊞ lau Off-site: 🏊R

Moulin du Pont d'Alies 11140 ☎ 468205327 📠 468205277
e-mail: contact@alies.fr website: www.alies.fr
In a picturesque location at the entrance to the Gorges de la
Pierre.
➲ *Junction of D117 and D118, 800m from Axat.*
Open: 15 Mar-11 Nov Site: 2HEC ⏚⏚⏚ ⚑ 🏠 Prices: ⚑4 ⚑4-
10 ⚑4-10 pitch 8-10 Facilities: ⟦ 🛒 ⊙ 🖭 🅿 Services: 🍴 ✗ ⊞
lau Leisure: 🏊 PR

BANDOL VAR

Vallongue 83150 ☎ 494294955 📠 494294955
e-mail: camping.vallongue@wanadoo.fr
Terraced site, parts of which have lovely sea views.
Camping Card Compulsory.
Open: Apr-Sep Site: 1.5HEC ⚪ ⌖ 🏠 Prices: ⚑4 ⚑1-1.50
pitch 12-15 Facilities: ⟦ ⊙ 🖭 🅿 Services: 🍴 ✗ lau
Leisure: 🏊 P Off-site: 🛒 ∅ 🚰

BARCARÈS, LE PYRÉNÉES-ORIENTALES

Bousigues av des Corbières, 66420
☎ 468861619 📠 468862844
e-mail: lesbousigues@wanadoo.fr
website: www.camping-barcares.com
Well equipped family site approx. 1km from the sea. Bar and
café etc open July and August only.
➲ *From D83 take exit 10.*
Open: Apr-1 Nov Site: 3HEC ⚇⚇⚇ ⚑ 🏠 Prices: pitch 14-
23.70 (incl 2 persons) Facilities: ⟦ 🛒 ⊙ 🖭 ∅ 🚰 🅿
Services: 🍴 ✗ ⊞ lau Leisure: 🏊 P Off-site: 🏊RS

California rte de St-Laurent, 66423
☎ 468861608 📠 468861820
e-mail: camping.california@wanadoo.fr
website: www.camping-california.fr
A friendly family site with regular organised entertainment
in a pleasant wooded location close to the beach.
➲ *1.5km SW via D90.*
Open: 3 Apr-18 Aug Site: 5HEC ⏚⏚⏚ ⚇⚇⚇ ⚑ 🏠 Prices: ⚑6.50
pitch 10-22.50 Facilities: ⟦ 🛒 ⊙ 🖭 🚰 🅿 Services: 🍴 ✗ ⊞ lau
Leisure: 🏊 P Off-site: ✗ 🏊RS

Europe rte de St-Laurent, 66420 ☎ 468861536 📠 468869788
e-mail: reception@europe-camping.com
website: www.europe-camping.com
A holiday village type of site with good recreational facilities,
500mtrs from the beach.
➲ *Via D90 2km SW, 200mtrs from Agly.*
Open: All year Site: 6HEC ⏚⏚⏚ ⚇⚇⚇ ⚑ 🏠 ⚑ Facilities: ⟦ 🛒
⊙ 🖭 ∅ 🅿 Services: 🍴 ✗ ⊞ lau Leisure: 🏊 P Off-site: ∅ 🏊RS

Presqu'île 66420 ☎ 468861280 📠 468862509
e-mail: camppresq@aol.com website: www.lapresquile.com
A well equipped family site on the edge of the Leucate lake
and close to the beach.
➲ *2km on rte de Leucate, turn right. Well-kept family site on
strip of land between large inlet and the Mediterranean*
Open: 28 Mar-3 Nov Site: 3HEC ⏚⏚⏚ ⚇⚇⚇ ⚑ 🏠
Prices: ⚑3.50-5 ⚑1.50-3 ⚑13.50-27.50 ⚑2-3 pitch 11-20
(incl 2 persons) Facilities: ⟦ 🛒 ⊙ 🖭 ∅ 🚰 🅿 Services: 🍴 ✗ ⊞
lau Leisure: 🏊 LP Off-site: ✗ 🏊RS

Sable d'Or r des Palombes, 66420
☎ 468861841 📠 466743730
A wooded site situated between the sea and the Lac Marin.
➲ *From Narbonne leave A9 at exit 40 and head towards
Grand Plage.*
Open: All year Site: 4HEC ⏚⏚⏚ ⚇⚇⚇ ⚑ 🏠 ⚑ Facilities: ⟦ 🛒
⊙ 🖭 ∅ 🅿 Services: 🍴 ✗ ⊞ lau Leisure: 🏊 PS Off-site: ∅ 🚰 🏊L

BAR-SUR-LOUP, LE ALPES-MARITIMES

Gorges du Loup 965 chemin des Vergers, 06620 ☎ 493424506
Terraced site divided into pitches, in an olive grove. Very
steep entrance.
➲ *Access from Grasse on D2085 towards Le Pré du Lac (NE),
then turn left on D2210 in the direction of Vence.*
Open: Mar-Sep Site: 2HEC ⏚⏚⏚ ⚑ ⚑ Facilities: ⟦ 🛒 ⊙ 🖭
∅ Services: 🍴 ✗ ⊞ lau Leisure: 🏊 P Off-site: 🏊R

BEAUCHASTEL ARDÈCHE

CM Voiliers 7800 ☎ 475622404
In a wooded location beside the River Rhône with good
recreational facilities.
➲ *1km E, 900mtrs S of N86.*
Open: Apr-Oct Site: 1.5HEC ⏚⏚⏚ ⚑ Facilities: ⟦ ⊙ 🖭 🅿
Services: 🍴 ✗ ⊞ lau Leisure: 🏊 P Off-site: ∅ 🏊R

Facilities: 🛒-shop ⟦-shower ⊙-electric points for razors 🖭-electric points for caravans 🅿-parking by tents permitted
🅿-compulsory separate car park Services: ✗-café/restaurant 🍴-bar ∅-Camping Gaz International 🚰-gas other than Camping
Gaz ⊞-first aid facilities lau-laundry Leisure: 🏊-swimming L-Lake P-Pool R-River S-Sea Off-site: All facilities within 2km

BEYNES ALPES-DE-HAUTE-PROVENCE

Célestine rte de Moustiers (D907), 4270
☎ 492355254 ▤ 492355007
e-mail: lacelestin@wanadoo.fr
A quiet site on flat ground in the heart of the Haute Provence
national park and surrounded by mountains. Facilities for
disabled people.
➪ *Situated on D907, before climb to the village*
Open: 15 Apr-29 Sep **Site:** 3HEC ▦ ⊕ 🏕 **Prices:** ♠3.90
♠3.90 pitch 3.90 **Facilities:** ⋒ ⅃ ⊙ 🗗 🕮 **Services:** ⏚
Leisure: ⇗ PR

BOISSON GARD

⼵Château de Boisson Boisson, 30500
☎ 466248561 ▤ 466248014
e-mail: reception@chateau-boisson.com
website: www.chateau-boisson.com
A peaceful, well equipped site in the beautiful Cevennes
region. Painting, bridge and cookery courses are available.
Camping Card Compulsory.
➪ *D7 in direction Fumades. Boisson is 10km on the right and
the campsite is signposted.*
Open: 10 Apr-Sep **Site:** 7.8HEC ▦ ⊕ 🏕 🐾
Prices: ♠5.40-6.50 ♠1.50-2 **Facilities:** ⋒ ⅃ ⊙ 🗗 🖉 🕮
Services: ⏚ ✕ ⊞ lau **Leisure:** ⇗ P

BOLLÈNE VAUCLUSE

Barry Lieu Dit St-Pierre, 84500 ☎ 490301320 ▤ 490404864
Well-kept site near ruins of Barry troglodite village.
➪ *Signposted from Bollène via D26.*
Open: All year **Site:** 3HEC ▦ ♣ 🏕 **Facilities:** ⋒ ⅃ ⊙ 🗗 🖉
🕮 **Services:** ⏚ ✕ ⊞ lau **Leisure:** ⇗ P **Off-site:** ⇗RS

Simioune Quartier Guffiage, 84500
☎ 490304462 ▤ 490304477
e-mail: la-simioune@wanadoo.fr
website: www.la-simioune.fr
In pleasant wooded surroundings close to the River Rhône.
➪ *From A7 follow signs for Carpentras, at 3rd x-roads turn
left towards Lambisque, then follow signposts to site.*
Open: All year **Site:** 2.5HEC ∷ ⊕ 🏕 🐾 **Prices:** ♠3.40
🐾3.10 ▲3 pitch 3.10 **Facilities:** ⋒ ⊙ 🗗 🕮 **Services:** ⏚ ✕ ⊞
lau **Leisure:** ⇗ PR **Off-site:** ⇗R

BORMES-LES-MIMOSAS VAR

Clau Mar Jo 895 chemin de Benat, 83230 ☎ 494715339
A well shaded site 1200mtrs from the sea with good facilities.
➪ *Access via N98, then D298.*
Open: Apr-Sep **Site:** 1HEC ♣ 🏕 **Facilities:** ⋒ ⊙ 🗗 🕮
Services: ⊞ lau **Off-site:** ⅃ ✕ 🖉 ⇗S

Manjastre 150 Chemin des Girolles, 83230
☎ 494710328 ▤ 494716362
e-mail: manjastre@infonie.fr
A peaceful site 6km from the Mediterranean beaches.
➪ *5km NW via N98 on road to La Môle/Cogolin.*
Open: All year **Site:** 8HEC ▦ ⊕ 🐾 **Prices:** pitch 19.65
(incl 2 persons) pp4.80 **Facilities:** ⋒ ⅃ ⊙ 🗗 🖉 🕮
Services: ⏚ ✕ ⊞ lau **Leisure:** ⇗ P

AT FAVIÈRE LA (3KM S)

Domaine 83230 ☎ 494710312 ▤ 494151867
e-mail: mail@campdudomaine.com
website: www.campdudomaine.com
In a very attractive setting with a long sandy beach and
numbered pitches. Fine views of sea. Sport facilities.
➪ *0.5km E of Bormes-Cap Bénat road.*
Open: 27 Apr-Oct **Site:** 38HEC ▦ ∷ ⊕ ♣ 🏕
Prices: ♠4.80-6.20 🐾2.80-3.50 pitch 16-29 **Facilities:** ⋒ ⅃ ⊙
🗗 🖉 🕮 **Services:** ⏚ ✕ ⊞ lau **Leisure:** ⇗ S

BOULOU, LE PYRÉNÉES-ORIENTALES

Mas Llinas 66165 ☎ 468832546
e-mail: info@camping-mas-llinas.com
website: www.camping-mas-llinas.com
A family site in wooded surroundings with a good variety of
leisure facilities.
➪ *3km N via N9.*
Open: Feb-Nov **Site:** 15HEC ∷ ⊕ 🏕 🏕 **Prices:** ♠4-4.70
🐾2 pitch 4.50-5.70 **Facilities:** ⋒ ⊙ 🗗 🕮 **Services:** ⏚ ✕ lau
Leisure: ⇗ P **Off-site:** 🛒 ✕ 🖉 🚿 🕮 ⊞

BOULOURIS-SUR-MER VAR

Ile d'Or P.N.44 BOULOURIS, 83700
☎ 494955213 ▤ 494955213
In a quiet location, 50mtrs from a private beach with well
equipped pitches.
➪ *E off N98.*
Open: Mar-Oct **Site:** 10HEC ▦ ⊕ 🏕 🐾 ▲ **Prices:** ♠5.25
🐾2.70 pitch 24.30 (incl 2 persons) **Facilities:** ⋒ ⅃ ⊙ 🗗 🖉 🕮
🕮 **Services:** ⏚ ✕ ⊞ lau **Leisure:** ⇗ S

Val Fleury RN 98, 83700 ☎ 494952152 ▤ 494190947
Terraced site with tarred drives set amongst pines and
mimosas close to the beach.
➪ *Off N98 at Km 93.1.*
Open: All year **Site:** 1HEC ⊕ ♣ 🏕 **Facilities:** ⋒ ⊙ 🗗 🚿 🕮 🅿 🖉
Services: ⏚ ✕ ⊞ lau **Off-site:** 🛒 🖉 ⇗PS

BOURDEAUX DRÔME

At POËT-CÉLARD, LE (3KM NW)

Couspeau Quartier Bellevue, 26460
☎ 475533014 ▤ 475533723
e-mail: info@couspeau.com
website: www.couspeau.com
In a beautiful natural setting with well maintained facilities.
➪ *1.3km SE via D328A.*
Open: 19 Apr- 14 Sep **Site:** 3HEC ▦ ♣ 🏕 🐾 **Facilities:** ⋒
⅃ ⊙ 🗗 🖉 🚿 🕮 **Services:** ⏚ ✕ ⊞ lau **Leisure:** ⇗ P

BOURG-ST-ANDÉOL ARDÈCHE

Lion 07700 ☎ 475545320
Large well-shaped park in wooded terrain, beside River
Rhône.
➪ *N86 in direction of Viviers, through the centre of town.*
Open: Apr-15 Sep **Site:** 8HEC ▦ ♣ 🐾 ▲ **Facilities:** ⋒ ⅃ ⊙
🗗 🕮 **Services:** ⏚ ✕ ⊞ lau **Leisure:** ⇗ PR **Off-site:** 🖉 🚿

BRISSAC HÉRAULT

Val d'Hérault St-Étienne d'Issensac, 34190
☎ 467737229 ▤ 467733081
A terraced site in a quiet location. Bar and restaurant
facilities available July and August only.
➪ *4km S via D4.*
Open: 15 Mar-12 Nov **Site:** 3.4HEC ∷ ⊕ ♣ 🏕 🐾
Facilities: ⋒ ⅃ ⊙ 🗗 🖉 🚿 🕮 **Services:** ⏚ ✕ lau **Leisure:** ⇗ PR
Off-site: ⊞

BROUSSES-ET-VILLARET AUDE

Martinet Rouge 11390 ☎ 468265198 ▤ 468265198
e-mail: martinet.bv.free.fr
website: www.camping-lemartinetrouge.com
A pleasant, well equipped site on gently sloping terrain.
Terraced, with well marked pitches.
➪ *Access via D48.*
Open: Apr-15 Oct **Site:** 2.8HEC ▦ ♣ 🏕 🐾 **Prices:** pitch
11.50-12 (incl 2 persons) **Facilities:** ⋒ ⅃ ⊙ 🗗 🖉 🕮
Services: ⏚ ✕ ⊞ lau **Leisure:** ⇗ P **Off-site:** ⇗R

Site: 6HEC-Site size ▦-grass ∷-sand ⬤-stone ⅍-little shade ⊕-partly shaded ♣-mainly shaded
🏕-bungalows for hire 🐾-caravans for hire ▲-tents for hire 🐾-no dogs **Prices:** ♠-adult per night ♠-car per night
pp-per person per night 🐾-caravan per night ▲-tent per night

CADENET VAUCLUSE

Val de Durance Les Routes, 84160
☎ 490683775 ▤ 490681634
e-mail: info@homair-vacances.fr
website: www.homair-vacances.fr
A well equipped family site on the shore of a lake and close to the River Durance.
Open: Apr-2 Oct Site: 3.5HEC ⚏ ⌺ ⌂ ♨ A Facilities: ☚
⚏ ⊙ ♨ 🅟 Services: ♟ ✕ 🕀 lau Leisure: ⋨ LP Off-site: 🛒 ♟
✕ ⌀ ♨ ⋨R

CAGNES-SUR-MER ALPES-MARITIMES

Colombier 35 chemin de Ste-Colombe, 06800
☎ 493731277 ▤ 493731277
e-mail: campinglecolombier06@wanadoo.fr
website: www.campinglecolombier.com
Well equipped site in a wooded location 2km from the sea.
Open: Apr-Sep Site: 0.6HEC ⚏ ⁙ ♠ 🔥 ⌀ 🅟 🅿 🅟
Services: ♟ ✕ 🕀 lau Leisure: ⋨ P Off-site: 🛒 ✕ ♨ ⋨S

Green Park 159 Vallon-des-Vaux, 06800
☎ 493070996 ▤ 493143655
e-mail: info@greenpark.fr website: www.greenpark.fr
A modern site with well defined pitches in pleasant wooded surroundings with good recreational facilities.
➲ From A8 exit Cagnes-sur-Mer take N7 towards Nice.
Open: 27 Mar-18 Oct Site: 5.4HEC ⚏ ⌺ ⌂ 🔥 A
Prices: ₳3.70-4.70 ♠3.50 ♨13.50-26 ▲12.50-26
Facilities: ☚ 🛒 ⊙ ♨ 🅟 🅟 Services: ♟ ✕ 🕀 lau Leisure: ⋨ P

Rivière 168 chemin des Salles, 06800
☎ 493206227 ▤ 493207253
In secluded wooded surroundings with good, modern facilities.
➲ 4km N beside River Cagne.
Open: All year Site: 1.2HEC ⚏ ♠ 🔥 🔥 Prices: ₳3.10
♠2.50 pitch 12.40 Facilities: ☚ 🛒 ⊙ ♨ ⌀ ♨ 🅟 Services: ♟
✕ 🕀 lau Leisure: ⋨ PR

Todos 159 Vallon des Vaux, 06800
☎ 493312005 ▤ 492128166
e-mail: info@letodos.fr website: www.letodos.fr
In a beautiful Mediterranean setting. Exceptionally shady with a mixture of flat and terraced sites. Evening entertainment. Use of car park compulsory after 11pm.
➲ Access via N7 towards Nice.
Open: 27 Mar-25 Sept Site: 6HEC ⚏ ♠ 🔥 🔥
Prices: ₳3.70-4.70 ♠3.50 ♨12-26 ▲12-26 Facilities: ☚ 🛒 ⊙
♨ 🅟 🅟 Services: ♟ ✕ 🕀 lau Leisure: ⋨ P

AT CROS-DE-CAGNES (2KM S)

Panoramer 30 chemin des Gros Buaux, 06800
☎ 493311615 ▤ 493311615
Pleasant terraced site with sea view. Separate sections for tents and caravans.
➲ 2km N of town.
Open: Mar-Oct Site: 1.4HEC ⚏ ⌺ Facilities: ☚ ⊙ ♨ ⌀ 🅟
Services: ♟ ✕ 🕀 lau Off-site: 🛒

CAMURAC AUDE

Sapins 11340 ☎ 468203811 ▤ 468207475
e-mail: yvan.dabouis@libertysurf.fr
website: www.paysdesauft.com/sapins
In a picturesque, wooded location on the edge of a forest with excellent views of the surrounding mountains.
➲ 1.5km from village.
Open: May-Sept Site: 3HEC ⚏ ⌺ ♠ 🔥 A Prices: ₳3.50
♠2.50 ♨2.50 ▲2.50 pitch 5 Facilities: ☚ ⊙ ♨ ⌀ 🅟
Services: ♟ ✕ 🕀 lau Leisure: ⋨ P Off-site: 🛒 ⌀ ⋨L

CANET-PLAGE PYRÉNÉES-ORIENTALES

Domino r des Palmiers, 66140 ☎ 468802725 ▤ 468734741
e-mail: camping.domino@wanadoo.fr
In a wooded location 150mtrs from the sea.
Open: Apr-Sep Site: 0.7HEC ⚏ ♠ 🔥 Prices: ₳3-4.50 pitch 16-26 (incl 2 persons) Facilities: ☚ ⊙ ♨ 🅟 Services: ♟ ✕ 🕀
lau Off-site: 🛒 ⌀ ⋨PRS

Mar Estang 1 rte de St-Cyprien, 66140
☎ 468803553 ▤ 468733294
e-mail: marestang@wanadoo.fr
website: www.marestang.com
Open: 30 Apr-26 Sep Site: 15HEC ⚏ ⌺ 🔥 A Prices: pitch 18-29 (incl 2 persons) Facilities: ☚ 🛒 ⊙ ♨ ♨ 🅟 Services: ♟
✕ 🕀 lau Leisure: ⋨ PS Off-site: ✕ ⌀

Facilities: 🛒-shop ☚-shower ⊙-electric points for razors ♨-electric points for caravans 🅟-parking by tents permitted 🅿-compulsory separate car park **Services:** ✕-café/restaurant ♟-bar ⌀-Camping Gaz International ♨-gas other than Camping Gaz 🕀-first aid facilities lau-laundry **Leisure:** ⋨-swimming L-Lake P-Pool R-River S-Sea **Off-site:** All facilities within 2km

AT CANET-VILLAGE (2KM W)

Brasilia Voie de la Crouste, Zone Technique du Port, 66140
☎ 468802382 ▤ 468733297
e-mail: camping-le-brasilia@wanadoo.fr
website: www.brasilia.fr
Near beach. Divided into pitches which are surrounded by bushes and flowerbeds.
➔ *Turn off main road in village and continue towards beach for 2km.*
Open: 30 Apr-25 Sep Site: 15HEC ⊞ ♠ ⊞ Prices: pitch 21-42 (incl 2 persons) pp4.50-7.50 Facilities: ⋔ ⅃ ⊙ ⬛ ∅ ☎ Services: ⬤ ✗ lau Leisure: ⬚ PS Off-site: ⌂

Peupliers Voie de la Crouste, 66140
☎ 468803587 ▤ 468733875
e-mail: camping.peupliers@clioz.net
Quiet, level site divided into pitches by hedges with a variety of leisure facilities. Reservations recommended for July and August.
Open: Jun-Sep Site: 4HEC ⊞ ♠ ⊞ Prices: ♦4.51-5.67 ♠2.73-3.04 pitch 10.40-14.38 Facilities: ⋔ ⅃ ⊙ ⬛ ∅ ☎ ▣ Services: ⬤ ✗ ⊞ lau Leisure: ⬚ PS

Ma Prairie Av des Coteaux, 66140
☎ 468732617 ▤ 468732882
e-mail: ma.prairie@wanadoo.fr
website: www.maprairie.com
Grassland site in a hollow surrounded by vineyards.
➔ *Access from D11 in the direction of Elne off N617 Perpignan-Canet-Plage road.*
Open: 05 May-25 Sep Site: 4.5HEC ⊞ ♠ ⊞ Prices: ♦3-6 pitch 17-28 (incl 2 persons) Facilities: ⋔ ⅃ ⊙ ⬛ ∅ ⌂ ☎ Services: ⬤ ✗ ⊞ lau Leisure: ⬚ P

CANNES ALPES-MARITIMES

Parc Bellevue 67 av M Chevalier, 6150
☎ 493472897 ▤ 493486625
e-mail: contact@parcbellevue.com
website: www.parcbellevue.com
➔ *leave A41 at the exit for Cannes, at the first set of traffic lights turn right.*
Open: Apr-Sep Site: 4HEC ⊞ ♠ ⊞ ⊞ Prices: ♦3-4 ♠2 pitch 7-10 Facilities: ⋔ ⅃ ⊙ ⬛ ∅ ☎ Services: ⬤ ✗ ⊞ lau Leisure: ⬚ PS Off-site: ⬚S

AT CANNET, LE

Grand Saule 24 bd J-Moulin, 06110
☎ 493905510 ▤ 493472455
e-mail: info@legrandsaule.com
website: www.legrandsaule.com
Separate sections for families and groups of young people. 5 mins to beach in peaceful surroundings with fine views and a variety of sports and leisure activities.
➔ *Access via A8 towards Ranguin.*
Open: May-Sept Site: 1HEC ⊞ ♠ ⊞ Prices: ♦16 ♠3 Facilities: ⋔ ⊙ ⬛ ∅ Services: ⬤ ✗ ⊞ lau Leisure: ⬚ P Off-site: ⅃ ⌂ ⬚S

Ranch chemin St-Joseph, L'Aubarède, 6110
☎ 493460011 ▤ 493464430   -
On a wooded hillside 2km from the local beaches with good facilities.
➔ *Access via A8 exit 41 & 42.*
Open: 15 Apr-15 Oct Site: 2HEC ⋰⋰ ⊙ ⊞ ⊞ Prices: ♦5-5 ♠2.50-2.50 pitch 10-13.50 Facilities: ⋔ ⅃ ⊙ ⬛ ∅ ☎ Services: ⊞ lau Leisure: ⬚ P Off-site: ⬤ ✗ ⬚S

CARCASSONNE AUDE

Breil d'Aude Le Breil d'Aude, rte de Limoux, Preixan, 11250
☎ 468268818 ▤ 468268507
e-mail: air-hotel.grand.sud@wanadoo.fr
website: www.camping-grandsud.com
In a wooded location beside a private lake where free fishing is allowed.
➔ *1.5km N via D118.*
Open: 15 Apr-15 Sep Site: 11HEC ⊞ ♠ ⊞ ⊞ ▲
Prices: pitch 16-21 (incl 2 persons) Facilities: ⋔ ⅃ ⊙ ⬛ ☎
Services: ⬤ ✗ lau Leisure: ⬚ LPR Off-site: ∅ ⌂ ⊞

Cité rte de St-Hilaire, 11000 ☎ 468251177
website: www.campeoles.fr
In wooded surroundings beside the River Aude in a prime position for exploring the surrounding region.
➔ *Access via A61 or A9.*
Open: 15 May-10 Oct Site: 7HEC ⊞ ♤ ⊞ Prices: pitch 13-19 Facilities: ⋔ ⅃ ⊙ ⬛ ∅ ☎ Services: ⬤ ✗ lau
Leisure: ⬚ P Off-site: ⬚R

CARPENTRAS VAUCLUSE

Lou Comtadou Route de St Didier, 881 av P-de-Coubertin, 84200 ☎ 490670316 ▤ 490866295
Near the Carpentras swimming pool in pleasant surroundings with good, modern facilities.
➔ *SE of town centre towards St-Didier.*
Open: Apr-Oct Site: 2.5HEC ⊞ ♠ ⊞ ⊞ ▲ Facilities: ⋔ ⅃ ⊙ ⬛ ∅ ☎ Services: ⬤ ✗ lau Off-site: ⌂ ⬚P ⊞

CARQUEIRANNE VAR

ⓑBeau-Vezé rte de la Moutonne, 83320
☎ 494576530 ▤ 494576530
In a beautiful wooded park with good, modern facilities.
➔ *2.5km NW via N559 and then D76 between Hyères and Toulon.*
Open: Jun-15 Sep Site: 7HEC ⊞ ♠ ⊞ ⊞ Facilities: ⋔ ⅃ ⊙ ⬛ ∅ ⌂ ☎ Services: ⬤ ✗ ⊞ lau Leisure: ⬚ P

CASTELLANE ALPES-DE-HAUTE-PROVENCE

International rte Napoléon, 04120 ☎ 492836667
Family site at the foot of the Col des Lèques and close to the Gorges du Verdon.
➔ *1km from the centre of the village. Signposted.*
Open: Apr-Sep Site: 6HEC ⊞ ⊙ ⊞ ⊞ Facilities: ⋔ ⅃ ⊙ ⬛ ⌂ ☎ Services: ⬤ ✗ lau Leisure: ⬚ P Off-site: ∅

Nôtre Dame rte des Gorges du Verdon, 04120
☎ 492836302 ▤ 492836302
website: www.castellane.org
In meadowland with deciduous and fruit trees.
➔ *200m W on D952.*
On D952, 600m away from the centre of village on the right.
Open: Apr-14 Oct Site: 0.6HEC ⊞ ♠ ⊞ Prices: pitch 9-13 (incl 2 persons) pp2.50-3 Facilities: ⋔ ⅃ ⊙ ⬛ ∅ ☎ Services: ⬤ lau Leisure: ✗ ⌂ ⬚PR

ⓑVerdon Domaine du Verdon, 4120
☎ 492836129 ▤ 492836937
e-mail: contact@camp-du-verdon.com
website: www.camp-du-verdon.com
Well-maintained site on meadowland on banks of River Verdon. Divided into pitches. Rooms in rustic style. Reservations recommended Jul-Aug.
➔ *Below the D952 towards the Gorges du Verdon.*
Open: 15 May-15 Sep Site: 14HEC ⊞ ♠ ⊞ ⊞
Prices: pitch 14-25 (incl 2 persons) Facilities: ⋔ ⅃ ⊙ ⬛ ∅ ☎ Services: ⬤ ✗ ⊞ lau Leisure: ⬚ PR

Site: 6HEC-Site size ⊞-grass ⋰⋰-sand ⬢-stone ⭙-little shade ⊙-partly shaded ♠-mainly shaded
⊞-bungalows for hire ⊞-caravans for hire ▲-tents for hire ⦸-no dogs Prices: ♦-adult per night ♠-car per night
pp-per person per night ⊞-caravan per night ▲-tent per night

AT CHASTEUIL (9KM W ON D952)

Gorges du Verdon Clos d'Arémus, 04120
☎ 492836364 ▤ 492837472
e-mail: aremus@camping-gorgesduverdon.com
website: camping-gorgesduverdon.com
Situated on bank of the Verdon, surrounded by mountains
and at an altitude of 660 metres. Fully divided into pitches
split into two by road. Bathing in river not advised due to
strong current.
➲ 0.5km S of village.
Open: May-15 Sep Site: 7HEC ⟁⟁⟁ ♦ ♣ ⊞ Prices: pitch
10.50-19.80 (incl 3 persons) pp3.50-4.30 Facilities: ⚑ ⌫ ☉
🔌 ⊘ 🅿 Services: ⚐ ✖ ⊞ lau Leisure: ⤳ PR

AT GARDE-CASTELLANE (7.5KM SE)

Collines de Castellane rte de Grasse Napoléon, 04120
☎ 492836896 ▤ 492837540
e-mail: rcnlescollines@wanadoo.fr
Terraced site on wooded grassland with mountain views and
fine recreational facilities.
➲ On Grasse road beyond La Garde.
Open: 15 May-15 Sep Site: 10HEC ⟁⟁⟁ ♦ ⊞ Facilities: ⚑ ⌫
☉ 🔌 🛆 🅿 Services: ⚐ ✖ lau Leisure: ⤳ P

CAVALAIRE-SUR-MER VAR

Cros de Mouton 83240 ☎ 494641087 ▤ 494054638
e-mail: campingcrosdemouton@wanadoo.fr
website: www.crosdemouton.com
Terraced site with individual pitches, separated for caravans
and tents. Good view of sea, 1.5km distance.
➲ Turn off N559 in town centre and continue inland for
1.5km.
Open: 15 Mar-Oct Site: 5HEC ♦ ♣ ⊞ 🔌 Prices: ⋔5.80-7.10
pitch 5.80-7.10 Facilities: ⚑ ⌫ ☉ 🔌 ⊘ 🅿 Services: ⚐ ✖ ⊞
lau Leisure: ⤳ P Off-site: ⤳S

Pinède Chemin des Mannes, 83240
☎ 494641114 ▤ 494641925
A family site with well defined pitches, 500mtrs from the sea.
➲ 300mtrs from the centre of the village.
Open: 15 Mar-15 Oct Site: 2HEC ⟁⟁⟁ ♣ Facilities: ⚑ ⌫ ☉
🔌 ⊘ 🅿 Services: ⊞ lau Off-site: ⌫ ⚐ ✖ ⤳S

CENDRAS GARD

Croix Clémentine rte de Mende, 30480
☎ 466865269 ▤ 466865484
e-mail: clementine@clementine.fr
website: www.clementine.fr
An extensive, partly terraced site, in wooded surroundings.
➲ Signposted W of town towards La Baume via D160.
Open: 28 Mar-14 Sep Site: 12HEC ⟁⟁⟁ ♣ ⊞ 🔌
Prices: ⋔2.50-7.20 pitch 12.60-22 (incl 2 persons)
Facilities: ⚑ ⌫ ☉ 🔌 ⊘ 🅿 Services: ⚐ ✖ ⊞ lau Leisure: ⤳ P
Off-site: ⤳R

CHABEUIL DRÔME

Grand Lierne 26120 ☎ 475598314 ▤ 475598795
e-mail: contact@grandlierne.com
website: www.grandlierne.com
On the edge of the Vercors Regional Park.
➲ Access via A7 exit 'Valence Sud' towards Chabeuil, then
follow signs for site.
Open: 24 Apr-11 Sep Site: 4.8HEC ⟁⟁⟁ ♦ ⊞ 🔌 ⊘
Prices: ⋔6.60-7.80 ⊕1-3 🔌1-4 ▲1-4 pitch 0.80-5.20
Facilities: ⚑ ⌫ ☉ 🔌 ⊘ 🅿 Services: ⚐ ✖ ⊞ lau Leisure: ⤳
P Off-site: ⤳LR

CHAPELLE-EN-VERCORS, LA DRÔME

Bruyères 26420 ☎ 475482146
e-mail: maine.levercos@wanadoo.fr
A well appointed municipal site in the centre of the Parc
Naturel Régional du Vercors.
Open: All year Site: 1HEC ⟁⟁⟁ ♦ ⊞ Facilities: ⚑ ☉ 🔌 🅿
Services: ⊞ lau Off-site: ⌫ ⚐ ✖ ⊘ 🛆 ⤳P

CHARLEVAL BOUCHES-DU-RHÔNE

Orée des Bois av du Bois, 13350 ☎ 442284175 ▤ 442284748
e-mail: campingclub@wanadoo.fr
website: www.campoclub.com
Spacious, well shaded pitches. Approx. 500mtrs from the
village.
➲ Access via A7 exit Sémas. From Charleval follow road
towards Cazan.
Open: All year Site: 5HEC ⟁⟁⟁ ┄┄ ♣ ⊞ Prices: ⋔3-4.30
▲4-6 pitch 4 Facilities: ⚑ ☉ 🔌 ⊘ 🅿 Services: ⚐ ✖ ⊞ lau
Off-site: ⌫ ✖ 🛆 ⤳P

CHÂTEAU-ARNOUX ALPES-DE-HAUTE-PROVENCE

Salettes 04160 ☎ 492640240 ▤ 492640240
e-mail: info@lessalettes.com
website: www.lessalettes.com
Some facilities (shop, café etc) available in summer only.
➲ 1km E beside the river.
Open: All year Site: 4HEC ⟁⟁⟁ ♣ ⊞ Facilities: ⚑ ⌫ ☉ 🔌 ⊘
🛆 🅿 Services: ⚐ ✖ ⊞ lau Leisure: ⤳ P

CHAUZON ARDÈCHE

Digue 07120 ☎ 475396357 ▤ 475397517
e-mail: info@camping-la-digue.fr
website: www.camping-la-digue.fr
In a beautiful wooded location with good recreational
facilities.
➲ 1km E, 100mtrs from the River Ardèche
Open: 20 Mar-Oct Site: 2.5HEC ⟁⟁⟁ ♣ ⊞ Facilities: ⚑ ⌫ ☉
🔌 ⊘ 🅿 Services: ⚐ ✖ ⊞ lau Leisure: ⤳ PR

CIOTAT, LA BOUCHES-DU-RHÔNE

Oliviers rte du Bord de Mer, 13600
☎ 442831504 ▤ 442839443
website: www.camping-lesolivers.com
A terraced family site between the N559 and the railway line
from Nice.
➲ Turn inland off the N559 at Km34, some 5km E of the
centre of town and drive for 150mtrs.
Open: Mar-Sep Site: 10HEC ⟁⟁⟁ ♦ ♣ ⊞ 🔌 Prices: ⋔5
⊕5.50 🔌5.50 ▲5.50 pitch 5.50 Facilities: ⚑ ⌫ ☉ 🔌 ⊘ 🅿
Services: ⚐ ✖ ⊞ lau Leisure: ⤳ P Off-site: ⤳S

St Jean 30 av de St-Jean, 13600
☎ 442831301 ▤ 442714641
e-mail: stjean@easynet.fr website: www.asther.com/stjean
Site on the right side of the coast road in an excellent
position with direct access to the beach.
➲ Between D559 and sea behind the motel in NE part of
town.
Open: Apr-Oct Site: 9.9HEC ⟁⟁⟁ ♣ ⊞ Prices: ▲4 pitch 19-
21 Facilities: ⚑ ☉ 🔌 🅿 Services: ⚐ ✖ ⊞ lau Leisure: ⤳ S
Off-site: ⌫

Soleil rte de Cassis, 13600 ☎ 442715532 ▤ 442839581
A small site, divided into pitches, 1.5km from the beach.
➲ Access via A50 exit 9 (La Ciotat).
Open: Apr-15 Oct Site: 0.5HEC ⟁⟁⟁ ♣ ⊞ 🔌 Prices: ⋔4-4.50
⊕4-4.50 ▲4-4.50 Facilities: ⚑ ☉ 🔌 🅿 Services: ✖ ⊞ lau
Off-site: ⌫ ⊘ 🛆 ⤳PS

Facilities: ⌫-shop ⚑-shower ☉-electric points for razors 🔌-electric points for caravans 🅿-parking by tents permitted
🅿-compulsory separate car park Services: ✖-café/restaurant ⚐-bar ⊘-Camping Gaz International 🛆-gas other than Camping
Gaz ⊞-first aid facilities lau-laundry Leisure: ⤳-swimming L-Lake P-Pool R-River S-Sea Off-site: All facilities within 2km

A QUIET GREEN OASIS BETWEEN NICE, CANNES, GRASSE and VENICE

*** Les Pinèdes
06480 La Colle sur Loup
Tel: 04.93.32.98.94 Fax: 04.93.32.50.20
www.lespinedes.com
e-mail: camplespinedes06@aol.com

Shade, peace, sparkling blue swimming pool, restaurant, clean modern toilets, constant hot water, marked pitches, a welcoming reception all in this family run campsite. Also comfortable bungalows and mobile homes for hire with service station for motorhomes.

Privileged tourist situation in the centre of the 'Alpes Maritimes', between the sea and the mountains (Gorges du Loup), near Saint Paul de Vence and villages of the Provence.

DISCOUNT IN LOW SEASON Open: 11/03 – 05/10

COGOLIN VAR

Argentière chemin de l'Argentière, 83310
☎ 494546363 ▤ 494540615
e-mail: camping-largentiere@wanadoo.fr
website: www.camping-argentiere.com
Landscaped, partly terraced site.
➲ *1500mtrs NW along D48 rte de St-Maur.*
Open: Apr-Sep Site: 8HEC ⃝⃠ ♣ ⊞ Prices: pitch 12-21.50 (incl 2 persons) Facilities: ♠ ⅀ ⊙ ⊠ ⌀ ⛐ ☎ Services: ⛤ ✕ ⊞ lau Leisure: ⁀ P

COLLE-SUR-LOUP, LA ALPES-MARITIMES

Castellas rte de Roquefort, 6480
☎ 493329705 ▤ 493329705
e-mail: lecastellas.camping@wanadoo.fr
website: www.camping-le-castellas.com
In a wooded location with direct access to the river.
Open: All year Site: 1.2HEC ⃝⃠ ♣ ⊞ ⊠ Facilities: ♠ ⊙ ⊠ ⌀ ⛐ ☎ Services: ⛤ ✕ ⊞ lau Leisure: ⁀ RS Off-site: ⁀P

Pinèdes rte du Pont de Pierre, Departementale No.6, 6480
☎ 493329894 ▤ 493325020
e-mail: camplespinedes06@aol.com
website: www.lespinedes.com
Well-kept terraced site on steep slope with woodland providing shade, interesting walks and beautiful views.
➲ *By the motorway A8 exit `Cagnes-sur-Mer' turn right off D6 towards La Colle-sur-Loup.*
Open: 15 Mar-5 Oct Site: 3.8HEC ⃝⃠ ⠒⠒ ♣ ⊞ ⊠ Prices: ⋔3.70-4.60 ⛌2-3 ⛐6.10-10.30 ⏚4.20-8.60 Facilities: ♠ ⅀ ⊙ ⊠ ⌀ ☎ Services: ⛤ ✕ ⊞ lau Leisure: ⁀ P Off-site: ⛐ ⁀R

Vallon Rouge rte Greolières, 06480
☎ 493328612 ▤ 493328009
e-mail: auvallonrouge@aol.com
website: www.auvallonrouge.com
In a picturesque forested location, close to the river, with good facilities.
➲ *3km W of town, 100mtrs to right of D6 towards Gréolières.*
Open: 3 Apr-25 Sep Site: 3HEC ⃝⃠ ♣ ⊞ Prices: ⋔3-4.30 pitch 9-19 Facilities: ♠ ⅀ ⊙ ⊠ ⌀ ⛐ ☎ Services: ⛤ ✕ ⊞ lau Leisure: ⁀ PR

COURONNE, LA BOUCHES-DU-RHÔNE

Mas Plage de Ste-Croix, La Couronne, 13500
☎ 442807034
e-mail: camping.le-mas@wanadoo.fr
website: www.camping-le-mas.com
A well equipped family site on a plateau with a fine view of the bay, and access to a sandy beach.

➲ *Access from A55, then D49.*
Open: 15 March-15 Oct Site: 6HEC ⃝⃠ ⌀ ♣ ⊞ ⛐ ☎ Services: ⛤ ✕ lau Leisure: ⁀ PS Off-site: ⊞

CRAU, LA VAR

Bois de Mont-Redon 480 chemin du Mont-Redon, 83260
☎ 494667408 ▤ 494660966
e-mail: mont.redon@wanadoo.fr
website: www.mont-redon.com
Set among oak and pine trees with well defined pitches and plenty of recreational facilities.
➲ *3km NE via D29*
Open: 15 Jun-15 Sep Site: 5HEC ⃝⃠ ♣ Facilities: ♠ ⅀ ⊙ ⊠ ☎ Services: ⛤ ✕ ⊞ lau Leisure: ⁀ P

CRESPIAN GARD

Mas de Reilhe 30260 ☎ 466778212 ▤ 466802650
e-mail: info@camping-mas-de-reilhe.fr
website: www.camping-mas-de-reilhe.fr
In the grounds of a château, surrounded by pine trees with good recreational facilities.
➲ *On N110. From A9 exit 25 to S of Nimes. Take N106 towards Alès. After 4km left onto D999 signed tl Le Vigan. Just before Vic-le-Fesq at 1st major x-rds, turn right onto N110 towards Lédignan. Site signed on right before village of Crespian.*
Open: May-26 Sep Site: 3HEC ⃝⃠ ♣ ⊞ ⏚ Prices: pitch 12.50-19 (incl 2 persons) Facilities: ♠ ⅀ ⊙ ⊠ ☎ Services: ⛤ ✕ ⊞ lau Leisure: ⁀ P Off-site: ⁀R

DIE DRÔME

Pinède Quartier du Pont-Neuf, 26150
☎ 475221777 ▤ 475222273
e-mail: info@camping-pinede.com
website: www.camping-pinede.com
In a picturesque mountain setting beside the River Drôme.
➲ *W via D93 then cross railway line and the river to site.*
Open: Apr-15 Sep Site: 5HEC ⃝⃠ ⠒⠒ ♣ ⊞ ⏚ Facilities: ♠ ⅀ ⊙ ⊠ ⌀ ⛐ ☎ Services: ⛤ ✕ ⊞ lau Leisure: ⁀ PR

DIEULEFIT DRÔME

Source du Jabron Jabron, 26220
☎ 475906130 ▤ 475906130
website: www.campinglasource.com
A terraced site in a pleasant location beside the River Jabron.
➲ *N of town on D538.*
Open: May-Sep Site: 5HEC ⃝⃠ ⌀ ♣ ⊞ ⊠ Facilities: ♠ ⅀ ⊙ ⊠ ☎ Services: ⛤ ✕ lau Leisure: ⁀ P

ENTRECHAUX VAUCLUSE

Bon Crouzet rte de St-Marcelin, 84340
☎ 490460162 ▤ 490460162
On level ground with modern facilities beside the river.
➲ *From Vaison-la-Romaine exit follow road towards St-Marcelin-les-Vaison for 6km.*
Open: Apr-Oct Site: 1.2HEC ⃝⃠ ♣ Prices: ⋔3.40-3.50 pitch 3.50-4 Facilities: ♠ ⅀ ⊙ ⊠ ☎ Services: ⛤ ✕ ⊞ lau Leisure: ⁀ R Off-site: ✕

ESPARRON-DE-VERDON ALPES-DE-HAUTE-PROVENCE

Soleil rte de la Tuilienne, 4800 ☎ 492771378 ▤ 492771045
e-mail: campinglesoleil@wanadoo.fr
website: www.multimania.com/campinglesoleil/
In wooded surroundings beside Lake Esparron with well defined pitches.
Open: Etr-Sep Site: 1.5HEC ⃝⃠ ⌀ ♣ ⊞ ⅋ Prices: ⋔4-5 ⛐5.50-6.50 Facilities: ♠ ⅀ ⊙ ⊠ ⌀ ⊡ Services: ⛤ ✕ ⊞ lau Leisure: ⁀ L

Site: 6HEC-Site size ⃝⃠-grass ⠒⠒-sand ⌀-stone ⅊-little shade ⅋-partly shaded ♣-mainly shaded
⊞-bungalows for hire ⛐-caravans for hire ⏚-tents for hire ⅋-no dogs Prices: ⋔-adult per night ⛌-car per night
pp-per person per night ⛐-caravan per night ⏚-tent per night

FLEURY AUDE

Aux Hamacs Les Cabanes de Fleury, 11560
☎ 468332222 🖩 468332223
e-mail: jhsilberman@wanadoo.fr
website: www.campingauxhamacs.com
A large site beside the River Aude and 1km from the coast.
➲ Access via A9 exit Béziers, then 15km W.
Open: 13 Apr-23 Sep Site: 10HEC ▦ ⁝⁝⁝ ◔ 🏕
Prices: ▲1.40-2.80 pitch 10.40-15.80 (incl 2 persons)
Facilities: ℟ 🖬 ⊙ 🖳 ∅ 🛆 🏤 Services: 🍴 ✕ 🗷 lau Leisure: ⇃
PR Off-site: ⇃S

FONTES HÉRAULT

Clairettes Route de Penet, 34320
☎ 467250131 🖩 467253864
e-mail: camping-clairettes@wanadoo.fr
website: www.campinglesclairettes.com
➲ D9 10km N of Pézenas, access via Adissan D128.
Open: Mar-Oct Site: 1.8HEC ▦ ◑ ♠ 🏕 🖳 Prices: pitch
17-20.50 (incl 2 persons) Facilities: ℟ ⊙ 🖳 🛆 🏤 Services: 🍴
✕ 🗷 lau Leisure: ⇃ P Off-site: 🖬 ✕

FONTVIEILLE BOUCHES-DU-RHÔNE

CM Pins r Michelet, 13990 ☎ 490547869 🖩 490548125
In a pine wood close to the Moulin d'Alphonse Daudet.
➲ 1km from village via D17.
Open: Apr-Sept Site: 3.5HEC ▦ ◑ ◔ Prices: ⋔7 pitch 10
(incl 2 persons) Facilities: ℟ ⊙ 🖳 🏤 Services: 🗷 lau
Off-site: 🖬 🍴 ✕ ∅ 🛆 ⇃P

FORCALQUIER ALPES-DE-HAUTE-PROVENCE

Indigo Forcalquier rte de Sigonce, 4300
☎ 492752794 🖩 492751810
e-mail: forcalquier@camping-indigo.com
website: www.camping-indigo.com
Open: Apr-Oct Site: 3HEC ▦ 𝄪 🏕 ♣ Prices: pitch
12.50-19 (incl 2 persons) Facilities: ℟ ⊙ 🖳 ∅ 🏤 Services: 🍴
✕ lau Leisure: ⇃ P Off-site: 🖬

FOS-SUR-MER BOUCHES-DU-RHÔNE

Estagnon Plage St-Gervais, 13270 ☎ 442050119
Level, rather dusty site. Public beach on other side of road.
Camping Card Compulsory.
➲ Situated S of an industrial zone-Quartier St-Gervais.
Open: May-Sep Site: 2HEC ▦ ◑ 🏕 🖳 Facilities: ℟ 🖬 ⊙
🖳 ∅ 🏤 Services: 🍴 ✕ 🗷 lau Leisure: ⇃ S

FRÉJUS VAR

Domaine de Colombier D4 Rue des Anciens Combattants,
d'Afrique du Nord, 83600 ☎ 494515601 🖩 494515557
e-mail: info@domaine-du-colombier.com
website: www.domaine-du-colombier.com
Widespread site on hill on some individual terraces under
pine trees. Good recreational facilities.
➲ Turn N off N7 onto D4 towards Bagnols and continue for
500mtrs. Access also via A8 exit 38.
Open: 15 Jun-2 Oct Site: 10HEC ▦ ♠ 🏕 Prices: pitch
17.70-38.50 (incl 3 persons) pp4.80-6.50 Facilities: ℟ 🖬 ⊙
🖳 ∅ 🏤 Services: 🍴 ✕ 🗷 lau Leisure: ⇃ P Off-site: 🛆

Fréjus rte de Bagnols, 83600 ☎ 494199460 🖩 494199469
e-mail: contact@lefrejus.com website: www.lefrejus.com
Well equipped site in wooded surroundings.
➲ Access via N7 and D4.
Open: 15 Jan-15 Dec Site: 8HEC ▦ ◑ 🏕 ♣
Prices: ♠3.20-5 pp4.50-6.30 Facilities: ℟ 🖬 ⊙ 🖳 ∅ 🛆 🏤 🅿
Services: 🍴 ✕ 🗷 lau Leisure: ⇃ P

Holiday Green

Holiday Green rte de Bagnols-en-Forêt, 83600
☎ 494198830 🖩 494198831
e-mail: info@holiday-green.com
website: www.holiday-green.com
A family site in a beautiful wooded location, offering fine
modern facilities and a wide variety of recreational and
entertainment facilities.
➲ 6km N via D4.
Open: 3 Apr-Sept Site: 15HEC ◈ ♠ 🏕 🖳 Prices: ⋔6-9 ♠6-9
▲9-12 pitch 15-20 Facilities: ℟ 🖬 ⊙ 🖳 ∅ 🛆 🏤 🅿 Services: 🍴
✕ 🗷 lau Leisure: ⇃ PS Off-site: ⇃L

Montourey

Montourey Quartier Montourey, 83600
☎ 494532641 🖩 494532675
e-mail: info@campingmontourey.com
website: www.campingmontourey.com
Comfortable, well equipped site within 10 minutes of the
beach.
➲ 2km N.
Open: Apr-Sep Site: 5HEC ▦ ◑ 🏕 Prices: ⋔3-30 pitch
18-200 (incl 3 persons) pp4-40 Facilities: ℟ 🖬 ⊙ 🖳 🛆 🏤
Services: 🍴 ✕ 🗷 lau Leisure: ⇃ P

Pierre Verte

Pierre Verte rte de Bagnols, 83.6
☎ 494408830 🖩 494407541
e-mail: camping.lapierre.verte@wanadoo.fr
website: www.campinglapierreverte.com
A large family site in a pine forest 8km from the coast.
➲ Access on A8 from Puget-sur-Argens.
Open: Apr-Sep Site: 28HEC ▦ 𝄪 ♠ 🏕 🖳 Prices: ⋔4.50-5.50
pitch 17-25 (incl 2 persons) Facilities: ℟ 🖬 ⊙ 🖳 ∅ 🛆 🏤
Services: 🍴 ✕ 🗷 lau Leisure: ⇃ P

Pins Parasols

Pins Parasols rte de Bagnols-en-Forêt, 83600
☎ 494408843 🖩 494408199
e-mail: lespinsparasols@wanadoo.fr
website: lespinsparasols.com
A modern family site shaded by oaks and pines with
spacious, well defined pitches and good recreational facilities.
➲ 4km N via D4.
Open: 12 Apr-Sep Site: 4.5HEC ▦ ◑ 🏕 Prices: ⋔4.40-5.90
pitch 17.40-24 (incl 2 persons) Facilities: ℟ 🖬 ⊙ 🖳 ∅ 🏤
Services: 🍴 ✕ 🗷 lau Leisure: ⇃ P Off-site: 🛆

FRONTIGNAN HÉRAULT

Soleil ☎ 467430202 🖩 467789002
Family site bordering the beach.
➲ NE via D60.
Open: May-Sep Site: 1.5HEC ▦ ◑ 🏕 🖳 Facilities: ℟ ⊙
🖳 🛆 🏤 🅿 Services: 🍴 ✕ 🗷 lau Leisure: ⇃ PS

Tamaris d'Ingril, 34110 ☎ 467434477 🖩 467189790
e-mail: les-tamaris@wanadoo.fr
website: www.les-tamaris.fr
A family site on level ground with direct access to the beach.
Good recreational facilities.
➲ From N112 take D129 and D60/D50 for 6km.
Open: Apr-Sep Site: 4.5HEC ⁝⁝⁝ ◑ 🏕 🖳 Prices: pitch 20-
32 (incl 2 persons) Facilities: ℟ 🖬 ⊙ 🖳 ∅ 🏤 Services: 🍴 ✕
🗷 lau Leisure: ⇃ PS

GALLARGUES-LE-MONTUEUX GARD

Amandiers 30660 ☎ 466352802
e-mail: campamandiers@wanadoo.fr
A family site with good facilities in a beautiful wooded
situation.
➲ Along N113 heading away from Lunel towards Nîmes.
Open: May-10 Sep Site: 3HEC ▦ ◑ 🏕 🖳 ♣ Facilities: ℟
🖬 ⊙ 🖳 ∅ 🛆 🏤 Services: 🍴 ✕ 🗷 lau Leisure: ⇃ P
Off-site: ✕ ⇃R

Facilities: 🖬-shop ℟-shower ⊙-electric points for razors 🖳-electric points for caravans 🏤-parking by tents permitted
🅿-compulsory separate car park Services: ✕-café/restaurant 🍴-bar ∅-Camping Gaz International 🛆-gas other than Camping
Gaz 🗷-first aid facilities lau-laundry Leisure: ⇃-swimming L-Lake P-Pool R-River S-Sea Off-site: All facilities within 2km

GALLICIAN GARD

Mourgues 30600 ☎ 466733088 📠 466733088
e-mail: info@masdemourgues.com
website: www.masdemourgues.com
Situated in an old vineyard with some vines retained to
separate pitches. Views overlooking the Camargue.
➲ On the N572 between St-Gilles and Vauvert at the junction
with the road to Gallician.
Open: Apr-Sep Site: 2HEC 〰 ☀ ♠ 🏠 Prices: pitch 10-12
(incl 2 persons) Facilities: 🌣 🏪 ⊙ 🍴 ∅ 🚿 🏧 Services: ♟ 🎪
lau Leisure: ⤳ P Off-site: ✗

GASSIN VAR

Moulin de Verdagne 83580 ☎ 494797821 📠 494542265
e-mail: moulindeverdagne@aol.com
Flat grassy site with a family atmosphere 4km from the beach.
➲ SE of town towards the coast.
Site: 5HEC 〰 ♃ 🏠 Prices: pitch 38-42 Facilities: 🌣 🏪 ⊙
🍴 ∅ 🚿 Services: ♟ ✗ 🎪 lau Leisure: ⤳ P

Parc St-James Gassin rte du Bourrian, 83580
☎ 494552020 📠 4945634877
Park-like site on slopes of a hill.
➲ 2.5km E of N559. Access from main road at Km84.5 and
84.9 on D89.
Site: 32HEC 〰 ∴ ♠ Facilities: 🌣 🏪 ⊙ 🍴 ∅ 🚿 🏧
Services: ♟ ✗ 🎪 lau Leisure: ⤳ P

GAUJAC GARD

Domaine de Gaujac Boisset, 30140
☎ 466618065 📠 466605390
e-mail: gravieres@clubinternet.fr
website: www.domaine.de.gaujac.com
A family site in wooded surroundings on the banks of a river.
➲ Access via D910.
Open: Apr-Sep Site: 10HEC 〰 ♠ 🏠 🚐 Facilities: 🌣 🏪 ⊙
🍴 ∅ 🚿 🏧 Services: ♟ ✗ 🎪 lau Leisure: ⤳ PR

GIENS VAR

Méditerranée-Les Cigales Quartier du Pousset, bd Alsace-
Lorraine, 83400 ☎ 494582106 📠 494589673
e-mail: aspicq@campinglmed.fr
website: www.campinglmed.fr
A well-kept site with numbered pitches. Special places for
caravans.
➲ 0.3km E of D97.
Open: Apr-end Sep Site: 1.5HEC 〰 ♠ 🏠 🚐
Prices: ▲3.05-4.85 pitch 11.40-16.05 (incl 2 persons) pp3.25-
4.05 Facilities: 🌣 🏪 ⊙ 🍴 🚿 🏧 Services: ♟ ✗ lau
Off-site: ∅ 🚿 ⤳S

GRANDE-MOTTE, LA HÉRAULT

Lou Gardian 603 allée de la Petite Motte, 34280
☎ 467561414 📠 467563103
A well run site with well defined pitches, 0.5km from the
beach. Advisable to book in advance in high season.
Open: 15 Apr-Sep Site: 2.6HEC 〰 ♠ 🏠 Facilities: 🌣 🏪 ⊙ 🍴
🏧 Services: ✗ 🎪 lau Off-site: ∅ 🚿 ⤳LPS

Lous Pibols 34280 ☎ 467565008
Well-organised. Divided into level pitches.
➲ W on D59, 0.4km from sea.
Open: Apr-Sep Site: 3HEC ∴ ♠ 🏠 ▲ Facilities: 🌣 🏪 ⊙ 🍴
∅ 🚿 🏧 Services: 🎪 lau Leisure: ⤳ P Off-site: ♟ ✗ ⤳S

GRASSE ALPES-MARITIMES

Paoute 160 rte de Cannes, 06130
☎ 493091142 📠 493400640
A family site in a wooded location close to the town centre.

➲ S of town centre, E of the Cannes road just beyond the
Centre Commercial.
Site: 2.5HEC 〰 ♠ 🏠 Facilities: 🌣 🏪 ⊙ 🍴 ∅ 🚿 🏧
Services: ♟ ✗ 🎪 lau Leisure: ⤳ P

AT OPIO (8KM E VIA D2085 & D3)

Caravan Inn 18 rte de Cannes, 6650
☎ 493773200 📠 493777189
A well equipped site in a wooded location between the sea
and the mountains
➲ 1.5km S of Opio on D3.
Open: Jun-15 Sep Site: 5HEC 〰 ♠ 🚐 Facilities: 🌣 ⊙ 🍴 ∅
🚿 🏧 Services: ♟ ✗ 🎪 lau Leisure: ⤳ P Off-site: 🏪

GRAU-DU-ROI, LE GARD

Abri de Camargue rte du Phare de l'Espiguette, Port
Camargue, 30240 ☎ 466515483 📠 466517642
e-mail: contact@abridecarmague.com
website: www.abridecarmague.com
A pleasant site near the beach on the edge of the Camargue
with well-marked pitches and modern installations.
➲ 2.5km S on L'Espiguette road.
Open: Apr-Sep Site: 4HEC 〰 ∴ ♠ 🏠 Prices: pitch 21-43
Facilities: 🌣 🏪 ⊙ 🍴 ∅ 🚿 🏧 Services: ♟ ✗ 🎪 lau Leisure: ⤳
P Off-site: ⤳S

Bon Séjour 30240 ☎ 466514711
Clean, tidy, well-kept site.
➲ 3km E of village off road to lighthouse.
Open: Apr-Sep Site: 5HEC 〰 ♃ 🚐 Facilities: 🌣 🏪 ⊙ 🍴 ∅
🚿 🏧 Services: ♟ ✗ 🎪 lau Leisure: ⤳ L

Eden Port-Camargue, 30240 ☎ 466514981 📠 466531320
e-mail: camping.eden@wanadoo.fr
website: www.campingeden.fr
Quiet site on both sides of access road. 300mtrs from beach.
➲ On D626 towards Espiguette.
Open: 4 Apr-3 Oct Site: 5.2HEC 〰 ∴ ♠ 🏠 Prices: ▲17-
32 🚗17-32 🚐17-32 Facilities: 🌣 🏪 ⊙ 🍴 ∅ 🚿 🏧 Services: ♟
✗ 🎪 lau Leisure: ⤳ P Off-site: 🏪 ♟ ✗ ⤳S 🎪

Elysée Résidence 980 rte de l'Espiguette, 30240
☎ 466535400 📠 466518512
e-mail: elysee.residence@elysee-residence.com
website: www.elysee-residence.com
Large family site on the edge of the Camargue with a good
variety of sporting and entertainment facilities.
➲ Access via A9.
Open: 15 May-12 Sep Site: 18HEC ∴ ♠ 🏠 Prices: pitch
8.80-37.80 (incl 2 persons) Facilities: 🌣 🏪 ⊙ 🍴 ∅ 🚿 🏧
Services: ♟ ✗ 🎪 lau Leisure: ⤳ LP Off-site: 🏪 ♟ ✗ ⤳S

Jardins de Tivoli rte de l'Éspiquette, 30240
☎ 466539700 📠 466510981
A modern site with well marked pitches in a wooded setting
600mtrs from the beach. There are good recreational facilities
including mountain bike hire.
➲ Access via A9 continuing SE through Le Grau-du-Roi.
Open: Apr-Sep Site: 7HEC 〰 ♠ 🏠 Prices: pitch 21-48
pp6 Facilities: 🌣 🏪 ⊙ 🍴 ∅ 🚿 🏧 Services: ♟ ✗ 🎪 lau
Leisure: ⤳ P Off-site: ⤳S

Mouettes av Jean-Jaurès, 30240 ☎ 466514400
On level ground, shaded by olive and poplar trees, this site is
well equipped and the beach is only 500mtrs away.
➲ 1.2km SE.
Open: Apr-Sep Site: 1HEC 〰 ♠ 🏠 Facilities: 🌣 ⊙ 🍴 ∅
🏧 Services: ♟ ✗ 🎪 lau Off-site: 🏪 ✗ ⤳S

Petits Camarguais rte de l'Espiguette, 30240
☎ 466511616 🖩 466511617
e-mail: petite.camargue@yellohvillage.com
website: www.les-petits-camarguais.fr
A comfortable family site in woodland with a wide range of
recreational facilities. Close to the beach.
Open: 3 Apr-19 Sep Site: 4HEC ⋅⋅⋅ ⊕ 🏕 ⊗ Facilities: ↟ 🏪
⊙ 🖥 🎪 Services: �!✗ 🎫 lau Leisure: ↖ P Off-site: ↖S

GRIGNAN DRÔME

Truffières Lieu-dit Nachony, 26230 ☎ 475469362
e-mail: info@lestruffieres.com
website: www.lestruffieres.com
A family site opposite the Château Grignan with good
facilities.
➲ Leave A7 at exit Montélimar Sud and follow N7 E.
Open: 20 Apr-Sep Site: 3HEC ⛺ ⊕ 🏕 🎪 ⊗ Prices: pitch
13-15.50 (incl 2 persons) Facilities: ↟ ⊙ 🖥 🎫 Services: !✗
🎫 lau Leisure: ↖ P Off-site: 🏪

HYÈRES VAR

AT AYGUADE-CEINTURON (4KM SE)

Ceinturon II 83400 ☎ 494663966 🖩 494664730
e-mail: camping.ceinturon2@wanadoo.fr
website: www.provence-campings.com
A popular site on level meadowland divided into pitches.
300yds from the sea. Some individual washing cubicles.
➲ 4km SE of Hyères on D42.
Open: Apr-Sep Site: 4.8HEC ⛺ ⊕ 🏕 Prices: ↟3.50-4 pitch
18.50 (incl 2 persons) pp3.60-6 Facilities: ↟ 🏪 ⊙ 🖥 🎫 🎫
Services: !✗ 🎫 lau Off-site: 🛁 ↖PRS

Ceinturon III L'Ayguade, 83400
☎ 494663265 🖩 494664843
e-mail: ceinturon3@securmail.net
website: www.provence-campings.com/azur/ceinturon3.htm
Well-kept site in wooded surroundings divided into
numbered pitches. Individual washing cubicles.
➲ 4km SE of Hyères on D42.
Open: Apr-Sep Site: 3HEC ⛺ ⊕ 🏕 Prices: ↟4.70 🚐4.70
pitch 5.80 Facilities: ↟ 🏪 ⊙ 🖥 🎫 🎫 🎫 Services: !✗ lau
Leisure: ↖ S Off-site: 🛁 ↖S 🎫

AT HYÈRES-PLAGE (4KM SE)

Pins Maritimes 1633 bd de la Marine, 83400 ☎ 494663357
Situated in a pine wood close to the beach.
➲ Turn off D42 between Hyères-Plage and L'Ayguade and
continue inland for 200mtrs.
Open: Apr-Sep Site: 37HEC ⛺ 🔲 🏕 Facilities: ↟ 🏪 ⊙ 🖥
🎫 🛁 🎫 Services: !✗ 🎫 lau Off-site: ↖S

ISLE-SUR-LA-SORGUE, L' VAUCLUSE

CM Sorguette rte d'Apt, 84800
☎ 490380571 🖩 490208461
e-mail: sorguette@wanadoo.fr
website: www.camping-sorguette.com
In tranquil wooded surroundings beside the River Sorguette
with good sports and entertainment facilities.
➲ Access via N100 towards Apt.
Open: 15 Mar-15 Oct Site: 2.5HEC ⛺ 🔲 🏕 🎪
Prices: ↟4.90-6.30 pitch 4.90-5.70 Facilities: ↟ 🏪 ⊙ 🖥 🎫 🛁
🎫 Services: !✗ 🎫 lau Leisure: ↖ R Off-site: ↖P

ISTRES BOUCHES-DU-RHÔNE

Vitou 31 rte de St-Chamas, 13800 ☎ 442565157
In a wooded location with a large area for tents.
➲ N of town on D16.
Open: All year Site: 6.5HEC ⛺ 🏕 🎪 Facilities: ↟ 🏪 ⊙ 🖥
🎫 Services: !✗ 🎫 Leisure: ↖ L Off-site: 🛁

LAROQUE-DES-ALBÈRES PYRÉNÉES-ORIENTALES

Planes 117 av du Vallespir, rte de Villelongue dels Monts,
66740 ☎ 468892136 🖩 468890142
e-mail: francois.camping.las.planes@libertysurf.fr
website: www.camping66.com
In a picturesque setting surrounded by trees, bushes and
flowers.
➲ Approach via Laroque towards Villelongue-del-Monts.
Open: 15 Jun-Aug Site: 2.5HEC ⛺ 🏕 Prices: ↟3.50 🚐2.50
pitch 8.30 Facilities: ↟ ⊙ 🖥 🛁 🎫 Services: ✗ 🎫 lau
Leisure: ↖ P Off-site: 🏪 !✗ 🛁

LÉZIGNAN-CORBIÈRES AUDE

CM Pinède av Gaston-Bonheur, 11200
☎ 468270508 🖩 468270508
website: www.campinglapinede.fr
Well-kept terraced site with numbered pitches and tarred
drives, decorated with bushes and flower beds. Shop available
July and August only.
➲ Signposted from N113.
Open: Mar-30 Oct Site: 3.5HEC 🔲 🏕 Prices: ↟3-4.20
pitch 5.50-7.30 Facilities: ↟ 🏪 ⊙ 🖥 🛁 🎫 Services: ✗ lau
Leisure: ↖ P Off-site: !✗ 🎫

LONDE-LES-MAURES, LA VAR

Moulières 83250 ☎ 494015321 🖩 494015322
e-mail: camping.les.moulieres@wanadoo.fr
website: www.provence-camping.com/azur/moulieres
Well tended level meadowland in quiet location. 1km from
the sea.
Camping Card Compulsory.
➲ On western outskirts towards the coast.
Open: 14 Jun-6 Sep Site: 3HEC ⛺ 🏕 Facilities: ↟ 🏪 ⊙ 🖥
🛁 🛁 🎫 🔲 Services: !✗ 🎫 lau Off-site: ↖S

Pansard 83250 ☎ 494668322 🖩 494665612
e-mail: pansardcamping@aol.com
website: www.provence-campings.com/azur/pansard
Beautiful, wide piece of land in a pine forest beside the
beach.
➲ Turn off N98.
Open: Apr-Sep Site: 6HEC ⛺ ⋅⋅⋅ 🏕 🎪 ⊗
Prices: ↟5.50 🚐3 pitch 22 (incl 3 persons) Facilities: ↟ 🏪 ⊙
🖥 🛁 🎫 Services: !✗ lau Leisure: ↖ S

Val Rose 83250 ☎ 494668136 🖩 494665267
e-mail: camping-valrose@wanadoo.fr
website: www.campingvalrose.com
In a rural setting at the foot of the Maures mountains, close
to a golf course. Well defined pitches and good modern
facilities.
➲ 4km NE on N98.
Open: Mar-01 Nov Site: 2.5HEC ⛺ 🏕 Facilities: ↟ 🏪
⊙ 🖥 🛁 🎫 Services: !✗ 🎫 lau Leisure: ↖ P

LUNEL HÉRAULT

Bon Port rte de la Petite Camargue, 34400
☎ 467711565 🖩 467836027
In a pleasant wooded location at the gateway to the
Camargue.
➲ Access via D24.
Open: Apr-Sep Site: 5HEC ⛺ 🏕 🎪 Facilities: ↟ 🏪 ⊙
🖥 🛁 🎫 Services: !✗ 🎫 lau Leisure: ↖ P

Mas de l'Isle 85 chemin du Clapas, 34400
☎ 467832652 🖩 467711388
A pleasant site between the Cévennes mountains and the
Mediterranean.

contd.

Facilities: 🏪-shop **↟**-shower **⊙**-electric points for razors **🖥**-electric points for caravans **🎫**-parking by tents permitted
🔲-compulsory separate car park **Services: ✗**-café/restaurant **!**-bar **🛁**-Camping Gaz International **🛁**-gas other than Camping
Gaz **🎫**-first aid facilities lau-laundry **Leisure: ↖**-swimming L-Lake P-Pool R-River S-Sea **Off-site:** All facilities within 2km

�» *1.5km SE via D34 near junction with the D61.*
Open: Apr-Aug Site: 4HEC ⬛⬛⬛⬛ ♣ 🏠 Prices: pitch 10-18
(incl 2 persons) Facilities: 🚿 ⊙ 🛢 🛒 🖭 🅿 Services: 🍴 ✕ lau
Leisure: 🟦 P Off-site: 🛒 ⊘ 🟦R ⊞

MALLEMORT BOUCHES-DU-RHÔNE

Durance Luberon Domaine du Vergon, 13370
☎ 490591336 📠 490574662
e-mail: duranceluberon@aol.com
website: www.campingduranceluberon.com
�» *2.5 km on D23c, 200mtrs from Canal.*
Open: Apr-15 Oct Site: 4.4HEC ⬛⬛⬛⬛ 🔾 🏠 Prices: ♠3.40-4
pitch 3.60-6 Facilities: 🚿 ⊙ 🛢 🛒 Services: 🍴 ✕ lau
Leisure: 🟦 P Off-site: 🛒 ✕ ⊘ 🟦R ⊞

MANDELIEU-LA-NAPOULE ALPES-MARITIMES

Cigales 505 av de la Mer, 06210
☎ 493492353 📠 493493045
e-mail: campingcigales@wanadoo.fr website: www.lescigales.com
A riverside site with well defined pitches, 800mtrs from the sea.
�» *S on N7.*
Open: All year Site: 2HEC ⬛⬛⬛⬛ ♣ 🏠 Prices: ♠5-5 ♠5-5
pitch 13.50-27 Facilities: 🚿 ⊙ 🛢 🛒 Services: 🍴 ✕ lau
Leisure: 🟦 P Off-site: 🛒 ⊘ 🟦S

Plateau des Chasses r J-Monnet, 6210 ☎ 493492593
Terraced land, on hill in a park.
�» *Turn off N7 at Km 4.2 and continue uphill for 1.2km.*
Open: Apr-Sep Site: 4HEC ⬛⬛⬛⬛ ♣ 🏠 🚐 Facilities: 🚿 ⊙ 🛢
🛒 Services: 🍴 ✕ ⊞ lau Leisure: 🟦 P Off-site: 🛒 ⊘ 🟦RS

MANOSQUE ALPES-DE-HAUTE-PROVENCE

Ubacs av de la Repasse, 4100 ☎ 492722808 📠 492877529
e-mail: lesubacs.manosque@ffcc.asso.fr
A well equipped site in the Durance valley, close to the town
centre.
�» *1.5 km W off D907, rte d'Apt.*
Open: Apr-Sep Site: 4HEC ⬛⬛⬛⬛ ♣ ♣ 🚐 Prices: ♠3-3.30 pitch
3.90-4.10 🛒 Services: ✕ lau
Leisure: 🟦 P Off-site: ⊞

MARSEILLAN-PLAGE HÉRAULT

Charlemagne av du Camping, 34340
☎ 467219249 📠 467218611
e-mail: info@charlemagne-camping.com
website: www.charlemagne-camping.com
200mtrs from the beach in quiet, wooded surroundings with
good sanitary and sporting facilities.
�» *Access via N112 at Marseillan Plage.*
Open: 3 Apr-25 Sep Site: 6.6HEC ⬛⬛⬛⬛ ∵∵ ♣ 🏠
Prices: pitch 15-41 (incl 3 persons) Facilities: 🚿 🛒 ⊙ 🛢 ⊘ 🟦
🛒 Services: 🍴 ✕ ⊞ lau Leisure: 🟦 PS

Languedoc-Camping 117 chemin du Pairollet, 34340
☎ 467219255 📠 467016375
A family site in wooded surroundings with direct access to
the beach.
�» *On the coast road between the Mediterranean and the
Bassin de Thau.*
Open: 15 Mar-Oct Site: 1.5HEC ⬛⬛⬛⬛ ∵∵ ♣ 🏠 🚐
Prices: pitch 25-32 (incl 3 persons) Facilities: 🚿 🛒 ⊙ 🛢 ⊘ 🟦
Services: ✕ ⊞ lau Leisure: 🟦 S Off-site: 🍴 ⊘ 🟦LPR

Plage 69 chemin du Pairollet, 34340
☎ 467219254 📠 467016357
e-mail: laplagecamping@aol.com
A family site with direct access to a sandy beach.
Open: 15 Mar-Oct Site: 1.3HEC ∵∵ ♣ 🏠 Prices: pitch 13-
27 (incl 2 persons) pp3.50-4 Facilities: 🚿 ⊙ 🛢 ⊘ 🟦
Services: 🍴 ✕ lau Leisure: 🟦 S Off-site: 🛒 ⊞

MAUREILLAS PYRÉNÉES-ORIENTALES

Val Roma Park Les Thermas du Boulou, 66480 ☎ 468831972
�» *2.5km NE on N9.*
Open: All year Site: 3.5HEC ⬛⬛⬛⬛ ♣ 🏠 🚐 Facilities: 🚿 🛒 ⊙
🛢 🛒 Services: 🍴 ✕ ⊞ lau Leisure: 🟦 PR

MENTON ALPES-MARITIMES

Fleur de Mai 67 rte du Val de Gorbio, 06500
☎ 493572236 📠 493572236
Terraced site in a peaceful situation by a stream in the heart
of the Côte-d'Azur.
�» *Exit from D23 at the Parc de la Madone.*
Open: 12 May-31 May, Jul-15 Sep Site: 2HEC ⬛⬛⬛⬛ 🔾
Prices: ♠3.50-4.50 ♠2.50-3.50 🚐12-13 🛖10-11 Facilities: 🚿
⊙ 🛢 🛒 🅿 Services: ⊞ lau Off-site: 🛒 🍴 ✕ ⊘ 🟦 🟦PS

MÉOLANS-REVEL ALPES-DE-HAUTE-PROVENCE

Domaine de Loisirs de l'Ubaye 4340
☎ 492810196 📠 492819253
e-mail: info@loisirsubaye.com
website: www.loisirsubaye.com
A large terraced site in a delightful wooded valley. There is a
small lake and direct access to the river and good sporting
and recreational facilities.
�» *7km NW of Barcelonnette.*
Site: 10HEC ⬛⬛⬛⬛ 🔾 🏠 🚐 Prices: ♠3-5 ♠2 🛖2 pitch 10.50-
17.50 (incl 2 persons) Facilities: 🚿 ⊙ 🛢 ⊘ 🛒 Services: 🍴
✕ ⊞ lau Leisure: 🟦 LPR

MIRABEL-ET-BLACONS DRÔME

Gervanne Camping 26400 ☎ 475400020 📠 475400397
e-mail: info@gervanne-camping.com
website: www.gervanne-camping.com
A pleasant site with scattered shade and plenty of facilities
beside the River Drôme.
�» *Access via D164 Crest-Die.*
Open: Apr-Oct Site: 3.8HEC ⬛⬛⬛⬛ ♣ 🏠 🚐 Prices: ♠3.40-4.70
♠2.10-2.50 🚐3-4 Facilities: 🚿 🛒 ⊙ 🛢 ⊘ 🟦 🛒 Services: 🍴
✕ ⊞ lau Leisure: 🟦 LPR

MONTBLANC HÉRAULT

Rebau 34290 ☎ 467985078 📠 467986863
e-mail: lerebau@club-internet.fr
website: www.club-internet.fr/perso/lerebau
Divided into pitches and surrounded by vineyards.
�» *From Pézenas follow N113; in La Bégude de Jordy turn off
main road and drive 2km on D18 towards Montblanc.*
Open: Mar-Oct Site: 3HEC ⬛⬛⬛⬛ ♣ 🏠 🚐 Prices: ♠3 pitch 18
(incl 2 persons) Facilities: 🚿 ⊙ 🛢 ⊘ 🟦 Services: 🍴 ✕ ⊞ lau
Leisure: 🟦 P

MONTCLAR AUDE

Au Pin d'Arnauteille Domaine d'Arnauteille, 11250
☎ 468268453 📠 468269110
e-mail: arnauteille@mnet.fr website: www.arnauteille.com
In a natural wooded park with fine views of the surrounding
mountains.
�» *2.2km SE via D43.*
Open: 10 Apr-26 Sep Site: 10HEC ⬛⬛⬛⬛ 🔾 🏠 Prices: ♠4-6.50
♠2-4 🚐3.50-6 🛖3.50-6 pitch 3.50-6 Facilities: 🚿 🛒 ⊙ 🛢 ⊘
🟦 🛒 Services: 🍴 ✕ ⊞ lau Leisure: 🟦 P Off-site: 🟦R

MONTÉLIMAR DRÔME

Deux Saisons Chemin des Alexis, 26200 ☎ 475018899
A well equipped site on the bank of River Roubion.
�» *From town centre follow D540 across Pont de la Libération;
then first turning right into chemin des Alexis.*
Open: Mar-Nov Site: 1.5HEC ⬛⬛⬛⬛ ∵∵ 🔾 🚐 Facilities: 🚿 ⊙
🛢 ⊘ 🛒 Services: 🍴 ✕ ⊞ lau Leisure: 🟦 R Off-site: 🟦 🟦P

Site: 6HEC-Site size ⬛⬛⬛⬛-grass ∵∵-sand ⬥-stone ✿-little shade 🔾-partly shaded ♣-mainly shaded
🏠-bungalows for hire 🚐-caravans for hire 🛖-tents for hire ⊘-no dogs Prices: ♠-adult per night ♠-car per night
pp-per person per night 🚐-caravan per night 🛖-tent per night

MONTPELLIER HÉRAULT

Floréal rte de Palavas, 34970 ☎ 467929305 ▤ 467929305
On level ground surrounded by vineyards.
➲ *500mtrs off Autoroute A9, exit Montpellier-Sud. From town centre follow road for Palavas (D986).*
Open: 15 Feb-Nov Site: 1.6HEC ▥ ♠ ⌂ ⌷ Prices: ⋔3.50-3.50 pitch 12-14.25 (incl 2 persons) Facilities: ↿ ⋤ ⊙ ⊟ ☎
Services: ⍟ ⊞ lau Off-site: ⋤ ⍟ ✕ ⌀ ⚏ ⋋PRS

MONTPEZAT ALPES-DE-HAUTE-PROVENCE

Coteau de la Marine 04500 ☎ 492775333 ▤ 492775934
A pleasant wooded site, providing easy access to the Verdon Gorges. There are good facilities, especially for boating.
➲ *Access via D11 and D211.*
Open: May-Sep Site: 10HEC ⬙ ♠ ⌂ ⌷ Facilities: ↿ ⋤ ⊙ ⊟ ⌀ ⚏ ☎ Services: ⍟ ✕ ⊞ lau Leisure: ⋋ PR

MONTRÉAL ARDÈCHE

Moulinage rte des Défilés de Ruoms, 7110 ☎ 475368620
Well-equipped family site with a variety of bungalows, caravans and timber chalets. Close to the famous Gorges de l'Ardèche.
Open: Apr-Sep Site: 3.5HEC ▥ ⬙ ⌂ ⌷ ⌰ Facilities: ↿ ⊙ ⊟ ☎ Services: ⍟ ✕ ⊞ lau Leisure: ⋋ PR

MOURIÈS BOUCHES-DU-RHÔNE

Devenson 13890 ☎ 490475201 ▤ 490476309
e-mail: devenson@libertysurf.fr
Terraced site amongst pine and olive trees in Provençal countryside.
➲ *Turn off N113 at La Samatane and continue N towards Mouriès. Site is in N part of village.*
Open: 30 Mar -15 Sep Site: 3.5HEC ⬙ ♠ ⌷ Prices: ⋔4.50 pitch 5 Facilities: ↿ ⋤ ⊙ ⊟ ⌀ ☎ Services: ⊞ lau Leisure: ⋋ P Off-site: ⍟ ✕ ⚏

MOUSTIERS-STE-MARIE ALPES-DE-HAUTE-PROVENCE

St-Jean rte de Riez, 04360 ☎ 492746685 ▤ 492746685
e-mail: camping-st-jean@wanadoo.fr
website: www.ville-moustiers-sainte-marie.fr
Quiet and relaxing site located at the gateway to the Gorges du Verdon, 5 minutes from Ste-Croix Lake.
➲ *Access D952.*
Open: 24 Apr -27 Sep Site: 1.6HEC ▥ ♠ ⌂ Prices: ⋔3.70 pitch 4 Facilities: ↿ ⋤ ⊙ ⊟ ⌀ ☎ Services: ⊞ lau Leisure: ⋋ R Off-site: ⍟ ✕ ⚏

Vieux Colombier Quartier St-Michel, 04360
☎ 492746189 ▤ 492746189
e-mail: camping.vieux.colombier@wanadoo.fr
website: http://perso.wanadoo.fr/camping-vieux.colombier/
A family site near the entrance to the Gorges du Verdon at an altitude of 630 metres.
➲ *0.8km S via D952 towards Castellane.*
Open: Apr-Sep Site: 2.7HEC ▥ ⬙ ⌂ Prices: ⋔3.80 pitch 3.90 Facilities: ↿ ⊙ ⊟ ⌀ ☎ Services: ⍟ ✕ ⊞ lau Off-site: ⋤ ⚏ ⋋R

MUY, LE VAR

Cigales 721 Chemin de Jas de la Paro, 83490
☎ 494451208 ▤ 494458280
e-mail: contact@les-cigales.com
website: www.les-cigales.com
A family site set among Mediterranean vegetation with excellent facilities and organised entertainment during the high season.

➲ *Exit 'Draguignan' off A8 onto N7. 0.8km to site. Well signposted.*
Open: Apr-Oct Site: 13.5HEC ▥ ♠ ⌂ Prices: ⋔3-5 ⬗2-3 pitch 4-8 Facilities: ↿ ⋤ ⊙ ⊟ ⌀ ☎ Services: ⍟ ✕ lau Leisure: ⋋ P

Sellig 41 chemin des Valettes, 83490 ☎ 494451171
A peaceful family site in a wooded location.
➲ *1.5km W on N7.*
Open: Mar-15 Oct Site: 1.6HEC ▥ ♠ ⌂ ⌷ Facilities: ↿ ⋤ ⊙ ⊟ ☎ Services: ⍟ ✕ lau Leisure: ⋋ P Off-site: ⋋LR

NAPOULE, LA ALPES-MARITIMES

Azur-Vacances bd du Bon Puits, 06120
☎ 493099216 ▤ 493499112
Site with many long terraces, on edge of mountain slope in mixed woodland.
➲ *Turn inland 200mtrs after fork at railway station and continue 600mtrs.*
Open: Apr-Sep Site: 6HEC ▥ ♠ Facilities: ↿ ⋤ ⊙ ⊟ ⌀ ⚏ ☎ Services: ⍟ ✕ ⊞ lau Off-site: ⋋RS

NARBONNE AUDE

Nautique La Nautique, 11100 ☎ 468904819 ▤ 468907339
e-mail: info@campinglanautique.com
website: www.campinglanautique.com
Situated on the salt water lake 'Étang de Bages et de Sigean', this site is particularly well appointed, each pitch having its own washing and toilet facilities. There are good recreational facilities and advance booking is recommended.
➲ *Access via Narbonne Sud exit on A9.*
Open: Feb-25 Nov Site: 16HEC ▥ ⫶ ♠ ⌂ ⌰ Prices: ⋔3.95-5.20 pitch 7.40-17.50 (incl 2 persons) Facilities: ↿ ⋤ ⊙ ⊟ ⋤ ☎ Services: ⍟ ✕ ⊞ lau Leisure: ⋋ P Off-site: ⌀ ⋋L

Camping La Nautique

11100 Narbonne - Languedoc - France
Tel (+33) 04 68 90 48 19 Fax (+33) 04 68 90 73 39
e-mail : info@campinglanautique.com
www.campinglanautique.com

Every plot, 130 m², has **PRIVATE SANITARY FACILITIES** (shower, WC and wash basin) with hot water and 10 amps electricity. Restaurant, bar and snackbar. A pool with waterslide and a paddling pool, children's club and many activities for all. Tennis, mini-golf etc. Ideal for windsurfing. Rental of fully equipped mobile-homes. Run by a Dutch family. English spoken.

Facilities: ⋤-shop ↿-shower ⊙-electric points for razors ⊟-electric points for caravans ☎-parking by tents permitted ⚏-compulsory separate car park Services: ✕-café/restaurant ⍟-bar ⌀-Camping Gaz International ⚏-gas other than Camping Gaz ⊞-first aid facilities lau-laundry Leisure: ⋋-swimming L-Lake P-Pool R-River S-Sea Off-site: All facilities within 2km

AT NARBONNE-PLAGE (15KM E D168)

CM de la Côte des Roses 11100 ☎ 468498365 ▤ 468494044
A modern site nestling at the foot of the Massif of the Calpe close to the sea.
➲ *3 km SW.*
Open: 25 May-Sep **Site:** 16HEC ⏛ ♣ **Facilities:** ℝ ⅃ ⊙ ⊠ ⊘ ⌂ **Services:** ⚊ ✗ ⊞ lau **Off-site:** ⸬ ⚘S

CM Falaise av des Vacances, 11100
☎ 468498077 ▤ 468494044
On level ground at the foot of the Massif of the Calpe with good modern facilities.
➲ *W of Narbonne Plage, 400mtrs from beach.*
Open: Apr-22 Sep **Site:** 8HEC ⏛ ♣ **Facilities:** ℝ ⅃ ⊙ ⊠ ⊘ ⌂ **Services:** ⚊ ✗ ⊞ lau **Off-site:** ⚘S

NÉBIAS AUDE

Fontaulié-Sud 11500 ☎ 468201762
e-mail: lefontauliesud@free.fr
website: www.fontaulie.com
In a beautiful setting in the heart of the Cathare region.
➲ *0.6km S via D117.*
Open: May-15 Sep **Site:** 4HEC ⏛ ♣ ⊞ **Prices:** ⚊4 pitch 6 **Facilities:** ℝ ⅃ ⊙ ⊠ ⊘ ⸬ ⌂ **Services:** ⚊ ✗ ⊞ lau **Leisure:** ⚘ P **Off-site:** ✗

NÎMES GARD

Domaine de la Bastide Rte de Generac, 30900
☎ 466380921 ▤ 466380921
In a rural setting with excellent facilities. Shop open summer only.
➲ *5km S of town centre on D13. Access via A9 exit 'Nîmes-Ouest'.*
Open: All year **Site:** 5HEC ⏛ ◊ ⚘ ⊞ **Facilities:** ℝ ⅃ ⊙ ⊠ ⊘ ⸬ ⌂ **Services:** ⚊ ✗ ⊞ lau **Off-site:** ⚘L

NIOZELLES ALPES-DE-HAUTE-PROVENCE

Moulin de Ventre 4300 ☎ 492786331 ▤ 492798692
In a rural setting with good facilities.
➲ *2.5km E via N100*
Open: 25 Mar-Sep **Site:** 2.8HEC ⏛ ♣ ⊞ ⚠ **Facilities:** ℝ ⅃ ⊙ ⊠ ⊘ ⌂ **Services:** ⚊ ✗ ⊞ lau **Leisure:** ⚘ P

NYONS DRÔME

CM Promenade de la Digue, 26110 ☎ 475262239
Situated on bank of river on level meadow with fruit trees. Sports ground and golf course in town.
Open: 15 Mar-7 Nov **Site:** 1.6HEC ⏛ ♣ **Facilities:** ℝ ⊙ ⊠ ⌂ **Services:** ⊞ lau **Off-site:** ⅃ ⚊ ✗ ⊘ ⸬ ⚘PR

Sagittaire Vinsobres, 26110 ☎ 475270000 ▤ 475270039
e-mail: camping.sagittaire@wanadoo.fr
website: www.le-sagittaire.com
Well-kept site divided by hedges in a beautiful Alpine setting.
➲ *S of town on D538 road to Vaison-la-Romaine.*
Open: All year **Site:** 14HEC ⏛ ⚘ ⊞ **Prices:** ⚊5.50 pitch 25 (incl 3 persons) **Facilities:** ℝ ⅃ ⊙ ⊠ ⊘ ⌂ **Services:** ⚊ ✗ ⊞ lau **Leisure:** ⚘ LP **Off-site:** ⚘R

OLLIÈRES-SUR-EYRIEUX, LES ARDÈCHE

⚑Domaine des Plantas 07360 ☎ 475662153 ▤ 475662365
e-mail: plantas.ardeche@wanadoo.fr
website: www.domainedesplantas.com
Games room, discotheque and other leisure activities.
Open: 8 May-18 Sep **Site:** 10IIEC ⏛ ◊ ♣ ⊞ **Prices:** ⚊4-7 pitch 18-28 (incl 2 persons) **Facilities:** ℝ ⅃ ⊙ ⊠ ⊘ ⸬ ⌂ **Services:** ⚊ ✗ ⊞ lau **Leisure:** ⚘ PR

CAMPING CLUB HOLIDAY MARINA

A bientôt

Site: 6HEC-Site size ⏛-grass ⸬-sand ◊-stone ⚘-little shade ⚘-partly shaded ♣-mainly shaded
⊞-bungalows for hire ⊞-caravans for hire ⚠-tents for hire ⊗-no dogs **Prices:** ⚊-adult per night ⚊-car per night
pp-per person per night ⊞-caravan per night ⚠-tent per night

ORANGE VAUCLUSE

Jonquier 1321 r Alexis-Carrel, 84100
☎ 490344948 ▤ 490511697
e-mail: joel.denis@wailea9.com
website: avignon-et-provence.com/le-jonquier
➪ *On the NW outskirts*
Open: Apr-Sep Site: 2HEC ⸗ ⚐ ☎ Prices: pitch 16.80-
21.40 (incl 2 persons) Facilities: ⋔ ⚍ ⊙ ⚑ ∅ ☎ Services: ✗
⊞ lau Leisure: ⸙ P Off-site: ⸙R

PALAVAS-LES-FLOTS HÉRAULT

Roquilles 267 bis av St-Maurice, 34250 ☎ 467680347
An attractive site 50mtrs from the sea.
Open: 15 Apr-25 Sep Site: 15HEC ⸗ ⸽⸽⸽ ⚡ ⚐ ☎ ⚑ ⫽
Facilities: ⋔ ⚍ ⊙ ⚑ ∅ ☎ Services: ⵖ ✗ ⊞ lau Leisure: ⸙ P
Off-site: ✗ ⸙S

PEYREMALE-SUR-CÈZE GARD

Drouilhèdes 30160 ☎ 466250480 ▤ 466251095
In a beautiful location beside the River Cèze surrounded by
pine and chestnut trees.
➪ *Access via A6 and D17.*
Open: Mar-Sep Site: 2HEC ⸗ ⚐ ☎ Facilities: ⋔ ⚍ ⊙ ⚑ ∅
☎ Services: ⵖ ✗ ⊞ lau Leisure: ⸙ R Off-site: ⸸

PEYRUIS ALPES-DE-HAUTE-PROVENCE

Cigales chemin de la Digue du Bevon, 04310
☎ 492681604 ▤ 492681604
website: www.lescigales.ifrance.com
A modern site in the heart of the Val de Durance.
➪ *Access via A51 and N96.*
Open: Apr-Sep Site: 1HEC ⸗ ⚐ Prices: ⸙3.75 pitch 3.75
Facilities: ⋔ ⊙ ⚑ ⸸ ☎ Services: lau Off-site: ⚍ ⵖ ✗ ⸙P ⊞

PONT-D'HÉRAULT GARD

Magnanarelles Le Rey, 30570 ☎ 467824013 ▤ 467825061
e-mail: info@maxfrance.fr website: www.maxfrance.fr
In a pleasant mountain setting with well defined pitches.
➪ *0.3km W via D999, beside the river.*
Open: All year Site: 2HEC ⸗ ⚐ ☎ ⚑ Prices: ⸙3.20 ⚑5.35
pitch 3.25 Facilities: ⋔ ⚍ ⊙ ⚑ ∅ ⸸ ☎ Services: ✗ ⊞ lau
Leisure: ⸙ PR

PONT-DU-GARD GARD

International des Gorges du Gardon rte de Uzès, 30210
☎ 466228181 ▤ 466229012
e-mail: camping.international@wanadoo.fr
website: www.le-camping-international.com
In a peaceful, wooded location beside the River Gardon.
➪ *1km from aqueduct on D981 Uzès road.*
Open: 15 Mar-30 Oct Site: 4.2HEC ⸗ ⸽⸽⸽ ⚐ ☎ ⚑
Facilities: ⋔ ⚍ ⊙ ⚑ ∅ ☎ Services: ⵖ ✗ ⊞ lau Leisure: ⸙ PR

PORT-GRIMAUD VAR

Club Holiday Marina RN 98 Le Ginestel, 83310
☎ 494560843 ▤ 494562388
e-mail: info@holiday-marina.com
Located close to beaches with diving tuition available.
➪ *on N98*
Open: Mar-Dec Site: 3.5HEC ⸗ ⚐ ⚑ Facilities: ⋔ ⚍ ⊙
⚑ ☎ Services: ⵖ ✗ lau Leisure: ⸙ PRS

Domaine des Naiades St-Pons-les-Mûres ☎ 94563008
Site on hilly land with terraces divided into pitches and with
many modern facilities.

Hôtel de plein air ★★★★
Golfe de Saint Tropez

DOMAINE
DES NAÏADES

Open from
27/03/2004 till
31/10/2004
Rental of
bungalows

Domaine des
Naïades • Saint
Pons les Mûres
83310 Grimaud

www.lesnaiades.com

GRIMAUD
Le Coeur du Golfe

Tel : + 33 (0)4 94 55 67 80
Fax : + 33 (0)4 94 55 67 81

➪ *Access via N98 and D244, then turn right and continue
uphill.*
Open: 5 Apr-2 Nov Site: 12HEC ⸗ ⚐ ☎ ⚑ Prices: pitch
25-41 (incl 3 persons) Facilities: ⋔ ⚍ ⊙ ⚑ ☎ Services: ⵖ ✗
⊞ lau Leisure: ⸙ P Off-site: ✗

Plage RN 98, 83310 ☎ 494563115 ▤ 494564961
e-mail: campingplagegrimaud@wanadoo.fr
website: www.camping-de-la-plage.net
Wide area of land on both sides of road beside sea. Partly
terraced and divided into pitches.
➪ *N on N98.*
Open: 4 Apr-26 Oct Site: 18HEC ⸗ ⸽⸽⸽ ⚐ Prices: pitch 19
(incl 2 persons) Facilities: ⋔ ⚍ ⊙ ⚑ ∅ ⸸ ☎ Services: ⵖ ✗ ⊞
lau Leisure: ⸙ S

PORTIRAGNES-PLAGE HÉRAULT

Mimosas 34420 ☎ 467909292 ▤ 467908539
e-mail: les.mimosas.portirgnes@wanadoo.fr
website: www.mimosas.com
A well equipped family site located in a leisure park on the
banks of the Canal du Midi, 1.3km from the sea.
➪ *Leave A9 at exit Béziers Est and continue towards coast via
N112 and D37.*
Open: May-15 Sep Site: 7HEC ⸗ ⚐ ☎ ⚑ ⋏ Prices: pitch
21-28 (incl 2 persons) pp4.50-7 Facilities: ⋔ ⚍ ⊙ ⚑ ∅ ⸸ ☎
Services: ⵖ ✗ ⊞ lau Leisure: ⸙ PR Off-site: ⸙S

Sablons rte de Portiragnes, 34420
☎ 467909055 ▤ 467908291
e-mail: les.sablons@wanadoo.fr. website: les-sablons.com
Large site subdivided into fields by fences. Beside beach.
Night club and discothèque.
➪ *0.5km N on D37.*
Open: Apr-Sep Site: 15HEC ⸗ ⸽⸽⸽ ⚐ ☎ Facilities: ⋔ ⚍ ⊙
⚑ ∅ ⸸ ☎ Services: ⵖ ✗ ⊞ lau Leisure: ⸙ PS

PRADET, LE VAR

Mauvallon chemin de la Gavaresse, 83220 ☎ 494213173
A well-kept site amidst young trees divided into pitches.
➪ *Turn off the N559 in Le Pradet and take the D86 for 2.5km
towards sea.*
Open: 15 Jun-15 Sep Site: 1.2HEC ⸗ ⚐ Prices: ⸙3.35 pitch
4.60 Facilities: ⋔ ⊙ ⚑ ∅ ☎ Services: ⊞ lau Off-site: ⚍ ⵖ ✗ ⸙S

PRAMOUSQUIER VAR

Pramousquier 83980 ☎ 494058395
A terraced site set in a wooded park 400mtrs from a fine
sandy beach. Good recreational facilities.
➪ *2km E via D559*
Open: May-Sep Site: 3HEC ⚐ ☎ Facilities: ⋔ ⚍ ⊙ ⚑ ∅ ☎
Services: ⵖ ✗ ⊞ lau Off-site: ⸙S

Facilities: ⚍-shop ⋔-shower ⊙-electric points for razors ⚑-electric points for caravans ☎-parking by tents permitted
⊞-compulsory separate car park Services: ✗-café/restaurant ⵖ-bar ∅-Camping Gaz International ⸸-gas other than Camping
Gaz ⊞-first aid facilities lau-laundry Leisure: ⸙-swimming L-Lake P-Pool R-River S-Sea Off-site: All facilities within 2km

PRIVAS ARDÈCHE

Ardeche rte de Montélimar, 07000
☎ 475640580 ▤ 475645968
e-mail: jcray@wanadoo.fr website: www.ardechecamping.fr
A comfortable municipal site with good facilities in the heart
of the Ardèche region.
Open: Apr-mid-Oct Site: 3.5HEC ﹏ ♣ ⊞ ▲ Prices: pitch
9-14 (incl 2 persons) Facilities: ⋔ ⊙ ☑ ☎ Services: ♀ lau
Leisure: ⇗ R Off-site: ☎ ♀ ✗ ⌀ ﹏ ⇗P ⊞

PUGET-SUR-ARGENS VAR

Aubrèdes 408 chemin des Aubrédes, 83480
☎ 494455146 ▤ 494452892
e-mail: campingaubredes@wanadoo.fr
website: campingaubredes.com
Situated on undulating meadowland surrounded by pine
trees with good, modern facilities.

↪ Leave autoroute A8 at exit Puget-sur-Argens, then site is
850mtrs. If approaching from Fréjus on N7 turn left before
Puget, cross motorway and follow road towards Lagourin.
Open: 01May-15 Sep Site: 3.8HEC ﹏ ♣ ⊞ Prices: ♠3.50-5
🚗2.57-3.67 🚐2.57-3.67 pitch 2.57-3.67 Facilities: ⋔ ☎ ⊙ ☑
⌀ ﹏ ☎ Services: ♀ ✗ ⊞ lau Leisure: ⇗ P

Bastiane 1056, chemin des Suvières, 83480
☎ 494455131 ▤ 494815055
e-mail: info@labastiane.com website: www.labastiane.com
Hilly site divided into numbered pitches in pine and oak
wood. Individual washing cubicles. Meals to take away.
Separate car park for arrivals after 23.00hrs.
↪ Access from A8.
Open: 8 Mar-25 Oct Site: 3.1HEC ﹏ ∷ ♣ ⊞ 🚐
Facilities: ⋔ ☎ ⊙ ☑ ☎ Services: ♀ ✗ ⊞ lau Leisure: ⇗ P
Off-site: ﹏ ⇗L

Parc St-James Oasis rte de la Bouverie, 83480
☎ 494454464 ▤ 494454499
Open: 27 Mar-25 Sep Site: 42HEC ﹏ ⊕ ⊞ Facilities: ⋔ ☎
⊙ ☑ Services: ♀ ✗ Leisure: ⇗ P

QUILLAN AUDE

Sapinette 21r René Delpech, 11500
☎ 468201352 ▤ 468202780
A comfortable site in a forest of fir trees with pitches
separated by hedges.
↪ Access W via D79, rte de Ginoles.
Open: Apr-Oct Site: 1.8HEC ﹏ ⊕ ⊞ Prices: ♠3.10-3.40
pitch 3.10-3.40 Facilities: ⋔ ⊙ ☑ ☎ Services: ⊞ lau
Off-site: ☎ ♀ ✗ ⌀ ﹏ ⇗LPRS

Site: 6HEC-Site size ﹏-grass ∷-sand ◢-stone ✹-little shade ⊕-partly shaded ♣-mainly shaded
⊞-bungalows for hire 🚐-caravans for hire ▲-tents for hire ⊘-no dogs Prices: ♠-adult per night 🚗-car per night
pp-per person per night 🚐-caravan per night ▲-tent per night

RACOU, LE PYRÉNÉES-ORIENTALES

Bois de Valmarie 66 ☎ 468810992 ▤ 468958058
e-mail: contact@camping-lasirene.fr
website: www.camping-lasirene.fr
A family site with plentiful recreational facilities.
➲ *Leave N114 at at Perpignan Sud exit.*
Open: 9 Apr-25 Sep Site: 7HEC ⬛ ⌖ Facilities: ⌂ ⬛ ⊙ ⬛
⌀ ⬛ Services: ⬛ ✕ ⊞ lau Leisure: ⬚ PS Off-site: ⬛

RAMATUELLE VAR

Cigale rte de L' Escalet, 83350 ☎ 494792253 ▤ 494791205
Site 800 metres from beach. *Off A8, exit Le Luc*
Open: 20 Mar-15 Oct Site: 1.5HEC ⬛ ⌖ ⬛ ▲ Prices: pitch
15-32 (incl 2 persons) Facilities: ⌂ ⬛ ⊙ ⬛ ⬛ ⬛ Services: ⬛
✕ ⊞ Leisure: ⬚ P Off-site: ⬚S

Tournels rte de Camarat, 83350 ☎ 494559090 ▤ 494559099
e-mail: info@tournels.com website: www.tournels.com
Lovely views to Pampelonne Bay from part of this site. 1km
to beach.
➲ *Access from D93 Croix-Valmer/St-Tropez road, follow the
signs to 'Cap Camarat'.*
Open: Mar-10 Jan Site: 20HEC ⬛ ⬛ ⬛ Prices: ⬛22.50-31
▲19.50-31 Facilities: ⌂ ⊙ ⬛ ⌀ ⬛ Services: ⬛ ✕ ⊞ lau
Off-site: ⬛ ⬚S

REMOULINS GARD

Soubeyranne rte de Beaucaire, 30210
☎ 466370321 ▤ 466371465
e-mail: soubeyranne@wanadoo.fr
website: www.soubeyranne.com
In a picturesque location close to the river Gard with good,
modern facilities.

➲ *S on D986.*
Open: 3 Apr-13 Sep Site: 6HEC ⸬ ⌖ ⬛ Prices: ▲12-22
Facilities: ⌂ ⬛ ⊙ ⬛ ⌀ ⬛ ⬛ Services: ⬛ ✕ ⊞ lau Leisure: ⬚
P Off-site: ⬚R

Sousta av du Pont-du-Gard, 30210
☎ 466371280 ▤ 466372369
e-mail: info@lasousta.fr website: www.lasousta.com
Picturesque forest site close to the Pont du Gard.
➲ *2km NW. From A9 exit for Remoulins, turn right after
bridge towards Pont de Gard.*
Open: Mar-Oct Site: 14HEC ⸬ ⬛ ⬛ ⬛ Prices: pitch 11-
21 (incl 2 persons) Facilities: ⌂ ⬛ ⊙ ⬛ ⌀ ⬛ Services: ⬛ ✕
⊞ lau Leisure: ⬚ PR

REVENS GARD

Lou Triadou Le Bourg, 30750 ☎ 467827358
e-mail: lou.triadou@wanadoo.fr
A well equipped site in the heart of the Causse Noir.
➲ *Access via D159/D151.*
Open: 20 Jun-1Sep Site: 0.8HEC ⬛ ⬚ ⬛ ▲ Prices: ▲3
pitch 4 Facilities: ⌂ ⊙ ⬛ ⌀ ⬛ ⬛ Services: ⬛ ✕ ⊞ lau

RIA PYRÉNÉES-ORIENTALES

Bellevue 8 r Bellevue, 66500 ☎ 468964896
Beautifully situated terraced site. Very well kept. Beside
former vineyard.
➲ *2km S on N116, take road to Sirach, turn right and
continue 600mtrs up drive which is difficult for caravans.*
Open: Apr-Sep Site: 2.2HEC ⬛ ⬛ ⬛ ⬛ Prices: ▲2.80
pitch 3.38 Facilities: ⌂ ⊙ ⬛ ⌀ ⬛ Services: ⊞ lau
Off-site: ⬛ ✕ ⬛ ⬚R

Leï SuveS
CAMPING CARAVANING
★★★★

In the middle of nature,
20 minutes from the
beaches of Fréjus
and Saint Raphaël

Quartier du Blavet
83520 ROQUEBRUNE sur Argens
Tel. (33) 04 94 45 43 95 • Fax. (33) 04 94 81 63 13
• www.camping-lei-suves.com

Roquebrune sur Argens . PROVENCE

Facilities: ⬛-shop ⌂-shower ⊙-electric points for razors ⬛-electric points for caravans ⬛-parking by tents permitted
⬛-compulsory separate car park **Services:** ✕-café/restaurant ⬛-bar ⌀-Camping Gaz International ⬛-gas other than Camping
Gaz ⊞-first aid facilities lau-laundry **Leisure:** ⬚-swimming L-Lake P-Pool R-River S-Sea **Off-site:** All facilities within 2km

ROQUEBRUNE-SUR-ARGENS VAR

Domaine de la Bergerie Valleé du Fournel, 83520
☎ 498114545 ▤ 498114546
e-mail: info@domainelabergerie.com
website: www.domainelabergerie.com
A large, well run family site set in pleasant Provençal countryside with fine recreational facilities.
➲ Access via A8 exit Le Muy N7 and D7.
Open: Jun-15 Sep Site: 60HEC ⬛⬛⬛ ♣ 🏠 🚐 Prices: pitch 16-26.50 (incl 2 persons) Facilities: 🏕 🔋 ⊙ 🚽 ⊘ ⌕ 🖻 Services: 🍴 ✕ 🔲 lau Leisure: ⬟ LP

Domaine J J Bousquet rte de la Bouverie, 83520
☎ 494454251 ▤ 494816106
In a quiet, wooded location with good, modern facilities.
➲ Access via N7 towards Le Muy.
Open: All year Site: 5HEC ⬛⬛⬛ ⚘ 🏠 Facilities: 🏕 🔋 ⊙ 🚽 ⊘ ⌕ 🖻 Services: 🍴 ✕ 🔲 lau Leisure: ⬟ P

Lei Suves Quartier du Blavet, 83520
☎ 494454395 ▤ 494816313
e-mail: camping.lei.suves@wanadoo.fr
website: www.camping-lei-suves.com
In a picturesque forested area with good recreational facilities.
➲ 4km N via N7.
Open: Apr-15 Oct Site: 7.4HEC ⬛⬛⬛ ♣ 🏠 🚐 Prices: ⚘4.50-6.60 pitch 19.50-30.50 (incl 2 persons) Facilities: 🏕 🔋 ⊙ 🚽 ⊘ ⌕ 🖻 Services: 🍴 ✕ 🔲 lau Leisure: ⬟ P
See advertisement on page 199

Moulin des Iscles Quartier La Valette, 83520
☎ 494457074 ▤ 494454609
e-mail: moulin.iscles@wanadoo.fr
In a picturesque location beside the River Argens with good, modern facilities.
➲ Access via D7 towards St-Aygulf.
Open: Apr-Sep Site: 1.3HEC ⬛⬛⬛ ♣ 🏠 🚐 Prices: ⚘3.20 pitch 18 (incl 3 persons) Facilities: 🏕 🔋 ⊙ 🚽 ⊘ ⌕ 🖻 Services: 🍴 ✕ 🔲 lau Leisure: ⬟ R Off-site: ⬟L

Pêcheurs 83520 ☎ 494457125 ▤ 494816513
e-mail: info@camping-les-pecheurs.com
website: www.camping-les-pecheurs.com
A pleasant site with direct access to the river in a wooded location at the foot of the Roquebrune crag.
➲ 0.5km NW via D7, near the lake
Open: Apr-15 Oct Site: 5HEC ⬛⬛⬛ ♣ 🚐 Prices: ⚘4-6 pitch 18-31 (incl 2 persons) Facilities: 🏕 🔋 ⊙ 🚽 ⊘ ⌕ 🖻 Services: 🍴 ✕ 🔲 lau Leisure: ⬟ LPR

ROQUE-D'ANTHÉRON, LA BOUCHES-DU-RHÔNE

Domaine les Iscles 13640 ☎ 442504425 ▤ 442505629
e-mail: campoclub@wanadoo.fr
➲ 1.8km N via D67c.
Open: Mar-15 Oct Site: 10HEC ⬛⬛⬛ ⚘ 🏠 Prices: ⚘3.60-5.50 ⚘2.40-5 pitch 4.30-14 Facilities: 🏕 🔋 ⊙ 🚽 ⊘ ⌕ 🖻 Services: 🍴 ✕ 🔲 lau Leisure: ⬟ LPR

Silvacane av de la Libération, 13640
☎ 442504054 ▤ 442504375
e-mail: campoclub@wanadoo.fr
Level gravelled ground with 100 sq m pitches. Heated common room with TV. Water sports centre and stables nearby. Site in wood on slopes of hill.
Open: Apr-15 Sep Site: 6HEC ⬛⬛⬛ ♣ 🏠 Prices: ⚘3.20-4.50 pitch 8-13 Facilities: 🏕 🔋 ⊙ 🚽 ⊘ ⌕ 🖻 Services: 🍴 ✕ 🔲 lau Leisure: ⬟ PR Off-site: ⬟LR

ROQUETTE-SUR-SIAGNE, LA ALPES-MARITIMES

Panoramic 1630 av de la République, Quartier St-Jean, 06550
☎ 492190777 ▤ 492190777
e-mail: campingpanoramic@wanadoo.fr
website: www.campingpanoramic.fr
A well equipped, modern site in a wooded location affording magnificent views of the surrounding hills.
➲ N of village off D9.
Open: All year Site: 1HEC ⬛⬛⬛ ♣ 🏠 🚐 ⚘ Prices: ⚘3.50 ⚘⚘1.50 pitch 12.50-14 (incl 1 persons) Facilities: 🏕 ⊙ 🚽 ⊘ ⌕ 🖻 Services: 🍴 ✕ 🔲 lau Leisure: ⬟ P Off-site: 🔋 ⬟R

St-Louis av de la République, 6550
☎ 492192313 ▤ 492192314
Well equipped site in a pleasant rural setting, backed by hills.
➲ On D9, 800mtrs from Pégomas towards La Bocca.
Open: Apr-1 Oct Site: 5HEC ⬛⬛⬛ ♣ 🏠 Facilities: 🏕 ⊙ 🚽 ⊘ 🖻 Services: 🔲 lau Leisure: ⬟ P Off-site: 🔋 🍴 ✕ ⊘ ⬟R ⬟

RUOMS ARDÈCHE

⬛Bastide 7120 ☎ 475396472 ▤ 475397328
e-mail: camping.bastide@wanadoo.fr
website: www.camping-la-bastide.fr
Well equipped family site in a pleasant wooded location.
➲ 4km SW on the banks of the Ardèche.
Open: Apr-14 Sep Site: 7HEC ⬛⬛⬛ ♣ 🏠 🚐 ⚘ Facilities: 🏕 🔋 ⊙ 🚽 ⊘ ⌕ 🖻 Services: 🍴 ✕ 🔲 lau Leisure: ⬟ PR

Ternis rte de Lagorce, 07120 ☎ 475939315 ▤ 475939090
e-mail: campternis@aol.com
website: www.camping.leternis.com
A terraced site in a delightful setting in the southern Ardèche region, with good recreational facilities. Separate car park for arrivals between 22.00 and 08.00hrs.
➲ Access via D559 towards Lagorce.
Site: 6HEC ⬛⬛⬛ ♣ 🏠 🚐 Facilities: 🏕 🔋 ⊙ 🚽 ⊘ ⌕ 🖻 🖻 Services: 🍴 ✕ 🔲 lau Leisure: ⬟ P Off-site: ⬟R

AT SAMPZON (6KM S)

Aloha-Plage 07120 ☎ 608988503 ▤ 475891026
e-mail: reception@camping-aloha-plage.fr
website: www.camping-aloha-plage.fr
In a fine situation beside the River Ardèche, midway between Ruoms and Vallon-Pont-d'Arc. The site now has two private swimming pools.
➲ 50mtrs from the river.
Open: Apr-20 Sep Site: 3HEC ⬛⬛⬛ ♣ 🏠 🚐 Facilities: 🏕 ⊙ 🚽 ⊘ ⌕ 🖻 Services: 🍴 ✕ 🔲 lau Leisure: ⬟ PR Off-site: 🔋

Soleil Vivarais 07120 ☎ 475396756 ▤ 475396469
e-mail: info@soleil.vivarais.com
website: www.camping-soleil-vivarais.com
An exceptionally well appointed, terraced site surrounded by the imposing scenery of the Ardèche Gorge. An excellent canoeing centre with opportunities for all kinds of outdoor/water activities and regular organised entertainment.
➲ From Vallon drive towards Ruoms on D579 for 5km and cross bridge over River Ardèche.
Open: 8 Apr-19 Sep Site: 14HEC ⬛⬛⬛ ♣ 🏠 Prices: ⚘4.50-7.50 pitch 15-38 (incl 2 persons) Facilities: 🏕 🔋 ⊙ 🚽 ⊘ 🖻 Services: 🍴 ✕ 🔲 lau Leisure: ⬟ PR Off-site: ⬟S

SAILLAGOUSE PYRÉNÉES-ORIENTALES

Cerdan 11 Route d'Estavar, 66800
☎ 468047046 ▤ 468040526
e-mail: lecerdan@lecerdan.com
website: www.lecerdan.com
Picturesque setting in meadow with some terraces. Hot meals served during peak season.
➲ Access via N116.

Open: All year Site: 0.8HEC 🏕 🔄 🏠 Prices: 🗪11.50
▲11.50 Facilities: 🌳 ⊙ 🖾 🚿 🅿 🄿 Services: lau
Off-site: 🛒 🍷 ✗ 🥘 ⁀PR 🚑

ST-ALBAN-AURIOLLES ARDÈCHE

Ranc Davaine 07120 ☎ 475396055 📠 475393850
e-mail: camping.ranc.davaine@wanadoo.fr
Well equipped, mainly level site with direct access to the
River Chassezac and a variety of entertainment facilities.
➲ 2.3km SW via D58.
Open: 3 Apr-26 Sep Site: 13HEC 🏕 ⠶ 🌢 🏠 🗪
Prices: 🅰6-9 pitch 20-34 (incl 2 persons) Facilities: 🌳 🛒 ⊙ 🗪
🥘 🄿 Services: 🍷 ✗ 🄴 lau Leisure: ⁀ PR

ST-AMBROIX GARD

Beau-Rivage Le Moulinet, 30500
☎ 466241017 📠 466242137
e-mail: mare@camping-beau-rivage.fr
website: www.camping-beau-rivage.fr
In a fine location between the sea and the Cevennes
mountains beside the River Cèze.
➲ 3.5km SE on D37.
Open: Apr-Sep Site: 3.5HEC 🏕 🌢 Prices: 🅰5 pitch 4-5
Facilities: 🌳 ⊙ 🗪 🥘 🄿 Services: 🄴 lau Leisure: ⁀ R
Off-site: 🛒 🍷

Clos 30500 ☎ 466241008 📠 466602562
A quiet site in a pleasant setting beside the River Cèze with
good, modern facilities.
➲ Access to the right of the church square.
Open: Apr-Oct Site: 1.8HEC 🏕 🌢 🏠 🗪 Facilities: 🌳 ⊙ 🗪
🥘 🚿 🄿 Services: 🍷 ✗ 🄴 lau Leisure: ⁀ PR Off-site: 🛒

ST-ANDIOL BOUCHES-DU-RHÔNE

St-Andiol 13670 ☎ 490950113
Well situated on the edge of the village. Divided into pitches.
➲ Access via A7.
Open: All year Site: 1HEC 🏕 🌢 Prices: 🗪16 pitch 13 (incl
2 persons) Facilities: 🌳 ⊙ 🗪 🄿 Services: 🍷 🄴 lau Leisure: ⁀
P Off-site: 🛒 ✗

ST-AYGULF VAR

Étoile d'Argens chemin des Étangs, 83370
☎ 494810141 📠 494812145
e-mail: letoiledargent@wanadoo.fr
website: www.provence-camping.com
In pleasant wooded surroundings 2km from the beach which
can be reached by a private boat service.
➲ 5km NW, beside the River Argens.
Open: Apr-Sep Site: 11HEC 🏕 🌢 🗪 Prices: pitch 15-50
(incl 2 persons) Facilities: 🌳 🛒 ⊙ 🗪 🥘 🚿 🄿 Services: 🍷 ✗ 🄴
lau Leisure: ⁀ PR Off-site: ⁀L

Paradis des Campeurs La Gaillarde Plage, 83380
☎ 494969355 📠 494496299
website: www.paradis-des-campeurs.com
A quiet family site in a picturesque location with direct
access to the beach.
➲ 2.5km towards Gaillarde-Plage between St-Aygulf and Ste-
Maxime.
Open: 19 Mar-15 Oct Site: 3.7HEC 🏕 🌢 🏠 Facilities: 🌳
🛒 ⊙ 🗪 🥘 🄿 Services: 🍷 ✗ 🄴 lau Leisure: ⁀ S

Pont d'Argens RN98, 83370 ☎ 494511497 📠 494512944
website: www.provence-campings.com/adherents/esterel/
pontargens
A pleasant site with good facilities beside the river.
Open: Apr-15 Oct Site: 7HEC 🏕 🔄 🏠 🗪 Prices: 🅰5-7 🚗2
pitch 13.50-23 Facilities: 🌳 🛒 ⊙ 🗪 🥘 🚿 🄿 Services: 🍷 ✗ 🄴
lau Leisure: ⁀ PRS

Ideally located in the heart of the Côte d'Azur,
exceptional site with friendly atmosphere on the
banks of the Argens river with direct access to the
fine sandy beaches (there is one for naturists). Bar,
restaurant, take away food, swimming-pool which is
heated in cool weather.
Entertainment: discotheque, giant barbecues,
cabarets, concerts, excursions and a miniclub for
children.
Mobile home and caravans available for hire.
Open from 1 April to 15 October.
Camping Caravanning Le Pont d'Argens
RN 98 Fréjus Saint Aygulf – FRANCE
Tél: 04 94 51 14 97 – Fax: 04 94 51 29 44

St-Aygulf 270 av Salvarelli, 83370
☎ 494176249 📠 494810316
e-mail: info@camping-cote-azur.com
A well equipped family site in wooded surroundings with
direct access to the beach.
➲ Inland from N98 at Km881.3 N of town. Entrance on right
of av Salvarelli.
Open: Apr-Oct Site: 22HEC 🏕 ⠶ 🌢 🏠 Facilities: 🌳 🛒 ⊙
🗪 🥘 🚿 🄿 Services: 🍷 ✗ 🄴 lau Leisure: ⁀ S

ST-CHAMAS BOUCHES-DU-RHÔNE

Canet Plage 13250 ☎ 490509689 📠 490509689
e-mail: canet-plage@wanadoo.fr
website: perso.wanadoo.fr/canet-plage/
A well equipped site beside the Étang de Berre with a wide
range of recreational facilities.
➲ On D10, S of Salon-de-Provence towards La Fare les
Oliviers.
Open: All year Site: 3HEC 🔄 🌢 🏠 🗪 Facilities: 🌳 🛒 ⊙ 🗪 🚿
🄿 Services: 🍷 ✗ 🄴 lau Leisure: ⁀ LP Off-site: 🥘

ST-CYPRIEN PYRÉNÉES-ORIENTALES

Roussillon chemin de la Mer, 66750
☎ 468216605 📠 0468210645
e-mail: chadotel@wanadoo.fr
Close to the Spanish border, flanked on one side by the
Mediterranean sea and on the other by the Pyrenees.
Open: Etr-Sep Site: 3HEC 🏕 🔄 🏠 🗪 Facilities: 🌳 🛒 ⊙ 🗪
🥘 🚿 🄿 Services: 🍷 ✗ 🄴 lau Leisure: ⁀ P Off-site: ✗ ⁀S

ST-CYR-SUR-MER VAR

Clos Ste-Thérèse rte de Bandol, 83270 ☎ 494321221
e-mail: camping@clos-therese.com
website: www.clos-therese.com
Located in the heart of the Bandol vinefields overlooking the
sea. A well shaded family camp site with well defined pitches
on terraces.
Open: Apr-Sep Site: 4HEC 🔄 🌢 🏠 Prices: 🅰3-4.40 🚗1.60-
2.90 🗪12.30-18 ▲1.50-1.90 pitch 11.80-17 (incl 2 persons)
Facilities: 🌳 🛒 ⊙ 🗪 🥘 🚿 🄿 Services: 🍷 ✗ 🄴 lau Leisure: ⁀ P
Off-site: 🥘

ST-JEAN-LE-CENTENIER ARDÈCHE

Arches Patrick Gaschet, 07580
☎ 475367545 📠 475367545
website: www.campinglesarches.htm
A family site in a wooded location with direct access to the
river.

contd.

Facilities: 🛒-shop 🌳-shower ⊙-electric points for razors 🗪-electric points for caravans 🄿-parking by tents permitted
🄿-compulsory separate car park Services: ✗-café/restaurant 🍷-bar 🥘-Camping Gaz International 🚿-gas other than Camping
Gaz 🄴-first aid facilities lau-laundry Leisure: ⁀-swimming L-Lake P-Pool R-River S-Sea Off-site: All facilities within 2km

CAMPING MONPLAISIR ★★
Chemin Monplaisir
13210 SAINT RÉMY DE PROVENCE
Tel: 00 33 (0)4 90 92 22 70
Fax: 00 33 (0)4 90 92 18 57
In beautiful surroundings, only 1km from the village centre.
Peaceful and green setting, in the countryside.
★ Marked and shady pitches.
★ Heated sanitary blocks in half season.
★ Launderette, snacks in season.
★ Groceries, drinks, swimming pool, French Boules,
table tennis.

➲ *A7 exit Montélimar Nord then follow N102 to exit Mirabel and take D458 for 500mtrs to site on right.*
Open: Etr-Sep **Site:** 1.8HEC ⊞ 🖩 Ⓐ 🏕 🚐 **Prices:** ⚡3 🚗2-3 🚐1-2 🏕1-2 pitch 2-3 pp1.20-2 **Facilities:** 🏪 ⊙ 🖳 🏤 **Services:** ⛴ ✗ lau **Leisure:** ⚓ R **Off-site:** 🏊 ✗ 🛆

ST-JEAN-PLA-DE-CORTS PYRÉNÉES-ORIENTALES

Casteillets 66490 ☎ 468832683 🗎 468833967
e-mail: je@campinglescasteillets.com
website: campinglescasteillets.com
A family site situated between the sea and the mountains close to the River Tech.
➲ *Access via A9 exit Le Boulu.*
Open: All year **Site:** 5HEC ⊞ Ⓐ 🏕 Ⓐ **Prices:** ⚡2.50-4 pitch 10-15 (incl 2 persons) **Facilities:** 🏪 🖳 ⊙ 🖳 🛆 🏤 **Services:** ⛴ ✗ 🖩 lau **Leisure:** ⚓ P **Off-site:** 🗗 ⚓LR

Deux Rivières rte de Maureillas, 66490
☎ 468832320 🗎 468830794
website: www.2rivieres.com
Situated on the banks of the River Tech with large roomy pitches.
➲ *0.5km SE via D13, beside the River Tech*
Open: Apr-15 Oct **Site:** 11HEC ⊞ 🖩 Ⓐ 🏕 🚐 **Facilities:** 🏪 🖳 ⊙ 🖳 🛆 🏤 **Services:** ⛴ ✗ lau **Leisure:** ⚓ PR **Off-site:** ⚓L 🖩

ST-JULIEN-DE-LA-NEF GARD

Isis en Cevennes Domaine de St-Julien, 30440
☎ 467738028 🗎 467738848
e-mail: info@isisencevennes.com
website: www.isisencevennes.com
In wooded surroundings with direct access to the River Hérault. Plenty of sporting facilities.
➲ *5km from Ganges towards Le Vigan.*
Open: 15 Mar-Oct **Site:** 4HEC ⊞ 🖩 Ⓐ 🏕 **Facilities:** 🏪 🖳 ⊙ 🖳 🗗 🛆 🏤 **Services:** ⛴ ✗ 🖩 lau **Leisure:** ⚓ PR

ST-LAURENT-DU-VAR ALPES-MARITIMES

Magali 1814 rte de la Baronne, 06700
☎ 493315700 🗎 492120133
website: www.camping-magali.com
A family site on level meadowland, surrounded by trees and bushes at the foot of the southern Alps.
➲ *Leave A8 at 'St-Laurent-du-Var' exit, cross industrial zone turn left for 100mtrs, then right and continue for 2km.*
Open: Feb-Oct **Site:** 1.2HEC ⊞ 🖩 Ⓐ 🏕 🚐 **Facilities:** 🏪 🖳 ⊙ 🖳 🗗 🛆 🏤 **Services:** ✗ 🖩 lau **Leisure:** ⚓ P **Off-site:** ⛴ ✗

ST-LAURENT-DU-VERDON ALPES-DE-HAUTE-PROVENCE

Farigoulette Lac de St Laurent, 4500
☎ 492744162 🗎 492740086
website: www.camping-la-farigoulette.com
➲ *1.5km NE near Verdon*
Open: 15 May-Sep **Site:** 14HEC ⊞ 🖩 ⧆ 🏕 🚐 **Facilities:** 🏪 🖳 ⊙ 🖳 🗗 🛆 🏤 **Services:** ⛴ ✗ 🖩 lau **Leisure:** ⚓ LP **Off-site:** ⚓S

ST-MAXIMIN-LA-STE-BAUME VAR

Provençal rte de Mazaugues, 83470
☎ 494781697 🗎 494780021
e-mail: camping.provencal@wanadoo.fr
A family site in wooded surroundings with plenty of recreational facilities. Bar, café and swimming pool are open Jul-Aug only.
➲ *2.5km S via D64.*
Open: All year **Site:** 5HEC ⊞ 🖩 🏕 🚐 **Facilities:** 🏪 🖳 ⊙ 🖳 🗗 🛆 🏤 **Services:** ⛴ ✗ 🖩 lau **Leisure:** ⚓ P **Off-site:** 🖩

ST-PAUL-EN-FORÊT VAR

Parc 83440 ☎ 494761535 🗎 494847184
e-mail: campingleparc@wanadoo.fr
website: www.campingleparc.com
Quiet, fairly isolated site surrounded by woodland.
➲ *3km N on D4.*
Open: Mar-Sept **Site:** 5HEC ⊞ 🖩 🏕 🚐 Ⓐ **Prices:** pitch 10-17.50 (incl 2 persons) **Facilities:** 🏪 🖳 ⊙ 🖳 🗗 🛆 🏤 🖩 **Services:** ⛴ ✗ 🖩 lau **Leisure:** ⚓ P

ST-PAUL-LES-ROMANS DRÔME

CM de Romans Les Chasses, 26100 ☎ 475723527
Shady pitches separated by hedges.
Open: May-Sep **Site:** 1HEC ⊞ 🖩 🏕 **Facilities:** 🏪 ⊙ 🖳 🗗 🏤 **Services:** 🖩 lau **Off-site:** 🏊 ⛴ ✗ 🗗 🛆 ⚓P

ST-RAPHAËL VAR

Douce Quiétude bd J-Baudino, 83700
☎ 494443000 🗎 494443030
e-mail: sunelia@douce-quietude.com
website: www.douce-quietude.com
Meadowland site in quiet location in attractively hilly countryside with good facilities.
➲ *Approach from Agay Plage past Esterel Camping in direction of Valescure.*
Open: Apr-Sep **Site:** 10HEC ⊞ 🖩 🏕 🚐 **Facilities:** 🏪 🖳 ⊙ 🖳 🗗 🛆 🏤 **Services:** ⛴ ✗ 🖩 lau **Leisure:** ⚓ P

Dramont 83700 ☎ 494820768 🗎 494827530
Located in a pine forest with direct access to the beach and good modern facilities.
➲ *Access via N98 at St-Raphaël. Between Boulouris and Agay.*
Open: 15 Mar-15 Oct **Site:** 6.5HEC ⊞ 🖩 🏕 🚐 **Prices:** pitch 15.50-30 (incl 2 persons) **Facilities:** 🏪 🖳 ⊙ 🖳 🗗 🏤 **Services:** ⛴ ✗ 🖩 lau **Leisure:** ⚓ S

Royal Camp Long, 83530 ☎ 494820020
Level site divided by walls and hedges. Ideal bathing for children. Bar and hall next to site.
➲ *On N98 towards Cannes.*
Open: 20 Jan-30 Oct **Site:** 0.6HEC ⊞ ⧆ 🏕 🚐 **Facilities:** 🏪 🖳 ⊙ 🖳 🗗 🛆 🏤 **Services:** ⛴ ✗ 🖩 lau **Leisure:** ⚓ S **Off-site:** 🏊 🖩

ST-REMÈZE ARDÈCHE

Domaine de Briange rte de Gras, 07700 ☎ 475041443
e-mail: briange07@aol.com
website: members.aol.com/briange07
In a wooded location close to the Gorges de l'Ardèche.
➲ *1.5km NE.*
Open: May-Sep **Site:** 4HEC ⊞ 🖩 🏕 🚐 Ⓐ **Facilities:** 🏪 🖳 ⊙ 🖳 🏤 **Services:** ⛴ ✗ 🖩 lau **Leisure:** ⚓ P **Off-site:** 🗗 🛆

ST-RÉMY-DE-PROVENCE BOUCHES-DU-RHÔNE

Monplaisir chemin Monplaisir, 13210
☎ 490922270 🗎 490921857
Open: Mar-10 Nov **Site:** 2.8HEC ⊞ Ⓐ 🏕 🚐 **Facilities:** 🏪 🖳 ⊙ 🖳 🗗 🏤 **Services:** ⛴ 🖩 lau **Leisure:** ⚓ P

Site: 6HEC-Site size ⊞-grass ⁖⁖-sand ⧆-stone ♨-little shade Ⓐ-partly shaded 🏕-mainly shaded 🏠-bungalows for hire 🚐-caravans for hire 🛆-tents for hire ⊘-no dogs **Prices:** ⚡-adult per night 🚗-car per night pp-per person per night 🚐-caravan per night 🛆-tent per night

Pégomas Av jean Moulin, 13210
☎ 490920121 ▦ 490925617
e-mail: campingpegomas@wanadoo.fr
website: www.campingpegomas.com
Well-tended grassland with trees and bushes. Divided into
several fields by high cedars providing shade.
➲ *500m E of village. Well signposted.*
Open: Mar-Oct Site: 2HEC ⬜⬜ ♠ 🏠 Prices: pitch 9-10.50
Facilities: 🏕 ⊙ 🔌 🖉 🕿 Services: ⽕ ✗ ⊞ lau Leisure: ⚡ P
Off-site: 🔋 ✗ 🛒

ST-ROMAIN-EN-VIENNOIS VAUCLUSE

Soleil de Provence rte de Nyons, 84110
☎ 490464600 ▦ 490464037
e-mail: info@camping-soleil-de-provence.fr
website: www.camping-soleil-de-provence.fr
4kms from Vaison-la-Romaine and 12 kms from the foot of
Mount Ventoux, this peaceful site is located uphill on
meadow with superb views of the surrounding mountains.
Large swimming pool with an island and palm trees.
Open: 15 Mar-30 Oct Site: 5HEC ⬜⬜ 🔌 🏠 Prices: ♠3.50-
5.50 🚐2.50-3 pitch 2.50-3 Facilities: 🏕 🔋 ⊙ 🔌 🖉 🕿
Services: ⽕ ✗ ⊞ lau Leisure: ⚡ P

ST-SAUVEUR-DE-MONTAGUT ARDÈCHE

Ardechois Le Chambon, Gluiras, 07190
☎ 475666187 ▦ 475666367
e-mail: ardechois.camping@wanadoo.fr
website: www.ardechois-camping.fr
In the grounds of a restored 18th-century farm set in rolling
countryside with fine views of the surrounding hills.
➲ *8.5km W on D102, beside the River Gluèyre.*
Open: 18 Apr-Oct Site: 5.5HEC ⬜⬜ 🔌 🏠 Prices: pitch 19-
24 (incl 2 persons) Facilities: 🏕 🔋 ⊙ 🔌 🖉 🕿 Services: ⽕
✗ ⊞ lau Leisure: ⚡ PR

ST-SORLIN-EN-VALLOIRE DRÔME

Château de la Pérouze 26210 ☎ 475317021 ▦ 475316274
e-mail: campingchateaudelaperouz@libertysurf.fr
A well appointed family site with a variety of recreational
facilities.
➲ *2.5km SE via D1.*
Open: 15 Jun-15 Sep Site: 14HEC ⬜⬜ 🔌 🏠 ⚙ Prices: ♠6
🚐6 🚐6 ♠6 Facilities: 🏕 ⊙ 🔌 🖉 🕿 🕿 P Services: ⽕ ✗ ⊞ lau
Leisure: ⚡ LP

ST-THIBÉRY HÉRAULT

Tane Le Causse, 34630 ☎ 467778429
In pleasant wooded surroundings, 1km from the River Hérault.
➲ *Access via A9 exit Agde-Pézenas.*
Open: Jun-Sep Site: 2.4HEC ⬜⬜ 🔌 🏠 ⚙ Facilities: 🏕 ⊙
🕿 Services: ⽕ ✗ lau Leisure: ⚡ P Off-site: 🔋 🖉 🛒 ⚡R ⊞

ST-VALLIER-DE-THIEY ALPES-MARITIMES

Parc des Arboins 755 RN85, 06460
☎ 493426389 ▦ 493096154
e-mail: reception@camping-des-arboins.com
Pleasantly situated terraced site on hillside with some oak trees.
➲ *Entrance at Km V36 on N85.*
Open: All year Site: 4HEC ⬜⬜ ⠿ ♠ 🏠 ⚙ Prices: ♠3.50
🚐8.50-11.50 ♠8.50-10 Facilities: 🏕 ⊙ 🔌 🖉 🕿 Services: ⽕
✗ ⊞ lau Leisure: ⚡ P Off-site: ⚡LRS

STE-MARIE PYRÉNÉES-ORIENTALES
AT TORREILLES (4KM NW ON D11)

Dunes de Torreilles 66440 ☎ 468283829 ▦ 468283257
e-mail: lesdunes@lesdunes.net website: www.lesdunes.net
A well equipped site in wooded surroundings with direct
access to the beach.
➲ *E of the village off D81.*
Open: 15 Mar-15 Oct Site: 16HEC ⠿⠿ ♠ 🔌 🏠 Prices: pitch
12.45-23.95 (incl 2 persons) Facilities: 🏕 🔋 ⊙ 🔌 🛒 🕿
Services: ⽕ ✗ ⊞ lau Leisure: ⚡ PS Off-site: ⚡R

Marisol Plage de Torreilles, 66440
☎ 468280407 ▦ 468281823
e-mail: marisol@camping-marisol.com
website: www.camping-marisol.com
A family site with a wide variety of sports and entertainment
facilities in a pleasant park-like setting 350 metres from the
beach.
➲ *Off D81 towards the sea.*
Open: Apr-15 Oct Site: 9HEC ⬜⬜ ⠿⠿ 🔌 🏠 ⚙ ♠
Facilities: 🏕 🔋 ⊙ 🔌 🖉 🛒 🕿 Services: ⽕ ✗ ⊞ lau Leisure: ⚡
PS Off-site: ⚡R

Trivoly bd des Plages, 66440 ☎ 468282028 ▦ 468281648
e-mail: chadotel@wanadoo.fr
website: camping-chadotel.fr
A modern site with excellent facilities and well defined
pitches, 800mtrs from the beach.
➲ *Access via autoroute exit `Perpignan Nord' towards Le
Barcarès.*
Open: Apr-Sep Site: 4.7HEC ⬜⬜ ♠ 🔌 ⚙ Prices: ♠5.50
pitch 14-22.50 (incl 2 persons) Facilities: 🏕 🔋 ⊙ 🔌 🖉 🛒 🕿
Services: ⽕ ✗ ⊞ lau Leisure: ⚡ P Off-site: ✗ ⚡RS

STES-MARIES-DE-LA-MER BOUCHES-DU-RHÔNE

CM Brise 13460 ☎ 490978467 ▦ 490977201
e-mail: labrise@laposte.net
A well equipped family site with direct access to the beach,
situated in the heart of the Camargue. The sanitary blocks are
modern and there are facilities for a wide variety of sports.
➲ *NE via D85A, towards the beach*
Site: 22HEC ⬜⬜ ⠿⠿ ⠿⠿ 🏠 ♠ Prices: ♠4.10-6.80 pitch
11.20-18.50 (incl 2 persons) Facilities: 🏕 🔋 ⊙ 🔌 🖉 🕿
Services: ⽕ ⊞ lau Leisure: ⚡ P Off-site: ✗ 🛒 ⚡RS

Clos-du-Rhône BP 74, 13460 ☎ 490978599 ▦ 490977885
e-mail: leclos@laposte.net
➲ *2km W via D38, near the beach*
Open: Apr-15 Nov Site: 7HEC ⬜⬜ ⠿⠿ 🏠 ♠ Prices: ♠4.60-
7.20 pitch 14.50-20 (incl 2 persons) Facilities: 🏕 🔋 ⊙ 🔌 🖉 🕿
Services: ⽕ ✗ ⊞ lau Leisure: ⚡ PRS

SALAVAS ARDÈCHE

Chauvieux 07150 ☎ 475880537 ▦ 475880537
e-mail: camping.chauvieux@wanadoo.fr
website: www.camping-le-chauvieux.com
A popular site in a wooded location close to the River
Ardèche with plenty of recreational facilities. Advance
booking recommended.
➲ *NE off D579.*
Open: 20 Apr-15 Sep Site: 1.8HEC ⬜⬜ ⠿⠿ ♠ 🏠
Prices: ♠4.50 🚐2 pitch 13-17 (incl 2 persons) Facilities: 🏕
🔋 ⊙ 🔌 🖉 🕿 Services: ⽕ ✗ ⊞ lau Leisure: ⚡ PR

**A full guide to the Symbols &
Abbreviations used in this book
can be found on page 6**

**A Guide to Caravan & Camping
in Great Britain is also available
from The AA**

Facilities: 🔋-shop 🏕-shower ⊙-electric points for razors 🔌-electric points for caravans 🕿-parking by tents permitted
🅿-compulsory separate car park **Services:** ✗-café/restaurant ⽕-bar 🖉-Camping Gaz International 🛒-gas other than Camping
Gaz ⊞-first aid facilities lau-laundry **Leisure:** ⚡-swimming L-Lake P-Pool R-River S-Sea **Off-site:** All facilities within 2km

SALERNES VAR

Arnauds Quartier des Arnauds, 83690
☎ 494675195 📋 494707557
e-mail: lesarnauds@ville-salernes.fr
website: www.ville-salernes.fr
Level site situated alongside a river and a lake.
➲ *Access via D560. Site entrance just beyond the village.*
Open: 2 May-Sep Site: 3HEC ⬛ ♣ 🏠 Prices: ♠4-5.50 pitch
7-9 Facilities: ⋒ ⊙ 🖳 🖗 ☎ Services: ⚋ ✗ 🖶 lau Leisure: ⭐ R
Off-site: 🖳 ✗ 🖉 🚿

SALINS-D'HYÈRES, LES VAR

Port Pothau 101 chemin les Ourledes, 83400
☎ 494664117 📋 494663309
e-mail: pothuau@free.fr
website: www.campingportpothuau.com
A peaceful holiday village, completely divided into pitches
with good leisure facilities.
➲ *6km E of Hyères on N98 and D12.*
Open: 4 Apr-19 Oct Site: 6HEC ⬛ 🖗 🏠 🖗
Prices: 🖗28.50-30 Facilities: ⋒ 🖳 ⊙ 🖳 🖉 🚿 ☎ Services: ⚋
✗ 🖶 lau Leisure: ⭐ P Off-site: ⭐RS

SALON-DE-PROVENCE BOUCHES-DU-RHÔNE

Nostradamus rte d'Eyguières, 13300
☎ 490560836 📋 490566505
e-mail: gilles.nostra@wanadoo.fr
In pleasant, wooded surroundings with good sporting
facilities.
➲ *5km W on D17 towards Eyguières and Arles.*
Open: Mar-Oct Site: 2.2HEC ⬛ ♣ 🏠 ⊙ 🖳
☎ Services: ⚋ ✗ 🖶 lau Leisure: ⭐ PR

SALVETAT, LA HÉRAULT

Goudal rte de Lacaune, 34330 ☎ 467976044 📋 467976044
e-mail: jnf@goudal.com website: www.goudal.com
Natural mountain setting in the Haut Lanquedoc Park.
➲ *Access via D907.*
Open: May-Sep Site: 5HEC ⬛ 🖗 🏠 🖗 ▲ Facilities: ⋒ 🖳
⊙ 🖳 🚿 ☎ Services: ⚋ ✗ 🖶 lau Leisure: ⭐ L Off-site: ⭐R

SANARY-SUR-MER VAR

Girelles chemin de Beaucours, 83110
☎ 494741318 📋 494746004
A modern family site with good facilities and direct access to
the sea.
Camping Card Compulsory.
➲ *3km NW via D539, beside the sea.*
Open: Etr-Sep Site: 2HEC ⬛ ♣ Prices: pitch 18-50 (incl 2
persons) Facilities: ⋒ 🖳 ⊙ 🖳 🖗 ☎ Services: ⚋ ✗ 🖶 lau
Leisure: ⭐ S

Mogador 83110 ☎ 494745316 📋 494741058
Situated 800mtrs from the sea. The site, divided into pitches
by hedges, is well managed and very well kept.
➲ *2km NW on N559 turn off at Km15 and take next left.*
Open: Etr-5 Oct Site: 2.7HEC ⬛ ♣ 🏠 ✗ Facilities: ⋒ 🖳
⊙ 🖳 🖉 🚿 ☎ Services: ⚋ ✗ 🖶 lau Leisure: ⭐ P
Off-site: ⭐S

Pierredon 652 Chemin Raoul Coletta, 83110
☎ 494742502 📋 494746142
e-mail: campasun@free.fr
website: www.campasun.fr
A well equipped, wooded site providing a variety of family
entertainment, 3km from the sea.

➲ *Access via A50 exit Bandol or Sanary.*
Open: 15 Mar-30 Oct Site: 4HEC ⬛ 🖗 🏠 ▲ Prices: ♠4.50-
5.90 pitch 5.90-10.55 Facilities: ⋒ 🖳 ⊙ 🖳 🚿 ☎ Services: ⚋
✗ lau Leisure: ⭐ P Off-site: 🖳 🖉 🖶

SAUVE GARD

Domaine de Bagard rte de Nîmes, 30610 ☎ 466775599
Shady site bordering the River Vidourle, surrounded by hedges.
➲ *1.2km SE via D999.*
Open: Apr-Sep Site: 16HEC ⬛ ♣ 🏠 🖗 Facilities: ⋒ 🖳 ⊙
🖗 🖉 ☎ Services: ⚋ ✗ lau Leisure: ⭐ PR Off-site: 🖶

SAUVIAN HÉRAULT

Gabinelle 34410 ☎ 467395087
website: www.gabinelle.com
A modern site in pleasant wooded surroundings with good
facilities.
➲ *Leave Sauvian in the direction of Valras Plage on D19.*
Open: 15 Apr-15 Sep Site: 4HEC ⬛ ♣ 🏠 🖗 ▲
Facilities: ⋒ ⊙ 🖳 ☎ 🖸 Services: ⚋ ✗ 🖶 lau Leisure: ⭐ P
Off-site: 🖉 🚿 ⭐R

SÉRIGNAN-PLAGE HÉRAULT

Clos Virgile 34410 ☎ 467322064 📋 467320542
e-mail: le.clos.virgile@wanadoo.fr
website: leclosvirgile.com
Situated 400mtrs from the beach, the site is on level
meadowland with large pitches and has two clean, well kept
sanitary blocks.
Open: May-15 Sep Site: 5HEC ⬛ ♣ 🏠 Prices: pitch 15-26
(incl 2 persons) Facilities: ⋒ 🖳 ⊙ 🖳 🖉 🚿 ☎ Services: ⚋ ✗ 🖶
lau Leisure: ⭐ PS

Grand Large 34410 ☎ 467397130 📋 467325815
e-mail: legrandlarge@wanadoo.fr
website: www.camping-grandlarge.com
Situated by the sea with private access to the beach. Good
facilities. Entertainment during high season.
Open: 26 Apr-14 Sep Site: 7HEC ⬛ ⸛ 🏠 ▲
Facilities: ⋒ 🖳 ⊙ 🖳 🖉 🚿 ☎ Services: ⚋ ✗ 🖶 lau Leisure: ⭐ PS

Sérignan-Plage 34410 ☎ 467323533 📋 467322636
e-mail: info@leserignanplage.com
website: www.leserignanplage.com
On a fine sandy beach, this is a family site with good
recreational facilities.
➲ *Access via A9 exit Béziers Est.*
Open: 10 Apr-22 Sep Site: 16HEC ⬛ ♣ 🏠 ▲ Facilities: ⋒
🖳 ⊙ 🖳 🖉 🚿 ☎ 🖸 Services: ⚋ ✗ 🖶 lau Leisure: ⭐ PS

SEYNE-SUR-MER, LA VAR

Mimosas av M-Paul, 83500 ☎ 494947315 📋 494873613
e-mail: camping_des_mimosas@yahoo.fr
website: www.camping-mimosas.com
Situated among pine trees facing the fortress of Six-Fours.
Bar and café available during high season only.
➲ *Access via A50 exit 13 towards 'La Seyne Centre', then
towards 'Sanary-Bandol'.*
Open: All year Site: 1.1HEC ⬛ ⍥ ♣ 🏠 🖗 Prices: ▲10.50-13.10
Facilities: ⋒ ⊙ 🖳 🚿 ☎ Services: ⚋ ✗ lau Off-site: 🖳 🖉 ⭐P 🖶

SILLANS-LA-CASCADE BOUCHES-DU-RHÔNE

Relais de la Bresque 15 chemin de la Piscine, 83690
☎ 494046489 📋 494046489
e-mail: relaisdelabresque@aol.com
In a beautiful setting among pine trees with good sanitary
and recreational facilities.
Open: All year Site: 3HEC ⍥ ♣ 🏠 🖗 Prices: ♠4.70 pitch
3.50 Facilities: ⋒ ⊙ 🖳 🚿 ☎ Services: ⚋ ✗ 🖶 lau
Off-site: ⭐PR

Site: 6HEC-Site size ⬛-grass ⸛-sand ⍥-stone ✗-little shade 🖗-partly shaded ♣-mainly shaded
🏠-bungalows for hire 🖗-caravans for hire ▲-tents for hire ✗-no dogs Prices: ♠-adult per night ♠-car per night
pp-per person per night 🖗-caravan per night ▲-tent per night

SIX-FOURS-LES-PLAGES VAR

Héliosports La Font de Fillol, 83140 ☎ 494256276
Between the town centre and the beach.
➲ *1km W*
Open: 25 Mar-15 Oct Site: 0.5HEC ⏛ ↻ ♠ Facilities: ↿ ⊙
⬛ 🏛 Services: lau Off-site: ⚑ ⍾ ✕ ⌀ ⼐ ↾PS

International St-Jean av de la Collégiale, 83140
☎ 494875151 ▤ 494062823
e-mail: info@campingstjean.com
website: www.campingstjean.com
Site with pitches, separated by hedges and reeds. Well
managed, and lies just below the Fort Six-Fours.
➲ *Access from N559 and D63 via chemin de St-Jean.*
Open: All year Site: 3HEC ⏛ ↻ ♠ ⬛ Prices: ↾6 pitch 20-
23 (incl 3 persons) Facilities: ↿ ⚑ ⊙ ⬛ ⌀ 🏛 Services: ⍾ ✕
⊞ lau Leisure: ↾ P Off-site: ✕

Playes 419 r Grand, 83140 ☎ 494255757 ▤ 494071990
e-mail: camping-les-playes.six-fours@wanadoo.fr
Terraced site on north side of town. Trees abound in this
excellent location.
➲ *Access from N559 and D63 via chemin de St-Jean.*
Open: All year Site: 1.5HEC ⏛ ♠ ⬛ ⬛ ▲ Prices: ↾3.50-5
♠2-3 ▲12-20 pitch 15-22 Facilities: ↿ ⚑ ⊙ ⬛ ⌀ ⼐ 🏛 ⬛
Services: ⍾ ✕ ⊞ lau Off-site: ↾PS

SOSPEL ALPES-MARITIMES

Domaine St-Madeleine rte de Moulinet, 06380
☎ 493041048 ▤ 493041837
e-mail: camp@camping-sainte-madeleine.com
website: camping-sainte-madeleine.com
A peaceful site in beautiful, unspoiled surroundings.
➲ *4.5km NW via D2566.*
Open: 27 Mar-Sep Site: 3.5HEC ⏛ ↻ ⬛ Prices: pitch
13.60-17 (incl 2 persons) Facilities: ↿ ⊙ ⬛ ⌀ ⼐ 🏛
Services: ⍾ ⊞ lau Leisure: ↾ P

SOUBÈS HÉRAULT

Les Rials rte de Poujols, 34700 ☎ 467441553
A terraced site in wooded surroundings on the banks of the
River Lergue.
➲ *4km from Lodève and 10km from Lac du Salagou.*
Open: 25 Jun-Aug Site: 3.5HEC ⏛ ↻ ⊙ ⬛ Prices: pitch 13-16
(incl 2 persons) Facilities: ↿ ⊙ ⬛ 🏛 Services: ⍾ ⊞ lau
Leisure: ↾ PR Off-site: ⚑ ✕

Sources Soubes, 34700 ☎ 467443202 ▤ 467443202
e-mail: jlsources@wanadoo.fr
website: www.campingdessources.cjb.net
A small, friendly site in a quiet location beside a river.
➲ *5km NE. Signposted from N9.*
Open: 15 May-15 Sep Site: 1.3HEC ⏛ ↻ ⬛ ⍟
Prices: pitch 14 (incl 2 persons) Facilities: ↿ ⊙ ⬛ 🏛
Services: ⍾ ✕ lau Leisure: ↾ PR Off-site: ✕ ⌀ ⼐ ↾L ⊞

TAIN-L'HERMITAGE DRÔME

CM Lucs 24 av Prés-Roosevelt, 26600
☎ 475083282 ▤ 475083206
e-mail: camping.tainlhermitage@wanadoo.fr
Good overnight stopping place but some traffic noise.
➲ *S of town near N7. Turn towards River Rhône at ESSO
garage.*
Open: 15 Mar-Oct Site: 1.5HEC ⏛ ♠ Prices: pitch 12.75-
15.30 (incl 2 persons) Facilities: ↿ ⊙ ⬛ 🏛 Services: ⍾ ✕ ⊞
lau Leisure: ↾ P Off-site: ⚑ ⌀

THOR, LE VAUCLUSE

Jantou Quartier le Bourdis, 84250
☎ 490339007 ▤ 490337984
e-mail: accueil@lejantou.com website: www.lejantou.com
In wooded surroundings beside a river. Separate car park for
arrivals after 22.00hrs.
➲ *Access via N100.*
Open: 15 Mar-Oct Site: 6HEC ⏛ ♠ ⬛ ⬛ Prices: ↾4.60-
5.50 pitch 5.60-6.70 Facilities: ↿ ⚑ ⊙ ⬛ ⌀ ⼐ 🏛 Services: ⍾
✕ ⊞ lau Leisure: ↾ PR Off-site: ⊞

TOURNON-SUR-RHÔNE ARDÈCHE

Manoir rte de Lamastre, 07300 ☎ 475080250 ▤ 475085710
e-mail: info@lemanoir-ardeche.com
website: www.lemanoir-ardeche.com
In picturesque wooded surroundings with good, modern
facilities.
➲ *From N86 (Lyon-Valence) take Lamastre road for 3km.*
Open: Apr-Sep Site: 2HEC ⏛ ♠ ⬛ ⬛ ▲ Prices: pitch
10.50-13.50 Facilities: ↿ ⚑ ⊙ ⬛ ⌀ ⼐ 🏛 ⬛ Services: ⍾ ✕ lau
Leisure: ↾ PR

Tournon 1 Promenade Roche de France, 07300
☎ 475080528 ▤ 475080528
e-mail: camping.tournon@wanadoo.fr
website: www.camping-tournon.com
Well laid-out site in town centre beside River Rhône.
➲ *NW on N86.*
Open: All year Site: 1HEC ⏛ ♠ ⬛ Prices: pitch 10-11.50
(incl 2 persons) Facilities: ↿ ⊙ ⬛ ⌀ ⼐ 🏛 Services: ⊞ lau
Leisure: ↾ R Off-site: ⚑ ⍾ ✕ ↾P

TOURRETTES-SUR-LOUP ALPES-MARITIMES

Camassade 523 rte de Pie Lombard, 06140
☎ 493593154 ▤ 493593181
e-mail: camassade@aol.com website: www.camassade.com
Quiet site under oak trees and pines with several terraces.
➲ *From Vence turn left immediately beyond Tourette.*
Open: All year Site: 2HEC ⏛ ◊ ♠ ⬛ ⬛ Prices: ↾3.70
♠2.60 pitch 8.40 Facilities: ↿ ⚑ ⊙ ⬛ ⌀ ⼐ 🏛 Services: ⊞
lau Leisure: ↾ P

Rives du Loup rte de la Colle, 6140
☎ 493241565 ▤ 493241565
e-mail: rdl@net-up.com website: www.rivesduloup.com
In a wooded riverside setting with good, modern facilities
adjacent to a small hotel.
➲ *Between Vence and Grasse, 3km from Pont-du-Loup on the
road to La Colle-sur-Loup.*
Open: Apr-Sep Site: 2.2HEC ⏛ ∴ ↻ ⬛ ⬛ Prices: ↾4
pitch 14-18.50 (incl 2 persons) Facilities: ↿ ⚑ ⊙ ⬛ ⌀ ⼐ 🏛
Services: ⍾ ✕ ⊞ lau Leisure: ↾ PR

UCEL ARDÈCHE

Domaine de Gil rte de Vals, 07200
☎ 475946363 ▤ 475940195
e-mail: raf.garcia@wanadoo.fr
website: www.domaine-de-gil.com
Pleasantly situated on the banks of the River Ardèche.
Surrounded by beautiful views of the countryside.
➲ *N of Aubenas off N104.*
Open: Apr-10 Sep Site: 4.5HEC ⏛ ∴ ♠ ⬛ Prices: ↾3.20-
5.50 ▲4.30-6.50 pitch 13-22.50 (incl 2 persons) Facilities: ↿
⚑ ⊙ ⬛ ⌀ 🏛 Services: ⍾ ✕ ⊞ lau Leisure: ↾ PR

> The AA cannot be held
> responsible for the content of
> third party websites

UR PYRÉNÉES-ORIENTALES

Gare d'Ur rte d'Espagne, UR, 66760 ☎ 468048095
In a pleasant mountainous setting with well defined pitches. 500mtrs from the village.
Site: 1HEC ⬛ ⊕ ⊞ 🏠 Prices: ⚹2.70 🚗3.30 🚙3.30 ⛺3.30 pitch 3.30 Facilities: ♠ ⊙ 🅿 𝄐 🚿 🏠 Services: lau
Off-site: ✗ ⊀R ⊞

UZÈS GARD

AT **ST-QUENTIN-LA-POTERIE** (4KM NE)

Moulin Neuf 30700 ☎ 466221721 ▤ 466229182
e-mail: le.moulin.neuf@wanadoo.fr
website: www.le-moulin-neuf.com
Quiet site on extensive meadowland within an estate.
➲ *4 km NE on D982.*
Open: Etr-Sep Site: 5HEC ⬛ ⦂⦂⦂ ♣ ⊞ Prices: pitch 12.50-18.20 pp3.50-4.50 Facilities: ♠ 🅛 ⊙ 🅿 𝄐 🏠 Services: 🍴 ✗ ⊞ lau Leisure: ⊀ P

VAISON-LA-ROMAINE VAUCLUSE

International Carpe Diem rte de St-Marcellin, 84110 ☎ 490360202 ▤ 490363690
e-mail: camping.carpe.diem@wanadoo.fr
website: www.guideweb.com/provence/camping/carpe.diem
In wooded surroundings close to Mont Ventoux, with a wide variety of leisure facilities.
➲ *S of town towards Malaucène.*
Open: 30 Mar-2 Nov Site: 10HEC ⬛ ♦ ⊕ ⊞ ⛺ Prices: ⚹4-5 pitch 14.50-26 (incl 3 persons) Facilities: ♠ 🅛 ⊙ 🅿 𝄐 🏠
Services: 🍴 ✗ ⊞ lau Leisure: ⊀ P Off-site: 𝄐 ⊀R

Théâtre Romain Quartier des Arts, chemin du Brusquet, 84110 ☎ 490287866 ▤ 490287876
e-mail: info@camping-theatre.com
website: www.camping-theatre.com
➲ *500mtrs from the town centre near the Roman Theatre.*
Open: 15 Mar-15 Nov Site: 1.5HEC ⬛ ⊕ Prices: ⚹4.70-5.50 🚗4.90-7.50 ⛺4.90-7.50 pitch 4.90-7.50 Facilities: ♠ ⊙
🅿 🏠 Services: ⊞ lau Leisure: ⊀ P Off-site: 🅛 🍴 ✗ 𝄐 ⊀R

VALENCE DRÔME

CM chemin de l'Epervière, 26000
☎ 475423200 ▤ 475562067
e-mail: eperviere@vacanciel.com
A well equipped site bordering the Rhône.
➲ *Access via exit Valence Sud off A7.*
Open: Feb-15 Dec Site: 3.5HEC ⬛ ⊕ Facilities: ♠ ⊙ 🅿 🏠
Services: 🍴 ✗ lau Leisure: ⊀ P Off-site: 🅛 𝄐 🚿 ⊞

VALLABRÈGUES GARD

Lou Vincen 30300 ☎ 466592129 ▤ 466590741
In a pleasant shady location in the heart of a Provençal village.
Open: 24 Mar-15 Oct Site: 1.4HEC ⬛ ♣ ⊞ Prices: ⚹3.30-4 pitch 11-13 (incl 2 persons) Facilities: ♠ ⊙ 🅿 𝄐 🏠
Services: ⊞ lau Leisure: ⊀ P Off-site: 🅛 🍴 ✗ 🚿 ⊀LR ⊞

VALLON-PONT-D'ARC ARDÈCHE

Ardechois 07150 ☎ 475880663 ▤ 475371497
e-mail: ardecamp@bigfoot.com
website: www.ardechois-camping.com
In a pleasant situation in the Ardèche Gorge. Good access for caravans and plentiful sporting facilities.
➲ *From Vallon take D290 towards St-Martin. Signposted.*
Open: Apr-Sep Site: 6HEC ⬛ ♣ ⊞ Prices: ⚹5.20-7.50 pitch 23-35 (incl 2 persons) Facilities: ♠ 🅛 ⊙ 🅿 𝄐 🏠
Services: 🍴 ✗ ⊞ lau Leisure: ⊀ PR Off-site: 🚿

ARDÈCHE

Mondial rte des Gorges de l'Ardèche, 7150
☎ 475880044 ▤ 475371373
Modernised site on the bank of the Ardèche with good sanitary arrangements.
➲ *Access from Vallon-Pont-d'Arc D290. 800mtrs towards Gorge d'Ardèche.*
Open: 15 Mar-10 Oct Site: 4.2HEC ⸺ ⠸⠆ ♠ ⌂ ▲ Facilities: ♠ ⅃ ⊙ ⊟ ∅ ≞ ☎ Services: ⅀ ✗ ⊞ lau Leisure: ⇃ LPR
See advertisement on page 206

Plage Fleurie Les Mazes, 7150 ☎ 475880115
website: www.laplagefleurie.com
Holiday site in unspoilt village beside river.
➲ *Take D579 towards Ruoms, turn left after 2.5km towards Les Mazes.*
Open: Apr-Sep Site: 12HEC ⸺ ⠸⠆ ♠ Facilities: ♠ ⅃ ⊙ ⊟ ∅ ☎ ▣ Services: ⅀ ✗ lau Leisure: ⇃ PR

VALRAS-PLAGE HÉRAULT

Lou Village chemin des Montilles, 34350
☎ 467373379 ▤ 467375356
e-mail: info@louvillage.com website: www.louvillage.com
Situated along a sandy beach, bordered by sand-dunes.
➲ *2km SW, 100mtrs from the beach*
Open: May-12 Sept 2004 Site: 8HEC ⸺ ♠ ⌂ ▦
Prices: pitch 18-30 (incl 2 persons) Facilities: ♠ ⅃ ⊙ ⊟ ∅ ≞ ☎ Services: ⅀ ✗ ⊞ lau Leisure: ⇃ PS Off-site: ⇃R

Occitanie 34350 ☎ 467395906 ▤ 467325820
e-mail: campingoccitanie@wanadoo.fr
website: www.campingoccitanie.com
Family site on rising ground to the north of town, 1km from the beach.
➲ *Access from A9 exit 'Béziers-Est' towards Valras.*
Open: 19 May-11 Sep Site: 6HEC ⸺ ♠ ⌂ ▲ Prices: pitch 16-22.75 (incl 2 persons) Facilities: ♠ ⅃ ⊙ ⊟ ☎ Services: ⅀ ✗ ⊞ lau Leisure: ⇃ P Off-site: ∅ ⇃RS

Vagues Vendres Plage, 34350 ☎ 467373312 ▤ 467375036
website: www.lesvagues.net
A well-organised family site 400mtrs from the sea with a variety of sporting and entertainment facilities.
Open: Apr-Sep Site: 7HEC ⠸⠆ ⌑ ⌂ ▦ Facilities: ♠ ⅃ ⊙ ⊟ ∅ ≞ ☎ Services: ⅀ ✗ ⊞ lau Leisure: ⇃ P Off-site: ⇃S

Yole 34350 ☎ 467373387 ▤ 467374489
e-mail: layole34@aol.com website: www.campinglayole.com
Very comfortable site divided into pitches. Good sanitary installations with individual washing cubicles. Hot water tap. Sailing boats for hire. Riding stables in village. Reservation recommended in July and August.
➲ *SW of D37E towards Vendres.*
Open: May-18 Sep Site: 20HEC ⸺ ⠸⠆ ♠ ⌂ ▦ Prices: ▦16.35-31.80 pitch 16.35-31.80 (incl 2 persons) Facilities: ♠ ⅃ ⊙ ⊟ ∅ ≞ ☎ Services: ⅀ ✗ ⊞ lau Leisure: ⇃ P Off-site: ⇃S

VAUVERT GARD

Tourrades chemin des Canaux, 30600
☎ 466888020 ▤ 466883380
A modern family site with a wide range of recreational facilities.
➲ *3km W via N572 and D135.*
Open: All year Site: 7.5HEC ⸺ ♠ ⌂ ▦ Facilities: ♠ ⅃ ⊙ ⊟ ≞ ☎ Services: ⅀ ✗ ⊞ lau Leisure: ⇃ P Off-site: ∅ ⊞

VEDÈNE VAUCLUSE

Flory rte d'Entraigues, 84270 ☎ 490310051 ▤ 490234679
e-mail: campingflory@wanadoo.fr
website: www.campingflory.com
Well-kept site on a pine covered hill with good facilities.

➲ *From motorway, do not head for Vedène but follow D942 for 800mtrs.*
Open: 15 Mar-15 Oct Site: 6.5HEC ⸺ ♠ ⌂ ▦ Prices: ⋔4.50 pitch 5 Facilities: ♠ ⅃ ⊙ ⊟ ∅ ☎ Services: ⅀ ✗ ⊞ lau Leisure: ⇃ P

VENCE ALPES-MARITIMES

Domaine de la Bergerie rte de la Sine, 06140
☎ 493580936 ▤ 493598044
Well-kept site on hilly land. Pitches near to a wood. Some facilities are only available in high season.
➲ *3km W on D2210.*
Open: 25 Mar-15 Oct Site: 13HEC ⸺ ⚭ ♠ ⌂ Prices: ⋔4.30 ⛺3.40 ▦1.70 ▲1.70 pitch 17.50-26 Facilities: ♠ ⅃ ⊙ ⊟ ∅ ≞ ☎ Services: ⅀ ✗ ⊞ lau Leisure: ⇃ P

VERCHENY DRÔME

Acacias 26340 ☎ 475217251 ▤ 475217398
e-mail: infos@campinglesacacias.com
website: campinglesacacias.com
Pleasant site beside the River Drôme.
Camping Card Compulsory.
➲ *Access via D93.*
Open: Apr-Sep Site: 3HEC ⸺ ♠ ⌂ ▦ Prices: pitch 10-12 (incl 2 persons) Facilities: ♠ ⅃ ⊙ ⊟ ∅ ≞ ☎ Services: ⅀ ✗ ⊞ lau Leisure: ⇃ R Off-site: ✗

VÉREILLES HÉRAULT

Sieste 34260 ☎ 467237296 ▤ 467237538
In a rural setting on the River Orb.
➲ *NE of Bédarieux, 10km from Lodève.*
Open: Jun-Aug Site: 2HEC ⸺ ♠ ⌂ ▦ Prices: ⋔12 Facilities: ♠ ⅃ ⊙ ⊟ ∅ ≞ ☎ Services: ⅀ ✗ ⊞ lau Leisure: ⇃ PR

Facilities: ⅃-shop ♠-shower ⊙-electric points for razors ⊟-electric points for caravans ☎-parking by tents permitted ▣-compulsory separate car park **Services:** ✗-café/restaurant ⅀-bar ∅-Camping Gaz International ≞-gas other than Camping Gaz ⊞-first aid facilities lau-laundry **Leisure:** ⇃-swimming L-Lake P-Pool R-River S-Sea **Off-site:** All facilities within 2km

La Carabasse

An excellently positioned parc on the sunny Mediterranean with two excellent pool complexes and its very own Beach Club.

■ 100m² standard pitch size
■ Superb spring & autumn prices
■ Ferry inclusive package
■ High standard facilities open all season
■ Free use of superb pool complex
■ Free use of 3 childrens clubs for all ages
■ Bilingual friendly staff
■ Site open from: 30 April - 19 September

La Carabasse, Route de Farinette, 34450 Vias-sur-Mer, France
Tel: 00 33 467 21 64 01 Fax: 00 33 467 21 76 87
To book please call the number above, quoting code TOAA01 or request a brochure by calling 0870 242 6666
V2819

CAMPING VILLAGE ★★★

LE MEDITERRANEE

MOBIL-HOMES CAMPING

SWIMMING-POOL
ANIMATIONS
SPORTS

www.mediterranee-plage.fr

LE MEDITERRANEE PLAGE - 34450 VIAS
Tél.: 04 67 90 99 07 • Fax : 04 67 90 99 17
e-mail : camping.med@wanadoo.fr

VIAS HÉRAULT

Air Marin 34450 ☎ 467216490 ▤ 467217679
e-mail: info@camping-air-marin
website: www.camping-air-marin
A well equipped family site in wooded surroundings 10 minutes walk from the beach.
➲ *E of Vias Plage.*
Open: 19 May-15 Sep Site: 7HEC ♣ ⬛ ⬛
Prices: ₳4.80-6 ⬛2.40-3 ▲2.40-3 pitch 22.40-28 (incl 2 persons) Facilities: ⬛ ⬛ ⊙ ⬛ ⬛ ⬛ Services: ⬛ ✕ lau
Leisure: ⬚ P Off-site: ⬛ ⬛ ⬚RS ⊞

Carabasse rte de Farinette, 34450
☎ 467216401 ▤ 467217687
website: www.haveneurope.com
A lively camping park with a wide range of activites, especially for young families and teenagers, centred around a lagoon pool complex and entertainment terrace.
➲ *1.5m NE of Vias.*
Open: 15 Apr-15 Sep Site: ⬚⬚ ⬛ ⬛ ⬛ ⬛ ⬛
Facilities: ⬛ ⬛ ⊙ ⬛ ⬛ ⬛ Services: ⬛ ✕ ⊞ lau Leisure: ⬚ P
Off-site: ⬚S

Cap Soleil Côte Ouest, 34450 ☎ 467216477 ▤ 467217066
website: www.capsoleil.fr
On level land near sea. Divided into pitches.
➲ *Cross Canal du Midi, S of town, then turn W.*
Open: All year Site: 5HEC ♣ ⬛ ⬛ Prices: pitch 15.25-29 Facilities: ⬛ ⬛ ⊙ ⬛ ⬛ ⬛ Services: ⬛ ✕ ⊞ lau
Leisure: ⬚ P Off-site: ⬚S

Hélios Vias-Plage, 34450 ☎ 467216366 ▤ 467216366
On level ground divided into pitches.
➲ *On D137 S of village signposted 'Farinette'.*
Open: May-Sep Site: 3HEC ⬚⬚ ♣ ⬛ ⬛ ⬛ Prices: pitch 10.70-15.30 (incl 2 persons) Facilities: ⬛ ⬛ ⊙ ⬛ ⬛ ⬛
Services: ⬛ ✕ ⊞ lau Off-site: ⬚RS

Mediterranee Plage ☎ 467909907 ▤ 467909917
Direct access to a fine sandy beach.
Open: 3 Apr-18 Sep Site: 10HEC ⬚⬚ ⬛ ⬛ Prices: pitch 25.30 (incl 2 persons) Facilities: ⬛ ⬛ ⬛ ⬛ ⬛ Services: ⬛ ✕
Leisure: ⬚ P

Napoléon av de la Mediterranée, 34450
☎ 467010780 ▤ 467010785
e-mail: reception@camping-napoleon.fr
website: www.camping-napoleon.fr
A well equipped family site surrounded by tropical vegetation with direct access to the beach.
➲ *Access via A9 exit Agde-Vias.*
Open: 26 Apr-Sep Site: 3HEC ⬚⬚ ♣ ⬛ ⬛ ▲
Prices: pitch 19-35 (incl 2 persons) pp4-6 Facilities: ⬛ ⬛ ⊙
⬛ ⬛ ⬛ ⬛ Services: ⬛ ✕ ⊞ lau Leisure: ⬚ P Off-site: ⬚RS

Yelloh Village Farret 34450 ☎ 467216445 ▤ 467217049
e-mail: farret@wanadoo.fr website: ww.farret.com
On level meadow beside flat sandy beach, ideal for children.
➲ *Access via A9 exit Agde-Vias.*
Open: 01 Apr-25 Sept Site: 7HEC ⬚⬚ ♣ ⬛ ⬛
Prices: pitch 15-38 (incl 2 persons) Facilities: ⬛ ⬛ ⊙ ⬛ ⬛ ⬛
⬛ Services: ⬛ ✕ ⊞ lau Leisure: ⬚ PS Off-site: ⬚R

VIC-LA-GARDIOLE HÉRAULT

Europe 34110 ☎ 467781150 ▤ 467784859
e-mail: campingdeleurope@wanadoo.fr
website: www.campingleurope.com
A pleasant site in peaceful surroundings.
➲ *1.5km W via D114.*
Open: 19 Jun-5 Sep Site: 5HEC ♣ ⬛ ⬛ Prices: pitch 15-24 (incl 2 persons) Facilities: ⬛ ⬛ ⊙ ⬛ ⬛ ⬛ ⬛ Services: ⬛ ✕ ⊞
lau Leisure: ⬚ P Off-site: ⬚LS

Site: 6HEC-Site size -grass ⬚⬚-sand ⬛-stone ⬚⬚-little shade ⬚-partly shaded ♣-mainly shaded
⬛-bungalows for hire ⬛-caravans for hire ▲-tents for hire ⬚-no dogs Prices: ₳-adult per night ⬛-car per night
pp-per person per night ⬛-caravan per night ▲-tent per night

VIGAN, LE GARD

Val de l'Arre rte de Ganges, 30120
☎ 467810277 ▤ 467817123
e-mail: valdelarre@wanadoo.fr
website: www.campingfrance.com/valdelarre
In wooded surroundings beside the River Arre. Compulsory separate carpark for late arrivals.
➲ *2.5km E on D999.*
Open: Apr-Sep Site: 4HEC ⊞ ♣ 🏠 Prices: ☎0.91-0.91 pitch 9.76-13.42 (incl 2 persons) pp5.18-6.71 Facilities: ⋔ ⅀ ⊙ ⌑ ⌀ 🏚 Services: ⏇ ✗ ⊞ lau Leisure: ⅂ PR Off-site: 🏔

VILLARS-COLMARS ALPES-DE-HAUTE-PROVENCE

Haut-Verdon 04370 ☎ 492834009 ▤ 492835661
e-mail: campinglehautverdon@wanadoo.fr
website: www.lehautverdon.com
A comfortable site in a picturesque wooded location beside the River Verdon.
➲ *N on D908.*
Open: May-Sep Site: 3.5HEC ⊞ ♦ ♣ 🏠 ⌑ Prices: ⍦3-4 pitch 6-10 Facilities: ⋔ ⅀ ⊙ ⌑ ⌀ 🏚 Services: ⏇ ✗ ⊞ lau Leisure: ⅂ PR Off-site: 🏔

VILLEMOUSTAUSSOU AUDE

Pinhiers chemin du Pont Neuf, 11620
☎ 468478190 ▤ 468714349
e-mail: campingdaspinhiers@wanadoo.fr
website: bienvenuedanslaude.com
➲ *A61 in the direction of Mazamet.*
Open: Apr-Sep Site: 2HEC ⊞ ⌑ 🏠 ⌑ Prices: ⍦3-3.60 pitch 3.30-3.70 Facilities: ⋔ ⅀ ⊙ ⌑ 🏚 Services: ⏇ lau Leisure: ⅂ P Off-site: ✗ ⌀ 🏔

VILLENEUVE-DE-BERG ARDÈCHE

Domaine de Pommier RN 102, 07170
☎ 475948281 ▤ 475948390
Holiday site in beautiful setting with terraces divided into pitches.
➲ *On winding private road off N102, 2km from village.*
Open: May-Sep Site: 30HEC ⫶⫶⫶ ♦ ⌑ 🏠 ⌑ Prices: pitch 29 (incl 2 persons) Facilities: ⋔ ⅀ ⊙ ⌑ ⌀ 🏚 Services: ⏇ ✗ ⊞ Leisure: ⅂ PR

VILLENEUVE-DE-LA-RAHO PYRÉNÉES-ORIENTALES

Rives-du-Lac chemin de la Serre, 66180
☎ 468558351 ▤ 468558637
e-mail: camping.villeneuve@worldonline.fr
A quiet family site beside the lake.
➲ *7km from Perpignan.*
Open: Mar-Nov Site: 2.5HEC ⊞ ⌇ ⌑ 🏠 ⍦ Prices: pitch 9.60-12.90 (incl 2 persons) Facilities: ⋔ ⅀ ⊙ ⌑ 🏚 Services: ⏇ ✗ lau Off-site: ⊞

VILLENEUVE-LÈS-AVIGNON GARD

Œle des Papes 30400 ☎ 490151590 ▤ 490151591
e-mail: ile.papes@wanadoo.fr website: www.campeoles.fr
A well equipped site situated on an island between the Rhône Canal and the River Rhône.
➲ *Access via N7 and D228.*
Open: 24 Mar-26 Oct Site: 20HEC ⊞ ♦ ⌑ 🏠 ⌑ ⍦
Prices: pitch 16-25 (incl 2 persons) Facilities: ⋔ ⅀ ⊙ ⌑ ⌀ 🏚 Services: ⏇ ✗ ⊞ lau Leisure: ⅂ P

> A full guide to the Symbols & Abbreviations used in this book can be found on page 6

Camping Domaine★★★★ "Le Pommier"

- Pleasant 7 ha family campsite on a 30 ha domain
- 275 spacious shady and sunny pitches
- hire of caravans and chalets
- grill restaurant/pizzeria, cafeteria / take-away meals
- bar with terrace, discotheque, campsite store
- aqua park, slides, paddling pool, children's shallow pool, whirlpool
- river, mini golf 18 holes, fitness, Internet corner
- playground, volleyball, bicycle hire, football, table tennis
- extensive entertainment programme with children's club, day and evening programmes organised by our CIOS and ALO qualified team
- special senior programme: jeu de boules matches, bridge drives, water colour classes

SPECIAL OFFERS: IN THE LOW SEASON

Camping Domaine "Le Pommier" ★★★★ - 07170 Villeneuve-de-Berg, France
Tel. (+) 33 4 75 94 82 81 - Fax (+) 33 4 75 94 83 90
www.campinglepommier.com - email: info@campinglepommier.com

Ardèche

heated sanitary building
heated swimming pool

Facilities: ⅀-shop **⋔**-shower **⊙**-electric points for razors **⌑**-electric points for caravans **🏚**-parking by tents permitted **▣**-compulsory separate car park **Services: ✗**-café/restaurant **⏇**-bar **⌀**-Camping Gaz International **🏔**-gas other than Camping Gaz **⊞**-first aid facilities lau-laundry **Leisure: ⅂**-swimming L-Lake P-Pool R-River S-Sea **Off-site:** All facilities within 2km

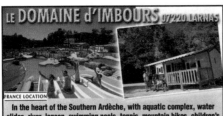

In the heart of the Southern Ardèche, with aquatic complex, water slides, river, lagoon, swimming pools, tennis, mountain bikes, children's club and evening entertainment. Your accommodation:**** campsite with 200 pitches, mobile homes and cottages.

info@domaine-imbours.com
www.domaine-imbours.com

VILLENEUVE-LOUBET-PLAGE ALPES-MARITIMES

Hippodrôme 5 av des Rives, 06270
☎ 493200200 ▤ 492132007
e-mail: blsced@aol.com
website: meublecamping-hippodrome.com
In a spacious park with pitches divided by hedges with good facilities.
➲ *Turn right off the N7 at ATLAS furniture store.*
Open: All year Site: 7.8HEC ⊞ ◕ ♠ ⬢ Prices: ♠3.50-4.50 ♠2.50-3.10 pitch 11.30-24.40 (incl 2 persons) Facilities: ⬡ ⊙ ⬢ ☜ Services: ⊞ lau Leisure: ⬩ P Off-site: ⬛ ⬤ ✗ ∅ ⬗ ⬩S

Panorama 6270 ☎ 493209153
Small terraced site mainly for tents 0.8km from the sea.
➲ *About 500mtrs from the Nice-Cannes Autoroute.*
Open: All year Site: 1HEC ⊞ ♠ ⬢ ⬤ Prices: ♠4 ♠2.80 ♠17.40-24.80 pitch 17.40 (incl 2 persons) Facilities: ⬡ ⊙ ⬢ ∅ ⬗ ☜ Services: ⬤ ✗ ⊞ lau Off-site: ⬩RS

Parc des Maurettes 730 av du Dr-Lefebvre, 06270
☎ 493209191 ▤ 493737720
Terraced site in a pine forest with good, modern facilities.
➲ *Access via A8: From Cannes take exit 'Villeneuve-Loubet-Plage', then N7 towards Antibes for 1km. From Nice, take Villeneuve exit and A8 for 2km.*
Open: 10 Jan-15 Nov Site: 2HEC ⊞ ♠ ⬢ Prices: ♠1-4.40 ▲14.20-21.05 pitch 17.90-26.65 (incl 2 persons) Facilities: ⬡ ⊙ ⬢ ∅ ☜ Services: ⊞ lau Off-site: ⬛ ✗ ⬗ ⬩S

Parc St-James Sourire rte de Grasse (D2085), 6270
☎ 493209611 ▤ 493220752
website: www.camping-parcsaintjames.com
Parkland dominated by an 11th-century monastery.
➲ *2km W on D2085*
Open: end Mar-end Sep Site: 8HEC ⊞ ◕ ◔ ⬢
Facilities: ⬡ ⬛ ⊙ ⬢ ∅ ⬗ ☜ Services: ⬤ ✗ lau Leisure: ⬩ P Off-site: ⬩R

Vieille Ferme 296 bd des Groules, 06270
☎ 493334144 ▤ 493333728
e-mail: vieilleferme@bigfoot.com website: www.vieilleferme.com
In a wooded park close to the sea. Shop and café open in summer only.
➲ *Access via A8/N7 from Antibes of Cagnes-sur-Mer.*
Open: All year Site: 2.8HEC ⊞ ♠ ⬢ Prices: pitch 17-27 (incl 2 persons) Facilities: ⬡ ⬛ ⊙ ⬢ ∅ ⬗ ☜ Services: ✗ ⊞ lau Leisure: ⬩ P Off-site: ⬩S

VILLEROUGE-LA-CRÉMADE AUDE

Pinada 11200 ▤ 468436861
e-mail: lepinada@libertysurf.fr
website: camping-le-pinada.com
In pleasant rural surroundings on edge of forest.

➲ *600mtrs NW on D106.*
Open: Apr-15 Oct Site: 4.5HEC ⊞ ⬙ ◕ ♠ ⬢ ⬤ Prices: ♠8-19 pitch 8-19 Facilities: ⬡ ⊙ ⬢ ☜ ⬗ ☜ Services: ⬤ ✗ ⊞ lau Leisure: ⬩ P

VILLES-SUR-AUZON VAUCLUSE

Verguettes rte de Carpentras, 84570
☎ 490618818 ▤ 490619787
e-mail: info@provence-camping.com
website: www.provence-camping.com
Lying at the foot of Mont Ventoux and Nesque Gorges in a pine forest
➲ *W via D942.*
Open: Apr-15 Oct Site: 2HEC ⊞ ◕ ⬢ Prices: ♠4.50-5 ♠6.50-7.10 ▲6.50-7.10 pitch 6.50-7.10 Facilities: ⬡ ⊙ ⬢ ☜ Services: ⬤ ✗ ⊞ lau Leisure: ⬩ P Off-site: ⬛ ✗ ∅

VITROLLES BOUCHES-DU-RHÔNE

Marina Plage 13127 ☎ 442893146 ▤ 442795990
e-mail: information@marina-plage.com
website: www.marina-plage.com
A family site in pleasant wooded surroundings with good recreational facilities.
➲ *Access via N113 towards Rognac, then turn S at exit after Marignane Airport.*
Open: All year Site: 10HEC ⊞ ⬙ ◕ ♠ ⬢ ⬤ Facilities: ⬡ ⬛ ⊙ ⬢ ☜ ⬗ Services: ⬤ ✗ ⊞ lau Leisure: ⬩ L

VIVIERS ARDÈCHE

Domaine d' Imbours 07220 ☎ 475543950 ▤ 475543920
e-mail: info@domaine-imbours.com
website: www.domaine-imbours.com
In wooded surroundings with a variety of recreational facilities.
➲ *Access via N86 and D4.*
Open: 15 Mar-Oct Site: 45HEC ⊞ ♠ ⬢ Prices: ♠4-5.50 ♠2 pitch 23 (incl 3 persons) Facilities: ⬡ ⬛ ⊙ ⬢ ∅ ⬗ ☜ Services: ⬤ ✗ ⊞ lau Leisure: ⬩ P

Rochecondrie Loisirs 07220 ☎ 475527466 ▤ 475527466
A level site with good facilities beside the River L'Escoutay.
➲ *N of town on N86.*
Open: Apr-Oct Site: 1.8HEC ⊞ ♠ ⬢ Prices: pitch 10-17.30 (incl 2 persons) Facilities: ⬡ ⊙ ⬢ ☜ ⬗ Services: ⬤ ⊞ lau Leisure: ⬩ PR Off-site: ⬛ ✗ ∅

VOGÜÉ ARDÈCHE

Domaine du Cros d'Auzon Hotellerie de Plein Air, 7200
☎ 475377586 ▤ 475370102
e-mail: cros.d.auzon@wanadoo.fr
website: www.guideweb.com/ardeche/camping/cros-auzon
In wooded surroundings close to the Gorges de l'Ardèche with good recreational facilities.
➲ *2.5km via D579 bordering the river.*
Open: 15 Apr-15 Sep Site: 20HEC ⊞ ⬙ ◕ ♠ ⬢ Prices: ♠2.10-5.20 pitch 12.40-21.60 Facilities: ⬡ ⬛ ⊙ ⬢ ∅ ⬗ ☜ Services: ⬤ ✗ ⊞ lau Leisure: ⬩ PR Off-site: ⬩LS

VOLONNE ALPES-DE-HAUTE-PROVENCE

Hippocampe rte Napoléon, 4290
☎ 492335000 ▤ 492335049
e-mail: camping@l.hippocampe.com
website: www.l-hippocampe.com
Several strips of land, interspersed with trees, and running down the edge of lake. Surrounded by fields and gardens.
➲ *On S edge of town. 2km E of N85.*
Open: Apr-Sep Site: 8HEC ⊞ ◕ ⬢ ▲ Prices: ▲2.50-6 pitch 15-31 (incl 2 persons) Facilities: ⬡ ⬛ ⊙ ⬢ ∅ ☜ Services: ⬤ ✗ ⊞ lau Leisure: ⬩ P

Site: 6HEC-Site size ⊞-grass ⬝⬝⬝-sand ⬙-stone ⬗-little shade ◕-partly shaded ♠-mainly shaded ⬢-bungalows for hire ⬤-caravans for hire ▲-tents for hire ⊘-no dogs **Prices:** ♠-adult per night ♠-car per night pp-per person per night ⬤-caravan per night ▲-tent per night

CORSICA

CORSE (CORSICA)

ALÉRIA HAUTE-CORSE

Marina d'Aléria rte de la Mer, 20270
☎ 495570142 ▧ 495570429
e-mail: info@marina-aleria.com website: www.marina-aleria.com
➲ *3km E of Cateraggio via RN200*
Open: 15 Apr-15 Oct Site: 10HEC ⁙ ♣ ⊞ ⊞
Prices: ⋔5.20-6.80 ⇔1.90-2.50 ⊞2.10-2.50 ⚑1.70-2
Facilities: ⋔ ⅃ ⊙ ⊞ ⌀ 瑥 Services: 甼 ✕ lau Leisure: ⤙ S

BONIFACIO CORSE-DU-SUD

Rondinara Suartone, 20169 ☎ 495704315 ▧ 495705679
e-mail: reception@rondinara.fr website: rondinara.fr
In a beautiful situation 300mtrs from the beach with modern facilities and fine opportunities for water sports.
➲ *Midway between Porto-Vecchio and Bonifacio on N198 in the direction of Suartone-La Rondinara.*
Open: 15 May-Sept Site: 6HEC ⁙ ⌿ ⊞ ⤝ Prices: ⋔5-6.50
⇔2.50-3 ⊞3-3.70 ⚑2.50-3 Facilities: ⋔ ⅃ ⊙ ⊞ ⌀ 瑥
Services: 甼 ✕ ⊞ lau Leisure: ⤙ PS

CALVI HAUTE-CORSE

Dolce Vita Ponte Bambino, 20260
☎ 495650599 ▧ 0495653125
website: www.dolce-vita-org/
In extensive woodland with well defined pitches and good, modern facilities.
➲ *4km SW of Calvi between N197 to L'Ile Rousse and the sea.*
Open: May-Sep Site: 6HEC ⁙ ♣ ⤝ Prices: ⋔6.90 ⇔2.55
⤝3.50 ⚑2.55 Facilities: ⋔ ⅃ ⊙ ⊞ ⌀ 瑥 Services: 甼 ✕ ⊞ lau
Leisure: ⤙ RS

CARGESE CORSE-DU-SUD

Torraccia Bagghiuccia, 20130 ☎ 495264239 ▧ 495204021
e-mail: contact@camping-torraccia.com
website: www.camping-torraccia.com
Terraced site close to the Chiuni and Pero beaches and backed by some fine mountain scenery.
➲ *4km N on N199.*
Open: May-Sep Site: 3.5HEC ♣ ⊞ Prices: ⋔4.80-5.80 ⇔2-2.50 ⊞2.10-2.80 ⚑2-2.50 Facilities: ⋔ ⅃ ⊙ ⊞ ⌀ 瑥
Services: 甼 ✕ ⊞ lau Off-site: 굛 ⤙S

CENTURI HAUTE-CORSE

Isulottu 20238 ☎ 495356281
A peaceful, shady site, 200mtrs from the beach.
➲ *1km from Centuri-Port towards Morsiglia.*
Site: 3HEC ♣ Prices: ⋔4.90 ⇔1.65 ⊞4.45 ⚑2.55 pitch 2.25
Facilities: ⋔ ⅃ ⊙ ⊞ ⌀ 瑥 ᠍ Services: 甼 ✕ ⊞ lau Off-site: ⤙S

GALÉRIA HAUTE-CORSE

Deux Torrents 20245 ☎ 495620067 ▧ 495620332
e-mail: 2torrents@corsica-net.com
website: www.corsica-net.com/2torrents
A spacious, well equipped site nestling between two torrents at the foot of the mountains.
➲ *5km E on D51 towards Calenzana.*
Open: Jun-Sep Site: 6.3HEC ⁙ ♣ ⊞ ⤝ Prices: ⋔4.95
⇔2.50 ⤝4.40 ⚑2.70 Facilities: ⋔ ⅃ ⊙ ⊞ ⌀ 굛 瑥
Services: 甼 ✕ lau Off-site: ⤙R

GHISONACCIA HAUTE-CORSE

Arinella-Bianca Arinella-Bianca, 20240
☎ 495560478 ▧ 495561254
e-mail: arinella@arinellabianca.com
website: www.arinellabianca.com
In wooded surroundings, directly on the beach with good recreational facilities.
Open: 3 Apr-16 Oct Site: 12HEC ⁙ ♣ ⊞ Prices: pitch 19-33 (incl 2 persons) pp6.50-9 Facilities: ⋔ ⅃ ⊙ ⊞ ⌀ 瑥
Services: 甼 ✕ ⊞ lau Leisure: ⤙ PRS

LOZARI HAUTE-CORSE

Clos des Chênes rte de Belgodère, 20226
☎ 495601513 ▧ 495602116
e-mail: cdc.lozari@wanadoo.fr
website: www.closdeschenes.fr
In a delightful wooded setting, 1km from a fine sandy beach.
➲ *1.5km S via N197 towards Belgodère*
Open: Etr-end Sep Site: 5.5HEC ⁙ ♣ ⊞ ⤝ Prices: ⋔5.70-6.90 ⤝4.25-5.70 Facilities: ⋔ ⅃ ⊙ ⊞ ⌀ 瑥 Services: 甼 ✕ ⊞
lau Leisure: ⤙ P Off-site: ⤙S

LUMIO HAUTE-CORSE

Panoramic rte de Lavataggio 1, 20260
☎ 495607313 ▧ 493991932
Very clean and tidy site divided into pitches.
➲ *From Calvi, 12km on N197, 200mtrs from main road.*
Open: Jun-15 Sep Site: 6HEC ⁙ ⌿ ⊞ ⊞ Facilities: ⋔ ⅃ ⊙
⊞ ⌀ 瑥 ᠍ Services: 甼 ✕ ⊞ lau Leisure: ⤙ P Off-site: ⤙S

OLMETO-PLAGE CORSE-DU-SUD

Esplanade 20113 ☎ 495760503 ▧ 495761622
e-mail: infos@camping-esplanade.com
website: www.camping-esplanade.com
In a pleasant natural park, 100mtrs from the sea.
Open: Apr-Oct Site: 4.8HEC ⁙ ♣ ⊞ ⤝ Prices: ⋔4.90-6
⇔2-2.70 ⤝2.50-3.20 ⚑2.50-3.20 pitch 2.50-3.20
Facilities: ⋔ ⅃ ⊙ ⊞ 瑥 Services: 甼 ✕ ⊞ lau Leisure: ⤙ S
Off-site: ⌀ 굛 ⤙R

PIANOTTOLI CORSE-DU-SUD

Kevano Plage Plage de Kevano, 20131
☎ 495718322 ▧ 495718383
In a beautiful setting in the middle of woodland with modern facilities, 400mtrs from the beach.
Open: May-Sep Site: 6HEC ◔ ♣ ⊞ Prices: ⋔5.40-7.20 ⇔2-2.50 ⤝3.30-4 ⚑2-2.50 Facilities: ⋔ ⅃ ⊙ ⊞ 瑥 Services: 甼 ✕
⊞ lau Off-site: ⌀ ⤙S

PISCIATELLO CORSE-DU-SUD

Benista 20166 ☎ 495251930 ▧ 495259370
e-mail: camping.benista@worldonline.fr
website: www.benista.com
In a beautiful wooded setting, 5 minutes from the local beaches. Pitches are divided by hedges and there are good sporting facilities.
Open: Apr-Oct Site: 5HEC ⁙ ♣ ⊞ ⤝ Facilities: ⋔ ⅃ ⊙
⊞ ⌀ 굛 瑥 Services: 甼 ✕ ⊞ lau Leisure: ⤙ PR Off-site: ⤙S

A full guide to the Symbols & Abbreviations used in this book can be found on page 6

The AA cannot be held responsible for the content of third party websites

---

Facilities: ⅃-shop ⋔-shower ⊙-electric points for razors ⊞-electric points for caravans 瑥-parking by tents permitted
᠍-compulsory separate car park Services: ✕-café/restaurant 甼-bar ⌀-Camping Gaz International 굛-gas other than Camping
Gaz ⊞-first aid facilities lau-laundry Leisure: ⤙-swimming L-Lake P-Pool R-River S-Sea Off-site: All facilities within 2km

Porto-Vecchio Corse-du-Sud

Pirellu rte de Palombaggia, 20137
☎ 495702344 ▤ 495706022
e-mail: v-pirellu@wanadoo.fr
A modern site situated in an oak grove 300mtrs from the beach.
⤳ *S of Porto-Vecchio, take road for Bonifacio. After Pont du Stabiacco take first road on the left.*
Open: Apr-Sep Site: 2.5HEC ⚏ ⬤ ♠ ⛺ Facilities: ⋔ ⚑ ⊙ ☒ ⊘ ♨ 🏛 Services: ⏣ ✕ lau Leisure: ⤳ P

Vetta rte de Bastia, 20137 ☎ 495700986 ▤ 495704321
e-mail: info@campinglavetta.com
website: www.campinglavetta.com
In natural parkland with good, modern facilities 3km from the sea.
⤳ *5.5km N on N198.*
Open: 15 May-15 Oct Site: 8HEC ⚏ ♠ ⛺ Facilities: ⋔ ⚑ ⊙ ☒ ⊘ ♨ 🏛 ⊞ Services: ⏣ ✕ ⊞ lau Leisure: ⤳ P Off-site: ⤳S

St-Florent Haute-Corse

U Pezzo chemin de la Plage, 20217
☎ 495370165 ▤ 495352816
e-mail: contact@upezzo.com website: www.upezzo.com
Pleasant site; partly level, partly terraced under eucalyptus trees. Private access to large beach.

⤳ *S of town on road to beach.*
Open: Apr-15 Oct Site: 2HEC ⚏ ♠ Prices: ⋔4.25-4.50 ⇐2.25-2.50 ⊞3.25-3.50 ▲2.25-3.50 pitch 2.25-2.50
Facilities: ⋔ ⚑ ⊙ ☒ ⊘ 🏛 Services: ⏣ ✕ ⊞ lau Leisure: ⤳ S
Off-site: ⤳R

Sotta Corse-du-Sud

U Moru 20114 ☎ 495712340 ▤ 495712619
e-mail: u-moru@wanadoo.fr
A quiet family site 5 minutes from the local beach.
⤳ *4km SW via D859.*
Open: 15 Jun-15 Sep Site: 6HEC ∴ ♠ ⛺ Prices: ⋔5.90 ⇐2 ⊞3.20 ▲2.30 pitch 2.30 Facilities: ⋔ ⚑ ⊙ ☒ ⊘ 🏛 Services: ⏣ ✕ ⊞ lau

Tiuccia Corse-du-Sud

Couchants rte de Casaglione, 20111
☎ 495522660 ▤ 495593177
e-mail: camping.les-couchants@wanadoo.fr
In a quiet location facing the vast Sagone Bay and close to the Liamone River.
⤳ *3km from the sea.*
Open: All year Site: 5HEC ⚏ ♠ ⛺ ⇐ Prices: ⋔5-5.50 ⇐2-2.50 ⊞3.50-4 ▲2-2.50 Facilities: ⋔ ⊙ ☒ ⊘ ♨ 🏛 Services: ⏣ ✕ ⊞ lau Off-site: ⤳RS

Fishing boats in the medieval port of Yvoire.

Site: 6HEC-Site size ⚏-grass ∴-sand ⬤-stone ѭ-little shade ⋪-partly shaded ♠-mainly shaded
⛺-bungalows for hire ⇐-caravans for hire ▲-tents for hire ⊘-no dogs Prices: ⋔-adult per night ⇐-car per night
pp-per person per night ⇐-caravan per night ▲-tent per night

GERMANY

Germany, an economic giant that offers a mix of fairytale castles, ancient towns, enormous forests and bustling modern cities, is a country of contrasts.

FACTS AND FIGURES
Area: 357,021 sq km (137,847 sq miles)
Population: 83,251,851 (2002 est)
Capital: Berlin
Language: German
IDD code: 49. To call the UK dial 00 44.
Currency: Euro
Local time: GMT + 1 (summer GMT + 2)

Emergency services: Fire and Ambulance 112; Police 110.
Banks: 0830-1230 & 1330-1530 Mon-Wed and Fri, 0830-1230 & 1330-1730 Thur. These are approximate, there are no uniform banking hours.

Shops: 0900-2000 Mon-Fri and 0900-1600 Sat These opening hours apply to city shops. Average daily temperatures:Munich
Jan 2°C	Sep15°C
Jul 18°C	May13°C
Mar 4°C	Nov 3°C
Tourist Information: National Tourist Office

UK PO Box 2695 London W1A 3TN Tel (020) 7317 0908 (09001 600100 premium rate information line)
USA 52nd Floor, 122 East 42nd Street, New York, NY10168 Tel (212) 661-7174.
Tourist website: www.germany-tourism.de

Germany is bordered by nine countries: Austria, Belgium, Czech Republic, Denmark, France, Luxembourg, Netherlands, Poland and Switzerland. The Rhine Valley boasts magnificent cliffs and woods whilst the Black Forest has some fine valley scenery with countless waterfalls and gorges. The climate is temperate and variable but Germany enjoys hotter summers than Britain.

OFF-SITE CAMPING

Permission to camp off an official campsite must be obtained from the landowner or local police. Overnight parking at parking places is tolerated for one night, unless otherwise indicated, provided nearby campsites and hotels are fully booked. However, make sure you do not contravene local regulations.

HOW TO GET THERE

For western Germany use the Channel Tunnel, or one of the short Channel crossings and travel via Belgium. For northern Germany take a direct ferry from **Harwich** to **Cuxhaven** (minimum sailing time 16hrs 45mins) or one of the North Sea crossings to the Netherlands.

For southern Germany use Eurotunnel, or one of the short Channel crossings and drive through northern France entering Germany near **Strasbourg**; this is also the route if using one of the longer Channel crossings to Caen (Ouistreham), Cherbourg, Dieppe or Le Havre.

DISTANCE

From the Continental Channel ports, Köln (Cologne) is about 414km (257 miles) and within a comfortable day's drive; routes to southern and eastern Germany usually require one or two overnight stops.

MOTORING & GENERAL

The information given here is specific to Germany. It must be read in conjunction with the Essential Motoring Information at the front of the book, which covers those regulations which are common to many countries.

BRITISH EMBASSY/CONSULATES*

The British Embassy, together with its consular section, is located at 10117 Berlin, Wilhelmstrasse 70 ☎ (030) 20457-0. There are British Consulates in Düsseldorf, Frankfurt am Main, Hamburg, München (Munich) and Stuttgart; there are British Consulates with Honorary Consuls in Bremen, Hanover, Kiel and Nürnberg (Nurenburg).

CHILDREN IN CARS

Children under 12 and/or 1.5 metres in height are not permitted to travel as front or rear seat passengers unless using suitable restraint system, if fitted. See Essential Motoring Information under 'Passengers' and 'Seat Belts'.

CURRENCY*

With the introduction of the Euro, the Deutsche Mark (DEM) ceased to be legal tender from 2002. However, DEM coins and notes can be exchanged at the German Central Bank (Deutsche Bundesbank) for an unlimited period.

DIMENSIONS AND WEIGHT RESTRICTIONS*

Private **cars** and **trailers** or **caravans** are restricted to the following dimensions - height, 4 metres; width, 2.55 metres; length, 12 metres. The maximum permitted overall length of vehicle/trailer or caravan combinations is 18 metres. A fully-laden trailer without brakes may have a total maximum weight of 750kg.

DRIVING LICENCE*

A valid UK or Republic of Ireland licence is accepted in Germany. The minimum age at which visitors from UK or Republic of Ireland may use a temporarily imported car or motorcycle is 17.

FIRST-AID KIT*

The German authorities recommend that visiting motorists equip their vehicles with a first-aid kit.

FOODSTUFFS*

If the imported foodstuff are for personal use, there are no limits when travelling between EU countries. Visitors entering Germany from outside the EU may import up to 1kg of meat and meat products and up to 30kg of game and poultry.

The importation of meat products and sheep and goat's cheese from the CIS, Turkey and all African and Asian countries is prohibited. Coffee (500g) and coffee extract (200g) are free of customs duties, but visitors under 15 cannot import coffee.

LIGHTS*

It is compulsory for motorcyclists to use dipped headlights during the day.

MOTORING CLUB

The principal motoring club is the **Allgemeiner Deutscher Automobil Club e.V.** (ADAC) based at 81373 München, Am Westpark 8 ☎(089) 7676-0. It has offices in the larger towns, and office hours are 08.00-17.00hrs Mon-Fri. ADAC also has offices at major frontier crossings. Website: **www.adac.de**

ROADS

Germany has a comprehensive motorway (*Autobahn*) network which takes most of the long-distance traffic. Emergency telephones are sited every 2km, the direction of the nearest telephone is indicated by the point of the black triangle on

A typical Bavarian landscape

The town of Berchtesgarden with the Bavarian Alps in the distance.

posts alongside the motorway.

The *Bundesstrassen,* or state roads, vary in quality. In the north and west, and in the touring Rhine Valley, Black Forest, and Bavaria, the roads are good and well-graded. Traffic at weekends increases considerably during the school holidays, which are from July to mid September. In order to ease congestion, lorries of more than 7,500kg and lorries towing trailers are subject to restrictions.

On all Saturdays from 1 July to 31 August such vehicles are not allowed on state roads or motorways betweeen 0700 and 2000 hours, and generally on all Sundays and public holidays between 0001 and 2200 hours.

SPEED LIMITS*

Car/Motorcycle
Built-up areas 50km/h (31mph)
Other roads inc dual-carriageways 100km/h
(62mph)
Motorways 130km/h (80mph)

Car/caravan/trailer
Built-up areas 50km/h (31mph)
Other roads 80km/h (49mph)
Motorways/dual-carriageways 80km/h (49mph)

Note:

Outside special built-up areas, motor vehicles to which a special speed limit applies, as well as vehicles with trailers with a combined length of more than 7 metres (23ft), must keep sufficient distance from the preceding vehicle so that an overtaking vehicle may pull in. Anyone driving so slowly that a line of vehicles has formed behind must permit the following vehicles to pass, by stopping at a suitable place if necessary.

WARNING TRIANGLE*

Although it is not compulsory for visiting motorists to equip their vehicles with a warning triangle, its use is compulsory in the event of accident or breakdown. The triangle must be placed on the road behind the vehicle to warn following traffic of any obstruction: 100 metres (109yds) on ordinary roads and 150 metres (164yds) on motorways.

*Additional information will be found in the Essential Motoring Information at the front of the book.

215

SOUTH EAST

AACH BEI OBERSTAUFEN   BAYERN

Aach 87534 ☎ 08386 363 ▤ 08386 961721
e-mail: camping-aach@t-online.de
website: www.camping-aach.de
A terraced site with beautiful views of the mountains. Sauna, solarium, games room.
➲ *From Oberstaufen follow B308 for 7km towards the Austrian border.*
Open: All year Site: 2.5HEC ⚌ ⚘ ⊞ Facilities: ℝ ℀ ⊙ ⚑ ⚛ ⚖ 🏠 Services: ⚥ ✕ lau Leisure: ⬚ P Off-site: ⬚R

AITRANG   BAYERN

Elbsee 3 Am Elbsee 3, 87648 ☎ 08343 248 ▤ 08343 1406
e-mail: info@elbsee.de website: www.elbsee.de
On the eastern shore of the lake with good bathing facilities. Section reserved for campers with dogs.
➲ *Take B12 from Marktoberdorf travel for 11km then turn N to Aitrang.*
Open: All year Site: 3.5HEC ⚌ ℀ ⊞ Prices: ♠3.50 ♠2.50 pitch 7.50 Facilities: ℝ ℀ ⊙ ⚑ ⚛ ⚖ 🏠 Services: ⊞ lau Leisure: ⬚ L Off-site: ✕ ⬚P

ARLACHING   BAYERN

Kupferschmiede Trostberger Str 4, 83339
☎ 086671 446 ▤ 08667 16198
e-mail: campingkupfer@aol.com
website: www.campingkupferschmiede.de
On meadowland. Partially gravel.
➲ *On Seebruck-Traunstein road.*
Open: Apr-Oct Site: 2.5HEC ⚌ ♠ Prices: ♠4.95-5.50 ♠1.50 ♠4 ▲3-4 Facilities: ℝ ℀ ⊙ ⚑ ⚛ ⚖ 🏠 Services: ⚥ ✕ ⊞ lau Leisure: ⬚ L Off-site: ⬚PR

AUGSBURG   BAYERN

Augusta Mühlhauser Str 54B, 86169
☎ 0821 707575 ▤ 0821 705883
e-mail: webmaster@campingplatzaugusta.de
website: www.campingplatz-augusta.de
Hard standings for caravans. Separate section for residential caravans.
➲ *Leave E11 by Augsburg-Ost exit. Continue N towards Neuburg and turn right after 400mtrs.*
Open: All year Site: 6.6HEC ⚌ ℀ ⚑ Prices: ♠4.10 ♠3.10 ♠4.10 ▲3.10 pitch 19 (incl 2 persons) Facilities: ℝ ℀ ⊙ ⚑ ⚛ ⚖ 🏠 Services: ✕ Leisure: ⬚ L Off-site: ⚥

BAMBERG   BAYERN

AT BUG (5KM S)

Insel 96049 ☎ 0951 56320 ▤ 0951 56321
e-mail: campinginsel@web.de website: www.campinginsel.de
The site lies on the bank of the River Regnitz, S of Bamberg. 'Park & Ride' scheme into Bamberg.
➲ *Leave A73 at Bamberg South exit and follow B505/B4 towards Bamberg until you see camping signs leading off left.*
Open: All year Site: 5HEC ⚌ ℀ Prices: ♠3.90 ♠3.40 ♠6.70 ▲3.40 pitch 6.70 Facilities: ℝ ℀ ⊙ ⚑ ⚛ ⚖ 🏠 Services: ⚥ ✕ ⊞ lau Leisure: ⬚ R

BERCHTESGADEN   BAYERN

Allweglehen 83471 ☎ 08652 2396 ▤ 08652 63503
A terraced site at the foot of the Untersalzberg Mountain surrounded by bushy woods. There is also a steep and narrow asphalt access road with passing places. A truck is available for towing caravans. The camp is closed between 12.30 and 14.30 hrs and from 21.00 hrs.

➲ *For access, take the B305, and drive approx. 3.5km towards Schellenberg.*
Open: All year Site: 3HEC ⚌ ∷ ⚘ ℀ ⊞ ⚖ Facilities: ℝ ℀ ⊙ ⚑ ⚛ 🏠 Services: ✕ ⊞ Leisure: ⬚ P Off-site: ⬚R

BERGEN   BAYERN

Wagnerhof Campingstr 11, 83346
☎ 08662 8557 ▤ 08662 5924
e-mail: info@camping-bergen.de
website: www.camping-bergen.de
Level site.
Camping Card Compulsory.
➲ *Access from München-Salzburg motorway, Bergen exit. Turn right at sawmill just before entering town.*
Open: All year Site: 2.8HEC ⚘ ℀ Prices: ♠4.25-5.25 pitch 5.50-7 Facilities: ℝ ℀ ⊙ ⚑ ⚛ ⚖ 🏠 Off-site: ⚥ ✕ ⬚LP ⊞

BRUNNEN FORGGENSEE   BAYERN

Brunnen Seestr 81, 87645 ☎ 08362 8273 ▤ 08362 8630
e-mail: info@camping-brunnen.de
website: www.camping-brunnen.de
Situated on eastern shore of Lake Forggensee.
➲ *From Füssen follow B17 to Schwangau, then continue N on minor road.*
Open: 21 Dec-2 Nov Site: 6HEC ⚌ ⚘ ℀ Facilities: ℝ ℀ ⊙ ⚑ ⚛ ⚖ 🏠 Services: ⚥ ✕ ⊞ lau Leisure: ⬚ L Off-site: ⬚P

CHIEMING   BAYERN

Chieming Möwenplatz Haupstr 3, 83335 ☎ 08664 361 & 653
Small site on shore of lake, with gravelly terrain.
Camping Card Compulsory.
➲ *5km S of Chieming.*
Open: Apr-Sep Site: 0.8HEC ⚌ ℀ Facilities: ℝ ⊙ ⚑ 🏠 Services: ✕ ⊞ lau Leisure: ⬚ L Off-site: ℀ ⚥ ✕ ⚛ ⬚P

DIESSEN   BAYERN

St-Alban 86911 ☎ 08807 7305 ▤ 08807 1057
e-mail: ivan.pavic@t-online.de
website: www.camping-ammersee.de
Clean site next to St-Alban, lakeside with private bathing beach and reserved section for residential campers. Good sanitary installations also used by the public.
➲ *From München follow B12 towards Landsberg/Lech. Near Greifenberg turn left, proceed via Utting to St-Alban.*
Open: Apr-Oct Site: 3.8HEC ⚌ ℀ ⊙ ⚑ ⚛ 🏠 Services: ✕ ⊞ Leisure: ⬚ L Off-site: ⚘

DINKELSBÜHL   BAYERN

Romantische Strasse 91550 ☎ 09851 7817 ▤ 09851 7848
e-mail: campdinkelsbuhl@aol.de
Terraced site with some hedges and trees. Separate field for young people. Good sporting facilities.
➲ *Signposted.*
Open: All year Site: 12HEC ⚌ ℀ Facilities: ℝ ℀ ⊙ ⚑ ⚛ 🏠 ⚑ Services: ✕ ⊞ lau Leisure: ⬚ L Off-site: ⚥

ENDORF, BAD   BAYERN

Stein Hintersee 10, 83093 ☎ 08053 9349 ▤ 08053 798745
A family site in wooded surroundings on the shore of the Simsee.
Open: 15 May-15 Sep Site: 2.5HEC ⚌ ∷ ⚒
Prices: ♠4.50 ♠2 ♠3.50 ▲3.50 Facilities: ℝ ℀ ⊙ ⚑ 🏠 Services: lau Leisure: ⬚ L Off-site: ✕

ERLANGEN   BAYERN

Rangau Campingstr 44, 91056
☎ 01935 8866 ▤ 01935 724743
e-mail: info@camping-rangau.de website: www.camping-rangau.de
Long stretch of land within the sportsground and next to the Dechsendorfer Weiher Lake in nature reserve.

Site: 6HEC-Site size ⚌-grass ∷-sand ⚘-stone ⚒-little shade ℀-partly shaded ♠-mainly shaded ⊞-bungalows for hire ⚑-caravans for hire ▲-tents for hire ⊘-no dogs **Prices:** ♠-adult per night ♠-car per night pp-per person per night ♠-caravan per night ▲-tent per night

⊃ *Leave motorway (A3/E5 Nürnberg-Würzburg) at exit Erlangen-West.*
Open: Apr-Sep Site: 18HEC ⚏ 🏕 Prices: ⚁4.50 pitch 4.50 Facilities: 🚿 ⊙ 🚻 🚮 🏕 Services: ✗ ⊞ lau Off-site: 🛒 ⟍L

ESCHERNDORF BAYERN

Escherndorf-Main 97332 ☎ 09381 2889 ▤ 09381 2889 website: www.camplingplatz-escherndorf.de Site lies on meadowland by the River Main, next to the ferry station (River Ferry Northeim). Lunchtime siesta 13.00-15.00 hrs.
⊃ *Site can be reached from motorway A7/E70 via exit Würzburg Estenfeld and follow road E towards 'Volkach'.*
Open: Apr-Oct Site: 1.5HEC ⚏ ♠ Prices: ⚁6 🚐5 ⚄4 Facilities: 🚿 🛒 ⊙ 🚻 🚮 🏕 Services: ✗ ⊞ lau Leisure: ⟍ PR

ESTENFELD BAYERN

Estenfeld Maidbronner Str 38, 97230 ☎ 09305 228 ▤ 09305 8006 e-mail: cplestenfeld@freenet.de website: www.camping-estenfeld.de On meadowland next to sportsground.
⊃ *From motorway A7/E70 leave at exit 'Würzburg/Estenfeld' and continue S on B19 for 1km.*
Open: Mar-23 Dec Site: 0.5HEC ⚏ 🏕 🚐 Prices: ⚁4.50 pitch 4 Facilities: 🚿 🛒 ⊙ 🚻 🚮 🏕 Services: ⚑ ✗ ⊞ lau Off-site: ✗ ⌀

FEILNBACH, BAD BAYERN

Tenda Reithof 2, 83075 ☎ 08066 533 ▤ 08066 8002 e-mail: info@tenda-camping.de website: www.tenda-camping.de Well organised site on level grassland with pitches laid out in circles and hardstandings for tourers near the entrance.
Camping Card Compulsory.
⊃ *Leave München-Salzburg motorway (A8/E11) at 'Bad Aibling' exit and continue S for 4km on unclass road.*
Open: All year Site: 14HEC ⚏ ♦ 🏕 Prices: ⚁4.50-5.50 🚐1.90-7 ⚄1.25-3 pitch 1.90-7 Facilities: 🚿 🛒 ⊙ 🚻 🚮 🏕 Services: ✗ ⊞ lau Leisure: ⟍ P Off-site: ⚑ ⟍L

FICHTELBERG BAYERN

Fichtelsee 95686 ☎ 09272 801 ▤ 09272 909045 e-mail: info@camping-fichtelsee.de website: www.camping-fichtelsee.de Gently sloping meadow amid pleasant woodland 100mtrs from Lake Fichtelsee.
⊃ *From A9/E6 Bad Berneck exit, take B303 to the Fichtelsee Leisure Centre turning.*
Open: 15 Dec-06 Nov Site: 2.6HEC ⚏ 🏕 Prices: ⚁5 pitch 6.50 Facilities: 🚿 🛒 ⊙ 🚻 ⌀ 🏕 Services: ⊞ lau Off-site: ⚑ ✗ 🚮 ⟍LP

FINSTERAU BAYERN

Nationalpark-Ost 94151 ☎ 08557 768 ▤ 08557 1062 e-mail: 085571062@t-online.de website: www.camping-nationalpark-ost.de Terraced site on edge of extensive woodland area at entrance to National Park.
⊃ *N of Freyung towards the frontier.*
Open: All year Site: 3HEC ⚏ 🏕 Prices: ⚁4.60 pitch 5 Facilities: 🚿 ⊙ 🚻 ⌀ 🚮 🏕 Services: ✗ ⊞ lau Off-site: 🛒 ⚑

A full guide to the Symbols & Abbreviations used in this book can be found on page 6

FRICKENHAUSEN BAYERN

KNAUS Camping Park Frickenhausen Ochsenfurter Strabe 49, 97252 ☎ 09331 3171 ▤ 09331 5784 e-mail: knauscamp.frickenhausen@freenet.de website: www.knauscamp.de On level meadow in a small poplar wood beside River Main. Lunchtime siesta 13.00-15.00 hrs.
⊃ *On N bank of Main 0.5km E of Ochsenfurt.*
Open: Jan-Oct & Dec Site: 3.4HEC ⚏ 🏕 🚐 ⚄ Prices: ⚁6 ⚄2 pitch 6-8 Facilities: 🚿 🛒 ⊙ 🚻 🚮 🏕 Services: ⚑ ✗ Leisure: ⟍ PR Off-site: ✗ ⊞

FÜRTH IM WALD BAYERN

Einberg Daberger Str 33, 93437 ☎ 09973 1811 ▤ 09973 803220 e-mail: camping@stadtwerke-furth.de website: www.stadtwerke-furth.de Municipal site in Dabergerstr, near swimming pool.
⊃ *NE of Cham on B20.*
Open: Mar-Oct Site: 2HEC ⚏ 🏕 Prices: ⚁3.60 🚐2.60 🚐3.10 ⚄2 Facilities: 🚿 ⊙ 🚻 ⌀ 🏕 Services: ⊞ lau Leisure: ⟍ R Off-site: 🛒 ⚑ ✗ ⌀ 🚮 ⟍P

FÜSSEN BAYERN

Hopfensee 87629 ☎ 08362 917710 ▤ 08362 917720 e-mail: info@camping-hopfensee.com website: www.camping-hopfensee.com In quiet situation beside lake. Private beach. Ski-ing lessons.
⊃ *4km N of Füssen.*
Open: 15 Dec-7 Nov Site: 8HEC ⚏ 🏕 Prices: ⚁7.45-8.50 pitch 11-12.20 Facilities: 🚿 🛒 ⊙ 🚻 🚮 🏕 Services: ⚑ ✗ ⊞ lau Leisure: ⟍ LP

FÜSSING, BAD BAYERN

Max I Falkenstr 12, Egglfing, 94072 ☎ 08537 96170 ▤ 08537 961710 e-mail: info@campingmax.de website: www.campingmax.de On a level meadow with some trees. Good modern facilities.
⊃ *Access via B12. Site S of Bad Füssing.*
Open: All year Site: 3HEC ⚏ ♠ 🏕 Facilities: 🚿 ⊙ 🚻 🚮 🏕 Services: ✗ ⊞ lau Off-site: ✗

Max II 94072 ☎ 08537 356 ▤ 08537 356 e-mail: CampingMax2@aol.com website: www.camping-max2.de On meadow divided into pitches and 1km from spa baths at Bad Füssing.
⊃ *Turn at Passau end of Tutling on B12 to Kircham then follow signs to site on Egglfinger Strasse, 2km from Bad Füssing.*
Open: All year Site: 1.5HEC ⚏ 🏕 🏕 🚐 Prices: ⚁4.50 ⚄4 pitch 5.50 Facilities: 🚿 🛒 ⊙ 🚻 🚮 🏕 Services: ⚑ ✗ ⊞ lau Off-site: ⟍PR

GADEN BAYERN

Schwanenplatz Schwanenpl 1, 83329 ☎ 08681 281 ▤ 08681 4276 e-mail: info@schwanenplatz.de website: www.schwanenplatz.de Site lies on a meadow, divided into sections beside one of Bavaria's warmest lakes, Waginger See.
⊃ *For access drive from Traunstein to Waging, then turn right in direction Freilassing 2km, then left to lake.*
Open: Apr-20 Oct Site: 4HEC ⚏ ⊙ 🚻 🚮 ⚗ Prices: ⚁4.65-5.65 pitch 5.50-8.80 Facilities: 🚿 ⊙ 🚻 🚮 🏕 Services: ⚑ ✗ ⊞ Leisure: ⟍ LR Off-site: 🛒 ⌀

GARMISCH-PARTENKIRCHEN BAYERN

Zugspitze Griesener Str 4, 82491 ☎ 08821 3180 ▤ 08821 947594 In beautiful setting at the foot of the Zugspitze between the road and the Loisach. *contd.*

Facilities: 🛒-shop 🚿-shower ⊙-electric points for razors 🚻-electric points for caravans 🏕-parking by tents permitted 🅿-compulsory separate car park Services: ✗-café/restaurant ⚑-bar ⌀-Camping Gaz International 🚮-gas other than Camping Gaz ⊞-first aid facilities lau-laundry Leisure: ⟍-swimming L-Lake P-Pool R-River S-Sea Off-site: All facilities within 2km

On the B24 towards the Austrian frontier.
Open: All year Site: 2.9HEC ⬛⬛⬛ ☘ Prices: ▲3-5
Facilities: ⋔ ⅄ ⊙ ⊡ ⌀ ☵ ⌂ Services: ⊞ lau Leisure: ⬎ R
Off-site: ⅄ ✕ ⬎LP

GEMÜNDEN AM MAIN BAYERN

Saaleinsel Duivenallee 7, 97737 ☎ 09351 8574 ▤ 09351 1093
This municipal site lies a short distance off the main road
bordering the River Fränkische Saale. It is in the grounds of a
sports field and has a swimming pool. Individual washing
cubicles with curtains for the ladies.
Access signposted off main B26 road.
Open: Apr-15 Oct Site: 5.1HEC ⬛⬛⬛ ⋇ Prices: ↟4.50 ⇜3
⇜3 ▲3 pitch 5.60 Facilities: ⋔ ⊙ ⊡ ⌀ ☵ ⌂ Services: ✕ ⊞
Leisure: ⬎ PR Off-site: ⅄ ⅄ ⌀

GEMÜNDEN-HOFSTETTEN BAYERN

Schönrain 97737 ☎ 09351 8645 ▤ 09351 8721
e-mail: info@spessart-camping.de
website: www.spessart-camping.de
Slightly sloping, partly terraced meadowland east of River
Main. Lunchtime siesta 13.00-15.00 hrs.
*From Gemünden/Main along the left bank of the River
Main about 3km downstream. Turn left of B26 through
Hofstetten to site.*
Open: Apr-Sep Site: 7HEC ⬛⬛⬛ ⋇ Facilities: ⋔ ⅄ ⊙ ⊡ ⌀ ☵
⌂ Services: ✕ ⊞ lau Leisure: ⬎ P

GOTTSDORF BAYERN

DUG-Ferienzentrum Bayerwald, Mitterweg 11, 94107
☎ 08593 880 ▤ 08593 88111
Extensive terrain in quiet location.
Access via A3 (Regensburg-Passau) and B388.
Open: 27 Mar-30 Oct Site: 12HEC ⬛⬛⬛ ♣ ⌸ Prices: ▲4.50-6
▲3.50-4.50 pitch 5.50-7.50 Facilities: ⋔ ⅄ ⊙ ⊡ ☵ ⌂
Services: ⊞ lau Off-site: ✕ ⬎LPR

GRIESBACH, BAD BAYERN

Kur-Und Feriencamping Dreiquellenbad 94086
☎ 08532 96130 ▤ 08532 961350
e-mail: info@camping-bad-griesbach.de
website: www.camping-bad-griesbach.de
In pleasant wooded surroundings with good, modern
facilities.
1km S of Griesbach Spa, on the Karpfham-Schwaim road.
Open: All year Site: 3.7HEC ⬛⬛⬛ ⌀ ⋇ ⌸ Prices: ↟4.90
⇜7.80-8.80 Facilities: ⋔ ⅄ ⊙ ⊡ ☵ ⌂ Services: ⅄ ✕ ⊞ lau
Leisure: ⬎ P

HASLACH BAYERN

Feriencenter Wertacher Hof 87466
☎ 08361 770 ▤ 08361 9344
Well-kept site on Lake Grüntensee.
Access road near the Wertach-Haslach railway station.
Open: All year Site: 3.5HEC ⬛⬛⬛ ⌀ ⋇ Prices: ↟5.50 pitch 5
Facilities: ⋔ ⅄ ⊙ ⊡ ⌀ ☵ ⌂ Services: ✕ lau Leisure: ⬎ L

HERSBRUCK BAYERN

AT HOHENSTADT (6KM E)

Pegnitz Eschenbacher Weg 4, 91224
☎ 09154 1500 ▤ 09154 91200
A quiet holiday site in set among wooded hills near the River
Pegnitz.
About 6km E of Hersbruck.
Open: Mar-Oct Site: 1.1HEC ⬛⬛⬛ ♣ Facilities: ⋔ ⊙ ⊡ ⌀ ⌂
Services: ✕ ⊞ lau Leisure: ⬎ R Off-site: ⅄ ⅄ ✕ ☵ ⬎LP

HOFHEIM BAYERN

Brugger am Riegsee 82418 ☎ 08847 728 ▤ 08847 228
e-mail: camping.brugger@t-online.de
website: www.camping-brugger.de
A lakeside site in a rural setting with good, modern facilities.
Site: 6HEC ⬛⬛⬛ ⌀ ♣ Prices: ↟4.50 ⇜2 ▲4.50-10 pitch 8-14
Facilities: ⋔ ⅄ ⊙ ⊡ ⌀ ☵ ⌂ Services: ⅄ ✕ ⊞ lau
Leisure: ⬎ L

HOHENWARTH BAYERN

Fritz-Berger-Comfort 93480 ☎ 09946 367 ▤ 09946 477
e-mail: cpl.hohenwarth@fritz-berger.de
website: www.fritz-berger.de
Meadowland in the valley of the Weissens Regens with views
of the mountain range and town above.
*Access from Cham on the B85 S to Miltach and continue
via Kotzing to Hohenwarth.*
Site: 12HEC ⬛⬛⬛ ⋇ Facilities: ⋔ ⅄ ⊙ ⊡ ⌀ ☵ ⌂ Services: ✕
Leisure: ⬎ LP

INGOLSTADT BAYERN

AZUR Camping Auwaldsee 85053
☎ 0841 9611616 ▤ 0841 9611617
Near to Auwaldsee, this site lies in a beautiful setting beside
the München-Ingolstadt motorway.
*Access via the Ingolstadt-Süd exit off the A9/E6 (Müchen-
Nürnberg motorway).*
Open: All year Site: 10HEC ⬛⬛⬛ ⋇ Facilities: ⋔ ⅄ ⊙ ⊡ ☵
⌂ Services: ✕ ⊞ lau Leisure: ⬎ L Off-site: ⬎P

ISSIGAU BAYERN

Schloss Issigau Altes Schloss 3, 95188
☎ 09293 7173 ▤ 09293 7050
e-mail: schloss_issigau@t.online.de
website: www.schloss-issigau.de
*About 5km W off A9/E6 (München-Berlin) road via the
Berg/Bad Steben exit.*
Open: 15 Mar-Oct Site: 2HEC ⬛⬛⬛ ⋇ ⌸ Prices: ↟4.50 ⇜5
▲4-5 pitch 5 Facilities: ⋔ ⊙ ⊡ ☵ ⌂ Services: ⅄ ✕ ⊞ lau
Off-site: ⅄

JODITZ BAYERN

Auensee 95189 ☎ 09295 381
Municipal site on partly terraced meadowland above lake.
*Leave München-Berlin motorway at Berg-Bad Steben exit
and drive E for 4km.*
Open: All year Site: 9HEC ⬛⬛⬛ ⋇ Facilities: ⋔ ⊙ ⊡ ☵ ⌂
Services: ⊞ lau Leisure: ⬎ L Off-site: ⅄ ✕ ⬎P

KIPFENBERG BAYERN

AZUR-Camping Altmühltal Campingstr, 85110
☎ 08465 905167 ▤ 08465 3745
e-mail: kipfenberg@azur-camping.de
website: www.azur-camping.de/kipfenberg
Well equipped site in an unspoilt wooded location with good
canoeing facilities.
Open: Apr-Oct Site: 5.5HEC ⬛⬛⬛ ♣ ⌸ Prices: ↟4.50-6
▲3.50-4.50 pitch 5.50-7.50 Facilities: ⋔ ⊙ ⊡ ☵ ⌂ Services: ⊞
lau Leisure: ⬎ R Off-site: ⅄ ⅄ ✕ ⬎P

KIRCHZELL BAYERN

AZUR-Camping Odenwald 63931
☎ 09373 566 ▤ 09373 7375
e-mail: kirchzell@azur-camping.de
website: www.azur-camping.de
In natural terraced meadowland in wooded hilly country. No
admission after 21.30 hrs. Lunchtime siesta 13.00-15.00 hrs.

Site: 6HEC-Site size ⬛⬛⬛-grass ∷∷-sand ⌀-stone ⋇-little shade ⋇-partly shaded ♣-mainly shaded
⌸-bungalows for hire ⇜-caravans for hire ▲-tents for hire ⊘-no dogs Prices: ↟-adult per night ⇜-car per night
pp-per person per night ⇜-caravan per night ▲-tent per night

➲ *From Amorbach follow the Eberbach road for 5km. Site 1km from town.*
Open: 15 Mar-15 Nov Site: 7HEC ▦ 🖧 Prices: ♦4.50-6 ▲3.50-4.50 pitch 5.50-7.50 Facilities: 🖍 🛋 ⊙ 🖳 ⚓ 🏕 Services: ☕ ✖ 🖭 lau Leisure: ⸰ P

KISSINGEN, BAD BAYERN

Bad Kissingen Euerdorfer Str 1, 97688
☎ 0971 5211 🗐 0971 5211
e-mail: info@campingpark-badkissingen.de
website: www.campingpark-badkissingen.de
In park beside River Saale. Lunchtime siesta 13.00-15.00 hrs.
➲ *Access near the southern bridge over the Saale.*
Open: Apr-15 Oct Site: 1.8HEC ▦ 🖧 Facilities: 🖍 🛋 ⊙ 🖳 ⚓ 🏕 Services: ✖ 🖭 lau Off-site: ⸰P

KITZINGEN BAYERN

Schiefer Turm Marktbreiter Str 20, 97318
☎ 09321 33125 🗐 09321 384795
e-mail: chr.schroeder@t-online.de
➲ *Access via A3 exit Biebelried/Kitzingen.*
Open: Apr-15 Oct Site: 2.3HEC ▦ 🖧 Facilities: 🖍 🛋 ⊙ 🖳 ⚓ 🏕 Services: ☕ ✖ lau Leisure: ⸰ R Off-site: ⸰P

KLINGENBRUNN BAYERN

NationalPark 94518 ☎ 08553 727 🗐 08553 6930
website: www.camping-nationalpark.de
In pleasant wooded surroundings attractively set out around the restaurant building.
➲ *For access, leave the B85, which turns from Cham to Passau, approx. 12km SE of Regen near Kirchdorf turn off E and drive about 6km towards Klingenbrunn.*
Open: All year Site: 5HEC ▦ 🖧 🐝 🖧 Prices: ♦3.60 ▲3.30 pitch 4.10 Facilities: 🖍 🛋 ⊙ 🖳 ⚓ 🏕 Services: ✖ 🖭 lau Off-site: ☕ ⸰LP

KÖNIGSDORF BAYERN

Königsdorf Am Bibisee, 82549
☎ 08171 81580 🗐 08171 81165
e-mail: mail@camping-koenigsdorf.de
website: www.camping-koenigsdorf.de
Unspoilt site in natural setting in meadowland. A number of individual pitches for tourers. Lunchtime siesta 12.30-14.30 hrs.
➲ *Off B11, 2km N of town just beyond the edge of the forest.*
Open: All year Site: 8.6HEC ▦ 🖧 🖧 Facilities: 🖍 🛋 ⊙ 🖳 ⚓ 🏕 Services: ✖ 🖭 lau Leisure: ⸰ L Off-site: ☕ ⸰PRS

KÖNIGSSEE BAYERN

Mühlleiten 83477 ☎ 08652 4584 🗐 08652 69194
e-mail: buchung@camping-muehlleiten.de
website: www.camping-muehlleiten.de
A pleasant site in wooded surroundings adjacent to a small guesthouse. Beautiful views of the Berchtesgaden mountains.
➲ *N of Königsee towards Berchtesgaden.*
Open: All year Site: 1.5HEC ▦ 🖧 Prices: ♦6.50 🖧2.50 🖧2.50 pitch 5 Facilities: 🖍 🛋 ⊙ 🖳 ⚓ 🏕 Services: ✖ lau Leisure: ⸰ R Off-site: ☕ ⸰LP

KRUN BAYERN

Tennsee 82493 ☎ 08825 170 🗐 08825 17236
e-mail: info@camping-tennsee.de
website: www.camping-tennsee.de
A partially terraced site with fine views of the Karwendel and Zugspitz mountains.
➲ *From München-Garmisch-Partenkirchen motorway take B2 to Mittenwald and follow signs "Tennsee".*
Open: 15 Dec-06 Nov Site: 5HEC ⠿ 🖧 ❀ ⁂ 🐝 Prices: ♦7 🖧3.50 pitch 19-20.50 (incl 2 persons) Facilities: 🖍 🛋 ⊙ 🖳 ⚓ 🏕 Services: ☕ ✖ 🖭 lau Off-site: ⸰L

KÜHNHAUSEN BAYERN

Stadler Strandbadstr 11, 83367
☎ 08686 8037 🗐 08685 919555
Level meadow on lake with private beach.
➲ *2m E shore of Lake Waginger.*
Open: Apr-Sep Site: 0.8HEC ▦ 🖧 🐝 🖧 Prices: ♦4.50 🖧1.50 🖧4-6 ▲2-5 pp4.50 Facilities: 🖍 ⊙ 🖳 🏕 Services: lau Leisure: ⸰ L Off-site: 🛋 ☕ ✖ ⚓ 🖭

LACKENHÄUSER BAYERN

KNAUS Lackenhäuser Lackenhauser 127, 94089
☎ 08583 311 🗐 08583 91079
e-mail: knaus-camping-lackenhaeuser@t-online.de
website: www.knauscamp.de
Extensive site with woodland parks, waterfalls. Siesta 13.00-15.00 hrs. Many health resort facilities. Garden chess. Curling.
Open: Dec-Oct Site: 14.5HEC ▦ 🖧 🐝 🖧 ▲ Prices: ♦6 ▲2 pitch 3-8 Facilities: 🖍 🛋 ⊙ 🖳 ⚓ 🏕 Services: ☕ ✖ Leisure: ⸰ P Off-site: 🖭

LANGLAU BAYERN

Langlau Seestr 30, Kleiner Brombachsee, 91738
☎ 09834 96969 🗐 09834 96968
e-mail: mail@seecamping-langlau.de
website: www.seecamping-langlau.de
On the shores of the Kleiner Brombachsee.
➲ *From Gunzenhausen 10km in the direction of Pleinfield.*
Open: Mar-Sept Site: 12.4HEC ▦ 🖧 🖧 Prices: ♦5.50 pitch 6.50 Facilities: 🖍 🛋 ⊙ 🖳 ⚓ 🏕 Services: ☕ ✖ lau Off-site: ✖ ⸰L 🖭

LECHBRUCK BAYERN

DCC Stadt Essen Oberer Lechsee, 8923
☎ 08862 8426 🗐 08862 7570
Terraced site, very tidy and well maintained on Oberen Lech lake. Separate section for dog owners. Closed 13.00-15.00 hrs and 22.00-07.00 hrs.
➲ *Signposted from town centre.*
Open: All year Site: 20HEC ▦ 🖧 Facilities: 🖍 🛋 ⊙ 🖳 ⚓ 🏕 Services: ✖ 🖭 lau Leisure: ⸰ L Off-site: ⸰P

LENGFURT BAYERN

Main-Spessart-Park 97855 ☎ 09395 1079 🗐 8295
e-mail: info@camping-main-spessart.de
website: www.camping-main-spessart.de
Site lies partly on terraced meadowland and partly on the eastern slopes of the Main Valley. Lunchtime siesta 13.00-15.00 hrs, Possibilities for water sports, nearby private mooring on the River Main.
➲ *From Frankfurt-Würzburg motorway A3/E5 leave at exit Markheidenfeld. In Altfled then E for 6km to Lengfurt. Site lies at NW edge of village.*
Open: All year Site: 10HEC ▦ 🖧 Prices: ♦5 🖧2 🖧3.50 ▲3 Facilities: 🖍 🛋 ⊙ 🖳 ⚓ 🏕 Services: ✖ lau Off-site: ⸰PR 🖭

LINDAU IM BODENSEE BAYERN

Gitzenweiler Hof 88131 ☎ 08382 94940 🗐 08382 949415
e-mail: info@gitzenweiler-hof.de
website: www.gitzenweiler-hof.de
Located in hilly meadow ground near Lake Constance surrounded with trees and hedges.
➲ *A96 Autobahn (Memmingen-Bregenz) exit Weissensberg*
Open: All year Site: 14HEC ▦ ❀ 🖧 Prices: ♦6.50 pitch 8 Facilities: 🖍 🛋 ⊙ 🖳 ⚓ 🏕 Services: ☕ ✖ 🖭 lau Leisure: ⸰ P

Facilities: 🛋-shop 🖍-shower ⊙-electric points for razors 🖳-electric points for caravans 🏕-parking by tents permitted 🅿-compulsory separate car park Services: ✖-café/restaurant ☕-bar ⚓-Camping Gaz International ⚒-gas other than Camping Gaz 🖭-first aid facilities lau-laundry Leisure: ⸰-swimming L-Lake P-Pool R-River S-Sea Off-site: All facilities within 2km

Waldcamping München-Obermenzing

To reach the site from Cross Münich West until the end at Mu-Lochhaüsen.
Set in a large park of 50,000 sq.m 900m from the end of the motorway Stuttgart-München.
350 spaces for caravans and tents, 130 with own electricity supply and separated by hedges. Individual washing cubicles, free hot water for washing, hot showers, washing machine, dryer, heated washrooms, self-service shop.
Opportunities for swimming 2.5km from site.
Locked from 22.00 hrs. Good connections to city centre by bus, tram or urban railway. Open from 15.3-31.10.
Farmer: A. Blenck Telephone 089/8 11 22 35 Fax 089/8 14 48 07
www.campingplatz-muenchen.de
email: campingplatz-obermenzing@t-online.de

AT ZECH (4KM SE)

Lindau am See Fraunhoferstr 20, 88131
☎ 08382 72236 ▤ 08382 976106
e-mail: info@park-camping.de
website: www.park-camping.de
Site lies on meadowland with trees, reaching down to the lake. Very large sanitary blocks. Common room, reading room, field for ball games and a separate common room for young people.
➲ *From Lindau, take the B31 towards Bregenz and turn right (signposted) just before the level crossing. The site is 500mtrs further down the road.*
Open: All year Site: 5HEC ▦ ⚭ ♣ ▦ Prices: ⋔4.50-5.50 ⋔2.40-3 ▲1.50-2.50 pitch 4.50-6 Facilities: ⋔ ⚑ ⊙ ⊒ ♨ ⚠ 🏛 Services: 🍴 ✕ ⊞ lau Leisure: ⋎ L Off-site: ⋎P

MEMMINGEN BAYERN

AT BUXHEIM (5KM NW)

See International Am Weiherhaus 7, 87740
☎ 08331 71800 ▤ 08331 63554
website: www.camping-buxheim.de
Terraced site beyond public bathing area.
➲ *Leave Um-Kempten motorway at Memminger Kreuz then right to Buxheim.*
Open: May-Sep Site: 42HEC ▦ ♣ Prices: ⋔4.20 ⋔3 ⋔7.50 ▲2.50 pitch 7.50 Facilities: ⋔ ⚑ ⊙ ⊒ ♨ 🏛 Services: 🍴 ✕ ⊞ lau Leisure: ⋎ L Off-site: ✕ ∅ ⋎P

MITTENWALD BAYERN

Isarhorn 82481 ☎ 08823 5216
In a loop of the River Isar with many pines. Lunchtime siesta 13.00-15.00 hrs.

➲ *3km N to the W of B2 (Garmisch-Partenkirchen-Mittenwald road).*
Open: All year Site: 7.5HEC ▦ ⚭ ♣ Facilities: ⋔ ⚑ ⊙ ⊒
∅ 🏛 Services: ✕ ⊞ Leisure: ⋎ R Off-site: 🍴 ✕ ⋎LP

MÖRSLINGEN BAYERN

Mörslingen 89435 ☎ 09074 4024 ▤ 09071 42
Camping Card Compulsory.
➲ *6km N of Dillengen.*
Open: All year Site: 1HEC ▦ ♣ ▦ ▦ Facilities: ⋔ ⊙ ⊒ ♨
🏛 Services: ⊞ lau Leisure: ⋎ L

MÜHLHAUSEN BEI AUGSBURG BAYERN

Lech Seeweg 6, 86444 ☎ 08207 2200 ▤ 08207 2202
e-mail: info@lech-camping.de
website: www.lech-camping.de
On level grassland with own swimming facilities on lakeside.
➲ *4km N in direction of Neuburg.*
Open: Apr-15 Sep Site: 3HEC ▦ ⚑ ▦ Prices: ⋔5-5.50
⋔1.50 ⋔7 ▲5-7 Facilities: ⋔ ⊙ ⊒ ∅ ♨ 🏛 Services: ✕ ⊞
lau Leisure: ⋎ L Off-site: 🐟 ⋎P

Ludwigshof am See Augsburger Str 36, 86444
☎ 08207 96170 ▤ 08207 961770
e-mail: info@bauer-caravan.de
website: www.bauer-caravan.de
Clean site with small lake away from motorway, near restaurant of the same name. Separate section for residential pitches.
➲ *1.5km from Augsburg Ost exit towards Neuberg.*
Open: Apr-Oct Site: 14HEC ▦ ⚑ Prices: ⋔4.50 ⋔5-9
Facilities: ⋔ 🐟 ⊙ ⊒ ∅ ♨ 🏛 Services: 🍴 ✕ ⊞ lau Leisure: ⋎
L Off-site: 🐟 ⋎PR

MÜNCHEN (MUNICH) BAYERN

AT OBERMENZING

München-Obermenzing Lochhausener Str 59, 81247
☎ 089 8112235 ▤ 089 8144807
e-mail: campingplatz-obermenzing@t-online.de
website: www.campingplatz-muenchen.de
Park-like site near motorway. Shop closed in winter and no campers accepted after 31 Oct.
Camping Card or Identification papers Compulsory.
➲ *Approx 1km from the end of Stuttgart-München motorway.*
Open: 15 Mar-Oct Site: 5.5HEC ▦ ∴ ⚭ ♣ ▦ ▦
Prices: ⋔4.35 ⋔6 ⋔6 ▲3.85 Facilities: ⋔ ⚑ ⊙ ⊒ ∅ 🏛
Services: 🍴 ✕ ⊞ lau Off-site: 🍴 ✕ ⋎LPR

NEUBÄU BAYERN

Seecamping Seestr 4, 93426 ☎ 09469 331
e-mail: seecamp-neubau@t-online.de
Meadowland site along lakeshore.
➲ *Access from Schwandorf on the B85 in direction of Cham.*
Site: 5HEC ▦ ♣ Facilities: ⋔ 🐟 ⊙ ⊒ ∅ ♨ 🏛 Services: 🍴 ✕
⊞ lau Leisure: ⋎ L

NEUSTADT BAYERN

Main-Spessart-Camping-International 97845
☎ 09393 639 ▤ 09393 1607
Beautifully situated site along the River Main. Watersports, including water skiing. Lunchtime siesta 12.00-14.00 hrs.
➲ *Access from Frankfurt-Würzburg motorway A3/E5, leave at Marktheidenfeld exit, and follow road towards Lohr.*
Open: Apr-Sep Site: 5.6HEC ▦ ⚑ Prices: ⋔4.50 pitch 6
Facilities: ⋔ 🐟 ⊙ ⊒ ∅ ♨ 🏛 Services: ✕ lau Leisure: ⋎ PR
Off-site: ✕

Site: 6HEC-Site size ▦-grass ∴-sand ⚭-stone ⚫-little shade ⚑-partly shaded ♣-mainly shaded
▦-bungalows for hire ▦-caravans for hire ▲-tents for hire ∅-no dogs Prices: ⋔-adult per night ⋔-car per night
pp-per person per night ▦-caravan per night ▲-tent per night

NÜRNBERG (NUREMBERG) BAYERN

Knaus Campingpark Nürnberg Hans-Kalb-Str 56, 90471
☎ 0911 9812717 ▤ 0911 9812718
e-mail: knaus.camp.nbg@freenet.de
website: www.knauscamp.de
Well-kept municipal site in beautiful situation in a forest
between a stadium with a swimming pool and the Trade Fair
Centre.
➲ *Leave A9 München motorway at Nürnberg-Fischbach exit,*
and continue towards the stadium.
Open: All year Site: 2.7HEC 👑 ♠ 🏕 🚐 ▲ Prices: ⚑6 ▲2
pitch 9.50 Facilities: 🏪 ⚐ ⊙ 🔌 🍴 🖽 Services: ♀ ✗
Off-site: ✗ ⚡LP 🖽

OBERAMMERGAU BAYERN

Oberammergau Ettaler Str 56, 82847
☎ 08822 94105 ▤ 08822 94197
e-mail: campingpark-oberammergau@t-online.de
website: www.campingpark-oberammergau.de
A year-round site with good, modern facilities providing fine
views of the Bavarian Alps.
➲ *Signposted from the town.*
Open: All year Site: 2.6HEC 👑 ♠ ⚑ 🏕 🚐 Prices: ⚑7.50-12
🚐7.50-12 ▲7.50-12 pitch 7.50-12 Facilities: 🏪 ⚐ ⊙ 🔌 ⚡ 🍴
🖽 Services: ♀ ✗ 🖽 lau Leisure: ⚡ R Off-site: ⚡P

OBERSTDORF BAYERN

Oberstdorf 87561 ☎ 08322 6525 ▤ 08322 809760
e-mail: camping-oberstdorf@t-online.de
website: www.camping-oberstdorf.de
Level grassland site with fine mountain views.
➲ *800m N of town centre near railway line.*
Open: Apr-Oct Site: 16HEC 👑 ♠ ⚑ 🏕 Prices: ⚑4.60-5.10
🚐2.60 🚐4.60-5.10 ▲2.60-4.60 Facilities: 🏪 ⚐ ⊙ 🔌 ⚡ 🍴 🖽
Services: ✗ 🖽 lau Off-site: ⚐ ⚡PR

OBERWÖSSEN BAYERN

Litzelau 83246 ☎ 08640 8704 ▤ 08640 5265
e-mail: camping-litzelau@t-online.de
website: www.camping-litzelau.de
Almost level meadowland surrounded by forested slopes.
➲ *Take B305 from Bernau exit on München-Salzburg*
motorway and continue through Marquartstein and
Unterwössen.
Open: All year Site: 4.5HEC 👑 ♠ ⚑ 🏕 Prices: ⚑4 🚐6.50
▲3.50 Facilities: 🏪 ⚐ ⊙ 🔌 ⚡ 🍴 🖽 Services: ♀ ✗ 🖽 lau
Leisure: ⚡ R Off-site: ⚡LP

PASSAU BAYERN

Dreiflüsse 94113 ☎ 08546 633 ▤ 08546 2686
e-mail: dreifluessecamping@t-online.de
website: www.dreifluessecamping.privat.t-online.de
A well equipped site in pleasant wooded surroundings.
➲ *From A3 exit 'Passau-Nord' follow signposts.*
Open: Apr-Oct Site: 5HEC 👑 ⁙⁙ ♠ 🏕 🚐 ▲ Prices: ⚑3
pitch 5-9 Facilities: 🏪 ⚐ ⊙ 🔌 ⚡ 🍴 🖽 🖪 Services: ♀ ✗ 🖽 lau
Leisure: ⚡ P

PFRAUNDORF BAYERN

Kratzmühle 85125 ☎ 08461 64170 ▤ 08461 641717
e-mail: kratzmuehle@t-online.de
website: www.kratzmuehle.de
Terraced site, divided into pitches, on a wooded hillside
overlooking the River Altmühl.
➲ *In village turn off to Kratzmühle.*
Open: All year Site: 9.6HEC 👑 ⚑ 🏕 Prices: ⚑5-5.50 pitch
5-7 Facilities: 🏪 ⚐ ⊙ 🔌 🍴 🖽 Services: ✗ 🖽 lau
Leisure: ⚡ LR

PIDING BAYERN

Staufeneck 83451 ☎ 08651 2134 ▤ 710450
e-mail: camping-staufeneck@t-online.de
website: www.camping-berchtesgadener-land.de
In beautiful and quiet situation beside River Saalach.
➲ *Leave motorway A8/E11 (München-Salzburg) via exit Bad*
Reichenall road for 2.5km and then turn right.
Open: Apr-Oct Site: 2.7HEC 👑 ♠ ⚑ Prices: ⚑5.50 pitch 5
Facilities: 🏪 ⚐ ⊙ ⚑ 🍴 🖽 Services: 🖽 lau
Off-site: ♀ ✗ ⚐

PIELENHOFEN BAYERN

Naabtal 93188 ☎ 09409 373 ▤ 723
e-mail: campingpielenhofen@t-online.de
website: www.camping-pielenhofen.de
The site is well-situated beside the River Nab, and has a
special section for overnight visitors.
➲ *Access from the Nittendorf turn off from A3/E5 Nürnberg-*
Regensburg N via Etterzhausen.
Open: All year Site: 6HEC 👑 ♠ 🏕 Prices: ⚑4.95 pitch 5.70
Facilities: 🏪 ⚐ ⊙ 🔌 ⚐ 🍴 🖽 Services: ♀ ✗ 🖽 lau
Leisure: ⚡ R

POTTENSTEIN BAYERN

Bärenschlucht 91278 ☎ 09243 206
The site lies on unspoilt meadowland in the narrow Püttlach
valley and is surrounded by the rocky hills of the Fränkische
Schweiz range.
➲ *From the München-Berlin motorway leave at the Pegnitz*
exit and drive W for 10km on the B470 towards Forchheim.
Open: All year Site: 5HEC 👑 ⚑ 🏕 🏕 Facilities: 🏪 ⚐ ⊙ ⚐
⚐ 🖽 Services: ✗ 🖽 lau Leisure: ⚡ R

PRIEN AM CHIEMSEE BAYERN

Hofbauer Bernauerstrasse 110, 83209
☎ 08051 4136 ▤ 08051 62657
e-mail: ferienhaus-campingpl.hofbauer@t-online.de
website: www.camping-prien-chiemsee.de
Situated in a peaceful location amid the Bavarian foothills of
the Alps with fine views of the nearby mountains. Site
divided into separate plots.
➲ *A8 motorway from Munich towards Salzburg, take exit 106*
for Bernau and turn right for Prien. Site approx 3km on left
Open: Apr-Oct Site: 2HEC 👑 ⚑ Facilities: 🏪 ⊙ ⚐ 🖽
Services: ♀ ✗ lau Leisure: ⚡ P Off-site: ⚐ ✗ ⚡L 🖽

ROSSHAUPTEN BAYERN

Warsitzka 87669 ☎ 08367 406 ▤ 08367 1256
e-mail: info@camping-warsitzka.de
website: www.camping-warsitzka.de
A well-kept site with good installations.
➲ *From Füssen follow road B16 for 10km towards*
Rosshaupten. About 2km before the village and before the
bridge turn right.
Open: All year Site: 4.5HEC 👑 ⚐ Prices: ⚑5-5.20 🚐6.20-
7.70 ▲6.20-7.70 pitch 6.20-7.70 Facilities: 🏪 ⚐ ⊙ ⚐ 🍴 🖽
Services: ♀ ✗ 🖽 lau Leisure: ⚡ LR

ROTHENBURG OB DER TAUBER BAYERN

Tauber-Idyll Detwang 28A, 91541
☎ 09861 3177 ▤ 09861 92848
e-mail: campingtauber-ldyll@t-online.de
website: www.rothenberg.de/tauber-idyll
This well-kept site lies on a meadow scattered with trees and
bushes, on the outskirts of the northern suburb of Detwang
and next to the River Tauber.

contd.

Facilities: 🏪-shop 🏕-shower ⊙-electric points for razors ⚐-electric points for caravans 🖽-parking by tents permitted
🖪-compulsory separate car park **Services:** ✗-café/restaurant ♀-bar ⚐-Camping Gaz International 🍴-gas other than Camping
Gaz 🖽-first aid facilities lau-laundry **Leisure:** ⚡-swimming L-Lake P-Pool R-River S-Sea **Off-site:** All facilities within 2km

⮑ *Access from all main roads is well signposted. The best route is from Nordinger Str (B25) heading W along the River Tauber in the direction of Bad Mergentheim.*
Open: 1 wk before Etr-Oct Site: 0.5HEC ⬛ ⌇ Prices: ⋔4 pitch 4.50-5 Facilities: ⌇ ⌇ ⊙ ⌇ ⌀ ⌇ ⌇ Services: ⊞ lau Off-site: ✕ ⌇R

Tauber-Romantik Detwang 39, 91541
☎ 09861 6191 ⦀ 09861 86899
e-mail: info@camping-tauberromantik.de
website: www.camping-tauberromantik.de
Open: 15 Mar-4 Nov Site: 1.2HEC ⬛ ♠ ⌇ ⌇
Prices: ⋔4.50 ⋔1.50 ⋔6 ⋔4.50 pitch 6 Facilities: ⌇ ⌇ ⊙ ⌇
⌀ ⌇ ⌇ Services: ⌇ ✕ lau Off-site: ⌇R

Terrassen-Camping am Richterbichl 82401
☎ 08867 1500 ⦀ 08867 8300
e-mail: christof.echtler@t-online.de
website: www.camping-rottenbuch.de
Several pleasant terraces with good views.
⮑ *On S outskirts on B23.*
Open: All year Site: 2.4HEC ⬛ ⌇ ⌇ Prices: ⋔4.70 pitch 4.70-5.50 Facilities: ⌇ ⌇ ⊙ ⌇ ⌀ ⌇ ⌇ Services: ⌇ ✕ lau Leisure: ⌇ L Off-site: ✕ ⌇PR ⊞

RUHPOLDING BAYERN

Ortnerhof Ort 5, 83324 ☎ 08663 1764 ⦀ 08663 5073
e-mail: camping-ortnerhof@t-online.de
website: www.ruhpolding.de/camping
Well-kept site on a meadow at the foot of the Rauschberg Mountain, opposite the cable-car station.
⮑ *Off Deutsche Alpenstr.*
Open: All year Site: 2.4HEC ⬛ ⌇ ⌇ ⌇ ♠ ⌇ ⌇ Prices: ⋔ 4.50 ⋔ 1.50 ⌇3 ⋔3 pitch 4.50 Facilities: ⌇ ⌇ ⊙ ⌇ ⌀ ⌇ ⌇ Services: ✕ ⊞ lau Off-site: ⌇

SCHECHEN BAYERN

Erlensee Rosenheimer Str 63, 83135
☎ 08039 1695 ⦀ 08039 9416
The site lies on the shores of an artificial lake.
⮑ *If approaching from Rosenheim, take the B15 approx 10km N of Rosenheim towards Wasserburg and turn right upon entering Schechen.*
Open: All year Site: 6HEC ⬛ ⌇ Prices: ⋔4.50 ⋔2 ⌇5 ⋔2.50-6 Facilities: ⌇ ⊙ ⌇ ⌇ ⌇ Services: ⊞ lau Leisure: ⌇ L Off-site: ⌇ ⌇ ✕

SCHÖNAU AM KÖNIGSSEE BAYERN

Grafenlehen Königsseer Fussweg 71, 83471
☎ 08652 4140 ⦀ 08652 690768
e-mail: camping-grafenlehen@t-online.de
website: www.camping-grafenlehen.de
Terraced and well drained site situated on the edge of the Berchtesgadener National Park. A quiet, peaceful location near Lake Königssee.
⮑ *From Munich leave motorway at Reichenhall and take B20 to Berchtesgaden. Turn right at railway station and remain on B20 to Königssee, turn right before large car park, site 20 mtrs on right*
Open: Jan-Oct & 11-31 Dec Site: 3HEC ⬛ ♠ ⌇
Facilities: ⌇ ⌇ ⊙ ⌇ Services: ⌇ ✕ lau Off-site: ⌇P

SEEFELD BAYERN

Strandbad Pilsensee Graf Toerringstr 11, 82229
☎ 08152 7232 ⦀ 08152 78473
e-mail: campingplatz@toerring-seefeld.de
website: www.toerring-seefeld.de
⮑ *S towards Pilsensee.*
Open: All year Site: 10HEC ⬛ ⌇ ⌇ Prices: ⋔4.20-5 ⋔1 ⌇6-7 ⋔5-6 Facilities: ⌇ ⌇ ⊙ ⌇ ⌀ ⌇ ⌇ Services: ✕ ⊞ lau Leisure: ⌇ L

SOMMERACH AM MAIN BAYERN

Katzenkopf am See 97334 ☎ 09381 9215 ⦀ 09381 6028
website: www.camping-katzenkopf.de
On level ground beside the river Main. Pitches divided by bushes and good recreational facilities.
⮑ *Leave A3 (Würzburg-Nürnberg) at exit 'Kitzingen-Schwarzach-Volkach' and continue towards Volkach for 7km.*
Open: Apr-07 Nov Site: 6HEC ⬛ ⌇ Prices: ⋔4.80-5 pitch 5-6 Facilities: ⌇ ⌇ ⊙ ⌇ ⌀ ⌇ Services: ⌇ ✕ ⊞ lau Leisure: ⌇ LR Off-site: ⌇ ⌇P ⊞

SONTHOFEN BAYERN

Iller Sinwagstr 2, 87527 ☎ 08321 2350 ⦀ 08321 71561
Site lies on the shore of the River Iller (too dangerous for swimming) near a swimming pool.
⮑ *1km on the B19 towards Obersdorf, before the bridge over the River Iller.*
Site: 2.1HEC ⬛ ⌇ Facilities: ⌇ ⌇ ⊙ ⌇ ⌀ ⌇ Services: ✕ ⊞ lau Leisure: ⌇ R Off-site: ✕ ⌇P

STADTSTEINACH BAYERN

Stadtsteinach 95346 ☎ 09225 800644 ⦀ 09225 800645
e-mail: info@campingplatz-stadsteinach.de
website: www.campingplatz-stadtsteinach.de
Terraced site on south-east facing slope with a view over the town and surrounding hills. Lunchtime siesta 13.00-15.00 hrs.

Site: 6HEC-Site size ⬛-grass ⌇-sand ♠-stone ⌇-little shade ⌇-partly shaded ♣-mainly shaded ⌇-bungalows for hire ⌇-caravans for hire ⌇-tents for hire ⌇-no dogs Prices: ⋔-adult per night ⋔-car per night pp-per person per night ⌇-caravan per night ⋔-tent per night

⮑ *Access via Badstr.*
Open: All year Site: 3.8HEC ⸝⸝⸝⸝⸝ ⬡ 💷 ⚠ Prices: ⚲4-6 💷5-7 ⚠3-4 pitch 5-7 Facilities: ⬥ ⚎ ⊙ 🖵 ≞ 🅿 Services: ✕ ⊞ lau Off-site: ⚡P

TETTENHAUSEN BAYERN

Gut Horn 83329 ☎ 08681 227 ▤ 08681 4282
e-mail: info@gut-horn.de website: www.gut-horn.de
Quiet site, divided into pitches on lake shore, sheltered by forest. Lunchtime siesta 13.00-14.00 hrs.
⮑ *SE on Wagingersee.*
Open: Mar-Nov Site: 5HEC ⸝⸝⸝⸝⸝ ⬡ 🚌 Prices: ⚲4.40-5 pitch 5.50-7 Facilities: ⬥ ⚎ ⊙ 🖵 ≞ 🅿 Services: ✕ lau Leisure: ⚡ L Off-site: ⬮ ⚡PR ⊞

TITTMONING BAYERN

Seebauer 84529 ☎ 08683 1216 ▤ 08683 7175
e-mail: campinseebauer@t-online.de
website: www.camping-seebauer.de
On meadow with a few terraces. Near a farm, beside a lake.
⮑ *3km NW towards Burghausen.*
Open: All year Site: 2.3HEC ⸝⸝⸝⸝⸝ ♠ 💷 Facilities: ⬥ ⚎ ⊙ 🖵 ⬮ ≞ 🅿 Services: ✕ ⊞ lau Leisure: ⚡ L Off-site: 💷 ⚡LP

TRAUSNITZ BAYERN

Trausnitz 92555 ☎ 09655 1304 ▤ 09655 1304
website: www.camping-trausnitz.de
In wooded surroundings on the shores of a lake with good, modern facilities.
⮑ *Access via A93 exit Pfreimd.*
Open: All year Site: 3.5HEC ⸝⸝⸝⸝⸝ ⬥ ⬡ 💷 Facilities: ⬥ ⚎ ⊙ 🖵 ≞ 🅿 Services: 💷 ✕ ⊞ Leisure: ⚡ LR

TÜCHERSFELD BAYERN

Fränkische Schweiz 91278
☎ 09242 1788 ▤ 09242 1040
e-mail: spaetling@t-online.de
website: www.cfs.via.t-online.de
⮑ *Access from motorway A9/E6, leave at exit 'Pegnitz' then 12km W on B470 towards Forchheim.*
Open: Apr-19 Oct Site: 2HEC ⸝⸝⸝⸝⸝ ⬡ Facilities: ⬥ ⚎ ⊙ 🖵 ⬮ ≞ 🅿 Services: 💷 ✕ ⊞ lau

VELBURG BAYERN

Hauenstein 92355 ☎ 09182 454 ▤ 09182 902251
A well-appointed site, lies on several terraces and is completely divided into individual pitches. All with electric points.
⮑ *From motorway A3 Nürnberg-Regensburg leave at exit Velberg, then continue through village towards the S following signs Naturbad.*
Open: All year Site: 5HEC ⸝⸝⸝⸝⸝ ⬡ Facilities: ⬥ ⚎ ⊙ 🖵 ≞ 🅿 Services: ✕ ⊞ lau Off-site: ⚡L

VIECHTACH BAYERN

KNAUS Viechtach Waldfrieden 22, 94234
☎ 09942 1095 ▤ 09942 902222
e-mail: knauscamp.viechtach@freenet.de
website: www.knauscamp.de
Site on slightly undulating meadow, divided by rows of trees. The site has modern facilities.
⮑ *For access, take the B85 which runs from the junction with the road towards Freibad Viechtach, and follow the signposts.*
Site: 5.7HEC ⸝⸝⸝⸝⸝ ⬡ 🚌 💷 ⚠ Prices: ⚠2 pitch 10-17.50 Facilities: ⬥ ⚎ ⊙ 🖵 ≞ 🅿 Services: ✕ ⊞ Leisure: ⚡ P

WAGING BAYERN

Strandcamping Am See 1, 83329
☎ 08681 552 ▤ 08681 45010
e-mail: strandcamp@aol.com website: strandcamp.de
Extensive, level grassland site divided in two by access road to neighbouring sailing club. The site lies near the Strandbad and Kurhaus bathing area and spa, and the Casino. There is a Kneipp (hydrotherapeutic) pool in the camp.
⮑ *Follow the signposts leading to the Strandbad bathing area.*
Open: Apr-Sep Site: 30HEC ⸝⸝⸝⸝⸝ ♠ 💷 ⬲ Facilities: ⬥ ⚎ ⊙ 🖵 ⬮ ≞ 🅿 Services: 💷 ✕ ⊞ lau Leisure: ⚡ L

WALTENHOFEN BAYERN

Insel-Camping am See 87448 ☎ 08379 881 ▤ 08379 7308
e-mail: insel-camping@t-online.de
website: www.insel-camping.de
A well equipped site situated directly on the lake shore with access to neighbouring ski slopes.
⮑ *Off B19, S of Memhölz.*
Open: All year Site: 1.5HEC ⸝⸝⸝⸝⸝ ⬡ Prices: ⚲4 ⬥1 💷4-6.50 ⚠3-5 pitch 4-6.50 Facilities: ⬥ ⊙ 🖵 ⬮ ≞ 🅿 Services: ✕ ⊞ lau Leisure: ⚡ L Off-site: 💷 💷 ⚡PR

WEISSACH BAYERN

Wallberg Rainerweg 10, 83700 ☎ 08022 5371 ▤ 08022 670274
e-mail: campingplatz-wallberg@web.de
This well-kept site lies on a level meadow with a few trees beside a stream.
⮑ *Take the B318 from Gmund to Tegernsee, drive through Bad Wiessee, and on to Wiessach, approx 9km further on.*
Open: All year Site: 3HEC ⸝⸝⸝⸝⸝ ⬡ 💷 Prices: ⚲4.50-5.20 💷2.50 💷5.50-6.50 ⚠4 Facilities: ⬥ ⚎ ⊙ 🖵 ⬮ ≞ 🅿 Services: ✕ Leisure: ⚡ R Off-site: ⚡L ⊞

WEISSENSTADT BAYERN

Weissenstädter See Badstr 91, 8687 ☎ 09253 288 ▤ 09253 8507
e-mail: st.weissenstadt@fichtelgebirge.org
website: www.weissenstadt.de
This municipal site is in close proximity to a swimming pool and a lake, so offering numerous sports facilities.
⮑ *1km NW of the town.*
Open: All year Site: 1.7HEC ⸝⸝⸝⸝⸝ ⬡ Facilities: ⬥ ⊙ 🖵 ⬮ ≞ Services: 💷 ✕ ⊞ Leisure: ⚡ LP Off-site: 💷

WEMDING BAYERN

AZUR Waldsee Wemding 86650
☎ 09092 90101 ▤ 09092 90100
In a wooded lakeside setting with excellent recreational facilities.
Open: 15 Mar-15 Nov Site: 9HEC ⸝⸝⸝⸝⸝ ⬥ ⬡ 💷 Facilities: ⬥ 💷 ⊙ 🖵 ⬮ 🅿 Services: ✕ ⊞ lau Leisure: ⚡ L Off-site: ≞ ⚡P

WERTACH BAYERN

Grüntensee Grüntenseestr 41, 87497
☎ 08365 375 ▤ 08365 1221
e-mail: info@gruentensee.de
website: www.gruentensee.de
A modern site beside Lake Grünten.
⮑ *If approaching from Kempten, turn right entering Nesselwerg, and follow the signposts.*
Open: All year Site: 5HEC ⸝⸝⸝⸝⸝ ⬥ ♠ Prices: ⚲5.40-6.20 💷5.20-6.20 ⚠3.10-5.20 Facilities: ⬥ ⊙ 🖵 ⬮ ≞ 🅿 Services: 💷 ✕ ⊞ lau Leisure: ⚡ L Off-site: ⚡P

The AA cannot be held responsible for the content of third party websites

Facilities: 💷-shop ⬥-shower ⊙-electric points for razors 🖵-electric points for caravans ≞-parking by tents permitted 💷-compulsory separate car park **Services:** ✕-café/restaurant 💷-bar ⬮-Camping Gaz International ≞-gas other than Camping Gaz ⊞-first aid facilities lau-laundry **Leisure:** ⚡-swimming L-Lake P-Pool R-River S-Sea **Off-site:** All facilities within 2km

WINKL BEI BISCHOFSWIESEN BAYERN

Winkllandthal 83483 ☎ 08652 8164 ▤ 08652 979831
e-mail: camping-winkl@t-online.de
website: www.camping-winkl.de
In meadow between the B20 and edge of woodland.
➲ From Bad Reichenhall to Berchtesgaden about 8km.
Open: Dec-Oct Site: 2.5HEC ⬛⬛⬛ ⋯⋯ ♨ ⚶ ♣ ▲
Prices: ₦5.85 pitch 5.15 Facilities: ⋔ ⚑ ⊙ ⚑ ∅ ⚶ ☎
Services: ⚓ ✗ ⊞ lau Leisure: ⚓ R

ZWIESEL BAYERN

AZUR-Ferienzentrum Bayerischer Wald Waldesruhweg 34,
94227 ☎ 09922 802595 ▤ 09922 802594
e-mail: info@azur-camping.de
website: www.azur-camping.de
A modern site. Clean sanitary installations.
Open: All year Site: 16HEC ⬛⬛⬛ ♨ Prices: ₦4.50-6 ♠2.80-
4.60 ▲3.50-4.50 pitch 5.50-7.50 Facilities: ⋔ ⊙ ⚑ ∅ ⚶ ☎
Services: ✗ ⊞ lau Off-site: ⚓PR

SOUTH WEST

ABTSGMÜND BADEN-WÜRTTEMBERG

AT POMMERTSWEILER (6KM N)

Hammerschmiede-See Hammerschmiede 6, 73453
☎ 07963 1205 & 415
e-mail: camping.hammerschmiede@t-online.de
website: www.camping-hammerschmiede.de
A terraced site in a wooded setting beside the lake. Partly
divided into pitches with concrete paths.
➲ From Abtsgmünd travel for 3km then turn N to
Pommertsweiler, site signposted.
Open: All year Site: 6HEC ⬛⬛⬛ ♨ Facilities: ⋔ ⚑ ⊙ ⚑ ∅ ☎
Services: ✗ ⊞ lau Leisure: ⚓ L

ACHERN BADEN-WÜRTTEMBERG

Staedtischer Campingplatz am Achernsee Am Achernsee 8,
77855 ☎ 07841 25253 ▤ 07841 508835
e-mail: camping@achern.de website: www.achern.de
Open: All year Site: 6.5HEC ⬛⬛⬛ ♨ Prices: ₦4.60 ▲6.20
pitch 6.20 Facilities: ⋔ ⚑ ⊙ ⚑ ∅ ⚶ ☎ Services: ✗ ⊞ lau
Leisure: ⚓ L Off-site: ⚑ ⚓P

ALPIRSBACH BADEN-WÜRTTEMBERG

Wolpert 72275 ☎ 07444 6313
On level land beside the River Kinzig.
➲ 1km N of town below B294.
Open: All year Site: 1.2HEC ⬛⬛⬛ ♣ ⚑ Facilities: ⋔ ⚑ ⊙ ⚑
∅ ⚶ ☎ Services: ⊞ lau Leisure: ⚓ R Off-site: ⚑ ✗

ALTENSTEIG BADEN-WÜRTTEMBERG

Schwarzwald 72213 ☎ 07453 8415
e-mail: info@schwarzwaldcamping.de
website: www.schwarzwaldcamping.de
Parkland site of motor sport club Altensteig beside the River
Nagold. Separate section for dog owners.
➲ On road to Garrweiler 1km from Altensteig.
Open: All year Site: 3.3HEC ⬛⬛⬛ ♨ Prices: ₦4.30 ♠2.30
⚑5.50 pitch 5.50 Facilities: ⋔ ⚑ ⊙ ⚑ ∅ ⚶ ☎ Services: ✗ ⊞
lau Leisure: ⚓ R Off-site: ⚓P

ALTNEUDORF BADEN-WÜRTTEMBERG

Steinachperle 69250
☎ 06228 467 ▤ 06228 8568
e-mail: campingplatz-steinachperle@t-online.de
The site lies in the narrow shady valley of the River Steinach.
Lunchtime siesta 13.00-15.00 hrs.

➲ The entrance to the camp lies next to the Gasthaus zum
Pflug, on the outskirts of Altneudorf.
Open: Apr-Sep Site: 3.5HEC ⬛⬛⬛ ♨ Facilities: ⋔ ⚑ ⊙ ⚑ ∅
⚶ ☎ Services: ✗ ⊞ lau Leisure: ⚓ R

BADENWEILER BADEN-WÜRTTEMBERG

Badenweiler Weilertalstr 73, 79410
☎ 07632 1550 ▤ 07632 5268
e-mail: info@camping-badenweiler.de
website: www.camping-badenweiler.de
On a level meadow surrounded by beautiful Black Forest
scenery. Good facilities for local walking etc.
➲ Access via A5 exit Neuenburg.
Open: 16 Jan-14 Dec Site: 1.6HEC ⬛⬛⬛ ♨ Prices: ₦5.90
pitch 8-8.50 Facilities: ⋔ ⚑ ⊙ ⚑ ∅ ⚶ ☎ Services: ✗ ⊞ lau
Leisure: ⚓ P Off-site: ✗

BUCHHORN BEI ÖHRINGEN BADEN-WÜRTTEMBERG

Seewiese Seestr 11, 74629 ☎ 07941 61568 ▤ 07941 38527
e-mail: campingseewiese@t-online.de
website: www.camping-seewiese.de
A well equipped site on a meadow beside a lake with fine
views of the surrounding mountains. Good recreational
facilities.
➲ 7km S of Öhringen via Pfedelbach. Access via A6.
Open: All year Site: 5.5HEC ⬛⬛⬛ ♨ Prices: ₦5 ♠3 ⚑3 ▲2-4
Facilities: ⋔ ⚑ ⊙ ⚑ ⚶ ☎ Services: ⚓ ✗ ⊞ lau Leisure: ⚓ LP

BÜHL BADEN-WÜRTTEMBERG

Adam Campingstr 1, 77185 ☎ 07223 23194 ▤ 07223 8982
e-mail: webmaster@campingplatz-adam.de
website: www.campingplatz-adam.de
On level grassland, by lake.
➲ 1km from the Bühl exit of the A5/E4-E11 (Karlsruhe-Basel)
in direction of Lichtenau.
Open: All year Site: 15HEC ⬛⬛⬛ ♨ ⬕ ⚑ Prices: ₦4.50-6.50
♠6-8 ⚑4.50-6.50 ▲4.50-5 Facilities: ⋔ ⚑ ⊙ ⚑ ∅ ⚶ ☎
Services: ⚓ ✗ ⊞ lau Leisure: ⚓ L Off-site: ⚓P

CREGLINGEN BADEN-WÜRTTEMBERG

Camping Romantische Strasse 97993
☎ 07933 20289 ▤ 07933 990019
e-mail: camping.hausotter@web.de
website: camping-romantische-strasse.de
A site completely divided into pitches, lying on the south
outskirts of Münster. Children's playground. Individual
washing cubicles.
➲ If approaching from Bad Mergentheim or from
Rothenburg/Tauber, take the 'Romantic road' up to Creglingen.
Then turn S and drive 3km up to Münster.
Open: 15 Mar-15 Nov Site: 6HEC ⬛⬛⬛ ♨ ⚑ Prices: ₦4.50-
5.50 ▲3-3.50 pitch 6-7 Facilities: ⋔ ⚑ ⊙ ⚑ ∅ ☎ Services: ✗
⊞ lau Leisure: ⚓ PR Off-site: ⚓L

DINGELSDORF BADEN-WÜRTTEMBERG

Fliesshorn 78465 ☎ 07533 5262
At a farm, on meadowland with fine trees.
➲ In town turn off Stadd-Dettingen road and follow signs to
NW for 1.3km.
Open: Apr-Sep Site: 5HEC ⬛⬛⬛ ♨ ⚿ Facilities: ⋔ ⚑ ⊙ ⚑
∅ ☎ Services: ⊞ lau Off-site: ✗ ⚓LS

DONAUESCHINGEN BADEN-WÜRTTEMBERG

Riedsee 78166 ☎ 0771 5511 ▤ 0771 5511
e-mail: info@riedsee-camping.de
website: www.riedsee-camping.de
Level meadow on lakeside.

Site: 6HEC-Site size ⬛⬛⬛-grass ⋯⋯-sand ♨-stone ♨-little shade ♨-partly shaded ♣-mainly shaded
⬕-bungalows for hire ⚑-caravans for hire ▲-tents for hire ⚿-no dogs Prices: ₦-adult per night ♠-car per night
pp-per person per night ⚑-caravan per night ▲-tent per night

➔ *Turn off A81 exit 'Geisingen' and continue 13km on B31 towards Pfohren, then turn left and continue for 1km.*
Open: All year Site: 8HEC ⏛ ⚘ ⚲ Prices: ⚑4.50 ⚓4-6 pitch 8 Facilities: ⚐ ⚍ ⊙ ☾ ⊘ ☵ ⚏ Services: ⚎ ✕ ⊞ lau Leisure: ⚑ L

DÜRRHEIM, BAD BADEN-WÜRTTEMBERG

Sunthauersee 78073 ☎ 07706 712 ▤ 07706 922906
e-mail: kurcamping@web.de
website: www.kurcamping.net
Open: All year Site: 10HEC ⏛ ⚘ ☾ Prices: ⚑3.60 ⚓3.80 ⚎7.65 ⚓2.30 Facilities: ⚐ ⊙ ☾ ⊘ ☷ Services: ✕ ⊞ lau
Off-site: ⚍ ✕

ELLWANGEN-JAGST BADEN-WÜRTTEMBERG

AZUR Ellwangen Rotenbacherstr 45, 73479
☎ 07961 7921 ▤ 07961 562330
e-mail: ellwangen@azur-camping.de
website: www.azur.camping.de/ellwangen
A modern site with good facilities in a wooded loaction on the banks of the River Jagst.
Open: All year Site: 3.5HEC ⏛ ⚘ Prices: ⚑4.50-6 ⚓3.50-4.50 pitch 5.50-7.50 Facilities: ⚐ ⚍ ⊙ ☾ ⊘ ☷ Services: ⚎ ✕ ⊞ lau Leisure: ⚑ R Off-site: ⚑LPR

ERPFINGEN BADEN-WÜRTTEMBERG

AZUR Schwäbische Alb (Rosencamping) 72820
☎ 07128 466 ▤ 07128 30137
e-mail: info@azur-camping.de
website: www.azur-camping.de
Extensive site on a hill.
➔ *Access from Reutlingen on B312 in SE direction to Grooengstingen, then S on Schwabische Albstr (B313) for 3.5km to Haid , then turn right to Erpfingen. Site on W outskirts.*
Open: All year Site: 9HEC ⏛ ⚘ ☾ Facilities: ⚐ ⚍ ⊙ ☾ ⊘ ☷ ☷ Services: ⚎ ✕ ⊞ lau Leisure: ⚑ P Off-site: ⚑L

ETTENHEIM BADEN-WÜRTTEMBERG

Oase 77955 ☎ 07822 445918 ▤ 07822 445919
e-mail: info@campingpark-oase.de
website: www.campingpark-oase.de
In a wooded location with good, modern facilities.
➔ *Access via A5 exit Ettenheim.*
Open: 02 Apr-04 Oct Site: 6HEC ⏛ ☾ ⚘ Prices: ⚑6 pitch 6 Facilities: ⚐ ⚍ ⊙ ☾ ⊘ ☷ Services: ✕ ⊞ lau Off-site: ⚑P

FREIBURG IM BREISGAU BADEN-WÜRTTEMBERG

Breisgau Seestr 20, 7801 ☎ 07665 2346
Extensive level grassland site on outskirts of town. Section reserved for campers with dogs.
➔ *500m E of autobahn exit 'Freiburg Nord'.*
Open: All year Site: 6.5HEC ⏛ ⚘ Facilities: ⚐ ⚍ ⊙ ☾ ⊘ ☷ ☷ Services: ✕ lau Leisure: ⚑ L

Ferien & Kurbad Mösle-Park Waldseestr 77, 79117
☎ 0761 72938 ▤ 0761 77578
e-mail: information@camping-freiburg.com
website: www.camping-freiburg.com
On outskirts of town near 'Busse's Waldschänke' inn.
➔ *Turn right after town hall across railway and follow Waldseestr towards Littenweiler.*
Open: 25 Mar-25 Oct Site: 0.7HEC ⏛ ⚘ Prices: ⚑5 ⚓2.50 pitch 5 Facilities: ⚐ ⚍ ⊙ ☾ ⊘ ☷ ☷ Services: ⚎ ✕ ⊞ lau Off-site: ⚑P

FREUDENSTADT BADEN-WÜRTTEMBERG

Langenwald Strassburgerstr 167, 72250
☎ 07441 2862 ▤ 07441 2893
e-mail: info@camping-langenwald.de
website: www.camping-langenwald.de
The site consists of several sections and lies next to a former mill beside the River Forbach.
➔ *4km W of Freudenstadt below the B28 (Freudenstadt-Strasbourg).*
Open: Apr-Nov Site: 2HEC ⏛ ⚘ ☾ Facilities: ⚐ ⚍ ⊙ ☾ ⊘ ☷ ☷ Services: ✕ ⊞ lau Leisure: ⚑ PR

HALLWANGEN BADEN-WÜRTTEMBERG

Königskanzel 72280 ☎ 07443 6730 ▤ 07443 4574
e-mail: info@camping-koenigskanzel.de
website: www.camping-koenigskanzel.de
In an elevated position in the centre of the Black Forest.
➔ *Follow B28 from Freudenstadt towards Altensteig past the Hallwangen junction to camping sign on left.*
Open: All year Site: 6HEC ⏛ ⚘ Prices: ⚑5-5.75 pitch 6.50 Facilities: ⚐ ⚍ ⊙ ☾ ⊘ ☷ ☷ Services: ⚎ ✕ ⊞ lau Leisure: ⚑ P Off-site: ✕

HAUSEN BADEN-WÜRTTEMBERG

Wagenburg 88637 ☎ 07579 559
On meadowland between the railway bank and the Danube. Site has spectacular view of surrounding landscape. Entrance through subway.
Open: May-Sep Site: 1.2HEC ⏛ ⚘ ☾ Prices: ⚑4.50 ⚓1 ⚎4.40 ⚓3.40-4.40 pitch 3.40-5.40 Facilities: ⚐ ⚍ ⊙ ☾ ⊘ ☷ ☷ Services: ⚎ ✕ ⊞ lau Leisure: ⚑ R Off-site: ✕

HEIDELBERG BADEN-WÜRTTEMBERG

Heidelberg-Neckartal Schlierbacher Landstr 151, 69118
☎ 06221 802506 ▤ 06221 802506
e-mail: mail@camping-heidelberg.de
website: www.camping-heidelberg.de
Open: 15 Mar-15 Oct Site: 3HEC ⏛ ⚘ ☾ ⚘ ☾ ⚘
Prices: ⚑5.50 ⚓2 ⚎3.50-8 ⚓2.50-8 Facilities: ⚐ ⚍ ⊙ ☾ ⊘ ☷ ☷ Services: ⚎ ✕ ⊞ lau Leisure: ⚑ R

HERBOLZHEIM BADEN-WÜRTTEMBERG

Herbolzheim Im Laue 1, 79336 ☎ 07643 1460 ▤ 07643 913382
e-mail: s.hugoschmidt@t-online.de
website: www.laue-camp.de
In a pleasant rural setting with good facilities, a short distance from the Europa Park Rust amusement park.
➔ *On B3 between Freiburgh and Offenburg.*
Open: 03 Apr-03 Oct Site: 8HEC ⏛ ⚘ Prices: ⚑5 ⚓7 ⚓6 Facilities: ⚐ ⚍ ⊙ ☾ ⊘ ☷ Services: ⚎ ✕ ⊞ lau Off-site: ⚍ ☷ ⚑LP

HÖFEN AN DER ENZ BADEN-WÜRTTEMBERG

Quellgrund 75339 ☎ 07081 6984 ▤ 07081 6984
Well maintained municipal site on grassland between the B294 and the River Enz.
➔ *Access from Pforzheim on the B294 in SW direction to the 'Quelle' inn with entrance to ARAL petrol station at entrance to Höfen, then turn right.*
Open: All year Site: 3.6HEC ⏛ ⚘ Prices: ⚑4.50 ⚓2 ⚎3.50-4 ⚓3-3.50 Facilities: ⚐ ⚍ ⊙ ☾ ⊘ ☷ Services: lau Leisure: ⚑ R Off-site: ✕ ⚑P ⊞

HORB BADEN-WÜRTTEMBERG

Schüttehof 72160 ☎ 07451 3951 ▤ 07451 1348
Situated on flat mountain top.

contd.

CAMP SITE SOUTHERN BLACK FORREST
79199 Kirchzarten
Tel. 07661 / 9040910
Fax. 07661 / 61624
E-mail: info@campingkirchzarten.de
www.camping-kirchzarten.de

Comfortable holiday site in the
southern Black Forrest near Freiburg.
New toilet facilities, 380 sites for visiting
holiday-makers. Heated outdoor pool 23°C
from 15.5 - 15.9 on the site itself.
Wide range of facilities for sports and games.
Walk in the magnificent
countryside. Trips to the higher parts
of the Black Forest, Switzerland
and France.

➲ *Access from Horb in direction of Freudenstadt. 1.5km
beyond the town boundary turn towards stables and site, and
onward for 1km.*
Open: All year Site: 6HEC ▩▩▩ ᢙ Facilities: ℝ ⅃ ⊙ ♨ ⌀ ⚎
⌂ Services: ✕ ⊞ lau Leisure: ⇥ P

ISNY BADEN-WÜRTTEMBERG

Waldbad Isny Lohbauerstr 59-69, 88316
☎ 07562 2389 ▤ 07562 2004
In wooded surroundings beside a lake.
➲ *S of town on B12. Signposted.*
Open: Jan-Oct Site: 3HEC ▩▩▩ ♣ ♨ Prices: ⚲5.50 ⚑5-8
pitch 8 Facilities: ℝ ⅃ ⊙ ♨ ⌀ ⚎ ⌂ Services: ✕ ⊞ lau
Leisure: ⇥ LP

KARLSRUHE BADEN-WÜRTTEMBERG
AT DURLACH (8KM SE)

AZUR Campingplatz Türmbergblick Tiengener Str 40,
D-76227 ☎ 0721 497236 ▤ 0721 497237
e-mail: karlsruhe@azur-camping.de
website: www.azur-camping.de/karlsruhe
On level ground amongst orchards. Lunchtime siesta 12.30-
15.00 hrs.
➲ *Access via Karlsruhe-Dürlach exit on A5/E4. Signposted.*
Open: 15 Mar-15 Nov Site: 3.5HEC ▩▩▩ ᢙ Prices: ⚲4.50-6
⚑3.50-4.50 pitch 5.50-7.50 Facilities: ℝ ⊙ ♨ ⚎ ⌂
Services: ✕ ⊞ lau Off-site: ⊞ ⅃ ✕ ⚎ ⇥LP

KEHL BADEN-WÜRTTEMBERG

Kehl-Strassburg 77694 ☎ 07851 2603 ▤ 07851 73076
Park-like site divided into separate sections for young
campers, transit and holiday campers. Lunchtime siesta
13.00-15.00 hrs.

➲ *Turn left at the Rhine dam on the outskirts of the town.*
Open: 15 Mar-Oct Site: 2.3HEC ▩▩▩ ᢙ Prices: ⚲4 pitch 8-10
Facilities: ℝ ⅃ ⊙ ♨ ⌀ ⚎ ⌂ Services: ✕ ⊞ lau Off-site: ⇥PR

KIRCHBERG BADEN-WÜRTTEMBERG

Christophorus 88486 ☎ 07354 663 ▤ 07354 91314
e-mail: info@camping-christophorus.de
website: www.camping-christophorus.de
Completely enclosed, clean site.
➲ *Leave motorway A7 (Ulm-Memmingen) at exit Illereichen
Allenstadt to town centre, then towards the railway station.*
Open: All year Site: 9.2HEC ▩▩▩ ᢙ Facilities: ℝ ⅃ ⊙ ♨ ⌀
⚎ ⌂ Services: ✕ ⊞ lau Leisure: ⇥ LP

KIRCHZARTEN BADEN-WÜRTTEMBERG

Kirchzarten Diefenbacher Str 17, 79199
☎ 07661 9040910 ▤ 07661 61624
e-mail: info@camping-kirchzarten.de
website: www.camping-kirchzarten.de
Extensive site with trees providing shade.
➲ *About 8km E of Freiburg im Breisgau off the B31.*
Open: All year Site: 5.9HEC ▩▩▩ ♣ ♨ Prices: ⚲5.20-8.20
⚑5.50-6.80 pitch 5.50-6.80 Facilities: ℝ ⅃ ⊙ ♨ ⌀ ⚎ ⌂
Services: ⅃ ✕ ⊞ lau Leisure: ⇥ P

KRESSBRONN BADEN-WÜRTTEMBERG

Gohren am See 88079 ☎ 07543 60590 ▤ 07543 605929
e-mail: info@campingplatz-gohren.de
website: www.campingplatz-gohren.de
A large site beside the lake. It has an older section divided by
many hedges reserved for residential campers, and a newer
section with fewer bushes.
➲ *3km from Kressbronn. Well signposted from B31.*
Open: 22 Mar-15 Oct Site: 38HEC ▩▩▩ ᢙ ♨ ⚑ Facilities: ℝ
⅃ ⊙ ♨ ⌀ ⚎ ⌂ Services: ⅃ ✕ ⊞ lau Leisure: ⇥ L
Off-site: ⇥P

LAICHINGEN BADEN-WÜRTTEMBERG

Heidehof Blaubeurer str 50, 89150
☎ 07333 6408 ▤ 07333 21463
e-mail: heidehof.camping@t-online.de
Well-cared for site on hillside with some high firs. Asphalt roads.
Separate section outside enclosure for overnight campers.
➲ *Leave Ulm-Stuttgart motorway at Merkingen exit, then
continue S via Machtolsheim to camp 2km S.*
Open: All year Site: 25HEC ▩▩▩ ᢙ Facilities: ℝ ⅃ ⊙ ♨ ⌀ ⚎
⌂ Services: ✕ ⊞ lau Leisure: ⇥ P

LAUTERBURG BADEN-WÜRTTEMBERG

Hirtenteich 73457 ☎ 07365 296 ▤ 07365 251
e-mail: campingplatz.hirtentiech@t-online.de
website: www.campingplatz-hirtentiech.de
This site lies on gently sloping terrain, near the Hirtenteich
recreation area.
➲ *Turn off the B29 (Aalen-Schwäbisch Gmünd) in Essingen
and drive S for a pprox. 5km.*
Open: All year Site: 4HEC ▩▩▩ ᢙ ⬛ ⚑ Prices: ⚲4 pitch 5-5.50
Facilities: ℝ ⅃ ⊙ ♨ ⌀ ⚎ ⌂ Services: ✕ ⊞ lau Leisure: ⇥ P

LENZKIRCH BADEN-WÜRTTEMBERG

Kreuzhof Bonndorfer Str 65, 79853
☎ 07653 700 ▤ 07653 6623
e-mail: info@brauerei-rogg.de
Grassland near former railton below Rogg Brewery on the B315.
➲ *Access from Freiburg on the B31 to Titisee, continue on the
B317 towards Schaffhausen junction then take the B315 via
Lenzkirch, site is some 2km from town.*
Open: All year Site: 2HEC ▩▩▩ ᢙ Facilities: ℝ ⅃ ⊙ ♨ ⌀ ⚎
⌂ Services: ⅃ ✕ ⊞ lau Leisure: ⇥ P

LIEBELSBERG BADEN-WÜRTTEMBERG

Erbenwald Neubulach 3, 75387
☎ 07053 7382 ▣ 07053 3274
e-mail: info@camping-erbenwald.de
website: www.camping-erbenwald.de
Pleasant site on edge of wood.
➲ *Approach via Calw on the B463 for about 6km travelling S, then turn right and shortly before Neubulach continue N about 2km.*
Open: All year Site: 7.2HEC ⛺ ⌇ 🏠 🚐 Prices: ⚡5 pitch 6
Facilities: 🚿 🛒 ⊙ 🔌 🔌 ⛽ 🏠 Services: 🍴 ✗ ⊞ lau
Leisure: ⚓ P

LIEBENZELL, BAD BADEN-WÜRTTEMBERG

Bad-Liebenzell Pforzheimerstr 34, 75378
☎ 07052 935680 ▣ 07052 935681
e-mail: campingpark-bl@gmx.de
website: www.abelundneff.de/campingpark
Municipal site with trees near tennis courts. Divided by hedges and internal asphalt roads.
➲ *Approach from Pforzheim on the B463 about 19km S. Turn left 500mtrs before Bad Liebenzell to site on the banks of the Nagold.*
Open: All year Site: 3HEC ⛺ ⌇ 🚐 ⚡ Prices: ⚡7-7.50 🚗6
⚡4-7 pitch 6 Facilities: 🚿 🛒 ⊙ 🔌 🔌 🏠 Services: 🍴 ✗ ⊞ lau
Leisure: ⚓ P Off-site: ✗

LÖRRACH BADEN-WÜRTTEMBERG

Grütt Grüttweg 8, 79539 ☎ 07621 82588 ▣ 07621 165034
Level, grassy site near frontier.
➲ *From motorway exit Lörrach on B316 then via Freiburger Str and bridge over the Wiesse and turn left after 100mtrs.*
Open: 18 Mar-Oct Site: 2.4HEC ⛺ ⌇ 🚿 ⊙ 🔌 🔌
🏠 Services: ✗ lau Off-site: 🛒 🍴 ✗ ⛽ ⚓PR ⊞

LUDWIGSHAFEN AM BODENSEE BADEN-WÜRTTEMBERG

See Ende 78346 ☎ 07773 5366 ▣ 07773 7375
website: www.see-ende.de
Meadowland with tall trees west of town, between railway and lake.
➲ *Access via Stuttgart-Singen-Lindau motorway. In Ludwigshafen turn off in direction of Radolfzell.*
Open: May-Sep Site: 2.6HEC ⛺ ⌇ ⚡ Facilities: 🚿 🛒 ⊙
🔌 🔌 🏠 Services: 🍴 ✗ ⊞ lau Leisure: ⚓ L

MANNHEIM BADEN-WÜRTTEMBERG

AT NECKARAU (5.5KM S)

Strandbad 68199 ☎ 0621 856240
A minicipal site in the grounds of a park beside the Rhine. At high water the site can get flooded.
➲ *From motorway exit 'Mannheim' to Neckarau, via the Freudenheim Bridge, then drive through Morchfeldstr, Friedrichstr, Rheingoldstr, Franzosenweg and Strandbadweg to the camp.*
Open: Mar-Oct Site: 0.9HEC ⛺ ⌇ 🚐 Facilities: 🚿 🛒 ⊙
🔌 🏠 Services: ⊞ lau Leisure: ⚓ R Off-site: 🍴 ✗ ⚓P

MARKDORF BADEN-WÜRTTEMBERG

Wirthshof 88677 ☎ 07544 96270 ▣ 07544 962727
e-mail: info@wirthshof.de website: www.wirthshof.de
Open: 15 Mar-30 Oct Site: 10HEC ⛺ ⌇ Prices: ⚡4.80-5.80
pitch 10-11 Facilities: 🚿 🛒 ⊙ 🔌 🔌 🏠 Services: ✗ ⊞ lau
Leisure: ⚓ P Off-site: 🍴 ✗ ⚓L

MERGENTHEIM, BAD BADEN-WÜRTTEMBERG

Willingertal 97980 ☎ 07931 2177
Site lies on a meadow between high green bank and wooded hillside.

➲ *From Bad Mergentheim follow B19 S towards Stuttgart, then left towards Wachbach after 2km. then left to Gaststätte.*
Open: All year Site: 15HEC ⛺ 🌿 Facilities: 🚿 🛒 ⊙ 🔌 🔌
⛽ 🏠 ▣ Services: ✗ ⊞ lau

MÖRTELSTEIN BADEN-WÜRTTEMBERG

Germania Mühlwiese 1, 6951 ☎ 06261 1795 ▣ 06261 37455
website: www.germania.bootswerft.de
Site is in Mörtelstein, 5km west of Obrigheim. Site lies between the left bank of the River Neckar and a wooded hillside.
➲ *Follow road B292 W towards 'Sinsheim' to just beyond Obrigheim, then N on a narrow, steep road into the Neckar Valley.*
Open: Apr-Oct Site: 0.8HEC ⛺ ⌇ 🚐 Facilities: 🚿 🛒 ⊙
🔌 🏠 Services: ✗ lau Leisure: ⚓ R Off-site: ✗ ⊞

MÜNSTERTAL BADEN-WÜRTTEMBERG

Münstertal Dietzelbachstr 6, 79244
☎ 07636 7080 ▣ 07636 7448
e-mail: info@camping-muenstertal.de
website: www.camping-muenstertal.de
Level, grassy site in pleasant situation with fine views.
Lunchtime siesta 13.00-15.00 hrs.
➲ *Leave Karlsruhe-Basel motorway at Bad Kroningen exit and continue SE via Stauffen to W outskirts of Untermünstertal.*
Open: All year Site: 7HEC ⛺ ⌇ ⚡ Prices: ⚡6.50-7.60
pitch 10-12 Facilities: 🚿 🛒 ⊙ 🔌 🔌 ⛽ 🏠 Services: ✗ ⊞ lau
Leisure: ⚓ P

MURRHARDT BADEN-WÜRTTEMBERG

AT FORNSBACH (6KM E)

Waldsee 71540 ☎ 07192 6436 ▣ 07192 5283
e-mail: waldsee@murrhardt.de
website: www.murrhardt.de
The site lies near Lake Waldsee. Asphalt paths and pitches, with gravel surface.
➲ *Drive through Murrhardt towards Fornsbach and the camp, which is on the eastern shore of the lake.*
Open: All year Site: 2HEC ⛺ ⌇ 🚐 Prices: ⚡3.50-4
🚗2.50-3.50 🚐3-3.50 ⚡3-3.50 pitch 3-3.50 Facilities: 🚿 🛒 ⊙
🔌 🔌 🏠 Services: ✗ ⊞ lau Leisure: ⚓ L

NECKARGEMÜND BADEN-WÜRTTEMBERG

Friedensbrücke 69151 ☎ 06223 2178
Campsite lies on the left bank of the River Neckar below the Frieden's bridge.
Open: Mar-Sep Site: 2.5HEC ⛺ ⌇ 🚐 Facilities: 🚿 🛒 ⊙ 🔌
🔌 ⛽ 🏠 ▣ Services: ✗ ⊞ lau Leisure: ⚓ R
Off-site: 🛒 ✗ ⚓P ⊞

Haide 69151 ☎ 06223 2111 ▣ 06223 71959
e-mail: info@camping-haide.de
website: www.camping-haide.de
A well appointed site in the picturesque Neckar Valley, directly on the river on the outskirts of Heidelberg.
➲ *Follow the river towards the castle and Neckarsteinach.*
Open: Apr-1 Nov Site: 3.6HEC ⛺ 🏠 🏠 Prices: ⚡4.70 🚗1
🚐4-6 ⚡3-6 Facilities: 🚿 ⊙ 🔌 🔌 🏠 Services: 🍴 ✗ ⊞ lau
Leisure: ⚓ R Off-site: 🛒 ⚓P ⊞

NECKARZIMMERN BADEN-WÜRTTEMBERG

Cimbria 74865 ☎ 06261 2562 ▣ 06261 35716
Site lies on level meadowland on the bank of the River Neckar.
➲ *Access to the site is signposted from road B27.*
Open: Apr-Oct Site: 3HEC ⛺ ⌇ Facilities: 🚿 ⊙ 🔌 🔌 🏠
Services: 🍴 ✗ lau Leisure: ⚓ PR Off-site: 🛒 ⊞

Facilities: 🛒-shop 🚿-shower ⊙-electric points for razors 🔌-electric points for caravans 🏠-parking by tents permitted
▣-compulsory separate car park **Services:** ✗-café/restaurant 🍴-bar 🔌-Camping Gaz International ⛽-gas other than Camping
Gaz ⊞-first aid facilities lau-laundry **Leisure:** ⚓-swimming L-Lake P-Pool R-River S-Sea **Off-site:** All facilities within 2km

NEUENBURG BADEN-WÜRTTEMBERG

Dreiländer Camping und Freizeitpark Oberer Wald, 79395
☎ 07631 7719 ▯ 07635 3393
e-mail: info@camping-gugel.de
website: www.camping-gugel.de
An excellent site, very extensive, providing many entirely
separate pitches.
➲ *Access via Karlsruhe-Basel motorway A5/E4, take the
Müllheim/Neuenburg exit, then about 3km to site.*
Open: All year Site: 12.8HEC ⸺ ⚘ Prices: ⋀5.75 ⬤4
⬤5.20 ▲3.50-5.20 Facilities: ⋔ ⅃ ⊙ ⬛ ⌀ ⩎ ⚐ Services: ✕
⊞ lau Leisure: ⬋ P Off-site: ⬋L

NUSSDORF BADEN-WÜRTTEMBERG

Nell Uberlinger See, 88662 ☎ 07551 4254
e-mail: info@campingplatz-nell.de
website: www.camping-nell.de
Site within orchard between farm of same name and the
lakeside promenade. Small private beach.
➲ *Under railway bridge, then turn right.*
Open: 1 wk before Etr -20 Oct Site: 0.6HEC ⸺ ⚘ ⬥
Prices: ⋀4.35-5.30 ⬤3 ⬤5 ▲5 Facilities: ⋔ ⊙ ⬛ ⚐
Services: ⊞ lau Leisure: ⬋ L Off-site: ⅃ ⍩ ✕ ⌀ ⩎ ⬋P

OSTRINGEN BADEN-WÜRTTEMBERG

Kraichgau Camping Wackerhof 76684
☎ 07259 361 ▯ 07259 2431
website: www.wackerhof.de
A modern terraced site. Lunchtime siesta 13.00-15.00 hrs
(except Saturdays).
➲ *From motorway A5 exit 'Kronau/Bad Schönborn' follow
road B292 to Östringen.*
Open: 25 Mar-15 Oct Site: 3HEC ⸺ ⚘ Prices: ⋀3 pitch 3
Facilities: ⋔ ⅃ ⊙ ⬛ ⌀ ⩎ ⚐ Services: lau

PFORZHEIM BADEN-WÜRTTEMBERG

International Schwarzwald Freibadweg 4, 75242
☎ 07234 6517 ▯ 07234 5180
e-mail: fam.frech@t-online.de
website: www.camping-schwarzwald.de
Site on edge of wood with southerly aspect. Separate fields
for residential, overnight and holiday campers.
➲ *S through Huchenfeld from Pforzheim to Schellbron (15km).*
Open: All year Site: 4HEC ⸺ ⚘ ⬤ ⬥ Facilities: ⋔ ⅃ ⊙
⬛ ⌀ ⩎ ⚐ Services: ✕ ⊞ lau Leisure: ⬋ P Off-site: ⬋R

RHEINMÜNSTER BADEN-WÜRTTEMBERG

AT STOLLHOFEN

Freizeitcenter-Oberrhein 77836 ☎ 07227 2500 ▯ 07227 2400
e-mail: info@freizeitcenter-oberrhein.de
website: www.freizeitcenter-oberrhein.de
Modern leisure complex next to Rhine.
Open: All year Site: 36HEC ⸺ ⚘ ⬤ Prices: ⋀5-7.50 pitch
5-7.50 Facilities: ⋔ ⅃ ⊙ ⬛ ⌀ ⩎ ⚐ Services: ⍩ ✕ ⊞ lau
Leisure: ⬋ L

ROSENBERG BADEN-WÜRTTEMBERG

Hüttenhof Hüttenhof 1, 73494 ☎ 07963 203 ▯ 07963 203
website: www.ecamp.com
Flat meadow on incline in quiet woodland area, next to large
farm.
➲ *From Ellwangen 3km N towards Crailsheim, turn W
towards Adelmannsfelden and continue for 8km to turn off to
N at Gaishardt.*
Open: 10 Apr-2 Nov Site: 4HEC ⸺ ⚘ Facilities: ⋔ ⅃ ⊙ ⬛
⌀ ⩎ ⚐ Services: ⊞ lau Leisure: ⬋ L Off-site: ✕

ST PETER BADEN-WÜRTTEMBERG

Steingrübenhof 79271 ☎ 07660 210 ▯ 07660 1604
e-mail: info@camping-steingrubenhof.de
website: www.camping-steingrubenhof.de
On a level plateau, surrounded by delightful mountain
scenery.
➲ *Access via A5 and B294.*
Open: All year Site: 2HEC ⸺ ⚘ ⬤ Prices: ⋀4 pitch 4
Facilities: ⋔ ⅃ ⊙ ⬛ ⌀ ⩎ ⚐ Services: ✕ lau Off-site: ⬋P

SCHAPBACH BADEN-WÜRTTEMBERG

Alisehof 77776 ☎ 07839 203 ▯ 07839 1263
e-mail: info@camping-online.de
website: www.camping-online.de
The site lies on well-kept ground with several terraces and is
separated from the road by the River Wolfach.
➲ *In Wolfach turn off the B924 at the Kinzighbrücke and
drive N for about 8km to Schapbach. Site is 1km N of village.*
Open: All year Site: 3HEC ⸺ ⚘ ⬤ Prices: ⋀5.80-6.20
⬤4.80-5.30 ⬤4.80-5.30 ▲4.80-5.30 pitch 4.80-5.30
Facilities: ⋔ ⅃ ⊙ ⬛ ⌀ ⩎ ⚐ Services: ⍩ ⊞ lau Leisure: ⬋ R
Off-site: ✕ ⬋LP

SCHILTACH BADEN-WÜRTTEMBERG

Schiltach 77761 ☎ 07836 7289 ▯ 07836 7466
e-mail: info@campingplatz-schittach.de
website: www.campingplatz-schittach.de
The site lies on meadowland on the banks of the River Kinzig
and is well placed for excursions.
Open: 24 Apr-03 Oct Site: 3.6HEC ⸺ ⚘ ⬤ ⬥ Prices: ⬤2
⬤3 pitch 3 pp3.50 Facilities: ⋔ ⅃ ⊙ ⬛ ⌀ ⩎ ⚐ Services: ✕
⊞ lau Leisure: ⬋ R Off-site: ⬋P

SCHÖMBERG BADEN-WÜRTTEMBERG

Höhen-Camping-Langenbrand 75328
☎ 07084 6131 ▯ 07084 931435
e-mail: eberhardt@hohencamping.de
website: www.hoehencamping.de
Open: All year Site: 1.6HEC ⸺ ⚘ Prices: ⋀4.50-5 ⬤5-6.50
⬤5-6.50 ▲5 pitch 5-6.50 Facilities: ⋔ ⊙ ⬛ ⌀ ⩎ ⚐
Services: ⊞ lau Off-site: ⅃ ⍩ ✕ ⬋P

SCHUSSENRIED, BAD BADEN-WÜRTTEMBERG

Reiterhof von Steinhausen Reiterhof, 88427
☎ 07583 3060 ▯ 07583 1004
e-mail: xschmid@t.online.de website: www.campingplatz1.de
In a pleasant rural setting.
➲ *Access via B30 Ulm-Bad Waldsee.*
Open: All year Site: 1HEC ⸺ ⚘ ⬤ Prices: ⋀2.10 ⬤9 ▲5-7
pitch 9 Facilities: ⋔ ⊙ ⬛ ⌀ ⩎ ⚐ Services: ✕ lau
Off-site: ⍩ ✕ ⬋LPR

SCHWÄBISCH GMÜND BADEN-WÜRTTEMBERG

AT RECHBERG (6KM S)

Schurrenhof 73072 ☎ 07165 8190 ▯ 07165 1625
The site lies in a beautiful setting on the edge of a forest, and
has a lovely view of the surrounding countryside.
➲ *Drive S on the B29 from Schwäbisch Gmünd, through
Strassdorf and Rechberg, and towards Reichenbach on the B10.
Then turn towards Schurrenhof.*
Open: All year Site: 3HEC ⸺ ⚘ ⬤ Facilities: ⋔ ⅃ ⊙ ⬛ ⌀
⩎ ⚐ Services: ✕ ⊞ lau Leisure: ⬋ P

> A full guide to the Symbols &
> Abbreviations used in this book
> can be found on page 6

Site: 6HEC-Site size ⸺-grass ⋱⋱-sand ⬤-stone ⅊-little shade ⚘-partly shaded ⬥-mainly shaded
⬛-bungalows for hire ⬤-caravans for hire ▲-tents for hire ⬥-no dogs Prices: ⋀-adult per night ⬤-car per night
pp-per person per night ⬤-caravan per night ▲-tent per night

SCHWÄBISCH HALL BADEN-WÜRTTEMBERG

Steinbacher See Mühlsteige 26, 74523
☎ 0791 2984 🗐 0791 9462758
e-mail: camping@hohenlohe2000.de
website: camping.hohenlohe2000.de
A modern site situated in the beautiful Kocher Valley. There
are good sporting facilities and many places of interest
nearby in the medieval town.
➱ *Access via B14/19 to Steinbach.*
Open: All year Site: 1.4HEC ⸺ 🔌 Prices: ♠4.60 pitch 5.10
Facilities: ↸ ⊙ 🖳 ♨ 🖺 Services: ♟ lau Off-site: 🏪 ✕ ⊞

STAUFEN BADEN-WÜRTTEMBERG

Belchenblick Münstertaler Str 43, 79219
☎ 07633 7045 🗐 07633 7908
e-mail: camping.belchenblick@t-online.de
website: www.camping-belchenblick.de
Well kept site on level ground.
➱ *Access from motorway exit Bad Krozingen/Staufen and
continue 4km SE.*
Open: All year Site: 2.5HEC ⸺ 🔌 Prices: ♠6-7.50 pitch 8-8
Facilities: ↸ 🏪 ⊙ 🖳 ♨ 🖺 Services: ♟ ✕ ⊞ lau Leisure: ⸰
PR Off-site: ✕

STEINACH BADEN-WÜRTTEMBERG

Kinzigtal 77790 ☎ 07832 8122 🗐 07832 6619
e-mail: webmaster@campingplatz-kinzigtal.de
website: www.campingplatz-kinzigtal.de
Site on level meadowland with tall trees, situated next to the
municipal heated swimming pool.
➱ *Signposted from Steinach.*
Open: All year Site: 2.6HEC ⸺ 🔌 🐞 Prices: ♠5 🏎5 🚐5
♠6.50 pitch 6.50 Facilities: ↸ 🏪 ⊙ 🖳 ♨ 🖺 Services: ♟ ✕
⊞ lau Off-site: ⸰PR

STUTTGART BADEN-WÜRTTEMBERG

Canstatter Wasen Mercedesstr 40, 70372
☎ 0711 556696 🗐 0711 557554
e-mail: info@campingplatz-stuttgart
website: www.campingplatz-stuttgart.de
Level site with tall poplar trees alongside the River Neckar.
Lunchtime siesta 12.30-14.00 hrs.
➱ *Access from Bad Cannstatt near sports stadium.*
Open: All year Site: 1.7HEC ⸺ ♨ 🐞 Prices: ♠5 🏎2.20
🚐5.50 ♠3.10-4.10 Facilities: ↸ 🏪 ⊙ 🖳 ♨ 🖺 Services: ✕ ⊞
lau Off-site: ⸰P

TITISEE-NEUSTADT BADEN-WÜRTTEMBERG

Bankenhof Bruderhalde 31a, 79822
☎ 07652 1351 🗐 07652 5907
e-mail: info@bankenhof.de website: www.bankenhof.de
A family site in a wooded location close to the lake.
➱ *From Titisee village follow signs 'Camping platz'. Access
road to site closed 22.00-06.00 hrs.*
Open: All year Site: 3.5HEC ⸺ ⁝⁝⁝ 🔌 🐞 ▲ Prices: ♠5.70
pitch 6.90 Facilities: ↸ 🏪 ⊙ 🖳 ♨ 🖺 Services: ♟ ✕ ⊞ lau
Leisure: ⸰ R Off-site: ⸰L

Bühlhof Bühlhofweg 13, 79822
☎ 07652 1606 🗐 07652 1827
e-mail: hertha-jaeger@t-online.de
website: www.camping-buehlhof.de
In pleasant situation on hillside above lake. Lunchtime siesta
13.00-14.30 hrs.
➱ *Well signposted.*
Site: 10HEC ⸺ ⁝⁝⁝ 🔌 Prices: ♠4.50-5 pitch 5.20-7
Facilities: ↸ 🏪 ⊙ 🖳 ♨ 🖺 Services: ♟ ✕ lau
Off-site: ✕ ⸰LP ⊞

Sandbank 79822
☎ 07651 8243 & 8166 🗐 07651 8286 & 88444
e-mail: info@camping-sandbank.com
website: www.camping-sandbank.com
On terrain rising from lakeside, upper part terraced,
landscaped with trees.
➱ *Access from Titisee, N bank of lake, turn into old
Feldbergstr. At SW end of lake turn left and continue along
narrow private road through Camping 'Bankenhof' (closed
22.00-06.00 hrs) to the site about 700mtrs on SE bank of lake.*
Open: Apr-20 Oct Site: 2HEC ⸺ ♨ 🔌 Prices: ♠3.40-
4.40 pitch 5.10-6.70 Facilities: ↸ 🏪 ⊙ 🖳 ♨ 🖺 Services: ✕
⊞ lau Leisure: ⸰ L Off-site: ⸰P

Wellerhof 79822 ☎ 07652 1468 🗐 07652 1478
Mainly level site with trees, bordering on lake shore for about
400mtrs.
➱ *Signposted from Titisee.*
Open: 15 May-Sep Site: 2HEC ⸺ ⁝⁝⁝ 🔌 Facilities: ↸ 🏪 ⊙
🖳 ♨ 🖺 Services: ✕ ⊞ lau Leisure: ⸰ L

TODTNAU BADEN-WÜRTTEMBERG

Hochschwarzwald 79674 ☎ 07671 1288 🗐 07671 95190
e-mail: camping.hochschwarzwald@web.de
website: www.camping-hochschwarzwald.de
Terraced site, partially grassland, by ski-lift.
➱ *6km NW of Todtnau.*
Open: All year Site: 2.5HEC ⸺ ⁝⁝⁝ ♨ 🔌 Prices: ♠4.10
🚐5.10 ▲3.30-5.10 pitch 5.10 Facilities: ↸ 🏪 ⊙ 🖳 ♨ 🖺
Services: ✕ ⊞ lau Leisure: ⸰ R

TÜBINGEN BADEN-WÜRTTEMBERG

Tübingen Fremdenverkehrsgesellschaft, Rappenberghalde 61,
72070 ☎ 07071 43145 🗐 07071 793391
e-mail: mail@neckarcamping.de
website: www.neckarcamping.de
A quiet site, well situated on the left bank of the River
Neckar.
➱ *For access from the town centre, cross the Neckar bridge,
then turn right and drive S through Uhlandstr or Bahnhofstr to
next bridge. Cross bridge and drive upstream to the
Rappenberghalde hill.*
Open: Apr-Oct Site: 1HEC ⸺ 🔌 Prices: ♠5.30 🏎2.50
🚐4.50 ▲3.80 Facilities: ↸ 🏪 ⊙ 🖳 ♨ 🖺 Services: ♟ ✕ ⊞ lau
Leisure: ⸰ R Off-site: ⸰LP

ÜBERLINGEN BADEN-WÜRTTEMBERG

West Bahnhofstr 57, 88662 ☎ 07551 64583 🗐 07551 945895
e-mail: info@campingpark-uberlingen.de
website: www.campingpark-uberlingen.de
The site lies on the western outskirts of the town, between
the railway line and the road on one side, and the concrete
shore wall on the other. It is divided into several sections by
low wooden barriers and has a very small beach. No
individual youths under 18.
➱ *Off B31 towards the lake.*
Open: Apr-5 Oct Site: 3HEC ⸺ 🔌 Prices: ♠4.50-5.50
▲3.80 pitch 9-10 Facilities: ↸ 🏪 ⊙ 🖳 ♨ 🖺 Services: ✕ ⊞
lau Leisure: ⸰ L Off-site: ♟ ⸰P

UHLDINGEN BADEN-WÜRTTEMBERG

AT SEEFELDEN (1KM W)

Seeperle 88690 ☎ 07556 5454 🗐 07556 966221
e-mail: info@camping-seeperle.de
website: www.camping-seeperle.de
This site has some large trees along the shore of the lake.
50metres-long boat landing stage. It is one of the few camps
that does not reserve its best pitches for residential campers.

contd.

Facilities: 🏪-shop **↸**-shower **⊙**-electric points for razors **🖳**-electric points for caravans **🖺**-parking by tents permitted
⊞-compulsory separate car park **Services: ✕**-café/restaurant **♟**-bar **♨**-Camping Gaz International **♨**-gas other than Camping
Gaz **⊞**-first aid facilities lau-laundry **Leisure: ⸰**-swimming L-Lake P-Pool R-River S-Sea **Off-site:** All facilities within 2km

Campingpark
»Wertheim-Bettingen«

No need to unhitch your caravan for the night!
On the A3/E5 Frankfurt-Würzburg motorway -
Wertheim exit - 2 km from the motorway

Familie Hupp • Tel. 09342 / 7077

➲ *Turn off B31 at Oberuhldingen and head towards Seefelden. Site 1km.*
Open: Apr-3 Oct **Site:** 0.7HEC ⬛ ⠿ ⍥ **Facilities:** ⋔ 🏪 ⊙ 🗜 ⌀ 🖻 **Services:** 🖃 **Leisure:** ⌇ L **Off-site:** 🍴 ✗

WALDKIRCH BADEN-WÜRTTEMBERG

Elztalblick 79183 ☎ 07681 4212 🗎 07681 4213
e-mail: eltztalblick@t-online.de
website: www.camping-elztalblick.de
Terraced pitches in the heart of the Black Forest.
➲ *Leave autobahn at 'Waldkirch/Ost' exit and follow signs for 3km.*
Open: 15 Mar-25 Oct **Site:** 2HEC ⬛ ⍥ **Prices:** ⚑5.50 ⚑5.50 ⚑5.50 pitch 5.50 **Facilities:** ⋔ 🏪 ⊙ 🗜 ⌀ ⍨ 🖻 **Services:** 🍴 ✗ 🖃 lau **Off-site:** ✗ ⌇P

WALDSHUT BADEN-WÜRTTEMBERG

Rhein-Camping Jahnweg 22, 79761
☎ 07751 3152 🗎 07751 3252
e-mail: rheincamping@t-online.de
website: www.rheincamping.de
In wooded surroundings beside the River Rhein.
➲ *1km from Waldshut towards the Swiss border.*
Open: All year **Site:** 8HEC ⬛ ◐ ⍥ ⚏ **Prices:** ⚑4.50 ⚑8 ⚑4.50-8 **Facilities:** ⋔ 🏪 ⊙ 🗜 ⌀ ⍨ 🖻 **Services:** 🍴 ✗ 🖃 lau **Leisure:** ⌇ R **Off-site:** ⌇P

WERTHEIM BADEN-WÜRTTEMBERG

AZUR Wertheim An den Christwiesen 35, 97877
☎ 09342 83111 🗎 09342 83171
e-mail: wertheim@azur-camping.de
website: www.azur-camping.de
Site lies on a level, long stretch of meadowland on the banks of the River Main next to a swimming pool. Lunchtime siesta 12.00-14.00 hrs.
➲ *Follow road towards 'Miltenberg', and in 1km turn right at the ARAL petrol station and head towards the site.*
Open: Apr-Oct **Site:** 7HEC ⬛ ⍥ **Prices:** ⚑4.50-6 pitch 5.50-7.50 **Facilities:** ⋔ 🏪 ⊙ 🗜 ⌀ ⍨ 🖻 **Services:** ✗ 🖃 lau **Leisure:** ⌇ R **Off-site:** 🏪 ⌇P

AT BETTINGEN (5KM E)

Wertheim-Bettingen Geiselbrunnweg 31, 97877
☎ 09342 7077 🗎 09342 913077
In a peaceful wooded area on the bank of a river.
➲ *M-way Frankfurt-Würzburg, exit Wertheim/Lengfurt, 1km.*
Open: Apr-Oct **Site:** 7.5HEC ⬛ ⍥ **Prices:** ⚑4 ⚑1.50 ⚑2.50 ⚑2.50 pitch 4 **Facilities:** ⋔ 🏪 ⊙ 🗜 ⌀ ⍨ 🖻 **Services:** ✗ 🖃 lau **Leisure:** ⌇ R

WILDBAD IM SCHWARZWALD BADEN-WÜRTTEMBERG

AZUR-Camping Schwarzwald 75323
☎ 07055 1320 🗎 07055 929081
e-mail: info@azur-camping.de
website: www.azur-freizeit.de
Long narrow site with some terraces, set between the River Enz and the wooded hillside. Separate section for young campers.
➲ *Access is from Pforzheim along B294 via Calmbach southwards.*
Open: All year **Site:** 2.5HEC ⬛ ⍥ **Facilities:** ⋔ 🏪 ⊙ 🗜 ⌀ ⍨ 🖻 **Services:** ✗ 🖃 lau **Leisure:** ⌇ R

Kleinenzhof 75323 ☎ 07081 3435 🗎 07081 3770
e-mail: info@kleinenzhof.de website: www.kleinenzhof.de
A family site with good, modern facilities.
➲ *Access via B294 3km S of Calmbach.*
Open: All year **Site:** 8HEC ⬛ ⍥ ⚏ **Prices:** ⚑5.60 pitch 7.30 **Facilities:** ⋔ 🏪 ⊙ 🗜 ⌀ ⍨ 🖻 **Services:** ✗ 🖃 lau **Leisure:** ⌇ PR

BERLIN AND EASTERN PROVINCES

ALT SCHWERIN MEKLENBURG-VORPOMMERN

See An der Schaftannen Nr 1, 17214
☎ 039932 42073 🗎 039932 42072
e-mail: info@camping-alt-schwerin.de
website: www.camping-alt-schwerin.de
A pleasant lakeside site with good, modern facilities.
➲ *Access via B192.*
Open: Apr-Oct **Site:** 3.6HEC ⬛ ⍥ ⚏ **Prices:** ⚑2.50-3 ⚑3 ⚑4.50-5.50 ⚑3-5 **Facilities:** ⋔ 🏪 ⊙ 🗜 ⌀ ⍨ 🖻 **Services:** ✗ lau **Leisure:** ⌇ L

BERLIN

Dreilinden Albrechts-Teerofen, 14109 ☎ 030 8051201
A transit site close to the city.
➲ *Access via A115.*
Open: Mar-Oct **Site:** 1HEC ⬛ **Facilities:** ⋔ ⊙ 🗜 **Services:** ✗

Gatow Kladower Damm 213-217, 14089
☎ 030 3654340 🗎 030 36808492
e-mail: info@lccberlin.de website: www.lccberlin.de
A good transit close to the river.
➲ *Access via B5.*
Open: All year **Site:** 2.7HEC ⬛ ⍥ ⚏ **Prices:** ⚑5.10 ⚑3.80 pitch 6.60 **Facilities:** ⋔ 🏪 ⊙ 🗜 ⍨ 🖻 **Services:** 🍴 ✗ lau **Off-site:** ⌇R 🖃

AT KLADOW

DCC Else-Eckert-Platz Krampnitzer Weg 111-117, 14089
☎ 030 3652797 🗎 030 3651245
e-mail: info@dccberlin.de
website: www.dccberlin.de
Large site in woodland close to the lake. Good, modern facilities.
➲ *Access via B5 and B2 exit Berlin Spandau.*
Open: All year **Site:** 7HEC ⬛ ⠿ ⍥ ⚏ **Prices:** ⚑5.10 ⚑3.80 pitch 6.60 **Facilities:** ⋔ 🏪 ⊙ 🗜 ⍨ 🖻 **Services:** ✗ lau **Off-site:** ⌇L 🖃

AT SCHMÖCKWITZ

Krossinsee Wernsdorfer Str 45, 12527 ☎ 030 6758687
In pleasant wooded surroundings on the shore of the Krossinsee with plenty of recreational facilities.
➲ *Access via A10 exit Berlin Köpenick.*
Open: All year **Site:** 7HEC ⬛ ◆ ⚏ **Facilities:** ⋔ 🏪 ⊙ 🗜 ⍨ 🖻 **Services:** ✗ 🖃 lau **Leisure:** ⌇ L

At Wannsee

Kohlhasenbrück Neue Kreisstr 36, 14109 ☎ 030 8051737
Very pleasantly situated site on shore of Lake Griebnitz, owned by Deutscher Camping Club. Bathing area.
➲ *From Wannsee railway station, drive through Königstr, past Rathaus, through Chausseestr, Kohlhasenbrückerstr, and Kreisstr.*
Open: Mar-Oct Site: 3.6HEC ⚏ ⚘ Facilities: �🏠 ☉ ⚑ ⚐
Services: ✗ lau

Bodstedt Mecklenburg-Vorpommern

Bodstedt Damm 1, 18356 ☎ 038231 4226 ▥ 038231 4820
A pleasant site on the shore of the Saaler Bodden with good boating facilities.
➲ *Access via B105 exit Zingst/Barth.*
Site: 3.5HEC ⚏ ♣ ⚘ ⚑ Facilities: �🏠 ☉ ⚑ ⚐
Off-site: ✗ ⌁LR

Caputh Brandenburg

Himmelreich Wentorfinsel, Geltow, 14542
☎ 033209 70475 ▥ 033209 20100
e-mail: himmelreich@campingplatz-caputh.de
website: www.campingplatz-caputh.de
Open: All year Site: 7.5HEC ⚏ ∷∷ ⚘ Prices: ⚒4-5 ⚗2
⚑6-6.50 ▲3 Facilities: �🏠 ⚒ ☉ ⚑ ⚑ 🚿 ⚐ ⚑ Services: 🍴 ✗ ⊞
lau Leisure: ⌁ LR

Colditz Sachsen

Waldbad 04680 ☎ 034381 43122 ▥ 034381 43122
In wooded surroundings with some shaded pitches.
➲ *Access via E176 exit Zschadras.*
Open: 28 May-7 Oct Site: 2HEC ⚏ ⚘ ⚑ Facilities: �🏠 ☉ ⚑
⚗ 🚿 ⚐ Services: ⊞ lau Leisure: ⌁ LPRS Off-site: ⚒ 🍴 ✗ ⌁P

Dresden Sachsen

Wostra Trieskestr 100, 01259 ☎ 0351 2013254 ▥ 0351 2013254
Café open May-Sep only.
➲ *Access via B172 towards Heidenau. Signposted.*
Open: Apr-Oct Site: 1.8HEC ⚏ ⚘ Prices: ⚒3.50 ⚗2.50
⚑5.50 ▲3-6 Facilities: �🏠 ☉ ⚑ ⚐ Services: ⊞
Off-site: ⚒ ✗ ⌁P

Falkenberg Brandenburg

Erholungsgebiet Kiebitz 04895
☎ 035365 2135 ▥ 035365 38533
e-mail: info@kiebitz-eg-urlaub.de
website: www.kiebitz-eg-urlaub.de
➲ *Access via E55 Duben exit, then B87/B101 towards Herzberg.*
Open: 28 Mar-2 Nov Site: 5.2HEC ⚏ ∷∷ ⚘ ⚘
Prices: ⚒2.50-4.40 ⚗3.50 ⚑2.50-3.85 ▲1.50-6.05 pitch 2.50-
6.60 Facilities: �🏠 ☉ ⚑ ⚐ Services: ⊞ lau Leisure: ⌁ L
Off-site: ⚒ ✗ ⚗

Freest Mecklenburg-Vorpommern

Waldcamp 17440 ☎ 038370 20538 ▥ 038370 20525
A modern site in wooded surroundings with good facilities.
➲ *300mtrs from Freest centre.*
Open: Apr-Oct Site: 2HEC ⚏ ∷∷ ⚘ ⚘ ⚑ Facilities: �🏠 ☉
⚑ ⚐ Services: lau Off-site: ⚒ 🍴 ✗ ⚗ 🚿 ⌁S

Georgenthal Thüringen

Georgenthal 99887 ☎ 036253 41314 ▥ 036253 25207
e-mail: campingplatz70@hotmail.com
website: www.campingplatz-georgenthal.de
Open: Apr-Oct Site: 1HEC ⚏ ⚘ ⚘ ⚑ Facilities: �🏠 ☉ ⚑ ⚗
⚐ ⚑ Services: ✗ lau Leisure: ⌁ P Off-site: ⚒ ⌁L ⊞

Gross-Leuthen Brandenburg

Spreewaldtor 15913 ☎ 035471 303 ▥ 035471 310
e-mail: eurocamp.spreewaldtor@t-online.de
website: www.eurocamp-spreewaldtor.de
On a level meadow beside the Gorss Leuthener See.
➲ *N of town off B179.*
Open: All year Site: 9HEC ⚏ ∷∷ ⚘ 🚿 ⚑ Facilities: �🏠 ⚒
☉ ⚑ ⚗ 🚿 ⚐ Services: ✗ ⊞ lau Off-site: ⌁L

Gross-Quassow Mecklenburg-Vorpommern

Havelberge am Woblitzsee 17237
☎ 03981 24790 ▥ 03981 247999
e-mail: info@haveltourist.de website: www.haveltourist.de
In a rural setting beside the lake. Restricted facilities during March.
➲ *1.5km S of town. Signposted.*
Open: All year Site: 14HEC ⚏ ∷∷ ♣ ⚘ ⚑ ▲ Facilities: �🏠
⚒ ☉ ⚑ ⚗ 🚿 ⚐ Services: 🍴 ✗ ⊞ lau Leisure: ⌁ L

Kamenz Sachsen

AZUR Waldbad Deutschbaselitz Grobteichstr 30, 01917
☎ 03578 301489 ▥ 03578 308316
e-mail: deutschbaselitz@azur.freizeit.de
website: www.azur-camping.de/deutschbaselitz
The site may close for a short time in the winter and the shop and café are only open between May and September.
Open: 15 Mar-Oct Site: 5HEC ⚏ ∷∷ ♣ ⚘ ⚑ Prices: ⚒3-5
▲2.50-3.50 pitch 4-6 Facilities: �🏠 ⚒ ☉ ⚑ ⚗ ⚐ Services: ✗
Leisure: ⌁ L

Kelbra Thüringen

Südharz Lange Str 150, 6537
☎ 034651 45290 & 45291 ▥ 034651 45292
e-mail: info@seecampingharz.de
website: www.seecampingharz.de
Open: All year Site: 6.5HEC ⚏ 🚿 ⚑ Prices: ⚒4 ⚗1.50
⚑5 ▲4 pitch 6 Facilities: �🏠 ⚒ ☉ ⚑ ⚗ 🚿 ⚐ Services: ✗ ⊞
Leisure: ⌁ LP Off-site: 🍴

Facilities: ⚒-shop ⚑-shower ☉-electric points for razors ⚑-electric points for caravans ⚐-parking by tents permitted
⚑-compulsory separate car park **Services:** ✗-café/restaurant 🍴-bar ⚗-Camping Gaz International 🚿-gas other than Camping
Gaz ⊞-first aid facilities lau-laundry **Leisure:** ⌁-swimming L-Lake P-Pool R-River S-Sea **Off-site:** All facilities within 2km

KLEINMACHNOW BRANDENBURG

Yacht-Caravan-Club Bäkehang 9a, 14532
☎ 033203 79684 📠 033203 77913
e-mail: citycamp-berlin@web.de
website: www.hettler-lange.de
A riverside site with an hotel SW of town off A115.
Open: All year Site: 2.2HEC ⊞⊞⊞ ⊕ Prices: ♠5 ♠2.50 ♠3
▲3 Facilities: 🏪 ⊙ 🖭 ⍉ 🏖 Services: ⚍ ✕ 🕂 lau Leisure: ⤳ R

KLEINRÖHRSDORF SACHSEN

LuxOase Arnsdorfer Str 1, 01900
☎ 035952 56666 📠 035952 56024
e-mail: camping.luxoase@t-online.de
website: www.luxoase.de
In beautiful, peaceful surroundings bordering a lake among
meadows and woods.
➲ Access via A4 (Dresden-Bautzen) exit Pulsnitz towards
Radeberg and continue for 4km through Leppersdorf then 1km
after the village turn right for site.
Open: Mar-9 Nov Site: 7.2HEC ⊞⊞⊞ ⋇ ⊕ 🖙 Prices: ♠4-
4.50 ♠1.70 ♠5.30-7.80 ▲4.50-5.60 Facilities: 🏪 🏖 ⊙ 🖭 ⍉
🏖 🏖 Services: ⚍ ✕ 🕂 lau Leisure: ⤳ L

KLEINSAUBERNITZ SACHSEN

Olbasee Olbaweg 16, 02694
☎ 035932 30232 📠 035932 30886
e-mail: natur@campingplatz-olbasee.de
website: www.campingplatz-olbasee.de
In a rural location on the Olbasee.
➲ Leave A4 at Bautzen Ost exit and take B156 N to
Kleinsaubernitz.
Open: 16 Apr- 24 Oct Site: 7HEC ⊞⊞⊞ ⠇⠇ ⊕ 🖙 🖙
Prices: ♠4.20 ♠2.50 ♠3 ▲2.50 Facilities: 🏪 🏖 ⊙ 🖭 ⍉ 🏖
Services: ✕ 🕂 lau Leisure: ⤳ L Off-site: ✕ 🏖

KÖNIGSTEIN SACHSEN

Königstein Schandauer Str 25e, 01822
☎ 035021 68224 📠 035021 60725
e-mail: camp.koenigstein@t-online.de
On level ground in a wooded location with fine views of the
surrounding mountains.
➲ Federal road B172 within Königstein near Dresden.
Site: 2.4HEC ⊞⊞⊞ ⊕ 🖙 Prices: ♠4.50 ♠3 ♠1.50-3 ▲1.50-
3 Facilities: 🏪 🏖 ⊙ 🖭 ⍉ 🏖 🏖 Services: ✕ lau
Off-site: ⚍ ⤳PR 🕂

LASSAN MEKLENBURG-VORPOMMERN

Lassan Garthof 5-6, 17440
☎ 038374 80373 📠 038374 80373
e-mail: naturcampingplatzlassan@gmx.de
website: www.campingplatz-lassan.de
A pleasant site on the Achterwasser.
➲ Access via B110.
Open: Apr-Sep Site: 1.4HEC ⊞⊞⊞ ⊕ Prices: ♠3.20-3.80
♠2-2 ♠4.50-5.50 ▲3.20-3.80 Facilities: 🏪 ⊙ 🖭 🏖
Services: ✕ lau Leisure: ⤳ LRS Off-site: 🏖 ⚍ ⍉ 🕂

LEHNIN BRANDENBURG

Seeblick am Klostersee 14797
☎ 03382 700274 📠 03382 700274
website: www.campingplatz-lehnin.de
➲ 50 miles from Berlin on E30.
Open: Apr-15 Oct Site: 1.5HEC ⊞⊞⊞ ⊕ Prices: ♠4.50 ♠1.50
♠4 ▲2.50 Facilities: 🏪 🏖 ⊙ 🖭 🏖 Services: 🕂 lau Leisure: ⤳
L Off-site: 🏖 ✕ ⍉

MÜHLBERG THÜRINGEN

Drei Gleichen 99869 ☎ 0236256 22715 📠 0236256 86801
e-mail: service@campingplatz-muehlberg.de
website: www.campingplatz-muehlberg.de
In pleasant wooded surroundings.
➲ Access via A4 exit Wandersleben, then follow signs for
Mühlberg.
Open: All year Site: 2.8HEC ⊞⊞⊞ ⋇ Prices: ♠3.60 ♠1
♠3.60 ▲2.60 Facilities: 🏪 ⊙ 🖭 ⍉ 🏖 🏖 Services: ✕ lau
Off-site: ✕ ⤳L 🕂

NIESKY SACHSEN

Tonschächte 02902 ☎ 03588 205771 📠 03588 205771
website: www.nol-kreis.de/ltonsee/indexton.htm
Open: May-Sep Site: 15HEC ⠇⠇ ♠ 🖙 Facilities: 🏪 ⊙ 🖭 ⍉
🏖 🏖 Services: ⚍ ✕ lau Leisure: ⤳ L Off-site: 🏖

NIEWISCH BRANDENBURG

Schwielochsee-Camping Uferweg Nord 16, 15848
☎ 033676 5186 📠 033676 5226
e-mail: fischer.camping@12move.de
website: www.fischer-camping.de
A family site in pleasant wooded surroundings on the banks
of the Schwielochsee.
Open: All year Site: 4.2HEC ⊞⊞⊞ ⠇⠇ ⊕ 🖙 Prices: ♠3.30
♠1.60 ▲3.20-4.70 pitch 6.20 (incl 2 persons) Facilities: 🏪 🏖
⊙ 🖭 ⍉ 🖭 Services: ✕ 🕂 lau Leisure: ⤳ L

PLÖTZKY SACHSEN

Ferienpark Plötzky Campingplatz Kleiner Waldsee, 39245
☎ 039200 50155 📠 039200 77120
e-mail: info@ferienpark-ploetzky.de
website: www.ferien-plotzky.de
In a wooded location beside a small lake with well defined
pitches.
➲ 20km S of Magdeburg. Access via A2 and B246.
Open: All year Site: 8HEC ⊞⊞⊞ ♠ 🖙 Facilities: 🏪 🏖 ⊙ 🖭 ⍉
🏖 🏖 Services: ✕ 🕂 lau Leisure: ⤳ L

POTSDAM BRANDENBURG

Sanssouci-Gaisberg An der Pirscheide, Templiner See 41,
14471 ☎ 0331 9510988 & 03327 55680
e-mail: info@recra.de website: www.recra.de
In wooded surroundings close to the Templiner See.
➲ Signposted from the B1.
Open: Apr-01 Nov Site: 6HEC ⊞⊞⊞ ⠇⠇ ⊕ Prices: ♠8.40
♠1.20 ♠8.20 pitch 8.20 Facilities: 🏪 🏖 ⊙ 🖭 ⍉ 🏖 🏖
Services: ⚍ ✕ 🕂 Leisure: ⤳ LR Off-site: ⤳P

REICHENBERG SACHSEN

Sonnenland Dresdner Str 115, 01468
☎ 0351 8305495 📠 0351 8305494
e-mail: bad-sonnenland@t-online.de
website: www.moritzburg.de
In a pleasant location beside the lake with good, modern
facilities.
➲ 3km S of Moritzburg, access via A4 exit Wilder Mann.
Open: Apr-Oct Site: 18HEC ⊞⊞⊞ ⊕ 🖙 Prices: ♠1.50 ♠5-6
▲2-4 Facilities: 🏪 🏖 ⊙ 🖭 🏖 Services: ✕ 🕂 lau Leisure: ⤳ L
Off-site: ⚍ ⤳P

SUHRENDORF MECKLENBURG-VORPOMMERN

Suhrendorf 18569 ☎ 038305 82234 📠 038305 8165
Open: All year Site: 90HEC ⊞⊞⊞ ⊕ 🖙 Facilities: 🏪 🏖 ⊙ 🖭
⍉ 🏖 🏖 Services: ⚍ ✕ lau Leisure: ⤳ S

Site: 6HEC-Site size ⊞⊞⊞-grass ⠇⠇-sand ♠-stone ⋇-little shade ⊕-partly shaded ♠-mainly shaded
🏠-bungalows for hire 🖙-caravans for hire ▲-tents for hire ⊗-no dogs Prices: ♠-adult per night ♠-car per night
pp-per person per night 🖙-caravan per night ▲-tent per night

ZINNOWITZ MECKLENBURG-VORPOMMERN

Pommernland Dr.Wachsmann-Strabe 40, 17454
☎ 038377 40348   ▤ 038377 40349
e-mail: camping-pommernland@m-vp.de
website: www.camping-pommernland.m-vp.de
In wooded surroundings on the north sea coast.
➲ *Access via B111.*
Open: All year Site: 7.7HEC � ᠅ ⌕ 🛅 Facilities: ⟡ ⌁ ⊙ 🖭 ⌀ 🛱 🖭 Services: ⟡ ✗ ⊞ lau Leisure: ⟡ S Off-site: ⟡P

CENTRAL

ASBACHERHÜTTE RHEINLAND-PFALZ

Harfenmühle 55758 ☎ 06786 7076   ▤ 06786 7570
e-mail: camping-harfenmuehle@t-online.de
website: www.camping-harfenmuehle.de
A quiet site, beautifully situated in Fischbach Valley. Level grassland, partly terraced.
➲ *3km NW of the B327 towards Kempfeld.*
Open: All year Site: 6.2HEC ᠅ ⌕ 🛅 Prices: ⌁4 ⟡1
🚐6 ⌁4-6 pitch 7.50 Facilities: ⟡ ⌁ ⊙ 🖭 ⌀ 🛱 🖭 Services: ⟡ ✗ ⊞ lau Leisure: ⟡ L

ATTENDORN NORDRHEIN-WESTFALEN

Biggesee-Waldenburg 57439 ☎ 02722 95500   ▤ 02722 955099
e-mail: camping-waldenburg@t-online.de
website: www.camping-biggesee.de
Generously terraced recreational site on the northern shore of the Bigge Reservoir, with adjoining public bathing area. Private sunbathing area. Lunchtime siesta 13.00-15.00 hrs.
➲ *From Attendorn follow road towards Heldren. Shortly after the railway turn right and follow the signs to the site, about 1.5km on.*
Open: All year Site: 6.5HEC ⌕ Facilities: ⟡ ⌁ ⊙ 🖭 ⌀ 🛱 🖭 Services: ⟡ ✗ ⊞ lau Leisure: ⟡ L Off-site: ⟡ ✗ ⟡P

Hof Biggen Finnentroper Str 131, 57439
☎ 02722 95530   ▤ 02722 955322
e-mail: info@hof-biggen.de website: www.hof-biggen.de
Well-equipped terraced site, surrounded by woodlands. Lunchtime siesta 13.00-15.00 hrs.
➲ *Follow Atterdorn road to Ahauser Reservoir. Entrance near 'Haus am See' inn.*
Open: All year Site: 18HEC ⚫ ⌕ Prices: ⌁3.50-5 ⟡1.75-2.50 🚐3.50-5 ⌁3.50-5 Facilities: ⟡ ⌁ ⊙ 🖭 ⌀ 🛱 🖭 Services: ⟡ ✗ ⊞ lau Off-site: ⟡R

BACHARACH RHEINLAND-PFALZ

Sonnenstrand Strandbadweg 9, 55422
☎ 06743 1752   ▤ 06743 3192
e-mail: info@camping-sonnenstrand.de
website: www.camping-sonnenstrand.de
On grassland beside the Rhine with some high trees. Close to a main road and two railway lines.
➲ *The turn off from B9 into the site can be difficult for caravans coming from the north, due to one way traffic.*
Open: 15 Mar-Oct Site: 1.4HEC ᠅ ⌕ 🛅 Prices: ⌁4.20 🚐6 Facilities: ⟡ ⌁ ⊙ 🖭 ⌀ 🖭 Services: ⟡ ✗ ⊞ lau Leisure: ⟡ R

BALHORN HESSEN

Erzeberg 34308 ☎ 05625 5274   ▤ 05625 7116
website: www.campingplatz-erzeberg.de
Site lies on meadowland on slightly sloping ground above the village. Lunchtime siesta 13.00-15.00 hrs.
➲ *On B450 between Istha and Fritzlar.*
Open: All year Site: 5HEC ⚫ 🛅 Prices: ⌁3.10 🚐6.20 ⌁6.20 pitch 6.20 Facilities: ⟡ ⌁ ⊙ 🖭 ⌀ 🖭 Services: ⟡ ✗ lau Leisure: ⟡ P Off-site: ⌁ 🛱 ⊞

BARNTRUP NORDRHEIN-WESTFALEN

Schwimmbad Fischteiche 4, 32683
☎ 05263 2221   ▤ 05263 2221
This well-kept site lies next to an open-air swimming pool, which is covered over in autumn and winter.
➲ *B66, near to junction with B1. Approach signposted from Barntrup.*
Open: All year Site: 2.4HEC ⌕ 🚐 ⌁ Facilities: ⟡ ⌁ ⊙ 🖭 ⌀ 🖭 Services: ⊞ lau Leisure: ⟡ P Off-site: ✗

BERNKASTEL-KUES RHEINLAND-PFALZ

Kueser Werth Am Hafen 2, 54470
☎ 06531 8200   ▤ 06531-8282
website: www.camping-kueser-werth.de
Grassy site near Mosel and boating marina, with view of Castle Landshut.
➲ *On S outskirts of town.*
Open: Apr-Oct Site: 2.2HEC ⌕ Prices: ⌁4.50 ⟡1.50 🚐4 ⌁2.50-4 Facilities: ⟡ ⌁ ⊙ 🖭 ⌀ 🛱 🖭 Services: ⟡ ✗ ⊞ lau

BIRKENFELD RHEINLAND-PFALZ

Waldwiesen 55765 ☎ 06782 5215   ▤ 06782 5219
e-mail: info@waldwiesen.de
website: www.waldwiesen.de
In a wooded location close to the lake.
➲ *Leave the B41 E of Birkenfeld. Signposted.*
Open: 15 Apr-14 Oct Site: 9.5HEC ⌕ 🛅 🚐
Prices: ⌁5.25 🚐6.75-8.25 ⌁5.75 pitch 6.75-8.25 Facilities: ⟡ ⊙ 🖭 ⌀ 🛱 🖭 Services: ⊞ lau Leisure: ⟡ L Off-site: ⌁ ⟡ ✗ ⟡P

BÖMIGHAUSEN HESSEN

Barenberg 34508 ☎ 05632 1044   ▤ 05632 1044
Beautifully terraced site at Neerdar reservoir.
➲ *Access from B251 between Korbach and Brilon.*
Open: All year Site: 1HEC ᠅ ⌕ Prices: ⌁3 🚐3 ⌁3 pitch 3 Facilities: ⟡ ⊙ 🖭 ⌀ 🖭 Services: lau Leisure: ⟡ LR

BRAUNFELS HESSEN

Braunfels Am Weiherstieg 2, 35619
☎ 06442 4366   ▤ 06442 6895
A terraced site surrounded by a forest of pine and deciduous trees. Separate meadow for touring campers. Lunchtime siesta 12.30-14.30 hrs.
➲ *Access from Köln-Frankfurt motorway, exit 'Limburg', then B49 towards town.*
Open: All year Site: 5.2HEC ⚫ ⌕ 🚐 Facilities: ⟡ ⊙ 🖭 ⌀ 🖭 Services: ✗ lau Off-site: ⌁ 🛱 ⟡P

BREISIG, BAD RHEINLAND-PFALZ

Rheineck 53498 ☎ 02633 95645   ▤ 02633 472008
e-mail: info@camping-rheineck.de
website: www.camping-rheineck.de
A quiet, well-kept site on a level meadow in Vinxtbach Valley.
➲ *From Koblenz follow B9 NW to Bad Breisig, then turn left, cross railway and continue for 400m.*
Open: All year Site: 5HEC ⌕ Prices: ⌁4.50 🚐3 🚐3.50 ⌁3 Facilities: ⟡ ⌁ ⊙ 🖭 ⌀ 🖭 Services: ⟡ ⊞ lau Off-site: ⟡PR

BULLAY RHEINLAND-PFALZ

Bären-Camp Am Moselüfer 1/3, 56859
☎ 06542 900097   ▤ 06542 900098
e-mail: info@baeren-camp.de
website: www.baeren-camp.de
On level meadow on right bank of the Mosel, next to the football ground. Fine view.

contd.

Facilities: ⌁-shop **⟡**-shower **⊙**-electric points for razors **🖭**-electric points for caravans **🖭**-parking by tents permitted **⊞**-compulsory separate car park **Services: ✗**-café/restaurant **⟡**-bar **⌀**-Camping Gaz International **🛱**-gas other than Camping Gaz **⊞**-first aid facilities lau-laundry **Leisure: ⟡**-swimming L-Lake P-Pool R-River S-Sea **Off-site:** All facilities within 2km

➲ *Access via B49 Cochem-Alf, then over the bridge and through the village. Signposted.*
Open: 15 Mar-5 Nov Site: 1.8HEC ⬛⬛⬛ ⚘ Prices: ⭢5.10 ⬛3.20 ⬛3.20 ⬛3.20 pitch 6.40-7 Facilities: ⬛ ⬛ ⊙ ⬛ ⬀ ⬛ Services: ⬛ ✗ ⊞ lau Leisure: ⬀ R Off-site: ⬀P

COBLENCE SEE KOBLENZ

COCHEM RHEINLAND-PFALZ

Freizeitzentrum Stadionstr, 56812
⬛ 02671 4409 ⬛ 02671 910719
e-mail: campingplatz-cochem.de
website: www.moselbad.de
Site lies on level meadowland with trees. On right bank of the Mosel, downstream from the swimming pool and sports ground.
➲ *From B49 in Cochem, follow 'Freizeitzentrum' signs, crossing the river on the downstream bridge. After swimming pool, turn left for site.*
Open: end Mar-Oct Site: 2.8HEC ⬛⬛⬛ ⚘ ⬛ Prices: ⭢4 pitch 4-7.50 Facilities: ⬛ ⬛ ⊙ ⬛ ⬀ ⬛ ⬛ ⬛ Services: ⬛ ✗ ⊞ lau Leisure: ⬀ R Off-site: ✗ ⬀P

AT LANDKERN (7KM N)

Altes Forsthaus Haupstr 2, 56814
⬛ 02671 8701 ⬛ 02671 8722
e-mail: camping.stern@t-online.de
website: www.landkern.com
The partly terraced site lies near woodland in the valley below Landkern.
➲ *From motorway A48 (Eifel motorway) leave at exit Kaisersesch, go S to Landkern, then follow signs to site.*
Open: All year Site: 10HEC ⬛⬛⬛ ⚘ Prices: ⭢3.25 ⬛1.75 ⬛5-7 ⬛5-7 Facilities: ⬛ ⊙ ⬛ ⬀ ⬛ ⬛ Services: ⬛ ✗ ⊞ lau Off-site: ⬛ ✗ ⬀P

COLOGNE SEE KÖLN

DAHN RHEINLAND-PFALZ

Büttelwoog 66994 ⬛ 06391 5622 ⬛ 06391 5326
e-mail: buettelwoog@t-online.de
website: www.camping-buettelwoog.de
Site lies in a magnificent pine forest, partly surrounded by steep hills and rocks. Section reserved for young people with tents. Lunchtime siesta 12.00-14.00 hrs.
➲ *From Pirmasens follow B10 up to Hinterweidenthal then S on B427 to Dahn.*
Open: All year Site: 6HEC ⬛⬛⬛ ⠿ ⚘ ⬛ Prices: ⭢5 ⬛3-6 ⬛6 ⬛3-6 pitch 6 Facilities: ⬛ ⬛ ⊙ ⬛ ⬀ ⬛ ⬛ Services: ⬛ ✗ ⊞ lau Off-site: ⬀P

DAUSENAU RHEINLAND-PFALZ

Lahn-Beach Hallgarten 16, 56132
⬛ 02603 13084 ⬛ 02603 13084
e-mail: info@althoff-freizeit.de
website: www.althoff-freizeit.de
A riverside site in a wooded setting.
Open: Apr-Oct Site: 3HEC ⬛⬛⬛ ⚘ ⬛ Facilities: ⬛ ⬛ ⊙ ⬛ ⬛ Services: ⬛ ✗ lau Leisure: ⬀ R

DIEMELSEE-HERINGHAUSEN NORDRHEIN-WESTFALEN

AZUR-Camping Hohes Rad 34519
⬛ 05633 99099 ⬛ 05633 99010
website: www.camping.diemelsee.de
A terraced site in the Sauerland hills overlooking Lake Diemel.
➲ *Access via B251 (Korbach-Beilon).*
Open: All year Site: 2.8HEC ⬛⬛⬛ ⬛ Facilities: ⬛ ⬛ ⊙ ⬛ ⬀ ⬛ ⬛ Services: ✗ lau Off-site: ✗ ⬀LP ⊞

DIEZ RHEINLAND-PFALZ

Ochsenwiese 65582 ⬛ 06432 2122 ⬛ 06432 2122
e-mail: info@camping-diez.de
website: www.camping-diez.de
On a meadow on the left bank of the River Lahn, below Schloss Oranienstein.
➲ *From N leave motorway A3 at Diez exit (from S at Limburg-Nord exit) then continue on B54 approx 7km.*
Open: Apr-Oct Site: 7HEC ⬛⬛⬛ ⬛ ⬛ Prices: ⭢3.30 ⬛2.80 ⬛3.80 ⬛2.20-3.80 Facilities: ⬛ ⬛ ⊙ ⬛ ⬀ ⬛ ⬛ Services: ⬛ ✗ lau Leisure: ⬀ R Off-site: ⬀L

DORSEL AN DER AHR RHEINLAND-PFALZ

Stahlhütte 53533 ⬛ 02693 438 ⬛ 02693 511
website: www.campingplatz-stahlhuette.de
Site with individual pitches, on meadowland with trees near River Ahr.
➲ *Off B258 (Aachen-Koblenz) road.*
Open: All year Site: 7HEC ⬛⬛⬛ ⬛ Prices: ⭢4 ⬛8 ⬛7 pp4 Facilities: ⬛ ⬛ ⊙ ⬛ ⬀ ⬛ ⬛ Services: ⬛ ✗ lau Leisure: ⬀ R

DORTMUND NORDRHEIN-WESTFALEN

Hohensyburg Syburger Dorfstr 69, 44265
⬛ 0231 774374 ⬛ 0231 7749554
e-mail: info@camping-hohensyburg.de
website: www.camping-hohensyburg.de
Terraced site on hilly grassland near Weitkamp inn.
➲ *Access via B54.*
Open: All year Site: 10HEC ⬛⬛⬛ ⬛ Prices: ⭢4.50 ⬛3 ⬛6 ⬛3.50 pitch 9 Facilities: ⬛ ⬛ ⊙ ⬛ ⬀ ⬛ Services: ⬛ ✗ ⊞ lau Leisure: ⬀ LR

DREIEICH-OFFENTHAL HESSEN

Offenthal Bahnhofstr 77, 63303
⬛ 06074 5629 ⬛ 06074 5629
e-mail: schoenweitz@t-online.de
website: www.t-online.de/home/schoenweitz/campa.htm
A well equipped site in wooded surroundings.
➲ *Exit B486 at Dreieich-Offenthal in direction of Dietzenbach.*
Open: All year Site: 3HEC ⬛⬛⬛ ⬛ ⬛ Prices: ⭢4 ⬛0.50-0.50 ⬛5 ⬛4 Facilities: ⬛ ⬛ ⊙ ⬛ ⬛ Services: ⊞ Leisure: ⬀ P Off-site: ✗ ⬀

DROLSHAGEN NORDRHEIN-WESTFALEN

Gut Kalberschnacke 57489 ⬛ 02763 7501 ⬛ 02763 7879
e-mail: camping-kalberschnacke@t-online.de
website: www.camping-kalberschnacke.de
Terraced site above Bigge-Lister Reservoir in wooded area.
➲ *Turn off A45 (E41) autobahn at Wegringhausen exit and continue NE for approx. 4km.*
Open: All year Site: 13.5HEC ⬛⬛⬛ ⬛ Facilities: ⬛ ⬛ ⊙ ⬛ ⬀ ⬛ ⬛ Services: ✗ lau Off-site: ⬀L

DÜLMEN NORDRHEIN-WESTFALEN

Tannenwiese Borkenbergestr 217, 48249 ⬛ 02594 991759
The site lies on meadowland in a well wooded country area, near the gliderdrome. Lunchtime siesta 12.30-14.30 hrs.
➲ *Take the B51 from Recklinghausen towards Münster as far as Hausdülmen, then follow signpost 'Segelflügplatz Borkenberge'.*
Open: Mar-30 Oct Site: 3.7HEC ⬛⬛⬛ ⚘ Prices: ⭢4 ⬛1 ⬛3.50 ⬛2.50-3.10 Facilities: ⬛ ⬛ ⊙ ⬛ ⬀ ⬛ Services: ⊞ lau Off-site: ⬛ ✗

Site: 6HEC-Site size ⬛⬛⬛-grass ⠿-sand ⬥-stone ⚘-little shade ⬤-partly shaded ✦-mainly shaded
⬛-bungalows for hire ⬛-caravans for hire ⬛-tents for hire ⊗-no dogs Prices: ⭢-adult per night ⬛-car per night pp-per person per night ⬛-caravan per night ⬛-tent per night

DÜRKHEIM, BAD RHEINLAND-PFALZ

KNAUS Bad Dürkheim In den Almen 3, 67098
☎ 06322 61356 ▦ 06322 8161
e-mail: knaus-camping-duerkheim@t-online.de
website: www.knauscamp.de
Lakeside site on level meadow between vineyards, adjoining a
sportsfield. Lunchtime siesta 12.00-15.00 hrs.
➲ *Access from E outskirts of town. Turn N at railway viaduct,
near JET petrol station.*
Open: Jan-Oct & Dec Site: 16HEC ㎜ ⌂ 🚐 ☕ 🅰 ⊗
Prices: ⚑6 ▲2 pitch 6-9 pp3 Facilities: ⬤ 🛍 ⊙ 🚰 ⛁ 🅿 🄿
Services: ⚑ ✗ 🞣 Leisure: ⌇ L Off-site: ⌇P

DÜSSELDORF NORDRHEIN-WESTFALEN

Unterbacher See Kleiner Torfbruch 31, 40627
☎ 0211 8992038 ▦ 0211 8929321
e-mail: service@uunterbachersee.de
website: www.unterbachersee.de
Site on sloping grassland.
➲ *From Düsseldorf B326 to 'Erkrath' exit. Turn left by
Unterbacher lake.*
Open: 03 Apr-24 Oct Site: 6.5HEC ㎜ ⌂ 🚐 ⊗
Prices: ⚑4.50 🚐8 ▲5 pitch 8 (incl 2 persons) Facilities: ⬤ ⊙
🚰 🄿 Services: ✗ 🞣 lau Leisure: ⌇ LP Off-site: 🛍 ⚑ ✗

EMS, BAD RHEINLAND-PFALZ

Bad Ems 56130 ☎ 02603 4679 ▦ 02603 4487
Level grassy site with isolated trees by the River Lahn.
➲ *On E outskirts on B260.*
Open: Apr-Oct Site: 16HEC ㎜ ⌂ 🚐 🚐 Facilities: ⬤ 🛍 ⊙
🚰 🄿 Services: ⚑ ✗ 🞣 lau Leisure: ⌇ PR

ESCHWEGE HESSEN

Knaus Campingpark Eschwege 37269
☎ 05651 338883 ▦ 05651 338884
e-mail: knaus.camp.esw@freenet.de
website: www.knauscamp.de
Site situated by the Werratalsee.
➲ *Leave A7 at exit for Eschwege, site signposted*
Open: Jan-Oct & Dec Site: 6.8HEC ㎜ ⠿ ⌂ 🚐 ▲
Prices: ⚑6 ▲2 pitch 3.50-8 Facilities: ⬤ 🛍 ⊙ 🚰 ⛁ 🅰
Services: ✗ 🞣 Leisure: ⌇ LR Off-site: ⚑ ✗ 🄿P

ESSEN NORDRHEIN-WESTFALEN

AT WERDEN (10KM S)

Essen-Werden Im Löwental 67, 45239
☎ 0201 492978 ▦ 0201 8496132
e-mail: stadtcamping@gmx.de
website: www.stadtcamping-essen.de
Several fields divided by bushes and surrounded by thick
hedges. Lunchtime siesta 13.00-15.00 hrs.
➲ *From centre of Essen towards Werden, then turn towards
railway station and follow signposts.*
Open: All year Site: 6HEC ㎜ ⠿ ⚭ ⌂ ⊗ Prices: ⚑4 🚐8
▲6 pitch 8 Facilities: ⬤ 🛍 ⊙ 🚰 🄿 Services: ⚑ ✗ 🞣 lau
Leisure: ⌇ R Off-site: 🛍 ⌇P

FÜRTH IM ODENWALD HESSEN

Tiefertswinkel Am Schwimmbad, 64658
☎ 06253 5804 ▦ 06253 3717
e-mail: info@camping-fuerth.de
website: www.camping-fuerth.de
Pleasantly landscaped site in beautiful setting next to the
municipal open-air swimming pool. Lunchtime siesta 13.00-
15.00 hrs.
Open: Mar-Nov Site: 4.2HEC ㎜ ⌂ 🚐 ⊗ Prices: ⚑3.30
🚐5.50 ▲3.50-5.50 Facilities: ⬤ 🛍 ⊙ 🚰 🄿 ⛁ 🅰 Services: ⚑ 🞣
lau Off-site: ✗ ⌇P

GAMMELSBACH HESSEN

Freienstein Neckartalstr 172, 64743
☎ 06068 1306 ▦ 06068 912121
The site lies just off the B45 in a landscaped preservation
area. It is terraced and divided into pitches. Lunchtime siesta
13.00-15.00 hrs.
Open: Apr-Sep Site: 5HEC ㎜ ♣ Facilities: ⬤ 🛍 ⊙ 🚰 ⛁ 🅰
Services: ⚑ ✗ lau

GEISENHEIM HESSEN

Geisenheim Postfach 1323, 65366
☎ 06722 75600 ▦ 06722 75600
Level grassland site.
➲ *Between B42 road and River Rhine.*
Open: Mar-Oct Site: 5HEC ㎜ ⌂ 🚐 Prices: ⚑3.95-5 🚐4
🚐5 ▲5 pitch 4-7 Facilities: ⬤ ⊙ 🚰 🅰 Services: ✗ lau
Leisure: ⌇ R Off-site: ⌀ ⌇P

GERBACH RHEINLAND-PFALZ

AZUR-Camping Pfalz 67813 ☎ 06361 8287 ▦ 06361 22523
e-mail: gerbach@azur-camping.de
website: www.azur-camping.de/gerbach
Lunchtime siesta 13.00-15.00 hrs.
➲ *Access from A8/E12 motorway at junction Enkenbach-
Hochspeyer. Then N on B48 via Rockenhausen and at
Dielkirchen continue E for 4.5km to Gerbach.*
Open: Apr-Oct Site: 8.5HEC ㎜ ⌂ Prices: ⚑4.50-6 pitch
5.50-7.50 Facilities: ⬤ 🛍 ⊙ 🚰 🄿 🅰 Services: ✗ 🞣 lau
Leisure: ⌇ P

GILLENFELD RHEINLAND-PFALZ

Feriedorf Pulvermaar 54558
☎ 06573 996500 ▦ 06573 996500
Partly terraced municipal site on a slightly sloping meadow
at Pulver Maar, surrounded by woods.
➲ *From motorway A48 (Eifel autobahn) leave at exit
Mehren/Daun, continue S on B421 and take the first turning
into Gillenfeld. On near side of village turn off towards Pulver
Maar.*
Open: All year Site: 3HEC ㎜ ⌂ 🚐 Prices: ⚑3-3.50 🚐1-2
🚐4.50-8 ▲4.50-6.50 Facilities: ⬤ ⊙ 🚰 ⛁ 🅰 Services: ⚑ ✗ 🞣
lau Off-site: 🛍 ⌇LP

GRÜNBERG HESSEN

Spitzer Stein Alsfelderstr, 6310 ☎ 06401 804
Beautifully situated site at a forest swimming pool.
➲ *From the Frankfurt-Kassel motorway (A5) leave at
Homberg junction. Campsite is 8km S.*
Open: All year Site: 4HEC ㎜ ⋇ Facilities: ⬤ 🛍 ⊙ 🚰 ⛁
🅰 Services: 🞣 lau Leisure: ⌇ P Off-site: 🛍 ✗

GRUNDMÜHLE BEI QUENTEL HESSEN

Grundmühle Quentel 37235
☎ 05602 3659 ▦ 05602 915811
A forest camp site with a sunny location. Lunchtime siesta
13.00-15.00 hrs.
➲ *From Melsungen follow road B83 to Röhrenfurth. Here turn
right towards 'Furstenhagen' and follow road via Eiterhagen to
Quentel.*
Open: All year Site: 1.8HEC ㎜ ⚭ ⌂ Prices: ⚑3.60 pitch
4.50 Facilities: ⬤ ⊙ 🚰 ⛁ 🅰 Services: ✗ lau Leisure: ⌇ R
Off-site: 🛍 ⚑ ✗

GULDENTAL RHEINLAND-PFALZ

Guldental 55452 ☎ 06707 633 ▦ 06707 18468
Site lies in a valley of the Guldenbach Valley. Some terraces
are reserved for tourers and there is a lake suitable for
bathing.
contd.

Facilities: 🛍-shop ⬤-shower ⊙-electric points for razors 🚰-electric points for caravans 🅰-parking by tents permitted
🄿-compulsory separate car park **Services:** ✗-café/restaurant ⚑-bar ⌀-Camping Gaz International ⛁-gas other than Camping
Gaz 🞣-first aid facilities lau-laundry **Leisure:** ⌇-swimming L-Lake P-Pool R-River S-Sea **Off-site:** All facilities within 2km

⮂ *From Bad Kreuznach N on road B48 to Langenlonsheim, and on nearside turn left to Guldental.*
Open: All year Site: 8HEC ⸬⸬⸬⸬ ⚘ Facilities: ↑ ⚍ ⊙ ⚑ ♨ 🏠
Services: ⚑ ✕ ⊞

HALDERN NORDRHEIN-WESTFALEN

Strandhaus Sonsfeld 46459 ☎ 02857 2247 ▤ 02857 7171
On meadowland at the 'Hagener-Meer' next to B8 and railway line.
Open: All year Site: 15HEC ⸬⸬⸬⸬ ⚘ Prices: ♠2.10 ♣2.10
♣2.10 ♠2.10 pitch 2.10 Facilities: ↑ ⊙ ⚑ ♨ 🏠 Services: ⚑
✕ ⊞ lau Leisure: ⟍ L

HAUSBAY RHEINLAND-PFALZ

AT PFALZFELD-HAUSBAY

Schinderhannes 56291 ☎ 06746 80280 ▤ 06746 802814
e-mail: info@countrycamping.de
website: www.countrycamping.de
Terraced site on south facing slope, broken up by trees and shrubs beside a small lake. Separate section for young people. Lunchtime siesta 13.00-15.00 hrs.
⮂ *E of B327. 29km S of Koblenz.*
Open: All year Site: 30HEC ⸬⸬⸬⸬ ♠ ⚘ Prices: ♠5 pitch 8
Facilities: ↑ ⚍ ⊙ ⚑ ♨ 🏠 Services: ✕ lau Leisure: ⟍ L
Off-site: ⚑ ✕ ⊞

HEIDENBURG RHEINLAND-PFALZ

Moselhöhe 54426 ☎ 06509 99016 ▤ 06509 99017
A small, well appointed site on a pure meadow.
⮂ *Access via A1 exit Mehring towards Thalfang am Erbestopf.*
Site: 3HEC ⸬⸬⸬⸬ ⚘ Prices: ♠4.50 ♣2.50 ♣4 ♠3
Facilities: ↑ ⊙ ⚑ ♨ 🏠 Services: ⚑ ✕ lau Off-site: ⚍ ⊞

HEIMBACH NORDRHEIN-WESTFALEN

Rurthal 52396 ☎ 02446 3377 ▤ 02446 911126
Site with individual pitches on meadowland beside the River Ruhr.
⮂ *From Düren follow road S via Nideggen and Abenden to Blens, then cross bridge and turn left.*
Site: 7HEC ⸬⸬⸬⸬ ⚘ ⚘ Facilities: ↑ ⚍ ⊙ ⚑ ♨ 🏠
Services: ✕ lau Leisure: ⟍ P Off-site: ✕ ⟍R

HEIMERTSHAUSEN HESSEN

Heimertshausen Ehringshauser Str, 36320
☎ 06635 206 ▤ 06635 918359
e-mail: info@campingplatz-heimertshausen.de
website: www.campingplatz-heimertshausen.de
Near swimming pool in extensive, grassy, wooded valley. Lunchtime siesta 13.00-15.00 hrs.
⮂ *From Kassel-Frankfurt motorway take Alsfeld-West exit, then continue via Romrod and Zell.*
Open: Apr-Sep Site: 3.6HEC ⸬⸬⸬⸬ ⚘ ⚘ Prices: ♠3.50 pitch
5.50-6.50 Facilities: ↑ ⚍ ⊙ ⚑ ♨ 🏠 Services: ⚑ ✕ ⊞ lau
Off-site: ⟍P

HELLENTHAL NORDRHEIN-WESTFALEN

Hellenthal Platiss 1, 53940 ☎ 02482 1500 ▤ 02482 2171
e-mail: info@camphellenthal.de website: www.camphellenthal.de
On extensive meadowland.
⮂ *0.5km S of town.*
Open: All year Site: 6HEC ⸬⸬⸬⸬ ⚘ Prices: ♠3.50 pitch 8
Facilities: ↑ ⊙ ⚑ 🏠 Services: ⚑ ✕ ⊞ lau Leisure: ⟍ P
Off-site: ⚍ ♨ ♨

HERINGEN HESSEN

Werra 36266 ☎ 06624 919043 ▤ 06624 915597
Municipal site on slightly sloping ground at the swimming pool. Lunchtime siesta 13.00-15.00 hrs.
Open: All year Site: 4HEC ⸬⸬⸬⸬ ♠ Facilities: ↑ ⚍ ⊙ ⚑ ♨ 🏠
Services: ✕ ⊞ lau Off-site: ⟍PR

HIRSCHHORN AM NECKAR HESSEN

Odenwald Langenthalerstr 80, 69430
☎ 06272 809 ▤ 06272 3658
e-mail: odenwald-camping-park@t-online.de
website: www.odenwald-camping-park.de
Extensive site in wooded valley. Divided by River Ülfenbach and hedges.
⮂ *Turn off B37 towards Wald-Michelbach and continue for 1.5km.*
Open: Apr-01 Oct Site: 8HEC ⸬⸬⸬⸬ ♠ ⚑ Prices: ♠4.50 pitch
6.20 Facilities: ↑ ⚍ ⊙ ⚑ ♨ 🏠 Services: ⚑ ✕ ⊞ lau
Leisure: ⟍ PR

HOFGEISMAR HESSEN

Parkschwimmbad Schöneberger Str 16, 3520 ☎ 05671 1215
Municipal site, subdivided by hedges. Next to a swimming pool. Lunchtime siesta 13.00-15.00 hrs. Mobile shop.
Open: All year Site: 1.5HEC ⸬⸬⸬⸬ ♠ Facilities: ↑ ⊙ ⚑ ♨ 🏠
Services: ✕ ⊞ lau Leisure: ⟍ P Off-site: ♨

AT LIEBENAU-ZWERGEN (9KM W)

Ponyhof Camping Club Teichweg 1, 34396
☎ 05676 1509 ▤ 05676 8880
e-mail: ponyhofcamping@t-online.de
website: www.ponyhofcamping.de
A terraced, south facing site, with magnificent scenery. 300mtrs from a swimming pool.
⮂ *Access from B83, at Hofgeismar turn W towards Liebenau, alternatively from B7 turn N at Obemeiser towards Liebenau.*
Site: 7HEC ⸬⸬⸬⸬ ♠ ⊞ ⚑ Facilities: ↑ ⚍ ⊙ ⚑ ♨ 🏠
Services: ⚑ ✕ ⊞ Leisure: ⟍ R Off-site: ⟍LP ⊞

HONNEF, BAD NORDRHEIN-WESTFALEN

AT HONNEF-HIMBERG, BAD (7KM E)

Jillieshof 53604 ☎ 02224 972066 ▤ 02224 972067
e-mail: hpfefferoth@t-online.de
Open: All year Site: 4HEC ⸬⸬⸬⸬ ♠ Prices: ♠4.50 ♣6 ♣6
Facilities: ↑ ⚍ ⊙ ⚑ ♨ 🏠 Services: ⊞ lau Off-site: ⚑ ✕

HORN-BAD MEINBERG NORDRHEIN-WESTFALEN

Eggewald Kempener Str 33, 32805
☎ 05255 236 ▤ 05255 1375
Site lies in well wooded countryside.
⮂ *Access via road B1. In Horn-Bad Meinberg turn off main road at the Waldschlosschen and follow the 'Altenbeken' road for about 8km up to Kempen.*
Open: All year Site: 2HEC ⸬⸬⸬⸬ ♠ Prices: ♠2.50 ♣5 ♠4-5
Facilities: ↑ ⊙ ⚑ ♨ 🏠 Services: ✕ ⊞ lau Leisure: ⟍ P

IDSTEIN HESSEN

AZUR-Camping Idstein 65510
☎ 06126 91299 ▤ 06126 990289
e-mail: idstein@azur-camping.de
website: www.azur-camping.de/idstein
In a peaceful rural setting close to the ancient town of Idstein.
⮂ *Access via A3 (Frankfurt-Limburg).*
Open: All year Site: 2.6HEC ⸬⸬⸬⸬ ♠ Facilities: ↑ ⊙ ⚑ ♨ 🏠
Services: ⊞ lau Leisure: ⟍ P Off-site: ⚍ ✕

Site: 6HEC-Site size ⸬⸬⸬⸬-grass ⋮⋮⋮-sand ♠-stone ⚘-little shade ♠-partly shaded ♣-mainly shaded
⚏-bungalows for hire ⚑-caravans for hire ⚍-tents for hire ⊘-no dogs Prices: ♠-adult per night ♣-car per night
pp-per person per night ♣-caravan per night ♠-tent per night

INGENHEIM RHEINLAND-PFALZ

SC Klingbachtal 76831 ☎ 06349 6278
Municipal site lies on level meadowland at the edge of the
village, next to the sports ground.
➲ *8km S of Landau via B38. Final approach well signposted.*
Open: Apr-Oct Site: 1.5HEC ⬛⬛ 🕭 Prices: ♦3.50 ♠2 ♣4
▲4 pitch 4 Facilities: 🏪 ⊙ ⊄ 🎦 🏕 Services: 🚻 Off-site: 🚻 🚻 ✗
⊄ 🎄 🕇P

IRREL RHEINLAND-PFALZ

Nimseck 54666 ☎ 06525 314 🖩 06525 1299
e-mail: info@camping-nimseck.de
website: www.camping-nimseck.de
Site on long grassy strip in wooded valley on the bank of
River Nims.
➲ *Approach from Bitburg via B257/E42 in SW direction. At
the turn-off from the bypass to Irrel, turn left.*
Open: 15 Mar-2 Nov Site: 7HEC ⬛⬛ 🕭 🏕 Prices: ♦3.75-
5.50 pitch 5.50-7.50 Facilities: 🏪 ⊙ ⊄ 🎦 🏕 Services: ✗ ⊞
lau Leisure: 🕇 PR Off-site: 🚻

KALLETAL-VARENHOLZ NORDRHEIN-WESTFALEN

Weser Freizeit-Zentrum 32689 ☎ 05755 444 🖩 05755 723
e-mail: info@camping-wfz-kalletal.de
website: www.camping-wfz-kalletal.de
Extensive site in Weser recreation area near River Weser
north of Schloss Varenholz. Separate field and common
room for young campers.
➲ *Leave A2/E8 motorway at Exter exit then continue via
Vlotho towards Rintein.*
Open: Feb-Oct Site: 12HEC ⬛⬛ 🕭 🏕 ✂ Prices: ♦2.30 ♣7
▲10 pitch 7 pp5 Facilities: 🏪 🚻 ⊙ ⊄ ⊄ 🎦 🏕 Services: 🚻 ✗
⊞ lau Leisure: 🕇 L

KELL RHEINLAND-PFALZ

Freibad Hochwald 54427 ☎ 06589 1695
On meadow on slightly sloping hillside, near a
public open-air swimming pool. **Advance booking necessary
in high season.**
➲ *2km from B407 towards Trier.*
Open: May-Sep Site: 2HEC ⬛⬛ 🕭 Prices: ♦5 ♠2.50 ♣5
▲5 Facilities: 🏪 ⊙ ⊄ 🏕 Services: ✗ ⊞ Leisure: 🕇 P

KIRCHHEIM HESSEN

Seepark Kirchheim 36275 ☎ 06628 1525 🖩 06628 8664
e-mail: info@campseepark.de
website: www.campseepark.de
This terraced site, with individual pitches, is part of an
extensive and well equipped leisure and recreation centre.
Open: All year Site: 10HEC ⬛⬛ 🕭 ⊄ ♣ Facilities: 🏪 🚻 ⊙
⊄ ⊄ 🏕 Services: 🚻 ✗ ⊞ lau Leisure: 🕇 LP

KIRN RHEINLAND-PFALZ

Papiermühle Krebsweilererstr 8, 55606 ☎ 06752 2267
➲ *Access via B41 exit Meisenheim*
Open: All year Site: 6HEC ⬛⬛ 🕭 Prices: ♦3.50 ♠3 ♣3 ▲3
pitch 6 Facilities: 🏪 ⊙ ⊄ ⊄ 🎦 🏕 Services: ✗ ⊞ Leisure: 🕇 R

KOBLENZ (COBLENCE) RHEINLAND-PFALZ

AT WINNINGEN (9KM SW)

Ziehfurt Fährstr 35, 56333 ☎ 02606 356 🖩 02606 2752
Site lies on level wooded meadowland.
➲ *From Koblenz follow road B416 for 11km towards Trièr.
Access to site at the Schwimmbad (swimming pool).*
Open: May-Sep Site: 7HEC ⬛⬛ ♣ Prices: ♦5 pitch 5
Facilities: 🏪 🚻 ⊙ ⊄ ⊄ 🏕 Services: 🚻 ✗ ⊞ lau Leisure: 🕇 R
Off-site: 🕇P

KÖLN (COLOGNE) NORDRHEIN-WESTFALEN

Berger Uferstr. 71, Rodenkirchen, 50996
☎ 0221 9355240 🖩 0221 9355246
e-mail: camping.berger@t-online.de
website: www.camping-berger-koeln.de
Situated on a meadow beside the River Rhine, the campsite
has fine views of the beautiful surrounding area and good,
modern facilities.
Open: All year Site: 6HEC ⬛⬛ 🕭 Prices: ♦4.50 ♠3 ♣3 ▲3
pitch 6 Facilities: 🏪 🚻 ⊙ ⊄ ⊄ 🏕 Services: 🚻 ✗ lau
Leisure: 🕇 R

KÖNEN RHEINLAND-PFALZ

Horsch Könenerstr 36, 54329 ☎ 06501 17571
Open: Apr-Oct Site: ⬛⬛ 🕭 Prices: ▲3 pitch 14-16 (incl 2
persons) Facilities: 🏪 🚻 ⊙ ⊄ ⊄ 🏕 Services: 🚻 ✗ ⊞
Leisure: 🕇 LPR

KÖNIGSTEIN IM TAUNUS HESSEN

AT EPPSTEIN (8KM SW)

Hubertushof Bezirksstr 2, 65817 ☎ 06198 7000 🖩 06198 7002
e-mail: info@taunuscamp.de website: www.taunuscamp.de
In the Taunus landscape preservation area.
➲ *Follow B455 from Königstein.*
Open: All year Site: 3HEC ⬛⬛ ♦ ♣ ♣ Facilities: 🏪 🚻 ⊙ ⊄
⊄ 🏕 Services: ⊞ Off-site: 🚻 ✗ 🕇P

KRÖV RHEINLAND-PFALZ

Kröver-Berg 54636 ☎ 06541 70040 🖩 06541 700444
website: www.kroverberg.de
Open: All year Site: 2HEC ⬛⬛ 🕭 Prices: ♠12 Facilities: 🏪
⊙ ⊄ 🎦 🏕 🅿 Services: 🚻 ✗ lau Off-site: 🕇P

LADBERGEN NORDRHEIN-WESTFALEN

Waldsee Waldseestr 81, 49549 ☎ 05485 1816 🖩 05485 3560
e-mail: info@waldsee-camping.de
website: www.waldsee-camping.de
Site lies at the inn, near the bathing area of the lake.
➲ *2km N. From motorway leave at 'Ladbergen' exit following
road towards Saerbeck/Emsdetten and after 100m turn right.*
Open: All year Site: 7HEC ⬛⬛ 🕭 ♣ Prices: ♦3.60 ▲6.20
pitch 6.60 Facilities: 🏪 🚻 ⊙ ⊄ ⊄ 🎦 🏕 Services: 🚻 ✗ ⊞ lau
Leisure: 🕇 LP Off-site: 🕇R

LAHNSTEIN RHEINLAND-PFALZ

Burg Lahneck 56112 ☎ 02621 2765 🖩 02621 18290
Level grassland site with sunny aspect and terraces which
provide shade. Situated next to Lahneck Castle. Pleasant view
of the Rhine Valley.
➲ *From Koblenz (8km distance) follow road B42. In
Lahnstein, leave main road and follow signs (Burg Lahneck),
1.5km to site.*
Open: Apr-Oct Site: 1.8HEC ⬛⬛ 🕭 Facilities: 🏪 🚻 ⊙ ⊄ ⊄
🏕 Services: ⊞ lau Off-site: ✗ 🕇P

If you want to tell us about your
experiences at a European
campsite, please use the Readers'
Report form at the back of the
book, or e-mail:
lifestyleguides@theAA.com

Facilities: 🚻-shop **🏪**-shower **⊙**-electric points for razors **⊄**-electric points for caravans **🏕**-parking by tents permitted
🅿-compulsory separate car park **Services: ✗**-café/restaurant **🚻**-bar **⊄**-Camping Gaz International **🎦**-gas other than Camping
Gaz **⊞**-first aid facilities lau-laundry **Leisure: 🕇**-swimming L-Lake P-Pool R-River S-Sea **Off-site:** All facilities within 2km

LEIWEN RHEINLAND-PFALZ

AEGON-Ferienpark Sonnenberg 54340
☎ 06507 93690 ▤ 06507 936936
e-mail: sonnenberg@landal.de website: www.landal.de
Extensive terraced site in one of the largest wine growing
areas of this district. Lies above the River Mosel.
➲ Access from main B53 (Mosel Valley road) cross the River
Mosel at Thornich then via Leiwen to site.
Site: 25HEC ⏚⏛ ◬ ♁ ✿ Prices: pitch 18-32 (incl 2 persons)
Facilities: ⚐ ⓩ ⊙ ⊞ ☎ Services: ♨ ✗ ⊞ lau Leisure: ⤳ PR
Off-site: ⌕ ♨ ✗ ∅

LEMGO NORDRHEIN-WESTFALEN

Alten Hansestadt Regenstorstr, 32657
☎ 05261 14858 ▤ 05261 188324
e-mail: info@camping-lemgo.de
website: www.camping-lemgo.de
The site lies by the swimming pool directly on the river.
Open: All year Site: 15HEC ⏚⏛ ◬ ✿ Facilities: ⚐ ⊙ ⊡ ∅
☎ Services: lau Leisure: ⤳ R Off-site: ⌕ ♨ ✗ ⤳P ⊞

LIBLAR NORDRHEIN-WESTFALEN

Liblarer See 50374 ☎ 02235 3899
This site lies at Lake Liblar, with its own bathing area.
Camping Card Compulsory.
➲ Access SW from Cologne on the B265 (for approx 15km)
1km before Liblar turn left towards the lake.
Open: All year Site: 10HEC ⏚⏛ ⫶⫶⫶ ◬ Prices: ⚹3.50 ⬤2
⬛4.50 ⬛3.50-5 Facilities: ⚐ ⓩ ⊙ ⊡ ∅ ☎ Services: ♨ ✗ ⊞
lau Leisure: ⤳ L

LINDENFELS HESSEN

Terrassencamping Schlierbach Am Zentbuckel 11, 64678
☎ 06255 630 ▤ 06255 3526
e-mail: info@terrassencampingschlierbach.de
website: www.terrassencampingschlierbach.de
Site is fenced and lies on sloping terrain. Lunchtime siesta
13.00-15.00 hrs.
➲ From Bensheim-Michelstadt road B47, turn off in
Lindenfels road go SW to Schlierbach.
Open: Apr-Oct Site: 3.2HEC ⏚⏛ ⫶⫶⫶ ◬ Prices: ⚹2.80-3.50
⬤3-5.50 pitch 4.40-5.50 Facilities: ⚐ ⓩ ⊙ ⊡ ∅ ☎
Services: ⊞ lau Off-site: ♨ ✗ ⤳P

LINGERHAHN RHEINLAND-PFALZ

Mühlenteich 56291 ☎ 067461 533 ▤ 067461 1566
e-mail: info@muehlenteich.de
website: www.muehlenteich.de
Site lies on slightly sloping meadowland, divided into
sections by a group of trees. Isolated situation at the edge of
woodland and adjoining the forest swimming pool (free
entry for campers). Lunchtime siesta 13.00-15.00 hrs. Trout
fishing.
➲ Access is from Koblenz-Bingen motorway A61 via exit
'Pfalzfeld' - or for caravans, an easier approach would be via
exit 'Laudert'.
Open: All year Site: 15HEC ⏚⏛ ♣ Prices: ⚹4 ⬤4 ⬛4 ⬛4
pitch 8 Facilities: ⚐ ⓩ ⊙ ⊡ ∅ ☎ Services: ♨ ✗ ⊞
Leisure: ⤳ P Off-site: ⤳R

LORCH HESSEN

Suleika 65382 ☎ 06726 9464 ▤ 06726 9440
website: www.suleika-camping.de
Well laid out terraced site in an ideal location for exploring
the historic Rhine Valley. Separate car park for users of the
smaller pitches.

➲ From Assmannshausen take B42 for 3km towards Lorch
then turn right into the Bodental - access to site through
railway underpass. Approach for larger caravans - turn right
1km before Lorch.
Open: 15 Mar-Oct Site: 4HEC ⏚⏛ ◬ ✿ Prices: ⚹4.50
⬤1.50 ⬛4.50 ◬3-4.50 Facilities: ⚐ ⓩ ⊙ ⊡ ∅ ⛟ ☎
Services: ♨ ✗ ⊞ lau Off-site: ✗ ⤳LR

LOSHEIM SAARLAND

AZUR-Camping Reiterhof Girtenmühle 66679
☎ 06872 90240 ▤ 06872 902411
e-mail: losheim@azur-camping.de
website: www.azur-camping.de/losheim
➲ Access via B268 (Trier-Losheim).
Open: All year Site: 5HEC ⏚⏛ ◬ Facilities: ⚐ ⊙ ⊡ ∅ ☎
Services: ✗ ⊞ lau Off-site: ⤳LP

MAINZ-KOSTHEIM HESSEN

Mainz-Wiesbaden Maarau 55246
☎ 06134 4383 ▤ 06134 4383
e-mail: info@kakg.de
website: www.knkg.de
Shop closed in April.
Open: 15 Mar-Oct Site: 2HEC ⏚⏛ ♣ Prices: ⚹4.20 ⬤2.70
⬛3.80 ◬3.20-4.30 pitch 4.30-6 Facilities: ⚐ ⓩ ⊙ ⊡ ☎
Services: ✗ lau Off-site: ⤳PR

MARBURG AN DER LAHN HESSEN

GC Lahnaue Tro je damm 47, 35037
☎ 06421 21331 ▤ 06421 21331
e-mail: info@lahnaue.de
website: www.lahnaue.de
Municipal site on level meadowland next to the 'Sommerbad'
(swimming pool) in the west part of this 'Town on the River
Lahn'.
Open: Apr-30 Oct Site: 1HEC ⏚⏛ ◬ Prices: ⚹4 ⬤2 ⬛3 ◬3
Facilities: ⚐ ⊙ ⊡ ∅ ☎ Services: ✗ lau Leisure: ⤳ R
Off-site: ⤳P

MEERBUSCH NORDRHEIN-WESTFALEN

AZUR-Camping Meerbusch Zur Rheinfähre 21, 40668
☎ 02150 911817 ▤ 02150 912289
e-mail: info@azur-camping.de
website: www.azur-camping.de
In a peaceful location on the banks of the Rhine within easy
reach of Dusseldorf.
➲ Access via A57 (Neuss-Krefeld).
Open: Apr-13 Oct Site: 3.8HEC ⏚⏛ ⚞ Facilities: ⚐ ⓩ ⊙
⊡ ⛟ ☎ Services: ✗ ⊞ lau Leisure: ⤳ R

MEHLEM NORDRHEIN-WESTFALEN

Genienau 53179 ☎ 0228 344949 ▤ 0228 3294989
e-mail: genienau@freenet.de
The site lies opposite the Drachenfels.
Open: All year Site: 1.8HEC ⏚⏛ ◬ Prices: ⚹5.10 ⬤1.60-
2.60 ⬛2.60-10.20 pitch 2.60-7.70 Facilities: ⚐ ⊙ ⊡ ∅ ☎
Services: ♨ ⊞ lau Leisure: ⤳ R Off-site: ⌕ ✗ ∅ ⛟ ⤳P

MEINHARD HESSEN

Werra-Meissner-Kreis 37276 ☎ 05651 6200 ▤ 05651 22272
e-mail: 0565113805-0001@t-online.de
website: www.eschwege.de/fez/index.htm
A lakeside site with facilities for water sports.
➲ Access via B27 and B249.
Open: Apr-Oct Site: 7HEC ⏚⏛ ◬ ⚘ Facilities: ⚐ ⊙ ⊡ ☎
Services: ♨ ✗ ⊞ lau Leisure: ⤳ L Off-site: ⌕ ⛟ ⤳P ⊞

Site: 6HEC-Site size ⏚⏛-grass ⫶⫶⫶-sand ◬-stone ⚞-little shade ◬-partly shaded ♣-mainly shaded
✿-bungalows for hire ⬛-caravans for hire ◬-tents for hire ⚘-no dogs Prices: ⚹-adult per night ⬤-car per night
pp-per person per night ⬛-caravan per night ◬-tent per night

MESCHEDE NORDRHEIN-WESTFALEN

Sauerland-Camp Hennesee 59872
☎ 0291 99950 📠 0291 999515
e-mail: info@hennesee.com website: www.hennesee.com
In pleasant wooded surroundings beside the Hennesee. Shop
and café only open during high season.
➲ *S via B55.*
Open: All year Site: 13HEC 🏕 ♔ Facilities: 🚿 🛒 ⊙ 🗲 ⌀ 🚻
🅿 Services: ⚐ ✗ 🖽 lau Leisure: ⚓ LP Off-site: ⚓L

MESENICH RHEINLAND-PFALZ

Family Camping Club 56820 ☎ 02673 4556 📠 02673 1751
A family site with plenty of recreational facilities beside the
River Moselle. Individual pitches are divided by trees and
hedges.
Open: May-Sep Site: 3HEC 🏕 ♔ ⚑ Facilities: 🚿 🛒 ⊙ 🗲
🚻 Services: ⚐ ✗ 🖽 lau Leisure: ⚓ PR

MICHELSTADT HESSEN

Odenwaldparadies 6120 ☎ 06061 74152/3256
Site is partly fenced in and lies next to the station and
swimming pool in the NE part of town.
➲ *Site is well signposted from the by-pass road of Michelstadt.*
Open: May-Sep Site: 1.2HEC 🏕 ⚞ ☼ Facilities: 🚿 ⊙ 🗲
⌀ 🚻 🅿 Services: ✗ 🖽 Off-site: ⚓P

MITTELHOF RHEINLAND-PFALZ

Eichenwald 57537
☎ 02742 931931/910643 📠 02742 9319931/910645
In oakwood, mainly divided into pitches.
Camping Card Compulsory.
➲ *From Siegen follow B62 towards Wissen. Turning to site
approximately 4km NE of Wissen.*
Open: All year Site: 10HEC 🏕 ♔ Prices: ♦3.50 🚗4 🚐4
🛖3 pitch 4 Facilities: 🚿 ⊙ 🗲 ⌀ 🅿 Services: ⚐ ✗ 🖽 lau
Off-site: 🛒 ⚓P

MONSCHAU NORDRHEIN-WESTFALEN

Perlenau Eifel, 52156 ☎ 02472 4136 📠 02472 4493
Open: Apr-Oct Site: 2HEC 🏕 ♔ 🚲 Facilities: 🚿 🛒 ⊙ 🗲 ⌀
🚻 🅿 Services: ⚐ ✗ lau Leisure: ⚓ PR Off-site: 🖽

MONTABAUR RHEINLAND-PFALZ

AT GIROD (4KM E)

Eisenbachtal 56412 ☎ 06485 766 📠 06485 4938
Situated in the 'Nassau Nature Park'.
➲ *From motorway exit 40 'Montabaur' turn right, before
Montabaur follow sign 5km towards Limburg. From motorway
exit 41 'Wallmerod/Diez' 5km towards Montabaur.*
Open: All year Site: 3HEC 🏕 ♣ ♔ Prices: ♦4 🚐6 pitch 6
Facilities: 🚿 🛒 ⊙ 🗲 ⌀ 🚻 🅿 Services: ⚐ ✗ 🖽 lau
Off-site: ⚓P

MÖRFELDEN-WALLDORF HESSEN

Arndt Mörfelden Am Zeltplatz 5, 64546
☎ 06105 22289 📠 06105 277459
website: www.campingplatz-moerfelden.de
Well laid out site in two sections near motorway. Lunchtime
siesta 13.00-15.00 hrs.
➲ *Well signposted 0.3km from Langen/Mörfelden exit on
A5/E4 Frankfurt-Darmstadt motorway.*
Open: All year Site: 6HEC 🏕 ⚞ ♔ Prices: ♦5.50 pitch
5.50-8 Facilities: 🚿 ⊙ 🗲 🚻 🅿 Services: ✗ lau Off-site: 🛒 ✗
⌀ ⚓LP 🖽

MÜLHEIM RHEINLAND-PFALZ

AZUR Camping Mülheim 54486
☎ 06534 940157 📠 06534 940157
Near Mülheim-Lieser bridge over the Mosel.
➲ *Access from Bernkastel, 5.5km along B53 towards Trier.*
Open: Etr-Oct Site: 1.5HEC 🏕 ♔ 🚐 Facilities: 🚿 ⊙ 🗲 ⌀
🚻 🅿 Services: ⚐ ✗ lau Leisure: ⚓ R Off-site: 🛒 🖽

MÜLHEIM AN DER RUHR NORDRHEIN-WESTFALEN

Entenfangsee 45481 ☎ 0203 760111 📠 0203 765162
Extensive site near lake. Touring pitches near railway line.
Adventure playground. Lunchtime siesta 13.00-15.00 hrs.
➲ *From motorway exit Duisburg-Wedau, continue towards
Bissingheim to lake.*
Open: All year Site: 12.5HEC 🏕 ♔ Prices: ♦3 🚐5.50
🛖5.50 Facilities: 🚿 🛒 ⊙ 🗲 ⌀ 🚻 🅿 Services: ✗ 🖽 lau
Leisure: ⚓ L Off-site: ⚓P 🖽

MÜLLENBACH RHEINLAND-PFALZ

Nürburgring 53520 ☎ 02692 224 📠 02692 1020
e-mail: rezeption@Camping-am-Nuerburgring.de
website: www.Camping-am-Nuerburgring.de
A large, well equipped site in a wooded location with direct
access to the Nürburgring Grand-Prix circuit.
➲ *Access via A61/A48 and B412.*
Open: All year Site: 30HEC 🏕 ⋮ ♔ 🚐 Prices: ♦10
Facilities: 🚿 🛒 ⊙ 🗲 ⌀ 🚻 🅿 Services: ✗ 🖽 lau

NEHREN RHEINLAND-PFALZ

Nehren 56820 ☎ 02673 4612 📠 02671 910754
On level terrain beside the River Moselle. Separate section for
teenagers. Lunchtime siesta 13.00-15.00 hrs. Liable to flood at
certain times of the year.
➲ *Turn off the B49 Cochem-Alf road in Nehren.*
Open: Apr-15 Oct Site: 5HEC 🏕 ♔ 🚐 Prices: ♦4 🚐7 🛖5
pitch 7 Facilities: 🚿 🛒 ⊙ 🗲 🚻 🅿 Services: ⚐ ✗ 🖽 lau
Leisure: ⚓ R Off-site: ⚐

NIEDEREISENHAUSEN HESSEN

Hinterland Ouotshauser Weg 32, Steffenberg, 35329
☎ 06464 7564
e-mail: camphinterland01@aol.com
Lunchtime siesta 13.00-14.30 hrs.
➲ *Follow signs to 'Schwimmbad'.*
Open: All year Site: 2HEC 🏕 ♔ ♣ 🚐 Prices: ♦4 pitch 4.50
Facilities: 🚿 ⊙ 🗲 🚻 🅿 Services: ⚐ ✗ 🖽 lau Off-site: 🛒 ⚓PR

NIEDERKRÜCHTEN NORDRHEIN-WESTFALEN

Lelefeld Lelefeld 4, 41372 ☎ 02163 81203 📠 02163 81203
e-mail: gblut@aol.com
website: www.camping-lelefeld.com
In a quiet, wooded, location on the outskirts of the village.
➲ *Signposted from Elmpt.*
Open: All year Site: 1.5HEC 🏕 ♔ 🚐 Prices: ♦3.10 🚗1.50
🚐3.10 🛖3.10 Facilities: 🚿 🛒 ⊙ 🗲 ⌀ 🚻 🅿 Services: ⚐ 🖽 lau
Off-site: ✗ ⚓LPR

OBERSGEGEN RHEINLAND-PFALZ

Reles-Mühle Kapellenstr 3, 54675
☎ 06566 8741 📠 06566 931064
e-mail: info@eifelcamping.com website: www.eifelcamping.com
In rural surroundings next to a farmhouse, set on a level
meadow at a brook with trees and bushes.
➲ *From Bitburg on road B50 towards Vianden. Site lies near
the Luxembourg frontier.*
Open: All year Site: 2HEC 🏕 ♔ 🚲 🚐 Prices: ♦2.10 🚗2.10
🚐2.10 🛖1.50-2.10 Facilities: 🚿 🛒 ⊙ 🗲 🅿 Services: 🖽 lau
Leisure: ⚓ R Off-site: 🛒 ⚐ ✗ ⌀ 🚻 ⚓P

OBERWEIS RHEINLAND-PFALZ

Prümtal-Camping In der Klaus 5, 54636
☎ 06527 92920 ▤ 06527 929232
e-mail: info@pruemtal.de website: www.pruemtal.de
A family site in pleasant wooded surroundings with good
sporting facilities.
➲ *Access from Bitburg on B50 towards Luxembourg border.*
Open: All year Site: 3HEC ⬛ ⚘ 🏠 Prices: ↟4.20-5.60
pitch 5.93-7.90 Facilities: ℝ ⅃ ⊙ ⊡ ⌀ 🛁 🏛 Services: ⚑ ✗
lau Leisure: ⬩ PR Off-site: ⊞

OLPE NORDRHEIN-WESTFALEN

AT KESSENHAMMER

Biggesee-Kessenhammer Kessenhammer 3, 57462
☎ 02761 94420 ▤ 02761 944299
e-mail: camping.kessenhammer@t-online.de
website: www.camping-biggesee.de
Long, narrow partly terraced site in quiet woodland setting
on eastern shore of Bigge-Reservoir. Lunchtime siesta 13.00-
15.00 hrs.
➲ *A45 exit Olpe continue B54 to Olpe eastwards on B55 and
turn off at exit Rhode.*
Open: All year Site: 5.7HEC ⬛ ⤳ Facilities: ℝ ⅃ ⊙ ⊡ ⌀
🛁 🏛 Services: ✗ ⊞ lau Leisure: ⬩ L Off-site: ✗

AT SONDERN

Biggesee-Sondern Sonderner Kopf 3, 57462
☎ 02761 944111 ▤ 02761 944141
e-mail: camping.sondern@t-online.de
website: www.camping-biggesee.de
A popular site in wooded surroundings on the shore of the
Biggersee.
➲ *Exit Olpe A45 in direction Attendorn. In 6km turn off for
Erholungsanlage Biggesee-Sondern.*
Open: All year Site: 6HEC ⬛ ⚘ ⚘ Facilities: ℝ ⅃ ⊙ ⊡ ⌀
🛁 🏛 Services: ✗ ⊞ lau Leisure: ⬩ L Off-site: ✗

PORTA WESTFALICA NORDRHEIN-WESTFALEN

Grosser Weserbogen 32457 ☎ 05731 6188 ▤ 05731 6601
e-mail: grosserweserbogen@t-online.de
website: www.grosserweserbogen.de
➲ *From A2 (travelling towards Dortmund), take exit Porta
Westfalica-Minden.*
Open: All year Site: 7HEC ⬛ ⤳ ⏦ Prices: ↟5.50 🚗1-
2.50 🚐7.50 ▲4.50 pitch 4.50 Facilities: ℝ ⅃ ⊙ ⊡ ⌀ ⊟
Services: ✗ ⊞ lau Leisure: ⬩ L Off-site: ⬩P

PRÜM RHEINLAND-PFALZ

Waldcampingplatz 54591 ☎ 06551 2481 ▤ 06551 6555
e-mail: info@waldcamping-pruem.de
website: www.waldcamping-pruem.de
Site lies on both side of the River Prüm and is surrounded by
woods. Divided into three sections of level meadowland.
➲ *Situated at the NW of Prüm.*
Open: All year Site: 3.5HEC ⬛ ⚘ Prices: ↟4 pitch 11
Facilities: ℝ ⅃ ⊙ ⊡ ⌀ 🛁 🏛 Services: ✗ ⊞ lau Leisure: ⬩ R
Off-site: ⅃ ✗ ⬩P

REINSFELD RHEINLAND-PFALZ

AZUR Camping Hunsrück 54421
☎ 06503 95123 ▤ 06503 95124
e-mail: reinsfeld@azur-camping.de
website: www.azur-camping.de/reinsfeld
In a peaceful location close to Trier on the Luxembourg
border, surrounded by hills.
➲ *Access via the B52 or B407.*
Open: All year Site: 20HEC ⬛ ⚘ Facilities: ℝ ⅃ ⊙ ⊡ 🛁
🏛 Services: ⚑ ✗ ⊞ lau Leisure: ⬩ P

ROTHEMANN HESSEN

Rothemann Maulkuppenstr 17, 36124 ☎ 06659 2285
A small, well-kept site surrounded by a hedge, lies next to the
main Fulda road.
➲ *From Fulda follow road B27 for 10km towards Bad
Brükenau; can also be reached from the Kassel-Würzburg
motorway leaving exit Fulda Süd, then 3km along B27 towards
Bad Brükenau.*
Open: Apr-Oct Site: 6.4HEC ⬛ ⚑ Prices: ↟3.60 🚗4.30
🚐4.30 Facilities: ℝ ⅃ ⊙ ⊡ ⌀ 🛁 🏛 Services: ⚑ ⊞ Off-site: ✗

RÜDESHEIM HESSEN

Rhein 65385
☎ 06722 2528 & 2582 ▤ 06722-941046 & 406783
website: www.campingplatz-ruedesheim.de
Near the open-air swimming pool and the River Rhine.
Open: May-3 Oct Site: 3HEC ⬛ ⚘ Prices: ↟4.30 🚗3.30
🚐4.30 ▲4.10-4.50 Facilities: ℝ ⅃ ⊙ ⊡ ⌀ 🛁 🏛 Services: ⚑ ✗
lau Off-site: ✗ ⬩P ⊞

SAARBURG RHEINLAND-PFALZ

Landal Greenpark Warsberg 54439
☎ 06581 91460 ▤ 06581 914646
website: www.landal.de
Open site in quiet situation on top of a hill. Chairlift
(700mtrs) leads down to the town.
➲ *At N end of the town leave the B51 'Trier' road and follow
signs. 3km uphill on good road.*
Open: 29 Mar-04 Nov Site: 11HEC ⬛ ⚘ 🏠 Prices: pitch
19-25 (incl 2 persons) Facilities: ℝ ⅃ ⊙ ⊡ ⌀ 🛁 🏛
Services: ⚑ ✗ ⊞ lau Leisure: ⬩ P

See advertisement on page 241

Leukbachtal 54439 ☎ 06581 2228 ▤ 06581 2228
e-mail: camping.leukbachtal@web.de
Municipal site on level meadows on both sides of the Leuk-
Bach (brook).
➲ *Leave Saarburg on road B51 towards Trassen, then after
crossroads, turn left off the B51.*
Open: Apr-Oct Site: 3HEC ⬛ ⚑ 🏠 Prices: ↟2.84-4.20
🚐7.50 ▲5 Facilities: ℝ ⊙ ⊡ ⌀ 🛁 🏛 Services: ⚑ ✗ ⊞ lau
Off-site: ⅃ ⬩P

Waldfrieden Im Fichtenhain 4, 54439
☎ 06581 2255 ▤ 06581 5809
e-mail: camping-waldfrieden@t-online.de
website: campingwaldfrieden.de
Site lies next to the Café Waldfrieden on unspoilt, slightly
rising meadowland in woods.
➲ *S of town leave B51 or B407 and follow road towards
Nennig (Luxembourg). 200mtrs to site.*
Open: Mar-3 Nov Site: 2HEC ⬛ ⚘ ⚘ Facilities: ℝ ⊙ ⊡ ⌀
🛁 🏛 Services: ⚑ ✗ ⊞ lau Off-site: ⅃ ⬩PR ⊞

SAARLOUIS SAARLAND

AZUR-Camping Saarlouis Marschall-Ney-Weg 2, 66740
☎ 06831 3691 ▤ 06831 122970
e-mail: chcibis@aol.com
A municipal site, divided into pitches, and set on level
meadowland with tall trees. Lunchtime siesta 13.00-14.30.
➲ *Turn off road B51 in suburb of Roden, cross new bridge
over the River Saar and continue to site, beyond sports hall.*
Open: 15 Mar-Oct Site: 2HEC ⬛ ⤳ Prices: ↟5 🚗3.30
🚐6 ▲3.50 Facilities: ℝ ⊙ ⊡ 🛁 🏛 Services: ⚑ ✗ ⊞ lau
Off-site: ⬩P

Site: 6HEC-Site size ⬛-grass ⁙-sand ◊-stone ⤳-little shade ⚘-partly shaded ⚑-mainly shaded
🏠-bungalows for hire 🚐-caravans for hire ▲-tents for hire ⊘-no dogs Prices: ↟-adult per night 🚗-car per night
pp-per person per night 🚐-caravan per night ▲-tent per night

ST GOAR RHEINLAND-PFALZ

Friedenau Gruendelbach 103, 35629
☎ 06741 368 📠 06741 368
On level, narrow stretch of meadowland at Gasthaus
Friedenau.
➲ *Leave B9 in St-Goar and continue through railway
underpass towards Emmelshausen for approx 1km.*
Open: Mar-01 Dec **Site:** 2HEC ⚏ ♣ 🖵 **Prices:** ⚑4.50
🛱2.50 🖵2.50 ▲2-2.50 **Facilities:** ⛺ 🖳 ⊙ 🖵 ⌀ 🚿 🏕
Services: ♀ ✗ ⊞ lau **Leisure:** ⸱⸱ R **Off-site:** ⸱⸱P

ST GOARSHAUSEN RHEINLAND-PFALZ

Loreleystadt 56346 ☎ 06771 2592 📠 02137 2637
Municipal site on level meadow beside the Rhine. Near a
sportsfield and opposite Rheinfels Castle.
➲ *Access via B42.*
Open: 15 Mar-Oct **Site:** 1.5HEC ⚏ 🖤 **Facilities:** ⛺ 🖳 ⊙ 🖵
⌀ 🏕 **Services:** ♀ ⊞ lau **Leisure:** ⸱⸱ R **Off-site:** ✗

SCHACHEN HESSEN

Hochrhön 36129 ☎ 06654 7836 📠 7836
e-mail: campinghochrhoen@aol.com
Lies 1.5km from the Kneipp (hydrotherapeutic) Spa area of
Gersfeld.
➲ *2km N of Gersfeld.*
Open: All year **Site:** 3HEC ⚏ 🖤 **Prices:** ⚑3.50 pitch 4.50
Facilities: ⛺ ⊙ 🖵 ⌀ 🚿 🏕 **Services:** lau **Off-site:** 🖳 ✗ ⸱⸱P ⊞

**A full guide to the Symbols &
Abbreviations used in this book
can be found on page 6**

SCHALKENMEHREN RHEINLAND-PFALZ

Camp am Maar Maarstr 22, 54552
☎ 06592 95510 📠 06592 955140
e-mail: hotelschneider@t-online.de
website: www.hotelschneider.de
Terraced lakeside site on meadowland at the
Schalkenmehrener Maar (water-filled crater). Towing help
for caravans.
➲ *From A48 (Eifelautobahn) leave at 'Mehren/Daun' exit and
follow B42 to Mehren. Turn off to the SW.*
Open: All year **Site:** 1HEC ⚏ ♣ **Prices:** ⚑2.50 🖵7-11
▲6.50-10 **Facilities:** ⛺ 🖳 ⊙ 🖵 ⌀ 🚿 🖵 **Services:** ♀ ✗ lau
Leisure: ⸱⸱ LP **Off-site:** ⊞

SCHLEIDEN NORDRHEIN-WESTFALEN

Schleiden Im Wiesengrund 39, 53937 ☎ 02445 7030
Site lies on hilly, well-wooded country.
➲ *On the B258 to Monschau, 1km to site.*
Open: All year **Site:** 5HEC ⚏ 🖤 ⚔ **Facilities:** ⛺ 🖳 ⊙ 🖵 ⌀
🚿 🏕 **Services:** ✗ ⊞ lau **Off-site:** 🖳 ♀ ✗ ⸱⸱P ⊞

SCHLÜCHTERN HESSEN

AT HUTTEN (8KM E)

Hutten Heiligenborn Helga Herzog-Gericke, 36381
☎ 06661 2424 📠 06661 917581
e-mail: helga.herzog-gericke@online.de
Site lies at Heiligenborn and has a pleasant southerly aspect.
Lunchtime siesta 13.00-15.00 hrs.
➲ *Approach from Fulda on B40 towards Frankfurt to Flieden
for 19km, then turn left via Rückers to Hutten (8km).*
Open: All year **Site:** 3.5HEC ⚏ ⚔ 🖵 **Prices:** ⚑4.64 pitch
5.08 **Facilities:** ⛺ 🖳 ⊙ 🖵 ⌀ 🚿 🏕 **Services:** ✗ ⊞ lau
Off-site: ⸱⸱P

Landal GreenParks Campsites

Three award-winning campsites with high
sanitary standards and privacy are awaiting
you in one of the most beautiful areas of
Germany. Open year-round in a natural,
quiet environment. Satellite-TV and
electricity hook-up available. Each park
offers indoor-swimming pool, restaurant,
snack bar, supermarket, children's
playgrounds, tennis, miniature golf, activity-
programmes for everyone etc. Panoramic
hiking-trails, bicycle-hire, wine tasting and a
large variety of things to do and see. Chalet
hire and English spoken.

"Wirfttal", distinctively located in a valley of the vulcanic Eifel-hills offers spacious pitches by the
Wirft-creek and lake. Rated in 2000 to be one of the best sites of Germany, and Top-Site by the
German Automobile Association ADAC.

"Warsberg", overlooking the valley of the river Saar, surrounded by vineyards and forests on top
of the hill. Chairlift from the campsite down to the romantic town of Saarburg. Near Luxembourg
and the Roman Trier, Germany's oldest city. 5-Star Rating and ADAC approved.

"Sonnenberg", terraced site with a stunning view down the romantic Moselle on top of vineyards
edged by forests above the wine-village of Leiwen. 5-star rating. Earned the ADAC Camping award
for 2002.

For further information or to order our free catalogue write or call:
Landal GreenParks, Postfach 1255, D-54432 Saarburg
Tel: 01805 700730, from GB dial 0049/1805 700730
e-mail: info@landal.de   www.landal.de

Facilities: 🖳-shop ⛺-shower ⊙-electric points for razors 🖵-electric points for caravans 🏕-parking by tents permitted
🖵-compulsory separate car park **Services:** ✗-café/restaurant ♀-bar ⌀-Camping Gaz International 🚿-gas other than Camping
Gaz ⊞-first aid facilities lau-laundry **Leisure:** ⸱⸱-swimming L-Lake P-Pool R-River S-Sea **Off-site:** All facilities within 2km

SCHÖNENBERG SAARLAND

Ohmbachsee 66901 ☎ 06373 4001 ▦ 06373 4002
Terraced site on sloping ground above eastern bank of the
Ohmabachsee. Separate field for young people. Lunchtime
siesta 13.00-15.00 hrs.
⊃ *Signposted.*
Open: All year Site: 7.8HEC ⊞ ⊙ ⌂ Facilities: ⋒ ⓛ ⊙ 🖳
⊘ ♨ ☎ Services: ⋔ ✗ ⊞ lau Leisure: ⋈ P Off-site: ⋈L

SCHOTTEN HESSEN

Nidda-Stausee Vogelsbergstr 184, 63679
☎ 06044 1418 ▦ 06044 6679 & 987995
e-mail: campingplatz@schotten.de website: www.schotten.de
A pleasant family site on the shore of a lake.
⊃ *Access via B455.*
Open: All year Site: 3.2HEC ⊞ ⊙ ⌂ Prices: ⋔4 🖳4.50 ▲3.50-
4.50 pitch 4.50 Facilities: ⋒ ⊙ 🖳 ⊘ ☎ Services: ✗ ⊞ lau
Off-site: ✗ ⋈LP

SECK RHEINLAND-PFALZ

Weiherhof 56479 ☎ 02664 8555 ▦ 02664 6388
Site lies on level meadowland next to a small lake in a
wooded nature reserve. Special section reserved for young
people. Many bathers at weekends.
⊃ *Take the B255 from Rennerod and drive to Hellenbahn-*
Schellenberg. Then turn S and continue for approx 2km.
Open: 15 Mar-15 Oct Site: 10HEC ⊞ ⊙ ⌂ Facilities: ⋒ ⓛ ⊙
🖳 ⊘ ♨ ☎ Services: ⋔ ✗ ⊞ lau Leisure: ⋈ L

SENHEIM RHEINLAND-PFALZ

Internationaler Holländischer Hof 56820
☎ 02673 4660 ▦ 02673 4100
e-mail: holl.hof@t-online.de
website: www.moselcamping.com
On level meadowland, divided into pitches beside the River
Mosel which has boatmooring facilities.
⊃ *Access from Cochem via B49 in direction of Zell as far as*
Senhals, then cross the bridge and turn left.
Open: 06 Apr-1 Nov Site: 4HEC ⊞ ⊙ 🖳 ⊗ Prices: ⋔3.46-
3.85 pitch 6.03-6.70 Facilities: ⋒ ⓛ ⊙ 🖳 ⊘ ♨ ☎ Services: ⋔
✗ ⊞ lau Leisure: ⋈ R

SENSWEILER MÜHLE RHEINLAND-PFALZ

Bauernhof Bundestr 422, 55758
☎ 06786 2395 ▦ 06781 35147
e-mail: info@sensweiler-muehle.de
website: www.sensweiler-muehle.de
On extensive grassland beside the Idar, partially terraced, in
rural area near a farm. Views of wooded range of hills. Next
to Camping Oberes Idartal. Separate section for young
groups.
⊃ *From Idar-Oberstein follow road B422 for about 10km to*
the NW. Site lies between Katzenloch and Allenbach.
Open: 03 Oct- 11 Feb Site: 4HEC ⊞ ⊙ ⌂ Facilities: ⋒ ⊙ 🖳
⊘ ☎ Services: ✗ ⊞ lau Leisure: ⋈ R Off-site: ⓛ ⋔ ⋈L

Oberes Idartal 55758 ☎ 06786 2114 ▦ 06786 2222
e-mail: cpoberesidartal@aol.com
website: www.oberes-idartal.de
Site lies on a farm by the Idar, set on several small meadows
and partly on terraced terrain next to Camping Sensweiler
Mühel. Blockhouse with facilities for spit-roasting.
⊃ *From Idar-Oberstein follow road B422 for about 10km to*
the NW. Site lies between Katzenloch and Allenbach.
Open: All year Site: 2HEC ⊞ ⊙ ⌂ 🖳 Facilities: ⋒ ⓛ ⊙ 🖳
⊘ ♨ ☎ Services: ⊞ lau Leisure: ⋈ R Off-site: ⋔ ✗

SOLINGEN NORDRHEIN-WESTFALEN

AT GLÜDER

Waldcamping Glüder 42659 ☎ 0212 242120 ▦ 0212 242123
Site on level terrain surrounded by woodland on banks of
the River Wupper.
⊃ *Access via Köln-Kamen Autobahn exit Burscheid, via*
Hilgen and Witzhelden to Glüder or from Solingen on
B299/B224 in direction of Witzhelden via Burg Hohenscheid.
Open: All year Site: 2HEC ⊞ ⊙ ⌂ Prices: ⋔3.60 ▲3.60-6.15
pitch 6.15 Facilities: ⋒ ⓛ ⊙ 🖳 ⊘ ♨ ☎ Services: ⋔ ✗ ⊞ lau
Off-site: ⋈P

STADTKYLL RHEINLAND-PFALZ

Landal Greenparks Wirftt 54589
☎ 06597 92920 ▦ 06597 929250
website: www.landal.de
Extensive, level grassland beside the upper of two small
reservoirs, approx 1km outside the town.
⊃ *Access S from Euskirchen on the A1, through Blankenheim*
and towards Stadtkyll.
Open: All year Site: 6.4HEC ⊞ ♨ ⊙ ⌂ Prices: pitch 13-26
(incl 2 persons) Facilities: ⋒ ⓛ ⊙ 🖳 ⊘ ♨ ☎ Services: ⋔ ✗ ⊞
lau Leisure: ⋈ P

STEINEN RHEINLAND-PFALZ

Hofgut Schönerlen 56244 ☎ 02666 207 ▦ 02666 8429
e-mail: camping-kopper@t-online.de
website: www.camping-westerwald.de
Beautiful and quiet site at Lake Hausweiher, has a special
section reserved for residential campers. Young campers
under 18 years old not accepted unless with adults.
⊃ *Take the B8 Limburg-Altenkirchen road. In Steinen turn*
left to the site.
Open: Dec-Oct Site: 15HEC ⊞ ♣ ⌂ 🖳 ⊗ Prices: ⋔4.10-
4.60 pitch 5.20-5.70 Facilities: ⋒ ⓛ ⊙ 🖳 ⊘ ♨ ☎ Services: ⊞
lau Leisure: ⋈ L Off-site: ⋔ ✗

STUKENBROCK NORDRHEIN-WESTFALEN

Furlbach Am Furlbach 33, 33758
☎ 05257 3373 ▦ 05257 940373
Extensive site, partly on level, open meadow and partly in
woodland. Separate section for dog owners. Old barn is used
as a common room for young campers. Lunchtime siesta
12.30-14.30 hrs.
⊃ *From the Dortmund-Hannover motorway (A2/E73) leave*
at exit 'Bielefeld/Sennenstadt' then follow B68 for about 12km
towards Paderborn. At Km44.2 turn off main road then 400m
to site.
Open: Apr-01 Nov Site: 9HEC ⊞ ⊙ ⌂ Prices: ⋔4 🖳2.50
🖳3.50 ▲3-3.50 pitch 6 Facilities: ⋒ ⓛ ⊙ 🖳 ♨ ☎ Services: ✗
⊞ lau Off-site: ⋔ ✗

TANN HESSEN

Ulstertal Dippach 4, 36142 ☎ 06682 8292 ▦ 06682 10086
Terraced site on slightly sloping meadowland.
⊃ *Leave the Bischofsheim-Tann road B278 in Wendershausen*
and go SE to Dippach.
Open: All year Site: 2.4HEC ⊞ ⊙ ⌂ 🖳 Facilities: ⋒ ⓛ ⊙
🖳 ⊘ ♨ ☎ Services: ✗ ⊞ lau

TREIS-KARDEN RHEINLAND-PFALZ

Mosel-Islands 56253 ☎ 02672 2613 ▦ 02672 912102
e-mail: mosel-boating-center@t-online.de
An extensive, level site on a grassy island in the Mosel next to
a yacht marina.

Site: 6HEC-Site size ⊞-grass ∴-sand ♦-stone ❀-little shade ⌂-partly shaded ♣-mainly shaded
⌂-bungalows for hire 🖳-caravans for hire ▲-tents for hire ⊗-no dogs Prices: ⋔-adult per night 🖳-car per night
pp-per person per night 🖳-caravan per night ▲-tent per night

⤴ *Turn off the B49 in Treis onto the southern coastal road.*
Open: Apr-Oct Site: 4.5HEC ⌶⌶⌶ 🛆 Prices: ⋔4 ⬛2.60
🚐5.50 🛆2.60 Facilities: 🏠 ⊙ 🖴 ⚑ Services: lau
Leisure: ⌇ R Off-site: 🛒 ⚑ ✗ ⌇P ⊞

TRENDELBURG HESSEN

Trendelburg 34388 ☎ 05675 301 ▦ 05675 5888
e-mail: conradi-camping@t-online.de
Site located at the foot of the castle, subdivided on the banks
of the River Diemel. Covered tennis court.
⤴ *Access from Kessel N via Hofgeismar (B83) to Trendelburg*
cross the bridge and turn sharp left, down to site.
Open: All year Site: 2.7HEC ⌶⌶⌶ 🛆 🏕 Facilities: 🏠 🛒 ⊙ 🖴
⌀ 🛆 ⚑ Services: ⚑ ✗ lau Leisure: ⌇ R Off-site: ⌇P

TRIER RHEINLAND-PFALZ

Trier-City Luxemburger Str 81, 54294
☎ 0651 86921 ▦ 0651 83079
Level site owned by the Rowing Club Treviris, on left bank of
the Mosel 1.6km from the city centre.
⤴ *Between the Romer bridge and Adenauer bridge on road*
towards Luxembourg.
Open: Apr-Oct Site: 1.5HEC ⌶⌶⌶ 🌢 Facilities: 🏠 ⊙ 🖴 ⚑
Services: ✗ Leisure: ⌇ R Off-site: 🛒 ⚑ ⌀ 🛆 ⌇P

TRIPPSTADT RHEINLAND-PFALZ

Sägmühle Sägmühle 1, 67705 ☎ 06306 92190 ▦ 06306 2000
e-mail: info@saegmuehle.de website: www.saegmuehle.de
The site lies in a wooded valley beside the Sägmühle Lake
(Saw Mill Lake). It consists of several unconnected sections,
some of them terraced. Lunchtime siesta 12.30-14.00 hrs.
⤴ *14km S of Kaiserslautern.*
Open: All year Site: 10HEC ⌶⌶⌶ 🛆 🏕 🚐 Prices: ⋔5.70-6.90
pitch 6.30-8 Facilities: 🏠 🛒 ⊙ 🖴 ⌀ 🛆 ⚑ Services: ⚑ ✗ lau
Leisure: ⌇ L Off-site: ⌇P

UTSCHEID RHEINLAND-PFALZ

Michelbach 54675 ☎ 06564 2097
A municipal site at the Michelbach, surrounded by meadows
and woods, 50% individual pitches.
⤴ *From the B50 Bittburg-Vianden road turn N in Sinspelt.*
Then continue via Niederraden to Utscheid.
Open: All year Site: 1.5HEC ⌶⌶⌶ 🏠 ⊙ 🖴 ⌀ ⚑
Services: ⚑ ✗ ⊞ lau Off-site: 🛒 🛆

VINKRATH BEI GREFRATH NORDRHEIN-WESTFALEN

SC Waldfrieden 47929 ☎ 02158 3855 ▦ 02158 3685
Site within nature reserve.
⤴ *From Grefrath N towards Wankum after 3km. Turn right.*
Site: 4.5HEC ⌶⌶⌶ 🛆 ⊘ Facilities: 🏠 ⊙ 🖴 ⌀ 🛆 ⚑
Services: ⊞ lau Off-site: 🛒 ⚑ ✗ ⌇LP

VLOTHO NORDRHEIN-WESTFALEN

Borlefzen Borlefzen 2, 32602
☎ 05733 80008 ▦ 05733 89728
e-mail: info@borlefzen.de website: www.borlefzen.de
Open: Apr-Oct Site: 40HEC ⌶⌶⌶ 🛆 🏕 Facilities: 🏠 🛒 ⊙ 🖴
⌀ ⚑ Services: ⚑ ✗ ⊞ lau Leisure: ⌇ LR

WARBURG NORDRHEIN-WESTFALEN

Eversburg 34414 ☎ 05641 8668
Site lies next to restaurant of the same name on the SE
outskirts of the town.
Open: All year Site: 4.5HEC ⌶⌶⌶ 🛆 🚐 Prices: ⋔4 ⬛1.50
🚐6 🛆3-6 pitch 6 Facilities: 🏠 🛒 ⊙ 🖴 ⌀ ⚑ Services: ⚑ ✗ ⊞
lau Leisure: ⌇ R Off-site: ⌇P

WASSERFALL NORDRHEIN-WESTFALEN

Wasserfall Aurorastr 9, 59909 ☎ 02905 332
Terraced site, surrounded by woodland, next to leisure centre
'Fort Fun'. Little room for touring campers during the winter.
⤴ *About 10km E of Meschedes, between Bestwig and Nuttlar,*
turn S off the B7. Driver past Gevelinghausen and up to
Wasserfall.
Open: All year Site: 0.7HEC ⌶⌶⌶ 🛆 🚐 🛆 Facilities: 🏠 ⊙ 🖴
🛆 ⚑ Services: ⚑ ✗ ⊞ Off-site: ⌇PR

WAXWEILER RHEINLAND-PFALZ

AEGON-Ferienpark Im Prümtal 54649
☎ 06554 92000 ▦ 06554 920029
e-mail: 0655492000-0001@t-online.de
website: www.ferierpark-waxweiler.de
Site lies on level terrain and is divided into pitches, with a
separate field on the opposite side of the River Prüm. Near
swimming pool. Lunchtime siesta between 13.00-15.00 hrs.
⤴ *From N end of Waxweiler, turn off towards the River Prüm.*
Open: 31 Mar-5 Nov Site: 3HEC ⌶⌶⌶ 🛆 🏕 Facilities: 🏠 🛒
⊙ 🖴 ⌀ 🛆 ⚑ Services: ✗ ⊞ lau Leisure: ⌇ P
Off-site: ⚑ ✗ ⌇P

WEILBURG HESSEN

AT ODERSBACH

Odersbach Runkler Str 5A, 35781
☎ 06471 7620 ▦ 06471 379603
e-mail: camping-odersbach@t-online.de
website: www.camping-odersbach.de
In attractive setting beside the River Lahn, next to a public
swimming pool. Lunchtime siesta 12.00-14.00 hrs.
⤴ *On S outskirts of town.*
Open: Apr-Oct Site: 6HEC ⌶⌶⌶ 🛆 Prices: ⋔3.25 ⬛2.40
🚐3.20 🛆1.90-12 Facilities: 🏠 ⊙ 🖴 ⌀ 🛆 ⚑ Services: ✗ ⊞ lau
Leisure: ⌇ PR Off-site: 🛒 ⚑ ✗

WINTERBERG NORDRHEIN-WESTFALEN

AT NIEDERSFELD (8.5KM N)

Vossmecke 59955 ☎ 02985 8418 ▦ 02985 553
e-mail: camping-vossmecke@t-online.de
website: www.camping-vossmecke.de
In a pleasant wooded location with facilities for winter camping.
⤴ *Off B480 towards Winterberg.*
Open: All year Site: 4HEC ⌶⌶⌶ 🛆 ❄ Prices: 🛆10.95-11.95
pitch 13.90-16.90 (incl 2 persons) Facilities: 🏠 🛒 ⊙ 🖴 ⌀ ⚑
⚑ Services: ✗ lau Off-site: 🛒 ✗ ⌇L

WISSEL NORDRHEIN-WESTFALEN

Wisseler See Zum Wisseler See 15, 47546
☎ 02824 96310 ▦ 02824 963131
e-mail: wisseler-see@t-online.de
website: www.wisseler-see.de
Well-kept municipal site with modern equipment beside
Lake Wissel. There is a separate car park next to the open-air
swimming pool. The pool belongs to the camp. The
washrooms are closed during lunchtimes and at night.
⤴ *From Kieve, take the B57 towards Xanten. After about 9km,*
turn left and drive a further 3km towards Wissel.
Open: All year Site: 40HEC ⌶⌶⌶ ⋰⋰ ⌀ ❄ Prices: ⋔5 ⬛3
🚐8 🛆6 Facilities: 🏠 🛒 ⊙ 🖴 ⌀ 🛆 ⚑ ⚑ Services: ⚑ ✗ ⊞ lau
Leisure: ⌇ L Off-site: ⌇P

WITZENHAUSEN HESSEN

Werratal Am Sande 11, 37213
☎ 05542 1465 ▦ 05542 72418
website: www.campingplatz-werratal.de
The site lies on meadow between the outskirts of
Witzenhausen and the banks of the Werra.   *contd.*

Facilities: 🛒-shop 🏠-shower ⊙-electric points for razors 🖴-electric points for caravans ⚑-parking by tents permitted
⚑-compulsory separate car park **Services:** ✗-café/restaurant ⚑-bar ⌀-Camping Gaz International 🛆-gas other than Camping
Gaz ⊞-first aid facilities lau-laundry **Leisure:** ⌇-swimming L-Lake P-Pool R-River S-Sea **Off-site:** All facilities within 2km

➲ *For access, leave Hannover-Kassel motorway at Werratal. 10km on B80 to Witzenhausen. From market place follow signs.*
Open: All year Site: 3HEC ⊞ ♣ ⌂ ⊞ Prices: ♠2.80-4 pitch 2.80-6 Facilities: ℾ ⅃ ⊙ ⊠ ∅ ≘ Services: ⾕ ⊞ lau
Leisure: ⸂ R Off-site: ✗ ⸂P

WOLFSTEIN RHEINLAND-PFALZ

AZUR Campingpark am Königsberg Am Schwimmbad 1, 67752 ☎ 06304 4143 ▤ 06304 7543
e-mail: benspruijt@gmx.de
website: www.camping-wolfstein.com
Municipal site, beside small River Lauter next to open air swimming pool.
➲ *Site lies at S end of Wolfstein to the right of B270 from Kaiserslautern.*
Open: All year Site: 1.5HEC ⊞ ⊕ ⌂ ⊞ Prices: ♠4.50-6 ♠2.10 pitch 5.50-7.50 Facilities: ℾ ⊙ ⊠ ≘ ⊞ ☐ Services: ⾕ ✗ lau Off-site: ⅃ ∅ ⸂LPR

ZERF RHEINLAND-PFALZ

Rübezahl 54314 ☎ 06587 814 ▤ 06587 814
e-mail: seyffardt-zerf@t-online.de
Meadowland site in natural grounds on wooded hillside.
➲ *Leave Zerf S on B268 towards Saarbrücken then turn towards Oberzerf 2.5km to site from turning. From Saarburg, follow B407 beyond Vierherrenhorn, turn right and follow track for 60m.*
Open: Apr-Oct Site: 2.5HEC ⊞ ⊕ Prices: ♠4 pitch 5 Facilities: ℾ ⊙ ⊠ ∅ ≘ Services: ⊞ Leisure: ⸂ P

ZWESTEN HESSEN

Waldcamping Hinter dem Wasser, 34596
☎ 05626 379 ▤ 06695 1320
e-mail: waldcamping@planet-interken.de
website: waldcamping-bad-zwesten.de
Site in bend of River Schwalm. Lunchtime siesta 13.00-15.00 hrs. For touring campers there is also an overflow site outside the actual campsite.
➲ *Access from Kassel in SW direction via Fritzlar to Zwesten.*
Open: All year Site: 5HEC ⊞ ⊕ Facilities: ℾ ⊙ ⊠ ≘ ⊞
Services: ⾕ ✗ ⊞ lau Leisure: ⸂ PR Off-site: ⅃ ✗

NORTH

ALTENAU NIEDERSACHSEN

Okertalsperre Kornhardtweg 1, 38707
☎ 05328 702 ▤ 05328 911708
e-mail: okercamping@t.online.de
website: www.camping-okertalsperre.harz.de
On a long stretch of grassland at the southern end of the Oker Reservoir. Lunchtime siesta 13.00-15.00 hrs.
➲ *Signposted from B498 (Oker-Altenau road).*
Open: All year Site: 4HEC ⊞ ⊕ ⌂ ⊞ ⊗ Facilities: ℾ ⅃
⊙ ⊠ ∅ ≘ ⊞ Services: ✗ ⊞ lau Leisure: ⸂ L

BLECKEDE NIEDERSACHSEN

Alt-Garge (ADAC) Am Waldbad 23, 21354
☎ 05854 311 ▤ 05854 1640
e-mail: adac-camping-altgarge@t-online.de
website: www.camping-urlaub.de
A modern site surrounded by tall trees, lying at the SE end of Alt-Garge next to a heated swimming pool in the woods. The camp has its own gas-filling station. Archery butts. Lunchtime siesta 13.00-14.30 hrs.
➲ *5km SE of Bleckede.*
Open: All year Site: 6.6HEC ⊞ ⠸ ⊕ Prices: pitch 17 (incl 2 persons) Facilities: ℾ ⅃ ⊙ ⊠ ≘ Services: ⊞
Off-site: ✗ ∅ ⸂LPR

BODENWERDER NIEDERSACHSEN

Himmelspforte Ziegeleiweg 1, 37619
☎ 05533 4938 ▤ 05533 4432
Site on grassland, with a fruit orchard, next to River Weser. Good possibilites for water sport. Separate section and common room for young campers.
➲ *Cross River Weser and turn right towards Rühle. Site is in about 2km.*
Open: All year Site: 8HEC ⊞ ♣ Facilities: ℾ ⅃ ⊙ ⊠ ≘ ⊞
Services: ⾕ ✗ lau Leisure: ⸂ R Off-site: ⸂P

Rühler Schweiz 37619 ☎ 05533 2827 ▤ 05533 5882
e-mail: info@brader-ruehler-schweiz.de
website: www.brader-ruehler-schweiz.de
This site lies on well-kept meadowland by the River Weser.
➲ *From the Weser Bridge in Bodenwerder and follow road for 4km towards Rühle.*
Open: Mar-Oct Site: 50HEC ⊞ ⠸ ⠼ ⅄ ⊞ Prices: ♠4 ♠4 pitch 4.50 Facilities: ℾ ⅃ ⊙ ⊠ ≘ ⊞ Services: ⾕ ✗ ⊞ lau
Leisure: ⸂ PR Off-site: ✗

BOTHEL NIEDERSACHSEN

Hanseat 27384 ☎ 04266 355
Open: All year Site: 20HEC ⊞ ⊕ Facilities: ℾ ⊙ ⊠ ∅ ≘
Services: ✗ ⊞ lau Off-site: ⅃ ⸂P

BRAUNLAGE NIEDERSACHSEN

Ferien vom Ich 38700 ☎ 05520 413
Quiet site, partly on different levels, near woodland inn.
➲ *2km from town centre on B27 towards Lauterberg.*
Open: All year Site: 5.5HEC ⊞ ⊕ ⊞ Facilities: ℾ ⅃ ⊙ ⊠
∅ ≘ ⊞ Services: ✗ ⊞ lau Off-site: ⸂P

At ZORGE (14KM S)

Harz Camping Im Waldwinkel 37449
☎ 05586 1048 ▤ 05586 8113
A site on different levels, surrounded by high trees, 200mtrs from an open-air woodland pool in Kunzen Valley.
Open: All year Site: 1.5HEC ⊞ ⠸ ⠼ ⊕ Prices: ♠4.50 pitch 9.70-13 (incl 2 persons) Facilities: ℾ ⅃ ⊙ ⊠ ∅ ≘ ⊞
Services: ⊞ lau Leisure: ⾕ ✗ ⸂P

BREMEN BREMEN

Freie Hansestadt Bremen Am Stadtwaldsee 1, 28359
☎ 0421 212002 ▤ 0421 219857
Situated in a Nature Reserve 700m from lake.
➲ *Access from autobahn A27 exit University Bremen.*
Open: All year Site: 5.8HEC ⊞ ⠼ ⊕ ⊞ Prices: ♠3.70-4.10
♣1.40 ♣6 pitch 4-6 Facilities: ℾ ⅃ ⊙ ⊠ ∅ ≘ Services: ⾕ ✗
lau Off-site: ⸂LP

BRIETLINGEN-REIHERSEE NIEDERSACHSEN

Reihersee 1 Alte Salzstr 8, 21382
☎ 04133 3671 & 3577 ▤ 04133 4391
Divided into pitches by hedges and pine trees. Private bathing area.
➲ *At car park, 2km beyond Brietlingen, turn E towards Reihersee and continue for 800m.*
Open: All year Site: 6.2HEC ⊞ ⊕ ⊞ Facilities: ℾ ⊙ ⊠ ≘
⊞ Services: ✗ ⊞ lau Leisure: ⸂ LR Off-site: ⅃

BÜCHEN SCHLESWIG-HOLSTEIN

Waldschwimmbad 21514 ☎ 04155 5360 ▤ 04155 499140
On gently sloping grassland. Lunchtime siesta 13.00-15.00 hrs.
➲ *From Lauenburg or Mölln follow road to Büchen then follow signposts to site.*
Open: All year Site: 1.6HEC ⊞ ⊕ ⊞ Facilities: ℾ ⅃ ⊙ ⊠
∅ ≘ ⊞ Services: ⾕ ✗ ⊞ lau Off-site: ✗ ⸂PR

Site: 6HEC-Site size ⊞-grass ⠼-sand ♦-stone ⠾-little shade ⊕-partly shaded ♣-mainly shaded
⠸-bungalows for hire ⊞-caravans for hire Δ-tents for hire ⊗-no dogs Prices: ♠-adult per night ♣-car per night
pp-per person per night ⊞-caravan per night Δ-tent per night

BURG (ISLAND OF FEHMARN) SCHLESWIG-HOLSTEIN
AT KLAUSDORF (5KM NW)

Klausdorfer Strand 23769 ☎ 04371 2549 ▤ 04371 2481
e-mail: info@camping-klausdorferstrand.de
website: www.camping-klausdorferstrand.de
A grassy site with sea views. Divided into pitches. Sandy
beach. Lunchtime siesta 12.30-14.30 hrs.
➲ *From Burg turn off the main road 2.5km before Klausdorf
onto a narrow asphalt road.*
Open: Apr-15 Oct Site: 12HEC ▥▥ ♁ ♨ Prices: ♠3.50-4.50
♣3 pitch 6-10 Facilities: ⋔ ⅏ ⊙ ♨ ∅ ≞ ☎ Services: ✕ ⊞ lau
Leisure: ⚲ PS Off-site: ⚲L

BURGWEDEL NIEDERSACHSEN

Erholungsgebiet Springhorstsee 30938
☎ 05139 3232 ▤ 05139 27070
e-mail: springhorstsee@aol.com
website: www.springhorstee.de
On level ground on the shores of a lake with well defined
pitches and modern facilities.
➲ *25km N of Hannover, 2km from Grossburgwedel motorway
exit.*
Open: All year Site: 29HEC ▥▥ ♨ ♁ ♨ ♨ Facilities: ⋔ ⊙
♨ ≞ ☎ Services: ♣ ✕ ⊞ lau Leisure: ⚲ LP Off-site: ∅

CLAUSTHAL-ZELLERFELD NIEDERSACHSEN

Prahljust 38678 ☎ 05323 1300 ▤ 05323 78393
website: www.prahljust.de
The site lies on slightly sloping grassland in an area of
woodland and lakes.
➲ *Follow road B242 SE from outskirts 2km in direction of
Braunlage, then turn right to site in 1.5km.*
Open: All year Site: 13HEC ▥▥ ♁ Prices: ♠4.40-5.20
♠2.40-2.80 ♨4.50-5.30 ♣2.40 Facilities: ⋔ ⅏ ⊙ ♨ ∅ ☎
Services: ♣ ✕ lau Leisure: ⚲ LP Off-site: ≞ ⊞

Waldweben Spiegelthalerstr 31, 38678
☎ 05323 81712 ▤ 05323 962134
website: www.campingplatz-waldweben.harz.de
Holiday village with individual pitches in open meadow and
coniferous woodland by three small lakes.
➲ *Signposted from B241 in direction of Goslar.*
Open: All year Site: 4.5HEC ▥▥ ♁ ♁ ♨ Prices: ♠3.50
♠2.40 ♨2.40 ♣2.40 pitch 4.80 Facilities: ⋔ ⅏ ⊙ ♨ ≞ ☎
Services: ✕ lau Off-site: ✕ ⚲LP ⊞

DAHRENHORST NIEDERSACHSEN

Irenensee Dahrenhorst, 31311
☎ 05173 98120 ▤ 05173 981213
e-mail: info@irenensee.de
website: www.irenensee.de
A lakeside site on meadowland, partly surrounded by woods,
with separate section for tourers, statics and residentials.
Lunchtime siesta 13.00-15.00 hrs.
➲ *From Burgdorf follow road B188 for about 15km towards
Uetze.*
Open: All year Site: 120HEC ▥▥ ♁ ♁ ♨ Facilities: ⋔ ⅏ ⊙
♨ ∅ ≞ ☎ Services: ✕ ⊞ lau Leisure: ⚲ L

DETERN NIEDERSACHSEN

Jümmesee 26847 ☎ 04957 1808 ▤ 04957 8112
e-mail: info@detern.com website: www.detern.com
➲ *Access via B72 (Aurich-Cloppenburg).*
Open: Mar-Oct Site: 11.5HEC ▥▥ ♁ ♨ Prices: ♠4.50
♣3.50 pitch 5 Facilities: ⋔ ⊙ ♨ ≞ ☎ Services: ✕ ⊞ lau
Leisure: ⚲ LR Off-site: ⚲PS

DORUM SCHLESWIG-HOLSTEIN

AZUR Nordseecamp Dorumer Tief 27632
☎ 04741 5020 ▤ 04741 914061
e-mail: dorum@azur-camping.de
website: www.azur-camping.de
Next to a small harbour. Separated from the beach by a dyke.
➲ *Access via A27 (Bremerhaven-Cuxhaven).*
Open: Apr-Sep Site: 7HEC ▥▥ ♨ Prices: ♠3-5 ♠3.50
♣2.50-3.50 pitch 4-6 Facilities: ⋔ ⅏ ⊙ ♨ ≞ ☎ Services: ✕
⊞ lau Leisure: ⚲ PS

EGESTORF NIEDERSACHSEN

AZUR-Camping Lüneburger Heide 21272
☎ 04175 661 ▤ 04175 8383
e-mail: egestorf@azur-camping.de
website: www.azurcamping.de/egestorf
Modern site on wooded heathland on the edge of the
Lüneburger Heath Nature Reserve 2km south of town on
slightly sloping terrain with asphalt internal roads.
➲ *Access via Hamburg-Hannover motorway A7/E4 Egestorf
or Evendorf exits.*
Open: All year Site: 22HEC ▥▥ ⁘ ♁ ♨ Prices: ♠4-6 ♣3-4
pitch 5-7 Facilities: ⋔ ⅏ ⊙ ♨ ∅ ≞ ☎ Services: ✕ ⊞ lau
Leisure: ⚲ P Off-site: ♣

EIMKE NIEDERSACHSEN

Eimke Im Extertal 32699 ☎ 05262 3307 ▤ 05262 992404
website: www.campingpark-eimke.de
Extensive, partly terraced site on slightly sloping meadowland
with two ponds.
Camping Card Compulsory.
➲ *From Dortmund-Hannover motorway (A2/E8) take 'Bad
Eilsen' exit and follow B238 S. 1km beyond Rinteln, turn left
and continue for 18km along External-Barntrup road.*
Open: All year Site: 20HEC ▥▥ ♁ ♨ Facilities: ⋔ ⅏ ⊙ ♨
∅ ≞ ☎ Services: ♣ ✕ ⊞ lau Leisure: ⚲ L Off-site: ✕ ⚲P

ELISABETH SOPHIENKOOG (ISLAND OF NORDSTRAND)
SCHLESWIG-HOLSTEIN

Elisabeth-Sophienkoog 25845 ☎ 04842 8534 ▤ 04842 8306
e-mail: camping-nordstrand@t-online.de
On meadowland behind the North Sea dyke. Lunchtime
siesta 12.00-14.00 hrs.
➲ *Access via Husum to Island of Nordstrand.*
Open: Apr-Oct Site: 1.7HEC ▥▥ ♨ Prices: ♠3.40 ♠2.10
♨3.90 ♣3.60 Facilities: ⋔ ⅏ ⊙ ♨ ∅ ☎ Services: ♣ ✕ ⊞ lau
Leisure: ⚲ S

ESENS-BENSERSIEL NIEDERSACHSEN

Benseriel Am Strand, 26427
☎ 04971 9150 ▤ 04971 4988
e-mail: campnig@bensersiel.de website: www.bensersiel.de
Well-managed, extensive leisure centre with harbour, good
fish restaurant and reading room. Swimming pools have sea
water and artificial waves.
➲ *Take B210 NE from Aurich to Ogenbargenn then via Esens.*
Open: Etr-15 Sep Site: 10HEC ▥▥ ⁘ ♨ ♨ ∅
Prices: ♠2.40 ♠1.60 ♨3.40 ♣5 pitch 5 Facilities: ⋔ ⅏ ⊙ ♨
☎ Services: ♣ ✕ ⊞ lau Leisure: ⚲ S Off-site: ∅ ⚲P

EUTIN-FISSAU SCHLESWIG-HOLSTEIN

Prinzenholz Prinzenholzweg 20, 23701
☎ 04521 5281 ▤ 04521 3601
e-mail: info@nc-prinzenholz.de
website: www.nc-prinzenholz.de
Terraced lakeside site divided by trees and bushes. Mobile
shop.

contd.

Facilities: ⅏-shop ⋔-shower ⊙-electric points for razors ♨-electric points for caravans ☎-parking by tents permitted
⊞-compulsory separate car park **Services:** ✕-café/restaurant ♣-bar ∅-Camping Gaz International ≞-gas other than Camping
Gaz ⊞-first aid facilities lau-laundry **Leisure:** ⚲-swimming L-Lake P-Pool R-River S-Sea **Off-site:** All facilities within 2km

⮑ *N of town take Malente road and turn right after 2km.*
Open: Apr-Oct Site: 2HEC ⊞⊞⊞ ♣ Prices: ♠5 🚗1.50
🚐6.50 ⛺5 Facilities: 🚿 🕊 ⊙ 🚻 ⌀ 🚮 🏪 Services: ✗ lau
Leisure: ⚓ L Off-site: 🍴 ✗ ⚓P ⊞

FALLINGBOSTEL NIEDERSACHSEN

Böhhmeschlucht Vierde 22, 29683 ☎ 05162 5604 ▤ 05162 5160
website: www.bohmeschlucht.de
Site located in a nature reserve beside the river Böhme.
⮑ *A7/E45, exit 46/47. signed about 3km N*
Open: All year Site: 4HEC ⊞⊞⊞ ♣ Prices: ♠2.50 pitch 11
Facilities: 🚿 🕊 ⊙ 🚻 🏪 🅿 Services: 🍴 ✗ lau Leisure: ⚓ R

FEHMARN (ISLAND OF)

FEHMARNSUND SCHLESWIG-HOLSTEIN

Miramar 23769 ☎ 04371 3220 ▤ 04371 868044
e-mail: campingmiramar@t-online.de
website: www.camping-miramar.de
A family site on meadowland situated at the southern end of
the island.
⮑ *Turn off the B207/E4 at the first turning after the
Sundbrücke (bridge) and drive towards Svendorf.*
Open: All year Site: 13HEC ⊞⊞⊞ ♣ 🚐 Prices: ♠4-6 pitch
8.50-11.50 Facilities: 🚿 🕊 ⊙ 🚻 ⌀ 🚮 🏪 Services: 🍴 ✗ ⊞ lau
Leisure: ⚓ LS

GANDERSHEIM, BAD NIEDERSACHSEN

DCC Kur-Campingpark Braunschweiger Str 12, 37581
☎ 05382 1595 ▤ 05382 1599
website: www.camping-bad-gandersheim.de
On level meadow, divided in two by a brook beside a public
park. Good sporting facilities. Separate section for young
people.
⮑ *Access from Hannover-Kassel motorway via exit Soesen.*
Open: All year Site: 9HEC ⊞⊞⊞ ♣ Prices: ♠3.70-4.50 🚐8.50
⛺6 pp4 Facilities: 🚿 🕊 ⊙ 🚻 🚮 🏪 Services: ✗ ⊞ lau
Off-site: ⚓P

GARTOW NIEDERSACHSEN

Gartow am See Am Helk, 29471 ☎ 05846 8250 ▤ 05846 2151
e-mail: campingpark@gartow.de
website: ww.campingpark-gartow.de
Situated in woodland with adjoining meadow.
Camping Card Compulsory.
⮑ *NE on A493 from Lüchow.*
Open: All year Site: 14HEC ⊞⊞⊞ ♣ 🚑 🚐 Prices: ♠3.40-4
⛺3.80-4.40 pitch 7.80-9 Facilities: 🚿 🕊 ⊙ 🚻 🚮 🏪
Services: lau Leisure: ⚓ P Off-site: 🕊 ✗ ⚓LR ⊞

GIFHORN NIEDERSACHSEN

AT RÖTGESBÜTTEL (8KM S)

Glockenheide 38531 ☎ 05304 1581 ▤ 05304 1581
e-mail: camping-glockenheide@T-online.de
website: www.glockenheide.de
Tranquil site in heathland. Lunchtime siesta 13.00-15.00 hrs.
Camping Card Compulsory.
⮑ *In Rötgesbüttel turn left, then turn left again after level
crossing.*
Open: All year Site: 5HEC ⊞⊞⊞ ♣ 🚑 🚐 Prices: ♠3.40 🚗2.60
🚐2.60 ⛺2.60 Facilities: 🚿 🕊 ⊙ 🚻 🚮 🏪 Services: lau
Off-site: 🕊 ✗

GLÜCKSBURG-HOLNIS SCHLESWIG-HOLSTEIN

AZUR Ostseecamp Grenzblick Am Kurstrand 3, 24960
☎ 04631 622071 ▤ 04631 622072
e-mail: info@azur-camping.de
website: www.azur-camping.de
Open: Apr-Oct Site: 6HEC ⊞⊞⊞ ☀ 🚐 Facilities: 🚿 ⊙ 🚻 🚮 🚮
🏪 Services: ✗ ⊞ lau Off-site: 🕊 ✗

GRUBE SCHLESWIG-HOLSTEIN

Rosenfelder Strand Textil 23749
☎ 04365 4112 ▤ 04365 1494
e-mail: info@rosenfelder-strand.de
website: www.rosenfelder-strand.de
Excellently managed family site beside the sea with a 1km
long beach. Divided into separate fields by rows of bushes.
Children's playground in woodland between site and sea.
Strict observance of lunchtime siesta 13.00-15.00 hrs.
⮑ *Take the B207/E4 from Lübeck and drive N to Lensahn,
then E to Grube.*
Open: Apr-Sep Site: 24HEC ⊞⊞⊞ ♣ 🚐 🚫 Prices: ♠4.20
pitch 9.50 Facilities: 🚿 🕊 ⊙ 🚻 ⌀ 🚮 🏪 Services: 🍴 ✗ ⊞
Leisure: ⚓ S Off-site: ⚓S

HADDEBY SCHLESWIG-HOLSTEIN

Haithabu 24866 ☎ 04621 32450 ▤ 04621 33122
e-mail: camping@uumail.de
website: www.campingplatz-haithabu.de
Clean, tidy site beside River Schlei.
⮑ *From Schleswig follow B76 towards Eckernförde.*
Open: Apr-Sep Site: 5HEC ⊞⊞⊞ ♣ 🚐 Prices: ♠3.50 🚗2
🚐7.50 ⛺5.50 Facilities: 🚿 🕊 ⊙ 🚻 🚮 🏪 Services: ✗ ⊞ lau
Leisure: ⚓ R

HADEMSTORF NIEDERSACHSEN

Waldhaus Allertal 29693 ☎ 05071 1872 ▤ 1912516
In a picturesque wooded setting with pitches separated by
hedges and bushes.
⮑ *Access via A27/A7.*
Open: Apr-Sep Site: 4HEC ⊞⊞⊞ ♠ Facilities: 🚿 🕊 ⊙ 🚻 ⌀ 🚮
🏪 Services: 🍴 ✗ lau Off-site: ⚓R ⊞

HAHNENKLEE NIEDERSACHSEN

Kreuzeck 38644 ☎ 05325 2570 ▤ 05325 3392
e-mail: kreuzeck@aol.com
website: www.campingground.de
In the forest beside a lake. Terraces and a separate section for
dog-owners.
⮑ *Beside Café am Kreuzeck at the junction of the B241 and
the Hahnenklee road.*
Open: All year Site: 5HEC ⊞⊞⊞ ∵∵ ☀ ♣ 🚑 🚐 ⛺
Prices: ♠4.05 🚗1.80 🚐4.45 ⛺4.45 Facilities: 🚿 🕊 ⊙ 🚻 🚮 🏪
🅿 Services: ✗ ⊞ lau Leisure: ⚓ LP Off-site: ⌀

HAMELN NIEDERSACHSEN

Waldbad Pfedeweg 2, 31787 ☎ 05158 2774 ▤ 05158 2774
A grassy terraced site on the edge of woodland beside a
public swimming pool.
Camping Card Compulsory.
⮑ *Follow 'swimming pool' signs from Havelstorf.*
Open: Apr-Oct Site: 2.8HEC ⊞⊞⊞ ♣ 🚐 Facilities: 🚿 ⊙ 🚻 🚮
🏪 Services: ✗ ⊞ lau Off-site: 🕊 ⚓P

Site: 6HEC-Site size ⊞⊞⊞-grass ∵∵-sand ◓-stone ☀-little shade ♣-partly shaded ♠-mainly shaded
🚑-bungalows for hire 🚐-caravans for hire ⛺-tents for hire 🚫-no dogs Prices: ♠-adult per night 🚗-car per night
pp-per person per night 🚐-caravan per night ⛺-tent per night

HANNOVER NIEDERSACHSEN
AT GARBSEN (10KM W)

Blauer See 30823 ☎ 05137 8996-0 🖳 05137 8996-77
e-mail: info@camping-blauer-see.de
website: www.camping-blauer-see.de
On a small lake beside the Garbsen service area on
Hannover-Bielefeld motorway A2/E8.
Open: All year Site: 22HEC ▦ ⚘ ♠ Prices: ♠5.50-7 ♣2
▲2.50-4 pitch 3.70-4.70 Facilities: ℹ 🛒 ⊙ 🔌 ∅ 🅿
Services: ✕ 🅘 lau Leisure: ⇗ L

AT ISERNHAGEN (16KM NE)

Parksee Lohne Alter Postweg 12, 30916
☎ 05139 88260 🖳 05139 891665
e-mail: parksee-lohne@t-online.de
website: www.parksee-lohne.de
Recreation area by a lake. On the flight approach path for
Hannover Langenhagen airport. Separate section for tourers.
⟳ From motorway exit 'Kirchorst' follow Altwarmbüchen road
to Isernhagen.
Open: All year Site: 16HEC ▦ ⚘ Facilities: ℹ ⊙ 🔌 ⚒ 🅿
Services: ♀ ✕ 🅘 lau Leisure: ⇗ L

HARDEGSEN NIEDERSACHSEN

Ferienpark Solling 37181 ☎ 05505 5585 🖳 05505 5585
Terraced site in forested area. Separate field for touring
pitches. Lunchtime siesta 13.00-15.00 hrs.
⟳ In town take 'Waldgebiet Gladeberg' road.
Open: All year Site: 2.4HEC ▦ ∅ ⚘ Prices: ♠4 pitch 6
Facilities: ℹ ⊙ 🔌 ⚒ 🅿 Services: ♀ ✕ 🅘 lau
Off-site: 🛒 ✕ ∅ ⇗P

HASSENDORF NIEDERSACHSEN

Stürberg 27367 ☎ 04264 9124 🖳 04264 821440
e-mail: campingpark-stuerberg@gmx.de
website: www.stuerberg.de
In pleasant wooded surroundings beside a lake.
⟳ From Ab1 exit Stuckenborstel take B75 towards Rotenburg
for 5km.
Open: Mar-Oct Site: 2HEC ▦ ⚘ Prices: ♠3 ♣7 ▲6
Facilities: ℹ ⊙ 🔌 ∅ ⚒ 🅿 Services: ♀ 🅘 Leisure: ⇗ L
Off-site: ✕

HATTEN NIEDERSACHSEN

Freizeitzentrum Hatten Kreyenweg 8, 26209
☎ 04482 677 🖳 04482 928027
e-mail: info@jzz.hatten.de
Open: All year Site: 2HEC ▦ ⚶ ▲ Prices: ♠5 ▲2.60 pitch
6 Facilities: ℹ 🛒 ⊙ 🔌 ∅ 🅿 Services: ✕ lau Leisure: ⇗ P
Off-site: ✕

HATTORF NIEDERSACHSEN

Oderbrücke 37197 ☎ 05521 4359 🖳 05521 4360
e-mail: oderbruecke@t-online.de
website: www.oderbruecke.top.ms
In a pleasant wooded location with good recreational and
sanitary facilities.
⟳ On the B27 towards Herzberg.
Open: All year Site: 2.5HEC ▦ ⚘ Prices: ♠3.15-3.50 pitch
5.20 Facilities: ℹ 🛒 ⊙ 🔌 ∅ ⚒ 🅿 Services: ♀ ✕ lau
Leisure: ⇗ R Off-site: 🅘

HEIKENDORF SCHLESWIG-HOLSTEIN

Möltenort 24226 ☎ 0431 241316 🖳 0431 2379920
e-mail: gronau.heikendorf@freenet.de
website: www.camping-ostree-online.de
Terraced site by the Kieler Förde.

⟳ 15km NE of Kiel to W of road B502.
Open: Apr-01 Oct Site: 2HEC ▦ ⚶ Prices: ♠4.50 ♣7-9
▲6-7 pitch 6-9 Facilities: ℹ 🛒 ⊙ 🔌 🅿 Services: 🅘 lau
Leisure: ⇗ S Off-site: ♀ ✕ ∅

HELMSTEDT NIEDERSACHSEN

Waldwinkel Maschweg 46, 38350 ☎ 05351 37161
In an orchard next to the Gasthaus Waldwinkel.
⟳ Signposted from autobahn exit 'Helmstedt'.
Open: All year Site: 10HEC ▦ ⚘ Facilities: ℹ 🛒 ⊙ 🔌 ∅ ⚒
🅿 Services: ✕ 🅘 lau Off-site: ⇗P

HEMELN NIEDERSACHSEN

Hemeln 34346 ☎ 05544 1414 🖳 05544 1414
e-mail: camping-hemeln@gmx.de
website: www.weserecamping.de
Well-kept site on northern outskirts of village, beside the
River Weser.
⟳ From Autobahn A7 take the Gothenburg exit & follow B3 to
Dransfeld then follow signposts.
Open: All year Site: 20HEC ▦ ⚶ ⚘ ♠ ♣ Prices: ♠3.50
♣2.10 ♣3.20 ▲2.20 Facilities: ℹ 🛒 ⊙ 🔌 ∅ ⚒ 🅿
Services: ✕ 🅘 lau Leisure: ⇗ R

HERMANNSBURG NIEDERSACHSEN

Örtzetal 29320 ☎ 05052 3072 & 1555
website: www.campingplatz-oldendorf.de
Site lies on meadows on the east bank of the River Örtze, set
in unspoilt woodlands of the Lüneburg Heath. Boat landing
stage. Lunchtime siesta 13.00-15.00 hrs.
⟳ From the B3 Celle-Soltau road turn off in Bergen and
follow road NE towards Hermannsburg, then continue towards
Eschwege.
Open: 15 Mar-Oct Site: 6HEC ▦ ⁚⁚⁚ ⚘ ♠ ♣ Prices: ♠4
♣1 ♣4.50 ▲2.50 Facilities: ℹ ⊙ 🔌 🅿 Services: ♀ ✕ 🅘 lau
Leisure: ⇗ R Off-site: 🛒 ♀ ⇗P

HOHEGEISS NIEDERSACHSEN

Bärenbache Barenbachweg 10, 38700
☎ 05583 1306 🖳 05583 1300
e-mail: info@campingplatz-hohegeiss.de
website: www.campingplatz-hohegeiss.de
Terraced site. Well-organised.
Open: All year Site: 2.8HEC ▦ ⚘ Prices: ♣4.35 pitch
4.70 Facilities: ℹ ⊙ 🔌 ∅ ⚒ 🅿 Services: ✕ Off-site: 🛒 ⇗P

HOLLE NIEDERSACHSEN
AT DERNEBURG (2KM NW ON UNCLASS ROAD)

Seecamp-Derneburg An der B6, 31188
☎ 05062 565 🖳 05062 8785
e-mail: info@campingplatz-derneburg.de
website: www.campingplatz-derneburg.de
A terraced lakeside site on a hill slope with a southerly
aspect. Separate towing field. Useful transit site near
autobahn.
⟳ From the motorway, leave at exit 'Derneburg' and continue
to road B6.
Open: Apr-15 Sep Site: 7.8HEC ▦ ⚘ ♣ Prices: ♠4 ♣2
♣4.50 ▲4-4.50 pitch 6.50 Facilities: ℹ 🛒 ⊙ 🔌 ∅ ⚒ 🅿
Services: ✕ 🅘 lau Leisure: ⇗ L Off-site: ⇗R

KLEINWAABS SCHLESWIG-HOLSTEIN

Ostsee Heide 24369 ☎ 04352 2530 🖳 04352 1398
e-mail: info@waabs.de website: www.waabs.de
Divided into pitches and pleasantly landscaped. Large games
room for teenagers. Lunchtime siesta 13.00-14.30 hrs.
Open: Mar-Oct Site: 21.5HEC ▦ ⚘ ♠ ♣ Facilities: ℹ 🛒
⊙ 🔌 ∅ ⚒ 🅿 Services: ♀ ✕ lau Leisure: ⇗ PS

Facilities: 🛒-shop **ℹ**-shower **⊙**-electric points for razors **🔌**-electric points for caravans **🅿**-parking by tents permitted
🅿-compulsory separate car park **Services: ✕**-café/restaurant **♀**-bar **∅**-Camping Gaz International **⚒**-gas other than Camping
Gaz **🅘**-first aid facilities lau-laundry **Leisure: ⇗**-swimming L-Lake P-Pool R-River S-Sea **Off-site:** All facilities within 2km

KLINT-BEI-HECHTHAUSEN NIEDERSACHSEN

Geesthof Am Ferienpark 1, 21755 ☎ 04774 512 📠 04774 9178
e-mail: ferienpark.geesthof@t-online.de
website: www.ferienpark-geesthof.de
On dry meadowland next to the River Oste, in quiet setting
with trees. Lunchtime siesta 13.00-15.00 hrs.
➲ *In Hechthausen leave road B73 and drive W towards*
'Lamstedt' for about 3 km.
Open: All year Site: 15HEC ⬛⬛⬛ ✦ 🏕 Prices: ♠3-6
Facilities: 🚻 🗲 ⊙ 🗔 ∅ 🚿 🍽 Services: ✗ ⊞ lau Leisure: ⇥ P

LANGHOLZ ÜBER ECKERNFÖRDE SCHLESWIG-HOLSTEIN

Langholz Fischerstr 9, 24369 ☎ 04352 2542
A holiday site surrounded by a belt of trees situated at a wide
natural beach, at the mouth of the Eckernförde Bay.
Camping Card Compulsory.
➲ *From the Eckernförde take the B203 towards the NE to the*
turn off for Langholz, then right and continue 3km to site.
Open: Apr-Sep Site: 20HEC ⬛⬛⬛ 🏕 Facilities: 🚻 🗲 ⊙
🗔 🍽 Services: 🍴 ✗ ⊞ lau Leisure: ⇥ S Off-site: ∅

LAUTERBERG, BAD NIEDERSACHSEN

Wiesenbeker Teich 37431 ☎ 05524 2510 📠 05524 932089
e-mail: info@campingwiesenbek.de
website: www.campingwiesenbek.de
In wooded surroundings on the Wiesenbeker Teich.
➲ *Approach via B243 SE of Bad Lauterberg.*
Open: All year Site: 10HEC ⬛⬛⬛ ✿ 🕌 🏕 Prices: ♠4-5.50
🚐1.30 🚃5-7 ⛺5-7 Facilities: 🚻 ⊙ 🗔 ∅ 🗔 Services: 🍴 ✗ ⊞
lau Leisure: ⇥ L Off-site: 🗲 🍽 ⇥P

LOOSE SCHLESWIG-HOLSTEIN

Gut Ludwigsburg 24369 ☎ 04358 1068 📠 04358 460370
This partly wooded holiday site lies between an inland lake and
the sea. 100m long private beach. It is divided into pitches.
➲ *From Eckernförde, head towards Klein-Wabbs up to Gut*
Ludwigsburg, then follow a dirt track for 2km.
Open: Apr-Sep Site: 10HEC 🕌 🏕 🏕 Facilities: 🚻 🗲 ⊙ 🗔 ∅
🍽 🗔 Services: 🍴 ✗ ⊞ lau Leisure: ⇥ L Off-site: ⇥S

MALENTE-GREMSMÜHLEN SCHLESWIG-HOLSTEIN

Schwentine Wiesenweg 14, 23714
☎ 04523 4327 📠 04523 202799
website: www.vcsh.de
A park-like setting with trees and bushes, at a river within
the village of Malente.
➲ *A17 18km NW of Eutin.*
Open: Apr-4 Oct Site: 2.5HEC ⬛⬛⬛ 🕌 Prices: ♠3.60-4.50
🚐1.60-2 🚃4.80-6 ⛺4.80-6 Facilities: 🚻 🗲 ⊙ 🗔 ∅ 🍽 🗔
Services: ✗ ⊞ lau Leisure: ⇥ R Off-site: ⇥LP

MELBECK NIEDERSACHSEN

Melbeck 21406 ☎ 04134 7311
Extensive site in woodland on the banks of the Ilmenau.
Centre of site free of trees and reserved for tourers.
➲ *On B4, 9km Lüneburg.*
Open: All year Site: 20HEC ⬛⬛⬛ 🕌 🏕 🏕 Facilities: 🚻 ⊙ 🗔
∅ 🗔 Services: ✗ lau Leisure: ⇥ R

NEUSTADT SCHLESWIG-HOLSTEIN

Strande Sandbergerweg, 23730 ☎ 04561 4188 📠 04361 7125
e-mail: am.strande@t-online.de website: www.amstrande.de
The site is divided into small sections and slopes down to the
sea. Narrow sandy beach.
➲ *Access from Neustadt towards Pelzerhaken, first site on the*
right after leaving Neustadt.
Open: Apr-Sep Site: 4.5HEC ⬛⬛⬛ 🕌 🏕 Prices: ♠4 pitch 6-
8.50 Facilities: 🚻 ⊙ 🗔 🍽 🗔 Services: ⊞ lau Leisure: ⇥ S
Off-site: 🗲 🍽 ✗ ∅

NORDSTRAND (ISLAND OF)

NORTHEIM NIEDERSACHSEN

Sultmer Berg Sultmerberg 3, 37154
☎ 05551 51559 📠 05551 5656
e-mail: campingplatzmajora@web.de
Grassland site with views of surrounding hills. Lunchtime
siesta 13.00-15.00 hrs.
➲ *Follow B3 from town centre.*
Open: All year Site: 5HEC ⬛⬛⬛ 🕌 🏕 Facilities: 🚻 🗲 ⊙ 🗔 ∅
🍽 🗔 Services: ✗ ⊞ lau Leisure: ⇥ P Off-site: 🍴 ✗ ⇥LR

OEHE-DRAECHT SCHLESWIG-HOLSTEIN

Oehe-Draecht 24376 ☎ 04642 6124 & 6029 📠 04642 69159
e-mail: Gut-oehe@T-online.de website: www.oehe-draecht.de
Grassy site, divided into pitches, on sandy ground behind a
sea dyke.
➲ *From Kappeln follow B199, turn towards Hasselberg and*
follow signs 'Strand'.
Open: 23 Mar-22 Sep Site: 6HEC ⬛⬛⬛ ⋮⋮⋮ 🕌 🏕 🏕
Facilities: 🚻 🗲 ⊙ 🗔 ∅ 🍽 🗔 Services: 🍴 ✗ ⊞ lau Leisure: ⇥ LS

AT ORSTEIL GOTTINGERODE

Freizeit Oase Harz Camp Kreisstr 66, Bad Harzburg, 38667
☎ 05322 81215 📠 05322 877533
e-mail: harz-camp@t-online.de website: www.harz-camp.de
On outskirts of village next to main road. Terraced site with
separate touring field. Lunchtime siesta 13.00-15.00 hrs.
➲ *On the B6 between Bad Harzburg and Goslar.*
Open: All year Site: 6.5HEC ⬛⬛⬛ 🕌 🏕 Prices: ♠4.70 pitch 5.80
Facilities: 🚻 🗲 ⊙ 🗔 ∅ 🍽 🗔 Services: ✗ ⊞ lau Leisure: ⇥ P

OSNABRÜCK NIEDERSACHSEN

Niedersachsenhof Nordstr 109, 49084
☎ 0541 77226 📠 0541 70627
e-mail: osnacamp@aol.com
website: www.osnabrueck.de/tourismus/1242.html
The site lies on a gently sloping meadow bordering a forest,
near a converted farmhouse with an inn.
➲ *On outskirts of town 5km from town centre NW on B51/65*
towards Bremen, turn right and continue 300mtrs.
Open: All year Site: 3HEC ⬛⬛⬛ 🕌 Prices: ♠3.50 pitch 7
Facilities: 🚻 ⊙ 🗔 🍽 🗔 Services: ✗ ⊞ lau Off-site: 🗲 🍴 ✗ ∅
⇥PRS ⊞

OSTERODE NIEDERSACHSEN

Sösestausee 37520 ☎ 05522 3319 📠 05522 72378
e-mail: harzcamp@t-online.de website: harzcamp.de
Terraced site on edge of woodland and by reservoir.
➲ *Follow road B498 from Osterode towards Altenau and after*
3km turn right to the site.
Open: All year Site: 4HEC ⬛⬛⬛ 🕌 Facilities: 🚻 🗲 ⊙ 🗔 ∅ 🍽
🗔 Services: ✗ ⊞ lau Leisure: ⇥ LR Off-site: 🍴 ✗

OSTRHAUDERFEHN NIEDERSACHSEN

AZUR-Camping Idasee 26842
☎ 04952 994297 📠 04952 994297
Situated beside a lake between Oldenburg and the Dutch
border with good water sports facilities.
➲ *Access via B27 (Cloppenburg-Aurich).*
Open: 15 Mar-15 Nov Site: 5HEC ⬛⬛⬛ 🕌 🏕 Facilities: 🚻 ⊙
🗔 ∅ 🗔 Services: ⊞ lau Leisure: ⇥ L

OTTERNDORF NIEDERSACHSEN

See Achtern Diek Deichstr 14, 21762
☎ 04751 2933 📠 04751 3016
e-mail: campingplatz@otterndorf.de website: www.otterndorf.de
A family site with good facilities close to the North Sea coast.

Site: 6HEC-Site size ⬛⬛⬛-grass ⋮⋮⋮-sand ✿-stone 🕌-little shade 🕌-partly shaded ✦-mainly shaded
🏕-bungalows for hire 🏕-caravans for hire ⛺-tents for hire ⊘-no dogs Prices: ♠-adult per night 🚐-car per night
pp-per person per night 🚃-caravan per night ⛺-tent per night

⊃ *Access via B73 Cuxhaven-Hamburg.*
Open: Apr-Oct Site: 13HEC ⊞ ⊛ Prices: ⋔4.50 ⇔2 ⊟5-
6.50 ⚑2-4 Facilities: ⋔ ⊙ ⊠ ☎ Leisure: ⊰ L Off-site: ⚊ ⚤ ✕
⊘ ⚌ ⊰LPRS ⊞

PLÖN SCHLESWIG-HOLSTEIN

Spitzenort Ascheberger Str 76, 24306
☎ 04522 2769 ▤ 04522 4574
A pleasantly situated site with hedges on the shore of Lake
Plön. Surrounded by the lake on three sides, it is ideal for
water sports.
⊃ *Access from Plön on B430 towards Neumünster.*
Open: Apr-15 Oct Site: 4.5HEC ⊞ ⊛ Prices: ⋔4.50 ⇔3
⊟5.50-8.50 ⚑3.50-6.50 Facilities: ⋔ ⚊ ⊙ ⊠ ⊘ ☎
Services: ✕ ⊞ lau Leisure: ⊰ L Off-site: ✕ ⊰P

PYRMONT, BAD NIEDERSACHSEN

AT LÜGDE-ELBRINXEN (3KM S)

Eichwald Obere Dorfstr 80, 32676 ☎ 05283 335 ▤ 05283 640
e-mail: campingeichwald@t-online.de
website: www.camping-eichwald.de
Pleasantly situated grassy site near woodland and pool.
⊃ *S of Lüdge in direction of Rischenau to Elbrinxen.*
Open: All year Site: 10HEC ⊞ ⊛ Prices: ⋔4.60 pitch 5.20
Facilities: ⋔ ⚊ ⊙ ⊠ ⊘ ⚌ ☎ Services: ⚤ ✕ lau Off-site: ⊰P

RIESTE NIEDERSACHSEN

Alfsee Am Campingpark 10, 49597
☎ 05464 92120 ▤ 05464 5837
e-mail: info@alfsee.de
website: www.alfsee.com
Open: All year Site: 15.5HEC ⊞ ⊛ ⚏ ⚑ Prices: ⋔3.20-5.20
pitch 7.60-10.70 Facilities: ⋔ ⚊ ⊙ ⊠ ⊘ ☎ Services: ⚤ ✕ ⊞
lau Leisure: ⊰ L

RINTELN NIEDERSACHSEN

Doktor-See Am Doktor-See8, 31722
☎ 05751 964860 ▤ 05751 964888
e-mail: info@doktorsee.de website: www.doktorsee.de
In a beautiful situation by a recreation area and beside the
Doktor See bathing beach. Section for touring campers.
Lunchtime siesta 13.00-15.00 hrs.
⊃ *In town turn downstream at the River Weser bridge and
continue along the left bank for 1.5km.*
Open: All year Site: 152HEC ⊞ ⊛ ⚏ Prices: ⋔4.41-6.30
pitch 5 Facilities: ⋔ ⚊ ⊙ ⊠ ⊘ ⚌ ☎ Services: ⚤ ✕ ⊞ lau
Leisure: ⊰ L Off-site: ⊰PR

ST ANDREASBERG NIEDERSACHSEN

Erikabrücke 37444 ☎ 05582 923056 ▤ 05582 1431
e-mail: camping@erikabruecke.de
website: www.erikabruecke.de
⊃ *Open site next to B27 NE of Oderstausee. Off B27 from
Bad Lauterberg towards Braunlage.*
Open: All year Site: 5.5HEC ⊞ ⸪ ◑ ⊛ ⚑ Prices: ⋔5.60
⇔1 ⊟4 ⚑4 Facilities: ⋔ ⚊ ⊙ ⊠ ⊘ ⚌ ☎ Services: ⚤ ✕ ⊞ lau
Leisure: ⊰ LR

SCHOBÜLL SCHLESWIG-HOLSTEIN

Seeblick 25875 ☎ 04841 3321 ▤ 04841 5773
e-mail: info@camping-seeblick.de
website: www.camping-seeblick.de
Beautifully situated beside the sea and divided into two
sections.
⊃ *Turn off the B5 on the northern outskirts of Husum, and
drive towards Insel Nordstrand for 4km up to Schobüll.*
Open: Apr-15 Oct Site: 3.4HEC ⊞ ⚑ Prices: ⋔3.30 ⇔6
⚑5 pitch 6.50 Facilities: ⋔ ⚊ ⊙ ⊠ ⊘ ⚌ ☎ Services: ⚤ ✕ ⊞
lau Off-site: ✕ ⊰PS

STELLE NIEDERSACHSEN

Steller See Zum Steller See 15, 28816
☎ 04206 6490 ▤ 04206 6668
e-mail: steller.see@t-online.de website: www.steller-see.de
⊃ *Delmenhorst-Ost exit off motorway. Site 300mtrs.*
Open: Apr-Sep Site: 16HEC ⊞ ⊛ ⚑ Prices: ⋔3-7.50 ⊟4
⚑3-7.50 Facilities: ⋔ ⚊ ⊙ ⊠ ⊘ ☎ ⊟ Services: ⚤ ✕ ⊞ lau
Leisure: ⊰ L

SUDERBURG NIEDERSACHSEN

AT HÖSSERINGEN (5KM SW)

Hardausee 29556 ☎ 05826 7676 ▤ 8303
e-mail: info@camping-hardausse.de
website: www.camping-hardausse.de
Grassland site without firm internal roads. Statics have
individual pitches and outbuildings. Separate fields for tourers.
⊃ *Approach from Uelzen S on B4. In 9km turn right, continue
via Suderburg to site on the right just before Hösseringen.*
Open: All year Site: 12HEC ⊞ ⸬ Prices: ⋔4 ⇔3 ⊟3 ⚑3
pitch 6 Facilities: ⋔ ⚊ ⊙ ⊠ ⊘ ⚌ ☎ Services: ✕ lau Off-site: ⊰L

TARMSTEDT NIEDERSACHSEN

Rethbergsee 27412 ☎ 04283 422 ▤ 04283 980139
e-mail: camping-rethbergsee@t-online.de
website: www.rethbergee-wochenendpark.de
Level site on a grand scale. Lunchtime siesta 13.00-15.00 hrs.
⊃ *About halfway between Bremen-Lilienthal and Zeven.*
Open: All year Site: 10HEC ⊞ ⊛ ⚑ Prices: ⋔4.50 pitch 5
Facilities: ⋔ ⚊ ⊙ ⊠ ⊘ ⚌ ☎ Services: ⚤ ✕ lau Leisure: ⊰ L
Off-site: ⊞

TELLINGSTEDT SCHLESWIG-HOLSTEIN

Tellingstedt Teichstr, 25789 ☎ 04838 657 ▤ 04838 786969
Divided by a row of high shrubs.
⊃ *Off B203 towards the swimming pool.*
Open: May-15 Sep Site: 1.2HEC ⊞ ⊛ Facilities: ⋔ ⊙ ⊠ ☎
Services: ✕ ⊞ lau Leisure: ⊰ P Off-site: ⚊ ⚤ ✕ ⊘

TINNUM (ISLAND OF SYLT) SCHLESWIG-HOLSTEIN

Südhörn 25980 ☎ 04651 3607 ▤ 04651 3619
Well-kept site divided into pitches.
⊃ *Well signposted from railway unloading ramp. No road
connections between the island and the mainland-rail from
Niebüll to Westerland.*
Open: All year Site: 2HEC ⊞ ⸬ ⚏ ⚑ Facilities: ⋔ ⚊ ⊙
⊠ ⊘ ☎ Services: ✕ Off-site: ⚤ ✕ ⊰PS ⊞

TÖNNING SCHLESWIG-HOLSTEIN

Lilienhof Katinger Landstr 5, 25832 ☎ 04861 439 ▤ 04861 439
e-mail: info@camping-lilienhof.de
website: www.camping-lilienhof.de
Well-maintained site in the woodland grounds of an old
manor house next to a quiet country road.
⊃ *Leave B202 at far end of Tönning, then 2km W towards Welt.*
Open: All year Site: 2HEC ⊞ ⊛ ⚏ ⚑ Prices: ⋔4.50 pitch 17
Facilities: ⋔ ⊙ ⊠ ⊘ ☎ Services: ⚤ ✕ ⊞ lau Off-site: ⚊ ✕ ⊘ ⊰PR

USLAR NIEDERSACHSEN

AT DELLIEHAUSEN SOLLING (8KM NE)

Bergsee Bergsee-Camp-Solling, 37170 ☎ 05573 1217 ▤ 05573 1613
Well-kept site on meadow beside lake, in Solling nature
reserve. Separate section for young campers. Lunchtime
siesta 13.00-15.00 hrs. Mobile shop.
⊃ *Access from motorway exit Nörten-Hardenberg, take the
B446 and then the B421 via Hardegsen to Volpriehausen, then
right to Delliehausen (2.5km).*
Open: Etr-Oct Site: 1HEC ⊞ ⊛ ⚏ Facilities: ⋔ ⊙ ⊠ ⊟
Services: ✕ ⊞ lau Leisure: ⊰ L Off-site: ⚊ ⚤

Facilities: ⚊-shop ⋔-shower ⊙-electric points for razors ⊠-electric points for caravans ☎-parking by tents permitted
⊟-compulsory separate car park **Services:** ✕-café/restaurant ⚤-bar ⊘-Camping Gaz International ⚌-gas other than Camping
Gaz ⊞-first aid facilities lau-laundry **Leisure:** ⊰-swimming L-Lake P-Pool R-River S-Sea **Off-site:** All facilities within 2km

WALKENRIED NIEDERSACHSEN

KNAUS Walkenried Ellricher Str 7, 37445
☎ 05525 778 📠 05525 2332
e-mail: knauscamp.walkenried@freenet.de
website: www.knauscamp.de
In an attractive location in the southern Harz area.
➲ *Access via A7 exit 'Seesen' and B243 via Herzberg and Bad Sachsa.*
Open: Dec-Oct Site: 5.4HEC ⫘ ♣ 🏕 🚐 Å Prices: 🏍6 Å2 pitch 3.50-8 Facilities: 🏪 🏬 ⊙ 🚿 ∅ 🛒 🏧 Services: ✗ lau Leisure: ⚓ P Off-site: ⚓LR ⊞

WEENER NIEDERSACHSEN

Weener Am Erholungsgebiet 4, 26826
☎ 04951 1740 📠 04951 8613
e-mail: weener@t-online.de website: www.weener.de
A municipal site, pleasantly landscaped and set inside a leisure centre with swimming pool and harbour. Lunchtime siesta 13.00-15.00 hrs.
➲ *From the main road B75 (E35) from Leer towards the Dutch frontier and turn off in the centre of Weener and follow signs to site.*
Open: 26 Mar-Oct Site: 3.2HEC ⫘ 🏕 Facilities: 🏪 ⊙ 🚿 🛒 🏧 Services: ⊞ lau Leisure: ⚓ P Off-site: 🏬 ✗ ∅ ⚓R

WIETZENDORF NIEDERSACHSEN

Südsee Soltau-Süd, 29649 ☎ 05196 980116/7 📠 05196 980299
e-mail: AA@sudseecamp.de website: www.suedsee-camp.de
This site is beautifully situated in a forest beside lake.
➲ *Leave the Hannover-Hamburg motorway at the Soltau-Süd exit, and take the B3 for 2km towards Bergen. At the underpass in Bokel, turn left and drive on for approx 4km towards Wietzendorf.*
Open: All year Site: 70HEC ⫘ 🏕 🚐 Prices: pitch 23.50-29.50 (incl 2 persons) Facilities: 🏪 🏬 ⊙ 🚿 ∅ 🛒 🏧 Services: 🍷 ✗ ⊞ lau Leisure: ⚓ LP

WILSUM NIEDERSACHSEN

AZUR-Ferienpark Wilsumer Berge 49849
☎ 05945 1029 📠 05945 511
e-mail: wilsum@azur-camping.de
website: www.azur-camping.de/wilsum
Parts of the site adjoin a large lake. The separate section for touring campers has its own sanitary building.
➲ *From Nordhorn follow road B403 via Uelsen to Wilsum. On nearside of Wilsum turn right.*
Open: All year Site: 88HEC ⫘ ∴ 🏕 Prices: 🏍4-6 Å3-4 pitch 5-7 Facilities: 🏪 🏬 ⊙ 🚿 🛒 🏧 Services: 🍷 ✗ ⊞ lau Leisure: ⚓ L

WINGST NIEDERSACHSEN

Knaus Wingst Schwimmbadallee 13, 21789
☎ 04778 7604 📠 04778 7608
e-mail: knauscamp.wingst@freenet.de
website: www.knauscamp.de
This modern comfortable site extends over several terraces, above a small artificial lake on the northern edge of an extensive forested area. Lunchtime siesta 13.00-15.00 hrs. Municipal recreation centre across the road.
➲ *Turn off the B73 between Stade and Cuxhaven, about 3km S of Cadenberge.*
Open: Mar-Oct Site: 8.7HEC ⫘ 🏕 🚐 Å Prices: 🏍6 Å2 pitch 4.50-9 Facilities: 🏪 🏬 ⊙ 🚿 🏧 🏭 Services: ✗ Off-site: 🍷 ⚓PS ⊞

WINSEN-ALLER NIEDERSACHSEN

Winsen 29308 ☎ 05143 93199 📠 05143 93144
e-mail: th-reiser@web.de website: www.camping-winsen.de
Site lies on meadowland at the River Aller. Watersports available. Lunchtime siesta 13.00-15.00 hrs.
➲ *From Celle go NW to Winsen.*
Open: All year Site: 12HEC ⫘ ⫘ 🏕 Prices: 🏍4-6 🚐2.10-3.30 🚐3-4 Å3-4 pitch 5-7 Facilities: 🏪 🏬 ⊙ 🚿 ∅ 🏧 Services: ✗ ⊞ lau Leisure: ⚓ R Off-site: 🛒 ⚓P

WITTENBORN SCHLESWIG-HOLSTEIN

Weisser Brunnen 23829
☎ 04554 1757 & 1413 📠 04554 4833
e-mail: gert.petzold@t-online.de
website: www.naturcamping-weisser-brunnen.de
A lakeside site consisting of several sections, hilly in parts, next to Lake Mözen. A public road, leading to the lake, passes through part of the site.
➲ *Turn off B206 at Km23.6 towards lake.*
Open: Apr-Oct Site: 7HEC ⫘ ⫘ 🚐 Prices: 🏍4.50 🚐6.50 Å4-5.50 pitch 6.50 Facilities: 🏪 🏬 ⊙ 🚿 ∅ 🛒 🏧 Services: 🍷 ✗ ⊞ lau Leisure: ⚓ L

WULFEN (ISLAND OF FEHMARN) SCHLESWIG-HOLSTEIN

Wulfener Hals 23769 ☎ 04371 8628-0 📠 04371 3723
e-mail: camping@wulfenerhals.de
website: www.wulfenerhals.de
Meadowland site beside the Baltic Sea and an inland lake (Burger Binnensee). 1700mtrs long private beach.
➲ *Turn off B20/E4 (Vogelfluglinie) after the 'Sundbrücke' and follow roads towards 'Avendorf', then 'Wulfen' and 'Wulfener Hals'.*
Open: All year Site: 34HEC ⫘ ⫘ 🏕 🚐 Prices: 🏍3.40-6.70 pitch 8.70-18 Facilities: 🏪 🏬 ⊙ 🚿 ∅ 🏧 Services: 🍷 ✗ ⊞ lau Leisure: ⚓ PS

Site: 6HEC-Site size ⫘-grass ∴-sand ♣-stone ❄-little shade ⫘-partly shaded ♣-mainly shaded 🏕-bungalows for hire 🚐-caravans for hire Å-tents for hire 🚫-no dogs **Prices:** 🏍-adult per night 🚗-car per night pp-per person per night 🚐-caravan per night Å-tent per night

ITALY

Italy, with its impressive culture and rich architectural heritage, has mountain ranges, beautiful coastal areas and bustling cities.

FACTS AND FIGURES
Area: 301,323 sq km
(116,341 sq miles)
Population: 57,587,985
(1998)
Capital: Roma (Rome)
Language: Italian
IDD code: 39. To call the
UK dial 00 44
Currency: Euro.

Local time: GMT + 1
(summer GMT + 2)
Emergency Services:
Police 113, Ambulance
113 or 118, Fire 115
(Carabinieri 112)
Banks: Mon-Fri 08.30-
13.30 and 15.30-16.30
Shops: Mon-Sat 08.30-
13.30 and 15.30-19.30

**Average daily
temperatures:** Roma
Jan 8°C   Jul 25°C
Mar 11°C   Sep21°C
May 18°C   Nov12°C
Tourist Information:
Italian State Tourist Office
(ENIT)
UK 1 Princess Street
London W1R 8AY
Tel (020) 7408 1254

USA 630 Fifth Avenue,
Suite 1565
New York, NY 10111
Tel(212) 245 5618
Tourist info website:
www.enit.it

The approaches to Italy are all dominated by mountains. The lakes of the north present a striking contrast with the sun-parched lands of the south and there is some beautiful countryside in the central Appenines. There are fine, sandy beaches on both the Tyrrhenian and Adriatic coasts. All this and the cities of Rome and Milan. Something for everyone, it seems.

The north has a typically Continental climate whilst the south has a temperate Mediterranean climate with extremely hot summers. The language is Italian, a direct development of Latin. There are several dialect forms such as Sicilian and Sardinian, but the accepted standard derives from the vernacular spoken in Florence 700 years ago. German is spoken, to a small extent, near the Austrian frontier and French in Valle d'Aosta.

The International Reservation Centre in Calenzano (near Florence) *Federcampeggio* provides a campsite information and reservation service ☎ 055-882391.

The *Assessorati Regionali per il Turismo* (ART) and the *Azienda Promozione Turistica* (APT) have regional and local information offices and can provide details of campsites within their locality. In northern Italy, especially by the lakes and along the Adriatic coast, sites tend to become very crowded and it is advisable to book in advance during the season which extends from May to the end of August.

Off-site camping is permitted provided the landowner's permission has been obtained, but is strictly prohibited in State forests and national parks. In built-up areas, if parking is allowed, the towing vehicle must remain connected to the trailer or caravan and the corner steadies must not be used.

HOW TO GET THERE

Although there are several ways of getting to Italy, entry will most probably be by way of France and Switzerland. Some passes, which are closed in winter, are served by road or rail-tunnels. For details of these, please consult the Contents Page.

DISTANCE

From the Channel ports Milano (Milan) is about 1100km (684 miles) requiring one or two overnight stops. Roma (Rome) is about 580km (360 miles) further south.

CAR-SLEEPER TRAINS

A summer service is available from **Denderleeuw** (Belgium) to Bologna.

MOTORING & GENERAL INFO

The information given here is specific to Italy. It **must** be read in conjunction with the Essential Motoring Information at the front of the book, which covers those regulations which are common to many countries.

Lush vineyards in the Chianti district, famed for its production of red wine.

British Embassy/Consulates*

The British Embassy together with its consular section is located at 00187 Roma, Via XX Settembre 80A ☎06-4220 0001. There are British Consulates in Firenze (Florence), Milano (Milan), and Napoli (Naples); there are British Consulates with honorary Consuls in Bari, Cagliari, Catania, Genova (Genoa), Palermo, Trieste, Torino (Turin) and Venezia (Venice).

Children in Cars

Child under 4 not permitted to travel as front or rear seat passenger unless using suitable restraint system. Child between 4 and 12 travelling in front seat must use suitable restraint system. See the Essential Motoring Information under 'Passengers' and 'Seat Belts'.

Currency

With the introduction of the Euro, the Italian Lira (ITL) ceased to be legal tender from 2002. However, ITL coins and notes may still be exchanged at the Italian Central Bank (**Banca d'Italia**) for 10 years.

Dimensions and Weight Restrictions*

Private **cars** and towed **trailers** or **caravans** are restricted to the following dimensions - car height, 4 metres: width, 2.55 metres: length (including tow-bar) 12 metres. Caravan/trailer height, must not exceed 1.8 times the distance between the wheels of the vehicle; width 2.3 metres; length (including tow-bar) with one axle 6.5 metres, with two axles 8 metres. The maximum permitted overall length of vehicle/trailer or caravan combination is 18.75 metres. Trailers with an unladen weight of over 750kg or 50% of the weight of the towing vehicle must have service brakes on all wheels.

A load may only overhang at the rear, and must be indicated by a special reflectorised square panel. The load must not exceed 30% of the length of the vehicle, nor should the combined length of vehicle and overhanging load exceed the length restrictions given above.

Driving Licence*

All valid UK or Republic of Ireland licences should be accepted in Italy. This includes the older all-green style UK licences, although the European Commission appreciates that these may be difficult to understand, and that drivers may wish to voluntarily update them before travelling abroad, if time permits. Application form D750 is available

252

from most Post Offices. Alternatively, older licences may be accompanied by an International Driving Permit (IDP). The minimum age at which visitors from UK or Republic of Ireland may use a temporarily imported car is 18 years. The minimum age for using a temporarily imported motorcycle of up to 125cc, not transporting a passenger, is 16 years; to carry a passenger, or use a motorcycle over 125cc, the minimum age is 18 years.

FISCAL RECEIPT

In Italy, the law provides for a special numbered fiscal receipt (*ricevuta fiscale*) to be issued after paying for a wide range of goods and services including meals and accommodation. This receipt indicates the cost of the various goods and services obtained, and the total charge after adding VAT. Tourists should ensure that this receipt is issued, as spot checks are made by the authorities, and both the proprietor and consumer are liable to an on-the-spot fine if the receipt cannot be produced.

FOODSTUFFS*

If the imported foodstuffs are for personal use, there are no limits when travelling between EU countries. Visitors entering Italy from outside the EU may import up to 1kg of meat or meat products. Coffee (500g), coffee extract (200g), tea (100g) and tea extract (40g) are free of customs duties, but visitors under 15 cannot import coffee.

LIGHTS*

It is compulsory for all vehicles to use dipped headlights during the day on motorways and main highways; motorcyclists must also use them on all other roads during the day.

MOTORING CLUBS

There are two motoring organisations in Italy. The **Touring Club Italiano** (TCI) which has its head office at 20122 Milano, 10 Corso Italia ☎02-85261 and the **Automobile Club d'Italia** (ACI) whose head office is at 00185 Roma, 8 Via Marsala ☎06-49981. Both clubs have branch offices in most leading cities and towns. Website: **www.touringclub.it** or **www.aci.it**

ROADS

Italy has over 4,000 miles of motorway (*autostrada*) with tolls payable on most sections. Emergency telephones are located every 2km on most motorways; there are two call buttons, one to call for technical assistance and one to alert the Red Cross services.

Main and secondary roads are generally good, and there are an exceptional number of by-passes. Mountain roads are usually well engineered; for details of mountain passes, see the contents page.

SPEED LIMITS*

The speed limit in *built-up areas* is 50km/h (31mph), *outside built-up areas* 90km/h (55mph) on ordinary roads, 110km/h (68mph) on dual carriageways and 130km/h (80mph) on motorways. NOTES: *i*) these limits also apply to vehicles towing one axle (two-wheeled) luggage trailers, *ii*) some three-lane (plus emergency lane) motorways may have a speed limit of 150km/h (93mph), *iii*) in wet weather speed limits on dual carriageways and motorways are reduced to 90km/h (55mph) and 110km/h (68mph) respectively.

For cars towing a caravan or trailer the speed limits are 70km/h (43mph) *outside built-up areas* and 80km/h (49mph) on motorways.

Motorcycles under 150cc are not allowed on motorways.

WARNING TRIANGLE*

It is compulsory for a vehicle to be equipped with a warning triangle and to use it in the event of an accident or breakdown outside built-up areas. The triangle must be placed 50 metres (55yds) behind the vehicle on ordinary roads and 100 metres (109yds) on motorways. Motorists who fail to do this are liable to an administrative fine of between €33.60 and €137.55.

*Additional information will be found in the Essential Motoring Information at the front of the book.

NORTH WEST/ALPS & LAKES

ANFO BRESCIA

Palafitte via Calcaterra, 25070
☎ 0365 809051 ▤ 0365 809051
Pleasant site divided into plots, sloping towards the lake where there are some trees.
⤷ *Access as for Pilù, then turn right.*
Open: 22 Apr-17 Sep Site: 20HEC ⏛ ♠ ⊞ Facilities: ⬧ ⅃ ⊙ ⬛ ⌀ ⚑ Services: ⅄ ✗ lau Leisure: �ɤ LP Off-site: ⅃ ✗

Pilù via Venturi 4, 25070 ☎ 0365 809037 ▤ 0365 809207
e-mail: info@pilu.it website: www.pilu.it
Well-maintained, slightly sloping site subdivided by trees and rows of shrubs on pebble beach from which it is separated by narrow public footpath.
⤷ *On southern outskirts; well signed.*
Open: Apr-Sep Site: 2HEC ⏛ ♠ ⊞ Prices: ⩘4.50-5.60 pitch 7.50-10.20 Facilities: ⬧ ⅃ ⊙ ⬛ ⌀ ⚑ ⚑ Services: ⅄ ✗ ⊞ lau Leisure: ɤ LPR Off-site: ✗

ANGERA VARESE

Città di Angera via Bruschera 99, 21021
☎ 0331 930736 ▤ 0331 960367
e-mail: info@campingcittadiangera.it
website: www.campingcittadiangera.it
Large family site with plenty of recreational facilities.
⤷ *Signposted.*
Open: All year Site: 6.7HEC ⏛ ♠ Prices: ⩘6-6.50 pitch 9-9.50 Facilities: ⬧ ⅃ ⊙ ⬛ ⌀ ⚑ ⚑ Services: ⅄ ✗ ⊞ lau Leisure: ɤ LP

ARONA NOVARA

AT **DORMELLETTO** (5KM S)

Lago Azzurro via E-Fermi 2, 28040
☎ 0322 497197 ▤ 0322 497197
e-mail: info@campinglagoazzuro.it
website: www.campinglagoazzuro.it
A lakeside site in beautiful surroundings with fine sporting facilities.
⤷ *S of Arona off SS Sempione 33.*
Open: All year Site: 2.5HEC ⏛ ♠ ⊞ ⚑ Prices: ⩘5.20-5.50 pitch 7.20-7.50 Facilities: ⬧ ⅃ ⊙ ⬛ ⌀ ⚑ Services: ⅄ ✗ ⊞ lau Leisure: ɤ LP

Lago Maggiore via L-da-Vinci 7, 28040
☎ 0322 497193 ▤ 0322 497193
e-mail: maggiore@azzurra.it website: www.lagomag.com
Well-maintained site divided into plots, pleasantly landscaped by the lakeside.
⤷ *Access from SS33, well signposted.*
Open: Apr-Sep Site: 5HEC ⏛ ♠ ⊞ ⚑ Prices: ⩘3.90-5.80 ⚗3.90 pitch 6.80-11.80 Facilities: ⬧ ⅃ ⊙ ⬛ ⚑ ⚑ Services: ⅄ ✗ lau Leisure: ɤ LP

Lido Holiday Inn via M-Polo 1, 28040
☎ 0322 497047 ▤ 0322 497047
e-mail: info@lidoholidayinn.com
website: www.lidoholidayinn.com
Site on bank of the lake, with some trees.
⤷ *Turn off the SS33 at Km60/VII and the IP petrol station.*
Open: Apr-29 Sep Site: 3.5HEC ⏛ ⚒ ⊞ Prices: ⩘4.80-6 pitch 6.80-9 Facilities: ⬧ ⅃ ⊙ ⬛ ⌀ ⚑ P Services: ⅄ ✗ lau Leisure: ɤ LP Off-site: ⌀

Smeraldo via Cavour 131, 28040
☎ 0322 497031 ▤ 0322 497031
e-mail: info@camping-smeraldo.com
website: www.camping-smeraldo.com
Well-landscaped site, divided into plots and situated in woodland by lakeside.

⤷ *Access from SS33.*
Open: Mar-Oct Site: 24HEC ⏛ ♠ ⊞ Prices: ⩘5-6.50 ⚗5.50-6.50 pitch 9-15 Facilities: ⬧ ⅃ ⊙ ⬛ ⌀ ⚑ Services: ⅄ ✗ ⊞ lau Leisure: ɤ L Off-site: ⅃ ⅄ ✗ ɤP

ARVIER AOSTA

Arvier via Chaussa 17, 11011 ☎ 0165 99088 ▤ 0165 99045
e-mail: campingarvier@yahoo.it
website: www.campingarvier.com
Wooded quiet site close to mountains and a peaceful village
Open: Jun-Aug Site: 1HEC ⏛ ♠ Prices: ⩘5.20-5.70 ⚗3.30-3.70 ⚗5-5.50 ⚑5-5.50 Facilities: ⬧ ⅃ ⊙ ⬛ ⚑ Services: lau Leisure: ɤ P Off-site: ⅃ ⅄ ✗ ⌀ ⚑ ɤR ⊞

BASTIA MONDOVI CUNEO

Cascina via Pieve 26, 12060 ☎ 0174 60181
e-mail: camping.lacascina@libero.it
A peaceful site on level land surrounded by mountains.
⤷ *Access via, then head towards Bastia.*
Open: Jan-Aug & Oct-Dec Site: 4HEC ⏛ ♠ Facilities: ⬧ ⅃ ⊙ ⬛ ⚑ ⚑ Services: ⅄ ✗ lau Leisure: ɤ PR Off-site: ⅃ ✗

BAVENO NOVARA

Tranquilla via Cave 2, 28831
☎ 0323 923452 ▤ 0323 923452
e-mail: info@tranquilla.com
website: www.tranquilla.com
In a peaceful location with fine panoramic views over the surrounding mountains and Lake Maggiore. Good, modern facilities.
⤷ *4 km from Stresa*
Open: Mar-Oct Site: 1.8HEC ⏛ ♠ ⚑ Prices: ⩘3.65-5 pitch 6-9 Facilities: ⬧ ⊙ ⬛ ⚑ Services: ⅄ ✗ lau Leisure: ɤ P Off-site: ⅃ ⌀ ⚑ ɤLR ⊞

BELLAGIO COMO

Azienda Agricola Clarke via Valassina 170/c, 22021
☎ 031 951325
e-mail: elizabethclarke@tin.it
A small, secluded site situated on a horsebreeding farm on the shores of Lake Bellagio.
Open: Jun-Sep Site: 0.5HEC ⏛ ⚑ Prices: ⩘6 pitch 10 Facilities: ⬧ ⊙ ⬛ ⚑ Services: ⅄ ⊞ Off-site: ⅃ ✗ ɤLP

BOLZANO-BOZEN BOLZANO

Moosbauer Moritzingerweg 83, 39100
☎ 0471 918492 ▤ 0471 204894
e-mail: info@moosbauer.com website: www.moosbauer.com
Small site in attractive valley at the "Gateway to the Dolomites."
Open: All year Site: 1HEC ⏛ ♠ ♠ Prices: ⩘5.50-6.50 ⚗5-5.50 ⚗12-15.50 ⚑5-5.50 pitch 12-15.50 Facilities: ⬧ ⅃ ⊙ ⬛ ⌀ ⚑ Services: ⅄ ✗ lau Leisure: ɤ P Off-site: ⊞

See advertisement on page 255

BRÉCCIA COMO

International via Cecilio, 22100
☎ 031 521435 ▤ 031 521435
e-mail: campingint@hotmail.com
website: www.camping-internationale.it
On a level meadow near the motorway. Lunchtime siesta 13.00-15.30 hrs.
⤷ *Off A9 Como-Milan motorway.*
Open: 28 Mar-15 Oct Site: 1.8HEC ⏛ ♠ ⊞ ⚑ Prices: ⩘5 ⚗3 ⚗4 ⚑3.50 Facilities: ⬧ ⅃ ⊙ ⬛ ⌀ ⚑ ⚑ Services: ⅄ ✗ ⊞ lau Leisure: ɤ P

Site: 6HEC-Site size ⏛-grass ⣿-sand ◈-stone ⋇-little shade ⚑-partly shaded ♠-mainly shaded ⊞-bungalows for hire ⚑-caravans for hire ⚑-tents for hire ⊗-no dogs Prices: ⩘-adult per night ⚗-car per night pp-per person per night ⚗-caravan per night ⚑-tent per night

BRENTONICO TRENTO

Polsa Polsa, 38060 ☎ 0464 867177 ▤ 0464 421003
Situated at 1300mtrs on Mount Baldo with easy access and
good, modern facilities.
⊃ *Access via Brenner Autostrada exit Rovereto Sud and
continue through Brentonico and Prada to Polsa.*
Open: 15 Jun-15 Sep Site: 33HEC ⬛⬛⬛ ⚆ 🏠 🚐
Facilities: 🏕 🏪 ⊙ 🚰 ⌀ 🛁 🅿 Services: 🍴 ✗ lau Off-site: ⚡P

BRESSANONE-BRIXEN BOLZANO

Löwenhof via Brennero 60, 39040
☎ 0472 836216 ▤ 0472 801337
e-mail: info@loewenhof.it website: www.loewenhof.it
Site offers rafting and canoeing school as well as sauna, pool
etc, which are avaliable in the Dolomiti resort 8km away.
⊃ *Exit Bolzano/Brennero motorway at Varna. Site is just
before Brixen.*
Open: Apr-Oct Site: 0.5HEC ⬛⬛⬛ ⚆ ⚡ Prices: ⚡7-8 🚗3.50-
5 🚐7-10 ▲5-8 pitch 10-15 Facilities: 🏕 🏪 ⊙ 🚰 ⌀ 🛁 🅿 P
Services: 🍴 ✗ lau Leisure: ⚡ PR Off-site: ⚡L ⊞

CALCERANICA TRENTO

Al Pescatore via dei Pescatori 1, 38050
☎ 0461 723062 ▤ 0461 724212
e-mail: trentino@campingpescatore.it
website: www.campingpescatore.it
The site consists of several sections of meadowland, inland
from the lake shore road to Lago di Caldonazzo. Well
maintained with private beach.
Open: 29 May-15 Sep Site: 3.8HEC ⬛⬛⬛ ⚆ Prices: ⚡6.50
pitch 8.70 Facilities: 🏕 🏪 ⊙ 🚰 ⌀ 🛁 Services: 🍴 ✗ lau
Leisure: ⚡ L Off-site: ⊞

Fleiola via Trento 20, 38050 ☎ 0461 723153 ▤ 0461 724386
e-mail: info@campingfleiola.it
website: www.campingfleiola.com
Site is divided into sectors beside lake.
⊃ *Exit the Verona/Brennero motorway at Trento, follow signs
for Pergine and Caldonazzo.*
Open: Apr-5 Oct Site: 1.2HEC ⬛⬛⬛ ⚆ ⌀ 🏠 🚐 Facilities: 🏕
🏪 ⊙ 🚰 ⌀ 🛁 Services: 🍴 ✗ lau Leisure: ⚡ L Off-site: ✗ 🛁 ⊞

Riviera viale Venezia 10, 38050
☎ 0461 724464 ▤ 0461 718689
e-mail: riviera@dnet.it
website: www.campingriviera.net
Open: Etr-15 Sep Site: 1.5HEC ⬛⬛⬛ ⚓ Prices: ⚡5-7.50 pitch
6-8.50 Facilities: 🏕 🏪 ⊙ 🚰 🛁 Services: 🍴 ✗ lau Leisure: ⚡ L
Off-site: 🛁 ⊞

CAMPITELLO DI FASSA TRENTO

Miravalle vicolo camping 15, 38031
☎ 0462 750502 ▤ 0462 751563
e-mail: info@campingmiravalle.it
website: www.campingmiravalle.it
In a wooded mountain setting beside the River Avisio and
close to the town centre.
⊃ *Signposted.*
Open: Jun-Sep & Dec-Apr Site: 3HEC ⬛⬛⬛ ⚆ 🏠
Facilities: 🏕 ⊙ 🚰 ⌀ 🛁 🅿 P Services: ⊞ lau Leisure: ⚡ R
Off-site: 🏪 🍴 ✗ ⌀ ⚡P

CANAZEI TRENTO

Marmolada via Pareda 60, 38032
☎ 0462 601660 ▤ 0462 601722
Grassland site extending to the river, part of it in spruce
woodland.

CAMPING ★★★★
Moosbauer

Via S.Maurizio, 83 • BOLZANO-South Tyrol
Tel. 0039/0471918492 • Fax 0039/0471204894
E-mail: info@moosbauer.com
Http: www.moosbauer.com

Encircled by orchards and vineyards, our campsite is only 4 km
away from the center of Bolzano (autobus). At your disposal
you will find: mini-market, bistro, comfortable toilet and shower
facilities, heated swimming pool with pool for children, play area
and a sunbathing area with chairs and deckchairs. Each pitch
(till 100 sqm) has an electricity point, water point and connection
for satellite TV. The campsite is a central starting point to visit
Bolzano "Ötzi, the man who came out of the ice" as well as to make
magnificent trips to the Alps of Siusi, Renon (with the pyramids)
and the lakes of Caldano and Monticcolo.

Further information: Camping Moosbauer, Family Egger
Via S. Maurizio 83, I-39100 Bolzano, Tel. 0039/0471918492
Fax 0039/0471204894, Internet: www.moosbauer.com
E-mail: info@moosbauer.com

Directions: A22, exit
Bolzano-Sud, then
follow directions for
the hospital.

⊃ *Located on S outskirts on the right of the road to Alba
Penia.*
Open: All year Site: 3HEC ⬛⬛⬛ ⚆ Facilities: 🏕 ⊙ 🚰 ⌀ 🛁 🅿
Services: 🍴 ✗ lau Leisure: ⚡ R Off-site: 🏪 ✗ ⚡P ⊞

CANNOBIO NOVARA

International Paradis via Casali Darbedo 12, 28052
☎ 0323 71227
A level site on the bank of a lake.
⊃ *Access from the SS34 at Km35/V.*
Open: 20 Mar-15 Oct Site: 1.2HEC ⬛⬛⬛ ⚓ 🚐 Facilities: 🏕
🏪 ⊙ 🚰 ⌀ 🛁 🅿 Services: 🍴 ✗ ⊞ lau Leisure: ⚡ L
Off-site: ✗ ⚡R

Residence Campagna via Casali Darbedo 20/22, 28822
☎ 0323 70100 ▤ 0323 72398
e-mail: info@campingcampagna.it
website: www.campingcampagna.it
A well equipped site in a pleasant lakeside location.
⊃ *Turn off SS34 to Locarno at Km35/V on N outskirts of
village. W of lake on road 21.*
Open: 20 Mar-04 Nov Site: 1.2HEC ⬛⬛⬛ ⚆ 🏠 🚐
Prices: ⚡5.50-6.50 🚗4.50-6 🚐4.50-6 ▲4.50-6 pitch 9-12
Facilities: 🏕 🏪 ⊙ 🚰 ⌀ 🛁 🅿 Services: 🍴 ✗ lau Leisure: ⚡ L
Off-site: ⚡R ⊞

Valle Romantica via Valle Cannobina, 28822
☎ 0323 71249 ▤ 0323 71249
e-mail: valleromantica@riviera-valleromantica.com
website: www.riviera-valleromantica.com
A pleasant site with trees, shrubs and flowers. Internal roads
are asphalted and a mountain stream provides bathing
facilities.

contd.

⊃ *1.5km w off road to Malesco.*
Open: 27 Mar-Sep **Site:** 25HEC ⸺ ♦ 🏠 ⊞ **Prices:** ⚑5.50-
6.50 ⇌4.50-5.50 ⊞9-11.50 ⚑2.50-3 pitch 9-11.50
Facilities: 🏕 ⚊ ⊙ 🛒 ∅ ☎ **Services:** ⚑ ✗ lau **Leisure:** ⥙ PR
Off-site: ⚏ ⥙L ⊞

CASTELLETTO TICINO NOVARA

Italia Lido via Cicognola 88, 28053
☎ 0331 923032   ▥ 0331 923032
e-mail: campingitalialido.campin@tin.it
website: www.campingitalialido.it
A large family site with its own private beach on Lake
Maggiore. The site is popular with families and there are
good recreational facilities.
⊃ *From A8 to Milan join A26 is then signposted.*
Open: Mar-Oct **Site:** 3HEC ⸺ ♦ 🏠 ⊞ **Prices:** ⚑3.75-4.85
⇌3.62 ⊞7-19.75 pitch 7-10.75 **Facilities:** 🏕 ⚊ ⊙ 🛒 ⚏ ☎
Services: ⚑ ✗ lau **Leisure:** ⥙ L **Off-site:** ⚊ ✗ ⊞

CHIUSA-KLAUSEN BOLZANO

Gamp Griesbruck 10, 39043 ☎ 0472 847425   ▥ 0472 845067
e-mail: info@camping-gamp.com
website: www.camping-gamp.com
The site lies next to the Gasthof Gamp, between the Brenner
railway line and the motorway bridge, which passes high
above the camp.
⊃ *Access from the motorway exit and the SS12 is well
signposted.*
Open: All year **Site:** 0.6HEC ⸺ ⥙ **Prices:** ⚑5.05-5.95
⇌3.35-4.35 ⊞5.45-6.45 ⚑4.15-5.55 **Facilities:** 🏕 ⚊ ⊙ 🛒 ☎
Services: ⚑ ✗ lau **Leisure:** ⥙ P **Off-site:** ∅ ⚏ ⥙P ⊞

COLFOSCO BOLZANO

Colfosco via Sorega 15, 39030 ☎ 0471 836515   ▥ 830801
e-mail: info@campingcolfosco.it
website: www.campingcolfosco.it
In a beautiful setting at the foot of the Sella mountains.
Open: 8 Jun-Sep & 7 Dec-10 Apr **Site:** 2.5HEC ⸺ ⸬ ⚇
⚘ 🏠 **Prices:** ⚑4.15-5.20 ⇌4.14-5.20 ⊞8-13 ⚑4-6
Facilities: 🏕 ⚊ ⊙ 🛒 ⚏ ☎ **Services:** ⚑ ✗ lau **Leisure:** ⥙ R
Off-site: ⥙L ⊞

COLOMBARE BRESCIA

Sirmione via Sirmioncino 9, 25010
☎ 030 919045   ▥ 030 919045
e-mail: info@camping-sirmione.com
website: www.camping-sirmione.com
A well equipped site in a beautiful location on the Sirmione
peninsula, with direct access to Lake Garda.
⊃ *From SS11 drive towards Sirmione and turn right after
approx. 0.4km.*
Open: 25 Mar-05 Oct **Site:** 3.5HEC ⸺ ♦ ⚇ 🏠 **Prices:** ⚑6-9
⇌3-5.50 ⊞8.50-13.50 ⚑5.50-8 pitch 8.50-13.50 **Facilities:** 🏕
⚊ ⊙ 🛒 ☎ **Services:** ⚑ ✗ ⊞ lau **Leisure:** ⥙ LP **Off-site:** ⚊ ∅ ⚏

CÚNEO CUNEO

Turistico Comunale Bisalta San Rocco Castagnaretta, 12100
☎ 0171 491334
Large site with well defined pitches and a wide variety of
sporting and recreational facilities.
⊃ *SW of town towards the French border.*
Open: All year **Site:** 4HEC ⸺ ♦ 🏠 **Facilities:** 🏕 ⚊ ⊙ 🛒 ☎
Services: ⚑ ✗ lau **Leisure:** ⥙ P **Off-site:** ⚏ ⊞

DESENZANO DEL GARDA BRESCIA

Vò via Vò 9, 25015 ☎ 030 9121325   ▥ 030 9120773
e-mail: vo@voit.it **website:** www.voit.it
Situated on Lake Garda, 1500mtrs from Desenzano,
surrounded by meadows and woods.

⊃ *On the banks of Lake Garda 2km from Desenzano, between
Padenghe and Sirmione.*
Open: Apr-Sep **Site:** 5HEC ⸺ ♦ 🏠 **Facilities:** 🏕 ⚊ ⊙ 🛒 ☎
Services: ⚑ ✗ lau **Leisure:** ⥙ LP **Off-site:** ∅

DIMARO TRENTO

Dolomiti di Brenta via Gole 105, 38025
☎ 0463 974332   ▥ 0463 973200
e-mail: dolomitibrenta@camping.it
website: www.camping.it/trentino/dolomiti
The campsite has large flat plots which are surrounded by tall
pine trees. The facilities for sport are excellent with special
lessons and tuition for canoeing and white water rafting.
⊃ *Turn off SS42, at Km173.5.*
Open: Jun-Sep & 6 Dec-15 Apr **Site:** 3HEC ⸺ ♦ 🏠
Facilities: 🏕 ⚊ ⊙ 🛒 ∅ ⚏ ☎ **Services:** ⚑ ✗ lau
Leisure: ⥙ P **Off-site:** ⥙R

DOMASO COMO

Gardenia via Case Sparse 164, 22013
☎ 0344 96262   ▥ 0344 83381
e-mail: campingardenia@interfree.it
website: www.campingardenia.it
⊃ *N at Case Sparse*
Open: Apr-29 Sep **Site:** 20HEC ⸺ ♦ 🏠 ∅ **Prices:** ⚑4.30
pitch 7.70-9.50 **Facilities:** 🏕 ⚊ ⊙ 🛒 ∅ ☎ **Services:** ⚑ ✗
lau **Leisure:** ⥙ L **Off-site:** ⥙R ⊞

EDOLO BRESCIA

Adamello via Campeggio 10, 25048
☎ 0364 71694   ▥ 0364 71694
e-mail: enrico.adamello@libero.it
A terraced site in wooded surroundings, 1km from the lake.
⊃ *1.5km W of SS39.*
Open: All year **Site:** 1.2HEC ⸺ ♦ 🏠 **Prices:** ⚑4.80 ⇌2
⊞6.50 ⚑4.50-6.50 pitch 10.50 **Facilities:** 🏕 ⚊ ⊙ 🛒 ∅ ☎
Services: ⚑ ✗ ⊞ lau **Off-site:** ✗ ⥙LPR

FERIOLO NOVARA

Orchidea via Repubblica dell'Ossola, 28835
☎ 0323 28257   ▥ 0323 28573
e-mail: camping.orchidea@libero.it
website: www.campingorchidea.it
A modern site on the extremity of Lake Maggiore with good
sports and entertainment facilities.
⊃ *Access via SS33.*
Open: 15 Mar-13 Oct **Site:** 4HEC ⸺ ♦ 🏠 ⊞ **Facilities:** 🏕
⚊ ⊙ 🛒 ∅ ⚏ ☎ **Services:** ⚑ ✗ ⊞ lau **Leisure:** ⥙ L

FONDOTOCE NOVARA

Continental Lido via 42 Martiri 156, 28924
☎ 0323 496300   ▥ 0323 496218
e-mail: info@campingcontinental.com
website: www.campingcontinental.com
By Lake Mergozzo and 1km from Lake Maggiore.
⊃ *On right hand side of road from Verbania Fondotoce to
Gravellona.*
Open: 5 Apr-20 Sep **Site:** 8HEC ⸺ ⥙ 🏠 ⊞ ⚑ **Facilities:** 🏕
⚊ ⊙ 🛒 ∅ ☎ **Services:** ⚑ ✗ lau **Leisure:** ⥙ L **Off-site:** ⚏ ⥙R

Lido Toce via per Feriolo 41, 28924
☎ 0323 496298   ▥ 0323 496220
e-mail: peruchinigiovanna@tiscali.it
website: tiscali.it.lidotoce
In a beautiful location on the eastern shore of the lake
offering spectacular views. Good recreational facilities.
Open: 20 Apr-Sep **Site:** 2HEC ⸺ ⸬ ♦ **Prices:** ⚑3.80-5
pitch 7.50-10 **Facilities:** 🏕 ⚊ ⊙ 🛒 ☎ **Services:** ⚑ ✗ ⊞ lau
Leisure: ⥙ LR **Off-site:** ∅ ⚏ ⥙P

Site: 6HEC-Site size ⸺-grass ⸬-sand ⚇-stone ⚘-little shade ⥙-partly shaded ♦-mainly shaded
🏠-bungalows for hire ⊞-caravans for hire ⚑-tents for hire ∅-no dogs **Prices:** ⚑-adult per night ⇌-car per night
pp-per person per night ⊞-caravan per night ⚑-tent per night

Village Isolino via Per Feriolo 25, 28924
☎ 0323 496080 ▤ 0323 496414
e-mail: info@isolino.com website: www.isolino.com.it
Open: 02 Apr-19 Sep **Site:** 12HEC ﹏ ♣ ⌂ **Prices:** pitch
17.20-29.25 (incl 2 persons) **Facilities:** ⋔ 🛓 ⊙ 🖫 ⊘ 📛 🏚
Services: ⏧ ✗ ⊞ lau **Leisure:** ⇃ LP **Off-site:** ⇃R

FUCINE DI OSSANA TRENTO

Cevedale 38026 ☎ 0463 751630 ▤ 0463 751630
e-mail: info@campingcevedale.it website: www.campingcevedale.it
A well equipped site in a peaceful location at an altitude of
900mtrs, close to the local ski resorts.
➲ *4km W of Savona.*
Open: All year **Site:** 3HEC ﹏ ♣ ⌂ ⌆ **Prices:** ⋔6-7.50
pitch 3.50-11 **Facilities:** ⋔ 🛓 ⊙ 🖫 ⊘ 🏚 **Services:** ⏧ ✗ ⊞ lau
Leisure: ⇃ LR **Off-site:** ✗

GERMIGNAGA VARESE

Il Boschetto via Mameli, 21010
☎ 0332 534740 ▤ 0332 500791
e-mail: boshol@tin.it website: www.boschettoholiday.it
In a pleasant location beside Lake Maggiore with a good
variety of facilities and opportunities for water sports.
Open: Apr-29Sep **Site:** 1HEC ﹏ ♣ ⌶ **Prices:** ⋔5-6.50
🚗2.50-3.50 ⌶8-9 ▲5-5.50 pitch 8-9 **Facilities:** ⋔ ⊙ 🖫 🏚
Services: ⏧ ✗ lau **Leisure:** ⇃ LPR **Off-site:** ⇃ ✗ ⊘ 📛 ⊞

IDRO BRESCIA

AZUR Idro Rio Vantone 25074
☎ 0365 83125 ▤ 0365 823663
e-mail: info@azur-freizeit.de website: www.azur-camping.de
The site lies at the mouth of the river of same name beside Lake
Idro. Subdivided into pitches (separate pitches for youths) on
grass and woodland at the foot of strange rock formations.

➲ *Approach from Idro direction of Vantone, well signed from
there.*
Open: 15 Mar-15 Nov **Site:** 4.5HEC ﹏ ♣ ⌂ **Facilities:** ⋔
🛓 ⊙ 🖫 ⊘ 📛 🏚 **Services:** ⏧ ✗ ⊞ lau **Leisure:** ⇃ LP

Vantone Pineta via Capovalle 11, 25074 ☎ 0365 823385
e-mail: campingpineta@libero.it
On eastern shore of lake. Grassland enclosed by rush and
willow fencing. Part of site in a small wood on the bank of a
stream.
➲ *Approach from Idro and follow signs for Camping Idro Rio
Vantone.*
Open: 31 Mar-30 Oct **Site:** 2HEC ﹏ ♣ ⌂ **Prices:** ⋔4.50-
5.60 pitch 7.50-10.20 **Facilities:** ⋔ 🛓 ⊙ 🖫 🏚 **Services:** ⏧ ✗
lau **Leisure:** ⇃ LP **Off-site:** ⊘ 📛 ⊞

ISEO BRESCIA

Iseo via Antonioli 57, 25049 ☎ 030 980213 ▤ 030 980213
e-mail: campeggioiseo@intelligenza.it
In a picturesque location directly on the lake shore with well
shaded pitches and modern installations.
➲ *Access via A4 Brescia-Bergamo.*
Open: Apr-Oct **Site:** 0.7HEC ﹏ ♣ ⌂ ⌶ **Facilities:** ⋔ 🛓 ⊙
🖫 ⊘ 📛 🏚 **Services:** ⏧ ✗ lau **Leisure:** ⇃ L **Off-site:** ✗ ⇃P ⊞

Punta d'Oro via Antonioli 51/53, 25049
☎ 030 980084 ▤ 030 980084
e-mail: info@puntadoro.com website: www.puntadoro.com
A well set out campsite with roads and paths reaching every
pitch.
➲ *From A4 exit at Rovato and follow signs Iseo.*
Open: Apr-Oct **Site:** 0.6HEC ﹏ ♣ ⌶ **Prices:** ⋔4.20-6.20
pitch 8.50-13.30 **Facilities:** ⋔ 🛓 ⊙ 🖫 🏚 **Services:** ⏧ ✗ lau
Leisure: ⇃ L **Off-site:** ✗ ⊘ 📛 ⇃P ⊞

Facilities: 🛓-shop ⋔-shower ⊙-electric points for razors 🖫-electric points for caravans 🏚-parking by tents permitted
🅿-compulsory separate car park **Services:** ✗-café/restaurant ⏧-bar ⊘-Camping Gaz International 📛-gas other than Camping
Gaz ⊞-first aid facilities lau-laundry **Leisure:** ⇃-swimming L-Lake P-Pool R-River S-Sea **Off-site:** All facilities within 2km

★★★ Camping STEINER

I-39055 Laives-Leifers (Bolzano)
Tel. +39 0471 950 105 • Fax +39 0471 951 572
campingsteiner@dnet.it • www.campingsteiner.com
Well-maintained, family-friendly campsite with good facilities. Located in the South Tyrol on the outskirts of Laives 8 km from Bolzano (highway A22, exit Bolzano Sud, towards Trento). Enter by Steiner Inn. Money change, safe-deposit boxes, table tennis, lending library, minimarket, pizza restaurant, cosy wine cellar on site. **Country-style wooden bungalows for 2 to 5 person.** Inn (50 rooms), restaurant and large covered terrace. **Open from 01.04 to 07.11.2004.**

SOUTH TYROL - DOLOMITES - ITALY

Quai via Antonioli 73, 25049 ☎ 0309 821610
e-mail: info@campingquai.it website: www.campingquai.it
Shady site close to the edge of Lake D'Iseo.
◆ *W of town. Signposted.*
Open: 08 Apr-26 Sep Site: 1.3HEC ⸺ ♣ ⌂ ⚘ Prices: ♠4.50 pitch 9-11 Facilities: ♠ ⊙ ⚙ 🏠 🄿 Services: ♀ ✗ lau Leisure: ⌁ L Off-site: ⚗ ✗ ⚗ ⌁P ⊞

Sassabanek via Colombera 2, 25049
☎ 030 980300   ▤ 030 9821360
e-mail: sassabanek@sassabanek.it website: www.sassabanek.it
In a pleasant wooded location on the shore of Lake Iseo with good recreational facilities.
Open: Apr-29 Sep Site: 3.5HEC ⸺ ♣ ⚘ ✗ Prices: ♠3.90-7.40 ▲2.10-4.70 pitch 7.80-14.30 Facilities: ♠ ⚗ ⊙ ⚙ 🄿 Services: ♀ ✗ ⊞ lau Leisure: ⌁ LP Off-site: ⚗

KALTERN BOLZANO

St Josef am Kalterer See Welnstr 75, 39052 ☎ 0471 960170
e-mail: camping.st.josef@dnet.it
website: www.kalterersee.com/camping
On level ground surrounded by trees close to the lake.
◆ *Signposted from the Kalten-Tramin road.*
Open: 15 Mar-10 Nov Site: 1.4HEC ⸺ ⋯ ⚘ Facilities: ♠ ⚗ ⊙ ⚙ 🄿 Services: ♀ ✗ ⊞ lau Leisure: ⌁ L

LAIVES-LEIFERS BOLZANO

Steiner Kennedystr 34, 39055
☎ 0471 950105   ▤ 0471 951572
e-mail: campingsteiner@olmet.it
website: www.campingsteiner.com
The site lies behind the Gasthof Steiner, the AGIP petrol station and a bungalow estate.
◆ *Off the SS12 on the northern outskirts of the village.*
Open: Apr-5 Nov Site: 2.5HEC ⸺ ♣ ⚘ ✗ Prices: pitch 11-13 pp5-6 Facilities: ♠ ⚗ ⊙ ⚙ 🄿 ⚗ 🏠 Services: ♀ ✗ ⊞ lau Leisure: ⌁ P

LATSCH BOLZANO

Latsch an der Etsch Reichstr 4, 39021
☎ 0473 623217   ▤ 0473 622333
e-mail: camping.latsch@dnet.it
website: www.camping-latsch.com
A terraced site beside the river.
◆ *Campsite is signposted on SS38.*
Open: All year Site: 1.6HEC ⸺ ♣ ⚘ Prices: ♠5.50-6.80 pitch 9.50-12.50 Facilities: ♠ ⚗ ⊙ ⚙ 🄿 ⚗ 🏠 Services: ♀ ✗ ⊞ lau Leisure: ⌁ PR

LECCO COMO

Rivabella via Alla Spiaggia 35, 23900 ☎ 0341 421143
On a private, guarded beach on the shore of Lake Como.

◆ *3km S towards Bergamo.*
Site: 2HEC ⸺ ♣ Prices: ♠4.50 pitch 8 Facilities: ♠ ⚗ ⊙ ⚙ 🄿 🏠 Services: ♀ ✗ ⊞ lau Leisure: ⌁ L Off-site: ✗

LEVICO TERME TRENTO

Due Laghi Loc Costa 3, 38056
☎ 0461 706290   ▤ 0461 707381
e-mail: info@campingclub.it website: www.campingclub.it
Aimed mainly at families, with 400 large flat grass pitches.
◆ *From Trento follow signs for Pergine and Lake Caldonazza.*
Open: 17 May- 13 Sep Site: 12HEC ⸺ ♣ ⌂ Prices: ♠6-8.50 ⚗4-6 pitch 11-14 Facilities: ♠ ⚗ ⊙ ⚙ 🄿 🏠 Services: ♀ ✗ ⊞ lau Leisure: ⌁ LP

Jolly Loc Pleina, 38056
☎ 0461 706934 & 701933   ▤ 0461 700227 & 701933
The site is divided into plots and lies 200 metres from the lake with three inside swimming pools.
Open: Apr-01 Oct Site: 2HEC ⸺ ♣ ⌂ Prices: ♠5.50-7 pitch 5.50-10.50 Facilities: ♠ ⚗ ⊙ ⚙ 🄿 🏠 Services: ♀ ✗ ⊞ lau Leisure: ⌁ P Off-site: ✗ ⌁LR

Levico 38056 ☎ 0461 706491   ▤ 0461 707735
e-mail: mail@campinglevico.com
website: www.campinglevico.com
Site is by a lake with a private beach.
◆ *Signposted from the Levico/Caldonazzo exit on SS47.*
Open: Apr-10 Oct Site: 4HEC ⸺ ♣ Prices: ♠5.70-7.50 pitch 6.30-14.10 Facilities: ♠ ⚗ ⊙ ⚙ 🄿 🏠 Services: ♀ ✗ ⊞ lau Leisure: ⌁ LR Off-site: ⌁P

LILLAZ AOSTA

Salasses 11012 ☎ 0165 74252
Pleasant site surrounded by mountains, grassland and conifers. The site lies at the end of the Val di Cogne.
◆ *Entrance to site before Camping al Sole.*
Open: All year Site: 1HEC ⸺ ⚘ Facilities: ♠ ⊙ ⚙ 🏠 🄿 Services: ♀ ✗ Leisure: ⌁ R Off-site: ⚗ ✗ ⚗ 🏠 ⊞

LIMONE PIEMONTE CUNEO

Luis Matlas 12015 ☎ 0171 927565   ▤ 0171 927565
This tidy site offers winter facilities and skiing lessons are provided by the owner. Fishing is also available.
◆ *It lies to the north of the town, off the Limone-Nice road.*
Open: All year Site: 1.5HEC ⸺ ⚘ ⚘ Prices: ♠4.70 ▲4 pitch 5.80 Facilities: ♠ ⊙ ⚙ 🄿 ⚗ 🏠 Services: ♀ ✗ lau Leisure: ⌁ R Off-site: ⚗ ✗ ⊞

LIMONE SUL GARDA BRESCIA

Nanzel via 4 Novembre 3, 25010
☎ 0365 954155   ▤ 0365 954468
e-mail: campingnanzel@cibero.it
Well managed site, with low terraces in olive grove.
◆ *Access from Km101.2 (Hotel Giorgiol).*
Open: 18 Oct Site: 0.7HEC ⸺ ⚘ ⌂ Prices: ♠4.70-6 pitch 9-11.50 Facilities: ♠ ⚗ ⊙ ⚙ 🄿 🏠 Services: ♀ ✗ lau Leisure: ⌁ L Off-site: ✗ 🏠 ⊞

MACCAGNO VARESE

AZUR-Lago Maggiore 21010
☎ 0332 560203   ▤ 0332 561263
A popular site on the shore of the lake.
◆ *In village turn off SS394 at Km43/III towards lake and after 500mtrs turn right.*
Open: 15 Mar-15 Nov Site: 1.5HEC ⋯ ⚘ ⌂ Facilities: ♠ ⚗ ⊙ ⚙ 🄿 Services: ✗ ⊞ lau Leisure: ⌁ LR Off-site: ✗

Brancheito via Pietraperzia 13, 21010 ☎ 045 6784029
Open: All year Site: 1.6HEC ⚗ ⚘ ⌂ 🏠 Facilities: ♠ ⚗ ⊙ ⚙ 🄿 🏠 Services: ♀ ✗ ⊞ lau Off-site: ✗

Lido via 6 Pietraperzia 13, 21010
☎ 0332 560250 ▤ 0332 560250
e-mail: campinglido.boschettoholiday.it
website: www.boschettoholiday.it
Lakeside site with good facilities, 200mtrs from the river.
Open: Apr-Sep Site: 0.8HEC ⊞ ♣ ⌁ Prices: ♦5-6.50 ♠2-3.50 ▲4-5 pitch 8-9 Facilities: ℕ ⊙ ◫ ⌂ ▯ Services: ▮ ✕ lau
Leisure: ⚐ LR Off-site: ⚑ ✕ ∅ ⍨ ⚐R ⊞

MANERBA DEL GARDA BRESCIA

Belvedere via Cavalle 5, 25080
☎ 0365 551175 ▤ 0365 552350
e-mail: info@camping-belvedere.it
website: www.camping.belvedere.it
Terraced site by Lake Garda.
⮱ *Signposted from SS572.*
Open: Etr-Oct Site: 2.1HEC ⊞ ∵ ⌁ ♀ ⌂ Prices: ♦3-6
♠2.60-4 ♠7.80-14 ▲1.80 pitch 7.80-14 Facilities: ℕ ⌢ ⊙
∅ ⍨ ⌂ Services: ▮ ✕ lau Leisure: ⚐ L Off-site: ✕ ⊞

Rio Ferienglück via del Rio 37, 25080
☎ 0365 551075 ▤ 0365 551044
⮱ *Follow SS572 Desenzano-Salo road, turn off between Km8 and 9, site 4km N.*
Open: Apr-Sep Site: 5HEC ⊞ ♣ ⌂ ⌁ Facilities: ℕ ⌢ ⊙
◫ ∅ ⍨ ⌂ Services: ▮ ✕ lau Leisure: ⚐ LPR

Rocca via Cavalle 22, 25080 ☎ 0365 551738 ▤ 0365 552045
e-mail: larocca@mtcomputer.it
website: www.mtcomputer.it/larocca
In a picturesque location with fine views over the Gulf of Manerba.
Open: Apr-Sep Site: 5HEC ⊞ ♣ ⌂ ⌁ Facilities: ℕ ⌢ ⊙
◫ ⍨ ⌂ Services: ▮ ✕ ⊞ lau Leisure: ⚐ LP Off-site: ✕

Zocco via del Zocco 43, 25080
☎ 0365 551605 ▤ 0365 552053
e-mail: info@campingzocco.it
website: www.campingzocco.it
The site consists of several, terraced sections. The section below the maintenance/supply building lies on a sloping olive grove and is somewhat obstructed by bungalows.
⮱ *500mtrs S of Gardonicino di Manerba.*
Open: 03 Apr-30 Sep Site: 5HEC ⊞ ♣ ⌂ ⌁ ⌁ ▲
Prices: ♦4.20-6.80 pitch 8.90-13.40 Facilities: ℕ ⌢ ⊙ ◫ ∅ ⌂
Services: ▮ ✕ ⊞ lau Leisure: ⚐ LP

MARONE BRESCIA

Riva di San Pietro via Cristini 9, 25054
☎ 030 9827129 ▤ 030 9827129
e-mail: rivasanpietro@hotmail.com
A good modern site on the eastern side of Lake Iseo. Plenty of recreational facilities.
⮱ *From Milano-Venezia road exit at Rovato or Palazzolo towards Iseo. Marone 10km N.*
Open: May-29 Sep Site: 2HEC ⊞ ♣ ⌂ Prices: ♦5-6 ♠7-11
▲7-9 Facilities: ℕ ⊙ ◫ ∅ ▯ Services: ▮ ✕ lau Leisure: ⚐ LP
Off-site: ⌢ ⍨

MOLINA DI LEDRO TRENTO

International Camping Al Sole via Maffei, 38060
☎ 0464 508496 ▤ 0464 508496
e-mail: info@campingalsole.it website: www.campingalsole.it
A family site with good, modern facilities situated on the shore of Lake Ledro at an altitude of 655mtrs.
⮱ *W of Molina beside the lake.*
Open: 20 Apr-Sep Site: 3HEC ⊞ ♀ Facilities: ℕ ⌢ ⊙ ∅
⌂ Services: ▮ ✕ ⊞ lau Leisure: ⚐ LP Off-site: ⍨

MOLVENO TRENTO

Spiaggia-Lago di Molveno via Lungolago 27, 38018
☎ 0461 586978 ▤ 0461 586330
e-mail: camping@molveno.it
website: www.molveno.it/camping
In a picturesque setting on the lake shore, at the foot of the Brenta Dolomites.
⮱ *Signposted from SS421.*
Open: All year Site: 4HEC ⊞ ♣ Facilities: ℕ ⌢ ⊙ ◫ ∅ ⍨
⌂ ▯ Services: ▮ ✕ lau Leisure: ⚐ LP Off-site: ⊞

MONIGA DEL GARDA BRESCIA

Fontanelle via Magone 13, 25080
☎ 0365 502079 ▤ 0365 503324/(557449 winter)
e-mail: info@campingfontanelle.it
website: www.campingfontanelle.it
Peaceful site on the shores of Lake Garda shaded by olive trees. All staff speak English.
Open: May-21 Sep Site: 45HEC ⊞ ♀ ⌂ Prices: ♦4.60-8.50
pitch 9.30-16 Facilities: ℕ ⌢ ⊙ ◫ ∅ ⌂ Services: ▮ ✕ ⊞ lau
Leisure: ⚐ LP Off-site: ⍨

San Michele via San Michele 8, 25080
☎ 0365 502026 ▤ 0365 503443
e-mail: gloriater@tiscalinet.it
A family site with good facilities and direct access to the lake via a private beach.
⮱ *Exit A4 at Desenzano. Site is 8km from Desenzano in direction of Salo.*
Open: 4 Apr- 29 Sep Site: 3HEC ⊞ ♣ ⌂ Prices: ♦4-6 pitch
8.50-14 Facilities: ℕ ⌢ ⊙ ◫ ∅ ⌂ Services: ▮ ✕ ⊞ lau
Leisure: ⚐ LP Off-site: ∅ ⍨

NATURNO-NATURNS BOLZANO

Wald Dornsbergweg 8, 39025
☎ 0473 667298 ▤ 0473 668072
e-mail: info@waldcamping.com
website: www.waldcamping.com
The site lies on gently rising ground, in a forest of pine and deciduous trees.
⮱ *For access, turn off the SS38 near the Gasthof Alderwirt in the village, and drive 0.8km S over the railway line.*
Open: 15 Mar-5 Nov Site: 3HEC ⊞ ♣ ♀ Prices: ♦5.50-6.50 ♠5.50-6 ♠5.50-6 ▲3-5.50 pitch 8-11 Facilities: ℕ ⌢ ⊙
◫ ⍨ ⌂ Services: ⊞ lau Leisure: ⚐ P Off-site: ▮ ✕ ∅ ⚐R

NOVATE MEZZOLA SONDRIO

El Ranchero via Nazionale 3, 23025
☎ 0343 44169 ▤ 0343 44169
Located on the edge of the Mezzola lake in front of a spectacular view of the mountains.
Open: May- 15 Oct Site: 1HEC ♀ ⌂ ⌁ ⌁ Prices: ♦5
♠4 ♠5-7 ▲5-7 Facilities: ℕ ⊙ ◫ ⌂ ▯ Services: ▮ ✕ lau
Leisure: ⚐ L Off-site: ⌢ ✕ ∅ ⍨ ⚐PR ⊞

ORTA SAN GIULIO NOVARA

Cusio Lago d'Orta, 28016 ☎ 0322 90290
website: www.orta.net/cusio
In a picturesque alpine valley, surrounded by woodland on the bank of Lake Orta. Good facilities.
⮱ *S of Omegna towards Borgomanero.*
Open: Apr-Nov Site: 2HEC ⊞ ♣ ⌂ ⌁ Prices: ♦4-5.50
♠3.60-4 ▲3-4.50 pitch 6.80-9.50 Facilities: ℕ ⊙ ◫
Services: ▮ ✕ lau Leisure: ⚐ P Off-site: ⌢ ⚐L ⊞

PADENGHE BRESCIA

Cá via S.Cassiano 12, 25080 ☎ 030 9907006 ▤ 030 9907693
e-mail: lacafab@tiscalinet.it website: www.laca.it
The site lies in a park-like setting on terraced ground.

contd.

Facilities: ⌢-shop ℕ-shower ⊙-electric points for razors ◫-electric points for caravans ⌂-parking by tents permitted
▯-compulsory separate car park **Services:** ✕-café/restaurant ▮-bar ∅-Camping Gaz International ⍨-gas other than Camping
Gaz ⊞-first aid facilities lau-laundry **Leisure:** ⚐-swimming L-Lake P-Pool R-River S-Sea **Off-site:** All facilities within 2km

➲ *For access, turn off the road along Lake Garda, 1.5km N turn for Padenghe, and drive down a very steep road towards the lake.*
Open: Mar-Oct Site: 2HEC ﷽ ♣ 🏠 🚐 Facilities: ⋔ ⅃ ⊙ 🗗 𝕒 🗎 Services: ⬜ ✗ lau Leisure: ↘ L

Villa Garuti via del Porto 5, 25080
☎ 030 9907134 ▤ 030 9907817
A camp site holiday village situated in the garden of the old Villa Garuti, directly on the lakeside with its own beach.
➲ *A4 from Brescia in direction of Verona, exit for Desenzano and follow SS572 to Padenghe.*
Open: Mar-Oct Site: 1.5HEC ﷽ ♣ 🏠 🚐 Facilities: ⋔ ⊙ 🗗 𝕒 🗎 Services: ⬜ ✗ ⊞ lau Leisure: ↘ LP Off-site: ⓶

Val di Sole Loc Dossi di Cavia, 38020
☎ 0463 753177 ▤ 0463 753176
e-mail: valdisole@camping.it
website: www.camping.it/trentino/valdisole
The site lies on terraced slopes at the foot of the Ortier mountain range.
➲ *400mtrs off SP87.*
Site: 2.3HEC ﷽ ⊕ 🏠 Prices: ♠4.50-6 ▲4.50-5.50 pitch 5.50-7 Facilities: ⋔ ⅃ ⊙ 🗗 𝕒 🗎 Services: ⬜ ✗ lau Off-site: ✗ ↘P

Soal via Dolomiti 32, 38030 ☎ 0462 764519 ▤ 0462 764609
e-mail: info@campingsoal.com
website: www.campingsoal.com
Breath-taking location among the Dolomites, ideal for skiing and walking.
Open: All year Site: 30HEC ﷽ ⊕ Facilities: ⋔ ⅃ ⊙ 🗗 𝕒 ᴬ 🗎 Services: ⬜ ✗ ⊞ lau Leisure: ↘ R

Punta Indiani Lago di Caldonazzo, 38058
☎ 0461 548062 ▤ 0461 548607
e-mail: info@campingpuntaindiani.it
website: www.campingpuntaindiani.it
On level ground surrounded by trees with direct access to 400mtrs of private beach on the banks of the lake.
➲ *From the A22 exit at Trento follow signs for Pergine, S. Cristoforo and Caldonazzo.*
Open: May-Sep Site: 1.5HEC ﷽ ⊕ 🕸 Prices: ♠7 pitch 7-12 Facilities: ⋔ ⊙ 🗗 🗎 Services: lau Leisure: ↘ L Off-site: ⓶ ⬜ ✗ 𝕒 ᴬ ⊞

San Cristoforo via dei Pescatori, 38057
☎ 0461 512707 ▤ 0461 707381
e-mail: info@campingclub.it website: www.campingclub.it
A family-run site in a prime position on the sunniest side of lake. Owned and run by family Oss with regular guests helping as staff.
➲ *Follow road 47 from Trento towards Venice for 14km. Site is in centre of S. Cristoforo village.*
Open: 17 May-14 Sep Site: 2.5HEC ﷽ ⊕ Facilities: ⋔ ⅃ ⊙ 🗗 𝕒 ᴬ 🗎 Services: ⬜ ✗ ⊞ lau Leisure: ↘ LP

Punta di Crabbia via Crabbia 2/A, 28028 ☎ 0323 89117
A well equipped site in a pleasant situation providing panoramic views over the surrounding area.
Open: Apr-Sep Site: 2HEC ﷽ ⊕ Facilities: ⋔ ⅃ ⊙ 🗗 🗎 Services: ⬜ ✗ ⊞ lau Leisure: ↘ L Off-site: ↘L

Faro via Repubblica 52, 25080
☎ 0365 651704 ▤ 0365 651704
e-mail: campeggioilfaro@virgilio.it
Situated in a peaceful rural area close to the sea.
➲ *Leave A4 at Desenzano and take N572 to Manerba del Garda.*
Open: 15 Apr-15 Sep Site: 1HEC ﷽ ♣ 🚐 Prices: ♠3.40-5.50 pitch 8-10.50 Facilities: ⋔ ⊙ 🗗 🗎 Leisure: ↘ P Off-site: ⓶ ⬜ ✗ 𝕒 ᴬ ↘L ⊞

Eden via Piangrande 3, 25055 ☎ 0364 880500 ▤ 0364 880500
The site lies on eastern lake shore with tall trees and a level beach.
➲ *Turn off SS510 at Km37/VII, over railway line towards lake.*
Open: 2 Apr-28 Sep Site: 2.5HEC ﷽ ♣ 🚐 Prices: ♠4.30-4.80 ▲3.60-5.20 pitch 7.50-11.50 Facilities: ⋔ ⅃ ⊙ 🗗 𝕒 Services: ⬜ ✗ ⊞ lau Leisure: ↘ L Off-site: ✗ 𝕒 ↘PR ⊞

Trelago via Trelago 20, 21030
☎ 0332 716583 ▤ 0332 719650
e-mail: info@3lagocamping.com
website: www.3lagocamping.com
Lakeside campsite with grassy pitches shaded by tall trees.
➲ *Follow signs from Milan to Varese and Ghirla. Site is 15km from Varese.*
Open: Apr-15 Sep Site: 3.3HEC ﷽ ⊕ 🏠 🚐 ᴬ Prices: ♠4.50 pitch 6.50 Facilities: ⋔ ⅃ ⊙ 🗗 𝕒 ᴬ 🗎 Services: ⬜ ✗ ⊞ lau Leisure: ↘ LP Off-site: ✗

Paradiso Via Calbiga,30, 22018 ☎ 0344 70393 ▤ 0344 70393
e-mail: info@campingoklarivetta.com
website: www.campingoklarivetta.com
The site lies in meadowland on the north eastern lake shore.
➲ *S from SS340.*
Open: Mar-15 Nov Site: 5HEC ﷽ ⊕ 🏠 Prices: ♠4-5 pitch 8-10 Facilities: ⋔ ⅃ ⊙ 🗗 𝕒 🗎 Services: ⬜ ✗ lau Leisure: ↘ LP Off-site: ✗ 𝕒 ᴬ ↘R

Caravan Garden Vidor Loc.Vidor, 5, 38036
☎ 0462 763247 ▤ 0462 764780
e-mail: info@campingvidor.it
website: www.campingvidor.it
This traditional family run site is set in a pine forest. Ideal for skiers, nature lovers and families all year round.
➲ *Signposted from SS48.*
Open: Jan-Apr & Jun-Dec Site: 2.5HEC ﷽ 🔆 🏠 Prices: ♠5-7 pitch 6-9 Facilities: ⋔ ⅃ ⊙ 🗗 𝕒 ᴬ 🗎 Services: ⬜ ✗ ⊞ lau Off-site: ✗ ↘R

Rosengarten via Avisio 15, Loc Puccia, 38036
☎ 0462 763305 ▤ 0462 763501
e-mail: campingcatinacciorosen@tin.it
In the heart of the Dolomites this well-tended site is an ideal base for a skiing or walking holiday.
➲ *Signposted from SS48.*
Open: Jun-Sep & Nov-Apr Site: 3HEC ﷽ ◊ ⊕ 🏠 🚐 Prices: ♠6.50-8.20 ▲5.17-6.72 pitch 7-7.25 pp7-7.25 Facilities: ⋔ ⊙ 🗗 𝕒 ᴬ 🗎 Services: ⬜ ✗ ⊞ lau Leisure: ↘ R Off-site: ⓶ ✗ ↘P

Site: 6HEC-Site size ﷽-grass ⋰⋰-sand ◊-stone 🔆-little shade ⊕-partly shaded ♣-mainly shaded 🏠-bungalows for hire 🚐-caravans for hire ᴬ-tents for hire 🕸-no dogs Prices: ♠-adult per night ♠-car per night pp-per person per night 🚐-caravan per night ᴬ-tent per night

RASUN BOLZANO

Corones 39030 ☎ 0474 496490 🖷 0474 498250
e-mail: info@corones.com website: www.corones.com
A modern site in an ideal mountain location with good
sporting facilities.
➲ *Exit Milan/Brenner motorway at Val Pusteria. Through
Brunico and Valdaora to Rasun.*
Open: All year Site: 2.7HEC ⏛ ♨ ♨ 🏠 Facilities: ♠ 🚾 ☉
🔌 🧺 🅿 Services: ♥ ✗ ⊞ lau Leisure: ⁂ P

RIVA DEL GARDA TRENTO

Bavaria viale Rovereto 100, 38066
☎ 0464 552524 🖷 0464 559126
e-mail: campingbavaria@yahoo.it
➲ *On SS240 towards Rovereto.*
Open: Apr-Oct Site: 6HEC ⏛ ⁙⁙⁙ 🕂 Facilities: ♠ ☉ 🔌 🅿
Services: ♥ ✗ ⊞ Leisure: ⁂ L Off-site: 🚾 🧺 🧺

Monte Brione via Brione 32, 38066
☎ 0464 520885 🖷 0464 520890
e-mail: campingbrione@rivadelgarda.com
This site is at the foot of a hill covered with olive trees with
good sports facilities.
➲ *250mtrs from San Nicolo' tourist centre.*
Open: Etr-early Oct Site: 3.3HEC ⏛ ♠ Facilities: ♠ 🚾 ☉
🔌 🅿 Services: ♥ ✗ lau Leisure: ⁂ P Off-site: ✗ ⁂L

RIVOLTELLA BRESCIA

San Francesco strada Vicinale San Francesco, 25010
☎ 030 9110245 🖷 030 9119464
e-mail: info@campingsanfrancesco.it
website: www.campingsanfrancesco.it
This well-kept site is divided into many sections by drives,
vineyards and orchards and has a private gravel beach.

➲ *At Km268 on SSN11.*
Open: Apr-Sep Site: 10.4HEC ⏛ ♠ 🏠 Prices: ⚹5.40-8.80
pitch 11.30-28.80 Facilities: ♠ 🚾 ☉ 🔌 🧺 🧺 🅿 Services: ♥ ✗
⊞ lau Leisure: ⁂ LP

SAN ANTONIO DI MAVIGNOLA TRENTO

Faé 38084 ☎ 0465 507178 🖷 0465 507178
e-mail: campingfae@campiglio.it
website: www.campiglio.it/campingfae
Situated in famous winter skiing region of Madonna di
Campiglio. Good base for climbing in Brenta mountain
range. On four gravel terraces, and alpine meadow in hollow
next to SS239.
Camping Card Compulsory.
Open: Jun-Sep & Dec-Apr Site: 2.1HEC ⏛ 🕂 Prices: ⚹6-
7.50 pitch 7.50-9 Facilities: ♠ 🚾 ☉ 🔌 🧺 🅿 Services: ♥ ✗
lau Off-site: ✗ ⊞

SAN FELICE DEL BENACO BRESCIA

Fornella via Fornella 1, 25010
☎ 0365 62294 🖷 0365 559418
e-mail: fornella@fornella.it
website: www.fornella.it
A quiet site in an ideal location on the shore of Lake Garda.
➲ *Signposted from SS572 (Salo-Desenzano).*
Open: 05 May-21 Sep Site: 7.5HEC ⏛ 🕂 🏠 🔌 🜊
Prices: ⚹4.60-7.60 🚐9.30-13.50 🛖9.30-13.50 pitch 9.30-13.50
Facilities: ♠ 🚾 ☉ 🔌 🧺 🅿 Services: ♥ ✗ ⊞ lau Leisure: ⁂ LP

Gardiola via Gardiola 36, 25010
☎ 0365 559240 🖷 0365 557625
e-mail: info@lagardiola.com
website: www.gruppobaiasilvella.com
A terraced site with a wide variety of good facilities on the
shore of Lake Garda. *contd.*

Facilities: 🚾-shop ♠-shower ☉-electric points for razors 🔌-electric points for caravans 🅿-parking by tents permitted
🅿-compulsory separate car park Services: ✗-café/restaurant ♥-bar 🧺-Camping Gaz International 🧺-gas other than Camping
Gaz ⊞-first aid facilities lau-laundry Leisure: ⁂-swimming L-Lake P-Pool R-River S-Sea Off-site: All facilities within 2km

...so unique!!
★★★★
camping villaggio
WEEKEND

Via Vallone della Selva, 2
25010 San Felice del Benaco
(BRESCIA) - Italy
Tel. 0039/036543712
Fax 0039/036542196
Http://www.weekend.it
E-mail: info@weekend.it

Quiet family site, well maintained. Modern sanitary facilities. Free hot water in the showers and basins. Washing machine, bar, restaurant, pizzeria, small shop. Very scenic. 2 swimming pools, children's playing area, volleyball, table tennis, music and dancing in the evenings. Ask for our brochure. Reservations accepted. Caravan, tent and bungalow for hire. New 6 person mobile-homes. Individual washing cubicles.

➲ *S of San Felice del Benaco off SS572.*
Open: Apr-29 Sep Site: 0.4HEC ⾵ 🗗 🏠 🚐 Prices: ⋏3.90-6.80 ⛺2.40-4 pitch 9.30-18 Facilities: 🏪 🏠 ☉ 🏠 🏠 Services: 🍴 ✗ lau Leisure: ⋏ L Off-site: 🏠 ✗ ⌀ 🛁 ⋏P ⊞

Ideal Molino 25010 ☎ 0365 62023 📠 0365 559395
e-mail: info@campingmolino.it
website: www.campingmolino.it
Situated right beside Lake Garda amid beautiful scenery. Charming and quiet site 1km from S. Felice. On the beach there is a pier and boat moorings. Pedal boats can be hired for lake trips.
Open: 23 Mar-Sept Site: 1.7HEC ⾵ 🗗 🏠 🚐 ⌀
Prices: ⋏4.50-7.50 pitch 9.30-15.50 Facilities: 🏪 🏠 ☉ 🏠 🏠
Services: 🍴 ✗ ⊞ lau Leisure: ⋏ L Off-site: ⌀ 🛁

Weekend via Vallone della Selva 2, 25010
☎ 0365 43712 📠 0365 42196
e-mail: info@weekend.it website: www.weekend.it
A quiet family site with modern facilities, situated in a olive grove overlooking Lake Garda.
➲ *Exit A4 at Desenzano following road to Cisano. Signposted S.Felice D/B.*
Open: 24 Apr-26 Sep Site: 9HEC ⾵ 🏠 🏠 Prices: ⋏5-7.50
⋏10.35-14.50 pitch 10.40-15 Facilities: 🏪 🏠 ☉ 🏠 🏠
Services: 🍴 ✗ ⊞ lau Leisure: ⋏ P Off-site: ⌀ 🛁 ⋏L

SAN MARTINO DI CASTROZZA TRENTO

Sass Maor via Laghetto 48, 38058
☎ 0439 68347 📠 0439 68347
e-mail: info@campingsassmaor.it
website: www.campingsassmaor.it
A winter sports site in a beautiful mountain setting.
➲ *From Trento travel to Ora, Cavalese and S.Martino di Castrozza.*
Open: All year Site: 0.2HEC ⋮⋮⋮ ⾴⾵ Prices: ⋏6-8 ⛺9-13
⋏6-8 Facilities: 🏪 🏠 ☉ 🏠 ⌀ 🛁 🏠 Services: 🍴 ✗ lau
Off-site: ⋏LPR ⊞

SAN PIETRO DI CORTENO GOLGI BRESCIA

Villaggio Aprica via Nazionale 507, 25040
☎ 0342 710001 📠 0342 710088
e-mail: apricamp@apricaonline.com
website: www.apricaonline.com/camping
A small natural park ideal for winter skiing and summer walking.
➲ *On SS39 (Aprica-Edolo).*
Open: All year Site: 2.1HEC ⾵ 🗗 🏠 🚐 Prices: ⋏4.80-6
pitch 5.20-10.50 Facilities: 🏪 🏠 ☉ 🏠 ⌀ 🛁 🏠 Services: 🍴 ✗
lau Leisure: ⋏ R Off-site: ⋏LPS ⊞

SAN VIGILIO DI MAREBBE BOLZANO

Al Plan 39030 ☎ 0474 501694 📠 0474 506550
e-mail: camping.alplan@rolmail.net
website: www.campingalplan.com
In a wooded Alpine setting at an altitude of 1200mtrs.
➲ *Access via A22 - Brenner Autostrada.*
Open: Dec-24 Apr & Jun-Nov Site: 1HEC ⾵ ⋮⋮⋮ ⾴ 🏠
Prices: ⋏4.50-7 ⋏5-7 pitch 10-12 Facilities: 🏪 🏠 ☉ 🏠 ⌀ 🛁 🏠
Services: 🍴 ✗ lau Off-site: ⋏PR ⊞

SARRE AOSTA

International Touring 11010
☎ 0165 257061 📠 0165 363907
Flat, wooded site set among the highest mountains in Europe.
➲ *4km W of Aosta on SS26.*
Open: 15 May-15 Sep Site: 6HEC ⾵ 🗗 🏠 🚐 Facilities: 🏪
🏠 ☉ 🏠 ⌀ 🛁 🏠 Services: 🍴 ✗ ⊞ lau Leisure: ⋏ PR

Monte Bianco Fraz St Maurice 3, 11010 ☎ 0165 257523
In wooded surroundings close to the town centre.
➲ *Access via SS26 towards Aosta and Courmayer.*
Open: Apr-Sep Site: 7.5HEC ⾵ 🗗 🏠 Prices: ⋏4.20-4.50
⛺2.03-2.50 ⛺3.60-3.90 ⋏3.60-3.90 Facilities: 🏠 ☉ 🏠 🏠
Services: ⊞ lau Leisure: ⋏ R Off-site: 🏠 🍴 ✗ ⌀ 🛁

SEXTEN BOLZANO

Sexten St-Josefstr 54, 39030 ☎ 0474 710444 📠 0474 710053
e-mail: info@caravanparksexten.it
website: www.caravanparksexten.it
Open: 6 Dec-2 Nov Site: 3HEC ⾵ ⾴ 🏠 Facilities: 🏪 🏠 ☉
🏠 ⌀ 🛁 🏠 Services: 🍴 ✗ lau Leisure: ⋏ PR

SORICO COMO

Au Lac De Como via C-Battisti 18, 22010
☎ 0344 84035 📠 0344 84802
The well-kept site lies on the right of the River Mera as it flows into Lake Como.
➲ *Turn off the SS340d at Km25 near TOTAL petrol station and drive 200mtrs towards the lake.*
Open: All year Site: 17HEC ⾵ 🗗 🏠 🚐 Prices: ⋏6.50 pitch
11 Facilities: 🏪 🏠 ☉ 🏠 ⌀ 🛁 Services: 🍴 ✗ ⊞ lau
Leisure: ⋏ LR

TORBOLE TRENTO

Porto 38069 ☎ 0464 505891 📠 0464 505891
e-mail: alporto@torbole.com
website: www.torbole.com/alporto
A new site with modern facilities, situated in a quiet position near the lake. Ideal for sports and families.
➲ *At Torbole join SS240 from there it is signposted.*
Open: Apr-06 Nov Site: 1.1HEC ⾵ 🗗 🏠 🚐 Prices: ⋏7 pitch 9.50
Facilities: 🏪 ☉ 🏠 ⌀ 🛁 Services: ✗ lau Off-site: 🏠 ✗ ⌀ ⋏LR

TORRE DANIELE TORINO

Mombarone via Nazionale 54, 10010
☎ 0125 757907 📠 0125 757396
➲ *13km N of Ivrea on SS26. Very close to River.*
Open: All year Site: 1.2HEC ⾵ 🗗 🏠 🚐 Prices: ⋏3.50-4
⛺2 ⛺3.50 ⋏3 Facilities: 🏪 ☉ 🏠 🏠 Services: 🍴 ✗ lau
Leisure: ⋏ PR Off-site: 🏠 ✗ ⌀ ⊞

TOSCOLANO MADERNO BRESCIA

Chiaro di Luna via Statale 218, 25088
☎ 0365 641179 📠 0365 641179
website: www.chiarodiluna.org
Open: Apr-29 Sep Site: 9HEC ⾵ ⾴ 🏠 🚐 Prices: ⋏4.30-6 ⛺7-10 ⋏7-10 Facilities: 🏪 🏠 ☉ 🏠 ⌀ 🛁 🏠 Services: 🍴 ✗ lau
Leisure: ⋏ L Off-site: ✗

Site: 6HEC-Site size ⾵-grass ⋮⋮⋮-sand ⾴-stone ⾴-little shade ⾴-partly shaded ⾴-mainly shaded
🏠-bungalows for hire 🚐-caravans for hire ⋏-tents for hire ⌀-no dogs Prices: ⋏-adult per night ⛺-car per night
pp-per person per night ⛺-caravan per night ⋏-tent per night

VALNONTEY AOSTA

Lo Stambecco 11012 ☎ 0165 74152 🖷 0165 749213
e-mail: campingstambecco@tiscali.it
website: www.campinglostambecco.com
Open: 15 May-20 Sep Site: 1.6HEC ⛺ 🏕 Prices: ⚑4.50-5
🚐2.50-3 🚐3.50-4 🛆2.50-4 Facilities: 🏚 ⊙ 🖳 ∅ 🛖 🏛
Services: 🍴 ✗ lau Off-site: 🛒 ✗ 🕀

VIVERONE VERCELLI

Rocca via Lungo Lago 35, 13886 ☎ 0161 98416 🖷 0161 98416
e-mail: Felicitaa@libero.it website: www.la-rocca.org
Open: 15 Mar-15 Oct Site: 1HEC ⛺ 🏕 🚐 Prices: ⚑5 pitch
6.50 Facilities: 🏚 🛒 ⊙ 🖳 🏛 Services: 🍴 ✗ 🕀 lau Leisure: ⚓
P Off-site: ∅ 🛖 ⚓L

VOLS BOLZANO

Seiseralm St Konstantin 16, 39050 ☎ 0471 706459
The site is avaliable all year round for skiers and climbers.
Horse riding/trekking is a major activity.
➲ From Bolzano motorway site is signposted from Fie.
Open: All year Site: 2.5HEC ⛺ 🏕 🏕 Facilities: 🏚 🛒 ⊙
🖳 ∅ 🛖 🏛 Services: 🍴 ✗ lau Off-site: ⚓L

VENICE/NORTH

ARSIE BELLUNO

Gajole Loc Soravigo, 32030 ☎ 0439 58505 🖷 0439 58505
website: www.campinggajole.it
In a delightful, peaceful setting on the shore of Lake Corlo.
➲ Access from SS50 bis.
Open: Apr-29 Sep Site: 1.5HEC ⛺ 🏕 Prices: ⚑4.80 pitch
4.80-5.50 Facilities: 🏚 🛒 ⊙ 🖳 ∅ 🏛 Services: 🍴 ✗ lau
Leisure: ⚓ L

ASIAGO VICENZA

Ekar Loc.Ta' Ekar, 36012 ☎ 0424 455157 🖷 0424 455161
e-mail: campingasiago@keycomm.itg-ekar
website: www.altopiano-asiago.com/camping-ekar
On a level meadow in a striking setting among wooded hills
in a popular skiing region.
Open: 18 May-Sep & 15 Nov-27 Apr Site: 3.5HEC ⛺ 🏕
Facilities: 🏚 🛒 ⊙ 🖳 ∅ 🛖 🏛 Services: 🍴 ✗ 🕀 lau

AURISINA TRIESTE

Imperial Aurisina Cave 55, 34011
☎ 040 200459 🖷 040 200459
e-mail: campimperial@libero.it
website: www.campingimperialcarso.it
A well maintained site in a secluded, wooded location.
➲ Access via SS14 in Sistiana-Aurisina direction.
Open: Jun-29 Sep Site: 1.5HEC ⛺ 🏕 🚐 Prices: ⚑3.50-6
🚐3.50-5 🚐3.50-5 🛆3.50-5 pitch 7-10 Facilities: 🏚 🛒 ⊙ 🖳
🛖 🏛 🅿 Services: ⚓ P Off-site: ✗

BARDOLINO VERONA

Continental Localita Reboin, 37011
☎ 045 7210192 🖷 045 7211756
e-mail: continental@campingarda.it
website: www.campingarda.it
A pleasant site directly on the lake with good, modern
facilities.
Open: Apr-5 Oct Site: 3.5HEC ⛺ 🏕 🚐 Prices: ⚑4.50-6.50
pitch 8.50-13.50 Facilities: 🏚 🛒 ⊙ 🖳 ∅ 🏛 Services: 🍴 ✗ 🕀
lau Leisure: ⚓ L Off-site: ⚓L

Rocca S Pietro, 37011 ☎ 045 7211111 🖷 045 7211300
Subdivided site in slightly sloping grassland broken up by
rows of trees. Separated from the lake by a public path (no
cars). Part of site on the other side of the main road is
terraced amongst vines and olives with lovely view of lake.
➲ Below the SS249 at Km40/IV
Open: 12 Apr-26 Sep Site: 80HEC ⛺ 🏕 🚐 Facilities: 🏚 🛒
⊙ 🖳 🏛 Services: 🍴 ✗ 🕀 lau Leisure: ⚓ LP Off-site: ∅

BIBIONE VENEZIA

Villagio Turistico Internazionale via Colonie 2, 30020
☎ 0431 442611 🖷 0431 43231
e-mail: info@vti.it website: www.vti.it
Mostly sandy terrain under pine trees. Some meadowland
with a few deciduous trees. Wide sandy beach. Tennis court.
➲ Access is well signed along approach.
Open: 12 Apr-23 Sep Site: 13HEC ⛺ 🏕 🏕 🚐
Prices: ⚑3.50-9 🚐3.10-4.70 🚐9-17 🛆9-17 pitch 9-22
Facilities: 🏚 🛒 ⊙ 🖳 ∅ 🛖 🏛 Services: 🍴 ✗ 🕀 lau
Leisure: ⚓ PS

BRENZONE VERONA

Primavera via Benaco 5, 37010 ☎ 045 7420421 🖷 045 7420421
e-mail: info@camping-primavera.com
website: www.camping-primavera.com
Small site on the shore of Lake Garda.
Open: Apr-15 Oct Site: 0.8HEC ⛺ 🏕 🏕 Facilities: 🏚 🛒 ⊙
🖳 ∅ 🛖 🏛 Services: 🍴 ✗ lau Leisure: ⚓ L Off-site: ✗ 🕀

CA'NOGHERA VENEZIA

Alba d'Oro via Triestina 214/B, 30030
☎ 041 5415102 🖷 041 5475971
e-mail: albadoro@tin.it website: www.ecvacanze.it
On level ground directly on the lagoon with good, modern
facilities including moorings for small boats. Regular bus
service to Venice.
➲ Access from SS14.
Open: Feb-Oct Site: 7HEC ⛺ 🏕 🏕 🛆 Facilities: 🏚 🛒 ⊙ 🖳
∅ 🛖 🏛 Services: 🍴 ✗ lau Leisure: ⚓ PR
Off-site: ⚓LS 🕀

CAORLE VENEZIA

San Francesco via Selva Rosata, 25080
☎ 0421 2982 🖷 299284
e-mail: info@villaggiosfrancesco.com
website: www.villaggiosfrancesco.com
This generously laid-out site, on level lawns with shady
poplars, lies in the midst of a holiday village.
➲ Follow signs from Caorle for access.
Open: 12 Apr-29 Sep Site: 32HEC ⛺ 🏕 🏕 🚐 Facilities: 🏚 🛒 ⊙ 🖳 ∅ 🛖 🏛 🅿 Services: 🍴 ✗ 🕀 lau
Leisure: ⚓ PS

CASSONE VERONA

Bellavista 37010 ☎ 045 7420244
In a fine position in an olive grove overlooking Lake Garda
with modern sanitary installations. Access to the lake is by an
underpass and good watersports facilities are available.
Open: All year Site: 27HEC ⛺ 🏕 🏕 🚐 🍽 Facilities: 🏚 🛒
⊙ 🖳 ∅ 🛖 🏛 Services: 🍴 ✗ 🕀 lau Leisure: ⚓ L Off-site: ⚓PR

CASTELLETTO DI BRENZONE VERONA

Maior VIA Croce N.10, 37010
☎ 045 7430333 🖷 045 7430333
A comfortable, modern site in a pleasant, quiet location.
Open: Etr-29 Sep Site: 8HEC ⛺ 🏕 🏕 🚐 Facilities: 🏚 🛒 ⊙
🖳 ∅ 🛖 🏛 Services: 🍴 ✗ lau Off-site: ✗ ⚓L 🕀

Facilities: 🛒-shop **🏚**-shower **⊙**-electric points for razors **🖳**-electric points for caravans **🏛**-parking by tents permitted
🅿-compulsory separate car park **Services: ✗**-café/restaurant **🍴**-bar **∅**-Camping Gaz International **🛖**-gas other than Camping
Gaz **🕀**-first aid facilities lau-laundry **Leisure: ⚓**-swimming L-Lake P-Pool R-River S-Sea **Off-site:** All facilities within 2km

San Zeno via A.Vespucci 91, 37010
☎ 045 7430231 ▓ 045 4430171
e-mail: info@campingsanzeno.it
Situated only a few metres from the lake surrounded by
hundred year old olive groves.
➲ *Exit the southbound motorway from Rovereto at Trento.
The site is 10km S of Malcesine*
Open: May-Sep Site: 1.4HEC ⸗ ♠ ⬛ Prices: ♠4.50-6.30
pitch 7.30-9.90 Facilities: ℝ ⅃ ⊙ ⬛ ⬚ ⬛ ℙ Services: ⬛ ✗ ⊞
Off-site: ✗ � ⅃

CAVALLINO VENEZIA

Cavallino via delle Batterie 164, 30013
☎ 041 966133 ▓ 041 5300827
e-mail: info@campingcavallino.com
website: www.gruppobaiasilvella.com
In a pinewood close to the sea with plenty of recreational
facilities.
Open: 03 Apr-10 Oct Site: 11.4HEC ⸗ ♠ ⬛ ⬛ ⬚
Prices: ♠3.30-8 pitch 9.30-19 Facilities: ℝ ⅃ ⊙ ⬛ ⬚ ⬛
Services: ⬛ ✗ ⊞ lau Leisure: ⬚ PS

Europa via Fausta 332, 30013 ☎ 041 968069 ▓ 041 5370150
e-mail: info@campingeuropa.com
website: www.campingeuropa.com
On grassland reaching to the sea, with some poplars.
Lunchtime siesta 13.00-15.00 hrs.
➲ *Well signposted on Punta Sabbioni road.*
Open: Apr-Sep Site: 11HEC ⸗ ∴ ♠ ⬛ ⬛ Prices: ♠4.10-
7.20 ♠2.90-5.10 ⬛7.90-18.50 ⬛2.90-5.10 pitch 7.90-18.50
Facilities: ℝ ⅃ ⊙ ⬛ ⬚ ⬛ Services: ⬛ ✗ lau Leisure: ⬚ S
Off-site: ⊞

Italy via Fausta 272, 30013 ☎ 041 968090 ▓ 041 5370076
e-mail: info@campingitaly.it website: www.campingitaly.it
Small family-type campsite 6km from Lido di Jesolo on a
peninsula. Venice can be reached by public ferry.
➲ *Brennero/Venezia motorway. Then follow signs for Jesolo-
Cavallino.*
Open: Etr-19 Sep Site: 3.9HEC ⸗ ♠ ⬛ ⬛ ⬚
Prices: ♠4.40-6.70 pitch 7.30-17.40 Facilities: ℝ ⅃ ⊙ ⬛ ⬚ ⬛
Services: ⬛ ✗ lau Leisure: ⬚ PS Off-site: ⊞

Joker via Fausta 318, 30013 ☎ 041 5370766 ▓ 041 968216
e-mail: jokercamping@iol.it website: www.jokercamping.it
Between coastal road and the sandy beach with tall poplars.
Partially subdivided.
Open: May-Sep Site: 4.4HEC ⸗ ♠ ⬛ Å ⬚ Facilities: ℝ
⅃ ⊙ ⬛ ⬚ ⬛ ⬛ Services: ⬛ ✗ ⊞ lau Leisure: ⬚ PS

Residence via F-Baracca 47, 30013
☎ 041 968027 ▓ 041 5370164
e-mail: info@campres.it website: www.campres.it
Well laid out site on level, wooded grassland, by a sandy
beach, between Jesolo and Cavallino. Lunchtime siesta 13.00-
15.00 hrs.
➲ *Signposted.*
Open: 24 Apr-21 Sep Site: 8HEC ∴ ♠ ⬛ ⬛ ⬚
Prices: ♠3.90-7.90 pitch 8.20-18.40 Facilities: ℝ ⅃ ⊙ ⬛ ⬚
⬛ Services: ⬛ ✗ ⊞ lau Leisure: ⬚ PS Off-site: ⬚R

Sant' Angelo via F-Baracca 63, 30013
☎ 041 968882 ▓ 041 5370242
e-mail: info@santangelo.it website: www.santangelo.it
A large beach site decorated by trees and flower beds. Good
entertainment, sports and eating facilities.
➲ *Outside Venice follow signs for Caposile and Jesolo. Crossing
the bridge just after Lido di Jesolo turn right and follow road
round to coast.*
Open: 4 May-21 Sep Site: 16HEC ⸗ ♠ ⬛ ⬛ ⬚
Facilities: ℝ ⅃ ⊙ ⬛ ⬚ ⬛ Services: ⬛ ✗ ⊞ lau Leisure: ⬚ PS

Silva via F-Baracca 53, 30013 ☎ 041 968087 ▓ 041 968087
The site lies on sand and grassland and is located between
road and beach, divided by a vineyard. The section of site
near the beach is quiet.
Open: 10 May-15 Sep Site: 3.3HEC ⸗ ∴ ♠ ⬛
Prices: ♠3-6 ⬛6.50-14 Å6-13 pitch 6.50-14 Facilities: ℝ ⅃
⊙ ⬛ ⬚ ⬛ Services: ⬛ ✗ lau Leisure: ⬚ S Off-site: ⊞

Union-Lido via Fausta 258, 30013
☎ 041 2575111 ▓ 041 5370355
e-mail: info@unionlido.com
website: www.unionlido.it
This large site lies on a long stretch of land next to a 1km-
long beach. Separate section for tents and caravans.
Minimum stay during peak period is one week. Ideal for
families.
➲ *From Tarvisio follow motorway via Udine, San Dona di
Piave then is signposted to Jesolo and Cavallino.*
Open: May-30 Sep Site: 60HEC ⸗ ♠ ⬛ ⬛ ⬚
Prices: ♠5.90-8.50 pitch 10.60-22 Facilities: ℝ ⅃ ⊙ ⬛ ⬚ ⬛
Services: ⬛ ✗ ⊞ lau Leisure: ⬚ PS

Villa al Mare via del Faro 12, 30013
☎ 041 968066 ▓ 041 5370576
e-mail: villaalmare@cavallino.net
website: www.cavallino.net/villaalmare
Level site divided into plots on a peninsula behind the
lighthouse. Direct access to a long, sandy beach.
Open: May-Sep Site: 2HEC ⸗ ♠ ⬛ ⬛ ⬚ Facilities: ℝ ⅃
⊙ ⬛ ⬚ ⬛ Services: ⬛ ✗ ⊞ lau Leisure: ⬚ PS

CHIOGGIA VENEZIA

Miramare via A-Barbarigo 103, 30019
☎ 041 490610 ▓ 041 490610
e-mail: campmir@tin.it
website: www.chioggiacamping.it/miramare
Longish site reaching as far as the beach, clean and well-
maintained.
➲ *Access from Strada Romeo (SS309) in direction of Chioggia
Sottomarina, turn right on reaching beach and continue
500mtrs.*
Open: May-20 Sep Site: 5HEC ⸗ ∴ ♠ ⬚ Facilities: ℝ
⅃ ⊙ ⬛ ⬚ ⬛ ⬛ Services: ⬛ ✗ lau Leisure: ⬚ PS Off-site: ⊞

Villaggio Turistico Isamar via Isamar 9, Isolaverde, 30015
☎ 041 5535811 ▓ 041 490440
e-mail: info@villaggioisamar.com
website: www.villaggioisamar.com
The site lies on level grassland at the mouth of the River
Etsch. Shade is provided by high poplars. Good beach.
➲ *Access via the SS309. Caravans are advised to approach via
Km84/VII near the Brenta village.*
Open: mid May-mid Sep Site: 33HEC ∴ ♠ ⬛ ⬛ ⬚
Prices: ♠3.50-8.80 ⬛5-21.50 pitch 4-21.50 (incl 2 persons)
Facilities: ℝ ⅃ ⊙ ⬛ ⬚ ⬛ Services: ⬛ ✗ ⊞ lau
Leisure: ⬚ PRS

CHIOGGIA SOTTOMARINA VENEZIA

Oasi via A-Barbarigo 147, 30019
☎ 041 490801 ▓ 041 490801
e-mail: info@campingoasi.com
website: www.campingoasi.com
A well equipped site situated on a wooded peninsula near the
mouth of the Brenta River with a wide private beach.
➲ *W of town centre towards the river and the beach.*
Open: Apr-Sep Site: 3HEC ⸗ ♠ ⬛ Prices: ♠4.50-6.50
pitch 8-15 Facilities: ℝ ⅃ ⊙ ⬛ ⬚ ⬛ ⬛ Services: ⬛ ✗ lau
Leisure: ⬚ PRS Off-site: ⊞

Site: 6HEC-Site size ⸗-grass ∴-sand ⬥-stone ⬚-little shade ⬚-partly shaded ♠-mainly shaded
⬛-bungalows for hire ⬛-caravans for hire Å-tents for hire ⬚-no dogs **Prices:** ♠-adult per night ♠-car per night
pp-per person per night ⬛-caravan per night Å-tent per night

CISANO VERONA

Cisano via Peschiera, 37011 ☎ 045 6229098 ▤ 045 6229059
e-mail: cisano@camping-cisano.it
website: www.camping-cisano.it
Quiet, partly terraced site beside Lake Garda with good
watersports facilities and entertainment.
➲ *AFFI exit on Brenner-Verona motorway, access 4km further.*
Open: 29 Mar-3 Oct **Site:** 14HEC ⸺ ♠ ⊞ ⊡ ⊗
Prices: ♠3-8 pitch 8-15.50 **Facilities:** ⚑ ⅃ ⊙ ⊠ ⌀ ᗰ ⊡
Services: ⊻ ✕ ⊞ lau **Leisure:** ⬩ LP

San Vito via Pralesi 3, 37010 ☎ 045 6229026 ▤ 045 6229059
e-mail: cisano@camping-cisano.it
website: www.camping-cisano.it
A tranquil and shady site with many modern facilities.
➲ *Off the Brennero motorway it is signposted to the south of
Cisano.*
Open: 29 Mar-4 Oct **Site:** 5HEC ⸺ ♠ ⊞ ⊡ ⊗ **Prices:** ♠3-
8 pitch 8-15.50 **Facilities:** ⚑ ⅃ ⊙ ⊠ ⌀ ᗰ ⊡ **Services:** ⊻ ✕ ⊞
lau **Leisure:** ⬩ LP

CORTINA D'AMPEZZO BELLUNO

Cortina via Campo 2, 32043 ☎ 0436 867575 ▤ 0436 867917
e-mail: campcortina@tin.it
This site lies amongst pine trees, several hundred metres
away from the edge of town, off the Dolomite road towards
Belluno.
➲ *Turn off road and drive 1km to the campsite which is
situated by a small river.*
Open: All year **Site:** 4.6HEC ⸺ ⦙⦙⦙ ♠ **Prices:** ♠4.50-7.50
pitch 7-9 **Facilities:** ⚑ ⅃ ⊙ ⊠ ⌀ ᗰ ⊡ **Services:** ⊻ ✕ lau
Leisure: ⬩ PR

Dolomiti via Campo di Sotto, 32043
☎ 0436 2485 ▤ 0436 5403
e-mail: campeggiodolomiti@tin.it
The site is beautifully situated on grassland with pine trees in
a hollow, not far from the Olympic ski-jump.
➲ *For access, follow the directions for Camping Cortina. The
camp is then 500mtrs further on 2.7km S of Cortina.*
Open: Jun-19 Sep **Site:** 5.4HEC ⸺ ♠ **Prices:** ♠4.50-7.50
pitch 7-9 **Facilities:** ⚑ ⅃ ⊙ ⊠ ⌀ ᗰ ⊡ **Services:** ⊻ lau
Leisure: ⬩ PR **Off-site:** ✕ ⬩L

Olympia Fiames 1, 32043 ☎ 0436 5057 ▤ 0436 5057
A very beautiful site set in the centre of the centre of the
magnificent Dolomite landscape.
➲ *It lies N of town off the SS51*
Open: 5 Dec-5 Nov **Site:** 4HEC ⸺ ♠ ⊞ ⊡ **Prices:** ♠4.50-
7.50 pitch 7-9 **Facilities:** ⚑ ⅃ ⊙ ⊠ ⌀ ᗰ ⊡ **Services:** ⊻ ✕ ⊞ lau
Leisure: ⬩ R **Off-site:** ⬩LP ⊞

Rocchetta via Campo 1, 32043 ☎ 0436 5063 ▤ 0436 5063
e-mail: camping@sunrise.it
website: www.cortinasunrise.it/oziende/camping
In beautiful wooded surroundings.
➲ *Access S from Cortina via SS51.*
Open: Jun-20 Sep & Dec-15 Apr **Site:** 2.5HEC ⸺ ♠
Facilities: ⚑ ⅃ ⊙ ⊠ ⌀ ᗰ ⊡ **Services:** ⊻ ✕ lau **Leisure:** ⬩ R
Off-site: ✕ ⬩LP

DUINO-AURISINA TRIESTE

AT SISTIANA

Marepinetá 34019 ☎ 040 299264 ▤ 040 299265
A modern site in a pleasant wooded location with a wide
range of recreational facilities. Free bus service to the beach.
➲ *On SS14 near the harbour and beach. Highway A4 Venice-
Trieste, exit Duino 1km on left.*
Open: May-Sep **Site:** 10.8HEC ♠ ♠ ⊞ ⊡ ⊗ **Facilities:** ⚑ ⅃
⊙ ⊠ ⌀ ᗰ ⊡ **Services:** ⊻ ✕ ⊞ lau **Leisure:** ⬩ P **Off-site:** ⬩S

ERACLEA MARE VENEZIA

Portofelice viale dei Fiori 15, 30010
☎ 0421 66021 ▤ 0421 66411
e-mail: info@portofelice.it **website:** www.portofelice.it
A well equipped family village site separated from the beach
by a pinewood. A wide variety of recreational facilities are
available.
➲ *Leave A4 at Venice/Mestre exit and follow signs for Carole
and Eraclea Mare.*
Open: 08 May-18 Sep **Site:** 19HEC ⸺ ♠ ⊞ ⊗
Prices: ♠2.80-7.90 pitch 6.40-17.90 **Facilities:** ⚑ ⅃ ⊙ ⊠ ᗰ
⊡ ⊞ **Services:** ⊻ ✕ ⊞ lau **Leisure:** ⬩ PS **Off-site:** ⬩R

FUSINA VENEZIA VENEZIA

Fusina via Moranzani 79, 30030 ☎ 041 5470055 ▤ 041 5470050
e-mail: info@camping-fusina.com
website: www.camping-fusina.com
This well-equipped site is ideal for those visiting Venice and
the Venetian Lagoon.
Open: All year **Site:** 5.5HEC ⸺ ♠ ⊞ ⊡ ♠ **Prices:** ♠7 ♠14
⊡14 pitch 14 **Facilities:** ⚑ ⅃ ⊙ ⊠ ⌀ ᗰ ⊡ **Services:** ⊻ ✕ ⊞
lau **Leisure:** ⬩ S

GEMONA DEL FRIÚLI UDINE

Ai Pioppi via del Bersaglio 118, 33013
☎ 0432 980358 ▤ 0432 980358
e-mail: bar-camping-taxi@aipioppi.it
website: www.aipioppi.it
Quiet, well equipped site in a pleasant mountain setting.
➲ *1km from town centre via N13.*
Open: 15 Mar-30 Oct **Site:** 11HEC ⸺ ♠ ⊞ ⊡ **Facilities:** ⚑
⊙ ⊠ ⌀ ᗰ ⊡ **Services:** ⊻ ✕ lau **Off-site:** ⬩ ⬩R ⊞

GRADO GORIZIA

Europa 34073 ☎ 0431 80877 ▤ 0431 82284
e-mail: info@villaggioeuropa.com
website: www.villaggioeuropa.com
In level terrain under half grown poplars. Partially in shade
in pine forest.
➲ *On road to Monfalcone, 20km from Palmanova via
Aquileia.*
Open: 10 Apr-26 Sep **Site:** 22HEC ⸺ ⦙⦙⦙ ♠ ⊞ ⊡
Prices: ♠5.50-8.50 pitch 8-17 **Facilities:** ⚑ ⅃ ⊙ ⊠ ⌀ ᗰ ⊡
Services: ⊻ ✕ ⊞ lau **Leisure:** ⬩ PS

Tenuta Primero via Monfalcone 14, 34073
☎ 0431 896900 ▤ 0431 896901
e-mail: info@tenuta-primero.com
website: www.tenuta-primero.com
The site lies in extensive level grassland between the road and
the dam, which is 2metres high along the narrow and level
beach. Tennis court.
➲ *Access from Monfalcone road. Signposted.*
Open: 15 May-Sep **Site:** 20HEC ⦙⦙⦙ ♠ ⊞ ⊗ **Prices:** ♠7-10
pitch 12-16 **Facilities:** ⚑ ⅃ ⊙ ⊠ ⌀ ᗰ ⊡ **Services:** ⊻ ✕ ⊞ lau
Leisure: ⬩ PS

JÉSOLO, LIDO DI VENEZIA

AT JÉSOLO PINETA (6KM E)

Malibu Beach viale Oriente 78, 30017
☎ 0421 362212 ▤ 0421 961338
e-mail: info@campingmalibubeach.com
In a pinewood facing the sea and a fine sandy beach.
➲ *From Venezia via Cavallino on coast road to Cortellazzo.*
Open: 16 May-15 Sep **Site:** 10HEC ⦙⦙⦙ ♠ ⊞ ⊡ ⊗
Prices: ♠4.55-7.25 ♠7.70-15.05 pitch 12.15-18.90
Facilities: ⚑ ⅃ ⊙ ⊠ ⌀ ᗰ ⊡ **Services:** ⊻ ✕ ⊞ lau
Leisure: ⬩ PS

Facilities: ⅃-shop ⚑-shower ⊙-electric points for razors ⊠-electric points for caravans ⊡-parking by tents permitted
⊞-compulsory separate car park **Services:** ✕-café/restaurant ⊻-bar ⌀-Camping Gaz International ᗰ-gas other than Camping
Gaz ⊞-first aid facilities lau-laundry **Leisure:** ⬩-swimming L-Lake P-Pool R-River S-Sea **Off-site:** All facilities within 2km

Waikiki viale Oriente 144, 30017 ☎ 0421 980186 🖷 0421 378040
e-mail: info@campingwaikiki.com
website: www.campingwaikiki.com
A family site in a pine wood with direct access to the beach.
Regular bus service to Venice passes the camp site.
Open: 15 May-12 Sep **Site:** 5.2HEC ▥ ⁙ ♣ ⊗
Prices: ⚑3.50-6.50 ⇌2.60-5.40 pitch 7.75-16.70 **Facilities:** �🖈
🟥 ⊙ 🟐 ∅ 🕋 **Services:** 🍸 ✕ ⊞ lau **Leisure:** 🕂 PS
Off-site: ∅ 🚿 🕂R

LAZISE VERONA

Parc Loc Sentieri, 37017 ☎ 045 7580127 🖷 045 6470150
e-mail: duparc@camping.it website: www.campingduparc.it
Well-kept, lakeside site off main road.
➲ *If approaching from Garda, the site is on S side of Lazise
just after turning for Verona.*
Open: 15 Mar-30 Oct **Site:** 6HEC ▥ ♣ 🟥 🟐
Prices: ⚑5.20-7.20 pitch 10.50-16 **Facilities:** 🖈 🟥 ⊙ 🟐 🕋
Services: 🍸 ✕ lau **Leisure:** 🕂 LP **Off-site:** ∅ 🚿 ⊞

LIDO DI JÉSOLO

LIGNANO SABBIADORO UDINE

Sabbiadoro via Sabbiadoro 8, 33054
☎ 0431 71455 🖷 0431 721355
e-mail: campsab@lignano.it website: www.campingsabbiadoro.it
A peaceful site situated in a pine grove close to the beach.
Open: 12 Apr-28 Sep **Site:** 13HEC ▥ ⁙ ♣ 🟥 🟐
Facilities: 🖈 🟥 ⊙ 🟐 ∅ 🕋 **Services:** 🍸 ✕ ⊞ lau
Leisure: 🕂 P **Off-site:** 🕂S

MALCESINE VERONA

Claudia via Molini 2, 37018 ☎ 045 7400786 🖷 045 7400786
website: www.campingclaudia.it
Flat grassy site only 30mtrs from the lake. Excellent facilities
available, especially for water sports.
➲ *From Rome/Brennero motorway, continue via Trento, Arco,
Torbole, and site is on outskirts of Malcestine.*
Open: Apr-20 Oct **Site:** 1HEC ▥ 🟐 **Prices:** ⚑4.60-5.30
🟥9.40-11 pitch 9.40-11 **Facilities:** 🖈 🟥 ⊙ 🟐 🕋 **Services:** 🍸
✕ lau **Off-site:** ✕ ∅ 🕂L

MALGA CIAPELA BELLUNO

Malga Ciapela Marmolada 32020 ☎ 0437 722064 🖷 0437 722064
e-mail: camping.mc.marmolada@dolomiti.com
A terraced site in tranquil wooded surroundings at the foot
on Mt. Marmolada.
➲ *Take the Bozen exit off the Brenner/Verona motorway.
Follow signs for Canazei, Malga Ciapela and finally the site,
Marmolada.*
Open: Jun-26 Sep, & Dec-25 Apr **Site:** 3HEC ▥ ⊿ 🟐
Prices: ⚑5.20-6.20 ⚖4.50-5.50 pitch 6-7 **Facilities:** 🖈 🟥 🟐
∅ 🚿 🕋 **Services:** 🍸 lau **Leisure:** 🕂 R **Off-site:** ✕

MARGHERA VENEZIA

Jolly delle Querce via A-de-Marchi 7, 30175
☎ 041 920312 🖷 041 920312
The site lies on meadowland scattered with poplars.
➲ *For access, turn off into the Autostrada in Venezia in the
direction of Chioggia on the SS309 and continue for 200mtrs.*
Open: Apr-Oct **Site:** 1.2HEC ▥ 🟐 **Facilities:** 🖈 🟥 ⊙
🟐 ∅ 🚿 🕋 **Services:** 🍸 ✕ ⊞ lau **Off-site:** 🕂PRS

MASARÈ BELLUNO

Alleghe 32022 ☎ 0437 723737 🖷 0437 723874
e-mail: alleghecamp@dolomites.com
website: www.camping.dolomites.com/alleghe
Several terraces on a wooded incline below a road.
Open: 14 Jun-29 Sep/6 Dec-Apr **Site:** 2HEC ▥ ⊿ 🟐 ⊗
Facilities: 🖈 ⊙ 🟐 ∅ 🚿 🟐 **Services:** 🍸 ✕ lau
Off-site: 🟥 ✕ 🕂LP

MESTRE VENEZIA

Venezia via Orlanda 8, 30030 ☎ 041 5312828
A well equipped site on the shore of the Lagoon close to the
causeway with a regular bus service to Venice within easy
reach.
Open: 15 Feb-Nov **Site:** 1.8HEC ▥ ♣ 🟐 **Facilities:** 🖈 🟥 ⊙
🟐 ∅ 🚿 **Services:** 🍸 ✕ lau

MONFALCONE GORIZIA

Isola Panzano Lido via dei Bagni Nuova 171, 34074
☎ 0481 411202 🖷 0481 45958
e-mail: itmargo@yahoo.it website: www.isolapanzanolido.com
Well equipped family site close to the beach.
➲ *A4 (Venezia-Trieste) exit at Monfalcone/Lisert and follow
signs for the sea. Site is signposted from coast.*
Open: 15 May-15 Sep **Site:** 13HEC ▥ ♣ 🟥 🟐 **Facilities:** 🖈
🟥 ⊙ 🟐 ∅ 🚿 🕋 **Services:** 🍸 ✕ ⊞ **Leisure:** 🕂 S

MONTEGROTTO TERME PADOVA

Sporting Center 35036 ☎ 049 793400 🖷 049 8911551
e-mail: sporting@sportingcenter.it
website: www.sportingcenter.it
A peaceful site in a pleasant setting in the Euganean hills
with good facilities including a thermal treatment centre.
Open: Mar-12 Nov **Site:** 6.5HEC ▥ 🟐 **Prices:** ⚑5.30-7.30
🟥9.70-13.60 ⚖7.20-10 **Facilities:** 🖈 ⊙ 🟐 🕋 **Services:** 🍸 ✕
lau **Leisure:** 🕂 P **Off-site:** 🟥 ∅

ORIAGO VENEZIA

Serenissima via Padana 334, 30030 ☎ 041 920286 🖷 041 920286
e-mail: campingserenissima@shineline.it
website: www.campingserenissima.com
A well looked after site with shade provided by the local
woodland. Local bus service every 20 minutes to Venice.

Site: 6HEC-Site size ▥-grass ⁙-sand ⊿-stone 🌿-little shade 🟐-partly shaded ♣-mainly shaded
🟐-bungalows for hire 🟥-caravans for hire ⚖-tents for hire ⊗-no dogs **Prices:** ⚑-adult per night ⇌-car per night
pp-per person per night 🟥-caravan per night ⚖-tent per night

➲ A4 to Venice, SS11 at Oriago.
Open: Etr-10 Nov Site: 2HEC ⚏ ♣ ⛺ 🚐 Prices: ⚑5.60-6.60 pitch 8.80-10.80 Facilities: ⛅ 🛒 ☉ 🚐 𝄕 🏕 Services: ⚑ ✕ lau Leisure: ⚓ R

PACENGO VERONA

Camping Lido via Peschiera 2, 37010
☎ 045 7590611 ▤ 045 7590030
e-mail: info@campinglido.it website: www.campinglido.it
Open: Apr-Oct Site: 10HEC ⚏ ⛺ ♣ Facilities: ⛅ 🛒 ☉ 🚐 𝄕 🏕 Services: ⚑ ✕ lau Leisure: ⚓ LP

PALAFAVERA BELLUNO

Palafavera 32010 ☎ 0437 788506 ▤ 0437 788857
e-mail: palafavera@sunrise.it
website: www.camping.dolomiti.com/palafavera
In a beautiful location in the heart of the Dolomites at an altitude of 1514mtrs. Good, modern sanitary installations and plenty of recreational facilities.
Open: Jun-Sep Site: 5HEC ⚏ 𝄕 ⚶ Prices: ⚑4.50-6 🚐5.50-7.50 ▲3.50-4.50 pitch 5.50-7.50 Facilities: ⛅ 🛒 ☉ 🚐 𝄕 🜲 🏕 Services: ⚑ ✕ 🖾 lau Leisure: ⚓ LPR Off-site: ⚓P

PESCHIERA DEL GARDA VERONA

Bella Italia via Bella Italia 2, 37019
☎ 045 6400688 ▤ 045 6401410
e-mail: bellaitalia@camping-bellaitalia.it
website: www.camping-bellaitalia.it
Extensive lakeside site. No animals or motorcycles allowed.
➲ Turn off Brescia road between Km276.2 and Km275.8 and head towards lake.
Open: 27 Mar-03 Oct Site: 30HEC ⚏ ♣ ⛺ 🚐 ▲ ⚶
Prices: ⚑4-9 pitch 9-18 Facilities: ⛅ 🛒 ☉ 🚐 𝄕 🜲 🏕 Services: ⚑ ✕ 🖾 lau Leisure: ⚓ P Off-site: 𝄕 ⚓LR

Bergamini via Bergamini 51, Porto Bergamini, 37010
☎ 045 7550283 ▤ 045 7550283
Ideal for young families as site has two children's pools and extensive play areas.
➲ Follow signs 'Porto Bergamini'.
Open: May-20 Sep Site: 1.4HEC ⚏ ♣ ⛺ 🚐 Prices: ⚑7-8.50 pitch 12-15 Facilities: ⛅ 🛒 ☉ 🚐 𝄕 🏕 Services: ⚑ ✕ 🖾 lau Leisure: ⚓ LP Off-site: 𝄕 🜲

Garda via Marzan, 37019
☎ 045 7550540 & 7551899 ▤ 045 6400711
A quiet, pleasant site with beach access on the shore of Lake Garda.
➲ Near the town centre, 2km from Milan/Venice motorway exit.
Open: Apr-Sep Site: 20.4HEC ⚏ ♣ ⛺ 🚐 ▲ ⚶ Facilities: ⛅ 🛒 ☉ 🚐 𝄕 🏕 Services: ⚑ ✕ lau Leisure: ⚓ LP Off-site: 𝄕 🜲 ⚓R 🖾

San Benedetto via Bergamini 14, 37010
☎ 045 7550544 ▤ 045 7551512
e-mail: info@campingsanbenedetto.it
website: www.campingsanbenedetto.it
A family site in a fine position overlooking the lake.
Open: Apr-Sep Site: 22HEC ⚏ ♣ ⛺ 🚐 ▲ Facilities: ⛅ 🛒 ☉ 🚐 𝄕 🏕 Services: ⚑ ✕ lau Leisure: ⚓ LP Off-site: 𝄕 🜲 🖾

PORTO SANTA MARGHERITA VENEZIA

Pra'delle Torri Viale Altanea 201, 30021
☎ 0421 299063 ▤ 0421 299035
e-mail: torri@vacanze-natura.it website: www.pradelletorri.it
Extensive site on flat ground.
➲ 3km W at edge of beach.
Open: 03 Apr-25 Sep Site: 65HEC ⚏ 𝄕 ⛺ 🚐 ▲ ⚶
Prices: ⚑3.55-8 pitch 6.80-20.50 Facilities: ⛅ 🛒 ☉ 🚐 𝄕 🜲 🏕 Services: ⚑ ✕ 🖾 lau Leisure: ⚓ PS

PUNTA SABBIONI VENEZIA

Marina di Venezia via Montello 6, 30010
☎ 041 5300955 ▤ 041 966036
Extensive, well-organised and well maintained holiday centre, extremely well appointed, with ample shade by trees. A section of the site is designated for dog owners, caravans and tents.
➲ Access from the coastal road, turn seawards about 500mtrs before the end then continue along narrow asphalt road. Well signposted approach.
Open: 15 Apr-Sep Site: 70HEC ⚏ ⸬ 𝄕 ⛺ 🚐 ▲ Facilities: ⛅ 🛒 ☉ 🚐 𝄕 🏕 Services: ⚑ ✕ 🖾 lau Leisure: ⚓ PS

Miramare Lungomare D-Alighieri 29, 30010
☎ 041 966150 ▤ 041 5301150
e-mail: info@camping-miramare.it
website: www.camping-miramare.it
In a magnificent location overlooking the lagoon.
Open: Apr-Nov Site: 1.8HEC ⚏ 𝄕 ⛺ ⚶ Prices: ⚑4.20-6.10 pitch 8.50-14.70 Facilities: ⛅ 🛒 ☉ 🚐 𝄕 🏕 Services: ⚑ ✕ 🖾 lau Off-site: ⚓S

ROSOLINA MARE ROVIGO

Margherita via Foci Adige 10, 45010 ☎ 0426 68212
A well equipped family site situated between the sea and a pine wood in the Po Delta Park.
Open: May-Sep Site: 6.4HEC ⚏ ⸬ ♣ ⛺ Facilities: ⛅ 🛒 ☉ 🚐 𝄕 🜲 🏕 Services: ⚑ ✕ 🖾 lau Leisure: ⚓ PRS

Rosapineta Strada Nord 24, 45010
☎ 0426 68033 ▤ 0426 68105
e-mail: info@rosapineta.it website: www.rosapineta.com
The site lies in the grounds of an extensive holiday camp. Pitches for caravans and tents are separate.
➲ Take Strada Romea towards Ravenna and drive to the bridge over the River Adige. Continue for 800mtrs, then turn off, cross bridge and head towards Rosolina Mare and Rosapineta (approx 8km).
Open: 9 May-13 Sep Site: 47HEC ⚏ ⸬ 𝄕 ⛺ 🚐 Facilities: ⛅ 🛒 ☉ 🚐 𝄕 🜲 🏕 Services: ⚑ ✕ 🖾 lau Leisure: ⚓ PS Off-site: ⚓R

TREPORTI VENEZIA

Ca' Pasquali Village via Poerio 33, 30010
☎ 041 966110 ▤ 041 5300797
e-mail: info@capasquali.it website: www.capasquali.it
Sandy, meadowland site with poplar and pine trees.
➲ Access from Cavallino-Punta Sabbioni coast road, along an asphalt road for 400mtrs.
Open: 30 Apr-18 Sep Site: 9HEC ⸬ ♣ ⚶ Prices: ⚑4.20-7.60 🚐3.40-7.90 🚐9-21.50 ▲3-8 pi   tch 7.20-16.20 Facilities: ⛅ 🛒 ☉ 🚐 𝄕 🏕 Services: ⚑ ✕ 🖾 lau Leisure: ⚓ PS Off-site: 𝄕 🜲

Facilities: 🛒-shop ⛅-shower ☉-electric points for razors 🚐-electric points for caravans 🏕-parking by tents permitted 🅿-compulsory separate car park **Services:** ✕-café/restaurant ⚑-bar 𝄕-Camping Gaz International 🜲-gas other than Camping Gaz 🖾-first aid facilities lau-laundry **Leisure:** ⚓-swimming L-Lake P-Pool R-River S-Sea **Off-site:** All facilities within 2km

Cá Savio via di Ca`Savio 77, 30010
☎ 041 966017   📠 041 5300707
e-mail: info@casavio.it website: www.casavio.it
A level site along the edge of the sea with private, sandy
beach. Separate pitches for caravans and tents.
⭢ *From Cá Savio, at traffic lights, turn towards the sea and
continue for 500mtrs to the beach.*
Open: May-Sep **Site:** 26.8HEC ∷∷ ♣ 🏠 🚐 ⌘
Prices: ⚦4.41-8.40 🚗9.03-18.37 ▲9.03-18.37 **Facilities:** ☞ 🌡
☉ 🚱 🖳 **Services:** ⛴ ✕ ⊞ **Leisure:** ⚓ PS **Off-site:** ∅

Fiori via Pisani 52, Ca`vio, 30010
☎ 041 966448   📠 041 966724
e-mail: fiori@vacanze-natura.it website: www.defiori.it
The site stretches over a wide area of sand dunes and pine
trees with separate sections for caravans and tents.
⭢ *From A4 at Venice follow coast road via Jesolo to Lido del
Cavallino.*
Open: 24 Apr-9 Oct **Site:** 11HEC ∷∷∷ ♣ 🏠 🚐 ⌘
Prices: ⚦4.30-8.70 ▲6.75-17 pitch 8.25-20.50 **Facilities:** ☞ 🌡
☉ 🚱 🖳 **Services:** ⛴ ✕ ⊞ lau **Leisure:** ⚓ PS **Off-site:** ∅

Mediterráneo via delle Batterie 38, Ca'Vio, 30010
☎ 041 966721   📠 041 966944
e-mail: mediterraneo@vacanze-natura.it
website: campingmediterraneo.it
Slightly hilly grassland site with trees and sunshade roofs.
Lunchtime siesta 13.00-15.00 hrs.
⭢ *Well signposted from Jesolo.*
Open: May-26 Sep **Site:** 17HEC ∷∷∷ ♣ 🏠 🚐 ⌘
Prices: ⚦3.85-8.25 pitch 5.80-20.55 **Facilities:** ☞ 🌡 ☉ 🚱 🖳
Services: ⛴ ✕ ⊞ lau **Leisure:** ⚓ PS **Off-site:** ∅ ⚱ ⚓R

Scarpiland via A-Poerio 14, 30010
☎ 041 966488   📠 041 966488
e-mail: info@scarpiland.com website: www.scarpiland.com
In a beautiful area surrounded by a pinewood with direct
access to the beach and beautiful views of the sea.
Open: 24 Apr-18 Sep **Site:** 4.5HEC ∷∷∷ ♣ 🏠 🚐 ⌘
Prices: ⚦3.60-6.70 pitch 6.70-15.50 **Facilities:** ☞ 🌡 ☉ 🚱 ∅ ⚱
🖳 **Services:** ⛴ ✕ ⊞ lau **Leisure:** ⚓ S

Vicenza Strada Pelosa 239, 36100
☎ 0444 582311   📠 0444 582434
e-mail: camping@.viest.it website: ascom.vi.it/camping
A modern, well-equipped site.
⭢ *Access via A4 exit `Vicenza-Est'.*
Open: Apr-Sep **Site:** 3HEC ∷∷∷ ♣ 🏠 🚐 **Prices:** ⚦5-6.50
🚗4.75-6.50 🚐10-13 **Facilities:** ☞ ☉ 🚱 🖳 **Services:** ⛴ ✕ lau
Off-site: 🌡 ✕ ∅ ⚓R

Pala Favera 32010 ☎ 0437 788506 & 789161   📠 0437 788857
e-mail: palafavera@sunrise.it
Site with some woodland, at the foot of Monte Pelmo.
Open: Dec-Apr & Jun-Sep **Site:** 5HEC ∷∷∷ ♣ 🔆 ⌘
Facilities: ☞ 🌡 ☉ 🚱 ∅ ⚱ 🖳 **Services:** ⛴ ✕ lau **Leisure:** ⚓ R
Off-site: ⚓P ⊞

NORTH WEST/MED COAST

Bella Vista Campochiesa, Reg Campore 23, 17031
☎ 0182 540213   📠 0182 554925
e-mail: info@campingbellavista.it
website: www.campingbellavista.it
A friendly, family orientated site with good facilities. Pitches
are divided by bushes and flowerbeds.

⭢ *1km from Km613.5 on SS1.*
Open: All year **Site:** 0.8HEC ∷∷∷ 🔆 🏠 🚐 **Prices:** ⚦2.20-4.50
🚗2.20-4.50 pitch 14-25 (incl 2 persons) **Facilities:** ☞ 🌡 ☉
🚱 🖳 **Services:** ⛴ ⊞ lau **Leisure:** ⚓ P **Off-site:** ✕ ⚓S

Roma Regione Foce, 17031 ☎ 0182 52317   📠 0182 555075
e-mail: info@campingroma.com
website: www.campingroma.com
The site is divided into pitches and laid out with many flower
beds.
⭢ *N of bridge over Centa, turn left.*
Open: Apr-29 Sep **Site:** 1HEC ∷∷∷ ♣ 🏠 **Prices:** ⚦4.50-6
▲5.50-8.50 pitch 11-17 **Facilities:** ☞ 🌡 ☉ 🚱 🖳 **Services:** ⛴ ✕
lau **Leisure:** ⚓ RS **Off-site:** ∅ ⚱ ⚓P ⊞

Acapulco via Aurelia Km155, 58010
☎ 0564 870165   📠 870165
e-mail: www.campeggioacapulco@virgilio.it
website: www.campeggioacapulco.interfree.it
Set on hilly terrain in pine woodland.
⭢ *Take coast road from via Aurelia at Km155.*
Open: May-14 Sep **Site:** 2HEC ∷∷∷ ♣ 🚐 ⌘ **Prices:** ⚦4.20-
8.50 pitch 6-12 **Facilities:** ☞ 🌡 ☉ 🚱 ∅ ⚱ 🖳 **Services:** ⛴ ✕ ⊞
lau **Leisure:** ⚓ S

Il Gabbiano 58010 ☎ 0564 870202   📠 0564 870470
Site in pine woodland and open meadowland with sunshade
roofing.
⭢ *Turn off SS at Km155.*
Open: Apr-Sep **Site:** 2.5HEC ∷∷∷ ♣ 🏠 🚐 **Facilities:** ☞
🌡 ☉ 🚱 ∅ 🖳 **Services:** ⛴ ✕ ⊞ lau **Leisure:** ⚓ S

Hawaii 58010 ☎ 0564 870164   📠 0564 872952
e-mail: hawaiigr@libero.it website: www.campinghawaii.it
The site lies in a pine forest on rather hilly ground.
⭢ *Turn off via Aurelia at Km154/V and drive towards the sea.*
Open: 16 Apr-27 Sep **Site:** 4HEC ∷∷∷ ♣ 🏠 ⌘
Facilities: ☞ 🌡 ☉ 🚱 ∅ 🖳 **Services:** ⛴ ✕ ⊞ lau **Leisure:** ⚓ S

Semifonte 50021 ☎ 055 8075454   📠 055 8075454
e-mail: semifonte@semifonte.it website: www.semifonte.it
Terraced site with pitches of varying sizes
Open: 15 Mar-20 Oct **Site:** 1.7HEC ∷∷∷ 🔆 🏠 **Facilities:** ☞
🚱 **Services:** lau **Leisure:** ⚓ P **Off-site:** 🌡 ✕

See also Forte di Bibbona
Capanne via Aurelia KM.273, 57020
☎ 0586 600064   📠 0586 600198
e-mail: info@campinglecapanne.it
website: www.campinglecapanne.it
A pleasant family site situated in a spacious wooded park
amid magnificent Tuscan scenery. The pitches are well
defined and there is a wide variety of recreational facilities.
⭢ *Access from Km273 via Aurelia travelling inland.*
Open: May-Sep **Site:** 6HEC ∷∷∷ 🔆 🏠 ☉ 🚱 ∅ ⚱ **Prices:** ⚦4.50-
8.30 pitch 7.80-13.60 **Facilities:** ☞ 🌡 ☉ 🚱 ∅ ⚱ 🖳
Services: ⛴ ✕ ⊞ lau **Leisure:** ⚓ P **Off-site:** ⚓S

Capannino via Cavalleggeri Sud 26, 57020
☎ 0586 600252   📠 0565 600720
e-mail: capannino@capannino.it website: www.capannino.it
Well tended park site in pine woodland with private beach.
⭢ *On via Aurelia by Km272/VII turn towards sea.*
Open: May-15 Sep **Site:** 3HEC ∷∷∷ 🔆 🏠 🚐 **Prices:** ⚦5-
9 🚗2-4 🚐8-11 ▲8-11 pitch 10-15 **Facilities:** ☞ 🌡 ☉ 🚱 ∅ ⚱
🖳 **Services:** ⛴ ✕ ⊞ lau **Leisure:** ⚓ S

Site: 6HEC-Site size ∷∷∷-grass ∷∷∷-sand ⬡-stone ⭹-little shade 🔆-partly shaded ♣-mainly shaded
🏠-bungalows for hire 🚐-caravans for hire ▲-tents for hire ⌘-no dogs **Prices:** ⚦-adult per night 🚗-car per night
pp-per person per night 🚐-caravan per night ▲-tent per night

Casa di Caccia via del Mare 40, La Calafornia, 57020
☎ 0586 600000 📠 0586 600000
e-mail: info@campingcasadicaccia.com
website: www.campingcasadicaccia.com
A tranquil site by the sea direct access to a private beach.
➲ From the A12 exit Rosignano and join SS follow signs for
Cecina. 6km exit "La California" site in a further 3km south.
Open: 15 Mar-30 Oct Site: 3.5HEC ∷∷ ♠ ⊞ ⊘ Prices: ♠4-
8.50 ♠3-4.50 ⊞6.50-10.50 ▲6.50-10.50 Facilities: ℕ ☎
⊞ ⊘ ≞ 🖭 Services: ▮ ✕ ⊞ lau Leisure: ⭐ S

Forte via dei Platani 58, 57020 ☎ 0586 600155 📠 0586 600123
e-mail: campeggiodelforte@campeggiodelforte.it
website: www.campeggiodelforte.it
Level site, grassy, sandy terrain.
Open: 29 Mar-22 Sep Site: 8HEC ⬛⬛⬛ ♠ ⊞ ⊘
Prices: ♠4.10-7 ♠2.20-3 ⊞7.10-10.70 ▲7.10-10.70
Facilities: ℕ ☎ ⊙ 🖭 ⊘ ≞ 🖭 Services: ▮ ✕ ⊞ lau Leisure: ⭐
P Off-site: ⭐S

Free Beach via Cavalleggeri Nord 88, 57020
☎ 0586 600388 📠 0586 602984
e-mail: umberto.free@tiscali.it
website: http://travel.to/freebeach
Situated 300mtrs from the sea through pine woods.
➲ From the SS206 at Cecina follow signs to S. Guido.
Open: 08 Apr-03 Oct Site: 9HEC ⬛⬛⬛ ∷∷ ☼ ⊞ Prices: ♠10
♠5 ⊞13 ▲8.50 pitch 13 Facilities: ℕ ☎ ⊙ 🖭 ⊘ ≞ 🖭
Services: ▮ ✕ lau Leisure: ⭐ LP Off-site: ⭐S

Il Gineprino via dei Platani 56a, 57020
☎ 0586 600550 📠 0586 600550
e-mail: ilgineprino@tiscalinet.it
website: www.ilgineprino.it
A modern site situated on the Tuscany coast and shaded by a
pine wood. There are good recreational facilities and the
beach is within 300mtrs.
➲ Access via motorway exit 'La California' for Marina di Bibbona.
Site: 1.5HEC ⬛⬛⬛ ♠ ⊞ 🖭 Prices: ♠6-10 ⊞8-13 ▲8-13 pitch
8-13 Facilities: ℕ ☎ ⊙ 🖭 ≞ 🖭 Services: ▮ ✕ lau Leisure: ⭐
P Off-site: ⊘ ⭐S ⊞

BOGLIASCO GENOVA

Genova Est via Marconi, Cassa, 16031
☎ 010 3472053 📠 010 3472053
e-mail: camping@dada.it
website: www.camping-genova-est.it
Quiet and shady site 1km from the sea. A free bus service
operates from the site to the railway station for links to
Genoa and Portofino.
➲ Exit A12 at Nervi, then 8km east.
Open: 10 Mar-2 Nov Site: 1.2HEC ⬛⬛⬛ ♠ ⊞ 🖭 Prices: ♠5-
5.30 ♠2.80 ⊞5.40-5.70 ▲4.60-7 Facilities: ℕ ☎ ⊙ 🖭 ⊘
Services: ▮ ✕ lau Off-site: ≞ ⭐PS ⊞

BORDIGHERA IMPERIA

Baia La Ruota via Madonna della Ruota 34, 18012
☎ 0184 265222
A well equipped holiday village with direct access to a private beach.
➲ Access via A10.
Open: Apr-Oct Site: 1.5HEC ◊ ♠ ⊞ ⊘ Facilities: ℕ ☎ ⊙
🖭 🖭 Services: ▮ ✕ ⊞ Leisure: ⭐ S

If you are dissatisfied with any
aspect of a campsite, discuss the
problem at the time with a
member of staff

BOTTAI FIRENZE

Internationale Firenze via S Cristoforo 2, 50029
☎ 055 2374704 📠 055 2373412
e-mail: internazionale@florencecamping.it
website: www.campingflorence.com
Situated on the welcoming Florentine hills this site offers a
restful atmosphere close to many historic places.
Open: Apr-29 Oct Site: 6HEC ⬛⬛⬛ ◊ ☼ ⊞ 🖭 Prices: ♠8.50
pitch 14 Facilities: ℕ ☎ ⊙ 🖭 ⊘ 🖭 Services: ▮ ✕ lau
Leisure: ⭐ P Off-site: ≞ ⭐LR ⊞

CALENZANO FIRENZE

Autosole via V-Emanuele 11, 50041
☎ 055 8827819 📠 055 8827819
➲ Motorway A1 exit "Calenzano-Sesto Fiorentino" at the
traffic light on the L - 200mtrs on L
Open: All year Site: 2.2HEC ⬛⬛⬛ ♠ Facilities: ℕ ☎ ⊙ 🖭 🖭
Services: lau Leisure: ⭐ P
Off-site: ☎ ℕ ✕ ≞

CAPALBIO GROSSETO

Costa d'Argento Monte Alzato, 58010
☎ 0564 893007 📠 0564 893107
e-mail: info@costadargento.it website: www.costadargento.it
A camping village in the middle of a nature park - 1km from
the Maremma coast.
Camping Card Compulsory.
➲ 12km from Orbetello via SS Aurelia.
Open: Apr-Sep Site: 6HEC ⬛⬛⬛ ♠ ⊞ 🖭 Facilities: ℕ ☎ ⊙
🖭 ⊘ 🖭 Services: ▮ ✕ ⊞ lau Leisure: ⭐ P Off-site: ⭐S

CAPANNOLE AREZZO

Chiocciola via G-Cesare 14, 52020
☎ 055 995776 📠 055 995776
e-mail: tourcountry@virgilio.it
website: www.campinglachiocciola.com
A modern site in a rural setting among chestnut trees at an
altitude of 250mtrs.
Open: 15 Mar-15 Oct Site: 3HEC ⬛⬛⬛ ♠ ⊞ ▲ Prices: ♠7-8
♠2.50-3 ⊞9-10 ▲8-9 Facilities: ℕ ☎ ⊙ 🖭 ⊘ ≞ 🖭
Services: ▮ ✕ ⊞ lau Leisure: ⭐ P Off-site: ⭐LR

CASALE MARITTIMO PISA

Valle Gaia 56040 ☎ 0586 681236 📠 0586 683551
e-mail: info@vallegaia.it website: www.vallegaia.it
Site amongst pines and olive trees in a quiet rural location.
➲ In Southern Cecina heading south from Livorno take the
autostrada/superstrada then take 2nd exit for Cecina (Casale
Marittimo - ignore first signpost for Cecina S Pietro). Camp is
signposted.
Open: 10 Apr-16 Oct Site: 4HEC ⬛⬛⬛ ♠ ⊞ Prices: ♠4.30-
7.40 pitch 8.10-13.40 Facilities: ℕ ☎ ⊙ 🖭 ⊘ 🖭 Services: ▮ ✕
⊞ lau Leisure: ⭐ P Off-site: ⭐S

CASTAGNETO CARDUCCI LIVORNO

Climatico Le Pianacce via Bolgherese, 57022
☎ 0565 763667 📠 0565 766085
e-mail: info@campinglepianacce.it
website: www.campinglepianacce.it
Terraced site on slopes of mountain in typical Tuscany
landscape, enhanced by site landscaping. Pleasant climate
due to height.
➲ Turn off via Aurelia at Km344/VIII in direction of
Castagneto Carducci/Sassetta. In 3.2km to left in direction of
Bolgheri, in 500mtrs turn right towards mountains.
Open: 13 Apr-11 Oct Site: 9HEC ∷∷ ♠ ⊞ ⊘ Prices: ♠4.80-
8.60 pitch 8.20-14 Facilities: ℕ ☎ ⊙ 🖭 ⊘ ≞ 🖭 Services: ▮ ✕
⊞ lau Leisure: ⭐ P

Facilities: ☎-shop ℕ-shower ⊙-electric points for razors 🖭-electric points for caravans 🖭-parking by tents permitted
🖭-compulsory separate car park **Services:** ✕-café/restaurant ▮-bar ⊘-Camping Gaz International ≞-gas other than Camping
Gaz ⊞-first aid facilities lau-laundry **Leisure:** ⭐-swimming L-Lake P-Pool R-River S-Sea **Off-site:** All facilities within 2km

CASTEL DEL PIANO GROSSETO

Amiata via Roma 15, 58033 ☎ 0564 955107 ▤ 0564 955107
e-mail: info@amiata.org website: www.amiata.org
A grassland site with a separate section for dog owners.
➲ *On the outskirts of Castel del Piano, on the national road
(SS) 323, towards Arcidosso.*
Open: All year Site: 4.2HEC ⊞ ♣ 🏠 Prices: ⚥5-6.20 pitch
5-6.20 Facilities: ⚑ ⚱ ⊙ 🖭 ⌀ ⚏ 🅿 Services: 🍽 ✕ 🖃 lau
Off-site: ⚥P 🖃

CASTIGLIONE DELLA PESCAIA GROSSETO

Santa Pomata Strada della Rocchette, 58043
☎ 0564 941037 ▤ 0564 941221
e-mail: info@campingsantapomata.it
website: www.campingsantapomata.it
Site in hilly woodland terrain with some pitches amongst
bushes. Flat clean sandy beach.
➲ *Turn off the SS322 at Km20, then in direction of Le
Rocchette 4.5km NW and continue towards the sea for 1km to
site on left.*
Open: Apr-20 Oct Site: 6HEC ⊞ ⠇⠇ ♣ 🏠 🚐 Prices: ⚥6-8
🚐7-13 ⚑7-13 Facilities: ⚑ ⚱ ⊙ 🖭 ⌀ ⚏ 🅿 Services: 🍽 ✕ 🖃
lau Leisure: ⚥ S

CERIALE SAVONA

Baciccia via Torino 19, 17023
☎ 0182 990743 ▤ 0182 993839
e-mail: info@campingbaciccia.it
website: www.campingbaciccia.it
An orderly site, lying inland off the via Aurelia, 500mtrs from
the sea.
➲ *Entrance 100mtrs W of Km612/V.*
Open: All year Site: 1.2HEC ⊞ ♣ 🏠 🚐 Facilities: ⚑ ⚱ ⊙
🖭 ⌀ ⚏ 🅿 Services: 🍽 ✕ lau Leisure: ⚥ P Off-site: ✕ ⚏ ⚥S 🖃

CERVO IMPERIA

Lino via N Sauro 4, 18010
☎ 0183 400087 ▤ 0183 400089
e-mail: info@campinglino.it website: www.campinglino.it
A seaside site shaded by grape vines, which is clean and well
managed. There is a knee-deep lagoon suitable for children.
➲ *Turn off via Aurelia at Km637/V near the railway
underpass and follow via Nazionale Sauro towards sea.*
Open: Apr-Oct Site: 1.1HEC ⠇⠇ ♣ 🏠 🚐 Prices: pitch 19-
43 (incl 2 persons) Facilities: ⚑ ⚱ ⊙ 🖭 ⌀ ⚏ 🏠 Services: 🍽
✕ 🖃 lau Off-site: ⚥PS

CUTIGLIANO PISTOIA

Betulle via Cantamaggio 6, 51024 ☎ 0573 68004
A pleasant year-round site with good facilities in a central
location with access to three popular ski stations.
Open: All year Site: 4HEC ⠿⠿ ♣ 🏠 Facilities: ⚑ ⚱ ⊙ 🖭 🏠
Services: 🍽 ✕ lau Leisure: ⚥ LR

DEIVA MARINA LA SPEZIA

La Sfinge Gea 5, 19013 ☎ 0187 825284 ▤ 0187 825464
e-mail: lasfinge@camping.it
website: www.camping.it/liguria/lasfinge
Partly terraced site in pleasant wooded surroundings. Ideal
for both nature lovers and families.
➲ *Access via A12 Genova-La Spezia.*
Open: All year Site: 1.8HEC ⠿⠿ ♣ Prices: ⚥6 🚗3 🚐8-13
⚑8-13 Facilities: ⚑ ⚱ ⊙ 🖭 ⌀ ⚏ 🏠 🅿 Services: 🍽 ✕ 🖃 lau
Leisure: ⚥ RS Off-site: ✕

Villaggio Turistico Arenella Arenella, 19013
☎ 0187 825259 ▤ 0187 815861 / 826884
e-mail: campingarenella@libero.it
website: www.campingarenella.it
In a beautiful, quiet valley 1.5km from the sea with good
facilities.
➲ *Access via A12 (Genoa-La Spezia).*
Open: Jan-Oct & Dec Site: 16.2HEC ⠇⠇ ♣ 🏠 Prices: ⚥6.20-
7.25 🚗1.55 🚐6.20-7.25 ⚑5.20-6.20 Facilities: ⚑ ⚱ ⊙ 🖭 🅿
Services: 🍽 ✕ lau Off-site: ⚏ 🍽 ✕ ⌀ ⚏ ⚥S 🖃

See advertisement on page 271

ELBA, ISOLA D' LIVORNO

LACONA

Lacona Pineta Lacona CP 186, 57037
☎ 0565 964322 ▤ 0565 964087
e-mail: info@campinglaconapineta.com
website: www.campinglaconapineta.com
In a picturesque location on a thickly wooded hillside sloping
gently towards a sandy beach with plenty of recreational
facilities.
Open: Apr-Oct Site: 4HEC ⚌ ♣ 🏠 Facilities: ⚑ ⚱ ⊙ 🖭 ⌀ 🅿
Services: 🍽 ✕ 🖃 lau Leisure: ⚥ S Off-site: ⌀

NISPORTO

Sole e Mare 57039 ☎ 0565 934907 ▤ 0565 961180
e-mail: gschezzini@tiscalinet.it
A well equipped, modern site in pleasant wooded
surroundings close to the beach. A wide variety of
recreational facilities are available.
➲ *From Portoferraio take Porto Azzurro road, then turn
towards Rio nell'Elba-Nisporto.*
Open: Apr-15 Oct Site: 2HEC ⠿⠿ ♣ 🏠 🚐 Facilities: ⚑ ⚱
⊙ 🖭 ⌀ ⚏ 🅿 Services: 🍽 ✕ 🖃 lau Leisure: ⚥ S

ORTANO

Canapai Loc Ortano, 57038 ☎ 0565 939165
Camping Card Compulsory.
Open: Apr-Sep Site: 4HEC ⬛ ∷ ♠ 🏠 🚐 Facilities: 🏪 🚿
⊙ 🔌 🅰 Services: ⚑ ✗ ⊞ Leisure: ⚓ P Off-site: ⚓S

OTTONE

Rosselba le Palme Ottone 3, 57037
☎ 0565 933101　🗐 0565 933041
e-mail: info@rosselbalepalme.it
website: www.rosselbalepalme.it
Pitches are on varying heights up from the beach. Shade is
provided by large palm trees.
➲ 8km from Portferraio around bay via Bivo Bagnaia.
Open: 25 Apr-Sep Site: 30HEC ⬛ ♠ 🏠 Prices: 🛏6-13 🚗2-
4.70 🚐9-17.50 🅰5-12.60 pitch 6.50-15 Facilities: 🏪 🚿 ⊙ 🔌
🅰 Services: ⚑ ✗ ⊞ lau Leisure: ⚓ PS

PORTO AZZURRO

Reale 57036 ☎ 0565 95678　🗐 0565 920127
e-mail: campingreale@tin.it
website: www.isolaelbacampingreale.com
A well equipped site in a wooded location with direct access
to the beach.
➲ From Portoferraio take the Porto Azzurro road for 13km,
then head towards Rio Marina for 2km and follow signposts.
Open: Apr-5 Oct Site: 2.5HEC ⬛ ♠ 🏠 Facilities: 🏪 🚿 ⊙
🔌 🅰 Services: ⚑ ✗ lau Leisure: ⚓ S Off-site: ⚓P ⊞

PORTOFERRAIO

Acquaviva Acquaviva, 57037 ☎ 0565 930674　🗐 0565 915592
e-mail: campingacquaviva@elbalink.it
website: www.campingacquaviva.it
This seafront site is surrounded by trees and has excellent
facilities for scuba diving, watersports etc.
➲ 3km W of town.
Open: Etr-Oct Site: 1.7HEC ⬛ ∷ ♠ 🏠 🚐 Prices: 🛏6-11
🚗1.30-2.50 🚐7.50-12 🅰7-12 Facilities: 🏪 🚿 ⊙ 🔌 🅰 🚽 ⊞ 🅿
Services: ⚑ ✗ lau Leisure: ⚓ S

Enfola Enfola, Casella Postale 147, 57037
☎ 0565 939001　🗐 0565 918613
e-mail: info@campingenfola.it
website: www.campingenfola.it
Located on the Isle of Elba, ideal for scuba-diving, sailing and
sunshine.
Open: Etr-Oct Site: 0.8HEC ⬛ ♠ 🏠 🚐 Prices: 🛏6-11 🚗2-
2.50 🚐8.50-14.50 🅰6-14.50 Facilities: 🏪 🚿 ⊙ 🔌 🅰 ⊞
Services: ⚑ ✗ lau Off-site: ⚓S

Scaglieri via Biodola 1, Casella Postale 158, 57037
☎ 0565 969940　🗐 0565 969834
e-mail: info@campingscaglieri.it
website: www.campingscaglieri.it
Sloping terraces 10mtrs from the sea make up this site.
Facilities such as tennis and golf are avaliable at the nearby
Hotel Hermitage.
➲ The island is accessable by plane and ferry. The site is on
the north coast 7km from Portoferraio.
Open: 12 Apr-17 Oct Site: 1.7HEC ∷ ♠ 🏠 Facilities: 🏪 🚿
⊙ 🔌 🅰 Services: ⚑ ✗ lau Leisure: ⚓ P Off-site: ⚓S

FIÉSOLE FIRENZE

Panoramico via Peramonda 1, 50014
☎ 055 599069　🗐 055 59186
e-mail: panoramico@florencecamping.com
website: www.florencecamping.com
Site stretches over wide terraces on the Fiesole hillside
surrounded by a variety of tall evergreens.
➲ Exit A1 at Firenze Sud, follow signs through the city to
Fiesole. Site is on SS Bolognese.
Open: All year Site: 5HEC ∷ 🔆 ♠ 🏠 🚐 Prices: 🛏9 🚗14.50
🚐14.50 pitch 14.50 Facilities: 🏪 🚿 ⊙ 🔌 🅰 🚽 Services: ⚑ ✗
lau Leisure: ⚓ P Off-site: 🚽

FIGLINE VALDARNO FIRENZE

Norcenni Girasole via Norcenni 7, 50063
☎ 055 915141　🗐 055 9151402
e-mail: girasole@ecvacanze.it
website: www.ecvacanze.it
Terraced site on partial slope. Separate section for young
people.
➲ From Florence take Roma A1/E35 autostrada & exit in
incisa - Turn L on rd 69 towards Figline, turn R for Greve &
look for Camping Girasole signs.
Site: 12HEC ⬛ 🔆 ♠ 🅰 Prices: 🛏6.80-9.70 🚗3.90-5.40
🚐6.10-8.40 🅰5.70-7.80 pitch 10-13.80 Facilities: 🏪 🚿 ⊙ 🔌
🅰 🚽 🚽 Services: ⚑ ✗ ⊞ lau Leisure: ⚓ PR

FIRENZE (FLORENCE) FIRENZE

See also Troghi

Semifonte via Ugo Foscolo 4, Barberino Val d'Elsa, 50021
☎ 055 8075454　🗐 055 8075454
e-mail: semifonte@semifonte.it website: www.semifonte.it
A peaceful, terraced site offering panoramic views over the
Chianti Hills. Regular bus services to Firenze and Siena.
➲ 25km S of Firenze and N of Barberino Val d'Elsa.
Open: 15 Mar-20 Oct Site: 1.6HEC ⬛ 🔆 Facilities: 🏪 🚿 ⊙
🔌 🅰 🚽 Services: lau Leisure: ⚓ P Off-site: ⚑ ✗ ⊞

Facilities: 🚿-shop 🏪-shower ⊙-electric points for razors 🔌-electric points for caravans 🚽-parking by tents permitted
🅿-compulsory separate car park Services: ✗-café/restaurant ⚑-bar 🅰-Camping Gaz International 🚽-gas other than Camping
Gaz ⊞-first aid facilities lau-laundry Leisure: ⚓-swimming L-Lake P-Pool R-River S-Sea Off-site: All facilities within 2km

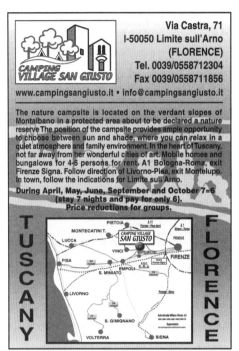

Via Castra, 71
I-50050 Limite sull'Arno
(FLORENCE)
Tel. 0039/0558712304
Fax 0039/0558711856
www.campingsangiusto.it • info@campingsangiusto.it

The nature campsite is located on the verdant slopes of Montalbano in a protected area about to be declared a nature reserve The position of the campsite provides ample opportunity to choose between sun and shade, where you can relax in a quiet atmosphere and family environment. In the heart of Tuscany, not far away from her wonderful cities of art. Mobile homes and bungalows for 4-6 persons for rent. A1 Bologna-Roma, exit Firenze Signa. Follow direction of Livorno-Pisa, exit Montelupo. In town, follow the indications for Limite sull'Arno.

During April, May, June, September and October 7=6
(stay 7 nights and pay for only 6).
Price reductions for groups.

AT **MARCIALLA**

Toscana Colliverdi via Marcialla 349, Certaldo, 50020
☎ 0571 669334 ▤ 0571 669334
e-mail: toscolverdi@virgilio.it
website: www.toscanacolliverdi.it
A sloping, terraced site with good facilities, surrounded by vineyards and olive groves.
➲ Access via 'Firenze-Certosa' exit on Autostrada del Sole or 'Tavarnelle Valpesa' exit on Autostrada del Palio.
Open: Apr-Sep Site: 2.2HEC ⏛ ⚘ Prices: ⋔6-6.50 ⇜1.50-2 ⊞7.50-8 ⛺5.50-8 pitch 7.50-8 Facilities: ⬟ ⚍ ☉ ⬙ ∅ ☒ Services: ⬤ ✕ ⊞ lau Leisure: ⇗ P Off-site: ⬙ ⬤ ✕

FLORENCE SEE **FIRENZE**

GROSSETO, MARINA DI GROSSETO

La Marze St Statale della Collacchie, 58046
☎ 0564 35501 ▤ 0564 35534
e-mail: lemarze@ecvacanze.it website: www.ecvacanze.it
➲ Access via SS322.
Open: May-03 Oct Site: 20HEC ⏛ ⣿ ⚘ ⛺ ⚑ Prices: ⋔5.90-9.90 ⇜3.50-5.40 ⊞5.40-7.50 ⛺5.10-7.90 Facilities: ⬟ ⚍ ☉ ⬙ ∅ ☒ ⬙ Services: ⬤ ✕ ⊞ lau Leisure: ⇗ PS

Rosmarina via delle Colonie 37, 58046
☎ 0564 36319 ▤ 0564 34758
e-mail: info@campingrosmarina.it
website: www.campingrosmarina.it
A modern site situated in a pine wood and close to the sea, with beautiful views. Various sports and entertainments for everyone to enjoy.
Open: May-Sep Site: 1.4HEC ⣿ ⚘ ⛺ ⚑ Prices: ⋔6-11 ⛺5-8 pitch 7-14 Facilities: ⬟ ⚍ ☉ ⬙ ∅ ☒ Services: ⬤ ✕ ⊞ lau Off-site: ⇗S

LERICI LA SPEZIA

Maralunga via Carpanini 61, Maralunga, 19032
☎ 0187 966589 ▤ 0187 966589
This terraced site is directly on the seafront and surrounded by olive groves.
➲ Access from Sarzana-La Spezia motorway.
Open: Jun-29 Sep Site: 10HEC ⬙ ⚘ Prices: ⋔7-9.20 ⇜6.30-7.70 ⊞11.80-13.80 ⛺8-13.20 Facilities: ⬟ ⚍ ☉ ⬙ ∅ ☒ Services: ⬤ ✕ ⊞ Leisure: ⇗ S Off-site: ✕

LIMITE FIRENZE

San Giusto via Castra 71, 50050
☎ 055 8712304 ▤ 055 8711856
A useful site on slightly sloping ground within easy reach of Florence by car or public transport.
Open: Etr-Oct Site: 2.5HEC ⏛ ⚑ ⣿ ⚑ Facilities: ⬟ ☉ ⬙ ∅ Services: ⬤ ✕ Off-site: ⇗P

MASSA, MARINA DI MASSA CARRARA

Giardino viale delle Pinete 382, 54037
☎ 0585 869291 ▤ 0585 240781
Site in pine woodland and on two meadows, shade provided by roof matting.
➲ On the island side of the SS328 to Pisa.
Open: Apr-Sep Site: 3.2HEC ⏛ ⚘ ⣿ ⚘ Prices: ⋔4-6 ⛺2-4 Facilities: ⬟ ⚍ ☉ ⬙ ∅ ☒ Services: ⬤ ✕ lau Off-site: ⇗S ⊞

MONÉGLIA GENOVA

Villaggio Smeraldo Preata, 16030
☎ 0185 49375 ▤ 0185 490484
A pleasant site in a pine wood overlooking the sea with good, modern facilities and direct access to the beach.
➲ Access via A12/SS1.
Open: All year Site: 1.5HEC ⬙ ⚘ ⣿ ⚘ Facilities: ⬟ ⚍ ☉ ⬙ ⬙ ☒ Services: ⬤ ✕ lau Leisure: ⇗ S Off-site: ∅

MONTECATINI TERME PISTOIA

Belsito via delle Vigne 1/A, Vico, 51016
☎ 0572 67373 ▤ 0572 67373
e-mail: cbelsito@tin.it website: www.campingbelsito.it
A quiet site at an altitude of 250mtrs with good sized pitches.
Open: 15 Feb-29 Nov Site: 3.5HEC ⏛ ⚘ ⣿ Prices: ⋔5-6 ⇜3-4 ⊞7-8.50 ⛺5.50-8.50 Facilities: ⬟ ⚍ ☉ ⬙ ∅ ☒ Services: ⬤ ✕ ⊞ lau Leisure: ⇗ P Off-site: ⇗L

MONTE DI FO FIRENZE

Sergente 50030 ☎ 055 8423018 ▤ 055 8423907
e-mail: info@campingilsergente.it
website: www.campingilsergente.it
The site is at 780mtrs above sea level on a hill. The pitches are flat. Ideal for walkers.
➲ Exit the SS65 at Barberino Mugello and follow signs for Monte di Fo.
Open: All year Site: 3HEC ⏛ ⚘ ⣿ ⚘ Facilities: ⬟ ⚍ ☉ ⬙ ∅ ☒ Services: ⬤ ✕ ⊞ lau

MONTERIGGIONI SIENA

Piscina Luxor Quies Loc. Trasqua, 53032
☎ 0577 743047 ▤ 0577 743047
e-mail: info@luxorcamping.com
website: www.luxorcamping.com
Lies on a flat-topped hill, partly in an oak wood, partly in meadowland.
➲ Turn off via Cassia (SS2) at Km239/II or Km238/IX and continue for further 2.5km, crossing railway line. Approach to site via very steep and winding road.
Open: 17 May-7 Sep Site: 1.5HEC ⏛ ⚘ Prices: ⋔6.65 ⇜2.90 ⊞3.40 ⛺3.50 Facilities: ⬟ ⚍ ☉ ⬙ ∅ ☒ Services: ⬤ ✕ ⊞ lau Leisure: ⇗ P

MONTESCUDÁIO LIVORNO

Montescudáio via del Poggetto, 56040
☎ 0586 683477 ▓ 0586 630932
e-mail: info@camping-montescudaio.it
website: www.camping-montescudaio.it
This modern site is situated on a hill and is completely
divided into individual pitches, some of which are naturally
screened. Children under 2 years are not accepted.
➲ *From Cecinia (on SS1, via Aurelia) follow road to
Guardistallo for 2.5km.*
Open: 14 May-19 Sep Site: 25HEC ▬▬ ♣ ▥ ▨ ⚘
Prices: ♠5.30-7.30 pitch 11.30-20.30 **Facilities:** ⋔ ☎ ⊙ ▣ ∅
♨ ▣ **Services:** ♀ ✗ lau **Leisure:** ⤸ PS **Off-site:** ⊞

MONTICELLO AMIATA GROSSETO

Lucherino Lucherino, 58047 ☎ 0564 992975 ▓ 992975
e-mail: meichu@tiscalinet.it website: www.lucherino.nl
A peaceful site 735mtrs above sea level on the slopes of
Mount Amiata. The shady but sloping site is ideal for walkers
and historians.
➲ *Access via SS223 to Paganico then follow signs to Monte
Amiata.*
Open: May-15 Oct Site: 2HEC ▬▬ ▵ ⊕ ▥ ▨ Prices: ♠7
pitch 8.50 **Facilities:** ⋔ ⊙ ▣ ∅ ♨ ▣ **Services:** ♀ ✗ lau
Leisure: ⤸ P **Off-site:** ▦

PEGLI GENOVA

Villa Doria via al Campeggio 15n, 16156
☎ 010 6969600 ▓ 010 6969600
e-mail: villadoria@camping.it
website: www.camping.it/liguria/villadoria
Quiet site in pleasant wooded surroundings.
➲ *Access via SS1. Singposted.*
Open: All year Site: 0.4HEC ▬▬ ♣ ▥ Prices: ♠3.45-6.85
pitch 7.65-11.85 pp3 **Facilities:** ⋔ ▦ ⊙ ▣ ▣ **Services:** ♀ ✗
lau **Off-site:** ✗ ∅ ⤸S

PISA PISA

Torre Pendente viale della Cascine 86, 56122
☎ 050 561704 ▓ 050 561734
e-mail: torrepen@campingtoscana.it
website: campingtoscana.it/torrependente
Pleasant, modern site on level ground in a rural setting. 1km
walk to the Leaning Tower.
➲ *Situated on the northern outskirts of Pisa.*
Open: Apr-15 Oct Site: 2.5HEC ▬▬ ♣ ▥ Prices: ♠7.50
🚗4.50 🚐6.80 ▲6.30 **Facilities:** ⋔ ▦ ⊙ ▣ ∅ ▣ **Services:** ♀ ✗
⊞ lau **Leisure:** ⤸ P **Off-site:** ♨ ⤸PR ⊞

POPULÓNIA LIVORNO

Sant'Albínia via della Principessa, 57025
☎ 0565 29389 ▓ 0565 221310
e-mail: arci.piobino@etruscan.li.it
A good overnight stopping place with plenty of facilities.
Ideally placed for the ferry ports.
➲ *10km N of Piombino on the San Vincenzo road.*
Open: May-15 Sep Site: 3HEC ▬▬ ♣ ▥ ▲ ⚘ **Facilities:** ⋔
▦ ⊙ ▣ ♨ ▣ **Services:** ♀ ✗ lau **Leisure:** ⤸ S

RIOTORTO LIVORNO

Orizzonte Perelli, 57020 ☎ 0565 28007 ▓ 0565 28033
In a fine coastal position overlooking the island of Elba.
Open: All year Site: 10HEC ▬▬ ♣ ▥ ▥ **Facilities:** ⋔ ▦ ⊙
▣ ∅ **Services:** ♀ ✗ ⊞ lau **Leisure:** ⤸ P **Off-site:** ⤸S

SAN BARONTO FIRENZE

Barco Reale via Nardini 11, 51030
☎ 0573 88332 ▓ 0573 856003
e-mail: info@barcoreale.com website: www.barcoreale.com
A well equipped site in a hilly, wooded location.
➲ *Signposted from Lamporecchio.*
Open: Apr-Sep Site: 10HEC ▬▬ ♣ ▥ Prices: ♠6.70-8.70
🚗3.70-4.80 🚐6.20-8 ▲5.50-7 **Facilities:** ⋔ ▦ ⊙ ▣ ∅ ▣
Services: ♀ ✗ lau **Leisure:** ⤸ P

SAN GIMIGNANO SIENA

Boschetto di Piemma Santa Lucia, 53037
☎ 0577 940352 ▓ 0577 941982
e-mail: bpiemma@tiscali.it
This small grassy site is well equipped and has many facilities
for both families and individuals.
Open: Apr-15 Oct Site: 1.5HEC ▬▬ ♣ ▥ **Facilities:** ⋔ ▦ ⊙
▣ ∅ ♨ ▣ **Services:** ♀ ✗ ⊞ **Leisure:** ⤸ P

SAN PIERO A SIEVE FIRENZE

Village Mugello Verde via Massorondinaio 39, 50037
☎ 055 848511 ▓ 055 8486910
e-mail: mugelloverde@florencecamping.com
website: www.florencecamping.com
Terraced site in wooded surroundings. Lunchtime siesta
14.00-16.00 hrs.
➲ *Leave motorway at exit 18 and follow signs.*
Open: All year Site: 12HEC ▬▬ ♣ ▥ Prices: ♠7.50-8 pitch 13-
13.50 **Facilities:** ⋔ ▦ ⊙ ▣ ∅ ▣ **Services:** ♀ ✗ ⊞ **Leisure:** ⤸ P
Off-site: ♨ ⤸R

IN THE HEART OF TUSCANY

CAMPING BARCO REALE

Via Nardini, 11/13 • 51030 S. Baronto (PT)
Tel. 0039/057388332 • Fax 0039/0573856003
info@barcoreale.com • www.barcoreale.com

2 Swimming pools (one for children, one for adults) - Volleyball - Internet point - Playroom - Skittle alley - Trekking - Football field - Boccia - Children's playground - Supermarket - Restaurant - Tennis (3 km)

The campsite lies on a hill in a pine and oak wood with a lovely panorama. The house where Leonardo da Vinci was born and the famous towns of Tuscany are not far away, excursions by bus are organised. Barco Reale is an ideal site for a pleasant holiday from April to Setember owing to guided walks among the olive groves and wine country, the wonderful scenery, the local culture and the climate.

Facilities: ▦-shop ⋔-shower ⊙-electric points for razors ▣-electric points for caravans ▨-parking by tents permitted
▣-compulsory separate car park **Services:** ✗-café/restaurant ♀-bar ∅-Camping Gaz International ♨-gas other than Camping
Gaz ⊞-first aid facilities lau-laundry **Leisure:** ⤸-swimming L-Lake P-Pool R-River S-Sea **Off-site:** All facilities within 2km

SAN VINCENZO LIVORNO

Park Albatros Pineta di Torre Nuova, 57027
☎ 0565 701018 ▓ 0565 703589
e-mail: info@parkalbatros.it website: www.parkalbatros.it
The site lies amongst beautiful, tall pine trees. 1km from sea.
⮑ *Turn off SP23 beyond San Vincenzo at Km7/III and drive 600mtrs inland.*
Open: 25 Mar-8 Sep Site: 11.4HEC ⦙⦙⦙⦙ ♣ ⛺ ⊘
Facilities: ⋔ ⅃ ⊙ ⊕ ⊘ ⚒ ☎ Services: ⊈ ✕ ⊞ lau Off-site: ⟨S

SARTEANO SIENA

Bagno Santo via del Bagno Santo 29, 53047
☎ 0578 26971 ▓ 0578 265889
e-mail: info@parcodellepiscine.it
website: www.parcodellepiscine.it
Open: Apr-Sep Site: 15HEC ⦙⦙⦙⦙ ♣ ⛺ ⊘ Prices: ⟨9.50-12
⟨3.50-6 ⛗9.50-12 ⚑9.50-12 Facilities: ⋔ ⊙ ⊕ ⚒ ☎
Services: ⊈ ✕ ⊞ lau Leisure: ⟨ P Off-site: ⅃

SARZANA LA SPEZIA

Iron Gate via XXV Aprile 54, 19038
☎ 0187 676370 ▓ 0187 675014
A modern site with good facilities attached to the Iron Gate Marina.
Open: All year Site: 2HEC ⦙⦙⦙⦙ ♣ ⛺ Facilities: ⋔ ⅃ ⊙ ⊕ ☎
Services: ⊈ ✕ ⊞ Leisure: ⟨ PR Off-site: ⊘ ⚒

SESTRI LEVANTE GENOVA

Fossa Lupara via Costa 31, 16039
☎ 0185 43992 ▓ 0185 43992
Open: All year Site: 1.5HEC ⦙⦙⦙⦙ ♣ ⛗ Prices: ⟨5 ⛗15 ⚑10
Facilities: ⋔ ⅃ ⊙ ⊕ ⊘ ⚒ ☎ Services: ⊈ ✕ ⊞ lau Off-site: ⟨S

SIENA SIENA

Montagnola Sovicille, 53018 ☎ 0577 314473 ▓ 0577 314473
e-mail: montagnolacamping@libero.it
Quiet site in an oak wood with individual plots separated by hedges. Facilities are modern and attractive.
⮑ *From the A1 westbound, exit at Siena, campsite is signposted towards Sovicille.*
Open: Etr-29 Sep Site: 2.5HEC ⦙⦙⦙⦙ ⠶⠶ ⊘ ♣ ⛺ ⛗
Prices: ⟨6 pitch 8 Facilities: ⋔ ⅃ ⊙ ⊕ ⚒ ☎ Services: ⊈ lau
Leisure: ⟨ R Off-site: ✕ ⊞

Siena Colleverde Strada di Scacciapensieri 47, 53100
☎ 0577 280044 ▓ 0577 333298
e-mail: campingsiena@terresiena.it website: www.terresiena.it
The site offers both large areas for caravans and mobile homes and a large grassy area for tents. There is a local bus service to the centre of Siena.
⮑ *The only campsite in Siena situated just to the north.*
Site: 4.5HEC ⦙⦙⦙⦙ ♣ Facilities: ⋔ ⊙ ⊕ ⚒ ☎ Services: ⊈ ✕
lau Leisure: ⟨ P Off-site: ⅃ ⊞

Soline Casciano di Murlo, 53010
☎ 0577 817410 ▓ 0577 817415
e-mail: camping@lesoline.it website: www.lesoline.it
Terraced hilly site surrounded by woodland. Offers a wide variety of sports facilities and family entertainment.
⮑ *Take the left turning at Fontazzi and ascend hill.*
Open: All year Site: 6HEC ⦙⦙⦙⦙ ⊘ ⛺ Prices: ⟨7 ⛗1.50
⛗6.50 ⚑5-6 Facilities: ⋔ ⅃ ⊙ ⊕ ⊘ ⚒ ☎ Services: ⊈ ✕ ⊞
lau Leisure: ⟨ PR

> The AA cannot be held
> responsible for the content of
> third party websites

STELLA SAN GIOVANNI SAVONA

Stella via Rio Basco 62, 17040 ☎ 019 703269 ▓ 019 703269
e-mail: campingdolcevita@libero.it
website: www.campingdolcevita.it
In wooded surroundings with well defined pitches, 5.5km from the coast.
⮑ *Access via SS334.*
Open: Apr-Sep Site: 10HEC ⦙⦙⦙⦙ ♣ Prices: ⟨4-5 pitch 10-17
(incl 2 persons) Facilities: ⋔ ⅃ ⊙ ⊕ ⊘ ⚒ ☎ Services: ⊈ ✕ ⊞
lau Leisure: ⟨ PR Off-site: ⊞

TORRE DEL LAGO PUCCINI LUCCA

Burlamacco viale G-Marconi Int, 55048
☎ 0584 359544 ▓ 0584 359387
e-mail: info@campingburlamacco.com
website: www.campingburlamacco.com
In a beautiful wooded location 1km from the sea on the Versilia Riviera and close to the former home of Puccini. A wide variety of facilities are available.
Open: Apr-29 Sep Site: 4HEC ⦙⦙⦙⦙ ⠶⠶ ♣ ⛺ ⛗ ⚑
Facilities: ⋔ ⅃ ⊙ ⊕ ⊘ ⚒ ⊞ Services: ⊈ ✕ Leisure: ⟨ P
Off-site: ⟨LS ⊞

Europa Viale dei Tigli, 55048
☎ 0584 350707 ▓ 0584 342592
e-mail: info@europacamp.it website: www.europacamp.it
Site in pine and poplar woodland.
⮑ *On the land side of the viale dei Tigli, coming from Viareggio.*
Open: 5 Apr-25 Oct Site: 60HEC ⦙⦙⦙⦙ ⠶⠶ ♣ ⛺ ⛗
Facilities: ⋔ ⅃ ⊙ ⊕ ⊘ ⚒ ☎ Services: ⊈ ✕ ⊞ lau Off-site: ⟨S

Italia 52 viale dei Tigli, 55048
☎ 0584 359828 ▓ 0584 341504
e-mail: info@campingitalia.net
website: www.campingitalia.net
This site is divided into pitches and lies in meadowland planted with poplar trees.
⮑ *Inland from the Viareggio road (viale dei Tigli).*
Open: 22 Apr-19 Sep Site: 9HEC ⦙⦙⦙⦙ ⠶⠶ ♣ ⛺ ⛗ ⊘
Prices: ⟨5.50-8.50 ⛗8-11.50 ⚑8-11.50 Facilities: ⋔ ⅃ ⊙ ⊕
⊘ ⚒ ☎ Services: ⊈ ✕ ⊞ lau Off-site: ⅃ ⊈ ✕ ⊘ ⚒ ⟨LS

Tigli Viale dei Tigli, 54, 55048 ☎ 0584 341278 ▓ 0584 341278
e-mail: info@campingdeitigli.com
website: www.campingdeitigli.com
Shady site close to a Regional Park, Lake Massaciuccoli, and the villa where Puccini wrote much of his music.
Open: Apr-15 Sep Site: 9HEC ⦙⦙⦙⦙ ⠶⠶ ♣ ⛺ Prices: ⟨5-9
⚑7-14 pitch 7-14 Facilities: ⋔ ⅃ ⊙ ⊕ ⊘ ⚒ ☎ Services: ⊈ ✕
⊞ lau Off-site: ⟨LS

TROGHI FIRENZE

Il Poggetto via il Poggetto 143, 50010
☎ 055 8307323 ▓ 055 8307323
e-mail: poggetto@tin.it
website: campingtoscana.it/ilpoggetto
A modern site with good facilities. Large, level, grassy pitches.
⮑ *5km from exit 'Incisa Valdarno' on the A1.*
Open: 27 Mar-17 Oct Site: 4.5HEC ⦙⦙⦙⦙ ⊘ ⛺ ⛗ ⚑
Prices: ⟨7.20 pitch 12.50 Facilities: ⋔ ⅃ ⊙ ⊕ ⊘ ⚒ ☎
Services: ⊈ ✕ ⊞ lau Leisure: ⟨ P

VADA LIVORNO

Flori 57018 ☎ 0586 770096 ▓ 0586 770323
e-mail: campofiori@multinet.it
website: www.campingcampodeifiori.it
Level grassland surrounded by fields. Shade provided by roof matting.

Site: 6HEC-Site size ⦙⦙⦙⦙-grass ⠶⠶-sand ⊘-stone ⠶⠶-little shade ⊘-partly shaded ♣-mainly shaded
⛺-bungalows for hire ⛗-caravans for hire ⚑-tents for hire ⊘-no dogs Prices: ⟨-adult per night ⟨-car per night
pp-per person per night ⛗-caravan per night ⚑-tent per night

➲ *Access from the SS1 S of Vada, after 1.5km turn right and continue for 500mtrs.*
Open: 10 Apr-19 Sep Site: 15HEC ⬛ ♠ ⬛ Prices: ♠6-11 ⬛6-10 ▲6-10 Facilities: ⬛ ⬛ ⊙ ⬛ ⬛ ⬛ ⬛ Services: ⬛ ✗ ⬛ lau Leisure: ⬚ P Off-site: ⬚S

VIAREGGIO LUCCA

Pineta via dei Lecci, 55049 ☎ 0584 383397
e-mail: campinglapineta@interfree.it
website: www.campinglapineta.com
A well organised site in a wooded location, 1km from a private beach.
➲ *Access via SSN1 between Km 354 and 355.*
Open: Etr-19 Sep Site: 3.2HEC ⬛ ♠ ⬛ ⬛ Facilities: ⬛ ⬛ ⊙ ⬛ ⬛ ⬛ Services: ⬛ ✗ ⬛ lau Leisure: ⬚ P Off-site: ⬚S

Viareggio via Comparini 1, 55049
☎ 0584 391012 ⬛ 0584 395462
e-mail: campingviareggio@tin.it
website: www.campingviareggio.it
The site lies in a poplar wood 700mtrs from beach.
➲ *1.5km S of town. At Km354/V head towards coast.*
Open: Apr-29 Sep Site: 2HEC ⬛ ⫶⫶⫶ ♠ Prices: ♠5-8 ⬛8-12 ▲8-12 Facilities: ⬛ ⬛ ⊙ ⬛ ⬛ ⬛ Services: ⬛ ✗ ⬛ lau Off-site: ⬚LPS

ZINOLA SAVONA

Buggi International via N S del Monte 15, 17049
☎ 019 860120 ⬛ 019 804573
A well equipped site with plenty of space for tents, approx. 900mtrs from the sea.
Open: All year Site: 2HEC ⬛ ♠ ⬛ ⬛ Prices: ♠5 ⬛5 ⬛7 ▲5 Facilities: ⬛ ⬛ ⊙ ⬛ ⬛ Services: ⬛ ✗ Off-site: ⬛ ⬛ ⬚S ⬛

NORTH EAST/ADRIATIC

ALBA ADRIATICA TERAMO
AT TORTORETO, LIDO (4KM S)

Salinello c da Piane a Mare, 64019
☎ 0861 786306 ⬛ 0861 786451
e-mail: salinello@camping.it
website: www.camping.it/salinello
Well-tended meadowland site with numerous rows of poplars. Private beach, siesta 13.30-16.00 hrs.
➲ *On southern outskirts, signposted from Km405 of the SS16.*
Open: May-Sep Site: 15HEC ⬛ ♠ ⬛ ⬛ Facilities: ⬛ ⬛ ⊙ ⬛ ⬛ ⬛ ⬛ Services: ⬛ ✗ ⬛ lau Leisure: ⬚ PS Off-site: ⬚R

ASSISI PERUGIA

Internationale Campiglione No. 110, 06081
☎ 075 813710 ⬛ 075 812335
e-mail: info@campingassisi.it
website: www.campingassisi.it
At the foot of the hill on which Assisi stands, this modern campsite is well-equipped and a good touring centre.
➲ *W via SS147.*
Open: Apr-19 Oct Site: 3HEC ⬛ ♠ ⬛ ⬛ ▲ Prices: ♠6-7 ⬛2-3 ⬛6-7 ▲5-6 Facilities: ⬛ ⬛ ⊙ ⬛ ⬛ ⬛ Services: ⬛ ✗ ⬛ lau Leisure: ⬚ PR

BARREA L'AQUILA

Grenziana Parco Nazionale d'Abruzzo, Tre Croci, 67030
☎ 0864 88101 ⬛ 0864 88101
e-mail: pasettanet@tiscalinet.it
website: www.campinglagenzianapasetta
In picturesque wooded surroundings on the shore of a lake.
Open: All year Site: 2HEC ⬛ ⫶⫶⫶ ⬛ ♠ ▲ Facilities: ⬛ ⬛ ⊙ ⬛ Services: ⬛ ✗ Off-site: ⬛ ⬛ ⬛ ⬚L ⬛

BELLARIA FORLI

Happy via Panzini 228, 47814
☎ 0541 346102 ⬛ 0541 346408
e-mail: happy@infotel.it website: www.happycamping.it
The campsite is in a quiet position on the sea shore close to the centre of town.
➲ *A14, SS16, exit for Bellaria Cagnona S. Mauro Mare, and follow signs for Acquabell. Over level crossing and site is on right.*
Open: All year Site: 4HEC ⬛ ⫶⫶⫶ ♠ ⬛ Prices: ♠4.60-8 pitch 8.78-14.98 Facilities: ⬛ ⊙ ⬛ ⬛ ⬛ ⬛ Services: ⬛ ✗ ⬛ lau Leisure: ⬚ PS Off-site: ⬛ ⬛ ✗ ⬚R

BEVAGNA PERUGIA

Pian di Boccio Pian di Boccio 10, 06031
☎ 0742 360164 ⬛ 0742 360691
e-mail: piandiboccio@tiscaliner.it
website: www.piandiboccio.com
In wooded surroundings in the centre of the Umbria region with good modern facilities. Popular with families.
Open: Apr-29 Sep Site: 8.5HEC ⬛ ♠ ⬛ ⬛ Facilities: ⬛ ⬛ ⊙ ⬛ ⬛ ⬛ Services: ⬛ ✗ lau Leisure: ⬚ LP

BOLOGNA BOLOGNA

Citta di Bologna via Romita 12/IVA, 40127
☎ 051 325016 ⬛ 051 325318
e-mail: info@hotelcamping.com
website: www.hotelcamping.com
Located in the northern part of this ancient town this site offers a cheap and convenient alternative to hotels.
Open: All year Site: 6.3HEC ⬛ ⬛ ⬛ Prices: ♠4-7 pitch 8-12 Facilities: ⬛ ⬛ ⊙ ⬛ ⬛ ⬛ Services: ⬛ ✗ ⬛ lau Leisure: ⬚ P Off-site: ✗ ⬛ ⬛

BORGHETTO PERUGIA

Badiaccia via Trasimenoi, no.91, 6061
☎ 075 9659097 ⬛ 075 9659019
e-mail: info@badiaccia.com website: www.badiaccia.com
A well equipped site with large grassy pitches and direct access to the lake.
➲ *From the A1 exit at Valdichiana and join the road to Perugia and follow signs for Lake Trasimeno.*
Open: Apr-Sep Site: 5.5HEC ⬛ ♠ ⬛ ⬛ Prices: ♠5-6.50 ⬛2 ⬛6-50 ▲5-6 Facilities: ⬛ ⬛ ⊙ ⬛ ⬛ Services: ⬛ ✗ lau Leisure: ⬚ LP Off-site: ⬛

CASAL BORSETTI RAVENNA

Adria via Spallazzi N30, 48010 ☎ 0544 445217
The site lies in a field behind the Ristorante Lugo.
➲ *Turn off the motorway at the Ravenna exit or take the SS309 (Romea) Km13 N of Ravenna.*
Open: May-20 Sep Site: 5.5HEC ⬛ ♠ ⬛ Facilities: ⬛ ⬛ ⊙ ⬛ ⬛ ⬛ Services: ⬛ ✗ ⬛ lau Leisure: ⬚ PS

Reno via Spallazzi 11, 48010 ☎ 0544 445020 ⬛ 0544 442056
e-mail: camping.reno@libero.it
website: www.camping.it/emiliaromagna/reno
Meadowland in sparse pine woodland and separated from the sea by dunes.
➲ *Turn off SS309 at Km8 or 14.*
Open: Apr-Oct Site: 33HEC ⬛ ♠ ⬛ ⬛ Prices: ♠4-6 7.15-9.50 (incl 4 persons) Facilities: ⬛ ⬛ ⊙ ⬛ ⬛ ⬛ Services: ⬛ ✗ ⬛ lau Off-site: ⬚S

A full guide to the Symbols & Abbreviations used in this book can be found on page 6

Facilities: ⬛-shop ⬛-shower ⊙-electric points for razors ⬛-electric points for caravans ⬛-parking by tents permitted ⬛-compulsory separate car park Services: ✗-café/restaurant ⬛-bar ⬛-Camping Gaz International ⬛-gas other than Camping Gaz ⬛-first aid facilities lau-laundry Leisure: ⬚-swimming L-Lake P-Pool R-River S-Sea Off-site: All facilities within 2km

CASTIGLIONE DEL LAGO PERUGIA

Listro via Lungolago, 6061 ☎ 075 951193 ▯ 075 951193
e-mail: listro@listro.it website: www.listro.it
Attractive site on a peninsula in Lake Trasimeno.
Open: Apr-29 Sep Site: 1HEC 〰〰 ♣ Facilities: ⟦ ⟧ ⊙ ⊙ 〓
⊡ Services: ⟐ ✗ lau Leisure: ⟲ L Off-site: ✗ ∅ ⟲P ⊞

CERVIA RAVENNA

Adriatico via Pinarella 90, 48015
☎ 0544 71537 ▯ 0544 72346
e-mail: info@campingadriatico.net
website: www.campingadriatico.net
Level meadowland site with plenty of shade, pleasantly
landscaped with olives, willows, elms and maples.
⊃ *Located shortly before Pinarella di Cervia. Access by via*
Caduti per le Liberta (SS16) 600mtrs from sea.
Open: 24 Apr-12 Sep Site: 3.4HEC 〰〰 Prices: ⋔4.40-7
⊞9.20-12.70 ⚠7.20-11 pitch 9.20-12.70 Facilities: ⟦ ⟧ ⊙ ⊙
∅ 〓 ⊡ Services: ⟐ ✗ ⊞ lau Leisure: ⟲ P Off-site: ⟧ ⟐ ✗ ∅
〓 ⟲L ⊞

CESENATICO FORLI

Cesenatico via Mazzini 182, 47042
☎ 0547 81344 ▯ 0547 672452
e-mail: campingcesenatico@gesturist.com
website: www.gesturist.com
The site stretches over an area of land belonging to the
Azienda di Soggiomo e Turismo.
⊃ *1.5km N at Km178 turn off the SS16 towards the sea.*
Open: All year Site: 17HEC 〰〰 ∴∴ ♣ ⊞ ⊞ Prices: ⋔4.80-
8.90 pitch 12.40-19.80 Facilities: ⟦ ⟧ ⊙ ⊙ 〓 ⊡ Services: ⟐
✗ lau Leisure: ⟲ PS Off-site: ⊞

Zadina via Mazzini 184, 47042
☎ 0547 82310 ▯ 0547 672802
e-mail: info@campingzadina.it
Very pleasant terrain in dunes on two sides of a canal.
Open: 23 Apr-16 Sep Site: 11HEC ∴∴ ♣ Facilities: ⟦ ⟧ ⊙
⊙ ∅ 〓 ⊡ Services: ⟐ ✗ ⊞ lau Leisure: ⟲ S

CITTA DI CASTELLO PERUGIA

La Montesca 06012 ☎ 075 8521420 ▯ 075 8520786
e-mail: villamontesca@sogepu.com
website: www.sogepu.com
In a large, wooded park with excellent facilities. An ideal base
for exploring the surrounding area.
⊃ *3km from the town, beside the River Tiber.*
Open: May-Sep Site: 5HEC 〰〰 ♣ Facilities: ⟦ ⊙ ⊙ ∅ ⊡
Services: ⟐ ✗ ⊞ lau Leisure: ⟲ P

CUPRA MARITTIMA ASCOLI PICENO

Calypso via Boccabianca 8, 63012
☎ 0735 778686 ▯ 0735 778106
e-mail: calypso@camping.it website: www.campingcalypso.it
Open: Apr-29 Sep Site: 26HEC 〰〰 ♣ ⊞ Prices: ⋔6-9
⊞8.50-14 Facilities: ⟦ ⟧ ⊙ ⊙ ∅ 〓 ⊡ Services: ⟐ ✗ ⊞ lau
Leisure: ⟲ PS

DANTE, LIDO DI RAVENNA

Classe viale Catone, 48100 ☎ 0544 492005 ▯ 0544 492058
e-mail: info@campingclasse.it website: www.campingclasse.it
Level meadowland in grounds of former farm.
⊃ *Access from the SS16 turning towards the sea at Km154/V*
and renewed 9km to site.
Open: 15 May-Sep Site: 7HEC 〰〰 ♣ ⊞ ⊞ ⚠ Facilities: ⟦
⟧ ⊙ ∅ ∅ 〓 ⊡ Services: ⟐ ✗ ⊞ lau Leisure: ⟲ PS
Off-site: ⟲LR

★★★★
Mare Pineta
International Camping - Bungalow - Appartamenti

♦ **Right by the sea**
♦ **Natural pine wood**
♦ **Right in the town centre**
♦ **4 Swimming pools**
♦ **Sporting events**
♦ **Entertainment ♦ Water sports**
♦ **Mobile homes for 6/4/2 persons**
♦ **Caravans for 4 persons**
♦ **Bungalows and apartments**
♦ **Excursions organized**
♦ **Bicycles ♦ Gymnasium**
♦ **Spinning ♦ Sauna**
♦ **Whirlpool ♦ Massages**
♦ **Solarium ♦ Doctor ♦ Mudtherapy**
♦ **Beautysalon ♦ Physiotherapy**

International Camping MAREPINETA
I-44024 Lido degli Estensi - Comacchio (FE)
Tel. 0039/0533330194-0533330110
Fax 0039/0533330052
Http: www.campingmarepineta.com
E-mail: info@campingmarepineta.com

Delta del Po
Struttura ricettiva
consigliata per l'impegno
in difesa dell'ambiente

Site: 6HEC-Site size 〰〰-grass ∴∴-sand ⧈-stone 𝔰-little shade ⊕-partly shaded ♣-mainly shaded
⊞-bungalows for hire ⊞-caravans for hire ⚠-tents for hire ⊘-no dogs Prices: ⋔-adult per night ⊟-car per night
pp-per person per night ⊞-caravan per night ⚠-tent per night

ESTENSI, LIDO DEGLI FERRARA

International Mare Pineta via delle Acacie 67, 44024
☎ 0533 330110 📠 0533 330052
e-mail: info@campingmarepineta.com
website: www.campingmarepineta.com
Extensive site on slightly hilly ground under pines and decidous trees, providing shade. Near the beach and has numerous mobile homes.
➲ *2km SE of Port Garibaldi.*
Open: 08 Apr-19 Sep Site: 16HEC ⬛ ⋮⋮ ♠ 🏠
Prices: ⚑3.70-7.95 🚗2.60-4.20 pitch 6.30-13.25 Facilities: ℟
🛂 ⊙ 🖾 ⌀ ♨ 🅿 Services: 🍴 ✗ lau Leisure: ⚓ PS
See advertisement on page 276

FANO PESARO & URBINO

Mare Blu 61032 ☎ 0721 884201 📠 0721 884389
The site is surrounded by tall poplars with direct access to a sandy beach. Facilities for most watersports and entertainment for children and families.
➲ *Exit A14 at Fano and travel south for 3km.*
Open: Apr-Sep Site: 2.5HEC ⬛ ♠ 🅿 Facilities: ℟ 🛂 ⊙ 🖾
⌀ ♨ 🅿 🖾 Services: 🍴 ✗ 🕀 lau Leisure: ⚓ S Off-site: ⚓PR

FERRARA FERRARA

Estense via Gramicia 76, 44100
☎ 0532 752396 📠 0532 752396
e-mail: camping.estense@libero.it
A good overnight stop on the way south.
➲ *NE outskirts of Ferrara*
Open: All year Site: 3.3HEC ⬛ ♠ 🅿 Prices: ⚑4.50 🚗6.50
⚑6.50 Facilities: ℟ ⊙ 🖾 🖾 Off-site: 🛂 🍴 ✗ ⌀ ⚓P 🕀

FIORENZUOLA DI FOCARA PESARO & URBINO

Panorama Strada Panoramica, 61010
☎ 0721 208145 📠 0721 208145
e-mail: info@campingpanorama.it
website: www.campingpanorama.it
Located in a park 100mtrs above sea level this site welcomes families, animals, cyclists and those wishing to relax.
➲ *Signposted off the SS16, 10km from Gabicce and 7km from Pesaro.*
Open: May-Sep Site: 2.2HEC ⬛ ♠ 🏠 🅿 Prices: ⚑5.50-
7.25 🚗2.50 🚗5.50-8 ⚑5.50-8 pitch 8-10.50 Facilities: ℟ 🛂
⊙ 🖾 ⌀ ♨ 🖾 Services: 🍴 ✗ 🕀 lau
Leisure: ⚓ LPS

GATTEO MARE FORLI

Rose via Adriatica 29, 47043 ☎ 0547 86213 📠 0547 87583
e-mail: baiocchi@villaggiorose.com
website: www.villaggiorose.com
In a peaceful setting close to the sea and the town centre.
➲ *Turn off SS16, at Km186.*
Open: May-25 Sep Site: 4HEC ⬛ ⋮⋮ ♠ 🏠 🅿
Prices: ⚑4.20-8.20 pitch 9-15.60 Facilities: ℟ 🛂 ⊙ 🖾 ⌀ ♨ 🖾
Services: 🍴 ✗ 🕀 lau Leisure: ⚓ PS Off-site: ⚓R

GIULIANOVA LIDO TERAMO

Baviera Lungomare Zara, 64022
☎ 085 8000053 📠 085 8004420
A family site in a wooded location with direct access to a private beach. A wide variety of sporting and entertainment facilities are available, particularly in July and August, when all cars must use the designated car park.
➲ *Access via A14 and SS80.*
Open: 31 May-15 Sep Site: 1.8HEC ⬛ ♠ 🏠 Facilities: ℟
🛂 ⊙ 🖾 ⌀ ♨ 🖾 Services: 🍴 ✗ lau Leisure: ⚓ PS

GUBBIO PERUGIA

Villa Ortoguidone Ortoguidone 214, 06020
☎ 075 9272037 📠 075 9276620
e-mail: info@gubbiocamping.com
website: www.gubbiocamping.com
One of two well equipped sites in the same location. Plenty of space for tents.
➲ *Access via SS298 (Gubbio-Perugia).*
Open: 07 Apr-19 Sep Site: 0.5HEC ⬛ ♠ 🏠 🅿
Prices: ⚑6.50-9 🚗9-10.50 ⚑7-9 Facilities: ℟ 🛂 ⊙ 🖾 🖾
Services: 🍴 ✗ lau Leisure: ⚓ P Off-site: 🛂 🍴 ✗ ⌀ ⚓P 🕀

MARCELLI DI NUMANA ANCONA

Conero Azzurro via Litoranea, 60026 ☎ 071 7390507
e-mail: coneroazzurro@camping.it
Well-equipped site situated between the Adriatic and Mount Canero.
Open: Jun-15 Sep Site: 5HEC ⬛ ♠ 🏠 ⌀ Prices: ⚑6-9
🚗3-5 🚗9-12 ⚑9-12 Facilities: ℟ 🛂 ⊙ 🖾 ⌀ Services: 🍴 ✗ 🕀
lau Leisure: ⚓ PS Off-site: ♨

MAROTTA PESARO & URBINO

Gabbiano via Faa' di Bruno 95, 61035
☎ 0721 96691 📠 0721 96691
e-mail: gabbiano.marche@camping.it
website: www.camping.it/marche/gabbiano
Quiet location surrounded by trees overlooking the sea.
➲ *Exit A14 at Marotta, join SS16 and site is 2.5km in the direction of Fano.*
Open: May-Sep Site: 1.9HEC ⬛ ♠ 🏠 ⌀ Facilities: ℟ 🛂
⊙ 🖾 ⌀ ♨ 🖾 Services: 🍴 ✗ 🕀 lau Leisure: ⚓ PS

MARTINISCURO TERAMO

Duca Amedeo Lungomare Europa 158, 64014
☎ 0861 797376 📠 0861 797264
e-mail: ducaamedeo@camping.it
website: www.camping.it/abruzzo.duca
In a pleasant location, surrounded by trees and lush vegetation. Close to the sea.
➲ *Access via A14 exit Martinsicuro.*
Open: May-28 Sep Site: 1.5HEC ⬛ ♠ 🏠 Prices: ⚑3.50-8
⚑5-8 pitch 8-14 Facilities: ℟ ⊙ 🖾 ⌀ 🖾 Services: 🍴 ✗ 🕀 lau
Leisure: ⚓ PS Off-site: 🛂 ✗

MILANO MARITTIMA RAVENNA

Romagna viale Matteotti 190, 48016
☎ 0544 949326 📠 0544 949345
Level and flat site with young trees.

contd.

➩ *Access via the SS16 (Strada Adriatica) turn off beyond Milano Marittima and follow signs.*
Open: 12 Apr-15 Sep Site: 40HEC ⊞ ⁖⁖ ♣ ⊗
Prices: ♠4.50-7.50 ♠4.50-7.50 ♠4.50-7.50 ▲6-11 pitch 7-12.50 Facilities: ♠ ⚍ ⊙ ⬤ ⊘ 🏠 Services: ⚎ ✗ lau Leisure: ⬦ S Off-site: ⬦P ⊞

MODENA MODENA

International via Cave di Ramo 111, 41100
☎ 059 332252 ▤ 059 823235
e-mail: ivanbompani@hotmail.com
website: www.internationalcamping.org
Open: All year Site: 2.6HEC ⊞ ⬥ ♣ Prices: ♠6 pitch 11
Facilities: ♠ ⚍ ⊙ ⬤ ⊘ 🏠 Services: ⚎ ✗ lau Leisure: ⬦ P
Off-site: ⚏

MONTENERO, MARINA DI CAMPOBASSO

Costa Verde 86036 ☎ 0873 803144
e-mail: info@costaverde.it website: www.costaverde.it
A level site with good facilities and direct access to the beach E of San Salvo Marino.
➩ *Leave the coast road, SS16, at Km525/VII and continue by a farm road for 300mtrs to the site.*
Open: 15 May-15 Sep Site: 1HEC ⊞ ⬥ 🏠 ♠ ▲ ⊗
Facilities: ♠ ⚍ ⊙ ⬤ ⊘ ⚏ 🏠 Services: ⚎ ✗ lau Leisure: ⬦ PRS Off-site: ⊞

NAZIONI, LIDO DELLE FERRARA

Tahiti viale Libia 133, 44020 ☎ 0533 379500 ▤ 0533 379700
e-mail: info@campingtahiti.com
website: www.campingtahiti.com
Pleasantly laid out site 650mtrs from sea. Has own private beach accessible via a miniature railway. Lunchtime siesta 13.30-15.30 hrs.
➩ *Turn off SS309 near Km32.5 then 2km to site. Signposted.*
Open: 03 Apr-26 Sep Site: 12HEC ⊞ ⁖⁖ ♣ 🏠 ♠ ⊗
Prices: ♠4.50-8.10 pitch 8.20-49.90 Facilities: ♠ ⚍ ⊙ ⬤ ⊘ 🏠 Services: ⚎ ✗ ⊞ lau Leisure: ⬦ P Off-site: ⬦S

OLMO PERUGIA

Rocolo strada Fontana la Trinita, 6074
☎ 075 5178550 ▤ 075 5177538
e-mail: ilrocolo@ilrocolo.it website: www.ilrocolo.it
Open: 15 Apr-Sep Site: 2.4HEC ⊞ ⬥ ▲ Prices: ♠5-6 ♠2-2.50 ♠5-6 ▲4.50-5 Facilities: ♠ ⚍ ⊙ ⬤ ⊘ 🏠 Services: ⚎ ✗ ⊞ lau Off-site: ⚏ ⬦P

PARMA PARMA

Cittadella parco Cittadella, 43100 ☎ 0521 961434
Camping Card Compulsory.
Site: 4HEC ⊞ ♣ Prices: ♠6.50 ♠5.50 ♠5.50 ▲5.50
Facilities: ♠ ⊙ ⬤ ⚏ Off-site: ⚍ ⚎ ✗ ⊘ ⚏ ⊞

PASSIGNANO PERUGIA

Europa Loc San Donato, 06065 ☎ 075 827405 ▤ 075 827405
e-mail: info@camping-europa.it website: www.camping-europa.it
Situated by Lake Trasimeno with private beach.
➩ *From the motorway take exit Passignano Est and campsite is signposted.*
Open: Etr-10 Oct Site: 3HEC ⊞ ♣ 🏠 ♠ Prices: ♠5.70-6.90 ♠2.50-3.50 ♠6-7 ▲5.30-6.30 Facilities: ♠ ⚍ ⊙ ⬤ ⊘ 🏠 Services: ⚎ ✗ ⊞ lau Leisure: ⬦ LP

Kursaal viale Europa 24, 06065
☎ 075 828085 ▤ 075 827182
e-mail: kursaalcamp@libero.it
website: www.camping.it/umbria/kursaal
The site is situated between the road and the lake, near the villa of the same name.

➩ *Access from SS75, Arezzo to Perugia road, from Km35.2.*
Open: Apr-29 Oct Site: 1HEC ⊞ ♣ Prices: ♠6-7 ♠2-2 ♠8-9 ▲8-9 pitch 8-9 Facilities: ♠ ⚍ ⊙ ⬤ ⊘ 🏠 Services: ⚎ ✗ lau Leisure: ⬦ LP Off-site: ⊞

PIEVEPELAGO MODENA

Fra Dolcino 41027 ☎ 0536 71229
Open: All year Site: 3.6HEC ⊞ ⬥ ♣ 🏠 Facilities: ♠ ⚍ ⊙ ⬤ ⚏ 🏠 Services: ⚎ ✗ lau Off-site: ✗ ⬦PR ⊞

Rio Verde via M-de-Canossa 34, 41027
☎ 0536 72204 ▤ 0536 72204
e-mail: info@abetour.it website: www.abetour.it
In a wooded mountain setting close to the river with good, modern facilities.
➩ *Access via A1 from Firenze via Pistoia, La Lima and Abetone.*
Open: All year Site: 1.8HEC ⊞ ⬥ 🏠 ♠ Prices: ♠4.65-5.70 ♠5.70-6.70 ▲3.60-4.65 pitch 5.70-6.70 Facilities: ♠ ⊙ ⬤ ⚏ Services: ⚎ ✗ lau Leisure: ⬦ R Off-site: ⚍ ⊘ ⚏ ⬦LP ⊞

PINARELLA RAVENNA

Pinarella viale Abruzzi 52, 48015
☎ 0544 987408 ▤ 0544 987408
e-mail: campingpinarella@libero,it
website: www.campingpinarella.com
Subdivided terrain surrounded by houses. Partially shaded, some young poplars. Private beach. Management request reservations day before arrival.
Site: 1.8HEC ⊞ ♣ ⊗ Facilities: ♠ ⊙ ⬤ 🏠 Services: ⚎ ✗ ⊞ lau Off-site: ⚍ ✗ ⊘ ⚏ ⬦S

Safari viale Titano 130, 48015 ☎ 0544 987356 ▤ 0544 987356
e-mail: csafari@cervia.com website: www.cervia.com
The site is divided into several sections. Only families are accepted.
Open: May-15 Sep Site: 3.1HEC ⊞ ♣ ⊗ Facilities: ♠ ⚍ ⊙ ⬤ ⊘ ⚏ 🏠 Services: ⚎ ✗ ⊞ lau Off-site: ✗ ⬦S

PINETO TERAMO

Heliopolis Contrada Villa Fumosa, 64025
☎ 085 9492720 ▤ 085 9492171
e-mail: info@heliopolis.it website: www.heliopolis.it
Situated near a golden sandy beach. Various activies for all to enjoy. Idyllic scenery for relaxing walks.
Open: Apr-Sep Site: 12HEC ⊞ ⁖⁖ ♣ ♠ Prices: ♠4-7 ▲7.80 Facilities: ♠ ⚍ ⊙ ⬤ ⊘ ⚏ Services: ⚎ ✗ ⊞ lau Leisure: ⬦ PS

International Loc Torre Cerrano, 64025
☎ 085 930639 ▤ 085 930639
e-mail: info@internationalcamping.it
website: www.internationalcamping.it
Site on level terrain with young poplars. Sunshade roofing on the beach.
➩ *Turn off SS16 at Km431.2 and continue under railway underpass. Adjoining railway line.*
Open: May-Sep Site: 1.5HEC ⊞ ♣ ♠ ⊗ Prices: ♠3.80-7 ♠7.60-14 ▲3-6 pitch 7.60-14 Facilities: ♠ ⚍ ⊙ ⬤ ⊘ ⚏ 🏠 ⚏ Services: ⚎ ✗ ⊞ lau Leisure: ⬦ S

Pineto Beach S.s 16 km425, 64025
☎ 085 9492724 ▤ 085 9492796
e-mail: pinetobeach@camping.it
website: www.camping.it/abruzzo/pinetobeach/
A well equipped site in wooded surroundings with direct access to the beach.
➩ *At Km425 on SS16 `Adriatica'.*
Open: 15 May-29 Sep Site: 3HEC ⊞ ⁖⁖ ♣ 🏠 ♠ Prices: ♠6-8 ♠1.50-2.50 ♠9.50-14 ▲7-14 Facilities: ♠ ⚍ ⊙ ⬤ ⊘ ⚏ Services: ⚎ ✗ ⊞ lau Leisure: ⬦ PS

Site: 6HEC-Site size ⊞-grass ⁖⁖-sand ⬥-stone ⬙-little shade ⬥-partly shaded ♣-mainly shaded
🏠-bungalows for hire ♠-caravans for hire ▲-tents for hire ⊗-no dogs Prices: ♠-adult per night ♠-car per night
pp-per person per night ♠-caravan per night ▲-tent per night

POMPOSA FERRARA

International Tre Moschettieri via Capanno Garibaldi 22, 44020 ☎ 0533 380376 ▤ 0533 380377
e-mail: info@tremoschettieri.com
website: www.tremoschettieri.com
Camp site set beneath pine trees next to sea.
➲ *Signposted from SS309.*
Open: 23 Apr-19 Sep Site: 11HEC ⬛ ⠿ ♠ ⏏ Prices: ⋔4-8 pitch 9-15 Facilities: ⋔ ⅀ ☉ ⬚ ⬭ ⫝ Services: ⏚ ✗ ⊞ lau
Leisure: ⋋ PS Off-site: ⫝ ⋋L ⊞

PORTO SANT'ELPÍDIO ASCOLI PICENO

Risacca via Gabbie 6, 63018 ☎ 0734 991423 ▤ 0734 997276
e-mail: info@larisacca.it website: www.larisacca.it
Clean, well-kept site on level meadowland, with some trees surrounded by fields.
➲ *Turn off main SS16 N of village, follow road seawards under railway (narrow underpass maximum height 3mtrs), then 1.2km along field paths to site. Caravan access is 400mtrs further S along SS16, then under railway and along field paths to site.*
Open: 22 May-11Sep Site: 8HEC ⬛ ♠ ⏏ ⫝ ⚑ ⚘
Prices: ⋔2.50-8 ⛟7-16 ⛺7-16 pitch 7-16 Facilities: ⋔ ⅀ ☉ ⬚ ⬭ ⫝ ⬚ Services: ⏚ ✗ ⊞ lau Leisure: ⋋ PS Off-site: ⋋R

PRECI PERUGIA

Il Collaccio Castelvecchio di Preci, 6047
☎ 0743 939005 ▤ 0743 939094
e-mail: info@ilcollaccio.com website: www.ilcollaccio.com
In beautiful natural surroundings with plenty of roomy pitches and good recreational facilities.
➲ *Access via SS 209.*
Open: Apr-Sep Site: 10HEC ⬛ ⚑ ⏏ Prices: ⋔5.50-7.25
⛟2-3 ⛟6.50-8.50 ⛺5.50-7.25 Facilities: ⋔ ⅀ ☉ ⬚ ⬭ ⬚ Services: ⏚ ✗ lau Leisure: ⋋ P Off-site: ⋋R

PUNTA MARINA RAVENNA

AT ADRIANO, LIDO (4.5KM S)

Adriano via dei Campeggi 7, 48020
☎ 0544 437230 ▤ 0544 438510
e-mail: info@campingadriano.com
website: www.campingadriano.com
300mtrs from the sea. A pleasantly landscaped site amidst the dunes of the Punta Marina.
➲ *On SS309 via Lido Adriano to Punta Marina.*
Open: 17 Apr-21 Sep Site: 14HEC ⬛ ⠿ ♠ ⏏ ⚑
Facilities: ⋔ ⅀ ☉ ⬚ ⬭ ⬚ Services: ⏚ ✗ ⊞ lau Leisure: ⋋ PS

Coop 3 via dei Campeggi 8, 48020
☎ 0544 437353 ▤ 0544 438144
e-mail: campingcoop3@libero.it
website: digilander.iol.it/campingcoop3
300mtrs to the sea. Level site under isolated high pines and poplars. Across flat dunes to the beach.
➲ *Signposted.*
Open: 25 Apr-16 Sep Site: 7HEC ⬛ ♠ ⚑ Facilities: ⋔ ⅀ ☉ ⬚ ⬭ ⬚ Services: ⏚ ✗ lau Off-site: ⫝ ⋋PS ⊞

RAVENNA, MARINA DI RAVENNA

International Piomboni via Lungomare 421, 48023
☎ 0544 530230 ▤ 0544 538618
e-mail: info@campingpiomboni.it
website: www.campingpiomboni.it
Site on slightly undulating mainly grassy terrain with pines and poplars. Separate section for tents. Lunchtime siesta 14.00-15.30 hrs.
➲ *Access is 1km S from town centre off coast road.*
Open: 25 Apr-12 Sep Site: 5HEC ⬛ ♠ ⏏ ⚑ Prices: ⋔4.50-6.50 pitch 7.50-10.40 Facilities: ⋔ ⅀ ☉ ⬚ ⬭ ⬚ Services: ⏚ ✗ ⊞ lau Leisure: ⋋ S

RICCIONE FORLI

Alberello via Torino 80, 47036
☎ 0541 615402 ▤ 0541 615248
e-mail: direzione@alberello.it website: www.alberello.it
On the seafront connected to the beach by a private subway. Popular with families, with a wide range of recreational facilities.
➲ *Access via A14 and SS16.*
Open: 18 May-15 Sep Site: 4HEC ⬛ ♠ ⚘ Facilities: ⋔ ⅀ ☉ ⬚ ⬭ ⬚ Services: ⏚ ✗ ⊞ lau Off-site: ⋋PRS

Fontanelle via Torino 56, 47838 ☎ 0541 615449 ▤ 0541 610193
e-mail: info@campingfontanelle.com
website: www.campingfontanelle.com
On southern outskirts separated from beach by coast road. Underpass to public beach.
Camping Card Compulsory.
➲ *Turn off SS16 between Km216 and 217.*
Open: 21 Apr-22 Sep Site: 6HEC ⬛ ♠ Facilities: ⋔ ⅀ ☉ ⬚ ⬭ ⬚ Services: ⏚ ✗ ⊞ lau Leisure: ⋋ S

Riccione via Marsala N10, 47838
☎ 0541 690160 ▤ 0541 690044
e-mail: info@campingriccione.it website: www.campingriccione.it
About 300mtrs from sea. Extensive flat meadowland, with poplars of medium height.
➲ *From SS16 turn seawards on the S outskirts of the town and continue for 200mtrs. Alternative access from coast road, turn inland on S outskirts at sign and continue for 700mtrs.*
Open: 18 Apr-20 Sep Site: 6.5HEC ⬛ ♠ Facilities: ⋔ ⅀ ☉ ⬚ ⬭ ⬚ Services: ⏚ ✗ lau Leisure: ⋋ P Off-site: ⋋S ⊞

Facilities: ⅀-shop **⋔**-shower **☉**-electric points for razors **⬚**-electric points for caravans **⬚**-parking by tents permitted **⬚**-compulsory separate car park **Services: ✗**-café/restaurant **⏚**-bar **⬭**-Camping Gaz International **⬭**-gas other than Camping Gaz **⊞**-first aid facilities lau-laundry **Leisure: ⋋**-swimming L-Lake P-Pool R-River S-Sea **Off-site:** All facilities within 2km

ROSETO DEGLI ABRUZZI TERAMO

Eurcamping-Roseto Lungomare Trieste Sud 90, 64026
☎ 085 8993179 ▤ 085 8930552
e-mail: eurcamping@camping.it
website: www.eurcamping.it
A meadow site at the S end of the beach road.
➲ *Leave the SS16 within the town, then continue for 500mtrs to the site.*
Open: Mar-Oct Site: 5HEC ⸬⸬⸬ ♣ 🏠 Facilities: 🏪 🛒 ⊙ 🖪 ⌀ 🚿 🚽 Services: 🍴 ✗ lau Leisure: ⚲ PS Off-site: ⚲R ⊞

Gilda viale Makarska, 64026 ☎ 085 8941023 ▤ 085 8941023
In a picturesque wooded setting with direct access to the beach and good, modern facilities.
Open: Jun-30 Aug Site: 1.5HEC ⸬⸬⸬ ♣ 🏠 🛒 Facilities: 🏪 🛒 ⊙ 🖪 🚿 🚽 Services: 🍴 ✗ ⊞ lau Leisure: ⚲ S Off-site: ⌀ ⚲P

SALSOMAGGIORE TERME PARMA

Arizona via Tabiano 42, 43030
☎ 0524 565648 ▤ 0524 567589
e-mail: info@camping-arizona.com
website: www.camping-arizona.com
Family site with plenty of activities, and close to two "thermal cures" establishments.
Open: Apr-15 Oct Site: 13HEC ⸬⸬⸬ ♣ 🏠 Prices: ♠5.50-7 🚐8-11 ▲5-10 Facilities: 🏪 🛒 ⊙ 🖪 ⌀ 🛒 Services: 🍴 ✗ lau Leisure: ⚲ P Off-site: 🚿 ⊞

See advertisement on page 279

S ARCANGELO SUL TRASIMENO PERUGIA

Polvese via Montivalle, 6060 ☎ 075 848078 ▤ 075 848050
e-mail: cpolvese@interfree.iti website: www.polvese.com
In a peaceful location beside Lake Trasimeno with plenty of recreational facilities.
Open: Apr-Sep Site: 5HEC ⸬⸬⸬ ♣ 🏠 Facilities: 🏪 🛒 ⊙ 🖪 ⌀ 🚿 🏠 Services: 🍴 ✗ lau Leisure: ⚲ LP

Villaggio Italgest via Martiri di Cefalonia, 06060
☎ 075 848238 ▤ 075 848085
e-mail: camping@italgest.com website: www.italgest.com
Situated by a lake and surrounded by woodland. There are good, modern facilities and all kinds of recreation are available.
Open: Apr-Sep Site: 5.5HEC ⸬⸬⸬ ♣ 🏠 ▲ Prices: ♠5.70-8 🚐1.80-2.50 🚐6-8.30 ▲6-8.30 Facilities: 🏪 🛒 ⊙ 🖪 ⌀ 🚿 🏠 Services: 🍴 ✗ ⊞ lau Leisure: ⚲ LP

SAN MARINO

Centro Turistico San Marino Strada San Michele 50, 47893
☎ 0549 903964 ▤ 0549 907120
e-mail: Info@centrovacanzesanmarino
website: www.centrovacanzesanmarino.com
In a quiet, wooded location close to the centre of the Republic of San Marino.
➲ *Access via 'Rimini Sud' exit on the A14.*
Open: All year Site: 100HEC ⸬⸬⸬ ♣ 🏠 ▲ Prices: ♠5-8 🚐2-4 🚐4-11 ▲3-8 Facilities: 🏪 🛒 ⊙ 🖪 ⌀ 🚿 🏠 Services: 🍴 ✗ ⊞ lau Leisure: ⚲ P Off-site: ⚲LRS

SAN PIERO IN BAGNO FORLI

Altosavio strada per Alfero 37c, 47026
☎ 0543 903409 ▤ 0543 903409/917397
e-mail: i4std@libero.it
website: www.bagnodiromagnaturismo.it
On level ground at an altitude of 600mtrs with good facilities.
➲ *Exit E45 at Bagno di Romagna for San Piero in Bagno*
Open: 24 Apr-Sep Site: 1.3HEC ⸬⸬⸬ ♣ Prices: ♠4.20-5 pitch 7.50 Facilities: 🏪 ⊙ 🖪 🛒 Services: 🍴 ✗ lau Off-site: 🛒 ✗ ⌀ 🚿 ⚲LR ⊞

SASSO MARCONI BOLOGNA

Piccolo Paradiso via Sirano, Marzabotto, 40037
☎ 051 842680 ▤ 051 6756581
Pleasant site with plenty of trees. A new sport centre less than 100mtrs from the site provides excellent facilities for sports and recreation.
➲ *Leave A1 autostrada (Milano-Roma) at town exit and continue towards Vado for 2km. Signposted.*
Open: All year Site: 6.5HEC ⸬⸬⸬ ♣ 🏠 🛒 Facilities: 🏪 🛒 ⊙ 🖪 ⌀ 🚿 🏠 Services: 🍴 ✗ lau Off-site: ⚲LPR

AT SAVIGNANO SUL RUBICONE

Rubicone via Matrice Destra 1, 47039
☎ 0541 346377 ▤ 0541 346999
e-mail: info@campingrubicone.com
website: www.campingrubicone.com
An extensive, level site divided into two sections by a narrow canal. It extends to the beach.
➲ *Situated about 0.8km from the road fork at Km187/0 off SS16 (Strada Adriatica).*
Open: 3 May-28 Sep Site: 13HEC ⸬⸬⸬ 🛒 ♣ 🏠 🛒
Prices: ♠4.60-8.50 pitch 9.80-14.70 Facilities: 🏪 🛒 ⊙ 🖪 ⌀ 🏠 Services: 🍴 ✗ ⊞ lau Leisure: ⚲ PS

SCACCHI, LIDO DEGLI FERRARA

Florenz via alpi Centrali 199, 44020
☎ 0533 380193 ▤ 0533 313166
e-mail: info@campingflorenz.com
website: www.campingflorenz.com
Site with sand dunes extending to the sea.
➲ *Turn off the Strada Romea in the direction of Lido Degli Scacchi, and continue along an asphalt road to the sandy beach.*
Open: 10 Apr-18 Sep Site: 8HEC ⸬⸬⸬ ♣ 🏠 🛒 Prices: ♠4-8 pitch 9.30-15.20 Facilities: 🏪 🛒 ⊙ 🖪 ⌀ 🚿 🏠 Services: 🍴 ✗ ⊞ lau Leisure: ⚲ PS

SENIGALLIA ANCONA

Summerland via Podesti 236, 60019
☎ 071 7926816 ▤ 071 7927758
website: www.camping.it/marche/summerland
A pleasant site with good facilities, 150mtrs from the sea.
➲ *3km from Senigallia exit on SS16.*
Open: Jun-15 Sep Site: 4.5HEC ⸬⸬⸬ ♣ 🏠 🛒 Facilities: 🏪 🛒 ⊙ 🖪 ⌀ 🏠 Services: 🍴 ✗ ⊞ lau Off-site: ⚲PS

SPINA, LIDO DI FERRARA

Spina via del Campeggio 99, 44024
☎ 0533 330179 ▤ 0533 333566
e-mail: spina@clubdesole.com website: www.clubdesole.com
Widespread site on level meadowland and on slightly hilly sand dune terrain. Separate section for dog owners.
➲ *Off SS309. Signposted.*
Open: Mar-Oct Site: 24HEC ⸬⸬⸬ ♣ 🏠 Prices: ♠3-8 pitch 8-13 Facilities: 🏪 🛒 ⊙ 🖪 ⌀ 🚿 🏠 Services: 🍴 ✗ lau Leisure: ⚲ PS Off-site: ⊞

SPOLETO PERUGIA

Girasole Loc. Petrognano, 6049
☎ 0743 51335 ▤ 0743 51335
website: www.campingilgirasole.com
Site on high ground with terraces and thick tree coverage.
Camping Carnet required for 1-2 nights stay.
➲ *S via SS3 towards Montefalco.*
Open: Apr-Sep Site: 2.5HEC ⸬⸬⸬ ♣ 🏠 🛒 ▲ Prices: ♠6.50 🚐3 🚐7-10 ▲5-6 Facilities: 🏪 🛒 ⊙ 🖪 ⌀ 🏠 Services: 🍴 ⊞ lau Off-site: ✗ 🚿

Site: 6HEC-Site size ⸬⸬⸬-grass ⁙-sand ◈-stone ☀-little shade ☘-partly shaded ♣-mainly shaded 🏠-bungalows for hire 🚐-caravans for hire ▲-tents for hire ⊘-no dogs Prices: ♠-adult per night 🚗-car per night pp-per person per night 🚐-caravan per night ▲-tent per night

Monteluco S.Pietro, 06049 ☎ 0743 220358 📳 0743 207146
e-mail: campeggiomonteluco@libero.it
website: www.geocities.com/monteluco2002
A modern site situated on the slopes of Monteluco.
➔ *From the SS75 towards Foligno exit on to the SS3 towards Spoleto. The Monteluco road leads to the site.*
Open: Apr-Sep Site: 6HEC ⛺ ⚘ ♣ ☂ Prices: ⭡5-6 ☗2-3 ☗4-5 ▲4-5 Facilities: ⬕ ⊙ ☕ ☵ 🏠 🅿 Services: ⬤ ✗
Off-site: 🛒 🚻

TORINO DI SANGRO MARINA CHIETI

Belvedere 66020 ☎ 0873 911381
Open: Jun-15 Sep Site: 1.5HEC ⛺ ♣ ☂ Facilities: ⬕ 🛒 ⊙ ☕ ⌀ ☵ 🏠 Services: ⬤ ✗ 🚻 lau Leisure: ⬝ S Off-site: ✗ ⬝P 🚻

VALLICELLA DI MONZUNO BOLOGNA

Le Querce Rioveggio, 40036 ☎ 051 6770248 📳 051 6770394
A well equipped site in a wooded mountain setting.
➔ *Access via Autostrada del Sole.*
Open: May-Sep Site: 12HEC ⛺ ♣ ☂ ☂ ▲ Prices: ⭡5 ☗7 ▲6 Facilities: ⬕ 🛒 ⊙ ☕ ⌀ ☵ 🏠 🅿 Services: ⬤ ✗ 🚻 lau
Leisure: ⬝ LPR

VASTO CHIETI

Europa 66055 ☎ 0873 801988 📳 0873 802553
Site on level terrain by the road with poplars.
➔ *At Km522 of road SS16.*
Open: May-Sep Site: 2.3HEC ⛺ ♣ ☂ Prices: ⭡4.80-7 pitch 7.30-12 Facilities: ⬕ 🛒 ⊙ ☕ ☵ Services: ⬤ ✗ lau
Leisure: ⬝ S

Grotta del Saraceno via Osca 6, loc Vignola, 66054
☎ 0873 310213 📳 0873 310295
e-mail: info@grottadelsaraceno.it
website: www.grottadelsaraceno.it
Site in olive grove on steep coastal cliffs with lovely views.
Steep path to beach. Siesta 14.00-16.00 hrs.
➔ *Turn off SS16 at Km512.200.*
Open: 15 Jun-15 Sep Site: 12HEC ⛺ ♣ Facilities: ⬕ ⊙ ☕ ☵ Services: ⬤ ✗ lau Leisure: ⬝ S Off-site: ⌀ ☵

Pioppeto 66055 ☎ 0873 801466 📳 0873 801466
Camping Card Compulsory.
Open: 15 May-14 Sep Site: 1.7HEC ⛺ ♣ Facilities: ⬕ 🛒 ⊙ ☕ ⌀ 🅿 Services: ⬤ ✗ Leisure: ⬝ S Off-site: 🚻

ZOCCA MODENA

Montequestiolo via Montequestiolo 184, 41059
☎ 059 985137 📳 059 985137
e-mail: monteq@tin.it
Site: 1.8HEC ⛺ ♣ ☂ ☂ ▲ Facilities: ⬕ 🛒 ⊙ ☕ ☵ 🅿 Services: ⬤ ✗ 🚻 lau Off-site: ⬝P

ROME

BOLSENA VITERBO

Blu International via Cassia, 01023
☎ 0761 798855 📳 0761 798855
e-mail: info@blucamping.it website: www.blucamping.it
A modern site with good facilities in a wooded location on the shore of Lake Bolsena. Compulsory separate car parking July and August.
➔ *Access via A1 exit Orvieto, then Via Cassia at Km111.650.*
Open: Apr-Sep Site: 3HEC ⛺ ♣ ☂ ☂ Prices: pitch 13 (incl 2 persons) Facilities: ⬕ 🛒 ⊙ ☕ 🅿 Services: ⬤ ✗ Leisure: ⬝ LP Off-site: ⌀ ☵ 🚻

Lido via Cassia km111, 01023 ☎ 0761 799258 📳 0761 796105
e-mail: info@atihotels.it website: www.bolsenacamping.it
A lakeside family site with good modern facilities.
➔ *Access via motorway exit 'Orvieto'.*
Open: Apr-Sep Site: 10HEC ⛺ ♣ ☂ ⌀ Prices: ⭡4.50-6.10 ☗1.70-2.60 pitch 8.50-10.50 Facilities: ⬕ 🛒 ⊙ ☕ ☵ 🅿 Services: ⬤ ✗ lau Leisure: ⬝ LP

BRACCIANO ROMA

Porticciolo via Porticciolo, 00062
☎ 06 99803060 📳 06 998803030
e-mail: info@porticciolo.it website: www.porticciolo.it
A family site in a pleasant location on the shore of a lake.
➔ *Access via SS493 to Bracciano.*
Open: Apr-Sep Site: 12HEC ⛺ ♣ ☂ ☂ Prices: ⭡4.10-5.50 ☗1.60-3 ☗4.40-6.40 ▲3.30-6.40 pitch 11 (incl 2 persons) Facilities: ⬕ 🛒 ⊙ ☕ ⌀ 🅿 Services: ⬤ ✗ lau Leisure: ⬝ L Off-site: 🚻

FIANO ROMANO ROMA

Bungalow Park I Pini via delle Sassete 1A, 00065
☎ 0765 453349 📳 0765 453057
e-mail: ipini@camping.it website: www.ecvacanze.it
A modern, well equipped site within easy reach of the centre of Rome which makes an excellent base for excursions.
➔ *From A1 Firenze-Roma take exit Fiano Romana.*
Open: 15 Mar-15 Nov Site: 5HEC ⛺ ⚘ ☂ Facilities: ⬕ 🛒 ⊙ ☕ ⌀ 🏠 Services: ⬤ ✗ 🚻 lau Leisure: ⬝ P

FORMIA LATINA

Gianola via delle Vigne, 04023 ☎ 0771 720223
e-mail: gianolacamping@tiscalinet.it
Situated in a narrow grassland area near a little stream and trees amidst agricultural land. Pleasantly sandy beach edged by rocks.
➔ *Access via Roma-Napoli road, from S Croce 800mtrs.*
Open: Apr-Sep Site: 4HEC ⛺ ⁝⁝⁝ ♣ ☂ Facilities: ⬕ 🛒 ⊙ ☕ ⌀ 🏠 Services: ⬤ ✗ Leisure: ⬝ S

MINTURNO, MARINA DI LATINA

Golden Garden via Dunale 74, 04020
☎ 0771 681425 📳 0771 614059
e-mail: servizio.clienti@goldengarden.it
website: www.goldengarden.it
Secluded quiet site within agricultural area by the sea.
Camping Card Compulsory.
➔ *Access from the SS7 across river bridge (Garigliano) and continue changing direction. Last km sandy field track.*
Open: Apr-15 Oct Site: 2.3HEC ⛺ ♣ ☂ ☂ ⌀ Prices: pitch 16-31 (incl 2 persons) pp4-8 Facilities: ⬕ 🛒 ⊙ ☕ ⌀ 🏠 🅿 Services: ⬤ ✗ lau Leisure: ⬝ S Off-site: ✗ ⬝PR 🚻

MONTALTO DI CASTRO, MARINA DI VITERBO

California 01014 ☎ 0766 802848 📳 0766 801210
Situated on the coast below an ancient pine grove with good facilities for sports and leisure.
Open: May-Sep Site: 1.4HEC ⛺ ⁝⁝⁝ ♣ ☂ ☂ Facilities: ⬕ 🛒 ⊙ ☕ ⌀ 🅿 Services: ⬤ ✗ 🚻 lau Leisure: ⬝ S

Internazionale Pionier Etrusco via Vulsinia, 01014
☎ 0766 802199 📳 0766 801214
e-mail: meleute@tin.it
website: www.campingpionieretrusco.com
Situated in a pine forest close to the beach. Various leisure and sports activities, also a relaxing atmosphere.
Camping Card Compulsory.
Open: Mar-15 Oct Site: 3HEC ⁝⁝⁝ ♣ ☂ ☂ Prices: pitch 17-32 (incl 2 persons) Facilities: ⬕ 🛒 ⊙ ☕ ⌀ ☵ 🅿 Services: ⬤ ✗ lau Off-site: ⬝PRS 🚻

Facilities: 🛒-shop ⬕-shower ⊙-electric points for razors ☕-electric points for caravans 🏠-parking by tents permitted 🅿-compulsory separate car park **Services:** ✗-café/restaurant ⬤-bar ⌀-Camping Gaz International ☵-gas other than Camping Gaz 🚻-first aid facilities lau-laundry **Leisure:** ⬝-swimming L-Lake P-Pool R-River S-Sea **Off-site:** All facilities within 2km

ROMA (ROME) ROMA

Flaminio Village via Flaminia Nuova 821, 00189
☎ 06 3332604   ▤ 06 3330653
e-mail: info@villageflaminio.com
website: www.villageflaminio.com
An exstensive site with good facilities, which lies in a quiet valley on narrow terraces on a hill.
➲ *From ring road follow via Flaminia, SS3, for 2.5km towards city centre.*
Open: All year Site: 8.4HEC ⸬ ♣ ⬛ Prices: ⚬8.90-10
⬤4.20-4.70 ⬤6.70-7.80 ▲4.90-6.40 Facilities: ⬧ ⚏ ⊙ ⬛ ⬢
⬚ ⬚ Services: ⬤ ✖ lau Leisure: ⬚ P Off-site: ⊞

Happy via Prato della Corte 1915, 123
☎ 06 33626401   ▤ 06 33613800
e-mail: info@happycamping.net
Conveniently placed in northern area of town. Modern installations, electricity and hot water free throughout.
➲ *Exit No.5 "Grande Raccordo Anulare" (ring road).*
Open: 15 Mar-5 Nov Site: 3.6HEC ⸬ ♣ ⬛ ⬤ Facilities: ⬧
⚏ ⊙ ⬛ ⬢ Services: ⬤ ✖ lau Leisure: ⬚ P

Roma via Aurelia 831, 00165 ☎ 06 6623018   ▤ 06 66418147
The site lies on terraces on a hill near the AGIP Motel. All kinds of excursions can be arranged.
➲ *From ring road follow SS1 (via Aurelia) for 1.5km towards town centre turn off to site at Km8/11.*
Open: All year Site: 3HEC ⸬ ♣ Facilities: ⬧ ⚏ ⊙ ⬛ ⬢ ⬚
⬚ Services: ⬤ ✖ lau Off-site: ⊞

Seven Hills via Cassia 1216, 00189
☎ 06 30310826   ▤ 06 30310039
e-mail: seven-hills@camping.it
website: www.camping.it/lazio/seven-hills
A fine, partly terraced site in beautiful rural surroundings yet ideally situated for access to the city by bus or underground.

➲ *2.5km NE of the outer ring road via exit '3'.*
Site: 5HEC ⸬ ⬢ ♣ ⬛ ▲ Facilities: ⬧ ⚏ ⊙ ⬛ ⬢ ⬚ ⬢
Services: ⬤ ✖ ⊞ lau Leisure: ⬚ P

See advertisement on page 283

Tiber via Tiberina Km1400, 188
☎ 06 33610733   ▤ 06 33612314
e-mail: info@campingtiber.com
website: www.campingtiber.com
On level grassland, shaded by poplars beside the Tiber.
➲ *N of city. Signposted from ringroad. Access from N via exit '3' or from S follow signs 'Prima Porta'.*
Open: 15 Mar-Oct Site: 5HEC ⸬ ♣ ⬛ Prices: ⚬8.50-9.60
⬤4.20-4.60 ⬤6.10-7.10 ▲4.20-4.70 Facilities: ⬧ ⚏ ⊙ ⬛ ⬢
⬢ Services: ⬤ ✖ ⊞ lau Leisure: ⬚ PR

SALTO DI FONDI LATINA

Fondi Holiday Camp via Flacca Km 6800, 04020
☎ 0771 555009
e-mail: info@holidayvillage.it website: www.holidayvillage.it
Well-shaded and well-equipped site only a few metres from the Mediterranean.
Open: Apr-Sep Site: 4HEC ⸬ ⸬ ♣ ⬛ ⬤ ⬥
Prices: pitch 26-50 (incl 2 persons) Facilities: ⬧ ⚏ ⊙ ⬛ ⬚
⬢ Services: ⬤ ✖ ⊞ lau Leisure: ⬚ PS

TERRACINA LATINA

Badino Porto Badino, 04019 ☎ 0773 764430   ▤ 0773 764430
In wooded surroundings with direct access to the beach.
➲ *From the main Roma-Napoli road head towards the canal (Porto Canale Badino) and the sea.*
Open: Apr-14 Oct Site: 1.8HEC ⸬ ⸬ ♣ ⬛ ⬤ ▲
Prices: ⚬4.25-6.85 ⬤2.60-5 ⬤7-12.70 Facilities: ⬧ ⊙ ⬛ ⬢
⬚ ⬢ Services: ⬤ ✖ lau Leisure: ⬚ S Off-site: ⚏ ✖

Site: 6HEC-Site size ⸬-grass ⸬-sand ⬢-stone ⬢-little shade ⬢-partly shaded ♣-mainly shaded
⬛-bungalows for hire ⬤-caravans for hire ▲-tents for hire ⬥-no dogs Prices: ⚬-adult per night ⬤-car per night
pp-per person per night ⬤-caravan per night ▲-tent per night

SOUTH

BAIA DOMIZIA CASERTA

Baia Domizia Camping Villaggio Baia Domizia, 81030
☎ 0823 930164 📠 0823 930375
e-mail: info@baiadomizia.it website: www.baiadomizia.it
Part of this extensive seaside site is laid out with flower beds.
Good sports and leisure facilities. Ideal for families. No
radios allowed.
➲ *Turn off the SS7 (qtr) at Km6/V, then 3km seawards.*
Open: May-19 Sep **Site:** 30HEC ⚏ ⁞⁞ ♣ 🏠 🚐 ⌦
Prices: ♦4.30-9.80 ♠2.80-5.50 ☎7.50-19 ▲2.60-7.60
Facilities: ℝ ⅃ ⊙ 🚱 ∅ ≞ 🏚 **Services:** ⅄ ✗ ⊞ lau **Leisure:** ↄ PS

BATTIPAGLIA SALERNO

Lido Mediterraneo via Litoranea, Salerno Paestum, 84091
☎ 0828 624097 📠 0828 624097
e-mail: mediterraneo.campania@camping.it
website: www.camping.it/campania/mediterraneo
In a pinewood with direct access to a private beach.
Open: 10 Mar-22 Sept **Site:** 1.2HEC ⚏ ♣ 🏠 🚐
Facilities: ℝ ⅃ ⊙ 🚱 ∅ ≞ 🏚 **Services:** ⅄ ✗ **Leisure:** ↄ S
Off-site: ✗ ↄP ⊞

BRIATICO CATANZARO

Dolomiti 89817 ☎ 0963 391355 📠 0963 393009
e-mail: dolmar@tin.it website: www.dolomitisulmare.com
The site is in a delightful setting on two terraces planted with
olive trees. It lies by the road and 150mtrs from railway.
➲ *Turn off road 522 between Km17 and Km18 and head
towards the sea.*
Open: 24 Jun-27 Sep **Site:** 5HEC ⚏ ♣ 🏠 🚐 **Prices:** ♦5-12
♠3-6 🚐10-17 ▲6-11 **Facilities:** ℝ ⅃ ⊙ 🚱 ∅ ≞ 🄿
Services: ⅄ ✗ lau **Leisure:** ↄ PS **Off-site:** ↄP ⊞

CAMEROTA, MARINA DI SALERNO

Risacca via delle Barche 11, Lentiscella, 84059
☎ 0974 932415 📠 0974 932415 & 0632 90973
e-mail: larisacca@its2001.it website: www.larisacca.com
On level ground, shaded by olive trees, with direct access to a
sandy beach.
➲ *Approach via SS18.*
Open: 20 May-25 Sep **Site:** 2HEC ⚏ ♣ 🏠 **Prices:** ♦8.50-12
pitch 10-18 **Facilities:** ℝ ⅃ ⊙ 🚱 🄿 **Services:** ⅄ ✗ ⊞
Leisure: ↄ S **Off-site:** ∅ ≞

CAPO VATICANO CATANZARO

Gabbiano San Nicolo di Ricadi, 89865
☎ 0963 663159 📠 0963 663384
Open: Apr-Oct **Site:** ⚏ ⁞⁞ ♣ 🏠 **Facilities:** ℝ ⅃ ⊙ 🚱 ∅ ≞
🄿 **Services:** ⅄ ✗ lau **Leisure:** ↄ PS **Off-site:** ⊞

CAROVIGNO BRINDISI

AT SPECCHIOLLA, LIDO

Pineta al Mare Lido Specchiolla, 72012
☎ 0831 987821 📠 0831 987826
e-mail: info@campingpinetamare.com
website: www.campingpinetamare.com
Site in pine woodland with sandy beach and some rocks.
➲ *E of Bari-Brindisi road at Km21.5.*
Open: All year **Site:** 5.5HEC ⚏ ♣ 🏠 🚐 **Prices:** ♦4.90-6.90
♠1.60-2.90 🚐5.20-6.90 ▲5.20-6.90 **Facilities:** ℝ ⅃ ⊙ 🚱 ∅
≞ 🏚 **Services:** ⅄ ✗ ⊞ lau **Leisure:** ↄ PS

CIRÒ MARINA CATANZARO

Punta Alice 88811 ☎ 0962 31160
The site lies on meadowland amidst lush Mediterranean
vegetation and borders a fine gravel beach, some 50mtrs wide.
contd.

★ ★ ★ ★
BUNGALOW PARK
SEVEN HILLS VILLAGE
BUNGALOW • CAMPING • MOBILHOME • APPARTAMENTS • RESORT

Via Cassia 1216 • I-00191 ROMA
Tel. 0039/0630362751-310826 • **Fax** 0039/0630310039
E-mail: seven_hills@camping.it
Http: www.camping.it/lazio/seven_hills
Village Seven Hills is located, 1,5 km. Form exit nr. 3 of the GRA in the direction
of Viterbo and is properly connected to the city centre of Rome, which can
be reached in 15 min. by metro or bus. The village squares for caravans and
campers are located on terraces plunged in the greenery of several varieties
of plants. Moreover it's possible to rent bungalows and mini-apartments (with
air conditioning, television and telephone) and mobile homes with bathrooms.
The village structure offers: supermarket, bazaar, bar, internet-room, restaurant,
pizzeria, tobacconist's shop, medical service and a magnificent swimming pool surrounded by palm trees and other exotic plants. The possible sports vary from squash, beach
volleyball to ping pong and golf (the Olgiata course is less than 2 km.). We mustn't
forget the typical guarded mini-zoo (www.sevenhills.it) located within the village. Group
accommodation possibilities are excellent and lots of fun guaranteed! Trips to Pompeii
and Capri are organized. It is possible for groups to stay with special prices, with free
stay for the guide and the bus driver, and free parking for the bus.

10% discount for a minimum stay of 5 days

Facilities: ⅃-shop ℝ-shower ⊙-electric points for razors 🚱-electric points for caravans 🏚-parking by tents permitted
🄿-compulsory separate car park **Services:** ✗-café/restaurant ⅄-bar ∅-Camping Gaz International ≞-gas other than Camping
Gaz ⊞-first aid facilities lau-laundry **Leisure:** ↄ-swimming L-Lake P-Pool R-River S-Sea **Off-site:** All facilities within 2km

➲ *2km from town. From SS106 (Strada Ionica) turn off at Km290 seaward to Cira Marina. Pass through village and follow beach road towards the lighthouse.*
Open: Apr-Sep Site: 5.5HEC ⦂⦂⦂ ♠ 🏠 Facilities: ⬚ 🌿 ⊙ ⬚ ⬚ 🏠 Services: 🍴 ✕ ⊞ lau Leisure: ⬚ PS

Villaggio Torrenova via Torrenova, 88811 ☎ 0962 31482
Directly on sea, with on site facilities to suit all the family.
Open: May-Sep Site: 1.2HEC ⦂⦂⦂ ♠ 🏠 🚐 Facilities: ⬚ 🌿 ⊙ 🚐 🏠 Services: 🍴 ✕ lau Leisure: ⬚ S

CORIGLIANO CÁLABRO COSENZA

Thurium Contrada Ricota Grande, 87060
☎ 0983 851101   📠 0983 851955
e-mail: info@campingthurium.com
website: www.campingthurium.com
The site is close to the beach and has all the facilites needed for an enjoyable camping break. It is just a walk away from the woodland and ideal for peaceful walks.
Open: 09 Apr-15 May Site: 16HEC ⦂⦂⦂ ♠ 🏠 🚐 Prices: ♟2.50-9.50 🚗0.50-4 🚐2.80-10 ⛺2.80-10 Facilities: ⬚ 🌿 ⊙ 🚐 ⬚ 🏠 ⬚ Services: 🍴 ✕ ⊞ lau Leisure: ⬚ PS

EBOLI SALERNO

Paestum Foce Sele, 84020 ☎ 0828 691003   📠 0828 691003
e-mail: info@campingpaestum.com
website: www.campingpaestum.com
Sandy, meadowland site in tall poplar wood by river mouth. Steps and bus service to private beach, 600mtrs from site.
➲ *Access from the Litoranea at Km20 from the road fork to Santa Cecilia and continue for 0.3km. Signposted.*
Open: 15 May-14 Sep Site: 8HEC ⦂⦂⦂ ♠ 🏠 🚐 Facilities: ⬚ 🌿 ⊙ 🚐 ⬚ 🏠 Services: 🍴 ✕ ⊞ lau Leisure: ⬚ P
Off-site: ⬚RS

GALLIPOLI LECCE

Baia di Gallipoli 73014 ☎ 0833 273210   📠 0833 262760
e-mail: info@baiadigallipoli.com
website: www.baiadigallipoli.com
A holiday village set amid pine woods close to the sea with good facilities.**Camping Card Compulsory.**
➲ *5km SE of Gallipoli.*
Open: Jun-Sep Site: 10HEC ⬛⬛ ♠ 🏠 Facilities: ⬚ 🌿 ⊙ 🚐 ⬚ 🏠 Services: 🍴 ✕ ⊞ Leisure: ⬚ P Off-site: ⬚S

Vecchia Torre 73014 ☎ 0833 209083
This well-kept and clean site lies amidst sand dunes in a pine wood. Small size pitches.
➲ *5km N of Gallipoli and 200mtrs S of Hotel Rivabella at seaward side of coast road.*
Open: Jun-Sep Site: 8HEC ⦂⦂⦂ ♠ 🏠 ⊘ Facilities: ⬚ 🌿 ⊙ 🚐 ⬚ 🏠 Services: 🍴 ✕ ⊞ lau Leisure: ⬚ S

GIOVINAZZO BARI

Campofreddo 70054 ☎ 080 3942112   📠 080 3942290
Site in level terrain by the sea, mainly under sunshade roofing. Siesta 14.00-16.00 hrs.
➲ *Turn off the SS16, 20km N of Bari at Km784,300.*
Open: May-Sep Site: 34HEC ⬛⬛ ⊙ 🏠 ⊘ Facilities: ⬚ 🌿 ⊙ 🚐 ⬚ 🏠 Services: 🍴 ✕ ⊞ lau Off-site: ✕ ⬚S

GUARDAVALLE, MARINA DI CATANZARO

Dello Ionio via Nazionale, 88065
☎ 0967 86002   📠 0967 86271
e-mail: calandrusa@yahoo.it **website:** www.calalandrusa.it
Site is situated on the seafront and along 4km of sandy beach. All pitches are under the shade of tall trees and have large grassy areas.

➲ *Situated 2km from Santa Caterina dello Jonio on the SS106.*
Open: Jun-15 Sep Site: 7HEC ⬛⬛ ♠ 🏠 Prices: 🚐4.80-10 ⛺4.80-10 pitch 4.80-10 pp4.50-9.30 Facilities: ⬚ 🌿 ⊙ ⬚ 🏠 Services: 🍴 ✕ ⊞ lau Leisure: ⬚ PS

LÁURA SALERNO

Hera Argiva 84063 ☎ 0828 851193
Site in sandy terrain in eucalyptus grove by the sea.
➲ *Signposted from Km88/VII SS18.*
Open: Apr-Sep Site: 40HEC ⦂⦂⦂ ♠ 🏠 🚐 Facilities: ⬚ 🌿 ⊙ 🚐 ⬚ 🏠 Services: 🍴 ✕ lau Leisure: ⬚ S Off-site: ⊞

LEPORANO, MARINA DI TARANTO

Porto Pirrone Litoranea Salentina, 74020
☎ 099 5334844   📠 099 5334844
e-mail: info@portopirrone.it **website:** www.portopirrone.it
Set in a pine wood offering flat large plots for both tents and caravans. Good sports and entertainment. No Animals.
➲ *From A14 at Massafra towards Taranto and Leporano. Site is near marina.*
Open: Jun-Sep Site: 3.2HEC ⬛⬛ ⦂⦂⦂ ♠ 🏠 ⊘ Facilities: ⬚ 🌿 ⊙ 🚐 ⬚ 🏠 ⬚ Services: 🍴 ✕ ⊞ Leisure: ⬚ S Off-site: ✕ ⬚ ⊞

MÁCCHIA FOGGIA

Monaco 71030 ☎ 0884 530280
In a pleasant situation with good facilities and direct access to the beach.
Open: Jun-Aug Site: 5.3HEC ⬛⬛ ♠ 🏠 🚐 ⊘ Facilities: ⬚ 🌿 ⊙ 🚐 ⬚ 🏠 Services: 🍴 ✕ ⊞ lau Leisure: ⬚ S

MANFREDONIA FOGGIA

Ippocampo SS 159, 71043
☎ 0884 571121   📠 0808724702 & 1782256192
e-mail: vitale@clarence.com
website: www.campingippocampo.too.it
In grounds of a holiday village.
Open: May -Sep Site: 8HEC ⬛⬛ ⦂⦂⦂ ♠ 🏠 ⛺ Prices: ♟3.10-5.50 🚗2-3.50 🚐3.10-8 ⛺1.80-5 Facilities: ⬚ 🌿 ⊙ 🚐 ⬚ 🏠 Services: 🍴 ✕ ⊞ Leisure: ⬚ S Off-site: ⬚P

MASSA LUBRENSE NAPOLI

Villa Lubrense via Partenope 31, 80061 ☎ 081 5339781
website: www.villalubrense.it
Open: All year Site: 2.5HEC ⬛⬛ ♠ 🏠 🚐 Facilities: ⬚ 🌿 ⊙ 🚐 ⬚ Services: 🍴 ✕ ⊞ Leisure: ⬚ PS

MATTINATA FOGGIA

Villaggio Turistico San Lorenzo 71030
☎ 0884 550152   📠 0884 552042
e-mail: info@sanlorenzo.it **website:** www.sanlorenzo.it
The site is situated above the coast road in direction of Viesta. Bungalows for hire.
Camping Card Compulsory.
Open: All year Site: 3HEC ⬛⬛ ♠ 🏠 Prices: ♟5.99-8 🚗3.49 ⛺5.99-7.99 Facilities: ⬚ ⊙ 🚐 ⬚ 🏠 Services: 🍴 ✕ lau Leisure: ⬚ PS Off-site: 🌿 ⬚ ⬚ ⬚S

METAPONTO, LIDO DI MATERA

Camel Camping Club viale Magna Grecia, 75010
☎ 0835 741926
A modern, well organised site. Sports and entertainment available all season. Ideal for both relaxing and sightseeing.
Open: Jun-Sep Site: 3.5HEC ⦂⦂⦂ ♠ 🚐 Facilities: ⬚ 🌿 ⊙ 🚐 Services: 🍴 ✕ Leisure: ⬚ P Off-site: 🌿 ⬚ ⬚S ⊞

Site: 6HEC-Site size ⬛⬛-grass ⦂⦂⦂-sand 🌊-stone 🌿-little shade ⊙-partly shaded ♠-mainly shaded
🏠-bungalows for hire 🚐-caravans for hire ⛺-tents for hire ⊘-no dogs Prices: ♟-adult per night 🚗-car per night
pp-per person per night 🚐-caravan per night ⛺-tent per night

NICÓTERA MARINA CATANZARO

Sabbia d'Oro 88033 ☎ 0963 886395 📠 0966 653312
Lies on level ground amidst farmland 100mtrs from a
beautiful lonely beach.
➲ *Turn off SS18 at Km453/VII and continue 15km.*
Open: 15 Jun-10 Sep Site: 2.7HEC ⸬⸪ ♠ 🏕 🚰 Facilities: ⋔
🗜 ⊙ 🟥 ∅ 🚿 🗒 Services: 🍴 ✗ 🏥 lau Leisure: ⏚ S

OTRANTO LECCE

Mulino d'Acqua via S Stefano, 73028
☎ 0836 802191 📠 0836 802196
e-mail: mulino.camping@anet.it
website: www.mulinodacqua.it
Shaded by olive trees, close to the beach and with plenty of
organised activities.
Open: Jun-10 Sep Site: 10HEC ⸬⸬ ♠ 🏕 🚰 ⚑ Prices: 🕮7-11
🚐3 🚐7-15 Facilities: ⋔ 🗜 ⊙ 🟥 🚿 🗒 Services: 🍴 ✗ lau
Leisure: ⏚ PS Off-site: 🏥

PALMI REGGIO DI CALABRIA

San Fantino via S-Fantino, 89015
☎ 0966 479430 📠 0966 479430
Site on several terraces with lovely views of the bay of Lido di
Palmi. 200mtrs to the beach. Siesta 13.00-16.00 hrs.
➲ *Turn off road SS18 seawards N of Palmi.*
Open: All year Site: 4HEC ⸬⸬ ♠ 🚰 ⚑ Facilities: ⋔ 🗜 ⊙ 🟥
∅ 🚿 🗒 Services: 🍴 ✗ lau Off-site: ⏚PS 🏥

PESCHICI FOGGIA

Centro Turistico San Nicola Loc San Nicola, 71010
☎ 0884 964024
Terraced site in lovely situation by the sea, in a bay enclosed
by rocks. Can become overcrowded.
➲ *Turn off coast road Peschici-Vieste, follow signs along
winding road to site in 1km.*
Open: Apr-15 Oct Site: 14HEC ⸬⸬ ♠ 🏕 Prices: 🕮6-9.50
🚐3-5 🚐9-13.50 Facilities: ⋔ 🗜 ⊙ 🟥 ∅ 🚿 🗒 Services: 🍴 ✗
🏥 lau Leisure: ⏚ S

Internazionale Manacore 71010
☎ 0884 911020 📠 0884 911049
Meadowland with a few terraces in attractive bay, surrounded
by wooded hills.
➲ *Turn off the coastal road (Peschici-Vieste) towards ths sea
in a wide U bend.*
Open: 4 May-20 Oct Site: 20HEC ⸬⸬ ♠ 🏕 🚰 Facilities: ⋔ 🗜
⊙ 🟥 🚿 Services: 🍴 ✗ 🏥 Leisure: ⏚ S

PIZZO CATANZARO

Pinetamare 89812 ☎ 0963 534871 📠 0963 534871
A sandy site surrounded by tall pine trees. Most watersports
are available along the private beach and families are
welcomed.
➲ *From the Salerno/Reggio motorway take the Pizzo exit and
site is north of town.*
Open: Jun-Sep Site: 10HEC ⸬⸪ ♠ 🏕 🚰 Facilities: ⋔ 🗜 ⊙
🟥 ∅ 🚿 🗒 Services: 🍴 ✗ 🏥 lau Leisure: ⏚ PS Off-site: ⏚L

POMPEI NAPOLI

Spartacus via Plinio 127, 80045 ☎ 081 8624078 📠 081 862407
e-mail: campingspartacus@tin.it
website: www.campingsspartacus.it
Site is on a level meadow with orange trees.
➲ *Lies near the motorway exit, Pompeii and access is from the
main Napoli road, opposite Scavi di Pompei near an IP petrol
station.*
Open: All year Site: 9HEC ⸬⸬ ♠ 🏕 🚰 ⚑ Prices: 🕮5.50-6
🚐2-3 🚐5.50-6 pitch 2.50 Facilities: ⋔ 🗜 ⊙ 🟥 ∅ 🚿 🗒
Services: 🍴 ✗ 🏥 lau Leisure: ⏚ P

POZZUOLI NAPOLI

Vulcano Solfatara via Solfatara 161, 80078
☎ 081 5267413 📠 081 5263482
e-mail: info@solfatara.it website: www.solfatara.it
Clean and orderly site situated in a deciduous forest near the
crater of the extinct Solfatara volcano.
➲ *Leave Nuova via Domiziana (SS7 qtr) at Km60/1 (at about
6km short of Napoli) and turn inland through stone gate.*
Open: Apr-Oct & 24 Dec-8 Jan Site: 3HEC ⸬⸬ ♠ 🏕 🚰
Prices: 🕮7-8.70 🚐4.60-6.50 🚐6.50-8.10 🅰4.10-6
Facilities: ⋔ 🗜 ⊙ 🟥 ∅ 🗒 Services: 🍴 ✗ 🏥 lau Leisure: ⏚ P
Off-site: 🚿 ⏚S

AT VARCATURO, MARINA DI (12KM N)

Partenope 80014 ☎ 081 5091076 📠 081 5096767
Partially undulating terrain in woodland of medium height.
Camping Card Compulsory.
➲ *Turn seawards for 300mtrs at Km45/II of the SS7 (via
Domiziana).*
Open: Jun-8 Sep Site: 6HEC ⸬⸬ ⸬⸪ ♠ 🏕 Prices: 🕮6.40-
7.50 pitch 7.50-10.50 Facilities: ⋔ 🗜 ⊙ 🟥 ∅ 🚿 🗒
Services: 🍴 ✗ 🏥 Leisure: ⏚ LRS

PRÁIA A MARE COSENZA

International Camping Village 87028
☎ 0985 72211 📠 0985 72211
e-mail: reception@campinginternational.it
website: www.campinginternational.it
In a beautiful location on the Gulf of Policastro with fine
recreational facilities.
➲ *Access via A3 to Falerna and then SS18.*
Open: May-Sep Site: 5.5HEC ⸬⸪ ♠ 🏕 🚰 Facilities: ⋔ 🗜 ⊙
🟥 ∅ 🗒 Services: 🍴 ✗ 🏥 lau Leisure: ⏚ PS

RODI GARGANICO FOGGIA

Ripa Contrada Ripa, 71012 ☎ 0884 965367 📠 0884 965695
e-mail: info@villaggioripa.it website: www.villaggioripa.it
Well-equipped and attractive site close to the beach.
Open: 15 Jun-Aug Site: 6HEC ⸬⸬ ♠ 🏕 Facilities: ⋔ 🗜 ⊙
🟥 ∅ 🗒 Services: 🍴 ✗ 🏥 lau Leisure: ⏚ PS Off-site: 🏥

ROSSANO SCALO COSENZA

Marina di Rossano Contrada Leuca, 87068
☎ 0983 516054 📠 0983 512069
e-mail: marina.club@tiscalinet.it
website: web.tiscalinet.it/marinadirossano
In wooded surroundings close to the beach, with good,
modern facilities.
➲ *Access via N106.*
Open: 15 May-29 Sep Site: 7HEC ⸬⸬ ♠ 🏕 Facilities: ⋔ 🗜
⊙ 🟥 🗒 Services: 🍴 ✗ 🏥 lau Leisure: ⏚ PS Off-site: ∅

SAN MENÁIO FOGGIA

Valle d'Oro via Degli Ulivi, 71010
☎ 0884 991580 & 991699 📠 0884 991699 & 991580
e-mail: campingvalledoro@libero.it
Site in olive grove surrounded by wooded hills with some
terraces.
➲ *Turn off the SS89 onto SS528 and to site at Km1.800. 2km
from the sea.*
Open: 15 Jun-15 Sep Site: 3HEC ⸬⸬ ♠ 🏕 Prices: 🕮2.50-5
pitch 4-6 Facilities: ⋔ ⊙ 🟥 🚿 🗒 Services: 🍴 ✗
Off-site: 🗜 ∅ ⏚PS 🏥

SANTA CESÁREA TERME LECCE

Scogliera 73020 ☎ 0836 949802 📠 0836 949794
Attractive site close to the sea.

contd.

Facilities: 🗜-shop ⋔-shower ⊙-electric points for razors 🟥-electric points for caravans 🗒-parking by tents permitted
🟥-compulsory separate car park Services: ✗-café/restaurant 🍴-bar ∅-Camping Gaz International 🚿-gas other than Camping
Gaz 🏥-first aid facilities lau-laundry Leisure: ⏚-swimming L-Lake P-Pool R-River S-Sea Off-site: All facilities within 2km

1km S on SS173.
Open: All year **Site:** 8HEC ⠿ ♣ ⊞ 🚐 **Prices:** ♠4-8 �car2-2.50 🚐4.50-7 ▲4-6.50 pitch 4-6.50 **Facilities:** ↟ 🆂 ⊙ 🖃 ∅ **Services:** ⍭ ✗ **Leisure:** ↘ P **Off-site:** 🍴 ↘S ⊞

SANTA MARIA DI CASTELLABATE SALERNO

Trezene 84072 ☎ 0974 965027 ▤ 0974 965013
e-mail: trezene@costacilento **website:** www.trezene.it
The site is partly divided into pitches and consists of two sections lying either side of the access road. Pitches between road and fine sandy beach are reserved for touring campers.
Open: Apr-Oct **Site:** 2.5HEC ⠿ ♣ ⊞ ✥ **Prices:** ♠4.75-7.50 ▲7-10 pitch 10.50-22 **Facilities:** ↟ 🆂 ⊙ 🖃 🖃 **Services:** ⍭ ✗ lau **Leisure:** ↘ S **Off-site:** 🆂 ∅ 🍴 ⊞

SORRENTO NAPOLI

Santa Fortunata Campogaio via Capo 39, 80067
☎ 081 8073579 ▤ 081 8073590
e-mail: info@santafortunata.com
website: www.santafortunata.com
A well appointed, terraced site shaded by olive trees and with direct access to the sea.
2km from town centre and 400mtrs beyond the turning from the SS145 on road towards Massa Lubrense and 50mtrs from sea.
Open: Apr-20 Oct **Site:** 20HEC ⠿ ⠿ ♣ ⊞ 🚐 **Prices:** ♠6-9 �car4-5 🚐9-11 ▲5-7 **Facilities:** ↟ 🆂 ⊙ 🖃 ∅ 🍴 🖃 **Services:** ⍭ ✗ lau **Leisure:** ↘ PS

Giardino delle Esperidi S.Agnello, 80065
☎ 081 8783255 ▤ 081 8785022
e-mail: info@esperidiresort.com
website: www.esperidiresort.com
In a pleasant park, surrounded by lemon and orange trees 2km from the centre of Sorrento and 250mtrs from La Marinella beach. There are good facilities and modern bungalows are available for hire.
Open: Apr-Sep **Site:** 3HEC ⠿ ♣ ⊞ ✥ **Prices:** ♠6.50-7.50 �car3-3.50 🚐5.50-6.50 ▲4-6.50 **Facilities:** ↟ ⊙ 🖃 🅿 **Services:** ⍭ ✗ **Off-site:** 🆂 ∅ 🍴 ↘PS ⊞

International Camping Nube d'Argento via Capo 21, 80067
☎ 081 8781344 ▤ 081 8073450
e-mail: info@nubedargento.com
The site lies on narrow terraces just off a steep concrete road between the beach and the outskirts of the town.
Access is rather difficult for caravans.
Open: All year **Site:** 1.5HEC ⠿ ♣ ⊞ 🚐 **Facilities:** ↟ 🆂 ⊙ 🖃 ∅ 🍴 🖃 **Services:** ⍭ ✗ ⊞ **Leisure:** ↘ PS

Santa Fortunata via Capo ☎ 081 8073579 ▤ 081 8073590
Extensive site lying on terraces in a shady olive grove with many small secluded pitches.
Camping Card Compulsory
1km from town and 50mtrs from sea.
Open: Apr-Sep **Site:** 12HEC ⠿ ♣ ⊞ 🚐 ▲ **Facilities:** ↟ 🆂 ⊙ 🖃 ∅ 🍴 🖃 **Services:** ⍭ ✗ ⊞ lau **Leisure:** ↘ PS

TORRE RINALDA LECCE

Torre Rinalda Litoranea Salentina, 73100
☎ 0832 652161 ▤ 0832 652165
On an extensive level meadow, separated from the sea by dunes. Discotheque. Lunchtime siesta 13.30-16.00 hrs.
Access via SS613 (Brindisi-Lecce) exit Trepuzzi then coastal road for 1.5km.
Open: All year **Site:** 23HEC ⠿ ♣ ⊞ ✥ **Facilities:** ↟ 🆂 ⊙ 🖃 🅿 **Services:** ⍭ ✗ ⊞ **Leisure:** ↘ PS **Off-site:** ∅ 🍴

UGENTO LECCE

Riva di Ugento Litoranea Gallipoli-SM diLeuca, 73059
☎ 0833 933600 ▤ 0833 933601
e-mail: info@rivadiugeuto.it **website:** www.rivadiugeuto.it
A well equipped site in wooded surroundings close to the beach.
Open: 15 May-29 Sep **Site:** 32HEC ⠿ ⠿ ♣ 🚐 ▲ ✥ **Prices:** pitch 16-34 (incl 3 persons) **Facilities:** ↟ 🆂 ⊙ 🖃 ∅ 🍴 🖃 **Services:** ⍭ ✗ ⊞ lau **Leisure:** ↘ PS

VICO EQUENSE NAPOLI

Sant' Antonio Marina d'Equa, 80069
☎ 081 8028570 ▤ 081 8028570
A modern site set among fruit trees, close to the beach with fine views over the Bay of Naples.
Camping Card Compulsory.
Open: 15 Mar-30 Oct **Site:** 1HEC ⠿ ♣ ⊞ 🚐 **Prices:** ♠6.70-7.75 �car2.60-3.20 🚐6.70-7.75 ▲4-6 **Facilities:** ↟ 🆂 ⊙ 🖃 ∅ 🍴 **Services:** ⍭ ✗ ⊞ lau **Leisure:** ↘ S **Off-site:** ↘PS

Seiano Spiaggia Marina Aequa, Castella-Postale, 38, 80069
☎ 081 8028560 ▤ 081 8028560
e-mail: info@campingseiano.it
website: www.campingseiano.it
Set in a plantation of evergreen and orange trees only a few metres from the sea. There are good facilities and the site is ideally situated for excursions to Pompeii, Naples, Vesuvius etc.
Motorway A3 (Naples-Pompeii-Salerno) leave m/way at Castellammare di Stabia-Highway 145 after Seiano tunnel and bridge turn R to Marina Aequa.
By Train: Naples-Sorrento Line, Stop at Seiano Station
Open: Apr-Sep **Site:** 1HEC ⠿ ♣ **Prices:** ♠5.90-6.90 �car3-3.50 🚐6.20-6.80 ▲5-5.70 **Facilities:** ↟ 🆂 ⊙ 🖃 ∅ 🍴 🖃 **Services:** ⍭ ✗ lau **Off-site:** ✗ ↘PS ⊞

Villagio Turistico Azzurro via Murrano 9, 80069
☎ 081 8029984 ▤ 081 8029176
e-mail: info@villaggioazzurro.net
website: www.villaggioazzurro.net
Shaded site among ancient olive groves, by the sea and in close proximity to the Isle of Capri.
Take Autostrada A3 Napoli-Pompei-Salerno, exit Castellammare and follow directions for Vico Equense. After 3rd tunnel and one bridge, turn right to Marina Aequa.
Open: Mar-Nov **Site:** ⠿ ♣ ⊞ 🚐 ▲ **Prices:** ♠6.50-7.50 �car3-4 🚐6-7 ▲5-6 **Facilities:** ↟ 🆂 ⊙ 🖃 ∅ 🍴 🖃 **Services:** ⍭ ✗ lau **Leisure:** ↘ S **Off-site:** ✗ ⊞

VIESTE FOGGIA

Baia Turchese 71019 Lungomare Europa, 71019
☎ 0884 708587
A family site in wooded surroundings with direct access to the sea.
1km N of Vieste on Strada Panoramica towards Peschici.
Open: May-Sep **Site:** 3.6HEC ⠿ ♣ ⊞ **Facilities:** ↟ 🆂 ⊙ 🖃 ∅ 🍴 🖃 **Services:** ⍭ ✗ ⊞ **Leisure:** ↘ S

Capo Vieste 71019 ☎ 0884 706326 ▤ 0884 705993
The site lies on a large area of unspoilt land, planted with a few rows of poplar and pine trees. It is by the sea and has a large bathing area.
Off coastal road to Peschici about 7km beyond Vieste.
Open: 20 Mar-Oct **Site:** 6HEC ⠿ ⠿ ♣ ⊞ 🚐 **Facilities:** ↟ 🆂 ⊙ 🖃 ∅ 🍴 🅿 **Services:** ⍭ ✗ ⊞ lau **Leisure:** ↘ S

Umbramare Santa Maria di Merino, 706174
☎ 0884 706174 ▤ 0884 706174
e-mail: umbramare@tiscali.it

Site: 6HEC-Site size ⠿-grass ⠿-sand ♣-stone ✥-little shade ✥-partly shaded ♣-mainly shaded ⊞-bungalows for hire 🚐-caravans for hire ▲-tents for hire ✥-no dogs **Prices:** ♠-adult per night 🚗-car per night pp-per person per night 🚐-caravan per night ▲-tent per night

➲ *On A14 leave at Poggio Imperiale and take route via Rodi Gargánico and Peschici.*
Open: All year Site: 10.5HEC ⟘⟘⟘ ⁝⁝⁝ ♠ 🅣 ⌀ Prices: ♦3-8.50 pitch 6-14.50 Facilities: ⋔ ⅃ ⊙ 🖾 ⌀ 🖻 🄿 Services: ⬤ ✕ Leisure: ⋋ S Off-site: ≞

Vieste Marina Litoranea Vieste, 71019
☎ 0884 706471 🗐 0884 706471
e-mail: viestemarina@tiscali.it
website: www.garganovecanze.it
Tree-lined level site adjacent to the coast road in a quiet situation with good facilities.
➲ *5km N of Vieste, signposted.*
Open: Jun-Sep Site: 5HEC ⟘⟘⟘ ♠ 🅣 Prices: ♦3.40-8.30 ♠2-3.50 pitch 19.30-37.70 (incl 4 persons) Facilities: ⋔ ⅃ ⊙ 🄯 Services: ⬤ ✕ 🞖 lau Leisure: ⋋ PS Off-site: ⌀ ≞ ⋋S

Village Punta Lunga Defensola, CP 339, 71019
☎ 0884 706031 🗐 0884 706910
e-mail: info@puntalunga.com
website: www.puntalunga.it
A terraced site in wooded surroundings encompassing two sandy bathing bays and a rocky peninsula.
➲ *2km N of Vieste, signposted from coast road.*
Open: 02 Apr-17 Oct Site: 6HEC ⁝⁝⁝ ♠ 🅣 ⌀ Prices: ♦3.70-9.70 ♠2-2.50 🄯4.50-9.90 🄰3.85-8.60 Facilities: ⋔ ⅃ ⊙ 🄯 ⌀ ≞ 🄿 Services: ⬤ ✕ 🞖 lau Leisure: ⋋ S

THE ISLANDS

SARDEGNA (SARDINIA)

AGLIENTU SASSARI

Baia Blu la Tortuga Pineta di Vignola Mare, 07020
☎ 079 602060 🗐 079 602040
e-mail: info@baiablu.com
website: www.gruppobaiasilvella.com
Site in pine forest by the sea.
Open: 03 Apr-Sep Site: 17HEC ⟘⟘⟘ ⁝⁝⁝ ♠ 🅣 🄯
Prices: ♦4.30-9.80 🄰6.70-18.60 pitch 8.30-21.20 Facilities: ⋔ ⅃ ⊙ 🄯 ⌀ 🖾 Services: ⬤ ✕ 🞖 lau Leisure: ⋋ S

ARBATAX NUORO

Telis Porto Frailis, 8041 ☎ 0782 667261 🗐 0782 667140
e-mail: telisca@tiscalinet.it
website: www.campingtelis.com
Terraced site by the sea.
➲ *SS125 between Cagliari and Olbia.*
Open: All year Site: 3HEC ♠ 🅣 🄯 Prices: ♦6-9.50 🄯7-9.50 🄰5-7 pitch 7-9.50 Facilities: ⋔ ⅃ ⊙ 🄯 ⌀ ≞ Services: ⬤ ✕ lau Leisure: ⋋ S

CÁGLIARI

AT SANT'ANTIOCO

Tonnara Loc Calasapone, 09017
☎ 0781 809058 🗐 0781 809036
e-mail: tonnaracamping@tiscali.it
website: www.campino.it/italy/sardegna/cagliari
Situated in the centre of Calasapone Bay with enclosed plots, good sporting facilities and access to a sandy beach.
➲ *Access is by road, south of Carbonia, to the small island of St Antioco.*
Open: Apr-Sep Site: 7HEC ⁝⁝⁝ ⊶ 🅣 🄯 Prices: ♦7.10-9.70 pitch 16 Facilities: ⋔ ⅃ ⊙ 🄯 ⌀ ≞ 🄿 Services: ⬤ ✕ lau Leisure: ⋋ S Off-site: ⋋P

CALASETTA CAGLIARI

Sardi Le Saline Le Saline, 9011 ☎ 0781 88615 🗐 0781 88615
e-mail: info@campinglesaline.com
website: www.campinglesaline.com
In wooded surroundings close to the beach and 500mtrs from the village with good recreational facilities.
Open: All year Site: 6HEC ⟘⟘⟘ ⁝⁝⁝ 🅣 🄯 Facilities: ⋔ ⅃ ⊙ 🄯 Services: ⬤ ✕ 🞖 lau Leisure: ⋋ S Off-site: ⌀ ≞ 🞖

CANNIGIONE DI ARZACHENA SASSARI

Isuledda 07020 ☎ 0789 86003 🗐 0789 86089
e-mail: informazioni@isuledda.it
website: www.isuledda.it
Near the sea on the beautiful Costa Smeralda with good, modern sanitary installations and plentiful sports and entertainment facilities.
Open: 08 May-15 Oct Site: 15HEC ⁝⁝⁝ ♠ 🅣 ⌀ Prices: ♦5-10 ♠2-4 🄯6.50-15 🄰4.50-15 Facilities: ⋔ ⅃ ⊙ 🄯 ⌀ 🄿 Services: ⬤ ✕ 🞖 lau Leisure: ⋋ S

LOTZORAI NUORO

Cernie via Case Sparse 17, 08040
☎ 0782 669472 🗐 0782 669612
Close to the beach with beautiful views on all sides. Varied sports and leisure activities.
Open: All year Site: 1.5HEC ⁝⁝⁝ ♠ 🅣 🄯 Prices: ♦9-12.90 🄯7 🄰6 pitch 7 Facilities: ⋔ ⅃ ⊙ 🄯 ⌀ 🄯 Services: ⬤ ✕ lau Leisure: ⋋ S Off-site: 🞖

PORTO ROTONDO SASSARI

Cugnana Loc Cugnana, 07026 ☎ 0789 33184 🗐 0789 33398
e-mail: info@campingcugnana.it
website: www.campingcugnana.it
A well appointed family site with good recreational facilities and offering free transport to the local beaches.
Open: 15 May-29 Sep Site: 5HEC ⟘⟘⟘ ♠ 🅣 Prices: ♦7.80-15 ♠2.60-3.60 Facilities: ⋔ ⅃ ⊙ 🄯 ⌀ ≞ 🄿 Services: ⬤ ✕ lau Leisure: ⋋ P Off-site: ⋋S 🞖

SANTA LUCIA NUORO

Cala-Pineta St Statale Orientale Sarde 125, 08029
☎ 0784 819184 🗐 0784 818128
e-mail: info@calapineta.it
website: www.calapineta.it
Well-equipped site 1.5km from a white sand beach.
Open: Jun-29 Sep Site: 5HEC ⟘⟘⟘ ♠ 🄯 🄰 Facilities: ⋔ ⅃ ⊙ 🄯 🖾 Services: ⬤ ✕ lau Leisure: ⋋ S

Selema 8029 ☎ 0784 819068 🗐 0784 819068
e-mail: info@selemacamping.com
website: www.selemacamping.com
Wooded beach site on the island of Sardinia.
Open: May-Oct Site: 7.5HEC ⟘⟘⟘ ⁝⁝⁝ ♠ 🅣 🄯 Facilities: ⋔ ⅃ ⊙ 🄯 ⌀ ≞ 🖾 Services: ⬤ ✕ lau Leisure: ⋋ RS Off-site: ≞ 🞖

SAN TEODORO NUORO

San Teodoro la Cinta via del Tirreno,89, 08020
☎ 0784 865777 🗐 0784 865777
e-mail: info@campingsanteodoro.com
website: www.campingsanteodoro.com
Situated in a large wooded, park the site faces the sea. Ideal for families with small children.
➲ *25km from Olbia.*
Open: 15 May-15 Oct Site: 3HEC ⟘⟘⟘ ⊶ 🅣 🄯 ⌀ Prices: ♦4.40-8.40 🄯7.80-12.20 🄰7.80-12.20 Facilities: ⋔ ⅃ ⊙ 🄯 ⌀ ≞ 🖾 Services: ⬤ ✕ 🞖 lau Leisure: ⋋ S Off-site: ✕ ⋋R

Facilities: ⅃-shop ⋔-shower ⊙-electric points for razors 🄯-electric points for caravans 🖾-parking by tents permitted 🄿-compulsory separate car park Services: ✕-café/restaurant ⬤-bar ⌀-Camping Gaz International ≞-gas other than Camping Gaz 🞖-first aid facilities lau-laundry Leisure: ⋋-swimming L-Lake P-Pool R-River S-Sea Off-site: All facilities within 2km

TEULADA CAGLIARI

Porto Tramatzu 09019 ☎ 070 9283027 ▤ 070 9283028
e-mail: coop.proturismo@libero.it
website: www.italiaabc.it/camping/sardegna/cagliari/
camping/cagliari2/portutramatzu
With extensive facilities and large individual plots. The site is
less than 100mtrs from the beautiful Port Tramatzu.
➲ SS195 from Cagliari.
Open: Etr-Oct Site: 3.5HEC ᚙᚚ ⚘ 🚐 Prices: ⚤5-8.50 🚐9-
11.50 ⚦6-8.50 Facilities: 📶 🖳 ⊙ 🖳 Services: 🍽 ✗ lau
Leisure: ⚓ S

TORRE SALINAS CAGLIARI

Torre Salinas 09043 ☎ 070 999032 ▤ 070 999001
e-mail: information@camping-torre-salinas.de
website: www.camping-torre-salinas.de
Open: Apr-14 Oct Site: 1.5HEC ⁙ ⚘ 🚐 ⚦ Facilities: 📶 🖳
⊙ 🖳 🏠 Services: 🍽 ✗ lau Leisure: ⚓ S

VALLEDORIA SASSARI

Foce via Ampurias1C.S., 07039 ☎ 079 582109 ▤ 079 582191
e-mail: lafoceuno@libero.it website: www.foce.it
In a delightful wooded setting separated from the main
beach by the River Coghinas which can be crossed by ferry.
Modern sanitary installations and plenty of recreational
facilities.
Open: 15 May-Sep Site: 20HEC ᚙᚚ ⁙ ⚘ 🖳 🚐 Prices: ⚤5-
13.50 🚗1.50-3.10 Facilities: 📶 🖳 ⊙ 🖳 🗑 🏠 🖳 Services: 🍽 ✗
lau Leisure: ⚓ PRS Off-site: ⊞

Valledoria 07039 ☎ 079 584070 ▤ 079 584058
e-mail: info@campingvalledoria.com
website: www.campingvalledoria.com
Located in a pine wood, this site has both white sand beaches
and rocky cliffs.
Open: 15 May- 29 Sep Site: 10HEC ⚘ 🖳 🚐 ⊘
Prices: ⚤6.50-11 🚗1.80-3 Facilities: 📶 🖳 ⊙ 🖳 🗑 🏠 🖳
Services: 🍽 ✗ lau Leisure: ⚓ S Off-site: ⊞

SICILIA (SICILY)

AVOLA SIRACUSA

Pantanello Lungomare di Avola, 96012 ☎ 0931 823275
Open: All year Site: 7.5HEC ᚙᚚ ⚘ 🖳 Facilities: 📶 ⊙ 🖳 🏠
Services: 🍽 ✗ Off-site: 🖳 ✗ 🗑 ⚓S ⊞

Sabbia d'Oro 96012 ☎ 0931 822415 ▤ 0931 822415 & 833233
e-mail: info@campeggiosabbiadoro.com
website: www.campeggiosabbiadoro.com
Situated close to the beach in a picturesque area surrounded
by trees with magnificient views.
Open: All year Site: 2.2HEC ⚘ 🖳 Prices: ⚤5.50 🚗2.50 🚐8
⚦7.50-9 Facilities: 📶 🖳 ⊙ 🖳 🗑 🖳 Services: 🍽 ✗ lau
Leisure: ⚓ S Off-site: ⚓R ⊞

CASTEL DI TUSA MESSINA

Scoglio S.S. 113-KM 164, 98070 ☎ 0921 334345 ▤ 0921 334303
e-mail: loscoglio@loscoglio.net website: www.loscoglio.net
A terraced site. No shade on the gravel beach.
➲ Turn off SS113 st Km164, 2km W of Castel di Tusa.
Open: All year Site: 1.5HEC ᚙᚚ ⚦ ⚘ 🖳 🚐 Prices: ⚤5-8
🚗2.50-3 🚐5.50-6 ⚦5.50-6 Facilities: 📶 🖳 ⊙ 🖳 🗑 🏠
Services: 🍽 ✗ lau Leisure: ⚓ S

CATÁNIA CATANIA

Ionio via Villini a Mare 2, 95126
☎ 095 491139 ▤ 095 492277
e-mail: jonio@camping.it website: camping.it/sicilia/jonio
On a clifftop plateau. Access to beach via steps. Lunchtime
siesta 14.00-17.00 hrs.

➲ Turn off SS14 N of town towards sea.
Open: All year Site: 1.2HEC ᚙᚚ ⚘ 🖳 🚐 Facilities: 📶 🖳 ⊙
🖳 🗑 🖳 🖳 Services: 🍽 ✗ ⊞ lau Leisure: ⚓ S

CEFALÚ PALERMO

Plaja degli Uccelli 90010 ☎ 0921 999068 ▤ 0921 999068
In wooded surroundings with good, modern equippment
close to a fine sandy beach.
Open: Apr-10 Oct Site: 1.8HEC ᚙᚚ ⁙ ⚘ 🖳 Prices: ⚤5-
6.50 🚗2.50-3.50 🚐11-14 ⚦6-9 Facilities: 📶 🖳 ⊙ 🖳 🗑 🖳 🖳
Services: 🍽 ✗ ⊞ lau Leisure: ⚓ S

FINALE DI POLLINA PALERMO

Rais Gerbi S.S.113KM 172,900, 90010
☎ 0921 426570 ▤ 0921 426577
e-mail: camping@raisgerbi.it
website: www.raisgerbi.it
A well equipped, modern site with its own private beach in
picturesque wooded surroundings.
➲ Take the SS113 Messina-Palermo road to Km172.9.
Open: All year Site: 5HEC ⁙ ⚘ 🖳 ⚦ Facilities: 📶 🖳 ⊙ 🖳
🗑 🏠 Services: 🍽 ✗ lau Leisure: ⚓ PS Off-site: 🖳 ⊞

FONDACHELLO CATANIA

Mokambo 95016 ☎ 095 938731
Level terrain, thickly wooded in parts not directly next to the
sea.
➲ For access leave A18 (Messina-Catania) at Giarre exit,
through Giarre and via Máscali to Fondachello on coast.
Open: Apr-Sep Site: 2.8HEC ⁙ ⚘ 🖳 🚐 Facilities: 📶 🖳 ⊙
🖳 🗑 🏠 Services: 🍽 ✗ ⊞ lau Leisure: ⚓ S

FÚRNARI MARINA MESSINA

Village Bazia Contrada Bazia, 98054
☎ 0941 800130 ▤ 0941 81006
e-mail: info@bazia.it website: www.bazia.it
A pleasant seaside site with plenty of recreational facilities.
Open: Jun-14 Sep Site: 40HEC ⚦ ⚘ 🖳 Prices: ⚤6.20 🚗2.10
🚐6.20 ⚦6.20 Facilities: 📶 🖳 ⊙ 🖳 🗑 🖳 Services: 🍽 ✗
Leisure: ⚓ PS

ÍSOLA DELLE FÉMMINE PALERMO

La Playa viale Marino 55, 90040
☎ 091 8677001 ▤ 091 8677001
e-mail: pigiambo@tin.it
website: www.tiscalinet.it/laplaya
A ideal site for a relaxing holiday with beautiful views and
quiet woodland walks. Direct access to the beach.
➲ A29 Palermo to Trapini and SS113.
Open: 21 Mar-30 Oct Site: 2.2HEC ⁙ ⚘ 🚐 Prices: ⚤3.90-
5.20 pitch 6.20-12.40 Facilities: 📶 🖳 ⊙ 🖳 🗑 🖳 🖳
Services: 🍽 ✗ lau Leisure: ⚓ S Off-site: ✗ ⚓S ⊞

MENFI AGRIGENTO

Palma via delle Palme n 29, 92013
☎ 0925 78392 ▤ 0925 78392
e-mail: campinglapalma@li bero.it
website: www.camping-lapalma.com
Camping Card Compulsory.
➲ 6km S.
Open: All year Site: 1HEC ᚙᚚ ⁙ ⚘ 🖳 🚐 ⚦ Facilities: 📶
🖳 ⊙ 🖳 🗑 🏠 Services: 🍽 ✗ lau Leisure: ⚓ S

NICOLOSI CATANIA

Etna via Goethe, 95030 ☎ 095 914309 ▤ 095 914309
e-mail: camping.etna@tiscalimet.it
Open: All year Site: 2.9HEC ⁙ ⚘ 🖳 🚐 ⚦ Facilities: 📶 ⊙
🖳 🏠 Services: 🍽 ✗ Leisure: ⚓ P Off-site: 🖳 ✗ 🗑

Site: 6HEC-Site size ᚙᚚ-grass ⁙-sand ⚦-stone ⚦-little shade ⚦-partly shaded ⚘-mainly shaded
🖳-bungalows for hire 🚐-caravans for hire ⚦-tents for hire ⊘-no dogs Prices: ⚤-adult per night 🚗-car per night
pp-per person per night 🚐-caravan per night ⚦-tent per night

OLIVERI MESSINA

Marinello Contrada Marinello, 98060
☎ 0941 313000   ▤ 0941 313702
e-mail: marinello@camping.it
website: www.camping.it/sicilia/marinello
Campsite consists of small pitches set in a woodland area
100mtrs from the sea. Dogs are not allowed during July and
August.
➲ *On the A20 motorway exiting at Falcone.*
Open: Apr-Oct **Site:** 3.2HEC ⸬ ♠ ☎ ⚲ **Prices:** ♦4.40-7
pitch 11.50-15.10 **Facilities:** ↑ ☒ ⊙ ☺ ∅ ▣ **Services:** ▼ ✕ lau
Leisure: ↑ S **Off-site:** ⚒ ⊞

PACHINO

AT PORTOPALO (6.6KM SE)

Capo Palssero 96010 ☎ 0931 842333
Site slightly sloping towards the sea with view of fishing
harbour of Portopalo. Discotheque.
➲ *Turn S on 115 in Noto or Iolspica in direction of Pachino.*
Open: 10 Mar-30 Oct **Site:** 3.5HEC ㎞ ♠ ☎ ▲ **Facilities:** ↑
☒ ⊙ ☺ ☎ ▣ **Services:** ▼ ✕ **Off-site:** ✕ ∅ ↑S ⊞

PALAZZOLO ACREIDE SIRACUSA

Torre Torre Tudica, 96010 ☎ 0931 32694
Open: All year **Site:** 2HEC ㎞ ♠ ☎ **Facilities:** ↑ ⊙ ☺ ☎
Services: ▼ ✕ **Leisure:** ↑ P **Off-site:** ☒ ⊞

PUNTA BRACCETTO RAGUSA

Rocca dei Tramonti 97017 ☎ 0932 918054   ▤ 0932 918054
e-mail: info@roccadeitramonti.com
website: www.roccadeitramonti.com
The site lies in a quiet setting on rather barren land near a
beautiful sandy bay surrounded by cliffs.
➲ *From Marina di Ragusa 10km W on coast road to Punta
Braccetto.*
Open: Easter-29 Sep **Site:** 3HEC ㎞ ⸬ ♠ ☎ ☺
Prices: ♦2.50-4.50 ☎3-4 ☎5-6 ▲5-6 **Facilities:** ↑ ⊙ ☺ ∅ ☎
Services: ✕ **Leisure:** ↑ S **Off-site:** ☒ ▼ ✕ ⚒

RAGUSA, MARINA DI RAGUSA

Baia del Sole Lungomare A-Doria, 97010
☎ 0932 239844   ▤ 0932 230341
e-mail: infobaiadelsole.it **website:** www.baiadelsole.it
Well tended level site. Pitches provided with roofs of straw
matting.
Open: All year **Site:** 3.5HEC ㎞ ♠ ☎ **Facilities:** ↑ ☒ ⊙ ☺
Services: ▼ ✕ **Leisure:** ↑ PS **Off-site:** ⊞

SANT' ALESSIO SICULO MESSINA

Focetta Sicula via Torrente Agrò, 98030
☎ 0942 751657   ▤ 0942 756708
e-mail: lafocetta@tin.it **website:** www.lafocetta.it
A well equipped site with a private beach in a quiet location.
➲ *From Messina take autostrada to 'Roccalumera' exit, then
SS114 towards Sant' Alessio and follow signs.*
Open: All year **Site:** 1.2HEC ㎞ ♠ ☎ ☺ **Facilities:** ↑ ⊙ ☺
∅ ⚒ **Services:** ▼ ✕ ⊞ lau **Leisure:** ↑ S **Off-site:** ☒

SANT' ANTONIO DI BARCELLONA MESSINA

Centro Vacanze Cantoni 98050 ☎ 090 9710165
website: http://members.xoom.it/cantoni93
Open: Jun-15 Sep **Site:** 1HEC ㎞ ♠ ☎ **Prices:** ♦5.16-6
☎2.58-3 ☎8.26-10.33 ▲5.16-6.20 pitch 12.50-14.50
Facilities: ↑ ☒ ⊙ ☺ ⚒ **Services:** ▼ ✕ ⊞ lau **Leisure:** ↑ PS

SECCAGRANDE AGRIGENTO

Kamemi Camping Village 92016
☎ 0925 69212   ▤ 0925 69212
e-mail: info@kamemicamping.it
website: www.kamemicamping.it
In wooded surroundings close to the beach with good
recreational facilities.
Open: All year **Site:** 5HEC ㎞ ♠ ☺ ▲ **Facilities:** ↑ ☒ ⊙ ☺
☎ **Services:** ▼ ✕ lau **Leisure:** ↑ PS **Off-site:** ∅ ⚒ ⊞

Statues at Isola Bella on Lake Maggiore.

Facilities: ☒-shop ↑-shower ⊙-electric points for razors ☺-electric points for caravans ☎-parking by tents permitted
▣-compulsory separate car park **Services:** ✕-café/restaurant ▼-bar ∅-Camping Gaz International ⚒-gas other than Camping
Gaz ⊞-first aid facilities lau-laundry **Leisure:** ↑-swimming L-Lake P-Pool R-River S-Sea **Off-site:** All facilities within 2km

LUXEMBOURG

Luxembourg, the tiny Grand Duchy only 999 square miles in size, offers a wide range of facilities to the visitor.

FACTS AND FIGURES
Area: 2,586 sq km (999 sq miles)
Population: 429,000 (1999)
Capital: Luxembourg City
Language: Luxembourgeois, French and German
IDD code: 352. To call

the UK dial 00 44
Currency: Euro
Local time: GMT + 1 (summer GMT + 2)
Emergency Services: Fire and ambulance 112; police 113
Banks: Mon-Fri 09.00-12.00 and 13.30-16.30
Shops: Mon-Sat 09.00-18.00

Average daily temperatures:
Luxembourg City
Jan 1°C   Jul 19°C
Mar 6°C   Sep15°C
May 13°C   Nov 5°C
Tourist Information:
Luxembourg National Tourist Office

UK 122 Regent Street London W1B 5SA
Tel (020) 7434 2800
USA 17 Beekman Place New York, NY 10022
Tel (212) 935 8888
Tourist info website:
www.luxembourg.co.uk

Luxembourg is entirely landlocked by France, Belgium and Germany. One third of the country is occupied by the hills and forests of the Ardennes, while the rest is mostly wooded farmland or the rich wine-growing area around the Moselle. The climate is temperate, with summer often extending from May to late October. Luxembourgeois is the everyday language but the official languages are French and German. English is widely spoken and understood.

There are over 100 officially recognised campsites throughout the country. Most open from April to October, but some function throughout the year. A booklet containing details of campsites is obtainable from the National Tourist Office (PO Box 1001, L-1010 Luxembourg. ☎ 42 82 82 1) or visit website at www.ont.lu. All campsites open to the public must be authorised by the Minister of Tourism.

Off-site camping. Caravans may only be parked on campsites. Non-coupled caravans may not be parked on the public highway or used as living accommodation. Casual camping with a tent is permitted, but permission must be obtained from the landowner. The owner is not allowed to give permission for more than 2 tents to be erected on his/her land. Casual camping is not allowed on the banks of Esch-sur-Sure.

How to Get There

Luxembourg is easily approached through either Belgium or France. Apart from crossing by Eurotunnel, the usual Continental Channel ports for this journey are Dunkerque or Calais in France, and Zeebrugge in Belgium.

Distance

Luxembourg City is just over 330km (205 miles) from the Belgian ports, or about 420km (260 miles) from the French ports, and is, therefore, within a day's drive of the Channel coast.

MOTORING & GENERAL INFO

The information given here is specific to Luxembourg. It **must** be read in conjunction with the Essential Motoring Information at the front of the book, which covers those regulations which are common to many countries.

British Embassy/Consulate*

The British Embassy together with its consular section is located at L-2450 Luxembourg, 14 Boulevard Roosevelt ☎229864/65/66

CHILDREN IN CARS

Children under 12 and/or 1.5 metres in height are not permitted to travel as front seat passengers unless using suitable restraint system. Children under 3 in rear must be seated in suitable restraint system. See Essential Motoring Information under 'Passengers' and 'Seat Belts'.

CURRENCY*

With the introduction of the Euro, the Luxembourg Franc (LUF) ceased to be legal tender from 2002. However, LUF coins and notes may still be exchanged at the Luxembourg Central Bank (Banque Central du Luxembourg) for an unlimited period (banknotes) and until the end of 2004 (coins).

DIMENSIONS AND WEIGHT RESTRICTIONS*

Private **cars** and towed **trailers** or **caravans** are restricted to the following dimensions - height, 4 metres; width, 2.5 metres; length, 12 metres. The maximum permitted overall length of vehicle/trailer or caravan combination is 25 metres.

The weight of a caravan must not exceed 75% of the weight of the towing vehicle.

DRIVING LICENCE*

A valid UK or Republic of Ireland licence is accepted in Luxembourg. The minimum age at which visitors from UK or Republic of Ireland may use a temporarily imported car or motorcycle is 17 years.

FOODSTUFFS*

The importation of meat is limited to 1kg, but there are no limits on other foodstuffs imported for personal use when travelling between EU countries.

LIGHTS*

It is compulsory for motorcyclists to use dipped headlights during the day.

MOTORING CLUB

The **Automobile Club du Grand-Duché de Luxembourg** (ACL) has its office at 8007 Bertrange, 54 route de Longwy ☎450045-1. ACL office hours are 08.30-12.00hrs and 13.30-18.00hrs from Monday to Friday; closed Saturday and Sunday.
Website: **www.acl.lu**

ROADS

There is a comprehensive system of good main and secondary roads. Luxembourg has 68 miles of toll-free motorway.

SPEED LIMITS*

Car/Motorcycle
Built-up areas 50km/h (31mph)
Other roads 90km/h (55mph)
Motorways 130km/h (80mph) reduced to
110km/h (68mph) in wet weather
Car/caravan/trailer
Built-up areas 50km/h (31mph)
Other roads 75km/h (46mph)
Motorways 90km/h (55mph)

All motorists who have held a full driving licence for less than one year 75kph (46mph) outside built-up areas, and 90kph (55mph) on motorways.

WARNING TRIANGLE*

Although it is not compulsory for visiting motorists to equip their vehicles with a warning triangle its use is compulsory in the event of accident or breakdown. The triangle must be placed on the road about 100 metres (109yds) behind the vehicle to on ordinary roads and 200-300 metres (219-328 yds) on motorways to warn following traffic of any obstruction.

*Additional information will be found in the International Motoring Information at the front of the book.

LUXEMBOURG

BERDORF

Parc Martbusch 3 Baim Maartbesch, 6552
☎ 79545
A comfortable, modern site in picturesque wooded surroundings.
➲ *NW of town centre.*
Open: All year Site: 3HEC ⸺ ⬭ ⬛ Facilities: ⬛ ⊙ ⬛ ⬛ ⬛
⬛ Services: ✕ lau Leisure: ⬩ P Off-site: ⬛ ✕

BOULAIDE

Haute-Sûre 34 r J-de-Busleyden, 9639 ☎ 993061 ⬛ 993604
e-mail: info@campinghautsure.com
website: www.campinghautsure.com
Open: 15 Apr-15 Sep Site: 2HEC ⸺ ⬛ Å Prices: pitch
23.60 (incl 2 persons) pp2.50 Facilities: ⬛ ⬛ ⊙ ⬛ ⬛ ⬛
Services: ⬛ ✕ ⬛ lau Leisure: ⬩ P

CLERVAUX

Official de Clervaux 33 r Klatzewee, 9714
☎ 920042 ⬛ 929728
e-mail: campingclervaux@internet.lu
website: www.camping-clervaux.lu
Situated next to the sports stadium, between the La Clervé
stream and the railway in a forested area. Trains only run
during the day and there is little noise. Separate field for tents.
➲ *0.5km SW from the village.*
Open: 15 Mar-30 Oct Site: 3HEC ⸺ ⬛ ⬛ ⬛ Prices: ⬥4.30
pitch 4.30 Facilities: ⬛ ⬛ ⊙ ⬛ ⬛ ⬛ ⬛ Services: ⬛ lau
Leisure: ⬩ P Off-site: ⬛ ✕

CONSDORF

Bel Air Burgkapp 15 r Burgkapp, 6211 ☎ 790353
The site is divided into pitches and lies on level meadowland
in the forest area of 'Petite Suisse Luxembourgeoise'.
➲ *On W outskirts of village. Turn right off E42. 6km S of
Echternach.*
Open: May-Aug Site: 2HEC ⸺ ⬛ Facilities: ⬛ ⊙ ⬛ ⬛ ⬛
Services: ⬛ lau Off-site: ⬛ ⬛ ✕

DIEKIRCH

Bleesbruck 9359 ☎ 803134
e-mail: info@camping-bleesbruck.lu
website: www.camping-bleesbruck.lu
A modern site in tranquil wooded surroundings.
Open: Apr-Oct Site: 5HEC ⸺ ⬛ ⬛ ⬛ Facilities: ⬛ ⬛ ⊙
⬛ ⬛ ⬛ Services: ⬛ ✕ ⬛ lau Leisure: ⬩ R Off-site: ✕ ⬩P

Op der Sauer rte de Gilsdorf, 9201
☎ 00352-808590 ⬛ 809470
e-mail: camsauer@pt.lu
website: www.campsauer.lu

➲ *500mtrs from town centre on Gilsdorf road near the sports
stadium.*
Open: All year Site: 5HEC ⸺ ⬭ ⬛ Facilities: ⬛ ⬛ ⊙ ⬛ ⬛
⬛ Services: ⬛ ✕ ⬛ lau Leisure: ⬩ P

DILLINGEN

Wies-Neu 12 r de la Sûre, 6350 ☎ 836110 ⬛ 26876438
A comfortable family site on the bank of the River Sûre.
➲ *Between Diekirch and Echternach.*
Open: Apr-30 Oct Site: 45HEC ⸺ ⬛ ⬛ Prices: ⬥3.50 pitch
4 Facilities: ⬛ ⬛ ⊙ ⬛ ⬛ ⬛ ⬛ Services: ⬛ lau Leisure: ⬩ R
Off-site: ⬛ ✕

ECHTERNACH

Official 5 rte de Diekirch, 6430 ☎ 720272 ⬛ 26720847
e-mail: info@camping_echternach.lu
website: www.mullerthal.lu
➲ *Take E42 to Echternach.*
Open: 15 Mar-1 Nov Site: 7HEC ⸺ ⬭ ⬛ ⬛ ⬛
Facilities: ⬛ ⊙ ⬛ ⬛ Services: ⬛ lau Leisure: ⬩ P Off-site: ⬛
⬛ ✕ ⬛ ⬩LPR

ENSCHERANGE

Val d'Or L-9747 ☎ 920691 ⬛ 929725
e-mail: valdor@pt.lu website: www.valdor.lu
Quiet family site in a beautiful natural setting beside the
River Clerve.
➲ *8km S of Clervaux between Drauffelt and Wilwerwiltz.*
Open: All year Site: 3HEC ⸺ ⬭ ⬛ ⬛ Prices: ⬥4.50 ⬛5.80
Å5.80 pitch 5.80 Facilities: ⬛ ⊙ ⬛ ⬛ ⬛ ⬛ Services: ⬛ ✕ ⬛
Leisure: ⬩ R Off-site: ⬛ ⬩LPS

ESCH-SUR-ALZETTE

Gaalgebierg L-4001 ☎ 541069 ⬛ 549630
e-mail: gaalcamp@pt.lu
A level park-like site with lovely trees on a hillock.
➲ *SE along N6 from the town centre in the direction of
Dudelange as far as the motorway underpass. Then turn right
and follow the steep climb uphill.*
Open: All year Site: 2.5HEC ⸺ ⬭ ⬛ Prices: pitch 6
Facilities: ⬛ ⬛ ⊙ ⬛ ⬛ ⬛ ⬛ Services: ⬛ ✕ ⬛ lau

HEIDERSCHEID

Fuussekaul 4 Fussekaul, 9156 ☎ 268888-1 ⬛ 268888-28
e-mail: info@fuussekaul.lu website: www.fuussekaul.lu
A level grassland family site adjoining a woodland area. Good
recreational facilities.
➲ *Turn off the N15 (Ettelbruck-Wiltz/Bastogne) S of
Heiderscheid in a westerly direction.*
Open: All year Site: 2HEC ⸺ ⬭ ⬛ ⬛ Å Prices: pitch
16.50-26.50 pp2 Facilities: ⬛ ⬛ ⊙ ⬛ ⬛ ⬛ ⬛ Services: ⬛ ✕
⬛ lau Leisure: ⬩ P Off-site: ⬩L

Site: 6HEC-Site size ⸺-grass ⸬-sand ⬥-stone ⬩-little shade ⬭-partly shaded ⬛-mainly shaded
⬛-bungalows for hire ⬛-caravans for hire Å-tents for hire ⬶-no dogs Prices: ⬥-adult per night ⬛-car per night
pp-per person per night ⬛-caravan per night Å-tent per night

INGLEDORF

Gritt r du Pont, 9161 ☎ 802018 🖹 802019
On southern bank of River Sûre between Ettelbruck and
Diekirch. In beautiful country setting ideal for fishing.
Open: Apr-Oct **Site:** 5HEC 🏕 ⬚ 🚐 **Prices:** ⚑4 pitch 4
Facilities: ⋔ ⊙ 🖨 🖉 ♨ 🏛 **Services:** ⚍ ✕ ⊞ lau **Leisure:** ⋨ R
Off-site: 🛒 ⋨LP

KOCKELSCHEUER

Kockelscheuer 22 rte de Bettembourg, 1899
☎ 471815 🖹 401243
e-mail: mail@camp-kockelscheuer.lu
website: www.camp-kockelscheuer.lu
A modern site on the edge of a forest.
➲ 4km from Luxembourg off N31.
Open: Etr-Oct **Site:** 3.8HEC 🏕 ⬚ **Prices:** ⚑3.50 pitch 4
Facilities: ⋔ 🛒 ⊙ 🖨 ♨ 🏛 **Services:** ⊞ lau **Off-site:** 🛒 ✕

LAROCHETTE

Kengert L-7633 ☎ 837186 🖹 878323
e-mail: info@kengert.lu
website: www.kengert.lu
On gently sloping meadow in a pleasant, rural location.
➲ Take the N8 towards Mersch, then the CR119 towards
Nommern and turn right after approx 2km.
Open: Mar-Nov **Site:** 4HEC 🏕 ♠ ⬚ 🚐 **Prices:** ⚑11-13
Facilities: ⋔ 🛒 ⊙ 🖨 🖉 ♨ 🏛 **Services:** ⚍ ✕ ⊞ lau **Leisure:** ⋨ P

MAULUSMÜHLE

Woltzdal Maison 12, 9974 ☎ 998938 🖹 979739
e-mail: info@camping-woltzdal.lu
website: www.campingwoltzdal.com
Quiet family site situated in the deep valley of the river
Woltz.
➲ From Liege take N30 to Bastogne, then N874 to Clervaux
and take N12
Open: Apr-Nov **Site:** 1.5HEC 🏕 ♠ ⬚ 🚐 **Prices:** ⚑5.30
⚑2.65 ⚑2.65 ⚑2.65 **Facilities:** ⋔ 🛒 ⊙ 🖨 🖉 ♨ 🏛
Services: ⚍ ✕ ⊞ lau **Leisure:** ⋨ R

MERSCH

Krounebierg rue du camping, 7572
☎ 329756 🖹 327987
e-mail: contact@campingkrounebierg.lu
website: www.campingkrounebierg.lu
A clean, well-kept site on five terraces, split into sections by
hedges.
➲ Approx 0.5km W of village church.
Open: 5 Apr-Sep **Site:** 5.5HEC 🏕 ♠ **Prices:** ⚑2.95 pitch
20.50-26.10 (incl 2 persons) **Facilities:** ⋔ 🛒 ⊙ 🖨 🖉 🏛
Services: ⚍ ✕ ⊞ lau **Leisure:** ⋨ P

MONDORF-LES-BAINS

Risette 4 rte de Burmerange, 5659 ☎ 660746 🖹 660758
e-mail: info@belhorizon.lu
website: www.belhorizon.lu
In pleasant wooded surroundings near the French and
German borders.
➲ 1km from Mondorf-les-Bains.
Open: Mar-Oct **Site:** 5HEC 🏕 ⬚ 🚐 **Facilities:** ⋔ 🛒 ⊙ 🖨
🖉 ♨ 🏛 **Services:** ⚍ ✕ ⊞ lau **Off-site:** ⋨LPR

NOMMERN

Europe Nommerlayen r Nommerlayen, 7465
☎ 878078 🖹 879678
e-mail: nommerlayen@vo.lu
website: www.nommerlayen-ec.lu
A terraced site in wooded surroundings with plenty of
recreational facilities.
Open: 16 Jan-15 Dec **Site:** 15HEC 🏕 ⬚ ⬚ 🚐 ⚑
Prices: ⚑4.25-4.25 ⚑3.50 ⚑3.50 pitch 18-35 **Facilities:** ⋔ 🛒
⊙ 🖨 🖉 ♨ 🏛 **Services:** ⚍ ✕ ⊞ lau **Leisure:** ⋨ P

OBEREISENBACH

Kohnenhof 1 Maison, 9838 ☎ 929464 🖹 929690
e-mail: kohnenho@pt.lu
website: www.campingkohnenhof.lu
Quiet site in a rural setting in the River Our valley.
Open: 28 Mar-3 Nov **Site:** 6HEC 🏕 ⬚ ⬚ 🚐 **Prices:** ⚑3.40-
4.50 pitch 7.20-9.80 **Facilities:** ⋔ 🛒 ⊙ 🖨 🖉 ♨ 🏛 **Services:** ⚍
✕ ⊞ lau **Leisure:** ⋨ R

ROSPORT

Barrage rte d'Echternach, 6580 ☎ 730160 🖹 735155
e-mail: campingrosport@pt.lu
website: www.campingrosport.com
Situated by Lake Sûre on the German border at the entrance
to Luxembourg's 'Little Switzerland'.
➲ Main road from Echternach to Wasserbillig.
Open: 15 Mar-Oct **Site:** 3.2HEC 🏕 ⬚ **Prices:** ⚑3.50 pitch 4
Facilities: ⋔ ⊙ 🖨 🏛 **Services:** ⊞ lau **Leisure:** ⋨ LR
Off-site: 🛒 ✕ 🖉 ♨

STEINFORT

Steinfort 72 rte de Luxembourg, 8440 ☎ 398827 🖹 397410
e-mail: campstei@pt.lu
website: www.camping-steinfort.lu
A small family site with good recreational and entertainment
facilities, well situated for exploring the 'Seven Castles' area.
➲ Access via E25 Steinfort exit.
Open: All year **Site:** 3.5HEC 🏕 ♠ ♠ ⬚ **Prices:** ⚑2.40-4
⚑2.40-4 pitch 4.50-7.50 **Facilities:** ⋔ 🛒 ⊙ 🖨 🖉 ♨ 🏛
Services: ⚍ ✕ ⊞ lau **Leisure:** ⋨ P

VIANDEN

AT WALSDORF (2KM SW)

Romantique Tandelerbaach, ☎ 834464 🖹 834440
A terraced grassland site in picturesque wooded
surroundings.
➲ W of Diekirch-Vianden road, access from the N17 and
CR354.
Open: 3 Mar-1 Nov **Site:** 6HEC 🏕 ⬚ **Facilities:** ⋔ ⊙ 🖨 🖉
🏛 **Services:** ⚍ ✕ ⊞ lau **Leisure:** ⋨ R **Off-site:** ⋨LP

WEILER-LA-TOUR

Ma Campagne 9 rte de Thionville, 5771
☎ 00352 369497 🖹 366912
Camp shop and bar available in August only.
➲ Access via main road Luxembourg-Thionville.
Open: All year **Site:** 0.5HEC 🏕 ⬚ 🚐 **Facilities:** ⋔ 🛒 ⊙ 🖨
🖉 🏛 **Services:** ⊞ lau **Off-site:** ✕

Facilities: 🛒-shop ⋔-shower ⊙-electric points for razors 🖨-electric points for caravans 🏛-parking by tents permitted
🖪-compulsory separate car park **Services:** ✕-café/restaurant ⚍-bar 🖉-Camping Gaz International ♨-gas other than Camping
Gaz ⊞-first aid facilities lau-laundry **Leisure:** ⋨-swimming L-Lake P-Pool R-River S-Sea **Off-site:** All facilities within 2km

NETHERLANDS

So much more than edam, tulips and windmills, the Netherlands has a rich history, stunning scenery and a vibrant capital city.

FACTS AND FIGURES
Area: 33,939 sq km (13,104 sq miles)
Population: 16,105,300 (2002)
Capital: Amsterdam
Language: Dutch, English
IDD code: 31. To call the UK dial 00 44
Currency: Euro
Local time: GMT + 1 (summer GMT + 2)

Emergency Services: Fire, Police and Ambulance 112
Banks: Mon-Fri 09.00-17.00
Shops: Mon-Fri 09.00-18.00, Supermarkets 08.00-20.00, Sat 08.00-17.00, Sun (Amsterdam and Rotterdam) 12.00-17.00.

Average daily temperature:
Amsterdam

Jan 2°C	Jul 18°C
Mar 5°C	Sep 15°C
May 13°C	Nov 7°C

Tourist Information: Netherlands Board of Tourism (postal/telephone enquiries only) UK PO Box 30783, London WC2B 6DH Tel: (020) 7539 7950

(Mon-Fri 09.30-17.30) or 09068 717777 (premium rate information line)
USA 355 Lexington Avenue, 19th Floor, New York, NY 10017 Tel (212) 370 7360
Tourist info website: www.holland.com/uk

A fifth of this flat, level country lies below sea-level. The areas reclaimed from the sea, the *polders,* are extremely fertile. The landscape is broken up by the forests of Arnhem, the bulbfields in the west, the lakes in the central and northern areas, and the impressive coastal dunes.

The climate is generally mild and tends to be damp. The summers are moderate with changeable weather and are seldom excessively hot. The language, Netherlandish (better known as Dutch!), is fairly guttural and closely allied to the Low German dialect. Other dialect forms exist throughout the Netherlands.

There are some 900 officially recognised and classifed campsites throughout the Netherlands. It is not generally possible to book sites in advance. Coastal sites tend to be crowded in June, July and August when the locals take their holidays. Local tourist information offices (VVV) can provide detailed information about sites in their area. The camping season is mainly from April to September, but some sites are open all year. Off-site camping is not possible and overnight stops are not permitted.

HOW TO GET THERE

There are direct ferry services to the Netherlands. The services and minimum sailing times are **Harwich to Hoek van Holland,** (6hrs 30mins or 3hrs 40mins by catamaran); **Hull to Rotterdam**

(Europoort) (12hrs 30mins); **Newcastle to Amsterdam** (terminal at Ijmuiden 29km from Amsterdam) (15hrs). Alternatively, use the Channel Tunnel, or take one of the short Channel crossings and drive through France and Belgium.

DISTANCE

From Calais to Den Haag (The Hague) is just over 340km (211 miles) (within a day's drive).

MOTORING & GENERAL INFO

The information given here is specific to The Netherlands. It **must** be read in conjunction with the Essential Motoring Information at the front of the book, which covers those regulations which are common to many countries.

BRITISH EMBASSY/CONSULATE*

The British Embassy is located at 2514 ED Den Haag, Lange Voorhout 10 ☎(070) 4270427, but the Embassy has no consular section. The British Consulate-General is located at 1075 AE Amsterdam, Koningslaan 44 ☎(020) 6764343.

CHILDREN IN CARS

Child under 12 and/or 1.5 metres* in height cannot travel as front seat passenger unless using a suitable restraint. Child under 3 in the rear does not have to wear a seat belt but must use child seat or restraint if fitted; child over 3 and under 12 must wear seat belt in the absence of such equipment. See Essential Motoring Information under 'Passengers' and 'Seat Belts'.
*A child of 10 eg 1.6 metres in height may sit in the front wearing normal seat belts.

CURRENCY*

With the introduction of the Euro, the Netherlands Guilder (NLG) ceased to be legal tender from 2002. However, NLG coins and notes may still be exchanged at the Netherlands Central Bank (De Nederlandsche Bank) until 1 January 2032 (banknotes) and 1January 2007 (coins).

DIMENSIONS AND WEIGHT RESTRICTIONS*

Private cars and towed trailers or caravans are restricted to the following dimensions - height, 4 metres; width†, 2.55 metres; length, car 12 metres, caravan 12 metres. The maximum permitted overall length of vehicle/trailer or caravan combination is 18 metres. The maximum weight of caravan/luggage trailers will be determined by the instructions of the manufacturer of the towing vehicle and/or the manufacturer of the caravan/luggage trailer.

†Some very small roads have a maximum width restriction of 2.2 metres.

DRIVING LICENCE*

A valid UK or Republic of Ireland licence is accepted in the Netherlands. The minimum age at which visitors from UK or Republic of Ireland may use an imported car or motorcycle is 18 years.

FIREARMS

Dutch laws concerning the possession of firearms are the most stringent in Europe. Any person crossing the frontier with any type of firearm will be arrested. The law applies also to any object which, on superficial inspection, shows any resemblance to real firearms (e.g. plastic imitations). If you wish to carry firearms, real or imitation, of any description into the Netherlands, seek the advice of the Netherlands Consulate.

FOODSTUFFS*

If the imported foodstuffs are for personal use, there are no limits when travelling between EU countries. However, importation of unpreserved meat products is forbidden and any other unpreserved foodstuffs must be declared.

MOTORING CLUB*

The **Koninklijke Nederlandse Toeristenbond ANWB** has its headquarters at 2596 EC 's-Gravenhage, Wassenaarseweg 220, tel (070) 31 47 14 7, and offices in numerous provincial towns. They will assist motoring tourists generally, and supply road and touring information. Offices are usually open 09.00-17.30hrs Mon-Fri and 09.00-14.00hrs on Saturday.
Website: **www.anwb.nl**

ROADS

The Netherlands has a dense network of motorways (*autosnelweg*) carrying most inter-city and long distance traffic. Yellow ANWB telephone pillars are located every 2km along highways.

Main roads usually have only two lanes, but are well-surfaced. The best way to see the countryside is to use minor roads, often by canals.

SPEED LIMITS*

Car/motorcycle
Built-up areas 50km/h (31mph)
Other roads 80km/h (49mph)
　　　or 100km/h (62mph)
Motorways 120km/h (74mph)
Car/caravan/trailer
Built-up areas 50km/h (31mph)
Other roads 80km/h (49mph)
Motorways 80km/h (49mph)

WARNING TRIANGLE/HAZARD WARNING*

In the event of accident or breakdown a motorist must use either a warning triangle or hazard-warning lights to warn approaching traffic of any obstruction. However, a warning triangle is recommended as hazard-warning lights may be damaged or inoperative. The triangle must be placed 30 metres (33yds) behind the vehicle on ordinary roads and 100 metres 109yds) on motorways: it must be visible at a distance of 100 metres (109yds).

*Additional information will be found in the Essential Motoring Information at the front of the book.

NORTH

AMEN DRENTHE

Reservaat Diana Heide 53 Amen, 9446
☎ 0592 389297 ▤ 0592 389432
e-mail: info@dianaheide.nl website: www.dianaheide.nl
An ideal site for relaxation, which lies away from the traffic
amongst forest and heathland.
➔ *If approaching from Assen along the E35, drive through
Amen and on towards Hooghalen.*
Open: Apr-1 Oct Site: 30HEC ⬛⬛⬛ ⁙⁙⁙ ⚜ 🕂 ♨ Å
Facilities: 🏠 🕿 ⊙ 🖙 🖉 🚿 🖀 Services: 🍴 ✕ 🖽 lau Leisure: 🕂
P Off-site: 🕂R

ANNEN DRENTHE

Hondsrug Annerweg 3, 9463 ☎ 0592 271292 ▤ 0592 271440
e-mail: info@hondsrug.nl website: www.hondsrug.nl
A family site in a pleasant rural setting with good
recreational facilities.
➔ *Access via N34 to site SE of Annen.*
Open: Apr-1 Oct Site: 18HEC ⬛⬛⬛ ⁙⁙⁙ ⚜ ♨ Å
Facilities: 🏠 🕿 ⊙ 🖙 🖉 🚿 🖀 Services: ✕ 🖽 lau Leisure: 🕂 P

ASSEN DRENTHE

Witterzomer Witterzomer 7, 9405
☎ 0592 393535 ▤ 0592 393530
e-mail: info@witterzomer.nl website: www.witterzomer.nl
A large site with asphalt internal roads, lying in mixed
woodland near nature reserve. Separate sections for dog
owners. Individual washing facilities for the disabled.
➔ *Turn off the E35 at Assen W exit into Europaweg Zuid and
continue for 100mtrs, then turn right. Continue through Witten
and follow signs.*
Open: All year Site: 75HEC ⬛⬛⬛ ⚜ 🕂 ♨ Å Prices: 🕿3.50
🚗5 ♨25 pitch 25 Facilities: 🏠 🕿 ⊙ 🖙 🖉 🚿 🖀 🖪 Services: 🍴
✕ lau Leisure: 🕂 LP

BERGUM FRIESLAND

Bergumermeer Solcamastr 30, 9262
☎ 0511 461385 ▤ 0511 463955
e-mail: info@bergumermeer.nl
website: www.bergumermeer.nl
In pleasant wooded surroundings close to the marina on the
Bergumermeer with good recreational facilities.
➔ *From N355 Groningen-Leeuwarden turn S via Bergum on
N356 then exit E to Sumar towards Oostermeer.*
Open: 27 Mar-16 Oct Site: 29HEC ⬛⬛⬛ ⚜ 🕂 ♨ Å
Prices: pitch 21-23 (incl 2 persons) Facilities: 🏠 🕿 ⊙ 🖙 🖉
🖪 Services: 🍴 ✕ 🖽 lau Leisure: 🕂 LP

BORGER DRENTHE

Hunzedal De Drift 3, 9531 ☎ 0599 234698 ▤ 0599 235183
e-mail: info@hunzedal.nl website: www.hunzedal.nl
The site is clean, well-kept and lies NE of the village.
➔ *For access, turn off the road towards Buinen, drive 200mtrs
E of the bridge over the Buinen-Schoondoord canal, then head
S for a further 1km.*
Open: 4 Apr-Oct Site: 30HEC ⬛⬛⬛ ⚜ 🕂 Facilities: 🏠 🕿 ⊙
🖙 🖉 🖀 Services: 🍴 ✕ 🖽 lau Leisure: 🕂 LP Off-site: 🚿

> A full guide to the Symbols &
> Abbreviations used in this book
> can be found on page 6

DIEVER DRENTHE

Hoeve AAn den Weg Bosweg 12, 8439 SN
☎ 0521 387269 ▤ 0521 387326
e-mail: camping@hoeveAAndenweg.nl
website: www.hoeveAAndenweg.nl
In pleasant wooded surroundings with good recreational
facilities.
Camping Card Compulsory.
Open: Apr-Oct Site: 5HEC ⬛⬛⬛ ⚜ 🕂 ♨ Facilities: 🏠 🕿 ⊙
🖙 🖉 🚿 🖀 🖪 Services: 🍴 ✕ 🖽 lau Leisure: 🕂 P

DWINGELOO DRENTHE

Noordster Noordster 105, 7991
☎ 0521 597238 ▤ 0521 597589
e-mail: noordster@rcn-centra.nl website: www.rcn-centra.nl
A large family site with static and touring pitches,
surrounded by woodland.
➔ *3km S on E35.*
Open: All year Site: 42HEC ⬛⬛⬛ ⚜ 🕂 ♨ Prices: pitch 17-28
(incl 6 persons) Facilities: 🏠 🕿 ⊙ 🖙 🖉 🚿 🖀 🖪 Services: 🍴 ✕
🖽 lau Leisure: 🕂 P

FRANEKER FRIESLAND

Bloemketerp Burg J Dykstraweg 3, 8801
☎ 0517 395099 ▤ 0517 395150
e-mail: bloemketerp@wxs.nl
website: www.bloemketerp.nl
In a well equipped leisure centre near the historic old city
centre of Franeker.
Open: All year Site: ⬛⬛⬛ ⚜ 🕂 ♨ Prices: 🕿10 🚗3 pitch 13.50-
22.50 (incl 2 persons) Facilities: 🏠 🕿 ⊙ 🖙 🖉 Services: 🍴 ✕
🖽 lau Leisure: 🕂 P Off-site: 🖉 🕂P

GRONINGEN GRONINGEN

Stadspark Campinglaan 6, 9727
☎ 050 5251624 ▤ 050 5250099
e-mail: camping_stadspark@planet.nl
website: www.grunopark.nl
A well-kept site on patches of grass between rows of bushes
and groups of pine and deciduous trees. Some of its pitches
are naturally screened.
➔ *For access from the SW outskirts of the town, take the road
towards Peize and Roden.*
Open: 15 Mar-15 Oct Site: 6HEC ⬛⬛⬛ ♣ Facilities: 🏠 🕿 ⊙
🖙 🖉 🖀 🖪 Services: 🍴 ✕ 🖽 lau Off-site: 🕂LP

HARKSTEDE GRONINGEN

Grunopark Hoofdweg 163, 9617
☎ 050 416371 ▤ 050 424521
website: www.grunopark.nl
Situated within a large waterpark with a great variety of
sporting facilities available.
Open: All year Site: 23HEC ⬛⬛⬛ ⚜ Å Facilities: 🏠 🕿 ⊙ 🖙 🖉
🚿 🖀 Services: 🍴 ✕ 🖽 lau Leisure: 🕂 L

HARLINGEN FRIESLAND

Zeehoeve 8862 ☎ 0517 413465 ▤ 0517 416971
e-mail: info@zeehoeve.nl
website: www.zeehoeve.nl
A well-kept meadow site which is divided into large sections
by rows of bushes.
➔ *1km S of Harlingen near a dyke.*
Open: Apr-Sep Site: 10HEC ⬛⬛⬛ ⚜ 🕂 ♨ Facilities: 🏠 ⊙
🖙 🖉 🖀 Services: 🍴 ✕ 🖽 lau Leisure: 🕂 S Off-site: 🕿

Site: 6HEC-Site size ⬛⬛⬛-grass ⁙⁙⁙-sand ⚜-stone ⚜-little shade ⚜-partly shaded ♣-mainly shaded
🕂-bungalows for hire ♨-caravans for hire Å-tents for hire ⊘-no dogs **Prices:** 🕿-adult per night 🚗-car per night
pp-per person per night ♨-caravan per night Å-tent per night

HEE (ISLAND OF TERSCHELLING) FRIESLAND

Kooi Hee 9, 8882 ☎ 0562 442743 ▤ 0562 442835
website: www.campingdekooi.nl
➲ *5km from the harbour.*
Open: 15 Apr-15 Sep Site: 8.5HEC ⛺ ⊶ Prices: ⋔4 ⇆2
⊞5 ▲2.25-5 Facilities: ⋒ ⊙ ⊟ ▣ Services: ⫛ ✕ ⊞ lau
Off-site: ⛴ ⌀ ⒵L

HINDELOOPEN FRIESLAND

Hindelopen Westerdijk 9, 8713 ☎ 0514 521452 ▤ 0514 523221
e-mail: info@campinghindeloopen.nl
website: www.campinghindeloopen.nl
A peaceful site on the Ysselmeer with fishing and watersports
facilities.
➲ *1km S.*
Open: Apr-Nov Site: 16HEC ⛺ ⊶ Facilities: ⋒ ⛴ ⊙ ⊟ ⌀
⛽ ⒵ ▣ Services: ⫛ ✕ ⊞ lau Leisure: ⒵ L

KOUDUM FRIESLAND

De Kuilart Kuilart 1, 8723 ☎ 0514 522221 ▤ 0514 523010
e-mail: info@kuilart.nl website: www.kuilart.nl
A camping and watersports centre on the shores of 'De
Fluessen' lake.
➲ *Access via N359.*
Open: All year Site: 30HEC ⛺ ⊶ ⓟ ⊞ Prices: ⋔3.50
⇆2.40 pitch 15-19.50 (incl 2 persons) Facilities: ⋒ ⛴ ⊙ ⊟
⌀ ⒵ ▣ Services: ⫛ ✕ ⊞ lau Leisure: ⒵ LP Off-site: ⒵S

LAUWERSOOG GRONINGEN

Lauwersoog Strandweg 5, 9976
☎ 0519 349133 ▤ 0519 349195
e-mail: info@lauwersoog.nl website: www.lauwersoog.nl
In a pleasant situation on the shores of Lauwersmeer. A good
excursion centre with fine water sports facilities.
Camping Card Compulsory.
Open: All year Site: 13HEC ⛺ ⫶⫶⫶ ⊶ Facilities: ⋒ ⛴ ⊙
⊟ ⌀ ⒵ ▣ Services: ⫛ ✕ ⊞ lau Leisure: ⒵ L Off-site: ⒵S

MAKKUM FRIESLAND

Holle Poarte Holle Poarte 2, 8754
☎ 0515 231344 ▤ 0515 231339
A modern site with fine water sports facilities on the Ijsselmeer.
Open: All year Site: 32HEC ⛺ ⫶⫶⫶ ⊶ ⓟ ⊞ Prices: pitch
14.55-16.10 (incl 2 persons) Facilities: ⋒ ⛴ ⊙ ⊟ ⌀ ⒵ ⒵
Services: ⫛ ✕ ⊞ lau Leisure: ⒵ L

ONNEN GRONINGEN

Fruitberg Dorpsweg 67, 9755 ☎ 050 4061282
A peaceful site situated in an orchard.
➲ *S of the village, and right of the Haren-Zuidlaren road.*
Open: 15 Mar-1 Nov Site: 5.5HEC ⛺ ⊶ ⊞ Facilities: ⋒ ⊙ ⊟
⌀ ⒵ ⒵ ▣ Services: ⫛ ✕ ⊞ lau Leisure: ⒵ P Off-site: ⛴ ✕ ⒵L

OPENDE FRIESLAND

'**T Strandheem** Parkweg 2, 9865
☎ 0594 659555 ▤ 0594 658592
e-mail: info@strandheem.nl website: www.strandheem.nl
A family site with modern sanitary blocks and a wide variety
of recreational facilities.
➲ *Access from A7 (Groningen-Afsluitdijk) exit 31.*
Open: Apr-1 Oct Site: 15HEC ⛺ ⊶ ⓟ ⊞ Prices: pitch
14.50-18.50 (incl 2 persons) Facilities: ⋒ ⛴ ⊙ ⊟ ⌀ ⒵ ⒵ ▣
Services: ⫛ ✕ ⊞ lau Leisure: ⒵ LP

RUINEN DRENTHE

Engeland Oude Benderseweg 11, 7963 ☎ 0522 471770
A family site in pleasant wooded surroundings with well
sheltered pitches on the edge of a National Park.

➲ *Access via A28 exit Ruinen-Pesse.*
Open: Apr-24 Oct Site: 25HEC ⛺ ⊶ ⓟ ▲ Facilities: ⋒ ⛴
⊙ ⊟ ⌀ ⒵ Services: ⫛ ✕ ⊞ lau Leisure: ⒵ P Off-site: ✕ ⛽

Wiltzangh Witteveen 2, 7963
☎ 0522 471227 ▤ 0522 472178
e-mail: wiltzangh@dwingelderveld.com
website: www.dwingelderveld.com/wiltzangh
North of the village in the middle of a coniferous and
deciduous forest, and within the grounds of a big holiday
village. Advance booking is necessary for the peak season.
➲ *For access, drive from Ruinen towards Ansen for 3km, then
turn and head N.*
Open: Apr-Oct Site: 13HEC ⛺ ⊶ ⓟ Prices: pitch 13-20
pp2.50 Facilities: ⋒ ⛴ ⊙ ⊟ ⌀ ⛽ ▣ Services: ✕ ⊞ lau
Leisure: ⒵ P

SONDEL FRIESLAND

Sondel Beuckenswijkstr 26, 8565 ☎ 0514 602300
website: www.campingsondel.nl
In a dense wood.
➲ *Just off the Sondel-Rijs road.*
Open: Apr-Oct Site: 5HEC ⛺ ⊶ ⚙ Prices: pitch 11.30
(incl 2 persons) pp3.80 Facilities: ⋒ ⊙ ⊟ ⒵ ▣ Services: ⫛ ✕
⊞ lau Leisure: ⒵ LPRS Off-site: ⛴ ⌀ ⛽

TERSCHELLING (ISLAND OF)

WEDDE GRONINGEN

Wedderbergen Molenweg 2, 9698
☎ 0597 561673 ▤ 0597 562595
e-mail: info@wedderbergen.nl
website: www.wedderbergen.nl
On meadowland divided by deciduous trees and bush
hedges.
➲ *On the E outskirts of the village take a narrow asphalt road,
and drive N for 3.2km. Then take Spanjaardsweg and
Molenweg to the camp.*
Open: Apr-1Nov Site: 40HEC ⛺ ⊶ ⊞ Prices: ⊞12.90-15
pitch 11.75-13.60 (incl 2 persons) Facilities: ⋒ ⛴ ⊙ ⊟ ⌀ ⛽
⒵ Services: ⫛ ✕ ⊞ lau Leisure: ⒵ LR

WEST TERSCHELLING (ISLAND OF TERSCHELLING)
FRIESLAND

Cnossen Hoofdweg 8, 8881 HA ☎ 0562 442321
Several patches of meadowland, left of the road towards
Formerum, and right of the forest.
➲ *For access, take the ferry from Harlingen.*
Open: Apr-1 Nov Site: 2.5HEC ⛺ ⊶ ⓟ ⊞ ▲ Facilities: ⋒
⛴ ⊙ ⊟ ⌀ ⛽ ▣ Services: ⫛ ✕ ⊞ Off-site: ⒵LP

CENTRAL

AALSMEER NOORD-HOLLAND

Amsterdamse Bos Kleine Noorddijk 1, 1432
☎ 020 6416868 ▤ 020 6402378
e-mail: camping@dab.amsterdam.nl
website: www.campingamsterdambos.nl
The site is in a park-like setting in the Amsterdam wood.
The camp is near the Airport flight path and is subject to
noise depending on the wind direction.
➲ *If approaching from The Hague along the motorway, turn at
the northern edge of the airport, and head towards Amstelveen.
Then follow directions for Aalsmeer. Alternatively, if approaching
from Utrecht, leave the motorway at the Amstelveen exit, and
drive towards Aalsmeer, passing through Bovenkerk.*
Open: Apr-14 Oct Site: 6.8HEC ⛺ ⊶ ⓟ Prices: ⋔5 ⇆3
⊞3.50 ▲3 Facilities: ⋒ ⛴ ⊙ ⊟ ⌀ ⒵ Services: ⫛ ✕ ⊞ lau
Off-site: ⛽ ⒵LS

Facilities: ⛴-shop ⋒-shower ⊙-electric points for razors ⊟-electric points for caravans ⒵-parking by tents permitted
▣-compulsory separate car park Services: ✕-café/restaurant ⫛-bar ⌀-Camping Gaz International ⛽-gas other than Camping
Gaz ⊞-first aid facilities lau-laundry Leisure: ⒵-swimming L-Lake P-Pool R-River S-Sea Off-site: All facilities within 2km

Gaasper Camping Amsterdam
Loosdrechtdreef 7,
NL-1108 AZ Amsterdam
Tel: +31 20 696 73 26
Fax: +31 20 696 93 69
GAASPER CAMPING
AMSTERDAM
www.gaaspercamping.nl
Just 20 minutes from the centre of Amsterdam there is a unique region of natural beauty, the "Gaasperpark" on the Gaasperplas. Within easy reach of a tube-station one of the finest camp sites of the Dutch capital is found: Gaasper Camping Amsterdam, situated on the verge of a park, with many trees and flowers.

ALKMAAR NOORD-HOLLAND

Alkmaar Bergerweg 201, 1817
☎ 072 5116924 ▦ 022 4216909
e-mail: johnbroers@planet.nl
The site is well-kept and divided into many sections by rows of trees and bushes.
Camping Card Compulsory.
➲ *Lies on the NW outskirts of the town, off the Bergen road.*
Open: Apr-Oct Site: 3HEC ▥ ⊕ ⊞ Prices: ♠5 ♣2.30 ♣4.50 ▲3.40 Facilities: ♠ ⚊ ⊙ ♥ ∅ ⊞ Services: ⊞ lau Off-site: ♠ ⚊ ✗ ∅ ⚊ ⚊LPS

AMSTERDAM NOORD-HOLLAND

See also Aalsmeer

Gaasper Loosdrechtdreef 7, 1108
☎ 020 6967326 ▦ 020 6969369
website: www.gaaspercamping-amsterdam.nl
Situated on the edge of the beautiful 'Gaasperpark' within easy reach of Amsterdam.
Camping Card Compulsory.
➲ *From A9 take Gaasperplas exit before city centre and follow camping signs.*
Open: 15 Mar-1 Nov Site: 5.5HEC ▥ ⊕ Prices: ♠4.25 ♣3.75 ♣6 ▲6 Facilities: ♠ ⚊ ⊙ ♥ ∅ ⚊ ⊞ Services: ⚊ ✗ ⊞ lau Off-site: ✗ ⚊L

Vliegenbos Meeuwenlaan 138, 1022 ☎ 020 6368855
This is a tent site for young people.
➲ *From main railway station through tunnel, then right and right again at traffic lights, then follow signposts.*
Open: Apr-Sep Site: 25HEC ▥ ♦ ⚊ ⊕ ♣ Facilities: ♠ ⚊ ⊙ ♥ ∅ ⚊ ⊞ Services: ⚊ ✗ ⊞ lau Off-site: ⚊P

Zeeburg Zuider Ijdijk 20, 1095
☎ 020 6944430 ▦ 020 6946238
e-mail: info@campingzeeburg.nl
website: www.campingzeeburg.nl
On an island in the Ijmeer, 15 minutes from the city centre, with good facilities. Popular with backpackers and holidaymakers alike.
➲ *Access via A10 exit S114 by second set of traffic lights.*
Open: All year Site: 3.8HEC ▥ ⚊ ⊞ Prices: ♠4.50 ♣4 ♣5 ▲3.50 pitch 3.50 Facilities: ♠ ⚊ ⊙ ♥ ∅ ⚊ ⊞ Services: ⚊ ✗ ⊞ lau Off-site: ⚊P

ANDIJK NOORD-HOLLAND

Vakantiedorp Het Grootslag Proefpolder 4, 1619
☎ 0228 592944 ▦ 0228 592457
e-mail: info@grootslag.nl website: www.grootslag.nl
One of the most well equipped sites in the area, situated on the Ijsselmeer. Individual bathrooms are allocated to each pitch and a wide range of recreational facilities are available.
➲ *From A7 exit Hoorn-Noord/Enkhuizen/Lelystad turn left for Andijk, then follow signs for Het Grootslag and Dijkweg.*
Open: Apr-Oct Site: 40HEC ▥ ⊕ ⊞ Prices: pitch 26 (incl 4 persons) Facilities: ♠ ⚊ ⊙ ♥ ∅ ⚊ ⚊ ⊞ Services: ⚊ ✗ ⊞ lau Leisure: ⚊ LP

APPELTERN GELDERLAND

Het Groene Eiland Lutenkampstr 2, 6629
☎ 0487 562130 ▦ 0487 561540
e-mail: info@hetgroeneeiland.nl
website: www.hetgroeneeiland.nl
In a 'Water Recreation' park with plenty of sporting facilities.
➲ *From A15 take Leeuwen turn and follow signs.*
Open: 15 Mar-Oct Site: 16HEC ▥ ⚊ ♥ Prices: ♠2.30 ♣2.60 ♣10.50 ▲10.50 Facilities: ♠ ⚊ ⊙ ♥ ∅ ⚊ ⊞ Services: ⚊ ✗ ⊞ lau Leisure: ⚊ LR Off-site: ✗

ARNHEM GELDERLAND

Arnhem Kemperbergerweg 771, 6816
☎ 026 4431600 ▦ 026 4457705
e-mail: arnhem@holiday.nl website: www.campingarnhem.nl
The site lies on grassland and is surrounded by trees.
➲ *NW of town and S of E36.*
Open: Apr-Oct Site: 36HEC ▥ ♥ Prices: pitch 15.75-24 (incl 2 persons) Facilities: ♠ ⚊ ⊙ ♥ ∅ ⚊ ⚊ Services: ⚊ ✗ ⊞ lau Leisure: ⚊ P

Hooge Veluwe Koningsweg 14, 6816
☎ 026 4432272 ▦ 026 4436809
e-mail: info@dehoogeveluwe
website: www.dehoogeveluwe.nl
Situated in a pleasant natural park with good facilities.
➲ *From Apeldoorn exit on E36 drive NW towards Hooge Veluwe.*
Open: 31 Mar-28 Oct Site: 18HEC ▥ ♥ ⊞ ♥ Prices: pitch 32.50-49.50 Facilities: ♠ ⚊ ⊙ ♥ ∅ ⚊ Services: ⚊ ✗ ⊞ lau Leisure: ⚊ P

Warnsborn Bakenbergseweg 257, 6816
☎ 026 4423469 ▦ 026 4421095
e-mail: info@campingwarnsborn.nl
website: www.campingwarnsborn.nl
The site is surrounded by woodland and lies on slightly sloping meadowland. Near zoo and open-air museum.
➲ *Near the E36 motorway NW of town in the direction of Utrecht. 200mtrs S of SHELL filling station, continue in W direction for 0.7km.*
Open: Apr-Oct Site: 3.5HEC ▥ ♥ ⊞ ♥ Facilities: ♠ ⚊ ⊙ ♥ ∅ ⚊ ⚊ Services: ⊞ lau Off-site: ⚊ ✗ ⚊P

BABBERICH GELDERLAND

Rivo Torto Beekseweg 8, 6909
☎ 0316 247332 ▦ 0316 246628
e-mail: rivotorto@hetnet.nl
website: www.rivotorto.nl
A riverside site with good recreational facilities.
➲ *3km W on E36.*
Open: 15 Mar-Oct Site: 8.5HEC ▥ ♥ Prices: ♠1.80 ♣2.35 ♣6 ▲3.65 pitch 3.65 Facilities: ♠ ⚊ ⊙ ♥ ∅ ⚊ ⚊ Services: ⚊ ⊞ lau Off-site: ✗ ⚊L

Site: 6HEC-Site size ▥-grass ∴-sand ⚊-stone ⚊-little shade ⊕-partly shaded ♠-mainly shaded ⊞-bungalows for hire ♥-caravans for hire ▲-tents for hire ♥-no dogs Prices: ♠-adult per night ♣-car per night pp-per person per night ♥-caravan per night ▲-tent per night

BEEKBERGEN GELDERLAND

Bosgraaf Kanaal Zuid 444, 7364 ☎ 055 5051359
Situated on hilly grassland and woodland, but the woodland pitches are mainly used by residential caravans.
➲ *For access from the N50, Arnhem-Apeldoorn road, turn N in West Hoeve onto the Loenen road, then follow signs for 2km.*
Site: 22HEC ⬛ 🚰 🚐 ⊘ Facilities: ☈ 🛢 ⊙ 🖾 ⊘ 🏕
Services: ✗ lau Leisure: ⤳ P

BERKHOUT NOORD-HOLLAND

Westerkogge Kerkebuurt 202, 1647
☎ 0229 551208   ▤ 0229 551390
e-mail: info@camping-westerkogge.nl
website: www.camping-westerkogge.nl
In a fine situation with well sheltered pitches and a good range of recreational facilities.
➲ *Access via A7 (Amsterdam-Leeuwarden) exit Hoorn-Berkhout or Berkhout-Avenhorn.*
Open: Apr-Oct Site: 11HEC ⬛ 🚰 🚐 Prices: ⋔2.75-3
⋔2.20-2.50 🚐7.40-8.30 ▲4.10 Facilities: ☈ 🛢 ⊙ 🖾 ⊘ 🚿 🏕
🅿 Services: 🍷 ✗ ⊞ lau Leisure: ⤳ P

BILTHOVEN UTRECHT

Bospark Bilthoven Burg v.d Borchlaan 7, 3722
☎ 030 2286777   ▤ 030 2293888
e-mail: bosparkbilthoven@wanadoo.nl
Family site in wooded surroundings with asphalt drives.
➲ *Signposted from town centre.*
Open: Apr-Oct Site: 20HEC ⬛ ⠂⠂⠂ 🚰 Facilities: ☈ ⊙ 🖾 ⊘
🏕 Services: 🍷 ✗ ⊞ lau Leisure: ⤳ P Off-site: 🛢 ✗

BLOKZIJL OVERIJSSEL

Tussen de Diepen Duinigermeerweg 1A, 8356
☎ 0527 291565   ▤ 0527 292203
e-mail: camping@tussendediepen.nl
website: www.tussendediepen.nl
Secluded site surrounded by water. Fishing, water-sports and sailing.
Open: Apr-Oct Site: 5.2HEC ⬛ 🚰 Facilities: ☈ 🛢 ⊙ 🖾 ⊘
🚿 🅿 Services: 🍷 ✗ ⊞ lau Leisure: ⤳ R Off-site: ⤳P

BUURSE OVERIJSSEL

't Hazenbos Oude Buurserdijk 1, 7481 ☎ 053 5696338
e-mail: info@hazenbos.nl website: www.hazenbos.nl
On several meadows, partially surrounded by trees.
➲ *7km from the German border.*
Open: All year Site: 6HEC ⬛ 🚰 Prices: ⋔2.50 🚐1.70
🚐2.55 ▲2.55 Facilities: ☈ ⊙ 🖾 ⊘ 🚿 🏕 🅿 Services: ⊞ lau
Off-site: 🛢 🍷 ✗ ⤳LP

CALLANTSOOG NOORD-HOLLAND

Recreatiecentrum de Nollen Westerweg 8, 1759
☎ 0224 581281   ▤ 0224 582098
e-mail: info@denollen.nl website: www.denollen.nl
A modern family site with plenty of facilities. Less than 1 mile from the beach.
➲ *E of town towards N9.*
Open: Apr-1 Nov Site: 9HEC ⬛ 🚰 🚐 ▲ Prices: pitch 18-24 Facilities: ☈ 🛢 ⊙ 🖾 ⊘ 🚿 🏕 🅿 Services: 🍷 ✗ ⊞ lau
Off-site: ⤳PS

Tempelhof Westerweg 2, 1759
☎ 0224 581522   ▤ 0224 582133
e-mail: tempelhof@planet.nl
website: www.tempelhof.nl
Well equipped site on level meadowland.
Open: All year Site: 12.7HEC ⬛ 🚰 Prices: ⋔3.67 pitch
24.34-28.34 (incl 2 persons) Facilities: ☈ 🛢 ⊙ 🖾 ⊘ 🚿 🏕
Services: 🍷 ✗ ⊞ lau Leisure: ⤳ P Off-site: ⤳LS

DALFSEN OVERIJSSEL

Buitenplaats Gerner Haersolteweg 9-17, 7722
☎ 0529 439191   ▤ 0529 439199
e-mail: info@gerner.nl website: www.gerner.nl
➲ *Turn off at Dalfsen and take second road on the left.*
Open: All year Site: 12HEC ⬛ 🚰 🚐 Facilities: ☈ 🛢 ⊙ 🖾
⊘ 🏕 🅿 Services: 🍷 ✗ ⊞ lau Leisure: ⤳ P

DENEKAMP OVERIJSSEL

Papillon Kanaalweg 30, 7591
☎ 05413 51670   ▤ 05413 55217
website: www.depapillon.nl
Predominantly a chalet site on meadowland in a tall coniferous and deciduous forest, about 2km N of Denekamp. It has a few naturally screened pitches.
➲ *For access, turn off the E72 towards Nordhorn (Germany), about 0.3km N of the signposts for Almelo-Nordhorn canal, and drive NE for 1.5km.*
Open: Apr-1 Oct Site: 11HEC ⬛ 🚰 🚐 🚐 Facilities: ☈ 🛢
⊙ 🖾 ⊘ 🏕 Services: 🍷 ✗ ⊞ lau Leisure: ⤳ LP

DIEPENHEIM OVERIJSSEL

Molnhofte Nyhofweg 5, 7478
☎ 0547 351514   ▤ 0547 351641
e-mail: molnhofte@planet.nl website: www.molnhofte.nl
A family site in a rural setting with modern bungalows for hire.
➲ *E of town.*
Open: All year Site: 6HEC ⬛ 🚰 🚐 🚐 Prices: ⋔2.75 🚐2.25
🚐2.75 ▲2.75 pitch 2.25 Facilities: ☈ 🛢 ⊙ 🖾 ⊘ 🚿 🏕 🅿
Services: 🍷 ✗ ⊞ lau Leisure: ⤳ P

DOESBURG GELDERLAND

Ijsselstrand Eekstr 18, 6984 ☎ 0313 472797   ▤ 0313 473376
e-mail: ijsselstrand@planet.nl website: www.ijsselstrand.nl
On level meadow with trees and hedges beside the River Ijssel. Separate field for young people. Water sports.
➲ *NE across river. Signposted.*
Open: All year Site: 45HEC ⬛ 🚰 🚐 🚐 Prices: ⋔3 🚐1.90
🚐3.40 ▲2.70 Facilities: ☈ 🛢 ⊙ 🖾 ⊘ 🏕 🅿 Services: 🍷 ✗ ⊞
lau Leisure: ⤳ LR

DOETINCHEM GELDERLAND

Wrange Rekhemseweg 144, 7004
☎ 0314 324852   ▤ 0314 324852
e-mail: info@dewrange.nl website: www.dewrange.nl
On the eastern outskirts of the town. It is set in meadowland and surrounded by bushes and deciduous trees.
➲ *200mtrs E of link road between roads to Varsseveld and Terborg.*
Open: Apr-1 Oct Site: 10HEC ⬛ 🚅 🚐 🚐 Prices: pitch
12.85-13.75 (incl 2 persons) Facilities: ☈ 🛢 ⊙ 🖾 ⊘ 🏕 🅿
Services: 🍷 ✗ ⊞ lau Leisure: ⤳ P

DOORN UTRECHT

Bonte Vlucht Leersumsestraatweg 23, 3941
☎ 0343 473232   ▤ 0343 414517
e-mail: info@bontevlucht.nl
website: www.bontevlucht.nl
➲ *3km E.*
Open: Apr-Oct Site: 17HEC ⬛ ⠂⠂⠂ 🚰 ⊘ Prices: pitch
17.50-19.50 (incl 2 persons) Facilities: ☈ ⊙ 🖾 ⊘ 🅿
Services: 🍷 ✗ ⊞ Off-site: ⤳P

Het Grote Bos Hydeparklaan 24, 3941
☎ 0343 513644   ▤ 0343 512324
Well layed out site on wooded grassland. Varied leisure activities for children and adults.

contd.

Facilities: 🛢-shop ☈-shower ⊙-electric points for razors 🖾-electric points for caravans 🏕-parking by tents permitted
🅿-compulsory separate car park Services: ✗-café/restaurant 🍷-bar ⊘-Camping Gaz International 🚿-gas other than Camping
Gaz ⊞-first aid facilities lau-laundry Leisure: ⤳-swimming L-Lake P-Pool R-River S-Sea Off-site: All facilities within 2km

⊃ *About 1km NW of Doorn.*
Open: All year Site: 80HEC ▦ ∷ ⊞ Facilities: ⋒ ⅃ ⊙ ⊠
⊘ ░ Services: ⅄ ✗ ⊞ lau Leisure: ⇥ P

DRONTEN GELDERLAND

AT BIDDINGHUIZEN (9KM S)

Riviera Park Spijkweg 15, 8256
☎ 0321 331344 ▤ 0321 331402
e-mail: info@riviera.nl website: www.riviera.nl
Situated on grassland near a forest of deciduous trees and
surrounded by shrubs.
⊃ *On the Polder beside the Veluwemeer, 5km S of
Biddinghuizen turn left.*
Site: 60HEC ▦ Ꭴ ⊠ ▲ Prices: pitch 22.80-29.70 (incl 4
persons) Facilities: ⋒ ⅃ ⊙ ⊠ ⊘ ░ ⊞ Services: ⅄ ✗ ⊞ lau
Leisure: ⇥ LP

EDAM NOORD-HOLLAND

Strandbad Zeevangszeedijk 7a, 1135
☎ 0299 371994 ▤ 0299 371510
e-mail: info@campingstrandbad.nl
website: www.campingstrandbad.nl
A friendly family site on the Ijssel Lake with plenty of
facilities and close to the historical town of Edam.
Open: Apr-Sep Site: 5HEC ▦ ⅊ ⊞ ⊘ Prices: ⋔2.95
⊶3.15 ⊠4.30 ▲4.30 Facilities: ⋒ ⅃ ⊙ ⊠ ⊘ ░ ⊞
Services: ⅄ ✗ ⊞ lau Leisure: ⇥ L Off-site: ⇥P

EERBEEK GELDERLAND

Landal Greenparks Coldenhove Boshoffweg 6, 6961
☎ 0313 659101 ▤ 0313 654776
website: www.landal.nl
In woodland.
⊃ *From Apeldoorn-Dieren road, drive 2km SW, then NW for
1km.*
Open: All year Site: 74HEC ▦ Ꭴ ⊞ ⊘ Facilities: ⋒ ⅃ ⊙
⊠ ⊘ ░ ⊞ ⊞ Services: ⅄ ✗ ⊞ lau Leisure: ⇥ P Off-site: ✗

Robertsoord Doonweg 4, 6961 ☎ 0313 651346 ▤ 0313 655751
e-mail: info@robertsoord.nl website: www.robertsoord.nl
In a wooded location with good recreational facilities.
⊃ *1km SE.*
Open: Apr-Oct Site: 2.5HEC ▦ Ꭴ ⊞ Facilities: ⋒ ⊙ ⊠ ⊘
░ ⊞ Services: ✗ ⊞ lau Off-site: ⇥P

EGMOND AAN ZEE NOORD-HOLLAND

Camping Egmond ann Zee Nollenweg 1, 1931 AV
☎ 072 5061702 ▤ 072 5067147
website: www.euroase.com
Part of a chain of family sites with excellent facilities. In a
wooded location 1500mtrs from the beach.
Open: Apr-Oct Site: 11HEC ▦ Ꭴ ⊠ ⊘ Facilities: ⋒ ⅃ ⊙
⊠ ⊘ ░ ⊞ Services: ⅄ ⊞ lau Leisure: ⇥ PS Off-site: ✗ ⇥P

ENSCHEDE OVERIJSSEL

De Twentse Es Keppelerdijk 200, 7534
☎ 053 4611372 ▤ 053 4618558
e-mail: info@twentse-es.nl website: www.twentse-es.nl
In a wooded location with good recreational facilities.
⊃ *E towards Glanerbrug.*
Open: All year Site: 10HEC ▦ Ꭴ Prices: pitch 19.40 (incl
5 persons) Facilities: ⋒ ⅃ ⊙ ⊠ ⊘ ░ ⊞ Services: ⅄ ✗ ⊞ lau
Leisure: ⇥ P

EPE GELDERLAND

Euroase Parc Epe Centrumweg 5, 8162 PT
☎ 05780 616204 ▤ 05780 627775
On level ground, surrounded by mature woodland, with fine
recreational facilities.

⊃ *SW of village.*
Open: Apr-1 Nov Site: 15HEC ▦ Ꭴ ⊞ Facilities: ⋒ ⅃ ⊙
⊠ ░ ⊞ Services: ⅄ ✗ ⊞ lau Leisure: ⇥ P

ERMELO GELDERLAND

Haeghehorst Fazantlaan 4, 3852
☎ 0341 553185 ▤ 0341 562751
e-mail: haeghehorst@vvc.nl website: www.haeghehorst.nl
Well equipped site in pleasant wooded surroundings.
Camping Card Compulsory.
⊃ *Access via A28/E35 towards Amersfoort, then N303.*
Open: All year Site: 10HEC ▦ ⅊ ⊞ ⊘ Prices: ⋔14-25
pitch 15.25-28.50 (incl 2 persons) Facilities: ⋒ ⅃ ⊙ ⊠ ⊘ ░
⊞ Services: ⅄ ✗ ⊞ lau Leisure: ⇥ P

GROET NOORD-HOLLAND

Groede Hargerweg 8, 1871 ☎ 072 5091555 ▤ 072 5092862
e-mail: campinggroede@planet.nl
website: www.camping-groede.nl
The site consists of a meadow enclosed by hedges.
Open: 15 Apr-15 Sep Site: 3HEC ▦ Ꭴ ⊘ Prices: ⋔11
⊠10.50 ▲10.50 Facilities: ⋒ ⅃ ⊙ ⊠ ⊘ ░ ⊞ Services: ⊞ lau
Off-site: ⅄ ✗

GROOTE KEETEN NOORD-HOLLAND

Callassande Voorweg 5A, 1759
☎ 0224 581663 ▤ 0224 582588
e-mail: info@callassande.nl website: www.callassande.nl
A large tourist site with fine facilities close to the sea.
Open: Apr-Oct Site: 12HEC ▦ Ꭴ ⊠ Prices: ⋔3.75 ⊠12
▲8-12 pitch 12 Facilities: ⋒ ⅃ ⊙ ⊠ ⊞ ⊞ Services: ⅄ ✗ ⊞
lau Leisure: ⇥ P Off-site: ⊘ ░ ⇥S

HAAKSBERGEN OVERIJSSEL

't Stien'nboer Scholtenhagenweg 42, 7481
☎ 053 5722610 ▤ 053 5729394
e-mail: info@stien-nboer.nl website: www.stien-nboer.nl
A family site with good recreational facilities lying S of the
town.
Open: 15 Mar-Nov Site: 10.5HEC ▦ Ꭴ ⊞ ⊠ ▲
Prices: ⋔11.45 ⊶17.55 pitch 11.45-17.55 (incl 2 persons)
Facilities: ⋒ ⅃ ⊙ ⊠ ⊘ ░ ⊞ Services: ⅄ ✗ ⊞ lau Leisure: ⇥
P Off-site: ⅃ ⅄ ✗

HALFWEG NOORD-HOLLAND

Houtrak Zuiderweg 2, 1165 NA
☎ 020 4972796 ▤ 020 4975887
e-mail: info@campinghoutrak.nl
website: www.campinghoutrak.nl
Grassy site on several levels subdivided by trees, hedges and
shrubs. Separate section for young campers.
⊃ *Signposted from Spaarwonde exit on A5.*
Open: Apr-Sep Site: 13HEC ▦ Ꭴ ⊞ Prices: ⋔3 ⊶2.40
⊠4.60 ▲3.60 Facilities: ⋒ ⅃ ⊙ ⊠ ⊘ ░ ⊞ Services: ✗ ⊞ lau
Leisure: ⇥ L Off-site: ⇥P

HATTEM GELDERLAND

Leemkule Leemkuilen 6, 8051 PN
☎ 038 4441945 ▤ 038 4446280
e-mail: info@leemkule.nl website: www.leemkule.nl
A holiday centre situated in one of the largest nature reserves
in the country.
⊃ *2.5km SW.*
Open: Apr-Oct Site: 16HEC ▦ Ꭴ ⊞ ⊘ Prices: ⋔3.50
pitch 15.50-21.50 (incl 2 persons) Facilities: ⋒ ⅃ ⊙ ⊠ ⊘ ⊞
Services: ⅄ ✗ ⊞ lau Leisure: ⇥ P

Site: 6HEC-Site size ▦ **-grass** ∷ **-sand** ⬥**-stone** ⅊**-little shade** Ꭴ**-partly shaded** ♣**-mainly shaded**
⊞**-bungalows for hire** ⊠**-caravans for hire** ▲**-tents for hire** ⊘**-no dogs Prices:** ⋔**-adult per night** ⊶**-car per night**
pp-per person per night ⊠**-caravan per night** ▲**-tent per night**

HEILOO NOORD-HOLLAND

Heiloo De Omloop 24, 1852 ☎ 072 5355555 ▤ 072 5355551
e-mail: info@campingheiloo.nl
website: www.campingheiloo.nl
One of the best sites in the area. It is divided into many large squares by hedges.
Open: Apr-Oct Site: 4HEC ⏛ ⛅ 🏠 🚐 ⌁
Prices: 🚐11.50-19.50 ▲9-16 pitch 11.50-19.50 (incl 2 persons) Facilities: 🏪 ⊙ 🚐 ⌀ 🚿 🅿 Services: 🍴 ✗ 🕀 lau
Off-site: 🛒 ⤳LP

Klein Varnebroek De Omloop 22, 1852
☎ 072 5331627 ▤ 072 5331620
e-mail: info@kleinvarnebroek.nl
website: www.kleinvarnebroek.nl
A grassy family campsite surrounded by trees.
➲ *Off the Alkmaar road towards the swimming pool.*
Open: 25 Mar-1 Nov Site: 4.9HEC ⏛ ⛅ ⌁ Prices: pitch 17-28 (incl 2 persons) Facilities: 🏪 🛒 ⊙ 🚐 ⌀ 🅿 Services: 🍴 ✗ 🕀 lau Off-site: 🛒 ⤳LPS

HELDER, DEN NOORD-HOLLAND

Donkere Duinen Jan Verfailleweg 616, 1783
☎ 0223 614731 ▤ 0223 615077
e-mail: info@donkereduinen.nl
website: www.donkereduinen.nl
A quiet, pleasant site with good facilities.
➲ *800mtrs towards the beach. Follow signs 'Nieuw-Den Helder' Strand.*
Open: 09 Apr-28 Aug Site: 7HEC ⏛ ⛅ Prices: 🅰4.10 pitch 20.70-23.20 (incl 2 persons) Facilities: 🏪 🛒 ⊙ 🚐 🅿 Services: 🕀 lau Leisure: ⤳ S Off-site: 🛒 🍴 ✗ ⌀ 🚿 ⤳PS

Noorder Sandt Noorder Sandt 2, Julianadorp aan Zee, 1787
☎ 0223 641266 ▤ 0233 645600
e-mail: info@noordersandt.com
website: www.noordersandt.com
A flat, well-maintained site on meadowland, with good sanitary blocks.
➲ *Access from the Den Helder to Callantsoog coastal road.*
Open: Etr-15 Sep Site: 10HEC ⏛ ⛅ Prices: 🅰3.93 pitch 23-29 (incl 2 persons) Facilities: 🏪 🛒 ⊙ 🚐 ⌀ 🚿 🅿 Services: 🍴 ✗ 🕀 lau Leisure: ⤳ P Off-site: ⤳S

HENGELO GELDERLAND

Kom-Es-An Handwijzersdijk 4, 7255 ☎ 0575 467242
A family site in wooded surroundings on the outskirts of the village.
➲ *NE of village in wooded area in the direction of Ruurlo.*
Open: Apr-Oct Site: 10.5HEC ⏛ ⛅ 🚐 Facilities: 🏪 🛒 ⊙ 🚐 ⌀ 🚿 🅿 🏠 Services: 🍴 ✗ 🕀 lau Leisure: ⤳ P

HENGELO OVERIJSSEL

Zwaaikom Kettingbrugweg 60, 7552
☎ 074 2916560 ▤ 074 2916785
A family site with good facilities situated on the Twente Canal.
➲ *SE towards Enschede between canal and road.*
Open: 15 Apr-15 Sep Site: 4HEC ⏛ ⛅ ⌁ Prices: 🅰3.30 🚐2.85 🚐2.88 ▲2.85 Facilities: 🏪 🛒 ⊙ 🚐 ⌀ 🏠 Services: 🍴 ✗ 🕀 Leisure: ⤳ P

HEUMEN GELDERLAND

Heumens Bos Vosseneindseweg 46, 6582
☎ 024 3581481 ▤ 024 3583862
e-mail: info@heumensbos.nl
website: www.heumensbos.nl
One of the best sites in the area with good, modern facilities and spacious pitches.

➲ *NW of village, 100mtrs N of the Wijchen road.*
Open: Apr-Oct Site: 16HEC ⏛ ⛅ 🏠 🚐 ▲ Prices: 🅰4 pitch 15-23.50 (incl 2 persons) Facilities: 🏪 🛒 ⊙ 🚐 ⌀ 🅿 Services: 🍴 ✗ 🕀 lau Leisure: ⤳ P

HOENDERLOO GELDERLAND

Pampel Woeste Hoefweg 33-35, 7351 TN
☎ 055 3781760 ▤ 055 3781992
e-mail: info@pampel.nl website: www.pampel.nl
A most attractive site in pleasant wooded surroundings with good facilities for families.
Open: All year Site: 14.5HEC ⏛ ⁞⁞⁞ ⛅ ⌁ Prices: pitch 19.20-23.50 (incl 2 persons) Facilities: 🏪 🛒 ⊙ 🚐 ⌀ 🚿 🏠 Services: 🍴 ✗ 🕀 lau Leisure: ⤳ P

't Veluws Hof Krimweg 154, 7351 ☎ 055 3781777
Comfortable site with good, modern facilities.
➲ *W of N93.*
Open: All year Site: 31HEC ⏛ ⛅ 🏠 🚐 Facilities: 🏪 🛒 ⊙ 🚐 ⌀ 🚿 🏠 Services: 🍴 ✗ 🕀 lau Leisure: ⤳ P

HOORN, DEN (ISLAND OF TEXEL) NOORD-HOLLAND

Loodsmansduin Rommelpot 19, 1797 ☎ 0222 317208
e-mail: info@rsttexel.nl website: www.rsttexel.nl
Extensive site, numerous large and small hollows between dunes, connected by paved paths. Several sanitary blocks. At the highest part there is a bungalow village in amongst a shopping and administrative complex. A section is reserved for naturists and there is a naturists beach 2km away.
➲ *From the ferry drive N towards Den Burg, then turn left at crossroads towards Den Hoorn.*
Open: 03 Mar-Oct Site: 38HEC ⏛ ⁞⁞⁞ ⛅ 🏠 Prices: 🅰2.25 pitch 9-19.45 Facilities: 🏪 🛒 ⊙ 🚐 ⌀ 🚿 Services: 🍴 ✗ 🕀 lau Leisure: ⤳ PS Off-site: ⤳S

KESTEREN GELDERLAND

Lede en Oudewaard Hogedijkseweg 40, 4041
☎ 0488 481477 ▤ 0488 482599
On level meadowland surrounded by bushy hedges and divided into individual pitches. 100mtrs from private beach and pool.
➲ *2km N of village, turn W off main Rhenen-Kesteren road, and continue for 2.7km.*
Open: All year Site: 30HEC ⏛ ⛅ Prices: 🅰3 ▲10 pitch 14 (incl 2 persons) Facilities: 🏪 🛒 ⊙ 🚐 ⌀ 🚿 🏠 🅿 Services: 🍴 ✗ 🕀 lau Leisure: ⤳ L

KOOG, DE (ISLAND OF TEXEL) NOORD-HOLLAND

Euroase Parc Texel Bosrandweg 395, 1796 NO
☎ 0222 817290 ▤ 0222 317194
website: www.euroase.nl
Part of a chain of family sites with excellent facilities.
Open: late Mar-Oct Site: ⏛ ⛅ 🏠 ⌁ Prices: pitch 35-50 (incl 4 persons) Facilities: 🏪 ⊙ 🚐 ⌀ Services: 🍴 ✗ lau Leisure: ⤳ P Off-site: 🛒

Shelter Boodtlaan 43, 1796 ☎ 0222 317475 ▤ 0222 31745
Small family site a short distance from the sea.
Open: 15 Mar-26 Aug Site: 1.1HEC ⏛ ⛅ Facilities: 🏪 ⊙ 🚐 🏠 Services: 🕀 lau Off-site: 🛒 🍴 ✗ ⌀ 🚿 ⤳S

KOOTWIJK GELDERLAND

Kerkendel Kerkendelweg 49, 3775
☎ 0577 456224 ▤ 0577 456545
e-mail: kerkendel@kerkendel.nl website: www.kerkendel.nl
A family site with good facilities situated in the heart of the Veluwe National Park.
Open: 27 Mar-Oct Site: 7.5HEC ⏛ ⛅ 🏠 ▲ Prices: 🅰17.50-25 Facilities: 🏪 🛒 ⊙ 🚐 ⌀ 🚿 🏠 Services: 🍴 ✗ 🕀 lau Leisure: ⤳ P Off-site: ⤳LR

Laag-Soeren Gelderland

Jutberg Jutberg 78, 6957 ☎ 0313 619220 ▥ 0313 619760
A well equipped site in the woods of the South East
Veluwezoom near Arnhem.
➲ *Access via A12 (Arnhem) towards Zulfa, then follow
signposts.*
Open: All year Site: ▦ ⠐⠂ ⊖ 🏠 🚐 Facilities: ⋔ 🛁 ⊙ 🚻 ∅
🍴 🛎 Services: 🍷 ✗ 🖂 lau Leisure: ⌇ P

Lathum Gelderland

Mars Marsweg 6, 6988 ☎ 0313 631131 ▥ 0313 631435
website: www.campingdemars.nl
Divided into pitches on level meadowland beside a dammed
tributary of River Ijssel.
➲ *Turn off Arnhem-Doesberg road N of village and continue
W for 1.7km.*
Open: Apr-Oct Site: 10HEC ▦ ⅊ Prices: ⋔3.60 🚗1.75
🚐3.25 ⛺3.25 Facilities: ⋔ 🛁 ⊙ 🚻 🍴 🛎 Services: 🍷 ✗ 🖂 lau
Leisure: ⌇ L

Luttenberg Overijssel

Luttenberg Heuvelweg 9, 8105
☎ 0572 301405 ▥ 0572 301757
e-mail: info@luttenberg.nl website: www.luttenberg.nl
A large holiday park with spacious, well defined pitches
separated by bushes. Wide variety of recreational facilities.
Camping Card Compulsory.
Open: Apr-Sep Site: 12HEC ▦ ⅊ 🏠 🚐 Prices: pitch 20-
23 (incl 2 persons) Facilities: ⋔ 🛁 ⊙ 🚻 ∅ 🍴 🛎 🅿
Services: 🍷 ✗ 🖂 lau Leisure: ⌇ P

Maarn Utrecht

Laag-Kanje Laan van Laag-Kanje 1, 3951
☎ 0343 441348 ▥ 0343 443295
e-mail: info@laagkanje.nl website: www.laagkanje.nl
Situated 500mtrs from the lake.
➲ *2km NE.*
Open: Apr-Sep Site: 28HEC ▦ ⅊ 🚷 Prices: 🚗2 🚐2
⛺3.20 pitch 11.60 (incl 2 persons) Facilities: ⋔ 🛁 ⊙ 🚻 ∅ 🅿
Services: 🍷 ✗ 🖂 lau Off-site: ⌇L

Markelo Overijssel

Hessenheem Potdijk 8, 7475 ☎ 0547 361200 ▥ 0547 363647
Situated near a swimming pool.
➲ *3km NE.*
Open: All year Site: 30HEC ▦ ⠐⠂ ⅊ 🏠 🚐 Facilities: ⋔ 🛁
⊙ 🚻 ∅ 🍴 🛎 Services: 🍷 ✗ 🖂 lau Leisure: ⌇ P

Mijnden Utrecht

Mijnden Bloklaan 22a, 1231 AZ
☎ 0294 233165 ▥ 0294 233402
e-mail: info@mijnden.nl website: www.mijnden.nl
Situated directly on the Loosdrechtse Plassen lake with good
sporting facilities.
➲ *Take A2 from Utrecht to Amsterdam. Exit at Hilversum,
after the bridge turn right, drive through Loenen and turn left*
Open: 27 Mar-3 Oct Site: 25HEC ▦ ⅊ Prices: ⋔4 🚗3
🚐6-14.50 ⛺6-14.50 pitch 2.50-5.50 (incl 2 persons)
Facilities: ⋔ 🛁 ⊙ 🚻 ∅ 🍴 🅿 Services: 🍷 ✗ 🖂 lau
Off-site: ⌇L

Neede Gelderland

Eversman Bliksteeg 1, 7161 ☎ 0545 291906
Situated in a quiet position, surrounded by trees.
➲ *W of town.*
Open: Apr-Sep Site: 3.8HEC ▦ ⅊ 🏠 🚐 Facilities: ⋔ ⊙ 🚻
∅ 🍴 🛎 Services: ✗ 🖂 lau Leisure: ⌇ P

Noord Scharwoude Noord-Holland

Molengroet Molengroet 1, 1723
☎ 0226 393444 ▥ 0226 391426
e-mail: info@molengroet.nl website: www.molengroet.nl
Site with modern facilities within easy reach of the beach and
the 'Geestmerambacht' water park.
➲ *Signposted on N245.*
Open: Apr-Oct Site: 11HEC ▦ ⅊ 🏠 Prices: pitch 21-24
(incl 2 persons) Facilities: ⋔ 🛁 ⊙ 🚻 ∅ 🍴 🛎 🅿 Services: 🍷 ✗
🖂 lau Off-site: ⌇LPS

Nunspeet Gelderland

Vossenberg Groenlaantje 25, 8071 ☎ 0341 252458
Open: Apr-1 Nov Site: 3.6HEC ▦ ⅊ 🏠 🚐 🚷 Facilities: ⋔
⊙ 🚻 ∅ 🍴 🛎 Services: 🍷 ✗ 🖂 lau Off-site: 🛁 ✗ ⌇LP

Putten Gelderland

Strand Nulde Strandboulevard 27, 3882
☎ 0341 361341 ▥ 0341 361210
Open: Apr-Oct Site: 8HEC ▦ ⅊ ⛺ 🚷 Facilities: ⋔ ⊙ 🚻
🅿 Services: 🍷 ✗ 🖂 lau Leisure: ⌇ L Off-site: 🛁 ∅ 🍴 ⌇P

Reutum Overijssel

De Molenhof Kleijsenweg 7, 7667
☎ 0541 661165 ▥ 0541 662032
e-mail: molenhof@wxs.nl website: www.demolenhof.nl
A large family site in wooded surroundings with plenty of
modern facilities.
➲ *S of Reutum off N343 towards Weersulo.*
Open: 3 Apr-3 Oct Site: 16HEC ▦ ⅊ 🏠 Prices: pitch
18.50-30 (incl 2 persons) Facilities: ⋔ 🛁 ⊙ 🚻 🍴 🛎
Services: 🍷 ✗ 🖂 lau Leisure: ⌇ P

Rhenen Utrecht

Thymse Berg Nieuwe Veenendaalseweg 229, 3911
☎ 0317 612384 ▥ 0317 618119
e-mail: thymseberg@planet.nl website: www.thymseberg.nl
➲ *N of town.*
Open: Apr-Sep Site: 10HEC ▦ ⅊ 🏠 🚐 🚷 Prices: ⋔4
🚗1.20 🚐5.50-9.50 ⛺3.50 pitch 5.50-9.50 Facilities: ⋔ 🛁 ⊙
🚻 ∅ 🅿 Services: 🍷 ✗ 🖂 lau Leisure: ⌇ P Off-site: 🍴 ⌇LR

Ruurlo Gelderland

't Sikkeler Sikkelerweg 8, 7261
☎ 0573 461221 ▥ 0573 461586
e-mail: info@sikkeler.nl website: www.sikkeler.nl
In a beautiful wooded location with good, modern facilities.
Popular with walkers.
➲ *4km SW.*
Open: All year Site: 7HEC ▦ ⅊ 🏠 Facilities: ⋔ 🛁 ⊙ 🚻 ∅
🛎 🅿 Services: ✗ 🖂 lau Off-site: 🍴 ⌇LP

St Maartenszee Noord-Holland

St Maartenszee Westerduinweg 30, 1753
☎ 0224 561401 ▥ 0224 561901
e-mail: info@campingsintmaartenszee.nl
website: www.campingsintmaartenszee.nl
Completely surrounded and divided into pitches by hedges,
lying on meadowland on the edge of a wide belt of sand
dunes.
➲ *For access, turn off the Alkmaar to Den Helder road at St
Maartensvlotburg and drive towards the sea. Take the road over
the dunes and follow it for about 1.5km, then turn right and
continue for a further 300mtrs.*
Open: 26 Mar-26 Sep Site: 5HEC ▦ ⅊ 🏠 🚷 Prices: ⋔4.25
pitch 8-12.85 Facilities: ⋔ 🛁 ⊙ 🚻 ∅ 🍴 🛎 Services: 🍷 ✗ 🖂
lau Off-site: ⌇LPS

Site: 6HEC-Site size ▦-grass ⠐⠂-sand 🔴-stone 🌿-little shade ⅊-partly shaded ♠-mainly shaded
🏠-bungalows for hire 🚐-caravans for hire ⛺-tents for hire 🚷-no dogs Prices: ⋔-adult per night 🚗-car per night
pp-per person per night 🚐-caravan per night ⛺-tent per night

SOEST UTRECHT

King's Home Birkstr 136, 3768
☎ 033 4619118   ▤ 033 4610808
e-mail: camping@kingshome.nl website: www.kingshome.nl
Well maintained site with modern facilities in a natural
setting on the edge of woodland.
⮑ *On N221 between Amersfoort and Soest.*
Open: All year Site: 5HEC ⬛ 4 🏕 🔌 Prices: ⋔2.75 ⬅2.25
🔌9.50 ▲7.50 Facilities: 🌧 ⊙ 🔌 🅓 🛏 🄿 Services: ⍾ ✕ 🄴 lau
Off-site: 🛒 ✕ ⭢P

STEENWIJK OVERIJSSEL

Kom Bultweg 25, 8346 ☎ 0521 513736   ▤ 0521 518736
e-mail: info@campingdekom.nl
website: www.campingdekom.nl
Split into two sections, lying near a country house, and
surrounded by a beautiful oak forest.
⮑ *The access road off the Steenwijk-Frederiksoord road is easy
to miss.*
Open: Apr-Sep Site: 12.5HEC ⬛ ⋮⋮⋮ 4 🏕 🏕 🔌
Prices: pitch 16.10-19.20 (incl 2 persons) Facilities: 🌧 🛒 ⊙
🔌 🅓 🛏 🄿 Services: ⍾ ✕ 🄴 lau Leisure: ⭢ P

TEXEL (ISLAND OF)

UITDAM NOORD-HOLLAND

Uitdam Zeedijk 2, 1154 ☎ 020 4031433   ▤ 020 4033692
e-mail: info@campinguitdam.nl
website: www.campinguitdam.nl
A well maintained site on the Markermeer adjoining the
marina.
⮑ *Access via N247 Amsterdam-Monnickendam.*
Open: Mar-Oct Site: 21HEC ⬛ ⭄ 🏕 🔌 Prices: ⋔4.50
pitch 16.80-20.50 (incl 2 persons) Facilities: 🌧 🛒 ⊙ 🔌 🅓 🛏
🅐 Services: ⍾ ✕ 🄴 lau Leisure: ⭢ L

URK FLEVOLAND

Hazevreugd Vormtweg 9, 8321 ☎ 0527 681785   ▤ 0527 686298
e-mail: info@hazevreugd.nl website: www.hazevreugd.nl
A modern family site in wooded surroundings with a wide
variety of recreational facilities.
⮑ *Access via A6.*
Open: Apr-Oct Site: 12HEC ⬛ 4 🏕 🔌 Prices: pitch
25.50-28.50 (incl 4 persons) Facilities: 🌧 🛒 ⊙ 🔌 🅓 🛏 🅐
Services: ⍾ ✕ 🄴 lau Leisure: ⭢ P Off-site: ⭢S

UTRECHT UTRECHT

Berekuil Arienslaan 5, 3573 ☎ 030 713870   ▤ 030 721436
In a wooded location beside a lake with well defined pitches
and good facilities.
⮑ *On N outskirts near motorway to Hilversum.*
Open: All year Site: 4.5HEC ⬛ 4 🏕 Facilities: 🌧 🛒 ⊙ 🔌
🅓 🛏 🄿 Services: ⍾ ✕ 🄴 lau Leisure: ⭢ P

VOGELENZANG NOORD-HOLLAND

Vogelenzang Tweede Doodweg 17, 2114 AP
☎ 023 5847014   ▤ 023 5849249
e-mail: camping@vogelenzang.nl website: www.vogelenzang.nl
⮑ *1km W.*
Open: Etr-15 Sep Site: 22HEC ⬛ 4 ⭄ Prices: ⋔2.90 pitch
13.10 Facilities: 🌧 🛒 ⊙ 🔌 🅓 🛏 🅐 Services: ⍾ ✕ 🄴 lau
Leisure: ⭢ P

WAGENINGEN GELDERLAND

Wielerbaan Zoomweg 7-9, 6705 ☎ 0317 413964
A friendly family site on the edge of a forest.
⮑ *Access via A12, then follow signposts.*
Open: All year Site: 7.5HEC ⬛ 4 🏕 🔌 Facilities: 🌧 🛒 ⊙
🔌 🅓 🛏 🅐 Services: ✕ 🄴 lau Leisure: ⭢ P

WEZEP GELDERLAND

Heidehoek Heidehoeksweg 7, 8091 ☎ 038 3761382
⮑ *0.5km W of railway station.*
Open: Apr-Oct Site: 16HEC ⬛ 4 Facilities: 🌧 🛒 ⊙ 🔌 🅓
🛏 🅐 Services: ⍾ ✕ 🄴 lau Leisure: ⭢ L

WIJDENES NOORD-HOLLAND

Het Hof Zuideruitweg 64, 1608
☎ 0229 501435   ▤ 0229 503244
e-mail: info@campinghefhof.nl
website: www.campinghethof.nl
A series of fields in a sheltered position on the shore of the
Ijsselmeer.
⮑ *From A7 exit 8 (Hoorn) follow N506 towards Enkhuizen,
then right to Wijdenes and follow camping signs.*
Open: 28 Mar-26 Oct Site: 3.9HEC ⬛ 4 Prices: ⋔3.50
🔌7.50 ▲7.50 Facilities: 🌧 🛒 ⊙ 🔌 🅓 🛏 🄿 Services: ⍾ ✕ 🄴
lau Leisure: ⭢ LP

WINTERSWIJK GELDERLAND

Twee Bruggen Meenkmolenweg 11, 7109
☎ 0543 565366   ▤ 0543 565222
e-mail: info@detweebruggen.nl
website: www.detweebruggen.nl
A family site in pleasant wooded surroundings with good,
modern facilities.
Open: All year Site: 34HEC ⬛ 4 🏕 🔌 Prices: pitch 9.50-
20 (incl 2 persons) Facilities: 🌧 🛒 ⊙ 🔌 🛏 🅐 🄿 Services: ⍾
✕ 🄴 lau Leisure: ⭢ LP

SOUTH

AFFERDEN LIMBURG

Klein Canada Dorpsstr 1, 5851
☎ 0485 531223   ▤ 0485 532218
e-mail: info@kleincanada.nl website: www.kleincanada.nl
Situated among heath and woodland close to the River
Meuse.
Open: All year Site: 12.5HEC ⬛ 4 🔌 Prices: ⋔3.50 pitch
9.80-19.90 (incl 2 persons) Facilities: 🌧 🛒 ⊙ 🔌 🅓 🛏
Services: ⍾ ✕ 🄴 lau Leisure: ⭢ P

ARCEN LIMBURG

Maasvallei Dorperheideweg 34, 5944 ☎ 077 4731564
In wooded surroundings near the beach, this family site has
varied sporting facilities and play areas for children.
⮑ *Off the N271.*
Open: All year Site: 11HEC ⬛ 4 🏕 🔌 ⭄ Facilities: 🌧 🛒
⊙ 🔌 🅓 🛏 🅐 Services: ⍾ ✕ 🄴 Leisure: ⭢ LP Off-site: ⭢R

ARNEMUIDEN ZEELAND

Witte Raaf Muidenweg 3, 4341
☎ 0118 601212   ▤ 0118 603650
A modern well-maintained site in meadowland, divided into
sections by rows of shrubs, ideal for sailing and motor boat
enthusiasts with yacht marina.
⮑ *Situated on the Veersmeer, N of the Goes-Vlissingen
motorway, from Arnemuiden exit follow signs for about 5km.*
Open: Apr-Sep Site: 20HEC ⬛ 4 🏕 ▲ ⭄ Facilities: 🌧 🛒
⊙ 🔌 🅓 🛏 🅐 Services: ⍾ ✕ 🄴 lau Leisure: ⭢ L

BAARLAND ZEELAND

Comfort Camping Scheldeoord Landingsweg 1, 4435
☎ 0113 639900   ▤ 0113 639500
e-mail: info@scheldeoord.nl website: www.scheldeoord.nl
A popular family site in a beautiful location by the Scheldt
River.

contd.

Facilities: 🛒-shop 🌧-shower ⊙-electric points for razors 🔌-electric points for caravans 🅐-parking by tents permitted
🄿-compulsory separate car park Services: ✕-café/restaurant ⍾-bar 🅓-Camping Gaz International 🛏-gas other than Camping
Gaz 🄴-first aid facilities lau-laundry Leisure: ⭢-swimming L-Lake P-Pool R-River S-Sea Off-site: All facilities within 2km

⊃ *S of town on the coast.*
Open: Apr-Oct Site: 16HEC ⊞ ⊕ ⊞ ⊞ Facilities: ⋒ ⅀ ⊙
⊟ ∅ ⊞ ⊟ Services: ⅀ ✗ ⊞ lau Leisure: ⊰ PS

BAARLE NASSAU NOORD-BRABANT

Heimolen Heimolen 6, 5111 EH
☎ 013 5079425 ⊠ 013 5077885
e-mail: info@deheimolen.nl website: www.deheimolen.nl
In a wooded location with good, modern facilities.
⊃ *1.5km SW.*
Open: All year Site: 15HEC ⊞ ⊕ ⊞ ⊞ Prices: ⋔3 ⊕1.50
⊞4.25 ⋀4.25 Facilities: ⋒ ⊙ ⊟ ∅ ⊞ ⊟ Services: ⅀ ✗ ⊞ lau
Off-site: ⊰P

BAARLO LIMBURG

Euroase Parc Napoleonsbaan Ned 4, 5991 ☎ 077 4771547
Part of a chain of family sites with excellent facilities.
⊃ *SW of Venlo.*
Open: 15 Mar-1 Nov Site: 32HEC ⊞ ⊕ ⊞ ⊞ ⊗
Facilities: ⋒ ⅀ ⊙ ⊟ ∅ ⊞ Services: ⅀ ✗ ⊞ lau Leisure: ⊰ P

BARENDRECHT ZUID-HOLLAND

Jachthaven de Oude Maas Achterzeedijk 1a, 2991
☎ 078 6772445 ⊠ 078 773013
e-mail: de.oudemaas@worldonline.nl
website: www.deoudemaas.com
On the banks of the Oude Maas, the site is particularly
suitable for families and hikers.
Open: Apr-15 Oct Site: 12HEC ⊞ ⊕ ⊞ Prices: ⋔3.35
⊕3.35 ⊞3.35 ⋀3.35 Facilities: ⋒ ⊙ ⊟ ∅ ⊞ ⊞ ⊟
Services: ⊞ lau Off-site: ⅀ ⅀ ✗

BERG EN TERBLIJT LIMBURG

Oriëntal Rijksweg 6, 6325 ☎ 043 6040075 ⊠ 043 6042912
e-mail: info@campingoriental.nl
website: www.campingoriental.nl
⊃ *On Maastricht-Valkenburg road 3km from Maastricht.*
Open: 08 Apr-24 Oct Site: 5.5HEC ⊞ ⊕ ⊞ Prices: ⋔2.25
pitch 19.50-24 (incl 2 persons) Facilities: ⋒ ⅀ ⊙ ⊟ ∅ ⊞ ⊞
Services: ⅀ ✗ ⊞ lau Leisure: ⊰ P Off-site: ✗

BERGEYK NOORD-BRABANT

Paal De Paaldreef 14, 5571 ☎ 0497 571977 ⊠ 0497 577164
e-mail: info@depaal.nl website: www.depaal.nl
Campsite especially catering for families with children.
Camping Card Compulsory.
⊃ *Signposted.*
Open: Mar-Oct Site: 41HEC ⊞ ⊕ Prices: pitch 22.50-33
(incl 2 persons) Facilities: ⋒ ⅀ ⊙ ⊟ ∅ ⊞ ⊟ Services: ⅀ ✗ ⊞
lau Leisure: ⊰ P Off-site: ⊰L

BOXTEL NOORD-BRABANT

Dennenoord Dennendreef 5, 5282
☎ 0411 601280 ⊠ 0411 601393
e-mail: info@dennenoord.nl website: www.dennenoord.nl
Level, grassy site with hedging and groups of trees. Leisure
activities organised for adults and young people. Soundproof disco.
⊃ *Turn off the N2 at Esch in direction of Osterwijk. Follow signs.*
Open: Apr-1 Oct Site: 7HEC ⊞ ⊕ Facilities: ⋒ ⅀ ⊙ ⊟ ∅
⊞ ⊞ Services: ⅀ ✗ ⊞ lau Leisure: ⊰ P

BRESKENS ZEELAND

Napoleon Hoeve Zandertje 30, 4511
☎ 0117 383838 ⊠ 0117 383550
e-mail: camping@napoleonhoeve.nl
website: www.napoleonhoeve.nl
A family site with access to the beach.
Open: All year Site: 13HEC ⊞ ⊕ ⊞ ⊞ Facilities: ⋒ ⅀ ⊙
⊟ ∅ ⊞ ⊞ ⊟ Services: ⅀ ✗ ⊞ lau Leisure: ⊰ PS

Schoneveld Schoneveld 1, 4511 HR
☎ 0117 383220 ⊠ 0117 383650
e-mail: schoneveld@zeelandnet.nl
website: www.zeelandnet.nl/schoneveld
Camping Card Compulsory.
⊃ *3km S at the beach.*
Open: All year Site: 14HEC ⊞ ⊕ ⋀ Prices: pitch 23-34
(incl 4 persons) Facilities: ⋒ ⅀ ⊙ ⊟ ∅ ⊞ ⊟ Services: ⅀ ✗ ⊞
lau Leisure: ⊰ PS

BRIELLE ZUID-HOLLAND

Krabbeplaat Oude Veerdam 4, 3231
☎ 0181 412363 ⊠ 0181 412093
e-mail: info@krabbeplaat.nl website: www.krabbeplaat.com
On level ground scattered with trees and groups of bushes.
has asphalt drives. Nearest campsite to the coast and ferries.
⊃ *Signposted.*
Open: Apr-Oct Site: 18HEC ⊞ ⊗ ⊗ Prices: pitch 13
(incl 2 persons) Facilities: ⋒ ⅀ ⊙ ⊟ ∅ ⊞ Services: ⅀ ✗ ⊞
lau Leisure: ⊰ L

BROEKHUIZENVORST LIMBURG

Kasteel Ooyen Blitterswijkseweg 2, 5871
☎ 077 4631307 ⊠ 077 4632765
e-mail: info@kasteelooijen.nl
website: www.kasteelooijen.nl
Open: Apr-Oct Site: 16HEC ⊞ ⊕ Prices: pitch 16.95
(incl 2 persons) Facilities: ⋒ ⅀ ⊙ ⊟ ∅ ⊟ Services: ⅀ ✗ ⊞
lau Leisure: ⊰ P

BROUWERSHAVEN ZEELAND

Osse Blankersweg 4, 4318 ☎ 0111 691513 ⊠ 0111 691058
e-mail: denosse@zeelandnet.nl
An attractive site with good watersports facilities.
Open: Apr-Oct Site: 8.3HEC ⊞ ⊗ ⊞ ⊞ Facilities: ⋒ ⊙
⊟ ∅ ⊟ Services: ⅀ ✗ ⊞ lau Leisure: ⊰ P
Off-site: ⅀ ∅ ⊰L

BURGH-HAAMSTEDE ZEELAND

Zeeland Camping Ginsterveld J J Boeijesweg 45, 4328 HA
☎ 0111 651590 ⊠ 0111 653040
e-mail: ginsterveld@zeelandcamping.nl
website: www.zeelandcamping.nl/ginsterveld
A family holiday centre with well defined pitches on level
ground and plenty of recreational facilities.
⊃ *NW of town, signposted from R107.*
Open: Apr-Sep Site: 14HEC ⊞ ⊕ ⊞ ⊗ Prices: pitch 18-27
(incl 2 persons) Facilities: ⋒ ⅀ ⊙ ⊟ ∅ ⊞ ⊟ Services: ⅀ ✗ ⊞
lau Leisure: ⊰ P Off-site: ⊰S

DELFT ZUID-HOLLAND

Delftse Hout Korftlaan 5, 2616
☎ 015 2130040 ⊠ 015 2131293
e-mail: info@delftsehout.nl website: www.delftsehout.nl
On a level meadow surrounded by woodland close to the
lake.
Camping Card Compulsory.
⊃ *1 mile E of A13. Signposted.*
Open: All year Site: 5.5HEC ⊞ ⊕ ⊞ ⊞ Prices: pitch
17.80-24 (incl 2 persons) Facilities: ⋒ ⅀ ⊙ ⊟ ∅ ⊞ ⊟
Services: ⅀ ✗ ⊞ lau Leisure: ⊰ P Off-site: ⊰L

ECHT LIMBURG

Marisheem Brugweg 89, 6102
☎ 04754 481458 ⊠ 04754 488018
e-mail: info@marisheem.nl
website: www.marisheem.nl
The site is well-kept and lies E of the village.

Site: 6HEC-Site size ⊞-grass ⋮⋮-sand ∅-stone ⊗-little shade ⊕-partly shaded ⊛-mainly shaded
⊞-bungalows for hire ⊞-caravans for hire ⋀-tents for hire ⊗-no dogs Prices: ⋔-adult per night ⊕-car per night
pp-per person per night ⊞-caravan per night ⋀-tent per night

➲ *From town drive approx 2.2km towards Echterbosch and the border, then turn left.*
Open: Apr-Oct **Site:** 12HEC ▥▥▥ ⌗ ⚮ **Prices:** ⚑7.85 ⇆8 ⇆8 **Facilities:** � 🛒 ⊙ 🚻 ⌀ ▦ 🅿 **Services:** ⛱ ✗ ⊞ lau **Leisure:** ⚓ P

EERSEL NOORD-BRABANT

Ter Spegelt Postelseweg 88, 5521
☎ 0497 512016 📠 0497 514162
e-mail: info@terspegelt.nl website: www.terspegelt.nl
A large family-orientated site with good recreational facilities.
Open: Mar-Nov **Site:** 63HEC ▥▥▥ ⚮ 🏠 ⇆ ⚮
Prices: ⇆14.50 **Facilities:** 🌲 🛒 ⊙ 🚻 ⌀ ▦ 🅿 **Services:** ⛱ ✗ ⊞ lau **Leisure:** ⚓ LP

'S-GRAVENZANDE ZUID-HOLLAND

Jagtveld Nieuwlandsedijk 41, 2691
☎ 0174 413479 📠 0174 422127
e-mail: info@jagtveld.nl website: www.jagtveld.nl
A quiet family site on level meadowland with good facilities.
➲ *Access via N220.*
Open: Apr-Sep **Site:** 3.3HEC ▥▥▥ ❄ ⚮ **Prices:** ⚑3 ⇆3 ⇆7.50 ⚑7.50 **Facilities:** 🌲 ⊙ 🚻 ⌀ ▦ 🅿 **Services:** ⛱ ✗ ⊞ lau **Off-site:** ⚓S

GROEDE ZEELAND

Groede Zeeweg 1, 4503
☎ 0117 371384 📠 0117 372277
e-mail: info@campinggroede.nl
website: www.campinggroede.nl
A large family site with a wide variety of leisure facilities and close to the beach.
Open: Apr-Oct **Site:** 20HEC ▥▥▥ ♣ **Prices:** pitch 14-26.25 **Facilities:** 🌲 🛒 ⊙ 🚻 ⌀ ▦ 🅿 **Services:** ⛱ ✗ ⊞ lau **Leisure:** ⚓ S

HAAG, DEN (THE HAGUE) ZUID-HOLLAND

Kijkduinpark Machiel Vrijenhoeklaan 450, 2555 NW
☎ 070 4482100 📠 070 3232457
e-mail: info@kijkduinpark.nl website: www.kijkduinpark.nl
A modern chalet and camping site in an extensive leisure park close to the beach with excellent recreational facilities
Open: All year **Site:** 40HEC ▥▥▥ ⚮ 🏠 **Prices:** pitch 13-33 (incl 6 persons) **Facilities:** 🌲 🛒 ⊙ 🚻 ⌀ ▦ **Services:** ⛱ ✗ lau **Leisure:** ⚓ P **Off-site:** ⚓S

HELLEVOETSLUIS ZUID-HOLLAND

'T Weergors Zuiddyk 2, 3221
☎ 0181 312430 📠 0181 311010
e-mail: weergors@publish-net.nl website: www.weergors.nl
A pleasant, peaceful site on a level meadow close to the beach. A good overnight stopping place or holiday site.
Open: Apr-Oct **Site:** 9.7HEC ▥▥▥ ⚮ 🏠 ⇆ **Prices:** ⚑3.50 ⇆2.50 ⇆6 ⚑6 **Facilities:** 🌲 🛒 ⊙ 🚻 ⌀ ▦ 🅿 **Services:** ⛱ ✗ ⊞ lau **Leisure:** ⚓ S

HENGSTDIJK ZEELAND

Vogel Vogelweg 4, 4585 ☎ 0114 681625 📠 0114 682527
e-mail: info@de-vogel.nl website: www.de-vogel.nl
Open: All year **Site:** 33HEC ▥▥▥ ⚮ 🏠 ⇆ **Facilities:** 🌲 🛒 ⊙ 🚻 ⌀ ▦ 🅿 **Services:** ⛱ ✗ ⊞ lau **Leisure:** ⚓ LP

HERPEN NOORD-BRABANT

Herperduin Schaykseweg 12, 5373
☎ 0486 411383 📠 0486 416171
e-mail: info@herperduin.nl website: www.herperduin.nl
Situated in extensive woodland.

➲ *Access from the 'S-Hertogenbosch-Nijmegen motorway. Take the Ravenstein exit and continue towards Herpen, then in direction Bergheim/Oss.*
Open: Apr-20 Oct **Site:** 7HEC ▥▥▥ ⚮ 🏠 ⚮ **Facilities:** 🌲 🛒 ⊙ 🚻 ⌀ ▦ **Services:** ⛱ ✗ ⊞ lau **Leisure:** ⚓ P

HILVARENBEEK NOORD-BRABANT

Beekse Bergen Beekse Bergen 1, 5081 NJ
☎ 031 5360032 📠 031 5366716
e-mail: beeksebergen@libema.nl
website: www.beeksebergen.com
Situated in a holiday centre in the Brabant afforestation on the edge of a safari park. Lake suitable for swimming. Various other facilities.
➲ *10km S of Tilburg.*
Open: 30 Mar-4 Nov **Site:** 400HEC ▥▥▥ ⚮ 🏠 ⇆ 👤 **Facilities:** 🌲 🛒 ⊙ 🚻 ⌀ ▦ 🅿 **Services:** ⛱ ✗ ⊞ lau **Leisure:** ⚓ LP

HOEK ZEELAND

Braakman Holiday Park Middenweg 1, 4542 PN
☎ 0115 481730 📠 0115 482077
e-mail: holidaypark@braakman.co.uk
website: www.braakman.co.uk
A large family site situated on the edge of extensive nature reserves. The pitches are shaded by woodland and there is direct access to the Braakman Lake. Plenty of recreational facilities.
➲ *4km W of town. Signposted from N61.*
Open: All year **Site:** 80HEC ▥▥▥ ⚮ 🏠 ⇆ **Facilities:** 🌲 🛒 ⊙ 🚻 ⌀ ▦ 🅿 **Services:** ⛱ ✗ ⊞ lau **Leisure:** ⚓ L

HOEK VAN HOLLAND ZUID-HOLLAND

Hoek van Holland Wierstraat 100, 3151
☎ 0174 382550 📠 0174 310210
e-mail: camping.hvh@hetnet.nl
website: www.campinghoekvanholland.nl
On grass, surrounded by bushes and paved drives.
➲ *If approaching from the N, turn off the E36 and drive to the beach.*
Open: 15 Mar-12 Oct **Site:** 5.5HEC ▥▥▥ ❄ ⚮ **Facilities:** 🌲 🛒 ⊙ 🚻 ⌀ ▦ 🅿 **Services:** ⛱ ✗ ⊞ lau **Off-site:** ⚓S

HOEVEN NOORD-BRABANT

Bosbad Hoeven Oude Antwerpse Postbaan 81b, 4741
☎ 0165 502570 📠 0165 504254
e-mail: info@bosbadhoeven.nl website: www.bosbadhoeven.nl
Extensive site with good, modern facilities.
➲ *Between Breda and Roosendaal W of Etten-Leur.*
Open: Apr-27 Oct **Site:** 35HEC ▥▥▥ ⚮ ♣ ⚮ **Prices:** pitch 12.85-21 (incl 2 persons) **Facilities:** 🌲 🛒 ⊙ 🚻 ⌀ ▦ **Services:** ⛱ ✗ ⊞ lau **Leisure:** ⚓ P

HOOGERHEIDE NOORD-BRABANT

FamilyLand Groene Papegaai 19, 4631
☎ 0164 613155 📠 0164 615216
In pleasant wooded surroundings, the site, as its name suggests has fine facilities for both adults and children with all kinds of sports and entertainments available.
➲ *2km from junction of A30 and A58.*
Open: All year **Site:** 25HEC ▥▥▥ ❄ ♣ 🏠 **Facilities:** 🌲 ⊙ 🚻 ⌀ ▦ **Services:** ⛱ ✗ ⊞ lau **Leisure:** ⚓ P

KAMPERLAND ZEELAND

Roompot Mariapolderseweg 1, 4493
☎ 0113 374000 📠 0113 374170
e-mail: info@roompot.nl website: www.roompot.nl
A level, well-maintained site with a private beach.

contd.

Facilities: 🛒-shop 🌲-shower ⊙-electric points for razors 🚻-electric points for caravans ▦-parking by tents permitted 🅿-compulsory separate car park **Services:** ✗-café/restaurant ⛱-bar ⌀-Camping Gaz International ▦-gas other than Camping Gaz ⊞-first aid facilities lau-laundry **Leisure:** ⚓-swimming L-Lake P-Pool R-River S-Sea **Off-site:** All facilities within 2km

⊃ *Turn off Kamperland-Wissenkerke road and drive N for 0.5km.*
Open: All year **Site:** 33HEC ⊞⊞ ᠉⅄ 🏠 🚐 Å **Prices:** pitch 22-34 (incl 5 persons) **Facilities:** 🏪 🖳 ⊙ 🚱 ⌀ 🚿 🖭 **Services:** 🍴 ✗ 🗗 lau **Leisure:** ⦂ PS

KATWIJK AAN ZEE ZUID-HOLLAND

Noordduinen Campingweg 1, 2221
☎ 071 4025295   🖹 071 4033977
Family site set among sand dunes close to the sea.
⊃ *Access via Hoorneslaan.*
Open: mid Mar-Oct **Site:** 11HEC ⊞⊞ ᠉⅄ 🏠 ⊗
Prices: pitch 21.50-32.50 **Facilities:** 🏪 🖳 ⊙ 🚱 🚿 🖭 **Services:** 🍴 ✗ 🗗 lau **Leisure:** ⦂ S

KORTGENE ZEELAND

Zeeland Camping de Paardekreek Havenweg 1, 4484
☎ 0113 302051   🖹 0113 302280
e-mail: paardekreek@zeelandcamping.nl
website: www.zeelandcamping.nl/paardekreek
A municipal site next to the Veerse Meer canal.
⊃ *For access, turn off the Zierikzee-Goes trunk road at the Chevron petrol station and drive towards Kortgene, continue through the village and drive SW.*
Open: Apr-Oct **Site:** 10HEC ⊞⊞ ⌕⅄ 🚐 **Prices:** pitch 16.80-30.90 **Facilities:** 🏪 🖳 ⊙ 🚱 ⌀ 🚿 🖭 **Services:** 🍴 ✗ 🗗 lau **Leisure:** ⦂ LP

KOUDEKERKE ZEELAND

Dishoek Dishoek 2, 4371 ☎ 0118 551348   🖹 0118 552990
e-mail: info@campingdishoek.nl **website:** www.roompot.nl
⊃ *W on Vlissingen-Dibhoek road.*
Open: Apr-Oct **Site:** 4.5HEC ⊞⊞ ⁚⁛⁚ ⌕⅄ 🚐 Å **Facilities:** 🏪 🖳 ⌀ 🖭 🖭 **Services:** 🍴 ✗ 🗗 lau **Leisure:** ⦂ S
Off-site: ✗

Duinzicht Strandweg 7, 4371 PK
☎ 0118 551397   🖹 0118 553222
e-mail: info@campingduinzicht.nl
website: www.campingduinzicht.nl
A small family site with good facilities.
⊃ *1.5km SW of Koudekerke.*
Open: Apr-Oct **Site:** 6.5HEC ⊞⊞ ⌕⅄ 🚐 **Prices:** pitch 15.30-16.35 (incl 2 persons) **Facilities:** 🏪 🖳 ⊙ 🚱 ⌀ 🖭 **Services:** 🗗 lau **Off-site:** 🍴 ✗ ⦂S

LAGE MIERDE NOORD-BRABANT

Vakantlecentrum de Hertenwei Wellenseind 7-9, 5094
☎ 013 5091295
website: www.hertenwei.nl
Pleasant wooded site with modern facilities.
Camping Card Compulsory.
⊃ *2km N on N269 (Tilburg-Reusel).*
Open: All year **Site:** 20HEC ⊞⊞ ⌕⅄ 🏠 🚐 **Prices:** pitch 18-30.25 (incl 2 persons) **Facilities:** 🏪 🖳 ⊙ 🚱 ⌀ 🚿 🖭 **Services:** 🍴 ✗ 🗗 lau **Leisure:** ⦂ P

LANDGRAAF LIMBURG

Bousberg Boomweg 10, 6370
☎ 045 5311213   🖹 045 5323143
⊃ *NW towards Kakert.*
Open: Apr-Oct **Site:** 7.5HEC ⊞⊞ ⌕⅄ 🏠 🚐 **Facilities:** 🏪 🖳 ⊙ 🚱 ⌀ 🚿 🖭 **Services:** 🍴 ✗ 🗗 lau **Leisure:** ⦂ P

LUYKSGESTEL NOORD-BRABANT

Zwarte Bergen Zwarte Bergen Dreef 1, 5575
☎ 0497 541373   🖹 0497 542673
e-mail: info@zwartebergen.nl **website:** www.zwartebergen.nl
The site is isolated and very quiet, and lies in a pine forest.

⊃ *From Eindhoven through Valkenswaard and Bergiejkl. Signposted.*
Open: All year **Site:** 25.5HEC ⊞⊞ ⌕⅄ 🏠 **Prices:** ⦉2.75-3.60 pitch 11.20-15 **Facilities:** 🏪 🖳 ⊙ 🚱 ⌀ 🖭 🖭 **Services:** 🍴 ✗ 🗗 lau **Leisure:** ⦂ P **Off-site:** ⦂L

MAASBREE LIMBURG

BreeBronne Lange Heide 9, 5993PB
☎ 077 4652360   🖹 077 4652095
e-mail: info@breebronne.nl **website:** www.breebronne.nl
A family site in quiet surroundings with good facilities.
⊃ *On the E3 just before Venlo, on the border with Germany.*
Open: All year **Site:** 23HEC ⊞⊞ ⌕⅄ 🏠 **Prices:** ⦉19 pitch 21.50-37 (incl 4 persons) **Facilities:** 🏪 🖳 ⊙ 🚱 ⌀ 🚿 🖭 🖭 **Services:** 🍴 ✗ 🗗 lau **Leisure:** ⦂ LP

MAASTRICHT LIMBURG

Dousberg Dousbergweg 102, 6216
☎ 043 3432171   🖹 043 3430556
e-mail: dousbergcamping@dousberg.nl
website: www.dousberg.nl
A modern site with good facilities.
⊃ *From the Eindhoven-Liège motorway follow sings for Hasselt, then pick up local signs to the site.*
Open: Apr-Oct **Site:** 10HEC ⊞⊞ ᠉⅄ **Facilities:** 🏪 🖳 ⊙ 🚱 ⌀ 🚿 🖭 **Services:** 🍴 ✗ 🗗 lau **Off-site:** ⦂P

MIDDELBURG ZEELAND

Middelburg Koninginnelaan 55, 4335
☎ 0118 625395   🖹 0118 625395
e-mail: campingmiddelburg@komnaarons.nl
website: www.campingmiddelburg.nl
On meadowlands surrounded by trees and bushes.
⊃ *On W outskirts of town.*
Open: Etr-15 Oct **Site:** 3.4HEC ⊞⊞ ⌕⅄ 🏠 🚐 **Prices:** ⦉3.70 🚗3.60 🚐4.50 Å3-4.50 **Facilities:** 🏪 ⊙ 🚱 🚿 🖭 **Services:** 🍴 ✗ 🗗 lau **Off-site:** 🖳 ⦂PS

MIERLO NOORD-BRABANT

Wolfsven Patrijslaan 4, 5731 ☎ 0492 661661
Large campsite with wooded areas and several lakes. Asphalt drives.
Open: All year **Site:** 70HEC ⊞⊞ ⁚⁛⁚ ᠉⅄ 🏠 ⊗ **Facilities:** 🏪 🖳 ⊙ 🚱 ⌀ 🖭 **Services:** 🍴 ✗ 🗗 lau **Leisure:** ⦂ LP

NIEUWVLIET ZEELAND

Pannenschuur Zeedijk 19, 4504
☎ 0117 372300   🖹 0117 371415
e-mail: info@pannenschuur.nl
website: www.pannenschuur.nl
A modern site with good facilities. Close to the beach.
⊃ *NW of town. Signposted.*
Open: All year **Site:** 14HEC ⊞⊞ ⌕⅄ 🏠 🚐 **Prices:** pitch 19-37 (incl 5 persons) **Facilities:** 🏪 🖳 ⊙ 🚱 ⌀ 🚿 🖭 **Services:** 🍴 ✗ 🗗 lau **Leisure:** ⦂ PS

NOORDWIJK AAN ZEE ZUID-HOLLAND

Club Soleil Kraaierslaan 7, 2204
☎ 0252 374225   🖹 0252 376450
e-mail: info@clubsoleil.nl
website: www.clubsoleil.nl
In a pleasant situation near the bulb fields and the sea.
⊃ *Signposted.*
Open: Apr-Nov **Site:** 5.5HEC ⊞⊞ ⌕⅄ 🏠 🚐 **Facilities:** 🏪 🖳 ⊙ 🚱 ⌀ 🖭 **Services:** 🍴 ✗ 🗗 lau **Leisure:** ⦂ P **Off-site:** ⦂LS

Site: 6HEC-Site size ⊞⊞-grass ⁚⁛⁚-sand ⬤-stone ᠉⅄-little shade ⌕⅄-partly shaded 🏠-mainly shaded
🏠-bungalows for hire 🚐-caravans for hire Å-tents for hire ⊗-no dogs **Prices:** ⦉-adult per night 🚗-car per night
pp-per person per night 🚐-caravan per night Å-tent per night

Jan de Wit Kapelleboslaan 10, 2204
☎ 0252 372485 ▯ 0252 340140
e-mail: camjam@xs4all.nl website: www.campingjandewit.nl
A well equipped family site in a wooded location 2km from the beach.
Open: 15 Mar-Sep Site: 6HEC ▦ ⊈ ⌘ Facilities: ↑ ⊙ ▢
∅ ⍾ ☎ Services: ⊞ lau Off-site: ⟲LS

OISTERWIJK NOORD-BRABANT

Reebok Duinenweg 4, 5062 ☎ 013 5282309 ▯ 013 5217592
e-mail: info@dereebok.nl website: www.dereebok.nl
Situated in a large pine forest, hardly fenced off and impossible to overlook. In attractive surroundings with numerous small lakes.
➲ SE of town.
Open: 15 Mar-Oct Site: 8HEC ▦ ⊈ ⌘ Prices: ⚡3.55
🚗3.20 pitch 3.80 Facilities: ↑ ⊾ ⊙ ▢ ∅ ⍾ ☎ Services: ⚊ ✕
⊞ lau Off-site: ⟲LP

OOSTERHOUT NOORD-BRABANT

Katjeskelder Katjeskelder 1, 4904
☎ 0162 453539 ▯ 0162 454090
e-mail: kkinfo@katjeskelder.nl website: www.katjeskelder.nl
A large, modern family site with good sanitary and recreational facilities.
➲ Access via A27 (Breda-Utrecht) exit 17 and follow signs.
Open: All year Site: 25HEC ▦ ⊈ ⬛ ⌘ Prices: ⚡24.50-38
Facilities: ↑ ⊾ ⊙ ▢ ∅ ☎ ▢ Services: ⚊ ✕ ⊞ lau Leisure: ⟲
P Off-site: ⍾

OOSTKAPELLE ZEELAND

Dennenbos Duinweg 64, 4356
☎ 0118 581310 ▯ 0118 583773
e-mail: dennenbos@zeelandnet.nl
website: www.dennenbos.nl
A well maintained family site in a wooded location, 500mtrs from the beach.
Open: Mar-Nov Site: 3HEC ▦ ⊈ ⬛ ⌘ Prices: pitch
17.50-25 (incl 2 persons) Facilities: ↑ ⊾ ⊙ ▢ ∅ ⍾ ☎
Services: ⊞ lau Leisure: ⟲ PS Off-site: ✕

In de Bongerd Brouwerijstr 13, 4356
☎ 0118 581510 ▯ 0118 581510
e-mail: info@bongerdzeeland.nl
website: www.campingindebongerd.nl
A well-kept family campsite, set in a meadow with hedges and apple trees. There are fine recreational facilities and the beach is within easy reach.
➲ 500mtrs S.
Open: 30 Mar-28 Oct Site: 7.4HEC ▦ ⊈ ⬛ ⌘
Facilities: ↑ ⊾ ⊙ ▢ ∅ ⍾ ☎ Services: ⚊ ✕ ⊞ lau Leisure: ⟲
PS Off-site: ✕

Ons Buiten Aagtekerkeseweg 2a, 4356
☎ 0118 581813 ▯ 0118 583771
e-mail: onsbuiten@zeelandcamping.nl
website: www.zeelandcamping.nl/onsbuiten
In a beautiful location with a wide choice of recreational activities.
➲ From church drive S towards Grijpskerke, turn W and continue 400mtrs.
Open: 22 Mar-Oct Site: 11.5HEC ▦ ⊈ ⌘ Prices: pitch
16.50-34.50 (incl 2 persons) pp4 Facilities: ↑ ⊾ ⊙ ▢ ∅ ⍾ ☎
▢ Services: ⚊ ✕ ⊞ lau Leisure: ⟲ PS

Pekelinge Landmetersweg 1, 4356
☎ 0118 582820 ▯ 0118 583782
e-mail: depekelinge@zeelandcamping.nl
website: www.zeelandcamping.nl/depekelinge
The on-site facilities have seasonal opening.
Open: Apr-Oct Site: 15HEC ▦ ⊈ ⌘ ⌘ Facilities: ↑ ⊾ ⊙
▢ ∅ ▢ Services: ⚊ ✕ ⊞ lau Leisure: ⟲ P Off-site: ∅ ⟲S

OOSTVOORNE ZUID-HOLLAND

Kruininger Gors Gorspl 2, 3233
☎ 0181 482711 ▯ 0181 485957
e-mail: info@kruiningers.nl
website: www.kruiningergors.nl
A small site, divided by hedges, close to the lake.
➲ Access via N15.
Open: Apr-Sep Site: 108HEC ▦ ⽔ ⌘ Prices: ⚡2.50 pitch
14.20 (incl 2 persons) Facilities: ↑ ⊾ ⊙ ▢ ∅ ▢
Services: ⚊ ✕ ⊞ lau Leisure: ⟲ LPR

OUDDORP ZUID-HOLLAND

Klepperstee Vrijheidsweg 1, 3253
☎ 0187 681511 ▯ 0187 683060
e-mail: info@klepperstee.com
website: www.klepperstee.com
On level meadow divided by hedges and trees.
➲ Access via N57 (Rotterdam-Vlissingen) exit Ouddorp.
Open: Apr-Oct Site: 40HEC ▦ ⊈ ⚠ ⌘ Prices: pitch 26-
31 (incl 4 persons) Facilities: ↑ ⊾ ⊙ ▢ ∅ ⍾ ☎ Services: ⚊
✕ ⊞ lau Leisure: ⟲ P Off-site: ⟲LPS

PLASMOLEN LIMBURG

Eldorado Witteweg 18, 6586 ☎ 024 6961914 ▯ 024 6963017
e-mail: info@eldorado-mook.nl
website: www.eldorado-mook.nl/eldorado-plasmolen.nl
Well equipped site in wooded surroundings on the Mooker See.
➲ S of N271.
Open: Apr-1 Oct Site: 6HEC ▦ ⊈ Prices: ⚡3.75 🚗2
🚐4.50 ⚠4.50 Facilities: ↑ ⊾ ⊙ ▢ ∅ ⍾ ☎ Services: ⚊ ✕ ⊞
lau Leisure: ⟲ L

RENESSE ZEELAND

Brem Hoogenboomlaan 11, 4325 ☎ 0111 461403
Well-kept site belonging to a trade union, but also accepting tourists. The last camping site in Hoogenboomlaan with numbered sections. It is advisable to reserve pitches between 21 Jun and 9 Aug.
Open: Apr-25 Oct Site: 12HEC ▦ ⊈ ⬛ ⌘ ⌘
Facilities: ↑ ⊙ ▢ ⍾ ▢ Services: ⚊ ✕ ⊞ lau Leisure: ⟲ P
Off-site: ⊾ ∅

International Scharendijkseweg 8, 4325
☎ 0111 461391 ▯ 0111 462571
e-mail: info@camping-international.net
website: www.camping-international.net
On grassland, between rows of tall shrubs and trees. Between dyke road and main road to Scharendijk on E outskirts of village.
Open: Mar-Nov Site: 3HEC ▦ ⊈ Prices: ⚡4.25 🚗2.50 🚐4
⚠4 Facilities: ↑ ⊾ ⊙ ▢ ∅ ☎ ▢ Services: ⚊ lau
Off-site: ✕ ⟲S

Wyde Blick Hagezoom 112, 4325
☎ 0111 468888 ▯ 0111 468889
e-mail: dewijdeblick@zeelandcamping.nl
website: www.zeelandcamping.nl/dewijdeblick
A family site with good facilities.
➲ Well signposted.
Open: All year Site: 10HEC ▦ ⊈ ⌘ ⌘ Prices: pitch 17-
27.50 (incl 2 persons) Facilities: ↑ ⊾ ⊙ ▢ ∅ ▢
Services: ⚊ ✕ ⊞ lau Leisure: ⟲ P Off-site: ⟲S

Facilities: ⊾-shop **↑**-shower **⊙**-electric points for razors **▢**-electric points for caravans **☎**-parking by tents permitted **▢**-compulsory separate car park **Services: ✕**-café/restaurant **⚊**-bar **∅**-Camping Gaz International **⍾**-gas other than Camping Gaz **⊞**-first aid facilities lau-laundry **Leisure: ⟲**-swimming L-Lake P-Pool R-River S-Sea **Off-site:** All facilities within 2km

---

RETRANCHEMENT ZEELAND

De Zwinhoeve Duinweg 1, 4525
☎ 0117 392120 📠 0117 392248
e-mail: info@zwinhoeve.net website: www.zwinhoeve.net
In a beautiful position backed by sandunes with easy access
to the fine beaches of the Zeeuws-Vlaanderen coast.
Open: All year Site: 9HEC ▦ ※ Prices: ✚5 ➡4 ➡4 ▲4
pitch 3 Facilities: ⋔ ♨ ⊙ ⌁ ∅ ▙ ⌺ ▣ Services: ⬮ ✕ ⊞ lau
Leisure: ⬮ S Off-site: ⬮P

RIJNSBURG ZUID-HOLLAND

Koningshof Elsgeesterweg 8, 2231
☎ 071 4026051 📠 071 4021336
e-mail: info@koningshofholland.nl
website: www.koningshofholland.nl
Modern site on level meadow near the flower fields.
⬧ 1km N. Signposted
Open: All year Site: 7.5HEC ▦ ⊈ ⬮ ⬮ Prices: pitch
19.50-29.50 (incl 2 persons) Facilities: ⋔ ♨ ⊙ ⬮ ∅ ▙ ⌺
Services: ⬮ ✕ ⊞ lau Leisure: ⬮ P Off-site: ⬮S

ROCKANJE ZUID-HOLLAND

Waterboscamping Duinrand 11, 3235
☎ 0181 401900 📠 0181 404233
e-mail: info@waterboscamping.nl
website: www.waterboscamping.nl
A small, pleasant site near the beach. **Motor caravans and
tents only.**
⬧ Access via N15.
Open: Apr-Sep Site: 7HEC ▦ ※ ⬮ Facilities: ⋔ ♨ ⊙ ⬮
∅ ▙ ⌺ ▣ Services: ⬮ ⊞ lau Off-site: ✕ ⬮S

ROERMOND LIMBURG

Hatenboer Hatenboer 51, 6041
☎ 0475 336727 📠 0475 310113
Situated in a `Waterpark' with access to all watersports.
Camping Card Compulsory
⬧ Leave A68 (Roermond-Eindhoven) at `Hatenboer' exit.
Open: Apr-1 Nov Site: 15HEC ▦ ※ Facilities: ⋔ ⊙ ⬮ ⌺
▣ Services: ⬮ ✕ ⊞ lau Leisure: ⬮ LR Off-site: ♨ ∅ ▙ ⬮P

Marina Oolderhuuske Oolderhuuske 1, 6041
☎ 0475 588686 📠 0475 582652
e-mail: info@oolderhuuske.nl
website: www.deooldies.nl/oolderhuuske.htm
A well equipped site within the marina area on the
Maasplassen.
Open: 28 Mar-01 Nov Site: 6HEC ▦ ※ ⬮ ⬮
Prices: ✚2.50 ▲12 pitch 18-23 Facilities: ⋔ ♨ ⊙ ⬮ ∅ ▙ ⌺ ▣
Services: ⬮ ✕ ⊞ lau Leisure: ⬮ LPR

ROOSENDAAL NOORD-BRABANT

Zonneland Tufvaartsestr 6, 4709 ☎ 01656 365429
e-mail: info@zonneland.nl website: www.zonneland.nl
⬧ S of town towards the Belgian border.
Open: Mar-15 Oct Site: 14HEC ▦ ➡ ⬮ Prices: ✚3 ➡2
➡5 ▲5 Facilities: ⋔ ♨ ⊙ ⬮ ⌺ Services: ⊞ lau Leisure: ⬮ P

ST ANTHONIS NOORD-BRABANT

Ullingse Bergen Bosweg 36, 5845
☎ 0485 388566 📠 0485 388569
e-mail: info@ullingsebergen.nl
website: www.ullingsebergen.nl
A family site in natural wooded surroundings with good
facilities for children.
⬧ W of town.
Open: Apr-Oct Site: 11HEC ▦ ⊈ ⬮ ⬮ Facilities: ⋔ ♨ ⊙
⬮ ∅ ▙ ⌺ ▣ Services: ✕ ⊞ lau Leisure: ⬮ P

ST OEDENRODE NOORD-BRABANT

Kienehoef Zwembadweg 35-37, 5491
☎ 0413 472877 📠 0413 477033
e-mail: info@kienehoef.nl website: www.kienehoef.nl
An exceptionally well appointed site in a peaceful rural
setting.
⬧ NW towards Boxtel.
Open: All year Site: 4HEC ▦ ⊈ ⬮ ▲ ⬮ Facilities: ⋔ ♨ ⊙
⬮ ∅ ▣ Services: ⬮ ✕ ⊞ lau Leisure: ⬮ P Off-site: ✕

SEVENUM LIMBURG

Schatberg Midden Peelweg 5, 5975
☎ 077 4677777 📠 077 4677799
e-mail: receptie@schatberg.nl website: www.schatberg.nl
A well appointed family site in wooded surroundings with
plenty of leisure facilities.
⬧ SW towards Eindhoven.
Open: All year Site: 86HEC ▦ ⊈ ⬮ ⬮ Prices: pitch 17-
29.80 (incl 4 persons) Facilities: ⋔ ♨ ⊙ ⬮ ∅ ▙ ⌺ ▣
Services: ⬮ ✕ ⊞ lau Leisure: ⬮ LP

SLUIS ZEELAND

Meldoorn Hoogstr 68, 4524 ☎ 0117 461662 📠 0117 461662
website: www.campingdemeidoorn.nl
In a meadow surrounded by rows of deciduous trees.
⬧ N on the road to Zuidzande.
Open: 26 Mar-15 Oct Site: 6.5HEC ▦ ⊈ Prices: ✚3.60
➡2.20 ➡4.25 ▲3.25-4.25 Facilities: ⋔ ⊙ ⬮ ▙ ⌺ ▣
Services: ⬮ ✕ ⊞ lau Off-site: ♨

VALKENBURG LIMBURG

Europa Couberg 29, 6301 ☎ 043 6013097 📠 043 6013525
A quiet family site within easy reach of the town.
⬧ SW of town.
Open: Apr-Oct Site: 10HEC ▦ ※ Facilities: ⋔ ♨ ⊙ ⬮ ∅
▙ ⌺ Services: ⬮ ✕ ⊞ lau Leisure: ⬮ P

VENRAY LIMBURG

de Oude Barrier Maasheseweg 93, 5802 ☎ 0478 582305
website: www.de-oude-barrier.nl
A quiet site recommended for young children.
⬧ NE of town.
Open: Apr-Sep Site: 14HEC ▦ ⊈ Facilities: ⋔ ⊙ ⬮ ∅ ⌺
Services: ⊞ lau Leisure: ⬮ P Off-site: ✕ ▙

VROUWENPOLDER ZEELAND

Oranjezon Koningin Emmaweg 16a, 4354
☎ 0118 591549 📠 0118 591920
e-mail: oranjezon@oranjezon.nl website: www.oranjezon.nl
Well-kept between tall, thick hedges and bushes. SW of the village.
Camping Card Compulsory.
⬧ For access drive towards Oostkapelle for approx 2.5km, then
turn N and continue for 300mtrs.
Open: Apr-Oct Site: 9.8HEC ▦ ⊈ ⬮ ▲ Prices: pitch 28
(incl 4 persons) Facilities: ⋔ ♨ ⊙ ⬮ ∅ ▙ ⌺ ▣ Services: ⬮ ✕
⊞ lau Leisure: ⬮ PS

Zandput Vroondijk 9, 4354 ☎ 0118 597210 📠 0118 591954
e-mail: info@roompot.nl website: www.roompot.nl
On level ground behind sand dunes and close to the beach.
⬧ 2km N.
Open: Apr-Oct Site: 12HEC ▦ ⊈ ⬮ ⬮ ▲ Facilities: ⋔ ♨
⊙ ⬮ ⌺ ▣ Services: ⬮ ✕ ⊞ lau Off-site: ∅ ▙ ⬮LS

> **The AA cannot be held
> responsible for the content of
> third party websites**

Site: 6HEC-Site size ▦-grass ⸬-sand ◈-stone ※-little shade ⊈-partly shaded ⬮-mainly shaded
⬮-bungalows for hire ⬮-caravans for hire ▲-tents for hire ⬮-no dogs Prices: ✚-adult per night ➡-car per night
pp-per person per night ➡-caravan per night ▲-tent per night

WASSENAAR ZUID-HOLLAND

Duinhorst Buurtweg 135, 2244
☎ 070 3242270 ▤ 070 3246053
A peaceful site in wooded surroundings with modern facilities and fine opportunities for sports and entertainment.
Open: Apr-1 Oct Site: 11HEC ⬜ ⠿ ⚬ ⚘ Facilities: ⋒ ⦰ ⊙ ⊞ ⌀ ♨ ⌂ Services: ⬍ ✗ ⊞ lau Leisure: ⦂ P

Duinrell Duinrell 1, 2242 ☎ 070 5155255 ▤ 070 5155371
website: www.duinrell.nl
Very well maintained site with additional recreation centre which is free for campers. NW in area of same name. Some noise from aircraft. Toilets for invalids. Area restricted to cars. Naturist beach nearby.
➲ *Turn off A44 (Den Haag-Leiden) at traffic lights in Wassenaar dorp' and camping signs.*
Open: All year Site: 110HEC ⬜ ⚬ ⊞ ⌷ ⋏ Prices: ⋏8.95 pitch 8.25-11.75 Facilities: ⋒ ⦰ ⊙ ⊞ ⌀ ♨ ⌂ ⊡ Services: ⬍ ✗ ⊞ lau Leisure: ⦂ P Off-site: ⦂LS

WEERT LIMBURG

Ijzeren Man Herenvennenweg 60, 6006 ☎ 0495 533202
Well-kept with asphalt drives, in a big nature reserve with zoo, heath and forest.
➲ *Off E9.*
Open: Apr-1 Oct Site: 11.5HEC ⬜ ⠿ ⚬ ⌷ Facilities: ⋒ ⦰ ⊙ ⊞ ⌀ ♨ ⌂ ⊡ Services: ⬍ ✗ ⊞ lau Leisure: ⦂ P

WELL LIMBURG

Leukermeer De Kamp 5, 5855 EG
☎ 0478 502444 ▤ 0478 501260
e-mail: info@leukermeer.nl website: www.leukermeer.nl
In beautiful surroundings on Lake Leukermeer with good modern installations and plenty of leisure facilities.

➲ *Signposted from N271.*
Open: 27 Mar-Oct Site: 12HEC ⬜ ⚬ ⊞ Prices: ⌷19-32.50 ⋏19-32.50 Facilities: ⋒ ⦰ ⊙ ⊞ ⌀ ♨ ⌂ Services: ⬍ ✗ ⊞ lau Leisure: ⦂ LP

WEMELDINGE ZEELAND

Linda Oostkanaalweg 4, 4424
☎ 0113 621259 ▤ 0113 622638
e-mail: info@campinglinda.nl website: www.campinglinda.nl
On meadowland surrounded by rows of tall shrubs.
➲ *Turn opposite bridge in town and continue 100mtrs, over bridge to camp.*
Open: Apr-Nov Site: 8HEC ⬜ ⥀ ⊞ ⌷ Prices: ⋏3.72 ⌷3.22 ⌷6.14 ⋏2.70 Facilities: ⋒ ⦰ ⊙ ⊞ ⌀ ♨ ⌂ Services: ⬍ ✗ ⊞ lau Leisure: ⦂ S

WESTKAPELLE ZEELAND

Boomgaard Domineeshofweg 1, 4361
☎ 0118 571377 ▤ 0118 572383
A flat grassy site.
➲ *For access turn off the Middleburg road on the S outskirts of the town, then follow signs.*
Open: 27 Mar-24 Oct Site: 8HEC ⬜ ⚬ ⌷ Facilities: ⋒ ⦰ ⊙ ⊞ ⌀ ♨ ⌂ ⊡ Services: ⬍ ✗ ⊞ lau Leisure: ⦂ P Off-site: ⦂S

ZOUTELANDE ZEELAND

Meerpaal Duinweg 133, 5375 ☎ 0118 561300
On meadowland hidden behind bushy hedges at the end of a cul-de-sac.
➲ *1km SE.*
Open: 27 Mar-1 Nov Site: 2HEC ⬜ ⥀ ⊞ ⌷ Facilities: ⋒ ⦰ ⊙ ⊞ ⌀ ♨ ⌂ ⊡ Services: ⊞ lau Leisure: ⦂ S Off-site: ⬍ ✗

Facilities: ⦰-shop ⋒-shower ⊙-electric points for razors ⊞-electric points for caravans ⌂-parking by tents permitted ⊡-compulsory separate car park Services: ✗-café/restaurant ⬍-bar ⌀-Camping Gaz International ♨-gas other than Camping Gaz ⊞-first aid facilities lau-laundry Leisure: ⦂-swimming L-Lake P-Pool R-River S-Sea Off-site: All facilities within 2km

PORTUGAL

This relatively small but once powerful country lies in the south western corner of the Iberian peninsula. Portugal's only land frontier is the Spanish border in the east and north.

FACTS AND FIGURES
Area: 92,345 sq km
35,655 sq miles
Population: 10,300,000
(2001)
Capital: Lisbon
Language: Portuguese
IDD code: 351. To call
the UK dial 00 44
Currency: Euro
Local time:
GMT(summer GMT+1)

Emergency Services:
Police, Fire and
Ambulance 112
Banks: Mon-Fri 08.30-
15.00
Shops: Mon-Fri 09.00-
13.00; 15.00-19.00, Sat
09.00-13.00;& Dec
15.00-19.00 ; shopping
centres Mon-Sun 10.00-
24.00

Average daily
temperature: Lisbon
Jan 11°C   Jul 21°C
Mar 13°C   Sep20°C
May 17°C   Nov14°C
Tourist Information:
ICEP/Portuguese Trade
and Tourism Office
UK 22-25A Sackville
Street
London W1S 3LY
Tel 09063 640610

(premium rate information
line)
USA 4th Floor, 590 Fifth
Avenue New York,
NY 10036
Tel (212) 719 3985
Tourist info website:
www.portugal.org/tourism

The country is perhaps, best known for its five hundred miles of coastline. The Algarve in the extreme south is one of the finest stretches of coastline in Europe, with unique caves and a remoteness which has been preserved despite the development of the area. Inland, the cool valleys and pastures of the Tagus contrast sharply with the wooded mountain slopes of the Minho area in the north.

Generally the country enjoys a mild climate with the Algarve being very hot in the summer. The language is Portuguese, which was developed from Latin and closely resembles Spanish, although English is often spoken in the Algarve.

Mainland Portugal has 198 campsites most of which are on the coast. A camping guide is available from Roteiro Campista, Rua do Griestal 5 1ºfte, 1300-274 Lisboa ☎ 213642370 (fax: 213619284 / e-mail: info@roteiro-campista.pt). There are about 22 Orbitur parks in the country which are privately owned and of a high standard, as indeed are the municipal parks. Orbitur parks are open throughout the year and most of them offer fully-equipped bungalows which accommodate four people. A booklet containing details of officially classified parks is produced by the Direcção Geral de Turismo, Palácio Foz, Praça dos Restauradores, Lisboa ☎ 213466307 or 213463624. The Oporto office is at Praça D João I, 25-4 L 222005805 and the

Coimbra office is at Largo da Portagem. Otherwise ask for Comissao Municipal de Turismo, Junta de Turismo or Câmara Municipal.

Off-site camping is prohibited. You must stay on an organised site. However, when stopping in a motorway rest or service area with a caravan, it is permissible to cook a meal.

HOW TO GET THERE

You can use one of the direct ferry services to Spain and then travel onwards by road. The services and minimum sailing times are **Plymouth to Santander** (24hrs) and **Portsmouth to Bilbao** (27hrs).

DISTANCE

From Santander to Lisboa (Lisbon) is about 920km (570 miles), normally requiring one or two overnight stops. Using the Channel ports, or the Channel tunnel, driving through France and Spain (enter Spain on the Biarritz to San Sebastian (Donostia) road at the western end of the Pyrénées).

From the Channel ports to Lisboa (Lisbon) is about 2,157km (1,340 miles). This will require 3 or 4 overnight stops.

CAR SLEEPER TRAINS

Summer services are available from **Calais** to Biarritz, Bordeaux, Brive, Narbonne, and Toulouse and **Denderleeuw** (Belgium) to Narbonne.
See Spain for location map

MOTORING & GENERAL INFO

The information given here is specific to Portugal. It **must** be read in conjunction with the Essential Motoring Information at the front of the book, which covers those regulations which are common to many countries. **Note**: Portuguese law requires that everyone carries photographic proof of identity at all times.

BRITISH EMBASSY/CONSULATES*

The British Embassy is located at 1249-082 Lisboa, rua de São Bernardo 33 ☎ 213924000; consular section ☎ 213924188. There is a British Consulate in Porto (Oporto) and one with an Honorary Consul in Portimão.

CHILDREN IN CARS

Child under 3 cannot travel as front seat passenger unless seated in approved child seat; child over 3 and under 12 must use approved restraint system unless the car is a two seater. See Essential Motoring Information under 'Passengers' and 'Seat Belts'.

CURRENCY

With the introduction of the Euro, the Portuguese Escudo (PTE) ceased to be legal tender from 28 2002. However, PTE banknotes may still be exchanged at the Portuguese Central Bank (Banco de Portugal) for 20 years.

DIMENSIONS AND WEIGHT RESTRICTIONS*

Private **cars** and towed **trailers** or **caravans** are restricted to the following dimensions - height, 4 metres; width, 2.55 metres; length, 12 metres. The maximum permitted overall length of vehicle/trailer or caravan combination is 18.75 metres.

Portuguese traffic regulations stipulate that the total permitted weight of a trailer or caravan may not exceed one and a half times the total permitted weight of the towing vehicle. For example, a car of 1000kg must not tow a trailer or caravan with a total laden weight of more than 1500kg.

DRIVING LICENCE*

A valid UK or Republic of Ireland licence is accepted in Portugal. The minimum age at which a visitor may use a temporarily imported motorcycle (over 50cc) or car is 18 years. See also Speed limits below.

FISCAL RECEIPT

Visiting motorists should ensure that they are able to provide proof of ownership of any goods and electrical equipment carried in the vehicle when entering Portugal. Both the Brigada de Trânsito (traffic police) and the Brigada Fiscal (fiscal police), part of the Guarda Nacional Republicana (GNR), have the authority to make spot checks on all roads within Portugal and at the frontier with Spain.

Proof of ownership in the form of fiscal receipts may be required for items such as computers, cameras, quantities of wine, cigarettes and groceries, carried in the vehicle.

FOODSTUFFS*

If the imported foodstuffs are for personal use, there are no limits when travelling between EU countries.

LIGHTS*

It is compulsory for motorcyclists to use dipped headlights during the day.

MOTORING CLUB

The **Automóvel Club de Portugal** (ACP) which has its headquarters at Lisboa 1250-195, rua Rosa Araüjo 24 ☎ 213180100 has offices in a number of provincial towns. ACP offices are normally open 09.00-17.00hrs Monday to Friday (to 17.30hrs from 1 April to 30 September); English and French are spoken. Offices are closed on Saturday and Sunday.
Website: **www.acp.pt**

ROADS

Main roads and most of the important secondary roads are good, as are the mountain roads to the north-east.

Portugal has about 700 miles of motorway (*auto-estrada*) with tolls payable on most sections. Emergency telephones are located every 2km on most motorways.

The Palace tower occupies a position overlooking the landscape of rich green forests which surround the town of Sintra.

SPEED LIMITS*

Car/motorcycle
Built-up areas 50km/h (31mph)
Other roads 90km/h (55mph)
 or 100km/h (62mph)
Motorways min† 40km/h (24mph)
max 120km/h (74mph)
Car/caravan/trailer
Built-up areas 50km/h (31mph)
Other roads 70km/h (43mph) or 80km/h (49mph)
Motorways min† 40km/h (24mph)
max 100km/h (62mph)
 †Minimum speeds on motorways apply,
except where otherwise signposted.
 Both Portuguese residents and visitors to
Portugal, who have held a full driving licence for
less than one year, must not exceed 90km/h
(55mph) when driving on any road or motorway
outside built-up areas.

WARNING TRIANGLE*

The use of a warning triangle or hazard-warning
lights is compulsory in the event of accident or
breakdown. As hazard warning lights may be
damaged or inoperative, it is recommended that a
warning triangle be carried. The triangle must be
placed on the road 30 metres (33yds) behind the
vehicle and must be clearly visible from 100
metres (109yds).

*Additional information will be found in the
Essential Motoring Information at the front of
the book.

SOUTH

ALBUFEIRA ALGARVE

Albufeira 8200-55 ☎ 351289 ▤ 289587633
e-mail: campingalbufeira@mail.telepac.pt
A modern, purpose-built site with excellent sanitary blocks
and a wide variety of sports and entertainment facilities.
➲ *1.5km from Albufeira. Signposted from N125*
Open: All year Site: 19HEC ⌖ ⠿ ⊙ ⊞ Prices: ⋔4.85
⛺4.35 ⛽4.85 ▲4.60 Facilities: ♠ ⅀ ⊙ ⊡ ⊞ Services: � ✗
⊞ lau Leisure: ⁀ P Off-site: ✗ ∅ ⨺ ⁀S ⊞

ALVITO BAIXO ALENTEJO

Markádia Barragem de Odivelas, 7920-999
☎ 284763141 ▤ 284763102
website: www.roteiro-campista.pt/Beja/ing/
markadia-info-uk.htm
Open savannah terrain beside a lake with good, modern
facilities.
➲ *Leave N121 (Beja-Lisboa) at Ferrera do Alentejo and
continue N towards Torrão. From Odivelas follow signposts.*
Open: All year Site: 10HEC ⌖ ∅ ⊙ ⊞ Prices: ⋔2.20-4.40
⛺2.20-4.40 ⛽2.20-4.40 ▲2.20-4.40 Facilities: ♠ ⅀ ⊙ ⊡ ∅
⨺ ⊡ Services: ⍩ ✗ ⊞ lau Leisure: ⁀ L Off-site: ⁀P

BEJA BAIXO ALENTEJO

CM de Beja Vasco da Gama, 7800-397
☎ 284311911 ▤ 284311911
website: www.embeja.pt/culturadesporto/parque.htm
Open: All year Site: 1HEC ⌖ ♠ Prices: ⋔1.03-2.05 ⛺0.76-
1.51 ⛽1.05-3.02 ▲0.76-1.51 Facilities: ♠ ⊙ ⊡ Services: ⍩
✗ ⊞ lau Off-site: ⅀ ✗ ∅ ⨺ ⁀LPRS ⊞

OLHÃO ARGARVE

Olhão Pinheiros de Marim, 8703
☎ 289700300 ▤ 289700390
e-mail: sbsicamping@mail.telepac.pt
Open: All year Site: 10HEC ♠ ▲ Facilities: ♠ ⅀ ⊙ ⊡ ∅ ⨺
Services: ⍩ ✗ ⊞ Leisure: ⁀ P Off-site: ⁀S

PORTIMÃO ALGARVE

Da Dourada Alvor, 8500 ☎ 282 459178 ▤ 458002
In a parklike area close to the beach with good facilities.
➲ *N off Portimão-Lagos road.*
Open: All year Site: 4HEC ⌖ ⠿ ♠ ⊞ ⛽ ▲ Prices: ⋔1.75-
3.50 ⛺1.50-3 ⛽2.15-4.25 ▲2-3.75 Facilities: ♠ ⅀ ⊙ ⊡ ∅ ⨺
⊡ Services: ⍩ ✗ ⊞ lau Leisure: ⁀ LRS Off-site: ⁀P

PRAIA DA LUZ ALGARVE

AT VALVERDE

Orbitur Estrada da Praia da Luz, 8600
☎ 282789211 ▤ 282789213
e-mail: info@orbitur.pt website: www.orbitur.pt
Well-equipped site with children's playground and tennis
courts.
➲ *Off N125 Lagos-Cape St Vincent road. 4km from Lagos.*
Open: All year Site: 9.1HEC ⌖ ♠ ⊞ ⛽ Prices: ⋔2.60-5
⛺2.20-4.50 ⛽3.80-6.60 ▲3.10-5.30 Facilities: ♠ ⅀ ⊙ ⊡ ∅
⊡ Services: ⍩ ✗ ⊞ lau Leisure: ⁀ P Off-site: ⅀ ✗ ⁀S

QUARTEIRA ALGARVE

Orbitur Estrada da Forte Santa, 8125
☎ 289302826 ▤ 289302822
e-mail: info@orbitur.pt website: www.orbitur.pt
A terraced site at the top of a hill.

★ ★ ★
Camping Olhão
Tel: 351 289 700 300 Fax: 351 289 700 390
Tennis
Football
Bar
Swimming
Pool
Restaurant
Bungalows
Mobil-Homes
Open All Year

➲ *Off M125 in Almoncil and follow signs to Quarteira. About
500mtrs before reaching the sea turn left into the camp.*
Open: All year Site: 9.7HEC ⌖ ♠ ⊞ Prices: ⋔2.60-5
⛺2.20-2.50 ⛽3.80-6.60 ▲3.10-5.30 Facilities: ♠ ⅀ ⊙ ⊡ ∅
⊡ Services: ⍩ ✗ ⊞ lau Leisure: ⁀ P Off-site: ⅀ ✗ ⁀S

SAGRES ALGARVE

Orbitur Cerro Das Moitas, 8650
☎ 282 624371 ▤ 282 624445
e-mail: info@orbitur.pt
website: www.orbitur.pt
Site situated in dune and forest area. *1.5km W of N268*
Open: All year Site: 6.7HEC ⌖ ♠ Prices: ⋔2.40-4.30
⛺2.10-3.80 ⛽3.20-5.50 ▲2.80-4.60 Facilities: ♠ ⅀ ⊙ ⊡ ⊡
Services: ⍩ ✗ ⊞ lau Off-site: ⁀S

SANTO ANDRE BAIXO ALENTEJO

Lagoa de Santo Andre 7500
☎ 269708550 ▤ 269708559
e-mail: info@fpcampismo.pt
website: www.fpcampismo.pt
In wooded surroundings with good facilities.
➲ *Signposted.*
Open: 18 Jan-30 Oct Site: 15HEC ⌖ ∅ ♠ ⊘ Facilities: ♠
⅀ ⊙ ⊡ ∅ ⊡ Services: ⍩ ✗ ⊞ lau Leisure: ⍩ ✗ ⁀LS

SINES BAIXO ALENTEJO

S. Tonnes S. Tonnes, 7520 ☎ 269 632105 ▤ 862430
In a pine wood on the Cabo de Sines peninsula, to the N of
the town.
➲ *Follow signs for Algarve/ S. Tonnes.*
Open: All year Site: 7.5HEC ⌖ ♠ ⊞ Prices: ⋔2.50 ⛽2.70-
7.40 ▲2.40 Facilities: ♠ ⊙ ⊡ ∅ ⨺ ⊡ Services: ⍩ ✗ ⊞ lau
Off-site: ⁀S

Facilities: ⅀-shop ♠-shower ⊙-electric points for razors ⊡-electric points for caravans ⊡-parking by tents permitted
⊡-compulsory separate car park **Services:** ✗-café/restaurant ⍩-bar ∅-Camping Gaz International ⨺-gas other than Camping
Gaz ⊞-first aid facilities lau-laundry **Leisure:** ⁀-swimming L-Lake P-Pool R-River S-Sea **Off-site:** All facilities within 2km

VILA DO BISPO ALGARVE

AT PRAIA DE SALEMA (7.5KM SE)

Quinta dos Carriços 8650 ☎ 282 695201 ▓ 282 65122
e-mail: quintacarrico@oninet.pt
A well equipped site with good facilities. There is a naturist
section in a separate valley with its own facilities.
Open: All year Site: 20HEC ⁙ ♣ ⛺ 🚐 Prices: ⋔4 ♠4
🚐5.70 ⛺4.11-5.20 Facilities: 🏪 🗟 ⊙ 🖂 ⌀ 🛒 ☎ Services: 🍴 ✗
⊞ lau Off-site: ⅋S

VILA NOVA DE MILFONTES BAIXO ALENTEJO

Parque de Campismo de Milfontes 7645
☎ 283 996104 ▓ 283 996104
e-mail: parquemilfontes@netc.pt
website: www.roteiro-campista.pt/Beja/milfontes-
morada.htm
Open: All year Site: 6.5HEC ♣ ⛺ 🚐 Facilities: 🏪 🗟 ⊙ 🖂 ⌀
🛒 ☎ Services: 🍴 ✗ lau Off-site: ⅋RS ⊞

NORTH

CAMINHA MINHO

Orbitur Mata do Camarido, 4910
☎ 258921295 ▓ 258921473
e-mail: info@orbitur.pt website: www.orbitur.pt
On undulating sandy ground with trees.
↪ Turn off N13 at Km89.7 and drive W, along the Rio Minho
for about 800mtrs, then turn left.
Open: 16 Jan-Nov Site: 2.1HEC ⁙ ⊄ Facilities: 🏪 🗟 ⊙ 🖂
⌀ ☎ Services: 🍴 ✗ lau Leisure: ⅋ S Off-site: 🗟 ✗ ⅋S

CAMPO DO GERES MINHO

Cerdeira 4840 ☎ 253 351005 ▓ 353315
e-mail: parque.cerdeira@portugalmail.pt
In a picturesque wooded location with mature oak trees
surrounding the pitches.
Camping Card Compulsory.
Open: All year Site: 5.1HEC ⅏ ⁙ ♣ ⛺ ⊘ Facilities: 🏪
🗟 ⊙ 🖂 ⌀ ☎ Services: 🍴 ✗ lau Off-site: 🖂 ⅋LR

MATOSINHOS DOURO LITORAL

AT ANGEIRAS (12KM N)

Orbitur Angeiras, 4455-039 ☎ 22 9270571 ▓ 22 9271178
e-mail: info@orbitur.pt website: www.orbitur.pt
A modern, well-kept site in a pine wood on a hill
overlooking the sea.
↪ W of the N13 at the X-roads at Km12.1, E of Vila do
Pinheiro and towards the sea for 5km.
Open: All year Site: 7HEC ⁙ ⊄ 🚐 Prices: ⋔2.20-4.30
♠1.90-3.80 🚐2.90-5.50 ⛺2.50-4.60 Facilities: 🏪 🗟 ⊙ 🖂 ⌀
☎ Services: 🍴 ✗ ⊞ lau Leisure: ⅋ P Off-site: ⅋S

MONDIM DE BASTO MINHO

Mondim de Basto 4880 ☎ 255381650 ▓ 255381650
e-mail: ccponto@mail.telepac.pt
website: www.tennavista.pt/pontosanto/2693
In wooded surroundings beside the River Olo.
↪ Signposted.
Open: Feb-Oct Site: 3HEC ⅏ ⊄ ⊘ Facilities: 🏪 ⊙ 🖂 ⌀ ☎
Services: 🍴 ✗ ⊞ lau Leisure: ⅋ R Off-site: 🖂 ✗

PÓVOA DE VARZIM DOURO LITORAL

Rio Alto Estela-Rio Alto, 4570-275
☎ 252615699 ▓ 252615599
e-mail: info@orbitur.pt website: www.orbitur.pt
Situated near dunes 150mtrs from the sea.

↪ Off NX111 towards Viana.
Open: All year Site: 7.9HEC ▦ ⁙ ⊄ ⛺ 🚐 Prices: ⋔2.40-
4.50 ♠2.20-4.40 🚐3.80-6.20 ⛺3.10-4.90 Facilities: 🏪 🗟 ⊙
🖂 ⌀ ☎ Services: 🍴 ✗ ⊞ lau Leisure: ⅋ PS Off-site: ⅋S

VIANA DO CASTELO MINHO

Orbitur Cabedelo, 4900-161 ☎ 258 322167 ▓ 258 321946
e-mail: info@orbitur.pt website: www.orbitur.pt
A well equipped site with direct access to a sandy beach.
↪ Approach via N13 Porto-Viana do Castelo.
Open: 16 Jan-Nov Site: 3HEC ⁙ ⊄ ⛺ Facilities: 🏪 🗟 ⊙
🖂 ⌀ ☎ Services: 🍴 ✗ ⊞ lau Leisure: ⅋ PS

VILA NOVA DE GAIA DOURO LITORAL

Orbitur Madalena, 4405-736 ☎ 227122520 ▓ 227122534
e-mail: info@orbitur.pt website: www.orbitur.pt
Well equipped site in a pinewood 500mtrs from Madalena
Beach.
Open: All year Site: 24HEC ⁙ ⊄ 🚐 Prices: ⋔2.20-4.30
♠1.90-3.80 🚐2.90-5.50 ⛺2.50-4.60 Facilities: 🏪 🗟 ⊙ 🖂 ⌀
☎ Services: 🍴 ✗ ⊞ lau Leisure: ⅋ P Off-site: ✗ ⅋S

VILA REAL TRAS-OS-MONTES ALTO DOURO

Parque Campismo de Vila Real r Dr-Manuel Cardona, 5000
☎ 259 324724
↪ In the E part of town off N2 by GALP petrol station. Site in
300mtrs near new school.
Open: 16 Jan-15 Dec Site: 4HEC ⁙ ⊄ Facilities: 🏪 🗟 ⊙ 🖂
⌀ ☎ Services: 🍴 ✗ ⊞ lau Off-site: ⅋PR

CENTRAL

ABRANTES RIBATEJO

Castelo do Bode Martinchel, 2200
☎ 241849262 ▓ 241849244
e-mail: info@fpcampismo.pt website: www.fpcampismo.pt
In natural wooded surroundings.
↪ Signposted.
Open: 18 Jan-Oct Site: 2HEC ⅏ ⊄ ⊘ Facilities: 🏪 ⊙ 🖂 ⌀
☎ Services: 🍴 ✗ ⊞ lau Leisure: ⅋ R Off-site: 🖂 ✗

ALENQUER ESTREMADURA

Alenquer Estrada Nacional No.9-KM94, 2580-330
☎ 263 710375 ▓ 263 710375
e-mail: dosdin@mail.telepac.pt
website: www.dosdin.pt/agirdin
A modern well equipped terraced site surrounded by walnut
trees.
**Reductions available to campers presenting this
publication.**
Open: All year Site: 1.5HEC ⅏ ⊄ ⛺ 🚐 ⛺ Facilities: 🏪 ⊙ 🖂
☎ Services: 🍴 ✗ ⊞ lau Leisure: ⅋ P Off-site: 🖂 ⌀ 🖂 ⅋R ⊞

ARGANIL BEIRA LITORAL

Arganil Sarzedo, 3300 ☎ 035 205706 ▓ 035 25423
e-mail: campingma@hotmail.com
website: www.cm-arganil.pt
In a pleasant situation among pine trees, close to the River Alva.
↪ On N342-4.
Open: All year Site: 2.5HEC ▦ ⊄ ⛺ Prices: ⋔1.50-1.70
♠1.50-2 🚐2-2.80 ⛺1.40-1.80 Facilities: 🏪 ⌀ ⊙ 🖂
Services: 🍴 ✗ ⊞ lau Leisure: ⅋ R Off-site: 🖂 ✗

> ## The AA cannot be held responsible for the content of third party websites

---

Site: 6HEC-Site size ▦▦▦-grass ⁙⁙-sand ⌀-stone ⊘-little shade ⊄-partly shaded ♣-mainly shaded
⛺-bungalows for hire 🚐-caravans for hire ⛺-tents for hire ⊘-no dogs Prices: ⋔-adult per night ♠-car per night
pp-per person per night 🚐-caravan per night ⛺-tent per night

CALDAS DA RAINHA ESTREMADURA

Orbitur Foz do Arelho Foz Do Arelho, 2500
☎ 262 978683   🖩 262 978685
e-mail: info@orbitur.pt **website:** www.orbitur.pt
Situated in a fine lagoon on the estuary of the Arelho.
➲ *3kms SE of Foz do Arelho*
Open: All year **Site:** 6HEC ⋯ ᐸ 🏕 **Prices:** ⋔2.10-4 ⇔1.80-
3.70 ⇔2.60-5.10 ▲2.25-4.20 **Facilities:** 🏾 ᴿ ⊙ 🚰 🏕
Services: ⟟ ✕ 🕀 lau **Leisure:** ⭲ P **Off-site:** ✕ ⭲S

CASFREIRES BEIRA LITORAL

Quinta Chava Grande 3560-043 ☎ 232 665552   🖩 232 665552
e-mail: bert@mail.telepac.pt
website: www.chave-grande.com
A terraced site overlooking a beautiful valley. There are
modern installations and leisure facilities.
Open: Apr-Oct **Site:** 10HEC ᐳᐳᐳ ᐸ 🚰 **Prices:** ⋔3.30 ⇔3
⇔3.30 ▲3.30 **Facilities:** 🏾 ⊙ 🚰 ∅ 🏕 **Services:** ⟟ 🕀 lau
Leisure: ⭲ P **Off-site:** ᴿ ✕

COJA BEIRA LITORAL

Coja 3305 ☎ 235 729666   🖩 235 728945
e-mail: coja@fpcampismo.pt
website: www.fpcampismo.pt
In a wooded location beside the River Alva.
➲ *Signposted.*
Open: 15 Mar-30 Oct **Site:** 3HEC ◕ ᐸ 🏕 ⌇ **Facilities:** 🏾 ᴿ
⊙ 🚰 ∅ 🏕 **Services:** ⟟ ✕ 🕀 lau **Leisure:** ⭲ R **Off-site:** ᴿ ⭲R

COSTA DA CAPARICA ESTREMADURA

Orbitur 2825 ☎ 21 2903894   🖩 21 2900661
e-mail: info@orbitur.pt **website:** www.orbitur.pt
This site has a small touring section and is situated 200mtrs
from a fine sandy beach.

➲ *After crossing the `Ponte Sul' on the road to Caparica, turn
right at first traffic light. Campsite is 1km on left.*
Open: All year **Site:** 5.7HEC ⋯ ● 🏕 🚰 **Facilities:** 🏾 ᴿ ⊙
🚰 ∅ 🏕 **Services:** ⟟ ✕ lau **Off-site:** ᴿ ✕ ∅ ⭲S

ÉVORA ALTO ALENTEJO

Orbitur Estrada de Alcacovas, 7000-703
☎ 266 705190   🖩 266 709830
e-mail: info@orbitur.pt **website:** www.orbitur.pt
In wooded surroundings with good, modern facilities.
➲ *2km S right of road near Km94.5.*
Open: All year **Site:** 3.3HEC ᐳᐳᐳ ⋯ ᐸ 🚰 **Prices:** ⋔2.20-
4.30 ⇔1.90-3.80 ⇔2.90-5.50 ▲2.50-4.60 **Facilities:** 🏾 ᴿ ⊙
🚰 ∅ 🏕 **Services:** ⟟ ✕ lau **Leisure:** ⭲ P **Off-site:** ᴿ ✕

ÉVORA DE ALCOBAÇA ESTREMADURA

Rural de Silveira Capuchos, 2460-479 ☎ 262 509573
e-mail: silveira.capuchos@clix.pt
In a wooded, rural location.
➲ *3km from Alcobaça on N86.*
Open: Jun-Sep **Site:** 0.5HEC ᐳᐳᐳ ● **Prices:** ⋔3 ⇔2 ⇔3-4 ▲2-
3 **Facilities:** 🏾 ⊙ 🚰 🏕 **Services:** 🕀 lau **Off-site:** ᴿ ⟟ ✕ ∅ ᐳ

FIGUEIRA DA FOZ BEIRA LITORAL

Foz do Mondego Cabedelo, Gala, 3080
☎ 233402740   🖩 233402749
e-mail: info@fpcampismo.pt **website:** www.fpcampismo.pt
Open: 19 Jan-30 Oct **Site:** 4HEC ⋯ ⌇ ⌇ **Facilities:** 🏾 ⊙
🚰 ∅ 🏕 **Services:** ⟟ ✕ lau **Leisure:** ⭲ RS **Off-site:** 🏾

Orbitur Gala, 3080 ☎ 233 431492   🖩 233 431231
e-mail: info@orbitur.pt **website:** www.orbitur.pt
In an enclosed area within a municipal park on top of
Guarda Hill.

contd.

Facilities: 🚰-shop 🏾-shower ⊙-electric points for razors 🚰-electric points for caravans 🏕-parking by tents permitted
🄿-compulsory separate car park **Services:** ✕-café/restaurant ⟟-bar ∅-Camping Gaz International ᴹ-gas other than Camping
Gaz 🕀-first aid facilities lau-laundry **Leisure:** ⭲-swimming L-Lake P-Pool R-River S-Sea **Off-site:** All facilities within 2km

⮩ *At Km177, on the NW outskirts of the town, turn left off the N16 Porto road and drive uphill for about 500mtrs.*
Open: All year **Site:** 6HEC ∷ ♣ 🏠 **Facilities:** ℕ 🔩 ☉ 🔊 ⌀
☎ **Services:** ⚒ ✗ ⊞ lau **Off-site:** ⌖S

GOUVEIA BEIRA LITORAL

Curral do Negro 6290 ☎ 238491008
e-mail: info@fpcampismo.pt **website:** www.fpcampismo.pt
In a mountainous setting, surrounded by woodland.
⮩ *Signposted.*
Open: 18 Jan-30 Oct **Site:** 2HEC ♠ ⊕ᵗ **Facilities:** ℕ ☉ 🔊 ⌀ ☎
Services: ⚒ ✗ ⊞ lau **Leisure:** ⌖ P

GUARDA BEIRA ALTA

Orbitur 6300 ☎ 071 211406 ▤ 071 221911
A well equipped site in a pleasant location.
⮩ *Access via N18 Guarda-Castelo Branco.*
Open: Mar-Oct **Site:** 2HEC ♠ ♣ **Facilities:** ℕ 🔩 🔊 ⌀ ☎
Services: ⚒ ✗ ⊞ lau

GUINCHO ESTREMADURA

Orbitur Areia-Guincho, 2750-053
☎ 21 4870450 ▤ 21 4872167
e-mail: info@orbitur.pt **website:** www.orbitur.pt
On hilly ground amidst a pine wood in the Parque du Guincho, near the Boca do Inferno.
⮩ *4km W of Cascais at Km98, turn right and follow road no 247-6 for 1km.*
Open: All year **Site:** 7HEC ∷ ♣ 🏠 🚐 **Prices:** 🛉2.40-4.50
🚗2.20-4.40 🚐3.80-6.20 ▲3.10-4.90 **Facilities:** ℕ 🔩 ☉ 🔊 ⌀
☎ **Services:** ⚒ ✗ ⊞ lau **Off-site:** 🔩 ✗ ⌖S

LOURIÇAL BEIRA LITORAL

De Klomp 11 Casas Brancas, 3100-231
☎ 236 952551 ▤ 236 952551
e-mail: campismo.o.tamanco@mail.telepac.pt
website: www.campismo-o-tamanco.com
In pleasant wooded surroundings.
⮩ *Access via N109 or A1.*
Open: Feb-Oct **Site:** 1.5HEC ⊞ ⊕ᵗ 🏠 🚐 **Prices:** 🛉3 🚗2.30
🚐3.30 ▲2.30-3 **Facilities:** ℕ 🔩 ☉ 🔊 ☎ **Services:** ⚒ ✗ lau
Leisure: ⌖ P **Off-site:** ⌀ ⊞

LUSO BEIRA LITORAL

Orbitur Pampilhosa, 3050-246
☎ 231 930916 ▤ 231 930917
e-mail: info@orbitur.pt **website:** www.orbitur.pt
Open: All year **Site:** 3HEC ∷ ⊕ᵗ 🏠 **Prices:** 🛉2-3.50 🚗1.80-
3.40 🚐2.40-4.70 ▲2.20-3.60 **Facilities:** ℕ 🔩 ☉ 🔊 ⌀ ☎
Services: ⚒ ✗ ⊞ lau **Off-site:** 🔩 ✗ ⌖P

MONTARGIL ALTO ALENTEJO

Orbitur Montargil, 7425-017 ☎ 242 901207 ▤ 242 901220
e-mail: info@orbitur.pt **website:** www.orbitur.pt
In a beautiful wooded location with good recreational facilities close to the River Alva.
⮩ *N off N2.*
Open: All year **Site:** 6HEC ⊞ ∷ ⊕ᵗ 🏠 **Facilities:** ℕ 🔩 ☉
🔊 ⌀ ☎ **Services:** ⚒ ✗ ⊞ lau **Off-site:** ✗ ⌖L

NAZARÉ ESTREMADURA

Orbitur Valado Valado, 2450-148
☎ 262 561111 ▤ 262 561137
e-mail: info@orbitur.pt **website:** www.orbitur.pt
In a pinewood 2km from the village with good facilities.
⮩ *300mtrs E of village, S of road 8-4 Nazaré-Alcobaça.*
Open: Feb-Nov **Site:** 6.3HEC ∷ ♣ 🏠 🚐 **Prices:** 🛉2-3.50
🚗1.80-2.50 🚐2.40-4.70 ▲2.20-3.60 **Facilities:** ℕ 🔩 ☉ 🔊 ⌀
☎ **Services:** ⚒ ✗ ⊞ lau **Off-site:** 🔩 ✗ ⌖S

Vale Paraiso Estrada Nacional 242, 2450-138
☎ 262 561800 ▤ 262 561900
e-mail: info@valeparaiso.com **website:** www.valeparaiso.com
Situated in a beautiful natural park amid tall pine trees, this site is exceptionally well appointed with very high standards of hygiene and varied recreational facilities.
Open: All year **Site:** 8.3HEC ⊞ ∷ ♣ 🏠 🚐 ▲
Prices: 🛉2.90-3.80 🚗2.50-3 🚐3.50-4.20 ▲2.50-4.70
Facilities: ℕ 🔩 ☉ 🔊 ⌀ ☎ **Services:** ⚒ ✗ ⊞ lau **Leisure:** ⌖ P
Off-site: 🎣 ⌖S

PALHEIROS DE MIRA BEIRA LITORAL

Orbitur 3070-792 ☎ 231 471234 ▤ 231 472047
e-mail: info@orbitur.pt **website:** www.orbitur.pt
Site lies in a dense forest.
⮩ *N off the N334 at KM2, towards Videira, opposite a road fork.*
Open: Feb-Nov **Site:** 3HEC ∷ ♣ 🏠 **Prices:** 🛉2.10-3.80
🚗1.80-3.50 🚐2.60-4.80 ▲2.25-3.90 **Facilities:** ℕ 🔩 ☉ 🔊 ⌀
☎ **Services:** ⚒ ✗ ⊞ lau **Off-site:** 🔩 ✗ ⌖LS

PENACOVA BEIRA LITORAL

Penacova est da Carvoeira, 3360
☎ 239477464 ▤ 239477464
e-mail: info@fpcampismo.pt **website:** www.fpcampismo.pt
A pleasant riverside site in wooded surroundings.
⮩ *Signposted.*
Open: 18 Jan-30 Dec **Site:** 1HEC ♠ ⊕ᵗ 🦮 **Facilities:** ℕ ☉ 🔊
⌀ ☎ **Services:** ⚒ ✗ ⊞ lau **Leisure:** ⌖ R **Off-site:** 🔩

PENICHE ESTREMADURA

CM Av. Monsenhor Bastos, 2520
☎ 262 789529 ▤ 262 789529
website: www.cm-peniche.pt
On a sandy hillock, partly wooded 0.5km from sea.
⮩ *2km E.*
Open: All year **Site:** 12.6HEC ⊞ ∷ ☆ **Prices:** 🛉2.05
🚗0.85-1.70 **Facilities:** ℕ 🔩 ☉ 🔊 ⌀ ☎ **Services:** ⚒ ✗ ⊞ lau
Off-site: 🔩 ⚒ ✗ ⌀ 🎣 ⌖PS

Peniche Praia 2520 ☎ 262783460 ▤ 262789447
e-mail: penichepraia@hotmail.com
website: www.roteiro-campista.pt
On level ground 500mtrs from the sea.
⮩ *N towards Cabo Carudeiro.*
Open: All year **Site:** 1.5HEC ⊞ ∷ ☆🦮 **Facilities:** ℕ 🔩
☉ 🔊 ☎ **Services:** ⚒ ✗ ⊞ lau **Off-site:** ⌀ 🎣 ⌖PS ⊞

PORTALEGRE ALTO ALENTEJO

Orbitur Quinta da Saude, 7300-435
☎ 245 308384 ▤ 245 308385
e-mail: info@orbitur.pt **website:** www.orbitur.pt
A hilltop site commanding magnificent views.
⮩ *Access via N18 Estremoz-Castelo Branco.*
Open: Apr-29 Sep **Site:** 2HEC ∷ ♠ ♣ **Prices:** 🛉1.90-3.40
🚗1.70-3.40 🚐2.30-4.50 ▲2.10-3.45 **Facilities:** ℕ ☉ 🔊 ⌀ ☎
Services: ⚒ ✗ lau **Off-site:** 🔩 ✗

SALVATERRA DE MAGOS RIBATEJO

Parque de Campismo de Escaroupim Mata Florestal de Escaroupim, 2120 ☎ 263595484 ▤ 263595484
e-mail: info@fpcampismo.pt **website:** www.fpcampismo.pt
Open: 18 Jan-30 Oct **Site:** 3HEC ♠ ♣ 🦮 **Facilities:** ℕ 🔩 ☉
🔊 ⌀ ☎ **Services:** ⚒ ✗ ⊞ lau **Leisure:** ⌖ P **Off-site:** 🎣 ⌖R

┌─────────────────────────────────────┐
A Guide to Caravan & Camping in Great Britain is also available from The AA
└─────────────────────────────────────┘

Site: 6HEC-Site size ⊞-grass ∷-sand ♠-stone ☆-little shade ⊕ᵗ-partly shaded ♣-mainly shaded
🏠-bungalows for hire 🚐-caravans for hire ▲-tents for hire 🦮-no dogs **Prices:** 🛉-adult per night 🚗-car per night
pp-per person per night 🚐-caravan per night ▲-tent per night

SÃO JACINTO BEIRA LITORAL

Orbitur 3800-901 ☎ 234 838284 📠 234838122
e-mail: info@orbitur.pt **website:** www.orbitur.pt
In a dense pine wood seawards from the uneven, paved road
from Ovar which runs alongside the lagoon.
➲ *1.5km from the sea.*
Open: Feb-Nov **Site:** 2.2HEC ⠿ ♣ 🛖 **Prices:** ⚡2-3.50
🚐1.80-3.40 🚙2.40-4.70 ▲2.20-3.60 **Facilities:** ⫞ 🛒 ⊙ 🔌 ⵁ
🅿 **Services:** 🍴 ✗ lau **Leisure:** ↘ R **Off-site:** ↘RS

SÃO PEDRO DE MOEL ESTREMADURA

Orbitur 2430 ☎ 244 599168 📠 244 599148
e-mail: info@orbitur.pt **website:** www.orbitur.pt
On a hill amidst pine trees.
➲ *Off road No 242-2 from Marinha Grande at the*
roundabout near the SHELL petrol station on the E outskirts of
the village and drive N for 100mtrs.
Open: All year **Site:** 7HEC ⠿ ♣ 🛖 🚙 **Prices:** ⚡2.20-4.30
🚐1.10-3.80 🚙2.90-5.50 ▲2.50-4.60 **Facilities:** ⫞ 🛒 ⊙ 🔌 ⵁ
🅿 **Services:** 🍴 ✗ 🏥 lau **Leisure:** ↘ P **Off-site:** 🛒 ✗ ↘PS

VISEU BEIRA ALTA

Orbitur Fontelo, 3500 ☎ 232 436146 📠 232 432076
e-mail: info@orbitur.pt
website: www.orbitur.pt
A pleasant, quiet site in a rural location.
➲ *Access via N2.*
Open: Apr-Sep **Site:** 3HEC ⠿ ◊ ♣ **Facilities:** ⫞ 🛒 ⊙ 🔌 ⵁ
🅿 **Services:** 🍴 ✗ 🏥 lau **Off-site:** 🛒 ✗

A rugged castle at the northern tip of Marao

Facilities: 🛒-shop ⫞-shower ⊙-electric points for razors 🔌-electric points for caravans 🅿-parking by tents permitted
🅿-compulsory separate car park **Services:** ✗-café/restaurant 🍴-bar ⵁ-Camping Gaz International ⵚ-gas other than Camping
Gaz 🏥-first aid facilities lau-laundry **Leisure:** ↘-swimming L-Lake P-Pool R-River S-Sea **Off-site:** All facilities within 2km

SPAIN

Rich in history and natural beauty, Spain is bordered by Andorra and France in the north and by Portugal in the west.

FACTS AND FIGURES
Capital: Madrid
Area: 504,782 sq km (194,897 sq miles)
Population: 39,371,147 (1998)
Language: Spanish (Castilian), Catalan, Galician, Basque
IDD code: 34. To call the UK dial 00 44

Currency: Euro
Local time: GMT + 1 (summer GMT + 2)
Emergency Services: Police, Fire and Ambulance 112.
Banks: Mon-Fri 08.30-14.30 (most banks are closed on Sats).
Shops: Mon-Sat 09.00-13.00 and 16.30-19.30.

Average daily temperatures: Madrid
Jan 4°C   Jul 24°C
Mar 9°C   Sep19°C
May 16°C   Nov 8°C
Tourist Information:
UK Spanish National Tourist Office, 22-23 Manchester Sq., London W1U 3PX
Tel (020) 7486 8077

USA 666 Fifth Avenue, 35th Floor, New York, NY 10103. Tel: (212) 265 8822
Tourist info website:
www.okspain.org

Central Spain is mountainous and barren while the coastline can be extremely rocky. Some of the most popular holiday areas in Europe are in Spain, the best known being the Costa Brava, the Costa Blanca, the Costa Dorada and the Costa del Sol. More recently, the island of Ibiza has become a very popular destination for young clubbers. All these regions offer fine, sandy and safe beaches. Spain has a varied climate; temperate in the north, dry and hot in the south and in the Balearic Islands. Languages spoken are Spanish, Catalan, Basque and Galician. Spanish has developed from Castilian and there are many local dialects spoken thoughout the provinces.

Sites are numerous on the Costa Brava and elsewhere along the coast, but there are not many inland. They are officially classified according to the facilities and services provided and their classification should be displayed at the site entrance and on any literature. If you intend visiting sites at popular resorts along the coast between late spring and mid-October, it is not generally possible to book in advance. The best advice is to arrive before midday when the new charge begins. Late spring is recommended, as the intense heat of mid-summer is avoided and sites and roads are less congested. Opening dates vary considerably and some sites are open all year. Information about campsites and a detailed guide book are available from the Spanish National Tourist Office (see *Tourist Information*) and local tourist information offices.

Hire of equipment is not generally possible, but some campsites have bungalow accommodation.

Off-site camping is generally prohibited. Permission to camp off an official campsite must be obtained from the landowner or local police. **Camp fires are absolutely forbidden.** Free camping near to beaches, rivers, towns or established campsites is forbidden.

How to Get There

There are direct ferry services to Spain. The services and minimum sailing times are **Plymouth** to **Santander** (24hrs) and **Portsmouth** to **Bilbao** (27hrs). Alternatively, using Eurotunnel or the Channel ports, approach Spain by passing either end of the Pyrenean mountains. For **central and southern Spain** take the Biarritz to San Sebastian (Donostia) road or motorway at the western end.

For **the Costa Brava and beyond** take the Perpignan to Barcelona road, or motorway, at the eastern end of the mountains. **For Andorra** from France via Pas de la Casa (6860ft) then over the Envalira Pass (7897ft). Nov - Apr roads through the central Pyrénées may sometimes be closed. From Spain, the approach via La Seu d'Urgell is always open.

Distance

From Calais to Madrid is about 1,600km (994 miles), usually requiring two or three overnight stops.

Car sleeper trains

Summer services are available from **Calais** to Biarritz, Bordeaux, Brive, Narbonne and Toulouse and **Denderleeuw** (Belgium) to Narbonne.

Travelling the AP132 road among the Mediterranean vegetation of Costa Blanca.

MOTORING & GENERAL INFO

The information given here is specific to Spain and/or Andorra. It **must** be read in conjunction with the Essential Motoring Information at the front of the book, which covers those regulations which are common to many countries.

BRITISH EMBASSY/CONSULATES*

The British Embassy is located at Madrid 28010, Calle de Fernando el Santo 16 ☎ 917008200; consular section, 28004 Madrid, Paseo de Recoletos 7-9, 4a ☎ 915249700. There are British Consulates in Alicante, Barcelona, Bilbao, Málaga and Palma (Majorca); there are British Consulates with Honorary Consuls in Santander and Vigo. There is a British Vice-Consulate in Ibiza and a British Vice-Consulate with Honorary Vice-Consul in Menorca.

CHILDREN IN CARS

Child under 12 not permitted to travel as front seat passengers unless using suitable restraint system. See Essential Motoring Information under 'Passengers' and 'Seat Belts'.

CURRENCY

With the introduction of the Euro, the **Spanish Peseta** (ESP) ceased to be legal tender from 2002. However, ESP coins and notes may still be exchanged at the Spanish Central Bank (**Banco de España**) for an unlimited period.

DIMENSIONS AND WEIGHT RESTRICTIONS*

Private **cars** and towed **trailers** or **caravans** are restricted to the following dimensions - height, 4 metres; width 2.5 metres; length 12 metres. The maximum permitted overall length of private vehicle/trailer or caravan combinations is 18.75 metres.

Trailers with an unladen weight exceeding 750kg must have an independent braking system.

DRIVING LICENCE*

All valid UK or Republic of Ireland licences should be accepted in Spain. This includes the older all-green style UK licences, although the European Commision appreciates that these may be more difficult to understand and that drivers may wish to voluntarily update them before travelling abroad, if time permits. Application form D750 is available from most Post Offices.

Alternatively, older licences may be accompanied by an International Driving Permit (IDP).The minimum age at which visitors from UK or Republic of Ireland may use a temporarily imported motorcycle (over 75cc) or car is 18 years.

FOODSTUFFS*

If the imported foodstuffs are for personal use there are no limits when travelling between EU countries.

LIGHTS*

Visitors must equip their vehicle with a spare set of bulbs. It is compulsory for motorcyclists to use dipped headlights during the day.

MOTORING CLUB

The **Real Automóvil Club de España** (RACE), which has its headquarters at 28760 Tres Cantos, Isaac Newton 4, Parque Technologico de Madrid ☎ 915947400, is associated with local clubs in a number of provincial towns. RACE has three offices in Madrid - 28013 Calle Elroy Gonzalo, 32; 28020 Calle General Peron, 32; 28045 Calle Mendez Alvaro, 33. These offices are open to the public from 08.30-17.30 Mon-Thu and 8.30-14.30 Fri during the summer (June to September) and from 08.30-17.30 Mon-Fri during the winter (Oct to May).
Website: **www.race.net**

ROADS, INC HOLIDAY TRAFFIC

Spain has an excellent network of motorways (mostly toll) and fast dual carriageways (*autovías*). Emergency telephones are located every 2km on both.

The surfaces of the other main roads vary, but on the whole are good. The roads are winding in many places, and at times it is not advisable to exceed 30-35mph. Secondary roads are often rough and winding. Holiday traffic, particularly on the coast road to Barcelona and Tarragona and in the San Sebastian-Donostia area, causes congestion which may be severe at weekends.

In the *Basque* and *Catalan* areas some place names appear on signposts as alternative spellings *eg* San Sebastian-Donostia and Gerona-Girona. The current AA directories and maps show both names.

SPEED LIMITS*

Car/motorcycle
Built-up areas 50km/h (31mph)
Other roads †90km/h (55mph)
††100km/h (62mph)
Motorways 120km/h (74mph)
Car/caravan/trailer
Built-up areas 50km/h (31mph)
Other roads †70km/h (43mph) or
††80km/h (49mph)
Motorways 80km/h (49mph)
†On ordinary roads
††On roads with more than one lane in each direction, a special lane for slow-moving vehicles or wide lanes.

WARNING TRIANGLES*

One warning triangle compulsory for non-Spanish registered vehicles (two for Spanish registered vehicles). The use of a warning triangle is compulsory outside built-up areas when the vehicle (or trailer) is stationary in an area where standing is prohibited. NOTE: Drivers of non-Spanish registered vehicles should consider carrying TWO triangles as, regardless of the regulations, local officials may impose on the spot fines if only one is available.

*Additional information will be found in the Essential Motoring Information at the front of the book.

ANDORRA

Andorra is an independent Principality located high in the
Pyrénées between France and Spain.

Andorra is administered by its own government and independent Legislative Assembly. The constitutional heads of state are its traditional co-princes, the President of France and the Bishop of Seu d'Urgell. Catalan is the official language, but French and Spanish are widely spoken. General regulations for France and Spain apply to Andorra with the following exceptions.

BRITISH CONSULATE*

The British Consulate with Honorary Consul is located at Casa Jacint Pons 3/2, La Massana, Andorra ☎83 98 40.

CHILDREN IN CARS

Child under 10 not permitted as front-seat passenger. See Continental ABC under 'Passengers' and 'Seat Belts'.

CURRENCY*

Andorra has no currency of its own and has traditionally used the French Franc (FRF) and Spanish Peseta (EPS). With the introduction of the Euro and withdrawal of FRF and EPS, Euro banknotes and coins came into circulation from 1 January 2002.

DIMENSIONS

The maximum height for vehicles going through tunnels is 3.5 metres.

DRIVING LICENCE*

A valid UK or Republic of Ireland driving licence is accepted. The minimum age at which a visitor may use a temporarily imported car or motorcycle is 18.

LIGHTS*

Visitors must equip their vehicle with a spare set of bulbs. It is compulsory for motorcyclists to use dipped headlights during the day.

MOTORING CLUB*

The **Automobil Club d'Andorra** (ACA) is the official **Motoring Club**, and has its head office at Andorra, Carrer Babot Camp 13 ☎ 803400. Website: **www.aca.ad**

ROADS

The three main roads in Andorra are prefixed 'N' and numbered; side roads are prefixed 'C'. Andorra has no motorways.

SPEED LIMITS*

Car/motorcycle/car towing caravan/trailer
Built-up areas 50km/h (31mph)
Other roads 90km/h (55mph)
Some villages have a speed limit of 20km/h (12mph).

WARNING TRIANGLE*

It is compulsory for a vehicle to be equipped with a warning triangle and to use it in the event of an accident or breakdown.

*Additional information will be found in the Essential Motoring Information at the front of the book.

NORTH EAST COAST

BEGUR GIRONA

Begur CTRA. D'Esclanya km2, 17255
☎ 972 623201 ▤ 972 624566
e-mail: info@campingbegur.com
website: www.campingbegur.com
A terraced site in a wooded valley.
⮑ 1.4kmtrs SE of town and right of the road to Palafrugell, 400mtrs after the turn towards Fornells and Aiguablava.
Open: 08 Apr-25 Sep Site: 8HEC ﹏ ∵∵ ♣ ⬛ 🚐
Prices: ♠2-3.50 pitch 9.50-18.40 Facilities: ♠ ⊙ 🖴 ﹏ 🖆 Services: 🍴 ✕ 🚻 lau Leisure: ⮑ P Off-site: 🖴 🌢 ⮑RS

Maset Playa de sa Riera, 17255 ☎ 972 623023 ▤ 972 623901
e-mail: campingelmaset@telefonica.net
website: www.campingelmaset.com
A well-kept terraced site, divided into pitches in a beautiful valley, 300mtrs from the sea.
⮑ 2km N of Begur. If entering from the W, turn left just before reaching the town.
Open: 02 Apr-25 Sep Site: 1.2HEC ∵∵ ♣ ⬛ 🚐 🌢
Prices: ♠4.20-5.80 🚗4-5.20 🚐5.30-7.40 ▲4.60-6.80
Facilities: ♠ 🖴 ⊙ 🖴 🌢 🖆 Services: 🍴 ✕ 🚻 lau Leisure: ⮑ P Off-site: ⮑S

BLANES GIRONA

Bella Terra av Villa de Madrid, 17300
☎ 972 348017 ▤ 972 348275
e-mail: cbellaterra@cbellaterra.com
website: www.cbelleterra.com
A large family site in a luxuriant pinewood beside the beach with good, modern facilities.
⮑ Access via main N11.
Open: Apr-Sep Site: 10.5HEC ﹏ ∵∵ ♣ ⬛ 🚐
Prices: ♠3.61 pitch 10.62-17.70 Facilities: ♠ 🖴 ⊙ 🖴 🌢 🖆
Services: 🍴 ✕ 🚻 lau Leisure: ⮑ PS

Blanes Avenida Villa de Madrid 33, 17300
☎ 972 331591 ▤ 972 337063
e-mail: info@campingblanes.com
website: www.campingblanes.com
In a pine forest bordering the beach, 1km from the town centre.
⮑ On left of the Paseo Villa de Madrid coast road towards town.
Open: All year Site: 2HEC ∵∵ ♣ Prices: ♠4.28-5.62 pitch 12.68-16.27 Facilities: ♠ 🖴 ⊙ 🖴 🌢 🖆 Services: 🍴 ✕ 🚻 lau Leisure: ⮑ PS Off-site: ⮑R

Masia c Colon 44, Los Pinos, 17300
☎ 972 331013 ▤ 972 333128
e-mail: info@campinglamasia.com
website: www.campinglamasia.com
A pleasant family site on level ground with shady pitches, 150mtrs from the sea.
⮑ 50mtrs inland from Paseo Villa de Madrid coast road.
Open: 16 Jan-14 Dec Site: 9HEC ﹏ ♦ ♣ ⬛ Prices: ♠4.10-5.50 ▲6.55-10.70 pitch 12-21.35 Facilities: ♠ 🖴 ⊙ 🖴 🌢 🖆
Services: 🍴 ✕ 🚻 lau Leisure: ⮑ PRS Off-site: 🖴 🍴 ✕ 🌢 ⮑P

Pinar av Villa de Madrid, 17300 ☎ 972 331083
Divided into two by the coastal road. Partially meadow under poplars.
⮑ 1km on Paseo Villa de Madrid coast road.
Open: Apr-Sep Site: 5HEC ﹏ ∵∵ ♣ ⬛ Facilities: ♠ 🖴 ⊙ 🖴 🌢 🖆 Services: 🍴 ✕ 🚻 lau Leisure: ⮑ S

S'Abanell av Villa Madrid 7-9, 17300
☎ 972 331809 ▤ 972 350506
e-mail: info@sabanell.com website: www.sabanell.com
Within a pine wood, a section of which is inland and open to the public.
⮑ On either side of the Avenida Villa de Madrid road. Off coast road S of Blanes.
Open: 8 Jan-23 Dec Site: 3.3HEC ∵∵ ♣ ⬛ 🚐 Facilities: ♠ 🖴 ⊙ 🖴 🌢 🖆 Services: 🍴 ✕ 🚻 lau Leisure: ⮑ S

CALELLA DE LA COSTA BARCELONA

Botanic Bona Vista Ctra. N2 KM 665, 08370
☎ 93 7692488 ▤ 93 7695804
e-mail: info@botanic-bonavista.net
website: www.botanic-bonavista.net
Totally subdivided and well tended terraced site on a hillside, beautifully landscaped. Internal roads steep. Access to beach via pedestrian underpass.
Camping Card Compulsory.
⮑ Turn off the N11 at Km665. Site immediately round a blind corner.
Open: All year Site: 3.4HEC ∵∵ 🔆 ♣ Facilities: ♠ 🖴 ⊙ 🖴 🌢 🖆 Services: 🍴 ✕ 🚻 lau Leisure: ⮑ S Off-site: ⮑P

Far 08370 ☎ 93 7690967 ▤ 93 7690967
e-mail: elfar@reset.es website: www.publintur.es/elfar.htm
Terraced site on a hillock under deciduous trees with lovely view of Calella and out to sea. Steep internal roads.
⮑ For access, travel S before reaching a major left hand bend at Km666 to the right of the N11.
Open: Apr-Sep Site: 2.5HEC ∵∵ 🔆 ⬛ Facilities: ♠ 🖴 ⊙ 🖴 🌢 🖆 Services: 🍴 ✕ 🚻 lau Off-site: ⛲ ⮑PS

CASTELL D'ARO GIRONA

Castell d'Aro crta S'Agaro, 17249 ☎ 972 819699 ▤ 972 819699
e-mail: campingcastelldaro@yahoo.es
A quiet family site, 2km from the beach, with good recreational facilities.
⮑ Access at Km1 on S'Agaró road.
Open: May-Sep Site: 8HEC ﹏ ♣ ⬛ Prices: ♠3.50-4.69 pitch 13-16.22 Facilities: ♠ 🖴 ⊙ 🖴 🌢 🖆 Services: 🍴 ✕ 🚻 lau Leisure: ⮑ P Off-site: ⮑S

CASTELLÓ D'EMPURIES GIRONA

Castell-Mar Platja de la Rubina, 17486
☎ 972 450822 ▤ 972 452330
e-mail: cmar@campingparks.com
website: www.campingparks.com
A modern family site close to the beach on the extremity of a National Park.
⮑ From A7 exit 3 or 4 (Figueres) follow C260 through Castello d'Empuries towards Roses.
Open: 15 May-26 Sep Site: 4HEC ﹏ ∵∵ 🔆 ⬛ ▲
Prices: ♠3 pitch 8-30 Facilities: ♠ 🖴 ⊙ 🖴 🌢 🖆 Services: 🍴 ✕ 🚻 lau Leisure: ⮑ PS

Mas-Nou Crta. Figueres a Roses, km38, 17486
☎ 972 454175 ▤ 972 454358
e-mail: info@masnou.com
website: www.campingmasnou.com
A family site with good recreational facilities, 2.5km from the coast.
⮑ Exit from the Figueres-Roses road at Km38.
Open: 3 Apr-26 Sep Site: 9.8HEC ﹏ 🔆 ⬛ Prices: ♠4.01-6.37 🚗4.01-6.37 🚐4.01-6.37 ▲4.01-6.37 Facilities: ♠ ⊙ 🖴 🖆 Services: 🍴 ✕ 🚻 lau Leisure: ⮑ P Off-site: 🖴 🌢 ⮑RS

Site: 6HEC-Site size ﹏-grass ∵∵-sand ♦-stone 🔆-little shade 🔆-partly shaded ♣-mainly shaded
⬛-bungalows for hire 🚐-caravans for hire ▲-tents for hire ✀-no dogs Prices: ♠-adult per night 🚗-car per night
pp-per person per night 🚐-caravan per night ▲-tent per night

Nautic Almanta 17486 ☎ 972 454477 ▤ 972 454686
e-mail: info@almata.com website: www.almata.com
Level meadowland, no shade, good facilities, reaching as far
as the sea. Alongside the River Fluvia which has been made
into a canal. Boating is possible in the canal which flows into
the sea.
⮕ *Turn S at Km11 on C260, approx, halfway along the road
and turn E along the track and continue 2.2km.*
Open: 15 May-19 Sep Site: 22HEC ▥▥▥ ⌕ ⌂ Å
Prices: ⭢1.60-3.20 pitch 17.50-35 Facilities: ⓝ ⚑ ☉ ◪ ⌀ ☎
Services: ⛆ ✗ ⊞ lau Leisure: ⭢ PRS

CUBELLES BARCELONA

La Rueda Ctra.C-31 KM146,2, 8880
☎ 938 950207 ▤ 938 950347
e-mail: larueda@la-rueda.com website: www.la-rueda.com
Level terrain between road and railway. Access to beach by
means of an underpass.
⮕ *The site lies about 1km N of Cunit near C-31, km 146.2*
Site: 6HEC ▥▥▥ ⌕ ⌂ Prices: ⭢3.20-5.33 pitch 9.59-15.99
Facilities: ⓝ ⚑ ☉ ◪ ⌀ ☎ Services: ⛆ ✗ ⊞ lau Leisure: ⭢ PS

ESCALA, L' GIRONA

Maite Playa Riells, 17310 ☎ 972 770544 ▤ 972 770599
e-mail: maite@campings.net
website: www.campings.net/maite
An extensive site, lying inland, but near the sea, at a small
lake. Partly on a hillock under pine trees.
⮕ *The access is well signed from the outskirts of L'Escala on
the road towards Cala Montgo.*
Site: 6HEC ▥▥▥ ⚑ Prices: ⭢4.50 ⛟4.50 Å4.50 Facilities: ⓝ ⚑
☉ ◪ ⌀ ☎ Services: ⛆ ✗ ⊞ Leisure: ⭢ LS

Neus Cala Montgó, 17130 ☎ 972 770403 ▤ 972 772751
e-mail: info@campingneus.com
website: www.campingneus.com
Peaceful situation among pine trees, 800 metres from the
beach.
Open: Jun-15 Sep Site: 4HEC ⋮⋮⋮ ⚑ Prices: ⭢3.85-5.02 pitch
11.23-16.74 Facilities: ⓝ ⚑ ☉ ◪ ⌀ ☎ Services: ⛆ ✗ ⊞ lau
Leisure: ⭢ P Off-site: ✗ ⭢S

ESTARTIT, L' GIRONA

Castell Montgri 17258 ☎ 972 751630 ▤ 972 750906
e-mail: c.montgri@campingparks.com
website: www.campingparks.com
On a large terraced meadow in pine woodlands.
⮕ *100mtrs N of GE road from Torroella de Montgri and
about 0.5km before L'Estartit on a hillock.*
Open: 08 May-3 Oct Site: 25HEC ▥▥▥ ⚑ ⌂ ⛟ Å Prices: ⭢3
pitch 9-2 Facilities: ⓝ ⚑ ☉ ◪ ⌀ ☎ Services: ⛆ ✗ ⊞ lau
Leisure: ⭢ P Off-site: ⭢S
See advertisement on page 324

Estartit Cap Villa Primavera 12, 17258
☎ 972 751909 ▤ 972 750991
In a valley on sloping ground which is rather steep in places.
Some terraces, shaded by pine trees.
⮕ *It is located about 200mtrs from the church and the road
from Torroella de Montgri.*
Open: Apr-Sep Site: 2.5HEC ⋮⋮⋮ ⚑ ⌂ Å ⚒ Prices: ⭢4.25
⛟4 ⛟4.70 Å4.50 Facilities: ⓝ ⚑ ☉ ◪ ☎ Services: ⛆ ✗ ⊞
lau Leisure: ⭢ LPRS Off-site: ⌀

Medes 17258 ☎ 972 751805 ▤ 972 750413
e-mail: campinglesmedes@cambrescat.es
website: www.campinglesmedes.com
Quiet holiday site in rural surroundings with clearly marked
pitches and good modern facilities.

CAMPING · CARAVANING
La Rueda
CUBELLES
**Catalonien Tourism
Merits Medal**

On the Costa Daurada, between BARCELONA and
TARRAGONA, near tourist sites and PORT
AVENTURA. Situated on the C-31, km 146,2,
between Cubellas and Cunit at only 100 m from the
beach. Hot water and swimming pool free.
Horseback riding, tennis etc. close by. Consult our
low-season fees. **20 % P/N red. with carnet CCI.**

INFORMATION and RESERVATION:

www.la-rueda.com
(in English)

Email: larueda@la-rueda.com
Aptdo. Correos 261 E-08880 Cubelles.
Tel. (0034) 938 950 207
Fax (0034) 938 950 347

⮕ *Turn right off GE641 from Torroella di Montgri by Km5
and continue for 1.5km .*
Open: Dec-Oct Site: 2.6HEC ▥▥▥ ⋮⋮⋮ ⌕ ⌂ ⚒
Prices: ⭢3.10-5.30 ⛟6.90-11.90 pitch 7.06-11.98
Facilities: ⓝ ⚑ ☉ ◪ ⌀ ☎ Services: ⛆ ✗ ⊞ lau Leisure: ⭢ P
Off-site: ⭢S

Molino 17258 ☎ 972 750629 ▤ 972 750629
e-mail: branders@teleline.es
Divided into several sections of open meadowland near the
beach on grassland with young poplars. The reconstructed
mill is a landmark.
⮕ *Approaching from Torroella de Montgri turn right on
entering L'Estartit and follow signs.*
Open: Apr-Sep Site: 10HEC ▥▥▥ ⌕ Facilities: ⓝ ⚑ ☉ ◪ ⌀
☎ ⊡ Services: ⛆ ✗ ⊞ lau Leisure: ⭢ S Off-site: ⭢R

GUARDIOLA DE BERGUEDA BARCELONA

El Bergueda 8694 ☎ 93 8227432 ▤ 93 8227432
e-mail: campingbergueda@worldonline.es
website: www.campingbergueda.com
A peaceful site in the middle of a forest at an altitude of
900mtrs with a wide variety of sporting facilities.
⮕ *On B400.*
Open: 24 Jun-1 Sep Site: 3HEC ▥▥▥ ⌕ ⚑ ⌂ ⛟ Prices: ⭢4.28
⛟4.28 ⛟4.28 Å4.28 Facilities: ⓝ ⚑ ☉ ◪ ⌀ ⚒ ☎
Services: ⛆ ✗ ⊞ lau Leisure: ⭢ P Off-site: ⭢R

GUILS DE CERDANYA GIRONA

Pirineus ctra Guils de Cerdanya, 17528
☎ 972 881062 ▤ 972 882471
e-mail: guils@stel.es website: www.stel.es
In a fine, level location at an altitude of 1200mtrs affording
fine views over the Cerdanya Valley.
contd.

Facilities: ⚑-shop ⓝ-shower ☉-electric points for razors ◪-electric points for caravans ☎-parking by tents permitted
⊡-compulsory separate car park Services: ✗-café/restaurant ⛆-bar ⌀-Camping Gaz International ⚒-gas other than Camping
Gaz ⊞-first aid facilities lau-laundry Leisure: ⭢-swimming L-Lake P-Pool R-River S-Sea Off-site: All facilities within 2km

➲ *On the main Puigcerda-Guils de Cerdanya road.*
Open: 18 Jun-12 Sep Site: 5HEC ⊞ ♣ 🏠 ⊗ Prices: ♠5.14
pitch 18.19 Facilities: 🏠 🗮 ⊙ 🗐 ⌀ 🎫 Services: 🍴 ✕ 🖽 lau
Leisure: ⌇ P

LLORET DE MAR GIRONA

Tucan Ctra. de Lloret a Blanes,S/N, 17310
☎ 972 369965 📠 972 360079
e-mail: info@campingtucan.com
website: www.campingtucan.com
A modern family site, close to the sea, with plenty of
recreational facilities.
➲ *Access via A7 exit 9 to Lloret de Mar.*
Open: May-Sep Site: 4HEC ⫶⫶⫶ ⊕ 🏠 🗮 🛆 Facilities: 🏠 🗮
⊙ 🗐 ⌀ 🎫 Services: 🍴 ✕ 🖽 lau Leisure: ⌇ P Off-site: 🎪 ⌇S

MALGRAT DE MAR BARCELONA

Naciones 08380 ☎ 93 7654153
Level site divided by a small stream. Partially dusty, another
part in meadow under high poplars.
➲ *Approach road passes through Camping Malgrat de Mar.*
Site: 9.7HEC ⊞ ⊕ ♣ 🗯 Facilities: 🏠 🗮 ⊙ 🗐 ⌀ 🎫 🎫
Services: 🍴 ✕ 🖽 lau Leisure: ⌇ PS

MASNOU, EL BARCELONA

Masnou ctra Nac 2, 8320 ☎ 93 5551503 📱 93 5551503
e-mail: campingmasnou@hotmail.com
A well equipped site in wooded surroundings, 150mtrs from
the beach on the Costa del Maresme.
➲ *Inland from the N11 at Km633.*
Open: Jun-Sep Site: 2HEC ⊞ ⊕ 🏠 🛆 Facilities: 🏠 🗮 ⊙ 🗐
⌀ 🎫 🎫 Services: 🍴 ✕ 🖽 lau Leisure: ⌇ PS

PALAFRUGELL GIRONA

AT LLAFRANC

Kim's Font d'En Xeco 1, 17211 ☎ 972 301156 📱 972 610894
e-mail: info@campingkims.com
website: www.campingkims.com/
Terraced site with winding drives, lying on the wooded slopes
of a narrow valley leading to the sea.
➲ *For access, turn right off the Palafrugell-Tamariu road,
follow a wide tarred road for 1km, past the El Paranso Hotel
and head towards Llafranc. 0.4km from sea.*
Open: May-Sep Site: 5.8HEC ⊞ ⫶⫶⫶ ⊕ 🏠 Prices: ♠2.25-
4.50 pitch 12-22.55 Facilities: 🏠 🗮 ⊙ 🗐 ⌀ 🎫 Services: 🍴 ✕
🖽 lau Leisure: ⌇ P Off-site: ⌇S

Site: 6HEC-Site size ⊞-grass ⫶⫶⫶-sand ⊕-stone ⋇-little shade ⊕-partly shaded ♣-mainly shaded
🏠-bungalows for hire 🗯-caravans for hire 🛆-tents for hire 🗯-no dogs Prices: ♠-adult per night 🗯-car per night
pp-per person per night 🗯-caravan per night 🛆-tent per night

At Montrás (3km SW)

Relax-Ge 17253 ☎ 972 301549 📠 972 601100
e-mail: campingpal@grn.es
website: www.campingrelaxge.com
Level meadow under poplars and olive trees.
⮕ *Turn off the C255 at Km38.7. 4km to the sea.*
Open: Jun-Aug Site: 3HEC ⛺ ⚍ 🏠 Prices: 🏕5 pitch 9-15
Facilities: ℞ ℟ ⊙ 🔌 🗓 Services: 🍴 ✗ 🏥 lau Leisure: 🏊 P
Off-site: 🏊S

At Playa De Ensueños

Tamariu 17212 ☎ 972 620422 📠 972 620422
e-mail: campingtamariu@teleline.es
Terraced site with mixture of high young pines. Direct access
to the beach.
⮕ *Turn towards site at beach parking area and continue
300mtrs.*
Open: May-Sep Site: 2HEC ⛺ ♠ ⚍ Facilities: ℞ ℟ ⊙ 🔌
🔌 🗓 Services: 🍴 ✗ 🏥 lau Leisure: 🏊 PS Off-site: ℟ 🍴 ✗ 🔌 🏥

Palamós Girona

Castell Park 17230 ☎ 972 315263 📠 972 315263
Level and gently sloping meadow with poplars and pine
woodland on a hill.
⮕ *At Km40 about 100mtrs to the right of the C255 to Palamós
and 3km S of Montras.*
Site: 4.5HEC ⛺ ♠ 🏠 Prices: 🏕2.70-4.40 pitch 10-17
Facilities: ℞ ℟ ⊙ 🔌 🔌 🗓 Services: 🍴 ✗ 🏥 lau Leisure: 🏊 P
Off-site: 🏊S

Coma Ronda Est, 17230 ☎ 972 314638 📠 972 315470
e-mail: lacoma@campinglacoma.com
website: www.campinglacoma.com
Sloping terraced terrain with young deciduous trees and
isolated pines. 0.8km from the sea.
⮕ *In N outskirts turn seawards off the C255 near the Renault
garage.*
Open: Apr-Sep Site: 5.2HEC ⛺ ♠ 🏠 Facilities: ℞ ℟ ⊙
🔌 🔌 🗓 Services: 🍴 ✗ 🏥 lau Leisure: 🏊 P Off-site: 🏊S

Internacional Palamós Playa de la Fosca, 17230
☎ 972 314736 📠 972 317626
A family site in a picturesque wooded location close to the
beach.
⮕ *Signposted.*
Open: Jul-Sep Site: 5.2HEC ⌗ ♠ 🏠 ⚍ ⅄ Facilities: ℞ ℟
⊙ 🔌 🗓 Services: 🍴 ✗ 🏥 lau Leisure: 🏊 PS Off-site: 🔌

Palamós ctra la Fosca 12, 17230
☎ 972 314296 📠 972 601100
e-mail: campingpal@grn.es
website: www.campingpalamos.com
In a picturesque situation on a wooded headland overlooking
the sea.
Open: 29 Mar-Sep Site: 5.5HEC ⛺ ⌗ ⚍ 🏠 ⚍ ⅄
Prices: 🏕4.75-5.25 pitch 10-18.50 Facilities: ℞ ℟ ⊙ 🔌 🔌 🗓
Services: 🍴 ✗ 🏥 lau Leisure: 🏊 PS Off-site: 🗑

Vilarromá calle del Mar-Avda catalunya, 17230
☎ 972 314375 📠 972 314375
e-mail: camping@vilarroma.es
website: www.campingvilarroma.com
Clean and tidy site, almost completely divided into pitches.
⮕ *Turn off on the eastern outskirts of Palamós near big petrol
station.*
Open: Apr-25 Sep Site: 1.8HEC ⛺ ♠ 🏠 ⚍ Prices: 🏕4.49-
4.81 ⛺4.81-6.09 ⚍4.70-8.34 ⅄4.70-8.34 Facilities: ℞ ℟ ⊙
🔌 🔌 🗓 Services: 🍴 ✗ 🏥 lau Off-site: ✗ 🗑 🏊LPS

camping - caravaning - bungalow

INTERNACIONAL PALAMÓS

ADAC 2003

Costa BRAVA

E-17230 PALAMOS
Apartado correos 100
Tel. 34+972 31 47 36
Fax 34+972 31 76 26

Modern, quiet family site, very near to the
beautiful **PLAYA DE FOSCA (La Fosca each) and in the
centre of the COSTA BRAVA.** Lots of shade from trees and many
flowers give you the impression of being in a garden. 3.000 sqm. of green
area with swimming pools, solarium and all install. of a good holiday site,
incl free hot water 24 hours a day. Bungalows tents 'Trigano' (4 pers.),
mobile homes (6 pers.) and wooden bungalows 'Campitel' for rent.
**There are more sites nearby, with mainly national campers.
Be sure to visit our site. Exemplary sanitary blocks.**

Acces: Take exit towards Palamós-Norte and continue
towards Playa de la Fosca.   Open: Easter - Sept.

At Calonge (5km W)

Cala Gogo 17251 ☎ 972 651564 📠 972 650553
e-mail: calagogo@calagogo.es website: www.calagogo.es
Terraced site in tall pine woodland and poplars with some
good views of the sea. Underpass across to section of site
with private beach. Some internal dusty roads
⮕ *Access from Palamós 4 km S on coastal road C253, entrance
to site on right shortly after Km47.*
Open: 12 Apr-28 Sep Site: 16HEC ⌗ 🏠 ⚍ ⅄ 🐾
Facilities: ℞ ℟ ⊙ 🔌 🔌 Services: 🍴 ✗ 🏥 lau Leisure: 🏊 PS

Internacional de Calonge 17250
☎ 972 651233 📠 972 652507
e-mail: intercalonge@intercalonge.com
website: www.intercalonge.com
Set on a pine covered hill overlooking the sea within easy
reach of a sandy beach.
⮕ *On the coast road between Platja d'Aro and Palamós.*
Open: All year Site: 13HEC ⌗ ♠ 🏠 ⅄ Prices: 🏕3.40-6.05
⅄11.75-21.10 pitch 12-22 Facilities: ℞ ℟ ⊙ 🔌 🔌 🗓
Services: 🍴 ✗ 🏥 lau Leisure: 🏊

See advertisement on page 326

Pals Girona

Cypsela 17256 ☎ 972 667696 📠 972 667300
e-mail: info@cypsela.com website: www.cypsela.com
Well-kept grassy site in a pine wood.
⮕ *For access, turn towards the sea N of Pals and follow road
towards Playa de Pals, then turn left after Km3.*
Open: 15 May-26 Sep Site: 20HEC ⌗ ♠ 🏠 ⚍ 🐾
Prices: 🏕5.30 pitch 16.47-28.56 Facilities: ℞ ℟ ⊙ 🔌 🔌 🗓 🅿
Services: 🍴 ✗ 🏥 lau Leisure: 🏊 P Off-site: 🏊S

Facilities: ℟-shop **℞**-shower **⊙**-electric points for razors **🔌**-electric points for caravans **🗓**-parking by tents permitted
🅿-compulsory separate car park **Services: ✗**-café/restaurant **🍴**-bar **🔌**-Camping Gaz International **🗑**-gas other than Camping
Gaz **🏥**-first aid facilities **lau**-laundry **Leisure: 🏊**-swimming **L**-Lake **P**-Pool **R**-River **S**-Sea **Off-site:** All facilities within 2km

Priviliged situation in the very heart of the famous COSTA BRAVA, between Palamós and Platja de Aro (follow indication signs "Sant Antoni, Platja d'Aro i Platges"), on a beautiful pine covered hill overlooking the sea, you will find one of the most beautiful camping and caravanning sites of Spain, 55 yards from a lovely sandy beach surrounded by rocks and with private access. Magnificent installations, including swimming pools (a new one is just completed), restaurant, bar, superm., tennis courts, hairdressers, free hot water, etc. Guarded day and night. English spoken.
Reservation and information:
Apto. Correos 272, E-17250 Platja d'Aro (Girona).
Tel. (34) 972 651 233
COMPLETELY EQUIPPED MOBILE HOMES, Fax 972 652 507
BUNGALOWS AND TENTS FOR HIRE.
www.intercalonge.com•intercalonge@intercalonge.com
OPEN THROUGHOUT THE YEAR.

Mas Patoxas 17256 ☎ 972 636928 ▤ 972 667349
e-mail: info@campingmaspatoxas.com
website: www.campingmaspatoxas.com
A family site in a quiet location close to the sea. Good, modern sanitary blocks and plenty of recreational facilities.
➲ *At Km5 on Palafrugell to Torroella.*
Open: Apr-Sep Site: 5.5HEC ⬛ ♣ 🏠 🚐 ⚓ Facilities: 🅿 ⚓ ⊙ 🚱 ⌀ 🏧 🏢 Services: 🍴 ✗ ⊞ lau Leisure: ⤳ P

AT PLAYA DE PALS

Playa Brava 17256 ☎ 972 636894 ▤ 972 636952
e-mail: info@playabrava.com website: www.playabrava.com
On level terrain adjoining pine woodlands, golf course, rivers and sea.
➲ *From N end of village of Pals turn towards sea and Playa de Pals.*
Open: 15 May-19 Sep Site: 11HEC ⬛ ⁛ ♣ ⚹
Prices: ⚹1.87-2.67 pitch 21.40-32.10 Facilities: 🅿 ⚓ ⊙ 🚱 🏢 Services: 🍴 ✗ ⊞ lau Leisure: ⤳ LPRS Off-site: ⚓ 🍴 ✗ ⌀

PINEDA DE MAR BARCELONA

Camell Ada de los Naranjos 12, 08397
☎ 93 7671520 ▤ 93 7670270
e-mail: campingcamell@teleline.es
Surrounded by deciduous trees next to a small wood owned by the Taurus Hotel.
➲ *Turn off the N11 at Km670 and drive along av de los Naranjos in direction of sea.*
Open: May-Sep Site: 2.2HEC ⁛ ♣ Prices: ⚹3.90 pitch 11.30 Facilities: 🅿 ⚓ ⊙ 🚱 ⌀ 🏢 Services: 🍴 ✗ ⊞ lau Leisure: ⤳ PS Off-site: ✗

PLATJA D'ARO, LA GIRONA

Valldaro ctra Santa Cristina 113, 17250
☎ 972 817515 ▤ 972 816662
e-mail: valldaro@valldaro.com website: www.valldaro.com
Extensive level meadowland under poplars, pines and eucalyptus trees. Some large pitches without shade.
➲ *Site lies on the left of the GE662 towards Castell and Santa Cristinia d 'Aro at Km4.*
Open: 26 Mar-03 Oct Site: 20HEC ⬛ ♣ 🏠 🚐
Prices: ⚹3.25-4.95 pitch 14.50-24.75 Facilities: 🅿 ⚓ ⊙ 🚱 ⌀ 🏢 Services: 🍴 ✗ ⊞ lau Leisure: ⤳ P Off-site: ⤳S

PUIGCERDÀ GIRONA

Stel ctra Llivia, 17520 ☎ 972 882361 ▤ 972 140419
e-mail: puigcerda@stel.es website: www.stel.es
Modern campsite in the Pyrenees on level land. Has wonderful views of the mountains and surrounding area. First class sanitary installations.
➲ *Access via N340 between Comarruga and Tarragona.*
Open: 28 May-26 Sep Site: 7HEC ⬛ ⚓ 🏠 Prices: ⚹5.14 pitch 18.19 Facilities: 🅿 ⚓ ⊙ 🚱 ⌀ 🏢 Services: 🍴 ✗ ⊞ lau Leisure: ⤳ P

RIPOLL GIRONA

Solana del Ter 17500 ☎ 972 701062 ▤ 972 714343
e-mail: hotel@solanadelter.com
website: www.solanadelter.com
In a peaceful location close to the local ski resorts at the foot of the Pyrenees. Part of a small hotel/restaurant complex.
Open: May-Oct Site: 8.5HEC ⬛ ⚓ Facilities: 🅿 ⊙ 🚱 🏢 Services: 🍴 ✗ ⊞ lau Leisure: ⤳ P Off-site: ⚓

SALDES BARCELONA

Repos del Pedraforca 08697 ☎ 93 8258044 ▤ 93 8258061
e-mail: pedra@campingpedraforca.com
website: www.campingpedraforca.com
A well equipped site sitauted in an area of natural beauty.
Open: All year Site: 4HEC ⬛ ♣ ⚓ 🏠 ⚓ Prices: ⚹3.94-4.92 pitch 9.97-12.97 Facilities: 🅿 ⚓ ⊙ 🚱 ⌀ 🏢 Services: 🍴 ✗ lau Leisure: ⤳ P Off-site: ⤳LR

SANTA CRISTINA D'ARO GIRONA

Mas St Josep 17246 Santa Cristina d'Aro, Costa Brava, 17246
☎ 972 835081 ▤ 972 837018
e-mail: info@campingmassantjosep.com
website: www.campingmassantjosep.com
A family site with plenty of recreational facilities.
➲ *At Km2 on the main Sta. Cristina d'Aro road.*
Open: 28 May-20 Sep Site: 35HEC ⁛ ♣ 🏠 Prices: ⚹5.90-6.90 🚐14.40-18.30 ⚓14.40-18.30 pitch 14.40-18.30 Facilities: 🅿 ⚓ ⊙ 🚱 ⌀ 🏢 Services: 🍴 ✗ ⊞ lau Leisure: ⤳ P

SANT ANTONI DE CALONGE GIRONA

Euro Ctra. Palamos-Platja d'Aro, 17252
☎ 972 650879 ▤ 972 661987
e-mail: info@euro-camping.com
website: www.euro-camping.com
A family site in a peaceful location close to the sea with fine recreational facilities.
➲ *Access via A7 exit 9.*
Open: 3 Apr-26 Sep Site: 13HEC ⬛ ♣ 🏠 Prices: ⚹2.19-5.46 pitch 15.62-25.68 Facilities: 🅿 ⚓ ⊙ 🚱 ⌀ 🏢 Services: 🍴 ✗ ⊞ lau Leisure: ⤳ P Off-site: ⚓ ⤳S

The AA cannot be held responsible for the content of third party websites

Site: 6HEC-Site size ⬛-grass ⁛-sand ♦-stone 🌿-little shade ⚓-partly shaded ♣-mainly shaded
🏠-bungalows for hire 🚐-caravans for hire ⚓-tents for hire ⚹-no dogs Prices: ⚹-adult per night ⚓-car per night
pp-per person per night 🚐-caravan per night ⚓-tent per night

Treumal Apartado de Correos 348, 17251
☎ 972 651095 ▤ 972 651674
e-mail: info@campingtreumal.com
website: www.campingtreumal.com
A peaceful family site in a beautiful location between a pine
wood and the beach.
➲ *Entrance on Sant Feliú-Platja d'Aro-Palamós road.*
Open: Apr-Sep Site: 7HEC ▒▒▒ ⁙⁙⁙ ♣ 🏠 Prices: ⋔3.79-6.85
⊞13.97-24.93 ▲13.35-23.86 Facilities: ⋔ ⒛ ⊙ 🕯 ∅ ⌂
Services: ⛉ ✕ ⊞ lau Leisure: ⋋ PS

SANTA SUSANA BARCELONA

Bon Répos 08398 ☎ 93 7678475 ▤ 93 7678526
e-mail: info@campingbonrepos.com
website: www.campingbonrepos.com
In pine woodland between railway and the beach with some
sunshade roofing.
➲ *Turn off the N11 at Km681 and approach via the
underpass (height 2.5mtrs) just before reaching the beach.*
Open: All year Site: 6HEC ▒▒▒ ⁙⁙⁙ ⚘ 🏠 Facilities: ⋔ ⒛ ⊙
🕯 ∅ ⌂ Services: ⛉ ✕ ⊞ lau Leisure: ⋋ PS Off-site: ⒛ ⛉ ⋋S

SANT CEBRIÁ DE VALLALTA BARCELONA

Verneda av Maresme, 08396 ☎ 93 7631185 ▤ 93 7631185
e-mail: lverneda@teleline.es
Inland and among tall trees.
➲ *Leave the N11 Girona-Barcelona road at the far end of
Sant Pol de Mar, turn inland at Km670. Continue for 2km to
edge of the village and short of the bridge over the River Vallala
turn right.*
Open: Apr-Sep Site: 1.6HEC ⁙⁙⁙ ♣ Facilities: ⋔ ⒛ ⊙ 🕯 ∅
⌂ Services: ⛉ ✕ ⊞ lau Leisure: ⋋ P

SANT FELIU DE GUIXOLS GIRONA

Sant Pol Doctor Fleming, 17220
☎ 972 327269 ▤ 972 327211
e-mail: info@campingsantpol.com
website: www.campingsantpol.com
In wooded surroundings near the beach with good facilities.
➲ *800mtrs from the town centre towards Palamos.*
Open: 20 Mar-Nov Site: 1.2HEC ▒▒▒ ♣ 🏠 Prices: ⋔3.40-
7.10 pitch 12-23.70 Facilities: ⋔ ⒛ ⊙ 🕯 ⌂ Services: ⛉ ✕ ⊞
lau Leisure: ⋋ P Off-site: ∅ ⋋S

SANT PERE PESCADOR GIRONA

Amfora av J-Terradellas 2, 17470
☎ 972 520540 ▤ 972 520539
e-mail: info@campingamfora.com
website: www.campingamfora.com
A pleasant site, directly on the beach, with good modern
sanitary facilities. There are plentiful leisure facilities and
English is spoken.
Open: 11 Apr-28 Sep Site: 12HEC ▒▒▒ ♣ 🏠 Prices: ⋔3.10-
3.95 pitch 18.51-29.96 Facilities: ⋔ ⒛ ⊙ 🕯 ∅ ⌂ Services: ⛉
✕ ⊞ lau Leisure: ⋋ PRS Off-site: ⋋L

Aquarius 17470 ☎ 972 520003 ▤ 550216
e-mail: camping@aquarius.es website: www.aquarius.es
Level meadowland. Partially in shade, quiet well organised
site by the lovely sandy beach of Bahia de Rosas.
➲ *Travel in direction of L'Escala and turn towards the beach
following signs.*
Open: 15 Mar-10 Jan Site: 6HEC ▒▒▒ ♣ Prices: ⋔2.94-3.53
pitch 11.24-29.96 Facilities: ⋔ ⒛ ⊙ 🕯 ∅ ♨ ⌂ Services: ⛉ ✕
⊞ lau Leisure: ⋋ S

Ballena Alegre 2 17470 ☎ 902 510520 ▤ 902 510521
e-mail: infb2@ballena-alegre.com
website: www.ballena-alegre.com
Extensive site near wide sandy beach with dunes. Large
shopping complex. Washing and sanitary facilities have
recently undergone extensive modernisation.
➲ *Access from L'Escala to San Martin de Ampurias, then
onward to site in 2km .*
Open: 15 May-28 Sep Site: 24HEC ⸺ ∷∷ ⊕ ⊞
Facilities: ⋔ ⅃ ⊙ ☒ ∅ ☎ Services: ⚓ ✗ ⊞ lau Leisure: ⚓ PS

Dunas 17470 ☎ 972 520400
Level extensive grassland site with young poplars, some of
medium height, on the beach, totally subdivided.
➲ *It lies 5km SE of village. If approaching from L'Escala follow
an asphalt road to San Martin, then follow a dusty earth track
for 2.5km.*
Open: 9 May-25 Sep Site: 30HEC ⸺ ⊕ ⊞ ☒ Å
Facilities: ⋔ ⅃ ⊙ ☒ ∅ ☎ Services: ⚓ ✗ ⊞ lau Leisure: ⚓ PS

Palmeras ctra de la Platja, 17470 ☎ 972 520506 ▤ 972 550285
e-mail: info@campinglaspalmeras.com
website: www.campinglaspalmeras.com
On level grassland with plenty of shade. Recently installed
modern sanitary blocks and heated swimming pool.
➲ *Off the road from Sant Pere Pescador to the beach about
200mtrs from the sea.*
Open: Apr-Oct Site: 5HEC ⸺ ♣ ⊞ Prices: ⚓2.14-3.21
pitch 12.62-29.74 Facilities: ⋔ ⅃ ⊙ ☒ ∅ ☎ Services: ⚓ ✗ ⊞
lau Leisure: ⚓ PS Off-site: ⚓R

SITGES BARCELONA

El Garrofer Ctra C-246a, 8870 ☎ 93 8941780 ▤ 93 8110623
e-mail: garroferpark@terra.es
website: www.garroferpark.com
Set in an area of 80,000 square metres with many pine trees.
Surrounded by a golf course and the Garraf Natural Park.
Close to the beach
Open: 17 Jan-17 Dec Site: 8HEC ⸺ ∷∷ ♣ ⊞ ☒
Facilities: ⋔ ⅃ ∅ ☎ Services: ⚓ ✗ ⊞ lau Leisure: ⚓ P
Off-site: ⚓S

Roca av de Ronda, 08870 ☎ 93 8940043 ▤ 93 8940150
e-mail: info@campingelroca.com
website: www.campingelroca.com
On three terraces with a view of Sitges. Shade is provided by
pines and deciduous trees. Separate section for young people.
1km from the sea.
Camping Card Compulsory.
➲ *Turn off the C246 (Barcelona-Tarragona) in the direction of
Sant Pere de Ribes/San Pedro de Ribas. In 15m turn right to site.*
Open: 28 Mar-12 Oct Site: 2HEC ∷∷ ⊕ ⊞ Prices: ⚓4.40-
5.10 ⚓4.40-5.10 Å4.40-5.10 Facilities: ⋔ ⅃ ⊙ ☒ ∅ ☎
Services: ⚓ ✗ ⊞ lau Off-site: ⚓ ⚓PS

TARADELL BARCELONA

Vall Cami de la Vallmitjana, 08552
☎ 93 8126336 ▤ 93 8126027
website: www.catalumya.net/campings/acmpc
In the mountains near the Guilleries-Montseny, with good
recreational facilities.
Site: 8HEC ⸺ ♣ ⊕ ⊞ Facilities: ⋔ ⅃ ⊙ ☒ ∅ ☵ ☎
Services: ⚓ ✗ ⊞ lau Leisure: ⚓ P

TORROELLA DE MONTGRI GIRONA

Delfin Verde 17257 ☎ 972 758450 ▤ 972 760070
e-mail: info@eldelfinverde.com
website: www.eldelfinverde.com
On undulating ground with some pine trees, and an open
meadow beside the long sandy beach.
contd.

El Garrofer

Str. C-31 (ex C-246a) km. 39
E- 08870 SITGES
Tel. (34) 93 894 17 80
Fax (34) 93 811 06 23
www.garroferpark.com
garroferpark@terra.es

Open: 17.1 - 17.12
Entertainment programme
Direct access to the sea (10 min.)
C-31, km 39 (C-246)
Special area for motor homes with
water connection and outlet.
Direct bus connection to
Barcelona, every hour Airport-
Sitges

Bungalows "gitötel"

SUNSHINE ALL YEAR ROUND

Special discount for pensioners (1.9/30.6)

www.sportnature.com

A first class site. **Fabulous situation**
in the most beautiful part of the Costa
Brava. Isolated and quiet. 4 beaches.
Swimming pool, children's
playground, bar, restaurant,
supermarket, laundry, hairdressing,
medical service. Exceptional sanitary
facilities with free hot water.
Numbered pitches. Open from 1st.
of May until 30th. of September.
Sports and animation:
Swimmingpool, tennis, basket ball,
windsurfing and diving school,
compressed air for divers, table
tennis, minigolf, mountain bike.
Special activities for the children in
July and August.
Reservation service. Caravans and
bungalows for hire.

Write to:
Camping **Cala Llevadó**
Postbus 34, E-17320 Tossa de Mar
COSTA BRAVA - Spain
Tel. 00 34 972 34 03 14
Fax 00 34 972 34 11 87
E-mail: info@calallevado.com
Web: www.calallevado.com

Cala Llevadó
camping ★★★

Facilities: ⅃-shop ⋔-shower ⊙-electric points for razors ☒-electric points for caravans ☎-parking by tents permitted
☒-compulsory separate car park **Services:** ✗-café/restaurant ⚓-bar ∅-Camping Gaz International ☵-gas other than Camping
Gaz ⊞-first aid facilities lau-laundry **Leisure:** ⚓-swimming L-Lake P-Pool R-River S-Sea **Off-site:** All facilities within 2km

⮑ *Turn left off the road to Begur approx 2km S of Torroella de Montgri, and head towards Maspinell following a wide asphalt road 4.8km towards the sea.*
Site: 35HEC ⚌ ⚘ ⊞ Prices: pitch 13-38 Facilities: ⚄ ⅀ ☉ ⚐ ∅ ⚎ Services: ⚍ ✗ ⊞ lau Leisure: ⇖ PRS

TOSSA DE MAR GIRONA

Cala Llevadó 17320 ☎ 972 340314 ▤ 972 341187
e-mail: info@calallevado.com website: www.calallevado.com
Magnificent terraced site with hairpin roads overlooking three bays, all suitable for bathing. Narrow, winding drives which are quite steep in parts. Separate section for caravans.
⮑ *Take the coast road for about 4km towards Lloret de Mar and turn towards the sea.*
Open: May-Sep Site: 14HEC ⚘ ♠ ⊞ ⚎ ⅄ Prices: ⚐5.03-7.81 ⚘5.03-7.81 ⚎5.78-8.35 ⚎5.03-7.81 Facilities: ⚄ ⅀ ☉ ⚐ ∅ ⚎ ⅂ Services: ⚍ ✗ ⊞ lau Leisure: ⇖ PS
See advertisement on page 329

Can Marti 17320 ☎ 972 340851 ▤ 972 342461
website: www.campingsgi.com
Pleasant, unspoilt site in a partly wooded location. Good modern facilities. English spoken.
⮑ *1km from the sea.*
Open: 14 May-19 Sep Site: 10HEC ⚌ ♠ Prices: ⚐6-7 ⚎6-7 ⚎6-7 Facilities: ⚄ ⅀ ☉ ⚐ ∅ ⚎ Services: ⚍ ✗ ⊞ lau Leisure: ⇖ PRS

Tossa ctra Llagostera, 17320 ☎ 972 340547 ▤ 972 341531
On a meadow in a quiet, isolated valley, in a deciduous forest. 3km from the sea.
⮑ *3km SW near the GE681 (Tossa de Mar-Llagostera), in 600mtrs to site along an unmade road.*
Open: Apr-Sep Site: 9.5HEC ⚋ ♠ ⊞ Facilities: ⚄ ⅀ ☉ ⚐ ∅ ⚎ ⅀ Services: ⚍ ✗ ⊞ lau Leisure: ⇖ PS

VALLROMANES BARCELONA

El Vedado 08188 ☎ 93 5729026 ▤ 93 5729621
website: www.campingsonline.com/vedado
Surrounded by wooded mountains in a valley location with the beach only a short drive away. Also ideal for visiting Barcelona. An award winning site with many facilities.
⮑ *A17 exit 13 in direction of Masnou/C32 exit 8 in direction of Granollers*
Open: Mar-15 Nov Site: 100HEC ⚌ ⚋ ⚘ ⊞ ⚎ ⅄ Prices: ⚐5.50 ⚎5.50 ⚎5.50 Facilities: ⚄ ⅀ ☉ ⚐ ∅ ⚎ Services: ⚍ ✗ ⊞ lau Leisure: ⇖ P Off-site: ⇖S

VILADECANS BARCELONA

Ballena Alegre I 08840 ☎ 93 902500526 ▤ 93 902500527
e-mail: ballena1@ballena-alegre.com
website: www.ballena-alegre.com
An exceptionally well run family site with a wide range of facilities and direct access to a fine, sandy beach.
⮑ *Access cia C246. Before entering Barcelona follow signs for 'Airport'.*
Open: Apr-Sep Site: 22HEC ⚌ ⚋ ♠ ⊞ Prices: ⚐3-5 pitch 15-30 Facilities: ⚄ ⅀ ☉ ⚐ ∅ ⚎ ⚎ ⅂ Services: ⚍ ✗ ⊞ lau Leisure: ⇖ PS

VILALLONGA DE TER GIRONA

Conca de Ter ctra Camprodon-Setcases s/n, 17869
☎ 972 740629 ▤ 972 130171
e-mail: concater@concater.com website: www.concater.com
A pleasant family site in wooded surroundings with a variety of recreational facilities.
⮑ *Between Camprodón and Setcases, 20km from the French border.*
Open: All year Site: 3.2HEC ⚌ ♠ ⊞ ⅄ Prices: ⚐4.50 pitch 12 Facilities: ⚄ ⅀ ☉ ⚐ ∅ ⚎ ⚎ Services: ⚍ ✗ ⊞ lau Leisure: ⇖ PR Off-site: ⅀ ⚍ ✗ ∅ ⚎ ⇖R

Site: 6HEC-Site size ⚌-grass ⚋-sand ⚘-stone ⚍-little shade ⚘-partly shaded ♠-mainly shaded ⊞-bungalows for hire ⚎-caravans for hire ⅄-tents for hire ⊘-no dogs Prices: ⚐-adult per night ⚎-car per night pp-per person per night ⚎-caravan per night ⅄-tent per night

VILANOVA I LA GELTRÚ BARCELONA

Vilanova Park 08800 ☎ 93 8933402 ▤ 93 8935528
e-mail: info@vilanovapark.es website: www.vilanovapark.es
A well equipped family site on the edge of a densely wooded
area close to the coast in the heart Catalonian wine
producing area. Modern sanitary block recently added.
➲ *Access via A7 exit 29.*
Open: All year Site: 51HEC ⶡⶡ ⸬⸬ ♠ 🏕 🚐 Prices: ♦4.15-
6.70 ▲4.15-6.70 pitch 12.30-17.60 Facilities: ℕ ⿰ ⊙ 🚱 𝑜 ⚒
🕿 Services: ♀ ✗ ⊞ lau Leisure: ⸙ P Off-site: ⸙LS

CENTRAL

ALBA DE TORMES SALAMANCA

Tormes av Dehesa Boyal, 37800 ☎ 923 160998
In a rural setting close to the River Tormes.*Camping Card
Compulsory.*
➲ *20km from Salamanca.*
Open: All year Site: 2.2HEC ⶡⶡ ⸾⸾ ▲ Facilities: ℕ ⊙ 🚱 🕿
Services: ♀ ✗ ⊞ lau Leisure: ⸙ R Off-site: ✗ 𝑜 ⚒ ⸙P

ALBARRACIN TERUEL

Ciudad de Albarracin Camino de Gea, Arrabal, 44100
☎ 978 710197 ▤ 978 710107
website: www.campingalbarracin.arrakis.es
A modern site on mainly level ground with good facilities.
➲ *Signposted from A1512.*
Open: Apr-Oct Site: 1.4HEC ⶡⶡ ♠ Prices: ♦2.88 🚐2.88
🚐2.94 ▲2.88 Facilities: ℕ ⊙ 🚱 𝑜 🕿 Services: ♀ ✗ ⊞ lau
Off-site: ⿰ ✗ ⸙LPR

ARANJUEZ MADRID

Soto del Castillo Soto Del Rebollo S/N, 28300
☎ 91 8911395 ▤ 91 8911395
Site developed into two parts with trees and lawns in large
castle park.
➲ *Turn off NIV at Km46. In the village 200mtrs beyond
Firestone petrol station turn sharp NE and continue for 1km.*
Open: All year Site: 33HEC ⶡⶡ ⸬⸬ 🏕 Prices: ♦3.20-4.15
🚐2.75-3.50 🚐3.70-4.65 ▲2.90-3.70 Facilities: ℕ ⿰ ⊙ 🚱 𝑜
🕿 Services: ♀ ✗ ⊞ lau Leisure: ⸙ PR

CABRERA, LA MADRID

Pico de la Miel 28751 ☎ 91 8688082 ▤ 91 8688541
e-mail: info@picodelamiel.com website: www.picodelamiel.com
Open: All year Site: 10HEC ⶡⶡ ♠ 🏕 Facilities: ℕ ⿰ ⊙ 🚱
𝑜 🕿 Services: ♀ ✗ ⊞ lau Leisure: ⸙ P Off-site: ⚒

CUENCA CUENCA

Cuenca Carretera Cuenca-Tragacete KM7, 16147
☎ 969 231656 ▤ 969 231656
A modern site in a peaceful wooded location.
➲ *N towards Mariana.*
Open: 18 Mar-12 Oct Site: 23HEC ⶡⶡ ♠ 🏕 Prices: ♦4
🚐3.50 🚐5 ▲4 Facilities: ℕ ⿰ ⊙ 🚱 𝑜 🕿 Services: ♀ ✗ ⊞
lau Leisure: ⸙ P Off-site: ⸙LR

ESCORIAL, EL MADRID

El Escorial ctra Guadarrama, km 3500, 28280
☎ 91 8902412 ▤ 91 8961062
e-mail: info@campingelescorial.com
website: www.campingescorial.com
In pleasant wooded surroundings with good recreational facilities.
Open: All year Site: 40HEC ⶡⶡ ♠ 🏕 Prices: ♦5.10 🚐5.10
🚐5.10 ▲5.10 pitch 14.50-15.25 Facilities: ℕ ⿰ ⊙ 🚱 𝑜 ⚒ 🕿
Services: ♀ ✗ ⊞ lau Leisure: ⸙ P

Facilities: ⿰-shop ℕ-shower ⊙-electric points for razors 🚱-electric points for caravans 🕿-parking by tents permitted
🅿-compulsory separate car park **Services:** ✗-café/restaurant ♀-bar 𝑜-Camping Gaz International ⚒-gas other than Camping
Gaz ⊞-first aid facilities lau-laundry **Leisure:** ⸙-swimming L-Lake P-Pool R-River S-Sea **Off-site:** All facilities within 2km

E-28906 CTA. N-IV Km 12.400
GETAFE (MADRID)
TEL. (34) 916 958 069
FAX: (34) 916 831 659

Alpha

Madrid

Visit us, we are in Madrid

www.campingalpha.com
info@campingalpha.com

Bungalows

CAMPING

Free hot water

Regular bus connection to Madrid

FUENTE DE SAN ESTEBAN, LA SALAMANCA

Cruce 37200 ☎ 923440130
e-mail: campingelcruce@yahoo.es
Useful transit site in a quiet location in typically Castillian countryside.
➲ *50mtrs from N620 at Km291.*
Open: 15 Jun-15 Sep Site: 0.5HEC ⚏ 🗲 🚐 Prices: ⋔3.50
🚗3 🚐4 🅰3 Facilities: 🌂 🚿 ⊙ 🚻 🍴 🏪 Services: 🍴 ⊞ lau
Leisure: ⚲ P Off-site: ✗ ⚲R

GARGANTILLA DE LOZOYA MADRID

Monte Holiday 28739 ☎ 91 8695278 🖷 91 8695278
e-mail: camp.m.holiday@teleline.es
website: www.vayacamping.net
A terraced site with good modern facilities in a beautiful mountain setting.

IN MADRID,
camp site & bungalows
ARCO IRIS

Heated and air-conditioned.
Swimming pools, jacuzzi, children's playgrounds, multi sports area, cafeteria, restaurant. Guarded 24 hours p. day… To visit Madrid: Arco Iris! Don't hesitate
Easy access by M-40, exit 36.

TEL: **34 - 91 616 03 87**
FAX: **34 - 91 616 00 59**
E-mail: madrid@bungalowsarcoiris.com
http: www.bungalowsarcoiris.com
BUNGALOWS ARCO IRIS, MADRID.

CAMPINGS DE CALIDAD DE MADRID

➲ *Turn off N1 (Burgos-Madrid) at Km69 towards Cotos and continue for 10km.*
Open: All year Site: 30HEC ⚏ ∵ ⚘ ᗺ 🚐 Prices: ⋔4.60
🚐4.60 🅰4.60 Facilities: 🌂 🚿 ⊙ 🚻 🍴 🏪 Services: 🍴 ✗ ⊞ lau
Leisure: ⚲ P Off-site: 🚿 🍴 ✗ ⚲LR

GETAFE MADRID

Alpha Ctra. N-4, km 12,400, 28906
☎ 91 6958069 🖷 91 6831659
e-mail: info@campingalpha.com
website: www.campingalpha.com
Surrounded by pine woods at approx. the geographical centre of Spain with well defined pitches and modern facilities. Direct bus service to Madrid.
➲ *Access via NIV at Km 12,400.*
Open: All year Site: 4.8HEC ∵ ᗺ 🚐 Prices: ⋔5.40 🚐5.80
🅰5.80 Facilities: 🌂 🚿 ⊙ 🚻 🍴 🏪 Services: 🍴 ✗ ⊞ lau
Leisure: ⚲ P

MADRID MADRID

Arco Iris 28670 ☎ 91 6160387 🖷 91 6160059
e-mail: madrid@bungalowsarcoiris.com
website: www.bungalowsarcoiris.com
A family site in a peaceful location, yet with easy access to Madrid.
➲ *From M40 (Madrid ring road) take exit 36 to Boadilla del Monte and continue towards Villaviciosa to Km12.*
Open: All year Site: 4HEC ⚏ ∵ ᗺ 🚐 Prices: ⋔5 🚗5
🚐5 🅰5 pitch 13.25 Facilities: 🌂 🚿 ⊙ 🚻 🍴 🏪 Services: 🍴
✗ ⊞ lau Leisure: ⚲ P

Osuna av de Logrono, 28042 ☎ 91 7410510 🖷 91 3206365
On long stretch of land, shade being provided by pines, acacias and maple. Some noise from airfield, road and railway.
➲ *If approaching from the town centre take N11 road and drive towards Barajas for about 7.5km. At Km1 in 300mtrs and after railway underpass turn right.*
Open: All year Site: 23HEC ⚏ ∵ 🚿 🏪 Facilities: 🌂 🚿 ⊙
🚻 🏪 Services: 🍴 ✗ ⊞ lau Off-site: ✗ 🍴 🚰 ⚲LP

MALPARTIDA DE PLASENCIA CÁCERES

Parque Natural de Monfrague Ctra Plasencia-Trujillo km-10, 10680 ☎ 927 459220 🖷 927 459233
A modern site with well defined pitches and good facilities.
➲ *10km from Plasencia on C524.*
Open: All year Site: 7HEC ⚏ 🚿 🏪 Prices: ⋔3.30 🚗3
🚐3.30 🅰3.30 Facilities: 🌂 🚿 ⊙ 🚻 🍴 🏪 Services: 🍴 ✗ ⊞ lau
Leisure: ⚲ P Off-site: 🚰

MÉRIDA BADAJOZ

Lago de Proserpina Apdo 121, 06800
☎ 924 123055 🖷 924 317555
e-mail: campingproserpina@estudiarte.com
website: www.campingproserpina.com
Open: May-Dec Site: 5.5HEC ⚏ ∵ ᗺ 🅰 Facilities: 🌂
🚿 ⊙ 🚻 🍴 🏪 Services: 🍴 ✗ ⊞ lau Leisure: ⚲ LP Off-site: ⚲P

MIRANDA DEL CASTAÑAR SALAMANCA

El Burro Blanco 37660 ☎ 923 161100 🖷 923 161100
e-mail: elbb@infonegocio.com
website: www.elbb.net
A well equipped site in an area of woodland overlooking the village.
➲ *Approx 1km from the village centre.*
Open: Apr-Sep Site: 3.5HEC ⚏ ᗺ 🗲 Prices: ⋔4 pitch 9
Facilities: 🌂 ⊙ 🚻 🏪 Services: 🍴 ✗ ⊞ lau Off-site: 🚿 ✗ 🍴
⚲PR

NAVALAFUENTE MADRID

Camping Piscis 28729 ☎ 91 8432268 ▤ 91 8471341
e-mail: campiscis@campiscis.com
website: www.campiscis.com
Spacious pitches surrounded by oak trees.
➲ *Turn off N1/E5 (Madrid-Burgos) at exit 50 and continue towards Guadalix de la Sierra.*
Open: All year Site: 23HEC ∷∷ ♠ ⚘ ♨ Prices: ♠4.50 ♠4.50 ♠4.50 ♠4.50 Facilities: ⚊ ⚌ ⊙ ⚒ ⌀ ♨ ☎
Services: ⚑ ✗ ⊞ lau Leisure: ⇌ P

SALAMANCA SALAMANCA

Don Quijote Cabrerizos, 37193 ☎ 923 209052 ▤ 923 251066
➲ *NE of the town towards Aldealengua.*
Open: All year Site: 4HEC ⚌ ∷∷ ⚒ Facilities: ⚊ ⚌ ⊙ ♨ ⌀ Services: ✗

SANTA MARTA DE TORMES SALAMANCA

Regio ctra Salamanca/Madrid Km4, 37900
☎ 923 138888 ▤ 923 138044
e-mail: recepcion@campingregio.com
website: www.campingregio.com
A pleasant site, divided into several fields, with good, modern facilities.
➲ *100mtrs from the N501 (Salamanca-Avila) behind Hotel Jardin-Regio.*
Open: All year Site: 3HEC ⚌ ⚒ ⚘ Prices: ♠3.21 ♠2.67-3.21 ♠2.67-3.21 pitch 9.30-10.70 Facilities: ⚊ ⚌ ⊙ ♨ ⌀ ☎
Services: ⚑ ✗ ⊞ lau Leisure: ⇌ PR

SEGOVIA SEGOVIA

Acueducto 40004 ☎ 921 425000 ▤ 921 425000
e-mail: campingsg@navegalia.com
website: www.campingacueducto.com
➲ *SE next to N601 at Km112*
Open: Apr-Sep Site: 3HEC ⚌ ♠ ⚘ ♠ Prices: ♠4.50-4.95 ♠4.50-4.95 ♠5-5.50 ♠4.50-4.95 pitch 14-15.40 Facilities: ⚊ ⚌ ⊙ ♨ ⌀ ☎ Services: ⚑ ✗ ⊞ lau Leisure: ⇌ P Off-site: ✗ ⇌L

TOLEDO TOLEDO

Greco 45004 ☎ 925 220090 ▤ 925 220090
e-mail: elgreco@retemail.es
website: www.accom.nct/elgreco
Few shady terraces on slope leading down to the River Tajo.
On SW outskirts of town.
➲ *Approaching from the town centre take the C401, Carretera Comarcal and drive SW for about 2km. Turn right at Km28 and drive 300mtrs towards Puebla de Montalban.*
Open: All year Site: 2.5HEC ∷∷ ⚒ ⚘ ♨ Prices: ♠4.75 ♠4.55 ♠4.55 ♠4.55 Facilities: ⚊ ⚌ ⊙ ♨ ⌀ ☎ Services: ⚑ ✗ ⊞ lau Leisure: ⇌ PR Off-site: ⛁

VALDEMAQUEDA MADRID

El Canto la Gallina 28295 ☎ 091 8984820 ▤ 091 8984823
e-mail: camping@elcantolagallina.com
website: www.elcantolagallina.com
In a wooded location at the foot of a mountain.
Open: All year Site: 12HEC ⚌ ∷∷ ⚒ ⚘ ♨ Prices: ♠5.35-6.42 ♠4.28 ♠5.35-6.42 ♠4.82-5.35 pitch 3.85 Facilities: ⚊ ⚌ ⊙ ♨ ⌀ ⛏ ☎ Services: ⚑ ✗ ⊞ lau Leisure: ⇌ P Off-site: ⇌R

VILLAMAYOR SALAMANCA

Ruta de la Plata ctra Villales a Villamayor, 37184
☎ 923 289574
e-mail: campingrutadelaplata@turisnet
website: www.turisnet.com salamanca
Open: All year Site: ⚌ ⚒ Facilities: ⚊ ⚌ ⊙ ♨ ⌀ ☎ Services: ⚑ ✗ ⊞ lau Leisure: ⇌ P Off-site: ✗

CAMPING
Don Quijote

Ctra. Aldealengua, km 4
E-37193 **CABRERIZOS** (Salamanca)
Tel./Fax: (34) 923 209 052 / (34) 923 209 801
Mobile phone: 669 850 391

SOUTH EAST COAST

ALCOCEBER CASTELLÓN

Playa Tropicana 12579 ☎ 964 412463 ▤ 964 412805
e-mail: info@playatropicana.com
website: www.playatropicana.com
On a 500mtrs long sandy beach 3km from the village.
➲ *For access, leave motorway at exit 44, then drive 3km N on the CN340 and turn towards the sea at Km1018.*
Open: All year Site: 3HEC ⚌ ♠ ⚘ ⚸ Prices: ♠6.80 pitch 26.75 Facilities: ⚊ ⚌ ⊙ ♨ ⌀ ☎ Services: ⚑ ✗ ⊞ lau Leisure: ⇌ PS

Ribamar Partida Ribamar s/n, 12579
☎ 964 761163 ▤ 964 761163
Quiet wooded site between sea and mountains. Individual pitches.
Open: 03 Apr-26 Sep Site: 2.2HEC ∷∷ ⚉ ⚒ ♠ ⚘ ♨
Prices: ♠2.89-3.96 ♠2.84-3.85 ♠3.70-5.08 ♠3.70-5.08
Facilities: ⚊ ⚌ ⊙ ♨ ⌀ ☎ Services: ⚑ ✗ ⊞ lau Leisure: ⇌ PS
Off-site: ⇌S

ALFAZ DEL PI ALICANTE

Excalibur Camino, Viejo del Albir s/n, 03580
☎ 96 6867139 ▤ 96 6866928
e-mail: c-m@camping-medieval.com
website: www.camping-medieval.com
Open: All year Site: 12HEC ⚌ ⚒ ⚘ Prices: ♠4.65-6.10 ♠4.85-6.60 ♠4.85-6.60 pitch 4.65-6.10 Facilities: ⚊ ⚌ ⊙ ♨ ⌀ ☎ Services: ⚑ ✗ ⊞ lau Leisure: ⇌ P Off-site: ⇌S

See advertisement on page 334

ALTEA ALICANTE

Cap Blanch Playa del Cap-Blanch, 3590 ☎ 96 5845946
A well equipped site on Albir beach backed by imposing mountains. Good sporting and recreational facilities.
➲ *Access via A7 exit 65 (Benidorm-Callosa).*
Open: All year Site: 4HEC ⚉ ♠ ⚘ Prices: ♠5.50 ♠6.50 ♠5.50 pitch 24 Facilities: ⚊ ⚌ ⊙ ♨ ⌀ ☎ Services: ✗ ⊞ lau Leisure: ⇌ S Off-site: ⚌ ⌀ ⊞

AMETLLA DE MAR, L' TARRAGONA

L'Ametlla Village Platja Paratge Santes Creus, 43860
☎ 977 267784 ▤ 977 267868
e-mail: info@campingametlla.com
website: www.campingametlla.com
A modern site with first class equipment. Direct access to two beaches. Substantial improvements have been made to the access road.
➲ *2km W, S of A7.*
Open: Apr-Oct Site: 8HEC ⚌ ∷∷ ⚒ ⚘ ♠ Facilities: ⚊ ⚌ ⊙ ♨ ⌀ ⛏ ☎ Services: ⚑ ✗ ⊞ lau Leisure: ⇌ PS

Facilities: ⚌-shop ⚊-shower ⊙-electric points for razors ♨-electric points for caravans ☎-parking by tents permitted ⚎-compulsory separate car park Services: ✗-café/restaurant ⚑-bar ⌀-Camping Gaz International ⛏-gas other than Camping Gaz ⊞-first aid facilities lau-laundry Leisure: ⇌-swimming L-Lake P-Pool R-River S-Sea Off-site: All facilities within 2km

BENICARLÓ CASTELLÓN

Alegria del Mar Playa Norte, 12580
☎ 964 470871 ▤ 964 470871
Open: All year Site: 10HEC ⸺ ⚄ ☎ Prices: ♦4.25 ⊞4.25 ▲4.25
Facilities: ⚘ ⚙ ⊙ ⚑ ∅ ☎ Services: ♟ ✗ ⊞ lau Leisure: ⚓ PS

BENICASIM CASTELLÓN

Bonterra Park av Barcelona 47, 12560
☎ 964 300007 ▤ 964 300008
e-mail: info@campingbonterra.com
website: www.campingbonterra.com
Between the railway line and avenida de Barcelona with a number of deciduous trees.
⮑ 300mtrs N towards Las Villas de Benicasim.
Open: All year Site: 5HEC ⸺ ⚄ ☎ Prices: ♦3.21-4.28 pitch 9.63-33.17 Facilities: ⚘ ⚙ ⊙ ⚑ ∅ ☎ Services: ♟ ✗ ⊞ lau Leisure: ⚓ P Off-site: ∅ ⚓PS

BENIDORM ALICANTE

Arena Blanca av Dr Severo Ochoa 44, 03500
☎ 96 5861889 ▤ 69 5861107
e-mail: arenablanca@ctv.es
website: www.camping-arenablanca.es
A modern site with plenty of good facilities.
⮑ Access via N332 Benidorm-Altea.
Open: All year Site: 2.2HEC ∵ ♣ ☎ Prices: ♦5.50 ⮜5.50 ⊞16 ▲5 pitch 16 Facilities: ⚘ ⚙ ⊙ ⚑ ∅ ⚒ ☎ Services: ♟ ✗ ⊞ lau Leisure: ⚓ PS

Armanello av Comunidad, 03500
☎ 96 5853190 ▤ 96 5853100
e-mail: armanello@camping-arenablanca.es
website: www.camping-arenablanca.es
Divided by bushes with large pitches on terraces under olive and palm trees next to a small orange grove.
⮑ For access turn off the N332 at Km123.1 N of the town.
Open: All year Site: 1.6HEC ⸺ ♣ ☎ Prices: ♦2-5.50 ▲4.40-5.50 pitch 7-16 (incl 2 persons) Facilities: ⚘ ⚙ ⊙ ⚑ ∅ ⚒ ☎ Services: ♟ ✗ ⊞ lau Leisure: ⚓ PS

Benisol av Comunidad Valenciana S/N, 3503
☎ 96 5851673 ▤ 96 5860895
A modern family site with plenty of facilities. The large pitches are separated by hedges and the centre of Benidorm is within easy reach.
⮑ NE of Benidorm off N332 towards Altea.
Open: All year Site: 7HEC ⚄ ♣ ⊞ Facilities: ⚘ ⚙ ⊙ ⚑ ∅ ⚒ ☎ Services: ♟ ✗ ⊞ lau Leisure: ⚓ P

BENISA ALICANTE

Fanadix ctra Calpe-Moraira Km 5, 03720
☎ 96 5747307 ▤ 96 5747307
e-mail: campingfanadix@campingfanadix.com
website: www.campingfanadix.com
Terraced site completely divided into pitches.
⮑ 10km E & 400mtrs from the sea. Access off AV-1445.
Site: 1.6HEC ⸺ ∵ ♣ Facilities: ⚘ ⊙ ⚑ ☎ Services: ♟ ✗ ⊞ lau Leisure: ⚓ P Off-site: ⚙ ∅ ⚒ ⚓S

CAMBRILS TARRAGONA

Playa Cambrils-Don Camilo Av Diputación 42, 43850
☎ 977 361490 ▤ 977 364988
e-mail: camping@playacambrils.com
website: www.playacambrils.com
Divided into pitches, lying on both sides of the coast road in a wooded location.

⊃ *Drive 2km N of the town towards Salou and W of the bridge over the river.*
Open: 15 Mar-12 Oct **Site:** 9HEC ∷ ✦ ⊞ **Prices:** ♦1.61-4.28 pitch 10.70-24.61 **Facilities:** ↑ 🕿 ⊙ 🖭 ⌀ 🖭 **Services:** ⏇ ✗ ⊞ lau **Leisure:** ⇲ P **Off-site:** 🚿 ⇲S

CAMPELLO ALICANTE

Costa Blanca c Convento 143, 03560
🕿 965 630670   ▤ 965 630670
e-mail: info@campingcostablanca.com
website: www.campingcostablanca.com
On most level ground scattered with old olive and eucalyptus trees. The Alicante-Denia railway line runs behind the camp.
⊃ *For access turn off the N332 at Km94.2 next to the big petrol station, and drive along a narrow gravel track towards the sea for 0.5km.*
Open: All year **Site:** 1.1HEC ∷ ✦ ✦ ⊞ 🅰 **Prices:** ♦4.30 ➔6.55 🅰4.30 pitch 13 **Facilities:** ↑ 🕿 ⊙ 🖭 ⌀ 🚿 🖭 **Services:** ⏇ ✗ ⊞ lau **Leisure:** ⇲ P **Off-site:** ⇲S

CANET D'EN BERENGUER VALENCIA

Canet de Mar Playa Canet d'en Berenguer, 46529
🕿 96 2608813   ▤ 96 2608089
e-mail: administracion@campingcanetmar.com
Surrounded by citrus fruit trees, 300mtrs from the beach.
Open: All year **Site:** 6.6HEC ▦ ∷ ◑ ✦ **Facilities:** ↑ 🕿 🖭 ⌀ 🖭 **Services:** ⏇ ✗ ⊞ lau **Off-site:** ⇲S

CUNIT TARRAGONA

Mar de Cunit Playa Cunit, 43881
🕿 977 674058   ▤ 977 675006
e-mail: mardecunit@seker.es website: www.mardecunit.com
A friendly site on level ground overlooking the beach.
Open: 15 May-1 Oct **Site:** 1.2HEC ∷ 🌿 ⊞ **Prices:** ♦3-3.50 ➔12 🖭12 🅰6 pitch 9-12 **Facilities:** ↑ 🕿 ⊙ 🖭 ⌀ 🖭 **Services:** ⏇ ✗ ⊞ lau **Leisure:** ⇲ LS **Off-site:** ⊞

DAIMUS VALENCIA

Aventura ctra Playa Daimus, 46710 🕿 96 2818330
Picturesque setting in wooded surroundings on a safe, sandy beach.
⊃ *Access via N332 Alicante-Valencia.*
Site: 1.8HEC ▦ ∷ ✦ ⊞ **Facilities:** ↑ 🕿 ⊙ 🖭 ⌀ 🖭 **Services:** ⏇ ✗ ⊞ lau **Leisure:** ⇲ PS

GUARDAMAR DEL SEGURA ALICANTE

Mare Nostrum 3140 🕿 96 5728073   ▤ 96 5728073
e-mail: cmarenostrum@cesser.com
website: www.costablanca.org/marenostrum.asp
Partially terraced meadow with some shade from roofing.
⊃ *Turn towards the sea off the N332 Alicante-Cartagena road at about Km38.5.*
Open: Apr-15 Sep **Site:** 20HEC ▦ ◑ 🖭 **Facilities:** ↑ 🕿 ⊙ 🖭 ⌀ 🚿 🖭 **Services:** ⏇ ✗ ⊞ lau **Leisure:** ⇲ PS **Off-site:** ✗ ⇲LS

Marjal Cartagena-Alicante Rd (N 332), 03140
🕿 966 725022   ▤ 966 726695
e-mail: camping@marjal.com website: www.marjal.com
Located in a national park called 'Dunas de Guardamar' next to the estuary of the Segura River, alongside pine and eucalyptus forests with access to fine sandy beaches.
Open: All year **Site:** 3.5HEC ▦ ◑ ⊞ **Prices:** ♦4-6 pitch 16-28 **Facilities:** ↑ 🕿 ⊙ 🖭 ⌀ 🚿 🖭 **Services:** ⏇ ✗ ⊞ lau **Leisure:** ⇲ P **Off-site:** 🕿 ⏇ ✗ ⇲S

Palm Mar 03140 🕿 96 5728856   ▤ 96 5728856
Open: Jun-Sep **Site:** 2HEC ∷ ✦ **Prices:** ♦4.50 pitch 12 **Facilities:** ↑ 🕿 ⊙ 🖭 ⌀ 🖭 **Services:** ⏇ ✗ ⊞ lau **Leisure:** ⇲ S **Off-site:** ✗ ⇲P

CAMPING · CARAVANING · BUNGALOWS

MARJAL

NL D GB F E

MARJAL SPORT
CENTRO DEPORTIVO Y DE SALUD

Mini Club   Club Junior

CTRA. N-332, Km. 73,4 • 03140 GUARDAMAR • (Alicante) ESPAÑA
Telfs.: (34) 96 672 50 22 - (34) 96 672 70 70 - Fax: (34) 96 672 66 95
www.marjal.com - E-mail: camping@marjal.com

HOSPITALET DE L'INFANT, L' TARRAGONA

El Templo del Sol Platja del Torn, 43890
☎ 977 810486 🖩 977 811306
A new site with modern sanitary installations and good recreational facilities on a 1.5km long beach.This is a naturist site and only families or holders of an International Naturism Carnet are allowed.
⊃ *Access via A3 (Barcelona-Valencia), 4km from exit 38 towards the sea.*
Open: Jun-Sep Site: ⛺ 🔌 🏠 ⊘ Facilities: 🕯 🛒 ☉ 🗬 ⊘ 🏚
Services: ⬤ ✕ 🔲 lau Leisure: ⬎ PS

JARACO VALENCIA

San Vincente Playa Xeraco, 46770
☎ 96 2888188 🖩 96 2888147
website: campingsanvincente.com
Level subdivided site with some trees.
⊃ *On leaving Jaraco at Km332 turn off at Km304 (Valencia-Alicante) in the direction of Playa to the site in 3.5km.*
Open: All year Site: 5HEC ⋰⋰ 🔌 🏠 Facilities: 🕯 ☉ 🗬 🏚
Services: ⬤ ✕ 🔲 lau Leisure: ⬎ S Off-site: 🛒 ⊘ 🏚 ⬎PR

MARINA, LA ALICANTE

International la Marina Ctra. N-332 KM76, 03194
☎ 96 5719200 🖩 96 5419110
e-mail: info@campinglamarina.com
website: www.campinglamarina.com
A modern site in a wooded setting, 500 metres from a sandy beach.
⊃ *At Km79 on Alicante-Cartagena road.*
Open: All year Site: 6.3HEC 🔌 🏠 Prices: ⬥1.55-7.70 pitch 5.93-30.17 Facilities: 🕯 🛒 ☉ 🗬 ⊘ 🏚 🏚 Services: ⬤ ✕ 🔲 lau Leisure: ⬎ P Off-site: ⬎S

MIRAMAR PLAYA VALENCIA

Coelius av del Mar, 46711 ☎ 96 2819574 🖩 96 2818733
e-mail: coelius@mx3.redestb.es website: www.coelius.com
A fine camp site 500mtrs from the Miramar beach with good, modern facilities.
⊃ *Access via N430.*
Open: All year Site: 2HEC 🔌 🏠 🏠 Facilities: 🕯 🛒 ☉ 🗬 🏚 🏚
Services: ⬤ ✕ 🔲 lau Leisure: ⬎ P Off-site: ⊘ ⬎S

MONTBLANC TARRAGONA

Montblanc Park 43400 ☎ 977 862544 🖩 977 860539
Prices: ⬥3-4 pitch 17-21 Facilities: 🕯 🛒 🗬 Services: ✕ lau Leisure: P

MONT-ROIG DEL CAMP TARRAGONA

Marius 43892 ☎ 977 810684 🖩 977 179658
e-mail: schmid@teleline.es
website: www.campingmarius.com
Pitches are planted with flowers and shrubs. Separate section for dog owners.
⊃ *For access, leave the N340, Tarragona to Valencia road, at Km1137 and drive through a 4.9mtr-wide railway underpass with a clearance of 3.65mtrs, then head towards the beach.*
Site: 4.5HEC ⛺ ⋰⋰ 🔌 🏠 Prices: ⬥5-7 pitch 12-17
Facilities: 🕯 🛒 ☉ 🗬 ⊘ 🏚 Services: ⬤ ✕ 🔲 lau Leisure: ⬎ S

Playa Montroig 43300 ☎ 977 810637 🖩 811411
e-mail: info@playamontroig.com
website: www.playamontroig.com
An ideal holiday centre for the whole family with sanitary installations of the highest quality. Situated on a fine sandy beach and surrounded by tropical gardens, this award winning site offers a wide range of sporting and recreational facilities and is noted for its helpful and friendly staff.

contd.

Facilities: 🛒-shop 🕯-shower ☉-electric points for razors 🗬-electric points for caravans 🏚-parking by tents permitted 🅿-compulsory separate car park **Services:** ✕-café/restaurant ⬤-bar ⊘-Camping Gaz International 🏚-gas other than Camping Gaz 🔲-first aid facilities lau-laundry **Leisure:** ⬎-swimming L-Lake P-Pool R-River S-Sea **Off-site:** All facilities within 2km

⮕ *Turn left off the N340 at Km1136. Exit 37 or 38.*
Open: 15 Mar-Oct Site: 35HEC ⬛⬛⬛ ♣ 🏠 ⊘ Prices: ⋔5
pitch 33-65 Facilities: 🌣 🏪 ⊙ 🔌 𝜕 🅿 Services: ▮ ✗ ⊞ lau
Leisure: ⚲ PS

Torre Del Sol 43892 ☎ 977 810486 📠 977 811306
e-mail: info@latorredelsol.com
website: www.latorredelsol.com
A level tidy grassland site on two levels, with young poplars
and some of medium height between a long stretch of beach
and the railway.
⮕ *For access, turn off the N340, Tarragona to Valencia road at
Km224.1 then follow the road towards the sea.*
Open: 15 Mar-23 Oct Site: 24HEC ⬛⬛⬛ ♣ ⊘ Prices: ⋔3-7.50
▲3-8 Facilities: 🌣 🏪 ⊙ 🔌 𝜕 🅿 Services: ▮ ✗ ⊞ lau
Leisure: ⚲ S

NAVAJAS CASTELLÓN

Altomira 12470 ☎ 964 713211 📠 964 713512
e-mail: reservar@campingaltomira.com
Situated in the valley of the Palancia river. Terraced campsite
with touring pitches on the higher levels.
⮕ *500mtrs W of Navajas. From N234 take exit for Sagunto*
Open: All year Site: 2.5HEC ⬛⬛⬛ 🏠 Prices: ⋔3.20 ⇆2.81
🚐4.12-5.24 ▲2.99 Facilities: 🌣 🏪 ⊙ 🔌 🅿 Services: ▮ ✗ ⊞ lau
Leisure: ⚲ P Off-site: ⚲R

OLIVA VALENCIA

Azul Apartado de Correos 96, 46780
☎ 96 2854106 📠 96 2854096
e-mail: campingazul@ctv.es website: www.campingazul.com
A well equipped site with direct access to the beach.
Open: All year Site: 2.5HEC ⠿⠿ 🞡 🏠 Prices: ⋔3.50 pitch 12
Facilities: 🌣 🏪 ⊙ 🔌 𝜕 🅿 Services: ▮ ✗ ⊞ lau Leisure: ⚲
S Off-site: ✗ ⚲R

Euro Camping 46780 ☎ 96 2854098 📠 96 2851753
e-mail: info@eurocamping-es.com
website: www.eurocamping-es.com
On a wide sandy beach between orange groves and well
shaded with poplar and eucalyptus trees.
⮕ *For access turn off the N332 at Km184.9, 600mtrs from
Oliva. Following signs for camp drive towards the sea for
3.3km. The access road has narrow stretches and some blind
corners so beware of oncoming traffic.*
Open: All year Site: 4.5HEC ⠿⠿ ♦ 🞡 🏠 Prices: ⋔3.70 pitch
22.20 Facilities: 🌣 🏪 ⊙ 🔌 𝜕 ⸬ 🅿 Services: ▮ ✗ ⊞ lau
Leisure: ⚲ S Off-site: ⚲R

Ferienplatz Olé 46780 ☎ 96 2857517
An extensive site with some pitches amongst dunes.
⮕ *Turn off the N332 at Km209.9 about 5km S of Oliva. In
about 3km continue to site on access road partially asphalt,
through an orchard.*
Open: Apr-Sep Site: 46HEC ⠿⠿ ♣ 🏠 Prices: ⋔4.52 🚐8.10
▲4.52 Facilities: 🌣 🏪 ⊙ 🔌 𝜕 🅿 Services: ▮ ✗ ⊞ lau
Leisure: ⚲ S Off-site: ⊞

Kiko Playa de Oliva, 46780 ☎ 96 2850905 📠 96 2854320
e-mail: kikopark@interbook.net website: www.kikopark.com
Family holiday camp, divided into pitches, lying between
marshland and vineyard. The sea can be reached by crossing
a dyke and there are sunshade roofs.
⮕ *Access from motorway A7 exit 61 and continue via CN332
towards Oliva.*
Open: All year Site: 4HEC ⠿⠿ 🞡 🏠 Facilities: 🌣 🏪 ⊙ 🔌 𝜕
⸬ 🅿 Services: ▮ ✗ ⊞ lau Leisure: ⚲ PS Off-site: ⚲P ⊞
See advertisement on page 340

OROPESA DEL MAR CASTELLÓN

Didota av de la Didota, 12594 ☎ 964 319551 📠 964 319557
e-mail: fenollosa@infonegocio.com
Open: 16 Mar-14 Oct Site: 1.7HEC ♦ ♣ 🏠 🚐 Facilities: 🌣
🏪 ⊙ 🔌 𝜕 🅿 Services: ▮ ✗ ⊞ lau Leisure: ⚲ P Off-site: ⚲S

PEÑISCOLA CASTELLÓN

Camping Eden Avda. Papa Luna, KM.6, 12598
☎ 964 480562 📠 964 489828
e-mail: camping@camping-eden.com
website: www.camping-eden.com
A modern, well appointed site on level ground close to the
seafront.
⮕ *Access via A7, then head for Peñiscola and turn towards
Benicarlo.*
Open: All year Site: 4HEC 🞡 🏠 🚐 Prices: ⋔2.70-5.20 pitch
7.80-13 Facilities: 🌣 🏪 ⊙ 🔌 𝜕 🅿 Services: ▮ ✗ ⊞ lau
Leisure: ⚲ PS Off-site: 🏪 ▮ ✗

Facilities: 🏪-shop 🌣-shower ⊙-electric points for razors 🔌-electric points for caravans 🅿-parking by tents permitted
🅿-compulsory separate car park **Services:** ✗-café/restaurant ▮-bar 𝜕-Camping Gaz International ⸬-gas other than Camping
Gaz ⊞-first aid facilities lau-laundry **Leisure:** ⚲-swimming L-Lake P-Pool R-River S-Sea **Off-site:** All facilities within 2km

PUEBLA DE FARNALS VALENCIA

Brasa 46137 ☎ 96 1460388
Level meadowland site with poplars near village centre.
➲ *For access leave motorway Barcelona-Valencia at exit 3, towards Playa Puebla de Farnals.*
Open: All year Site: 3.9HEC ⏚⏚⏚ ⊕ ⊞ Facilities: ⋔ ⊙ ⊞ ⊞ ⊞
Services: ⍩ ✗ ⊞ lau Leisure: ⊰ P Off-site: ⊠ ⊰S

SALOU TARRAGONA

Cambrils Park Apartado de Correos 123, 43840
☎ 977 351031 ⊞ 977 352210
e-mail: mail@cambrilspark.es website: www.cambrilspark.es
A large, well equipped holiday park in a wooded location. Abundant facilities for all types of recreation.
➲ *Leave main Barcelona/Valencia road at exit 35 Reus/Salou. In Salou head for seafront, then right towards harbour and Cambrils.*
Open: 11 Apr-12 Oct Site: 17HEC ⏚⏚⏚ ⊞ ⊞ ⊗ Facilities: ⋔
⊠ ⊙ ⊞ ⊘ ⊞ Services: ⍩ ✗ ⊞ lau Leisure: ⊰ P Off-site: ⊰S

Pineda de Salou Playa de la Pineda, 43840
☎ 977 373080 ⊞ 977 373081
e-mail: info@campingglapineda.com
website: www.campingglapineda.com
A well equipped site close to the sea.
➲ *At Km5 on the Tarragona-Salou road.*
Open: All year Site: 4HEC ⏚⏚⏚ ⊞ ⊞ ⊞ Facilities: ⋔ ⊠ ⊙ ⊞
⊘ ⊞ ⊞ Services: ⍩ ✗ ⊞ lau Leisure: ⊰ P
Off-site: ⊠ ⍩ ✗ ⊰ ⊰S

Sanguli-Salou 43840 ☎ 977 381641 ⊞ 977 384616
e-mail: mail@sanguli.es website: www.sanguli.es
A large, family site in pleasant wooded surroundings, 50mtrs from the beach, with extensive sports and entertainment facilities.

contd.

Site: 6HEC-Site size ⏚⏚⏚-grass ∴∴-sand ◕-stone ⋇-little shade ⊕-partly shaded ◆-mainly shaded
⊞-bungalows for hire ⊞-caravans for hire ⚠-tents for hire ⊗-no dogs Prices: ⋔-adult per night ◆-car per night
pp-per person per night ⊞-caravan per night ⚠-tent per night

PARC DE VACANCES

Sanguli Salou

CAMPING & BUNGALOW PARK

Prolongació carrer E, s/n
Apartat de Correus 123
43840 SALOU • Costa Daurada
Tarragona • España
tel. +34 977 38 16 41
fax +34 977 38 46 16

Better is Impossible...

mail@sanguli.es • www.sanguli.es

Salou • Costa Daurada • Catalunya • España

3km from Port Aventura on SW outskirts, 50mtrs inland from coast road to Cambrils
Open: 19 Mar-01 Nov Site: 23HEC ⚏ ∷ ♠ 🏠
Prices: ♠5.35 pitch 12.84-37.45 Facilities: 🏕 🛁 ⊙ 🍴 ⌀ 🏪
Services: 🍸 ✗ ⊞ lau Leisure: ⚓ PS

Siesta 43840 ☎ 977 380852
Divided into pitches and planted with young deciduous trees and old olive trees. Sunshade roofs.
If approaching from Tarragona, turn right off the main road on outskirts of Salou and drive a further 150mtrs to the camp. The site is between the railway and road 0.4km from the sea.
Open: 16 Mar-3 Nov Site: 6HEC ∷ ♠ 🏠 Facilities: 🏕 🛁 ⊙ 🍴 ⌀ 🏪 Services: 🍸 ✗ ⊞ lau Leisure: ⚓ P
Off-site: 🏖 ⚓S

See advertisement on page 340

Union c Pompeu Fabra 37, 43840
☎ 977 384816 ▤ 977 351444
e-mail: launion@campings.net
A well equipped site in wooded surroundings, 350mtrs from the sea.
On southern outskirts, 1km from the Port Aventura theme park.
Open: Apr-Sep Site: 3.8HEC ⚏ ♠ 🚐 Facilities: 🏕 🛁 ⊙ 🍴 ⌀ 🏪 Services: 🍸 ✗ ⊞ lau Leisure: ⚓ PS

SANTA OLIVA TARRAGONA

Santa Oliva Jaume Balmes 122, 43710
☎ 977 679546 ▤ 977 679228
At Km3 on Vendrell-Santa Oliva road.
Open: All year Site: 2HEC ∷ ♠ Prices: ♠3.50 ♠3.50 🚐3.50 ▲3.50 Facilities: 🏕 ⊙ ⌀ 🏖 🏪 Services: 🍸 ✗ lau Leisure: ⚓ P Off-site: 🛁 ✗ ⚓S

TAMARIT TARRAGONA

Caledonia 43008 ☎ 977 650098 ▤ 977 652867
A well appointed site in wooded surroundings, 800mtrs from the sea.
At Km1172 on N340.
Open: 18 Jun-20 Sep Site: 3.5HEC ∷ ♠ 🏠 Facilities: 🏕 🛁 ⊙ 🍴 ⌀ 🏪 Services: 🍸 ✗ ⊞ lau Leisure: ⚓ P Off-site: ⚓S

Trillas Platja Tamarit 43008 ☎ 977 650249
About 50mtrs from the sea. On several terraces planted with olive trees next to a farm.
For access, turn off the N340 at Km1.172, about 8km N of Tarragona. Follow road and cross a narrow railway bridge. (Beware of oncoming traffic).
Open: Apr-17 Oct Site: 4HEC 🏠 Facilities: 🏕 🛁 ⊙ 🍴 ⌀ 🏖 🏪 Services: 🍸 ✗ ⊞ lau Leisure: ⚓ PRS

TARRAGONA TARRAGONA

Tamarit-Park Platja Tamarit, 43008
☎ 977 650128 ▤ 977 650451
e-mail: tamaritpark@tamarit.com website: www.tamarit.com
Well-kept site at the sea beneath Tamarit Castle. One section lies under tall shady trees, and a new section lies in a meadow with some trees.
Turn off N340 at Km1171.5 towards the beach, turn left at end of road.
Open: All year Site: 17HEC ⚏ ∷ ♠ 🏠 ▲ Prices: ♠4.55 pitch 16.05-48.15 Facilities: 🏕 🛁 ⊙ 🍴 ⌀ 🏪 Services: 🍸 ✗ ⊞ lau Leisure: ⚓ PRS

TAMARIT PARK CAMPING BUNGALOWS

7km north of Tarragona ("Patrimony of Humanity"), ideal for wonderful holidays in the midst of nature, under a wonderful, mild sun and a perfect beach with shallow waters. Exceptional situation at the foot of Tamarit castle - very quiet and isolated, 1,2km from road and railway. from famous Universal's and Port Aventura theme park.

Restaurant, pizzeria and bar directly alongside the beach, barbecue grill, swimming-pool. Animation and activity programmes for adults and children. Extensive sporting area with 2 tennis courts, 2 paddle pools (illuminated), footbal, handball, volley ball, table tennis and petanq. Amphitheatre with animation activities (disco, aerobics, cultural events...) Social club with TV, cinema, internet, terrace bar. Out-of-season offers with up to 50% discounts.

Platja Tamarit • CN 340, km 1172 • E-43008 TARRAGONA
Tel. (34) 977 65 01 28 ~ Fax (34) 977 65 04 51 • www.tamarit.com • tamaritpark@tamarit.com

TORREBLANCA CASTELLÓN

Mon Rossi Carrasa Mon Rossi, Torrenostra, 12596
☎ 964 425096 📠 964 421147
e-mail: campingmonrossi@hotmail.com
Open: All year Site: 0.8HEC ♣ ⚐ 🚐 Prices: ⚐4 🚐5 ▲4
Facilities: 🏾 ⊕ 🖳 🅿 Services: 🍴 ✕ 🗷 lau Leisure: ⚓ P
Off-site: 🛒 ∅ 🍴 ⚓S

VALENCIA VALENCIA

Saler 46012 ☎ 96 1830023 📠 96 1830024
Amongst pines providing shade with its own entrance to
sandy beach in 300mtrs. The site has recently undergone
many improvements and has modern sanitary and
recreational facilities.
➲ *Access from Valencia via coastal road towards Cullera as far
as El Saler, then turn left at SE end of village and turn right.*
Open: All year Site: 80HEC ⋮⋮ 🔶 Facilities: 🏾 ⊕ 🖳 ∅ 🅿
Services: 🍴 ✕ 🗷 lau Leisure: ⚓ P Off-site: 🛒 ✕ ⚓LS

VENDRELL, EL TARRAGONA

San Salvador av Palfuriana 68, 43880
☎ 977 680804 📠 977 680804
e-mail: campingsantsalvador@trx.com
website: www.campingsantsalvador.com
On two large grassy terraces and has some sunshade roofs.
Near the sea in the centre of the town.
➲ *Access via A7 exit 31 (Barcelona-Tarragona). Site in centre
of Comarruga-Sant Salvador.*
Open: 6 Apr-Sep Site: 2.9HEC ⋮⋮ 🔶 🏫 Facilities: 🏾 🛒 ⊕
🖳 ∅ 🅿 Services: 🍴 ✕ 🗷 lau Off-site: ⚓PS

Vendrell Platja 43820 ☎ 977 694009 📠 977 694106
e-mail: vendrell@camping-vendrellplatja.com
website: www.camping-vendrellplatja.com
A large family site in a pleasant wooded location close to the
beach.
Open: 4 Apr-17 Oct Site: 7.3HEC ⋮⋮ 🔶 🏫 Prices: ⚐1.28-
6.42 🚐3.21-6.42 🚐3.21-6.42 ▲3.21-6.42 Facilities: 🏾 🛒 ⊕
🖳 ∅ 🅿 Services: 🍴 ✕ 🗷 lau Leisure: ⚓ P Off-site: ⚓S 🗷

VILANOVA DE PRADES TARRAGONA

Serra de Prades Sant Antoni, 43439
☎ 977 869050 📠 977 869050
e-mail: info@serradeprades.com
website: www.serradeprades.com
A fine site close to the beach and within easy reach of
Barcelona and the Port Aventura theme park.
Open: All year Site: 5HEC ⚏⚏⚏ ⋮⋮ 🔶 🏫 ▲ Prices: ⚐5.30
🚐5.30 🚐5.30 ▲5.30 Facilities: 🏾 🛒 ⊕ 🖳 ∅ 🍴 🅿
Services: 🍴 ✕ 🗷 lau Leisure: ⚓ P Off-site: 🛒 🍴 ✕ ∅ 🍴 ⚓LR

VILLAJOYOSA ALICANTE

Hércules CN 332 KM 141, 3570
☎ 96 5891343 📠 96 5891500
Section near sea is well shaded. Asphalt interior road,
separate section for caravans with numbered pitches.
➲ *Turn E off N332 near Km141 then turn S.*
Open: All year Site: 6.3HEC ⋮⋮ 🔷 🔶 🏫 🅿 Prices: ⚐4.54
🚐4.54 🚐4.86 ▲4.86 pitch 15.05 Facilities: 🏾 🛒 ⊕ 🖳 ∅ 🍴 🅿
Services: 🍴 ✕ 🗷 lau Leisure: ⚓ PS

Facilities: 🛒-shop 🏾-shower ⊕-electric points for razors 🖳-electric points for caravans 🅿-parking by tents permitted
🅿-compulsory separate car park Services: ✕-café/restaurant 🍴-bar ∅-Camping Gaz International 🍴-gas other than Camping
Gaz 🗷-first aid facilities lau-laundry Leisure: ⚓-swimming L-Lake P-Pool R-River S-Sea Off-site: All facilities within 2km

Sertorium N332.PK 141, 03570
☎ 96 965891599 ▤ 96 6851114
e-mail: sertorium@ctv.es website: www.sertorium.es
On level ground on the seaward side of the N332. Small stony beach, suitable for non-swimmers.
⮞ *On N332 at Km141.*
Open: All year Site: 69.7HEC ⬙ ⊕ ▲ Prices: ⭢4.59 ⬙4.59 ▲4.59 Facilities: ⬧ ⬙ ⊙ ⬙ ⬙ ▤ ⬙ Services: ⬙ ✕ ⊞ lau Leisure: ⬙ PS

Vinaroz Castellón

Garoa-Sol de Riu Playa 12500 ☎ 964 496356 ▤ 964 496368
In wooded surroundings close to the sea with good, modern facilities.
Open: All year Site: 5.5HEC ⬛⬛ ⬙ ⊕ Prices: ⭢4.20 pitch 15.80 Facilities: ⬧ ⬙ ⊙ ⬙ ⬙ ▤ Services: ⬙ ✕ ⊞ lau Leisure: ⬙ PRS Off-site: ⬙R

NORTH COAST

Ajo-Bareyo Cantabria

Cabo de Ajo ctra al Faro, 39170
☎ 942 670624 ▤ 942 630725
e-mail: losmolinos@ceoecant.es
On level ground 2km from the coast.
⮞ *Access via A8/E70 exit beranga Km185.*
Open: 15 Jun-15 Sep Site: ⬛⬛ ⊕ Prices: ⭢3.40 ⬙7.50 ▲3.50 pitch 2.40 Facilities: ⬧ ⊙ ⬙ ⬙ ▤ Services: ⬙ lau Leisure: ⬙ P Off-site: ⬙ ✕ ⬙S

Camping • Caravaning
LAS HORTENSIAS
33590 Colombres-Ribadedeva (Prin. Asturias)
Tel. 985 41 24 42 - 985 41 21 45
Leave the N-634 motorway (Santander-Oviedo) at km 28 (Playa de la Franca) and follow for 500 more meters.

www.campinglashortensias.com
lashortensias@campinglashortensias.com

1st quality camp site with excellent amenities, right on the sandy beach of Playa de la Franca. Only 30 min. away from the mountain range of the Picos de Europa and 1 hr. from Santander and Oviedo. **Very quiet, safe, terraced site with asphalt-paved paths and tennis courts. Ideal for fishing and excursions in the beautiful surroundings.**

Bareyo Cantabria

Los Molinos de Bareyo ctra Bareyo-Güemes, 39190
☎ 942 670569 ▤ 942 630725
e-mail: losmolinosdebareyo@ceoecant.es
website: www.campinglosmolinosdebareyo.com
In a quiet position with fine views.
Open: Jun-Sep Site: 12HEC ⬛⬛ ⊕ ⬙ Facilities: ⬧ ⬙ ⊙ ⬙ ⬙ ▤ Services: ⬙ ✕ ⊞ lau Leisure: ⬙ P Off-site: ⬙S

Barreiros Lugo

Gaivota Playa de Barreiros, 27793
☎ 982 124451 ▤ 982 124451
Site leads down to a sandy beach with windsurfing. The main buildings have been designed and built by the owner, who is a painter.
Open: 10 Jun-20 Sep Site: 1HEC ⬛⬛ ⬙ ⬙ ▲ Prices: ⭢3.50 ⬙3.50 ⬙4 ▲3.50 Facilities: ⬧ ⬙ ⊙ ⬙ ⬙ ▤ Services: ⬙ ✕ ⊞ lau Leisure: ⬙ S Off-site: ⬙PR

Bergondo La Coruña

Santa Marta-Coruña 15166 ☎ 981 795826
e-mail: info@campingsantamarta.com
website: www.campingsantamarta.com
Open: 15 May-15 Sep Site: 2.8HEC ⬛⬛ ⊕ ⬙ ▲ Prices: ⭢4.30 ⬙4.30 ⬙4.30 pitch 3.25 Facilities: ⬧ ⬙ ⊙ ⬙ ⬙ ▤ Services: ⬙ ✕ ⊞ lau Leisure: ⬙ PS

Cadavedo Asturias

Regalina ctra de la Playa, 33788
☎ 98 5645056 ▤ 98 5645014
e-mail: laregalina@la-regalina.com website: www.laregalina.com
A modern site with good facilities noted for its mountain and sea views.
⮞ *On N632 between Luarca and Avilés.*
Open: All year Site: 1HEC ⬛⬛ ⬙ ⬙ ▲ Facilities: ⬧ ⬙ ⊙ ⬙ ⬙ ▤ Services: ⬙ ✕ ⊞ lau Leisure: ⬙ P Off-site: ⬙ ⬙ ✕ ⬙ ⬙S ⊞

Castro-Urdiales Cantabria

Castro Barrio Campijo s/n, 39700
☎ 942 867423 ▤ 942 630725
e-mail: losmolinios@ceoecant.es
In a quiet location with terraces.
⮞ *Access via A8 exit Castro-Urdiales Km151.*
Open: Jun-Sep Site: 3HEC ⬛⬛ ⬙ ⬙ Prices: ⭢4.20 pitch 8.70 Facilities: ⬧ ⬙ ⊙ ⬙ ⬙ ▤ Services: ⬙ ✕ ⊞ lau Leisure: ⬙ P Off-site: ⬙S

Cóbreces Cantabria

Cóbreces Playa de Cóbreces, 39320 ☎ 942 725120
A peaceful site on level ground with modern facilities.
⮞ *50mtrs from the Luaña beach.*
Open: 15 Jun-15 Sep Site: 1.5HEC ⬛⬛ ⬙ Facilities: ⬧ ⬙ ⊙ ⬙ ⬙ ▤ Services: ⬙ lau Leisure: ⬙ S

Comillas Cantabria

Comillas ctra M-Noriga, 39520
☎ 942 720074 ▤ 942 720074
Level grassland site to the right of the road to the beach.
⮞ *E on C6316 at Km23.*
Open: Jun-Sep Site: 3HEC ⬛⬛ ⊕ Facilities: ⬧ ⬙ ⊙ ⬙ ⬙ ▤ Services: ⬙ ✕ ⊞ lau Leisure: ⬙ S Off-site: ✕ ⬙P

A full guide to the Symbols & Abbreviations used in this book can be found on page 6

Site: 6HEC-Site size ⬛⬛-grass ⋯-sand ⬙-stone ⬙-little shade ⊕-partly shaded ⬙-mainly shaded ⬙-bungalows for hire ⬙-caravans for hire ▲-tents for hire ⬙-no dogs Prices: ⭢-adult per night ⬙-car per night pp-per person per night ⬙-caravan per night ▲-tent per night

CUDILLERO ASTURIAS

Amuravela El Pito, 33150 ☎ 985 590995 ▤ 985 590995
e-mail: www.camping@lamuravela.com
website: www.lamuravela.com
Open: Jun-15 Sep Site: 2.5HEC ▦ ⚘ ⌂ Prices: ⚐4-4.22
⚘4-4.22 ⚑4.55-4.76 ▲3.75-4.33 Facilities: ⚐ ⚌ ⊙ ⚐ ⌀ Services: ⚑ ✗ ⊞ lau Leisure: ⚑ P Off-site: ⚏ ⚑RS

FOZ LUGO

San Rafael Playa de Peizas, 27789 ☎ 982 132218 ▤ 982 13221
e-mail: info@campingsanrafael.com
website: www.campingsanrafael.com
A small site on open, level ground 50mtrs from the beach.
⊃ 2km from the town centre.
Open: May-29 Sep Site: 1.2HEC ▦ ⚘ ⚑ ▲ Prices: ⚐2.97-
3.18 ⚘2.97-3.18 ⚑3.97-4.25 ▲3.37-3.61 Facilities: ⚐ ⚌ ⊙
⚐ ⌀ 🅿 Services: ⚑ ✗ ⊞ lau Off-site: ⚏ ⚑LPRS

FRANCA, LA ASTURIAS

Las Hortensias Playa de la Franca, 33590
☎ 98 5412442 ▤ 98 5412153
e-mail: lashortensias@campinglashortensias.com
website: www.campinglashortensias.com
A well maintained site with good facilities beside the La
Franca Beach.
Open: Jun-Sep Site: 2.8HEC ▦ ⚘ Prices: ⚐3.74-4.15
⚘3.42-3.80 ⚑4.90-5.45 ▲3.69-4.10 Facilities: ⚐ ⚌ ⊙ ⚐ ⌀
🅿 Services: ⚑ ✗ ⊞ lau Leisure: ⚑ RS Off-site: ⚏

ISLARES CANTABRIA

Playa Arenillas 39798 ☎ 942 863152 ▤ 942 863152
e-mail: cueva@mundivia.es
website: www.cantabria.com/arenillas.asp
Well equipped site in meadowland with some pine trees,
100mtrs from the beach.
⊃ On N634 at Km155.8 turn N and continue 100mtrs. The
entrance is rather steep.
Open: Apr-Sep Site: 2.5HEC ▦ ⚘ ▲ ⚋ Prices: ⚐4.26
pitch 10.90 Facilities: ⚐ ⚌ ⊙ ⚐ ⌀ 🅿 Services: ⚑ ✗ ⊞ lau
Leisure: ⚑ S

LAREDO CANTABRIA

Carlos V pl de Carlos V, 39770 ☎ 942 605593
Camp surrounded by walls and buildings on W outskirts of
Laredo.
⊃ Turn off N634 at Km171.6 into an avenue and drive
towards the sea. Turn left before reaching the beach and drive
around rdbt on the plaza Carlos V.
Open: Apr-Oct Site: 10HEC ▦ ⚘ ⌂ ⚑ ▲ Facilities: ⚐ ⚌
⊙ ⚐ ⌀ 🅿 Services: ⚑ ✗ ⊞ lau Off-site: ✗ ⚏ ⚑LPRS

LLANES ASTURIAS

Barcenas Antigua CN 634, 33500
☎ 98 5402887 ▤ 98 5400175
100mtrs from the town centre and beaches beside the
Carrocedo River.
⊃ SW of town beyond the hospital.
Open: Jun-Sep & Easter Site: 2.2HEC ▦ ⚘ ⌂ ▲
Prices: ⚐3.75-4.28 ⚘3.75-4.01 ⚑5.35-5.88 Facilities: ⚐ ⚌ ⊙
⚐ ⌀ 🅿 Services: ⚑ ✗ ⊞ lau Off-site: ✗ ⚏ ⚑S

Palacio de Garaña 33591 ☎ 98 5410075 ▤ 98 5410298
e-mail: info@campingpalacio.com
website: www.campingpalacio.com
Situated in the grounds of the former Palace of the Marquis
of Argüelles, the site is enclosed by stone walls and has good
facilities.
Open: May-15 Sep Site: 2.8HEC ▦ ⚒ ⌂ ⚑ Facilities: ⚐
⚌ ⊙ ⚐ ⌀ 🅿 🅿 Services: ⚑ ✗ ⊞ lau Leisure: ⚑ PRS
Off-site: ⚑L

LUARCA ASTURIAS

Cantiles 33700 ☎ 98 5640938 ▤ 98 5640938
e-mail: cantiles@conectia.net
website: www.conectica.es/cantiles
Meadowland beautifully situated high above the cliffs with
little shade from bushes. Footpath to bay 70mtrs below.
⊃ At Km308.5 turn off the N634 from Oviedo, turn towards
Faro de Luarca beyond the Firestone filling station. In Villar de
Luarca turn right and onwards 1km to site.
Open: All year Site: 2.3HEC ▦ ⚒ ⌂ Facilities: ⚐ ⚌ ⊙ ⚐
⌀ 🅿 Services: ⚑ ✗ ⊞ lau Off-site: ✗ ⚑PRS ⊞

MOTRICO (MUTRIKU) GUIPÚZCOA

Aitzeta 20830 ☎ 943 603356
On two sloping meadows, partially terraced. Lovely view of
the sea 1km away.
⊃ 0.5km NE on C6212 turn at KmSS56.1.
Open: All year Site: 1.5HEC ▦ ⚘ Facilities: ⚐ ⚌ ⊙ ⚐ ⌀
🅿 Services: ⚑ ✗ ⊞ lau Leisure: ⚑ S Off-site: ✗

NOJA CANTABRIA

Los Molinos c,la Ria S/N, 39180 ☎ 942 630426 ▤ 942 63072
e-mail: losmolinos@ceoecant.es
website: www.campinglosmolinos.com
In pleasant surroundings close to the Esmerald Coast with its
fine beaches. Various leisure and sports activities.
Open: Jun-Sep & Etr Site: 18HEC ▦ ⚘ ⌂ Prices: ⚐3.45-
4.50 ▲4.50-5.50 pitch 6.80-9.70 Facilities: ⚐ ⚌ ⊙ ⚐ ⌀ 🅿
Services: ⚑ ✗ ⊞ lau Leisure: ⚑ P Off-site: ⚑S

Playa Joyel Playa de Ris, 39180 ☎ 942 630081 ▤ 942 631294
e-mail: playajoyel@telefonica.net
website: www.cantabria.com/playajoyel.asp
On a level meadow on a peninsula with direct access to the
beach.
⊃ Between Laredo and Solares.
Open: 3 Apr-30 Sep Site: 24HEC ▦ ⚘ ⌂ ⚑ ⚋
Prices: ⚐3.70-5.50 ▲4-5 pitch 10-15.25 Facilities: ⚐ ⚌ ⊙ ⚐
⌀ 🅿 Services: ⚑ ✗ ⊞ lau Leisure: ⚑ PS

ORIO GUIPÚZCOA

CM Playa de Orio 20810 ☎ 943 834801 ▤ 943 133433
e-mail: kanpina@terra.es
website: www.oriora.com
On two flat terraces along cliffs and surrounded by hedges.
⊃ Turn off the N634 San Sebastian-Bilbao road at about
Km12.5 in Orio. Shortly before the bridge over the River Orio
turn towards the sea and continue for 1.5km.
Open: Mar-02 Nov Site: 5.4HEC ▦ ⚒ ⚋ Prices: ⚐2.50-
3.90 pitch 13.55-22.25 Facilities: ⚐ ⚌ ⊙ ⚐ ⌀ 🅿 Services: ⚑
✗ ⊞ lau Leisure: ⚑ P Off-site: ⚑RS

PECHÓN CANTABRIA

Arenas 39594 ☎ 942 717188 ▤ 942 717188
e-mail: lasarenas@ctv.es website: www.ctv.es/users/lasarenas
On numerous terraces between rocks, reaching down to the
sea.

---

contd.

⮣ *Turn off N634 E of Unquera at Km74 towards sea and take road towards S.*
Open: Jun-Sep **Site:** 12HEC ⊞ ∴ ⊕ **Prices:** ⋔3.90 ⊕3.90 ⊕5.50 ▲3.30-3.90 **Facilities:** ⋔ 🏠 ⊙ 🔁 ⊘ 🏧 **Services:** 🍽 ✕ ⊞ lau **Leisure:** ⬩ PRS

PERLORA-CANDAS ASTURIAS

Perlora 33491 ☎ 98 5870048
On top of a large hill on a peninsula with a few terraced pitches.
⮣ *Access 7km W of Gijon, turn off N632 in direction Luanco and continue for 5km.*
Open: All year **Site:** 1.4HEC ⊞ ⬥⬥ **Prices:** ⋔4.39 ⊕3.10 ⊕4.17 ▲3.75 **Facilities:** ⋔ 🏠 ⊙ 🔁 ⊘ 🏧 **Services:** 🍽 ✕ ⊞ lau **Leisure:** ⬩ S **Off-site:** ⛲

REINANTE LUGO

Reinante 27279 ☎ 982 134005 ▤ 982 134005
Longish site beyond a range of dunes on lovely sandy beach.
⮣ *On N634 at Km391.7.*
Open: All year **Site:** ⊞ ⬥⬥ 🏠 **Prices:** ⋔3.50 ⊕3.50 **Facilities:** ⋔ 🏠 ⊙ 🔁 ⊘ 🏧 **Services:** 🍽 ✕ ⊞ lau **Leisure:** ⬩ LRS

SAN SEBASTIÁN (DONOSTIA) GUIPÚZCOA

AT IGUELDO

Garoa Camping Igueldo Aita Orkolaga Pasealekua 69, 20008 ☎ 943 214502 ▤ 943 280411
e-mail: info@campingigueldo.com
website: www.campingigueldo.com
Terraced site on Monte Igualdo divided by hedges.
⮣ *Follow signs Monte Igualdo from town, and beach road, about 4.5km.*
Open: All year **Site:** 5HEC ⊞ 🏠 **Prices:** pitch 12-23.80 (incl 2 persons) **Facilities:** ⋔ 🏠 ⊙ 🔁 ⊘ 🏧 **Services:** 🍽 ✕ ⊞ lau

SANTIAGO DE COMPOSTELA LA CORUÑA

As Cancelas r do 25 de Xulls 35, 15704 ☎ 981 580266 ▤ 981 575553
Open: All year **Site:** 1.8HEC ⊞ ♣ 🏠 ▲ **Facilities:** ⋔ 🏠 ⊙ 🔁 ⊘ 🏧 **Services:** 🍽 ✕ ⊞ lau **Leisure:** ⬩ P

SANTILLANA DEL MAR CANTABRIA

Santillana 39330 ☎ 942 818250 ▤ 942 840183
e-mail: campingsantillana@ceocatnt.es
Slightly sloping meadow with bushes on a hillock within the area of a restaurant adjoining a swimming pool.
⮣ *Access from Santander via C6316 turn off shortly after the Santillana sign and continue up the hill.*
Open: All year **Site:** 70HEC ⊞ ♣ 🏠 🏠 ▲ **Facilities:** ⋔ 🏠 ⊙ 🔁 ⊘ 🏧 **Services:** 🍽 ✕ ⊞ lau **Leisure:** ⬩ P

VALDOVIÑO LA CORUÑA

Valdoviño ctra de la Playa, 15552 ☎ 981 487076 ▤ 981 486131
Six gently sloping fields partly in shade. Located behind Cafeteria Andy and block of flats with several villas beyond.
⮣ *Turn off the C646 towards Cedeira seawards and continue 700mtrs to site.*
Open: All year **Site:** 2HEC ⊞ ♣ 🏠 **Prices:** ⋔4.40-4.60 ⊕4.60-4.80 ⊕4.80-5 ▲4.60-4.80 pitch 12.40-12.80 **Facilities:** ⋔ 🏠 ⊙ 🔁 ⊘ 🏧 **Services:** 🍽 ✕ ⊞ lau **Off-site:** ⬩LPRS

VIVEIRO LUGO

Vivero 27850 ☎ 982 560004
In tall woodland near beach road and sea.
⮣ *Turn off the C642 Barreois-Ortueire road at Km443.1 and follow signs.*
Open: Jun-Sep **Site:** 1.2HEC ⊞ ♣ **Prices:** ⋔3.42 ⊕3.42 ⊕4.28 ▲3.42 **Facilities:** ⋔ 🏠 ⊙ 🔁 ⊘ 🏧 **Services:** 🍽 ⊞ lau **Off-site:** 🏠 🍽 ✕ ⬩RS

ZARAUZ (ZARAUTZ) GUIPÚZCOA

Talai Mendi 20800 ☎ 943 830042
In meadowland on hillside divided by interior roads without shade. 0.5km from the sea.
⮣ *On outskirts of town at FIRESTONE filling station at Km17.5 on N634 turn towards the sea and continue for 350mtrs along narrow asphalt road.*
Open: Jul-10 Sep **Site:** 3.8HEC ⊞ ⬥⬥ **Prices:** ⋔3.50 ⊕3.50 ▲4.18 pitch 18.95 **Facilities:** ⋔ 🏠 ⊙ 🔁 ⊘ 🏧 **Services:** 🍽 ✕ ⊞ lau **Leisure:** ⬩ S **Off-site:** ⬩PR

Zarauz Monte "Talai-Mendi" Mountain, 20800 ☎ 943 831238 ▤ 943 132486
Site with terraces separated by hedges.
⮣ *1.8km from the N634 San Sebastian-Bilbao road. Asphalt access road from Km15.5.*
Open: All year **Site:** 5HEC ⊞ 🏠 ▲ **Facilities:** ⋔ 🏠 ⊙ 🔁 ⊘ 🏧 **Services:** 🍽 ✕ ⊞ lau **Off-site:** ⬩RS

NORTH EAST

ARANDA DE DUERO BURGOS

Costajàn 9400 ☎ 947 502070
In a wooded setting with good facilities.
⮣ *Turn off N1 (Burgos-Madrid) at Km162.1 N of town.*
Open: All year **Site:** 1.8HEC ∴ 🏠 🏠 ⊕ **Facilities:** ⋔ 🏠 ⊙ 🔁 ⊘ 🏧 **Services:** 🍽 ✕ ⊞ lau **Leisure:** ⬩ P **Off-site:** 🏠 🍽 ✕ ⬩LR

BELLVER DE CERDANYA LLEIDA

Solana del Segre CTRA N-260 km198, 25720 ☎ 973 510310 ▤ 973 510698
e-mail: info@solanadelsegre.com
website: www.solanadelsegre.com
A well equipped site on the River Segre, known for its trout fishing.
⮣ *Off N260.*
Open: All year **Site:** 6.5HEC ⊞ ♣ 🏠 **Facilities:** ⋔ 🏠 ⊙ 🔁 ⊘ ⛲ 🏧 **Services:** 🍽 ✕ ⊞ lau **Leisure:** ⬩ PR **Off-site:** ⬩L

BIESCAS HUESCA

Edelweiss 22630 ☎ 974 485084
In meadow with deciduous trees on a hill in a pleasant situation.
⮣ *Turn right off C138 at Km97.*
Open: 15 Jun-15 Sep **Site:** 50HEC ⊞ ♣ **Facilities:** ⋔ 🏠 ⊙ 🔁 ⊘ 🏧 **Services:** 🍽 ✕ ⊞ lau **Off-site:** ⬩PR

BONANSA HUESCA

Baliera Cruce ctra Castejon de Sos, 22486 ☎ 974 554016 ▤ 974 554099
e-mail: info@baliera.com
website: www.baliera.com
A well equipped site in a beautiful Pyrenean location on the bank of a river.
⮣ *At Km365.5 on N260.*
Open: All year **Site:** 5HEC ⊞ 🏠 🏠 **Prices:** ⋔3.60-4.50 ⊕3.60 ▲3.60 pitch 10.50 **Facilities:** ⋔ 🏠 ⊙ 🔁 ⊘ ⛲ 🏧 **Services:** 🍽 ✕ ⊞ lau **Leisure:** ⬩ LPR **Off-site:** ✕

Site: 6HEC-Site size ⊞-grass ∴-sand ⬩-stone ⬥⬥-little shade 🏠-partly shaded ♣-mainly shaded 🏠-bungalows for hire 🏠-caravans for hire ▲-tents for hire ⊗-no dogs **Prices:** ⋔-adult per night ⊕-car per night pp-per person per night ⊕-caravan per night ▲-tent per night

BORDETA, LA LLEIDA

Prado Verde 25551 ☎ 973 647172
e-mail: euroci@hotmail.com
Level meadowland on River Garona with sparse trees and
sheltered by high hedges from traffic noise.
➲ *On the N230, Puente de Rey (French border)-Lleida road,
at Km199 behind Pirelli General filling station.*
Open: All year Site: 1.7HEC ⸛⸛⸛ ♣ Prices: ⋔4-4.20 ♣4-4.20
♣4-4.20 ⚑2 Facilities: ⋒ ⓧ ⊙ ⚑ ⌀ 🅰 Services: ⓨ ✕ ⊞ lau
Leisure: ⤳ LPR

BOSSOST LLEIDA

Bedurá-Park 25551 ☎ 73 648293 🗏 73 648293
e-mail: bedurapark@ibercom.com
website: aramweb.com/bedurapark
A terraced site in the Aran Valley offering spectacular views
over the surrounding mountains. The site, in wooded
surroundings, offers all modern facilities and a wide variety
of sporting opportunities.
➲ *Access via N230 Km174.4.*
Open: Apr-15 Sep Site: 5HEC ⸛⸛⸛ ♣ ⚐ ⌁ Prices: ⋔4.30
pitch 8-12 Facilities: ⋒ ⓧ ⊙ ⚑ ⌀ 🅰 Services: ⓨ ✕ ⊞ lau
Leisure: ⤳ PR Off-site: ⤳L

CALATAYUD ZARAGOZA

Calatayud ctra Madrid-Barcelona KM239, 50300
☎ 976 880592 🗏 976 880592
Open: 15 Mar-15 Oct Site: 1.7HEC ⸛⸛⸛ Ⓠ Prices: ⋔3.37-
5.08 ♣3.21-4.17 ♣4.49-8.35 ⚑4.49-8.35 Facilities: ⋒ ⓧ ⊙
⚑ ⌀ 🅰 Services: ⓨ ✕ ⊞ lau Leisure: ⤳ P Off-site: ✕

ESPOT LLEIDA

Sol I Neu ctra d'Espot, 25597 ☎ 973 624001 🗏 973 624107
e-mail: camping@solineu.com
A peaceful site in a beautiful mountain setting with good,
modern facilities. Organised Land Rover excursions available.
Open: Jun-15 Sep Site: 1.5HEC ⸛⸛⸛ ♣ Prices: ⋔4.20 pitch
11.30 Facilities: ⋒ ⓧ ⊙ ⚑ ⌀ 🅰 Services: ⓨ ✕ ⊞ lau
Leisure: ⤳ PR Off-site: ⓧ ⓨ ✕ ⤳L

ESTELLA NAVARRA

Lizarra Paraje de Ordoiz, 31200
☎ 948 551733 🗏 948 554755
Open: All year Site: 4HEC ⸛⸛⸛ Ⓠ ⚑ 🅰 Prices: ⋔4.07 ⚑4.07
pitch 11.02 Facilities: ⋒ ⓧ ⊙ ⚑ ⌀ 🅰 Services: ⓨ ✕ ⊞ lau
Leisure: ⤳ P

GUINGUETA, LA LLEIDA

Vall d'Aneu 25597 ☎ 973 626390
In meadowland on rising ground on both sides of the road,
partially in shade. No shade on terrace between road and
lake.
➲ *On outskirts of town near the by-pass, C147.*
Open: May-Sep Site: 0.5HEC ⸛⸛⸛ ♣ Facilities: ⋒ ⓧ ⊙ ⚑ 🗷 🅰
Services: ⓨ ✕ ⊞ lau Leisure: ⤳ P Off-site: ⓧ ⓨ ✕ ⌀ ⤳LR

HUESCA HUESCA

San Jorge Ricardo del Arco, 22004 ☎ 974 227416
website: www.camping-sanjorge.com
Site with sports field surrounded by high walls. Subdivided
by hedges, sparse woodland.
➲ *From town centre, about 1.5km along M123 towards
Zaragoza direction and follow signs.*
Open: Apr-15 Oct Site: 0.7HEC ⸛⸛⸛ Ⓠ Prices: ⋔3.75 ♣3.75
⚑3.75 Facilities: ⋒ ⓧ ⊙ ⚑ 🅰 Services: ⓨ ✕ ⊞ lau Leisure: ⤳ P
Off-site: ⓧ ⌀

JACA HUESCA

AT GUASA

Peña Oroel ctra Jaca-Sabiñanigo, 22700 ☎ 974 360215
Grassland site with rows of high poplars.
➲ *At Km13.8 of the C134 Jaca-Sabiñanigo road.*
Open: 15 Jun-15 Sep Site: 50HEC ⸛⸛⸛ ♣ Facilities: ⋒ ⓧ ⊙
⚑ ⌀ 🅰 Services: ⓨ ✕ ⊞ lau Leisure: ⤳ P

LABUERDA HUESCA

Peña Montañesa ctra Aínsa-Francia,KM2, 22360
☎ 974 500032 🗏 974 500991
e-mail: info@penamontanesa.com
website: www.penamontanesa.com
A well equipped family site in a wooded location near the
entrance to the Ordesa and Monte Perdido National Park.
Open: All year Site: 10HEC ⸛⸛⸛ ♣ ⛺ ⚑ Prices: ⋔5.75 pitch
16.50 Facilities: ⋒ ⓧ ⊙ ⚑ ⌀ 🅰 Services: ⓨ ✕ ⊞ lau
Leisure: ⤳ P Off-site: ⤳LR

MENDIGORRIA NAVARRA

El Molino ctra N111, 31150 ☎ 948 340604 🗏 948 340082
e-mail: molino@cmn.navaua.net
website: www.navaua.net/molino
Open: All year Site: 15HEC ⸛⸛⸛ Ⓠ ♣ ⛺ ⚑ 🅰 Facilities: ⋒
ⓧ ⊙ ⚑ ⌀ 🅰 Services: ⓨ ✕ ⊞ lau Leisure: ⤳ PR
Off-site: ⚌ ⤳R

NÁJERA LA RIOJA

Ruedo ps San Julian 24, 26300 ☎ 941 360102
Amongst poplars and the area of the bullring, almost no
shade.
➲ *Turn off the N120 Logroño-Burgos road in Nájera and then
continue along the river banks just before the stone bridge
across the River Majerilla, then turn left.*
Site: 0.5HEC ⸛⸛⸛ Ⓠ Prices: ⋔3.75 ♣3.50 ♣3.75 ⚑3.75
Facilities: ⋒ ⓧ ⊙ ⚑ ⌀ 🅰 Services: ⓨ ✕ ⊞ lau
Off-site: ⚌ ⤳PR

NUEVALOS ZARAGOZA

Lago Park ctra Alhama de Aragón-Nuevalos, 50210
☎ 976 849038
In a pleasant location, 100mtrs from the Laguna de la
Tranquera.
➲ *NE towards Alhama de Aragon.*
Open: Apr-Sep Site: 3HEC ⸛⸛⸛ ♣ ♣ ⛺ Facilities: ⋒ ⓧ ⊙ ⚑
⌀ 🅰 Services: ⓨ ✕ ⊞ lau Leisure: ⤳ LPR

ORICAIN NAVARRA

Ezcaba ctra Francia-Irun km7, 31194
☎ 948 330315 🗏 948 331316
e-mail: info@campingezcaba.com
website: www.campingezcaba.com
Gently sloping meadowland and a few terraces on a flat
topped hill.
➲ *N of Pamplona. Turn off N121 at Km7.3 and drive towards
Berriosuso. Turn right and drive uphill after crossing the bridge
over the River Ulzama.*
Open: All year Site: 2HEC ⸛⸛⸛ Ⓠ ⛺ ⚑ 🅰 Prices: ⋔3.89
♣3.89 ⚑4.78 ⚑3.89 Facilities: ⋒ ⓧ ⊙ ⚑ ⌀ 🅰 🗷
Services: ⓨ ✕ ⊞ lau Leisure: ⤳ PR Off-site: ⤳R

PANCORBO BURGOS

Desfiladero 9280 ☎ 947 354027
A well appointed site close to the river.
➲ *Off N1 at Km305.2.*
Open: All year Site: 13HEC ⸛⸛⸛ ⚱ Ⓠ ⛺ ⚑ Prices: ⋔3.50
♣3.50 ⚑3.50 Facilities: ⋒ ⓧ ⊙ ⚑ ⌀ 🅰 Services: ⓨ ✕ ⊞ lau
Leisure: ⤳ L Off-site: ⤳PR

Facilities: ⓧ-shop ⋒-shower ⊙-electric points for razors ⚑-electric points for caravans 🅰-parking by tents permitted
⚑-compulsory separate car park Services: ✕-café/restaurant ⓨ-bar ⌀-Camping Gaz International ⚌-gas other than Camping
Gaz ⊞-first aid facilities lau-laundry Leisure: ⤳-swimming L-Lake P-Pool R-River S-Sea Off-site: All facilities within 2km

---

PUEBLA DE CASTRO, LA HUESCA

Lago Barasona crta Nacional 123 A KM25, 22435
☎ 974 545148 ▥ 974 545228
e-mail: info@lagobarasona.com
website: www.lagobarasona.com
A well equipped, terraced site in a beautiful setting beside the lake and backed by mountains.
Open: Apr-Sep Site: 5HEC ⌸ ⌺ ⌺ Prices: ⋔3.95-5.19
⌗3.95-5.56 ⌗3.95-5.56 ⌗3.95-5.56 Facilities: ⌔ ⌸ ⊙ ⌺ ⌀
⌺ Services: ⌺ ✕ ⊞ lau Leisure: ⌇ P Off-site: ⌇LR

RIBERA DE CARDÓS LLEIDA

Cardós 25570 ☎ 973 623112 ▥ 973 623183
website: www.campingdelcardos.com
Long stretch of meadowland divided by four rows of poplars.
Camping Card Compulsory.
⮕ *Near the electricity plant in Llavorsi turn NE onto the Ribera road and follow it for 9km. Entrance near hostel Soly Neu.*
Open: Apr-29 Sep Site: 3HEC ⌸ ⌺ ⌺ ⌺ Prices: ⋔4.20-4.50 ⌗4.20-4.50 ⌗4.20-4.50 Facilities: ⌔ ⌸ ⊙ ⌺ ⌀ ⌺
Services: ⌺ ✕ ⊞ lau Leisure: ⌇ PR

SANTO DOMINGO DE LA CALZADA LA RIOJA

Bañares 26250 ☎ 941 342804 ▥ 941 340131
Open: All year Site: 12HEC ⌸ ⌺ ⌺ ⌺ ⌺ Prices: ⋔5.35
⌗5.35 ⌗5.35 ⌗5.35 Facilities: ⌔ ⌸ ⊙ ⌺ ⌀ ⌺ ⌺
Services: ⌺ ✕ ⊞ lau Leisure: ⌇ P

SAVIÑAN ZARAGOZA

Saviñan Park 50299 ☎ 976 825423 ▥ 976 825423
On meadowland in the Jalón Valley with plenty of trees for shade.
⮕ *Access via NII Zaragoza-Calatayud, exit El Frasno towards Illueca.*
Open: All year Site: 6HEC ⌸ ⌺ Facilities: ⌔ ⌸ ⊙ ⌺ ⌀
Services: ⌺ ✕ Leisure: ⌇ P

SOLSONA LLEIDA

Solsonès 25280 ☎ 973 482861 ▥ 973 481300
e-mail: info@campingsolsones.com
website: www.campingsolsones.com
A well equipped site in a picturesque mountain setting with facilities for both summer and winter holidays.
Open: All year Site: 6.3HEC ⌸ ⌺ ⌺ ⌺ ⌺ Prices: ⋔4.92
⌗4.92 ⌗4.92 ⌗4.92 Facilities: ⌔ ⌸ ⊙ ⌺ ⌀ ⌺ ⌺
Services: ⌺ ✕ ⊞ lau Leisure: ⌇ P Off-site: ⌇LR

TIERMAS ZARAGOZA

Mar del Pirineo 50682 ☎ 948 398073 ▥ 948 887177
e-mail: aytosigues@teleline.es
On broad terraces sloping down to the banks of the Embalse de Yese. Roofing provides shade for tents and cars.
⮕ *Situated on the N240 Huesca-Pamplona road at Km317.7.*
Open: May-Sep Site: 2.9HEC ⌸ ⋮⋮⋮ ⌀ ⌸ ⌺ Facilities: ⌔
⌺ ⊙ ⌺ ⌀ ⌺ Services: ⌺ ✕ ⊞ lau Leisure: ⌇ LP

TORLA HUESCA

Ordesa ctra de Ordesa, 22376 ☎ 974 486146 ▥ 974 486381
e-mail: hotelordesa@ibercom.com
website: www.staragon.com/campingordesa
On three terraces between well-kept hedges.
⮕ *2km N of the village at Km96 and N of the C138.*
Open: Easter-Oct Site: 3.5HEC ⌸ ⌺ ⌺ Prices: ⋔3.75
⌗3.75 ⌗4.39 ⌗3.75 Facilities: ⌔ ⌺ ⊙ ⌺ ⌀ ⌺ Services: ⌺ ✕
⊞ lau Leisure: ⌇ P Off-site: ⌇R

VILLOSLADA DE CAMEROS LA RIOJA

Los Cameros ctra La Virgen, 26125
☎ 941 747021 ▥ 941 742091
e-mail: info@camping-loscameros.com
website: www.camping-loscameros.com
Situated in the National Park of the Sierra Cebollera in the Iberian mountain range.
⮕ *Access via N111, turn off 50km before Logroño towards Soria and on to Villoslada.*
Open: All year Site: 4HEC ⌸ ⌺ ⌺ ⌺ Prices: ⋔3.70
⌗3.70 ⌗3.70 ⌗3.70 Facilities: ⌔ ⌺ ⊙ ⌺ ⌀ ⌺ Services: ⌺ ✕
lau Leisure: ⌇ R

NORTH WEST

BAIONA PONTEVEDRA

Baiona Playa ctra Vigo-Baiona (km 19.4), 36393
☎ 986 350035 ▥ 986 352952
e-mail: campingbayona@bme.es
website: www.campingbayona.com
On a long sandy peninsula on the Galicia coast with direct access to the beach. The site has good, modern facilities and a variety of watersports can be enjoyed there.
Open: All year Site: 4HEC ⌸ ⌺ ⌺ ⌺ Facilities: ⌔ ⌺ ⊙ ⌺
⌀ ⌺ ⌺ Services: ⌺ ✕ ⊞ lau Leisure: ⌇ PRS

CUBILLAS DE SANTA MARTA VALLADOLID

Cubillas 47290 ☎ 983 585002 ▥ 983 585016
e-mail: campingcubillas@verial.es
website: www.varial.es/valladolid/campingcubillas.htm
Meadowland with young trees, subdivided by hedges.
⮕ *Entrance on the right of the N620 from Burgos between Km100 & 101.*
Open: All year Site: 4HEC ⌸ ⌺ ⌀ ⌸ ⌺ Prices: ⋔3.40-3.80
pitch 6.40-7.25 Facilities: ⌔ ⌺ ⊙ ⌺ ⌀ ⌺ ⌺ Services: ⌺ ✕ ⊞
lau Leisure: ⌇ P Off-site: ⌇R

NIGRÁN PONTEVEDRA

Playa America 36350 ☎ 986 365404 ▥ 986 365404
e-mail: oficina@campingplayaamerica.com
website: www.campingplayaamerica.com
A modern site in a poplar wood, 300mtrs from a magnificent beach.
⮕ *Access at Km 9.250 on the Vigo-Bayona road.*
Open: 15 Jun-15 Sep Site: 4HEC ⌸ ⌺ ⌺ ⌺ Prices: ⋔3.85-4.35 ⌗3.85-4.35 ⌗3.90-4.45 ⌗3.90-4.45 Facilities: ⌔ ⌺ ⊙
⌺ ⌀ ⌺ ⌺ Services: ⌺ ✕ ⊞ lau Leisure: ⌇ PS Off-site: ⌇R

PORTONOVO PONTEVEDRA

Paxariñas 36970 ☎ 986-72 723055
website: www.sauxenxotur/paxarinas.com
Slightly sloping towards a bay, in amongst dunes, with high pines and young deciduous trees. Lovely beach.
Camping Card Compulsory.
Open: All year Site: 3HEC ⌸ ⌺ ⌺ ⌺ Facilities: ⌔ ⌺ ⊙ ⌺
⌀ ⌺ Services: ⌺ ✕ ⊞ lau Leisure: ⌇ S

SANTA MARINA DE VALDEON LÉON

El Cares 24915 ☎ 987 742676 ▥ 987 742676
e-mail: cares@elcares.com website: www.elcares.com
In a wooded mountain setting with good facilities.
⮕ *N off N621 from Portilla de la Reina.*
Open: Apr-Sep Site: 15HEC ⌸ ⌺ ⌺ Facilities: ⌔ ⌺ ⊙ ⌺
⌀ ⌺ ⌺ Services: ⌺ ✕ ⊞ lau Leisure: ⌇ R Off-site: ⌇L

Site: 6HEC-Site size ⌸-grass ⋮⋮⋮-sand ⌀-stone ⌺-little shade ⌸-partly shaded ⌺-mainly shaded ⌺-bungalows for hire ⌺-caravans for hire ⌺-tents for hire ⌀-no dogs Prices: ⋔-adult per night ⌺-car per night pp-per person per night ⌺-caravan per night ⌺-tent per night

SAN VICENTE DO MAR PONTEVEDRA

Siglo XXI 36988 ☎ 986 738100 ▤ 986 738113
e-mail: info@campingsiglo21.com
website: www.campingsiglo21.com
A popular modern site with individual sanitary facilities
attached to each pitch.
Open: May-Sep Site: 1.5HEC ⊞ ⊶ Facilities: ℝ ⅃ ⊙ ⊕ ⌀
🅿 Services: ⅒ ✕ ⊞ lau Leisure: ⅂ PS Off-site: ⅂S

SIMANCAS VALLADOLID

Plantió 47130 ☎ 983 590082
In a poplar wood, on the river bank.
⮑ *On outskirts turn off N620 at Km132.2 and continue
500mtrs on narrow asphalt road and a long single track stone
bridge over the River Pisverga.*
Open: 15 Jun-25 Sep Site: 1HEC ⊞ ⁖⁖ ♣ ▲ Facilities: ℝ ⅃
⊙ ⊕ ⌀ 🏛 🅿 Services: ⅒ ✕ ⊞ lau Leisure: ⅂ PR Off-site: 🏛

TORDESILLAS VALLADOLID

Astral Camino de Pollos 8, 47100
☎ 983 770953 ▤ 983 770953
e-mail: info@campingelastral.com
website: www.campingelastral.com
A well equipped site in a pleasant rural location close to the
River Duero.
⮑ *Leave motorway at Tordesillas exit and follow signs.*
Open: Apr-Sep Site: 3HEC ⊞ ⁖⁖ ♣ 🏠 Prices: ⅃3.65-4.65
⚗3.12 ⚘3.65 ▲3.65-4.65 Facilities: ℝ ⅃ ⊙ ⊕ ⌀ 🅿
Services: ⅒ ✕ ⊞ lau Leisure: ⅂ P Off-site: 🏛 ⅂R

VALENCIA DE DON JUAN LÉON

Pico Verde Ctra C-621 Mayorga-Astorga, 24200
☎ 987 750525 ▤ 987 750525
e-mail: campingpicoverde@terra.es
⮑ *Turn E off the N630 (Léon-Madrid) at Km32.2 and
continue for 4km.*
Open: 15 Jun-13 Sep Site: 2.7HEC ⊞ ♣ Prices: ⅃3.53
⚗3.53 ⚘3.53 ▲3.53 Facilities: ℝ ⅃ ⊙ ⊕ ⌀ 🅿 Services: ⅒ ✕
⊞ lau Leisure: ⅂ P Off-site: ⅂R

VILLAMEJIL LÉON

Rio Tuerto 24711 ☎ 987 605076
Open: Jul-Aug Site: 0.6HEC ⊞ ♣ Facilities: ℝ ⅃ ⊙ ⊕ 🅿
Services: ⅒ ✕ ⊞ lau Leisure: ⅂ R Off-site: ⅃ ⅒ ✕

SOUTH

ADRA ALMERIA

Las Gaviotas 04770 ☎ 950 400660 ▤ 950 400660
e-mail: info@campinglasgaviotas.com
website: www.campinglasgaviotas.com
A modern site close to the beach with good facilities.
⮑ *2km W on N340 (Almeria-Málaga)*
Open: All year Site: 2HEC ⁖⁖ ♣ 🏠 ⚘ Prices: ⅃2.67-3.70
⚗2.67-3.70 ⚘2.73-4.02 ▲2.67-3.70 Facilities: ℝ ⊙ ⊕ ⌀ 🏛
🅿 Services: ⅒ ✕ ⊞ lau Leisure: ⅂ PS Off-site: ⅂PS

Habana 4770 ☎ 619454134 ▤ 950522274
A quiet site with good facilities and direct access to the sea.
⮑ *2km W at Km58.3 on N340 (Almeria-Málaga).*
Open: All year Site: 1.5HEC ⁖⁖ ♣ ⚘ ▲ Facilities: ℝ ⅃ ⊙
⚘ ⌀ 🅿 Services: ⅒ ✕ ⊞ lau Leisure: ⅂ S

> ### A Guide to Caravan & Camping
> ### in Great Britain is also available
> ### from **The AA**

AGUILAS MURCIA

Calarreona ctra de Aguilas a Vera, 30880
☎ 968 413704 ▤ 968 413704
e-mail: info@campingcalarreona.com
website: www.campingcalarreona.com
A quiet site, 50mtrs from the sea.
⮑ *Near Km4 on N332 (Aguilas-Murcia).*
Open: All year Site: 3.6HEC ⁖⁖ ⊶ 🏠 ⚘ Prices: ⅃3.42
⚗3.81 ▲3.42 Facilities: ℝ ⅃ ⊙ ⊕ ⌀ 🅿 Services: ⅒ ✕ ⊞ lau
Leisure: ⅂ S

ALCAZARES, LOS MURCIA

Cartagonova 30710 ☎ 968 575100 ▤ 968 575225
⮑ *On CN332 between Los Alcazares and La Union.*
Open: All year Site: 30HEC ⁖⁖ ⊶ ⚘ ▲ Facilities: ℝ ⅃ ⊙
⚘ ⌀ 🅿 Services: ⅒ ⊞ lau Leisure: ⅂ PS Off-site: ✕ 🏛

ALMAYATE MÁLAGA

Almayate Costa 29749 ☎ 952 556289 ▤ 952 556310
e-mail: almayatecosta@campings.net
website: www.campings.net/almayatecosta
Open: Apr-Sep Site: 2.4HEC ⊞ ⁖⁖ ⚹ Facilities: ℝ ⅃ ⊙
⚘ ⌀ 🅿 Services: ⅒ ✕ ⊞ lau Leisure: ⅂ P Off-site: ⅂S

ALMERIMAR ALMERIA

Mar Azul Playa de San Miguel, 04700
☎ 950 497505 ▤ 950 497294
e-mail: info@campingmarazul.com
website: www.campingmarazul.com
On level ground surrounded by palm trees and tamarins.
Sports and recreational facilities available.
⮑ *6km from village.*
Open: All year Site: 22HEC ⁖⁖ ⚹ ⊶ 🏠 Prices: ⅃3.90-5.08
⚗3.90-5.08 ⚘3.90-5.08 ▲3.90-5.08 Facilities: ℝ ⅃ ⊙ ⊕ ⌀
🏛 🅿 Services: ⅒ ✕ ⊞ lau Leisure: ⅂ PS

BAÑOS DE FORTUNA MURCIA

Fuente 30326 ☎ 968 685017 ▤ 968 685125
e-mail: campingfuente@terra.es
website: www.campingfuente.com
A camping ground within a hotel complex with individual
bathroom facilities attached to each pitch and good
recreational facilities.
⮑ *Take C3223 from Fortuna à Pinoso to Balncario de
Fortuna. Signposted.*
Open: All year Site: 1.9HEC ⁖⁖ ⚹ ⊶ Prices: ⅃2.25 pitch
8.50-9.50 Facilities: ℝ ⅃ ⊙ ⊕ ⌀ 🏛 🅿 Services: ⅒ ✕ ⊞ lau
Leisure: ⅂ LP

Facilities: ⅃-shop ℝ-shower ⊙-electric points for razors ⊕-electric points for caravans 🏛-parking by tents permitted
🅿-compulsory separate car park **Services:** ✕-café/restaurant ⅒-bar ⌀-Camping Gaz International 🏛-gas other than Camping
Gaz ⊞-first aid facilities lau-laundry **Leisure:** ⅂-swimming L-Lake P-Pool R-River S-Sea **Off-site:** All facilities within 2km

BOLNUEVO MURCIA

Garoa Camping Playa de Mazarrón 30877
☎ 968 150660 ▤ 968 150837
On level ground divided by a footpath and partly bordered
by palm trees.
➔ *Turn W off N332 in Puerto de Mazarrón at approx Km111
and head towards Bolnuevo. Then take the MU road and drive
4.6km to site entrance which is 1km E of Punta Bela.*
Open: All year Site: 8.5HEC ∷∴ ۹ ⊞ Facilities: ⋔ 🖫 ⊙ 🖭
𝓸 🏠 Services: 🍴 ✕ ⊞ lau Leisure: ⤳ PS

CABO DE GATA ALMERIA

Cabo de Gata 04150 ☎ 950 160443 ▤ 950 160044
In a natural parkland location near the beach.
➔ *N340 (E15), exit 467/471.*
Open: All year Site: 3.60HEC ∷∴ ⤳₶ Prices: ⋔3.40 ⋔🚗3.70
🚐3.70 ▲3.70 Facilities: ⋔ 🖫 𝓸 Services: 🍴 ✕ Leisure: P
See advertisement on page 349

CARCHUNA GRANADA

Don Cactus Carchuna-Motril, 18730
☎ 958 623109 ▤ 958 624294
e-mail: info@campingcastillo.com
website: www.campingcastillo.com
Modern site adjoining the beach. Dogs not allowed in July
and August.
➔ *At Km343 on N340 (Carchuna-Motril).*
Open: All year Site: 4HEC ∷∴ ۹ ⊞ Prices: ⋔1.38-4.60 pitch
2.57-8.56 Facilities: ⋔ 🖫 ⊙ 🖭 𝓸 🏠 Services: 🍴 ✕ lau
Leisure: ⤳ PS

CARLOTA, LA CORDOBA

Carlos III Ctra N-4 km430, 14100
☎ 957 300697 ▤ 957 300697
e-mail: camping@campingcarlosIII.com
website: www.campingcarlosIII.com
In wooded surroundings with modern facilities.
➔ *Access via 'La Carlota' exit on NIV.*
Open: All year Site: 7HEC ∷∴ ♣ ⊞ 🚐 Prices: ⋔4.30 ⋔🚗3.90
🚐4.30 ▲4.10 Facilities: ⋔ 🖫 ⊙ 🖭 𝓸 🏠 Services: 🍴 ✕ lau
Leisure: ⤳ LP Off-site: ⛁ ⤳PS

CASTILLO DE BAÑOS GRANADA

Castillo de Baños Castillo de Baños, La Mamola, 18750
☎ 958 829528 ▤ 958 829768
e-mail: castillo@doucactus.com website: www.doucactus.com
Well equipped site next to the beach.
➔ *At Km360 on N340 (Castillo de Baños-La Mamola).*
Open: All year Site: 3HEC ∷∴ ♣ Facilities: ⋔ 🖫 ⊙ 🖭 𝓸 🏠
Services: 🍴 ✕ ⊞ lau Leisure: ⤳ PS

CONIL DE LA FRONTERA CÁDIZ

Fuente del Gallo Fuente del Gallo, 11140
☎ 956 440137 ▤ 956 442036
e-mail: camping@campingfuentedelgallo.com
website: www.campingfuentedelgallo.com
A well equipped site in a wooded location 300mtrs from the beach.
➔ *Signposted from N340, Km21.6.*
Open: Apr-Sep Site: 3HEC ∷∴ ♣ ⊞ ▲ Facilities: ⋔ 🖫 ⊙ 🖭
𝓸 🏠 Services: 🍴 ✕ ⊞ lau Leisure: ⤳ P Off-site: ⤳S

Roche Pago del Zorro, 11149 ☎ 956 442216 ▤ 956 232319
e-mail: info@campingroche.com
website: www.campingroche.com
Spread among pine groves with well defined pitches close to
the beach.
Open: All year Site: 3.3HEC ∷∴ ∷∴ ♣ ⊞ Prices: ⋔4.50
⋔🚗3.70 🚐9.50 ▲4.30 pitch 21.20 Facilities: ⋔ 🖫 ⊙ 🖭 𝓸 🏠
Services: 🍴 ✕ ⊞ lau Leisure: ⤳ P Off-site: ⤳S ⊞

ESTEPONA MALÁGA

Parque Tropical 29680 ☎ 95 2793618 ▤ 95 2793618
A modern site situated at the foot of the Sierra Bermeja
mountains, five minutes walk from the sea.
➔ *Access via N340 at Km162.*
Open: All year Site: 12.4HEC ♠ ۹ ⊞ Facilities: ⋔ 🖫 ⊙ 🖭 𝓸
🏠 Services: 🍴 ✕ ⊞ lau Leisure: ⤳ PS Off-site: ⤳S

GALLARDOS, LOS ALMERIA

Gallardos 04280 ☎ 950 528324 ▤ 950 469596
e-mail: campinglosgallardos@hotmail.com
website: www.campinglosgallardos.com
Level site with individual pitches, 11km from the sea and
10km from the old Moorish village of Mojacar. English
management.
➔ *500mtrs from km 525 on CN340.*
Open: All year Site: 3.5HEC ∷∴ ۹ Prices: ⋔3.75 ⋔🚗3.75
🚐3.75 ▲3.75 Facilities: ⋔ 🖫 ⊙ 🖭 𝓸 ⛺ 🏠 Services: 🍴 ✕
⊞ lau Leisure: ⤳ P

GRANADA GRANADA

Sierra Nevada ctra de Jaen 107, 18014
☎ 958 150062 ▤ 958 150954
e-mail: campingmotel@terra.es
website: www.campingsierranevada.com
Almost level grassy site, in numerous sections, within motel
complex.
Open: Mar-1 Nov Site: 3HEC ▬ ♣ ⊞ Prices: ⋔480 ▲4.80
pitch 10.90 Facilities: ⋔ 🖫 ⊙ 🖭 𝓸 🏠 Services: 🍴 ✕ ⊞ lau
Leisure: ⤳ P Off-site: ⤳LRS

GUIJARRO, LA CORDOBA

Campiña 14547 ☎ 957 315303 ▤ 957 315158
e-mail: camping_campina@bch.vodafone.es
In a quiet location in a rural setting surrounded by olive trees
and elms with good, modern facilities.
➔ *Access via N4 turn off at Km424 or Km441 and follow signs
to Santaella and campsite.*
Open: All year Site: 0.7HEC ∷∴ ۹ ⊞ ▲ Prices: ⋔3.96
⋔🚗3.96 🚐4.12 ▲3.75 Facilities: ⋔ 🖫 ⊙ 🖭 𝓸 🏠 Services: 🍴 ✕
⊞ lau Leisure: ⤳ P

ISLA CRISTINA HUELVA

Giralda 21410 ☎ 959 343318 ▤ 959 343318
e-mail: campinggiralda@infonegocio.com
On level ground dotted with trees within easy reach of the
beach. Good, modern facilities and plenty of entertainment.
➔ *On Isla Cristina-La Antilla road.*
Open: All year Site: 15HEC ∷∴ ♣ ⊞ Prices: ⋔5.50 ⋔🚗4.60
🚐6.50 ▲5.10-6.95 Facilities: ⋔ 🖫 ⊙ 🖭 𝓸 🏠 Services: 🍴 ✕ ⊞
lau Leisure: ⤳ PR Off-site: ⤳S

ISLA PLANA MURCIA

Madrilles ctra de la Azohia Km45, 30868
☎ 968 152151 ▤ 968 152092
A large family site with a wide variety of recreational
facilities.
➔ *Access via Mazarron-Cartagena road.*
Open: All year Site: 5.5HEC ▬ ۹ ⊞ ⌀ Prices: ⋔3.12-3.69
⋔🚗3.12-3.69 🚐3.55 ▲3.12-3.69 pitch 10.65 Facilities: ⋔ 🖫 ⊙
🖭 𝓸 ⛺ 🏠 Services: 🍴 ✕ ⊞ lau Leisure: ⤳ PS Off-site: ✕

MANGA DEL MAR MENOR, LA MURCIA

La Manga 30370 ☎ 968 563014 ▤ 968 563426
e-mail: lamanga@caravaning.es website: www.caravaning.es
A large family site on the Mar Menor lagoon. Pitches
separated by hedges or trees. Good recreational facilities.

➲ *Off the Cartagena motorway.*
Open: All year Site: 32HEC ♨ ⚤ ⊞ Facilities: ↑ ⅃ ⊙ ⊡ ∅
♨ ☎ Services: ⚐ ✗ ⊞ lau Leisure: ⇌ PS

MARBELLA MÁLAGA

Buganvilla 29600 ☎ 95 2831973 ▤ 95 2831974
A well equipped site in a pine forest close to the beach.
Camping Card Compulsory.
➲ *E of Marbella off the N340 coast road towards Mijas.*
Open: All year Site: 4HEC ⏛ ∴∴ ⚤ ⊞ ⊡ Facilities: ↑ ⅃
⊙ ⊡ ∅ ♨ ☎ Services: ⚐ ✗ ⊞ lau Leisure: ⇌ PS

MAZAGÓN HUELVA

Mazagón cuesta de la Barca s/n, 21130
☎ 959 376208 ▤ 959 536256
e-mail: info@campingplayamazagon.com
website: www.campingplayamazagon.com
Undulating terrain amongst dunes in sparse pine forest. Long
sandy beach.
➲ *Turn off the N431 Sevilla-Huelva road just before San Juan
del Puerto in direction of Moguer and continue S via Palso de
la Frontera.*
Open: All year Site: 8HEC ∴∴ ⚤ Prices: ⚐4.28 ⊞4.28 ⊼4
pitch 16 Facilities: ↑ ⅃ ⊙ ⊡ ∅ ☎ Services: ⚐ ✗ lau
Leisure: ⇌ P Off-site: ⇌S

MOJÁCAR ALMERIA

Sopalmo Sopalmo, 04637 ☎ 950 478413
Open: All year Site: 1.7HEC ∴∴ ♨ ⚤ Facilities: ↑ ⊙ ⊡ ♨ ☎
Services: ⚐ ✗ ⊞ lau Off-site: ✗ ⇌S

MOTRIL GRANADA

Playa de Poniente 18613 ☎ 958820303 ▤ 958604191
e-mail: camplapo@infonegocio.com
website: www.infonegocio.com/camplapo
Open: All year Site: 2.4HEC Facilities: ↑ ⅃ ⊙ ⊡ ♨
Services: ✗ lau Leisure: ⇌ P Off-site: ⇌S

OTURA GRANADA

Suspiro del Moro 18630 ☎ 958 555105 ▤ 958 555105
A modern site with good facilities, 5 minutes from the town centre.
➲ *10km S of Granada via N323.*
Open: All year Site: 1HEC ∴∴ ⚤ ⊞ Facilities: ↑ ⅃ ⊙ ⊡ ∅
☎ Services: ⚐ ✗ ⊞ lau Leisure: ⇌ P Off-site: ♨ ⇌R

PELIGROS GRANADA

Granada Cerro de la Cruz, 18210 ☎ 958 340548
In a wooded location with panoramic views.
➲ *Access via N323 Jaen-Granada exit 123 towards Peligros.*
Site: 2.2HEC ⏛ ♨ ⚤ Prices: ⚐4.49 pitch 9.95 Facilities: ↑
⅃ ⊙ ⊡ ☎ Services: ⚐ ✗ ⊞ lau Leisure: ⇌ P

PUERTO DE SANTA MARÍA, EL CÁDIZ

Playa Las Dunas de San Anton
ps Maritimo de la Puntilla, 11500
☎ 956 872210 ▤ 956 860117
e-mail: campinglasdunas@terra.es
website: www.lasdunascamping.com
Large site with good recreational facilities close to the beach.
Open: All year Site: 13.2HEC ⚤ ⊞ ⊼ Prices: ⚐3.83-4.26
⊞4.17-4.63 ⊼4.17-4.63 Facilities: ↑ ⅃ ⊙ ⊡ ∅ ☎ Services: ⚐
✗ ⊞ lau Leisure: ⇌ P Off-site: ⅃ ⚐ ✗ ♨ ⇌RS ⊞

CAMPING
PLAYA DE PONIENTE
Playa de Poniente, s/n.
Costa Tropical • E-18600 Motril
Granada
Tel: (34) 958 820 303
Fax: (34) 958 60 41 91

Open
all year

Situated in the Tropical Coast, it is
45 minutes from Granada and
65 minutes from Sierra Nevada, where
you can practise ski and with an agreable weather all the year. You can
enjoy excursions and all kind of sports. The following facilities are available:

- Cafeteria
- Restaurante
- Terrace
- Swimming pool
- Tennis court
- Animation
- Solarium
- Park
- Washing machine
- Supermarket

- Hot free water
- Car wash
- Telephone box
- Medicine cabinet
- Fridge
- Safe
- Aerobic
- Canoas
- Bungalows
- Football

- Mountain bike.
In the surroundings you
also can practise:
- Windsurfing (100mts.)
- Golf (500m.)
- Scuba diving clases
(800m.)
- Paragliding (3km.)
- Water skiing (100mts.)

RONDA MÁLAGA

El Sur ctra de Algeciras, 29400 ☎ 95 2875939 ▤ 95 2877054
e-mail: info@campingelsur.com
website: www.campingelsur.com
In a beautiful location in the heart of the Serrania of Ronda.
Open: All year Site: 4HEC ∴∴ ⚤ ⊞ Prices: ⚐3.85 ⊞3.30
⊼3.30 Facilities: ↑ ⅃ ⊙ ⊡ ∅ ☎ Services: ⚐ ✗ ⊞ lau
Leisure: ⇌ P

ROQUETAS-DE-MAR ALMERIA

Roquetas Los Parrales, 04740 ☎ 950 343809 ▤ 950 342525
e-mail: roquetas@campings.net
website: www.campings.net/roquetas
➲ *Access by road No 340. 1.7km from Km428.6.*
Open: All year Site: 8HEC ∴∴ ⚤ ⊞ Prices: ⚐3.80 ⊞3.80
⊞3.80 ⊼3.80 Facilities: ↑ ⅃ ⊙ ⊡ ∅ ♨ ☎ Services: ⚐ ✗ ⊞
lau Leisure: ⇌ LPS

SANTA ELENA JAÉN

Despeñaperros 23213 ☎ 953 664192 ▤ 953 664192
e-mail: campingdesp@navegalia.com
A clean, restful site, in a nature reserve with fine views of the
surrounding mountains.
➲ *At Km257 on NIV-E5.*
Open: All year Site: 5HEC ∴∴ ⚤ Prices: ⚐3.30 ⊞3.30
⊞3.30 ⊼3.50 Facilities: ↑ ⅃ ⊙ ⊡ ∅ ☎ Services: ⚐ ✗ ⊞ lau
Leisure: ⇌ P

SEVILLA (SEVILLE) SEVILLA

Sevilla 41008 ☎ 954 514379 ▤ 954 514379
e-mail: campingsevilla@turinet.net
website: es.turinet.net/empresa/campingsevilla
Level site near airfield, road and railway.

contd.

Facilities: ⅃-shop ↑-shower ⊙-electric points for razors ⊡-electric points for caravans ☎-parking by tents permitted
⊟-compulsory separate car park Services: ✗-café/restaurant ⚐-bar ∅-Camping Gaz International ♨-gas other than Camping
Gaz ⊞-first aid facilities lau-laundry Leisure: ⇌-swimming L-Lake P-Pool R-River S-Sea Off-site: All facilities within 2km

⊃ *About 2km from airfield, 100mtrs from the NIV (Madrid-Sevilla) at Km533.8.*
Open: All year Site: 2HEC :⋅⋅: ⊶ ⊞ Prices: ⋔3.25 ⊶3.25 ⊕3.25 ▲3.25 pitch 8 Facilities: ⋔ ⅀ ⊙ ⊕ ∅ ☎ Services: ⍱ ✕ ⊞ lau Leisure: ⋋ P

Tarifa Cádiz

Paloma 11380 ☎ 956 684203 ▥ 956 681880
A modern site in a secluded situation 400mtrs from the beach and next to the Bronze Age Necrolopis de los Algarbes. Fine views of the African coast across the Straits of Gibraltar.
⊃ *Access via N340 Cádiz-Málaga at Km 74.*
Open: All year Site: 4.9HEC ⊔⊔⊔ ⊶ ⊞ Facilities: ⋔ ⅀ ⊙ ⊕ ∅ ☎ Services: ⍱ ✕ ⊞ lau Leisure: ⋋ P Off-site: ⋋RS

Rió Jara 11380 ☎ 956 680570 ▥ 956 680570
e-mail: campingriojara@terra.es
Extensive site on meadowland with good tree coverage. Long sandy beach.
⊃ *On the N340 Málaga-Cádiz road at Km79.7 turn towards the sea.*
Open: All year Site: 3HEC ⊔⊔⊔ ♣ Facilities: ⋔ ⅀ ⊙ ⊕ ∅ ☎ Services: ⍱ ✕ ⊞ lau Leisure: ⋋ RS

Tarifa 11380 ☎ 956 684778 ▥ 956 684778
e-mail: camping-tarifa@camping-tarifa.com
website: www.camping-tarifa.com
A terraced site in wooded surroundings, 100mtrs from the sea.
⊃ *At Km78 on Málaga-Cádiz road.*
Open: All year Site: 3.2HEC :⋅⋅: ♣ Facilities: ⋔ ⅀ ⊙ ⊕ ∅ ☎ Services: ⍱ ✕ ⊞ lau Leisure: ⋋ P Off-site: ⋋RS

At Torre De La Peña (7km NW)

Torre de la Peña 11380 ☎ 956 684903 ▥ 956 681473
e-mail: info@campingtp.com website: www.campingtp.com
Terraced, on both sides of through road. Upper terraces are considerably quieter. Roofing provides shade. View of the sea, Tarifa and on clear days N Africa (Tangier).

⊃ *Entrance on the N340 Cádiz-Málaga, at Km76.5 turn inland by the old square tower.*
Open: All year Site: 3HEC ⊔⊔⊔ :⋅⋅: ⊶ ⊞ Facilities: ⋔ ⅀ ⊙ ⊕ ∅ ☎ Services: ⍱ ✕ ⊞ lau Leisure: ⋋ PS

Torre Del Mar Málaga

Torre del Mar 29740 ☎ 95 2540224
A fine site on a beautiful beach, with good facilities. Shop open June-September only.
⊃ *SW of town. Access via N340 (Almeria-Málaga).*
Open: All year Site: 2.4HEC ⊔⊔⊔ :⋅⋅: ♣ Facilities: ⋔ ⅀ ⊙ ⊕ ∅ ☎ Services: ⍱ ✕ ⊞ lau Leisure: ⋋ P Off-site: ⋋S

Vejer De La Frontera Cádiz

Vejer ctra National (N340), 11150
☎ 956 450098 ▥ 956 450098
e-mail: info@campingvejer.com
website: www.campingvejer.com
A quiet family site in a pleasant shady location.
⊃ *At Km39.5 on N340 Cádiz-Málaga.*
Open: Etr-end Sep Site: 0.8HEC :⋅⋅: ♣ ⊞ ⊕ ▲ Facilities: ⋔ ⅀ ⊙ ⊕ ☎ Services: ⍱ ✕ ⊞ lau Leisure: ⋋ P

Andorra

Sant Julià De Lúria

Huguet ctra de Fontaneda ☎ 376 843718 ▥ 376 843718
On level strip of meadowland with rows of fruit and deciduous trees.
⊃ *Off La Seu d'Urgell road N1, S of village and drive W across river.*
Open: All year Site: 1.5HEC ⊔⊔⊔ ⊶ ♣ Prices: ⋔4-4.50 ⊕4-4.50 ▲4-4.50 Facilities: ⋔ ⊙ ⊕ ☎ Services: ⊞ lau Leisure: ⋋ R Off-site: ⅀ ⍱ ✕ ∅ ⌂ ⋋LP

A cable car climbing the Picos de Europe

Site: 6HEC-Site size ⊔⊔⊔-grass :⋅⋅:-sand ♣-stone ⅃⅄-little shade ⊶-partly shaded ♣-mainly shaded
⊞-bungalows for hire ⊕-caravans for hire ▲-tents for hire ⊘-no dogs Prices: ⋔-adult per night ⊶-car per night
pp-per person per night ⊕-caravan per night ▲-tent per night

SWITZERLAND

Bordered by France in the west, Germany in the north, Austria in the east, and Italy in the south, Switzerland is considered by many to be one of the most beautiful countries in Europe.

FACTS AND FIGURES
Area: 41,285 sq km (15,940 sq miles)
Population: 7,283,274 (1998)
Capital: Bern (Berne)
Language: German, French, Italian, Romansh
IDD code: 41. To call the UK dial 00 44
Currency: Swiss Franc (CHF)

Local time: GMT + 1 (summer GMT + 2)
Emergency Services: Police 117; Fire 118; Ambulance 144.
Business Hours-Banks: Mon-Fri 08.30-16.30 (in towns)
Shops: Mon-Fri 08.00/08.30-12.00 and 13.30-18.30/19.00 (no lunchtime closure in large cities); Saturday until 16.00/17.00.
Average daily temperatures: Zurich

Jan 0°C	Jul 19°C
Mar 5°C	Sep 15°C
May 9°C	Nov 5°C

Tourist Information:
Switzerland Travel Centre
UK Swiss Centre, 10 Wardour Street, London W1D 6QF

Tel 00800 100 200 30 (freephone)
USA 608 Fifth Avenue New York, NY 10020
Tel (212) 757 5944
Tourist info website: www.myswitzerland.com

It has the highest mountains in Europe and some of the most awe-inspiring waterfalls and lakes, features that are offset by picturesque villages set amid green pastures and an abundance of Alpine flowers covering the valleys and lower mountain slopes during the spring. The highest peaks are Monte Rosa (15,217ft) on the Italian border, the Matterhorn (14,782ft), and the Jungfrau (13,669ft). Some of the most beautiful areas are the Via Mala Gorge, the Falls of the Rhine near Schaffhausen, the Rhône Glacier, and the lakes of Luzern and Thun.

The Alps cause many climatic variations throughout Switzerland, but generally the climate is said to be the healthiest in the world. In the higher Alpine regions temperatures tend to be low, whereas the lower land of the northern area has higher temperatures and hot summers. French is spoken in the western cantons (regions), Swiss-German dialects (although German is understood) in the central and northern cantons and Italian in Ticino. Romansch is spoken in Grisons.

Switzerland has 340 campsites, 43 of them are run by the Touring Club Suisse (TCS) who publish details of classified sites annually. Information can also be obtained from tourist offices, which are to be found in most provincial towns and resorts. The season extends from April or May to September or October, although some sites are open all year, particularly at winter sports resorts.

Off-site camping regulations differ from canton (region) to canton. However, permission to camp off an official campsite must be obtained from the landowner or local police. Overnight parking may be tolerated in rest areas of some motorways, but at all times the high standard of hygiene regulations must be observed. Make sure you do not contravene local laws.

HOW TO GET THERE

From Britain, Switzerland is usually approached via France.

DISTANCE

From the Channel ports to Bern is approximately 810km (503 miles), a distance which will normally require only one overnight stop.

If you intend to use Swiss motorways, you will be liable for a tax of CHF 40 - see 'Motorway tax' below for full details.

CAR SLEEPER TRAINS

Summer services are available from Calais to Avignon and Paris to Geneva.

MOTORING & GENERAL INFORMATION

The information given here is specific to Switzerland. It **must** be read in conjunction with the Essential Motoring Information at the front of the book, which covers those regulations which are common to many countries.

BRITISH EMBASSY/CONSULATES*

The British Embassy together with its consular section is located at 3005 Berne, Thunstrasse 50 ☎ 031 359 77 41. There is a British Consulate in Genève (Geneva) and British Consulate with Honorary Consul in Montreux/Vevey (St Légier) and Vice-Consulates with Honorary Consuls in Basel, Lugano, Valais (Mollens) and Zurich.

CHILDREN IN CARS

It is recommended that children do not travel as front seat passengers. Children under 12 travelling in the rear must use seat belts or restraint system appropriate to size. See Essential Motoring Information under 'Passengers' and 'Seat Belts'.

CURRENCY

The currency is the Swiss Franc (CHF), which is divided into 100 centimes. Banknotes have denominations of CHF 10, 20, 50, 100, 200, and 1000; the coins are CHF 1, 2, and 5, and centimes 5, 10, 20 and 50.

There are no restrictions on the import or export of foreign or Swiss currency. In addition to banks there are exchange offices at the border, railway stations in large towns, airports and in travel agencies and hotels which are usually open 08.00-20.00hrs.

Although the Euro is not the Swiss currency, many sites may quote prices in Euros, rather than Swiss Francs. Please contact the site directly to check prices.

DIMENSIONS AND WEIGHT RESTRICTIONS*

Private cars and towed trailers or caravans are restricted to the following dimensions - car height, 4 metres; width, 2.55 metres; length, 12 metres.

Trailer/caravan height, 4 metres; width, 2.55 metres; length, 12 metres (including tow bar). The maximum permitted overall length of vehicle/trailer or caravan combination is 18.75 metres.

Note: It is dangerous or forbidden to use a vehicle towing a trailer or caravan on some mountain roads; motorists should ensure that roads on which they are about to travel are suitable for the conveyance of vehicle/trailer or caravan combinations.

The fully-laden weight of trailers which do not have an independent braking system should not exceed 50% of the unladen weight of the towing vehicle, but trailers which have an independent braking system can weigh up to 100% of the unladen weight of the towing vehicle.

DRIVING LICENCE*

A valid UK or Republic of Ireland licence is accepted in Switzerland. The minimum age at which visitors from UK or Republic of Ireland may use a temporarily imported car is 18 years and a temporarily imported motorcycle of between 50-125cc (not exceeding 40kph) 16 years, exceeding 125cc 18 years.

FOODSTUFFS*

Visitors may import foodstuffs and non-alcoholic drinks duty-free, for private use up to the value of CHF300 per person per day. Subject to certain prohibitions and restrictions, meat and meat products may be imported duty free up to 500g per person per day (beef, veal etc.) and up to 3.5kg per person per day (chicken etc.).

LIGHTS*

It is recommended that motorcyclists use dipped headlights during the day.

MOTORING CLUB

The **Touring Club Suisse** (TCS) has branch offices in all important towns, and has its head office at 1214 Vernier/Genève, Chemin de Blandonnet 4, ☎ 022 417 27 27. The TCS will extend a courtesy service to all motorists but their major services will have to be paid for. The opening hours of TCS offices vary according to location and time of year, but generally they are 08.00/09.00-11.45/12.30hrs and 13.30/14.00-17.00/18.30hrs Monday to Friday and 08.00/09.00-11.45/12.00hrs Saturday (summer only).

MOTORWAY TAX

The Swiss authorities levy an annual motorway tax and substantial fines are imposed for non-payment (CHF100 plus cost of *vignette*). A vehicle sticker, costing CHF40 for vehicles up to 3.5 tonnes

Estaveyer-Le-Lac on the shores of Lake Neuchatel.

maximum total weight and known locally as a *vignette,* must be displayed by vehicles using Swiss motorways including motorcycles, trailers and caravans. Motorists may purchase the stickers in the UK from Switzerland Tourism, Swiss Centre, 10 Wardour Street, London W1D 6QF, ; in Switzerland from customs offices, post offices, service stations and garages.

Vehicles over 3.5 tonnes maximum total weight are taxed on all roads in Switzerland. For coaches and caravans a licence for one day, 10 days, one month and one year periods can be obtained. For lorries the tax depends on weight and distance. There are no stickers, and the tax must be paid at the Swiss frontier.

PETROL*

See Essential Motoring Information under 'Petrol/Diesel'.

ROADS

Switzerland has about 1,000 miles of motorway (*Autobahn* or *autoroute*). Tolls are not payable but see *Motorway Tax* above. Emergency telephones, which connect you to the motorway control police, are located every 2km.

The road surfaces are generally good, but some main roads are narrow in places. Traffic congestion may be severe at the beginning and end of the German school holidays.

On any stretch of mountain road, the driver of a private car may be asked by the driver of a postal bus, which is painted yellow, to reverse, or otherwise manoeuvre to allow the postal bus to pass. Postal bus drivers often sound a distinctive three note horn; no other vehicles may use this type of horn in Switzerland.

SPEED LIMITS*

Car/motorcycle
Built-up areas 50km/h (31mph)
Other roads 80km/h (49mph)
semi-motorways 100km/h (62mph)
Motorways 120km/h (74mph)

Car/caravan/trailer
Built-up areas 50km/h (31mph)
Other roads, including semi-motorways 80km/h (49mph)
Motorways 80km/h (49mph)

These limits do not apply if another limit is indicated by signs, or if the vehicle is subject to a lower general speed limit.

WARNING TRIANGLE/HAZARD WARNING

It is compulsory for a vehicle to be equipped with a warning triangle and to use it in the event of accident or breakdown. The triangle must be placed on the road at least 50 metres (55yds) behind the vehicle on ordinary roads, and at least 100 metres (109yds) on high speed roads. If in an emergency lane the triangle must be placed on the right. Hazard warning lights may be used in conjunction with the triangle or when traffic slows due to accident or traffic jam.

*Additional information will be found in the Essential Motoring Information at the front of the book.

NORTH

KÜNTEN AARGAU

Sulz 5444 ☎ 079 6607426 ▤ 056 4964879
e-mail: camping.sulz@bluewin.ch
Situated by a river.
⮕ *From motorway A1 turn off at Baden in the direction of Bremgarten.*
Open: 15 Mar-Oct Site: 3HEC ⤒⤒⤒ 🔾 🚐 Prices: ♦6 🚗2
🚐8-12 ▲6-10 Facilities: 🏪 🛁 ⊙ 🚻 ⌀ 🛁 🅿 Services: ✕ ⊞ lau
Leisure: ⅂ PR

LÄUFELFINGEN BASEL

Läufelfingen 4448 ☎ 062 2991189
⮕ *On road from Basel to Olten.*
Open: Apr-Oct Site: 0.5HEC ⤒⤒⤒ 🔾 🚐 Facilities: 🏪 ⊙ 🚻 🛁
Services: ⊞

MÖHLIN AARGAU

Bachtalen (TCS) 4313 ☎ 061 815095 ▤ 061 853 9494
e-mail: camping.moehlin@bluewin.ch
website: www.campingtcs.ch
A pleasant site in a wooded rural setting.
⮕ *2km N towards the River Rhine.*
Open: Apr-Sep Site: 1HEC ⤒⤒⤒ ☙ Facilities: 🏪 ⊙ 🚻 ⌀ 🛁
Services: ⊞ lau Off-site: 🛁 🍽 ✕ ⅂PR

REINACH BASEL

Waldhort Heideweg 16, 4153 ☎ 061 7116429 ▤ 061 7139835
e-mail: camp.waldhort@gmx.ch
website: camping-waldhort.ch
In pleasant wooded surroundings close to the
Basle/Delémont road.
Open: Mar-25Oct Site: 3.3HEC ⤒⤒⤒ 🔾 Prices: ♦7 🚐17 ▲11
Facilities: 🏪 🛁 ⊙ 🚻 ⌀ 🛁 Services: ✕ ⊞ lau Leisure: ⅂ P
Off-site: ✕

ZURZACH AARGAU

Oberfeld 8437 ☎ 056 2492575
Open: Apr-Oct Site: 2HEC ⤒⤒⤒ ♨ 🔾 🚐 Facilities: 🏪 🛁 ⊙ 🚐
⌀ 🛁 Services: ✕ ⊞ Leisure: ⅂ PR

NORTH EAST

ALTNAU THURGAU

Ruderbaum 8595 ☎ 071 6952965
e-mail: camping@ruderbaum.ch
website: www.ruderbaum.ch
A small tourist site with ample facilities.
⮕ *Close to the railway station by Lake Bodensee between Constance and Romanshorn.*
Open: Apr-Oct Site: 7.5HEC ⤒⤒⤒ 🔾 Facilities: 🏪 ⊙ 🚐 ⌀ 🛁
🛁 Services: ✕ ⊞ lau Leisure: ⅂ L Off-site: 🛁 🍽

APPENZELL APPENZELL

Kau Appenzell 9050 ☎ 071 7875030
A woodland site with good modern installations.
Camping Card Compulsory.
⮕ *S of Appenzell towards Wattwil.*
Open: All year Site: 2HEC ⤒⤒⤒ ☙ 🐾 Facilities: 🏪 🛁 ⊙ 🚐
🚻 🛁 Services: ✕ ⊞ lau

ESCHENZ THURGAU

Hüttenberg Hüttenberg, 8264
☎ 052 7412337 ▤ 052 7415671
e-mail: info@huettenberg.ch website: www.huettenberg.ch
Terraced site lying above village.
⮕ *1km SW.*
Open: All year Site: 6HEC ⤒⤒⤒ ☙ ▲ Facilities: 🏪 🛁 ⊙ 🚐
⌀ 🚻 🛁 Services: ⊞ Leisure: ⅂ P Off-site: ✕ ⅂LR ⊞

GOLDINGEN ST-GALLEN

Atzmännig 8638 ☎ 055 2846434 ▤ 055 2846435
e-mail: info@atzmaennig.ch website: www.atzmaennig.ch
Suitable for summer and winter holidays, the site is situated
close to the main cable car and ski lift stations and the giant
mountainside slide.
Open: All year Site: 1.5HEC ⤒⤒⤒ ☙ Prices: ♦6-6 🚐7-7 ▲7-
7 Facilities: 🏪 ⊙ 🚐 🚻 🛁 Services: ✕ ⊞ lau

KRUMMENAU ST-GALLEN

Adler 9643 ☎ 071 9941030
⮕ *On edge of village.*
Open: All year Site: 0.8HEC ⤒⤒⤒ ☙ Facilities: 🏪 🛁 ⊙ 🚐
Services: ✕ ⊞ lau

LEUTSWIL BEI BISCHOFFZELL THURGAU

Sitterbrücke 9220 ☎ 071 4226398
⮕ *Signposted from Bischoffzell on the Konstanz-St Gallen road.*
Open: Apr-15 Oct Site: 1HEC ⤒⤒⤒ ☙ Facilities: 🏪 ⊙ 🚐 ⌀ 🚻
🛁 Services: ⊞ lau Leisure: ⅂ R

MAMMERN THURGAU

Guldifuss Guldifusstr 1, 8265 ☎ 052 7411320
A terraced site directly on the Untersee.
Open: All year Site: 1.6HEC ⤒⤒⤒ ☙ Facilities: 🏪 🛁 ⊙ 🚐 ⌀
🚻 🅿 Services: ✕ lau Leisure: ⅂ L Off-site: 🍽 ⊞

OTTENBACH ZÜRICH

Reussbrücke (TCS) Muristr 32, 8913
☎ 01 7612022 ▤ 01 7612042
e-mail: reussbruecke@tcs-ccz.ch website: www.tcs-ccz.ch
By river of same name.

Site: 6HEC-Site size ⤒⤒⤒-grass ∴∴-sand ♦-stone ☙-little shade 🔾-partly shaded 🌳-mainly shaded
🏠-bungalows for hire 🚐-caravans for hire ▲-tents for hire 🐾-no dogs Prices: ♦-adult per night 🚗-car per night
pp-per person per night 🚐-caravan per night ▲-tent per night

⮩ *Access from Zürich via road 126 in SW direction, via Affoltern to Ottenbach.*
Open: Apr-Oct Site: 1.5HEC ⛺ 🄌 🖵 A Prices: 🏕5.50-6.60 ⛺11-16 🚐10-14 A8-11 Facilities: ⟟ 🟂 ⊙ 🖵 🄌 ⚏ 🅿 Services: ✗ 🕀 lau Leisure: ⟋ R Off-site: 🍴 ✗

SCHÖNENGRUND APPENZELL

Kronenfeld 9105 ☎ 071 3611268 ▤ 071 3611166
e-mail: hotel.krone.schoenengrund@bluewin.ch
website: www.gasthaus-krone.ch.tf
A comfortable, partly residential site with well defined touring pitches.
Open: All year Site: 1HEC ⛺ 🄌 Prices: 🏕3.70-5.50 ⛺2-3 🚐3-4.50 A3-4.50 Facilities: ⟟ ⊙ 🖵 🄌 ⚏ 🅿 Services: lau Off-site: 🟂 ✗ ⟋P 🕀

WAGENHAUSEN SCHAFFHAUSEN

Wagenhausen Hauptstr 82, 8259
☎ 052 7414271 ▤ 052 7414157
e-mail: campingwagenhausen@bluewin.ch
website: www.campingwagenhausen.ch
In a delightful wooded location beside the River Rhein.
Open: Apr-Oct Site: 4.5HEC ⛺ 🄌 Prices: 🏕7 ⛺4 A7 pitch 11 Facilities: ⟟ 🟂 ⊙ 🖵 🄌 ⚏ 🅿 Services: ✗ 🕀 lau Leisure: ⟋ PR

WALENSTADT ST-GALLEN

See-Camping 8880 ☎ 081 7351212 ▤ 081 7351841
e-mail: see-camping@bluewin.ch
A well equipped family site with direct access to the Walensee.
⮩ *Access via Zürich-Chur motorway*
Open: May- Sep Site: 1.2HEC ⛺ 🄌 ⚗ Prices: 🏕8 ⛺4 🚐8-12 A6-12 Facilities: ⟟ 🟂 ⊙ 🖵 🅿 Services: ✗ lau Leisure: ⟋ L Off-site: 🍴 ✗ 🄌 ⚏ 🕀

WILDBERG ZÜRICH

Weid 8321 ☎ 052 3853388 ▤ 052 3853477
e-mail: seiler.camping@bluewin.ch
On a terraced meadow in a very peaceful situation surrounded by woods.
⮩ *In Winterthur, follow Tösstal signs, then turn right after spinning-mill in Turbenthal.*
Open: All year Site: 6.1HEC ⛺ 🄌 🚽 🖵 Prices: 🏕6 A6-8 pitch 10-12 Facilities: ⟟ 🟂 ⊙ 🖵 🄌 ⚏ 🅿 Services: 🍴 ✗ 🕀 lau Off-site: ⟋PR

WINTERTHUR ZÜRICH

Winterthur Eichliwaldstr 4, 8400
☎ 052 2125260 ▤ 052 2125260
⮩ *To the left of the Schaffhausen road, near the Schützenhaus restaurant.*
Open: All year Site: 1HEC ⛺ 🄌 🖵 ⚗ Facilities: ⟟ ⊙ 🖵 🄌 ⚏ 🅿 Services: 🕀 lau Off-site: 🟂 🍴 ✗ ⟋P

NORTH WEST/CENTRAL

AESCHI BERN

Panorama 3703 ☎ 033 2233615 ▤ 033 22333656
e-mail: postmaster@camping-aeschi.ch
website: www.camping-aeschi.ch
⮩ *400m SE of Camping Club Bern.*
Site: 1HEC ⛺ 🄌 🚽 Prices: 🏕5.60 ⛺3 🚐10-12 A8-12 Facilities: ⟟ 🟂 ⊙ 🖵 🅿 Services: 🕀 lau Off-site: 🍴 ✗ 🄌

ALTDORF URI

Moosbad Flülerstr, 6460 ☎ 041 8708541
In a delightful mountain setting.

⮩ *Access via Altdorf exit on A2.*
Open: All year Site: 0.9HEC ⣿ 🄌 🚽 🖵 Facilities: ⟟ 🟂 ⊙ 🖵 🄌 🅿 Services: 🕀 lau

BERN (BERNE) BERN

AT WABERN

SC Eichholz Strandweg 49, 3084
☎ 031 9612602 ▤ 031 9613526
e-mail: info@campingeichholz.ch
website: www.campingeichholz.ch
In municipal parkland. Separate section for caravans.
⮩ *Approach via Gossetstr and track beside river.*
Open: 20 Apr-Sep Site: 2HEC ⛺ 🄌 🚽 Prices: 🏕6.90 ⛺3.20 🚐9-9 A5-8.50 Facilities: ⟟ ⊙ 🖵 🄌 🅿 Services: 🍴 ✗ 🕀 lau Leisure: ⟋ R Off-site: 🟂 🍴 ✗ ⚏ ⟋P

BRENZIKOFEN BERN

Wydeli (TCS) Wydeli 60, 3671 ☎ 031 7711141
e-mail: info@camping-brenzikofen.ch
website: www.camping-brenzikofen.ch
⮩ *8km N of Thun.*
Open: Jul-Aug Site: 1.3HEC ⛺ ⚗ 🖵 Prices: 🏕5.80-6.40 ⛺2-3 🚐12-14 Facilities: ⟟ ⊙ 🖵 🄌 ⚏ 🅿 Services: ✗ lau Leisure: ⟋ P Off-site: 🟂 🕀

BRUNNEN SCHWYZ

Hopfreben 6440 ☎ 041 8201873
website: www.camping-brunnen.ch
On the right bank of the Muotta stream 100mtrs before it flows into the lake.
⮩ *1km W.*
Open: May-29 Sep Site: 1.5HEC ⛺ 🟂 🄌 Prices: 🏕5.50 pitch 12-16 Facilities: ⟟ 🟂 ⊙ 🖵 🄌 ⚏ 🅿 Services: 🍴 ✗ 🕀 lau Leisure: ⟋ LRS

COLOMBIER NEUCHÂTEL

Paradis-Plage 2013 ☎ 032 8412446 ▤ 032 8414305
e-mail: paradisplage@freesurf.ch website: www.paradisplage.ch
In a delightful setting beside Lake Neuchâtel with good, modern facilities.
Open: Mar-Oct Site: 4HEC ⛺ 🄌 🖵 Facilities: ⟟ 🟂 ⊙ 🖵 🄌 ⚏ 🅿 Services: 🍴 ✗ 🕀 Leisure: ⟋ L

ERLACH BERN

Mon Plaisir 3235 ☎ 032 3381358 ▤ 032 3381305
e-mail: info@camping24.ch website: www.camping24.ch
Well equipped site beside the lake.
Open: All year Site: 0.6HEC ⛺ 🄌 🚽 🖵 Prices: pitch 24-50 Facilities: ⟟ 🟂 ⊙ 🖵 🄌 ⚏ 🅿 Services: ✗ 🕀 lau Leisure: ⟋ L Off-site: ✗ ⟋PR

EUTHAL SCHWYZ

Euthal 8844 ☎ 055 4122718 ▤ 055 4127673
e-mail: hotel.post@sihlnet.ch
website: www.hotelposteuthal.ch
On the shore of the Sihlsee in a beautiful mountain setting.
The site is reserved for tents only.
Open: Apr-Oct Site: 1HEC ⛺ ⚗ ⚗ Prices: 🏕7.50 ⛺2.50 A6-8 Facilities: ⟟ ⊙ 🅿 Services: ✗ Leisure: ⟋ L Off-site: 🟂 🍴 🄌 🕀

FLÜELEN URI

Urnersee 6454 ☎ 041 8709222 ▤ 041 8709216
e-mail: info@windsurfing-urnersee.ch
website: www.windsurfing-urnersee.ch
On level ground on the shore of the Vierwaldstättersee with plenty of sporting facilities.
Open: 15 Apr-Oct Site: 4.5HEC ⛺ ⚗ Facilities: ⟟ 🟂 ⊙ 🖵 🅿 Services: 🍴 ✗ 🕀 Leisure: ⟋ LR Off-site: 🄌 ⟋P

Facilities: 🟂-shop ⟟-shower ⊙-electric points for razors 🖵-electric points for caravans 🄌-parking by tents permitted 🅿-compulsory separate car park **Services:** ✗-café/restaurant 🍴-bar 🄌-Camping Gaz International ⚏-gas other than Camping Gaz 🕀-first aid facilities lau-laundry **Leisure:** ⟋-swimming L-Lake P-Pool R-River S-Sea **Off-site:** All facilities within 2km

Camping Grassi Frutigen

Located off the road, alongside the Engstligen Stream, this is the location for the quiet and well equipped site in the summer holiday resort of Frutigen, about 15 km from Spiez, Adelboden and Kandersteg

- Inexhaustible choice of excursions
- Free loan of bicycles, guided mountainbike tours

Winter camping: to skiing resorts of Adelboden, Kandersteg, Elsigenalp, Swiss ski-school, only 10–12 km.

Infos: W. Glausen, CH-3714 Frutigen
Tel. 0041-(0)33-671 11 49, Fax 0041-(0)33-671 13 80
E-mail: campinggrassi@bluewin.ch
www.campinggrassi.ch

FRUTIGEN BERN

Grassi 3714 ☎ 033 6711149 ▤ 033 6711380
e-mail: campinggrassi@bluewin.ch
Scattered with fruit trees beside a farm on the right bank of the River Engstilgern.
➲ *From the Haupstr, turn right at the Simplon Hotel.*
Open: All year Site: 1.5HEC ⃝⃝⃝⃝ ⊕ 🏠 🚐 Prices: ⋏6.40 pitch 8-14 Facilities: 🅿 🔋 ⊙ 🚱 ⌀ ♨ 🏧 Services: 🚻 lau Off-site: 🍴 ✕ ⤳P

GAMPELEN BERN

Fanel (TCS) 3236 ☎ 032 3132333 ▤ 032 3131407
e-mail: camping.gampelen@tcs.ch
website: www.campingtcs.ch
A level site on the shore of Lake Neuchâtel protected by trees and bushes.

Camping Aareschlucht,
Innertkirchen

A reasonably priced, charming little camping site in the centre of the Swiss Alps. (**www.alpenregion.ch**). Large network of marked walking tracks, awesome natural scenery. On top of our very affordable prices, for stays of one week or longer in May/June and September/October you receive **an additional discount of 25% per plot and person.**

Camping Aareschlucht, CH-3862 Innertkirchen
Tel. 0041-(0)33-971 53 32, Fax 0041-(0)33-971 53 44
E-mail: campaareschlucht@bluewin.ch

➲ *Access via A5 towards Gampelen.*
Open: 02 Apr-03 Oct Site: 11.3HEC ⃝⃝⃝⃝ ⃝⊕ 🚐 Prices: ⋏6.10-8.10 🚐14-21 ▲6-9 Facilities: 🅿 🔋 ⊙ 🚱 ⌀ ♨ 🏧 Services: 🍴 ✕ 🞐 lau Leisure: ⤳ L Off-site: ⤳R

GISWIL OBWALDEN

Giswil 6074 ☎ 041 6752355
Open: Apr-20 Oct Site: 1.9HEC ⃝⃝⃝⃝ ⸬ ♠ Facilities: 🅿 🔋 ⊙ 🚱 ⌀ ♨ 🏧 Services: ✕ 🞐 lau Leisure: ⤳ L

GOLDAU SCHWYZ

Bernerhöhe 6410 ☎ 041 8551887 ▤ 041 8555970
On the edge of a forest with a beautiful view of Lake Lauerz. Separate field for tents.
➲ *1.5km SE and turn left.*
Open: All year Site: 2.5HEC ⃝⃝⃝⃝ ⃝ ⃝ ⊘ Prices: ⋏5.30 🚗1 🚐3 ▲3 Facilities: 🅿 🔋 ⊙ 🚱 ⌀ 🏧 Services: 🞐 lau

GRINDELWALD BERN

Aspen 3818 ☎ 033 8531124 ▤ 033 534157
Sunny hill terraces.
Open: Jun-15 Oct Site: 2.5HEC ⃝⃝⃝⃝ ⃝ Facilities: 🅿 ⊙ 🚱 ⌀ 🏧 Services: lau Off-site: ✕ 🞐

GSTAAD BERN

Bellerive 3780 ☎ 033 7446330 ▤ 033 7446345
e-mail: bellerive.camping@bluewin.ch
Open: All year Site: 0.8HEC ⃝⃝⃝⃝ ⃝⊕ 🏠 🚐 Prices: ⋏6.40-7.50 pitch 13-15 Facilities: 🅿 ⊙ 🚱 ⌀ Services: ✕ 🞐 lau Leisure: ⤳ R Off-site: ⤳P

INNERTKIRCHEN BERN

Aareschlucht Hauptstr 6/11, 3862
☎ 033 9715532 ▤ 033 9715344
e-mail: campaareschlucht@bluewin.ch
website: www.swisscamps.ch
In a beautiful Alpine location with superb mountain views.
Open: May-Oct Site: 0.5HEC ⃝⃝⃝⃝ ⃝⊕ 🚐 Prices: ⋏5.70 pitch 7-14 Facilities: 🅿 🔋 ⊙ 🚱 ⌀ ♨ 🏧 Services: 🞐 lau Off-site: 🍴 ✕ ⤳R

Grund 3862 ☎ 033 9714409 ▤ 033 9714767
e-mail: camping_grund@bluewin.ch
website: www.camping-grund.ch
Next to a farm on southern outskirts of village.
➲ *Turn S off main road in centre of village at hotel Urweider. Drive for 0.3km, turn right.*
Open: All year Site: 120HEC ⃝⃝⃝⃝ ⃝⊕ 🏠 ▲ Prices: ⋏3.90-4.50 🚐15-19 ▲10-15 Facilities: 🅿 ⊙ 🚱 🏧 Services: 🞐 lau Off-site: 🔋 🍴 ✕ ⌀ ⤳R

INTERLAKEN BERN

Hobby 3 Lehnweg 16, 3800
☎ 033 8229652 ▤ 033 8229657
e-mail: info@campinghobby.ch
website: www.campinghobby.ch
Family site with first class sanitary facilities, quietly situated with fine views of the surrounding mountains and within easy walking distance of Interlaken.
➲ *Access via A8 (Spiez-Interlaken) towards Gunten/Beatenberg.*
Open: Apr-Sep Site: 1.5HEC ⃝⃝⃝⃝ ♠ Prices: ⋏5.50-6.90 pitch 12.50-26 Facilities: 🅿 🔋 ⊙ 🚱 ⌀ 🏧 Services: 🞐 lau Off-site: 🍴 ✕ ⤳LPRS

Site: 6HEC-Site size ⃝⃝⃝⃝-grass ⸬-sand ⃝-stone ⃝-little shade ⃝-partly shaded ♠-mainly shaded
🏠-bungalows for hire 🚐-caravans for hire ▲-tents for hire ⊘-no dogs Prices: ⋏-adult per night 🚗-car per night
pp-per person per night 🚐-caravan per night ▲-tent per night

Manor Farm	...1	.033 822 22 64
Alpenblick	2	.033 822 77 57
Hobby	3	.033 822 96 52
Lazy Rancho	...4	.033 822 87 16
Jungfrau Camp	5	.033 822 57 30
Sackgut TCS	...6	.033 822 44 34
Jungfraublick	..7	.033 822 44 14
Oberei	8	.033 822 13 35

Jungfrau Steindlerstr 50, 3800
☎ 033 8227107 ▦ 033 8225730
e-mail: info@jungfraucamp.ch website: www.jungfraucamp.ch
Has a beautiful view of the Eiger, the Mönch and the Jungfrau.
➲ *Turn right at Unterseen, drive through the Schulhaus and Steinler Str to site.*
Open: May-Sep Site: 2.5HEC ▤▥▥ ⊕ ☎ Prices: ♠6.50 pitch 8-25 Facilities: ↟ 🕊 ⊙ 🖾 ⌀ ⚒ ☎ Services: ♀ ✗ lau
Leisure: ⚓ P Off-site: ⚓LR ⊞

Jungfraublick Gsteigstr 80, 3800
☎ 033 8224414 ▦ 033 8221619
e-mail: info@jungfraublick.ch website: www.jungfraublick.ch
A family site with clean, modern facilities in a fine central situation.
➲ *Take Autobahn A8 through tunnel, leave at Lauterbrunnen-Grindelwald exit, site on left, 300mtrs from A8 sliproad.*
Open: May-25 Sep Site: 1.3HEC ▤▥▥ ⊕ Prices: ♠7.40-8.40 pitch 14-28 Facilities: ↟ 🕊 ⊙ 🖾 ⌀ ☎ Services: ⊞ lau
Leisure: ⚓ P Off-site: ♀ ✗ ⚓R

Lazy Rancho 4 3800 ☎ 033 8228716 ▦ 033 8231920
e-mail: info@lazyrancho.ch website: www.lazyrancho.ch
A family campsite in a magnificent position with views of the Eiger, Mönch and Jungfrau with fine facilities.
➲ *Motorway A8: exit Unterseen, turn toward Gunten. After 2km turn right, then at Landhotel Golf turn left.*
Open: 15 Apr-15 Oct Site: 16HEC ▤▥▥ ⊕ Prices: ♠6-7.50 pitch 7-28 Facilities: ↟ 🕊 ⊙ 🖾 ⌀ ☎ Services: ⊞ lau
Leisure: ⚓ P Off-site: ♀ ✗ ⚓LR

Manor Farm 3800 ☎ 033 8222264 ▦ 033 8222279
e-mail: manorfarm@swisscamps.ch
website: www.manorfarm.ch
A well equipped site in a beautiful mountain setting.

➲ *From motorway A8 (Bern-Speiz-Interlaken-Brienz), exit Gunten/Beatenberg; follow signposts.*
Open: All year Site: 7.5HEC ▤▥▥ ⋮⋮⋮ ⊕ ☎ 🖾 ▲ Prices: ♠6-10 pitch 7.80-38 Facilities: ↟ 🕊 ⊙ 🖾 ⌀ ⚒ ☎ Services: ♀ ✗ ⊞ lau Leisure: ⚓ LR

Rendez-Vous 3718 ☎ 033 6751534 ▦ 033 6751737
e-mail: rendez-vous.camping@bluewin.ch
website: www.camping-kandersteg.ch
In a delightful mountain setting with good modern facilities.
➲ *750m E of town.*
Open: All year Site: 1HEC ▤▥▥ ⊕ Prices: ♠7.50 ♠3 ▲6-12 pitch 8-16 Facilities: ↟ 🕊 ⊙ 🖾 ⌀ ⚒ ☎ Services: ♀ ✗ ⊞ lau
Off-site: ⚓P

Camping Rendez-vous, CH-3718 Kandersteg

Situated in an ideal position and basecamp for various beautiful walks. On our terraced camping site you'll find a modern infrastructure as well as an in house shop. Our little village at 1200m above sea-level, the surrounding mountains, the fresh air, a great number of sports facilities and our friendly hospitality will make your holiday refreshing for body and soul.
Tel. 0041-(0)33-675 15 34, Fax 0041-(0)33-675 17 37
www.camping-kandersteg.ch, rendez-vous.camping@bluewin.ch

Facilities: 🕊-shop ↟-shower ⊙-electric points for razors 🖾-electric points for caravans ☎-parking by tents permitted ▣-compulsory separate car park Services: ✗-café/restaurant ♀-bar ⌀-Camping Gaz International ⚒-gas other than Camping Gaz ⊞-first aid facilities lau-laundry Leisure: ⚓-swimming L-Lake P-Pool R-River S-Sea Off-site: All facilities within 2km

Modern camping site, especially suitable for families, ideal for walking/biking tours, paragliding and golf, possibilities for horse-riding in the village. **First-class facilities:** heated swimming pool, children's paddling pool and large play-ground, 2 tennis courts, volley/soccer-playground, boule-alleys, ping-pong, chess etc. Shop with restaurant, size of units 100m2.

FRASO RANCH
CH-2523 Lignières
Tel. 0041-32-751 46 16
Fax 0041-32-751 46 14

LANDERON, LE NEUCHÂTEL

Peches 2525 ☎ 032 7512900 ▤ 032 7516354
e-mail: info@camping-lelanderon.ch
website: www.camping-lelanderon.ch
A small site at the meeting point of the River Thielle and the Lac de Bienne.
Open: Apr-15 Oct Site: 2.1HEC ⛛ ⥷ 🚍 Facilities: ⬗ ⭒
☉ 🖭 🖉 ♨ 🏠 Services: ⊞ lau Leisure: ⭢ L
Off-site: ⬤ ✗ ⭢PR

LAUTERBRUNNEN BERN

Schützenbach (TCS) 3822 ☎ 033 8551268
In an fine Alpine location close to the main skiing areas and about 300mtrs from the lake.
⮑ *S of village to the left of road leading to Stechelberg opposite B50. 0.8km SE towards Stechelberg.*
Open: All year Site: 3HEC ⛛ ⥷ 🚍 🚍 ⛺ Prices: ⬤4.60-6
⛺5-8 pitch 10-16 Facilities: ⬗ ⭒ ☉ 🖭 🖉 ♨ 🏠 Services: ⬤ ✗
⊞ lau Off-site: ✗ ⭢P

Camping site with most modern comfort in the heart of beautiful surroundings.

Superb for summer and winter camping, for relaxing family holidays in a unique scenery, ideal for skiing, walking and trekking. Magnificent nature with high mountains, glaciers valleys and gorges. Sport and recreation facilities such as a climbing hall, tennis centre, swimming pool and mountain cable cars are directly accessible in front of the camping grounds. Ask for more printed information!

Camping Balmweid
Balmweidstrasse 22, P.O.box 543
CH-3860 Meiringen, Switzerland
Phone 0041-(0)33-971 51 15, Fax 0041-(0)33-971 51 17
E-mail: info@camping-meiringen.ch
www.camping-meiringen.ch

LIGNIÈRES NEUCHÂTEL

Fraso-Ranch 2523 ☎ 032 7514616 ▤ 032 7514614
e-mail: camping.fraso-ranch@bluewin.ch
website: mypage.bluewin.ch/camping_lignieres
A modern family site with good recreational facilities and a separate section for tourers.
⮑ *NE of Lignières on Nods road. Signposted.*
Open: All year Site: 8.7HEC ⛛ ⥷ Prices: ⬤6-8 pitch 11-15
Facilities: ⬗ ⭒ ☉ 🖭 🖉 🏠 Services: ✗ lau Leisure: ⭢ P

LOCLE, LE NEUCHÂTEL

Communal (TCS) 2400 ☎ 032 9317493 ▤ 032 9317408
e-mail: camping.lelode@tcs.ch
website: www.campingtcs.ch
On a level meadow surrounded by woodland. Good recreational facilities.
⮑ *S of town off the La Sagne road.*
Open: 17Apr-19Oct Site: 1.2HEC ⛛ ⥷ Facilities: ⬗ ☉ 🖭
🖉 ♨ 🏠 Services: ⬤ ✗ ⊞ lau Leisure: ⭢ P Off-site: ⭒ ✗

LUCERNE

LUNGERN OBWALDEN

Obsee 6078 ☎ 041 6781463 ▤ 041 6782163
e-mail: camping@obsee.ch website: www.obsee.ch
In a beautiful setting between the lake and the mountains with good facilities for watersports.
⮑ *1km W.*
Open: All year Site: 1.5HEC ⛛ ⥷ Facilities: ⬗ ☉ 🖭 🖉 ♨
🏠 Services: ⬤ ✗ ⊞ lau Leisure: ⭢ LPR Off-site: ⭒

LUZERN (LUCERNE) LUZERN

Steinibachried (TCS) Horw, 6048
☎ 041 3403558 ▤ 041 3403556
e-mail: camping.horw@tcs.ch website: www.campingtcs.ch
In gently sloping meadow next to the football ground and the beach, separated from the lake by a wide belt of reeds.
⮑ *3.2km S of Luzern.*
Open: 2 Apr-3 Oct Site: 2HEC ⛛ ⥷ 🚍 Prices: ⬤5-7.60
🚍14-19 ⛺6-19 pitch 14-19 Facilities: ⬗ ⭒ ☉ 🖭 🖉 🅿
Services: ✗ ⊞ lau Off-site: ⬤ ⭢L

MEIRINGEN BERN

Balmweid Balmweidstrasse 22, 3860
☎ 033 9715115 ▤ 033 9715117
e-mail: camping.balmweid@popnet.ch
Mainly flat meadowland site with mountain views.
Open: All year Site: 2.2HEC ⛛ ⥷ Facilities: ⬗ ⭒ ☉ 🖭 ♨
🏠 Services: ✗ lau

MOSEN LUZERN

Seeblick 6295 ☎ 041 9171666 ▤ 041 9171666
e-mail: mptrunz@gmx.ch website: www.swisscamps.ch
In two strips of land on edge of lake, divided by paths into several squares.
⮑ *N on the A26.*
Open: Apr-Oct Site: 3HEC ⛛ ⥷ Facilities: ⬗ ⭒ ☉ 🖭 🖉
🏠 Services: ⊞ lau Leisure: ⭢ L Off-site: ✗

Campsites in popular areas can get very crowded at busy times – it is advisable to book well in advance

Site: 6HEC-Site size ⛛-grass ⸬-sand ◐-stone ⥷-little shade ⥶-partly shaded ♣-mainly shaded
🏠-bungalows for hire 🚍-caravans for hire ⛺-tents for hire ⊘-no dogs Prices: ⬤-adult per night ⬤-car per night
pp-per person per night 🚍-caravan per night ⛺-tent per night

NOTTWIL LUZERN

St Margrethen 6207 ☎ 041 9371404 ▦ 041 9371865
e-mail: st.margrethen@swisscamps.ch
website: www.swisscamps.ch
Natural meadowland under fruit trees, with own access to
lakeside.
➲ *Turn off road to Sursee 400mtrs NW of Nottwil and drive
towards lake for 100mtrs.*
Open: Apr-Oct **Site:** 1HEC ▥ ⚐ **Prices:** ⚑6.50-7 ⚗4 ⚙4-
4.50 ▲3-5 **Facilities:** ⚐ ⚒ ⊙ ⚙ ∅ ⚏ ⚐ **Services:** ⊞ lau
Leisure: ⚐ L **Off-site:** ⚏ ✗ ⚐LP

PRÊLES BERN

Prêles 2515 ☎ 032 3151716 ▦ 032 3155160
e-mail: info@camping-jura.ch
website: www.camping-jura.ch
On a wooded plateau overlooking Lake Biel.
➲ *Turn off the main Biel-Neuchâtel road at Twann and follow
signs for Prêles. Pass through village, site on left.*
Open: All year **Site:** 6HEC ▥ ⚐ ⚏ **Prices:** ⚑8 ⚗2.50
⚙13-15 ▲7-10 **Facilities:** ⚐ ⚒ ⊙ ⚙ ∅ ⚐ **Services:** ✗ ⊞ lau
Leisure: ⚐ P

SAANEN BERN

Beim Kappeli (TCS) 3792 ☎ 033 7446191 ▦ 033 7446184
e-mail: camping.saaren@tcs.ch website: www.campingtcs.ch
In a long meadow between railway and River Saane.
➲ *1km SE.*
Open: Jan-Oct, 11 Dec-31 Dec **Site:** 0.8HEC ▥ ∆ ⚐
Prices: ⚑7.70-8.30 ⚙14-15 ▲8-11 **Facilities:** ⚐ ⊙ ⚙ ∅ ⚐
Services: ⊞ lau **Leisure:** ⚐ R **Off-site:** ⚒ ⚏ ✗ ∅ ⚐P

SACHSELN OBWALDEN

Ewil CH-6072 ☎ 041 6663270 ▦ 041 6663279
e-mail: m.k.berlinger@pop.agri.ch website: www.camping.ch
On a level meadow on the SW shore of the Sarnersee.
➲ *W of the main Sachseln-Ewil road towards the lake.*
Open: Apr-Sep **Site:** 1.5HEC ▥ ⚐ ⚏ **Prices:** ⚑5.80-6.50
⚗3 ⚙8 ▲4-8 **Facilities:** ⚐ ⚒ ⊙ ⚙ ∅ ⚐ **Services:** ⚏ ⊞ lau
Leisure: ⚐ LS **Off-site:** ⚐R

SEMPACH LUZERN

Seeland (TCS) 6204 ☎ 041 4601466 ▦ 041 4604766
e-mail: camping.sempad@tcs.ch
website: www.tcs.ch
Rectangular, level site on SW shore of lake.
➲ *700mtrs S on Luzern road by lake.*
Open: Apr-Nov **Site:** 5.2HEC ▥ ⚐ ⚘ ▲ **Facilities:** ⚐ ⚒ ⊙
∅ ⚏ ⚐ **Services:** ⚏ ✗ ⊞ lau **Leisure:** ⚐ L

STECHELBERG BERN

Breithorn 3824 ☎ 033 8551225 ▦ 033 8553561
e-mail: breithorn@stechelberg.ch
In a beautiful location in the Lauterbrunnen valley.
➲ *3km S of Lauterbrunnen.*
Open: All year **Site:** 1HEC ▥ ⚐ ⚏ **Prices:** ⚑6.70
Facilities: ⚐ ⚒ ⊙ ⚙ ∅ ⚐ **Services:** ⊞ lau

SURSEE LUZERN

Sursee Waldheim, 6216 ☎ 041 9211161 ▦ 041 9211160
e-mail: campingsursee@bluewin.ch
website: www.camping-sursee.ch
Next to Waldheim Country Estate.
➲ *0.8km W of Sursee, 100mtrs from Sursee-Basel road.*
Open: Apr-Sep **Site:** 1.7HEC ▥ ⚐ **Prices:** ⚑6.80 ⚗4 ⚙4
▲4 **Facilities:** ⚐ ⚒ ⊙ ⚙ ∅ ⚐ **Services:** ⚏ ✗ ⊞ lau
Off-site: ⚐L

VITZNAU LUZERN

Vitznau 6354 ☎ 041 3971280 ▦ 041 3972457
e-mail: camping-vitznau@bluewin.ch
website: www.swisscamps.ch
Well tended terraced site, in lovely countryside with fine
views of lake.
➲ *Approaching from N, turn towards mountain at church and
follow signs.*
Open: Apr-26 Oct **Site:** 1.8HEC ▥ ⚐ ⚏ ⚙ **Prices:** ⚑8-9.50
pitch 14-22 **Facilities:** ⚐ ⚒ ⊙ ⚙ ∅ ⚏ ⚐ **Services:** ⊞ lau
Leisure: ⚐ P **Off-site:** ⚏ ✗ ⚐L

WILDERSWIL BERN

Oberei 3812 ☎ 033 8221335 ▦ 033 8221335
e-mail: oberei8@swisscamps.ch
A peaceful site in a picturesque village with fine views of the
Jungfrau and surrounding mountains. There are good
facilities and reservations are recommended during July and
August.
Open: 15 Apr-15 Oct **Site:** 0.6HEC ▥ ⚐ ⚏ **Facilities:** ⚐ ⚒
⊙ ⚙ ∅ ⚏ ⚐ **Services:** ⊞ lau **Off-site:** ⚏ ✗ ⚐LPR

ZUG ZUG

Innere Lorzenallmend (TCS) Chamer Fussweg 36, 6300
☎ 041 7418422 ▦ 041 7418130
e-mail: tcscamping.zug@tcs.ch website: www.campingtcs.ch
Pleasantly situated with beautiful view of Lake Zug and
surrounding mountains. Much traffic on railway which
passes the site.
➲ *1km NW by lake.*
Open: 02 Apr-03 Oct **Site:** 1.1HEC ▥ ⚐ **Prices:** ⚑6-7.20
⚗3-3 ⚙6-7.50 pitch 12-18 **Facilities:** ⚐ ⊙ ⚙ ∅ ⚐
Services: ✗ ⊞ lau **Leisure:** ⚐ LRS **Off-site:** ⚒ ⚏ ✗

EAST

ANDEER GRAUBÜNDEN

Sut Baselgia (TCS) 7440 ☎ 081 6611453 ▦ 081 6611080
e-mail: camping.andeer@bluewin.ch
website: www.viamalaferien.ch
In a pleasant, peaceful setting N towards Chur.
Open: Dec-Oct **Site:** 1.2HEC ▥ ⚐⚏ ⚏ **Prices:** ⚑8.30 ⚗3
⚙13 ▲8-13 **Facilities:** ⚐ ⊙ ⚙ ∅ ⚏ ⚐ **Services:** ✗ ⊞ lau
Off-site: ⚒ ⚏ ✗ ⚐PR

AROSA GRAUBÜNDEN

Arosa Tourismus 7050 ☎ 081 3771745 ▦ 081 3773005
Open: All year **Site:** 0.6HEC ▥ ⚐ **Facilities:** ⚐ ⊙ ⚙ ∅ ⚐
Off-site: ⚒ ⚏ ✗ ⚐LP ⊞

CHUR (COIRE) GRAUBÜNDEN

Camp Au Felsenaustr 61, 7000
☎ 081 2842283 ▦ 081 2845683
e-mail: info@camping-chur.ch website: www.camping-chur.ch
A summer and winter site on level ground with fine views of
the surrounding mountains. Good recreational facilities.
➲ *Take exit Chur-Süd from A13. 2km NW of town centre on
bank of Rhein. Access is via outskirts of town.*
Open: All year **Site:** 2.6HEC ▥ ⚐ **Facilities:** ⚐ ⚒ ⊙ ⚙ ∅
⚏ ⚐ **Services:** ✗ ⊞ lau **Off-site:** ⚐P

CHURWALDEN GRAUBÜNDEN

Pradafenz 7075 ☎ 081 3821921 ▦ 081 3821921
e-mail: camping@pradafenz.ch website: www.pradafenz.ch
A year round site in a beautiful mountain area close to the
local ski slopes.
Open: Jan-22 Apr & 28 May-Oct **Site:** 1.5HEC ▥ ⚐
Facilities: ⚐ ⊙ ⚙ ∅ ⚏ ⚐ **Services:** ⚏ ✗ ⊞ lau **Off-site:** ⚐PR

Facilities: ⚒-shop ⚐-shower ⊙-electric points for razors ⚙-electric points for caravans ⚐-parking by tents permitted
⚐-compulsory separate car park **Services:** ✗-café/restaurant ⚏-bar ∅-Camping Gaz International ⚏-gas other than Camping
Gaz ⊞-first aid facilities lau-laundry **Leisure:** ⚐-swimming L-Lake P-Pool R-River S-Sea **Off-site:** All facilities within 2km

LENZ GRAUBÜNDEN

St Cassian 7083 ☎ 081 3842472 ▤ 081 3842489
e-mail: camping.st.cassian@bluwin.ch
A level, shady site in a beautiful location at an altitude of
1415mtrs above sea level. There are good facilities and the
site is 1km from the town.
➲ *Leave motorway at 'Chur-Süd' exit and follow signs for*
Lenzerheide/St.Moritz up a well constructed mountain road.
Open: All year Site: 25HEC ⬛ ⅊ Prices: ⚲8 ⊕2.50
⊕9.50 ⚲9.50 Facilities: ⬧ ⊙ ⬤ ⬤ ⬤ ⬤ Services: ✗ ⊞ lau
Off-site: ⬤ ✗

MÜSTAIR GRAUBÜNDEN

Clenga 7537 ☎ 081 8585410 ▤ 081 8585422
website: www.campclenga.ch
Next to small river near the Italian frontier.
Open: 15 May-20 Oct Site: 1.5HEC ⬛ ⅊ ⊕ Prices: ⚲5.50-
6 pitch 10-12 Facilities: ⬧ ⬤ ⊙ ⬤ ⬤ ⬤ ⬤ Services: ⅊ ⊞ lau
Leisure: ⬧ R

PONTRESINA GRAUBÜNDEN

Plauns (TCS) 7504 ☎ 081 8426285 ▤ 081 8345136
e-mail: a.brueli@bluewin.ch website: www.pontresina.ch
Beautiful situation at foot of Pit Palü.
➲ *Access from road towards Bernina pass about 4.5km beyond*
Pontresina. Turn off main road 29 towards Hotel Morteratsch
then 0.5km to site.
Open: Jun-15 Oct/15 Dec-15 Apr Site: 4HEC ⬛ ⋮⋮⋮ ◈ ⬤
⅊ ⊕ Facilities: ⬧ ⬤ ⊙ ⬤ ⬤ ⬤ ⬤ Services: ✗ ⊞ lau

POSCHIAVO GRAUBÜNDEN

Boomerang 7745 ☎ 081 8440713
In a quiet setting.
➲ *2km SE.*
Open: All year Site: 1.5HEC ⬛ ⅊ Facilities: ⬧ ⬤ ⊙ ⬤ ⬤
⬤ Services: ⅊ ⊞ lau Off-site: ⬧LP

SAMEDAN GRAUBÜNDEN

Punt Muragl (TCS) 7503 ☎ 081 8428197 ▤ 081 8428197
e-mail: camping.samedan@tcs.ch website: www.campingtcs.ch
A summer and winter site in a pleasant alpine setting.
➲ *Near Bernina railway halt, to the right of the fork of the*
two roads Samedan and Celerina/Schlarigna to Pontresina.
Open: Jun-6 Oct / 1 Dec- 15 Apr Site: 2HEC ⬛ ⅊ ⊕
Prices: ⚲6.75-8.35 ⊕13-18 ⚲6-8 Facilities: ⬧ ⬤ ⊙ ⬤ ⬤ ⬤ ⬤
Services: ⅊ ✗ ⊞ lau Off-site: ✗ ⬧L

SPLÜGEN GRAUBÜNDEN

Sand 7435 ☎ 081 6641476 ▤ 081 6641460
e-mail: camping@splugen.ch
website: www.campingsplugen.ch
On left bank of River Hinterrhein.
➲ *Turn off the main trunk road in the village and follow*
signposts.
Open: All year Site: 0.8HEC ⬛ ⬤ Prices: ⚲6.50 ⊕3.20
⊕13-16 Facilities: ⬧ ⬤ ⊙ ⬤ ⬤ ⬤ ⬤ Services: ⅊ ✗ ⊞ lau
Leisure: ⬧ R Off-site: ✗

SUSCH GRAUBÜNDEN

Muglinas 7542 ☎ 081 8561927
➲ *200mtrs W.*
Open: Jun-15 Sep Site: 1HEC ⬛ ⅊ Facilities: ⬧ ⊙ ⬤ ⬤ ⬤
⬤ Services: ⊞ lau Leisure: ⬧ R Off-site: ⬤ ⅊ ✗

THUSIS GRAUBÜNDEN

Viamala 7430 ☎ 081 6512472
In pleasant wooded surroundings near the River Hinterrhein
and close to the beautiful Viamala Gorge.

➲ *NE towards Chur.*
Open: May-Sep Site: 4.5HEC ⬛ ⬤ ⬤ Facilities: ⬧ ⬤ ⊙ ⬤
⬤ ⬤ Services: ⅊ ✗ lau Off-site: ⬧PR

TSCHIERV GRAUBÜNDEN

Sternen (TCS) Chasa Maruya, 7532 ☎ 081 8585628
e-mail: maruya@tiscalinet.ch website: www.muenstertal.ch
In village behind the Sternen Hotel.
➲ *Between Ofen Pass and Santa Maria.*
Open: All year Site: 1HEC ⬛ ⊕ Prices: ⚲5 ⊕3 ⊕5 ⚲3
Facilities: ⬧ ⬤ ⊙ ⬤ ⬤ ⬤ Services: ⅊ ✗ ⊞ lau Leisure: ⬧ PR

ZERNEZ GRAUBÜNDEN

Cul 7530 ☎ 081 8561456 ▤ 081 8561462
e-mail: a.filli@camping-cul.ch website: www.camping-cul.ch
In a delightful mountain setting close to the Swiss National
Park.
➲ *Off road 27 W of Zernez.*
Open: May-15 Oct Site: 3.6HEC ⬛ ⊕ Facilities: ⬧ ⬤ ⊙ ⬤
⬤ ⬤ ⬤ Services: ⅊ ✗ ⊞ lau Leisure: ⬧ R Off-site: ✗ ⬧P

SOUTH

ACQUACALDA TICINO

Ai Cembri Lukmanierstr, 6718 ☎ 091 8722610
In a beautiful mountain location with good hiking facilities.
Open: Apr-Oct Site: 5HEC ⬛ ⊕ ⬤ ⬤ ⬤ Facilities: ⬧ ⊙
⬤ ⬤ ⬤ Services: ⅊ ✗ ⊞ lau Leisure: ⬧ R

AGNO TICINO

Eurocampo 6982 ☎ 091 6052114 ▤ 091 6053187
Part of site is near its own sandy beach and is divided by
groups of trees.
➲ *600mtrs E on road from Lugano to Ponte Tresa. Entrance*
opposite Aeroport sign and Alfa Romeo building.
Open: Apr-Oct Site: 4HEC ⬛ ⊕ Prices: ⚲9 ⊕2.50 pitch 8
Facilities: ⬧ ⬤ ⊙ ⬤ ⬤ ⬤ Services: ⅊ ✗ ⊞ lau Leisure: ⬧
LR Off-site: ✗

Golfo del Sole via Rivera 8, 6982
☎ 091 6054802 ▤ 091 6052319
e-mail: info@golfodelsole.ch website: www.golfodelsole.ch
By lake. Separate play area for children.
Open: Apr-Oct Site: 6HEC ⬛ ⊕ ⊕ Prices: ⚲8-9 ⊕2 ⊕10-
13 ⚲8-10 Facilities: ⬧ ⬤ ⊙ ⬤ ⬤ ⬤ ⬤ ⬤ Services: ⅊ ✗ ⊞
Leisure: ⬧ L Off-site: ✗ ⬧P

CUGNASCO TICINO

Park-Camping Riarena 6516
☎ 091 8591688 ▤ 091 8592885
e-mail: camping.riarena@bluwin.ch
website: www.camping-riarena.ch
Beautiful park-like family site in level, natural woodland. All
facilities are well maintained and Lake Maggiore is within
easy reach.
➲ *1.5km NW. Turn off road 13 at BP filling station 9km NE*
of Locarno and continue 0.5km.
Open: Mar-Oct Site: 3.2HEC ⬛ ⋮⋮⋮ ⬤ ⬤ ⬤ Prices: ⚲6-8
⊕2-3 pitch 27-38 (incl 2 persons) Facilities: ⬧ ⬤ ⊙ ⬤ ⬤ ⬤
⬤ Services: ⅊ ✗ ⊞ lau Leisure: ⬧ P Off-site: ⬧R

GORDEVIO TICINO

Bellariva 6672 ☎ 091 7531444 ▤ 091 7531764
e-mail: camping.gerdevio@tcs.ch
website: www.campingtcs.ch
In quiet location between the road and the left bank of the
River Maggia.
Open: Apr-Oct Site: 2.5HEC ⬛ ⊕ Facilities: ⬧ ⬤ ⊙ ⬤ ⬤
⬤ ⬤ ⬤ Services: ⅊ ✗ ⊞ lau Leisure: ⬧ PR

Site: 6HEC-Site size ⬛-grass ⋮⋮⋮-sand ◈-stone ⅊-little shade ⊕-partly shaded ⬤-mainly shaded
⬤-bungalows for hire ⊕-caravans for hire ⚲-tents for hire ⬰-no dogs Prices: ⚲-adult per night ⊕-car per night
pp-per person per night ⊕-caravan per night ⚲-tent per night

LOCARNO TICINO

Delta via Respini 7, 6600 ☎ 091 7516081 ▥ 091 7512243
e-mail: info@campingdelta.com
website: www.campingdelta.com
A beautiful, well-equipped and well-organised site at Lake
Maggiore.
⮕ *2km away from the city.*
Open: Mar-Oct Site: 60HEC ▦ ♣ 🚐 ⚡ Prices: ⵜ11-18
pitch 21-57 Facilities: ♠ ⅃ ⊙ ⨀ ≞ ☎ Services: ⛾ ✗ ⊞ lau
Leisure: ⵜ LR Off-site: ⵜP

AT LOSONE (4KM W)

Zandone 6616 ☎ 091 7916563 ▥ 091 7910047
In a quiet, picturesque location beside the River Melezza with
fine views of the Tessin mountains.
⮕ *Situated between the Losone-Golino road and the river.*
Open: Etr-Oct Site: 2.1HEC ▦ ⚓ 🌀 Facilities: ♠ ⅃ ⊙ ⨀
⚫ ≞ ☎ Services: ⊞ Leisure: ⵜ R Off-site: ⛾ ✗

MOLINAZZO DI MONTEGGIO TICINO

Tresiana 6995 ☎ 091 6083342 ▥ 091 6083142
e-mail: mail@camping-tresiana
website: www.camping-tresiana.ch
A family site on meadowland with trees on riverbank.
⮕ *Turn right after bridge in Ponte Tresa, then 5km to site.*
Site: 1.5HEC ▦ ⚓ 🚐 Facilities: ♠ ⅃ ⊙ ⨀ ⚫ ☎ Services: ✗
⊞ lau Leisure: ⵜ PR Off-site: ⛾

TENERO TICINO

Campofelice Lago Maggiore, 6598
☎ 091 7451417 ▥ 091 7451888
e-mail: camping@campofelice.ch website: www.campofelice.ch
Beautifully situated and extensive site completely divided
into pitches, and crossed by asphalt drives.
⮕ *1.9km S. Signposted.*
Open: 26 Mar-23 Oct Site: 15HEC ▦ ⠒⠒ ♣ 🏠 🚐 ⚡
Prices: (incl 2 persons) Facilities: ♠ ⅃ ⊙ ⨀ ⚫ ≞
☎ Services: ⛾ ✗ ⊞ lau Leisure: ⵜ LR

Lido Mappo Via Mappo, 6598 ☎ 091 7451437 ▥ 091 745480
e-mail: lidomappo@bluewin.ch website: www.lidomappo.ch
Beautifully situated, well appointed site on lakeside.
Teenagers not accepted on their own. Minimum stay, 1 week
in Jul-Aug.
⮕ *700mtrs SW. Signposted.*
Open: 26 Mar- 17 Oct Site: 6.5HEC ▦ ♣ ⚡ Prices: pitch
32-49 (incl 2 persons) Facilities: ♠ ⅃ ⊙ ⨀ ≞ ☎
Services: ⛾ ✗ ⊞ lau Leisure: ⵜ L Off-site: ⵜPR

Tamaro via Mappo, 6598 ☎ 091 7452161 ▥ 091 7456636
e-mail: info@campingtamaro.ch
website: www.campingtamaro.ch
Well equipped site with direct access to the lake. Groups of
young persons not admitted unless accompanied by adults.
⮕ *4km from Locano. Signposted from motorway.*
Open: 25 Mar-24 Oct Site: 6HEC ▦ ♣ ⚡ Prices: 🚐5
⛺15-30 pitch 33-62 (incl 2 persons) Facilities: ♠ ⅃ ⊙ ⨀ ⚫
≞ ☎ Services: ⛾ ✗ ⊞ lau Leisure: ⵜ L Off-site: ⵜP

SOUTH WEST

AGARN VALAIS

Gemmi Briannenstr, 3952 ☎ 027 4731154 ▥ 027 4734295
e-mail: info@campgemmi.ch website: www.campgemmi.ch
In a very pleasant location on the outskirts of the town,
providing outstanding views of the surrounding mountains.
There are clean, modern facilities and individual bathrooms
are available for weekly hire.

⮕ *Exit from A9 at Agarn. Signposted*
Open: 24 Apr-16 Oct Site: 0.9HEC ▦ ⚓ Prices: ⵜ7-8 pitch
11-19 Facilities: ♠ ⅃ ⊙ ⨀ ⚫ ≞ ☎ Services: ✗ ⊞ lau
Off-site: ⅃ ⛾ ✗ ⵜP

AIGLE VAUD

Glariers (TCS) 1860 ☎ 024 4662660 ▥ 024 4662660
e-mail: camping.aigle@tcs.ch website: www.campingtcs.ch
On level ground with trees and bushes near railway line and
the avenue des Glariers. Fine mountain views.
⮕ *800mtrs NE off the A9 near Shell Migrol petrol station.*
Open: 2 Apr-3 Oct Site: 1HEC ▦ ⤳ Prices: ⵜ6.20-8.20
⛺7-10 pitch 14-18 Facilities: ♠ ⅃ ⊙ ⨀ ≞ ☎ Services: ⛾ ✗
⊞ lau Leisure: ⵜ PR Off-site: ✗ ⚫

AROLLA VALAIS

Petit Praz 1986 ☎ 027 2832295
e-mail: camping@arolla.com
In an imposing mountain setting.
Open: Jun-Sep Site: 1HEC ▦ ⚫ ⤳ Prices: ⵜ6 ⵜ3 🚐7
⛺5-7 Facilities: ♠ ⅃ ⊙ ⨀ ⚫ ≞ ☎ Services: lau

BALLENS VAUD

Bois Gentil 1144 ☎ 021 8095120
⮕ *200mtrs S of station.*
Open: Apr-Sep Site: 2.5HEC ▦ ⚓ Prices: ⵜ5.50 🚐2
🚐6.50 ⛺5 Facilities: ♠ ⅃ ⊙ ⨀ ⚫ ☎ Services: ⊞
Leisure: ⵜ P

BOURG-ST-PIERRE VALAIS

Grand St-Bernard 1946 ☎ 027 7871411 ▥ 027 7871411
e-mail: grand-st-bernard@swisscamps.ch
website: www.campinggrand-st-bernard.ch
In beautiful mountain scenery with easy access to winter
sports areas.
⮕ *Near the Italian border, between Martigny and Aosta.*
Open: May-Sep Site: 1HEC ▦ ⤳ Facilities: ♠ ⊙ ⨀ ⚫ ☎
Services: ⊞ lau Leisure: ⵜ P Off-site: ⅃ ⛾ ✗ ⵜR

BOUVERET, LE VALAIS

Rive Bleue 1897 ☎ 024 4812161
e-mail: info@camping-rive-bleue.ch
website: www.camping-rive-bleue.ch
Beside lake with a natural sandy beach and good, modern
facilities.
⮕ *Turn off the A37 to Monthey in the SW district of Bouveret
and drive NE for about 0.8km.*
Open: Apr-Sep Site: 3HEC ▦ ⚓ 🏠 🚐 Prices: ⵜ7.60-9.30
🚐1.90 🚐8.30-11.40 ⛺6.50-11.40 Facilities: ♠ ⅃ ⊙ ⨀ ⚫ ≞
🅿 Services: ⊞ lau Leisure: ⵜ LP Off-site: ⛾ ✗ ⵜR

BULLET VAUD

Cluds 1453 ☎ 024 4541440 ▥ 024 4541440
e-mail: vd28@campings-ccyverdon.ch
website: www.campings-ccyverdon.ch
In beautiful mountain setting among pine trees.
⮕ *1.5km NE.*
Open: All year Site: 1.2HEC ▦ ⤳ Prices: ⵜ7 ⵜ3 🚐7-11
⛺5-11 Facilities: ♠ ⊙ ⨀ ⚫ ≞ 🅿 Services: ✗ ⊞ lau

CHÂTEAU-D'OEX VAUD

Berceau (TCS) 1837
☎ 026 9246234 ▥ 026 9246234/ 026 9242526
e-mail: info@chateau-doex.ch website: www.chateau-doex.ch
On level strip of grass between the mountain and the river
bank.
⮕ *1km SE at junction of roads 77 and 76.*
Open: All year Site: 1HEC ▦ ⤳ Facilities: ♠ ⊙ ⨀ ⚫ ≞ ☎
Services: ✗ ⊞ lau Leisure: ⵜ PR Off-site: ⅃ ⛾

Facilities: ⅃-shop ♠-shower ⊙-electric points for razors ⨀-electric points for caravans ☎-parking by tents permitted
🅿-compulsory separate car park Services: ✗-café/restaurant ⛾-bar ⚫-Camping Gaz International ≞-gas other than Camping
Gaz ⊞-first aid facilities lau-laundry Leisure: ⵜ-swimming L-Lake P-Pool R-River S-Sea Off-site: All facilities within 2km

CHÂTEL-ST-DENIS FRIBOURG

Bivouac rte des Paccots, 1618 ☎ 021 9487849 ▤ 021 9487849
e-mail: bivouac@swissonline.ch
website: www.le-bivouac.ch
Beautiful views of the rolling Swiss countryside. Various
sports and leisure activities.
➲ Turn E in Chatel-St Denis and continue for 2km.
Open: Apr-Sep Site: 2HEC ▥▥ ⌀ Prices: ♠5-6 pitch 10-15
Facilities: ♠ ⚍ ⊙ ⚑ ⌀ ⚏ ☎ Services: ⬥ ✗ ⊞ lau Leisure: ⬩
PR Off-site: ✗

CHESSEL VAUD

Grands Bois 1846 ☎ 024 4814225 ▤ 024 4815113
e-mail: au.grand-bois@bluewin.ch
On a level meadow close to a canal and only a few kilometres
from Lake Geneva.
➲ N of town towards the lake.
Open: All year Site: 4HEC ▥▥ ⌀ ⚏ ⚑ Prices: ♠4.50-6
⚗2.50-3 ⚑6.50-9 ▲3.50-9 Facilities: ♠ ⚍ ⊙ ⚑ ⌀ ⚏ ☎
Services: ⬥ ✗ lau Leisure: ⬩ PR

CUDREFIN VAUD

Chablais 1588 ☎ 026 6773277
500mtrs from the town centre, directly on the lake.
Open: 15 Mar-Oct Site: 228HEC ▥▥ ⌀ Facilities: ♠ ⊙ ⚑
⚑ Services: lau Leisure: ⬩ L Off-site: ⚍ ⬥ ✗ ⌀ ⬩R ⊞

DÜDINGEN FRIBOURG

Schiffenensee 3186 ☎ 026 493486
➲ Leave the A12 (Bern-Fribourg) at Düdingen and proceed
N towards Murten.
Open: Apr-Oct Site: 9HEC ▥▥ ⌀ Facilities: ♠ ⚍ ⊙ ⚑ ⚏
Services: ⬥ ✗ ⊞ lau Leisure: ⬩ LP Off-site: ⌀ ⚍

EVOLÈNE VALAIS

Evolène 1983 ☎ 027 2831144 ▤ 027 2833255
e-mail: evolene@swisscamps.ch
website: www.camping-evolene.ch
On a level meadow with fine views of the surrounding
mountains.
➲ 200mtrs from town
Open: All year Site: 10HEC ▥▥ ✲ ⚑ Prices: ♠6 ⚗3 ⚑7
▲5-7 Facilities: ♠ ⊙ ⚑ ⌀ ⚍ ☎ Services: ⊞ lau Leisure: ⬩ P
Off-site: ⚍ ⬥ ✗ ⬩R

FOREL VAUD

Forel 1606 ☎ 021 7811464 ▤ 021 7813126
A family site in a pleasant rural setting with good
recreational facilities.
➲ Leave the A9 at Chexbres in the direction of Forel and take
left turning to Savigny.
Open: All year Site: 4HEC ▥▥ ⌀ ⚏ ⚑ Facilities: ♠ ⚍ ⊙ ⚑
⌀ ⚍ ☎ Services: ⬥ ✗ ⊞ lau Leisure: ⬩ P

FOULY, LA VALAIS

Glaciers 1944 ☎ 027 7831735 ▤ 027 7833605
e-mail: camping.glaciers@st-bernard.ch
website: www.camping-glaciers.ch
At end of village in a beautiful Alpine location with fine
views of the surrounding mountains.
Open: 15 May-Sep Site: 8HEC ▥▥ ⌀ Prices: ♠6.50 pitch
14-16 Facilities: ♠ ⚍ ⊙ ⚑ ⌀ ⚍ ☎ Services: ⊞ lau
Off-site: ⬩R

GENÈVE (GENEVA) GENÈVE

AT SATIGNY (6KM SW)

Bois-de-Bay 1242 ☎ 022 3410505 ▤ 022 3410606

➲ Leave A1 at Bernex and follow campsite signs.
Open: All year Site: 2.8HEC ▥▥ ⌀ Facilities: ♠ ⚍ ⊙ ⚑ ⌀
⚍ ☎ Services: ⬥ ⊞

AT VÉSENAZ (6KM NE)

Pointe á la Bise (TCS) 12223
☎ 022 7521296 ▤ 022 7523767
e-mail: camping.geneve@tcs.ch
In a pleasant wooded setting on the shore of Lake Léman.
➲ NE between Vésenaz and Collonge-Bellerive.
Open: Etr-mid Oct Site: 3.2HEC ▥▥ ⌀ ⚏ Facilities: ♠ ⚍
⊙ ⚑ ⌀ ⚍ ☎ Services: ⬥ ✗ ⊞ Leisure: ⬩ L

GRANDSON VAUD

Pécos VD24, 1422 ☎ 024 4454969 ▤ 024 4462904
e-mail: vd24@campings-ccyverdon.ch
website: www.campings-ccyverdon.ch
➲ 400mtrs SW of railway station between railway and lake.
Open: Apr-Sep Site: 2HEC ▥▥ ✲ ⚏ Facilities: ♠ ⚍ ⊙ ⚑
⌀ ⚍ ⚑ Services: ✗ ⊞ lau Leisure: ⬩ L

GUMEFENS FRIBOURG

Lac 1643 ☎ 026 9152162 ▤ 026 9152162
e-mail: campingdulac@planet.ch
On the borders of the lake.
Open: 15 May-15 Sep Site: 1.5HEC ▥▥ ✲ ⊗
Prices: ♠7.20 ⚗2.50 ⚑8.50 ▲6.50-8.50 Facilities: ♠ ⚍ ⊙ ⚑
⌀ ☎ Services: ⬥ ✗ ⊞ lau Leisure: ⬩ L

LAUSANNE VAUD

Vidy chemin du Camping 3, 1007
☎ 021 6225000 ▤ 021 6225001
e-mail: info@campinglausannevidy.ch
website: www.campinglausannevidy.ch
In a delightful location amid trees and flowerbeds
overlooking Lac Léman. Shop and restaurant open May-Sep
only.
Open: All year Site: 4.5HEC ▥▥ ⌀ ⚏ Prices: ♠7.80 ⚗3.50
pitch 12 Facilities: ♠ ⚍ ⊙ ⚑ ⌀ ⚍ ☎ Services: ⬥ ✗ ⊞ lau
Leisure: ⬩ L

LEYSIN VAUD

Sémiramis 1854 ☎ 024 4943939 ▤ 024 4942121
e-mail: info@hoteldusoleil.ch website: camping-leysin.ch
In a picturesque Alpine setting.
➲ After entering the village turn left at SHELL filling station
and continue for 400mtrs.
Open: All year Site: 1.1HEC ▥▥ ✲ Prices: ♠5-6.50 ⚗3-5
⚑6-7.20 ▲2-4 Facilities: ♠ ⚍ ⊙ ⚑ ⌀ ⚍ ☎ Services: ⬥ ✗ ⊞
lau Off-site: ⚍ ⬩P

MORGINS VALAIS

Morgins (TCS) 1875 ☎ 024 4772361 ▤ 024 4773708
e-mail: touristoffice@morgins.ch website: www.morgins.ch
A terraced site below pine forest.
➲ Turn left at end of village towards Pas de Morgins near
Swiss Customs.
Open: All year Site: 1.3HEC ▥▥ ✲ Prices: ♠6.70 pitch 10
Facilities: ♠ ⊙ ⚑ ☎ Services: ⊞ lau Off-site: ⚍ ⬥ ✗ ⌀ ⚍
⬩PR

PAYERNE VAUD

Piscine de Payerne 1530 ☎ 037 614322
Camping Card compulsory
Open: Apr-Sep Site: 8HEC ▥▥ ⌀ Facilities: ♠ ⊙ ⚑ ⌀ ⚍ ☎
Services: ✗ ⊞ lau Leisure: ⬩ P

Site: 6HEC-Site size ▥▥-grass ░-sand ◈-stone ✲-little shade ⌀-partly shaded ⬥-mainly shaded
⚏-bungalows for hire ⚑-caravans for hire ▲-tents for hire ⊗-no dogs **Prices:** ♠-adult per night ⚗-car per night
pp-per person per night ⚑-caravan per night ▲-tent per night

RARON VALAIS

Camping Simplonblick 3942 ☎ 027 9341274 ▤ 027 9342600
e-mail: simplon-blick@bluewin.ch
website: www.camping-simplonblick.ch
➲ *300mtrs W of Turtig.*
Open: All year Site: 6HEC ⬛⬛⬛ 🇶 🚐 🇦 Prices: ♠5.50
🚙1.50 🚐10 🇦9 Facilities: 🇮 🇱 ☉ 🇶 🇵 🖴 🇦 Services: ♈ ✗
🇵 lau Leisure: ⇃ P Off-site: 🇱

Santa Monica 3942 ☎ 027 9342424
Open: All year Site: 4HEC ⬛⬛⬛ 🇶 🇺 Facilities: 🇮 🇱 ☉ 🇶 🇵
🇦 Services: ✗ lau Leisure: ⇃ P Off-site: ♈ ⇃LR

RECKINGEN VALAIS

Ellbogen (TCS) CH-3998 ☎ 027 9731395 ▤ 027 9732677
e-mail: augenstern1@bluewin.ch
On an alpine meadow close to the River Rhône.
➲ *400mtrs S on bank of Rhône.*
Open: 10 Dec-01 Apr & 10 May-24 Oct Site: 1.5HEC ⬛⬛⬛
🇷 Prices: ♠7.30 🇦7.50 pitch 8.50 Facilities: 🇮 🇱 ☉ 🇶 🇦
Services: ✗ 🇵 lau Off-site: ⇃P

RIED-BRIG VALAIS

Tropic 3911 ☎ 027 9232537
➲ *To the left of Simplon road near entrance to village. 3km above Brig.*
Open: May-15 Sep Site: 1.5HEC ⬛⬛⬛ 🍀 🇺 🇷 Prices: ♠5.50
🚙4 🇷6-7 🇦4-7 pitch 4 Facilities: 🇮 🇱 ☉ 🇶 🇵 🇦
Services: ♈ ✗ 🇵 lau Off-site: ⇃P

SAAS-GRUND VALAIS

Kapellenweg 3910 ☎ 027 9574997 ▤ 027 9573316
e-mail: camping@kapellenweg.ch
website: www.kapellenweg.ch
On a level meadow in a picturesque mountain setting in the Saas Valley. Good, modern facilities.
➲ *Turn right over bridge towards Saas-Almagell.*
Open: May-Oct Site: 1.5HEC ⬛⬛⬛ 🇶 🇷 Prices: ♠5.90-7.10
🚙3.60-4.50 🇷3.60-4.50 🇦3.60-4.50 Facilities: 🇮 🇱 ☉ 🇶 🇵
🖴 🇦 Services: lau Leisure: ⇃ R Off-site: ♈ ✗

SALGESCH VALAIS

Swiss Plage 3970 ☎ 027 4556608 ▤ 027 4813215
e-mail: info@swissplage.ch website: http://swissplage.ch
Situated beside a small lake and surrounded by vineyards.
Good recreational facilities.
Open: Etr-1 Nov Site: 10HEC ⬛⬛⬛ ⋮⋮⋮ 🌢 🇶 🇺 🇷
Prices: ♠6.50-7.20 pitch 13.50-15 Facilities: 🇮 🇱 ☉ 🇶 🇵 🖴
🇦 Services: ♈ ✗ 🇵 lau Leisure: ⇃ LR

SEMBRANCHER VALAIS

Prairie (TCS) 1933 ☎ 027 7852206 ▤ 027 7852131
e-mail: prairie01@bluewin.ch
➲ *12km from Martigny and 500mtrs from town.*
Open: June-Sept Site: 50HEC ⬛⬛⬛ 🌣 Facilities: 🇮 🇱 ☉ 🇶
🇵 🖴 🇦 Services: ♈ ✗ lau Off-site: ⇃R 🇵

SIERRE (SIDERS) VALAIS

Bois de Finges (TCS) 3960 ☎ 027 4550284 ▤ 027 4553351
e-mail: camping.sierre@tcs.ch
website: www.campingtcs.ch
Situated in a pine forest with well defined pitches set on terraces.
➲ *Access via motorway exit Sierre-Ouest towards Sierre.*
Open: 28 Apr-3 Oct Site: 5HEC ⬛⬛⬛ ⋮⋮⋮ 🌢 🍀 🇺
Prices: ♠6.40-6.80 pitch 15-18 Facilities: 🇮 🇱 ☉ 🇶 🇵 🖴 🇦
Services: ♈ ✗ 🇵 lau Leisure: ⇃ P Off-site: ✗ ⇃LR

Rhonetal Simplonblick, Raron
4****-Camping in a park-like situation
• 3 play grounds, soccer, net ball, trampoline, table tennis,
etc. • heated swimming pool • centrally located for
excursions to Zermatt,
Saas Fee, etc.

Phone 0041-(0)27-934 12 74
Fax 0041-(0)27-934 26 00
Phone 0041-(0)27-967 75 75
Fax 0041-(0)27-967 50 12
www.camping-simplonblick.ch
simplonblick@bluewin.ch

SORENS FRIBOURG

Forêt 1642 ☎ 026 9151882 ▤ 026 9150363
e-mail: camping.laforet@caramail.com
A pleasant site on a level meadow surrounded by woodland and with pleant of vegetation.
➲ *Turn right off the A12 in Gumefens and drive on to the village.*
Open: All year Site: 4HEC ⬛⬛⬛ 🇶 🇷 Prices: ♠6 🚙2.50 🇷5
🇦5 pitch 4 Facilities: 🇮 🇱 ☉ 🇶 🇵 🖴 🇦 Services: ✗ 🇵 lau
Leisure: ⇃ P

SUSTEN VALAIS

Bella Tola (TCS) Waldstrosse 57, CH 3952
☎ 027 4731491 ▤ 027 4733641
e-mail: info@bella-tola.ch website: www.bella-tola.ch
A peaceful, terraced site at an altitude of 750mtrs, sheilded by a belt of woodland. Good, clean modern facilities.
➲ *2km from village.*
Open: 11 May-28 Sep Site: 3.6HEC ⬛⬛⬛ 🇶 Prices: ♠6.53
pitch 10.71-33.33 Facilities: 🇮 🇱 ☉ 🇶 🇵 🖴 🇦 Services: ♈ ✗
🇵 lau Leisure: ⇃ P

Rhodania Kantonstr, 3952 ☎ 027 4731312
Open: May-Oct Site: 0.2HEC ⬛⬛⬛ 🍀 Facilities: 🇮 ☉ 🇶 🇦
Services: ♈ ✗ Off-site: 🇱 🇵 ⇃PR 🇵

ULRICHEN VALAIS

Nufenen 3988 ☎ 027 9731437 ▤ 027 9741433
e-mail: camping-nufenen@rhone.ch
website: www.rhone.ch/camping-nufenen
➲ *1km SE to right of road to Nufenen Pass.*
Open: Jun-Sep Site: 8HEC ⬛⬛⬛ 🇶 Prices: ♠6 🚙3 🇷6-8
🇦4.50-5.50 Facilities: 🇮 ☉ 🇶 🇵 🖴 🇦 Services: 🇵 lau
Leisure: ⇃ R Off-site: 🇱 ♈ ✗

VALLORBE VAUD

Pré sous Ville (TCS) 1337 ☎ 021 8432309
In a wooded riverside location. Neighbouring swimming pool available to campers free of charge.
➲ *On left bank of River Orbe.*
Open: May-Oct Site: 1HEC ⬛⬛⬛ 🇶 Prices: ♠6 🇷8-9.50
🇦3.50-9.50 Facilities: 🇮 ☉ 🇶 🇵 🖴 🇦 Services: lau
Leisure: ⇃ P Off-site: 🇱 ♈ ✗

VERS-L'ÉGLISE VAUD

Murée (TCS) 1864 ☎ 021 6345284 ▤ 021 6345284
e-mail: dagonch@bluewinch.
website: www.camping-caravaningvd.com
Partially terraced site by a stream.
➲ *Signposted on the right at the entry to the village.*
Open: All year Site: 1.1HEC ⬛⬛⬛ 🇶 🇺 Prices: ♠4.80-5.30
🇦6-9 pitch 9-10 Facilities: 🇮 ☉ 🇶 🇵 🖴 🇦 Services: lau
Leisure: ⇃ R Off-site: 🇵

Botza (TCS) 1963 ☎ 027 3461940
e-mail: info@botza.ch
website: www.botza.ch
On a level meadow with pitches divided by hedges. Fine panoramic views and good leisure facilities.
Open: All year Site: 3HEC ⛺ ♠ ⊞ Å Prices: ♠4.70-7.80
pitch 7.50-19.50 Facilities: ♠ ☎ ⊙ ♨ ⌀ ♨ ☎ Services: ♥ ✕
⊞ lau Leisure: ⇃ P

Yverdon 1462 ☎ 024 4301655 🗐 024 4302463
e-mail: vd8@campings-ccyverdon.ch
website: www.campings-ccyverdon.ch
6km NE of Yverdon bordering Lake Neuchâtel with private beach 1km away, boat moorings, private jetty and boat hire.
⊃ *3km W. Signposted.*
Open: Apr-Sep Site: 5HEC ⛺ ⣿ ♠ ⊞ ♣ ⊘
Prices: ♠6.90-8.90 ♠3.50 ♠7-15 Facilities: ♠ ☎ ⊙ ♨ ⌀ ♨
🄿 Services: ♥ ✕ ⊞ lau Leisure: ⇃ L

The old Zunfthaus der Waldleute (Guild-House of the Foresters), Biel

Site: 6HEC-Site size ⛺**-grass** ∷**-sand** ♠**-stone** ♨**-little shade** ⊶**-partly shaded** ♠**-mainly shaded**
⣿**-bungalows for hire** ♠**-caravans for hire** Å**-tents for hire** ⊘**-no dogs Prices:** ♠**-adult per night** ♠**-car per night**
pp-per person per night ♠**-caravan per night** Å**-tent per night**

INDEX

INDEX

INDEX

INDEX

INDEX

INDEX

INDEX

INDEX

INDEX

INDEX

INDEX

INDEX

INDEX

INDEX

INDEX

SWITZERLAND

INDEX

PICTURE CREDITS

The Automobile Association would like to thank the following libraries and agencies for their assistance in the preparation of this book:
Nova Development Corp. 6cbl; Photodisc 35bc

The remaining images are held in the Association's own library (AA World Travel Library) with contributions by:
Adrian Baker 2, 6lcbl, 9br, 10bl, 12bc, 14, 15bl, 16t, 17t, 17b, 18t, 18bl, 19, 21br, 22t, 23t, 2 27br, 28b, 30bl, 57, 215; Peter Baker 37; M Birkitt 29b; Pete Bennett 23br, 31bc; Michelle Chaplow 321; Roger Day 6t; Steve Day 4, 5, 6cb, 8, 11, 18b, 355, 366; Philip Enticknap 13, 32t, 33, 34t, 35t, 36t; Jim Holmes 21bl; Caroline Jones 34b; Max Jourdan 289, 352; Alex Kouprianoff 28t, 30t, 30bc, 30br, 31t, 32br, 36bl, 72, 79, 314, 317; Rob Moore 12bl, 15bc, 54, 212; Simon McBride 36br; Dario Mitidieri; 9bl, 36bc; David Noble 35br; Ken Paterson 6rcbr, 16bc, 27bc, 32bc, 252; Clive Sawyer 6cbr, 22bc, 23bl, 82; Neil Setchfield 23bc, 29bl; M Siebert 1, 10r 15t, 15br; Tony Souter 3t, 16bl, 35br, 214; Rick Strange 18b, 27bl; David Tarn 24bc; James Tims; 3c

Cover credits:
F/C AA World Travel Library/Steve Day
B/C t AA World Travel Library/Alex Kouprianoff
B/C b AA World Travel Library/Steve Day

COUNTRY MAP SECTION

AUSTRIA

1

BELGIUM & LUXEMBOURG

2

FRANCE

FRANCE

GERMANY

5

GERMANY

NETH

Aachen ■

BELGIUM

LUXEMBOURG

FRANCE

SWITZERLAND

AUSTRIA

Drolshagen   Attendorn
Olpe
● KÖLN
Liblar   Niedereisenhausen   Zwesten   Grundmühle
Heimbach   Marburg   bei Quentel
BONN ■   Bad Honnef   Mittelhof   Heimertshausen Kirchheim Heringen
Mehlem   Steinen Seck
Schleiden   Bad Breisig   Braunfels Grünberg   Tann
Hellenthal Monschau   Montabaur Weilburg   Schotten Rothemann Schachen
Stadtkyll   Dorsel an der Ahr   Koblenz   Schlüchtern
Prüm   Lahnstein Bad Ems Diez Dausenau
Waxweiler Schalkenmehren   Treis- C E N T R A L   Bad
Gillenfeld Cochem Karden Hausbay St Goarshausen Königstein   Kissingen
Utscheid   Nehren Mesenich St.Goar Idstein FRANKFURT
Oberweis   Bullay Senheim Lingerhahn Lorch Mainz-Kostheim AM MAIN   Gemünden am Main
Obersgegen Kröv   Bacharach   Dreieich-Offenthal Gemünden-Hofstetten
Irrel   Mülheim Kirn   Geisenheim Rüdesheim Mörfelden-Walldorf   Neustadt
Leiwen Bernkastel-   Asbacherhütte   SOUTH EAST
Heidenburg Kues Sensweiler Mühle Guldental   Lengfurt
Könen Trier Reinsfeld   Gerbach Lindenfels   Wertheim
Kell   Zerf   Birkenfeld   Michelstadt
Saarburg   Wolfstein   Fürth im Odenwald Kirchzell Bad Mergentheim
Losheim   Altneudorf Gammelsbach
Schönenburg   Bad Dürkheim MANNHEIM Flirschhorn Creglingen
Saarlouis   am Neckar
Trippstadt   Heidelberg Neckargemünd Neckarzimmern
Mörtelstein 2
Dahn Ingenheim   Ostringen   Buchhorn
bei Ohringen
Karlsruhe   Schwäbisch Hall
Pforzheim   Murrhardt Ellwangen
Höfen an der Enz Schömberg
Rheinmünster Wildbad im Bad Liebenzell   STUTTGART Schwäbisch
Kehl Bühl Schwarzwald Liebelsberg   Gmünd
Achern Altensteig
Hallwangen Horb Tübingen Laichingen
Schapbach Freudenstadt Erpfingen   Bad
Steinach Alpirsbach S O U T H W E S T Schussenried
Ettenheim   Schiltach
Herbolzheim
Waldkirch   Hausen
Freiburg im St Peter Bad Dürrheim
Breisgau Kirchzarten Titisee-Neustadt Donaueschingen Ludwigshafen
Staufen Münstertal Lenzkirch Badenweiler am Bodensee Markdorf
Neuenburg Todtnau   Überlingen Nussdorf
Dingelsdorf Uhldingen Isny
Waldshut   Kressbronn
Lörrach   Lindau im Bodensee Aach bei
Oberstaufen

■ Town names
● Gazetteer location

0   10   20   30 miles
0   20   40   60 kilometres

6

NETHERLANDS

Legend:
- ■ Town names
- ● Gazetteer location

Scale: 0 — 20 — 40 — 60 miles / 0 — 50 — 100 kilometres

NORTH

Hee, West Terschelling, Lauwersoog, Groningen, Harkstede, Harlingen, Leeuwarden, Bergum, Franeker, Opende, Onnen, Wedde, De Koog, Makkum, Annen, Assen, Amen, Borger, Den Hoorn, Hindeloopen, Den Helder, Groote Keeten, Koudum, Diever, Dwingeloo, Callantsoog, St Maartenszee, Sondel, Steenwijk, Ruinen, Groet, Andijk, Egmond aan Zee, Noord Scharwoude, Urk, Blokzijl, Heiloo, Alkmaar, Berkhout, Wijdenes

CENTRAL

Edam, Uitdam, Dronten, Hattem, Dalfsen, Reuturn, Haarlem, Nunspeet, Wezep, Luttenberg, Denekamp, Vogelenzang, Haltweg, AMSTERDAM, Putten, Ermelo, Hengelo, Noordwijk aan Zee, Aalsmeer, Mijnden, Apeldoorn, Markelo, Enschede, Rijnsburg, Beekbergen, Diepenheim, Buurse, Katwijk aan Zee, Ruurlo, Haaksbergen, Wassenaar, Leiden, Blithoven, Soest, Kootwijk, Epe, Eerbeek, Neede, Utrecht, Maarn, Hoenderloo, Laag-Soeren, Hengelo, 's-Gravenzande, DEN HAAG, Delft, Doorn, Arnhem, Lathum, Winterswijk, Hoek Van Holland, Rotterdam, Rhenen, Doesburg, Doetinchem, Oostvoorne, Brielle, Wageningen, Babberich, Rockanje, Barendrecht, Kesteren, Nijmegen, Ouddorp, Hellevoetsluis, Appeltern

SOUTH

Renesse, Brouwershaven, Herpen, Heumen, Plasmolen, Burgh-Haamstede, Hoeven, Breda, Oosterhout, St Anthonis, Afferden, Vrouwenpolder, Kamperland, Oostkapelle, Kortgene, Roosendaal, Tilburg, Boxtel, St Oedenrode, Well, Broekhuizenvorst, Westkapelle, Middelburg, Oisterwijk, Eindhoven, Venray, Arcen, Zoutelande, Wemeldinge, Hilvarenbeek, Sevenum, Koudekerke, Arnemuiden, Baarle Nassau, Mierlo, Nieuwvliet, Hoogerheide, Lage Mierde, Eersel, Maasbree, Baarlo, Breskens, Baarland, Bergeyk, Groede, Hengstdijk, Retranchement, Hoek, Luyksgestel, Weert, Roermond, Sluis, Echt

Berg en Terblijt, Landgraaf, Maastricht, Valkenburg

BELGIUM

GERMANY

FRANCE

LUX

ITALY

NORTH EAST & ADRIATIC

Cutigliano
Montecatini Terme
Pievepelago
Sarzana
Viareggio
Lerici
Moneglia
Deiva Marina
Marina di Massa
Torre del Lago Puccini
Sestri Levante
Bogliasco
Genova
Pegli

Golfo di Genova

Stella
San Giovanni
Diano
Ceriale
Albenga
Cervo

NORTH WEST & ALPS & LAKES

Bastia Mondovì
Cuneo
Limone Piemonte
Bordighera

FRANCE

MONACO

ROMANIA

HUNGARY

SERBIA & MONTENEGRO

ALBANIA

CROATIA

BOSNIA AND HERCEGOVINA

SLOVENIA

25 Marina di Ravenna
26 Punta Marina
27 Lido di Dante
28 Cervia
29 Milano Marittima
30 Pinarella
31 Cesenatico
32 Gatteo Mare

GERMANY

AUSTRIA

18 Naturno-Naturns
19 Kaltern
20 Lawes-Leifers
21 Bolzano-Bozen
22 Campitello di Fassa
23 Chiusa-Klausen
24 Colfosco

LIECHTENSTEIN

SWITZERLAND

FRANCE

1 Calenzano
2 Barberino Val d'Elsa
3 San Gimignano
4 Castagnetto Carducci
5 Montescudaio
6 Lacona
7 Porto Azzurro
8 Ortano
9 Nisporto
10 Ottone
11 Portoferraio
12 Castiglione della Pescaia
13 Casale Marittimo
14 Castel del Piano
15 Citta di Castello
16 Castiglione del Lago
17 S Arcangelo sul Trasimeno

CORSE (Fr)

ADRIATIC

ROME

NORTH EAST & SAN MARINO

VENICE & NORTH

NORTH WEST & MED COAST

8

SPAIN AND PORTUGAL

Viveiro
Foz
La Coruña/ Valdoviño
A Coruña
Barreiros Reinante Cadavedo
Bergondo
Luarca Cudillero Perlora-Candas
La Franca
Pechón Cornillas
Cóbreces Santillana del Mar
Ajo Bareyo
Gijón
Islares
Noja Laredo
Castro-Urdiales
San Sebastián/
Donostia
Santiago de
Compostela
Oviedo
Llanes
Santa Marina
de Valdeon
Santander Bareyo
Bilbao/Bilbo
Motrico
Zarauz
Orio
San Vicente do Mar
Portonovo
Vigo
León
Villamejil
Vitoria/
Gasteiz
Mendigorria
Estella
Baiona
Nigrán
Valencia
de Don
Juan
Burgos
Pancorbo
Santa
Domingo de
la Calzada
Nájera
N O
Caminha
Viana do Castelo
Campo do Geres
Bragança
Cubillas
de Santa
Marta
Villoslada de
Cameros
Póvoa de Varzim
Braga
Mondim de Basto
Simancas
Valladolid
Aranda
de Duero
Matosinhos
Vila Nova de
Gaia
Porto
Vila Real
Tordesillas
São Jacinto
Casfreires
Villamayor
La Fuente
de San
Esteban
Salamanca
Gargantilla
de Lozoya
Segovia
Navalafuente
La Cabrera
Aveiro
Viseu
Santa Marta
de Tormes
Alba de Tormes
C E N T R A L
Palheiros de Mira
Luso
Coimbra
Guarda
Gouveia
Miranda del
Castañar
El Escorial
MADRID
Figueira da Foz
Peñacova
Coja
Arganil
Valdemaqueda
Getafe
Aranjuez
Cuenca
Lourical
São Pedro de Moel
Leiria
Malpartida
de Plasencia
Toledo
Nazaré
C E N T R A L
Castelo
Branco
Peniche
Évora de
Alcobaça
Caldas da
Rainha
Santarém
Abrantes
Montargil
Portalegre
Alenquer
Salvaterra
de Magos
LISBOA
Guincho
Costa
da Caparica
Setúbal
Badajoz
Mérida
Albacete
Évora
Alvito
Santa Elena
Sines
Vila Nova de
Milfontes
Beja
Córdoba
La Carlota
S O U T H
Santo Andre
S O U T H
La Guijarrosa
Vila do Bispo
Portimão
Mazagón
Peligros
Sagres
Praia
da Luz
Albufeira
Quarteira
Isla Cristina
Sevilla
Los Gallardos
Faro
Olhão
Granada
Otura
Ronda
Málaga
Torre
del Mar
Motril
Castillo
de Baños
Roquetas-
de-Mar
Cabo de
Gata
El Puerto de
Santa María
Jerez de
la Frontera
Almayate
Carchuna
Adra
Almerimar
Cádiz
Marbella
Estepona
Conil de la Frontera
Vejer de la Frontera
Gibraltar
Tarifa

MOROCCO

■ Town names
● Gazetteer location

0   50   100 miles
0   50   100   150   200 kilometres

FRANCE

Oricain
Pamplona/
Iruñea
Tiermas
Tunnel de
Somport
Bossost
La Bordeta
La Guingueta
Espot
Torla
Biescas
Jaca
Labuerda
Ribera de Cardós
Bonansa
ANDORRA
Huesca
La Puebla
de Castro
R T H   E A S T
NORTH EAST
COAST
Saviñan
Zaragoza
Calatayud
Vilanova
de Prades
BARCELONA
Nuevalos
Salou
Mont-Roig del Camp
Cambrils
L'Hospitalet de l'infant
L'Ametlla de Mar
See enlarged area
Albarracin
Vinaroz
Peñiscola
Benicarló
Alcoceber
Torreblanca
Oropesa del Mar
Benicasim
Navajas
Islas Baleares
Palma
Puebla de Farnals
Canet d'en Berenguer
Valencia
Jaraco
Miramar Playa
Daimus
Oliva
Benisa
Alfaz del Pi
Altea
Campello
Benidorm
Villajoyosa
Alicante/Alacant
Baños
de Fortuna
La Marina
Guardamar del Segura
Murcia
Los Alcazares
La Manga del
Mar Menor
Isla Plana
Bolnuevo
Cartagena
Aguilas
Mojácar

FRANCE

ANDORRA
Guils de Cerdanya
Santa Juliá
de Loria
Bellver de
Cerdanya
Puigcerdá
Vilallonga de Ter
Túnel
del Cadi
Guardiola de
Bergueda
NORTH
EAST
Ripoll
NORTH EAST
COAST
Castelló d'Empuries
Sant Pere Pescador
l'Escala
L'Estartit
Torroella de Montgri
Pals
Begur
Solsona
Saldes
Taradell
Sant Antoni
de Calonge
Palafrugell
Palamós
Castell d'Aro
La Platja d'Aro
Santa Cristina d'Aro
Sant Feliu de Guixols
Tossa de Mar
Santa Susana
Lloret de Mar
Sant Cebriá de Vallalta
Blanes
Malgrat de Mar
Sabadell
Vallromanes
Calella
de la
Costa
Pineda de Mar
El Masnou
Badalona
BARCELONA
Viladecans
SOUTH
EAST
COAST
Santa
Oliva
Vilanova
i la Geltrú
Sitges
El Vendrell
Cunit Cubelles
Tamarit
Tarragona

0	20	40 miles
0	20	40	60 kilometres

SWITZERLAND

GERMANY

AUSTRIA

LIECHTENSTEIN

ITALY

FRANCE

NORTH EAST

NORTH WEST & CENTRAL

NORTH

SOUTH EAST

SOUTH WEST

SOUTH

Müstair
Scuol
Tschierv
Zernez
Susch
Pontresina
Poschiavo
Arosa
Samedan
Chur
Churwalden
Lenz
Thusis
Andeer
Splügen
Tunnel del San Bernardino
Acquacalda
Cugnasco
Locarno
Agno
Lugano
Gordevio
Tenero
Molinazzo di Monteggio
Altnau
Leutswil bei Bischoffzell
Appenzell
Kummenau
Schöningrund
Walenstadt
Wegenhausen
Mammern
Eschenz
Winterthur
Wildberg
Goldingen
Euthal
Schaffhausen
Zürich
Zug
Schwyz
Brunnen
Flüelen
Altdorf
Goldau
Vitznau
Gotthard Tunnel
Urnächen
Zurzach
Ottenbach
Luzern (Lucerne)
Sachseln
Sachseln
Reckingen
Künten
Mosen
Sursee
Nottwil
Sempach
Giswil
Lungern
Meiringen
Innertkirchen
Grindelwald
Stechelberg
Raron
Rhäb-Brig
SaasGrund
Zermatt
Aarau
Reinach
Läufelfingen
Brenzikofen
Wilderswil
Aeschi
Kandersteg
Susten
Agarn
Evolène
Arolla
Basel (Basle)
Solothurn
Thun
Frutigen
Sierre
Salgesch
Sembrancher
Bourg-St-Pierre
Tunnel du Grand-St-Bernard
Biel (Bienne)
Prêles
Erlach
Le Landeron
Gampelen
Düdingen
Bern (Berne)
Fribourg
Château-d'Oex
Gstaad
Saanen
Vers-l'Eglise
Vétroz
Aigle
Morgins
La Folly
Lignières
Cudrefin
Payerne
Gumefens
Sorens
Frasel
Chessel
Leysin
Neuchâtel
Colombier
Yvonand
Châtel-St-Denis
Montreux
Le Bouveret
Le Locle
Lausanne
Grandson
Bullet
Valorbe
Ballens
Genève (Geneva)

■	Town names
●	Gazetteer location

10

Please send this form to:
    Editor, Caravan & Camping Europe
    AA Lifestyle Guides,
    Fanum House,
    Basingstoke RG21 4EA

    or fax: 01256 491647
    or e-mail: lifestyleguides@theAA.com

Readers' Report form

Please use this form to recommend any caravan and camping park where you have stayed, whether it is included in the guide or not. You can also help us to improve the guide by completing the short questionnaire on the reverse.

The AA does not undertake to arbitrate between guide readers and campsites, or to obtain compensation or engage in correspondence.

Date:

Your name (block capitals)

Your address (block capitals)

....

....

....

.... e-mail address:

Name of Park:

Comments

....

....

....

....

....

....

....

(please attach a separate sheet if necessary)

Please tick here if you DO NOT wish to receive details of AA offers or products

PTO

Readers' Report Form

Readers' Report Form

How often do you visit a caravan park or camp site?

Once a year ☐   Twice a year ☐   3 times a year ☐   More than 3 times ☐

How long do you generally stay at a park or site?

One night ☐   Up to a week ☐   1 week ☐   2 weeks ☐   Over 2 weeks ☐

Do you have a: tent ☐   caravan ☐   motorhome ☐

Which of the following in most important when choosing a site?

☐ Location   ☐ Toilet/Washing facilities
☐ Personal Recommendation   ☐ Leisure facilities
☐ Other

Do you prefer self-contained, cubicled washrooms with WC, shower and washhand basin to open-plan separate facilities?

Yes ☐   No ☐   Don't Mind ☐

Do you buy any other camping guides? If so, which ones?

....

Have you read the introductory pages and features in this guide? ....

Do you use the location atlas in this guide? ....

Which of the following most influences your choice of park from this guide?

Gazetteer entry information and description ☐

Photograph ☐   Advertisement ☐

Do you have any suggestions to improve the guide?

....

....

....

....

....

Thank you for taking the time to complete this form